Volume 10

Highways, Streets and Bridges
Housing
Insurance
Judgments
Juries
Landlord and Tenant

Volume 11

Licensing and Liquor Duties
Local Government

Volume 12

Matrimonial Law
Medicine and Pharmacy

Volume 13

Mental Health
Mines, Minerals and Quarries
Money

Volume 14(1)

National Health Service
Nationality and Immigration
Northern Ireland

Volume 14(2)

Open Spaces and National Heritage
Parliament
Partnership
Patents and Designs
Pensions and Superannuation

Volume 15

Petroleum
Police
Postal Services

Volume 16

Public Health
Real Property
Registration Concerning the Individual

Volume 17

Sale of Goods and Consumer Protection
Savings Banks
Sheriffs and Bailiffs
Shipping, Ports and Harbours

Volume 18(1)

Social Security (Part 1)

Volume 18(2)

Social Security (Part 2)

Volume 19

Stamp Duties
Taxation
Telecommunications and Broadcasting
Time
Tort

Volume 20

Town and Country Planning
Trade and Industry

Volume 21

Trade Marks and Trade Names
Transport
Trusts

Volume 22

Value Added Tax
War and Emergency
Water
Weights and Measures
Wills

Halsbury's Statutory Instruments Volume 21 (2009 Issue)

We have pleasure in sending you Volume 21 (2009 Issue) which replaces your present Volume 21 (2007 Issue). The new volume, which contains the titles TRADE MARKS AND TRADE NAMES, TRANSPORT and TRUSTS, has been completely revised so as to take into account the effect of over 190 new instruments.

Volume 21 includes statutory instruments which were available before 2 October 2009, although later changes have been noted wherever possible. Instruments which ceased to have effect between April 2007 and September 2009 are recorded in the lists of Instruments No Longer in Operation at the beginning of the titles.

October 2009

Reference Numbers

Please note that this volume includes an individual reference number for:

(a) each statutory instrument which is summarised; and

(b) where a statutory instrument is printed in full, each article, regulation or rule and each Schedule.

The reference numbers are indicated as a bold number in square brackets on the right hand side of the page, either beneath the summary of an instrument or the relevant provision of a full text instrument.

It should be noted that the index in the back of this volume refers to these reference numbers and not to page numbers.

Halsbury's Statutory Instruments

VOLUME 21

2009 Issue

ISSUE DATE

This volume contains the Statutory Instruments which became available before 2 October 2009

Volume 21 (2007 Issue), published in May 2007, should be discarded.

Members of the LexisNexis Group worldwide

United Kingdom	LexisNexis, a Division of Reed Elsevier (UK) Ltd, Halsbury House, 35 Chancery Lane, London, WC2A 1EL, and London House, 20–22 East London Street, Edinburgh EH7 4BQ
Australia	LexisNexis Butterworths, Chatswood, New South Wales
Austria	LexisNexis Verlag ARD Orac GmbH & Co KG, Vienna
Benelux	LexisNexis Benelux, Amsterdam
Canada	LexisNexis Canada, Markham, Ontario
China	LexisNexis China, Beijing and Shanghai
France	LexisNexis SA, Paris
Germany	LexisNexis Deutschland GmbH Munster
Hong Kong	LexisNexis Hong Kong, Hong Kong
India	LexisNexis India, New Delhi
Italy	Giuffrè Editore, Milan
Japan	LexisNexis Japan, Tokyo
Malaysia	Malayan Law Journal Sdn Bhd, Kuala Lumpur
New Zealand	LexisNexis NZ Ltd, Wellington
Poland	Wydawnictwo Prawnicze LexisNexis Sp, Warsaw
Singapore	LexisNexis Singapore, Singapore
South Africa	LexisNexis Butterworths, Durban
USA	LexisNexis, Dayton, Ohio

Published by LexisNexis

This is a Butterworths title

A CIP Catalogue record for this book is available from the British Library.

ISBN for the complete set of volumes: 978 0 4069 9617 6
ISBN for this Volume: 978 1 4057 4393 8

ISBN 978-1-4057-4393-8

9 781405 743938

Typeset by Letterpart Ltd, Reigate, Surrey

Printed and bound in Great Britain by CPI Antony Rowe, Chippenham and Eastbourne

Visit LexisNexis at www.lexisnexis.co.uk

Halsbury's Statutory Instruments

VOLUME 21

2009 Issue

TRADE MARKS AND TRADE NAMES
TRANSPORT
TRUSTS

Publishing Manager

CRAIG ROSE, of Lincoln's Inn, Barrister

Assistant Editors

MADELEINE JONES, LLB, Solicitor
REBECCA MITCHELL, LLB

Editors

MADELEINE JONES, LLB, Solicitor
REBECCA MITCHELL, LLB
TRACY ROBINSON, LLB, MA

Indexer
TRACY ROBINSON, LLB, MA

Table of Contents

References and Abbreviations used in this work

A list of references and abbreviations used in this work will be found in the preliminary pages of Volume 1.

Trade Marks and Trade Names

CHRONOLOGICAL LIST OF INSTRUMENTS

SR & O	*Description*	*Remarks*	*Page*
SR & O 1927/1059	Chartered Associations (Venerable Order of Saint John of Jerusalem) Protection Order 1927	See Preliminary Note "Use of particular emblems, badges, uniforms etc"	—
SR & O 1931/929	Chartered Associations (British Legion) Protection Order 1931	See Preliminary Note "Use of particular emblems, badges, uniforms etc"	—
SR & O 1931/1099	Chartered Associations (Royal Life Saving Society) Protection Order 1931	See Preliminary Note "Use of particular emblems, badges, uniforms etc"	—

SI	*Description*	*Remarks*	*Page*
SI 1967/1673	Chartered Associations (Scout Association) Protection Order 1967	See Preliminary Note "Use of particular emblems, badges, uniforms etc"	—
SI 1970/1944	Chartered Associations (Girl Guides Association) Protection Order 1970	See Preliminary Note "Use of particular emblems, badges, uniforms etc"	—
SI 1973/1952	Crystal Glass (Descriptions) Regulations 1973	—	12
SI 1975/1883	Hallmarking (Exempted Articles) (Amendment) Order 1975	Made under Hallmarking Act 1973, s 21(3), Sch 1, Pt IV, para 1(1)(b); substitutes paras 5, 10, 12, 13 of Pt II of Sch 1 to the 1973 Act and inserts para 14A thereof (paras 12 and 14A subsequently substituted by SI 1982/256); revokes SI 1975/1 (in force on 18 December 1975)	—
SI 1978/639	Sheffield Assay Office Order 1979	—	13
SI 1978/1587	Gun Barrel Proof Act 1978 (Commencement No 1) Order 1978	—	13
SI 1979/1088	Motor Vehicles (Designation of Approval Marks) Regulations 1979	—	13
SI 1979/1587	Edinburgh Assay Office Order 1979	—	13
SI 1980/582	Motor Vehicles (Designation of Approval Marks) (Amendment) Regulations 1980	Amend SI 1979/1088	—
SI 1980/640	Gun Barrel Proof Act 1978 (Commencement No 2) Order 1980	See note "Further commencement order" to SI 1978/1587	—
SI 1980/2027	Motor Vehicles (Designation of Approval Marks) (Amendment) (No 2) Regulations 1980	Amend SI 1979/1088	—
SI 1981/122	Trade Descriptions (Country of Origin) (Cutlery) Order 1981	—	14
SI 1981/126	Motor Vehicles (Designation of Approval Marks) (Amendment) Regulations 1981	Amend SI 1979/1088	—

SI	*Description*	*Remarks*	*Page*
SI 1981/1732	Motor Vehicles (Designation of Approval Marks) (Amendment) (No 2) Regulations 1981	Amend SI 1979/1088	—
SI 1982/256	Hallmarking (Exempted Articles) Order 1982	Made under Hallmarking Act 1973, Sch 1, Pt IV, para 1(1)(b); substitutes paras 12, 14A of Pt II of Sch 1 to the 1973 Act and repeals para 14B thereof (in force on 31 March 1982)	—
SI 1982/1479	Motor Vehicles (Designation of Approval Marks) (Amendment) Regulations 1982	Amend SI 1979/1088	—
SI 1983/1602	Motor Vehicles (Designation of Approval Marks) (Amendment) Regulations 1983	Amend SI 1979/1088	—
SI 1985/113	Motor Vehicles (Designation of Approval Marks) (Amendment) Regulations 1985	Amend SI 1979/1088	—
SI 1985/611	Chartered Associations (National Society for the Prevention of Cruelty to Children) Protection Order 1985	See Preliminary Note "Use of particular emblems, badges, uniforms etc"	—
SI 1986/26	Textile Products (Indications of Fibre Content) Regulations 1986	—	14
SI 1986/369	Motor Vehicles (Designation of Approval Marks) (Amendment) Regulations 1986	Amend SI 1979/1088	—
SI 1986/1274	Patents, Designs and Marks Act 1986 (Commencement No 1) Order 1986	—	15
SI 1986/1757	Hallmarking (Approved Hallmarks) Regulations 1986	Made under Hallmarking Act 1973, ss 4(7), 21(1); amends s 4 of, and paras 4, 6 of Sch 2 to, the 1973 Act (in force on 10 November 1986)	—
SI 1986/1758	Hallmarking (Exempted Articles) Order 1986	Made under Hallmarking Act 1973, Sch 1, Part IV, para 1(1)(b); amends paras 11, 12, 13, 14, 14A of Pt II of Sch 1 to the 1973 Act and inserts para 14AA thereof (in force partly on 10 November 1986 and fully on 1 May 1987)	—
SI 1987/1892	Hallmarking (International Convention) (Amendment) Order 1987	Revokes 1983/1389; spent in so far as amended 1976/730 (revoked)	—
SI 1988/1350	Textile Products (Indications of Fibre Content) (Amendment) Regulations 1988	Amend SI 1986/26; partially revoked by SI 2006/3297 (itself revoked)	—
SI 1989/900	Birmingham Assay Office Order 1989	—	15
SI 1989/992	Transfer of Functions (Economic Statistics) Order 1989	See title Constitutional Law (Pt 2); amends SI 1979/1587	—
SI 1989/1014	Motor Vehicles (Designation of Approval Marks) (Amendment) Regulations 1989	Amend SI 1979/1088	—
SI 1989/1292	Copyright, Designs and Patents Act 1988 (Isle of Man) (No 2) Order 1989	See title Patents and Designs	—
SI 1990/1458	Register of Trade Mark Agents Rules 1990	—	15
SI 1990/1838	Motor Vehicles (Designation of Approval Marks) (Amendment) Regulations 1990	Amend SI 1979/1088	—
SI 1991/1979	Motor Vehicles (Designation of Approval Marks) (Amendment) Regulations 1991	Amend SI 1979/1088	—

SI	*Description*	*Remarks*	*Page*
SI 1991/1997	Companies Act 1989 (Eligibility for Appointment as Company Auditor) (Consequential Amendments) Regulations 1991	See title Companies; amend SI 1978/639, SI 1979/1587, SI 1989/900	—
SI 1992/634	Motor Vehicles (Designation of Approval Marks) (Amendment) Regulations 1992	Amend SI 1979/1088	—
SI 1992/3086	Motor Vehicles (Designation of Approval Marks) (Amendment) (No 2) Regulations 1992	Amend SI 1979/1088	—
SI 1993/1710	Motor Vehicles (Designation of Approval Marks) (Amendment) Regulations 1993	Amend SI 1979/1088	—
SI 1993/2135	Edinburgh Assay Office (Amendment) Order 1993	Amends SI 1979/1587	—
SI 1994/363	Registered Trade Mark Agents (Mixed Partnerships and Bodies Corporate) Rules 1994	—	16
SI 1994/450	Textile Products (Indications of Fibre Content) (Amendment) Regulations 1994	Amend SI 1986/26	—
SI 1994/2550	Trade Marks Act 1994 (Commencement) Order 1994	—	16
SI 1994/2625	Trade Marks (Customs) Regulations 1994	—	16
SI 1994/2803	Trade Marks (Claims to Priority from Relevant Countries) Order 1994	—	17
SI 1995/2472	Olympic Symbol etc (Protection) Act 1995 (Commencement) Order 1995	Made under s 19(2) of the 1995 Act; brought the whole Act into force on 20 September 1995	—
SI 1995/2997	Trade Marks (Claims to Priority from Relevant Countries) (Amendment) Order 1995	Amends SI 1994/2803	—
SI 1995/3175	Community Trade Marks (Fees) Regulations 1995	See Preliminary Note "Trade marks"	—
SI 1995/3325	Olympics Association Right (Infringement Proceedings) Order 1995	—	18
SI 1995/3342	Motor Vehicles (Designation of Approval Marks) (Amendment) Regulations 1995	Amend SI 1979/1088	—
SI 1996/729	Trade Marks Act 1994 (Isle of Man) Order 1996	Made under Trade Marks Act 1994, s 108(2); amended by 2002/3148, 2004/1497; specifies the exceptions and modifications subject to which the 1994 Act extends to the Isle of Man (in force on 1 April 1996)	—
SI 1996/1576	Deregulation (Gun Barrel Proving) Order 1996	—	18
SI 1996/2757	Trade Descriptions (Place of Production) (Marking) (Revocation) Order 1996	Made under Trade Descriptions Act 1968, ss 8 (repealed), 38(1), (2); revokes SI 1988/1771 (in force on 9 December 1996)	—
SI 1997/58	Motor Vehicles (Designation of Approval Marks) (Amendment) Regulations 1997	Amend SI 1979/1088	—
SI 1998/2978	Hallmarking (Hallmarking Act Amendment) Regulations 1998	Made under European Communities Act 1972, s 2(2) and Hallmarking Act 1973, s 4(7); amend ss 2, 4, 22 of, and Sch 2 to, the 1973 Act; spent in so far as amended SI 1976/730 (revoked)	—

SI	*Description*	*Remarks*	*Page*
SI 1998/2979	Hallmarking (Hallmarking Act Amendment) Order 1998	Made under Hallmarking Act 1973, Sch 1, Pt IV, para 1(1)(b); amends para 10(b) of Pt II of Sch 1 to that Act (in force on 1 January 1999)	—
SI 1999/983	Register of Patent Agents and the Register of Trade Mark Agents (Amendment) Rules 1999	Amend SI 1990/1458 (and SI 1990/1457, in title Patents and Designs)	—
SI 1999/1899	Patents and Trade Marks (World Trade Organisation) Regulations 1999	Made under the European Communities Act 1972, s 2(2); amend the Trade Marks Act 1994, ss 6, 55–59; see also title Patents and Designs	—
SI 2002/506	Hallmarking (International Convention) Order 2002	—	18
SI 2002/3148	Trade Marks Act 1994 (Isle of Man) (Amendment) Order 2002	Amends SI 1996/729	—
SI 2004/946	Trade Marks (Proof of Use, etc) Regulations 2004	Made under European Communities Act 1972, s 2(2); amend Trade Marks Act 1994, ss 5, 10, 40, 47 and inserts s 6A thereof	—
SI 2004/1473	Goods Infringing Intellectual Property Rights (Customs) Regulations 2004	See title Customs and Excise; revoke SI 1995/1444, SI 1999/1618	—
SI 2004/1497	Trade Marks Act 1994 (Isle of Man) (Amendment) Order 2004	Amends SI 1996/729	—
SI 2004/2332	Trade Marks (International Registrations Designating the European Community, etc) Regulations 2004	Made under European Communities Act 1972, s 2(2) and Trade Marks Act 1994, s 52; amend ss 5(3), 6(1), 53, 104 of the 1994 Act; revoked by SI 2006/1027 in so far as amended SI 1996/1908 (revoked)	—
SI 2005/240	Institute of Trade Mark Attorneys Order 2005	See title Courts and Legal Services	—
SI 2006/1027	Community Trade Mark Regulations 2006	—	21
SI 2006/1119	Olympics and Paralympics Association Rights (Appointment of Proprietors) Order 2006	—	25
SI 2006/1120	Paralympics Association Right (Paralympic Symbol) Order 2006	See Preliminary Note "Olympics and Paralympics association rights"	—
SI 2007/872	Hallmarking Act 1973 (Amendment) Regulations 2007	Made under Hallmarking Act 1973, s 4(7) and European Communities Act 1972, s 2(2); substitutes s 2(2A) of, and Pts II, III of Sch 2 to, the 1973 Act; inserts s 4(3A) thereof and paras 12(3), 14A(3) of Pt II of Sch 1 thereto; renumbers para 27 of Pt IV of Sch 2 thereto as para 20 (in force on 6 April 2007)	—

SI	*Description*	*Remarks*	*Page*
SI 2007/880	Hallmarking Act 1973 (Exemption) (Amendment) Order 2007	Made under Hallmarking Act 1973, Sch 1, Pt IV, para 1(1)(b); amends para 10(b) of Pt II of Sch 1 to that Act (in force on 6 April 2007)	—
SI 2007/1508	Goods Infringing the Olympics and Paralympics Association Rights (Customs) Regulations 2007	—	25
SI 2007/1976	Trade Marks (Relative Grounds) Order 2007	—	26
SI 2007/2493	Hallmarking Act 1973 (Exemption) (Amendment No 2) Order 2007	Made under the Hallmarking Act 1973, Sch 1, Pt 4, para 1(1)(b); amends Sch 1, Pt 2 thereto	—
SI 2008/6	Textile Products (Indications of Fibre Content) (Amendment) Regulations 2008	Amend SI 1986/26; revoke SI 2006/3297	—
SI 2008/15	Textile Products (Determination of Composition) Regulations 2008	—	26
SI 2008/948	Companies Act 2006 (Consequential Amendments etc) Order 2008	See title Companies; amends SI 1978/639, SI 1979/1587, SI 1989/900	—
SI 2008/1067	Trade Marks (Earlier Trade Marks) Regulations 2008	Made under the European Communities Act 1972, s 2(2); amend the Trade Marks Act 1994, ss 6A, 47, subject to transitional provisions	—
SI 2008/1797	Trade Marks Rules 2008	—	26
SI 2008/1958	Trade Marks (Fees) Rules 2008	—	54
SI 2008/1959	Community Trade Mark (Amendment) Regulations 2008	Amend SI 2006/1027	—
SI 2008/2206	Trade Marks (International Registration) Order 2008	—	56
SI 2008/2207	Trade Marks (Fees) Revocation Rules 2008	Revoke SI 2000/137 in so far as they relate to fees payable in respect of matters arising under SI 1996/714 (revoked and replaced by SI 2008/2206)	—
SI 2008/2297	Veterinary Medicines Regulations 2008	See title Medicine and Pharmacy; revoke SI 1988/1586	—
SI 2008/2300	Trade Marks (Amendment) Rules 2008	Amend SI 2008/1797	—
SI 2008/2683	Tribunals, Courts and Enforcement Act 2007 (Transitional and Consequential Provisions) Order 2008	See title Courts; amends SI 2008/1797	—
SI 2009/546	Patents, Trade Marks and Designs (Address for Service) Rules 2009	See title Patents and Designs; amend SI 2008/1797	—
SI 2009/1034	Textile Products (Indications of Fibre Content) (Amendment) (No 2) Regulations 2009	Amend SI 1986/26; revoke SI 2009/551	—
SI 2009/2089	Trade Marks and Trade marks and Patents (Fees) (Amendment) Rules 2009	Amend SI 2008/1797, SI 2008/1958; also amend SI 2007/3292, in the title Patents and Designs	

INSTRUMENTS NO LONGER IN OPERATION

The following instruments, which were formerly contained in this title, are no longer in operation:

SI 1980/1150	lapsed[1]		SI 2006/763	revoked by	SI 2008/2206
SI 1988/1586	revoked by	SI 2008/2297[2]	SI 2006/1029	revoked by	SI 2008/1797
SI 1996/714	revoked by	SI 2008/2206	SI 2006/1080	revoked by	SI 2008/2206
SI 2000/136	revoked by	SI 2008/1797	SI 2006/3039	revoked by	SI 2008/1797
SI 2000/137	revoked[3]		SI 2006/3297	revoked by	SI 2008/6
SI 2000/138	revoked by	SI 2008/2206	SI 2006/3298	revoked by	SI 2008/15
SI 2001/3832	revoked by	SI 2008/1797	SI 2007/2076	revoked by	SI 2008/1797
SI 2002/692	revoked by	SI 2008/2206	SI 2007/2077	revoked by	SI 2008/1958
SI 2004/947	revoked by	SI 2008/1797	SI 2008/11	revoked by	SI 2008/1958
SI 2004/948	revoked by	SI 2008/2206	SI 2009/551	revoked by	SI 2009/1034

1 Lapsed on repeal of enabling power (Trade Descriptions Act 1968, ss 8, 9) by SI 2008/1277, reg 30(1), (3), Sch 2, Pt 1, paras 7, 8(d), Sch 4, Pt 1
2 In the title Medicine and Pharmacy
3 Revoked by the combined effect of SI 2008/1958 and SI 2008/2207

CROSS REFERENCES

Aircraft	Aviation
Coinage	Constitutional Law (Pt 1)
Copyright	Copyright
Dangerous drugs	Medicine and Pharmacy
Fertilisers and feeding stuffs	Agriculture
Imported livestock	Animals
Labelling of food and wine	Food
Marking of agricultural produce	Agriculture
Milk, protection of designation	Food
Patents and registered designs	Patents and Designs
Poisons	Medicine and Pharmacy
Prices, misleading indications	Sale of Goods and Consumer Protection
Registration marks on road vehicles	Transport
Registration of business names	Companies
Stamping of weights and measures	Weights and Measures
Medicinal products	Medicine and Pharmacy
Transfer of ministerial functions	Constitutional Law (Pt 2)
Vehicles carrying dangerous goods, marking	Health and Safety at Work
Statutory instruments generally, their validity, effect and termination	Statutory Instruments, Vol 1 of this work

PRELIMINARY NOTE

The instruments in this title are primarily concerned with: (a) trade marks; (b) trade descriptions; (c) approval marks under the Road Traffic Act 1988, s 80; (d) the use of particular emblems, badges, uniforms etc; and (e) assaying and hallmarking. Instruments within these categories are briefly discussed in the following paragraphs of this Preliminary Note.

The title also includes instruments relating to merchandise marks and trade descriptions that stem directly from the European Communities Act 1972, s 2; see SI 1973/1952, SI 1986/26, and SI 2008/15.

[2]

Trade marks

The statute law relating to trade marks is now contained in the Trade Marks Act 1994 (as to the commencement of which, see SI 1994/2550). The 1994 Act:

(a) repeals and replaces the Trade Marks Act 1938 and the enactments which amended and supplemented it including, in particular, the Trade Marks (Amendment) Act 1984, the Patents, Designs and Marks Act 1986, s 2, Sch 1, paras 1, 2, Sch 2, and the Copyright, Designs and Patents Act 1988, ss 282–284, 300;

(b) implemented Council Directive 89/104/EEC to approximate the laws of the Member States relating to trade marks (OJ L40, 11.02.1989, p 1), which has now been revoked and replaced by Directive 2008/95/EC of the European Parliament and of the Council to approximate the laws of the Member States relating to trade marks (OJ L299, 8.11.2008, p 25).

(c) made provision in connection with Council Regulation (EC) 40/94 on the Community trade mark (OJ L11, 14.01.1994, p 1), which has been repealed and replaced by Council Regulation (EC) 207/2009 (OJ L78, 24.03.2009, p 1);

(d) enables effect to be given in the United Kingdom to the Protocol to the Madrid Agreement concerning the International Registration of Trade Marks, adopted at Madrid on 27 June 1989 ("the Madrid Protocol") so as to enable the United Kingdom to ratify it; and

(e) meets other international obligations in relation to trade marks under the Paris Convention for the Protection of Industrial Property of 20 March 1883, as revised or amended from time to time ("the Paris Convention").

Pt I (ss 1–50 and Schs 1, 2) of the Act establishes a new code for the registration of trade marks in implementation of Council Directive 89/104/EEC (OJ L40, 11.02.1989, p 1) (repealed). S 1 defines "trade mark" as any sign capable of being represented graphically which is capable of distinguishing goods or services of one undertaking from those of other undertakings and a trade mark may, in particular, consist of words (including personal names), designs, letters, numerals or the shape of goods or their packaging. That section further provides that throughout the Act "trade mark" includes a collective mark (defined in s 49) or certification mark (defined in s 50). S 2 provides that a registered trade mark is a property right obtained by the registration of the trade mark under the Act and the proprietor of a registered trade mark has the rights and remedies provided by the Act. It also provides that the Act does not affect the right of the proprietor of an unregistered trade mark under the law relating to passing off. The remainder of Pt I makes provision as to the grounds for refusal of registration; the effects of registered trade marks; infringement proceedings; registered trade marks as objects of property; licensing; applications for registered trade mark; claims for priority; the registration procedure; the duration, renewal and alteration of registered trade marks; surrender, revocation and invalidity; and collective and certification marks. The principal rules relating to trade marks are the Trade Marks Rules 2000, SI 2008/1797, which make provision in respect of a number of matters under Pt I of the 1994 Act. For fees in respect of matters arising out of those rules, see SI 2008/1958.

Under s 36 of the Act, Her Majesty may by Order in Council make provision for conferring a right to priority on a person who has duly filed an application for protection of a trade mark in any of the Channel Islands or a colony or in a country or territory in relation to which a treaty, convention, arrangement or engagement for the reciprocal protection of trademarks has been entered; see SI 1994/2803.

Pt II (ss 51–60) concerns Community trade marks and international matters. Ss 51, 52 relate to Community trade marks. S 51 provides that "Community trade mark" has the meaning given by Art 1(1) of Council Regulation (EC) 40/94 on the Community trade mark (OJ L11, 14.01.1994, p 1) (repealed and replaced by Council Regulation (EC) 207/2009); and s 52 empowers the Secretary of State to make regulations making such provision as he considers appropriate in connection with Council Regulation (EC) 40/94; see SI 2006/1027. The registrar of trade marks is enabled, by SI 1995/3175 (made under s 52 and in force on 1 January 1996) to charge a fee of £15 for receiving and forwarding applications for a Community trade mark to the Office for Harmonisation in the Internal Market by way of the Patent Office.

Ss 53, 54 make provision with respect to the Madrid Protocol (i e the Protocol to the Madrid Agreement concerning the International Registration of Trade Marks, adopted at Madrid on 27 June 1989). S 53 provides that "international trade mark (EC)" means a trade mark which is entitled to protection in the European Community under the Madrid Protocol, and "international trade mark (UK)" means a trade mark which is entitled to international protection in the United Kingdom under that Protocol. S 54 empowers the Secretary of State, by order, to make such provision as he thinks fit for giving effect in the United Kingdom to the provisions of the Madrid Protocol; see SI 2008/2206. This order also sets out fees payable in relation to international registration.

Ss 55–60 make provision in respect of the Paris Convention.

Pt III (ss 62–98) contains administrative and other supplementary provisions. Provision is made as to the registrar (ie the Comptroller-General of Patents, Designs and Trade Marks) and the register to be maintained by him; the powers and duties of the registrar; legal proceedings and appeals; rules, fees and hours of business; trade mark agents (including registration etc); the importation of infringing goods, material or articles; offences; and forfeiture of counterfeit goods, material or articles. Further administrative and supplementary provision is made by SI 2008/1797. Fees in respect of matters arising out of SI 2008/1797 are prescribed by SI 2008/1958.

In relation to the registration of trade mark agents, see SI 1990/1458 (taking effect under s 83); and as to conditions imposed on certain partnerships and companies in order for them to be entitled to describe themselves as registered trade mark agents, see SI 1994/363 (taking effect under s 85 (repealed by the Legal Services Act 2007, ss 18491), (5), 210, Sch 23 as from a day to be appointed)).

Under s 89 a proprietor or licensee of a registered trade mark may give notice to the Commissioners for Revenue and Customs, where goods which are infringing goods in relation to that trade mark are expected to arrive in the United Kingdom from certain areas, that he wishes the Commissioners to treat them as prohibited goods. S 90 empowers the Commissioners to make regulations in respect of the form of notice and for related matters; see SI 1994/2625.

Pt IV (ss 99–110 and Schs 3–5) contains miscellaneous and general provisions, including provision in respect of offences, interpretation, consequential amendments, repeals and transitional matters. The territorial extent of the Act is defined in ss 107 and 108; by s 108(2), the Act extends to the Isle of Man, subject to such exceptions and modifications as may be specified by Order in Council; SI 1996/729, as amended by SI 2002/3148 and SI 2004/1497 (made under s 108(2)), specifies such exceptions and modifications. S 109 makes provision as to the commencement of the Act; see further SI 1994/2550.

[3]

Trade descriptions

The Trade Descriptions Act 1968 (which replaced the Merchandise Marks Acts 1887 to 1953) prohibited the application of false trade descriptions to goods and prohibits false or misleading statements as to services, accommodation or facilities provided in the course of trade. These provisions have been largely repealed and replaced by the Consumer Protection from Unfair Trading Regulations 2008, SI 2008/1277, in the title Sale of Goods.

"Trade description" continues to be defined in s 2 of the 1968 Act and, by virtue of the Road Traffic Act 1988, s 80(1), includes approval marks for motor vehicles and parts of vehicles (as to which, see the head "Approval marks"). However, by s 2(4) of the 1968 Act, it does not include:

(a) any description or mark applied in pursuance of:
   (1) the Agricultural Produce (Grading and Marking) Act 1928, s 2 (as amended by the Agricultural Produce (Grading and Marking) Amendment Act 1931);
   (2) the Plant Varieties and Seeds Act 1964;
   (3) the Agriculture and Horticulture Act 1964 or any Community grading rules within the meaning of Pt III of that Act;
   (4) the Consumer Protection Act 1987;
   (5) the Plant Varieties Act 1997;

(b) any statement made in respect of, or mark applied to, any material in pursuance of the Agriculture Act 1970, Pt IV, or any name or expression to which a meaning has been assigned under s 70 of that Act when applied to any material in the circumstances specified in that section;

(c) any mark prescribed by a system of classification compiled under the Agriculture Act 1967, s 5; and

(d) any designation, mark or description applied in pursuance of a scheme brought into force under the Agriculture Act 1970, s 6(1) (repealed) or an order made under s 25(1) (repealed) of that Act.

Under s 34 of the 1968 Act, a trade mark or part of a trade mark may constitute a false trade description. Under s 7 of that Act, power exists to make "definition orders", ie orders defining expressions when used in a trade description of goods. At the issue date of this volume no such order had been made. Under s 36(2) there is a power by order to specify: (a) what treatment or process is to be regarded as resulting or not resulting in a substantial change (see SI 1981/122), and (b) in relation to goods different parts of which were manufactured or produced in different countries or goods assembled in a country different from that in which their parts were manufactured or produced, in which country the goods are to be regarded as having been manufactured or produced (at the issue date of this volume no such order had been made).

[4]

Approval marks

The Road Traffic Act 1988, s 80(1) provides that, where any international agreement to which the United Kingdom is a party or a Community obligation provides:

(a) for markings to be applied:
   (1) to motor vehicle parts to indicate conformity with a type approved by any country, or
   (2) to a motor vehicle to indicate that the vehicle is fitted with motor vehicle parts which conform with a type approved by any country or that the vehicle is such that as so fitted it conforms with a type so approved; and

(b) for motor vehicle parts or, as the case may be, motor vehicles, bearing those markings to be recognised as complying with the requirements imposed by the law of another country,

the Secretary of State may by regulations designate the markings as approval marks. An international agreement, with the substantive provisions set out in regulations annexed ("the annexed regulations"), was concluded at Geneva on 20 March 1958 (Cmnd 2535), as amended (Cmnd 3562) and acceded to by the United Kingdom on 15 January 1963. S 80(1) of the 1988 Act further provides that any markings so designated are to be deemed for the purposes of the Trade Descriptions Act 1968 to be a trade description, whether or not those markings fall within the definition of the expression in s 2 of the 1968 Act. For the current regulations as to approval marks, which now have effect as if made under the said s 80(1), see SI 1979/1088.

[5]

Use of particular emblems, badges, uniforms etc

A number of Acts make provision to protect the use of certain emblems, symbols, badges, uniforms etc, from misleading usage or commercial exploitation. In some cases provision is also made by statutory instrument and these are discussed under the various headings below.

[6]

Geneva Conventions The Geneva Conventions Act 1957 was substantially amended and extended, as from 20 July 1998, by the Geneva Conventions (Amendment) Act 1995, so as to make the necessary changes to the law to enable the United Kingdom to ratify the Protocols done at Geneva on 10 June 1977, which are additional to the 1949 Geneva Conventions. The Act is also amended by the Geneva Conventions and United Nations Personnel (Protocols) Act 2009 as from a day to be appointed, to give effect to the Third Additional Protocol to the Geneva Conventions, adopted on 8 December 2005, which introduced a new humanitarian emblem, the Red Crystal.

The Geneva Conventions Act 1957, s 6(1)(a)–(f) makes it unlawful to use, for any purpose whatsoever, without the authority of the Secretary of State: the emblem of a red cross, or the designation "Red Cross" or "Geneva Cross; a red crescent moon, or the designation "Red Crescent"; a red lion and sun on a white ground, or the designation "Red Lion and Sun"; the sign of an equilateral blue triangle on an orange ground (being the international distinctive sign of civil defence); any of the signals specified in Chapter III of Annex I to the first protocol (being the signals of identification for medical units and transports); the emblem of a red frame in the shape of a square on edge on a white ground, conforming to the illustration in Article 1 of the Annex to the third protocol (and whether or not incorporating another emblem, or a combination of emblems, in accordance with Article 3 of the protocol), or the designation "Red Crystal" or "third Protocol emblem. S 6(2) of the 1957 Act makes it unlawful to use, for any purpose whatsoever, without the authority of the Secretary of State, any design, wording or signal so nearly resembling any of the emblems, designations, signs or signals specified in s 6(1)(a)–(f) as to be capable of being mistaken for them, or any design consisting of a white or silver cross on a red ground (being the heraldic emblem of the Swiss Confederation) or any other design so nearly resembling that emblem as to be capable of being mistaken for it. As respects the emblems and designations "Red Crescent" and "Red Lion and Sun", there is, however, a saving in certain circumstances for trade marks registered before 31 July 1957 (see s 6(4)), in respect of any designs reproducing or resembling the sign specified in s 6(1)(d), there is a similar saving for trade marks registered before 19 July 1995 (see s 6(4A)); and in respect of a similar saving regarding any designs reproducing or resembling the sign specified in s 6(1)(f), see (s 6(4B) (not yet in force)).

[7]

Chartered associations Under the Chartered Associations (Protection of Names and Uniforms) Act 1926, provision is made for the protection of names, uniforms and badges of various associations incorporated by Royal Charter. Such names, uniforms and badges may be protected by Order in Council on application by the association, and the matter to be protected must be clearly specified in the order. Before the order is made, the Lord Chancellor must consider any objections by persons or societies affected or likely to be affected. On such protection becoming effective, the unauthorised use of the protected matter is a criminal offence punishable on summary conviction with a fine not exceeding level 1 on the standard scale.

Six Orders in Council have been made under the 1926 Act, as follows:

(a) SR & O 1927/1059, which protects the badges worn without uniform by the Venerable Order of St John of Jerusalem;
(b) SR & O 1931/929, which protects the name "British Legion" and the two badges to be worn without uniform by members of the British Legion;
(c) SR & O 1931/1099, which protects the name "The Royal Life Saving Society" and certain badges to be worn without uniform;
(d) SI 1967/1673, which protects the name "The Scout Association", various names and designations used by the association for its members or for members of organisations constituted by the association, and certain badges to be worn with or without uniform;
(e) SI 1970/1944, which protects the name "The Girl Guides Association", various names and designations used by the association for its members or for members of organisations constituted by the association, and certain badges to be worn with or without uniform; and
(f) SI 1985/611, which protects the names "National Society for the Protection of Cruelty to Children" and "NSPCC Young League", the designation "NSPCC", and three badges described in the order.

[8]

Olympics and Paralympics association rights The relevant enactments relating to Olympics and Paralympics association rights are the Olympic Symbol etc (Protection) Act 1995 (which was brought into force on 20 September 1995 by SI 1995/2472), and the London Olympic Games and Paralympic Games Act 2006 (which makes provision in connection with the Olympic Games and Paralympic Games that are to take place in London in the year 2012, and amends the 1995 Act). The 2006 Act comes into force partly on 30 March 2006 (date of royal assent) and partly on a day or days to be appointed by order under s 40 thereof; at the issue date of this volume, a number of provisions of the Act had been brought into force by SI 2006/1118 and SI 2007/1064, in the title Culture Entertainment and Sport. All the provisions of the 2006 Act mentioned in this note are fully in force.

As originally enacted, the 1995 Act made provision to protect the Olympic symbol (i e the symbol of the International Olympic Committee consisting of five interlocking rings; see s 18(1) of the 1995 Act) and the Olympic motto (i e the motto of the International Olympic Committee "Citius, altius, fortius"; see s 18(1) of the 1995 Act) from unauthorised commercial exploitation, in order to enable the Secretary of State to grant the British Olympic Association an exclusive licence to exploit the Olympic symbols commercially. As amended by the London Olympic Games and Paralympic Games Act 2006, s 32, Sch 3, the 1995 Act now makes parallel provision to protect the Paralympic symbol and the Paralympic motto. By s 18(1) of the 1995 Act (as amended by paras 1, 7 of Sch 3 to the 2006 Act), "Paralympic symbol" means the symbol of the International Paralympic Committee set out in an order made by Secretary of State under s 18(1) of the 1995 Act; and "Paralympic motto" means the motto of the International Paralympic Committee—"Spirit in Motion". SI 2006/1120 (made under s 18(1) of the 1995 Act and in force on 12 May 2006) sets out in the Schedule thereto the symbol of the International Paralympic Committee.

S 1 of the 1995 Act (as amended by paras 1, 2 of Sch 3 to the 2006 Act) introduces the Olympics association right and makes provision for it to be exercised by such person or persons as the Secretary of State may by order appoint. S 5A(1) of the 1995 Act (as inserted by paras 1, 6 of Sch 3 to the 2006 Act) creates the Paralympics association right. By s 5A(2) (as so inserted) the provisions of the 1995 Act are applied to the Paralympics association right as they apply to the Olympics association right (and for that purpose references to the Olympic motto and the Olympic symbol are to be treated as references to the Paralympic motto and the Paralympic symbol respectively). SI 2006/1119 (made under ss 1, 5A of the 1995 Act) appoints the British Olympic Association and the London Organising Committee as the proprietors of the Olympics association right, and appoints the British Paralympic Association and the London Organising Committee as the proprietors of the Paralympics association right. (The London Organising Committee was set up under the Host City Contract for the Olympic Games and Paralympic Games to be held in London in 2012; see s 1(3)(d) of the 2006 Act.)

Ss 2–5 of the 1995 Act (as amended by paras 1, 3–5 of Sch 3 to the 2006 Act), as read with s 5A thereof, specify, or make provision for specifying, the rights conferred by the Olympics association right and the Paralympics association right; the activities that amount to infringement of those rights; and the limits of those rights (which may be extended by order under s 5; at the issue date of this volume this power had not been exercised). S 5A of the 1995 Act (as inserted by paras 1, 6 of Sch 3 to the 2006 Act) creates the Paralympics association right and extends the 1995 Act to that right as it applies to the Olympics association right. S 6 makes provision for an infringement of rights to be actionable by the proprietor. S 7 defines infringing goods, material and articles and empowers the Secretary of State to make regulations specifying the court's powers to make orders in infringement proceedings and containing other procedural provision for such proceedings; see SI 1995/3325. The remainder of the 1995 Act includes provision for: offences of infringing the Olympics association right and the Paralympics association right (s 8); the enforcement of s 8 by a local weights and measures authority (s 8A, as inserted by paras 1, 12 of Sch 3 to the 2006 Act); the forfeiture of counterfeit goods, material and articles (s 11); the detention of infringing goods, material and articles by the Commissioners for Her Majesty's Revenue and Customs (s 12A, as inserted by paras 1, 14 of Sch 3 to the 2006 Act); and restrictions on the acquisition of competing rights (ss 13, 14).

S 33 of, and Sch 4 to, the 2006 Act create the London Olympics association right in relation to the London Olympics (defined by s 1(1) of that Act as the Games of the Thirtieth Olympiad that are to take place in 2012 and the Paralympic Games that are to take place in that year). The right confers exclusive rights in relation to the use of any representation (of any kind) in a manner likely to suggest to the public that there is an association between the London Olympics and goods or services or a person who provides goods or services (para 1 of Sch 4). Para 2 of Sch 4 sets out the circumstances in which a person infringes the London Olympics association right, and para 3 thereof sets out specific expressions which, when used in combination, may be taken into account by a court when considering whether the London Olympics association right has been infringed. Paras 4–9 of Sch 4 provide exceptions to infringement of the right, including an exception for authorised use. Para 10 of Sch 4 provides that specified provisions of the 1995 Act (i e ss 2 (part), 3 (part), 4 (part), 5, 6, 7, 15 and 16) have effect in relation to the London Olympics association right as they have effect in relation to the Olympics association right. S 33 of, and Sch 4 to, the 2006 Act cease to have effect at the end of 31 December 2012; see s 40(8) of that Act.

[9]

Assaying and hallmarking

The Hallmarking Act 1973, which came fully into force on 1 January 1975 (see s 24(2)), and which repealed the bulk of the previous enactments relating to assaying and hallmarking, implements certain recommendations of the Departmental Committee on Hallmarking (Cmnd 663), published in 1959. It makes provision for the composition, assaying, marking and description of articles of, or containing, precious metals, and for connected purposes.

S 2(1) of the 1973 Act defines approved hallmarks as:

(a) marks struck by an assay office in the United Kingdom;

(b) marks struck by the Wardens and Commonalty of Goldsmiths of the City of Dublin before 1 April 1923;

(c) marks struck by an assay office under the law of a country outside the United Kingdom, being marks designated by order of the Secretary of State as marks recognised pursuant to any international convention or treaty to which the United Kingdom is a party; or

(d) marks struck in an EEA State other than the United Kingdom, being marks which: (i) have been struck by an independent body in accordance with the law of that state, and (ii) provide information which is equivalent to the information provided by the marks mentioned in s 4(1)(a)(i), (ii) of the 1973 Act and which is intelligible to consumers in the United Kingdom.

In relation to s 2, see further SI 2002/506.

S 16 of the Act empowers the making of orders: (a) constituting or closing and dissolving etc assay offices (see the definition in s 22(1) of the Act), or (b) varying or abolishing etc the duties or powers of assay offices and repealing or amending the statutory provisions relating to them. SI 1978/639, SI 1979/1587 and SI 1989/900, made under that section, vary existing statutory provisions relating to assay offices. Sch 1 to the Act sets out exemptions to the prohibition under s 1 on describing unhallmarked articles as made of gold, silver or platinum, and Pt IV of that Schedule gives the Secretary of State power to amend those exemptions. That power has been exercised in SI 1975/1883, SI 1982/256, SI 1986/1758, SI 1998/2979, SI 2007/880 and SI 2007/2493. S 4 of, and Sch 2 to, the 1973 Act make provision as to the form of approved hallmarks; those provisions have been amended by SI 1986/1757, SI 1998/2978 and SI 2007/872.

[10]

CRYSTAL GLASS (DESCRIPTIONS) REGULATIONS 1973
SI 1973/1952

Authority Made by the Secretary of State under the European Communities Act 1972, s 2 and SI 1972/1811, in the title Constitutional Law (Pt 5).

Date made 20 November 1973.

Commencement 19 December 1973.

Summary These regulations implement Council Directive 69/493/EEC on the approximation of the laws of the Member States relating to crystal glass (OJ L326, 29.12.1969, p 36). They do not apply in relation to glass that is intended for export from the United Kingdom to a country other than a member state of the European Community.

The regulations prohibit the supply of glassware to which is applied a description specified in the Schedule to the regulations unless the glass is of the chemical composition and has the physical properties mentioned in relation to the description in British Standard 3828 published on 28 February 1973 (as amended). British Standards are issued by, and are available from, the British Standards Institution, 389 Chiswick High Road, London W4 4AL (tel: 020 8996 9001; fax: 020 8996 7001; email: cservices@bsi-global.com; internet: www.bsonline.bsi-global.com). It should be noted that British Standards may be withdrawn or superseded from time to time; information as to the status of British Standards may be obtained from the British Standards Institution.

Disclosure of Information These regulations have been specified by SI 2003/1400, in the title Trade and Industry, for the purposes of the Enterprise Act 2002, ss 238(1) and 241(3). S 238(1) defines "specified information" for the purposes of Pt 9 of the 2002 Act as including information which comes to a public authority in connection with the exercise of any function it has under or by virtue of such subordinate legislation as is specified by order. Specified information is subject to the restrictions on disclosure and permitted disclosures set out in Pt 9 of the 2002 Act. By s 241(3) of that Act, a public authority may disclose specified information to any other person for the purpose of facilitating the exercise by that person of any function he has under or by virtue of such subordinate legislation as is specified by order.

[11]

SHEFFIELD ASSAY OFFICE ORDER 1978
SI 1978/639

Authority Made by the Secretary of State under the Hallmarking Act 1973, s 16(1)(c), (3), Sch 6, para 6.
Date made 19 April 1978.
Commencement 20 April 1978.
Amendment Amended by SI 1991/1997 and SI 2008/948.
Summary This order was made on the application of the Guardians of the Standard of Wrought Plate within the Town of Sheffield ("the Company") (referred to in the Hallmarking Act 1973 as the Sheffield Assay Office: see s 22(1) thereof) under s 16(1)(c) of the 1973 Act. It confers powers upon, and varies existing statutory provisions relating to, the Company, so as to alter the constitution of the Company, establish an Executive Committee responsible for the general management of the assay office, and provide for the appointment of officers, acquisition and disposal of land, accounts and audit, borrowing and investment, pensions and disposal of historical articles. Certain provisions of the Plate Assay (Sheffield and Birmingham) Act 1772 and the Sheffield Assay Act 1906 are amended or repealed.

[12]

GUN BARREL PROOF ACT 1978 (COMMENCEMENT NO 1) ORDER 1978
SI 1978/1587

Authority Made by the Secretary of State under the Gun Barrel Proof Act 1978, s 9(3).
Date made 1 November 1978.
Summary This order brought into force on 1 December 1978 the Gun Barrel Proof Act 1978, except for those provisions relating to the Convention for the Reciprocal Recognition of Proof Marks of Small Arms (Cmnd 5942), that is except for ss 1, 8(1) (in part), (3) and Schs 1, 2 and 3 (in part).
Further commencement order The provisions of the Act relating to the Convention specified above were brought into force on 5 June 1980 by SI 1980/640.

[13]

MOTOR VEHICLES (DESIGNATION OF APPROVAL MARKS) REGULATIONS 1979
SI 1979/1088

Authority Made by the Minister of Transport under the Road Traffic Act 1972, s 63(1) (repealed); now take effect as if made under the Road Traffic Act 1988, s 80(1), by virtue of the Interpretation Act 1978, ss 17(2)(b), 23(2), in the title Statutory Instruments (Pt 2), Vol 1 of this work.
Date made 30 August 1979.
Commencement 1 October 1979.
Amendment Amended by SI 1980/582, SI 1980/2027, SI 1981/126, SI 1981/1732, SI 1982/1479, SI 1983/1602, SI 1985/113, SI 1986/369, SI 1989/1014, SI 1990/1838, SI 1991/1979, SI 1992/634, SI 1992/3086, SI 1993/1710, SI 1995/3342 and SI 1997/58.
Summary The Road Traffic Act 1988, s 80(1) provides for the making of regulations designating as vehicle approval marks markings recognised under any international agreement to which the United Kingdom is a party or under any Community obligation (see further the Preliminary Note "Approval marks").

The regulations revoke and replace with amendments the Motor Vehicles (Designation of Approval Marks) Regulations 1976, SI 1976/2226, and the amending SI 1977/1400, SI 1978/1111 and SI 1978/1870. Reg 4 designates approval marks required by specified ECE Regulations (i e regulations annexed to the International Agreement concluded at Geneva on 20 March 1958). The markings, which are listed in Sch 2, relate to headlamps and other lamps; reflex reflectors; devices for illumination of rear registration plates; direction indicators; head restraints; advance-warning triangles; audible warning devices; tyres; rear-view mirrors; windscreens and other glass; child restraints; pneumatic tyres for commercial vehicles; motor vehicles approved in respect of radio interference suppression; door latches and hinges; brakes; protection against impact; safety-belts and anchorages; emission of pollutants; seats and anchorages; unauthorised use; interior fittings; external projections; fire prevention; foot control arrangement; speedometers; installation of lights and light-signalling devices; structural fittings; structural features; noise emissions; rear marking plates.

Reg 5 designates approval marks required by specified Community instruments. The markings, which are listed in Sch 4, relate to audible warning devices; rear-view mirrors; road transport recording equipment; reflex reflectors; headlamps; centre-mounted stop lamps and other lamps; direction indicators; devices for illuminating rear registration plates; safety belts; head restraints; spray suppression devices; windscreens; windows other than windscreens; tyres; alarm systems or immobilisers; electrical/electronic sub-assemblies; replacement exhaust systems or components; and materials used in the internal construction vehicles. Schs 3 and 5 specify permitted variations on the markings and certain further requirements.

[14]

EDINBURGH ASSAY OFFICE ORDER 1979
SI 1979/1587

Authority Made by the Secretary of State under the Hallmarking Act 1973, s 16(1)(c), (3), Sch 6, para 6.

Date made 4 December 1979.
Commencement 5 December 1979.
Amendment Amended by SI 1989/992, SI 1991/1997, SI 1993/2135 and SI 2008/948.
Summary This order was made on the application of the Incorporation of Goldsmiths of the City of Edinburgh ("the Incorporation") (referred to in the Hallmarking Act 1973 as the Edinburgh Assay Office: see s 22(1) thereof) under s 16(1)(c) of the 1973 Act. It confers powers upon, and varies existing statutory provisions relating to, the Incorporation, so as to alter the constitution of the Incorporation and the Court of Wardens responsible for the general management of the assay office, and provides for the appointment of officers, acquisition and disposal of land, accounts and audit, borrowing and investment pensions and annuities, disposal of historical articles and the siting of offices. Enactments of 1587 and 1687, relating to the Incorporation, are repealed with a saving.

[15]

TRADE DESCRIPTIONS (COUNTRY OF ORIGIN) (CUTLERY) ORDER 1981
SI 1981/122

Authority Made by the Secretary of State under the Trade Descriptions Act 1968, s 36(2)(a).
Date made 2 February 1981.
Commencement 1 January 1982.
Summary This order applies to cutlery (i e knives, forks, spoons, ladles, servers, slicers, sharpening steels and similar articles) wholly or partly made of silver-plated stainless steel, which would have been suitable for retail supply for domestic use without having been silver plated. It provides that the process of silver plating or any ancillary process is to be regarded as not resulting in a substantial change for the purposes of the Trade Descriptions Act 1968, s 36.

[16]

TEXTILE PRODUCTS (INDICATIONS OF FIBRE CONTENT) REGULATIONS 1986
SI 1986/26

Authority Made by the Secretary of State under the European Communities Act 1972, s 2(2) and the Medicines Act 1968, s 103(3).
Date made 13 January 1986.
Commencement Partly on 1 March 1986; fully on 29 May 1987.
Amendment Amended by SI 1988/1350 (itself amended by SI 2006/3297 (revoked)), SI 1994/450, SI 2008/6 and SI 2009/1034, and by virtue of the Commissioners for Revenue and Customs Act 2005, s 50(1). Also amended by SI 1998/1169, SI 2005/1401 SI 2006/3297 and SI 2009/551 (all revoked).
Summary These regulations revoke and replace the Textile Products (Indications of Fibre Content) Regulations 1973, SI 1973/2124, as amended by SI 1975/928, SI 1984/1640, as from 29 May 1987 (the 1973 regulations were amended by these regulations for the period between 1 March 1986 and 29 May 1987). The regulations implement Directive 2008/121/EC of the European Parliament and of the Council on textile names (OJ L19, 23.01.2009, p 29)).

The regulations require that when textile products are supplied or offered for supply in the course of a trade or business, or are described in certain advertisements, an indication of their fibre content must be given, except in specified circumstances. Such indications must contain specified names for the fibres concerned, and the use of the expressions "100 per cent", "pure" and "all" is restricted; the use of the phrases "virgin wool" and "fleece wool" is also limited. Manners of specifying proportional fibre content of products which contain more than one textile are prescribed, and the terms "mixed fibres" and "unspecified textile composition" are permitted in certain circumstances. Indications must be given clearly, legibly and in uniform lettering, and separate from all other information, subject to certain exceptions. Provision is also made as to the language to be used, and as to the use of abbreviations.

Nothing in the regulations applies in relation to textile products:

(a) which are intended for export from the United Kingdom to any destination except a destination in another member state;
(b) which are imported into the United Kingdom for transit through the United Kingdom under the control of the Commissioners for Her Majesty's Revenue and Customs;
(c) which are imported into the United Kingdom for the purposes of re-export after processing; and
(d) in respect of a supply to or from outworkers or other persons who are to carry out or who have carried out work on the products on commission.

Failure to comply with the requirements of these regulations is an offence, which, by virtue of reg 11 (referring to the Trade Descriptions Act 1968, s 18), is punishable with a fine not exceeding the prescribed sum or imprisonment for a term not exceeding two years, or both. In all matters relating to the prosecution of offences under these regulations, certain provisions of the 1968 Act are applied with such modifications as are necessary.
Disclosure of information These regulations have been specified by SI 2003/1400, in the title Trade and Industry, for the purposes of the Enterprise Act 2002, ss 238(1) and 241(3); see further the corresponding note to SI 1973/1952.

[17]

PATENTS, DESIGNS AND MARKS ACT 1986 (COMMENCEMENT NO 1) ORDER 1986
SI 1986/1274

Authority Made by the Secretary of State under the Patents, Designs and Marks Act 1986, s 4(6).
Date made 21 July 1986.
Summary This order brought into force on 1 October 1986 the following provisions of the Patents, Designs and Marks Act 1986: s 1 and Sch 1, paras 1, 2, and s 3(1) and Sch 3, Pt I (so far as they related to the repeal of the Trade Marks Act 1938, ss 57, 58).

S 4 of the Act came into force on 8 July 1986 (the date of royal assent). Ss 2, 3(2) of, and Sch 2 and Pt II of Sch 3 to, the Act came into force on the same date as the Trade Marks (Amendment) Act 1984 (which was brought into force on 1 October 1986 by SI 1986/1273, made under s 2(2) of the 1984 Act). Ss 2, 3(4) of, and paras 1, 2 of Sch 1 and Sch 2 to, the 1986 Act, and the whole of the 1984 Act, were repealed by the Trade Marks Act 1994, s 106(2), Sch 5 (and SI 1986/1273 has consequently lapsed).

[18]

BIRMINGHAM ASSAY OFFICE ORDER 1989
SI 1989/900

Authority Made by the Secretary of State for Trade and Industry under the Hallmarking Act 1973, s 16(2), (3), Sch 6, para 6.
Date made 25 May 1989.
Commencement 1 July 1989.
Amendment Amended by SI 1991/1997 and SI 2008/948.
Summary This order was made on the application of the Guardians of the Standard of Wrought Plate in Birmingham ("the Company") (referred to in the Hallmarking Act 1973 as the Birmingham Assay Office: see s 22(1) thereof) under s 16(1)(c) of the 1973 Act. It confers powers upon, and varies existing statutory provisions relating to, the Company, so as to alter the constitution of the Company and the Wardens' Committee responsible for the general management of the assay office, and provide for the appointment of officers and employees, acquisition and disposal of land, accounts and audit, borrowing and investment, pensions and annuities, disposal of historical articles and the siting of offices elsewhere than in Birmingham. The order also provides for the amendment or repeal of certain provisions of the Birmingham Assay Office Acts 1824 and 1902.

[19]

REGISTER OF TRADE MARK AGENTS RULES 1990
SI 1990/1458

Authority Made by the Secretary of State for Trade and Industry under the Copyright, Designs and Patents Act 1988, s 282. The said s 282 was repealed by the Trade Marks Act 1994, s 106(2), Sch 5; by virtue of s 105 of, and para 22(1) of Sch 3 to, the 1994 Act, these rules now take effect under s 83 thereof.
Date made 18 July 1990.
Commencement 1 October 1990.
Amendment Amended by SI 1999/983.
Summary These rules regulate the registration of persons who act as agents for others for the purpose of applying for or obtaining the registration of trade marks.

The Institute of Trade Mark Attorneys is to keep a register containing the name of each person who is entitled to be registered, together with their business address, the date of registration, qualifications for registration and such other particulars as the Registrar (appointed to maintain the register by the Institute) may think fit to include. A special record is to be kept of names erased from the register (together with the reason for erasure). That record and the register are to be open to public inspection as and when the Registrar may direct, subject to any general directions of the Comptroller-General of Patents, Designs and Trade Marks; and the register is to be printed, published and placed on sale by the Institute not later than 1 April in each year.

The Institute is required to make provision for such educational qualifications, training and qualifying examinations (to be offered at least once in every year) as it considers appropriate for the registration of persons under the rules. The Institute, subject to certain conditions, has the entire management and control of such examinations.

The following persons qualify for registration:

(a) a person who has passed the qualifying examinations and has at least two years' (or four years' without supervision) full-time practice in the field of intellectual property, including substantial experience in trade mark agency work;
(b) until 1 October 1993, a Fellow or an ordinary member of the Institute;
(c) until 1 October 1994, a person, being a registered patent agent, or barrister, solicitor, or in Scotland or the Isle of Man, an advocate, who has in the eight years prior to the application completed a total of three years' practice in trade mark agency work;
(d) until 1 October 1992, a person who has in the eleven years prior to the application completed a total of eight years of full-time practice in trade mark agency work; and
(e) a person who passed, in March 1990, the Advanced Trade Marks Practice (T3) examination and
    (1) becomes a registered patent agent before 31 December 1992, or

(2) passed, before 31 December 1991, a special advanced trade mark examination set by the Institute.

A person who qualifies for registration is entitled to be registered on production of evidence of qualification and payment of the registration fee.

Provision is made with regard to the amendment and correction of the register and erasure of registration for failure to pay any annual practice fee that may be prescribed. In addition, where the Secretary of State is satisfied, after due enquiry, that a person has been guilty of misconduct, he may direct that the name of that person be erased from the register. The Secretary of State must serve on such persons a notice informing them of the grounds and the substance of any allegations and inviting them to submit representations in writing and requiring them to serve notice, if they wish, of their intention to make oral representations. Provision is made with regard to the hearing of representations, the decision of the Secretary of State and directions as to the restoration of names and particulars to the register. Persons aggrieved by any decision of the Institute or the Registrar under these rules may appeal to the Comptroller (whose decision on any appeal is final).

Provision is also made conferring on the Institute the power to make regulations, with the approval of the Comptroller, regarding the payment of examination, registration and annual practice fees; for the Comptroller to give directions to the Institute; and as to the form of the annual report which the Institute must make to the Comptroller.

[20]

REGISTERED TRADE MARK AGENTS (MIXED PARTNERSHIPS AND BODIES CORPORATE) RULES 1994
SI 1994/363

Authority Made by the Secretary of State for Trade and Industry under the Copyright, Designs and Patents Act 1988, s 283(4). The said s 283 was repealed by the Trade Marks Act 1994, s 106(2), Sch 5; by virtue of s 105 of, and para 22(1) of Sch 3 to, the 1994 Act, these rules now take effect under s 85 thereof. The said s 85 is repealed by the Legal Services Act 2007, ss 18491), (5), 210, Sch 23 as from a day to be appointed.

Date made 17 February 1994.

Commencement 24 March 1994.

Summary These rules prescribe, for the purposes of the Trade Marks Act 1994, s 84, the conditions to be satisfied by partnerships or bodies corporate where all the partners or, as the case may be, directors, are not registered trade mark agents in order for the partnership or body corporate to carry on business under the name or any description containing the words "registered trade mark agents", or describe itself or permit itself to be described as such. The conditions to be satisfied are:

(a) that each partner or, as the case may be, director must be a person whose name is entered in at least one of the registers kept pursuant to rules made under s 83 of the 1994 Act (register of trade mark agents; see SI 1990/1458), or the Copyright, Designs and Patents Act 1988, s 275 (register of patent agents; see SI 1990/1457, in the title Patents and Designs); and

(b) that at least one-quarter of the partners or, as the case may be, the directors must be registered trade mark agents.

[21]

TRADE MARKS ACT 1994 (COMMENCEMENT) ORDER 1994
SI 1994/2550

Authority Made by the Secretary of State for Trade and Industry under the Trade Marks Act 1994, s 109.

Date made 29 September 1994.

Summary This order brought into force on 31 October 1994 all the provisions of the Trade Marks Act 1994. However the following provisions of the 1994 Act were brought into force on 29 September 1994 for the purpose only of enabling the making of subordinate legislation thereunder, expressed to come into force on 31 October 1994: ss 4(4), 13(2), 25(1), (5), (6), 34(1), 35(5), 38(1), (2), 39(3), 40(4), 41(1), (3), 43(2), (3), (5), (6), 44(3), 45(2), 63(2), (3), 64(4), 65(1), (3), (4), (5), 66(2), 67(1), (2), 68(1), (3), 69, 76(1), 78, 79, 80(3), 81, 82, 88, Sch 1, para 6(2), Sch 2, para 7(2), Sch 3, paras 10(2), 11(2), 12, 14(5). The order also brought into force on 29 September 1994 ss 66(1), 80(1), (3) of the 1994 Act to enable the Registrar to exercise his powers to require forms and give directions as to their use and to specify business hours and business days of the Patent Office, effective from 31 October 1994.

[22]

TRADE MARKS (CUSTOMS) REGULATIONS 1994
SI 1994/2625

Authority Made by the Commissioners of Customs and Excise under the Trade Marks Act 1994, s 90(1), (2), (3).

Date made 11 October 1994.

Commencement 31 October 1994; see reg 1.

General These regulations, which revoke and replace the Trade Marks (Customs) Regulations 1970, SI 1970/212, prescribe the form in which the proprietor or licensee of a registered trade mark may give notice under the Trade Marks Act 1994, s 89 to the Commissioners for Her Majesty's Revenue and Customs of the expected arrival of infringing goods, material or articles which he wishes to be treated as prohibited. The regulations also specify the fee to be paid and the conditions to be observed by the person giving the notice.

[23]

1 These Regulations may be cited as the Trade Marks (Customs) Regulations 1994 and shall come into force on 31st October 1994.

[24]

2 If notice is given under section 89(1) of the Trade Marks Act 1994 by the proprietor or licensee of a registered trade mark in respect of certain goods it shall be in the form set out in the Schedule to these Regulations or a form to the like effect approved by the Commissioners; and separate notices shall be given in respect of each arrival of such goods.

[25]

3 A fee of £30 (plus value added tax) in respect of each notice shall be paid to the Commissioners at the time it is given.

[26]

4 The person giving the notice shall give to the Commissioners such security or further security within such time and in such manner, whether by deposit of a sum of money or guarantee, as the Commissioners may require, in respect of any liability or expense which they may incur in consequence of the notice by reason of the detention of any goods or anything done to goods so detained: and if such security or further security is not given within the time specified by the Commissioners, then (but without prejudice to the operation of regulation 5 below) the notice shall have no effect.

[27]

5 In every case, whether any security or further security is given or not, the person who has given the notice shall keep the Commissioners indemnified against all such liability and expense as is mentioned in regulation 4 above.

[28]

6 (1) The person giving the notice shall, either on giving notice or when the goods are imported, furnish the Commissioners with the certificate of registration (or a copy of it) issued by the Registrar of Trade Marks on the registration of the trade mark specified in the notice, together with evidence that such registration was duly renewed at all such times as it may have expired.

(2) If such a certificate or copy and, where applicable, evidence of renewal is not furnished in accordance with paragraph (1) above then the goods shall not be detained, or, if detained, shall be released, and (but without prejudice to the operation of regulation 5 above) any notice given in respect of them shall have no effect.

[29]

7 (*Revokes the Trade Marks (Customs) Regulations 1970, SI 1970/212.*)

SCHEDULE

NOTES
This Schedule sets out the form of notice requesting infringing goods, material or articles to be treated as prohibited goods (referred to in reg 2).

[30]

TRADE MARKS (CLAIMS TO PRIORITY FROM RELEVANT COUNTRIES) ORDER 1994
SI 1994/2803

Authority Made under the Trade Marks Act 1994, s 36(1), (2).
Date made 2 November 1994.
Commencement 5 December 1994.
Amendment Amended by SI 1995/2997.

Summary This Order in Council specifies, for the purposes of the Trade Marks Act 1994, s 36, the following countries as relevant countries in which an application for the protection of a trade mark will confer a right to priority for the purpose of registering the same trade mark in the UK under the 1994 Act: Antigua and Barbuda, Bahrain, Belize, Bolivia, Botswana, Brunei Darussalam, Colombia, Djibouti, Dominica, Ecuador, Guatemala, Hong Kong, India, Jamaica, Kuwait, Macau, Maldives, Mozambique, Myanmar, Namibia, Nicaragua, Pakistan, Sierra Leone and Thailand. The period within which the claim to priority must be made is six months from the date of filing the application in the relevant country. The order also makes provisions corresponding to s 35(2), (4)–(6) of the 1994 Act, which confer the right to priority in respect of applications filed in Convention countries (i e countries which are party to the Paris Convention for the Protection of Industrial Property of 20 March 1883 or the Agreement establishing the World Trade Organisation signed at Marrakesh on 15 April 1994 (see s 55(1) of the 1994 Act)).

[31]

OLYMPICS ASSOCIATION RIGHT (INFRINGEMENT PROCEEDINGS) REGULATIONS 1995
SI 1995/3325

Authority Made by the Secretary of State for National Heritage and the Secretary of State for Scotland under the Olympic Symbol etc (Protection) Act 1995, s 7(1).
Date made 20 December 1995.
Commencement 12 January 1996.
Summary These regulations make provision with respect to the orders that a court may make in an action for infringement of the Olympics association right (consisting of the rights and remedies conferred by the Olympic Symbol etc (Protection) Act 1995 in relation to controlled representations).

The regulations provide:

(a) that the court may order the erasure of the offending controlled representation from any infringing goods, material or articles or the destruction of the infringing goods, material or articles in question;
(b) that the proprietor of the Olympics association right may apply to the court for an order that any infringing goods, material or articles be delivered up to him or such other person as the court directs; and
(c) that the proprietor of the Olympics association right may apply to the court for an order that infringing goods, material or articles which have been delivered up in pursuance of an order under these regulations may be destroyed or forfeited.

The regulations make provision for the periods beyond which an application for such an order may not be brought; enable the making of rules of court providing for the notification of any persons who might have an interest in any such goods, material or articles; and provide that the orders specified in these regulations may be made by the High Court in England, Wales and Northern Ireland, and the Court of Session in Scotland. Orders made under heads (b) and (c) above may also be made by the sheriff court in Scotland or a county court in Northern Ireland.

It should be noted that s 5A of the 1995 Act (as inserted by the London Olympic Games and Paralympic Games Act 2006, s 32, Sch 3, paras 1, 6) creates the Paralympics association right and applies the provisions of the 1995 Act to that right as they apply to the Olympics association right. In addition, para 1 of Sch 4 to the 2006 Act creates the London Olympics association right; provisions of the 1995 Act are applied to the London Olympics association right until the end of 31 December 2012 (see s 40(8) of, and para 10 of Sch 4 to, the 2006 Act, and the Preliminary Note "Olympics and Paralympics association rights").

[32]

DEREGULATION (GUN BARREL PROVING) ORDER 1996
SI 1996/1576

Authority Made by the Secretary of State for Trade and Industry under the Deregulation and Contracting Out Act 1994, s 1 (repealed by the Regulatory Reform Act 2001, s 12(1)). This order continued in force by virtue of s 12(4) of the 2001 Act (repealed by the Legislative and Regulatory Reform Act 2006, s 30(1), Schedule), and now continues in force by virtue of s 30(5) of the 2006 Act.
Date made 17 June 1996.
Commencement 15 July 1996.
Summary This order, which extends to Northern Ireland, amends the Gun Barrel Proof Act 1868, s 118, so as to remove the requirement that the sums charged by the London and Birmingham Proof Houses for the proving of civilian small arms should not exceed the sums laid down in the Schedules to the 1868 Act. The order also repeals the Gun Barrel Proof Act 1950, ss 3, 4 and the Schedule, and the Gun Barrel Proof Act 1978, Sch 3, para 20, which are spent in consequence of the amendment to s 118 of the 1868 Act.

[33]

HALLMARKING (INTERNATIONAL CONVENTION) ORDER 2002
SI 2002/506

Authority Made by the Secretary of State for Trade and Industry under the Hallmarking Act 1973, ss 2(1)(c), (3), 21(1). It is thought that the reference to s 21(1) of the 1973 Act in the Queen's Printer's copy of this order should be to s 22(1) of that Act.

Date made 7 March 2002.
Commencement 1 April 2002; see art 1(1).
Interpretation By the preamble to this order (not printed in this work), any reference in the order to "the Act" is a reference to the Hallmarking Act 1973.
General This order, which revokes the Hallmarking (International Convention) Order 1976, SI 1976/730 (the amending SI 1981/559, SI 1983/1608, SI 1984/1131, SI 1988/2286 and SI 1995/2488 are spent), implements the Convention on the Control and Marking of Articles of Precious Metals done at Vienna on 15 November 1972. The order recognises convention hallmarks and sponsors' marks applied in another convention country; as a consequence articles bearing such marks will be hallmarked for the purposes of the Hallmarking Act 1973 and can therefore be described in the United Kingdom as being of the precious metal (gold, silver or platinum) of which they are made. The order also provides for the application in the United Kingdom of similar marks which will be recognised in other convention countries.

[34]

1 (1) This Order may be cited as the Hallmarking (International Convention) Order 2002, and shall come into force on the 1st April 2002.

(2) The Hallmarking (International Convention) Order 1976 is hereby revoked.

NOTES
Hallmarking (International Convention) Order 1976 SI 1976/730 (the amending SI 1981/559, SI 1983/1608, SI 1984/1131, SI 1988/2286 and SI 1995/2488 are spent).

[35]

2 In this Order "the Convention" means the Convention on the Control and Marking of Articles of Precious Metals done at Vienna on 15th November 1972.

[36]

3 (1) The following marks are designated for the purposes of section 2 of the Act as marks recognised pursuant to the Convention, that is to say—

(a) except in a case in which the number is applied to the article by a person other than an assay office authorised as mentioned in sub-paragraph (b) below, a number in Arabic numerals indicating the standard of fineness of an article being—
  (i) in the case of gold, 750, 585 or 375;
  (ii) in the case of silver, 800 or 925; and
  (iii) in the case of platinum, 950;
(b) a mark which has been notified in accordance with the Convention as being the mark of an assay office authorised for the purposes of the Convention in the territory of a Contracting State other than the United Kingdom;
(c) The Common Control Mark comprising a number specified in sub-paragraph (a) above.

(2) The Common Control Mark consists of the representation of a balance together with the number in Arabic numerals showing the standard of fineness of the article in relief on a lined background surrounded by a shield indicating the nature of the precious metal. The shields are illustrated in Part 1 of Schedule 1 hereto; and examples of the Common Control Mark are illustrated in Part II of that Schedule.

(3) The marks referred to in paragraph (1)(b) are illustrated in Schedule 2 hereto.

[37]

4 Every mark, being the name of a person who submits articles for hallmarking, or an abbreviation thereof or a symbol indicating such a person which has been entered in the official register of a Contracting State other than the United Kingdom, or in the official register of an authorised assay office in the territory of such a Contracting state, is designated—

(a) as a mark recognised pursuant to the Convention; and
(b) as a sponsor's mark for the purposes of the Act.

[38]

5 (1) A person submitting an article for hallmarking to an assay office in the United Kingdom authorised for the purposes of the Convention may request the assay office to strike the article with the marks specified in Article 3(1)(a) and (c) above whether or not the article bears or is to bear other approved hallmarks, and (subject to the provisions of the Act and, in particular, section 4 as having effect in the manner indicated in paragraph (2) of this Article) the assay office shall give effect to any such request; and the following provisions of this Article shall apply:

Provided that nothing in this paragraph shall require an assay office to strike an article with the mark specified in Article 3(1)(a) if the article already bears approved hallmarks struck in the United Kingdom which include the mark so specified.

(2) Section 4 of the Act shall have effect in relation to the striking of such specified marks as if—

(a) subsection (1)(a)(ii) required the striking on the article of the marks specified in Article 3(1)(a) (subject to the proviso in paragraph (1) of this Article), and in Article 3(1)(c), instead of the standard mark;
(b) subsection (1)(a)(iii) were omitted;
(c) the words in subsection (1)("and, as respects all such articles" to the end of the subsection and Part IV of Schedule 2 to the Act, did not apply in relation to the Common Control Mark;
(d) in subsection (2) the reference to subsection (1)(a)(iii) were omitted;
(e) in subsection (3), in head (c) of the proviso to paragraph b(i) "585" were substituted for "500", and in paragraph (b)(iii), "995" were substituted for "the standard of fineness of the article";
(f) in paragraph 4 of Part II of Schedule 2 to the Act—
    (i) in subparagraph (c), for the words "struck only with the standard mark for the metal of which those parts are made" there were substituted the words "stamped or engraved with a specific designation of the metal";
    (ii) the words "and in relation to any article" to the end of paragraph 4 were omitted; and
(g) in Part III of Schedule 2 to the Act, for paragraph 6(b)(ii) there were substituted the following—

"(ii) these materials are used for filling the handle of a knife, fork or spoon and only in such a quantity as is necessary for joining."

[39]

6 (1) A person may submit to an assay office an article wholly or partly of silver with a written request that it be marked as being of a fineness of 830 as respects the article as a whole or its silver parts; and in such a case the following provisions of this Article shall have effect.

(2) Article 5 shall apply as if—

(a) the number 830 were specified in relation to silver in Article 3(1)(a);
(b) a new sub-paragraph were added after paragraph 2(e) substituting in section 4(3)(b)(ii) of the Act "550" for "650".

(3) Where a silver article is struck with the mark indicating a standard of fineness of 830 the article shall be struck with the relevant assay office mark set out below instead of the mark set out in column (2) or (3), as the case may be, of paragraph 1 of Part 1 of Schedule 2 to the Act.

London	A silversmith's hammer with the figure 1 in the bottom left hand corner of the shield
Edinburgh	A silversmith's hammer with the figure 11 in the top right hand corner of the shield
Birmingham	A silversmith's hammer with the figure 1 in the top right hand corner of the shield
Sheffield	A silversmith's hammer with the figure 11 in the bottom left hand corner of the shield

(4) Marks struck by an assay office on an article in accordance with sub-paragraph (1) above shall not be approved hallmarks for the purposes of section 2(4)(a) of the Act; and accordingly the article shall be unhallmarked.

[40]

SCHEDULES 1, 2

NOTES

Sch 1, mentioned in art 3(2), contains illustrations of the shields used for the purposes of the common control mark for gold, silver or platinum articles, together with examples of the mark.

Sch 2, mentioned in art 3(3), contains illustrations of the foreign assay office marks recognised for the purposes of the Convention. The contracting states are Austria, the Czech Republic, Denmark, Finland, Ireland, the Netherlands, Norway, Portugal, Sweden and Switzerland.

[41]

COMMUNITY TRADE MARK REGULATIONS 2006
SI 2006/1027

Authority Made by the Secretary of State for Trade and Industry under the Trade Marks Act 1994, s 52.

Date made 5 April 2006.

Commencement 29 April 2006; see reg 1(1).

Amendment Amended by SI 2008/1959, and by virtue of the Commissioners for Revenue and Customs Act 2005, s 50(1).

Interpretation See reg 2.

General These regulations make provision for the operation of Council Regulation (EC) 40/94 on the Community trade mark (OJ L11, 14.01.1994, p 1) ("the Community Trade Mark Regulation") (repealed and replaced by Council Regulation (EC) 207/2009 (OJ L78, 24.03.2009, p 1). They revoke and replace the Community Trade Mark Regulations 1996, SI 1996/1908, and the amending SI 2004/949, and the Community Trade Mark (Designation of Community Trade Mark Courts) Regulations 2005, SI 2005/440, and revoke SI 2004/2332 in so far as it amended SI 1996/1908.

A Community trade mark registered at the Office for Harmonisation in the Internal Market (trade marks and designs) under the Community Trade Mark Regulation has effect throughout the Community. Following the Community's accession to the Madrid Agreement concerning the International Registration of Trade Marks, adopted at Madrid on 27 June 1989, holders of an international registration under the Protocol to that Agreement ("the Madrid Protocol") may apply for protection of their marks under the Community trade mark system. Similarly, applicants for, or proprietors of, a Community trade mark may apply for international protection of their marks under the Madrid Protocol. The provision made by these regulations in respect of the Community trade mark also extends to marks protected under the Madrid Protocol in the territory of the Community.

[42]

Citation, commencement, extent and revocations

1 (1) These Regulations may be cited as the Community Trade Mark Regulations 2006 and shall come into force on 29th April 2006.

(2) These Regulations extend to England and Wales, Scotland and Northern Ireland.

(3) The instruments set out in the Schedule (revocations) shall be revoked to the extent specified.

[43]

Interpretation

2 (1) In these Regulations—

"Community trade mark court" means a court designated by regulation 12;

"international application" means an application to the International Bureau for registration of a trade mark in the International Register;

"international application designating the European Community" means an international application in which a request has been made for extension of protection to the European Community under Article 3*ter* (1) of the Madrid Protocol;

"International Register" means the register of trade marks maintained by the International Bureau for the purposes of the Madrid Protocol;

"international registration" means the registration of a trade mark in the International Register;

"international registration designating the European Community" means an international registration in relation to which a request has been made (either in the relevant international application or subsequently) for extension of protection to the European Community under Article 3*ter* (1) or (2) of the Madrid Protocol.

(2) In regulations 3 to 9, a reference to a Community trade mark includes a reference to an international trade mark (EC), and in that case—

(a) a reference to a revocation or declaration of invalidity of the mark is a reference to a revocation or declaration of invalidity of the protection of the mark;

(b) a reference to the goods or services for which the mark is registered is a reference to the goods or services in respect of which the mark is protected.

(3) In these Regulations "the Act" means the Trade Marks Act 1994, and any reference to a section is, unless the context otherwise requires, a reference to a section of that Act.

[44]

Determination of invalidity and liability to revocation in relation to claims of seniority

3 (1) Where the proprietor of a Community trade mark claims the seniority of a registered trade mark which—

(a) has been removed from the register under section 43, or

(b) has been surrendered under section 45,

any person may apply to the registrar or to the court for the declaration set out in paragraph (3).

(2) Where such a proprietor claims the seniority of an international trade mark (UK) which has been removed from the International Register or surrendered, any person may apply to the registrar or to the court for the declaration set out in paragraph (3).

(3) The declaration is that if the trade mark had not been so removed or surrendered, it would have been liable to be revoked under section 46 or declared invalid under section 47.

(4) An address for service in the United Kingdom shall be filed by—

(a) the person making an application under paragraph (1) or (2); and

(b) the proprietor of the Community trade mark,

unless in a particular case the registrar otherwise directs.

(5) Where the trade mark has been surrendered in respect of some only of the goods or services for which it is registered (or protected), paragraph (1) or (2) shall apply in relation to those goods or services only.

[45]

Procedure for declaration that trade mark would have been liable to be revoked or declared invalid

4 (1) In proceedings on an application under regulation 3(1) or (2) the registration of a person as proprietor of a trade mark shall be prima facie evidence of the validity of the original registration.

(2) In the case of such proceedings before the registrar, the provisions of [rules 38 to 43, 45, 62 to 79 and 82 of the Trade Marks Rules 2008], with necessary modifications, shall apply.

(3) In the case of such proceedings before the court, the registrar is entitled to appear and be heard, and shall appear if so directed by the court.

(4) Unless otherwise directed by the court, the registrar may instead of appearing submit to the court a statement in writing signed by him, giving particulars of—

(a) any proceedings before him in relation to the matter in issue,

(b) the grounds of any decision given by him affecting it,

(c) the practice of the Patent Office in like cases, or

(d) such matters relevant to the issues and within his knowledge as registrar as he thinks fit;

and the statement shall be deemed to form part of the evidence in the proceedings.

(5) Anything which the registrar is or may be authorised or required to do under this regulation may be done on his behalf by a duly authorised officer.

NOTES

Amendment Para (2): words in square brackets substituted by SI 2008/1959.

Trade Marks Rules 2008 SI 2008/1797.

[46]

Remedies in infringement proceedings

5 (1) This regulation is without prejudice to the duties of the Community trade mark court under Article 98(1) of the Community Trade Mark Regulation.

(2) In an action for infringement of a Community trade mark all such relief by way of damages, injunctions, accounts or otherwise is available to the proprietor of the Community trade mark as is available in respect of the infringement of any other property right.

(3) The provisions of sections 15 to 19 apply in relation to a Community trade mark as they apply to a registered trade mark; and any reference to the court shall be construed as meaning the Community trade mark court.

[47]

Groundless threats of infringement proceedings

6 (1) The provisions of section 21 apply in relation to a Community trade mark as they apply to a registered trade mark.

(2) However, in the application of those provisions in relation to an international trade mark (EC)—

(a) the reference in section 21(3) to the registration of the trade mark shall be treated as a reference to the protection of the international trade mark (EC);

(b) the reference in section 21(4) to notification that a trade mark is registered, shall be treated as a reference to notification that a trade mark is an international trade mark (EC); and

(c) the reference in section 21(4) to notification that an application for registration has been made, shall be treated as a reference to notification that a trade mark is the subject of an international application or international registration designating the European Community.

[48]

Importation of infringing goods, material or articles

7 (1) The provisions of—

(a) section 89 (infringing goods, material or articles may be treated as prohibited goods);

(b) section 90 and section 91 (power of [Commissioners for Revenue and Customs] to disclose information),

apply in relation to a Community trade mark as they apply in relation to a registered trade mark.

(2) The Trade Marks (Customs) Regulations 1994 shall apply in relation to notices given under section 89 as applied by paragraph (1).

NOTES

Amendment Para (1)(b): words in square brackets substituted by virtue of the Commissioners for Revenue and Customs Act 2005, s 50(1).

Trade Marks (Customs) Regulations 1994 SI 1994/2625.

[49]

Offences and forfeiture

8 (1) The provisions of—

(a) section 92 (unauthorised use of trade mark, etc, in relation to goods);

(b) section 92A (search warrants);

(c) section 93 (enforcement function of local weights and measures authority);

(d) section 97 (forfeiture: England and Wales or Northern Ireland); and

(e) section 98 (forfeiture: Scotland),

apply in relation to a Community trade mark as they apply in relation to a registered trade mark.

(2) For the purposes of those provisions, references to goods in respect of which a trade mark is registered shall include goods in respect of which an international trade mark (EC) confers protection in the European Community.

[50]

Falsely representing trade mark as a Community trade mark

9 (1) It is an offence for a person—

- (a) falsely to represent that a mark is a Community trade mark, or
- (b) to make a false representation as to the goods or services for which a Community trade mark is registered,

knowing or having reason to believe that the representation is false.

(2) A person guilty of an offence under this regulation is liable on summary conviction to a fine not exceeding level 3 on the standard scale.

[51]

Conversion

10 (1) This regulation applies where, pursuant to Article 108 of the Community Trade Mark Regulation—

- (a) the applicant for or the proprietor of a Community trade mark requests the conversion of his Community trade mark application or Community trade mark into an application for registration of a trade mark under the Act; or
- (b) the holder of an international registration designating the European Community requests (in accordance with Article 154(1)(a) of that Regulation) the conversion of that designation into an application for registration of a trade mark under the Act.

(2) Where the request has been transmitted to the registrar under Article 109(3) of the Community Trade Mark Regulation, it shall be treated as an application for registration of a trade mark under the Act.

(3) A decision of the registrar in relation to the request shall be treated as a decision of the registrar under the Act.

[52]

Privilege for communications with those on the list of professional trade marks representatives

11 (1) This regulation applies to communications as to any matter relating to the protection of any trade mark or as to any matter involving passing off.

(2) Any such communication—

- (a) between a person and his professional trade marks representative, or
- (b) for the purposes of obtaining, or in response to a request for, information which a person is seeking for the purpose of instructing his professional trade marks representative,

is privileged from, or in Scotland protected against, disclosure in legal proceedings in the same way as a communication between a person and his solicitor or, as the case may be, a communication for the purpose of obtaining, or in response to a request for, information which a person is seeking for the purpose of instructing his solicitor.

(3) In paragraph (2) a person's "professional trade marks representative" means a person who is retained by him and is on the special list of professional representatives for trade marks matters referred to in Article 89 of the Community Trade Mark Regulation.

[53]

Designation of Community trade mark courts

12 (1) For the purposes of Article 91 of the Community Trade Mark Regulation, the following courts are designated as Community trade mark courts—

- (a) in England and Wales—
  - (i) the High Court;

(ii) any county court designated as a patents county court under section 287(1) of the Copyright, Designs and Patents Act 1988; and
(iii) the county courts listed in paragraph (2);

(b) in Scotland, the Court of Session; and
(c) in Northern Ireland, the High Court.

(2) The county courts referred to in paragraph (1)(a)(iii) are the county courts at—

(a) Birmingham;
(b) Bristol;
(c) Cardiff;
(d) Leeds;
(e) Liverpool;
(f) Manchester; and
(g) Newcastle upon Tyne.

(3) For the purpose of hearing appeals from judgments of the courts designated by paragraph (1), the following courts are also designated as Community trade mark courts—

(a) in England and Wales, the Court of Appeal;
(b) in Scotland, the Court of Session; and
(c) in Northern Ireland, the Court of Appeal.

[54]

SCHEDULE

NOTES
This Schedule sets out the regulations revoked by reg 1(3), namely the Community Trade Mark Regulations 1996, SI 1996/1908, and the amending SI 2004/949, and the Community Trade Mark (Designation of Community Trade Mark Courts) Regulations 2005, SI 2005/440, and SI 2004/2332, regs 7–14 (ie in so far as it amended SI 1996/1908).

[55]

OLYMPICS AND PARALYMPICS ASSOCIATION RIGHTS (APPOINTMENT OF PROPRIETORS) ORDER 2006
SI 2006/1119

Authority Made by the Secretary of State for Culture, Media and Sport under the Olympic Symbol etc (Protection) Act 1995, ss 1(2), (2A), (3), 5A(2).
Date made 19 April 2006.
Commencement 12 May 2006.
Summary This order, which revokes the Olympics Association Right (Appointment of Proprietor) Order 1995, SI 1995/2473, appoints the proprietors of the Olympics and Paralympics association rights for the purposes of the Olympic Symbol etc (Protection) Act 1995, s 1(2), and provides for the exercise of the proprietors' rights under that Act. Those association rights entitle their respective proprietors to use, and control the use by others of, the Olympic and Paralympic symbols and mottos; protected Olympic- and Paralympic-related words; and any symbols, mottos or words which are confusingly similar to such symbols, mottos or words.

The order appoints the British Olympic Association and the London Organising Committee as the proprietors of the Olympics association right, and appoints the British Paralympic Association and the London Organising Committee as the proprietors of the Paralympics association right. (The London Organising Committee was set up under the Host City Contract for the Olympic Games and Paralympic Games that are to take place in London in the year 2012.) Provision is made as to the exercise of the rights of the proprietors of the Olympics and Paralympics association rights; the right of those proprietors to consent to an act under s 2(2)(b) of the 1995 Act (consent to use the Olympic and Paralympic symbols and mottos and the protected words under that Act); and the rights of the proprietors of the Olympics and Paralympics association rights to bring an action for infringement of the Olympics and Paralympics association rights under s 6 of the 1995 Act. See further the Preliminary Note "Olympics and Paralympics association rights".

[56]

GOODS INFRINGING THE OLYMPICS AND PARALYMPICS ASSOCIATION RIGHTS (CUSTOMS) REGULATIONS 2007
SI 2007/1508

Authority Made by the Commissioners for Her Majesty's Revenue and Customs under the Olympic Symbol etc (Protection) Act 1995, s 12B(1), and the Trade Marks Act 1994, s 90.
Date made 22 May 2007.
Commencement 13 June 2007.

Summary These regulations prescribe the forms of the notices to be given to the Commissioners for HM Revenue and Customs by the proprietor of the Olympics association right and the Paralympics association right under the Olympic Symbol etc (Protection) Act 1995, s 12A(1), (8)(a) which allow the Commissioners to detain or continue to detain certain goods that have been or are expected to be imported and that infringe the proprietor's intellectual property rights in relation to the symbols. The regulations also require a person giving such notice to indemnify the Commissioners.

[57]

TRADE MARKS (RELATIVE GROUNDS) ORDER 2007
SI 2007/1976

Authority Made by the Secretary of State for Innovation, Universities and Schools under the Trade Marks Act 1994, s 8(5).
Date made 10 July 2007.
Commencement 1 October 2007.
Summary The Trade Marks Act 1994, s 5 (relative grounds for refusal) provides that a trade mark shall not be registered if it is identical or similar to and earlier trade mark or earlier right. Under s 37 of the 1994 Act the registrar must examine whether an application for the registration of a trade mark satisfies the requirements of the Act, and is therefore, required to carry out a search on earlier trade marks. If the registrar is of the opinion that requirements are not met he must inform the applicant who then has the opportunity to amend the application, otherwise he must accept the application and publish it. After publication any person may oppose the application within a prescribed period.

Under s 8 of the 1994 Act the Secretary of State may make an order to this effect following the expiry of a period of ten years beginning with the date on which applications for Community trade marks may first be filed in pursuance of the Community Trade Mark Regulation (Council Regulation (EC) 207/2009 (OJ L78, 24.03.2009, p 1) which repealed and replaced Council Regulation 40/94/EEC).

This order provides that the registrar shall not refuse to register a trade mark on a ground mentioned in s 5 of the 1994 Act unless objection on that ground is raised in opposition proceedings by the proprietor of the earlier trade mark or other earlier right. Provision is also made in respect of the carrying out by the registrar of searches of earlier trade marks and as to the persons by whom an application for a declaration of invalidity may be made on the grounds specified in s 47(2) of the Act. The order also repeals s 37(2) of the Act.

[58]

TEXTILE PRODUCTS (DETERMINATION OF COMPOSITION) REGULATIONS 2008
SI 2008/15

Authority Made by the Secretary of State for Business, Enterprise and Regulatory Reform under the European Communities Act 1972, s 2(2), Sch 2, para 1A.
Date made 8 January 2008.
Commencement 2 February 2008.
Summary These regulations, which revoke and replace the Textile Products (Determination of Composition) Regulations 2006, SI 2006/3298, implement Council Directive 73/44/EEC on the approximation of the laws of the Member States relating to the quantitative analysis of ternary fibre mixtures (OJ L83, 30.03.1973, p 1) and Directive 96/73/EC of the European Parliament and of the Council on certain methods for the quantitative analysis of binary textile fibre mixtures (OJ L32, 03.02.1997, p 1), as amended by Commission Directive 2006/2/EC (OJ L5, 10.01.2006, p 10) and Commission 2007/4/EC (OJ L28, 03.02.2007, p 14.

The regulations apply for the purposes of SI 1986/26 for determining in the course of any official test (ie a test carried out by or on behalf of a person whose duty it is to enforce SI 1986/26) the composition of any textile product comprising a binary textile fibre mixture or a ternary textile fibre mixture. Under the regulations, test samples and test specimens must be prepared for analysis in accordance with Annex I to Directive 96/73/EC. The following provision is made for test processes:

(a) the analysis of a binary textile fibre mixture which is specified in Annex II of Directive 96/73/EC must be carried out, and the results calculated and expressed, in accordance with that Annex;
(b) the analysis of a binary textile fibre mixture other than one for which a method of analysis is specified in Annex II of Directive 96/73/EC must be carried out by the use of any valid method of analysis; and the test report must set out the result obtained and, so far as is known, the degree of accuracy and the method used;
(c) the analysis of a ternary fibre mixture must be carried out in accordance with Annexes I and II of Directive 73/44/EEC and the results calculated and expressed in accordance with Annex I.

[59]

TRADE MARKS RULES 2008
SI 2008/1797

Authority Made by the Secretary of State for Innovation, Universities and Skills under the Trade Marks Act 1994, ss 4(4), 13(2), 25(1), (5), (6), 34(1), 35(5), 38(1), (2), 39(3), 40(4), 41(1), (3), 43(2), (3), (5), (6), 44(3), 45(2), 63(2), (3), 64(4), 65(1), (2), 66(2), 67(1), (2), 68(1), (3), 69, 76(1), 78, 80(3), 81, 82, 88, Sch 1, para 6(2), Sch 2, para 7(2).

Date made 7 July 2008.
Commencement 1 October 2008.
Amendment Printed as amended by SI 2008/2300, SI 2008/2683, SI 2009/546 and SI 2009/2089.
Interpretation See r 2.
General These rules revoke and replace the Trade Marks Rules 2000, SI 2000/136 and the amending SI 2001/3832, SI 2004/947, SI 2006/1029, SI 2006/3039, SI 2007/2076, subject to transitional provisions. They make provision as to the classification and registration of trade marks and other supplementary and procedural matters. The rules also amend SI 2008/11 (revoked), and SI 2006/760, in the title Patents and Designs.
Application to international trade marks (UK) By SI 2008/2206, these rules (except rr 6, 8, 9, 12(4)(a), 13, 46, 47, 56) apply, with modifications to international trade marks (UK) and requests for extension of time; see art 3 thereof.
Fees For fees in respect of matters arising out of this order, see SI 2008/1958.

[60]

Preliminary

Citation and commencement

1 These Rules may be cited as the Trade Marks Rules 2008 and shall come into force on 1st October 2008.

[61]

Interpretation

2 (1) In these Rules—

"the Act" means the Trade Marks Act 1994;

"the Journal" means the Trade Marks Journal published in accordance with rule 81;

"the "Nice Agreement" means the Nice Agreement Concerning the International Classification of Goods and Services for the Purposes of the Registration of Marks of 15th June 1957, which was last amended on 28th September 1979;

"the "Nice Classification" means the system of classification under the Nice Agreement;

["the Office" means the Patent Office which operates under the name "UK Intellectual Property Office";]

"send" includes give;

"specification" means the statement of goods or services in respect of which a trade mark is registered or proposed to be registered;

"transformation application" means an application to register a trade mark under the Act where that mark was the subject of an international registration prior to that registration being cancelled.

(2) In these Rules a reference to a section is a reference to that section in the Act and a reference to a form is a reference to that form as published under rule 3.

(3) In these Rules references to the filing of any application, notice or other document, unless the contrary intention appears, are to be construed as references to its being delivered to the registrar at the Office.

NOTES
Amendment Para (1): definition "the Office substituted by SI 2009/2089.

[62]

Forms and directions of the registrar; section 66

3 (1) Any forms required by the registrar to be used for the purpose of registration of a trade mark or any other proceedings before the registrar under the Act pursuant to section 66 and any directions with respect to their use shall be published on the Office website and any amendment or modification of a form or of the directions with respect to its use shall also be published on the Office website.

(2) Except in relation to Forms TM6 and TM7A a requirement under this rule to use a form as published is satisfied by the use either of a replica of that form or of a form which is acceptable to the registrar and contains the information required by the form as published and complies with any directions as to the use of such a form.

NOTES

Office website The website of the Patent Office which operates under the name "the UK Intellectual Property Office": see www.ipo.gov.uk/types/tm/t-formsfees.htm.

[63]

Requirement as to fees

4 (1) The fees to be paid in respect of any application, registration or any other matter under the Act and these Rules shall be those (if any) prescribed in relation to such matter by rules under section 79 (fees).

(2) Any form required to be filed with the registrar in respect of any specified matter shall be subject to the payment of the fee (if any) prescribed in respect of that matter by those rules.

[64]

Application for Registration

Application for registration; section 32 (Form TM3)

5 [(1) An application for the registration of a trade mark (other than a transformation application, which shall be filed on Form TM4) shall be filed on Form TM3 or, where the application is filed in electronic form using the filing system provided on the Office website, on Form e-TM3.

[(1A) An application for the registration of a trade mark (other than a transformation application, which shall be filed on Form TM4) shall be filed on Form TM3 or, where the application is filed in electronic form using the filing system provided on the Office website, on Form e-TM3.

[(1B) Where an application is filed on Form e-TM3 (an "electronic application") the application shall be subject to the payment of the e-filed application fee and such class and series fees as may be appropriate, which shall be payable at the time the electronic application is made and if they are not so paid the application shall be subject to the payment of the standard application fee referred to in paragraph (1A) and such class and series fees as may be appropriate.]

(2) [Subject to paragraph (6)] where an application is for the registration of a single trade mark, an applicant may request the registrar to undertake an expedited examination of the application.

(3) A request for expedited examination shall be made on [Form e-TM3] and shall be subject to payment of the prescribed fee.

(4) Where an applicant makes a request for expedited examination, the application fee and any class fees payable in respect of the application shall be payable at the time the application is made and accordingly rule 13 shall not apply insofar as it relates to the failure of an application to satisfy the requirements of section 32(4).

(5) In this rule and rule 15 a "request for expedited examination" means a request that, following an examination under section 37, the registrar notify the applicant within a period of ten business days (as specified in a direction given by the registrar under section 80) beginning on the business day after the date of filing of the application for registration whether or not it appears to the registrar that the requirements for registration are met.

[(6) Where it appears to the registrar that the period (the "routine period") within which applicants are routinely notified of the outcome of an examination under section 37 is equal to or less than the period specified in paragraph (5), the registrar may suspend the right of applicants to file a request for expedited examination until such time as the routine period exceeds the period specified in paragraph (5) and the registrar shall, in each case, publish a notice on the Office website to this effect.]

NOTES

Amendment Paras (1), (1A), (1B): substituted for para (1) by SI 2009/2089.
Para (2): words in square brackets inserted by SI 2009/2089.
Para (3): words in square brackets substituted by SI 2009/2089
Para (6): inserted by SI 2009/2089.
Office website See the note to r 3.

[65]

Claim to priority; sections 35 & 36

6 (1) Where a right to priority is claimed by reason of an application for protection of a trade mark duly filed in a Convention country under section 35 or in another country or territory in respect of which provision corresponding to that made by section 35 is made under section 36 (an "overseas application"), the application for registration under rule 5 shall specify—

(a) the number accorded to the overseas application by the registering or other competent authority of the relevant country;
(b) the country in which the overseas application was filed; and
(c) the date of filing.

(2) The registrar may, in any particular case, by notice require the applicant to file, within such period of not less than one month as the notice may specify, such documentary evidence as the registrar may require certifying, or verifying to the satisfaction of the registrar, the date of the filing of the overseas application, the country or registering or competent authority, the representation of the mark and the goods or services covered by the overseas application.

[66]

Classification of goods and services; section 34

7 (1) The prescribed system of classification for the purposes of the registration of trade marks is the Nice Classification.

(2) When a trade mark is registered it shall be classified according to the version of the Nice Classification that had effect on the date of application for registration.

[67]

Application may relate to more than one class and shall specify the class (Form TM3A)

8 (1) An application may be made in more than one class of the Nice Classification.

(2) Every application shall specify—

(a) the class in the Nice Classification to which it relates; and
(b) the goods or services which are appropriate to the class and they shall be described in such a way as to indicate clearly the nature of those goods or services and to allow them to be classified in the classes in the Nice Classification.

(3) If the application relates to more than one class in the Nice Classification the specification contained in it shall set out the classes in consecutive numerical order and the specification of the goods or services shall be grouped accordingly.

(4) If the specification contained in the application lists items by reference to a class in the Nice Classification in which they do not fall, the applicant may request, by filing Form TM3A, that the application be amended to include the appropriate class for those items, and upon the payment of such class fee as may be appropriate the registrar shall amend the application accordingly.

[68]

Determination of classification

9 (1) Where an application does not satisfy the requirements of rule 8(2) or (3), the registrar shall send notice to the applicant.

(2) A notice sent under paragraph (1) shall specify a period, of not less than one month, within which the applicant must satisfy those requirements.

(3) Where the applicant fails to satisfy the requirements of rule 8(2) before the expiry of the period specified under paragraph (2), the application for registration, insofar as it relates to any goods or services which failed that requirement, shall be treated as abandoned.

(4) Where the applicant fails to satisfy the requirements of rule 8(3) before the expiry of the period specified under paragraph (2), the application for registration shall be treated as abandoned.

[69]

Prohibition on registration of mark consisting of arms; section 4

10 Where having regard to matters coming to the notice of the registrar it appears to the registrar that a representation of any arms or insignia as is referred to in section 4(4) appears in a mark, the registrar shall refuse to accept an application for the registration of the mark unless satisfied that the consent of the person entitled to the arms has been obtained.

[70]

Address for service

11 (1) For the purposes of any proceedings under the Act or these Rules, an address for service shall be filed by—

- (a) an applicant for the registration of a trade mark;
- (b) any person who opposes the registration of a trade mark in opposition proceedings;
- (c) any person who applies for revocation, a declaration of invalidity or rectification under the Act;
- (d) the proprietor of the registered trade mark who opposes such an application.

(2) The proprietor of a registered trade mark, or any person who has registered an interest in a registered trade mark, may file an address for service on Form TM33 or, in the case of an assignment of a registered trade mark, on Form TM16.

(3) Where a person has provided an address for service under paragraph (1) or (2), that person may substitute a new address for service by notifying the registrar on Form TM33.

[(4) An address for service filed under this Rule shall be an address in the United Kingdom, another EEA state or the Channel Islands.]

(5) …

NOTES

Amendment Para (4): substituted by SI 2009/546.
Para (5): revoked by SI 2009/546.

[71]

Failure to provide an address for service

12 (1) Where—

- (a) a person has failed to file an address for service under rule 11(1); and
- (b) the registrar has sufficient information enabling the registrar to contact that person,

the registrar shall direct that person to file an address for service.

(2) Where a direction has been given under paragraph (1), the person directed shall, before the end of the period of one month beginning with the date of the direction, file an address for service.

(3) Paragraph (4) applies where—

- (a) a direction was given under paragraph (1) and the period prescribed by paragraph (2) has expired; or
- (b) the registrar had insufficient information to give a direction under paragraph (1),

and the person has failed to provide an address for service.

(4) Where this paragraph applies—

- (a) in the case of an applicant for registration of a trade mark, the application shall be treated as withdrawn;
- (b) in the case of a person opposing the registration of a trade mark, that person's opposition shall be treated as withdrawn;
- (c) in the case of a person applying for revocation, a declaration of invalidity or rectification, that person's application shall be treated as withdrawn; and
- (d) in the case of the proprietor opposing such an application, the proprietor shall be deemed to have withdrawn from the proceedings.

(5) In this rule an "address for service" means an address which complies with the requirements of rule 11(4) …

NOTES
Amendment Para (5): words omitted revoked by SI 2009/546.

[72]

Deficiencies in application; section 32

13 (1) Where an application for registration of a trade mark does not satisfy the requirements of section 32(2), (3) or (4) or rule 5(1), the registrar shall send notice to the applicant to remedy the deficiencies or, in the case of section 32(4), the default of payment.

(2) A notice sent under paragraph (1) shall specify a period, of not less than [14 days], within which the applicant must remedy the deficiencies or the default of payment.

(3) Where, before the expiry of the period specified under paragraph (2), the applicant—

(a) fails to remedy any deficiency notified to the applicant in respect of section 32(2), the application shall be deemed never to have been made; or

(b) fails to remedy any deficiency notified to the applicant in respect of section 32(3) or rule 5(1) or fails to make payment as required by section 32(4), the application shall be treated as abandoned.

NOTES
Amendment Para (2): words in square brackets substituted by SI 2009/2089.

[73]

Notifying results of search

14 (1) Where, following any search under article 4 of the Trade Marks (Relative Grounds) Order 2007, it appears to the registrar that the requirements for registration mentioned in section 5 are not met, the registrar shall notify this fact to—

(a) the applicant; and
(b) any relevant proprietor.

(2) In paragraph (1), "relevant proprietor" means—

(a) the proprietor of a registered trade mark or international trade mark (UK) which is an earlier trade mark in relation to which it appears to the registrar that the conditions set out in section 5(1) or (2) obtain but does not include a proprietor who does not wish to be notified and who has notified the registrar to this effect; and

(b) the proprietor of a Community trade mark or international trade mark (EC) which is an earlier trade mark in relation to which it appears to the registrar that the conditions set out in section 5(1) or (2) obtain and who has filed a request to be notified in relation to that mark in accordance with paragraph (4) below.

(3) References in paragraph (2) to the proprietor of a trade mark include a person who has applied for registration of a trade mark which, if registered, would be an earlier trade mark by virtue of section 6(1)(a) or (b).

(4) The proprietor of a Community trade mark or international trade mark (EC) may file a request to be notified in relation to that mark of the results of a notifiable search on Form TM6, which shall be filed electronically using the filing system provided on the Office website, or by such other means as the registrar may permit in any particular case, and shall be subject to payment of the prescribed fee.

(5) In paragraph (4) a "notifiable search" means any search under article 4 of the Trade Marks (Relative Grounds) Order 2007 conducted within the period of three years beginning with the date on which the request was filed.

(6) The filing of any request under paragraph (4) shall be subject to such terms or conditions as the registrar may specify generally by published notice or in any particular case by written notice to the person desiring to file the request otherwise than by electronic means.

(7) Rule 63 shall not apply to any decision made in pursuance of this rule.

(8) No decision made in pursuance of this rule shall be subject to appeal.

[74]

Compliance with request for expedited examination

15 Where the registrar receives a request for expedited examination under rule 5, the date on which the registrar shall be deemed to have notified the applicant whether or not it appears to the registrar that the requirements for registration are met shall be the date on which notice is sent to the applicant.

[75]

Publication, Observations, Oppositions and Registration

Publication of application for registration; section 38(1)

16 An application which has been accepted for registration shall be published in the Journal.

[76]

Opposition proceedings: filing of notice of opposition; section 38(2) (Form TM7)

17 (1) Any notice to the registrar of opposition to the registration, including the statement of the grounds of opposition, shall be filed on Form TM7.

(2) Unless paragraph (3) applies, the time prescribed for the purposes of section 38(2) shall be the period of two months beginning with the date on which the application was published.

(3) This paragraph applies where a request for an extension of time for the filing of Form TM7 has been made on Form TM7A, before the expiry of the period referred to in paragraph (2) and where this paragraph applies, the time prescribed for the purposes of section 38(2) in relation to any person having filed a Form TM7A (or, in the case of a company, any subsidiary or holding company of that company or any other subsidiary of that holding company) shall be the period of three months beginning with the date on which the application was published.

(4) Where a person makes a request for an extension of time under paragraph (3), Form TM7A shall be filed electronically using the filing system provided on the Office website or by such other means as the registrar may permit.

(5) Where the opposition is based on a trade mark which has been registered, there shall be included in the statement of the grounds of opposition a representation of that mark and—

- (a) the details of the authority with which the mark is registered;
- (b) the registration number of that mark;
- (c) the goods and services in respect of which—
  - (i) that mark is registered, and
  - (ii) the opposition is based; and
- (d) where the registration procedure for the mark was completed before the start of the period of five years ending with the date of publication, a statement detailing whether during the period referred to in section 6A(3)(a) the mark has been put to genuine use in relation to each of the goods and services in respect of which the opposition is based or whether there are proper reasons for non-use (for the purposes of rule 20 this is the "statement of use").

(6) Where the opposition is based on a trade mark in respect of which an application for registration has been made, there shall be included in the statement of the grounds of opposition a representation of that mark and those matters set out in paragraph (5)(a) to (c), with references to registration being construed as references to the application for registration.

(7) Where the opposition is based on an unregistered trade mark or other sign which the person opposing the application claims to be protected by virtue of any rule of law (in particular, the law of passing off), there shall be included in the statement of the grounds of opposition a representation of that mark or sign and the goods and services in respect of which such protection is claimed.

(8) The registrar shall send a copy of Form TM7 to the applicant and the date upon which this is sent shall, for the purposes of rule 18, be the "notification date".

(9) In this rule "subsidiary" and "holding company" have the same meaning as in the Companies Act 2006.

[77]

Opposition proceedings: filing of counter-statement and cooling off period (Forms TM8, TM9c & TM9t)

18 (1) The applicant shall, within the relevant period, file a Form TM8, which shall include a counter-statement.

(2) Where the applicant fails to file a Form TM8 or counter-statement within the relevant period, the application for registration, insofar as it relates to the goods and services in respect of which the opposition is directed, shall, unless the registrar otherwise directs, be treated as abandoned.

(3) Unless either paragraph (4), (5) or (6) applies, the relevant period shall begin on the notification date and end two months after that date.

(4) This paragraph applies where—

- (a) the applicant and the person opposing the registration agree to an extension of time for the filing of Form TM8;
- (b) within the period of two months beginning on the notification date, either party files Form TM9c requesting an extension of time for the filing of Form TM8; and
- (c) during the period beginning on the date Form TM9c was filed and ending nine months after the notification date, no notice to continue on Form TM9t is filed by the person opposing the registration and no request for a further extension of time for the filing of Form TM8 is filed on Form TM9e,

and where this paragraph applies the relevant period shall begin on the notification date and end nine months after that date.

(5) This paragraph applies where—

- (a) a request for an extension of time for the filing of Form TM8 has been filed on Form TM9c in accordance with paragraph (4)(b);
- (b) during the period referred to in paragraph (4)(c), either party files Form TM9e requesting a further extension of time for the filing of Form TM8 which request includes a statement confirming that the parties are seeking to negotiate a settlement of the opposition proceedings; and
- (c) the other party agrees to the further extension of time for the filing of Form TM8,

and where this paragraph applies the relevant period shall begin on the notification date and end eighteen months after that date.

(6) This paragraph applies where—

- (a) a request for an extension of time for the filing of Form TM8 has been filed on Form TM9c in accordance with paragraph (4)(b); and
- (b) the person opposing the registration has filed a notice to continue on Form TM9t,

and where this paragraph applies the relevant period shall begin on the notification date and end one month after the date on which Form TM9t was filed or two months after the notification date, whichever is the later.

(7) The registrar shall send a copy of Form TM8 to the person opposing the registration.

[78]

Opposition proceedings: preliminary indication (Form TM53)

19 (1) This rule applies if—

- (a) the opposition or part of it is based on the relative grounds of refusal set out in section 5(1) or (2); and
- (b) the registrar has not indicated to the parties that the registrar thinks that it is inappropriate for this rule to apply.

(2) After considering the statement of the grounds of opposition and the counter-statement the registrar shall send notice to the parties ("the preliminary indication") stating whether it appears to the registrar that—

(a) registration of the mark should not be refused in respect of all or any of the goods and services listed in the application on the grounds set out in section 5(1) or (2); or

(b) registration of the mark should be refused in respect of all or any of the goods and services listed in the application on the grounds set out in section 5(1) or (2).

(3) The date upon which the preliminary indication is sent shall be the "indication date".

(4) Where it appeared to the registrar under paragraph (2) that registration of the mark should not be refused in respect of all or any of the goods or services listed in the application on the grounds set out in section 5(1) or (2), the person opposing the registration shall, within one month of the indication date, file a notice of intention to proceed with the opposition based on those grounds by filing a Form TM53, otherwise that person's opposition to the registration of the mark in relation to those goods or services on the grounds set in section 5(1) or (2) shall be deemed to have been withdrawn

(5) Where it appeared to the registrar under paragraph (2) that registration of the mark should be refused in respect of all or any of the goods or services listed in the application on the grounds set out in section 5(1) or (2), the applicant shall, within one month of the indication date, file a notice of intention to proceed on Form TM53, otherwise the applicant shall be deemed to have withdrawn the request to register the mark in respect of the goods or services for which the registrar indicated registration should be refused.

(6) A person who files a Form TM53 shall, at the same time, send a copy to all other parties to the proceedings.

(7) The registrar need not give reasons for the preliminary indication nor shall the preliminary indication be subject to appeal.

[79]

Opposition proceedings: evidence rounds

20 (1) Where—

(a) Form TM53 has been filed by either party;

(b) the opposition or part of it is based on grounds other than those set out in section 5(1) or (2) and the applicant has filed a Form TM8; or

(c) the registrar has indicated to the parties that it is inappropriate for rule 19 to apply,

the registrar shall specify the periods within which evidence and submissions may be filed by the parties.

(2) Where—

(a) the opposition is based on an earlier trade mark of a kind falling within section 6(1)(c); or

(b) the opposition or part of it is based on grounds other than those set out in section 5(1) or (2); or

(c) the truth of a matter set out in the statement of use is either denied or not admitted by the applicant,

the person opposing the registration ("the opposer") shall file evidence supporting the opposition.

(3) Where the opposer files no evidence under paragraph (2), the opposer shall be deemed to have withdrawn the opposition to the registration to the extent that it is based on—

(a) the matters in paragraph (2)(a) or (b); or

(b) an earlier trade mark which has been registered and which is the subject of the statement of use referred to in paragraph (2)(c).

(4) The registrar may, at any time, give leave to either party to file evidence upon such terms as the registrar thinks fit.

[80]

Procedure for intervention

21 (1) If the opposition or part of it is based on the relative grounds for refusal set out in section 5(1), (2) or (3), any person in paragraph (3) may file an application to the registrar on Form TM27 for leave to intervene and the registrar may, after hearing the parties concerned if so required, refuse such leave or grant leave upon such terms and conditions (including any undertaking as to costs) as the registrar thinks fit.

(2) Any person granted leave to intervene shall, subject to any terms and conditions imposed in respect of the intervention, be treated as a party to the proceedings for the purposes of the application of the provisions of rules 19, 20 and 62 to 73.

(3) The persons referred to in paragraph (1) are—

(a) where the opposition is based on an earlier trade mark, a licensee of that mark; and

(b) where the opposition is based on an earlier collective mark or certification mark, an authorised user of that mark.

[81]

Observations on application to be sent to applicant; section 38(3)

22 The registrar shall send to the applicant a copy of any document containing observations made under section 38(3).

[82]

Publication of registration; section 40

23 On the registration of the trade mark the registrar shall publish the registration on the Office website, specifying the date upon which the trade mark was entered in the register.

[83]

Amendment of Application

Amendment of application; section 39 (Form TM21)

24 A request for an amendment of an application to correct an error or to change the name or address of the applicant or in respect of any amendment requested after publication of the application shall be made on Form TM21.

[84]

Amendment of application after publication; section 39 (Form TM7)

25 (1) Where, pursuant to section 39, a request is made for amendment of an application which has been published in the Journal and the amendment affects the representation of the trade mark or the goods or services covered by the application, the amendment or a statement of the effect of the amendment shall also be published in the Journal.

(2) Any person claiming to be affected by the amendment may, within one month of the date on which the amendment or a statement of the effect of the amendment was published under paragraph (1), give notice to the registrar of objection to the amendment on Form TM7 which shall include a statement of the grounds of objection which shall, in particular, indicate why the amendment would not fall within section 39(2).

(3) The registrar shall send a copy of Form TM7 to the applicant and the procedure in rules 17, 18 and 20 shall apply to the proceedings relating to the objection to the amendment as they apply to proceedings relating to opposition to an application for registration, but with the following modifications—

(a) any reference to—

(i) an application for registration shall be construed as a reference to a request for amendment of an application,

(ii) the person opposing the registration shall be construed as a reference to the person objecting to the amendment of an application,

(iii) the opposition shall be construed as a reference to the objection;

(b) the relevant period, referred to in rule 18(1), shall for these purposes be the period of two months beginning with the date upon which the registrar sent a copy of Form TM7 to the applicant; and

(c) rules 18(3) to (6), 20(2) and (3) shall not apply.

[85]

Division, Merger and Series of Marks

Division of application; section 41 (Form TM12)

26 (1) At any time before registration an applicant may send to the registrar a request on Form TM12 [to divide the specification] of the application for registration (the original application) into two or more separate applications (divisional applications), indicating for each division the specification of goods or services.

(2) Each divisional application shall be treated as a separate application for registration with the same filing date as the original application.

(3) Where the request to divide an application is sent after publication of the application, any objections in respect of, or opposition to, the original application shall be taken to apply to each divisional application and shall be proceeded with accordingly.

(4) Upon division of an original application in respect of which notice has been given to the registrar of particulars relating to the grant of a licence, or a security interest or any right in or under it, the notice and the particulars shall be deemed to apply in relation to each of the applications into which the original application has been divided.

NOTES

Amendment Para (1): words in square brackets substituted by SI 2009/2089.

[86]

Merger of separate applications or registrations; section 41 (Form TM17)

27 (1) An applicant who has made separate applications for registration of a mark may, at any time before preparations for the publication of any of the applications have been completed by the Office, request the registrar on Form TM17 to merge the separate applications into a single application.

(2) The registrar shall, if satisfied that all the applications which are the subject of the request for merger—

(a) are in respect of the same trade mark;
(b) bear the same date of application; and
(c) are, at the time of the request, in the name of the same person,

merge them into a single application.

(3) The proprietor of two or more registrations of a trade mark may request the registrar on Form TM17 to merge them into a single registration and the registrar shall, if satisfied that the registrations are in respect of the same trade mark, merge them into a single registration.

(4) Where any registration of a trade mark to be merged under paragraph (3) is subject to a disclaimer or limitation, the merged registration shall also be restricted accordingly.

(5) Where any registration of a trade mark to be merged under paragraph (3) has had registered in relation to it particulars relating to the grant of a licence or a security interest or any right in or under it, or of any memorandum or statement of the effect of a memorandum, the registrar shall enter in the register the same particulars in relation to the merged registration.

(6) The date of registration of the merged registration shall, where the separate registrations bear different dates of registration, be the latest of those dates.

[87]

Registration of a series of trade marks; section 41 (Form TM12)

28 [(1) An application may be made in accordance with rule 5 for the registration of a series of trade marks in a single registration provided that the series comprises of no more than six trade marks.

(1A) Where an application for registration of a series of trade marks comprises three or more trade marks, the application shall be subject to the payment of the prescribed fee for each trade mark in excess of two trade marks]

(2) Following an application under paragraph (1) the registrar shall, if satisfied that the marks constitute a series, accept the application.

(3) …

(4) …

(5) At any time the applicant for registration of a series of trade marks or the proprietor of a registered series of trade marks may request the deletion of a mark in that series and, following such request, the registrar shall delete the mark accordingly.

(6) Where under paragraph (5) the registrar deletes a trade mark from an application for registration, the application, in so far as it relates to the deleted mark, shall be treated as withdrawn.

(7) …

NOTES

Amendment Paras (1), (1A): substituted for para (1) by SI 2009/2089.
Paras (3), (4), (7): revoked by SI 2009/2089.

[88]

Collective and Certification Marks

Filing of regulations for collective and certification marks; Schedules 1 & 2 (Form TM35)

29 Where an application for registration of a collective or certification mark is filed, the applicant shall, within such period of not less than three months as the registrar may specify, file Form TM35 accompanied by a copy of the regulations governing the use of the mark.

[89]

Amendment of regulations of collective and certification marks; Schedule 1 paragraph 10 and Schedule 2 paragraph 11 (Forms TM36 & TM7)

30 (1) An application for the amendment of the regulations governing the use of a registered collective or certification mark shall be filed on Form TM36.

(2) Where it appears to be expedient to the registrar that the amended regulations should be made available to the public the registrar shall publish a notice in the Journal indicating where copies of the amended regulations may be inspected.

(3) Any person may, within two months of the date of publication of the notice under paragraph (2), make observations to the registrar on the amendments relating to the matters referred to in paragraph 6(1) of Schedule 1 to the Act in relation to a collective mark, or paragraph 7(1) of Schedule 2 to the Act in relation to a certification mark and the registrar shall send a copy of those observations to the proprietor.

(4) Any person may, within two months of the date on which the notice was published under paragraph (2), give notice to the registrar of opposition to the amendment on Form TM7 which shall include a statement of the grounds of opposition indicating why the amended regulations do not comply with the requirements of paragraph 6(1) of Schedule 1 to the Act, or, as the case may be, paragraph 7(1) of Schedule 2 to the Act.

(5) The registrar shall send a copy of Form TM7 to the proprietor and the procedure in rules 18 and 20 shall apply to the proceedings relating to the opposition to the amendment as they apply to proceedings relating to opposition to an application for registration, but with the following modifications—

- (a) any reference to—
  - (i) the applicant shall be construed as a reference to the proprietor,
  - (ii) an application for registration shall be construed as a reference to an application for the amendment of the regulations,
  - (iii) the person opposing the registration shall be construed as a reference to the person opposing the amendment of the regulations;
- (b) the relevant period, referred to in rule 18(1), shall for these purposes be the period of two months beginning with the date upon which the registrar sent a copy of Form TM7 to the proprietor;
- (c) rules 18(3) to (6), 20(2) and (3) shall not apply.

[90]

Registration subject to disclaimer or limitation; section 13

31 Where the applicant for registration of a trade mark or the proprietor by notice in writing sent to the registrar—

(a) disclaims any right to the exclusive use of any specified element of the trade mark; or

(b) agrees that the rights conferred by the registration shall be subject to a specified territorial or other limitation,

the registrar shall make the appropriate entry in the register and publish such disclaimer or limitation.

[91]

Alteration of registered trade marks; section 44 (Forms TM25 & TM7)

32 (1) The proprietor of a registered trade mark may request the registrar on Form TM25 for such alteration of the mark as is permitted under section 44 and following such request the registrar may require evidence as to the circumstances in which the application is made.

(2) Where, upon the request of the proprietor, the registrar proposes to allow such alteration, the registrar shall publish the mark as altered in the Journal.

(3) Any person claiming to be affected by the alteration may, within two months of the date on which the mark as altered was published under paragraph (2), give notice to the registrar of objection to the alteration on Form TM7 which shall include a statement of the grounds of objection.

(4) The registrar shall send a copy of Form TM7 to the proprietor and the procedure in rules 18 and 20 shall apply to the proceedings relating to the objection to the alteration as they apply to proceedings relating to opposition to an application for registration, but with the following modifications—

(a) any reference to—

(i) the applicant shall be construed as a reference to the proprietor,

(ii) an application for registration shall be construed as a reference to a request for alteration,

(iii) the person opposing the registration shall be construed as a reference to the person objecting to the alteration,

(iv) the opposition shall be construed as a reference to the objection;

(b) the relevant period, referred to in rule 18(1), shall for these purposes be the period of two months beginning with the date upon which the registrar sent a copy of Form TM7 to the proprietor;

(c) rules 18(3) to (6), 20(2) and (3) shall not apply.

[92]

Surrender of registered trade mark; section 45 (Forms TM22 & TM23)

33 (1) Subject to paragraph (2), the proprietor may surrender a registered trade mark, by sending notice to the registrar—

(a) on Form TM22 in respect of all the goods or services for which it is registered; or

(b) on Form TM23, in respect only of those goods or services specified by the proprietor in the notice.

(2) A notice under paragraph (1) shall be of no effect unless the proprietor in that notice—

(a) gives the name and address of any person having a registered interest in the mark; and

(b) certifies that any such person—

(i) has been sent not less than three months' notice of the proprietor's intention to surrender the mark, or

(ii) is not affected or if affected consents to the surrender.

(3) The registrar shall, upon the surrender taking effect, make the appropriate entry in the register and publish the date of surrender on the Office website.

[93]

Renewal and Restoration

Reminder of renewal of registration; section 43

34 (1) Subject to paragraph (2) below, at any time not earlier than six months nor later than one month before the expiration of the last registration of a trade mark, the registrar shall (except where renewal has already been affected under rule 35) send to the registered proprietor notice of the approaching expiration and inform the proprietor at the same time that the registration may be renewed in the manner described in rule 35.

(2) If it appears to the registrar that a trade mark may be registered under section 40 at any time within six months before or at any time on or after the date on which renewal would be due (by reference to the date of application for registration), the registrar shall be taken to have complied with paragraph (1) if the registrar sends to the applicant notice to that effect within one month following the date of actual registration.

[94]

Renewal of registration; section 43 (Form TM11)

35 Renewal of registration shall be effected by filing a request for renewal on Form TM11 at any time within the period of six months ending on the date of the expiration of the registration.

[95]

Delayed renewal and removal of registration; section 43 (Form TM11)

36 (1) If on the expiration of the last registration of a trade mark the renewal fee has not been paid, the registrar shall publish that fact.

(2) If, within six months from the date of the expiration of the last registration, a request for renewal is filed on Form TM11 accompanied by the appropriate renewal fee and additional renewal fee, the registrar shall renew the registration without removing the mark from the register.

(3) Where no request for renewal is filed, the registrar shall, subject to rule 37, remove the mark from the register.

(4) Where a mark is due to be registered after the date on which it is due for renewal (by reference to the date of application for registration), the request for renewal shall be filed together with the renewal fee and additional renewal fee within six months after the date of actual registration.

(5) The removal of the registration of a trade mark shall be published on the Office website.

[96]

Restoration of registration; section 43 (Form TM13)

37 (1) Where the registrar has removed the mark from the register for failure to renew its registration in accordance with rule 36, the registrar may, following receipt of a request filed on Form TM13 within six months of the date of the removal of the mark accompanied by the appropriate renewal fee and appropriate restoration fee—

(a) restore the mark to the register; and

(b) renew its registration,

if, having regard to the circumstances of the failure to renew, the registrar is satisfied that it is just to do so.

(2) The restoration of the registration, including the date of restoration, shall be published on the Office website.

[97]

Revocation, Invalidation and Rectification

Application for revocation (on the grounds of non-use); section 46(1)(a) or (b) (Forms TM8(N) & TM26(N))

38 (1) An application to the registrar for revocation of a trade mark under section 46, on the grounds set out in section 46(1)(a) or (b), shall be made on Form TM26(N).

(2) The registrar shall send a copy of Form TM26(N) to the proprietor.

(3) The proprietor shall, within two months of the date on which he was sent a copy of Form TM26(N) by the registrar, file a Form TM8(N), which shall include a counter-statement.

(4) Where the proprietor fails to file evidence of use of the mark or evidence supporting the reasons for non-use of the mark within the period specified in paragraph (3) above the registrar shall specify a further period of not less than two months within which the evidence shall be filed.

(5) The registrar shall send a copy of Form TM8(N) and any evidence of use, or evidence supporting reasons for non-use, filed by the proprietor to the applicant.

(6) Where the proprietor fails to file a Form TM8(N) within the period specified in paragraph (3) the registration of the mark shall, unless the registrar directs otherwise, be revoked.

(7) Where the proprietor fails to file evidence within the period specified under paragraph (3) or any further period specified under paragraph (4), the registrar may treat the proprietor as not opposing the application and the registration of the mark shall, unless the registrar directs otherwise, be revoked.

(8) The registrar may, at any time, give leave to either party to file evidence upon such terms as the registrar thinks fit.

[98]

Application for revocation (on grounds other than non-use); section 46(1)(c) or (d) (Forms TM8 & TM26(O))

39 (1) An application to the registrar for revocation of a trade mark under section 46, on the grounds set out in section 46(1)(c) or (d), shall be made on Form TM26(O) and shall include a statement of the grounds on which the application is made and be accompanied by a statement of truth.

(2) The registrar shall send a copy of Form TM26(O) and the statement of the grounds on which the application is made to the proprietor.

(3) The proprietor shall, within two months of the date on which he was sent a copy of Form TM26(O) and the statement by the registrar, file a Form TM8 which shall include a counter-statement, otherwise the registrar may treat the proprietor as not opposing the application and the registration of the mark shall, unless the registrar directs otherwise, be revoked.

(4) The registrar shall send a copy of Form TM8 to the applicant.

[99]

Application for revocation (on grounds other than non-use): evidence rounds

40 (1) Where the [proprietor] has filed a Form TM8, the registrar shall specify the periods within which further evidence may be filed by the parties.

(2) Where the applicant files no further evidence in support of the application the applicant, shall, unless the registrar otherwise directs, be deemed to have withdrawn the application.

(3) The registrar shall notify the proprietor of any direction given under paragraph (2).

(4) The registrar may, at any time give leave to either party to file evidence upon such terms as the registrar thinks fit.

NOTES

Amendment Para (1): word in square brackets substituted by SI 2008/2300.

[100]

Application for invalidation: filing of application and counter-statement; section 47 (Forms TM8 & TM26(I))

41 (1) An application to the registrar for a declaration of invalidity under section 47 shall be filed on Form TM26(I) and shall include a statement of the grounds on which the application is made and be accompanied by a statement of truth.

(2) Where the application is based on a trade mark which has been registered, there shall be included in the statement of the grounds on which the application is made a representation of that mark and—

- (a) the details of the authority with which the mark is registered;
- (b) the registration number of that mark;
- (c) the goods and services in respect of which—
  - (i) that mark is registered, and
  - (ii) the application is based; and
- (d) where neither section 47(2A)(a) nor (b) applies to the mark, a statement detailing whether during the period referred to in section 47(2B)(a) it has been put to genuine use in relation to each of the goods and services in respect of which the application is based or whether there are proper reasons for non-use (for the purposes of rule 42 this is the "statement of use").

(3) Where the application is based on a trade mark in respect of which an application for registration has been made, there shall be included in the statement of the grounds on which the application is made a representation of that mark and those matters set out in paragraph (2)(a) to (c), with references to registration being construed as references to the application for registration.

(4) Where the application is based on an unregistered trade mark or other sign which the applicant claims to be protected by virtue of any rule of law (in particular, the law of passing off), there shall be included in the statement of the grounds on which the application is made a representation of that mark or sign and the goods and services in respect of which such protection is claimed.

(5) The registrar shall send a copy of Form TM26(I) and the statement of the grounds on which the application is made to the proprietor.

(6) The proprietor shall, within two months of the date on which a copy of Form TM26(I) and the statement was sent by the registrar, file a Form TM8, which shall include a counter-statement, otherwise the registrar may treat the proprietor as not opposing the application and registration of the mark shall, unless the registrar otherwise directs, be declared invalid.

(7) The registrar shall send a copy of Form TM8 to the applicant.

[101]

Application for invalidation: evidence rounds

42 (1) Where the proprietor has filed Form TM8, the registrar shall send notice to the applicant inviting the applicant to file evidence in support of the grounds on which the application is made and any submissions and to send a copy to all the other parties.

(2) The registrar shall specify the periods within which evidence and submissions may be filed by the parties.

(3) Where—

- (a) the application is based on an earlier trade mark of a kind falling within section 6(1)(c); or
- (b) the application or part of it is based on grounds other than those set out in section 5(1) or (2); or
- (c) the truth of a matter set out in the statement of use is either denied or not admitted by the proprietor,

the applicant shall file evidence supporting the application.

(4) Where the applicant files no evidence under paragraph (3), the applicant shall be deemed to have withdrawn the application to the extent that it is based on—

- (a) the matters in paragraph (3)(a) or (b); or
- (b) an earlier trade mark which has been registered and is the subject of the statement of use referred to in paragraph (3)(c).

(5) The registrar may, at any time give leave to either party to file evidence upon such terms as the registrar thinks fit.

[102]

Setting aside cancellation of application or revocation or invalidation of registration; (Form TM29)

43 (1) This rule applies where—

(a) an application for registration is treated as abandoned under rule 18(2);
(b) the registration of a mark is revoked under rule 38(6) or rule 39(3); or
(c) the registration of a mark is declared invalid under rule 41(6),

and the applicant or the proprietor (as the case may be) claims that the decision of the registrar to treat the application as abandoned or revoke the registration of the mark or declare the mark invalid (as the case may be) ("the original decision") should be set aside on the grounds set out in paragraph (4).

(2) Where this rule applies, the applicant or the proprietor shall, within a period of six months beginning with the date that the application was refused or the register was amended to reflect the revocation or the declaration of invalidity (as the case may be), file an application on Form TM29 to set aside the decision of the registrar and shall include evidence in support of the application and shall copy the form and the evidence to the other party to the original proceedings under the rules referred to in paragraph (1).

(3) Where the applicant or the proprietor demonstrates to the reasonable satisfaction of the registrar that the failure to file Form TM8 within the period specified in the rules referred to in paragraph (1) was due to a failure to receive Form TM7, Form TM26(N), Form TM26(O) or Form TM26(I) (as the case may be), the original decision may be set aside on such terms and conditions as the registrar thinks fit.

(4) In considering whether to set aside the original decision the matters to which the registrar must have regard include whether the person seeking to set aside the decision made an application to do so promptly upon becoming aware of the original decision and any prejudice which may be caused to the other party to the original proceedings if the original decision were to be set aside.

[103]

Procedure on application for rectification; section 64 (Form TM26(R))

44 (1) An application for rectification of an error or omission in the register under section 64(1) shall be made on Form TM26(R) together with:

(a) a statement of the grounds on which the application is made; and
(b) any evidence to support those grounds.

(2) Where any application is made under paragraph (1) by a person other than the proprietor of the registered trade mark the registrar—

(a) shall send a copy of the application and the statement, together with any evidence filed, to the proprietor; and
(b) may give such direction with regard to the filing of subsequent evidence and upon such terms as the registrar thinks fit.

[104]

Procedure for intervention

45 (1) Any person, other than the registered proprietor, claiming to have an interest in proceedings on an application under rule 38, 39, 41 or 44, may file an application to the registrar on Form TM27 for leave to intervene, stating the nature of the person's interest and the registrar may, after hearing the parties concerned if they request a hearing, refuse leave or grant leave upon such terms and conditions (including any undertaking as to costs) as the registrar thinks fit.

(2) Any person granted leave to intervene shall, subject to any terms and conditions imposed in respect of the intervention, be treated as a party to the proceedings for the purposes of the application of the provisions of rules 38 to 40, 41 and 42 or 44 (as appropriate) and rules 62 to 73.

[105]

The Register

Form of register; section 63(1)

46 The register required to be maintained by the registrar under section 63(1) need not be kept in documentary form.

[106]

Entry in register of particulars of registered trade marks; section 63(2) (Form TM24)

47 In addition to the entries in the register of registered trade marks required to be made by section 63(2)(a), there shall be entered in the register in respect of each trade mark the following particulars—

(a) the date of registration as determined in accordance with section 40(3) (that is to say, the date of the filing of the application for registration);
(b) the date of completion of the registration procedure;
(c) the priority date (if any) to be accorded pursuant to a claim to a right to priority made under section 35 or 36;
(d) the name and address of the proprietor;
(e) the address for service (if any) filed under rule 11;
(f) any disclaimer or limitation of rights under section 13(1)(a) or (b);
(g) any memorandum or statement of the effect of any memorandum relating to a trade mark of which the registrar has been notified on Form TM24;
(h) the goods or services in respect of which the mark is registered;
(i) where the mark is a collective or certification mark, that fact;
(j) where the mark is registered pursuant to section 5(5) with the consent of the proprietor of an earlier trade mark or other earlier right, that fact;
(k) where the mark is registered pursuant to a transformation application,
  (i) the number of the international registration, and
  (ii) either:—
    (aa) the date accorded to the international registration under Article 3(4), or
    (bb) the date of recordal of the request for extension to the United Kingdom of the international registration under Article 3*ter*,

  as the case may be, of the Madrid Protocol;
(l) where the mark arises from the conversion of a Community trade mark or an application for a Community trade mark, the number of any other registered trade mark from which the Community trade mark or the application for a Community trade mark claimed seniority and the earliest seniority date.

NOTES

Initial Commencement Specified date: 1 October 2008: see r 1.

[107]

Entry in register of particulars of registrable transactions; section 25

48 Upon application made to the registrar by such person as is mentioned in section 25(1)(a) or (b) there shall be entered in the register in respect of each trade mark the following particulars of registrable transactions together with the date on which the entry is made—

(a) in the case of an assignment of a registered trade mark or any right in it—
  (i) the name and address of the assignee,
  (ii) the date of the assignment, and
  (iii) where the assignment is in respect of any right in the mark, a description of the right assigned;
(b) in the case of the grant of a licence under a registered trade mark—
  (i) the name and address of the licensee,
  (ii) where the licence is an exclusive licence, that fact,
  (iii) where the licence is limited, a description of the limitation, and
  (iv) the duration of the licence if the same is or is ascertainable as a definite period;
(c) in the case of the grant of any security interest over a registered trade mark or any right in or under it—
  (i) the name and address of the grantee,
  (ii) the nature of the interest (whether fixed or floating), and
  (iii) the extent of the security and the right in or under the mark secured;

(d) in the case of the making by personal representatives of an assent in relation to a registered trade mark or any right in or under it—

(i) the name and address of the person in whom the mark or any right in or under it vests by virtue of the assent, and

(ii) the date of the assent;

(e) in the case of a court or other competent authority transferring a registered trade mark or any right in or under it—

(i) the name and address of the transferee,

(ii) the date of the order, and

(iii) where the transfer is in respect of a right in the mark, a description of the right transferred; and

(f) in the case of any amendment of the registered particulars relating to a licence under a registered trade mark or a security interest over a registered trade mark or any right in or under it, particulars to reflect such amendment.

[108]

Application to register or give notice of transaction; sections 25 & 27(3) (Form TM16, TM24, TM50 & TM51)

49 (1) An application to register particulars of a transaction to which section 25 applies or to give notice to the registrar of particulars of a transaction to which section 27(3) applies shall be made—

(a) relating to an assignment or transaction other than a transaction referred to in sub-paragraphs (b) to (d) below, on Form TM16;

(b) relating to a grant of a licence, on Form TM50;

(c) relating to an amendment to, or termination of a licence, on Form TM51;

(d) relating to the grant, amendment or termination of any security interest, on Form TM24; and

(e) relating to the making by personal representatives of an assent or to an order of a court or other competent authority, on Form TM24.

(2) An application under paragraph (1) shall—

(a) where the transaction is an assignment, be signed by or on behalf of the parties to the assignment;

(b) where the transaction falls within sub-paragraphs (b), (c) or (d) of paragraph (1), be signed by or on behalf of the grantor of the licence or security interest,

or be accompanied by such documentary evidence as suffices to establish the transaction.

(3) Where an application to give notice to the registrar has been made of particulars relating to an application for registration of a trade mark, upon registration of the trade mark, the registrar shall enter those particulars in the register.

[109]

Public inspection of register; section 63(3)

50 (1) The register shall be open for public inspection at the Office during the hours of business of the Office as published in accordance with rule 80.

(2) Where any portion of the register is kept otherwise than in documentary form, the right of inspection is a right to inspect the material on the register.

[110]

Supply of certified copies etc; section 63(3) (Form TM31R)

51 The registrar shall supply a certified copy or extract or uncertified copy or extract, as requested on Form TM31R, of any entry in the register.

[111]

Request for change of name or address in register; section 64(4) (Form TM21)

52 The registrar shall, on a request made on Form TM21 by the proprietor of a registered trade mark or a licensee or any person having an interest in or charge on a registered trade mark which has been registered under rule 48 ("the applicant"), enter a change in the applicant's name or address as recorded in the register.

[112]

Removal of matter from register; sections 25(5)(b) and 64(5) (Form TM7)

53 (1) Where it appears to the registrar that any matter in the register has ceased to have effect, before removing it from the register—

(a) the registrar may publish in the Journal the fact that it is intended to remove that matter, and

(b) where any person appears to the registrar to be affected by the removal, notice of the intended removal shall be sent to that person.

(2) Within two months of the date on which the intention to remove the matter is published, or notice of the intended removal is sent, as the case may be—

(a) any person may file notice of opposition to the removal on form TM7; and

(b) the person to whom a notice is sent under paragraph (1)(b) may file in writing their objections, if any, to the removal,

and where such opposition or objections are made, rule 63 shall apply.

(3) If the registrar is satisfied after considering any objections or opposition to the removal that the matter has not ceased to have effect, the registrar shall not remove it.

(4) Where there has been no response to the registrar's notice the registrar may remove the matter and where representations objecting to the removal of the entry have been made the registrar may, if after considering the objections the registrar is of the view that the entry or any part of it has ceased to have effect, remove it or the appropriate part of it.

[113]

Change of Classification

Change of classification; sections 65(2) & 76(1)

54 (1) The registrar may at any time amend an entry in the register which relates to the classification of a registered trade mark so that it accords with the version of the Nice Classification that has effect at that time.

(2) Before making any amendment to the register under paragraph (1) the registrar shall give the proprietor of the mark written notice of the proposed amendments and shall at the same time advise the proprietor that—

(a) the proprietor may make written objections to the proposals, within two months of the date of the notice, stating the grounds of those objections; and

(b) if no written objections are received within the period specified the registrar shall publish the proposals and the proprietor shall not be entitled to make any objections to the proposals upon such publication.

(3) If the proprietor makes no written objections within the period specified in paragraph (2)(a) or at any time before the expiration of that period decides not to make any objections and gives the registrar written notice to this effect, the registrar shall as soon as practicable after the expiration of that period or upon receipt of the notice publish the proposals in the Journal.

(4) Where the proprietor makes written objections within the period specified in paragraph (2)(a), the registrar shall, as soon as practicable after having considered the objections, publish the proposals in the Journal or, where the registrar has amended the proposals, publish the proposals as amended in the Journal; and the registrar's decision shall be final and not subject to appeal.

[114]

Opposition to proposals; sections 65(3), (5) & 76(1) (Form TM7)

55 (1) Any person may, within two months of the date on which the proposals were published under rule 54, give notice to the registrar of opposition to the proposals on Form TM7 which shall include a statement of the grounds of opposition which shall, in particular, indicate why the proposed amendments would be contrary to section 65(3).

(2) If no notice of opposition under paragraph (1) is filed within the time specified, or where any opposition has been determined, the registrar shall make the amendments as proposed and shall enter in the register the date when they were made; and the registrar's decision shall be final and not subject to appeal.

[115]

Request for Information, Inspection of Documents and Confidentiality

Request for information; section 67(1) (Form TM31C)

56 A request for information relating to an application for registration or to a registered trade mark shall be made on Form TM31C

[116]

Information available before publication; section 67(2)

57 (1) Before publication of an application for registration the registrar shall make available for inspection by the public the application and any amendments made to it and any particulars contained in a notice given to the registrar under rule 49.

(2) Nothing in section 67(2) relating to publication of information shall be construed as preventing the publication of decisions on cases relating to trade marks decided by the registrar.

[117]

Inspection of documents; sections 67 & 76(1)

58 (1) Subject to paragraphs (2) and (3), the registrar shall permit all documents filed or kept at the Office in relation to a registered mark or, where an application for the registration of a trade mark has been published, in relation to that application, to be inspected.

(2) The registrar shall not be obliged to permit the inspection of any such document as is mentioned in paragraph (1) until the completion of any procedure, or the stage in the procedure which is relevant to the document in question, which the registrar is required or permitted to carry out under the Act or these Rules.

(3) The right of inspection under paragraph (1) does not apply to—

(a) any document prepared in the Office solely for its own use;
(b) any document sent to the Office, whether at its request or otherwise, for inspection and subsequent return to the sender;
(c) any request for information under rule 56;
(d) any document received by the Office which the registrar considers should be treated as confidential;
(e) any document in respect of which the registrar issues directions under rule 59 that it be treated as confidential.

(4) Nothing in paragraph (1) shall be construed as imposing on the registrar any duty of making available for public inspection—

(a) any document or part of a document which in the registrar's opinion disparages any person in a way likely to cause damage to that person; or
(b) any document or information filed at or sent to or by the Office before 31st October 1994; or
(c) any document or information filed at or sent to or by the Office after 31st October 1994 relating to an application for registration of a trade mark under the Trade Marks Act 1938.

(5) No appeal shall lie from a decision of the registrar under paragraph (4) not to make any document or part of a document available for public inspection.

[118]

Confidential documents

59 (1) Where a document (other than a form required by the registrar and published in accordance with rule 3) is filed at the Office and the person filing it requests at the time of filing that it or a specified part of it be treated as confidential, giving reasons for the request, the registrar may direct that it or part of it, as the case may be, be treated as confidential, and the document shall not be open to public inspection while the matter is being determined by the registrar.

(2) Where such direction has been given and not withdrawn, nothing in this rule shall be taken to authorise or require any person to be allowed to inspect the document or part of it to which the direction relates except by leave of the registrar.

(3) The registrar shall not withdraw any direction given under this rule without prior consultation with the person at whose request the direction was given, unless the registrar is satisfied that such prior consultation is not reasonably practical.

(4) The registrar may where the registrar considers that any document issued by the Office should be treated as confidential so direct, and upon such direction that document shall not be open to public inspection except by leave of the registrar.

(5) Where a direction is given under this rule for a document to be treated as confidential a record of the fact shall be filed with the document.

[119]

Agents

Proof of authorisation of agent may be required; section 82 (Form TM33)

60 (1) Where an agent has been authorised under section 82, the registrar may in a particular case require the personal signature or presence of the agent or the person authorising the agent to act as agent.

(2) Subject to paragraph (3), where a person appoints an agent for the first time or appoints one agent in substitution for another, the newly appointed agent shall file Form TM33.

(3) Where after a person has become a party to proceedings involving a third party before the registrar, the person appoints an agent for the first time or appoints one agent in substitution for another, the newly appointed agent shall file Form TM33P.

(4) Any act required or authorised by the Act in connection with the registration of a trade mark or any procedure relating to a trade mark may not be done by or to the newly appointed agent until on or after the date on which the newly appointed agent files Form TM33 or TM33P as appropriate.

(5) The registrar may by notice in writing require an agent to produce evidence of his authority under section 82.

[120]

Registrar may refuse to deal with certain agents; section 88

61 The registrar may refuse to recognise as agent in respect of any business under the Act—

- (a) a person who has been convicted of an offence under section 84;
- (b) an individual whose name has been erased from and not restored to, or who is suspended from, the register of trade mark agents on the ground of misconduct;
- (c) a person who is found by the Secretary of State to have been guilty of such conduct as would, in the case of an individual registered in that register, render that person liable to have their name erased from it on the ground of misconduct;
- (d) a partnership or body corporate of which one of the partners or directors is a person whom the registrar could refuse to recognise under paragraph (a), (b) or (c).

[121]

Proceedings Before and Decision of Registrar, Evidence and Costs

General powers of registrar in relation to proceedings

62 (1) Except where the Act or these Rules otherwise provide, the registrar may give such directions as to the management of any proceedings as the registrar thinks fit, and in particular may—

(a) require a document, information or evidence to be filed within such period as the registrar may specify;
(b) require a translation of any document;
(c) require a party or a party's legal representative to attend a hearing;
(d) hold a hearing by telephone or by using any other method of direct oral communication;
(e) allow a statement of case to be amended;
(f) stay the whole, or any part, of the proceedings either generally or until a specified date or event;
(g) consolidate proceedings;
(h) direct that part of any proceedings be dealt with as separate proceedings;
(i) exclude any evidence which the registrar considers to be inadmissible.

(2) The registrar may control the evidence by giving directions as to—

(a) the issues on which evidence is required; and
(b) the way in which the evidence is to be placed before the registrar.

(3) When the registrar gives directions under any provision of these Rules, the registrar may—

(a) make them subject to conditions; and
(b) specify the consequences of failure to comply with the directions or a condition.

(4) The registrar may at any stage of any proceedings direct that the parties to the proceedings attend a case management conference or pre-hearing review.

[122]

Decisions of registrar to be taken after hearing

63 (1) Without prejudice to any provisions of the Act or these Rules requiring the registrar to hear any party to proceedings under the Act or these Rules, or to give such party an opportunity to be heard, the registrar shall, before taking any decision on any matter under the Act or these Rules which is or may be adverse to any party to any proceedings, give that party an opportunity to be heard.

(2) The registrar shall give that party at least fourteen days' notice, beginning on the date on which notice is sent, of the time when the party may be heard unless the party consents to shorter notice.

[123]

Evidence in proceedings before the registrar; section 69

64 (1) Subject to rule 62(2) and as follows, evidence filed in any proceedings under the Act or these Rules may be given—

(a) by witness statement, affidavit, statutory declaration; or
(b) in any other form which would be admissible as evidence in proceedings before the court.

(2) A witness statement may only be given in evidence if it includes a statement of truth.

(3) The general rule is that evidence at hearings is to be by witness statement unless the registrar or any enactment requires otherwise.

(4) For the purposes of these Rules, a statement of truth—

(a) means a statement that the person making the statement believes that the facts stated in a particular document are true; and
(b) shall be dated and signed by—
    (i) in the case of a witness statement, the maker of the statement,
    (ii) in any other case, the party or legal representative of such party.

(5) In these Rules, a witness statement is a written statement signed by a person that contains the evidence which that person would be allowed to give orally.

(6) Under these Rules, evidence shall only be considered filed when—

(a) it has been received by the registrar; and
(b) it has been sent to all other parties to the proceedings.

[124]

Registrar to have power of an official referee; section 69

65 The registrar shall have the powers of an official referee of the Supreme Court as regards—

(a) the attendance of witnesses and their examination on oath; and
(b) the discovery and production of documents,

but the registrar shall have no power to punish summarily for contempt.

[125]

Hearings before registrar to be in public

66 (1) The hearing before the registrar of any dispute between two or more parties relating to any matter in connection with an application for the registration of a mark or a registered mark shall be in public unless the registrar, after consultation with those parties who appear in person or are represented at the hearing, otherwise directs.

(2) …

NOTES
Amendment Para (2): revoked by SI 2008/2683.

[126]

Costs of proceedings; section 68

67 The registrar may, in any proceedings under the Act or these Rules, by order award to any party such costs as the registrar may consider reasonable, and direct how and by what parties they are to be paid.

[127]

Security for costs; section 68

68 (1) The registrar may require any person who is a party in any proceedings under the Act or these Rules to give security for costs in relation to those proceedings; and may also require security for the costs of any appeal from the registrar's decision.

(2) In default of such security being given, the registrar, in the case of the proceedings before the registrar, or in the case of an appeal, the person appointed under section 76 may treat the party in default as having withdrawn their application, opposition, objection or intervention, as the case may be.

[128]

Decision of registrar (Form TM5)

69 (1) The registrar shall send to each party to the proceedings written notice of any decision made in any proceedings before the registrar stating the reasons for that decision and for the purposes of any appeal against that decision, subject to paragraph (2), the date on which the notice is sent shall be taken to be the date of the decision.

(2) Where a statement of the reasons for the decision is not included in the notice sent under paragraph (1), any party may, within one month of the date on which the notice was sent to that party, request the registrar on Form TM5 to send a statement of the reasons for the decision and upon such request the registrar shall send such a statement, and the date on which that statement is sent shall be deemed to be the date of the registrar's decision for the purpose of any appeal against it.

[129]

Appeals

Decisions subject to appeal; section 76(1)

70 (1) Except as otherwise expressly provided by these Rules an appeal lies from any decision of the registrar made under these Rules relating to a dispute between two or more parties in connection with a trade mark, including a decision which terminates the proceedings as regards one of the parties or a decision awarding costs to any party ("a final decision") or a decision which is made at any point in the proceedings prior to a final decision ("an interim decision").

(2) An interim decision (including a decision refusing leave to appeal under this paragraph) may only be appealed against independently of any appeal against a final decision with the leave of the registrar.

[130]

Appeal to person appointed; section 76

71 (1) Notice of appeal to the person appointed under section 76 shall be filed on Form TM55 which shall include the appellant's grounds of appeal and his case in support of the appeal.

(2) Such notice shall be filed with the registrar within the period of 28 days beginning with the date of the registrar's decision which is the subject of the appeal ("the original decision").

(3) The registrar shall send the notice and the statement to the person appointed.

(4) Where any person other than the appellant was a party to the proceedings before the registrar in which the original decision was made ("the respondent"), the registrar shall send to the respondent a copy of the notice and the statement and the respondent may, within the period of 21 days beginning with the date on which the notice and statement was sent, file a notice responding to the notice of appeal.

(5) The respondent's notice shall specify any grounds on which the respondent considers the original decision should be maintained where these differ from or are additional to the grounds given by the registrar in the original decision.

(6) The registrar shall send a copy of the respondent's notice to the person appointed and a copy to the appellant.

[131]

Determination whether appeal should be referred to court; section 76(3)

72 (1) Within 28 days of the date on which the notice of appeal is sent to the respondent by the registrar under rule 71(4);

(a) the registrar; or
(b) any person who was a party to the proceedings in which the decision appealed against was made,

may request that the person appointed refer the appeal to the court.

(2) Where the registrar requests that the appeal be referred to the court, the registrar shall send a copy of the request to each party to the proceedings.

(3) A request under paragraph (1)(b) shall be sent to the registrar following which the registrar shall send it to the person appointed and shall send a copy of the request to any other party to the proceedings.

(4) Within 28 days of the date on which a copy of a request is sent by the registrar under paragraph (2) or (3), the person to whom it is sent may make representations as to whether the appeal should be referred to the court.

(5) In any case where it appears to the person appointed that a point of general legal importance is involved in the appeal, the person appointed shall send to the registrar and to every party to the proceedings in which the decision appealed against was made, notice to that effect.

(6) Within 28 days of the date on which a notice is sent under paragraph (5), the person to whom it was sent may make representations as to whether the appeal should be referred to the court.

[132]

Hearing and determination of appeal; section 76(4)

73 (1) Where the person appointed does not refer the appeal to the court, the person appointed shall send written notice of the time and place appointed for the oral hearing of the appeal—

(a) where no person other than the appellant was a party to the proceedings in which the decision appealed against was made, to the registrar and to the appellant; and
(b) in any other case, to the registrar and to each person who was a party to those proceedings.

(2) The person appointed shall send the notice at least fourteen days before the time appointed for the oral hearing.

(3) If all the persons notified under paragraph (1) inform the person appointed that they do not wish to make oral representations then—

(a) the person appointed may hear and determine the case on the basis of any written representations; and

(b) the time and place appointed for the oral hearing may be vacated.

(4) Rules 62, 65, 67 and 68 shall apply to the person appointed and to proceedings before the person appointed as they apply to the registrar and to proceedings before the registrar.

(5) If there is an oral hearing of the appeal then rule 66 shall apply to the person appointed and to proceedings before the person appointed as it applies to the registrar and to proceedings before the registrar.

(6) A copy of the decision of the appointed person shall be sent, with a statement of the reasons for the decision, to the registrar and to each person who was a party to the appeal.

[133]

Correction of Irregularities, Calculation and Extension of Time

Correction of irregularities in procedure

74 (1) Subject to rule 77, the registrar may authorise the rectification of any irregularity in procedure (including the rectification of any document filed) connected with any proceeding or other matter before the registrar or the Office.

(2) Any rectification made under paragraph (1) shall be made—

(a) after giving the parties such notice; and

(b) subject to such conditions,

as the registrar may direct.

[134]

Interrupted day

75 (1) The registrar may certify any day as an interrupted day where—

(a) there is an event or circumstance causing an interruption in the normal operation of the Office; or

(b) there is a general interruption or subsequent dislocation in the postal services of the United Kingdom.

(2) Any certificate of the registrar made under paragraph (1) shall be displayed in the Office and published on the Office website.

(3) The registrar shall, where the time for doing anything under these Rules expires on an interrupted day, extend that time to the next following day not being an interrupted day (or an excluded day).

(4) In this rule—

"excluded day" means a day which is not a business day as specified in a direction given by the registrar under section 80; and

"interrupted day" means a day which has been certified as such under paragraph (1).

[135]

Delays in communication services

76 (1) The registrar shall extend any time limit in these Rules where the registrar is satisfied that the failure to do something under these Rules was wholly or mainly attributed to a delay in, or failure of, a communication service.

(2) Any extension under paragraph (1) shall be—

(a) made after giving the parties such notice; and

(b) subject to such conditions,

as the registrar may direct.

(3) In this rule "communication service" means a service by which documents may be sent and delivered and includes post, facsimile, email and courier.

[136]

Alteration of time limits (Form TM9)

77 (1) Subject to paragraphs (4) and (5), the registrar may, at the request of the person or party concerned or at the registrar's own initiative extend a time or period prescribed by these Rules or a time or period specified by the registrar for doing any act and any extension under this paragraph shall be made subject to such conditions as the registrar may direct.

(2) A request for extension under this rule may be made before or after the time or period in question has expired and shall be made—

(a) where the application for registration has not been published and the request for an extension [relates to a time or period other than one specified under rule 13 and] is made before the time or period in question has expired, in writing; and

(b) in any other case, on Form TM9.

(3) Where an extension under paragraph (1) is requested in relation to proceedings before the registrar, the party seeking the extension shall send a copy of the request to every other person who is a party to the proceedings.

(4) The registrar shall extend a flexible time limit, except a time or period which applies in relation to proceedings before the registrar or the filing of an appeal to the Appointed Person under rule 71, where—

(a) the request for extension is made before the end of the period of two months beginning with the date the relevant time or period expired; and

(b) no previous request has been made under this paragraph.

(5) A time limit listed in Schedule 1 (whether it has already expired or not) may be extended under paragraph (1) if, and only if—

(a) the irregularity or prospective irregularity is attributable, wholly or in part, to a default, omission or other error by the registrar, the Office or the International Bureau; and

(b) it appears to the registrar that the irregularity should be rectified.

(6) In this rule—

"flexible time limit" means—

(a) a time or period prescribed by these Rules, except a time or period prescribed by the rules listed in Schedule 1, or

(b) a time or period specified by the registrar for doing any act or taking any proceedings; and

"proceedings before the registrar" means any dispute between two or more parties relating to a matter before the registrar in connection with a trade mark.

NOTES

Amendment Para (2)(a): words in square brackets inserted by SI 2009/2089.

[137]

Filing of Documents, Hours of Business, Trade Marks Journal and Translations

Filing of documents by electronic means

78 The registrar may permit as an alternative to the sending by post or delivery of the application, notice or other document in legible form the filing of the application, notice or other document by electronic means subject to such terms or conditions as the registrar may specify either generally by published notice or in any particular case by written notice to the person desiring to file any such documents by such means.

[138]

Electronic communications

79 (1) The delivery using electronic communications to any person by the registrar of any document is deemed to be effected, unless the registrar has otherwise specified, by transmitting an electronic communication containing the document to an address provided or made available to the registrar by that person as an address for the receipt of electronic communications; and unless the contrary is proved such delivery is deemed to be effected immediately upon the transmission of the communication.

(2) In this rule "electronic communication" has the same meaning as in the Electronic Communications Act 2000.

[139]

Directions on hours of business; section 80

80 Any directions given by the registrar under section 80 specifying the hours of business of the Office and business days of the Office shall be published on the Office website.

[140]

Trade Marks Journal; section 81

81 The registrar shall publish a journal, entitled "The Trade Marks Journal" containing such information as is required to be published in the Journal under these Rules and such other information as the registrar thinks fit.

[141]

Translations

82 (1) Where any document or part thereof which is in a language other than English is filed or sent to the registrar in pursuance of the Act or these Rules, the registrar may require that there be furnished a translation into English of the document or that part, verified to the satisfaction of the registrar as corresponding to the original text.

(2) The registrar may refuse to accept any translation which the registrar considers to be inaccurate in which event there shall be furnished another translation of the document in question verified in accordance with paragraph (1).

[142]

Transitional Provisions and Revocations

Revocation of previous rules and proceedings commenced under previous rules

83 (1) The instruments set out in Schedule 2 ("the previous rules") are revoked to the extent specified.

(2) Where immediately before these Rules come into force, any time or period prescribed by the previous rules has effect in relation to any act or proceeding and has not expired, the time or period prescribed by the previous rules and not by these Rules shall apply to that act or proceeding.

(3) Except as provided by paragraph (4) where a new step is to be taken on or after 1st October 2008 in relation to any proceedings commenced under the previous rules these Rules shall apply to such proceedings from that date.

(4) Subject to paragraph (5) where prior to the entry into force of these Rules-

(a) a Form TM8 and counter-statement have been filed in-

(i) opposition proceedings, or

(ii) proceedings for the revocation of a trade mark on the grounds set out in section 46(1)(c) or (d); or

(iii) invalidation proceedings; or

(b) an application for revocation of a trade mark on the grounds set out in section 46(1)(a) or (b) has been filed,

the previous rules shall apply with regard to the filing of any evidence in relation to those proceedings.

(5) Where proceedings as described in paragraph (4) are consolidated with proceedings commenced on or after 1st October 2008 these Rules shall apply with regard to the filing of any evidence in relation to those consolidated proceedings.

[143]

SCHEDULE 1
EXTENSION OF TIME LIMITS

Rule 77

rule 17(2) (filing notice of opposition)
rule 17(3) (filing notice of opposition: request for extension of time)
rule 18(1) (counter-statement in opposition proceedings)
rule 19(4) (responding to preliminary indication)
rule 25(2) (opposition to amendment after publication)
rule 30(4) (opposition to amendment of regulations of collective and certification marks)
rule 32(3) (opposition to alteration of mark)
rule 35 (renewal of registration)
rule 36(2) (delayed renewal)
rule 37(1) (restoration of registration)
rule 38(3) (counter-statement for revocation on grounds of non-use)
rule 39(3) (counter-statement for revocation on grounds other than non-use)
rule 41(6) (counter-statement for invalidity)
rule 43(2) (setting aside cancellation of application or revocation or invalidation of registration)
rule 53(2) (opposition to removal of matter from register)
rule 55(1) (opposition to proposals for change of classification)
rule 77(4) (period for making a retrospective request to extend a flexible time period).

[144]

SCHEDULE 2

Rule 83

NOTES

This Schedule lists the following rules revoked by reg 83: the Trade Marks Rules 2000, SI 2000/136, and the amending SI 2001/3832, SI 2004/947, SI 2006/3039, SI 2007/2076, and the Trade Marks and Designs (Address for Service)(Amendment) Rules 2006, SI 2006/1029. SI 2006/760 and SI 2008/11 (now revoked) are amended.

[145]

TRADE MARKS (FEES) RULES 2008
SI 2008/1958

Authority Made by the Secretary of State for Innovation, Universities and Skills under the Trade Marks Act 1994, s 79, and Department of Trade and Industry (Fees) Order 1988, SI 1988/93.
Date made 21 July 2008.
Commencement 1 October 2008.
Amendment Printed as amended by SI 2009/2089.
General These rules revoke and replace the Trade Marks (Fees) Rules 2000, SI 2000/137 (except in so far as they related to fees payable under SI 1996/714) and the amending SI 2007/2077, SI 2008/11 and prescribe fees payable under the Trade Marks Act 1994 and SI 2008/1797.
Fees for international registration SI 2000/137 had continued to prescribe fees in relation to matters arising under SI 1996/714, but this order has now been revoked and accordingly the 2000 rules were fully revoked by SI 2008/2207; in relation to fees for international registration, see now SI 2008/2206.

[146]

Citation, commencement and interpretation

1 (1) These Rules may be cited as the Trade Marks (Fees) Rules 2008 and shall come into force on 1st October 2008.

(2) These Rules shall be construed as one with the Trade Marks Rules 2008 ("the 2008 Rules").

[147]

NOTES

Trade Marks Rules 2008 SI 2008/1797.

Fees payable

2 (1) The fees to be paid in respect of any matters arising under the Act and the 2008 Rules shall be those specified in the Schedule to these Rules.

(2) In any case where a form specified in the Schedule as the corresponding form in relation to any matter is specified in the 2008 Rules, that form shall be accompanied by the fee specified in respect of that matter (unless the 2008 Rules otherwise provide).

[148]

Repayment of fee

3 (1) Where the registrar—

(a) has received a request for expedited examination of an application for registration of a trade mark under rule 5(2) of the 2008 Rules; and

(b) following the expiry of a period of ten business days (as specified in a direction given by the registrar under section 80 of the Act) beginning on the business day after the date of filing of the application for registration, notifies the applicant, in accordance with rule 15 of the 2008 Rules, whether or not it appears to the registrar that the requirements for registration are met,

the registrar shall repay the fee specified in the Schedule in respect of a request for expedited examination.

(2) Where a fee has been paid in error, the registrar shall repay the same; and where a fee is paid in excess of the amount specified, the registrar shall remit the amount paid in excess.

[149]

4 (*Revokes the Trade Mark (Fees) Rules 2000, SI 2000/137, and the amending SI 2007/2077, SI 2008/11.*)

SCHEDULE
FEES PAYABLE

Rule 3

(In this section references to a rule are references to that rule in the 2008 Rules)

Number of corresponding form	*Item*	*Amount*
		£
TM3	[Standard] Application for registration of a trade mark (rule 5) or a series of trade marks (rule 28)	200
[e-TM3]	Request to the Registrar for expedited examination of [electronic] application for registration of a trade mark (rule 5(2))	300
TM3	Class fee (rule 5), for each class over one [contained in a standard application]	50
[TM3	Series fee (rule 28(1A)), for each trade mark over two contained in a standard application	50
e-TM3	Electronic application for registration of a trade mark (rule 5(1B)) or a series of trade marks (rule 28)	170
e-TM3	Class fee (rule 5), for each class over one contained in an electronic application	50
e-TM3	Series fee (rule 28(1A)), for each trade mark over two contained in an electronic application	50]
TM3A	Application for additional classes following examination of a mark (rule 8(4)), for each additional class	50
TM5	Request to the registrar for a statement of the reasons for his decision (rule 69(2))	100
TM6	Request to the registrar by the proprietor of a Community trade mark or international trade mark (EC) to be notified of the results of a search of the register (rule 14(4))	50

Number of corresponding form	*Item*	*Amount*
		£
TM7	Notice of opposition to the registration of a mark (rule 17(1)), to the amendment of an application (rule 25(2)), or to the amendment of the regulations relating to a certification or collective trade mark (rule 30(4)), to the alteration of a registered trade mark (rule 32(3)), to the removal of matter from the register (rule 53(2)(a)), to the reclassification of a mark in accordance with the relevant Nice Classification (rule 55(1))	200
TM9	Request for extension of time (rule 77(2))	[100]
TM11	Renewal of registration (rule 35)	200
TM11	Class fee for each class over one (rule 35)	50
TM11	Delayed renewal of registration (rule 36(2))	50
TM12	Request for division of an application (rule 26(1))	100
TM13	Request for the restoration and renewal of a registration removed from the register for failure to renew (rule 37(1))	100
TM16	Request to enter details of an assignment (rule 49(1)(a))	50
TM26 (N)	Request for the revocation of a registration (on grounds of non-use) (rule 38)	200
TM26 (O)	Request for the revocation of a registration (on grounds other than non-use) (rule 39)	200
TM26 (I)	Request for the invalidation of a registration (rule 41)	200
TM31C	Request for information about applications and registered trade marks (rule 56)	20
TM31R	Request for certified copy of an entry on the register (rule 51), per certificate	20
TM35	Filing of regulations governing the use of a certification or collective mark (rule 29)	200
TM36	Request to amend regulations governing the use of a certification or collective mark (rule 30(1))	100

NOTES

Amendment In first entry, word in square brackets in column 2 substituted by SI 2009/2089; in second entry, words in square brackets in columns 1 and 2 substituted by SI 2009/2089; third, fourth, fifth and sixth entries, inserted by SI 2009/2089; in entry relating to TM9, sum in square brackets in column 3 substituted by SI 2009/2089.
2008 Rules Trade Marks Rules 2008, SI 2008/1797.

[150]

TRADE MARKS (INTERNATIONAL REGISTRATION) ORDER 2008
SI 2008/2206

Authority Made by the Secretary of State for Innovation, Universities and Skills under the Trade Marks Act 1994, s 54, and Department of Trade and Industry (Fees) Order 1988, SI 1988/93.
Date made 13 August 2008.
Commencement 1 October 2008.
Amendment Printed as amended by SI 2009/2464.
Interpretation See art 2.
General This order, which revokes and replaces the Trade Marks (International Registration) Order 1996, SI 1996/714 and the amending SI 2000/138; SI 2002/692; SI 2004/948; SI 2006/763, SI 2006/1080, gives effect in the United Kingdom to the Protocol relating to the Madrid Agreement concerning the International Registration of Marks adopted at Madrid on 27 June 1989 (the Madrid Protocol) which the United Kingdom ratified on 6 April 1995.

[151]

Citation and commencement

1 This Order may be cited as the Trade Marks (International Registration) Order 2008 and shall come into force on 1st October 2008.

[152]

Interpretation

2 In this Order—

"the Act" means the Trade Marks Act 1994 and "section" means a section of that Act;

"Common Regulations" means the regulations adopted under article 10 of the Madrid Protocol with effect from 1 April 1996 and as amended with effect from 1 April 2002;

"concurrent registered trade mark" means a trade mark as defined in Schedule 4, paragraph 2;

"date of the international registration" means the date of the international registration under Article 3(4) of the Madrid Protocol;

"international application" means an application by way of the Patent Office as office of origin to the International Bureau for registration of a trade mark in the International Register;

"International Register" means the register of trade marks maintained by the International Bureau for the purposes of the Madrid Protocol;

"international registration" means a registration of a trade mark in the International Register;

"protected international trade mark (UK)" means an international registration which is the subject of a request for extension and which is protected in accordance with section 38 as modified by Schedule 2, paragraph 6 and references to "protection" and "protected" shall be construed accordingly;

"request for extension" means a request for an extension of protection to the United Kingdom under Article 3*ter* (1) or (2) of the Madrid Protocol which has been notified by the International Bureau;

"the Relative Grounds Order" means the Trade Marks (Relative Grounds) Order 2007;

"supplementary register" means the register of international trade marks (UK) required to be maintained under section 63 as modified by Schedule 2, paragraph 8;

"the Trade Marks Rules" means the Trade Marks Rules 2008 and "trade marks rule" shall be construed accordingly.

NOTES

Trade Marks (Relative Grounds) Order 2007 SI 2007/1976.
Trade Marks Rules 2008 SI 2008/1797.

[153]

International trade marks (UK)

3 (1) An international registration which is the subject of a request for extension shall be entitled to protection subject to the provisions of the Act, the Relative Grounds Order and the Trade Marks Rules as applied by this Order if the particulars of the request for extension were contained in an application for registration of a trade mark under the Act and such application would satisfy the requirements of the Act (including any imposed by the Trade Mark Rules).

(2) Subject to paragraph (3) a protected international trade mark (UK) shall be treated as if it were a trade mark registered under the Act and the holder shall have the same rights and remedies but shall be subject to the same conditions as the proprietor of a registered trade mark.

(3) The provisions of the Act (except those listed in Schedule 1, Part 1), the Relative Grounds Order and the Trade Marks Rules (except those listed in Schedule 1, Part 2) shall apply to international trade marks (UK) and requests for extension with the following modifications;

(a) references to a registered trade mark shall include references to a protected international trade mark (UK);

(b) references to a proprietor of a registered trade mark shall include references to the holder of a protected international trade mark (UK);
(c) references to an application for registration of a trade mark shall include references to a request for extension;
(d) references to an applicant for registration shall include references to the holder of an international registration in respect of which a request for extension has been made;
(e) references to registration of a trade mark shall include the conferring of protection on an international registration which is the subject of a request for extension;
(f) references to the goods or services for which a trade mark is registered shall include references to the goods or services in respect of which a protected international trade mark (UK) confers protection;
(g) references to the publication of the application include references to the publication of the notice of details of the international registration in the Journal;
(h) references to the register are to the supplementary register;
(i) the modifications set out in Schedule 2; and
(j) such further modifications as the context requires for the purpose of giving effect to those provisions as applied by this Order.

[154]

International applications originating in the United Kingdom

4 The provisions set out in Schedule 3 shall apply in relation to the making of applications for international registration by way of the Patent Office as office of origin.

[155]

Concurrent registrations and transformation applications

5 The provisions set out in Schedule 4 shall apply in relation to—

(a) the effects of international registration where a trade mark is also registered under the Act; and
(b) the transformation of an application for an international registration, or an international registration, into an application for registration of a trade mark under the Act.

[156]

Miscellaneous and General Provisions

6 The provisions set out in Schedule 5 shall apply.

[157]

Fees

7 The fees to be paid in respect of any matters arising under this Order shall be those specified in Schedule 6.

[158]

Revocations and transitional provisions

8 (1) The instruments set out in Schedule 7 are revoked ("the previous Orders").

(2) Where immediately before this Order comes into force any time period prescribed by the previous Orders has effect in relation to any act or proceeding and has not expired, the time or period prescribed by the previous Orders and not by this Order shall apply to that act or proceeding.

(3) Except as provided by paragraph (4), where a new step is to be taken on or after 1st October 2008 in relation to any proceedings commenced under the previous Orders this Order shall apply to such proceedings from that date.

(4) Subject to paragraph (5), where prior to the entry into force of this Order:

(a) A Form TM8 and counter-statement have been filed in

(i) opposition proceedings; or

(ii) proceedings for the revocation of a trade mark on the grounds set out in section 46(1)(c) or (d); or

(iii) invalidation proceedings; or

(b) an application for revocation of a trade mark on the grounds set out in section 46(1)(a) or (b) has been filed,

the previous Orders shall apply with regard to the filing of any evidence in relation to those proceedings.

(5) Where proceedings as described in paragraph (4) are consolidated with proceedings commenced on or after 1st October 2008 this Order shall apply with regard to the filing of any evidence in relation to those consolidated proceedings.

[159]

SCHEDULE 1
PROVISIONS OF THE ACT AND TRADE MARKS RULES WHICH DO NOT APPLY TO INTERNATIONAL TRADE MARKS (UK) OR REQUESTS FOR EXTENSION

Article 3(3)

PART 1

section 24(2)(b) (assignment or other transmission in relation to use of the trade mark in a particular manner or locality)

section 32(1), (2) and (4) (application for registration)

section 33(1) (date of filing)

section 34 (classification of trade marks)

section 39(2) (withdrawal, restriction or amendment of application)

section 40 (registration)

section 41 (registration: supplementary provisions)

section 42 (duration of registration)

section 43 (renewal of registration)

section 44 (alteration of registered trade mark)

section 45 (surrender of registered trade mark)

section 64(4) (change of name and address by proprietor or licensee)

section 65 (adaptation of entries to new classification)

section 79 (fees)

section 94 (falsification of register)

[160]

PART 2

trade marks rule 6 (claim to priority; sections 35 & 36)

trade marks rule 8 (application may relate to more than one class and shall specify the class (Form TM31C))

trade marks rule 9 (determination of classification)

trade marks rule 12(4)(a) (failure to provide an address for service)

trade marks rule 13 (deficiencies in application; section 32)

trade marks rule 46 (form of register; section 63(1))

trade marks rule 47 (entry in register of particulars of registered trade marks; section 63(2) (Form TM24))

trade marks rule 56 (request for information; s 67(1) (Form TM31C))

[161]

SCHEDULE 2
MODIFICATIONS TO PROVISIONS OF THE ACT APPLIED TO INTERNATIONAL TRADE MARKS (UK)

Article 3(3)(i)

1 (1) Section 25 (registration of transactions affecting registered trade mark) is modified as follows.

(2) Omit paragraph (a) of subsection (1) and substitute—

"(a) a person claiming to be entitled to any security interest (whether fixed or floating) over a protected international trade mark (UK) or any right in or under it, or".

(3) Omit paragraphs (a), (b) and (c) of subsection (2) and substitute—

"(a) a change to the ownership of a registration recorded by the International Bureau in the International Register pursuant to article 9 of the Madrid Protocol;

(b) the grant of a licence recorded by the International Bureau in the International Register pursuant to rule 20 *bis* of the Common Regulations;".

(4) After subsection (2)(e) insert—

"(f) any matter other than as is referred to in paragraphs (a) and (b) above that is recorded in the International Register pursuant to article 9 *bis* of the Madrid Protocol.".

(5) In subsection (3) omit "Until an application has been made for registration of the prescribed particulars of a registrable transaction" and substitute "Until an application for registration of a matter in the supplementary register pursuant to subsection (1) has been made or an application for registration of a registrable transaction in the International Register (in accordance with Article 9 *bis* of the Madrid Protocol and rule 20 *bis* of the Common Regulations) has been made".

(6) In subsection (4)(a) omit "the prescribed particulars of the transaction" and substitute "a transaction in the International Register (in accordance with Article 9 *bis* of the Madrid Protocol and rule 20 *bis* of the Common Regulations)".

2 In section 33 (date of filing), for subsection (1), substitute—

"**33** (1) The date of filing of a request for extension shall be the date of the international registration except—

(a) where at the time protection is conferred on an international trade mark (UK) there is a concurrent registered trade mark, the date of filing shall be the date of filing of the registered trade mark; and

(b) where a request for extension is made in accordance with Article 3*ter*(2) of the Madrid Protocol, the date of filing shall be the date that the request for extension was recorded in the International Register.".

3 In section 35 (claim to priority of convention application), for subsection (5), substitute—

"(5) The manner of claiming priority shall be determined in accordance with the Madrid Protocol and the Common Regulations.".

4 In section 37 (examination of application) omit subsections (3) to (5) and substitute—

"(3) If it appears to the registrar that the requirements for registration are not met, the registrar shall give notice of provisional refusal to the International Bureau.

(4) Where the International Bureau notifies the registrar or the registrar considers that a particular term used to indicate any of the goods or services included in the international registration is—

(a) too vague for the purposes of classification; or

(b) incomprehensible or linguistically incorrect,

the registrar may give notice of provisional refusal to the International Bureau in respect of that term.

(5) Where a decision of the registrar has been notified to the International Bureau pursuant to subsection (3) or (4), the registrar shall give the holder of the international registration an opportunity, within such period as the registrar may specify, to make representations or amend the request for extension by limiting the goods and services.".

5 In section 38(2) (publication, opposition proceedings and observations) after "opposition to the registration" insert "in which event the registrar shall give notice of provisional refusal to the International Bureau".

6 After section 38, insert—

"38A Notices of provisional refusal

(1) A notice of provisional refusal must set out the matters required by Article 5 of the Madrid Protocol and Rule 17 of the Common Regulations.

(2) Except as provided in subsection (3), a notice of provisional refusal may not be given after the expiry of the relevant period.

(3) Where before the expiry of the relevant period the registrar has given notice to the International Bureau—

(a) that the period prescribed for the purposes of section 38(2) expires after the end of the relevant period; or

(b) that the period prescribed for the purposes of section 38(2) expires less than one month before the end of the relevant period;

a notice of provisional refusal may be given after the expiry of the relevant period provided that it is given before the end of the period of one month beginning immediately after the period prescribed for the purposes of section 38(2).

(4) Where the registrar sends the International Bureau a notice of provisional refusal, the registrar must notify the International Bureau as to the final decision (meaning a decision from which no appeal may be brought) on whether the refusal should be upheld.

(5) The relevant period is the period of 18 months beginning with the date the International Bureau sent the registrar the request for extension.

38B Protection

(1) Where no notice of provisional refusal is given to the International Bureau following publication under section 38(1), the international registration which is the subject of the request for extension shall be protected as a protected international trade mark (UK) with effect from the first day immediately following the end of the period prescribed for the purposes of section 38(2).

(2) Where notice of provisional refusal is given following publication under section 38(1), the international registration which is the subject of the request for extension shall be protected as a protected international trade mark (UK) with effect from the date on which the registrar notifies the International Bureau that the final decision is that the provisional refusal should not be upheld in accordance with section 38A(4).

(3) The reference to the completion of the registration procedure in section 46(1) shall be construed as a reference to the conferring of protection on an international registration in accordance with this section.

(4) When an international registration becomes protected as a protected international trade mark (UK), the registrar shall—

(a) notify the International Bureau that the international registration is protected in the United Kingdom; and

(b) publish a notice specifying the number of the international registration in respect of that trade mark, the date on which protection is conferred and the date and place of publication of the request for extension under section 38(1) in relation to that trade mark.".

7 In section 39 (Withdrawal, restriction or amendment of application) for subsection (1) substitute—

"(1) The goods and services covered by a request for extension may be restricted at any time by the applicant provided that if the request for extension has been published, the restriction must also be published in the Journal . . . ".

8 (1) Section 63 (the register) shall be modified as follows.

(2) For subsection (1) substitute—

"(1) The registrar shall maintain a register for the purpose of entering transactions under section 25(1) (as modified by paragraph 1 of Schedule 2 to the Trade Marks International Registration) Order 2008) and disclaimers and limitations relating to international trade marks (UK).".

(3) In subsection (3) for the words "shall be kept in such manner as may be prescribed" substitute "need not be kept in documentary form".

(4) After subsection (3) insert—

"(4) Following notification from the International Bureau under rule 28(2) of the Common Regulations the registrar may correct an error or omission in the information entered in the register required to be maintained under subsection (1).".

9 In section 67(2)(a) (Information about applications and registered trade marks) before "in such cases" insert "any information recorded in the International Register or".

NOTES

Amendment Para 7: in the Trade Marks Act 1994, s 39(1) (as set out) words omitted revoked by SI 2009/2464.

[162]

SCHEDULE 3
INTERNATIONAL APPLICATIONS ORIGINATING IN THE UNITED KINGDOM

Article 4

Application for international registration at the Patent Office

1 (1) An applicant for the registration of a trade mark, or the proprietor of a registered trade mark, may, subject to the provisions of this paragraph, apply by way of the Patent Office as office of origin for the international registration of the trade mark.

(2) For the purposes of this paragraph an applicant shall be—

(a) a British citizen, a British overseas territories citizen, a British overseas citizen, a British subject or a British protected person;

(b) an individual domiciled in the United Kingdom;

(c) a body incorporated under the law of a part of the United Kingdom; or

(d) a person who has a real and effective industrial or commercial establishment in the United Kingdom.

(3) Where the registrar has reasonable doubts about whether an applicant is eligible, the registrar—

(a) must inform the applicant of the reason for those doubts; and

(b) may require that applicant to file evidence in support of his eligibility.

(4) Where—

(a) the registrar has no doubts or is satisfied as to the applicant's eligibility; and

(b) the particulars appearing in the application for an international registration correspond with the particulars at that time in the basic application or, as the case may be, the basic registration,

the registrar must submit the application to the International Bureau.

(5) In this Schedule—

(a) "basic application" means an application for registration of a trade mark in the United Kingdom in respect of which application is made for international registration;

(b) "basic registration" means a trade mark registered in the United Kingdom in respect of which application is made for international registration.

Termination of basic application or basic registration

2 (1) This paragraph applies where the registrar submits an application to the International Bureau in accordance with paragraph 1 and the basic application or basic registration is terminated.

(2) Where, before the end of the relevant period, a basic application or basic registration is terminated, the registrar shall request that the International Bureau cancel the International Registration.

(3) A basic application is terminated where it is—

(a) not accepted;

(b) refused; or

(c) withdrawn (including deemed as such).

(4) A basic registration is terminated where the rights in the registered trade mark cease to have effect.

(5) Where a basic application or basic registration is terminated in respect of some only of the goods or services for which the trade mark is registered (or is sought to be registered), the request must relate only to those goods and services.

(6) The relevant period is the period of 5 years beginning with the date of the international registration.

(7) But if during that period the registrar becomes aware of proceedings which may result in the termination of the basic application or basic registration, the registrar must notify the International Bureau accordingly, stating that no final decision has been made.

(8) On completion of the proceedings referred to in paragraph (7) the registrar must promptly notify the International Bureau of their outcome.

Division or merger of basic application or basic registration

3 (1) This paragraph applies where the registrar submits an application to the International Bureau in accordance with paragraph 1 and—

(a) the basic application is divided into two or more applications; or

(b) two or more basic applications or basic registrations are merged into a single application or registration.

(2) Where, before the end of the relevant period, a basic application is divided or two or more basic applications or basic registrations are merged, the registrar shall notify the International Bureau and shall indicate—

(a) the number of the international registration or, where the mark has not been registered, the number of the basic application;

(b) the name of the applicant or the holder of the relevant trade mark; and

(c) the number of each application resulting from the division or the number of the application or registration resulting from the merger.

(3) The relevant period is the period of 5 years beginning with the date of the international registration.

[163]

SCHEDULE 4
TRANSFORMATION APPLICATIONS AND CONCURRENT REGISTRATIONS

Article 5

Transformation applications

1 (1) A transformation application is an application to register a trade mark under the Act where—

(a) the mark was the subject of an international registration and the international registration was the subject of a request for extension; and

(b) the international registration was cancelled at the request of the Office of origin under Article 6(4) of the Madrid Protocol.

(2) But an application shall only be treated as a transformation application where the goods and services cited in it are identical to some or all of the goods and services included in the international registration.

(3) Any application made under the Act which is a transformation application shall state that it is made by way of transformation.

(4) Such an application may only be made before the end of the period of three months beginning with the date on which the international registration was cancelled.

(5) A transformation application may only be made by the person who was the holder of the international registration immediately before it was cancelled.

(6) Where on or before the date the transformation application was made, the trade mark is protected as an international trade mark (UK), the mark shall be registered under the Act; and it shall have the date of filing of the cancelled international trade mark (UK).

(7) Where on that date the trade mark is not so protected, the transformation application shall be treated as an application to register under the Act and it shall have the date of filing of the request for extension relating to that mark.

(8) Where in relation to the international registration a right of priority was claimed on the basis of a Convention application, the transformation application shall have the same right of priority.

Concurrent registrations

2 (1) This paragraph applies where at the time protection is conferred on an international trade mark (UK) there is a concurrent registered trade mark.

(2) A registration is concurrent where—

(a) the proprietor of the registered trade mark is the holder of the protected international trade mark (UK);
(b) the registered trade mark is the same as the protected international trade mark (UK);
(c) the goods and services in relation to which protection is conferred by the international trade mark (UK) include all those for which the registered trade mark is registered.

(3) The protected international trade mark (UK) shall be treated as being registered under the Act as of the date of registration of the registered trade mark.

(4) The priorities claimed in respect of the registered trade mark may also be claimed in respect of the international trade mark (UK).

(5) The provisions of this paragraph shall continue to apply after the registered trade mark lapses or is surrendered, but shall cease to apply if or to the extent that it is revoked or declared invalid.

(6) On the application of the holder of the protected international trade mark (UK) the registrar shall note the international registration in the register against the registered trade mark.

(7) For the purposes of paragraph (6), the holder of the international trade mark (UK) shall make an application to the registrar using Form TM28.

[164]

SCHEDULE 5
MISCELLANEOUS AND GENERAL PROVISIONS

Article 6

Correction of international registration

1 (1) Where the International Bureau notifies the registrar that it has corrected an international registration and the correction either—

(a) substantially affects the identity of the trade mark; or
(b) alters the goods or services covered by the international registration,

the registrar may treat the notification as a new request for extension.

(2) Where paragraph (1)(a) applies, any earlier request for protection shall be deemed to have been withdrawn and any resulting protection granted to the international trade mark (UK) shall be treated as having been declared invalid.

(3) Where paragraph (1)(b) applies and—

(a) the correction extends the goods and services covered by the request for extension, the new request for extension shall apply only to the additional goods and services; or
(b) the correction restricts the goods and services covered by the international registration, to the extent it relates to goods and service outside the restriction, an earlier request for protection shall be treated as having been withdrawn, and any resulting protection granted to the international trade mark (UK) shall be treated as having been declared invalid.

Assignment

2 (1) A protected international trade mark (UK) may only be assigned to an eligible person.

(2) An eligible person is—

(a) a national of any country which is a party to the Madrid Protocol;
(b) an individual domiciled in such a country;
(c) a body incorporated under the law of such a country; and

(d) a person who has a real and effective industrial or commercial establishment in such a country.

Judicial notice

3 (1) Judicial notice shall be taken of the following—

(a) the Madrid Protocol and the Common Regulations;

(b) copies issued by the International Bureau of entries in the International Register;

(c) copies of the periodical gazette published by the International Bureau in accordance with rule 32 of the Common Regulations.

(2) Any document mentioned in paragraph (1)(b) or (c) shall be admissible as evidence of any instrument or other act of the International Bureau so communicated.

(3) Where in relation to the international registration a right of priority was claimed on the basis of a Convention application, the transformation application shall have the same right of priority.

Revocation

4 Where the protection of a protected international trade mark (UK) is revoked or declared invalid to any extent, the registrar shall notify the International Bureau, and—

(a) in the case of a revocation, the rights of the proprietor shall be deemed to have ceased to exist to that extent as from—

(i) the date of the application for revocation, or

(ii) if the registrar or court is satisfied that the grounds for revocation existed at an earlier date, that date;

(b) in the case of a declaration of invalidity, the trade mark shall to that extent be deemed never to have been a protected international trade mark (UK).

Requests for Information

5 A request for information relating to a protected international trade mark (UK) must be made on Form TM31M.

Communication of information to the International Bureau

6 Notwithstanding any other enactment or rule of law, the registrar may communicate to the International Bureau any information which the United Kingdom is required to communicate by virtue of this Order or pursuant to the Madrid Protocol or Common Regulations.

Transmission of fees to the International Bureau

7 The registrar may accept for transmission to the International Bureau fees payable to the International Bureau in respect of an application for international registration originating in the United Kingdom or a renewal of such an international registration, subject to such terms and conditions as the registrar may specify, either generally by published notice, or in any particular case by written notice to the applicant desiring to make payment by such means.

[165]

SCHEDULE 6
FEES

Article 7

Matter in respect of which fee payable	*Amount*
Notice of opposition to the conferring of protection on an international registration (trade marks rule 17)	£200
Request for the revocation of a protected international trade mark (UK) (on grounds other than non-use) (trade marks rule 39)	£200
Request for the revocation of a protected international trade mark (UK) (on grounds of non-use) (trade marks rule 38)	£200
Request for the invalidation of a protected international trade mark (UK) (trade marks rule 41)	£200
Submission fee for an international application (Schedule 3, paragraph 1)	£40
Handling fee for the transmission by the Patent Office of fees payable to the International Bureau for renewal of an international registration (Schedule 5, paragraph 7)	£20
Request to the Registrar for a statement of reasons for his decision (trade mark rule 69(2))	£20
Request for an extension of time (trade marks rule 77(2))	[£100]
Request for information in relation to an international mark (UK)	£50

Matter in respect of which fee payable	*Amount*
Filing of regulations governing the use of a certification or collective mark (trade mark rules 29)	£200
Request to amend regulations governing the use of a certification or collective mark (trade mark rules 30)	£100
Notice of opposition to the amendment of regulations relating to a certification or collective mark (trademark rules 30(4))	£200

NOTES
Amendment In entry "Request for an extension of time (trade marks rule 77(2))" in the second column sum in square brackets substituted by SI 2009/2464.

[166]

SCHEDULE 7
REVOCATIONS

Article 8

NOTES
Amendment This Schedule lists the following instruments revoked by art 8: the Trade Marks (International Registration) Order 1996, SI 1996/714, and the amending SI 2000/138, SI 2002/692, SI 2004/948, SI 2006/763, SI 2006/1080.

[167]

Trade Unions and Employers' Associations

See the title Employment

Traffic

See the titles Aviation; Highways, Streets and Bridges; Shipping and Navigation; Transport

Tramways

See the title Transport

Transport

CHRONOLOGICAL LIST OF INSTRUMENTS

Date made	*Description*	*Remarks*	*Page*
20 March 1878	Canal Boats Regulations 1878	—	158
7 March 1889	Order prescribing the date for forwarding bye-laws and regulations of canal companies under the Railway and Canal Traffic Act 1888	Prescribed 10 August 1889 for the purposes of s 40(1) of the 1888 Act	—
January 1892	Rules with respect to provisional Orders and other matters under the Tramways Act 1870	See Preliminary Note "Construction and operation of railways etc" (under main head Railways, tramways and inland waterways")	—
1895 (undated)	Form of Coroner's Return as to Death caused by Railway accidents	See Preliminary Note "Safety" (under main head "Nationalisation, reorganisation and subsequent privatisation")	—

SR & O	*Description*	*Remarks*	*Page*
SR & O 1933/634	London Passenger Transport Act 1933 (Appointed Day) Order (No 1) 1933	See Preliminary Note "London Passenger Transport Board" (under main head "London")	—
SR & O 1933/934	London Passenger Transport Act 1933 (Appointed Day) Order (No 2) 1933	See Preliminary Note "London Passenger Transport Board" (under main head "London")	—
SR & O 1933/964	London Passenger Transport Act 1933 (Appointed Day) Order (No 3) 1933	See Preliminary Note "London Passenger Transport Board" (under main head "London")	—
SR & O 1933/1051	London Passenger Transport Act 1933 (Appointed Day) Order (No 4) 1933	See Preliminary Note "London Passenger Transport Board" (under main head "London")	—
SR & O 1933/1082	London Passenger Transport Act 1933 (Appointed Day) Order (No 5) 1933	See Preliminary Note "London Passenger Transport Board" (under main head "London")	—
SR & O 1933/1115	London Passenger Transport Act 1933 (Appointed Day) Order (No 6) 1933	See Preliminary Note "London Passenger Transport Board" (under main head "London")	—
SR & O 1933/1139	London Passenger Transport Act 1933 (Appointed Day) Order (No 7) 1933	See Preliminary Note "London Passenger Transport Board" (under main head "London")	—
SR & O 1933/1181	London Passenger Transport Act 1933 (Appointed Day) Order (No 8) 1933	See Preliminary Note "London Passenger Transport Board" (under main head "London")	—

SR & O	*Description*	*Remarks*	*Page*
SR & O 1933/1191	London Passenger Transport Act 1933 (Appointed Day) Order (No 9) 1933	See Preliminary Note "London Passenger Transport Board" (under main head "London")	—
SR & O 1934/82	London Passenger Transport Act 1933 (Appointed Day) Order (No 10) 1934	See Preliminary Note "London Passenger Transport Board" (under main head "London")	—
SR & O 1934/161	London Passenger Transport Act 1933 (Appointed Day) Order (No 11) 1934	See Preliminary Note "London Passenger Transport Board" (under main head "London")	—
SR & O 1934/563	London Passenger Transport Act 1933 (Appointed Day) Order (No 12) 1934	See Preliminary Note "London Passenger Transport Board" (under main head "London")	—
SR & O 1934/627	London Passenger Transport Act 1933 (Appointed Day) Order (No 13) 1934	See Preliminary Note "London Passenger Transport Board" (under main head "London")	—
SR & O 1934/628	London Passenger Transport Act 1933 (Appointed Day) Order (No 14) 1934	See Preliminary Note "London Passenger Transport Board" (under main head "London")	—
SR & O 1934/827	London Passenger Transport Act 1933 (Appointed Day) Order (No 15) 1934	See Preliminary Note "London Passenger Transport Board" (under main head "London")	—
SR & O 1934/931	London Passenger Transport Act 1933 (Appointed Day) Order (No 16) 1934	See Preliminary Note "London Passenger Transport Board" (under main head "London")	—
SR & O 1934/975	London Passenger Transport Act 1933 (Appointed Day) Order (No 17) 1934	See Preliminary Note "London Passenger Transport Board" (under main head "London")	—
SR & O 1934/1202	London Passenger Transport Act 1933 (Appointed Day) Order (No 18) 1934	See Preliminary Note "London Passenger Transport Board" (under main head "London")	—
SR & O 1934/1346	London Cab Order 1934	—	159
SR & O 1934/1365	London Passenger Transport Act 1933 (Appointed Day) Order (No 19) 1934	See Preliminary Note "London Passenger Transport Board" (under main head "London")	—
SR & O 1947/2192	Motor Vehicles (Variation of Speed Limit) Regulations 1947	—	160

SI	*Description*	*Remarks*	*Page*
SI 1948/1585	Transferred Undertakings (Pensions of Employees losing Employment) Regulations 1948	—	161
SI 1949/584	Pension Schemes (Employees in Northern Ireland) Regulations 1949	—	161

SI	*Description*	*Remarks*	*Page*
SI 1949/603	Railway and Canal Commission (Abolition) Act 1949 (Commencement) Order 1949	Made under s 8(1) of the 1949 Act; brought that Act into force on 1 April 1949	—
SI 1952/1159	Transferred Undertakings (Pensions of Employees) (No 1) Regulations 1952	—	162
SI 1952/1612	Transferred Undertakings (Pensions of Employees) (No 2) Regulations 1952	—	162
SI 1953/1445	British Transport Commission (Pensions of Employees) Regulations 1953	—	162
SI 1954/139	Railway Clearing House Scheme Order 1954	—	162
SI 1954/898	British Transport Commission (Male Wages Grades Pensions) Regulations 1954	—	163
SI 1954/943	Motor Vehicles (Variation of Speed Limit) (Amendment) Regulations 1954	Amend SI 1947/2192	—
SI 1954/1428	British Transport Commission (Amendment of Pension Schemes) Regulations 1954	—	163
SI 1955/1853	London Cab Order 1955	Amends SR & O 1934/1346	—
SI 1956/732	National Insurance (Modification of the London Transport and Railway Pension Schemes) Regulations 1956	—	164
SI 1957/438	Transferred Undertakings (Pensions of Employees) (Amendment) Regulations 1957	Amend SI 1952/1612	—
SI 1957/1455	British Transport Commission (Male Wages Grades Pensions) (Amendment) Regulations 1957	Amend SI 1954/898	—
SI 1960/784	British Transport Commission (Male Wages Grades Pensions) (Amendment) Regulations 1960	Amend SI 1954/898	—
SI 1961/559	National Insurance (Modification of Transport Undertaking Superannuation Funds) Regulations 1961	—	164
SI 1962/289	London Cab Order 1962	Amends SR & O 1934/1346	—
SI 1962/898	British Transport Commission Group Pension Funds Regulations 1962	—	164
SI 1962/1788	Transport Act 1962 (Commencement No 1) Order 1962	—	165
SI 1962/2634	Transport Act 1962 (Vesting Date) Order 1962	Made under s 31(1) of the 1962 Act; appointed 1 January 1963 as the vesting date for the purposes of that Act	—
SI 1962/2714	British Transport Reorganisation (Pensions of Employees) (No 1) Order 1962	—	165
SI 1962/2715	British Transport Reorganisation (Pensions of Employees) (No 2) Order 1962	—	165
SI 1962/2758	British Transport Reorganisation (Pensions of Employees) (No 3) Order 1962	—	166
SI 1962/2790	Pipe-lines Act 1962 (Commencement) Order 1962	Made under s 70(3) of the 1962 Act; brought the whole Act (except s 41 (repealed)) into force on 1 January 1963	—
SI 1962/2793	British Transport Reorganisation (Pensions of Employees) (No 4) Order 1962	—	166
SI 1962/2834	British Transport Reorganisation (Compensation to Employees) Regulations 1962	—	166
SI 1963/151	Pipe-lines (Notices) Regulations 1963	—	167
SI 1963/2023	British Transport Commission (Transfer of Functions) (Appointments and Nominations) Order 1963	—	167

SI	*Description*	*Remarks*	*Page*
SI 1963/2126	Vehicles (Conditions of Use on Footpaths) Regulations 1963	—	168
SI 1964/448	British Transport Reorganisation (Commencing Capital Debts) Order 1964	—	169
SI 1964/489	Defence (Transfer of Functions) (No 2) Order 1964	See title Constitutional Law (Pt 2); amends SI 1947/2192	—
SI 1964/1329	British Transport Reorganisation (Pensions of Employees) (No 1) Order 1964	—	169
SI 1965/43	British Transport (Closed Railway Pension Scheme) Order 1965	—	170
SI 1966/864	Vehicles (Conditions of Use on Footpaths) (Amendment) Regulations 1966	Amend SI 1963/2126	—
SI 1966/1145	National Insurance (Modification of Transport Undertaking Superannuation Funds) (Amendment) Regulations 1966	Amend SI 1961/559	—
SI 1966/1465	British Transport (Pensions of Employees Transferred to Harbour Authorities) Order 1966	—	170
SI 1966/1556	London Transport (Alteration of Wages Grades Pension Schemes) Order 1966	Modifies SI 1954/898; also modified SI 1966/1164 (revoked)	—
SI 1967/819	Carriage of Goods by Road Act 1965 (Commencement) Order 1967	Made under s 14 of the 1965 Act; brought the Act into force on 5 June 1967	—
SI 1967/820	Carriage of Goods by Road (Gibraltar) Order 1967	See Preliminary Note "International carriage by road" (under main head "Road traffic")	—
SI 1967/929	British Railways (Alteration of Pension Schemes) Order 1967	—	171
SI 1967/1683	Carriage of Goods by Road (Parties to Convention) Order 1967	—	171
SI 1968/597	London Cab Act 1968 (Commencement) Order 1968	Made under s 4(6) of the 1968 Act; brought s 4(1)–(5) into force on 15 July 1968 (s 4 of the 1968 Act is repealed by Private Hire Vehicles (London) Act 1998, ss 29, 39(2), Sch 2, except in relation to vehicles used for funerals or weddings)	—
SI 1968/825	British Transport (Transfers from British Waterways Board Pension Schemes) Order 1968	—	172
SI 1968/1021	British Transport (Closed Railway Pension Schemes) Order 1968	See note "Further order" to SI 1965/43	—
SI 1968/1217	British Transport Docks Board (Alteration of Pension Schemes) Order 1968	—	173
SI 1968/1249	British Transport (Male Wages Grades Pensions) (Amendment) Order 1968	Amends SI 1954/898	—
SI 1968/1498	British Transport Police (Transfers from Pension Schemes) Order 1968	—	173
SI 1968/1822	Transport Act 1968 (Commencement No 1) Order 1968	—	173
SI 1968/2011	British Transport (Pensions of Employees) (No 1) Order 1968	—	174
SI 1968/2012	British Transport (Pensions of Employees) (No 2) Order 1968	—	174
SI 1969/94	Merseyside Passenger Transport Area (Designation) Order 1969	—	174
SI 1969/95	South East Lancashire and North East Cheshire Passenger Transport Area (Designation) Order 1969	—	175

SI	*Description*	*Remarks*	*Page*
SI 1969/96	Tyneside Passenger Transport Area (Designation) Order 1969	—	175
SI 1969/97	West Midlands Passenger Transport Area (Designation) Order 1969	—	176
SI 1969/507	Transport Act 1968 (Commencement No 2) Order 1969	See note "Further orders" to SI 1968/1822	—
SI 1969/1130	Transport (London) Act 1969 (Commencement No 1) Order 1969	—	176
SI 1969/1510	Transport (London) Act 1969 (Commencement No 2) Order 1969	See note "Further orders" to SI 1969/1130	—
SI 1969/1613	Transport Act 1968 (Commencement No 3) Order 1969	See note "Further orders" to SI 1968/1822	—
SI 1969/1695	British Transport (Closed Railway Pension Scheme) Order 1969	—	177
SI 1969/1824	British Transport (Pensions of Employees) (No 1) Order 1969	—	177
SI 1969/1825	British Transport (Pensions of Employees) (No 2) Order 1969	—	177
SI 1969/1858	British Transport (Alteration of Pension Schemes) Order 1969	—	178
SI 1970/22	British Transport (Southern Railway Superannuation Fund) Order 1970	—	178
SI 1970/41	Transport Act 1968 (Commencement No 4) Order 1970	See note "Further orders" to SI 1968/1822	—
SI 1970/145	Drivers' Hours (Passenger Vehicles) (Exemptions) Regulations 1970	—	178
SI 1970/187	British Transport (Compensation to Employees) Regulations 1970	—	178
SI 1970/188	Transport Act 1968 (Commencement No 5) Order 1970	See note "Further orders" to SI 1968/1822	—
SI 1970/257	Drivers' Hours (Goods Vehicles) (Modifications) Order 1970	—	179
SI 1970/259	Transport Act 1968 (Commencement No 6) Order 1970	See note "Further orders" to SI 1968/1822	—
SI 1970/385	Transport Act 1968 (Commencement No 7) Order 1970	See note "Further orders" to SI 1968/1822	—
SI 1970/477	British Transport (Amalgamation of Railways' Pension Funds) (No 1) Order 1970	—	179
SI 1970/649	Drivers' Hours (Passenger Vehicles) (Exemptions) (Amendment) Regulations 1970	Amend SI 1970/145	—
SI 1970/749	Passenger Transport (Compensation to Officers) Regulations 1970	—	179
SI 1970/1151	Transport Act 1968 (Commencement No 8) Order 1970	See note "Further orders" to SI 1968/1822	—
SI 1970/1298	British Transport (Amalgamation of Railways' Pension Funds) (No 2) Order 1970	—	180
SI 1970/1299	British Transport Docks Board (Alteration of Pension Schemes) Order 1970	—	180
SI 1970/1631	Transport Act 1968 (Commencement No 9) Order 1970	See note "Further orders" to SI 1968/1822	—
SI 1970/1767	Transport Act 1968 (Commencement No 10) Order 1970	See note "Further orders" to SI 1968/1822	—
SI 1970/1958	Functions of Traffic Wardens Order 1970	—	180

SI	*Description*	*Remarks*	*Page*
SI 1970/1990	London Transport (Alteration of Pension Schemes) Order 1970	—	183
SI 1970/1997	Vehicle and Driving Licences Records (Evidence) Regulations 1970	—	184
SI 1970/2019	London Transport (Compensation to Employees) Regulations 1970	—	185
SI 1971/116	National Freight Corporation (Alteration of Pension Schemes) (No 1) Order 1971	—	186
SI 1971/117	National Freight Corporation (Alteration of Pension Schemes) (No 2) Order 1971	—	186
SI 1971/189	Transport Pension Schemes (Decimal Currency) Order 1971	Made under Decimal Currency Act 1969, s 11(1); amends Port of London Act 1968 and SI 1954/898, SI 1956/732, SI 1961/559; also amended SI 1966/1164 (revoked)	—
SI 1971/333	London Cab Order 1971	Amends SR & O 1934/1346	—
SI 1971/629	British Waterways Board (Alteration of Pensions Schemes) Order 1971	—	186
SI 1971/818	Drivers' Hours (Passenger and Goods Vehicles) (Modifications) Order 1971	—	187
SI 1971/1128	British Transport (Pensions of Employees) Order 1971	—	187
SI 1971/1491	Chronically Sick and Disabled Persons Act 1970 (Commencement No 2) Order 1971	Made under s 21(9) of the 1970 Act; brought s 21 into force on 1 December 1971	—
SI 1971/1780	British Waterways Board (Alteration of Pension Schemes) (No 2) Order 1971	—	187
SI 1972/51	British Transport (Male Wages Grades Pensions) (Amendment) Order 1972	Amends SI 1954/898	—
SI 1972/632	Transport Holding Company (Compensation to Employees) Regulations 1972	—	187
SI 1972/1018	Road Traffic (Foreign Vehicles) Act 1972 Commencement Order 1972	Made under s 8(2) of the 1972 Act; brought the Act into force on 31 July 1972	—
SI 1972/1023	National Bus Company (Commencing Capital Debt) Order 1972	Made under Transport Act 1968, Sch 2, paras 1, 4; fixed the commencing capital debt of the National Bus Company at £97,625,178 (as from 4 August 1972)	—
SI 1972/1047	London Cab Order 1972	—	188
SI 1973/337	Transport Holding Company (Pensions) Order 1973	—	188
SI 1973/338	Transport Holding Company (Dissolution) Order 1973	—	188
SI 1973/366	Transport Holding Company (Commencing Capital Debt) (Extinguishment) Order 1973	—	189
SI 1973/1390	British Railways and London Transport Pension Schemes (Amendment) Order 1973	Amends SI 1970/1298, SI 1970/1990	—
SI 1973/1671	London Cab (No 2) Order 1973	—	189
SI 1973/1727	Greater Manchester Passenger Transport Area (Adaptation of Enactments and Instruments) Order 1973	—	189
SI 1973/1728	South Yorkshire Passenger Transport Area (Establishment of Executive) Order 1973	—	189

SI	*Description*	*Remarks*	*Page*
SI 1973/1729	West Yorkshire Passenger Transport Area (Establishment of Executive) Order 1973	—	190
SI 1973/1730	West Midlands Passenger Transport Area (Adaptation of Enactments and Instruments) Order 1973	—	190
SI 1973/1731	Merseyside Passenger Transport Area (Adaptation of Enactments and Instruments) Order 1973	—	190
SI 1973/1732	Tyne and Wear Passenger Transport Area (Adaptation of Enactments and Instruments) Order 1973	—	191
SI 1973/2019	British Railways Board (Alteration of Pension Schemes) Order 1973	—	191
SI 1974/407	Transport (London) Act 1969 (Commencement No 5) Order 1974	See note "Further orders" to SI 1969/1130	—
SI 1974/502	Motorways Traffic (Speed Limit) Regulations 1974	—	191
SI 1974/1986	Pipe-lines Act 1962 (Repeals and Modifications) Regulations 1974	—	192
SI 1974/2001	British Railways Board (Central Trust) Order 1974	—	192
SI 1974/2045	British Transport (Male Wages Grades Pensions) (Amendment) Order 1974	Amends SI 1954/898	—
SI 1974/2075	Road Traffic Act 1974 (Commencement No 1) Order 1974	—	192
SI 1975/489	Road Traffic Act 1974 (Commencement No 3) Order 1975	See note "Further orders" to SI 1974/2075	—
SI 1975/756	Road Traffic Act 1974 (Commencement No 4) Order 1975	See note "Further orders" to SI 1974/2075	—
SI 1975/1154	Road Traffic Act 1974 (Commencement No 5) Order 1975	See note "Further orders" to SI 1974/2075	—
SI 1975/1208	Motor Vehicles (International Circulation) Order 1975	—	193
SI 1975/1479	Road Traffic Act 1974 (Commencement No 6) Order 1975	See note "Further orders" to SI 1974/2075	—
SI 1975/1653	Road Traffic Act 1974 (Commencement No 7) Order 1975	See note "Further orders" to SI 1974/2075	—
SI 1975/2111	International Carriage of Dangerous Goods (Rear Marking of Motor Vehicles) Regulations 1975	—	194
SI 1976/329	National Freight Corporation (Commencing Capital Debt) Order 1976	Made under Transport Act 1968, Sch 2, paras 1, 4; fixed the commencing capital debt of the National Freight Corporation at £98,096,733 (as from 29 March 1976)	—
SI 1976/555	Goods Vehicles (Ascertainment of Maximum Gross Weights) Regulations 1976	—	194
SI 1977/276	Carriage of Goods (Prohibition of Discrimination) Regulations 1977	—	194
SI 1977/699	British Railways Board (Pension Funds Investment Provisions) Order 1977	—	195
SI 1977/1316	Vehicle and Driving Licences (Compensation to Officers) Regulations 1977	—	195

Date made	*Description*	*Remarks*	*Page*
25 May 1977	70 miles per hour, 60 miles per hour and 50 miles per hour (Temporary Speed Limit) Order 1977	—	195

SI	*Description*	*Remarks*	*Page*
SI 1978/1150	Transport Act 1978 (Commencement No 1) Order 1978	—	196
SI 1978/1180	Weighing of Motor Vehicles (Use of Dynamic Axle Weighing Machines) Regulations 1978	—	196
SI 1978/1187	Transport Act 1978 (Commencement No 2) Order 1978	See note "Further orders" to SI 1978/1150	—
SI 1978/1290	National Freight Corporation (Central Trust) Order 1978	—	196
SI 1978/1358	British Railways Board (Winding Up of Closed Pension Funds) Order 1978	—	197
SI 1978/1535	Control of Off-Street Parking (England and Wales) Order 1978	—	197
SI 1978/1548	70 miles per hour, 60 miles per hour and 50 miles per hour (Temporary Speed Limit) (Continuation) Order 1978	Continues Order of 25 May 1977	—
SI 1978/1684	Public Service Vehicles (Lost Property) Regulations 1978	—	198

Date made	*Description*	*Remarks*	*Page*
16 Aug 1978	70 miles per hour, 60 miles per hour and 50 miles per hour (Temporary Speed Limit) (Variation) Order 1978	Amends Order of 25 May 1977	—

SI	*Description*	*Remarks*	*Page*
SI 1979/236	Control of Off-Street Parking outside Greater London (Appeals Procedure) (England and Wales) Regulations 1979	See note "Appeals procedure" to SI 1978/1535	—
SI 1979/1746	Passenger and Goods Vehicles (Recording Equipment) Regulations 1979	—	198
SI 1980/588	London Cab Order 1980	Amends SR & O 1934/1346	—
SI 1980/657	National Freight Corporation (Central Trust) (Amendment) Order 1980	See note "Further order" to SI 1978/1290	—
SI 1980/697	Carriage of Goods by Road (Parties to Convention) (Amendment) Order 1980	Amends SI 1967/1683	—
SI 1980/765	Motorcycles (Sound Level Measurement Certificates) Regulations 1980	—	199
SI 1980/913	Transport Act 1980 (Commencement No 1) Order 1980	—	199
SI 1980/1095	Motor Vehicles (International Circulation) (Amendment) Order 1980	Amends SI 1975/1208; partially revoked by SI 1989/993	—
SI 1980/1182	Motor Vehicles (Type Approval) Regulations 1980	—	200
SI 1980/1351	British Transport (Pensions of Employees) Order 1980	—	201
SI 1980/1353	Transport Act 1980 (Commencement No 2) Order 1980	See note "Further orders" to SI 1980/913	—
SI 1980/1380	National Freight Corporation (Transfer of Undertaking) Order 1980	Made under Transport Act 1980, s 45; nominated the National Freight Company Ltd, and appointed 1 October 1980 as the appointed day, for the purposes of s 45 of that Act	—
SI 1980/1460	Road Transport (Northern Ireland Passenger Services) Regulations 1980	—	201

SI	*Description*	*Remarks*	*Page*
SI 1980/1966	Carriage by Air and Road Act 1979 (Commencement No 1) Order 1980	—	201
SI 1981/256	Transport Act 1980 (Commencement No 4) Order 1981	See note "Further orders" to SI 1980/913	—
SI 1981/257	Public Service Vehicles (Conditions of Fitness, Equipment, Use and Certification) Regulations 1981	—	201
SI 1981/346	British Railways Pension Schemes (Unfunded Proportions) (No 1) Order 1981	—	203
SI 1981/347	National Freight Company Pension Schemes (Unfunded Proportions) Order 1981	See note "Further orders" to SI 1981/346	—
SI 1981/462	Road Transport (Northern Ireland Passenger Services) (Amendment) Regulations 1981	Amend SI 1980/1460	—
SI 1981/493	Motor Vehicles (Type Approval) (EEC Manufacturers) Regulations 1981	—	203
SI 1981/604	Carriage of Goods by Road (Gibraltar) (Amendment) Order 1981	Amends SI 1967/820	—
SI 1981/1331	Transport Act 1981 (Commencement No 1) Order 1981	—	203
SI 1981/1373	Road Traffic Acts 1960 and 1972, Road Traffic Regulation Act 1967, and Transport Act 1968 (Metrication) Regulations 1981	See Preliminary Note "Metrication" (under main head "Road traffic")	—
SI 1981/1374	Road Traffic Acts 1960 and 1972, and Road Traffic Regulation Act 1967 (Metrication) (No 2) Regulations 1981	See Preliminary Note "Metrication" (under main head "Road traffic")	—
SI 1981/1387	Public Passenger Vehicles Act 1981 (Commencement) Order 1981	Made under s 89(2) of the 1981 Act; brought the Act into force on 30 October 1981	—
SI 1981/1543	Carriage of Goods by Road (Isle of Man) Order 1981	See Preliminary Note "International carriage by road" (under main head "Road traffic")	—
SI 1981/1646	British Railways Pension Schemes (Unfunded Proportions) (No 2) Order 1981	See note "Further orders" to SI 1981/346	—
SI 1981/1694	Motor Vehicles (Tests) Regulations 1981	—	204
SI 1982/7	Motor Vehicles (Type Approval) (Amendment) Regulations 1982	Amend SI 1980/1182; amended by SI 1986/1501	—
SI 1982/20	Public Service Vehicles (Conditions of Fitness, Equipment, Use and Certification (Amendment) Regulations 1982	Amend SI 1981/257	—
SI 1982/310	Transport Act 1981 (Commencement No 4) Order 1982	See note "Further orders" to SI 1981/1331	—
SI 1982/311	London Cab Order 1982	Amends SR & O 1934/1346	—
SI 1982/814	Motor Vehicles (Tests) (Amendment) (No 2) Regulations 1982	Amend SI 1981/1694	—
SI 1982/1058	Public Service Vehicles (Conditions of Fitness, Equipment, Use and Certification) (Amendment) (No 2) Regulations 1982	Amend SI 1981/257	—
SI 1982/1271	Motor Vehicles (Type Approval for Goods Vehicles) (Great Britain) Regulations 1982	—	207
SI 1982/1451	Transport Act 1981 (Commencement No 7) Order 1982	See note "Further orders" to SI 1981/1331	—
SI 1982/1477	Motor Vehicles (Tests) (Amendment) (No 3) Regulations 1982	Amend SI 1981/1694	—
SI 1982/1555	Driving Licences (Community Driving Licence) Regulations 1982	—	207

SI	*Description*	*Remarks*	*Page*
SI 1982/1561	Transport Act 1982 (Commencement No 1) Order 1982	—	208
SI 1982/1715	Motor Vehicles (Tests) Amendment (No 4) Regulations 1982	Amend SI 1981/1694	—
SI 1982/1804	Transport Act 1982 (Commencement No 2) Order 1982	See note "Further orders" to SI 1982/1561	—
SI 1983/276	Transport Act 1982 (Commencement No 3) Order 1983	See note "Further orders" to SI 1982/1561	—
SI 1983/576	Transport Act 1981 (Commencement No 9) Order 1983	See note "Further orders" to SI 1981/1331	—
SI 1983/910	Road Vehicles (Marking of Special Weights) Regulations 1983	—	208
SI 1983/930	Transport Act 1981 (Commencement No 10) Order 1983	See note "Further orders" to SI 1981/1331	—
SI 1983/1089	Transport Act 1981 (Commencement No 11) Order 1983	See note "Further orders" to SI 1981/1331	—
SI 1983/1168	Electrically Assisted Pedal Cycles Regulations 1983	—	208
SI 1983/1176	Pedal Cycles (Construction and Use) Regulations 1983	—	209
SI 1983/1434	Motor Vehicles (Tests) (Amendment) (No 2) Regulations 1983	Amend SI 1981/1694	—
SI 1984/144	Passenger and Goods Vehicles (Recording Equipment) (Amendment) Regulations 1984	See note "Further regulations" to SI 1979/1746	—
SI 1984/175	Transport Act 1982 (Commencement No 5) Order 1984	See note "Further orders" to SI 1982/1561	—
SI 1984/672	Driving Licences (Exchangeable Licences) Order 1984	—	212
SI 1984/697	Motor Vehicles (Type Approval for Goods Vehicles) (Great Britain) (Amendment) Regulations 1984	Amend SI 1982/1271	—
SI 1984/748	Road Transport (International Passenger Services) Regulations 1984	—	212
SI 1984/811	Road Traffic Act 1974 (Commencement No 8) Order 1984	See note "Further orders" to SI 1974/2075	—
SI 1984/981	Motor Vehicles (Type Approval) (Great Britain) Regulations 1984	—	213
SI 1984/1126	Motor Vehicles (Tests) (Amendment) (No 4) Regulations 1984	Amend SI 1981/1694	—
SI 1984/1401	Motor Vehicles (Type Approval) (Great Britain) (Amendment) Regulations 1984	Amend SI 1984/981	—
SI 1984/1402	Motor Vehicles (Type Approval for Goods Vehicles) (Great Britain) (Amendment) (No 2) Regulations 1984	Amend SI 1982/1271	—
SI 1984/1406	Public Service Vehicles (Carrying Capacity) Regulations 1984	—	214
SI 1984/1761	Motor Vehicles (Type Approval) (Great Britain) (Amendment) (No 2) Regulations 1984	Amend SI 1984/981	—
SI 1984/1763	Public Service Vehicles (Conditions of Fitness, Equipment, Use and Certification) (Amendment) Regulations 1984	Amend SI 1981/257	—
SI 1984/1996	Motor Vehicles (Payments in Respect of Applicants for Exemption from Wearing Seat Belts) Order 1984	Made under Transport Act 1982, s 70(3); amends s 70(2) of that Act (as from 1 February 1985)	—
SI 1985/45	Motor Vehicles (Tests) (Amendment) Regulations 1985	Amend SI 1981/1694	—

SI	*Description*	*Remarks*	*Page*
SI 1985/46	Motor Vehicles (Type Approval for Goods Vehicles) (Great Britain) (Amendment) Regulations 1985	Amend SI 1982/1271	—
SI 1985/65	Driving Licences (Exchangeable Licences) Order 1985	See note "Further orders" to SI 1984/672	—
SI 1985/459	Motor Vehicles (International Circulation) (Amendment) Order 1985	Amends SI 1975/1208; partially revoked by SI 1989/993	—
SI 1985/610	Motor Vehicles (International Circulation) Regulations 1985	—	214
SI 1985/713	Traffic Signs (Welsh and English Language Provisions) Regulations and General Directions 1985	See note "Welsh versions" to SI 2002/3113	—
SI 1985/722	Motor Vehicles (Exemption from Vehicles Excise Duty) Order 1985	—	215
SI 1985/933	London Cab Order 1985	Amends SR & O 1934/1346	—
SI 1985/1461	Driving Licences (Exchangeable Licences) (No 2) Order 1985	See note "Further orders" to SI 1984/672	—
SI 1985/1651	Motor Vehicles (Type Approval) (Great Britain) (Amendment) Regulations 1985	Amend SI 1984/981	—
SI 1985/1887	Transport Act 1985 (Commencement No 1) Order 1985	—	215
SI 1985/1901	Public Transport Companies (Permitted Maximum and Required Minimum Number of Directors) Order 1985	—	219
SI 1985/1902	Transport Act 1985 (Exclusion of Bus Operating Powers and Exemption for Councils Running Small Bus Undertakings) Order 1985	—	219
SI 1985/1903	Transport Act 1985 (Modifications in Schedule 4 to the Transport Act 1968) Order 1985	—	220
SI 1985/1921	Service Subsidy Agreements (Tendering) Regulations 1985	See note "Wales" to SI 2002/2090	—
SI 1985/1923	Motor Vehicles (Tests) (Amendment) (No 3) Regulations 1985	Amend SI 1981/1694	—
SI 1986/77	Travel Concession Schemes Regulations 1986	—	222
SI 1986/80	Transport Act 1985 (Commencement No 2) Order 1986	See note "Summary" to SI 1985/1887	—
SI 1986/81	Public Passenger Transport Policies (Anticipatory Exercise of Powers) Order 1986	—	222
SI 1986/225	Control of Off-Street Parking (England and Wales) (Metropolitan Districts) Order 1985	—	223
SI 1986/262	Control of Off-Street Parking in Greater London (Appeals Procedure) Regulations 1986	—	223
SI 1986/264	Control of Off-Street Parking (Appeals Procedure) (England and Wales) (Metropolitan Districts) Regulations 1986	See note "Appeals procedure" to SI 1986/225	—
SI 1986/414	Transport Act 1985 (Commencement No 3) Order 1986	See note "Summary" to SI 1985/1887	—
SI 1986/427	Motor Vehicles (Type Approval for Goods Vehicles) (Great Britain) (Amendment) Regulations 1986	Amend SI 1982/1271	—
SI 1986/566	Local Services (Operation by Taxis) (London) Regulations 1986	—	224
SI 1986/567	Local Services (Operation by Taxis) Regulations 1986	—	224
SI 1986/739	Motor Vehicles (Type Approval) (Great Britain) (Amendment) Regulations 1986	Amend SI 1984/981	—
SI 1986/1078	Road Vehicles (Construction and Use) Regulations 1986	—	224
SI 1986/1088	Transport Act 1985 (Commencement No 4) Order 1986	See note "Summary" to SI 1985/1887	—

SI	*Description*	*Remarks*	*Page*
SI 1986/1089	Motor Vehicles (Type Approval for Goods Vehicles) (Great Britain) (Amendment) (No 2) Regulations 1986	Amend SI 1982/1271	—
SI 1986/1175	Motor Vehicles (Variation of Speed Limits) Regulations 1986	Made under Road Traffic Regulation Act 1984, s 86(2), (3); amend Pts I, IV of Sch 6 to that Act (as from 22 July 1986)	—
SI 1986/1188	London Taxis (Licensing Appeals) Regulations 1986	—	290
SI 1986/1326	Transport Act 1982 (Commencement No 6) Order 1986	See note "Further orders" to SI 1982/1561	—
SI 1986/1328	Functions of Traffic Wardens (Amendment) Order 1986	Amends SI 1970/1958	—
SI 1986/1330	Fixed Penalty (Procedure) Regulations 1986	—	290
SI 1986/1385	Transport Act 1985 (Extension of Eligibility for Travel Concessions) Order 1986	—	294
SI 1986/1386	Licensed Taxis (Hiring at Separate Fares) Order 1986	—	294
SI 1986/1387	Licensed Taxis (Hiring at Separate Fares) (London) Order 1986	—	295
SI 1986/1428	Vehicle Licences (Duration of First Licences and Rate of Duty) Order 1986	—	295
SI 1986/1450	Transport Act 1985 (Commencement No 5) Order 1986	See note "Summary" to SI 1985/1887	—
SI 1986/1457	Community Drivers' Hours and Recording Equipment Regulations 1986	See note "Further regulations" to SI 1979/1746	—
SI 1986/1458	Drivers' Hours (Harmonisation with Community Rules) Regulations 1986	—	295
SI 1986/1459	Drivers' Hours (Goods Vehicles) (Modifications) Order 1986	—	295
SI 1986/1492	Drivers' Hours (Goods Vehicles) (Exemptions) Regulations 1986	—	296
SI 1986/1501	Motor Vehicles (Type Approval) (Amendment) Regulations 1986	Amend SI 1980/1182, SI 1982/7; revoke SI 1982/1623, SI 1984/1927, SI 1985/1072	—
SI 1986/1597	Road Vehicles (Construction and Use) (Amendment) Regulations 1986	Amend SI 1986/1078	—
SI 1986/1628	Operation of Public Service Vehicles (Partnership) Regulations 1986	—	296
SI 1986/1629	Public Service Vehicles (Traffic Commissioners: Publications and Inquiries) Regulations 1986	—	296
SI 1986/1648	Tyne and Wear Passenger Transport Executive (Exclusion of Bus Operating Powers) Order 1986	—	297
SI 1986/1649	Greater Manchester Passenger Transport Executive (Exclusion of Bus Operating Powers) Order 1986	See note "Further orders" to SI 1986/1648	—
SI 1986/1650	Merseyside Passenger Transport Executive (Exclusion of Bus Operating Powers) Order 1986	See note "Further orders" to SI 1986/1648	—
SI 1986/1651	South Yorkshire Passenger Transport Executive (Exclusion of Bus Operating Powers) Order 1986	See note "Further orders" to SI 1986/1648	—
SI 1986/1652	West Midlands Passenger Transport Executive (Exclusion of Bus Operating Powers) Order 1986	See note "Further orders" to SI 1986/1648	—
SI 1986/1653	West Yorkshire Passenger Transport Executive (Exclusion of Bus Operating Powers) Order 1986	See note "Further orders" to SI 1986/1648	—

SI	*Description*	*Remarks*	*Page*
SI 1986/1671	Public Service Vehicles (Registration of Local Services) Regulations 1986	—	297
SI 1986/1691	Public Service Vehicles (London Local Service Licences) Regulations 1986	—	298
SI 1986/1779	Taxis (Schemes for Hire at Separate Fares) Regulations 1986	—	298
SI 1986/1794	Transport Act 1985 (Commencement No 6) Order 1986	See note "Summary" to SI 1985/1887	—
SI 1986/1801	Airports Act 1986 (Modifications in Sch 4 to the Transport Act 1968) Order 1986	See title Aviation	—
SI 1986/1812	Public Service Vehicles (Conditions of Fitness, Equipment, Use and Certification) (Amendment) (No 2) Regulations 1986	Amend SI 1981/257	—
SI 1986/1882	Carriage of Goods by Road (Guernsey) Order 1986	See Preliminary Note "International carriage by road" (under main head "Road traffic")	—
SI 1986/2076	Passenger and Goods Vehicles (Recording Equipment) (Amendment) Regulations 1986	Amend SI 1979/1746	—
SI 1986/2128	Passenger and Goods Vehicles (Recording Equipment) (Approval of fitters and workshops) (Fees) Regulations 1986	See note "Fees" to SI 1979/1746	—
SI 1987/337	Transport Act 1985 (Modifications in Schedule 4 to the Transport Act 1968) (Amendment) Order 1987	Amends SI 1985/1903	—
SI 1987/676	Road Vehicles (Construction and Use) (Amendment) Regulations 1987	Amend SI 1986/1078	—
SI 1987/1133	Road Vehicles (Construction and Use) (Amendment) (No 2) Regulations 1987	Amend SI 1986/1078	—
SI 1987/1228	Transport Act 1985 (Commencement No 7) Order 1987	See note "Summary" to SI 1985/1887	—
SI 1987/1229	Section 19 Minibus (Designated Bodies) Order 1987	—	299
SI 1987/1326	Road Vehicles (Marking of Special Weights) (Amendment) Regulations 1987	Amend SI 1983/910	—
SI 1987/1421	Drivers' Hours (Goods Vehicles) (Keeping of Records) Regulations 1987	—	299
SI 1987/1508	Motor Vehicles (Type Approval for Goods Vehicles) (Great Britain) (Amendment) Regulations 1987	Amend SI 1982/1271	—
SI 1987/1509	Motor Vehicles (Type Approval) (Great Britain) (Amendment) Regulations 1987	Amend SI 1984/981	—
SI 1987/1535	London Taxi Sharing Scheme Order 1987	—	299
SI 1987/1755	Road Transport (International Passenger Services) (Amendment) Regulations 1987	Amend SI 1984/748	—
SI 1988/271	Road Vehicles (Construction and Use) (Amendment) Regulations 1988	Amend SI 1986/1078	—
SI 1988/340	Public Service Vehicles (Conditions of Fitness, Equipment, Use and Certification) (Amendment) Regulations 1988	Amend SI 1981/257	—
SI 1988/370	International Carriage of Dangerous Goods by Road (Fees) Regulations 1988	—	299
SI 1988/371	International Transport of Goods under Cover of TIR Carnets (Fees) Regulations 1988	—	300
SI 1988/408	Public Service Vehicles (London Local Service Licences) (Amendment) Regulations 1988	Amend SI 1986/1691	—
SI 1988/643	Department of Transport (Fees) Order 1988	—	300
SI 1988/962	British Transport (Alteration of Pension Schemes) (Amendment) Order 1988	Amends SI 1969/1858	—
SI 1988/989	Motor Vehicles (Tests) (Amendment) (No 2) Regulations 1988	Amend SI 1981/1694	—
SI 1988/1103	Motor Vehicles (Type Approval) (Amendment) Regulations 1988	Amend SI 1980/1182	—

SI	*Description*	*Remarks*	*Page*
SI 1988/1177	Road Vehicles (Construction and Use) (Amendment) (No 3) Regulations 1988	Amend SI 1986/1078; revoke SI 1988/1102	—
SI 1988/1178	Road Vehicles (Construction and Use) (Amendment) (No 4) Regulations 1988	Amend SI 1986/1078	—
SI 1988/1287	Road Vehicles (Construction and Use) (Amendment) (No 5) Regulations 1988	Amend SI 1986/1078	—
SI 1988/1478	Goods Vehicles (Plating and Testing) Regulations 1988	—	301
SI 1988/1522	Motor Vehicles (Type Approval) (Great Britain) (Amendment) Regulations 1988	Amend SI 1984/981	—
SI 1988/1523	Motor Vehicles (Type Approval for Goods Vehicles) (Great Britain) (Amendment) Regulations 1988	Amend SI 1982/1271	—
SI 1988/1524	Road Vehicles (Construction and Use) (Amendment) (No 6) Regulations 1988	Amend SI 1986/1078	—
SI 1988/1640	Motorcycles (Sound Level Measurement Certificates) (Amendment) Regulations 1988	Amend SI 1980/765	—
SI 1988/1809	Road Transport (International Passenger Services) (Amendment) Regulations 1988	Amend SI 1984/748	—
SI 1988/1871	Road Vehicles (Construction and Use) (Amendment) (No 7) Regulations 1988	Amend SI 1986/1078	—
SI 1988/1879	Public Service Vehicles (Registration of Local Services) (Amendment) Regulations 1988	Amend SI 1986/1671	—
SI 1988/1894	Motor Vehicles (Tests) (Amendment) (No 3) Regulations 1988	Amend SI 1981/1694	—
SI 1988/2268	Use of Invalid Carriages on Highways Regulations 1988	—	302
SI 1988/2294	Transport Act 1985 (Commencement No 6) (Amendment) Order 1988	Amends 1986/1794	—
SI 1989/495	Transfer of Functions (Transport Tribunal) Order 1989	See title Constitutional Law (Pt 2)	—
SI 1989/713	Motorcycles (Sound Level Measurement Certificates) (Amendment) Regulations 1989	Amend SI 1980/765	—
SI 1989/993	Motor Vehicles (International Circulation) (Amendment) Order 1989	Amends SI 1975/1208; partially revokes SI 1980/1095, SI 1985/459	—
SI 1989/1064	Public Service Vehicles (Registration of Local Services) (Amendment) Regulations 1989	Amend SI 1986/1671	—
SI 1989/1226	Recovery Vehicles (Number of Vehicles Recovered) Order 1989	—	302
SI 1989/1478	Road Vehicles (Construction and Use) (Amendment) Regulations 1989	Amend SI 1986/1078	—
SI 1989/1579	Motor Vehicles (Type Approval for Goods Vehicles) (Great Britain) (Amendment) Regulations 1989	Amend SI 1982/1271	—
SI 1989/1580	Motor Vehicles (Type Approval) (Great Britain) (Amendment) Regulations 1989	Amend SI 1984/981	—
SI 1989/1591	Motorcycles (Sound Level Measurement Certificates) (Amendment) (No 2) Regulations 1989	Amend SI 1980/765	—
SI 1989/1693	Goods Vehicles (Plating and Testing) (Amendment) (No 2) Regulations 1989	Amend SI 1988/1478	—
SI 1989/1694	Motor Vehicles (Tests) (Amendment) (No 3) Regulations 1989	Amend SI 1981/1694	—
SI 1989/1695	Road Vehicles (Construction and Use) (Amendment) (No 2) Regulations 1989	Amend SI 1986/1078	—
SI 1989/1796	Road Vehicles Lighting Regulations 1989	—	303
SI 1989/1843	Road Traffic (Driver Licensing and Information Systems) Act 1989 (Commencement No 1) Order 1989	—	303
SI 1989/1865	Road Vehicles (Construction and Use) (Amendment) (No 3) Regulations 1989	Amend SI 1986/1078	—

SI	*Description*	*Remarks*	*Page*
SI 1989/2121	Passenger and Goods Vehicles (Recording Equipment) Regulations 1989	See note "Further regulations" to SI 1979/1746	—
SI 1989/2262	Motor Vehicles (Type Approval) (Amendment) (No 2) Regulations 1989	Amend SI 1980/1182	—
SI 1989/2288	All-Terrain Motor Vehicles (Safety) Regulations 1989	See title Sale of Goods and Consumer Protection	—
SI 1989/2293	Transport Act 1985 (Extension of Eligibility for Travel Concessions) (Amendment) Order 1989	Amends SI 1986/1385; partially revoked by Transport Act 2000, s 274, Sch 31, Pt II	—
SI 1989/2359	Public Service Vehicles (Conditions of Fitness, Equipment, Use and Certification) (Amendment) (No 2) Regulations 1989	Amend SI 1981/257	—
SI 1989/2360	Road Vehicles (Construction and Use) (Amendment) (No 4) Regulations 1989	Amend SI 1986/1078	—
SI 1990/94	Motor Vehicles (Type Approval) (Great Britain) (Amendment) Regulations 1990	Amend SI 1984/981	—
SI 1990/144	Driving Licences (Community Driving Licence) Regulations 1990	—	305
SI 1990/317	Road Vehicles (Construction and Use) (Amendment) Regulations 1990	Amend SI 1986/1078	—
SI 1990/335	Fixed Penalty Offences Order 1990	—	306
SI 1990/448	Goods Vehicles (Plating and Testing) (Amendment) Regulations 1990	Amend SI 1988/1478; supersede SI 1989/320	—
SI 1990/802	Road Traffic (Driver Licensing and Information Systems) Act 1989 (Commencement No 2) Order 1990	See note "Summary" to SI 1989/1843	—
SI 1990/865	Driver Information Systems (Exemption) Order 1990	—	307
SI 1990/933	Parking Act 1989 (Commencement) Order 1990	Made under s 5(2) of the 1989 Act; brought the whole Act into force on 16 May 1990	—
SI 1990/1020	Public Service Vehicles (Conduct of Drivers, Inspectors, Conductors and Passengers) Regulations 1990	—	307
SI 1990/1103	Road Transport (International Passenger Services) (Amendment) Regulations 1990	Amend SI 1984/748	—
SI 1990/1131	Road Vehicles (Construction and Use) (Amendment) (No 2) Regulations 1990	Amend SI 1986/1078	—
SI 1990/1163	Road Vehicles (Construction and Use) (Amendment) (No 3) Regulations 1990	Amend SI 1986/1078	—
SI 1990/1192	Goods Vehicles (Community Cabotage Authorisations) (Fees) Regulations 1990	—	317
SI 1990/1285	Local Government Finance (Miscellaneous Amendments and Repeal) Order 1990	See title Local Government; amends SI 1973/1727, SI 1973/1728, SI 1973/1729, SI 1973/1730	—
SI 1990/1656	Secretary of State's Traffic Orders (Procedure) (England and Wales) Regulations 1990	—	317
SI 1990/1708	Section 19 Minibus (Designated Bodies) (Amendment) Order 1990	Amends SI 1987/1229	—
SI 1990/1839	Motor Vehicles (Type Approval) (Great Britain) (Amendment) (No 2) Regulations 1990	Amend SI 1984/981	—
SI 1990/1850	Operation of Public Service Vehicles (Partnership) (Amendment) Regulations 1990	Amend SI 1986/1628	—

SI	*Description*	*Remarks*	*Page*
SI 1990/1851	Public Service Vehicle Operators (Qualifications) Regulations 1990	Made under European Communities Act 1972, s 2(2); amend Public Passenger Vehicles Act 1981, Sch 3 (as from 11 October 1990)	—
SI 1990/1981	Road Vehicles (Construction and Use) (Amendment) (No 4) Regulations 1990	Amend SI 1986/1078	—
SI 1990/2003	London Cab (No 2) Order 1990	Amends SR & O 1934/1346	—
SI 1990/2212	Road Vehicles (Construction and Use) (Amendment) (No 5) Regulations 1990	Amend SI 1986/1078	—
SI 1990/2228	Road Traffic (Driver Licensing and Information Systems) Act 1989 (Commencement No 3) Order 1990	See note "Summary" to SI 1989/1843	—
SI 1990/2610	Road Traffic (Driver Licensing and Information Systems) Act 1989 (Commencement No 4) Order 1990	See note "Summary" to SI 1989/1843	—
SI 1991/252	Goods Vehicles (Plating and Testing) (Amendment) (No 1) Regulations 1991	Amend SI 1988/1478	—
SI 1991/253	Motor Vehicles (Tests) (Amendment) (No 1) Regulations 1991	Amend SI 1981/1694	—
SI 1991/288	Traffic Areas (Reorganisation) Order 1990	—	318
SI 1991/455	Motor Vehicles (Tests) (Amendment) (No 2) Regulations 1991	Amend SI 1981/1694	—
SI 1991/458	International Carriage of Dangerous Goods by Road (Fees) (Amendment) Regulations 1991	Amend SI 1988/370	—
SI 1991/459	International Transport of Goods under Cover of TIR Carnets (Fees) (Amendment) Regulations 1991	Amend SI 1988/371	—
SI 1991/486	Driving Licences (Community Driving Licence) (Amendment) Regulations 1991	Partially revoke SI 1982/1555; repeal Road Traffic (Driving Licences) Act 1983, s 2(3)	—
SI 1991/510	National Bus Company (Dissolution) Order 1991	—	318
SI 1991/634	Traffic Areas (Reorganisation) Order 1991	Amends SI 1991/288	—
SI 1991/771	Motor Vehicles (International Circulation) (Amendment) Order 1991	Amends SI 1975/1208	—
SI 1991/811	Department of Transport (Fees) (Amendment) Order 1991	Amends SI 1988/643	—
SI 1991/1021	Motor Vehicles (Type Approval for Goods Vehicles) (Great Britain) (Amendment) Regulations 1991	Amend SI 1982/1271	—
SI 1991/1022	Motor Vehicles (Type Approval) (Great Britain) (Amendment) Regulations 1991	Amend SI 1984/981	—
SI 1991/1129	Motor Cars (Driving Instruction) (Amendment) Regulations 1991	Made under Road Traffic Act 1988, ss 125(3), 127(2), 132(1)(a), (2)(b), 134, 141 and SI 1988/643; insert s 128(8) of the 1988 Act (as from 3 June 1991) (s 128 of the 1988 Act is substituted by the Road Safety Act 2006, s 42, Sch 6, paras 1, 10, as from a day to be appointed by order); revoked by SI 2005/1902 in so far as amended SI 1989/2057	—

SI	*Description*	*Remarks*	*Page*
SI 1991/1212	Channel Tunnel Rail Link (Effective Joining) Order 1991	See Preliminary Note "Channel Tunnel" (under main head "Railways, tramways and inland waterways")	—
SI 1991/1525	Motor Vehicles (Tests) (Amendment) (No 3) Regulations 1991	Amend SI 1981/1694	—
SI 1991/1526	Road Vehicles (Construction and Use) (Amendment) (No 1) Regulations 1991	Amend SI 1986/1078	—
SI 1991/1527	Road Vehicles (Construction and Use) (Amendment) (No 2) Regulations 1991	Amend SI 1986/1078	—
SI 1991/1727	Motor Vehicles (International Circulation) (Amendment) (No 2) Order 1991	Amends SI 1975/1208	—
SI 1991/1970	Motor Vehicles (Type Approval for Goods Vehicles) (Great Britain) (Amendment) (No 2) Regulations 1991	Amend SI 1982/1271	—
SI 1991/1971	Motor Vehicles (Type Approval) (Great Britain) (Amendment) (No 2) Regulations 1991	Amend SI 1984/981	—
SI 1991/1997	Companies Act 1989 (Eligibility for Appointment as Company Auditor) (Consequential Amendments) Regulations 1991	See title Companies; amend SI 1991/510	—
SI 1991/2003	Road Vehicles (Construction and Use) (Amendment) (No 3) Regulations 1991	Amend SI 1986/1078	—
SI 1991/2054	Road Traffic Act 1991 (Commencement No 1) Order 1991	—	318
SI 1991/2125	Road Vehicles (Construction and Use) (Amendment) (No 4) Regulations 1991	Amend SI 1986/1078	—
SI 1991/2229	Motor Vehicles (Tests) (Amendment) (No 4) Regulations 1991	Amend SI 1981/1694	—
SI 1991/2684	Solicitors' Incorporated Practices Order 1991	See title Courts and Legal Services; modifies SI 1979/236, SI 1986/262, SI 1986/264	—
SI 1991/2710	Road Vehicles (Construction and Use) (Amendment) (No 5) Regulations 1991	Amend SI 1986/1078	—
SI 1991/2791	Motor Vehicles (Tests) (Amendment) (No 5) Regulations 1991	Amend SI 1981/1694	—
SI 1991/2830	Motor Vehicles (Type Approval) (Amendment) (No 3) Regulations 1991	Amend SI 1980/1182	—
SI 1992/25	Motor Vehicles (Type Approval for Goods Vehicles) (Great Britain) (Amendment) (No 3) Regulations 1992	Amend SI 1982/1271	—
SI 1992/56	Agricultural or Forestry Tractors and Tractor Components (Type Approval) (Fees) (Revocation) Regulations 1992	Made under Finance Act 1973, s 56(1), (2); revoke SI 1991/2098 (as from 10 February 1992)	—
SI 1992/199	Road Traffic Act 1991 (Commencement No 2) Order 1991	See note "Summary" to SI 1991/2054	—
SI 1992/345	Fixed Penalty Offences Order 1992	See note "Further orders" to SI 1990/335	—
SI 1992/352	Road Vehicles (Construction and Use) (Amendment) Regulations 1992	Amend SI 1986/1078	—
SI 1992/386	Vehicles (Charges for Release from Immobilisation Devices) Regulations 1992	—	321
SI 1992/421	Road Traffic Act 1991 (Commencement No 3) Order 1992	See note "Summary" to SI 1991/2054	—
SI 1992/422	Road Vehicles (Construction and Use) (Amendment) (No 2) Regulations 1992	Amend SI 1986/1078	—

SI	*Description*	*Remarks*	*Page*
SI 1992/449	Pipe-lines (Metrication) Regulations 1992	Made under European Communities Act 1972, s 2(2), (4); amend Pipe-lines Act 1962, s 66, Sch 1, Pt I, Sch 2, Pt I (and other provisions all now repealed) (as from 1 January 1995)	—
SI 1992/510	Retention of Registration Marks Regulations 1992	See note "Previous regulations" to SI 1993/987	—
SI 1992/566	Motor Vehicles (Tests) (Amendment) Regulations 1992	Amend SI 1981/1694	—
SI 1992/646	Road Vehicles (Construction and Use) (Amendment) (No 3) Regulations 1992	Amend SI 1986/1078	—
SI 1992/1209	Road Traffic Offenders (Prescribed Devices) Order 1992	—	321
SI 1992/1215	Road Traffic (Temporary Restrictions) Procedure Regulations 1992	—	322
SI 1992/1217	Tramcars and Trolley Vehicles (Modification of Enactments) Regulations 1992	—	322
SI 1992/1218	Road Traffic (Temporary Restrictions) Act 1991 (Commencement) Order 1992	Made under s 2(7) of the 1991 Act; brought the whole Act into force, subject to transitional provisions, on 1 July 1992	—
SI 1992/1285	Road Vehicles (Prohibition) Regulations 1992	—	323
SI 1992/1286	Road Traffic Act 1991 (Commencement No 4 and Transitional Provisions) Order 1992	See note "Summary" to SI 1991/2054	—
SI 1992/1341	Motor Vehicles (Type Approval) (Great Britain) (Amendment) Regulations 1992	Amend SI 1984/981	—
SI 1992/1342	Motor Vehicles (Type Approval for Goods Vehicles) (Great Britain) (Amendment) (No 2) Regulations 1992	Amend SI 1982/1271	—
SI 1992/1347	Transport and Works Act 1992 (Commencement No 1) Order 1992	—	325
SI 1992/1410	Road Traffic Act 1991 (Commencement No 4 and Transitional Provisions) (Amendment) Order 1992	Amends SI 1992/1286	—
SI 1992/1609	Motor Vehicles (Tests) (Amendment) (No 2) Regulations 1992	Amend SI 1981/1694	—
SI 1992/2010	Road Traffic Act 1991 (Commencement No 5 and Transitional Provisions) Order 1992	See note "Summary" to SI 1991/2054	—
SI 1992/2016	Road Vehicles (Construction and Use) (Amendment) (No 4) Regulations 1992	Amend SI 1986/1078	—
SI 1992/2043	Transport and Works Act 1992 (Commencement No 2) Order 1992	See note "Further orders" to SI 1992/1347	—
SI 1992/2044	Transport (Guided Systems) Order 1992	—	326
SI 1992/2137	Road Vehicles (Construction and Use) (Amendment) (No 5) Regulations 1992	Amend SI 1986/1078	—
SI 1992/2161	Motor Vehicles (Type Approval) (Great Britain) (Amendment) (No 2) Regulations 1992	Amend SI 1984/981	—
SI 1992/2784	Transport and Works Act 1992 (Commencement No 3 and Transitional Provisions) Order 1992	See note "Further orders" to SI 1992/1347	—
SI 1992/2789	Transport Levying Bodies Regulations 1992	—	326
SI 1992/2843	Road Traffic Offenders (Prescribed Devices) (No 2) Order 1992	See note "Further orders" to SI 1992/1209	—

SI	*Description*	*Remarks*	*Page*
SI 1992/2908	Motor Vehicles (Type Approval) (Great Britain) (Amendment) (No 3) Regulations 1992	Amend SI 1984/981; amended by SI 1992/3173	—
SI 1992/2909	Road Vehicles (Construction and Use) (Amendment) (No 6) Regulations 1992	Amend SI 1986/1078	—
SI 1992/3013	Road Traffic (Courses for Drink-Drive Offenders) Regulations 1992	—	327
SI 1992/3077	Goods Vehicles (Community Authorisations) Regulations 1992	—	327
SI 1992/3084	Motor Vehicles (Type Approval for Goods Vehicles) (Great Britain) (Amendment) (No 3) Regulations 1992	Amend SI 1982/1271	—
SI 1992/3088	Road Vehicles (Construction and Use) (Amendment) (No 7) Regulations 1992	Amend SI 1986/1078	—
SI 1992/3105	Road Traffic Act 1988 (Amendment) Regulations 1992	Made under European Communities Act 1972, s 2(2); amend Road Traffic Act 1988, ss 14, 15, 195 (as from 2 February 1993)	—
SI 1992/3107	Motor Vehicles (EC Type Approval) Regulations 1992	Made under European Communities Act 1972, s 2(2); amend Road Traffic Act 1988, ss 57, 63, 65, 66, 85, 86, 183, and insert ss 64A, 65A of that Act; and amend Road Traffic Offenders Act 1988, Sch 2, Pt I (partly as from 1 January 1993 and fully as from 1 January 1996); remainder revoked by SI 1998/2051 (previously amended by SI 1993/1221, SI 1993/2198, SI 1994/617, SI 1994/1570, SI 1995/2328, SI 1997/191, SI 1997/1501 (all revoked by SI 1998/2051))	—
SI 1992/3138	Transport and Works Applications (Listed Buildings, Conservation Areas and Ancient Monuments Procedure) Regulations 1992	—	328
SI 1992/3144	Transport and Works Act 1992 (Commencement No 4) Order 1992	See note "Further orders" to SI 1992/1347	—
SI 1992/3160	Motor Vehicles (Tests) (Amendment) (No 3) Regulations 1992	Amend SI 1981/1694	—
SI 1992/3173	Motor Vehicles (Type Approval) (Great Britain) (Amendment) (No 4) Regulations 1992	Amend SI 1992/2908	—
SI 1992/3230	Transport and Works (Descriptions of Works Interfering with Navigation) Order 1992	—	328
SI 1992/3231	Transport and Works (Guided Transport Modes) Order 1992	—	328
SI 1992/3285	Road Vehicles (Construction and Use) (Amendment) (No 8) Regulations 1992	Amend SI 1986/1078	—
SI 1993/31	Motor Vehicles (Wearing of Seat Belts by Children in Front Seats) Regulations 1993	—	329

SI	*Description*	*Remarks*	*Page*
SI 1993/35	Road Traffic Regulation Act 1984 (Amendment) Order 1993	Made under Road Traffic Regulation Act 1984, s 124, Sch 9, para 15; amends para 13 of Sch 9 to that Act (as from 23 January 1993)	—
SI 1993/158	Drivers' Hours (Passenger and Goods Vehicles) (Exemption) (Revocation) Regulations 1993	Made under Transport Act 1968, s 96(10); revoke SI 1993/66 (as from 2 February 1993)	—
SI 1993/176	Motor Vehicles (Wearing of Seat Belts) Regulations 1993	—	333
SI 1993/987	Retention of Registration Marks Regulations 1993	—	341
SI 1993/988	Retention of Registration Marks Regulations 1992 (Amendment) Regulations 1993	Amend SI 1992/510	—
SI 1993/1119	Transport and Works Applications (Inland Waterways Procedure) Regulations 1993	—	342
SI 1993/1202	Road Traffic (Parking Adjudicators) (London) Regulations 1993	—	342
SI 1993/1334	Functions of Traffic Wardens (Amendment) Order 1993	Amends SI 1970/1958	—
SI 1993/1450	Parking Attendants (Wearing of Uniforms) (London) Regulations 1993	—	342
SI 1993/1461	Road Traffic Act 1991 (Commencement No 6 and Transitional Provisions) Order 1993	See note "Summary" to SI 1991/2054	—
SI 1993/1686	Road Traffic Act 1991 (Commencement No 6 and Transitional Provisions) (Amendment) Order 1993	Amends SI 1993/1461	—
SI 1993/1698	Road Traffic Offenders (Prescribed Devices) Order 1993	See note "Further orders" to SI 1992/1209	—
SI 1993/1946	Road Vehicles (Construction and Use) (Amendment) (No 1) Regulations 1993	Amend SI 1986/1078	—
SI 1993/2048	Goods Vehicles (Plating and Testing) (Amendment) Regulations 1993	Amend SI 1988/1478	—
SI 1993/2199	Road Vehicles (Construction and Use) (Amendment) (No 2) Regulations 1993	Amend SI 1986/1078	—
SI 1993/2200	Motor Vehicles (Type Approval for Goods Vehicles) (Great Britain) (Amendment) Regulations 1993	Amend SI 1982/1271	—
SI 1993/2201	Motor Vehicles (Type Approval) (Great Britain) (Amendment) Regulations 1993	Amend SI 1984/981	—
SI 1993/2229	Road Traffic Act 1991 (Commencement No 7 and Transitional Provisions) Order 1993	See note "Summary" to SI 1991/2054	—
SI 1993/2754	Public Service Vehicles (Traffic Commissioners: Publication and Inquiries) (Amendment) Regulations 1993	Amend SI 1986/1629	—
SI 1993/2797	Transport Act 1985 (Modifications in Schedule 4 to the Transport Act 1968) (Further Modification) Order 1993	—	343
SI 1993/2803	Road Traffic Act 1991 (Commencement No 8 and Transitional Provisions) Order 1993	See note "Summary" to SI 1991/2054	—
SI 1993/2909	Transport Act 1985 (Modifications in Schedule 4 to the Transport Act 1968) (Further Modification) (Amendment) Order 1993	Amends SI 1993/2797	—
SI 1993/3011	Motor Vehicles (Tests) (Amendment) Regulations 1993	Amend SI 1981/1694	—
SI 1993/3013	Goods Vehicles (Plating and Testing) (Amendment) (No 2) Regulations 1993	Amend SI 1988/1478	—
SI 1993/3048	Road Vehicles (Construction and Use) (Amendment) (No 3) Regulations 1993	Amend SI 1986/1078	—

SI	*Description*	*Remarks*	*Page*
SI 1993/3237	Railways Act 1993 (Commencement No 1) Order 1993	—	345
SI 1993/3238	Road Traffic Act 1991 (Commencement No 9 and Transitional Provisions) Order 1993	See note "Summary" to SI 1991/2054	—
SI 1994/14	Road Vehicles (Construction and Use) (Amendment) Regulations 1994	Amend SI 1986/1078	—
SI 1994/81	Road Traffic Act 1991 (Commencement No 10 and Transitional Provisions) Order 1994	See note "Summary" to SI 1991/2054	—
SI 1994/202	Railways Act 1993 (Commencement No 2) Order 1994	See note "Summary" to SI 1993/3237	—
SI 1994/328	Goods Vehicles (Plating and Testing) (Amendment) Regulations 1994	Amend SI 1988/1478	—
SI 1994/329	Road Vehicles (Construction and Use) (Amendment) (No 2) Regulations 1994	Amend SI 1986/1078	—
SI 1994/447	Railways Act 1993 (Commencement No 3) Order 1994	See note "Summary" to SI 1993/3237	—
SI 1994/571	Railways Act 1993 (Commencement No 4 and Transitional Provision) Order 1994	See note "Summary" to SI 1993/3237	—
SI 1994/572	Railways (Licence Application) Regulations 1994	—	349
SI 1994/573	Railways (London Regional Transport) (Exemptions) Order 1994	—	351
SI 1994/574	Railways (Heathrow Express) (Exemptions) Order 1994	See note "Further exemptions" to SI 1994/573	—
SI 1994/575	Railways (Registers) Order 1994	—	354
SI 1994/576	Railways (Penalty Fares) Regulations 1994	—	354
SI 1994/606	Railways (Class and Miscellaneous Exemptions) Order 1994	See note "Further exemptions" to SI 1994/573	—
SI 1994/607	Railways (Alternative Closure Procedure) Order 1994	—	358
SI 1994/718	Transport and Works Act 1992 (Commencement No 5 and Transitional Provisions) Order 1994	See note "Further orders" to SI 1992/1347	—
SI 1994/857	Railways Act 1993 (Consequential Modifications) Order 1994	—	358
SI 1994/970	Channel Tunnel (Application of Road Traffic Enactments) Order 1994	—	359
SI 1994/1432	Railway Pensions (Protection and Designation of Schemes) Order 1994	—	359
SI 1994/1433	Railways Pension Scheme Order 1994	—	360
SI 1994/1482	Road Traffic Act 1991 (Commencement No 11 and Transitional Provisions) Order 1994	See note "Summary" to SI 1991/2054	—
SI 1994/1484	Road Traffic Act 1991 (Commencement No 12 and Transitional Provisions) Order 1994	See note "Summary" to SI 1991/2054	—
SI 1994/1648	Railways Act 1993 (Commencement No 5 and Transitional Provisions) Order 1994	See note "Summary" to SI 1993/3237	—
SI 1994/1649	Railways Act 1993 (Consequential Modifications) (No 2) Order 1994	See note "Further orders" to SI 1994/857	—
SI 1994/1667	Channel Tunnel (Application of Road Traffic Enactments) (No 2) Order 1994	See note "Further order" to SI 1994/970	—
SI 1994/2005	Railway Pensions (Transfer and Miscellaneous Provisions) Order 1994	—	361
SI 1994/2142	Railways Act 1993 (Commencement No 6) Order 1994	See note "Summary" to SI 1993/3237	—
SI 1994/2150	Railways Pensions Guarantee (Prescribed Persons) Order 1994	—	361
SI 1994/2190	Motor Vehicles (Type Approval) (Great Britain) (Amendment) Regulations 1994	Amend SI 1984/981	—
SI 1994/2191	Motor Vehicles (Type Approval for Goods Vehicles) (Great Britain) (Amendment) Regulations 1994	Amend SI 1982/1271	—

SI	*Description*	*Remarks*	*Page*
SI 1994/2192	Road Vehicles (Construction and Use) (Amendment) (No 3) Regulations 1994	Amend SI 1986/1078	—
SI 1994/2229	Railways Act 1993 (Consequential Modifications) (No 3) Order 1994	See note "Further orders" to SI 1994/857	—
SI 1994/2280	Road Vehicles Lighting (Amendment) Regulations 1994	Amend SI 1989/1796	—
SI 1994/2388	Railway Pensions (Substitution) Order 1994	—	361
SI 1994/2520	Railways Act 1993 (Consequential Modifications) (No 4) Order 1994	See note "Further orders" to SI 1994/857	—
SI 1994/2567	Coal Industry Act 1994 (Consequential Modifications of Subordinate Legislation) Order 1994	See title Mines, Minerals and Quarries; amends SI 1986/1078, SI 1989/1796	—
SI 1994/2976	Retention of Registration Marks (Amendment) Regulations 1994	Amend SI 1992/510, SI 1993/987	—
SI 1994/3095	Vehicle Licences (Duration of First Licences and Rate of Duty) (Amendment) Order 1994	Amends SI 1986/1428	—
SI 1994/3117	Motor Vehicle Tyres (Safety) Regulations 1994	See title Sale of Goods and Consumer Protection	—
SI 1994/3270	Road Vehicles (Construction and Use) (Amendment) (No 4) Regulations 1994	Amend SI 1986/1078	—
SI 1994/3271	Public Service Vehicles (Registration of Local Services) (Amendment) Regulations 1994	Amend SI 1986/1671	—
SI 1995/185	Public Service Vehicles (Lost Property) (Amendment) Regulations 1995	Amend SI 1978/1684	—
SI 1995/186	Public Service Vehicles (Conduct of Drivers, Inspectors, Conductors and Passengers) (Amendment) Regulations 1995	Amend SI 1990/1020	—
SI 1995/305	Public Service Vehicles (Conditions of Fitness, Equipment, Use and Certification) (Amendment) Regulations 1995	Amend 1981/257	—
SI 1995/430	Railway Pensions (Substitution And Miscellaneous Provisions) Order 1995	See note "Further orders" to SI 1994/2388	—
SI 1995/551	Road Vehicles (Construction and Use) (Amendment) Regulations 1995	Amend SI 1986/1078; amended by SI 1995/737	—
SI 1995/737	Road Vehicles (Construction and Use) (Amendment) (No 2) Regulations 1995	Amend SI 1995/551	—
SI 1995/889	Road Traffic Accidents (Payments for Treatment) Order 1995	Made under Public Expenditure and Receipts Act 1968, s 5, Sch 3; amends Road Traffic Act 1988, ss 157(2), 158(2) (as from 17 April 1995)	—
SI 1995/1201	Road Vehicles (Construction and Use) (Amendment) (No 3) Regulations 1995	Amend SI 1986/1078	—
SI 1995/1239	Pipe-lines (Inquiries Procedure) Rules 1995	—	362
SI 1995/1290	Goods Vehicles (International Road Haulage Permits) (Revocation) Regulations 1995	Revoke SI 1975/2234; revoke SI 1992/3077 in so far as amended SI 1975/2234	—
SI 1995/1322	Motor Vehicles (Type Approval) (Great Britain) (Amendment) Regulations 1995	Amend SI 1984/981	—
SI 1995/1323	Motor Vehicles (Type Approval for Goods Vehicles) (Great Britain) (Amendment) Regulations 1995	Amend SI 1982/1271	—
SI 1995/1371	Motor Vehicles (Off Road Events) Regulations 1995	—	370
SI 1995/1397	Vehicle Excise Duty (Designation of Small Islands) Order 1995	—	370
SI 1995/1455	Vehicle Excise (Design Weight Certificate) Regulations 1995	—	371

SI	*Description*	*Remarks*	*Page*
SI 1995/1456	Goods Vehicles (Plating and Testing) (Amendment) Regulations 1995	Amend SI 1988/1478	—
SI 1995/1457	Motor Vehicles (Tests) (Amendment) Regulations 1995	Amend SI 1981/1694	—
SI 1995/1458	Road Vehicles (Construction and Use) (Amendment) (No 4) Regulations 1995	Amend SI 1986/1078	—
SI 1995/1540	Section 19 Minibus (Designated Bodies) (Amendment) Order 1995	Amends SI 1987/1229	—
SI 1995/1684	Department of Transport (Fees) (Amendment) Order 1995	Amends SI 1988/643	—
SI 1995/2181	Goods Vehicles (Licensing of Operators) Act 1995 (Commencement and Transitional Provisions) Order 1995	Made under s 61 of the 1995 Act; brought the Act, except s 50 and Sch 5, into force on 1 January 1996, and made transitional provision	—
SI 1995/2210	Road Vehicles (Construction and Use) (Amendment) (No 5) Regulations 1995	Amend SI 1986/1078	—
SI 1995/2367	Motor Cycle Noise Act 1987 (Commencement) Order 1995	Made under s 2(3) of the 1987 Act; brought the Act into force on 1 August 1996	—
SI 1995/2370	Motor Cycle Silencer and Exhaust Systems Regulations 1995	—	371
SI 1995/2438	Motor Vehicles (Tests) (Amendment) (No 2) Regulations 1995	Amend SI 1981/1694	—
SI 1995/2803	National Park Authorities (Wales) Order 1995	See title Open Spaces and National Heritage; modifies SI 1992/3270 (revoked and replaced by SI 2006/1954)	—
SI 1995/2869	Goods Vehicles (Licensing of Operators) Regulations 1995	—	371
SI 1995/2880	Sale of Registration Marks Regulations 1995	—	390
SI 1995/2908	Public Service Vehicles (Operators' Licences) Regulations 1995	—	390
SI 1995/2909	Public Service Vehicles (Operators' Licences) (Fees) Regulations 1995	—	391
SI 1995/3000	Goods Vehicles (Licensing of Operators) (Fees) Regulations 1995	—	391
SI 1995/3051	Road Vehicles (Construction and Use) (Amendment) (No 6) Regulations 1995	Amend SI 1986/1078	—
SI 1996/16	Road Vehicles (Construction and Use) (Amendment) Regulations 1996	Amend SI 1986/1078	—
SI 1996/163	Road Vehicles (Construction and Use) (Amendment) (No 2) Regulations 1996	Amend SI 1986/1078	—
SI 1996/167	Public Service Vehicles (Carrying Capacity) (Amendment) Regulations 1996	Amend SI 1984/1406	—
SI 1996/252	Gas Act 1995 (Consequential Modifications of Subordinate Legislation) Order 1996	See title Energy; amends SI 1986/1078	—
SI 1996/420	Railways Act 1993 (Consequential Modifications) (No 5) Order 1996	See note "Further orders" to SI 1994/857	—
SI 1996/664	Railways Act 1993 (Extinguishment of Relevant Loans) (Railtrack plc) Order 1996	—	392
SI 1996/1008	Local Government Reorganisation (Wales) (Consequential Amendments No 2) Order 1996	See title Local Government; amends SI 1978/1535, SI 1979/236, SI 1995/1239	—
SI 1996/1356	Railways (Closure Provisions) (Exemptions) Order 1996	See note "Further exemptions" to SI 1994/573	—
SI 1996/1553	Deregulation (Parking Equipment) Order 1996	See title Highways, Streets and Bridges	—

SI	*Description*	*Remarks*	*Page*
SI 1996/1609	Transport and Works Act 1992 (Commencement No 6) Order 1996	See note "Further orders" to SI 1992/1347	—
SI 1996/1700	Deregulation (Motor Vehicles Tests) Order 1996	Made under Deregulation and Contracting Out Act 1994, s 1 (repealed by Regulatory Reform Act 2001, s 12(1)–(3), with a saving in s 12(4) of the 2001 Act for existing orders made under s 1 of the 1994 Act; s 12 of the 2001 Act was itself repealed by Legislative and Regulatory Reform Act 2006, s 30(1), Schedule, with a saving in s 30(5) thereof for existing orders made under s 1 of the 1994 Act continued in force by virtue of s 12(4) of the 2001 Act); amends Road Traffic Act 1988, s 48 (as from 1 July 1996)	—
SI 1996/1786	Private Crossings (Signs and Barriers) Regulations 1996	—	392
SI 1996/1929	Motor Vehicles (International Circulation) (Amendment) Order 1996	Amends SI 1975/1208	—
SI 1996/1943	Transport Act 1982 (Commencement No 7 and Transitional Provisions) Order 1996	See note "Further orders" to SI 1982/1561	—
SI 1996/1961	Department of Transport (Fees) (Amendment) Order 1996	Amends SI 1988/643	—
SI 1996/1974	Driving Licences (Community Driving Licence) Regulations 1996	—	393
SI 1996/1980	Road Traffic (Driving Instruction by Disabled Persons) Act 1993 (Commencement) Order 1996	Made under s 7(2) of the 1993 Act; brought the Act into force on 9 September 1996	—
SI 1996/2008	Vehicle Excise Duty (Fee for Temporary Licences) Regulations 1996	Made under Vehicle Excise and Registration Act 1994, s 9(4); amend s 9(3) of that Act (as from 2 September 1996)	—
SI 1996/2064	Road Vehicles (Construction and Use) (Amendment) (No 3) Regulations 1996	Amend SI 1986/1078	—
SI 1996/2085	Road Vehicles (Construction and Use) (Amendment) (No 4) Regulations 1996	Amend SI 1986/1078	—
SI 1996/2186	Goods Vehicles (Licensing of Operators) (Temporary Use in Great Britain) Regulations 1996	—	393
SI 1996/2329	Road Vehicles (Construction and Use) (Amendment) (No 5) Regulations 1996	Amend SI 1986/1078	—
SI 1996/2330	Motor Vehicles (Type Approval) (Great Britain) (Amendment) Regulations 1996	Amend SI 1984/981	—
SI 1996/2331	Motor Vehicles (Type Approval for Goods Vehicles) (Amendment) Regulations 1996	Amend SI 1982/1271	—
SI 1996/2489	Local Authorities' Traffic Orders (Procedure) (England and Wales) Regulations 1996	—	394
SI 1996/2551	Railtrack Group PLC (Target Investment Limit) Order 1996	See note "Target investment limit" to SI 1996/664	—

SI	*Description*	*Remarks*	*Page*
SI 1996/2711	Travel Concession Schemes (Amendment) Regulations 1996	Amend SI 1986/77	—
SI 1996/3014	Motor Vehicles (Type Approval for Goods Vehicles) (Great Britain) (Amendment) (No 2) Regulations 1996	Amend SI 1982/1271; amended by SI 1997/1365 (amendment superseded by SI 1997/2936)	—
SI 1996/3015	Motor Vehicles (Type Approval) (Great Britain) (Amendment) (No 2) Regulations 1996	Amend SI 1984/981; amended by SI 1997/1367 (amendment superseded by SI 1997/2933)	—
SI 1996/3016	Road Vehicles Lighting (Amendment) Regulations 1996	Amend SI 1989/1796	—
SI 1996/3017	Road Vehicles (Construction and Use) (Amendment) (No 6) Regulations 1996	Amend SI 1986/1078; amended by SI 1997/1458	—
SI 1996/3033	Road Vehicles (Construction and Use) (Amendment) (No 7) Regulations 1996	Amend SI 1986/1078	—
SI 1996/3133	Road Vehicles (Construction and Use) (Amendment) (No 8) Regulations 1996	Amend SI 1986/1078	—
SI 1996/3206	Driving Licences (Designation of Relevant External Law) Order 1996	—	394
SI 1997/8	Channel Tunnel Rail Link (Qualifying Authorities) Order 1997	See title Town and Country Planning	—
SI 1997/81	Motor Vehicles (Tests) (Amendment) Regulations 1997	Amend SI 1981/1694	—
SI 1997/82	Goods Vehicles (Plating and Testing) (Amendment) Regulations 1997	Amend SI 1988/1478	—
SI 1997/83	Road Vehicles (Prohibition) (Amendment) Regulations 1997	Amend SI 1992/1285	—
SI 1997/165	Local Government Changes for England (Transport Levying Bodies) Regulations 1997	Modify SI 1992/2789	—
SI 1997/263	Goods Vehicles (Plating and Testing) (Amendment) (No 2) Regulations 1997	Amend SI 1988/1478	—
SI 1997/267	Road Traffic (New Drivers) Act 1995 (Commencement) Order 1997	—	394
SI 1997/384	Road Traffic Offenders (Additional Offences and Prescribed Devices) Order 1997	See note "Further orders" to SI 1992/1209	—
SI 1997/487	Level Crossings Regulations 1997	—	395
SI 1997/530	Road Vehicles (Construction and Use) (Amendment) Regulations 1997	Amend SI 1986/1078	—
SI 1997/535	Section 19 Minibus (Designated Bodies) (Amendment) Order 1997	Amends SI 1987/1229	—
SI 1997/553	Railway Safety (Miscellaneous Provisions) Regulations 1997	—	395
SI 1997/712	Electricity Generating Stations and Overhead Lines and Pipe-lines (Inquiries Procedure) (Amendment) Rules 1997	Amend SI 1995/1239 (and SI 1990/528 (revoked))	—
SI 1997/1096	Road Vehicles (Construction and Use) (Amendment) (No 2) Regulations 1997	Amend SI 1986/1078	—
SI 1997/1098	New Drivers (Appeals Procedure) Regulations 1997	—	399
SI 1997/1340	Road Vehicles (Construction and Use) (Amendment) (No 3) Regulations 1997	Amend SI 1986/1078	—
SI 1997/1458	Road Vehicles (Construction and Use) (Amendment) (No 4) Regulations 1997	Amend SI 1996/3017	—
SI 1997/1502	Motor Vehicles (Type Approval) (Great Britain) (Amendment) (No 2) Regulations 1997	Amend SI 1984/981	—
SI 1997/1544	Road Vehicles (Construction and Use) (Amendment) (No 5) Regulations 1997	Amend SI 1986/1078	—
SI 1997/1679	Motor Vehicles (Tests) (Amendment) (No 2) Regulations 1997	Amend SI 1981/1694; supersede SI 1996/1751	—

SI	*Description*	*Remarks*	*Page*
SI 1997/1951	Transport and Works (Guided Transport Modes) (Amendment) Order 1997	Amends SI 1992/3231	—
SI 1997/2392	Finance Act 1997 (Commencement No 1) Order 1997	Made under s 20(4) of the 1997 Act; brought s 20 thereof (removal and disposal of vehicles) into force on 8 October 1997	—
SI 1997/2439	Vehicle Excise Duty (Immobilisation, Removal and Disposal of Vehicles) Regulations 1997	—	399
SI 1997/2565	Carriage by Air and Road Act 1979 (Commencement No 2) Order 1997	See note "Further orders" to SI 1980/1966	—
SI 1997/2906	Transport and Works (Descriptions of Works Interfering with Navigation) (Amendment) Order 1997	Amends SI 1992/3230	—
SI 1997/2935	Road Vehicles (Construction and Use) (Amendment) (No 6) Regulations 1997	Amend SI 1986/1078	—
SI 1997/3053	Traffic Signs (Temporary Obstructions) Regulations 1997	See note "Other traffic signs" to SI 2002/3113	—
SI 1997/3063	Vehicle Excise Duty (Immobilisation, Removal and Disposal of Vehicles) (Amendment) Regulations 1997	Amend SI 1997/2439	—
SI 1998/1	Road Vehicles (Construction and Use) (Amendment) Regulations 1998	Amend SI 1986/1078	—
SI 1998/111	Temporary Traffic Signs (Prescribed Bodies) (England and Wales) Regulations 1998	—	400
SI 1998/274	Transport and Works Act 1992 (Commencement No 7) Order 1998	See note "Further orders" to SI 1992/1347	—
SI 1998/494	Health and Safety (Enforcing Authority) Regulations 1998	See title Health and Safety at Work; amend SI 1997/553	—
SI 1998/560	Finance Act 1997 (Commencement No 2) Order 1998	Made under para 9 of Sch 3 to the 1997 Act; brought Sch 3 (vehicle excise duty: exempt vehicles) into force on 1 April 1998	—
SI 1998/948	Local Authorities (Transport Charges) Regulations 1998	—	400
SI 1998/967	Road Traffic Act 1991 (Commencement No 15 and Transitional Provisions) Order 1998	See note "Summary" to SI 1991/2054	—
SI 1998/1000	Road Vehicles (Construction and Use) (Amendment No 2) Regulations 1998	Amend SI 1986/1078	—
SI 1998/1005	Motor Vehicles (Type Approval) (Great Britain) (Amendment) Regulations 1998	Amend SI 1984/981; supersede SI 1997/2933	—
SI 1998/1006	Motor Vehicles (Type Approval for Goods Vehicles) (Great Britain) (Amendment) Regulations 1998	Amend SI 1982/1271; supersede SI 1997/2936	—
SI 1998/1188	Road Vehicles (Construction and Use) (Amendment) (No 3) Regulations 1998	Amend SI 1986/1078	—
SI 1998/1217	Vehicle Excise Duty (Immobilisation, Removal and Disposal of Vehicles) (Amendment) Regulations 1998	Amend SI 1997/2439	—
SI 1998/1281	Road Vehicles (Construction and Use) (Amendment) (No 4) Regulations 1998	Amend SI 1986/1078	—
SI 1998/1420	Driving Licences (Community Driving Licence) Regulations 1998	—	401
SI 1998/1445	Channel Tunnel Rail Link (Qualifying Authorities) Order 1998	See title Town and Country Planning	—
SI 1998/1563	Road Vehicles (Construction and Use) (Amendment) (No 5) Regulations 1998	Amend SI 1986/1078	—
SI 1998/1670	Public Service Vehicles (Conditions of Fitness, Equipment, Use and Certification) (Amendment) Regulations 1998	Amend SI 1981/257	—

SI	*Description*	*Remarks*	*Page*
SI 1998/1672	Motor Vehicles (Tests) (Amendment) Regulations 1998	Amend SI 1981/1694	—
SI 1998/1807	Motor Cycles (Protective Helmets) Regulations 1998	—	401
SI 1998/1917	Deregulation (Exchangeable Driving Licences) Order 1998	Made under Deregulation and Contracting Out Act 1994, s 1 (repealed by Regulatory Reform Act 2001, s 12(1)–(3), with a saving in s 12(4) of the 2001 Act for existing orders made under s 1 of the 1994 Act; s 12 of the 2001 Act was itself repealed by Legislative and Regulatory Reform Act 2006, s 30(1), Schedule, with a saving in s 30(5) thereof for existing orders made under s 1 of the 1994 Act continued in force by virtue of s 12(4) of the 2001 Act); amends Road Traffic Act 1988, s 108 and Road Traffic Offenders Act 1988, s 36 (as from 31 August 1998)	—
SI 1998/1946	Deregulation (Taxis and Private Hire Vehicles) Order 1998	Made under Deregulation and Contracting Out Act 1994, s 1 (repealed; see SI 1998/1917 above); amends Local Government (Miscellaneous Provisions) Act 1976, ss 51, 59 (as from 5 September 1998)	—
SI 1998/2197	Service Subsidy Agreements (Tendering) (Amendment) Regulations 1998	Amend SI 1985/1921; supersede SI 1994/1227; revoked in relation to England only by SI 2002/2090	—
SI 1998/2429	Road Vehicles (Construction and Use) (Amendment) (No 6) Regulations 1998	Amend SI 1986/1078	—
SI 1998/2456	Rail Vehicle Accessibility Regulations 1998	—	401
SI 1998/2457	Rail Vehicle (Exemption Applications) Regulations 1998	See note "Applications for exemption" to SI 1998/2456	—
SI 1998/3092	Finance Act 1998 (Commencement No 1) Order 1998	Made under para 17(1) of Sch 1 to the 1998 Act; brought paras 3–14 of Sch 1 thereto (rates of vehicle excise duty where pollution reduced) into force in relation to licences issued on or after 1 January 1999	—
SI 1998/3093	Motor Vehicles (Type Approval of Reduced Pollution Adaptations) Regulations 1998	—	402
SI 1998/3111	Road Vehicles (Authorised Weight) Regulations 1998	—	403
SI 1998/3112	Road Vehicles (Construction and Use) (Amendment) (No 7) Regulations 1998	Amend SI 1986/1078	—

SI	*Description*	*Remarks*	*Page*
SI 1998/3113	Goods Vehicles (Plating and Testing) (Amendment) (No 2) Regulations 1998	Amend SI 1988/1478	—
SI 1999/162	Road Traffic Offenders (Prescribed Devices) Order 1999	See note "Further orders" to SI 1992/1209	—
SI 1999/357	Motor Cars (Driving Instruction) (Admission of Community Licence Holders) Regulations 1999	Made under Road Traffic Act 1988, s 134; amend ss 125, 125A, 128, 130, 142 of that Act (as from 1 April 1999); revoked by Road Safety Act 2006, s 59, Sch 7(14), in so far as amend ss 125, 128, 130, 142, as from a day to be appointed by order under s 61(1) thereof	—
SI 1999/535	Motor Cycles (Eye Protectors) Regulations 1999	—	403
SI 1999/742	Deregulation (Pipe-lines) Order 1999	—	403
SI 1999/786	Road Traffic (NHS Charges) (Reviews and Appeals) Regulations 1999	—	404
SI 1999/1204	Traffic Areas (Reorganisation) (Wales) Order 1999	See note "Wales" to SI 1991/288	—
SI 1999/1205	Road Traffic (Parking Adjudicators) (London) (Amendment) Regulations 1999	Amend SI 1993/1202	—
SI 1999/1322	Public Service Vehicles (Community Licences) Regulations 1999	—	405
SI 1999/1443	Railways Act 1993 (Consequential Modifications) Order 1999	See note "Further orders" to SI 1994/857	—
SI 1999/1608	Road Traffic Regulation Act 1984 (Amendment) Order 1999	—	405
SI 1999/1641	Driving Licences (Exchangeable Licences) Order 1999	See note "Further orders" to SI 1984/672	—
SI 1999/1851	Fixed Penalty Offences Order 1999	See note "Further orders" to SI 1990/335	—
SI 1999/1985	Channel Tunnel Rail Link (Nomination) (London Underground Works) Order 1999	See note "Previous order" to SI 2008/3076	—
SI 1999/1998	Railways Act 1993 (Consequential Modifications) (No 2) Order 1999	See note "Further orders" to SI 1994/857	—
SI 1999/2024	Quarries Regulations 1999	See title Mines, Minerals and Quarries; amend SI 1997/553; also amended SI 1994/299 (revoked)	—
SI 1999/2149	Motor Vehicles (Type Approval and Approval Marks) (Fees) Regulations 1999	—	405
SI 1999/2198	Channel Tunnel Rail Link (Nomination) (London Underground Works) (Amendment) Order 1999	Amends SI 1999/1985	—
SI 1999/2244	Railway Safety Regulations 1999	—	406
SI 1999/2430	Goods Vehicle Operators (Qualifications) Regulations 1999	Made under European Communities Act 1972, s 2(2); amend Goods Vehicles (Licensing of Operators) Act 1995, Sch 3 (as from 1 October 1999)	—
SI 1999/2431	Public Service Vehicle Operators (Qualifications) Regulations 1999	Made under European Communities Act 1972, s 2(2); insert Public Passenger Vehicles Act 1981, s 16A and amend Sch 3 thereto (superseding previous amendments to Sch 3 by SI 1990/2641) (as from 1 October 1999)	—

SI	*Description*	*Remarks*	*Page*
SI 1999/2864	Motor Vehicles (Driving Licences) Regulations 1999	—	410
SI 1999/2920	Motor Cycles Etc (EC Type Approval) Regulations 1999	—	414
SI 1999/2932	Rail Vehicle Accessibility (Serco Metrolink T68A Vehicles) Exemption Order 1999	See note "Exemption from rail vehicle accessibility regulations" to SI 1998/2456	—
SI 1999/2978	Road Vehicles (Brake Linings Safety) Regulations 1999	See title Sale of Goods and Consumer Protection	—
SI 1999/3111	Docklands Light Railway (Miscellaneous Closure Exemptions) Order 1999	See note "Further exemptions" to SI 1994/573	—
SI 1999/3112	Docklands Light Railway (Lewisham Extension) (Exemptions) Order 1999	See note "Further exemptions" to SI 1994/573	—
SI 1999/3113	Railways (Alternative Closure Procedure) (Amendment) Order 1999	Amends SI 1994/607	—
SI 1999/3413	Road Transport (Passenger Vehicles Cabotage) Regulations 1999	—	415
SI 2000/253	National Assembly for Wales (Transfer of Functions) Order 2000 (W 5)	See title Constitutional Law (Pt 3); modified 1992/2817 (revoked and replaced by SI 2004/2018)	—
SI 2000/412	Greater London Authority Act 1999 (Hackney Carriages and Private Hire Vehicles) (Transitional and Consequential Provisions) Order 2000	—	415
SI 2000/524	Rail Vehicle Accessibility (North Western Trains Class 175/0 and Class 175/1 Vehicles) Exemption Order 2000	See note "Exemption from rail vehicle accessibility regulations" to SI 1998/2456	—
SI 2000/555	Railtrack plc (Rateable Value) (Wales) Order 2000 (W 22)	See title Local Government	—
SI 2000/682	Disabled Persons (Badges for Motor Vehicles) (England) Regulations 2000	—	416
SI 2000/683	Local Authorities' Traffic Orders (Exemptions for Disabled Persons) (England) Regulations 2000	—	416
SI 2000/735	Road Traffic Reduction Act 1997 (Commencement) (England and Wales) Order 2000	Made under s 4(3) of the 1997 Act; brought the whole Act into force on 10 March 2000	—
SI 2000/949	Railways (Rateable Values) (England) Order 2000	See title Local Government	—
SI 2000/1045	Transport for London (Preliminary Arrangements) Order 2000	—	416
SI 2000/1349	Rail Vehicle Accessibility (The Chiltern Railway Company Limited Class 168/1 Vehicles) Exemption Order 2000	See note "Exemption from rail vehicle accessibility regulations" to SI 1998/2456	—
SI 2000/1432	Motor Vehicles (Tests) (Amendment) Regulations 2000	Amend SI 1981/1694	—
SI 2000/1433	Goods Vehicles (Plating and Testing) (Amendment) Regulations 2000	Amend SI 1988/1478; supersede SI 1998/1671	—
SI 2000/1434	Road Vehicles (Construction and Use) (Amendment) Regulations 2000	Amend SI 1986/1078	—
SI 2000/1441	Rail Vehicle Accessibility (Central Trains Class 170/5 and Class 170/6 Vehicles) Exemption Order 2000	See note "Exemption from rail vehicle accessibility regulations" to SI 1998/2456	—
SI 2000/1442	Greater London (Penalty Fares) (Croydon Tramlink Designation) Order 2000	See Preliminary Note "Fares and penalty fares" (under main head "London")	—

SI	*Description*	*Remarks*	*Page*
SI 2000/1462	Regulation of Bus Services in Greater London (Transitional Provisions) Order 2000	—	416
SI 2000/1484	London Transport Users' Committee (Transitional Provisions) Order 2000	—	417
SI 2000/1488	Motor Cycles (Protective Helmets) (Amendment) Regulations 2000	Amend SI 1998/1807	—
SI 2000/1489	Motor Cycles (Eye Protectors) (Amendment) Regulations 2000	Amend SI 1999/535	—
SI 2000/1507	Disabled Persons (Badges for Motor Vehicles) (England) (Amendment) Regulations 2000	Amend SI 2000/682	—
SI 2000/1547	Greater London Highways and Road Traffic (Various Provisions) Order 2000	—	417
SI 2000/1548	Transport for London (Specified Activities) Order 2000	—	417
SI 2000/1552	GLA Roads and Side Roads (Transfer of Property etc) Order 2000	See title Highways, Streets and Bridges	—
SI 2000/1666	London Cab Order 1934 (Modification) Order 2000	Amends and modifies SR & O 1934/1346	—
SI 2000/1770	Rail Vehicle Accessibility (Anglia Railways Class 170/2 Vehicles) Exemption Order 2000	See note "Exemption from rail vehicle accessibility regulations" to SI 1998/2456	—
SI 2000/1785	Local Authorities' Traffic Orders (Exemptions for Disabled Persons) (Wales) Regulations 2000 (W 122)	See note "Wales" to SI 2000/683	—
SI 2000/1786	Disabled Persons (Badges for Motor Vehicles) (Wales) Regulations 2000 (W 123)	See note "Wales" to SI 2000/682	—
SI 2000/1970	Public Service Vehicles Accessibility Regulations 2000	—	418
SI 2000/1971	Road Vehicles (Construction and Use) (Amendment) (No 2) Regulations 2000	Amend SI 1986/1078	—
SI 2000/2050	Rail Vehicle Accessibility (Connex South Eastern Class 375 Vehicles) Exemption Order 2000	See note "Exemption from rail vehicle accessibility regulations" to SI 1998/2456	—
SI 2000/2237	Road Traffic Regulation Act 1984 (GLA Side Roads Amendment) Order 2000	Made under s 124A(6) of the 1984 Act; amends s 124A and inserts ss 124B, 124C (as from 1 October 2000)	—
SI 2000/2397	Rail Vehicle Accessibility (The Chiltern Railway Company Limited Class 168/1 Vehicles) Exemption (No 2) Order 2000	See note "Exemption from rail vehicle accessibility regulations" to SI 1998/2456	—
SI 2000/2493	GLA Roads and Side Roads (Transfer of Property etc) (Modification) (College Farm, Finchley) Order 2000	See title Highways, Streets and Bridges	—
SI 2000/2546	Road Traffic (Owner Liability) Regulations 2000	—	418
SI 2000/2615	GLA Roads (Continuity of Orders etc) Order 2000	See title Highways, Streets and Bridges	—
SI 2000/2766	Motor Vehicles (Driving Licences) (Amendment) Regulations 2000	Amend SI 1999/2864	—
SI 2000/2768	Carriage by Air and Road Act 1979 (Commencement No 4) Order 2000	See note "Further orders" to SI 1980/1966	—
SI 2000/2792	Fixed Penalty Order 2000	—	419
SI 2000/2953	Rail Vehicle Accessibility (South West Trains Class 170/3 Vehicles) Exemption Order 2000	See note "Exemption from rail vehicle accessibility regulations" to SI 1998/2456	—
SI 2000/2990	Disability Discrimination Act 1995 (Taxis) (Carrying of Guide Dogs etc) (England and Wales) Regulations 2000	—	419

SI	*Description*	*Remarks*	*Page*
SI 2000/3114	Road Transport (Passenger Vehicles Cabotage) (Amendment) Regulations 2000	Amend SI 1999/3413	—
SI 2000/3115	Community Drivers' Hours (Tankers) (Temporary Exception) (Revocation) Regulations 2000	Made under European Communities Act 1972, s 2(2); revoke SI 2000/2960 (as from 24 November 2000)	—
SI 2000/3144	Private Hire Vehicles (London) Act 1998 (Commencement No 1) Order 2000	—	419
SI 2000/3146	Private Hire Vehicles (London) (Operators' Licences) Regulations 2000	—	421
SI 2000/3157	Motor Vehicles (Driving Licences) (Amendment) (No 2) Regulations 2000	Amend SI 1999/2864	—
SI 2000/3197	Road Vehicles (Construction and Use) (Amendment) (No 3) Regulations 2000	Amend SI 1986/1078	—
SI 2000/3199	Transport and Works (Assessment of Environmental Effects) Regulations 2000	See title Environment	—
SI 2000/3215	Rail Vehicle Accessibility (Amendment) Regulations 2000	Amend SI 1998/2456	—
SI 2000/3217	Rail Vehicle Accessibility (South West Trains Class 170/3 Vehicles) Exemption (Amendment) Order 2000	Amends SI 2000/2953	—
SI 2000/3218	Rail Vehicle Accessibility (The Chiltern Railway Company Limited Class 168/1 Vehicles) Exemption (No 2) (Amendment) Order 2000	Amends SI 2000/2397	—
SI 2000/3224	Road Vehicles (Authorised Weight) (Amendment) Regulations 2000	Amend SI 1998/3111; amended by SI 2001/1125	—
SI 2000/3226	Transport Tribunal Rules 2000	—	421
SI 2000/3229	Transport Act 2000 (Commencement No 1 and Transitional Provisions) Order 2000	—	422
SI 2000/3275	Motor Vehicles (Type Approval of Reduced Pollution Adaptations) (Amendments) Regulations 2000	Amend SI 1998/3093	—
SI 2000/3318	Public Service Vehicles Accessibility (Amendment) Regulations 2000	Amend SI 2000/1970	—
SI 2000/3376	Transport Act 2000 (Commencement No 2) Order 2000	See note "Further orders" to SI 2000/3229	—
SI 2000/3386	London Transport Pension Arrangements Order 2000	—	432
SI 2001/25	Motor Vehicles (Approval) Regulations 2001	—	433
SI 2001/53	Motor Vehicles (Driving Licences) (Amendment) Regulations 2001	Amend SI 1999/2864; amended by SI 2001/236	—
SI 2001/57	Transport Act 2000 (Commencement No 3) Order 2001	See note "Further orders" to SI 2000/3229	—
SI 2001/93	Graduated Vehicle Excise Duty (Prescribed Types of Fuel) Regulations 2001	—	434
SI 2001/115	Transport Act 2000 (Commencement No 3) (Amendment) Order 2001	Amends SI 2001/57	—
SI 2001/217	British Railways Board (Reduction of Membership) Order 2001	See Preliminary Note "Privatisation of the railway system" (under main head "Reorganisation of transport undertakings")	—
SI 2001/218	Strategic Rail Authority (Licence Exemption) Order 2001	See note "Further exemptions" to SI 1994/573	—
SI 2001/236	Motor Vehicles (Driving Licences) (Amendment) (No 2) Regulations 2001	Amend SI 1999/2864, SI 2001/53	—
SI 2001/242	Transport Act 2000 (Commencement No 4) Order 2001	See note "Further orders" to SI 2000/3229	—

SI	*Description*	*Remarks*	*Page*
SI 2001/250	Rail Vehicle Accessibility (Connex South Eastern Class 375 Vehicles) Exemption (Amendment) Order 2001	Amends SI 2000/2050	—
SI 2001/262	Strategic Rail Authority (Capital Allowances) Order 2001	—	434
SI 2001/277	Rail Vehicle Accessibility (ScotRail Class 334 Vehicles) Exemption Order 2001	See note "Exemption from rail vehicle accessibility regulations" to SI 1998/2456	—
SI 2001/306	Road Vehicles (Construction and Use) (Amendment) Regulations 2001	Amend SI 1986/1078	—
SI 2001/307	Goods Vehicles (Plating and Testing) (Amendment) Regulations 2001	Amend SI 1988/1478	—
SI 2001/319	Competition Act 1998 (Public Transport Ticketing Schemes Block Exemption) Order 2001	See title Trade and Industry	—
SI 2001/368	Motor Cycles Etc (EC Type Approval) (Amendment) Regulations 2001	Amend SI 1999/2920	—
SI 2001/492	Transport Act 2000 (Amendment) Order 2001	Made under Transport Act 2000, s 77(5); amends s 77(3)(a) and inserts s 77(3A) (as from 1 April 2001)	—
SI 2001/499	Rail Vehicle Accessibility (Midland Mainline Class 170/1 Vehicles) Exemption Order 2001	See note "Exemption from rail vehicle accessibility regulations" to SI 1998/2456	—
SI 2001/560	Road Vehicles Lighting (Amendment) Regulations 2001	Amend SI 1989/1796	—
SI 2001/561	Road Vehicles (Display of Registration Marks) Regulations 2001	—	434
SI 2001/690	Transport for London (Bus Lanes) Order 2001	Made under Greater London Authority Act 1999, ss 405, 406; amends London Local Authorities Act 1996, ss 2, 4, 8, 9, Schs 1, 2; repeals London Local Authorities Act 2000, s 48 (in so far as it relates to s 4 of the 1996 Act), Sch 2, para 1 (s 8 of the 1996 Act is substituted in relation to England by SI 2007/2053 for a transitional period; and ss 4, 8, 9 of the 1996 Act are repealed by Transport Act 2000, s 274, Sch 31, Pt II, as from a day to be appointed by order)	—
SI 2001/785	Rail Vehicle Accessibility (Midland Metro T69 Vehicles) Exemption Order 2001	See note "Exemption from rail vehicle accessibility regulations" to SI 1998/2456	—
SI 2001/847	Rail Vehicle Accessibility (Gatwick Express Class 460 Vehicles) Exemption Order 2001	See note "Exemption from rail vehicle accessibility regulations" to SI 1998/2456	—
SI 2001/869	Transport Act 2000 (Commencement No 5) Order 2001	See note "Further orders" to SI 2000/3229	—
SI 2001/926	Fixed Penalty (Procedure) (Amendment) Regulations 2001	Amend SI 1986/1330	—
SI 2001/936	Vehicle Excise Duty (Immobilisation, Removal and Disposal of Vehicles) (Amendment) Regulations 2001	Amend SI 1997/2439	—

SI	*Description*	*Remarks*	*Page*
SI 2001/937	Motor Vehicles (Driving Licences) (Amendment) (No 3) Regulations 2001	Amend SI 1999/2864	—
SI 2001/1043	Road Vehicles (Construction and Use) (Amendment) (No 2) Regulations 2001	Amend SI 1986/1078	—
SI 2001/1054	British Waterways Board (Limit for Borrowing) Order 2001	—	446
SI 2001/1079	Road Vehicles (Display of Registration Marks) (Amendment) Regulations 2001	Amend SI 2001/561	—
SI 2001/1125	Road Vehicles (Authorised Weight) (Amendment) Regulations 2001	Amend SI 1998/3111, SI 2000/3224	—
SI 2001/1149	Postal Services Act 2000 (Consequential Modifications No 1) Order 2001	See title Postal Services; amends SI 1986/1078, SI 1995/2908, SI 1996/2186, SI 1997/2439; spent in so far as amended SI 1971/450, SI 1986/1456 (revoked), SI 1992/2902, SI 2000/2190 (all revoked)	—
SI 2001/1222	Road Traffic (Owner Liability) (Amendment) (No 2) Regulations 2001	Amend SI 2000/2546; revoke SI 2001/925	—
SI 2001/1498	Transport Act 2000 (Commencement No 6) Order 2001	See note "Further orders" to SI 2000/3229	—
SI 2001/1547	Motor Cycles Etc (EC Type Approval) (Amendment) (No 2) Regulations 2001	Amend SI 1999/2920	—
SI 2001/1747	Rail Vehicle Accessibility (Great Western Trains Company Class 180 Vehicles) Exemption Order 2001	See note "Exemption from rail vehicle accessibility regulations" to SI 1998/2456	—
SI 2001/1814	Road Traffic Offenders (Additional Offences and Prescribed Devices) Order 2001	See note "Further orders" to SI 1992/1209	—
SI 2001/1825	Road Vehicles (Construction and Use) (Amendment) (No 3) Regulations 2001	Amend SI 1986/1078	—
SI 2001/1896	Road Traffic (Vehicle Testing) Act 1999 (Commencement No 1) Order 2001	—	446
SI 2001/2264	Railway Pensions (Designation, Substitution and Miscellaneous Provisions) Order 2001	See note "Further orders" to SI 1994/2388	—
SI 2001/2285	Road User Charging (Charges and Penalty Charges) (London) Regulations 2001	—	446
SI 2001/2303	Trunk Road Charging Schemes (Bridges and Tunnels) (England) Procedure Regulations 2001	—	447
SI 2001/2313	Road User Charging (Enforcement and Adjudication) (London) Regulations 2001	—	447
SI 2001/2486	Motor Vehicles (Approval) (Fees) Regulations 2001	See note "Fees" to SI 2001/25	—
SI 2001/2788	Transport Act 2000 (Commencement No 1) (Wales) Order 2001 (W 238)	See note "Further orders" to SI 2000/3229	—
SI 2001/2793	Road User Charging and Workplace Parking Levy (Classes of Motor Vehicles) (England) Regulations 2001	—	447
SI 2001/3208	Road Vehicles (Construction and Use) (Amendment) (No 4) Regulations 2001	Amend SI 1986/1078	—
SI 2001/3215	Vehicles (Crime) Act 2001 (Commencement No 1) Order 2001	—	447
SI 2001/3291	Railway Safety (Miscellaneous Amendments) Regulations 2001	Amend SI 1999/2244; revoked by SI 2006/599 in so far as amended SI 1998/1340, SI 2000/2688 (both revoked)	—

SI	*Description*	*Remarks*	*Page*
SI 2001/3317	Quality Partnership Schemes (Existing Facilities) Regulations 2001	—	448
SI 2001/3330	Motor Vehicles (Tests) (Amendment) (No 2) Regulations 2001	Amend SI 1981/1694; supersede SI 2000/2322	—
SI 2001/3342	Transport Act 2000 (Commencement No 7) Order 2001	See note "Further orders" to SI 2000/3229	—
SI 2001/3343	Motor Vehicles (Access to Driver Licensing Records) Regulations 2001	—	449
SI 2001/3352	Railway Administration Order Rules 2001	See title Bankruptcy and Insolvency	—
SI 2001/3434	Rail Vehicle Accessibility (North Western Trains Class 175/0 and Class 175/1 Vehicles) Exemption Order 2001	See note "Exemption from rail vehicle accessibility regulations" to SI 1998/2456	—
SI 2001/3606	Goods Vehicles (Authorisation of International Journeys) (Fees) Regulations 2001	—	449
SI 2001/3649	Financial Services and Markets Act 2000 (Consequential Amendments and Repeals) Order 2001	See title Financial Services; amends SI 1969/1858, SI 1978/1358	—
SI 2001/3764	Mandatory Travel Concessions (Reimbursement Arrangements) (Wales) Regulations 2001 (W 312)	—	450
SI 2001/3908	Drivers' Hours (Goods Vehicles) (Milk Collection) (Temporary Exemption) (Revocation) Regulations 2001	Made under Transport Act 1968, s 96(10); revoke SI 2001/629 (as from 31 December 2001)	—
SI 2001/3952	Rail Vehicle Accessibility (Croydon Tramlink Class CR4000 Vehicles) Exemption Order 2001	See note "Exemption from rail vehicle accessibility regulations" to SI 1998/2456	—
SI 2001/3953	Rail Vehicle Accessibility (ScotRail Class 170/4 Vehicles) Exemption Order 2001	See note "Exemption from rail vehicle accessibility regulations" to SI 1998/2456	—
SI 2001/3954	Rail Vehicle Accessibility (Gatwick Express Class 460 Vehicles) Exemption (Amendment) Order 2001	Amends SI 2001/847	—
SI 2001/3955	Rail Vehicle Accessibility (C2C Class 357/0 Vehicles) Exemption Order 2001	See note "Exemption from rail vehicle accessibility regulations" to SI 1998/2456	—
SI 2001/3981	Goods Vehicles (Enforcement Powers) Regulations 2001	—	450
SI 2001/4041	Transport Tribunal (Amendment) Rules 2001	Amend SI 2000/3226	—
SI 2001/4051	Driving Licences (Disqualification until Test Passed) (Prescribed Offence) Order 2001	—	451
SI 2001/4059	Vehicles (Crime) Act 2001 (Commencement No 2) Order 2001	See note "Further orders" to SI 2001/3215	—
SI 2002/182	Public Service Vehicles (Registration of Local Services) (Amendment) (England and Wales) Regulations 2002	Amend SI 1986/1671	—
SI 2002/227	Road Vehicles (Construction and Use) (Amendment) Regulations 2002	Amend SI 1986/1078	—
SI 2002/335	Public Service Vehicles (Conditions of Fitness, Equipment, Use and Certification) (Amendment) Regulations 2002	Amend SI 1981/257	—
SI 2002/487	Goods Vehicles (Plating and Testing) (Amendment) Regulations 2002	Amend SI 1988/1478	—
SI 2002/488	Motor Vehicles (Tests) (Amendment) Regulations 2002	Amend SI 1981/1694	—

SI	*Description*	*Remarks*	*Page*
SI 2002/520	Service Subsidy Agreements (Tendering) (Amendment) (Wales) Regulations 2002 (W 63)	Amend SI 1985/1921	—
SI 2002/643	Transport Tribunal (Amendment) Rules 2002	Amend SI 2000/3226	—
SI 2002/656	Rail Vehicle Accessibility (South West Trains Class 458 Vehicles) Exemption Order 2002	See note "Exemption from rail vehicle accessibility regulations" to SI 1998/2456	—
SI 2002/658	Transport Act 2000 (Commencement No 8 and Transitional Provisions) Order 2002	See note "Further orders" to SI 2000/3229	—
SI 2002/673	Travel Concessions (Eligibility) Act 2002 (Commencement) (England) Order 2002	Made under s 2(1) of the 2002 Act; brought s 1 thereof into force on 1 April 2003 in England (as to Wales, see SI 2002/3014)	—
SI 2002/745	Vehicle Excise Duty (Immobilisation, Removal and Disposal of Vehicles) (Amendment) Regulations 2002	Amend SI 1997/2439; supersede SI 1999/35	—
SI 2002/846	Transport Act 2000 (Commencement No 8 and Transitional Provisions) (Amendment) Order 2002	Amends SI 2002/658	—
SI 2002/1014	Transport Act 2000 (Commencement No 9 and Transitional Provisions) Order 2002	See note "Further orders" to SI 2000/3229	—
SI 2002/1015	Bus Service Operators Grant (England) Regulations 2002	—	451
SI 2002/1016	Travel Concessions (Eligible Services) Order 2002	—	451
SI 2002/1072	Vehicle Excise Duty (Designation of Small Islands) (Amendment) Order 2002	Amends SI 1995/1397	—
SI 2002/1092	Radioactive Material (Road Transport) (Definition of Radioactive Material) Order 2002	See title Energy	—
SI 2002/1415	Goods Vehicles (Community Authorisations) (Modification of the Road Traffic (Foreign Vehicles) Act 1972) Regulations 2002	Made under European Communities Act 1972, s 2(2); amend Road Traffic (Foreign Vehicles) Act 1972, Schs 1, 2 (as from 1 July 2002)	—
SI 2002/1474	Road Vehicles (Construction and Use) (Amendment) (No 2) Regulations 2002	Amend SI 1986/1078	—
SI 2002/1593	Driving Licences (Exchangeable Licences) (Amendment) Order 2002	Amends SI 1984/672	—
SI 2002/1617	Rail Vehicle Accessibility (South Central Class 375/3 Vehicles) Exemption Order 2002	See note "Exemption from rail vehicle accessibility regulations" to SI 1998/2456	—
SI 2002/1694	Rail Vehicle Accessibility (Isle of Wight Railway LCDR No 2515 Vehicle) Exemption Order 2002	See note "Exemption from rail vehicle accessibility regulations" to SI 1998/2456	—
SI 2002/1698	Motor Vehicles (Tests) (Amendment) (No 2) Regulations 2002	Amend SI 1981/1694	—
SI 2002/1724	Public Service Vehicles (Conduct of Drivers, Inspectors, Conductors and Passengers) (Amendment) Regulations 2002	Amend SI 1990/1020	—
SI 2002/1762	Rail Vehicle Accessibility (South West Trains Class 458 Vehicles) Exemption (Amendment) Order 2002	Amends SI 2002/656	—
SI 2002/1808	Road Traffic (Vehicle Emissions) (Fixed Penalty) (England) Regulations 2002	—	452
SI 2002/1914	Vehicles (Crime) Act 2001 (Commencement No 3) Order 2002	See note "Further orders" to SI 2001/3215	—

SI	*Description*	*Remarks*	*Page*
SI 2002/2022	Bus Service Operators Grant (Wales) Regulations 2002 (W 206)	See note "Wales" to SI 2002/1015	—
SI 2002/2023	Travel Concessions (Eligible Services) (Wales) Order 2002 (W 207)	See note "Wales" to SI 2002/1016	—
SI 2002/2024	Transport Act 2000 (Commencement No 2) (Wales) Order 2002 (W 208)	See note "Further orders" to SI 2000/3229	—
SI 2002/2090	Service Subsidy Agreements (Tendering) (England) Regulations 2002	—	452
SI 2002/2126	Road Vehicles (Construction and Use) (Amendment) (No 3) Regulations 2002	Amend SI 1986/1078	—
SI 2002/2377	Vehicles (Crime) Act 2001 (Commencement No 4) Order 2002	See note "Further orders" to SI 2001/3215	—
SI 2002/2379	Driving Licences (Exchangeable Licences) Order 2002	See note "Further orders" to SI 1984/672	—
SI 2002/2426	Road Vehicles (Testing) (Disclosure of Information) (Great Britain) Regulations 2002	—	453
SI 2002/2535	Public Service Vehicles (Operators' Licences) (Fees) (Amendment) Regulations 2002	Amend SI 1995/2909	—
SI 2002/2590	Driving Licences (Designation of Relevant External Law) Order 2002	—	453
SI 2002/2687	Road Vehicles (Display of Registration Marks) (Amendment) Regulations 2002	Amend SI 2001/561	—
SI 2002/2703	Railways (Heathrow Express) (Exemptions) (Amendment) Order 2002	Amends SI 1994/574	—
SI 2002/2742	Road Vehicles (Registration and Licensing) Regulations 2002	—	453
SI 2002/2873	Rail Vehicle Accessibility (Summerlee Tramcar No 392) Exemption Order 2002	See note "Exemption from rail vehicle accessibility regulations" to SI 1998/2456	—
SI 2002/2957	Vehicles (Crime) Act 2001 (Commencement No 5) Order 2002	See note "Further orders" to SI 2001/3215	—
SI 2002/2975	Functions of Traffic Wardens (Amendment) Order 2002	Amends SI 1970/1958	—
SI 2002/2981	Public Service Vehicles Accessibility (Amendment) Regulations 2002	Amend SI 2000/1970	—
SI 2002/3002	Rail Vehicle Accessibility (C2C Class 357/0 Vehicles) Exemption (Amendment) Order 2002	Amends SI 2001/3955	—
SI 2002/3014	Travel Concessions (Eligibility) Act 2002 (Commencement) (Wales) Order 2002 (W 286)	Made under s 2(1) of the 2002 Act; brought s 1 thereof into force on 1 April 2003 in Wales (as to England, see SI 2002/673)	—
SI 2002/3017	Quality Partnership Schemes (Existing Facilities) (Wales) Regulations 2002 (W 287)	See note "Wales" to SI 2001/3317	—
SI 2002/3113	Traffic Signs Regulations and General Directions 2002	—	490
SI 2003/108	Road User Charging (Enforcement and Adjudication) (London) (Amendment) Regulations 2003	Amend SI 2001/2313	—
SI 2003/109	Road User Charging (Charges and Penalty Charges) (London) (Amendment) Regulations 2003	Amend SI 2001/2285	—
SI 2003/110	Road User Charging and Workplace Parking Levy (Net Proceeds) (England) Regulations 2003	—	491
SI 2003/166	Motor Vehicles (Driving Licences) (Amendment) Regulations 2003	Amend SI 1999/2864	—
SI 2003/182	Road Vehicles (Construction and Use) (Amendment) Regulations 2003	Amend SI 1986/1078	—

SI	*Description*	*Remarks*	*Page*
SI 2003/222	Motor Vehicles (Driving Licences) (Amendment) (No 2) Regulations 2003	Amend SI 1999/2864	—
SI 2003/298	Trunk Road Charging Schemes (Bridges and Tunnels) (Keeping of Accounts) (England) Regulations 2003	—	491
SI 2003/300	Road Traffic (Vehicle Emissions) (Fixed Penalty) (Wales) Regulations 2003 (W 42)	See note "Wales" to SI 2002/1808	—
SI 2003/393	Traffic Signs (Amendment) General Directions 2003	Amend SI 2002/3113	—
SI 2003/580	Private Hire Vehicles (London) Act 1998 (Commencement No 2) Order 2003	See note "Summary" to SI 2000/3144	—
SI 2003/582	Motor Vehicles (Type Approval for Goods Vehicles) (Great Britain) (Amendment) Regulations 2003	Amend SI 1982/1271	—
SI 2003/636	Motor Vehicles (Driving Licences) (Amendment) (No 3) Regulations 2003	Amend SI 1999/2864	—
SI 2003/655	Private Hire Vehicles (London) (Transitional and Saving Provisions) Regulations 2003	—	491
SI 2003/943	Bus Service Operators Grant (Amendment) (Wales) Regulations 2003 (W 124)	Amend SI 2002/2022	—
SI 2003/1036	Bus Service Operators Grant (Amendment) (England) Regulations 2003	Amend SI 2002/1015	—
SI 2003/1094	Department of Transport (Fees) (Amendment) Order 2003	Amends SI 1988/643	—
SI 2003/1095	Road Traffic (Vehicle Testing) Act 1999 (Commencement No 2) Order 2003	See note "Summary" to SI 2001/1896	—
SI 2003/1099	Motor Cycles Etc (EC Type Approval) (Amendment) Regulations 2003	Amend SI 1999/2920 and Road Traffic Act 1988, s 85 (also amend Road Traffic (Northern Ireland) Order 1981, SI 1981/154 (NI 1) (outside the scope of this work))	—
SI 2003/1113	Motor Vehicles (Tests) (Amendment) Regulations 2003	Amend SI 1981/1694	—
SI 2003/1118	Road Transport (International Passenger Services) (Amendment) Regulations 2003	Amend SI 1984/748	—
SI 2003/1253	Fixed Penalty Offences Order 2003	See note "Further orders" to SI 1990/335	—
SI 2003/1254	Fixed Penalty (Amendment) Order 2003	Amends SI 2000/2792	—
SI 2003/1436	Rail Vehicle Accessibility (Furness Railway Trust North London Coach) Exemption Order 2003	See note "Exemption from rail vehicle accessibility regulations" to SI 1998/2456	—
SI 2003/1545	Regulatory Reform (British Waterways Board) Order 2003	Made under Regulatory Reform Act 2001, s 1 (repealed by Legislative and Regulatory Reform Act 2006, s 30(1), (3)(a), Schedule, with saving for orders made under s 1 of the 2001 Act); inserts Transport Act 1962, s 10(3)(dd) and Transport Act 1968, s 50(8A) (as from 13 June 2003)	—
SI 2003/1562	Rail Vehicle Accessibility (Great Eastern Railway Class 360 Vehicles) Exemption Order 2003	See note "Exemption from rail vehicle accessibility regulations" to SI 1998/2456	—
SI 2003/1613	Transport for London (Reserved Services) (London Underground Limited) Exception Order 2003	—	492

SI	*Description*	*Remarks*	*Page*
SI 2003/1615	Transport for London (Consequential Provisions) Order 2003	—	492
SI 2003/1633	Uncertificated Securities (Amendment) (Eligible Debt Securities) Regulations 2003	See title Money; modify SI 1994/2005	—
SI 2003/1687	Rail Vehicle Accessibility (Festiniog Railway Company Vehicle Number 122) Exemption Order 2003	See note "Exemption from rail vehicle accessibility regulations" to SI 1998/2456	—
SI 2003/1690	Road Vehicles (Construction and Use) (Amendment) (No 2) Regulations 2003	Amend SI 1986/1078	—
SI 2003/1694	Transport Act 2000 (Commencement No 10) Order 2003	See note "Further orders" to SI 2000/3229	—
SI 2003/1695	Railways (Rail Passengers' Council and Rail Passengers' Committees) (Exemptions) Order 2003	—	493
SI 2003/1698	Motor Vehicles (Tests) (Amendment) (No 2) Regulations 2003	Amend SI 1981/1694	—
SI 2003/1704	Rail Vehicle Accessibility (South West Trains Class 444 and Class 450 Vehicles) Exemption Order 2003	See note "Exemption from rail vehicle accessibility regulations" to SI 1998/2456	—
SI 2003/1811	International Carriage of Dangerous Goods by Road (Fees) (Amendment) Regulations 2003	Amend SI 1988/370	—
SI 2003/1815	Motor Vehicles (Tests) (Amendment) (No 3) Regulations 2003	Amend SI 1981/1694	—
SI 2003/1816	Goods Vehicles (Plating and Testing) (Amendment) Regulations 2003	Amend SI 1988/1478	—
SI 2003/1866	Motor Vehicles (Type Approval for Goods Vehicles) (Great Britain) (Amendment) (No 2) Regulations 2003	Amend SI 1982/1271	—
SI 2003/1913	London Regional Transport (Dissolution) Order 2003	Made under Greater London Authority Act 1999, s 302; dissolves London Regional Transport as from 16 July 2003	—
SI 2003/1946	Road Vehicles (Construction and Use) (Amendment) (No 3) Regulations 2003	Amend SI 1986/1078	—
SI 2003/1959	Motor Cycles Etc (Single Vehicle Approval) Regulations 2003	—	493
SI 2003/1960	Motor Cycles Etc (Single Vehicle Approval) (Fees) Regulations 2003	See note "Fees" to SI 2003/1959	—
SI 2003/1985	Transport Act 1968 (Commencement No 11) Order 2003	See note "Further orders" to SI 1968/1822	—
SI 2003/1998	Road Vehicles (Authorisation of Special Types) (General) Order 2003	—	494
SI 2003/2003	Motor Vehicles (Driving Licences) (Amendment) (No 4) Regulations 2003	Amend SI 1999/2864; partially revoked by SI 2007/698	—
SI 2003/2096	Enterprise Act 2002 (Insolvency) Order 2003	See title Bankruptcy and Insolvency; amends SI 1986/1078, SI 1995/2869	—
SI 2003/2154	Road Vehicles (Registration and Licensing) (Amendment) Regulations 2003	Amend SI 2002/2742	—
SI 2003/2155	Communications Act 2003 (Consequential Amendments) Order 2003	See title Telecommunications and Broadcasting; amends SI 1970/145, SI 1986/1078, SI 1986/1492, SI 2002/3113; also amended SI 2000/2190 (revoked)	—

SI	*Description*	*Remarks*	*Page*
SI 2003/2335	Road Vehicles (Registration and Licensing) (Amendment) (No 2) Regulations 2003	Revoke SI 2003/1814; superseded by SI 2004/1872 (itself superseded) in so far as amended SI 2002/2742	—
SI 2003/2408	Rail Vehicle Accessibility (Bristol Harbour Railway Vehicle Number DB978121) Exemption Order 2003	See note "Exemption from rail vehicle accessibility regulations" to SI 1998/2456	—
SI 2003/2462	Registered Health Care Profession (Designation No 2) Order 2003	Made under Road Traffic Act 1988, s 11(2) and Transport and Works Act 1992, ss 31(9A), 38(2A); enables paramedics registered under Pt 8 of the register maintained by the Health Professions Council under SI 2002/254, in title Medicine and Pharmacy, to take samples under s 7 of the 1988 Act and ss 31, 38 of the 1992 Act (as from 1 November 2003)	—
SI 2003/2635	End-of-Life Vehicles Regulations 2003	See title Environment; amend SI 2002/2742	—
SI 2003/2681	Railways and Transport Safety Act 2003 (Commencement No 1) Order 2003	—	495
SI 2003/2695	Road Vehicles (Construction and Use) (Amendment) (No 4) Regulations 2003	Amend SI 1986/1078	—
SI 2003/2981	Road Vehicles (Registration and Licensing) (Amendment) (No 3) Regulations 2003	Amend SI 2002/2742	—
SI 2003/2994	Department for Transport (Driver Licensing and Vehicle Registration Fees) Order 2003	See note "Further orders" to SI 1988/643	—
SI 2003/3028	Private Hire Vehicles (London) (Transitional and Saving Provisions) (Amendment) Regulations 2003	Amend SI 2003/655	—
SI 2003/3073	Road Vehicles (Registration and Licensing) (Amendment) (No 4) Regulations 2003	Amend SI 2002/2742	—
SI 2003/3086	Finance Act 2002, Section 19 (Appointed Days etc) Order 2003	Made under Finance Act 2002, s 19(2), (4)(a); provides that (subject to transitional provision) the appointed day on which s 19(1) of that Act comes into force, so far as that section is not already in force by virtue of s 19(3), is: (a) for the purpose of giving effect to paras 8–10, 12–15 of Sch 5 to the 2002 Act, 19 December 2003; and (b) for all other purposes, 30 November 2003 (the said s 19(1) introduces Sch 5 to the 2002 Act, which amends Vehicle Excise and Registration Act 1994)	—
SI 2003/3122	Disability Discrimination Act 1995 (Private Hire Vehicles) (Carriage of Guide Dogs etc) (England and Wales) Regulations 2003	—	496

SI	*Description*	*Remarks*	*Page*
SI 2003/3123	Private Hire Vehicles (Carriage of Guide Dogs etc) Act 2002 (Commencement No 1) Order 2003	—	496
SI 2003/3145	Road Vehicles (Construction and Use) (Amendment) (No 5) Regulations 2003	Amend SI 1986/1078	—
SI 2003/3313	Motor Vehicles (Driving Licences) (Amendment) (No 5) Regulations 2003	Amend SI 1999/2864	—
SI 2004/9	Bus Service Operators Grant (Amendment) (England) Regulations 2004	Amend SI 2002/1015	—
SI 2004/10	Public Service Vehicles (Registration of Local Services) (Amendment) (England and Wales) Regulations 2004	Amend SI 1986/1671	—
SI 2004/129	Cableway Installations Regulations 2004	—	497
SI 2004/238	Road Vehicles (Registration and Licensing) (Amendment) Regulations 2004	Amend SI 2002/2742	—
SI 2004/241	Private Hire Vehicles (London) Act 1998 (Commencement No 3) Order 2004	See note "Summary" to SI 2000/3144	—
SI 2004/242	Private Hire Vehicles (London) (Transitional Provisions) Regulations 2004	—	498
SI 2004/265	Motor Vehicles (Driving Licences) (Amendment) Regulations 2004	Amend SI 1999/2864	—
SI 2004/301	Driving Licences (Exchangeable Licences) Order 2004	See note "Further orders" to SI 1984/672	—
SI 2004/462	Goods Vehicles (Licensing of Operators) (Temporary Use in Great Britain) (Amendment) Regulations 2004	Amend 1996/2186	—
SI 2004/609	Service Subsidy Agreements (Tendering) (England) (Amendment) Regulations 2004	Amend SI 2002/2090	—
SI 2004/623	Motor Vehicles (Approval) (Amendment) Regulations 2004	Amend SI 2001/25	—
SI 2004/696	Health and Social Care (Community Health and Standards) Act 2003 (Supplementary and Consequential Provision) (NHS Foundation Trusts) Order 2004	See title National Health Service; amends SI 1996/2489, SI 1999/2864; also amended SI 1986/1456 (revoked)	—
SI 2004/827	Railways and Transport Safety Act 2003 (Commencement No 2) Order 2004	See note "Summary" to SI 2003/2681	—
SI 2004/915	Railway Safety Accreditation Scheme Regulations 2004	—	498
SI 2004/954	Rail Vehicle Accessibility (Midland Mainline Class 222 Vehicles) Exemption Order 2004	See note "Exemption from rail vehicle accessibility regulations" to SI 1998/2456	—
SI 2004/955	Rail Vehicle Accessibility (CrossCountry Trains Class 220 and Class 221) Exemption Order 2004	See note "Exemption from rail vehicle accessibility regulations" to SI 1998/2456	—
SI 2004/1037	Driver and Vehicle Licensing Agency Trading Fund Order 2004	See title Constitutional Law (Pt 2)	—
SI 2004/1205	Rail Vehicle Accessibility (Seaton Tramway Tramcars 9, 10 and 11) Exemption Order 2004	See note "Exemption from rail vehicle accessibility regulations" to SI 1998/2456	—
SI 2004/1230	Cableway Installations (Amendment) Regulations 2004	Amend SI 2004/129	—
SI 2004/1275	Traffic Signs (Amendment) General Directions 2004	Amend SI 2002/3113	—
SI 2004/1302	Rail Vehicle Accessibility (South Eastern Trains Class 376) Exemption Order 2004	See note "Exemption from rail vehicle accessibility regulations" to SI 1998/2456	—
SI 2004/1410	Rail Vehicle Accessibility (Hull Trains Class 170/3) Exemption Order 2004	See note "Exemption from rail vehicle accessibility regulations" to SI 1998/2456	—
SI 2004/1519	Motor Vehicles (Driving Licences) (Amendment) (No 2) Regulations 2004	Amend SI 1999/2864	—

SI	*Description*	*Remarks*	*Page*
SI 2004/1522	British Transport Police (Police Services Agreement) Order 2004	—	498
SI 2004/1572	Railways and Transport Safety Act 2003 (Commencement No 3) Order 2004	See note "Summary" to SI 2003/2681	—
SI 2004/1573	British Transport Police (Transitional and Consequential Provisions) Order 2004	—	499
SI 2004/1773	Road Vehicles (Registration and Licensing) (Amendment No 2) Regulations 2004	Amend SI 2002/2742	—
SI 2004/1827	Bus Service Operators Grant (Wales) (Amendment) Regulations 2004 (W 203)	Amend SI 2002/2022	—
SI 2004/1873	Goods Vehicles (Plating and Testing) (Amendment) Regulations 2004	Amend SI 1988/1478	—
SI 2004/1879	Motor Vehicles (Tests) (Amendment) (No 2) Regulations 2004	Amend SI 1981/1694	—
SI 2004/1882	Road Transport (International Passenger Services) (Amendment) Regulations 2004	Amend SI 1984/748	—
SI 2004/1896	Motor Vehicles (Evidence of Test Certificates) Regulations 2004	See note "Obligatory test certificates" to SI 1981/1694	—
SI 2004/1948	Motor Cycles Etc (EC Type Approval) (Amendment) Regulations 2004	Amend SI 1999/2920	—
SI 2004/1992	Motor Vehicles (International Circulation) (Amendment) Order 2004	Amends SI 1975/1208	—
SI 2004/2018	Transport and Works (Inquiries Procedure) Rules 2004	—	499
SI 2004/2102	Road Vehicles (Construction and Use) (Amendment) (No 2) Regulations 2004	Amend SI 1986/1078	—
SI 2004/2149	Rail Vehicle Accessibility (South West Trains Class 458 Vehicles) Exemption (Amendment) Order 2004	Amends SI 2002/656	—
SI 2004/2150	Rail Vehicle Accessibility (Gatwick Express Class 460 Vehicles) Exemption (Amendment) Order 2004	Amends SI 2001/847	—
SI 2004/2180	Rail Vehicle Accessibility (Hull Trains Class 222) Exemption Order 2004	See note "Exemption from rail vehicle accessibility regulations" to SI 1998/2456	—
SI 2004/2380	Traffic Management Act 2004 (Commencement No 1 and Transitional Provision) (England) Order 2004	—	511
SI 2004/2539	Motor Cycles Etc (EC Type Approval) (Amendment) (No 2) Regulations 2004	Amend SI 1999/2920	—
SI 2004/2577	Goods Vehicles (Evidence of Test Certificates) Regulations 2004	See note "Evidence of test certificates" to SI 1988/1478	—
SI 2004/2682	Public Service Vehicles (Traffic Regulation Conditions) (England and Wales) Regulations 2004	—	521
SI 2004/2759	Railways and Transport Safety Act 2003 (Commencement No 4) Order 2004	See note "Summary" to SI 2003/2681	—
SI 2004/2922	Fixed Penalty Offences Order 2004	See note "Further orders" to SI 1990/335	—
SI 2004/3028	Motor Vehicles (Driving Licences) (Amendment) (No 3) Regulations 2004	Amend SI 1999/2864	—
SI 2004/3110	Traffic Management Act 2004 (Commencement No 2) (England) Order 2004	See note "Further commencement orders" to SI 2004/2380	—
SI 2004/3139	Rail Vehicle Accessibility (South West Trains Class 444 and Class 450 Vehicles) Exemption (Amendment) Order 2004	Amends SI 2003/1704	—

SI	*Description*	*Remarks*	*Page*
SI 2004/3168	Fire and Rescue Services Act 2004 (Consequential Amendments) (England) Order 2004	See title Fire and Rescue Services; amends SI 1986/1078, SI 1989/1796, SI 1990/1656, SI 1992/1215, SI 1993/176, SI 1995/2869, SI 1996/2489, SI 1999/2864, SI 2001/2303, SI 2002/3113	—
SI 2004/3198	Rail Vehicle Accessibility (South Central Class 377/4) Exemption Order 2004	See note "Exemption from rail vehicle accessibility regulations" to SI 1998/2456	—
SI 2004/3222	Goods Vehicle Operators (Qualifications) (Amendment) Regulations 2004	Made under European Communities Act 1972, s 2(2); amend Goods Vehicles (Licensing of Operators) Act 1995, Sch 3, para 6(2) (as from 1 January 2005)	—
SI 2004/3223	Public Service Vehicle Operators (Qualifications) (Amendment) Regulations 2004	Made under European Communities Act 1972, s 2(2); amend Public Passenger Vehicles Act 1981, Sch 3, para 2(2) (as from 1 January 2005)	—
SI 2004/3298	Road Vehicles (Registration and Licensing) (Amendment) (No 5) Regulations 2004	Amend SI 2002/2742	—
SI 2005/27	Motor Vehicles (Wearing of Seat Belts) (Amendment) Regulations 2005	Amend SI 1993/176	—
SI 2005/56	Transport for London (Consequential Provisions) Order 2005	Made under Greater London Authority Act 1999, ss 405(2), 406, 420(1); amends London Local Authorities Act 1995, s 9 and London Local Authorities Act 2000, ss 6, 9–13, 16 (as from 14 February 2005); also amended s 4 of the 1995 Act and ss 4, 5, 7, 8 of the 2000 Act (repealed) (ss 6, 9–13 of the 2000 Act are repealed by Traffic Management Act 2004, s 98, Sch 12, Pt 1, as from a day to be appointed by order)	—
SI 2005/75	Transport Act 2000 (Commencement of Quality Contracts Schemes) (England) Order 2005	See Preliminary Note "Public service vehicles: bus services"" (under main head "Road traffic")	—
SI 2005/86	Rail Vehicle Accessibility (Heathrow Express Class 360/2) Exemption Order 2005	See note "Exemption from rail vehicle accessibility regulations" to SI 1998/2456	—
SI 2005/329	Rail Vehicle Accessibility (Virgin West Coast Class 390) Exemption Order 2005	See note "Exemption from rail vehicle accessibility regulations" to SI 1998/2456	—
SI 2005/390	Tractor etc (EC Type-Approval) Regulations 2005	—	521

SI	*Description*	*Remarks*	*Page*
SI 2005/395	Rail Vehicle Accessibility (Croydon Tramlink Class CR4000 Vehicles) Exemption (Amendment) Order 2005	Amends SI 2001/3952; supersedes SI 2002/3001	—
SI 2005/549	Non-Domestic Rating (Communications and Light Railways) (England) Regulations 2005	See title Local Government	—
SI 2005/617	Courts Act 2003 (Consequential Provisions) (No 2) Order 2005	See title Courts and Legal Services; amends SI 1986/1330, SI 2000/682, SI 2001/3981	—
SI 2005/639	Road Transport (Working Time) Regulations 2005	—	522
SI 2005/1095	Railways (Penalty Fares) (Amendment) Regulations 2005	Amend SI 1994/576	—
SI 2005/1140	Passenger and Goods Vehicles (Recording Equipment) (Tachograph Card Fees) Regulations 2005	—	533
SI 2005/1403	Public Service Vehicles (Conditions of Fitness, Equipment, Use and Certification) (Amendment) Regulations 2005	Amend SI 1981/257	—
SI 2005/1404	Rail Vehicle Accessibility (Heathrow Express Class 360/2) Exemption (Amendment) Order 2005	Amends SI 2005/86	—
SI 2005/1444	Railways Act 2005 (Commencement No 1) Order 2005	—	533
SI 2005/1670	Traffic Signs (Amendment) Regulations and General Directions 2005	Amend SI 2002/3113	—
SI 2005/1737	Railways (Rail Passengers' Council and Rail Passengers' Committees) (Exemptions) (Amendment) Order 2005	Amends SI 2003/1695	—
SI 2005/1738	Railways Act 2005 (Transitional Provisions and Savings) Order 2005	—	542
SI 2005/1832	Motor Vehicles (Tests) (Amendment) Regulations 2005	Amend SI 1981/1694; supersede SI 2004/1632	—
SI 2005/1902	Motor Cars (Driving Instruction) Regulations 2005	—	542
SI 2005/1904	Passenger and Goods Vehicles (Recording Equipment) Regulations 2005	See note "Further regulations" to SI 1979/1746	—
SI 2005/1909	Railways Act 2005 (Commencement No 2) Order 2005	See note "Summary" to SI 2005/1444	—
SI 2005/1975	Motor Vehicles (Driving Licences) (Amendment) Regulations 2005	Amend SI 1999/2864	—
SI 2005/1991	Railways and Transport Safety Act 2003 (Commencement No 5) Order 2005	See note "Summary" to SI 2003/2681	—
SI 2005/1992	Railways (Accident Investigation and Reporting) Regulations 2005	—	543
SI 2005/2060	Fire (Scotland) Act 2005 (Consequential Provisions and Modifications) Order 2005	See title Constitutional Law (Pt 3); amends SI 1995/2869	—
SI 2005/2092	Railways (Convention on International Carriage by Rail) Regulations 2005	—	562
SI 2005/2185	Railways Act 1993 (Determination of Turnover) Order 2005	Made under Railways Act 1993, ss 55(7B), 57A(3); makes provision for the determination of turnover of a relevant operator for the purposes of ss 55(7B), 57A(3) of the 1993 Act (as from 3 August 2005)	—
SI 2005/2252	Railways Act 2005 (Commencement No 3) Order 2005	See note "Summary" to SI 2005/1444	—
SI 2005/2290	Transport (Guided Systems) (England) (Amendment) Order 2005	Amends SI 1992/2044	—

SI	*Description*	*Remarks*	*Page*
SI 2005/2343	Goods Vehicles (Plating and Testing) (Amendment) Regulations 2005	Amend SI 1988/1478	—
SI 2005/2356	Finance Act 2004, Section 18 (Appointed Day) Order 2005	Made under s 18(4) of the 2004 Act; appointed 14 October 2005 as the day on which s 18 is to have effect in relation to vehicle licences or trade licences issued on or after that day	—
SI 2005/2460	Road Vehicles (Payment of Duty by Credit Card) (Prescribed Fee) Regulations 2005	Made under Vehicle Excise and Registration Act 1994, ss 19C(2), (4), 57(1), (2)(b); prescribe the fee payable under s 19C of the 1994 Act and the meaning of "credit card" for the purposes of that section (as from 14 October 2005)	—
SI 2005/2559	Road Vehicles Lighting (Amendment) Regulations 2005	Amend SI 1989/1796	—
SI 2005/2560	Road Vehicles (Construction and Use) (Amendment) (No 2) Regulations 2005	Amend SI 1986/1078	—
SI 2005/2628	Railways (Provision etc of Railway Facilities) (Exemptions) Order 2005	See note "Further exemptions" to SI 1994/573	—
SI 2005/2713	Road Vehicles (Registration and Licensing) (Amendment) (No 2) Regulations 2005	Amend SI 2002/2742	—
SI 2005/2716	Motor Cars (Driving Instruction) (Amendment) Regulations 2005	Amend SI 2005/1902	—
SI 2005/2717	Motor Vehicles (Driving Licences) (Amendment) (No 2) Regulations 2005	Amend SI 1999/2864	—
SI 2005/2756	Bus Lanes (Approved Devices) (England) Order 2005	See note "Approved devices" to SI 2005/2757	—
SI 2005/2757	Bus Lane Contraventions (Penalty Charges, Adjudication and Enforcement) (England) Regulations 2005	—	562
SI 2005/2812	Railway Act 2005 (Commencement No 4) Order 2005	See note "Summary" to SI 2005/1444	—
SI 2005/2833	Disclosure of Vehicle Insurance Information Regulations 2005	—	578
SI 2005/2862	Transport Act 2000 (Commencement No 11) Order 2005	See note "Further orders" to SI 2000/3229	—
SI 2005/2905	Railway Heritage Scheme Order 2005	—	578
SI 2005/2929	Fire and Rescue Services Act 2004 (Consequential Amendments) (Wales) Order 2005 (W 214)	See title Fire and Rescue Services; amends SI 1986/1078, SI 1989/1796, SI 1990/1656, SI 1992/1215, SI 1993/176, SI 1995/2869, SI 1996/2489, SI 1999/2864, SI 2002/3113	—
SI 2005/2986	Public Service Vehicles (Conditions of Fitness, Equipment, Use and Certification) (Amendment) (No 3) Regulations 2005	Amend SI 1981/257	—
SI 2005/2987	Road Vehicles (Construction and Use) (Amendment) (No 3) Regulations 2005	Amend SI 1986/1078	—
SI 2005/2988	Public Service Vehicles Accessibility (Amendment) Regulations 2005	Amend SI 2000/1970	—

SI	*Description*	*Remarks*	*Page*
SI 2005/3049	Railways Infrastructure (Access and Management) Regulations 2005	—	578
SI 2005/3050	Railway (Licensing of Railway Undertakings) Regulations 2005	—	604
SI 2005/3128	Public Service Vehicles (Conditions of Fitness, Equipment, Use and Certification) (Amendment) (No 4) Regulations 2005	Amend SI 1981/257	—
SI 2005/3165	Road Vehicles (Construction and Use) (Amendment) (No 4) Regulations 2005	Amend SI 1986/1078	—
SI 2005/3169	Road Vehicles Lighting (Amendment) (No 2) Regulations 2005	Amend SI 1989/1796	—
SI 2005/3170	Road Vehicles (Construction and Use) (Amendment) (No 5) Regulations 2005	Amend SI 1986/1078	—
SI 2005/3190	Disability Discrimination (Transport Vehicles) Regulations 2005	—	605
SI 2005/3225	Wales Tourist Board (Transfer of Functions to the National Assembly for Wales and Abolition) Order 2005 (W 237)	See title Trade and Industry; amends SI 2002/3113	—
SI 2005/3261	Railways (Accident Investigation and Reporting) (Amendment) Regulations 2005	Amend SI 2005/1992	—
SI 2006/5	Public Contracts Regulations 2006	See title Local Government; amend SI 2003/1615	—
SI 2006/91	Transport for London (Best Value) (Contracting Out of Investment and Highway Functions) Order 2006	—	605
SI 2006/266	Railways Act 2005 (Commencement No 5) Order 2006	See note "Summary" to SI 2005/1444	—
SI 2006/397	Railways (Interoperability) Regulations 2006	—	605
SI 2006/524	Motor Cars (Driving Licences) (Amendment) Regulations 2006	Amend SI 1999/2864	—
SI 2006/525	Motor Cars (Driving Instruction) (Amendment) Regulations 2006	Amend SI 2005/1902	—
SI 2006/556	Railways Act 2005 (Amendment) Regulations 2006	Made under Railways Act 2005, Sch 3, para 1(4); amend Sch 3, para 1(3), (7) thereto (as from 1 April 2006)	—
SI 2006/557	Health and Safety (Enforcing Authority for Railways and Other Guided Transport Systems) Regulations 2006	See title Health and Safety at Work; amend SI 1997/553, SI 1999/2244, SI 2005/1992; also amended SI 1994/157, SI 1994/299, SI 2000/2688 (all revoked)	—
SI 2006/582	Tyne and Wear Passenger Transport Authority (Increase in Number of Members) Order 2006	Made under Local Government Act 1985, ss 29(2), 103(1); as from 1 April 2006, amends Pt V of Sch 10 to the 1985 Act so as to alter the composition of the Tyne and Wear Passenger Transport Authority (now the Tyne and Wear Integrated Transport Authority; see the Local Transport Act 2008, s 77(2))	—
SI 2006/584	Private Hire Vehicles (London) (Transitional and Saving Provisions) (Amendment) Regulations 2006	Amend SI 2003/655	—

SI	*Description*	*Remarks*	*Page*
SI 2006/594	Serious Organised Crime and Police Act 2005 (Consequential and Supplementary Amendments to Secondary Legislation) Order 2006	See title Police; amends SI 1981/1694, SI 1986/1078, SI 1989/1796, SI 1993/176, SI 1995/2869, SI 2002/3113	—
SI 2006/598	Railways (Access to Training Services) Regulations 2006	—	607
SI 2006/599	Railways and Other Guided Transport Systems (Safety) Regulations 2006	—	607
SI 2006/680	Lord Chancellor (Transfer of Functions and Supplementary Provisions) Order 2006	See title Constitutional Law (Pt 2); amends SI 1952/1612, SI 1953/1445, SI 1954/139, SI 1962/2793, SI 1968/2012	—
SI 2006/933	Rail Vehicle Accessibility (Gatwick Express Class 458 Vehicles) Exemption Order 2006	See note "Exemption from rail vehicle accessibility regulations" to SI 1998/2456	—
SI 2006/958	Transport and Works (Assessment of Environmental Effects) Regulations 2006	See title Environment	—
SI 2006/1010	Railway Safety Levy Regulations 2006	—	637
SI 2006/1016	Lord Chancellor (Transfer of Functions and Supplementary Provisions) (No 2) Order 2006	See title Constitutional Law (Pt 2); amends 1962/2834	—
SI 2006/1057	Railways and Other Guided Transport Systems (Safety) (Amendment) Regulations 2006	Amend SI 2006/599	—
SI 2006/1117	Passenger and Goods Vehicles (Recording Equipment) (Fitting Date) Regulations 2006	See note "Further regulations" to SI 1979/1746	—
SI 2006/1177	Restricted Byways (Application and Consequential Amendment of Provisions) Regulations 2006	See title Open Spaces and National Heritage; amend SI 1992/1215; also amended SI 2000/2190 (revoked)	—
SI 2006/1403	Transport (Wales) Act 2006 (Commencement) Order 2006 (W 140)	Made under ss 12, 13 of the 2006 Act; brought ss 1–11 thereof into force on 26 May 2006	—
SI 2006/1466	Transport and Works (Applications and Objections Procedure) (England and Wales) Rules 2006	—	637
SI 2006/1616	Disability Discrimination Act 1995 (Taxis) (Carrying of Guide Dogs etc) (England and Wales) (Amendment) Regulations 2006	Amend SI 2000/2990	—
SI 2006/1617	Disability Discrimination Act 1995 (Private Hire Vehicles) (Carriage of Guide Dogs etc) (England and Wales) (Amendment) Regulations 2006	Amend SI 2003/3122	—
SI 2006/1638	Motor Vehicles (Type Approval and Approval Marks) (Fees) (Amendment) Regulations 2006	Amend SI 1999/2149	—
SI 2006/1736	Traffic Management Act 2004 (Commencement No 3) (England) Order 2006	See note "Further commencement orders" to SI 2004/2380	—

SI	*Description*	*Remarks*	*Page*
SI 2006/1892	Motor Vehicles (Wearing of Seat Belts) (Amendment) Regulations 2006	Made under European Communities Act 1972, s 2(2) and Road Traffic Act 1988, ss 14(1), (2), 15(3), (5); amend s 15 of, and insert s 15B of, and Sch 2A to, the 1988 Act; amend Road Traffic Offenders Act 1988, Schs 1, 2 (as from 18 September 2006); also amend SI 1993/176	—
SI 2006/1914	Medical Act 1983 (Amendment) and Miscellaneous Amendments Order 2006	See title Medicine and Pharmacy; amends SI 1989/1796	—
SI 2006/1933	Transport Act 2000 (Commencement No 12) Order 2006	See note "Further orders" to SI 2000/3229	—
SI 2006/1935	Railways (Substitute Road Services) (Exemptions) Order 2006	—	638
SI 2006/1937	Passenger and Goods Vehicles (Recording Equipment) (Tachograph Card) Regulations 2006	—	639
SI 2006/1951	Railways Act 2005 (Commencement No 6) Order 2006	See note "Summary" to SI 2005/1444	—
SI 2006/1954	Transport and Works (Model Clauses for Railways and Tramways) Order 2006	—	639
SI 2006/1998	Motor Vehicles (Tests) (Amendment) Regulations 2006	Amend SI 1981/1694	—
SI 2006/2082	Quiet Lanes and Home Zones (England) Regulations 2006	—	640
SI 2006/2083	Traffic Signs (Amendment) Regulations 2006	Amend SI 2002/3113	—
SI 2006/2190	Transport Security (Electronic Communications) Order 2006	Made under Electronic Communications Act 2000, ss 8, 9; amends Aviation Security Act 1982, ss 24, 24A, Aviation and Maritime Security Act 1990, ss 45, 46, and inserts Railways Act 1993, s 149A (also amends SI 1994/570, in title Criminal Law, and SI 2004/1495, in title Shipping, Ports and Harbours) (as from 30 September 2006)	—
SI 2006/2213	Motor Vehicles (Wearing of Seat Belts by Children in Front Seats) (Amendment) Regulations 2006	Amend SI 1993/31	—
SI 2006/2215	School Crossing Patrol Sign (England and Wales) Regulations 2006	See note "Other traffic signs" to SI 2002/3113	—
SI 2006/2320	Road Vehicles (Registration and Licensing) (Amendment) Regulations 2006	Amend SI 2002/2742	—
SI 2006/2533	Tractor etc (EC Type-Approval) (Amendment) Regulations 2006	Amend SI 2005/390; revoke SI 1988/1567, SI 1989/2275, SI 1990/2336, SI 1992/80, SI 2000/828, SI 2001/1710, SI 2002/1890	—
SI 2006/2565	Road Vehicles (Construction and Use) and Motor Vehicles (Type Approval for Goods Vehicles) (Great Britain) (Amendment) Regulations 2006	Amend SI 1982/1271, SI 1986/1078	—

SI	*Description*	*Remarks*	*Page*
SI 2006/2826	Traffic Management Act 2004 (Commencement No 1) (Wales) Order 2006 (W 249)	See note "Further commencement orders" to SI 2004/2380	—
SI 2006/2836	Closures Guidance (Railway Services in England and Wales) Order 2006	Made under Railways Act 2005, ss 43(3)(a), 56(5); specifies that the closures guidance dated 18 October 2006 and laid before Parliament on 24 October 2006 is to have effect in relation to the proposals referred to in s 42(3), (4) of the 2005 Act	—
SI 2006/2837	Closures Guidance (Railway Services in Scotland and England) Order 2006	Made under Railways Act 2005, ss 43(3)(a), 56(5); specifies that the closures guidance dated 18 October 2006 and laid before Parliament on 24 October 2006 is to have effect in relation to the proposals referred to in s 42(1) of the 2005 Act and in s 42(2) thereof, in so far as they relate to proposals to discontinue any cross-border services in relation to which the Secretary of State provides funding or both the Scottish Ministers and the Secretary of State provide funding	—
SI 2006/2911	Railways Act 2005 (Commencement No 7, Transitional and Saving Provisions) Order 2006	See note "Summary" to SI 2005/1444	—
SI 2006/2925	Railways (Abolition of the Strategic Rail Authority) Order 2006	Made under Railways Act 2005, s 1(10); abolishes the Strategic Rail Authority on 1 December 2006	—
SI 2006/2935	Motor Cycles Etc (EC Type Approval) (Amendment) Regulations 2006	Amend SI 1999/2920	—
SI 2006/2993	Regional Transport Planning (Wales) Order 2006 (W 280)	—	641
SI 2006/3276	Passenger and Goods Vehicles (Community Recording Equipment Regulation) Regulations 2006	See note "Further regulations" to SI 1979/1746	—
SI 2007/58	Road Tolling (Interoperability of Electronic Road User Charging and Road Tolling Systems) Regulations 2007	—	641
SI 2007/62	Railways Act 2005 (Commencement No 8) Order 2007	See note "Summary" to SI 2005/1444	—
SI 2007/95	Driving Licences (Exchangeable Licences) Order 2007	See note "Further orders" to SI 1984/672	—
SI 2007/96	Driving Licences (Exchangeable Licences) (Amendment) Order 2007	Amends SI 1999/1641	—
SI 2007/237	Road Safety Act 2006 (Commencement No 1) Order 2007	—	641
SI 2007/339	Traffic Management (Guidance on Intervention Criteria) (England) Order 2007	See Preliminary Note "Regulation of traffic" (under main head "Road traffic")	—

SI	*Description*	*Remarks*	*Page*
SI 2007/361	Motor Vehicles (Type Approval for Goods Vehicles) (Great Britain) (Amendment) Regulations 2007	Amend SI 1982/1271, SI 1986/1078 and make transitional provisions	—
SI 2007/466	Road Safety Act 2006 (Commencement No 1) (England and Wales) Order 2007	See note "Further commencement orders" to SI 2007/237	—
SI 2007/495	Motor Vehicles (Approval) (Fees) (Amendment) Regulations 2007	Amend SI 2001/2486	—
SI 2007/506	Motor Vehicles (Tests) (Amendment) Regulations 2007	Amend SI 1981/1694	—
SI 2007/605	Vehicle Drivers (Certificates of Professional Competence) Regulations 2007	—	642
SI 2007/634	International Carriage of Dangerous Goods by Road (Fees) (Amendment) Regulations 2007	Amend SI 1988/370; supersede SI 2005/2456	—
SI 2007/697	Motor Cars (Driving Instruction) (Amendment) Regulations 2007	Amend SI 2005/1902	—
SI 2007/698	Motor Cars (Driving Licences) (Amendment) Regulations 2007	Amend SI 1999/2864, SI 2003/2003	—
SI 2007/853	Road Transport (Working Time) (Amendment) Regulations 2007	Amend SI 2005/639	—
SI 2007/1018	Road Vehicles (Registration and Licensing) (Amendment) (No 2) Regulations 2007	Amend SI 2002/2742	—
SI 2007/1161	Motor Vehicles (Tests) (Amendment) (No 2) Regulations 2007	Amend SI 1981/1694	—
SI 2007/1520	Road Tunnel Safety Regulations 2007	—	643
SI 2007/1595	Railways Pensions Guarantee (Prescribed Persons) Order 2007	See note "Further order" to SI 1994/2150	—
SI 2007/1712	Traffic Management (Guidance on Intervention Criteria) (Wales) Order 2007 (W 149)	See Preliminary Note "Regulation of traffic" (under main head "Road traffic")	—
SI 2007/1790	Railways (North and West London Lines) Exemption Order 2007	See note "Further exemptions" to SI 1994/573	—
SI 2007/1819	Community Drivers' Hours and Recording Equipment Regulations 2007	—	655
SI 2007/1890	Traffic Management Act 2004 (Commencement No 4 and Transitional Provisions) (England) Order 2007	See note "Further commencement orders" to SI 2004/2380	—
SI 2007/1898	Mental Capacity Act 2005 (Transitional and Consequential Provisions) Order 2007	See title Mental Health; amends SI 1981/1694, SI 1986/1078, SI 1986/1628, SI 1995/2869	—
SI 2007/1993	Railways Act 2005 (Commencement No 9) Order 2007	See note "Summary" to SI 2005/1444	—
SI 2007/2053	Traffic Management Act 2004 (Commencement No 5 and Transitional Provisions) (England) Order 2007	See note "Further commencement orders" to SI 2004/2380	—
SI 2007/2205	Railway Pensions (Transfer of Pension Schemes) Order 2007	—	655
SI 2007/2370	Drivers' Hours (Goods Vehicles) (Milk Collection) (Temporary Exemption) Regulations 2007	—	656
SI 2007/2472	Road Safety Act 2006 (Commencement No 2) Order 2007	See note "Further commencement orders" to SI 2007/237	—
SI 2007/2531	Disabled Persons (Badges for Motor Vehicles) (England) (Amendment) Regulations 2007	Amend SI 2000/682; amended by SI 2007/2600	—
SI 2007/2542	National Park Authorities' Traffic Orders (Procedure) (England) Regulations 2007	See title Open Spaces and National Heritage	—
SI 2007/2544	Road Vehicles (Construction and Use) (Amendment) (No 2) Regulations 2007	Amend SI 1986/1078	—

SI	*Description*	*Remarks*	*Page*
SI 2007/2553	Road Vehicles (Registration and Licensing) (Amendment) (No 3) Regulations 2007	Amend SI 2002/2742	—
SI 2007/2600	Disabled Persons (Badges for Motor Vehicles) (England) (Amendment No 2) Regulations 2007	Amend SI 2007/2531	—
SI 2007/2656	Motor Cycles Etc (EC Type Approval) (Amendment) Regulations 2007	Amend SI 1999/2920	—
SI 2007/2799	Concessionary Bus Travel Act 2007 (Commencement and Transitional Provisions) Order 2007	—	656
SI 2007/2935	Transport for London (Consequential Provisions) Order 2007	Made under Greater London Authority Act 1999, ss 405(2), 406(1); amends London Local Authorities Act 1995, s 9(8) (from 30 November 2007)	—
SI 2007/3132	Road Vehicles (Construction and Use) (Amendment) (No 3) Regulations 2007	Amend SI 1986/1078	—
SI 2007/3174	Traffic Management Act 2004 (Commencement No 2 and Transitional Provisions) (Wales) Order 2007 (W 279)	See note "Further commencement orders" to SI 2004/2380	—
SI 2007/3184	Traffic Management Act 2004 (Commencement No 6) (England) Order 2007	See note "Further commencement orders" to SI 2004/2380	—
SI 2007/3372	Traffic Management Permit Scheme (England) Regulations 2007	See title Highways, Streets and Bridges	—
SI 2007/3386	Railways (Interoperability) (Amendment) Regulations 2007	Amend SI 2006/397	—
SI 2007/3453	Private Hire Vehicles (London) (Transitional Provisions) (Amendment) Regulations 2007	Amend SI 2004/242	—
SI 2007/3482	Civil Enforcement of Parking Contraventions (England) Representations and Appeals Regulations 2007	—	657
SI 2007/3483	Civil Enforcement of Parking Contraventions (England) General Regulations 2007	—	674
SI 2007/3485	Civil Enforcement Officers (Wearing of Uniforms) (England) Regulations 2007	—	687
SI 2007/3486	Civil Enforcement of Parking Contraventions (Approved Devices) (England) Order 2007	—	687
SI 2007/3487	Civil Enforcement of Parking Contraventions (Guidelines on Levels of Charges) (England) Order 2007	—	688
SI 2007/3492	Road Safety Act 2006 (Commencement No 2) (England and Wales) Order 2007	See note "Further commencement orders" to SI 2007/237	—
SI 2007/3531	Channel Tunnel (Safety) Order 2007	—	691
SI 2008/198	Passenger and Goods Vehicles (Recording Equipment) (Downloading and Retention of Data) Regulations 2008	Made under Transport Act 1968, ss 95(1), (1A), 101(2) and European Communities Act 1972, s 2(2); amend Transport Act 1968, ss 96, 97, 103, insert ss 97C–97H, 102B, 102C, and repeal s 97A (from 5 February 2008)	—
SI 2008/417	Concessionary Bus Travel (Permits) (England) Regulations 2008	—	692
SI 2008/419	Motor Cars (Driving Instruction) (Amendment) Regulations 2008	Amend SI 2005/1902	—
SI 2008/506	Vehicle Drivers (Certificates of Professional Competence) (Amendment) Regulations 2008	Amend SI 2007/605	—

SI	*Description*	*Remarks*	*Page*
SI 2008/508	Motor Vehicles (Driving Licences) (Amendment) Regulations 2008	Amend SI 1999/2864	—
SI 2008/608	Civil Enforcement of Parking Contraventions (Representations and Appeals) (Wales) Regulations 2008	See note "Wales" to SI 2007/3482	—
SI 2008/609	Civil Enforcement of Parking Contraventions (Penalty Charge Notices, Enforcement and Adjudication) (Wales) Regulations 2008	See note "Wales" to SI 2007/3483	—
SI 2008/613	Civil Enforcement of Parking Contraventions (Guidelines on Levels of Charges) (Wales) Order 2008 (W 65)	See note "Wales" to SI 2007/3487	—
SI 2008/615	Civil Enforcement of Parking Contraventions (Representations and Appeals) Removed Vehicles (Wales) Regulations 2008 (W 67)	See note "Wales" to SI 2007/3482	—
SI 2008/616	Civil Enforcement Officers (Wearing of Uniforms) (Wales) Regulations 2008 (W 68)	See note "Wales" to SI 2007/3485	—
SI 2008/642	Road Vehicles (Registration and Licensing) (Amendment) Regulations 2008	Amend SI 2002/2742	—
SI 2008/757	Traffic Management Act 2004 (Commencement No 5 and Transitional Provisions) (England) (Amendment) Order 2008	Amends SI 2007/2053	—
SI 2008/908	Department for Transport (Driver Licensing and Vehicle Registration Fees) (Amendment) Order 2008	Amends SI 2003/2994	—
SI 2008/913	Civil Enforcement of Parking Contraventions (Penalty Charge Notices, Enforcement and Adjudication) (Wales) (Amendment) Regulations 2008	Amend SI 2008/609	—
SI 2008/925	Rail Vehicle Accessibility (B2007 Vehicles) Exemption Order 2008	See note "Exemption from rail vehicle accessibility regulations" to SI 1998/2456	—
SI 2008/960	Legislative Reform (Health and Safety Executive) Order 2008	See title Health and Safety at Work; amends SI 2004/129	—
SI 2008/1214	Civil Enforcement of Parking Contraventions (General Provisions) (Wales) (No 2) Regulations 2008 (W 122)	See note "Wales" to SI 2007/3483	—
SI 2008/1215	Civil Enforcement of Parking Contraventions (Approved Devices) (Wales) (No 2) Order 2008 (W 123)	See note "Wales" to SI 2007/3486	—
SI 2008/1277	Consumer Protection from Unfair Trading Regulations 2008	See title Sale of Goods and Consumer Protection; amend SI 1986/1078, SI 1989/1796, SI 1995/2370, SI 1998/1807	—
SI 2008/1312	Motor Vehicles (Driving Licences) (Amendment No 3) Regulations 2008	Amend SI 1999/2864; revoke SI 2008/1038	—
SI 2008/1332	Road Traffic Offenders (Prescribed Devices) Order 2008	See note "Further orders" to SI 1992/1209	—
SI 2008/1435	Motor Vehicles (Driving Licences) (Amendment) (No 4) Regulations 2008	Amend SI 1999/2864	—
SI 2008/1443	Motor Vehicles (Approval) (Fees) (Amendment) Regulations 2008	Amend SI 2001/2486	—
SI 2008/1444	Road Vehicles (Registration and Licensing) (Amendment) (No 2) Regulations 2008	Amend SI 2002/2742; supersede SI 2005/2344	—
SI 2008/1458	Public Service Vehicles (Conditions of Fitness, Equipment, Use and Certification) (Amendment) Regulations 2008	Amend SI 1981/257; supersede SI 2007/502	—

SI	*Description*	*Remarks*	*Page*
SI 2008/1460	Goods Vehicles (Plating and Testing) (Amendment) Regulations 2008	Amend SI 1988/1478; partially supersede SI 2007/503	—
SI 2008/1576	Goods Vehicles (Authorisation of International Journeys) (Fees) (Amendment) Regulations 2008	Amend SI 2001/3606; supersede SI 2004/1883	—
SI 2008/1577	Road Transport (International Passenger Services) (Amendment) Regulations 2008	Amend SI 1984/748	—
SI 2008/1660	Cross-border Railway Services (Working Time) Regulations 2008	—	692
SI 2008/1715	Vehicles Crime (Registration of Registration Plate Suppliers) Regulations 2008	—	704
SI 2008/1746	Rail Vehicle Accessibility (Interoperable Rail System) Regulations 2008	Made under European Communities Act 1972, s 2(2), Disability Discrimination Act 1995, s 46(1), Transport Act 2000, s 247; amend Disability Discrimination Act 2005, s 6 and SI 1998/2456, SI 2006/397	—
SI 2008/1862	Road Safety Act 2006 (Commencement No 3) (England and Wales) Order 2008	See note "Further commencement orders" to SI 2007/237	—
SI 2008/1864	Road Safety Act 2006 (Commencement No 3) Order 2008	See note "Further commencement orders" to SI 2007/237	—
SI 2008/1879	Employment and Support Allowance (Consequential Provisions) (No 3) Regulations 2008	See title Social Security (Pt 1); amend SI 2002/1015, SI 2002/2022	—
SI 2008/1918	Road Safety Act 2006 (Commencement No 4) Order 2008	See note "Further commencement orders" to SI 2007/237	—
SI 2008/1956	Road User Charging (Enforcement and Adjudication) (London) (Amendment) Regulations 2008	Amend SI 2001/2313	—
SI 2008/1965	Vehicle Drivers (Certificates of Professional Competence) (Amendment) (No 2) Regulations 2008	Amend SI 2001/3343, SI 2007/605	—
SI 2008/1980	Tractor etc (EC Type-Approval) (Amendment) Regulations 2008	Amend SI 2005/390	—
SI 2008/2034	Crossrail (Qualifying Authorities) Order 2008	See title Town and Country Planning	—
SI 2008/2036	Crossrail (Nomination) Order 2008	Made under Crossrail Act 2008, s 39(1); specifies Cross London Rail Links Limited and London Underground Limited as nominated undertakers for all purposes of s 1 of the 2008 Act in relation to specified works, and for the purposes of any other provision of the 2008 Act so far as connected with or related to specified works (in force on 24 July 2008)	—
SI 2008/2091	Concessionary Bus Travel (Permits) (England) (Amendment) Regulations 2008	Amend SI 2008/417	—
SI 2008/2142	Transport Tribunal (Amendment) Rules 2008	Amend SI 2000/3226	—

SI	*Description*	*Remarks*	*Page*
SI 2008/2177	Traffic Signs (Amendment) Regulations and General Directions 2008	Amend SI 2002/3113	—
SI 2008/2266	Vehicle Excise Duty (Immobilisation, Removal and Disposal of Vehicles) (Amendment) Regulations 2008	Amend SI 1997/2439	—
SI 2008/2372	Sale of Registration Marks (Amendment) Regulations 2008	Amend SI 1995/2880	—
SI 2008/2508	Motor Vehicles (Driving Licences) (Amendment) (No 5) Regulations 2008	Amend SI 1999/2864	—
SI 2008/2683	Tribunals, Courts and Enforcement Act 2007 (Transitional and Consequential Provisions) Order 2008	See title Courts and Legal Services; amends SI 1986/1629, SI 1993/1202, SI 1999/786, SI 2001/2313, SI 2001/3981, SI 2005/2757 (also amended SI 1999/1918 (lapsed))	—
SI 2008/2831	Housing and Regeneration Act 2008 (Consequential Provisions) (No 2) Order 2008	See title Housing; amends SI 1995/1239, SI 2006/1954	—
SI 2008/2849	Road Vehicles (Registration and Licensing) (Amendment No 3) Regulations 2008	Amend SI 2002/2742	—
SI 2008/2850	Retention of Registration Marks (Amendment) Regulations 2008	Amend SI 1993/987	—
SI 2008/2908	Crossrail (Planning Appeals) (Written Representations Procedure) (England) Regulations 2008	See title Town and Country Planning	—
SI 2008/2969	Rail Vehicle Accessibility (London Underground Victoria Line 09TS Vehicles) Exemption Order 2008	See note "Exemption from rail vehicle accessibility regulations" to SI 1998/2456	—
SI 2008/2975	Rail Vehicle Accessibility Exemption Orders (Parliamentary Procedures) Regulations 2008	—	708
SI 2008/3010	Mutual Recognition of Driving Disqualifications (Great Britain and Ireland) Regulations 2008	—	711
SI 2008/3076	Channel Tunnel Rail Link (Nomination) Order 2008	—	712
SI 2008/3164	Road Safety Act 2006 (Commencement No 5) Order 2008	See note "Further commencement orders" to SI 2007/237	—
SI 2009/64	Road Tunnel Safety (Amendment) Regulations 2009	Amend SI 2007/1520	—
SI 2009/107	Local Transport Act 2008 (Commencement No 1 and Transitional Provisions) Order 2009	—	712
SI 2009/109	Regional Transport Planning (Wales) (Amendment) Order 2009 (W 22)	Amends SI 2006/2993; supersedes SI 2008/1286	—
SI 2009/141	Public Service Vehicles (Conditions of Fitness, Equipment, Use and Certification) (Amendment) Regulations 2009	Amend SI 1981/257	—
SI 2009/142	Road Vehicles (Construction and Use) (Amendment) Regulations 2009	Amend SI 1986/1078 (and implement Directive 2007/38/EC (OJ L184, 14.07.2007, p 25))	—
SI 2009/143	Public Service Vehicles Accessibility (Amendment) Regulations 2009	Amend SI 2000/1970	—
SI 2009/269	Harbour Works (Environmental Impact Assessment) (Amendment) (England and Wales) Regulations 2009	See title Environment	—
SI 2009/365	Section 19 Permit Regulations 2009	—	716
SI 2009/366	Community Bus Regulations 2009	—	717

SI	*Description*	*Remarks*	*Page*
SI 2009/443	Public Service Vehicles (Registration Restrictions) (England and Wales) Regulations 2009	—	718
SI 2009/445	Quality Partnership Schemes (England) Regulations 2009	—	721
SI 2009/478	Civil Enforcement of Parking Contraventions (England) General (Amendment) Regulations 2009	Amend SI 2007/3483; revoke SI 2008/1513	—
SI 2009/483	Fixed Penalty Offences Order 2009	See note "Further orders" to SI 1990/335	—
SI 2009/488	Fixed Penalty (Amendment) Order 2009	Amends SI 2000/2792	—
SI 2009/491	Road Safety (Financial Penalty Deposit) Order 2009	—	733
SI 2009/492	Road Safety (Financial Penalty Deposit) (Appropriate Amount) Order 2009	—	741
SI 2009/493	Road Safety (Immobilisation, Removal and Disposal of Vehicles) Regulations 2009	—	756
SI 2009/494	Fixed Penalty (Procedure) (Amendment) Regulations 2009	Amend SI 1986/1330	—
SI 2009/495	Fixed Penalty (Procedure) (Vehicle Examiners) Regulations 2009	—	761
SI 2009/498	Road Safety (Financial Penalty Deposit) (Interest) Order 2009	See note "Financial penalty deposit: interest" to SI 2009/491	—
SI 2009/575	Travel Concessions (Eligible Services) (Amendment) Order 2009	Amends SI 2002/1016	—
SI 2009/579	Local Transport Act 2008 (Commencement No 1 and Transitional Provisions) (Wales) Order 2009 (W 55)	See note "Further commencement orders" to SI 2009/107	—
SI 2009/643	Motor Vehicles (Tests) (Amendment) Regulations 2009	Amend SI 1981/1694; supersede SI 2008/1402	—
SI 2009/711	Department for Transport (Fees) Order 2009	See note "Further orders" to SI 1988/643	—
SI 2009/717	Road Vehicles (Approval) Regulations 2009	—	764
SI 2009/718	Road Vehicles (Individual Approval) (Fees) Regulations 2009	—	766
SI 2009/719	Motor Vehicles (Type Approval and Approval Marks) (Fees) (Amendment) Regulations 2009	Amend SI 1999/2149	—
SI 2009/721	Contracting Out (Highway Functions) Order 2009	See title Highways, Streets and Bridges; amends SI 2006/91	—
SI 2009/786	Public Service Vehicles (Operators' Licences) (Amendment) Regulations 2009	Amend SI 1995/2908	—
SI 2009/787	Public Service Vehicles (Operators' Licences) (Fees) (Amendment) Regulations 2009	Amend SI 1995/2909; supersede SI 2008/1473	—
SI 2009/788	Motor Vehicles (Driving Licences) (Amendment) Regulations 2009	Amend SI 1999/2864	—
SI 2009/799	Goods Vehicles (Plating and Testing) (Amendment) Regulations 2009	Amend SI 1988/1478; partially supersede SI 2007/503	—
SI 2009/802	Motor Vehicles (Tests) (Amendment) (No 2) Regulations 2009	Amend SI 1981/1694; supersede SI 2008/1461	—
SI 2009/804	Goods Vehicles (Licensing of Operators) (Fees) (Amendment) Regulations 2009	Amend SI 1995/3000; supersede SI 2008/1474	—
SI 2009/811	Road Vehicles (Display of Registration Marks) (Amendment) Regulations 2009	Amend SI 2001/561	—
SI 2009/815	Motor Vehicles (Approval) (Amendment) Regulations 2009	Amend SI 2001/25	—

SI	*Description*	*Remarks*	*Page*
SI 2009/818	Road Vehicles (Approval) (Consequential Amendments) Regulations 2009	Made under European Communities Act 1972, s 2(2); amend Public Passenger Vehicles Act 1981, s 6, Road Traffic Act 1988, ss 64A, 65A, 85, 86; repeal Road Traffic (Consequential Provisions) Act 1988, Sch 3, para 22, Vehicle Excise and Registration Act 1994, Sch 3, para 24(3)(b), (4)(b), Fire and Rescue Services Act 2004, Sch 1, para 69 (as from 29 April 2009)	—
SI 2009/844	Motor Cars (Driving Instruction) (Amendment) Regulations 2009	Amend SI 2005/1902	—
SI 2009/855	Goods Vehicles (Authorisation of International Journeys) (Fees) (Amendment) Regulations 2009	Amend SI 2001/3606	—
SI 2009/856	International Carriage of Dangerous Goods by Road (Fees) (Amendment) Regulations 2009	Amend SI 1988/370; supersede SI 2008/1578	—
SI 2009/861	International Transport of Goods under Cover of TIR Carnets (Fees) (Amendment) Regulations 2009	Amend SI 1988/371; supersede SI 2008/1580	—
SI 2009/863	Motor Vehicles (Approval) (Fees) (Amendment) Regulations 2009	Amend SI 2001/2486	—
SI 2009/865	Motor Cycles Etc (Single Vehicle Approval) (Fees) (Amendment) Regulations 2009	Amend SI 2003/1960; supersede SI 2008/1462	—
SI 2009/866	Passenger and Goods Vehicles (Recording Equipment) (Approval of Fitters and Workshops) (Fees) (Amendment) Regulations 2009	Amend SI 1986/2128; supersede SI 2008/1581	—
SI 2009/876	Public Service Vehicles Accessibility (Amendment) Regulations 2009	Amend SI 2000/1970; supersede SI 2008/1459	—
SI 2009/877	Public Service Vehicles (Conditions of Fitness, Equipment, Use and Certification) (Amendment) (No 2) Regulations 2009	Amend SI 1981/257	—
SI 2009/878	Public Service Vehicles (Registration of Local Services) (Amendment) (England and Wales) Regulations 2009	Amend SI 1986/1671; supersede SI 2008/1470; partially supersede SI 2007/690 (remainder superseded by SI 2008/1470)	—
SI 2009/879	Road Transport (International Passenger Services) (Amendment) Regulations 2009	Amend SI 1984/748	—
SI 2009/880	Road Vehicles (Registration and Licensing) (Amendment) Regulations 2009	Amend SI 2002/2742	—
SI 2009/881	Vehicle Excise (Design Weight Certificate) (Amendment) Regulations 2009	Amend SI 1995/1455	—
SI 2009/1095	Traffic Management Act 2004 (Commencement No 3) (Wales) Order 2009 (W 98)	See note "Further commencement orders" to SI 2004/2380	—
SI 2009/1116	Local Authorities' Traffic Orders (Procedure) (England and Wales) (Amendment) (England) Regulations 2009	Amend SI 1996/2489	—
SI 2009/1122	Railways Infrastructure (Access and Management) (Amendment) Regulations 2009	Made under European Communities Act 1972, s 2(2), Sch 2, para 1A; amend Railways Act 1993, s 145(2)(gb), Greater London Authority Act 1999, s 235, and SI 2005/3049	—

SI	*Description*	*Remarks*	*Page*
SI 2009/1267	Traffic Management Permit Scheme (Wales) Regulations 2009 (W 114)	See title Highways, Streets and Bridges	—
SI 2009/1307	Transfer of Tribunal Functions (Lands Tribunal and Miscellaneous Amendments) Order 2009	See title Courts and Legal Services; amends SI 1995/2869	—
SI 2009/1348	Carriage of Dangerous Goods and Use of Transportable Pressure Equipment Regulations 2009	See title Health and Safety at Work	—
SI 2009/1487	Fixed Penalty (Amendment) (No 3) Order 2009	Amends SI 2000/2792	—
SI 2009/1806	Road Vehicles (Construction and Use) (Amendment) (No 2) Regulations 2009	Amend SI 1986/1078; supersede SI 2008/1702	—
SI 2009/1885	Transfer of Functions (Transport Tribunal and Appeal Panel) Order 2009	See title Courts and Legal Services; amends SI 1988/643, SI 1992/3077, SI 1999/1322, SI 1999/3413, SI 2001/3981, SI 2007/605, SI 2009/711; revokes SI 2002/614	—
SI 2009/1896	Motor Cycles Etc (Replacement of Catalytic Converters) Regulations 2009	—	766
SI 2009/1899	Motor Vehicles (Replacement of Catalytic Converters and Pollution Control Devices) Regulations 2009	—	767
SI 2009/1914	Heavy Goods Vehicles (Charging for the Use of Certain Infrastructure on the Trans-European Road Network) Regulations 2009	See title Highways, Streets and Bridges	—
SI 2009/1964	Public Service Vehicles (Enforcement Powers) Regulations 2009	—	767
SI 2009/1965	Goods Vehicles (Enforcement Powers) (Amendment) Regulations 2009	Amend SI 2001/3981	—
SI 2009/2054	Armed Forces Act 2006 (Consequential Amendments) Order 2009	See title Armed Forces; amends SI 2005/3050	—
SI 2009/2084	Motor Vehicles (Type Approval for Goods Vehicles) (Great Britain) (Amendment) Regulations 2009	Amend SI 1982/1271	—
SI 2009/2085	Workplace Parking Levy (England) Regulations 2009	—	768
SI 2009/2194	Motor Vehicles (Refilling of Air Conditioning Systems by Service Providers) Regulations 2009	—	773
SI 2009/2196	Road Vehicles (Construction and Use) (Amendment) (No 3) Regulations 2009	Amend SI 1986/1078	—
SI 2009/2362	Motor Vehicles (Driving Licences) (Amendment) (No 2) Regulations 2009	Amend SI 1999/2864	—

[168]

INSTRUMENTS NO LONGER IN OPERATION

The following instruments, formerly included in this title, are no longer in operation:

SI 1983/559	spent[1]	
SI 1984/522	lapsed[2]	
SI 1986/1245	revoked by	SI 2009/366
SI 1986/1456	revoked by	SI 2007/1819
SI 1986/1669	revoked by	SI 2007/1819
SI 1986/1672	lapsed[3]	
SI 1986/1673	lapsed[3]	
SI 1986/1674	lapsed[3]	
SI 1986/1675	lapsed[3]	
SI 1986/1676	lapsed[3]	
SI 1986/1677	lapsed[3]	
SI 1987/805	revoked by	SI 2007/1819
SI 1987/1230	revoked by	SI 2009/365
SI 1988/760	revoked by	SI 2007/1819
SI 1988/1567	revoked by	SI 2006/2533
SI 1989/2275	revoked by	SI 2006/2533
SI 1990/2336	revoked by	SI 2006/2533
SI 1992/80	revoked by	SI 2006/2533
SI 1995/1437	lapsed[4]	
SI 1996/500	lapsed[5]	
SI 1996/960	revoked[6]	
SI 1996/3087	revoked by	SI 2009/366
SI 1996/3088	revoked by	SI 2009/365
SI 1997/2916	revoked by	SI 2009/365

SI 1997/2917	revoked by	SI 2009/366	SI 2005/2981	revoked by	SI 2008/1715
SI 1998/459	spent[7]		SI 2005/3224	revoked[11]	
SI 1998/2006	revoked by	SI 2007/1819	SI 2006/142	revoked by	SI 2009/717
SI 1998/2051	revoked by	SI 2009/717	SI 2006/1695	revoked by	SI 2009/717
SI 1999/391	revoked by	SI 2008/3076	SI 2006/1756	superseded by	SI 2007/1817
SI 1999/778	revoked by	SI 2009/717	SI 2006/2409	revoked by	SI 2009/717
SI 1999/1521	superseded by	SI 2000/1434	SI 2006/2680	superseded by	SI 2008/1402
SI 1999/1918	lapsed[8]		SI 2006/2816	revoked by	SI 2009/717
SI 1999/1959	spent[9]		SI 2007/498	superseded[22]	
SI 1999/2324	revoked by	SI 2009/717	SI 2007/500	superseded[23]	
SI 2000/828	revoked by	SI 2006/2533	SI 2007/502	superseded by	SI 2008/1458
SI 2000/869	revoked by	SI 2009/717	SI 2007/503	superseded[24]	
SI 2000/2730	revoked by	SI 2009/717	SI 2007/507	superseded[25]	
SI 2001/1710	revoked by	SI 2006/2533	SI 2007/606	superseded by	SI 2008/1581
SI 2001/2809	revoked by	SI 2009/717	SI 2007/632	superseded[26]	
SI 2001/3486	spent[10]		SI 2007/687	superseded[27]	
SI 2001/3765	revoked[11]		SI 2007/689	superseded[28]	
SI 2002/537	superseded[12]		SI 2007/690	superseded[29]	
SI 2002/614	revoked by	SI 2009/1885[13]	SI 2007/691	revoked by	SI 2009/365
SI 2002/539	superseded[14]		SI 2007/693	superseded by	SI 2008/1465
SI 2002/1835	revoked by	SI 2009/717	SI 2007/855	revoked by	SI 2009/717
SI 2002/1890	revoked by	SI 2006/2533	SI 2007/1817	superseded by	SI 2008/1702
SI 2002/2641	spent[10]		SI 2007/2904	spent[30]	
SI 2002/2743	revoked by	SI 2009/717	SI 2007/2920	spent[18]	
SI 2002/2977	revoked by	SI 2008/1715	SI 2007/3135	revoked by	SI 2009/717
SI 2003/228	revoked by	SI 2008/1715	SI 2007/3143	spent[30]	
SI 2003/859	lapsed[15]		SI 2008/614	revoked by	SI 2008/1214
SI 2003/1019	revoked by	SI 2009/717	SI 2008/620	revoked by	SI 2008/1215
SI 2003/1818	superseded[16]		SI 2008/1038	revoked by	SI 2008/1312
SI 2003/2258	spent[17]		SI 2008/1286	superseded by	SI 2009/109
SI 2003/2306	spent[18]		SI 2008/1402	superseded by	SI 2009/643
SI 2003/2428	revoked by	SI 2009/717	SI 2008/1459	superseded by	SI 2009/876
SI 2003/2834	spent[18]		SI 2008/1461	superseded by	SI 2009/802
SI 2004/73	revoked by	SI 2009/717	SI 2008/1462	superseded by	SI 2009/865
SI 2004/1706	superseded by	SI 2005/1641	SI 2008/1465	revoked by	SI 2009/366
SI 2004/1872	superseded[19]		SI 2008/1470	superseded by	SI 2009/878
SI 2004/1878	superseded[20]		SI 2008/1473	superseded by	SI 2009/787
SI 2004/1883	superseded by	SI 2008/1576	SI 2008/1474	superseded by	SI 2009/804
SI 2004/2106	spent[17]		SI 2008/1513	revoked by	SI 2009/478
SI 2004/2186	revoked by	SI 2009/717	SI 2008/1578	superseded by	SI 2009/856
SI 2005/1641	superseded by	SI 2006/1756	SI 2008/1580	superseded by	SI 2009/861
SI 2005/2341	superseded by	SI 2007/506	SI 2008/1581	superseded by	SI 2009/866
SI 2005/2344	superseded by	SI 2008/1444	SI 2008/1702	superseded by	SI 2009/1806
SI 2005/2345	superseded[21]		SI 2008/2844	revoked by	SI 2009/717
SI 2005/2454	revoked by	SI 2009/717			

1 Spent on the amendment of the Transport Act 1981, s 10(1), (2) by SI 2008/948, in the title Companies
2 Lapsed on the repeal of its enabling power (Harbours Act 1964, s 9(1), (14)) by the Ports (Finance) Act 1985, s 6(2), Schedule
3 Lapsed on the repeal of the enabling power (Transport Act 1985, s 60(2), (4)) by the Local Transport Act 2008, ss 66(5), 131, Sch 7, Pt 3
4 Lapsed on the repeal of the enabling power (Road Traffic Act 1991, s 76(4)) by the Traffic Management Act 2004, s 98, Sch 12, Pt 1
5 Lapsed on the repeal of the enabling power (Road Traffic Act 1991, Sch 3, paras 1(5), 2(5)) by the Traffic Management Act 2004, s 98, Sch 12, Pt 1
6 Revoked by the London Cab Order 2007 (outside the scope of this work)
7 SI 1998/459 (spent) amended provisions of SI 1988/643 which are no longer in force
8 Lapsed on the repeal of the enabling power (Road Traffic Act 1991, s 73(11), (12)) by the Traffic Management Act 2004, s 98, Sch 12, Pt 1
9 SI 1999/1959 (spent) amended SI 1999/1521, which has been superseded by SI 2000/1434
10 SI 2001/3486 and SI 2002/2641 (both spent) made amendments to SI 1999/2864 which are no longer in force
11 Revoked by the Concessionary Bus Travel Act 2007, s 13(2), Sch 3
12 Superseded by the combined effect of SI 2003/1811 and SI 2005/2456
13 In the title Courts and Legal Services
14 Superseded by the combined effect of SI 2003/1813 and SI 2005/2457
15 Lapsed on the repeal of the enabling power (Road Traffic Act 1991, s 76(4), Sch 3, para 2(5)) by the Traffic Management Act 2004, s 98, Sch 12, Pt 1
16 Superseded by the combined effect of SI 2004/1881 and SI 2008/1459

17 SI 2003/2258 and SI 2004/2106 (both spent) made amendments to SI 1999/2149 which are no longer in force
18 SI 2003/2306, SI 2003/2834, SI 2007/2920 amended SI 1999/391 (revoked) and are accordingly spent
19 Superseded by the combined effect of SI 2007/498 and SI 2008/1444
20 Superseded by the combined effect of SI 2005/2345 and SI 2007/687
21 Superseded by the combined effect of SI 2007/687 and SI 2008/1474
22 Superseded by the combined effect of SI 2008/1444 and SI 2009/880
23 Superseded by the combined effect of SI 2008/1459 and SI 2009/876
24 Superseded by the combined effect of SI 2008/1460 and SI 2009/799
25 Superseded by the combined effect of SI 2008/1462 and SI 2009/865
26 Superseded by the combined effect of SI 2008/1580 and SI 2009/861
27 Superseded by the combined effect of SI 2008/1474 and SI 2009/804
28 Superseded by the combined effect of SI 2008/1473 and SI 2009/787
29 Superseded by the combined effect of SI 2008/1470 and SI 2009/878
30 SI 2007/2904 ceased to have effect on 19 November 2007 (see reg 1(1) of SI 2007/2904, as amended by SI 2007/3143); both SI 2007/2904 and SI 2007/3143 are now spent

CROSS REFERENCES

Air navigation	Aviation
Animals, transport of	Animals
Aviation security	Aviation
Bridges	Highways, Streets and Bridges
Carriage of dangerous substances generally	Health and Safety at Work
Control of pollution, air quality	Environment
Crown roads, Royal Parks	Open Spaces and National Heritage
Dockyard ports	Shipping, Ports and Harbours
GLA roads and side roads	Highways, Streets and Bridges
Harbours	Shipping, Ports and Harbours
Highways	Highways, Streets and Bridges
Hovercraft	Shipping, Ports and Harbours
Hydrocarbon oil, excise duty	Customs and Excise
Mines and quarries, railway lines	Mines, Minerals and Quarries
Motor fuel, composition	Petroleum
Motor salvage operators, regulation of	Trade and Industry
Motor vehicle parts, approval marks	Trade Marks and Trade Names
Motor vehicles, safety	Sale of Goods and Consumer Protection
Motorway traffic regulations	Highways, Streets and Bridges
NHS charges	National Health Service
Oil in navigable waters	Shipping, Ports and Harbours
Passenger cars, fuel consumption	Petroleum
Pedestrian crossings	Highways, Streets and Bridges
Ports	Shipping, Ports and Harbours
Public transport ticketing schemes, block exemption from competition prohibition	Trade and Industry
Radioactive material, carriage by road	Energy
Railway premises, safety and welfare of employees	Health and Safety at Work
Railways, administration order	Bankruptcy and Insolvency
Railways, rateable values	Local Government
Road Transport Board (abolition), industrial training	Employment
Roads	Highways, Streets and Bridges
Shipping	Shipping, Ports and Harbours
Submarine pipe-lines	Petroleum
Third party insurance	Insurance
Transfer of ministerial functions	Constitutional Law (Pts 2, 3)
Transport and works, assessment of environmental effects	Environment
Vehicles, competitions and trials	Highways, Streets and Bridges
Vehicles, importation of	Customs and Excise
Vehicles, removal and disposal of	Highways, Streets and Bridges

PRELIMINARY NOTE

The instruments in this title relate principally to the following matters:

(a) the reorganisation of transport undertakings;

(b) road traffic;

(c) railways, tramways, inland waterways and pipe-lines;

(d) transport in London; and

(e) miscellaneous matters.

Matters connected with transport, but within the scope of other titles, are indicated in the list of cross references. Note that instruments concerning ports and harbours, previously dealt with in this title, are now in the title Shipping, Ports and Harbours. **[169]**

Reorganisation of transport undertakings

The structure and finances of the nationalised transport undertakings carried on by the British Transport Commission under the Transport Act 1947 were reorganised, and most of the provisions of that Act (as well as various related enactments) were repealed, subject to certain savings, by the Transport Act 1962 which, with certain exceptions, came into force on 1 September 1962 (see SI 1962/1788). Under Pt I of the 1962 Act, the British Transport Commission was succeeded by four public authorities, namely:

(a) the British Railways Board (as to which, see further below);

(b) the London Transport Board (replaced by the London Transport Executive and subsequently reconstituted as London Regional Transport (London Regional Transport Act 1984, s 1 (repealed)); as to the transition from London Regional Transport to Transport for London and the dissolution of LRT (by SI 2003/1913), see the Greater London Authority Act 1999 and the main head "London" below);

(c) the British Transport Docks Board (reconstituted as Associated British Ports under a holding company by the Transport Act 1981, Pt II (see further below); as to the dissolution of the holding company (called the Transport Holding Company), see SI 1973/338); and

(d) the British Waterways Board.

On 1 January 1963 (ie "the vesting date" appointed by SI 1962/2634), the property and functions of the British Transport Commission were distributed among those bodies in accordance with the Transport Act 1962, Pt II. Under s 36 of that Act, the Commission's rights and liabilities in relation to the transport stock created and issued under the Transport Act 1947, s 89 were taken over by the Treasury. As from the same date, the British Transport Stock Regulations 1947, SR & O 1947/2686, as amended by SI 1949/183, SI 1955/1192, which were formerly included in this title, ceased to have effect by virtue of s 36(8) (repealed) of the 1962 Act, without prejudice, however, to the rights and liabilities transferred to the Treasury under s 36(1) and subject to the transitional provisions contained in Pt I of Sch 7 to the 1962 Act. The British Transport Commission was dissolved as from 1 January 1964, having been continued until that date by orders under s 80 of the 1962 Act (repealed), the last of which was SI 1963/1554 (now spent).

Further provision with respect to the nationalised or publicly-owned transport undertakings was made by the Transport Act 1968. That Act was brought into force by a series of orders under s 166; see SI 1968/1822 and the further orders noted thereto. In so far as the organisation of transport is concerned, attention is drawn particularly to the following provisions of the 1968 Act. Pt I (ss 1–8 (repealed)) of the 1968 Act established a new public authority, called the National Freight Corporation (now dissolved; see below), with the duty, in conjunction with the British Railways Board, to provide a comprehensive publicly-owned freight transport service. Pt II (ss 9–23A) of the Act empowered the Minister of Transport (now the Secretary of State) by order to designate in any given area, outside Greater London, a passenger transport area and to establish for that area a Passenger Transport Authority and a Passenger Transport Executive. Passenger transport areas and authorities have been renamed integrated transport areas and Integrated Transport Authorities respectively by the Local Transport

Act 2008, s 77(1), (2), and consequential amendments have been made to the 1968 Act by Pt 1 of Sch 4 to the 2008 Act. As to integrated transport areas etc, see now the provisions of the Transport Act 1985, as amended by Pt 2 of Sch 4 to the 2008 Act, discussed below. Pt III (ss 24–37 (largely repealed)) of the 1968 Act related to bus and ferry services and under which a National Bus Company and a Scottish Transport Group were formed. As to the transfer of the operations of the National Bus Company to the private sector, see the provisions of the Transport Act 1985 discussed below. The Scottish Transport Group was dissolved, and ss 24, 26–29 of the 1968 Act were repealed in relation to Scotland, on 7 June 2002 by the Scottish Transport Group (Dissolution) Order 2002, SSI 2002/263 (outside the scope of this work). S 24 of the 1968 Act (establishment and general duties of the National Bus Company and the Scottish Transport Group) was repealed in relation to England and Wales by the Local Transport Act 2008, ss 66(6)(b), 131, Sch 7, Pt 3, on 9 February 2009 (see SI 2009/107).

Further reorganisation was effected by the Transport Act 1980, Pt II (ss 45–51), which dissolved the National Freight Corporation on 1 October 1980 (see SI 1980/1380, made under s 45) and transferred its undertaking to a successor company limited by shares (the National Freight Company Ltd). Ss 47 (transitional provisions), 48 (dissolution of the Corporation) of the 1980 Act have been repealed by the Statute Law (Repeals) Act 2004, s 1(1), Sch 1, Pt 5, Group 14.

The Transport Act 1981 provided for the introduction of private capital into subsidiaries of the British Railways Board and into a reconstituted British Transport Docks Board. Pt I (ss 1–4) (repealed) of the Act empowered the British Railways Board to sell shares in any of its subsidiaries, with the consent or at the direction of the Secretary of State, and to dispose of any part of the undertaking or property of a subsidiary. Pt II (ss 5–14) of the 1981 Act provides for the reconstitution of the British Transport Docks Board under the name Associated British Ports and under the control of a holding company limited by shares on 31 December 1982; see SI 1982/1887 (made under s 5(3), (4) of the 1981 Act), in the title Shipping, Ports and Harbours.

Further provisions concerning the National Bus Company were made by the Transport Act 1982, Pt I (ss 1–7) (repealed), providing for the introduction of private capital into the Company. Operations of the Company were transferred to the private sector under the Transport Act 1985, Pt III (ss 47–56) (now largely repealed by SI 1991/510), and the company was dissolved and all outstanding property, rights and liabilities transferred to the Secretary of State for Transport, on 1 April 1991, by SI 1991/510, in accordance with the said Pt III.

Pt IV (ss 57–87) of the 1985 Act, as originally enacted, made new provision for local passenger transport services, amending provisions of the Transport Act 1968 relating to the designation of passenger transport areas and the establishment of Passenger Transport Authorities and Executives (see further SI 1969/94, SI 1969/95, SI 1969/96, SI 1969/97 and SI 1973/1728, SI 1973/1729, SI 1973/1730, SI 1973/1731, SI 1973/1732) and providing for the formation of public transport companies. Pt IV (ss 57–87) of the 1985 Act has been amended by the Local Transport Act 2008, s 77(5), Sch 4, Pt 2, in consequence of the renaming of passenger transport areas and Passenger Transport Authorities as integrated transport areas and Integrated Transport Authorities respectively by s 77(1), (2) of the 2008 Act. As to the establishment of metropolitan county integrated transport authorities, see the Local Government Act 1985, s 28 (as amended by para 53 of Pt 4 of Sch 4 to the 2008 Act).

As to the present organisation of passenger transport in the London area, see the main head "London" below.

The Local Government Finance Act 1988 introduced a complete reorganisation of local government finance; s 117 removed the statutory powers of certain bodies to issue levies to local authorities in respect of their expenses. Certain transport bodies have, however, been given a general power to issue such levies by SI 1992/2789.

The Local Government Act 2003, Pt 1, Chapter 1 (ss 1–20) makes new provision for the capital finance of local authorities. S 18(1) of that Act enables the Secretary of State to provide by regulations for things done by or to a body mentioned in s 18(2), which includes Passenger Transport Executives, to be treated as done by or to a local authority specified in, or determined in accordance with, the regulations. As at the issue date of this volume, no such regulations had been made.

As to the winding down and abolition of the British Railways Board, see the head "Privatisation of the railway system" below.

[170]

Transport (Wales) Act 2006 This Act provides additional powers to the National Assembly for Wales to exercise strategic control over transport services to, from and within Wales. It grants to the Assembly a general duty to develop policies for the promotion and encouragement of safe, integrated, sustainable, efficient and economic transport facilities in Wales and to carry out its functions so as to implement those policies (s 1). As part of this duty, the Assembly must publish a Wales Transport Strategy, setting out the policies developed by the Assembly under s 1 and how it proposes to discharge its duty under s 1 (s 2). The Assembly is given a power to provide financial assistance to local transport authorities (s 6) and air transport services (s 11) and may enter into direct agreements with providers of public passenger transport services (s 7). The Act also establishes a Public Transport Users' Committee for Wales (s 8) which may consider and make recommendations about any matter relating to public passenger transport services or facilities to, from and within Wales (s 9). The Act, which received royal assent on 16 February 2006, generally comes into force by order of the Assembly under s 12 thereof; see SI 2006/1403. SI 2006/2993, made under provisions of the Transport Act 2000 amended by the 2006 Act, deals with regional transport planning in Wales; see further the head "Bus services" below.

[171]

Privatisation of the railway system The Railways Act 1993 effected the privatisation of the railway system by means of franchising. As to the commencement of the Act, see SI 1993/3237 and the further orders noted thereto. As originally enacted, Pt I (ss 1–83) of the 1993 Act introduced a system of licensing of the operators of railway assets. S 1 of the 1993 Act, which related to the Rail Regulator and the Director of Passenger Rail Franchising, has been repealed by the Railways and Transport Safety Act 2003, and the functions of the Rail Regulator were transferred to the Office of Rail Regulation by s 16 of the 2003 Act. Ss 2, 3 of the 1993 Act, which related to Rail Passengers' Committees and the Rail Passengers' Council, have been repealed by the Railways Act 2005. S 19 of the 2005 Act creates a new body corporate to be known as the Rail Passengers' Council in place of the Rail Passengers' Council established by s 3(2) of the 1993 Act, and s 21 of the 2005 Act abolishes Rail Passengers' Committees established under s 2(2) of the 1993 Act; see further the head "Railways Act 2005" below.

Pt II (ss 84–116) of the 1993 Act provided for the reorganisation of the railways. The British Railways Board is empowered to form companies for the purposes of, inter alia, facilitating the disposal of its undertaking and for such other purposes as may be specified by the Secretary of State in a direction to the Board (s 84). The Board may also make schemes for the transfer of its undertaking to certain persons, including the Franchising Director (now abolished; see below) or a franchise company (s 85(1)). The powers conferred by s 85(1) may only be exercisable for certain specified purposes, including the purpose of effecting or facilitating the disposal of such property, rights or liabilities as the Secretary of State may direct (s 85(3)(b)). Under s 86, the Franchising Director may make schemes for the transfer of franchise assets at or after the end of the franchise period, and under s 89 the Secretary of State may direct the disposal of the undertaking and securities of the Board. Provision is made by ss 98–108 concerning successor companies. Pt II of the 1993 Act is repealed by the Transport Act 2000, s 274, Sch 31, Pt IV, partly (i e except the repeal of s 113) as from a day to be appointed by order under s 275(1) thereof.

The 1993 Act has been extensively amended by the Transport Act 2000 and the Railways Act 2005. With minor exceptions, the 2000 Act comes into force on days to be appointed by order under s 275 (see SI 2000/3229 and the further orders noted thereto). The 2000 Act established the Strategic Rail Authority (now abolished as noted below) and abolished the office of the Franchising Director and the British Railways Board. Chapter I (ss 201–222 and Schs 14–21) of Pt IV to the 2000 Act concerned the Strategic Rail Authority and is now largely repealed by the Railways Act 2005. The remaining provisions of the said Chapter I are ss 212, 215–217 and Sch 16 (in part), Sch 17, Pts I, II, Sch 18, Pt I. S 215 and Sch 16 of the 2000 Act transferred the functions, property, rights and liabilities of the Franchising Director to the Strategic Rail Authority and the office of Franchising Director was abolished by s 215(8). S 216 of, and Pt I of Sch 17 to, the 2000 Act made further amendments to Pt I of the 1993 Act for the purpose of transferring to the Strategic Rail Authority certain functions of the Office of Rail Regulation (formerly the Rail Regulator). S 217(1) of, and Sch 18 to, the 2000 Act transferred to the Strategic Rail Authority the functions of the British Railways Board relating to the British Transport Police and associated property, rights and liabilities (see further the head "British Transport Police" under the main head "Railways, tramways and inland waterways" below) The Strategic Rail Authority and every wholly owned subsidiary of the Authority were exempt from the requirement of the Railways Act 1993, s 6 to be licensed to be the operator of any railway asset; see SI 2001/218, noted to SI 1994/573.

Chapter II (ss 223–251 and Schs 22–26) of Pt IV to the 2000 Act makes further provision about the railways. S 240 and Sch 25 enable the Secretary of State to make a scheme for the transfer to him of any property, rights and liabilities of the British Railways Board (other than property etc transferred under Sch 18). S 241 provides for the winding down and abolition of the Board. S 241(3) enables the Secretary of State by order to reduce the membership of the Board; SI 2001/217, made under s 241(3) and in force on 1 February 2001, provides that the membership of the Board is to consist of a chairman and one or more other persons appointed by the Secretary of State. When the Secretary of State considers that it is no longer necessary for the Board to exist, he must by order provide for its dissolution (s 241(4)). S 250 and Sch 26 provide for the taxation of various transfers under the 2000 Act; see SI 2001/262 (made under Sch 26, Pt II, para 5, Pt III, para 13). The remaining functions of the British Railways Board are now discharged by BRB (Residuary) Ltd, which reports to the Department for Transport.

Instruments made under the 1993 Act are mentioned under the main head "Railways, tramways and inland waterways" below.

Both the Railways Act 1993 and the Transport Act 2000 are extensively amended by the Railways Act 2005 (as to the commencement of the 2005 Act, see SI 2005/1444 and the orders noted thereto). S 1(1) of the 2005 Act introduces Sch 1 thereto, which amends Pt I of the 1993 Act and repeals ss 213, 214, 219 of the 2000 Act, so as to transfer consumer protection functions of the Strategic Rail Authority to the Office of Rail Regulation, transfer other functions of the Authority to the Secretary of State and devolved authorities and abolish some functions of the Authority. S 1(2) enables the Secretary of State to make a scheme for the transfer of property, rights and liabilities from the Strategic Rail Authority to a person specified in s 1(3) (including the Secretary of State, the Scottish Ministers, the National Assembly for Wales, the Office of Rail Regulation and the Rail Passengers' Council established by s 19(1) of the 2005 Act). As to supplemental provisions about transfer schemes, see s 1(6) and Sch 2. S 1(10) provides that where, after consulting the Strategic Rail Authority, the Secretary of State is satisfied: (a) that all such transfers have been provided for as will secure that the dissolution of the Authority will not extinguish any of its liabilities, and (b) that it is no longer necessary, for any other reason, for that Authority to continue to exist, the Secretary of State may by order provide for it to cease to exist; see SI 2006/2925, abolishing the Authority as from 1 December 2006.

[172]

Road traffic

The law relating to road traffic generally is now contained in the 1988 consolidating legislation, i e the Road Traffic Act 1988, the Road Traffic Offenders Act 1988 and the Road Traffic (Consequential Provisions) Act 1988. Those Acts have been amended and extended by, in particular, the Road Traffic (Driver Licensing and Information Systems) Act 1989, the Motor Vehicles (Safety Equipment for Children) Act 1991, the Road Traffic Act 1991, the Road Traffic (Driving Instruction by Disabled Persons) Act 1993, the Road Traffic (New Drivers) Act 1995, the Road Traffic Reduction Act 1997, the Road Traffic Reduction (National Targets) Act 1998, the Road Traffic (Vehicle Testing) Act 1999, the Greater London Authority Act 1999, the Transport Act 2000, the Vehicles (Crime) Act 2001, the Serious Organised Crime and Police Act 2005, ss 152–155, the Road Safety Act 2006, the Concessionary Bus Travel Act 2007 and the Local Transport Act 2008.

The regulation of public service vehicles is provided for by the Public Passenger Vehicles Act 1981 (a consolidating Act), the Transport Act 1985, Pts I, II (as to the repeal of Pt II of the 1985 Act, see the head "Public service vehicles" below), the Greater London Authority Act 1999, Pt IV, Chapter V and the Transport Act 2000, Pt II. The licensing of operators of goods vehicles is governed by the Goods Vehicles (Licensing of Operators) Act 1995 (a consolidating Act). Provision concerning drivers' hours is made by the Transport Act 1968, Pt VI. Traffic regulation is governed mainly by the Road Traffic Regulation Act 1984 (a consolidating Act); the Road Traffic (Driver Licensing and Information Systems) Act 1989, Pt II; provisions of the Greater London Authority Act 1999, Pt IV; the Transport Act 2000, Pt III; and the Traffic Management Act 2004, Pts 1, 2, 6 (as to the provisions of the 2004 Act which had been brought into force at the issue date of this volume, see SI 2004/2380 and the further orders noted thereto). Instruments relating to traffic regulation are also dealt with in the title Highways, Streets and Bridges.

Instruments in this title concerning road traffic are principally made or have effect under the above-mentioned Acts (instruments under the Greater London Authority Act 1999 are dealt with under the main head "London" below). Such instruments relate in particular to the licensing of drivers and the licensing and registration of vehicles under provisions of the Road Traffic Act 1988 and the Vehicle Excise and Registration Act 1994, operators' licences for goods vehicles under the Goods Vehicles (Licensing of Operators) Act 1995 and the hours and records of drivers under the Transport Act 1968, Pt VI. In addition, instruments are made relating to such matters as the construction, use, lighting, marking and speed of vehicles; seat belts, protective helmets etc; the type approval of vehicles and vehicle parts; traffic signs; traffic wardens; and the fixed penalty procedure for certain traffic offences.

As is explained in the Preliminary Note to the title Highways, Streets and Bridges, that title deals, broadly speaking, with the creation, maintenance, classification and general use of roads and bridges, and this title deals with the regulation of vehicular traffic and the construction of vehicles which may be used on the roads. However, the borderline between the two titles has been arbitrarily drawn in some cases. Among the instruments made under traffic regulating powers which are included in the title Highways, Streets and Bridges because they affect the user of roads are those relating to pedestrian crossings, traffic regulation on motorways, the removal and disposal of vehicles, and cycle racing on highways. Instruments regulating or restricting the user of highways are considered more fully in the Preliminary Note to the title Highways, Streets and Bridges, under the head "User of highways".

[173]

Driving licences

The Road Traffic Act 1988, Pts III (ss 87–109C), IV (ss 110–122) provide for the licensing of drivers of vehicles, and enable regulations to be made in connection with such matters as minimum ages for holding licences, provisional licences, fees, driving tests, disabilities etc. These matters are provided for in SI 1999/2864; see also SI 1976/555, SI 1996/3206, SI 2004/301. The 1988 Act now provides for a unified driver licensing system in Great Britain. In this context Pt IV of the 1988 Act makes general provision regarding the licensing of drivers of large goods vehicles and passenger-carrying vehicles, further provision being made by SI 1999/2864. By the Criminal Justice and Court Services Act 2000, s 71, the Secretary of State may make any information held by him for the purposes of Pt III of the 1988 Act available to the National Policing Improvement Agency for use by constables and members of the staff of the Serious Organised Crime Agency; as to the purposes for which constables may be given access to such information, see SI 2001/3343.

Pt III of the 1988 Act should be read subject to the Road Traffic (New Drivers) Act 1995 (brought into force by SI 1997/267), which makes provision for the retesting of inexperienced drivers who commit traffic offences. The Act contains powers to make regulations in connection with appeals against disqualification and the temporary restoration of licences in such cases. SI 1997/1098, made under s 5 of, and para 11 of Sch 1 to, the 1995 Act, provides for the procedure to be followed when a person whose licence has been revoked under the 1995 Act appeals against his conviction.

This title also contains instruments which provide for the recognition of driving licences issued by other EC states, by Gibraltar and by other non-member state territories; see SI 1982/1555, SI 1984/672 and the orders noted thereto. As to the introduction of a Community driving licence, see SI 1990/144, SI 1996/1974, SI 1998/1420.

[174]

Driving instruction

Driving instruction is governed generally by the Road Traffic Act 1988, Pt V (ss 123–142), including registration of approved instructors, examinations and tests. See further SI 2005/1902. Pt V of the 1988 Act has been amended by the Road Traffic (Driving Instruction by Disabled Persons) Act 1993, which was brought into force on 9 September 1996 by SI 1996/1980. Pt V of the 1988 Act is extensively amended by the Road Safety Act 2006, s 42, Sch 6, paras 1–26, largely as from a day to be appointed by order.

[175]

Driver information systems

The Road Traffic (Driver Licensing and Information Systems) Act 1989, Pt II (ss 8–15) provides for the introduction of systems giving drivers of motor vehicles information on routes, traffic conditions etc. Providers of such systems are to be licensed and regulated; for exemptions, see SI 1990/865.

[176]

Licensing and registration of vehicles

Under the Vehicle Excise and Registration Act 1994, excise duty is payable:

(a) in respect of every mechanically propelled vehicle that:
  (1) is registered under the 1994 Act (s 1(1)(a)), or
  (2) is not registered but is used, or kept, on a public road (s 1(1)(b));
(b) in respect of every thing (whether or not it is a vehicle) that has been, but has ceased to be, a mechanically propelled vehicle and:
  (1) is registered under the 1994 Act (s 1(1A)(a)), or
  (2) is not so registered but is used, or kept, on a public road (s 1(1A)(b)).

For the current annual rates of duty, see Sch 1 to the 1994 Act (and see also SI 1989/1226, SI 1995/1397, SI 2001/93, SI 2002/2742). S 1(1C), (1D) of the 1994 Act provide for:

(a) duty charged by s 1(1)(a) or (1A)(a) to be paid on a licence to be taken out by the person in whose name the vehicle is registered, or if that person is not the person keeping the vehicle, by either of those persons (s 1(1C));
(b) duty charged by s 1(1)(b) or (1A)(b) to be paid on a licence to be taken out by the person keeping the vehicle (s 1(1D)).

Provision as regards the periods for which a vehicle licence may be taken out, and the amount of duty payable in respect of licences for such periods, is made by ss 3 and 4 of the 1994 Act. By s 5, no vehicle excise duty is charged in respect of a vehicle if it is an exempt vehicle; descriptions of vehicles which are exempt vehicles are specified by Sch 2 (see further below). As to the issue etc of vehicle licences, see ss 7–10; and as to trade licences, see ss 11–14. S 19C applies where a person applies for a vehicle licence or a trade licence, and the Secretary of State, or an authorised body, accepts a credit card payment in respect of the duty payable on the licence; SI 2005/2460 prescribes the fee payable under s 19C and the meaning of "credit card" for the purposes of that section.

Licensing and registration are governed by SI 2002/2742. The duration of first licences and the rates of duty applicable thereto are provided for by SI 1986/1428. Reduced rates of vehicle excise duty are applicable to certain buses, haulage vehicles and heavy goods vehicles adapted so as to reduce pollution. The reduced pollution requirements to be satisfied are prescribed by SI 2002/2742, reg 5, Sch 2 (as to reduced pollution certificates, see s 61B referred to below).

S 61A of the 1994 Act enables regulations to make provision for the issue of a "design weight certificate", which states the design weight of a vehicle (used for calculating the rate of vehicle excise duty payable in respect of certain classes of goods vehicle), and for various related matters; SI 1995/1455 has been made for these purposes. S 61B enables regulations to be made in respect of the issue of a reduced pollution certificate when the reduced pollution requirements are satisfied; see SI 2002/2742, reg 5, Sch 2.

Certain vehicles (eg certain old vehicles, electrically assisted pedal cycles, police vehicles, fire engines, ambulances and vehicles for disabled people) are exempt from duty under s 5 of, and Sch 2 to, the 1994 Act. By SI 1975/1208, art 5 provision is made for the exemption from duty of vehicles brought temporarily into the United Kingdom. Certain other exemptions are provided for by SI 1985/722, SI 2002/2742 (see reg 34 of, and Sch 5 to, SI 2002/2742). By SI 1999/1736, art 8(8), in the title Armed Forces, duty is not chargeable on any vehicle in the service of a visiting force as defined in that order. Provision relating to the registration of exempt (non-dutiable) vehicles is made by reg 32 of SI 2002/2742.

By SI 2002/2742, reg 47, Sch 8, contravention of regs 16(1), 17, 17A, 18(1), 19(1), 21, 22, 23, 24, 25, 26 (and Sch 4), 40(5), 42 of SI 2002/2742 attracts a maximum penalty of a fine not exceeding level 3 on the standard scale. Regulations not prescribed by SI 2002/2742 and other regulations made or having effect under the 1994 Act continue to attract a lesser penalty; see s 59.

As to the fee for registration of a vehicle, see s 21 of the 1994 Act and SI 2002/2742, reg 10. As to the disclosure of registration and licensing particulars by the Secretary of State for use by certain bodies, see SI 2002/2742, reg 27. As to the sale by the Secretary of State of information derived from particulars contained in the register, see s 22(1A) and reg 28 of SI 2002/2742. As to the particulars to be furnished by a person who surrenders a vehicle licence, does not renew a licence or keeps an unlicensed vehicle, see s 22(1D) and reg 26 of, and Sch 4 to, SI 2002/2742. Provision concerning registration marks is made by ss 23–27; as to the display of registration marks, see SI 2001/561. Ss 26, 27 provide for the retention of registration marks pending transfer to other vehicles and for the sale by the Secretary of State of rights to particular registration marks (see SI 1992/510, SI 1993/987, now having effect under s 26, and SI 1995/2880, made under s 27).

Pt III (ss 29–46A) of the 1994 Act relates to offences. S 29(1) makes it an offence to use or keep on a public road a vehicle (other than an exempt vehicle) which is unlicensed. S 32A and Sch 2A enable regulations to be made providing for the immobilisation, removal and disposal of vehicles as regards which it appears that an offence under s 29 is being committed; see SI 1997/2439.

[177]

Goods vehicle operators' licences

Users of certain goods vehicles are required to hold licences under the Goods Vehicles (Licensing of Operators) Act 1995, which was brought into force (except for s 50 and Sch 5) on 1 January 1996 by SI 1995/2181, and which repealed and replaced the Transport Act 1968, Pt V (ss 59–94), and the Deregulation and Contracting Out Act 1994, Pt I, Chapter III (ss 41–57). Provisions as to such licences formerly contained in regulations relating to standard and restricted licences, certificates of qualification, the attachment of conditions to, and the variation and revocation of, standard licences etc are now contained in the 1995 Act. Various other matters in relation to operators' licensing, such as applications for licences, objections and representations, operating centres, inquiries, applications and decisions etc, are dealt with by SI 1995/2869. The payment of fees in respect of licences is provided for by SI 1995/3000. As to regulations permitting an authorised person to detain a heavy goods vehicle and its contents where the person using the vehicle does not hold an operator's licence, see SI 2001/3981 (made under Sch 1A to the 1995 Act). For special provisions applicable in relation to certain foreign goods vehicles and Northern Ireland goods vehicles, see SI 1996/2186.

[178]

Drivers' hours and record-keeping

The Transport Act 1968, Pt VI (ss 95–103) imposes restrictions on the hours which may be worked by drivers of passenger-carrying vehicles and goods vehicles and provides for certain records to be kept with respect to matters relevant to the enforcement of these restrictions. These provisions were extensively amended by the Road Traffic (Drivers' Ages and Hours of Work) Act 1976 (the relevant provisions of which were brought into force (so far as not in force on royal assent) by SI 1978/6 (lapsed), made under s 4(2), (3), (4) of the 1976 Act (repealed)) to take account of Community provisions on the subject. Further, the effect of the requirements concerning drivers' hours, contained in s 96 of the 1968 Act, has been considerably modified, and exclusions and exemptions have been made, by regulations and orders under that section; see SI 1970/145, SI 1970/257, SI 1971/818, SI 1986/1459, SI 1986/1492, SI 2007/2370, and see also SI 1986/1458, SI 2007/1819. Exemptions from directly applicable Community provisions are granted by SI 2007/1819. S 99A(1) of the 1968 Act empowers an authorised person to prohibit the driving of a vehicle where there has been a contravention of provisions about drivers' hours; as to the immobilisation, removal and disposal of a vehicle which has been prohibited from being driven under s 99A(1), see SI 2009/493 (made under the Road Safety Act 2006, s 11(3), Sch 4).

SI 1987/1421 deals with the keeping of record books of their working time by drivers of goods vehicles in cases where Community rules do not apply. The installation and use of recording equipment (tachographs) in accordance with various EC Regulations is provided for in SI 1979/1746 and the further regulations noted thereto. As to the issue and use of driver cards, company cards, workshop cards and control cards with digital tachographs, see SI 2005/1140, SI 2006/1937.

[179]

International circulation

For the purpose of enabling effect to be given to certain international agreements, SI 1975/1208 (made under the Motor Vehicles (International Circulation) Act 1952, s 1(1), (4), as extended by SI 1973/2163, in the title Northern Ireland) makes provision as respects motor vehicles and drivers going abroad from the United Kingdom and coming to the United Kingdom from abroad. See also SI 1985/610, made under SI 1975/1208 and taking effect under provisions of the Vehicle Excise and Registration Act 1994.

[180]

International carriage by road

The Carriage of Goods by Road Act 1965 (which was brought into force on 5 June 1967 by SI 1967/819) gives effect to the Convention on the Contract for the International Carriage of Goods by Road signed at Geneva on 19 May 1956 (Cmnd 2260); the Convention is scheduled to the Act. SI 1967/1683 certifies who are the parties to the Convention and in respect of what territories they are respectively parties. By SI 1967/820, as amended by SI 1981/604, made under s 9 of the 1965 Act, ss 1–6, 7(1), 13 and 14(2) of the Act have been extended to Gibraltar with modifications; and by SI 1981/1543, SI 1986/1882, also made under s 9, the Act has been extended, with exceptions and modifications, to the Isle of Man and Guernsey, respectively.

Fees payable in connection with the issue of certificates relating to the international carriage of dangerous goods by road are prescribed by SI 1988/370; fees payable in connection with the issue of various documents authorising certain international journeys are prescribed by SI 2001/3606; and fees payable in connection with approvals and the issue of certificates relating to the international transport of goods are prescribed by SI 1988/371.

Effect is given to a directly applicable Community provision prohibiting the carriage of goods by road between member states without Community authorisation by SI 1992/3077.

[181]

Construction and use of vehicles; equipment and lighting; type approval

The Road Traffic Act 1988, Pt II (ss 40A–86) makes provision in relation to the construction and use of vehicles and equipment. Under s 41 of that Act, the Secretary of State has power to make regulations generally as to the use of motor vehicles on roads, their construction and equipment and the conditions under which they may be so used, and in particular with respect to a number of specified matters. The principal instrument having effect under that section is SI 1986/1078. However, that instrument should be read subject to SI 2003/1998, which authorises, subject to conditions and restrictions, the use on roads of various vehicles constructed for special purposes, notwithstanding that they do not comply with certain of the requirements of SI 1986/1078. See also SI 1998/3111, made under s 41. Among the matters with respect to which regulations may be made under the said s 41 are: (a) the particulars to be marked on motor vehicles (see SI 1975/2111); and (b) lighting equipment and reflectors (see SI 1989/1796).

As to the conditions of use of certain vehicles on footpaths, footways, bridleways or restricted byways by local authorities, see SI 1963/2126 (now having effect under the Highways Act 1980, s 300); and as to the use of invalid carriages on the highway, see SI 1988/2268 (made under the Chronically Sick and Disabled Persons Act 1970, s 20).

This title also contains a number of instruments relating to the testing of vehicles, which derive mainly from the enabling powers conferred by the Road Traffic Act 1988, ss 45–53; in particular, note SI 1981/1694, SI 1988/1478. Other instruments concerning tests are noted to the said SI 1981/1694 (under the head "Obligatory test certificates"), and SI 1988/1478 (under the head "Evidence of test certificates").

The requirements to be complied with as respects the construction and use of pedal cycles are prescribed by SI 1983/1176.

Provision for the type approval of vehicles and vehicle parts conforming with specified requirements as to design, construction, equipment and marking is contained in ss 54–65A of the 1988 Act (relating to the national type approval scheme) and in various EC directives (relating to Community schemes). As to instruments made or having effect under those provisions of the 1988 Act, see SI 1982/1271, SI 1984/981, SI 1998/3093, SI 2001/25, SI 2003/1959 (as to fees payable in connection with SI 2001/25, SI 2003/1959, see SI 2001/2486, SI 2003/1960 respectively). The national type approval scheme is extended to vehicles and vehicle parts made in other member states by SI 1981/493. As to instruments made under the European Communities Act 1972, s 2(2) in implementation of various EC Directives, see eg SI 1980/765, SI 1980/1182, SI 1999/2920, SI 2005/390, SI 2009/717. Fees in respect of type approval of vehicles and vehicle parts are prescribed by SI 1999/2149; and fees in respect of individual approval of vehicles under SI 2009/717 are prescribed by SI 2009/718.

S 64 of the 1988 Act relates to the marking of special authorised weights on vehicles, in addition to the determined plated weights for such vehicles; as to the authorised weights for the purposes of s 64, see SI 1983/910. S 67 of the Act relates to the testing of condition of vehicles on roads; and s 68 thereof provides for the inspection of public passenger vehicles and goods vehicles. As to the disclosure of information obtained from tests and inspections carried out under s 67 or 68 to competent authorities in member states, see SI 2002/2426 (made under the European Communities Act 1972, s 2(2)). Ss 69–73 of the 1988 Act make provision concerning the prohibition of unfit vehicles; see SI 1992/1285. As to the immobilisation, removal and disposal of a vehicle which has been prohibited from being driven under s 69 or 70 of the 1988 Act (unfit or overloaded vehicles), see SI 2009/493 (made under the Road Safety Act 2006, s 11(3), Sch 4). As to regulations under s 78 of the 1988 Act relating to the weighing of vehicles and trailers, see SI 1978/1180.

The Motor Cycle Noise Act 1987, s 1 prohibits the supply of motor cycle exhaust systems, silencers and components which do not comply with requirements prescribed by regulations made by the Secretary of State; see SI 1995/2370.

[182]

Seat belts, protective helmets etc

The Road Traffic Act 1988, s 14 provides that the Secretary of State may make regulations requiring persons who are driving or riding in motor vehicles on a road to wear seat belts of a prescribed description, subject to prescribed exceptions. As to regulations for these purposes, see SI 1993/176. Under s 15(1) of the 1988 Act, except as provided by regulations, where a child under the age of 14 years is in the front of a motor vehicle, a person must not without reasonable excuse drive the vehicle on a road unless the child is wearing a seat belt in conformity with regulations; as to regulations for these purposes, see SI 1993/31. Under s 15(1A) (inserted by SI 2006/1892), where: (a) a child is in the front of a motor vehicle other than a bus, (b) the child is in a rear-facing child restraining device, and (c) the passenger seat where the child is placed is protected by a front air bag, a person must not without reasonable excuse drive the vehicle on a road unless the air bag is deactivated. Under s 15(3) (substituted by SI 2006/1892), except as provided by regulations, where: (a) a child under the age of three years is in the rear of a motor vehicle, or (b) a child of or over that age but under the age of 14 years is in the rear of a motor vehicle and any seat belt is fitted in the rear of that vehicle, a person must not without reasonable excuse drive the vehicle on a road unless the child is wearing a seat belt in conformity with regulations. Under s 15(3A), except as provided by regulations, where: (a) a child under the age of 12 years and less than 150 cm in height is in the rear of a passenger car, (b) no seat belt is fitted in the rear, and (c) a seat in the front is provided with a seat belt but is not occupied, a person must not without reasonable excuse drive the passenger car on a road. As to regulations for these purposes, see SI 1993/176. By the Transport Act 1982, s 70, as amended by, inter alia, SI 1984/1996, the Secretary of State may make payments in respect of the examination of certain applicants for medical certificates required as a condition of any exception prescribed by regulations under s 14 or 15 of the 1988 Act.

Under ss 16, 17 of the 1988 Act, regulations may be made concerning the wearing of protective headgear by persons driving or riding on motor cycles; see SI 1998/1807. Under s 18, regulations may be made concerning appliances designed or adapted for use: (a) with any headgear; or (b) by being attached to or placed upon the head, by persons driving or riding on motor cycles; see SI 1999/535.

[183]

Public service vehicles

The statute law relating to public service vehicles is now to be found principally in the Public Passenger Vehicles Act 1981, the Transport Act 1985, Pts I, II (as to the repeal of Pt II of the 1985 Act, see below), the Road Traffic Act 1988, Pt IV (ss 110–122), the Greater London Authority Act 1999, Pt IV, Chapter V (ss 179–195) and the Transport Act 2000, Pt II (ss 108–162). Certain of these enactments have been extensively amended by the Local Transport Act 2008, partly as from a day to be appointed by order under s 134 thereof, as noted to the provisions concerned.

The Public Passenger Vehicles Act 1981, Pt I (ss 1–5) defines (in s 1) the expression "public service vehicle", and includes provision (in s 4) for the appointment by the Secretary of State of a traffic commissioner for each traffic area specified in s 3(1) with the responsibility for issuing licences. The traffic areas specified in the said s 3(1) have now been replaced by those specified in SI 1991/288 (and see also SI 1999/1204 noted thereto). S 4 of the 1981 Act is amended by the Local Transport Act 2008, s 2, as from a day to be appointed by order, so as to provide for the appointment by the Secretary of State of such number of traffic commissioners as he considers appropriate; and to enable a traffic commissioner to exercise his functions in any traffic area. Ss 4A–4D of the 1981 Act (inserted by s 3(1) of the 2008 Act as from 4 March 2009 (see SI 2009/107), except s 4B, which comes into force a day to be appointed by order) provide for the appointment and functions of a senior traffic commissioner.

Pt II (ss 6–29) of the 1981 Act contains general provision as to the fitness of public service vehicles, the licensing of vehicles, seating capacity and conduct on board vehicles. Under s 6 of the 1981 Act, as amended by SI 2009/818, a vehicle used as a public service vehicle is required to be issued with a certificate of initial fitness or a certificate of type approval under s 10, or an EC certificate of conformity, a national small series certificate of conformity or an individual approval certificate under SI 2009/717. As to the required conditions of fitness, see SI 1981/257. S 12(1) provides that a public service vehicle may not be used on a road for carrying passengers for hire or reward except under a PSV operator's licence issued in accordance with ss 12–21. S 12A and Sch 2A (inserted by the Local Transport Act 2008, s 47, Sch 3) provide for the detention, removal and disposal of certain PSVs in respect of which s 12(1) of the 1981 Act is contravened; as to regulations under Sch 2A, see SI 2009/1964. For general regulations relating to PSV operators' licences, and for conditions which may be attached to such licences, see SI 1995/2908. Fees in respect of such licences are prescribed by SI 1995/2909. The carrying capacity of public service vehicles is regulated by SI 1984/1406, and the conduct of drivers, conductors and passengers is regulated by SI 1990/1020. SI 1999/1322, made under the European Communities Act 1972, s 2(2), relates to the carriage of passengers in public service vehicles between member states under a Community licence. SI 1999/3413, also made under s 2(2) of the 1972 Act, implements Council Regulation (EC) 12/98 (OJ L4, 08.01.1998, p 10) laying down the conditions under which non-resident carriers may operate national road passenger transport services within a member state.

The requirement for special licences to drive public service vehicles formerly contained in the Public Passenger Vehicles Act 1981, s 22 (repealed) was abolished by the Road Traffic (Driver Licensing and Information Systems) Act 1989, s 1. Licences authorising the driving of such vehicles are now granted under the general licensing provisions of the Road Traffic Act 1988, Pt III (see above), as supplemented by Pt IV in relation to passenger-carrying vehicles. For regulations made under the 1988 Act in relation to such licences, see SI 1999/2864.

SI 2007/605 implements Directive 2003/59/EC of the European Parliament and of the Council (OJ L226, 10.09.2003, p 4) (made under the European Communities Act 1972, s 2(2)), on the initial qualification and periodic training of drivers of certain road vehicles for the carriage of goods or passengers.

Other instruments in this title relating to public service vehicles and road passenger transport generally include those concerning: lost property (SI 1978/1684); Northern Ireland passenger services (SI 1980/1460); international passenger services (SI 1984/748); service subsidies (SI 1985/1921, SI 2002/2090); the formulation of policies by metropolitan county passenger transport authorities (SI 1986/81); taxis (SI 1986/567, SI 1986/1386, SI 1986/1779); modifications of the Public Passenger Vehicles Act 1981 and the Transport Act 1985 with respect to partnerships (SI 1986/1628); and publication of the statement known as "Notices and Proceedings" by traffic commissioners and inquiries (SI 1986/1629).

[184]

Bus services The system of road service licensing formerly contained in the Public Passenger Vehicles Act 1981, Pt III (repealed) was abolished by the Transport Act 1985, s 1. It was replaced in London with a system of London local service licences (see Pt II (ss 34–46) of the 1985 Act) which broadly retained the existing pattern of regulation with minor modifications (as to the repeal of Pt II, see below). It was replaced outside London with a system of registration of local services under which no such service may be provided in any traffic area unless the prescribed particulars of the service have been registered with the traffic commissioner, the period of notice in relation to the registration has expired, and the service is operated in accordance with the registered particulars (see ss 6–9 of the 1985 Act, as amended by the Local Transport Act 2008, ss 48–51, partly (s 49) as from a day to be appointed by order). As to the registration of local services in an area outside London where a quality partnership scheme containing registration restrictions has been made, see s 6A of the 1985 Act (inserted by s 48 of the 2008 Act) and SI 2009/443. In relation to London local service licensing, see SI 1986/1691 (and the paragraph below), and in relation to the registration of local services outside London, see SI 1986/1671, SI 2004/2682.

Bus services in Greater London are now regulated by the Greater London Authority Act 1999, Pt IV, Chapter V (ss 179–195), which introduces a system of London service permits. SI 2000/1462 makes provision for the transition from London local service licensing of bus services under Pt II of the 1985 Act to London service permits under Chapter V of Pt IV of the 1999 Act. S 180(1) of the 1999 Act provides that no London local service may be provided except in accordance with the provisions of the said Chapter V. However, s 180(1) is modified by SI 2000/1462 for the duration of the transitional period (i e the period beginning with 3 July 2000 and ending with the last day on which a London local service licence granted under the 1985 Act ceases to be in force), so as to allow holders of London local service licences to continue operating under those licences after the introduction of London service permits. By SI 2000/1462, Pt II of the 1985 Act ceases to have effect immediately after the end of the transitional period. Pt II of the 1985 Act is repealed by s 423 of, and Pt II of Sch 34 to, the 1999 Act, as from a day to be appointed by order under s 425(2) thereof. S 185(1) of the 1999 Act prohibits a person from operating a London local service which is not part of the London bus network unless he has been granted a London service permit by Transport for London (TfL).

S 19 of the 1985 Act provides for the granting by certain bodies of permits in relation to the use of buses by educational and other bodies. A number of such bodies are designated in SI 1987/1229, and general regulations relating to vehicles used under permits issued under s 19 are contained in SI 2009/365. S 22 of the 1985 Act enables the granting by traffic commissioners of community bus permits to bodies concerned for the social and welfare needs of one or more communities. Regulations relating to vehicles used under such permits are contained in SI 2009/366.

Provision is made by ss 93–101 of the 1985 Act for the establishment of travel concession schemes for the provision of travel concessions on journeys on public passenger transport services. The nature etc of such schemes is provided for by s 93 of the 1985 Act. S 93(7) sets out the persons eligible to receive travel concessions under a scheme, including persons who have attained the age of 60 years, the disabled and such other classes of persons as may be specified by order; as to an order extending the classes of eligible persons in Wales, see SI 1986/1385. As to eligible services for the purposes of schemes under s 93, see SI 2002/1016, SI 2002/2023 (both made partly under s 94 of the 1985 Act). SI 1986/77 makes provision for the arrangements between authorities administering travel concession schemes and operators of public passenger transport services participating in such schemes, and for certain other connected matters.

The Transport Act 2000, ss 145A–150 (as amended by the Concessionary Bus Travel Act 2007, ss 1–3, 13(1), Sch 2, paras 10–14) introduce a system of mandatory travel concessions for journeys not beginning on the London bus network. S 145A of the 2000 Act (substituted for the original s 145 of that Act by s 1 of the 2007 Act) provides that any person to whom a current statutory travel concession permit has been issued by a travel concession authority in England (ie elderly or disabled persons) and who travels on an eligible journey (between places in England) on an eligible service is entitled to a concession consisting of a waiver of the fare for the journey by the operator of the service. As to the form and duration of a travel concession permit in England, see SI 2008/417. S 145B of the 2000 Act (inserted by s 13(1) of, and paras 10, 11 of Sch 2 to, the 2007 Act) makes similar provision for mandatory travel concessions in Wales. "Elderly person" for the purposes of ss 145A, 145B means a person who has attained the age of 60 years (s 146). "Eligible service" means a bus service of a class specified in an order under s 146; see SI 2002/1016, SI 2002/2023. S 149 of the 2000 Act (as amended by s 3 of the 2007 Act) requires travel concession authorities to reimburse operators for providing concessions in accordance with arrangements agreed with the operators or determined by the authorities; s 150 provides for the procedure for reimbursement arrangements determined by the authorities. As to regulations applying in Wales under ss 149, 150, see SI 2001/3764. As to travel concessions in Greater London, see the Greater London Authority Act 1999, Pt IV, Chapter VIII (ss 240–244, as amended by ss 4–7, 13 of, and paras 7, 8 of Sch 2 and Sch 3 to, the 2007 Act) and SI 2008/417. SI 1998/948, made under the Local Government and Housing Act 1989, s 150, authorises local authorities to impose charges on persons dealing with the local authority in connection with specified matters relating to, inter alia, travel concessions.

Further provisions relating to bus services are made by the Transport Act 2000, Pt II (ss 108–162) (amended by the Local Transport Act 2008, ss 7–44, 131, Sch 7, Pts 1, 2, partly as from a day to be appointed by order; as to the commencement of the 2008 Act, see the table to SI 2009/107). Ss 108–113B of the 2000 Act (amended by ss 7–12, 131 of, and Pt 1 of Sch 7 to, the 2008 Act) provide a statutory basis for local transport plans and bus strategies in England and Wales outside London; see SI 2006/2993. London has its own transport planning system under the Greater London Authority Act 1999; see the head "Transport for London" under the main head "London" below. Ss 114–123 of the 2000 Act (amended by ss 13–18 of the 2008 Act, partly as from a day to be appointed by order) enable local transport authorities to make quality partnership schemes as part of the process of implementing their current bus strategy. Under s 119, regulations may make provision about the specifying in quality partnership schemes of facilities which are already being provided before the schemes are proposed; see SI 2001/3317, SI 2002/3017. As to regulations making provision about quality partnership schemes, including requirements as to frequencies, timings and maximum fares as a standard of services, see SI 2009/445 (made under s 122). Ss 124–134 enable local transport authorities to make a quality contracts scheme if they are satisfied that it is the only practicable way to implement their bus strategy and that the scheme will implement that policy in a way which is economic, efficient and effective. S 127 relates to the making of a quality contracts scheme. Under s 127(2)(b), such a scheme must specify the date on which it is to come into operation, which must not be earlier than 21 months after the date on which it is made; that period may be varied by order. SI 2005/75, made under s 127(10), varies s 127(2)(b) so that, as respects quality contracts schemes relating to areas wholly in England, the reference to 21 months is a reference to six months. Ss 124–134 of the 2000 Act (quality contracts schemes) are extensively amended by ss 19–44, 131 of, and Pt 2 of Sch 7 to, the 2008 Act, as from a day to be appointed by order.

Ss 135–138 of the 2000 Act enable local transport authorities to make ticketing schemes whereby operators of local bus services are required to make and implement arrangements to accept each other's tickets or provide integrated ticketing in ways specified in the scheme. In doing so, the authorities must be satisfied that this is in the public interest and implements their bus strategy. Ss 139–141 concern the provision of information about bus services by local transport authorities. Ss 142–144 contain miscellaneous provisions relating to bus services, including civil penalties for bus lane contraventions. SI 2005/2757 makes provision for the enforcement of bus lane contraventions by local authorities in England (exclusive of Greater London) which are approved for the purposes of s 144, and SI 2005/2756 noted thereto provides that a device which is of a specified description is an approved device for the purposes of regulations under s 144 (s 144 is repealed in relation to England by the Traffic Management Act 2004, s 98, Sch 12, Pt 1, as from a day to be appointed by order). S 154 of the 2000 Act enables grants to be made to operators of eligible bus services towards their costs in operating those services and supersedes the previous eligibility rules for fuel duty rebates under the Finance Act 1965, s 92 (repealed); as to "eligible bus services" for the purposes of s 154, see SI 2002/1015, SI 2002/2022.

[185]

Disabled access

The Disability Discrimination Act 1995, Pt V (ss 32–49) makes provision requiring operators of bus, taxi, train and tram services to comply with specified "minimum access requirements" to facilitate the use of those services by disabled persons. As at the issue date of this volume, ss 32–36 had not been brought into force, and s 49 had been brought partly into force by SI 2005/1122, in the title Civil Rights and Liberties. S 32 of the 1995 Act empowers the Secretary of State to make "taxi accessibility regulations" for the purpose of securing that it is possible for disabled persons to get in and out of taxis and to travel in such vehicles safely and in reasonable comfort. Taxi provisions (including any such regulations) may be extended to apply to vehicles used as hire cars by order under s 33. Under s 34 a taxi may not be licensed to ply for hire unless the vehicle in question conforms with provisions of the taxi accessibility regulations with which it would be required to conform if licensed. This requirement does not apply if a licence was in force with respect to the vehicle at any time during a period of 28 days immediately before the day on which the licence is granted, although the Secretary of State may provide that this exclusion ceases to have effect on a specified day. Regulations may be made under s 35 enabling licensing authorities to apply for orders exempting them from the requirements of s 34. As to regulations made under s 37 in connection with the carrying in taxis of guide dogs, hearing dogs or other categories of dogs, see SI 2000/2990. Provision relating to the carrying of assistance dogs in private hire vehicles is made by s 37A of the 1995 Act, inserted by the Private Hire Vehicles (Carriage of Guide Dogs etc) Act 2002, s 1(1) (brought into force by SI 2003/3123, made under s 6(2) of the 2002 Act). S 37A imposes a duty on the operator and driver of a private hire vehicle to carry, without additional charge, an assistance dog which is accompanying a disabled person. This duty does not apply to the driver of a private hire vehicle if a certificate of exemption on medical grounds is in force in respect of the vehicle and the prescribed notice is exhibited on the vehicle in the prescribed manner (s 37A(8)). As to the prescribed form of notice of exemption and the manner in which it must be displayed, see SI 2003/3122 (which also prescribes charities for the purposes of the definition "assistance dog" in s 37A(9)).

S 40 of the 1995 Act empowers the Secretary of State to make "PSV accessibility regulations" for the purpose of securing that it is possible for disabled persons to get on to and off regulated public service vehicles and to travel in such vehicles safely and in reasonable comfort. S 41 provides that a registered public service vehicle may not be used on a road unless there has been issued in respect of it an "accessibility certificate" certifying that it complies with prescribed provisions of the PSV accessibility regulations or that an approval certificate (ie a certificate that the vehicle conforms with a type of vehicle that complies with prescribed provisions of the PSV accessibility regulations) has been issued in respect of the vehicle under s 42. Regulations in connection with applications for and grants of approval certificates may be made under s 42. S 44 makes provision in connection with reviews of, and appeals against, decisions in connection with applications for approval under s 42; regulations may be made in connection with such appeals. S 43 empowers the Secretary of State by order to authorise the use of specified public service vehicles notwithstanding ss 40–42. Fees may be prescribed under s 45. As to regulations under ss 40–45, see SI 2000/1970.

SI 2005/3190 disapplies certain vehicles from the exemptions provided by the Disability Discrimination Act 1995, s 21ZA (application of ss 19–21 to transport vehicles), so that specified transport services providers must now comply with certain provisions of ss 19 (discrimination in relation to goods, facilities and services) and 21 (duty of providers of services to make adjustments) of the 1995 Act.

Provisions of the 1995 Act concerned with the accessibility of rail vehicles are dealt with in the corresponding note under the main head "Railways, tramways and inland waterways".

[186]

Speed limits for vehicles; quiet lanes and home zones

The speed limits of different classes of motor vehicles are prescribed by the Road Traffic Regulation Act 1984, s 86, Sch 6. However, the said Sch 6 must be read subject to the variations contained in SR & O 1947/2192 (vehicles used for naval, military or air force purposes etc) and has been amended by SI 1986/1175. By virtue of SI 1974/502 (now having effect under s 17(2) of the 1984 Act), the driving of motor vehicles on motorways is subject to a maximum speed limit of 70 mph, except for certain lengths of motorways where lower speed limits apply; and, in relation to other roads, maximum speed limits of 70 mph, 60 mph and 50 mph are imposed by the Order of 25 May 1977 (now having effect under s 88 of the 1984 Act).

Under the Transport Act 2000, s 268, a local traffic authority may designate any road for which it is the traffic authority as a quiet lane or a home zone and the appropriate national authority may make regulations authorising local traffic authorities which have designated roads as quiet lanes or home zones to make use orders (ie orders permitting the use of a road for purposes other than passage) and speed orders (ie orders authorising the local traffic authority by which it is made to take measures with a view to reducing the speed of motor vehicles or cycles (or both) on a road to below that specified in the order) of such descriptions as are prescribed by the regulations in relation to any roads designated by them as quiet lanes or home zones; see SI 2006/2082.

[187]

Traffic signs

The main statutory provisions relating to the placing of traffic signs are those contained in the Road Traffic Regulation Act 1984, s 64 et seq. SI 2002/3113 prescribes the size, colour and type of signs which may be erected by a traffic authority and contains general directions subject to which they may be erected. Other regulations and directions relating to traffic signs are considered in the note "Other traffic signs" to SI 2002/3113, and equivalent signs and permitted variants to be used in Wales are prescribed by SI 1985/713. SI 1998/111, made under s 65(3A), prescribes certain bodies as appearing to the Secretary of State to be representative of certain classes of road users.

[188]

Road user charging and workplace parking levy

The Transport Act 2000, Pt III (ss 163–200) concerns road user charging and workplace parking levy. Chapter I (ss 163–177A) (road user charging) of Pt III imposes charges in respect of the use or keeping of motor vehicles on roads. The said Chapter I has been extensively amended by the Local Transport Act 2008, ss 103–117, Sch 5, paras 1–7. S 163(3) of the 2000 Act sets out the charging schemes which may be made, including local charging schemes and trunk road charging schemes. Under s 167, a trunk road charging scheme may only be made in respect of a road if: (a) the road is carried by a bridge, or passes through a tunnel, of at least 600 metres in length, or (b) a local traffic authority, an Integrated Transport Authority or Transport for London has requested the charging authority to make the trunk road charging scheme in connection with a charging scheme made or proposed by that body. As to the procedures for the making, variation and revocation of orders for trunk road charging schemes, see s 168 and SI 2001/2303. S 171(1)(c) requires a charging scheme to specify the classes of motor vehicles in respect of which charges are imposed; as to specified classes, see SI 2001/2793. S 172A (inserted by the Local Transport Act 2008, s 114) makes provision for the suspension of charging schemes. Ss 173–175 relate to the enforcement of charging schemes. S 173(1) enables regulations to be made for or in connection with the imposition and payment of penalty charges in respect of charging schemes. By s 173(4), regulations may be made about the enforcement of charging scheme penalty charges; at the issue date of this volume, the only regulations which have been made under s 173(4) are of local application only and are outside the scope of this work.

Chapter II (ss 178–190) (workplace parking levy) of Pt III of the 2000 Act concerns licensing schemes for imposing charges in respect of the provision of workplace parking places. As to the payment of charges imposed in respect of any premises by a licensing scheme, see s 178 and SI 2009/2085. By s 184(1), a licensing scheme does not come into force unless the order making it has been confirmed by the appropriate national authority; as to exemptions, see s 184(2) and SI 2009/2085. S 186(3)(d) provides that the charges that may be imposed by a licensing scheme include different charges for different cases, including different classes of motor vehicles; as to specified classes, see SI 2001/2793. Regulations under s 189 may make provision in connection with the imposition and payment of licensing scheme penalty charges in respect of acts, omissions, events or circumstances relating to licensing schemes; see SI 2009/2085. S 195 enables regulations to be made in connection with appeals and the determination of disputes; see SI 2009/2085.

Chapter III (ss 191–200) of Pt III of the 2000 Act contains general and supplementary provisions. S 191 and Sch 12 contain financial provisions about charging schemes and licensing schemes. As to provision for the determination by charging and licensing authorities of the net proceeds of road user charging schemes and workplace parking levy schemes, see SI 2003/110 (made under para 2 of Sch 12); and as to the keeping of accounts in relation to a trunk road charging scheme and the calculation of the annual net proceeds of a scheme, see SI 2003/298 (made under paras 2, 5 of Sch 12).

As to road user charging and workplace parking levy in London, see the head "Traffic regulation" under the main head "London" below.

SI 2007/58, made under the European Communities Act 1972, s 2(2), implements the provisions of an EC Directive which require the use of certain technical standards for the interoperability of electronic road toll systems in the Community.

[189]

Regulation of traffic

The principal powers under which the Secretary of State (or, in relation to Wales, the National Assembly for Wales) and local traffic authorities are authorised to make orders and regulations restricting the use of roads and otherwise regulating traffic are discussed in the Preliminary Note to the title Highways, Streets and Bridges, under the head "Powers for regulating traffic". Such instruments are mainly local in character and are outside the scope of this work, but one instrument, SI 1963/1172, is included in that title. As to the regulation of traffic using special roads, see SI 1982/1163, also in that title. The principal powers under which the Secretary of State (or the National Assembly for Wales) and local authorities are authorised to make parking place orders are also cited in the Preliminary Note to that title, under the head "Parking places". Such orders are local in character and are outside the scope of this work. However, note SI 2000/2546 which prescribes the forms to be used in connection with the enforcement of excess parking charges.

The procedure to be followed in connection with the making of various types of traffic orders and parking place orders under the Road Traffic Regulation Act 1984 is prescribed by SI 1990/1656, SI 1996/2489. See also SI 2000/683, SI 2000/1785 (exemptions for disabled persons), made under para 23 of Pt III of Sch 9 to the 1984 Act, as extended by the Chronically Sick and Disabled Persons Act 1970, s 21(1)(b). SI 2000/682, SI 2000/1786, made under s 21 of the 1970 Act, prescribe various matters in connection with the issue of badges to disabled persons entitling them to special parking facilities. SI 1992/1215 relates to the regulation of traffic under the 1984 Act for temporary periods.

Provision for the regulation of traffic is also made by the Traffic Management Act 2004. Pt 1 (ss 1–15) of that Act (brought into force as noted in the table to SI 2004/2380) makes provision for the designation of a force of traffic officers by the appropriate national authority (the Secretary of State in relation to England and the National Assembly for Wales in relation to Wales). Under ss 6, 7 traffic officers have powers to stop or direct traffic (s 6) and powers to place temporary traffic signs (s 7). Further powers may be conferred on traffic officers by order made by the appropriate national authority (s 8).

Pt 2 (ss 16–31) of the 2004 Act provides for network management by local traffic authorities. S 16 requires a local traffic authority to manage its road network with a view to achieving the following objectives: (a) securing the expeditious movement of traffic on the authority's road network; and (b) facilitating the expeditious movement of traffic on road networks for which another authority is the traffic authority. By s 17 a local traffic authority must make such arrangements as it considers appropriate for planning and carrying out the action to be taken in performing the network management duty. The arrangements must include provision for the appointment of a traffic manager to perform such tasks as the authority considers will assist it to perform its network management duty. Provision for the enforcement of the network management duty is made by ss 20–31. Ss 20–22 relate to the giving of intervention notices and the making of intervention orders by the appropriate national authority where a local traffic authority is failing properly to perform any duty under ss 16, 17. An intervention order under s 21 is an order made by statutory instrument making provision for or in connection with the appointment of a traffic director. Ss 23–25 concern the general powers which may be conferred on a traffic director by an intervention order. Under s 26, the appropriate national authority may by order made by statutory instrument provide for the application of ss 20–25 (with or without modifications) in cases where to any extent the performance of the duties under ss 16, 17 is carried out jointly by two or more local traffic authorities. S 27 requires the appropriate national authority to give guidance about the criteria which it proposes to apply for the purpose of deciding whether to give an intervention notice or make an intervention order. The guidance must be appended to an order made by the authority by statutory instrument; see SI 2007/339 (which applies in relation to England only and comes into force on 12 March 2007), and SI 2007/1712 (which applies in relation to Wales only and comes into force on 10 July 2007).

Pt 6 (ss 72–93 and Schs 7–11) of the 2004 Act (brought into force, subject to transitional provisions, by SI 2006/2826 (Wales), SI 2007/2053 (England)) provides a single national framework for regulations to be made for the civil enforcement by local authorities of road traffic contraventions (ie parking contraventions, bus lane contraventions, London lorry ban contraventions and moving traffic contraventions). The following regulations have been made under Pt 6 of the 2004 Act so as to implement that Part in so far as it provides for the civil enforcement of parking contraventions by local authorities. The effect of the regulations is to replace the Road Traffic Act 1991, Pt II, which has largely been repealed by s 98 of, and Pt 1 of Sch 12 to, the 2004 Act, subject to transitional provisions (see SI 2007/2053 (England), SI 2007/3174 (Wales)).

(a) SI 2007/3482 (England) (made under s 80 of the 2004 Act and the Road Traffic Regulation Act 1984, s 101B), provides for representations and appeals: (i) against penalty charge notices given under SI 2007/3483 and in relation to vehicles which have been immobilised under SI 2007/3483, and (ii) in relation to vehicles which have been removed under the 1984 Act and regulations thereunder (corresponding provision for representations and appeals in Wales is made by the combined effect of SI 2008/608, SI 2008/615);

(b) SI 2007/3483 (England) (made under ss 72, 73(3), 78, 79, 81, 82, 88, 89 of, and para 6 of Sch 9 to, the 2004 Act), provides for penalty charges, the immobilisation of vehicles, the appointment of adjudicators by enforcement authorities, and the enforcement of penalty charges (corresponding provision for Wales is made by the combined effect of SI 2008/609, SI 2008/1214);

(c) SI 2007/3485 (England), SI 2008/616 (Wales) (both made under s 76(4) of the 2004 Act), specify functions of civil enforcement officers appointed under Pt 6 of the Act which may only be exercised by such officers when in uniform;

(d) SI 2007/3486 (England), SI 2008/1215 (Wales) (both made under s 92(1) of the 2004 Act), specify approved devices for the purposes of regulations relating to the civil enforcement of parking contraventions under s 72(4)(a) of the 2004 Act;

(e) SI 2007/3487 (England), SI 2008/613 (Wales) (both made under para 8 of Sch 9 to the 2004 Act), set out the guidelines given by the Secretary of State for Transport and the Welsh Ministers for the setting by enforcement authorities in England (outside Greater London) and Wales respectively of the level of charges for parking contraventions.

[190]

Penalties

Provision governing sentence for road traffic offences is now made by the Road Traffic Offenders Act 1988, Pt II (ss 27–50). S 20 of the 1988 Act makes provision for the admissibility of certain evidence in relation to speeding offences; see SI 1992/1209 and the further orders noted thereto. Under s 34A of that Act (which is substituted by the Road Safety Act 2006, s 35, as from a day to be appointed by order), a period of disqualification may in certain circumstances be reduced if the offender completes an approved course. As to certificates to be given on completion of such a course, see SI 1992/3013. S 36(1) of the 1988 Act requires the court, where that subsection applies to a person, to order him to be disqualified until he passes the appropriate driving test; s 36(1) applies to a person who is disqualified under s 34 of that Act on conviction of certain offences (s 36(2)). As to other offences involving obligatory endorsement to which s 36(1) is to apply, see s 36(3) and SI 2001/4051.

Provisions governing fixed penalties for road traffic offences are now made by the Road Traffic Offenders Act 1988, Pt III (ss 51–90). By s 51(1), fixed penalty offences for the purposes of Pt III are offences in respect of a vehicle under an enactment specified in Sch 3 to that Act, including specified provisions of: (a) the Greater London Council (General Powers) Act 1974; (b) the Highways Act 1980; (c) the Road Traffic Regulation Act 1984; (d) the Road Traffic Act 1988; and (e) the Vehicle Excise and Registration Act 1994.

This is subject to the Road Traffic Offenders Act 1988, s 51(2), which provides that an offence under an enactment specified in Sch 3 to that Act is not a fixed penalty offence if it is committed by causing or permitting a vehicle to be used by another person in contravention of any provision made or restriction or prohibition imposed by or under any enactment. S 51(3) of that Act enables orders to be made providing for offences to become, or to cease to be, fixed penalty offences, and making necessary modifications to the said Pt III; as to such orders, see SI 1990/335 and the further orders noted thereto. As to the procedure to be followed under the fixed penalty system, see SI 1986/1330; as to the procedure to be followed where a fixed penalty notice is issued by a vehicle examiner, see SI 2009/495.

By the Road Traffic Offenders Act 1988, s 53(1), the fixed penalty for an offence is: (a) such amount as the Secretary of State may by order prescribe, or (b) one-half of the maximum amount of the fine to which a person committing that offence would be liable on summary conviction, whichever is the less. By s 53(2) (as substituted by the Road Safety Act 2006, s 3(1), (2)), any order made under s 53(1)(a) may make provision for the fixed penalty for the offence to be different depending on the circumstances, including (in particular) the nature of the contravention or failure constituting the offence, how serious it is, the area, or sort of place, where it takes place, and whether the offender appears to have committed any offence of a description specified in the order during a period so specified. As to the fixed penalty amounts and graduated fixed penalty amounts which have been prescribed by order under s 53, see SI 2000/2792.

As to fixed penalty notices fixed to vehicles, see the Road Traffic Offenders Act 1988, ss 62–68 and the forms prescribed by SI 2000/2546.

The Road Traffic Offenders Act 1988, Pt 3A (ss 90A–90F) (inserted by the Road Safety Act 2006, s 11(1)) provides for a constable or vehicle examiner to impose a financial penalty deposit requirement on a person without a satisfactory United Kingdom address on any occasion if he reasonably believes that: (a) the person is committing or has on that occasion committed an offence relating to a motor vehicle, and (b) the person, the offence and the circumstances in which the offence is committed are of a description specified by order (see s 90A). As to the specified persons, offences and circumstances, see SI 2009/491. A financial penalty deposit requirement is a requirement to make a payment of the appropriate amount to the Secretary of State in a manner specified in an order under s 90B. As to the manner of payment of the appropriate amount under s 90B, see SI 2009/491, and as to the appropriate amount, see SI 2009/492 (also made under s 90B). S 90C applies where a person on whom a financial penalty deposit requirement is imposed makes a payment of the appropriate amount in accordance with s 90B(1), and provides for an appropriate refund to be made in certain circumstances. As to the steps to be taken by the Secretary of State when making an appropriate refund, see SI 2009/491; and as to the interest payable in respect of an appropriate refund, see SI 2009/498. S 90D contains a power to prohibit the driving of a vehicle where a person on whom a financial penalty deposit requirement is imposed does not make an immediate payment of the appropriate amount. As to the immobilisation, removal and disposal of a vehicle which has been prohibited from being driven under s 90D, see SI 2009/493 (made under the Road Safety Act 2006, s 11(3), Sch 4).

Note also SI 2002/1808, SI 2003/300, made under the Environment Act 1995, s 87, Sch 11, para 5, enabling designated local authorities to issue fixed penalty notices in relation to certain vehicle emissions.

[191]

Vehicle crime

The Vehicles (Crime) Act 2001 regulates motor salvage operators and registration plate suppliers; makes further provision for preventing or detecting vehicle crime; and enables the Secretary of State to make payments in respect of certain expenditure relating to vehicle crime. The Act comes into force partly on 10 April 2001 (date of royal assent) and fully on days to be appointed by order (see s 44). The Act has largely been brought into force by SI 2001/3215 and the further orders noted thereto. Pt 2 (ss 17–31) of the Act requires any person carrying on business as a registration plate supplier in England or Wales to be registered. Provision concerning registration is made by ss 17–23, including provision as to the requirement to register, the register of registration plate suppliers, and applications for registration. As to the keeping of records by registered persons, see s 24; and as to the provision of information by prospective purchasers of registration plates, see s 25. SI 2002/1715, made under ss 17, 18, 19, 24, 25, prescribes an activity which is exempt from registration; the particulars to be entered on the register of registration plate suppliers; the requirements for applications for registration; and the information to be obtained by a registered person before selling a registration plate.

[192]

Traffic wardens

Under the Road Traffic Regulation Act 1984, s 95, police authorities may appoint traffic wardens to undertake certain functions in connection with the control and regulation of, or the enforcement of the law relating to, traffic (including pedestrians) or stationary vehicles. The functions which may be discharged by such wardens are prescribed by SI 1970/1958.

[193]

The highway code

Guidance for all road users is contained in the Highway Code, which may be obtained from The Stationery Office. As to the revision and issue to the public of the code by the Secretary of State, see the Road Traffic Act 1988, s 38. By virtue of that section, a failure to observe the code may be relied on in any legal proceedings as tending to establish or negative any liability which is in question.

[194]

Metrication

References to imperial units of measurement in the Road Traffic Act 1960, s 253 and the Transport Act 1968, s 103(6) have been altered so as to refer to metric units by SI 1981/1373, SI 1981/1374. Those instruments originally also altered such references in provisions of:

(a) the Road Traffic Regulation Act 1967 and the Road Traffic Act 1972, which have since been repealed and consolidated in, respectively, the Road Traffic Regulation Act 1984 and the Road Traffic Act 1988; and

(b) the Transport Act 1968, which have since been repealed and consolidated in the Goods Vehicles (Licensing of Operators) Act 1995. SI 1981/1373 has been revoked by s 60(2) of, and Pt II of Sch 8 to, the 1995 Act to the extent that it amended the provisions consolidated in that Act, and the amending SI 1984/177 has been wholly revoked.

[195]

Railways, tramways, inland waterways and pipe-lines

Nationalisation, reorganisation and subsequent privatisation

On 1 January 1948 the undertakings of the principal railway and canal companies, of the London Passenger Transport Board and of certain other railway and light railway undertakers vested, by virtue of the Transport Act 1947, ss 12, 13, Sch 3 (repealed), in the British Transport Commission, and the rights and obligations of those companies and bodies under any statutory provision passed to the Commission under s 14(4) of the 1947 Act. In 1954 the railways operated by the Commission were reorganised by the setting up of area authorities under the provisions of the Transport Act 1953, ss 16, 17 (both now repealed), and the British Transport Commission (Organisation) Scheme 1954 (which was made and approved under those sections and embodied in SI 1954/1579). On the reorganisation of the nationalised transport undertakings by the Transport Act 1962, the Commission was succeeded by four statutory boards and a statutory holding company (among which the Commission's property and functions were distributed in accordance with Pt II of that Act), and the Commission was subsequently dissolved; see the head "Reorganisation of transport undertakings" above. By s 31 of the 1962 Act, the Commission's railways system was divided, except as respects certain harbours, between the British Railways Board (see below) and the London Transport Board. The London Transport Board was subsequently dissolved by the Transport (London) Act 1969 and replaced by the London Transport Executive. The Executive was reconstituted as London Regional Transport by the London Regional Transport Act 1984 (now repealed). As to the transition from London Regional Transport to Transport for London and the dissolution of LRT, see the Greater London Authority Act 1999 and the head "Transport for London" under the main head "London" below.

Instruments concerning various matters arising in connection with the above-mentioned Acts will be found mainly under the main head "Reorganisation of transport undertakings" above. Further provisions with respect to the nationalised or publicly-owned transport undertakings, the subsequent privatisation of the railway system by the Railways Act 1993, and the winding down and abolition of the British Railways Board under the Transport Act 2000 are also mentioned under that head. Instruments made under the Railways Act 1993 and included in this title are: SI 1994/572 (applications for a licence to operate a railway asset); SI 1994/573 and the further orders noted thereto (exemptions from provisions of the 1993 Act); SI 1994/575 (registers under the 1993 Act to be available for inspection); SI 1994/576 (penalty fares); SI 1994/607 (discontinuance of railway passenger services); SI 1994/857 and the further orders noted thereto (consequential modifications); SI 1994/1432, SI 1994/1433, SI 1994/2005, SI 1994/2150, SI 2007/1595, SI 2007/2205 (pensions of railway staff); SI 1996/664 (extinguishment of liabilities of

Railtrack plc); SI 1996/2551 (target investment limit for the government shareholding in Railtrack plc); SI 2003/1695 (duties of the Rail Passengers' Council); and see also SI 2005/2905 (Railway Heritage Scheme, made under the Railway Heritage Act 1996).

[196]

Construction and operation of railways etc

The Transport and Works Act 1992, Pt I (ss 1–25) provides for a system of orders relating to the construction or operation of railways, tramways and other guided transport systems and inland waterways, and works interfering with navigation. As to the commencement of the 1992 Act, see SI 1992/1347 and the further orders noted thereto. This new procedure is intended to replace the private Bill procedure and the order-making procedures under certain Acts such as the Tramways Act 1870, which are fully or partly repealed by the 1992 Act in relation to the previously mentioned matters. The Secretary of State was enabled by s 8 of the 1870 Act to make provisional orders on the application of local authorities and other bodies and persons specified in s 4 of that Act authorising the construction of tramways. Provisional orders were applied for and granted in accordance with the 1870 Act and the Rules of January 1892. The Tramways Act 1870 (including ss 4, 8 thereof) is largely repealed by the Transport and Works Act 1992; some provisions of Pts II, III of the 1870 Act remain unrepealed only in so far as they have been incorporated in, or otherwise applied by, any Act of Parliament or provisional order, but Pt I thereof, which made provision for the making of provisional orders, is fully repealed. The Rules of January 1892 are accordingly now of very limited effect.

S 1 of the 1992 Act enables orders to be made concerning the construction and operation of railways, tramways, trolley vehicle systems and other guided transport systems, and s 2 enables modes of guided transport to be prescribed for the purposes of s 1; see SI 1992/3231, which prescribes eight such modes. Orders under s 1 (for example the Docklands Light Railway (Capacity Enhancement) Order 2005, SI 2005/3105) are of local application only and therefore outside the scope of this work. As to works interfering with navigation, see SI 1992/3230 (made under s 4). Ss 6–14 relate to applications for orders, cases where other member states are affected and orders made otherwise than on application (ss 6, 6A, 7), model clauses (s 8), schemes of national significance (s 9), objections (s 10), inquiries and hearings (s 11), special parliamentary procedure (s 12), the making or refusal of orders (s 13) and publicity relating to such making or refusal (s 14). As to the procedures for the making of applications for orders under Pt I of the 1992 Act and for objections to such applications, see SI 2006/1466 (made under ss 6, 6A, 7, 10). As to model clauses for railways and tramways, see SI 2006/1954 (made under s 8). As to the procedure for inquiries under s 11, see SI 2004/2018. Ss 15–25 deal with consents etc under other enactments and miscellaneous matters; SI 1992/3138, SI 1993/1119, made under s 15, provide for the assimilation of procedures under the 1992 Act with those under other enactments.

[197]

Safety

The Transport and Works Act 1992, Pt II (ss 26–59) makes provision as to safety on railways and tramways. New offences involving drink or drugs are created by Chapter I (ie ss 26–39) of Pt II. In particular, s 27 makes it a criminal offence to perform certain functions on a transport system specified by virtue of s 26 while unfit through drink or drugs to carry out those functions, or with more than a prescribed limit of alcohol in the body. SI 1992/2044, made under s 26, specifies certain systems of guided transport for the purposes of Chapter I of Pt II, which also deals with police enforcement powers, provision of specimens, related offences, penalties etc. Chapter II (ss 41–56) of Pt II of the 1992 Act makes other safety provisions in respect of regulations requiring the approval of works, plant and equipment (s 41); the making of directions limiting speeds and loads and requiring insurance (ss 45, 46); orders requiring operators to provide tunnels or bridges where footpaths, bridleways or restricted byways cross railways (s 48); regulations requiring the placing of signs and barriers (s 52; see SI 1996/1786); rights to enter land (s 53); and the default powers of the Secretary of State (s 54).

By the Coroners Act 1988, s 11(8), a return must be made to the Secretary of State by the coroner within seven days of holding an inquest on the body of any person proved to have been killed on a railway or to have died in consequence of injuries received on a railway. The particulars to be given in this return are prescribed by a form dated 1895, which now takes effect under s 11(8) of the 1988 Act.

This title also contains a number of instruments made under provisions of the Health and Safety at Work etc Act 1974 relating to safety on the railways:

(a) SI 1997/487 relates to the provision, maintenance and operation of level crossings;
(b) SI 1997/553 makes provision with regard to the safe operation of transport systems (i e railways, tramways, trolley vehicles and other systems using guided transport);
(c) SI 1999/2244 makes provision with respect to the use of a train protection system, Mark I rolling stock and rolling stock with hinged doors;
(d) SI 2006/599 imposes prohibitions in relation to the operation of trains or vehicles on railways and other guided transport systems and the management and use of infrastructure unless a person has established and is maintaining a safety management system and in specified cases has a safety certificate in relation to the operation of vehicles or a safety authorisation in relation to the management and use of infrastructure; and
(e) SI 2006/1010 requires persons who provide railway services to pay a levy to the Office of Rail Regulation to meet the expenses it incurs in performing activities relating to railway safety.

The Office of Rail Regulation is generally responsible for the enforcement of the relevant statutory provisions to the extent that they relate to the operation of a railway, a tramway and any other system of guided transport (whether or not that activity is the main activity carried out in premises); see SI 2006/557, in the title Health and Safety at Work.

SI 2004/915 (made under the Police Reform Act 2002) enables the chief constable of the British Transport Police Force (see below) to establish and maintain a railway safety accreditation scheme in England and Wales.

[198]

Railways and Transport Safety Act 2003 The Railways and Transport Safety Act 2003 makes provision concerning safety on the railways, and other connected matters. The Act, which received royal assent on 10 July 2003, comes into force largely on a day or days to be appointed by order in accordance with s 120 thereof; see SI 2003/2681 and the further orders noted thereto.

Pt 1 (ss 1–14) of the 2003 Act, which concerns the investigation of railway accidents, provides for the creation of an independent body of accident inspectors known as the Rail Accident Investigation Branch (RAIB), whose primary purpose is to find out the cause of railway accidents. The RAIB is established by s 3, which also provides for the appointment of one of the inspectors as the Chief Inspector of Rail Accidents. The general aims of the RAIB are to improve the safety of railways and to prevent railway accidents and railway incidents (s 4). The Secretary of State must make regulations requiring the Chief Inspector of Rail Accidents to produce an annual report in connection with the activities of the RAIB (s 6). S 7 relates to investigations by the RAIB, and s 8 sets out the powers of inspectors for the purpose of conducting investigations. By s 9, the Secretary of State may make regulations about the conduct of investigations by the RAIB. S 10 enables the Chief Inspector of Rail Accidents to direct that railway accidents or railway incidents should be investigated by managers or controllers of railway property. S 11 enables the Secretary of State to make regulations in connection with the investigation of railway accidents and railway incidents and sets out the requirements which may be included in such regulations. SI 2005/1992 has been made under ss 2, 6, 7, 9, 11, 13 of the 2003 Act, and sets out the procedures for dealing with specified accidents and incidents, including notification requirements, dealing with evidence and publishing reports and recommendations.

[199]

Disabled access

The Disability Discrimination Act 1995, s 46 empowers the Secretary of State to make "rail vehicle accessibility regulations" for the purpose of securing that it is possible for disabled persons to get on to and off regulated rail vehicles and to travel in such vehicles safely and in reasonable comfort. As to such regulations, see SI 1998/2456. S 46(4A) of the 1995 Act, inserted by the Disability Discrimination Act 2005, s 6(1), as from a day to be appointed by order under s 20(3) thereof, provides that the Secretary of State must exercise the power to make rail vehicle accessibility regulations so as to secure that on and after 1 January 2020 every rail vehicle is a regulated rail vehicle, but not so as to affect the powers conferred by s 46(5), 47(1) or 67(2) of the 1995 Act. Under s 47(1), (1A) of the 1995 Act, the Secretary of State may by order (an "exemption order") authorise the use of a regulated rail vehicle even though the vehicle does not conform with the provisions of rail vehicle accessibility regulations with which it is required to conform and authorise a regulated rail vehicle to be used for carriage otherwise than in conformity with the provisions of rail vehicle accessibility regulations with which use of the vehicle is required to conform. Numerous exemption orders and regulations (SI 1998/2457) made under s 47 as originally enacted or as amended are noted to SI 1998/2456. As to parliamentary procedures in connection with the making of rail vehicle accessibility exemption orders, see SI 2008/2975 (made under ss 67(2), (3)(b), 67A(3) of the 1995 Act).

Ss 47A–47C of the 1995 Act are inserted by the Disability Discrimination Act 2005, s 7(1), as from a day to be appointed by order under s 20(3) thereof. S 47A(1), (2) provide that a regulated rail vehicle which is prescribed or is of a prescribed class or description, must not be used for carriage unless a rail vehicle accessibility compliance certificate is in force for the vehicle. An accessibility compliance certificate is a certificate that the Secretary of State is satisfied that the regulated rail vehicle conforms with those provisions of rail vehicle accessibility regulations with which the vehicle is required to conform (s 47A(3)). S 47B enables regulations to be made with respect to rail vehicle accessibility compliance certificates. Fees are payable in respect of applications for, and the issue of, compliance certificates; see s 47C. Ss 47D–47M of the 1995 Act are inserted by s 8(1) of the 2005 Act, as from a day to be appointed by order under s 20(3) thereof. These provisions impose penalties for using a rail vehicle without an accessibility compliance certificate, for using a rail vehicle which does not conform with a provision of rail vehicle accessibility regulations and for using a rail vehicle otherwise than in conformity with rail vehicle accessibility regulations (ss 47D–47F). S 47G confers powers of inspection on authorised persons where the Secretary of State reasonably suspects that a regulated rail vehicle may not conform with provisions of rail vehicle accessibility regulations. Ss 47J–47L concern the amount and recovery of penalties, the procedure for the imposition of penalties and appeals against penalties.

Provisions of the 1995 Act concerned with the accessibility of taxis and public service vehicles are dealt with in the corresponding note under the main head "Road traffic" above.

The Transport Act 2000, s 248 applies where a person who provides services for the carriage of passengers by railway provides or secures the provision of substitute road services, or the provision of such services is secured by the Secretary of State, the Scottish Ministers or the National Assembly for Wales (s 248(1)). In providing or securing the provision of the services, the person providing them, the Secretary of State, the Scottish Ministers or the National Assembly for Wales must ensure, so far as is reasonably practicable, that the substitute road services allow disabled passengers to undertake their journeys safely and in reasonable comfort (s 248(2)). In the event of any failure by a person to comply with s 248(2), he is liable to pay damages in respect of any expenditure reasonably incurred, or other loss sustained, by a disabled passenger in consequence of the failure (s 248(3)). The Secretary of State may by order grant exemptions from this provision; see s 248(4) and SI 2006/1935.

[200]

Railway charges and conditions of carriage

Under the Transport Act 1947, s 76 and the Transport Act 1953, s 20(1), the British Transport Commission (now dissolved) was required to prepare, and submit to the Transport Tribunal for confirmation, drafts of schemes for determining the charges which were to be made by the Commission for various services and facilities provided by it, and, where necessary, the other terms and conditions which were to be applicable to the provision of those services and facilities. Such schemes did not constitute statutory instruments but any scheme confirmed by the Transport Tribunal was required to be published. In so far as this part of the Preliminary Note is concerned, the British Transport Commission (Railway Merchandise) Charges Scheme 1957 and the British Transport Commission (Passenger) Charges Scheme 1959 were the last schemes to be made under these powers.

On the transfer of the Commission's railway system to the British Railways Board and the London Transport Board (subsequently reconstituted as London Regional Transport (now dissolved)) by the Transport Act 1962, the Commission's charges schemes ceased to have effect, subject to certain savings, by virtue of s 43(1) of the 1962 Act, and the relevant provisions of the 1947 and 1953 Acts were repealed. In general the British Railways Board and London Regional Transport were empowered to make such charges for their services and facilities, and to make the use of those services and facilities subject to such terms and conditions, as they thought fit; see s 43(3) of the 1962 Act, as originally enacted, and the London Regional Transport Act 1984, Sch 2, para 7 (now repealed). The same applies in the case of independent railway undertakings and independent inland waterway undertakings (see further the head "Canal boats and inland waterway charges" below); see s 52(2) of the 1962 Act. Provision for the winding down and abolition of the British Railways Board is made by the Transport Act 2000; see further the head "Privatisation of the railway system" under the main head "Reorganisation of transport undertakings" above. S 43(1), (3) of the 1962 Act were subsequently amended by s 252 of, and para 1 of Sch 27 to, the 2000 Act so as to refer to the Strategic Rail Authority instead of the Board and have now been amended by the Railways Act 2005, s 59(1), (6), Sch 12, para 1(1), (2), Sch 13, Pt 1, so as to omit the references to the Authority. Provision as to the charging of fares on franchised passenger services and approved discount fare schemes is now made by the Railways Act 1993, s 28. As to the transition from London Regional Transport to Transport for London and the dissolution of LRT, see the Greater London Authority Act 1999 and the head "Transport for London" under the main head "London" below. The London Regional Transport Act 1984 has been repealed by s 423 of, and Pt II of Sch 34 to, the 1999 Act. As to the structure of fares to be charged for public passenger transport services provided by Transport for London, see generally Chapter IV (ss 173–178) of Pt IV of the 1999 Act.

[201]

British Transport Police

The Railways and Transport Safety Act 2003, Pt 3 (ss 18–77) creates an independent police authority for the British Transport Police Force and transfers responsibility for the Force from the Strategic Rail Authority to the new Police Authority. Pt 3 of the Act was brought into force by SI 2004/1572 (largely on 1 July 2004). Ss 18, 19 (and Sch 4) provide for the establishment and functions of the British Transport Police Authority ("the Authority"), and s 20 requires the Authority to secure the maintenance of the British Transport Police Force ("the Police Force") to police the railways. Ss 21–30 provide for the ranks to be held in the Police Force (including that of chief constable), and for the employment of civilians. Ss 31, 32 provide for the jurisdiction of a constable of the Police Force. Ss 33–35 provide for agreements (police services agreements) to be made between the Authority and a person providing railway services; empower the Secretary of State to make orders requiring such persons to enter into a police services agreement; and make provision for disputes. As to an order under s 34 requiring specified persons to enter into a police services agreement, see SI 2004/1522.

The regulation of the Police Force is dealt with by ss 36–49. Ss 36–39 enable the Authority to make regulations about the government, administration and conditions of persons in the Police Force, and about the British Transport Police Federation (provision for the approval in draft of such regulations is made by s 40). Regulations made by the Authority are not made by statutory instrument and are accordingly outside the scope of this work. The Secretary of State may direct the Authority to prepare draft regulations under any of ss 36–39 for a specified purpose and may make them if approved (s 41). Provision is made enabling the Secretary of State to make regulations (by statutory instrument) relating to the Police Force in respect of any matter about which he could make regulations under the Police Act 1996, s 50, 51, 52 or 60 (s 42 of the 2003 Act); equipment (s 44); procedure and practice (s 45), and service outside the Police Force (s 49). The Secretary of State may issue codes of practice relating to the performance by the Authority and the Chief Constable of any of their functions (ss 47, 48). Ss 50–55 relate to policing objectives, railways policing plans, performance targets and directions, and a three-year strategy plan. Ss 56–62 (information) include provision for the making of reports by the Chief Constable; annual reports by the Authority; reports by the Authority and the Chief Constable to the Secretary of State; and provision for inquiries into matters connected with the Police Force. Ss 63–67 provide for the inspection of the Police Force and the action which may taken after an adverse inspection report. Miscellaneous and general provisions are made by the remaining provisions of Pt 3. In particular, s 73 enables the Secretary of State by order to make consequential and transitional provision or savings for the purposes of or in connection with a provision of Pt 3; see SI 2004/1573.

SI 2004/915 (made under the Police Reform Act 2002) enables the chief constable of the British Transport Police Force to establish and maintain a railway safety accreditation scheme in England and Wales.

[202]

Railways Act 2005

The Railways Act 2005 amends the law relating to the provision and regulation of railway services, and gives effect to the proposals set out in the White Paper "The Future of Rail" (July 2004) (Cm 6233). With the exception of ss 56(1), 60, which came into force on 7 April 2005 (the date of royal assent), the Act comes into force on days to be appointed by order under s 60(2); see SI 2005/1444 and the orders noted thereto.

Pt 1 (ss 1–5 and Schs 1–4) provides for the transfer of functions and for railway strategy. S 1 and Schs 1, 2, which provide for the transfer etc of the functions of the Strategic Rail Authority and its abolition, are dealt with under the head "Privatisation of the railway system" under the main head "Reorganisation of transport undertakings" above. S 2 introduces Sch 3, which makes provision for and in connection with the transfer to the Office of Rail Regulation of the safety functions of the Health and Safety Executive and the (former) Health and Safety Commission in respect of the railway industry conferred by or under the Health and Safety at Work etc Act 1974. Ss 3, 4 and Sch 4, which concern railway strategy, amend provisions of the Railways Act 1993.

Pt 2 (ss 6–18) provides for the giving of financial assistance by the Secretary of State for purposes connected with the railways. In particular, s 6 enables the Secretary of State to provide financial assistance to any person for the purpose of securing the provision, improvement or development of railway services or railway assets, or for any other purpose relating to a railway or to railway services. S 8 gives the Scottish Ministers similar powers to provide financial assistance in Scotland and s 10 concerns the involvement of the National Assembly for Wales in relation to financial assistance in Wales. Ss 7, 9, 11 provide for the notification between the Secretary of State, the Scottish Ministers and the National Assembly for Wales of any new or modified financial assistance schemes aimed at freight services. S 12 provides for the making of transfer schemes where a franchise agreement terminates in order to transfer the franchise assets of the previous franchisee to the new franchisee, or in certain circumstances to the Secretary of State or the Scottish Ministers.

Pt 3 (ss 19–21 and Schs 5, 6) relates to the Rail Passengers' Council and Rail Passengers' Committees. S 19 and Sch 5 provide for the establishment of a body corporate to be known as the Rail Passengers' Council, which is to replace the council known as the Rail Passengers' Council established by the Railways Act 1993, s 3(2) (repealed). By s 19(7), references in enactments, instruments and other documents to the Rail Passengers' Council established by s 3(2) of the 1993 Act have effect from the commencement of s 19(7) as references to the Council established by s 19(1) of the 2005 Act. S 21 and Sch 6 abolish the Rail Passengers' Committees established under s 2(2) of the 1993 Act (repealed), and provide for the London Transport Users' Committee to continue to have functions it previously had by virtue of being treated as a Rail Passengers' Committee. (As to transitional provisions and savings in connection with the coming into force of s 21(1), see SI 2005/1738, made under s 60 of the 2005 Act.)

Pt 4 (ss 22–45 and Schs 7, 8) concerns network modifications etc and replaces the procedures contained in the Railways Act 1993, ss 37–49 (repealed). It provides for the procedures to be followed by operators and public sector funders when discontinuing passenger services, networks and stations. Ss 22, 23 set out the procedures which apply when a service operator (s 22) or a railway funding authority (s 23) proposes to discontinue all non-franchised services on a line or from a station (subject to certain specified exceptions). S 24 sets out the procedures which apply when a railway funding authority proposes to discontinue all franchised or secured services on a particular line or from a particular station (subject to certain specified exceptions). S 25 concerns proposals to discontinue excluded services. Ss 26–28 set out the procedures which apply when an operator (s 26) or a railway funding authority (s 27) proposes to close all or part of its passenger network, or where a railway funding authority proposes to discontinue all or part of a secured network (s 28). Ss 29–31 set out the procedures which apply where the operator of a station (s 29) or a railway funding authority (s 30) proposes to close all or part of a station, or where a railway funding authority proposes to discontinue the operation of all or part of a secured station (s 31). S 32 concerns the reference of a proposal under Pt 4 to the Office of Rail Regulation. S 33 enables the Office of Rail Regulation to impose specific requirements in connection with a closure. Ss 34–38 relate to proposals which are excluded from the closure requirements of Pt 4. Ss 34, 35 concern minor modifications and closures eligible to be treated as minor modifications. Under s 36 passenger services may be designated by the Secretary of State, the Scottish Ministers or the National Assembly for Wales as experimental services (for a period not exceeding five years) and s 37 sets out the procedure to be followed for the discontinuance of experimental passenger services. S 38 enables services, networks and stations to be excluded by order from the application of ss 22–24, 26–28 or 29–31. S 41 sets out the circumstances in which a railway funding authority may make a proposal for the discontinuance of a railway passenger service or for the discontinuance of the operation of a network or part of a network or a station or part of a station. S 42 requires the Secretary of State, the Scottish Ministers and the National Assembly for Wales to publish guidance on closure proposals for the purposes of Pt 4, and s 43 relates to the publication and modification of such guidance; see SI 2006/2836, SI 2006/2837.

Pt 5 (ss 46–52 and Sch 9) contains further miscellaneous provisions relating to the railways. S 46 and Sch 9 empower railway operators to make bye-laws. S 51 imposes a duty on the Office of Rail Regulation to provide information and advice to the Secretary of State, the Scottish Ministers and the National Assembly for Wales in connection with their railway functions. S 52 requires Passenger Transport Executives to provide advice to the Secretary of State where requested to do so.

Pt 6 (ss 53–60 and Schs 10–13) contains general and supplementary provisions relating to the Act. S 60(3) enables the Secretary of State by order to make transitional provisions and savings in connection with the bringing into force of s 21 of the 2005 Act (abolition of Rail Passengers' Committees) and the repeal of the Railways Act 1993, ss 37–49, Sch 5 (railway closures); as to such an order, see SI 2005/1738.

[203]

International conventions

The International Transport Conventions Act 1983 gave the force of law in the United Kingdom to the Convention concerning International Carriage by Rail, signed by the United Kingdom on 9 May 1980. That Act repealed the Carriage by Railway Act 1972, and two earlier international conventions were superseded by the 1980 Convention. 1 May 1985 was certified by SI 1985/612 (revoked) as the day on which the Convention came into force in the United Kingdom.

The Railways and Transport Safety Act 2003, s 103 and Sch 6 empower the Secretary of State to make regulations to give effect to the Convention concerning International Carriage by Rail signed at Berne on 9 May 1980 as set out in the Annex to the modifying Protocol signed at Vilnius on 3 June 1999; see SI 2005/2092, which repeals and largely replaces most of the International Transport Conventions Act 1983 and revokes SI 1985/612.

[204]

Canal boats and inland waterway charges

The Canal Boats Act 1877, s 1 provided that no canal boat might be used as a dwelling unless it had been registered in accordance with that Act. Under s 2 thereof the Local Government Board was required to make regulations:

(a) with respect to registration and the lettering, numbering and marking of boats, and

(b) for fixing the number, age and sex of persons who may be allowed to live in them, and certain ancillary matters relating to public health.

The 1877 Act was wholly repealed by the Public Health Act 1936 but, by virtue of s 346(1) of that Act, the Canal Boats Regulations 1878, made under s 2 of the 1877 Act, were continued in force and had effect as if made under s 251(1) of the 1936 Act. In 1966 registration of canal boats ceased on the repeal (by the Local Government Act 1966) of s 250 of the 1936 Act (which replaced s 1 of the 1877 Act), and of s 251(1)(a), (b) of the 1936 Act, which related to the matters in head (a). The 1878 Regulations accordingly became spent with respect to matters in head (a). S 251 of the 1936 Act was fully repealed by the Public Health (Control of Disease) Act 1984, and the 1878 Regulations, in so far as they are not spent, now take effect under s 49 of the 1984 Act. S 49(1) of the 1984 Act is repealed by the Health and Social Care Act 2008, ss 130(2), 166, Sch 11, paras 1, 8(b), Sch 15, Pt 3, as from a day to be appointed by order, in so far as it enables regulations to be made for preventing the spread of infectious disease by canal boats.

All the principal canal and inland navigation undertakings were transferred to the British Transport Commission on 1 January 1948 under the Transport Act 1947, s 12, Sch 3, Pt II. Under s 76 of that Act and the Transport Act 1953, s 20(1), the Commission was required to prepare for confirmation by the Transport Tribunal schemes for determining the charges to be made by the commission for various services and facilities provided by them, including tolls for the use of inland waterways. Under the Transport Charges &c (Miscellaneous Provisions) Act 1954, ss 3, 4, the appropriate charges scheme could be applied by order made by the Minister of Transport to certain independent inland waterway undertakings. The last relevant scheme and order made under these powers were the British Transport Commission (Inland Waterways Charges Scheme Application) Order 1958, SI 1958/1801. Pending the preparation of a charges scheme the minister was empowered under s 82 of the 1947 Act to authorise by regulations the making of charges additional to those in operation under any statutory provision. This power was exercised in relation to canals by the Canals (Increase of Charges) Regulations 1947, SR & O 1947/2428 and the Canals (Additional Charges) Regulations 1950, SI 1950/704 (as modified by subsequent instruments). These regulations lapsed in 1959 on the repeal of s 82 by the Statute Law Revision Act 1959; and the said charges scheme order ceased to have effect in 1962 by virtue of the Transport Act 1962, ss 43(1)(a), 52(1). That Act transferred most of the inland waterways comprised in the Commission's undertaking to the British Waterways Board established under that Act (see s 31(5)) and empowered the Board and certain independent waterway undertakings to make such charges as they thought fit for the use of any inland waterway owned or managed by them (see ss 43(3), (8), 52(2)).

Provisions relating to the revision of certain charges made by other independent inland waterway undertakings are contained in the Transport Charges &c (Miscellaneous Provisions) Act 1954, s 6, but orders revising charges under this power, being local, are outside the scope of this work.

As to the new system of authorising the construction or operation of inland waterways and works interfering with navigation, see the head "Construction and operation of railways etc" above.

[205]

Channel Tunnel

The Channel Tunnel Act 1987 provides for the construction and operation of a fixed rail tunnel link between the United Kingdom and France, in accordance with the Treaty between the two countries signed at Canterbury on 12 February 1985 and pursuant to agreements between the governments of those countries and the private concessionaires who are to carry out the work. S 10 of the 1987 Act provides, inter alia, that if any part of the tunnel system constructed by or on behalf of the concessionaires working from England extends beyond the frontier between England and France (as defined in s 49(1)) before it effectively joins the part of the tunnel system constructed by or on behalf of the concessionaires working from France, until the English section effectively joins the French section, any such cross-frontier extension is to be treated as being in England and, except for rating purposes, as forming part of the county of Kent and the law of England is to apply there. Art 10 of the Treaty established an Intergovernmental Commission to fix a date of effective connection of the two sections of the tunnel, which, pursuant to s 10(8) of the 1987 Act, the Secretary of State may by order certify as being that date; SI 1991/1212 certified 30 November 1992 as that date.

S 11 of the 1987 Act enables orders to be made providing for the regulation of the tunnel system; in so far as relevant to this title, see SI 2007/3531, which brings into effect for the Channel Tunnel Directive 2004/49/EC of the European Parliament and of the Council on safety on the Community's railways (OJ L220, 21.06.2004, p 16).

[206]

Miscellaneous

This title also contains several instruments relating to railways made wholly or partly under the European Communities Act 1972, s 2(2); see:

(a) SI 2005/1992 (setting out the procedures for dealing with specified railway accidents and incidents) (also made under the Railways and Transport Safety Act 2003, ss 2, 6, 7, 9, 11, 13);

(b) SI 2005/3049 (granting access rights to the entire rail network in Great Britain (including access to terminals and ports linked to the rail network) to railway undertakings for the purpose of the operation of any type of rail freight service or international passenger service);

(c) SI 2005/3050 (licensing of railway undertakings which provide train services and are established or to be established in an EEA state);

(d) SI 2006/397 (interoperability of the trans-European high speed rail system and the trans-European conventional rail system) (also made under the Transport Act 2000, s 247, which enables provision to be made for the setting of standards to be complied with in relation to railway assets, railway vehicles or railway services);

(e) SI 2006/598 (access to training services for train drivers and staff of railway undertakings applying for a safety certificate in accordance with SI 2006/599 (see the head "Safety" above) and for infrastructure managers etc); and

(f) SI 2008/1660 (implements Council Directive 2005/47/EC on the Agreement between the Community of European Railways (CER) and the European Transport Workers' Federation (ETF) on certain aspects of the working conditions of mobile workers engaged in interoperable cross-border services in the railway sector (OJ L195, 27.07.2005, p 15)).

[207]

Pipe-lines

The Pipe-lines Act 1962 regulates and facilitates the construction, and secures the safe operation, of pipe-lines. The Act has been heavily amended by SI 1999/742 (and by SI 2000/1937, in the title Energy). This title contains an instrument affecting the 1962 Act made under the Health and Safety at Work etc Act 1974 (SI 1974/1986); and rules made under the Tribunals and Inquiries Act 1992, s 9 (SI 1995/1239).

[208]

Control of construction

The Pipe-lines Act 1962 distinguishes two types of pipe-line (as defined in s 65): (a) a cross-country pipe-line, which is one more than 16.093 kilometres long; and (b) a local pipe-line, which is a pipe-line other than a cross-country one (s 66(1)). S 1 of the Act makes it unlawful to construct a cross-country pipe-line except under a pipe-line construction authorisation granted by the Secretary of State (formerly the Minister of

Power) (s 1(1)). This is subject to the Planning Act 2008, s 33(1), which provides that authorisation under s 1(1) of the 1962 Act is not required to the extent that development consent is required for the construction concerned (s 1(1ZA) of the 1962 Act, inserted by s 36 of, and paras 5, 6(1), (2) of Sch 2 to, the 2008 Act, as from a day to be appointed by order). The provisions of Pt I of Sch 1 to the 1962 Act govern the making of applications for authorisations (s 1(3)). The Secretary of State may by order direct that s 1 is to apply to specified local pipe-lines (s 6). Orders under this power are outside the scope of this work. The application of s 1 may be excluded by order in relation to certain pipe-lines in particular localities (s 64). Such orders are also outside the scope of this work. S 2 of the Act, which made it unlawful to construct a local pipe-line unless the required notice of intention to do so was given to the Secretary of State, has been repealed by SI 1999/742 (SI 1962/2845, which was made under s 2 of the 1962 Act, has accordingly lapsed). S 3, under which a pipe-line diversion authorisation from the Secretary of State was required if a cross-country pipe was to be diverted outside permitted limits of deviation, has also been repealed by SI 1999/742. However, by s 1(1A) of the 1962 Act, as inserted by SI 1999/742:

(a) the construction of a diversion to a pipe-line is to be treated as the construction of a separate pipe-line for the purposes of s 1 of the Act; and
(b) if the diversion is to a pipe-line which is the subject of a pipe-line construction authorisation but the length of that pipe-line which is being diverted has not been constructed, the construction of the diversion is to be treated as the construction of a cross-country pipe-line whatever the length of the diversion (amended as from a day to be appointed by the Planning Act 2008, s 36, Sch 2, paras 5, 6(1), (3), so as to refer to a nationally significant pipe-line instead of a pipe-line which is the subject of a pipe-line construction authorisation).

SI 1999/742 also repealed s 7 of the 1962 Act, under which, if a new pipe-line was to be added to another pipe-line, or was to connect two other pipe-lines, such that their combined length exceeded 16.093 kilometres, the new pipe-line had to be authorised by the Secretary of State under s 1 of the Act. As to the avoidance of the construction of superfluous pipe-lines, see ss 9–10F (as amended or inserted by SI 1999/742, SI 2000/1937 (the latter in the title Energy)).

By s 58B(1) of the 1962 Act, in relation to the construction, by any person other than a gas transporter, of a pipe to which that section applies: (a) references in ss 1–14 of that Act to a pipe-line are to be construed as not including references to such a pipe; (b) references in those sections to pipe-line works are to be construed as not including references to works executed in connection with the construction of such a pipe. S 58B(1) applies to any pipe by which any premises are proposed to be connected to a distribution main of a gas transporter and by which gas is proposed to be conveyed to premises at a rate not expected to exceed 75,000 therms in any period of 12 months (s 58B(2)).

The provisions of the 1962 Act relating to the granting of a pipe-line construction should be read in conjunction with regs 10, 48 et seq, 75–78 of SI 1994/2716, in the title Environment.

As to regulations prohibiting the Secretary of State from granting a pipe-line construction authorisation in respect of relevant pipe-line works unless requirements relating to environmental impact are satisfied, see SI 2000/1928, in the title Environment.

[209]

Compulsory acquisition of land or rights over land

Under the Pipe-lines Act 1962, s 11, a person proposing to lay a pipe-line may be authorised, by a compulsory purchase order, to purchase the land concerned compulsorily. Such a person may also be authorised by a compulsory rights order to exercise the necessary rights over the land (s 12). The provisions of Sch 2 to the Act govern applications for such orders (ss 11(3), 12(3)). By s 13(2) the Secretary of State may by order vary a compulsory rights order; such orders are local and accordingly outside the scope of this work. Forms for use in connection with applications for compulsory purchase and compulsory rights orders and proposals to make an order under s 13(2) are prescribed by SI 1963/151. A compulsory rights order may give rise to a right to compensation (s 14). Questions as to compensation are to be determined, in default of agreement, by the Upper Tribunal (established under the Tribunals, Courts and Enforcement Act 2007, s 3); see s 48 of the 1962 Act and the Land Compensation Act 1961, s 1, as modified by Sch 3 to the 1962 Act (all amended by SI 2009/1307, in the title Courts and Legal Services). For the procedure on references to the Upper Tribunal, see Pts IV, VII of SI 1996/1022, in the title Compulsory Acquisition.

[210]

Public inquiries and hearings

The Secretary of State is required to hold a public inquiry, or afford the objector an opportunity of a hearing before a person appointed by him, when objection is duly made (and not withdrawn) to an application for a pipe-line construction (Pipe-lines Act 1962, Sch 1, Pt I, para 4(1)) or a compulsory purchase or compulsory rights order (Sch 2, Pt I, para 4(1), Pt II, para 10). The Secretary of State is also required to hold a public inquiry when objection is made (and not withdrawn) to a pipe-line construction authorising the execution of works for the placing of a proposed pipe-line along a modified route (Sch 1, Pt I, para 6A). He may, if he thinks fit, hold a public inquiry with respect to an application for the grant of a pipe-line construction whether or not any objection to the application, or to any modification of the route proposed in it, is made or maintained (Sch 1, Pt I, para 6B). The procedure to be followed in connection with such inquiries or hearings is laid down by SI 1995/1239 (made under the Tribunals and Inquiries Act 1992, s 9). The Local Government Act 1972, s 250(2)–(5) applies, with modifications, to all public inquiries under the 1962 Act (s 47(1) of the 1962 Act).

[211]

Safety

Following the coming into operation of the Health and Safety at Work etc Act 1974, various provisions of the Pipe-lines Act 1962 were superseded by provisions of that Act, and it became necessary to transfer certain functions under the 1962 Act from the Secretary of State to the Health and Safety Executive. Amendments were therefore made to the 1962 Act by SI 1974/1986. Provisions of the 1962 Act concerning safety of pipe-lines have been repealed and replaced by SI 1996/825, in the title Petroleum, made under the 1974 Act.

[212]

London

This title contains a number of instruments which are limited in their application to the London area or to vehicles and premises under the control of Transport for London (formerly London Regional Transport). Of particular importance are instruments made under the Greater London Authority Act 1999, which, inter alia, provides for the transition from London Regional Transport to Transport for London. Many of the instruments mentioned elsewhere in this Preliminary Note apply as much in the London area as elsewhere. Note, however, that the regulation of bus services in Greater London is dealt with under the head "Bus services" under the main head "Road traffic" above (see SI 1986/1691).

[213]

London Passenger Transport Board

The ownership and operation of public transport in the London Passenger Transport Area was entrusted by the London Passenger Transport Act 1933 to a body established by that Act and known as the London Passenger Transport Board. Sch 7 to the 1933 Act defines the London Passenger Transport Area, and Sch 2 specifies the numerous transport undertakings operating in the area which, under s 5, were transferred to the Board. The date of transfer for the underground, metropolitan and local authorities' undertakings specified in Pts I, II, III of Sch 2 was 1 July 1933; and the dates of transfer for the Tilling undertakings, the independent undertakings and the Lewis undertaking specified in Pts IV, V, VI of Sch 2 were dates between 1 July 1933 and 5 December 1934 fixed by various London Passenger Transport Act 1933 (Appointed Day) Orders, beginning with SR & O 1933/634 and ending with SR & O 1934/1365 (see the chronological list of instruments at the beginning of this title), which were made under s 107(1) of the 1933 Act.

The undertaking of the London Passenger Transport Board vested (along with many other undertakings) in the British Transport Commission on 1 January 1948 under the Transport Act 1947 (repealed), and the Board was finally dissolved on 23 December 1949. Subsequently, on the reorganisation of the nationalised transport undertakings under the Transport Act 1962 (see the main head "Reorganisation of transport undertakings" above), the relevant part of the Commission's undertaking was transferred to the London Transport Board. That Board was later succeeded by a new London Transport Executive established under the Transport (London) Act 1969 (largely repealed), which was itself reconstituted as London Regional Transport (now dissolved).

[214]

Transport for London

The Transport (London) Act 1969 was largely repealed as from 29 June 1984 by the London Regional Transport Act 1984; that date was the day appointed by SI 1984/877 (lapsed). The London Transport Executive, established under the 1969 Act, was reconstituted as London Regional Transport (LRT) as from that date. LRT was under a general duty to provide or secure the provision of public passenger transport services for Greater London (s 2 of the 1984 Act (repealed)), and a specific duty to establish companies to run London bus and underground services (s 4 thereof (repealed)). The functions, powers and duties of LRT were set out in the London Regional Transport Act 1984 and included the financing of LRT; pensions; consultation with passengers; railway closures; and travel concessions.

The Greater London Authority Act 1999, Pt IV (ss 141–303) of which contains provisions relating to transport, established on 8 May 2000 a new body called Transport for London to carry on the undertakings vested in London Regional Transport and to perform other functions. As to the commencement of the 1999 Act, see SI 1999/3271 and the note "Further orders" thereto, in the title Local Government. Provisions of the London Regional Transport Act 1984 were amended by SI 2000/1504 (revoked by SI 2003/1615) during the transitional period (ie the period beginning with 3 July 2000 and ending with the day on which LRT ceased to provide or secure the provision of public passenger transport services). The 1984 Act was repealed by s 423 of, and Pt II of Sch 34 to, the 1999 Act on 15 July 2003, and LRT was dissolved on 16 July 2003 by SI 2003/1913, made under s 302 of the 1999 Act. S 154(1), which established Transport for London (TfL), was brought into force on 8 May 2000 by SI 2000/801, in the title Local Government, and the provisions of the Act relating to the principal functions of TfL were brought into force on 3 July 2000 by SI 2000/801.

As to the grant of exemptions to Transport for London (formerly LRT) and its subsidiaries from provisions of the Railways Act 1993, see SI 1994/573.

SI 2006/91 (made under the Deregulation and Contracting Out Act 1994, s 70) enables Transport for London to contract out certain investment and highway functions.

Chapter I of Pt IV (ss 141–153) of the 1999 Act sets out the transport functions of the Greater London Authority. S 141 requires the Mayor of London to develop and implement policies for the promotion and encouragement of safe, integrated, efficient and economic transport facilities and services to, from and within Greater London; and s 142 requires him to prepare and publish a transport strategy. Chapter II (ss 154–169) relates to Transport for London. S 154(1) established on 8 May 2000 a new body called Transport for London (TfL) to carry on the undertakings vested in LRT and to perform other functions. General provision as to the functions of TfL is made by ss 156–158. As to restrictions on TfL carrying out specified activities, see s 157 and SI 2000/1548. S 163 prohibits TfL from disposing of certain land without the consent of the Secretary of State, which is to be given by order; such orders, being local in nature, are outside the scope of this work. S 165 (and Sch 12) enables TfL to make schemes for the transfer of property, rights and liabilities between TfL and any of its subsidiaries, and between its subsidiaries. These schemes must be confirmed by order made by the Secretary of State; such orders, being local in nature, are outside the scope of this work.

Chapter IV of Pt IV (ss 173–178) concerns public passenger transport. Under s 173, TfL may provide or secure the provision of public passenger transport services to, from or within Greater London. S 174 relates to the structure of fares and services. Chapter VI (ss 198–209) (repealed in part by the Railways Act 2005, ss 16(1), 59(6), Sch 13, Pt 1) relates to railways. S 207 imposes restrictions on TfL contracting out certain reserved services; as to an exception order made under that section, see SI 2003/1613. Chapter VII (ss 210–239) concerns public-private partnership agreements. Chapter VIII (ss 240–244) relates to travel concessions in Greater London; as to the form of concessionary travel permits, see SI 2008/417 (also mentioned in the head "Bus services" under the main head "Road traffic" above). Chapter X (ss 246–252E) abolishes the London Regional Passengers' Committee (s 246) and replaces it with the London Transport Users' Committee (LTUC), established under s 247. As to transitional provisions relating to LTUC, see SI 2000/1484. Ss 252A–252E (inserted by the Railways Act 2005, s 21(3), Sch 6, paras 2–4) require LTUC to keep railway matters under review (s 252A) and to investigate and report on railway matters (ss 252B–252D). S 252E enables the Secretary of State by order to make exclusions from the duties under ss 252A–252D.

Chapter XVI of Pt IV (ss 297–303) provides for the transition from London Regional Transport (LRT) to TfL, and for the two bodies to operate side by side during a transitional period (ie the period beginning with 3 July 2000 and ending with the day on which LRT ceases to provide or secure the provision of public passenger transport services). S 297 requires the Secretary of State to prepare programmes for the transfer to TfL of property, rights and liabilities of LRT: (a) for the purpose of enabling TfL to perform its functions as they become exercisable; or (b) in preparation for the dissolution of LRT. S 298 provides for the functions of LRT and TfL during the transitional period. S 302 provides that the Secretary of State may by order dissolve LRT; by SI 2003/1913 LRT was dissolved on 16 July 2003.

Ss 405–407 of the 1999 Act enable consequential and transitional provisions to be made in relation to the Act. As to orders made partly under those sections, see eg SI 2000/412 (provision consequent on the alteration of the metropolitan police district); SI 2000/1045 (preliminary arrangements in relation to the exercise of certain of TfL's functions); SI 2001/690 (amending provisions of the London Local Authorities Acts 1996 and 2000); and SI 2003/1615 (provision consequent on completion of the transfer of the undertaking of LRT to TfL and the abolition of TfL). Orders made partly under ss 405–407 of the 1999 Act relating to GLA roads and side roads are dealt with in the title Highways, Streets and Bridges.

Provision protecting the pension arrangements of persons who were employed by LRT and become employees of private sector companies is made by s 411 of, and Sch 32 to, the 1999 Act, and by SI 2000/3386.

[215]

Fares and penalty fares

Under the Transport Act 1962, s 45 (repealed), the Transport Tribunal was empowered to make orders with respect to passenger fares chargeable in London by the London Transport Board and the British Railways Board (as to the winding down and abolition of the British Railways Board, see the Transport Act 2000 and the head "Privatisation of the railway system" under the main head "Reorganisation of transport undertakings" above). Such orders (the last of which were the London Fares (London Transport) Order 1968 and the London Fares (British Railways) Order 1968) did not constitute statutory instruments but were published by HM Stationery Office. This control over London passenger fares ceased on 8 August 1969 with the repeal of the relevant provisions (ss 44–49) of the 1962 Act by the Transport (London) Act 1969, ss 27(1), 47(2), Sch 6, and the responsibility for setting fares passed to the London Transport Executive. That body was reconstituted as London Regional Transport (now dissolved and replaced by Transport for London) by the London Regional Transport Act 1984, s 1(2) (repealed). Fares were subsequently determined by London Regional Transport under s 3(9) of, and para 7 of Sch 2 to, the 1984 Act (repealed). Provisions as to penalty fares, which were formerly contained in the London Regional Transport Act 1984, were subsequently dealt with by the London Regional Transport (Penalty Fares) Act 1992. Both the 1984 Act and the 1992 Act were repealed by the Greater London Authority Act 1999, as from 15 July 2003.

The Greater London Authority Act 1999 provides for the transition from London Regional Transport to Transport for London; see above. Under s 174 of the 1999 Act, the Mayor of London must ensure that the following matters are determined:

(a) the general level and structure of fares to be charged for public passenger transport services provided by Transport for London or by any other person in pursuance of any agreement entered into by Transport for London by virtue of s 156(2) or (3)(a) of that Act or in pursuance of a transport subsidiary's agreement; and

(b) the general level of charges to be made for other facilities provided as mentioned in head (a).

S 178 requires Transport for London to inform specified bodies of the general level and structure of fares to be charged for the provision of transport services. S 245 of, and Sch 17 to, the 1999 Act provide for the payment of penalty fares on local services or train services provided by:

(a) Transport for London or any of its subsidiaries, or

(b) any other person in pursuance of an agreement by London Transport under s 156(2) or (3)(a) of that Act, or in pursuance of a transport subsidiary's agreement, which provides that Sch 17 is to apply to services provided under that agreement (para 2(1) of Sch 17).

By para 9 of Sch 17, that Schedule may be applied to services for the carriage of passengers by railway which do not fall within para 2(1) but are provided wholly within Greater London and are designated in an order as qualifying train services. As to such an order, see SI 2000/1442, designating services on Croydon Tramlink.

[216]

Taxis

The licensing authority within the metropolitan police district and the City of London is now Transport for London (formerly an assistant commissioner of police of the metropolis); see SR & O 1934/1346, in accordance with which cab and cab-drivers' licences are issued and fares are fixed. The Transport Act 1985, Pt I contains provision in relation to taxis; see ss 10–17 thereof. In particular, taxis may now be operated under taxi-sharing schemes. Such a scheme was brought into force by SI 1987/1535, made under s 10 of the 1985 Act (as to further such schemes, see the note "Summary" to SI 1987/1535); see also SI 1986/1387, made under s 13 thereof, which disapplies certain provisions of the "taxi code" to taxis which are to be hired at separate fares. S 12 of the 1985 Act makes provision in relation to special licences granted to holders of taxi licences who intend to use taxis to provide local services; in this regard, see SI 1986/566. See also SI 1986/1188, made under s 17 of the 1985 Act. (SI 1986/567, SI 1986/1386 make provision corresponding to SI 1986/566, SI 1986/1387 in relation to taxis other than in London. See also SI 1986/1779, made under s 10, which prescribes the description of the provisions which are required to be included in a scheme outside London.) S 13A (inserted by the Local Transport Act 2008, s 54(8)) enables Transport for London by order to provide that s 12 of the 1985 Act is to apply to private hire vehicles in London.

In Greater London the traffic authority (i e the Secretary of State, London borough council or the Common Council of the City of London) is empowered to make orders governing cabs and hackney carriages not hired and being in a street elsewhere than on a cab rank by the Road Traffic Regulation Act 1984, s 6, Sch 1, para 16. Such orders however are treated as local and are outside the scope of this work.

[217]

Traffic regulation

Wide powers to make orders for controlling or regulating traffic in Greater London lie with the traffic authorities (i e the Secretary of State, London borough council or the Common Council of the City of London) under the Road Traffic Regulation Act 1984, s 6. Such orders, being local, are outside the scope of this work.

Traffic in London was also regulated by the Road Traffic Act 1991, Pt II (ss 64–82), which was largely repealed on 31 March 2008 (see SI 2007/2053), subject to transitional provisions, by the Traffic Management Act 2004, s 98, Sch 12, Pt 1, and replaced by Pt 6 (ss 72–93 and Schs 7–11) of the 2004 Act. Pt 6 of the 2004 Act provides a single national framework for regulations to be made for the civil enforcement by local authorities of road traffic contraventions (i e parking contraventions, bus lane contraventions, London lorry ban contraventions and moving traffic contraventions). A number of regulations have been made under Pt 6 of the 2004 Act so as to implement that Part in so far as it provides for the civil enforcement of parking contraventions by local authorities; these regulations are dealt with in the head "Regulation of traffic" under the main head "Road traffic" above.

The Road Traffic Act 1991, ss 66–77 related to parking in London. S 73 enabled regulations to be made making provision as to the procedure to be followed in relation to proceedings before parking adjudicators in London; as to such regulations, see SI 1993/1202 (made under s 73(11), (12)). As noted above, ss 66–77 have been repealed by the Traffic Management Act 2004, s 98, Sch 12, Pt 1. Notwithstanding the repeal of s 73(11), (12), SI 1993/1202 is continued in force for a transitional period for the purpose of applying in relation to:

(a) proceedings before traffic adjudicators under the London Local Authorities Act 1996, and for that purpose s 73(11)–(13) of the 1991 Act continue to have effect (see s 6(2) of the 1996 Act, as substituted by SI 2007/2053); and

(b) proceedings before traffic adjudicators under the London Local Authorities and Transport for London Act 2003, and for that purpose s 73(11)–(13) of the 1991 Act continue to have effect (see para 10(2) of Sch 1 to the 2003 Act, as substituted by SI 2007/2053).

Local authorities may provide parking attendants under the Road Traffic Regulation Act 1984, s 63A; in this connection, see SI 1993/1450.

The Greater London Authority Act 1999, Pt IV, Chapters XIV (ss 271–294) and XV (ss 295, 296 and Schs 23, 24) also provide for road traffic in London. Chapter XIV amends provisions of the Road Traffic Regulation Act 1984, the Road Traffic Act 1988, the Road Traffic Act 1991 and the Road Traffic Reduction Act 1997 relating to traffic control systems, road safety and traffic reduction, parking and school crossing patrols etc. Chapter XV provides for road user charging and workplace parking levy. As to the imposition of charges and penalty charges under road user charging schemes, see SI 2001/2285; and as to the enforcement and adjudication of such schemes, see SI 2001/2313 (both made under Sch 23 to the 1999 Act). As to the determination of the net proceeds of road user charging and workplace parking levy schemes, see SI 2003/110 (made under Schs 23, 24 to the 1999 Act).

[218]

Private Hire Vehicles (London) Act 1998

This Act provides for the licensing and regulation of private hire vehicles and their drivers and operators within the metropolitan police district and the City of London. The Act (except s 40, which came into force on 28 July 1998 (date of royal assent)) has been brought into force by order under s 40(2). Provisions relating to the licensing of private hire vehicle operators were brought into force by SI 2000/3144; provisions relating to the licensing of private hire vehicle drivers were brought into force by SI 2003/580; and the remainder of the Act was brought into force by SI 2004/241. As to regulations concerning operators' licences, see SI 2000/3146. As to transitional provisions in connection with the introduction of the licensing of private hire vehicle drivers, see SI 2003/655, SI 2004/242 (both made under s 37 of the Act). Further regulations have been made relating to licensing of private hire vehicles by Transport for London (the licensing authority). These regulations are not statutory instruments and are therefore outside the scope of this work; however they can be found at www.tfl.gov.uk.

[219]

Miscellaneous

This title contains a number of instruments which do not fall directly within the scope of the previous heads of this Preliminary Note and, with some exceptions, are not mentioned elsewhere in the Note. The majority of these instruments were made under the European Communities Act 1972, s 2(2):

(a) SI 2004/129, which implements Council Directive 2000/9/EC relating to cableway installations (OJ L106, 03.05.2000, p 21) by introducing standards for the construction and putting into service of cableway installations, including safety components and subsystems incorporated into such installations;

(b) SI 2005/639, which implements the provisions of Directive 2002/15/EC of the European Parliament and of the Council on the organisation of the working time of persons performing mobile road transport activities (OJ L80, 23.03.2002, p 35);

(c) SI 2007/1520, which implements Directive 2004/54/EC of the European Parliament and of the Council on minimum safety requirements for tunnels in the Trans-European Road Network (OJ L167, 30.04.2004, p 39), and ensures a minimum level of safety for road users in tunnels in the trans-European road network;

(d) SI 2009/1896, SI 2009/1899, which together impose requirements and prohibitions in relation to the supply and installation of replacement catalytic converters and pollution control devices in respect of certain vehicles; and

(e) SI 2009/2194, which implements in part Directive 2006/40/EC of the European Parliament and of the Council relating to emissions from air conditioning systems in motor vehicles (OJ L161, 14.06.2006, p 12).

Note also SI 2008/3010 (made under the Crime (International Co-operation) Act 2003, s 57), which relates to the mutual recognition of driving disqualifications between the United Kingdom and Ireland.

This title includes the Transport Tribunal Rules 2000, SI 2000/3226 (made under the Transport Act 1985, Sch 4, para 11(1)), which make provision concerning applications and appeals to the Transport Tribunal. The relevant functions of the Transport Tribunal have largely been transferred to the First-tier Tribunal or the Upper Tribunal (established under the Tribunals, Courts and Enforcement Act 2007, s 3) by SI 2009/1885, in the title Courts and Legal Services, and SI 2000/3226 is largely spent. However, the Transport Tribunal was not abolished by SI 2009/1885, and SI 2000/3226 is retained in this title although it has very limited application.

Note also SI 1999/786, which was made under the Road Traffic (NHS Charges) Act 1999, ss 6(1), 7(4), 9, 16(2), and contained procedural matters relating to reviews and appeals for the purposes of that Act. The whole of the 1999 Act has been repealed by the Health and Social Care (Community Health and Standards) Act 2003, ss 169(1), 196, Sch 14, Pt 3, as from 29 January 2007 (see SI 2006/3397, in the title National Health Service), except in relation to injuries to which the Act applied which occurred before that date. SI 1999/786 (as partially revoked and amended by SI 2008/2683, in the title Courts and Legal Services) is retained in this title in the light of that saving.

The title also includes numerous commencement orders relating to various enactments, and instruments relating to employees' pensions and providing for compensation for persons adversely affected by the nationalisation or reorganisation of transport.

[220]

CANAL BOATS REGULATIONS 1878

Authority Made by the Local Government Board under the Canal Boats Act 1877, ss 2, 9 (repealed). Now take effect under the Public Health (Control of Disease) Act 1984, s 49(1), by virtue of the Interpretation Act 1978, s 17(2)(b), printed in the title Statutory Instruments (Pt 2), Vol 1 of this work. S 49(1) of the 1984 Act is repealed by the Health and Social Care Act 2008, ss 130(2), 166, Sch 11, paras 1, 8(b), Sch 15, Pt 3, as from a day to be appointed by order, in so far as it enables regulations to be made for preventing the spread of infectious disease by canal boats.

Date made 20 March 1878.

Commencement 30 June 1878.

Amendment Amended by SR & O 1925/843, SR & O 1931/444, but, as a result of the repeal of the Public Health Act 1936, s 25(a), (b), those regulations are now spent.

Interpretation By reg 14 words used in these regulations have the same meaning as in the Canal Boats Act 1877; see now the Public Health (Control of Disease) Act 1984, s 53, for interpretation provisions corresponding to those in the 1877 Act.

Summary These regulations contain provisions as to the number and age etc of persons who may live in canal boats, cleanliness, and the prevention of the spreading of infectious disease.

Number, age and sex of occupants The maximum number of persons who may live in a canal boat is determined by reference to air space per person; a minimum of 60 cubic feet is required for persons over 12 and 40 cubic feet for children under 12. Provision is also made for separation of the sexes in sleeping accommodation.

Cleanliness The paint on all interior surfaces must be renewed at least once in three years, cabins must be kept clean and habitable, and bilge water must be removed as often as is necessary to prevent any collection beneath the floor of a cabin and at least once in every 24 hours.

Prevention of spread of disease Notification of any serious illness or infectious disease on board must be given to the local sanitary authority (now the local authority or port health authority) wherever the boat may be, and, if it is in port or at its destination, also to the owner. If the boat is detained for cleansing or disinfection under the Public Health (Control of Disease) Act 1984, s 51(1), the sanitary authority must obtain a certificate of cleansing and disinfection from their medical officer of health, which must be given to the master of the boat, before allowing it to proceed. S 51(1) of the 1984 Act is repealed by the Health and Social Care Act 2008, ss 130(2), 166, Sch 11, paras 1, 10(a), Sch 15, Pt 3, as from a day to be appointed by order.

These regulations are spent in so far as they provided for the registration, lettering, marking and numbering of canal boats; see the Preliminary Note "Canal boats and inland waterway charges" (under the main head "Railways, tramways and inland waterways").

[221]

LONDON CAB ORDER 1934
SR & O 1934/1346

Authority Made by the Secretary of State under the Metropolitan Public Carriage Act 1869 and the London Cab and Stage Carriage Act 1907.

Date made 11 December 1934.

Commencement 1 January 1935.

Amendment Amended by SI 1955/1853, SI 1962/289, SI 1971/333, SI 1980/588, SI 1982/311, SI 1985/933, SI 1990/2003, SI 2000/1666. Also currently amended by the London Cab (No 2) Order 2001 and the London Cab Orders 2002, 2004, 2007 and 2008. These orders, made by Transport for London, are not statutory instruments and are outside the scope of this work; however, they may be found at www.tfl.gov.uk.

Previously amended by SI 1950/650, SI 1950/863, SI 1951/956, SI 1951/1352, SI 1957/1620, SI 1958/2148, SI 1964/105, SI 1968/1929, SI 1973/519, SI 1974/601, SI 1975/1216, SI 1976/1956, SI 1977/2030, SI 1979/706, SI 1980/939, SI 1981/843, SI 1982/610, SI 1983/653, SI 1984/707, SI 1985/1023, SI 1986/857, SI 1987/999, SI 1988/996, SI 1989/848, SI 1990/1076, SI 1991/1301, SI 1992/1169, SI 1993/1093, SI 1994/1087, SI 1995/1181, SI 1996/1176, SI 1997/1116, SI 1998/1043, SI 1999/1117, SI 1999/3250, SI 2000/1276 (all now revoked or superseded).

Modification Modified by SI 1986/1387 in relation to obligatory hiring and fares, so that certain provisions of this order do not apply when a taxi is being used for hire at separate fares.

Also modified by SI 2000/1666 so that:

(a) any reference to the Assistant Commissioner, the Commissioner of Police or the Secretary of State is to be treated as a reference to Transport for London; and

(b) a document which is required to be in the form contained in Sch A, B, C or D may be modified so far as may be necessary in consequence of any provision of the Greater London Authority Act 1999, Sch 20 (hackney carriages) or of this order.

Application This order applies only within the Metropolitan Police District and the City of London.

Summary This order is divided into ten Parts which are briefly summarised in the following note.

Pt I sets out the short title and defines terms which are used throughout the order.

Pt II (so far as still in force) provides that any appointment made or approval or direction given by Transport for London (formerly the Assistant Commissioner) under the order may be revoked or varied by that body.

Pts III and IV govern the grant and revocation of cab licences and cab-drivers' licences and deal with ancillary matters. No person under the age of 21 years may receive a licence and Transport for London has discretionary power to refuse licences in other cases. All cabs must be certified by a public carriage examiner to conform with prescribed conditions of fitness. Conditions subject to which licences are issued are specified. Provision is made as to a cab owner's liability to third parties.

Pt V lays down that no person other than the driver may be carried on any cab in excess of the number of persons which it is licensed to carry. An infant in arms does not, however, count as a person and two children under the age of 10 years count as only one person. Normally only the driver may travel on the driving box or platform of a cab. Luggage must not be carried on the roof unless the cab is fitted for that purpose and is so licensed. A driver is not compelled to accept a hiring for a distance of more than 12 miles.

Pt VI contains regulations as to taximeters and fares for motor cabs. The owner must cause the cab to be fitted with a taximeter of a type approved by Transport for London and sealed by an authorised person. Thereafter while the cab is licensed no unauthorised person may remove or tamper with the meter. Plying for hire without a meter, or with an unsealed meter, is prohibited and meters must be lighted in the manner prescribed. The driver must, as soon as the cab is hired, set the mechanism of the meter in motion and must stop it as soon as the hiring is terminated. Fares payable for the hiring of a motor cab are prescribed.

Pt VII regulated fares for horse cabs (there are now, however, no horse cabs in the metropolis).

Pt VIII deals with the care and disposal of property accidentally left in cabs. The finder is required to hand such property to the driver immediately, and an obligation is placed on the driver to search the cab after each hiring or as soon as practicable after the termination of a hiring. Within 24 hours of finding property the driver must deposit it at a police station unless he has previously given it to a person whom he is satisfied is the owner. Provision is made for the disposal by Transport for London of property deposited at a police station.

Pt IX prescribes a penalty not exceeding £2 for any breach of the order. Earlier orders are revoked and provision is made for the reprinting of the order complete with subsequent amendments.

Pt X contains transitory provisions and provided for the order to come into force on 1 January 1935.

The order contains three Schedules:

Sch A (*Revoked by the London Cab Order 2007*)
Sch B Description of plates etc to be affixed to cabs
Sch C Form of cab licence
Sch D Form of cab-driver's licence.

Cases relating to this order See *R v Metropolitan Police Commissioner, ex parte Parker* [1953] 2 All ER 717, [1953] 1 WLR 1150.
Further orders See also SI 1972/1047, SI 1973/1671.

[222]

MOTOR VEHICLES (VARIATION OF SPEED LIMIT) REGULATIONS 1947
SR & O 1947/2192

Authority Made by the Minister of Transport under the Road Traffic Act 1930, s 121(2). On the repeal of that subsection by the Road Traffic Act 1960, these regulations continued in force under the saving provisions of s 267(2) of, and para 1 of Sch 19 to, the 1960 Act as if made under ss 250(4), 251 thereof; and on the repeal of the said ss 250(4), 251 by the Road Traffic Regulation Act 1967, they continued in force under the saving provisions of s 110(2) of, and para 1 of Sch 8 to, the 1960 Act as if made under ss 97(3), 98 thereof. Since the repeal of those provisions of the 1967 Act by the Road Traffic Regulation Act 1984, the regulations now continue in force (by virtue of the Interpretation Act 1978, s 17(2)(b), printed in the title Statutory Instruments (Pt 2), Vol 1 of this work) as if made under s 130(3) of the 1984 Act and under that subsection as extended by s 133 thereof.
Date made 13 October 1947.
Commencement 23 October 1947; see reg 1.
Amendment Printed as amended by SI 1954/943, SI 1964/489.
General These regulations, as construed in accordance with the Road Traffic Regulation Act 1984, s 144(1), Sch 10, para 2, vary Sch 6 to that Act (which now replaces the Road Traffic Act 1930, Sch 1), so that no speed limit is imposed in relation to certain vehicles used for naval, military or air force purposes. Sch 6 to the 1984 Act has also been amended by SI 1986/1175.

[223]

1 These Regulations shall come into force on the twenty-third day of October, 1947, and may be cited as "The Motor Vehicles (Variation of Speed Limit) Regulations, 1947".

[224]

2 The Motor Vehicles (Variation of Speed Limit) Provisional Regulations, 1940, dated April 1st, 1940, are hereby revoked.

[225]

[2A In these Regulations the expression "vehicle in the service of a visiting force" has the same meaning as it has in the Visiting Forces (Application of Law) Order, 1954.]

NOTES
Amendment Inserted by SI 1954/943.
Visiting Forces (Application of Law) Order 1954 SI 1954/635; revoked and replaced by SI 1999/1736, in the title Armed Forces.

[226]

3 The provisions of the First Schedule to the Act are hereby varied in manner following, that is to say, they shall have effect as though they imposed no speed limit in relation to:—

(a) motor vehicles of the types specified in the Schedule to these Regulations which are owned by [the Secretary of State for Defence] and used for naval, military or air force purposes or which are so used whilst being driven by persons for the time being subject to the orders of any member of the armed forces of the Crown [or which are vehicles in the service of a visiting force]; or
(b) motor vehicles used for salvage purposes, pursuant to Part IX of the Merchant Shipping Act, 1894.

NOTES
Amendment Words in first pair of square brackets substituted by SI 1964/489; words in second pair inserted by SI 1954/943.

First Schedule to the Act Ie the Road Traffic Act 1930, Sch 1 (as defined in the preamble (not printed) to the regulations). This is now to be construed as a reference to the Road Traffic Regulation Act 1984, Sch 6.
Merchant Shipping Act 1894, Pt IX Repealed; see now the Merchant Shipping Act 1995, Pt IX.

[227]

4 The Interpretation Act, 1889, shall apply to the interpretation of these Regulations as it applies to the interpretation of an Act of Parliament.

NOTES
Interpretation Act 1889 Repealed and replaced by the Interpretation Act 1978, printed in the title Statutory Instruments (Pt 2), Vol 1 of this work.

[228]

SCHEDULE

1 Motor vehicles constructed or adapted
- (a) for actual combative purposes, or, for naval, military or air force training in connection therewith, or
- (b) for the conveyance of personnel, or
- (c) for use with, or for the carriage or drawing of, guns or machine guns.

2 Mobile cranes constructed or adapted for the raising of aircraft.

3 Motor track laying vehicles constructed or adapted
- (a) for actual combative purposes, or
- (b) for use with, or for the carriage or drawing of guns, machine guns, ammunition, equipment or stores in connection therewith.

4 Fire tenders.

5 Ambulances.

[229]

TRANSFERRED UNDERTAKINGS (PENSIONS OF EMPLOYEES LOSING EMPLOYMENT) REGULATIONS 1948
SI 1948/1585

Authority Made by the Minister of Transport under the Transport Act 1947, s 98. That section was repealed by the Transport Act 1962, but these regulations were saved; see s 75 of, and para 17(1) of Pt IV of Sch 7 to, the 1962 Act.
Date made 7 July 1948.
Commencement 31 July 1948; however, the regulations have retroactive effect from 31 December 1947.
Summary These regulations provide for the continuation of pension schemes affecting persons who were officers or servants of railway and canal undertakings transferred to the British Transport Commission (now dissolved) under the Transport Act 1947, or officers and servants of the railway clearing house (as to which, see SI 1954/139), and for the preservation of the accrued pension rights of any such person who suffered loss of employment in consequence of any transfer under that Act. On 1 January 1963 the Commission was succeeded by new authorities and a holding company (now dissolved) under Pt I of the Transport Act 1962; see the Preliminary Note "Reorganisation of transport undertakings". As to the continued application of pension schemes see s 75 of, and para 12 of Pt IV of Sch 7 to, that Act.

For regulations relating to the payment of pensions in respect of persons formerly employed in connection with the Caledonian and Crinan Canals or Holyhead Harbour, see SI 1952/1159.

[230]

PENSION SCHEMES (EMPLOYEES IN NORTHERN IRELAND) REGULATIONS 1949
SI 1949/584

Authority As noted to SI 1948/1585.
Date made 28 March 1949.
Commencement 31 March 1949.
Summary These regulations enabled officers or servants of the British Transport Commission (now dissolved) who were participants in pension schemes to continue to be participants therein on becoming officers or servants of the Ulster Transport Authority. The British Transport Commission was succeeded in 1963 by new authorities and a holding company (now dissolved) under Pt I of the

Transport Act 1962; see the Preliminary Note "Reorganisation of transport undertakings". As to the continued application of pension schemes, see s 75 of, and para 12 of Pt IV of Sch 7 to, that Act.

[231]

TRANSFERRED UNDERTAKINGS (PENSIONS OF EMPLOYEES) (NO 1) REGULATIONS 1952
SI 1952/1159

Authority As noted to SI 1948/1585.
Date made 12 June 1952.
Commencement 26 June 1952; however, the regulations have retroactive effect from 1 April 1948.
Summary These regulations provide for the payment of pensions on civil service superannuation terms to or in respect of persons who on 1 April 1948 became employed as officers and servants by the British Transport Commission (now dissolved) and who were immediately before that date employed by the minister as successor to the Commissioners of the Caledonian Canal or the Board of Trade, in connection with the Caledonian and Crinan Canals or Holyhead Harbour. The British Transport Commission was succeeded in 1963 by new authorities and a holding company (now dissolved) under Pt I of the Transport Act 1962; see the Preliminary Note "Reorganisation of transport undertakings".

[232]

TRANSFERRED UNDERTAKINGS (PENSIONS OF EMPLOYEES) (NO 2) REGULATIONS 1952
SI 1952/1612

Authority As noted to SI 1948/1565.
Date made 1 September 1952.
Commencement 15 September 1952; however, the regulations have retroactive effect as from 1 January 1948.
Amendment Amended by SI 1957/438, SI 2006/680.
Summary These regulations (which superseded the Transferred Undertakings (Pensions of Employees) Regulations 1951, SI 1951/1952) provide for the preservation of the pension rights of employees of road haulage undertakings acquired by the British Transport Commission (now dissolved), and for those rights to continue during employment by the Commission. The Commission was succeeded in 1963 by new authorities and a holding company (now dissolved) under Pt I of the Transport Act 1962; see the Preliminary Note "Reorganisation of transport undertakings". As to the continued application of pension schemes, see s 75 of, and para 12 of Pt IV of Sch 7 to, that Act.

The Commission was required to dispose of its road haulage undertakings under the Transport Act 1953, s 1 et seq, and provision for pension rights of employees who were adversely affected is made under SI 1953/1445.

[233]

BRITISH TRANSPORT COMMISSION (PENSIONS OF EMPLOYEES) REGULATIONS 1953
SI 1953/1445

Authority Made by the Minister of Transport under the Transport Act 1953, s 27. That section was repealed by the Transport Act 1962, but these regulations were saved; see s 75 of, and para 17(1) of Pt IV of Sch 7 to, the 1962 Act.
Date made 29 September 1953.
Commencement 13 October 1953; however the regulations have retroactive effect from 6 May 1953.
Amendment Amended by SI 2006/680.
Summary These regulations provide for the preservation of the pension rights of employees of the British Transport Commission (now dissolved; see the Preliminary Note "Reorganisation of transport undertakings") who ceased to be in the employment of the Commission, or suffered a change in the nature or terms of their employment in consequence of the denationalisation of road haulage, or the modifications of the functions of the Commission or the reorganisation of the railways, provided for by the Transport Act 1953.

[234]

RAILWAY CLEARING HOUSE SCHEME ORDER 1954
SI 1954/139

Authority Made by the Minister of Transport and Civil Aviation under the Transport Act 1947, s 38. That section was repealed as from 1 January 1963, but not so as to affect this order, by the Transport Act 1962, s 95, Sch 12, Pt II (repealed) and this saving is continued by the Statute Law (Repeals) Act 1974, Schedule, Pt VI, note.
Date made 4 February 1954.
Commencement 4 February 1954 (but the scheme embodied in the order took effect on 18 February 1954).
Amendment Amended by SI 2006/680.

Summary This order brought into effect as from 18 February 1954 the Railway Clearing House Scheme 1954 (set out in the Schedule to the order), which was prepared by the British Transport Commission (now dissolved) and submitted to the minister under the Transport Act 1947, s 38 (as to which, see the note "Authority" above). The scheme provided for the transfer, as from 24 May 1954, of the property, rights, powers and liabilities of the Railway Clearing House to the British Transport Commission (except in relation to the Railway Clearing System Superannuation Fund), and for the dissolution of the Clearing House. The rights and powers of the Clearing House in the management of the Railway Clearing Systems Superannuation Fund were transferred to the Railway Clearing System Superannuation Council, which was constituted by the scheme. The following were repealed as from 24 May 1954: the Railway Clearing System Superannuation Fund Association Act 1873 (c lxxxviii), and certain rules (not included in this work) made thereunder; the Railway Clearing System Superannuation Fund Incorporation Act 1897 (c cxx); the Railway Clearing House Extension Act 1874 (c xvi); the Railway Clearing Committee Incorporation Act 1897 (c cxvi); the Railways Act 1921, s 14(1)–(3); and the Railway Clearing House Scheme 1922, SR & O 1922/1443.

The dissolution of the Railway Clearing House took place on 8 April 1955 (i e when the minister's certificate to that effect was published in the *London Gazette* in accordance with clause 8 of the scheme).

[235]

BRITISH TRANSPORT COMMISSION (MALE WAGES GRADES PENSIONS) REGULATIONS 1954
SI 1954/898

Authority Made by the Minister of Transport and Civil Aviation under the Transport Act 1947, s 98. That section was repealed by the Transport Act 1962, but these regulations were saved; see s 75 of, and para 17(1) of Pt IV of Sch 7 to, the 1962 Act.

Date made 1 July 1954.

Commencement 8 July 1954 (but the pension scheme was established on 1 October 1954; see the note "Summary" below).

Amendment and modification etc Rules of the scheme set out in these regulations amended by SI 1957/1455, SI 1960/784, SI 1968/1249, SI 1971/189, SI 1972/51, SI 1974/2045.

The pension scheme established by these regulations was modified, and partly superseded, by the scheme contained in SI 1966/1164; the said SI 1966/1164 has been revoked by SI 2000/3386 and the scheme contained therein has ceased to have effect.

The application of the pension scheme established by these regulations has also been restricted by SI 1966/1556 (which provided for the exclusion from the scheme of members opting to join the London Transport Pension Fund, introduced by the London Transport Board on 1 January 1967), SI 1967/929, SI 1968/1217, SI 1970/1298, SI 1970/1299, SI 1971/116, SI 1971/117, SI 1971/629, SI 1971/1780. See also SI 1966/1465, SI 1974/2001.

Summary These regulations provided for the establishment by the British Transport Commission (now dissolved) on 1 October 1954 of a pension scheme, to be known as the British Transport Commission (Male Wages Grades) Pension Scheme, for male employees in whole time employment with the Commission in a wages grade other than employment:

(a) of a casual or seasonal nature;
(b) for a specific purpose for a limited period; or
(c) in the Commission's existing road haulage undertaking as defined in the Transport Act 1953, s 1 (now repealed).

The Commission was succeeded in 1963 by new authorities and a holding company under the Transport Act 1962, Pt I; see the Preliminary Note "Reorganisation of transport undertakings". As to the continued application of pension schemes, see s 75 of, and para 12 of Pt IV of Sch 7 to, that Act.

The scheme is to be in accordance with the detailed rules set out in the regulations, as amended and modified, and is to be administered as provided for in those rules.

[236]

BRITISH TRANSPORT COMMISSION (AMENDMENT OF PENSION SCHEMES) REGULATIONS 1954
SI 1954/1428

Authority As noted to SI 1954/898.

Date made 27 October 1954.

Commencement 4 November 1954.

Summary These regulations provide for the preservation of the accrued pension rights of certain members of railway salaried staff pension schemes who were employed by the British Transport Commission (now dissolved) (or by the Ulster Transport Authority immediately after ceasing to be employed by the Commission) and who transferred to the employment of the British European Airways Corporation or to railway employment in a country (other than a foreign country as defined in the British Nationality Act 1948, s 32(1) (repealed)) outside the United Kingdom. The pension rights accrued up to the date of transfer are normally payable when the employee retires from the employment to which he transfers, or when an event occurs which would have given rise to benefit under the rules of his pension scheme. If an employee who transfers to railway employment retires (otherwise than on the grounds of ill health) at an earlier age than that at which he could have retired on pension if he had not transferred, the retirement benefits will be reduced by the percentage prescribed by the regulations.

[237]

NATIONAL INSURANCE (MODIFICATION OF THE LONDON TRANSPORT AND RAILWAY PENSION SCHEMES) REGULATIONS 1956

SI 1956/732

Authority Made by the Minister of Transport and Civil Aviation under the National Insurance Act 1946, s 69(4) (repealed). Now have effect, by virtue of the National Insurance Act 1965, s 117(1), as if made under s 110 of that Act; by virtue of SI 1974/2057, in the title Social Security (Pt 1), the said s 110 continues in force, despite its repeal by the Social Security Act 1973, for the purpose of facilitating the winding up of the system of insurance under the 1965 Act.
Date made 15 May 1956.
Commencement 1 September 1956.
Amendment Amended by SI 1971/189.
Summary These regulations modified the London Transport and railway salaried staff superannuation schemes to take account of the fact that members of those schemes were insured persons under the National Insurance Acts (now repealed but continued in force for the purpose of the winding up of the old system of national insurance; see the Social Security (Consequential Provisions) Act 1975). Provision was made, subject to certain conditions and exceptions, for reduction of the future contributions payable under the schemes by the members and their employers and for corresponding reduction of the pensions payable under the schemes. These reductions were compulsory in respect of existing and future members of railways schemes who entered railway service after 31 December 1947 or became employed by the Railway Clearing House after 1 January 1948 and (with certain exceptions) in respect of persons who became members of the London Transport scheme on or after 29 July 1947 or become members in the future. Other members could elect to have the reductions applied. In certain cases, members could elect for further reduction of future contributions, with correspondingly greater reduction of pension within the maximum.

For further modifications under the National Insurance Act 1965, s 110 of the schemes affected by these regulations (and certain other schemes), see SI 1961/559.

[238]

NATIONAL INSURANCE (MODIFICATION OF TRANSPORT UNDERTAKING SUPERANNUATION FUNDS) REGULATIONS 1961

SI 1961/559

Authority Made by the Minister of Transport under the National Insurance Act 1946, s 69(4) (repealed), as extended by the National Insurance Act 1959, s 15 (repealed). Now have effect, by virtue of the National Insurance Act 1965, s 117(1), as if made under s 110 of that Act; by virtue of SI 1974/2057, in the title Social Security (Pt 1), the said s 110 continues in force, despite its repeal by the Social Security Act 1973, for the purpose of facilitating the winding up of the system of insurance under the 1965 Act.
Date made 23 March 1961.
Commencement 30 March 1961.
Amendment Amended by SI 1966/1145, SI 1971/189.
Summary By virtue of the National Insurance Act 1965, s 56(1) (repealed, but continued in force for the purpose of the winding up of the old system of national insurance; see the Social Security (Consequential Provisions) Act 1975), an employment could not be contracted out of the graduated national insurance pension scheme unless those employed in it qualified for "equivalent pension benefits", and s 57(1) of that Act laid down the conditions which must be satisfied if an occupational pension scheme was to be treated as providing equivalent pension benefits. These regulations accordingly modified the rules of the London Transport, British Road Services and railway salaried staff superannuation schemes, and of certain superannuation schemes of the Hay's Wharf Companies and Regent's Canal and Dock Company, to meet those requirements The regulations also provided for the modification of benefits payable to, and contributions payable by and in respect of, members of these schemes who were or had been in "participating employment" (i e employment in which they were required to pay graduated contributions under the 1965 Act or would be required to pay such contributions if their remuneration exceeded the amount mentioned in s 4(1) of that Act).

For other modifications under the National Insurance Act 1965, s 110 of certain of the schemes affected by these regulations, see SI 1956/732.

[239]

BRITISH TRANSPORT COMMISSION GROUP PENSION FUNDS REGULATIONS 1962

SI 1962/898

Authority Made by the Minister of Transport under the Transport Act 1947, s 98. That section has been repealed by the Transport Act 1962, but without prejudice to the continued operation of these regulations; see s 75 of, and para 17(1) of Pt IV of Sch 7 to, that Act.
Date made 30 April 1962.
Commencement 11 May 1962; however, the regulations have retroactive effect from earlier dates (see below).

Summary These regulations were made for the purpose of providing pensions to or in respect of certain employees of the British Transport Commission (now dissolved and succeeded by new bodies; see the Preliminary Note "Reorganisation of transport undertakings"), being members of specified pension funds, namely:

(a) the British Road Services (Salaried Staff) Group Superannuation Fund, established by a deed made on 1 April 1957;

(b) the British Road Services (Male Wages Grades) Group Pension Fund, established by a deed made on 1 July 1957;

(c) the Scottish Omnibuses Group Pension Fund, established by an agreement and deed of trust made on 16 January 1946; and

(d) the Tilling Group Pension Fund established by a deed made on 3 December 1952.

Provision is made for the Commission to make appropriate contributions to these funds and to comply generally with the obligations imposed on the Commission by the provisions of the trust deeds and rules of the funds. The regulations have effect in relation to the four funds concerned from 1 April 1957, 1 July 1952, 1 June 1952 and 24 September 1951 respectively.

[240]

TRANSPORT ACT 1962 (COMMENCEMENT NO 1) ORDER 1962 SI 1962/1788

Authority Made by the Minister of Transport under the Transport Act 1962, s 96.
Date made 14 August 1962.
Summary This order brought the Transport Act 1962 into force on 1 September 1962, except as is otherwise expressly provided in the Act and with the exception of s 65(4)–(6) and s 71 (repealed). The order brought s 65(4)–(6) into force on the vesting date, ie on 1 January 1963 (see SI 1962/2634). S 71 was brought into force on 1 January 1965 by SI 1964/2025 (now spent).

[241]

BRITISH TRANSPORT REORGANISATION (PENSIONS OF EMPLOYEES) (NO 1) ORDER 1962
SI 1962/2714

Authority Made by the Minister of Transport under the Transport Act 1962, ss 74, 75, Sch 7, Pt IV, para 13. S 74 has been repealed by the Railways Act 1993, s 134(2), (3) in so far as relating to the British Railways Board and its subsidiaries, but without prejudice to the continuing validity of any orders made under that section.
Date made 12 December 1962.
Commencement 28 December 1962; however, the order has effect from 1 September 1962.
Summary This order applies in relation to persons who became employees of the British Railways Board, the London Transport Board (subsequently London Regional Transport, now dissolved and replaced by Transport for London), the British Transport Docks Board (now Associated British Ports), the British Waterways Board, the Transport Holding Company (now dissolved), or British Transport Hotels Limited before 1 January 1963 (ie the vesting date for the purposes of the Transport Act 1962; see SI 1962/2634). It enables such persons to be eligible to join the pension schemes which they would have been entitled to join had they continued in, or entered, comparable employment with the British Transport Commission (which was succeeded, as from 1 January 1963, by the said Board and Holding Company). Pensionable employees of the Commission who became members of the Boards or of the Holding Company or directors of the Hotel Company are entitled to count their service as members or directors for pension purposes under their pension schemes.

As to the winding down and abolition of the British Railways Board, see the Transport Act 2000 and the Preliminary Note "Privatisation of the railway system" (under the main head "Reorganisation of transport undertakings"). As to the transition from London Regional Transport to Transport for London and the dissolution of LRT, see the Greater London Authority Act 1999 and the Preliminary Note "Transport for London" (under the main head "London").

[242]

BRITISH TRANSPORT REORGANISATION (PENSIONS OF EMPLOYEES) (NO 2) ORDER 1962
SI 1962/2715

Authority Made by the Minister of Transport under the Transport Act 1962, Sch 7, Pt IV, para 16.
Date made 13 December 1962.
Commencement 20 December 1962.
Summary This order directed the British Transport Commission (now dissolved) to prepare a scheme under the Transport Act 1962, Sch 7, Pt IV, para 15 to distribute, among the British Railways Board, the London Transport Board (subsequently London Regional Transport, now dissolved and replaced by Transport for London), the British Transport Docks Board (now Associated British Ports), the British Waterways Board and the Transport Holding Company (now dissolved), responsibility for making payments on and after 1 January 1963 (ie the vesting date, fixed by SI 1962/2634, on which the property, rights and liabilities of the Commission were transferred to and vested in those bodies), under specified pension arrangements under which the Commission had been making payments to certain persons or classes of persons as of grace.

As to the winding down and abolition of the British Railways Board, see the Transport Act 2000 and the Preliminary Note "Privatisation of the railway system" (under the main head "Reorganisation of transport undertakings"). As to the transition from London Regional Transport to Transport for London and the dissolution of LRT, see the Greater London Authority Act 1999 and the Preliminary Note "Transport for London" (under the main head "London").

[243]

BRITISH TRANSPORT REORGANISATION (PENSIONS OF EMPLOYEES) (NO 3) ORDER 1962
SI 1962/2758

Authority Made by the Minister of Transport under the Transport Act 1962, ss 74, 75, Sch 7, Pt IV, para 14(1), (2)(b). S 74 has been repealed by the Railways Act 1993, s 134(2), (3) in so far as relating to the British Railways Board and its subsidiaries, but without prejudice to the continuing validity of any orders made under that section.
Date made 18 December 1962.
Commencement 31 December 1962.
Amendment Amended by SI 1969/1824, SI 1971/1128.
Modification Modified by SI 1968/2011.
Summary This order provided for the transfer of the rights, liabilities and functions of the British Transport Commission (now dissolved) relating to pensions or pension schemes, and of any securities or other property held by the Commission on trust for a pension scheme, to the British Railways Board, the London Transport Board (subsequently London Regional Transport, now dissolved and replaced by Transport for London), the British Transport Docks Board (now Associated British Ports), the British Waterways Board and the Transport Holding Company (now dissolved) on 1 January 1963 (ie the vesting date, fixed by SI 1962/2634, on which the other property, rights and liabilities of the Commission were transferred to and vested in those bodies). The order modified existing contributory pension schemes so as to give employees entering the service of any of the Boards, the Holding Company and their subsidiaries on and after the vesting date eligibility to join those schemes.

As to the winding down and abolition of the British Railways Board, see the Transport Act 2000 and the Preliminary Note "Privatisation of the railway system" (under the main head "Reorganisation of transport undertakings"). As to the transition from London Regional Transport to Transport for London and the dissolution of LRT, see the Greater London Authority Act 1999 and the Preliminary Note "Transport for London" (under the main head "London").

[244]

BRITISH TRANSPORT REORGANISATION (PENSIONS OF EMPLOYEES) (NO 4) ORDER 1962
SI 1962/2793

Authority Made by the Minister of Transport under the Transport Act 1962, ss 74, 75, Sch 7, Pt IV, para 14(2)(a). S 74 has been repealed by the Railways Act 1993, s 134(2), (3) in so far as relating to the British Railways Board and its subsidiaries, but without prejudice to the continuing validity of any orders made under that section.
Date made 19 December 1962.
Commencement 1 January 1963; however, the order has effect from 1 September 1962.
Amendment Amended by SI 2006/680.
Summary This order provides for the preservation of the pension rights of persons who, in consequence of the reorganisation effected by the Transport Act 1962, left the employment of the British Transport Commission (now dissolved) at any time after the passing of the Act (1 August 1962) and did not become employees of the British Railways Board, the London Transport Board (subsequently London Regional Transport, now dissolved and replaced by Transport for London), the British Transport Docks Board (now Associated British Ports), the British Waterways Board, the Transport Holding Company (now dissolved), or one of their subsidiaries, or who, having become employees of any of these bodies, suffered diminution of emoluments or a change in the nature of terms of their employment in consequence of the reorganisation effected by the Act.

As to the winding down and abolition of the British Railways Board, see the Transport Act 2000 and the Preliminary Note "Privatisation of the railway system" (under the main head "Reorganisation of transport undertakings"). As to the transition from London Regional Transport to Transport for London and the dissolution of LRT, see the Greater London Authority Act 1999 and the Preliminary Note "Transport for London" (under the main head "London").

[245]

BRITISH TRANSPORT REORGANISATION (COMPENSATION TO EMPLOYEES) REGULATIONS 1962
SI 1962/2834

Authority Made by the Minister of Transport under the Transport Act 1962, s 81.
Date made 20 December 1962.
Commencement 1 January 1963; however, the regulations have effect from 1 September 1962.
Amendment Amended by SI 2006/1016.

Summary These regulations provide for the payment by the British Railways Board, the London Transport Board (subsequently London Regional Transport, now dissolved and replaced by Transport for London), the British Transport Docks Board (now Associated British Ports), the British Waterways Board and the Transport Holding Company (now dissolved) of compensation to persons who were, at the passing of the Transport Act 1962 on 1 August 1962, officers or servants of the British Transport Commission (now dissolved) and who, in consequence of the reorganisation effected by that Act, suffered loss of employment or loss or diminution of emoluments or pension rights or whose position was worsened.

The regulations prescribe the conditions which must be satisfied before entitlement to compensation is established, the procedure to be followed when making and dealing with claims, and the manner in which compensation is to be assessed. Provision is also made as to appeals by claimants who are aggrieved by a decision or the failure of the appropriate body to notify their decisions. Appeals originally lay to a referee or boards of referees appointed by the Minister of Labour, but by the Employment Protection (Consolidation) Act 1978, s 130, Sch 10 (repealed), this jurisdiction was transferred to an employment tribunal (formerly known as an industrial tribunal) established under s 128 of that Act (repealed); see now the Employment Tribunals Act 1996, s 1.

As to the winding down and abolition of the British Railways Board, see the Transport Act 2000 and the Preliminary Note "Privatisation of the railway system" (under the main head "Reorganisation of transport undertakings"). As to the transition from London Regional Transport to Transport for London and the dissolution of LRT, see the Greater London Authority Act 1999 and the Preliminary Note "Transport for London" (under the main head "London").

Set-off of redundancy payments By virtue of SI 1965/1988, in the title Employment, the amount of the redundancy payment to be paid to an employee is to be set off against the compensation payable to him under these regulations.

[246]

PIPE-LINES (NOTICES) REGULATIONS 1963
SI 1963/151

Authority Made by the Minister of Power under the Pipe-lines Act 1962, ss 13(3), 53, Sch 2, paras 3, 7, 10.

Date made 24 January 1963.

Commencement 6 February 1963.

Summary These regulations provide that the forms set out in the Schedule thereto or forms substantially to the like effect are the forms to be used in the cases to which they are applicable for the purposes of the Pipe-lines Act 1962, s 13(3), Sch 2. The list of forms is as follows:

1 Form of Advertisement of the making of an Application for a Compulsory Purchase Order
2 Form of Notice to Owners, Lessees and Occupiers of the making of an Application for a Compulsory Purchase Order
3 Form of Notice of the making of a Compulsory Purchase Order
4 Form of Advertisement of the making of an Application for a Compulsory Rights Order
5 Form of Notice to Owners, Lessees and Occupiers of the making of an Application for a Compulsory Rights Order
6 Form of Notice of the making of a Compulsory Rights Order
7 Form of Notice of Proposal to make an Order varying a Compulsory Rights Order.

[247]

BRITISH TRANSPORT COMMISSION (TRANSFER OF FUNCTIONS) (APPOINTMENTS AND NOMINATIONS) ORDER 1963
SI 1963/2023

Authority Made by the Minister of Transport under the Transport Act 1962, s 32(5).

Date made 9 December 1963.

Commencement 10 December 1963.

Summary The Transport Act 1962, s 32 provides for the distribution among the Boards set up under that Act of those statutory functions formerly exercised by the British Transport Commission. S 32(5) provides that, if the statutory provision concerned authorises the Commission to appoint, nominate, or concur in or approve the appointment or nomination of, a member of some body or the holder of some other office, the functions of the Commission under the statutory provision are to be transferred to such Board as the minister (now the Secretary of State) may by order direct. This order provides for the distribution among the British Railways Board, the British Transport Docks Board (now Associated British Ports) and the British Waterways Board of such functions under a number of local enactments and orders. As to the winding down and abolition of the British Railways Board, see the Transport Act 2000 and the Preliminary Note "Privatisation of the railway system" (under the main head "Reorganisation of transport undertakings").

[248]

VEHICLES (CONDITIONS OF USE ON FOOTPATHS) REGULATIONS 1963

SI 1963/2126

Authority Made by the Minister of Transport and the Minister of Power under the Public Health Act 1961, s 49 (repealed). Now have effect (by virtue of the Interpretation Act 1978, s 17(2)(b), printed in the title Statutory Instruments (Pt 2), Vol 1 of this work) as if made under the Highways Act 1980, s 300.

Date made 19 December 1963.

Commencement 20 January 1964; see reg 1.

Amendment Printed as amended by SI 1966/864.

General The Highways Act 1980, s 300 (which replaced the Public Health Act 1961, s 49) confers on local authorities rights to use appliances or vehicles on footpaths, footways, bridleways or restricted byways for the cleansing, maintenance or improvement thereof, for preventing or removing obstructions to them or otherwise preventing or abating nuisances or other interferences with them, or for maintaining or altering structures or other works situated therein. These regulations prescribe the conditions under which such rights may be exercised.

[249]

1 Section 49 of the Public Health Act 1961 shall come into force on the 20th January 1964, and these Regulations shall come into operation on that date and may be cited as the Vehicles (Conditions of Use on Footpaths) Regulations 1963.

NOTES

Public Health Act 1961, s 49 Repealed by the Highways Act 1980, s 343(3), Sch 25 and replaced by s 300 of that Act; s 49 of the 1961 Act had provided for regulations to specify the date of its coming into force.

[250]

2 The Interpretation Act 1889 shall apply for the interpretation of these Regulations as it applies for the interpretation of an Act of Parliament.

NOTES

Interpretation Act 1889 Repealed and replaced by the Interpretation Act 1978, printed in the title Statutory Instruments (Pt 2), Vol 1 of this work.

[251]

3 The conditions under which the rights conferred by section 49 of the Public Health Act 1961 on authorities as therein specified may be exercised shall be those contained in the following Regulations.

NOTES

Public Health Act 1961, s 49 See the notes to reg 1.

[252]

[4 (1) Subject to the provisions of the next succeeding paragraph, an authority specified in the said section 49 shall not use a restricted appliance or vehicle on any footpath, footway or bridleway under which there is a gas pipe maintainable by an Area Gas Board unless prior to such use the authority have consulted with that Board and are satisfied having regard to any representations made to them by the Board that the use of the restricted appliance or vehicle as aforesaid is not likely to cause any damage to any such gas pipe.

(2) Nothing in the foregoing paragraph shall apply so as to render unlawful the use by an authority specified in the said section 49 of any restricted appliance or vehicle on a footpath, footway or bridleway if a direction has been given by the Minister of Power under these Regulations before the 1st August 1966 to that authority and the weight of the restricted appliance or vehicle, whether laden or not, does not exceed three tons.

(3) In this Regulation "restricted appliance or vehicle" means any appliance or vehicle, whether mechanically operated or propelled or not and whether laden or not, to which any one or more of the following sub-paragraphs applies, that is to say—

- (a) the weight of the appliance or vehicle exceeds one ton;
- (b) the weight transmitted to any strip of the surface of the ground on which the appliance or vehicle rests contained between any two parallel lines drawn two feet apart on that surface at right angles to the longitudinal axis of the appliance or vehicle exceeds twelve hundredweight and a half;
- (c) the weight transmitted to the surface of the ground by any one wheel of the appliance or vehicle where no other wheel is in the same line

transversely in the case of a road roller exceeds either twelve hundredweight and a half, or half a hundredweight per inch width of wheel in contact with such surface, whichever is the less, or in any other case exceeds eight hundredweight.

For the purposes of sub-paragraph (c) of this paragraph any two wheels of the appliance or vehicle shall be regarded as one wheel if the distance between the centres of the areas of contact between such wheels and such surface is less than eighteen inches.]

NOTES

Amendment Substituted by SI 1966/864.

S 49 Ie the Public Health Act 1961, s 49, as to which, see the notes to reg 1.

Area Gas Board Area gas boards were dissolved and their rights and obligations etc were vested in the British Gas Corporation by the Gas Act 1972, s 1(1) (repealed) and SI 1972/1440 (lapsed). The Corporation's privilege with respect to the supply of gas through pipes under the 1972 Act has been abolished by the Gas Act 1986, s 3 (repealed by the Utilities Act 2000, s 108, Sch 8). Provision is made by ss 7, 7A of the 1986 Act for the authorisation of gas transporters to convey gas through pipes and gas suppliers to supply to premises gas which has been conveyed to those premises. The property, rights and liabilities of the British Gas Corporation were transferred on 24 August 1986 to British Gas plc by s 49 of the 1986 Act and SI 1986/1317 and SI 1986/1318, in the title Energy, and the Corporation itself was dissolved on 28 February 1990 by s 57 of the 1986 Act (repealed by the Statute Law (Repeals) Act 2004, s 1(1), Sch 1, Pt 5, Group 7) and SI 1990/147 (lapsed).

Minister of Power The powers formerly exercised by the Minister of Power are now generally exercised by the Secretary of State for Energy and Climate Control; see the title Constitutional Law (Pt 2).

[253]

5 No appliance or vehicle when used on any footpath, footway or bridleway shall travel thereon at a speed exceeding five miles per hour.

[254]

6 Where a person other than an authority specified in the said section 49 is responsible for the maintenance of either the surface of, or of any work supporting, a footpath, footway or bridleway, no such authority shall use any appliance or vehicle on that footpath, footway or bridleway without the consent of that person.

NOTES

S 49 Ie the Public Health Act 1961, s 49, as to which, see the notes to reg 1.

[255]

7 *(Revoked by SI 1966/864.)*

BRITISH TRANSPORT REORGANISATION (COMMENCING CAPITAL DEBTS) ORDER 1964

SI 1964/448

Authority Made by the Minister of Transport, with the approval of the Treasury, under the Transport Act 1962, s 39(4), (5) and under s 40(2), (5) (repealed) of that Act.

Date made 20 March 1964.

Commencement 26 March 1964.

Summary This order prescribed the amounts of the commencing capital debts for the purposes of the Transport Act 1962 of the British Railways Board (£1,562,061,697 17s 11d); the London Transport Board (£161,830,904); the British Transport Docks Board (£84,116,192); the British Waterways Board (£19,252,298); and the Transport Holding Company (now dissolved) (£122,503,436). The commencing capital debt of the Transport Holding Company (which was reduced by SI 1972/1024 to £4,648,946 and by SI 1973/290 to £4,647,805) has been extinguished by SI 1973/366.

As to the winding down and abolition of the British Railways Board, see the Transport Act 2000 and the Preliminary Note "Privatisation of the railway system" (under the main head "Reorganisation of transport undertakings").

[256]

BRITISH TRANSPORT REORGANISATION (PENSIONS OF EMPLOYEES) (NO 1) ORDER 1964

SI 1964/1329

Authority Made by the Minister of Transport under the Transport Act 1962, s 74. S 74 has been repealed by the Railways Act 1993, s 134(2), (3) in so far as relating to the British Railways Board and its subsidiaries, but without prejudice to the continuing validity of any orders made under that section.

Date made 21 August 1964.
Commencement 31 August 1964. However, the order has retroactive effect from 1 January 1963 (ie the vesting date; see SI 1962/2634).
Amendment Amended by SI 1969/1824.
Modification Modified by SI 1968/2011, SI 1969/1824, SI 1994/2005 (in the case of SI 1994/2005 so as to apply the provisions of the order, so far as applicable, in relation to the Railways Pension Scheme established by SI 1994/1433 as if that scheme were an established scheme as defined in SI 1969/1824).
Application of order Applied by SI 1970/1298, SI 1970/1299, SI 1971/116, SI 1971/117, SI 1971/629, SI 1971/1780. By the British Railways (No 2) Act 1986, s 48(4), this order is applied in relation to "the new scheme" within the meaning of s 48(1) of that Act (ie the BR Pension Scheme constituted by the trust deed dated 25 November 1985 made by the British Railways Board and the British Rail Pension Trustee Company Limited).
Summary This order provides for staff of the nationalised transport bodies specified in the order (ie the British Railways Board, the London Transport Board (subsequently London Regional Transport, now dissolved and replaced by Transport for London), the British Transport Docks Board (now Associated British Ports), the British Waterways Board, the Transport Holding Company (now dissolved), and their subsidiaries), who move from one body to another within the nationalised transport industry, to continue in membership of their pension schemes. As to the winding down and abolition of the British Railways Board, see the Transport Act 2000 and the Preliminary Note "Privatisation of the railway system" (under the main head "Reorganisation of transport undertakings"). As to the transition from London Regional Transport to Transport for London and the dissolution of LRT, see the Greater London Authority Act 1999 and the Preliminary Note "Transport for London" (under the main head "London").

A person who leaves a nationalised transport body and immediately enters the employment of another such body is entitled to remain in membership of his pension scheme unless he gives notice to the contrary within three months of the date of transfer, and provided the terms of the scheme (other than those requiring membership to cease on transfer) permit. Where there is an intervening period, not exceeding 12 months, between a person's leaving a nationalised transport body and his re-entering the employment of that body or entering the employment of another such body, the trustees of, or the persons administering, the appropriate pension scheme are empowered to re-admit that person to membership on such terms and conditions as they may prescribe. These provisions apply to all persons who transfer after 1 January 1963 (ie the vesting date, fixed by SI 1962/2634, on which all the property, rights and liabilities of the British Transport Commission were vested in the previously mentioned Boards and Holding Company), and also to those persons who left the British Transport Commission before that date but who, before the expiry of a period of 12 months, entered the employment of a nationalised transport body. Members of non-contributory pension schemes are included.

[257]

BRITISH TRANSPORT (CLOSED RAILWAY PENSION SCHEME) ORDER 1965
SI 1965/43

Authority Made by the Minister of Transport under the Transport Act 1962, s 74. S 74 has been repealed by the Railways Act 1993, s 134(2), (3) in so far as relating to the British Railways Board and its subsidiaries, but without prejudice to the continuing validity of any orders made under that section.
Date made 15 January 1965.
Commencement 1 February 1965.
Summary This order provided for the functions of the managing committee of the Lancashire and Yorkshire Railway Pension Fund to be transferred to and exercised by the British Railways Board; for existing provisions of the scheme relating to the election or appointment of members of the managing committee to cease to have effect; and for the audit of the funds of the scheme to be carried out by auditors appointed by the Board. Provision was also made for the disposal of surplus funds on the winding up of the scheme. As to the winding down and abolition of the British Railways Board, see the Transport Act 2000 and the Preliminary Note "Privatisation of the railway system" (under the main head "Reorganisation of transport undertakings").
Further order SI 1968/1021, which was made under the same power as SI 1965/43 and came into force on 11 July 1968, made similar provision in relation to the Great Eastern Railway New Pension Fund Scheme, the Great Eastern Railway New Pension Supplemental Fund Scheme and the London Brighton and South Coast Railway Pension Fund.

[258]

BRITISH TRANSPORT (PENSIONS OF EMPLOYEES TRANSFERRED TO HARBOUR AUTHORITIES) ORDER 1966
SI 1966/1465

Authority Made by the Minister of Transport under the Transport Act 1962, s 74. S 74 has been repealed by the Railways Act 1993, s 134(2), (3) in so far as relating to the British Railways Board and its subsidiaries, but without prejudice to the continuing validity of any orders made under that section.
Date made 18 November 1966.
Commencement 5 December 1966.

Summary This order provides for the apportionment of and transfer of assets from funded pension schemes of the nationalised bodies specified in the order (i e the British Railways Board, the London Transport Board (subsequently London Regional Transport, now dissolved and replaced by Transport for London), the British Transport Docks Board (now Associated British Ports), the British Waterways Board, the Transport Holding Company (now dissolved), and their subsidiaries; and for the payment of transfer values from the British Transport Commission (Male Wages Grades) Pension Scheme (established by SI 1954/898) and the London Transport (Male Wages Grades) Pension Scheme (established by SI 1966/1164 (revoked by SI 2000/3386, which wound up the pension scheme thereunder)) in cases where a participant in one of these schemes is transferred to a harbour authority outside the nationalised transport industry by virtue of a harbour revision order or a harbour reorganisation scheme under the Harbours Act 1964 (see ss 14(1), 18(1) of that Act), or a local Act having the same effect, and becomes eligible to participate in a pension scheme established by that harbour authority.

The order also provides for ascertaining the portion of any transferred assets or payment which is to be regarded as the employer's contribution for the purposes of the harbour authority's pension scheme, for excluding from any other benefits under the terms of the nationalised transport pension scheme a participant on whose behalf such a transfer or payment has been made, and for determining questions arising in connection with such transfers or payments to a harbour authority's pension scheme.

As to the winding down and abolition of the British Railways Board, see the Transport Act 2000 and the Preliminary Note "Privatisation of the railway system" (under the main head "Reorganisation of transport undertakings"). As to the transition from London Regional Transport to Transport for London and the dissolution of LRT, see the Greater London Authority Act 1999 and the Preliminary Note "Transport for London" (under the main head "London").

[259]

BRITISH RAILWAYS (ALTERATION OF PENSION SCHEMES) ORDER 1967
SI 1967/929

Authority Made by the Minister of Transport under the Transport Act 1962, s 74. S 74 has been repealed by the Railways Act 1993, s 134(2), (3) in so far as relating to the British Railways Board and its subsidiaries, but without prejudice to the continuing validity of any orders made under that section.
Date made 20 June 1967.
Commencement 13 August 1967.
Summary This order provides for termination of membership of, and rights in, the British Transport Commission (Male Wages Grades) Pension Scheme (established by SI 1954/898), and certain other pension and insurance schemes, in the case of members in the service of the British Railways Board who joined the British Railways (Wages Grades) Pension Fund (established by the Board, with the consent of the Minister of Transport, under the terms of a Trust Deed executed by the Board on 5 May 1967). Provision is also made for relieving new entrants to the service of the Board and certain other persons of any obligation to enter the British Transport Commission (Male Wages Grades) Pension Scheme; that scheme is modified accordingly. The order provides, in addition, for the ascertainment of transfer values and for certain other consequential matters.

As to the winding down and abolition of the British Railways Board, see the Transport Act 2000 and the Preliminary Note "Privatisation of the railway system" (under the main head "Reorganisation of transport undertakings").

[260]

CARRIAGE OF GOODS BY ROAD (PARTIES TO CONVENTION) ORDER 1967
SI 1967/1683

Authority Made under the Carriage of Goods by Road Act 1965, s 2(1).
Date made 13 November 1967.
Commencement 13 November 1967; i e date when made (but see the dates in the third column of the Schedule).
Amendment Printed as amended by SI 1980/697.
General See the Preliminary Note "International carriage by road" (under main head "Road traffic").

[261]

1 It is hereby certified that the High Contracting Parties to the said Convention and the territories in respect of which they are respectively parties are as specified in the Schedule to this Order.

NOTES
Convention Ie the Convention on the Contract for the International Carriage of Goods by Road (signed at Geneva on 19 May 1956), as stated in the preamble (not printed) to this order.

[262]

2 This Order may be cited as the Carriage of Goods by Road (Parties to Convention) Order 1967.

[263]

[SCHEDULE

The High Contracting Parties to the Convention, the territories in respect of which they are respectively parties and the dates of entry into force of the Convention in regard to such territories are as follows:—

High Contracting Parties to the Convention	*Territories in respect of which they are respectively parties*	*Dates of entry into force of the Convention*
The United Kingdom of Great Britain and Northern Ireland	The United Kingdom of Great Britain and Northern Ireland	19th October 1967
	Gibraltar	29th January 1969
	Bailiwick of Guernsey	1st June 1972
	Isle of Man	10th February 1970
The Republic of Austria	Austria	2nd July 1961
The Kingdom of Belgium	Belgium	17th December 1962
The People's Republic of Bulgaria	Bulgaria	18th January 1978
The Czechoslovak Republic	Czechoslovakia	3rd December 1974
The Kingdom of Denmark	Denmark	26th September 1965
The Republic of Finland	Finland	25th September 1973
The French Republic	Metropolitan France, Martinique, Guadeloupe, French Guiana, Réunion, Saint-Pierre and Miquelon, French Polynesia, New Caledonia	2nd July 1961
The Federal Republic of Germany	The Federal Republic of Germany and Berlin (West)	5th February 1962
The German Democratic Republic	German Democratic Republic	27th March 1974
The Hellenic Republic	Greece	22nd August 1977
The Hungarian People's Republic	Hungary	28th July 1970
The Italian Republic	Italy	2nd July 1961
The Grand Duchy of Luxembourg	Luxembourg	19th July 1964
The Kingdom of the Netherlands	The Netherlands	2nd July 1961
The Kingdom of Norway	Norway	29th September 1969
The Polish People's Republic	Poland	11th September 1962
The Portuguese Republic	Portugal	21st December 1969
The Socialist Republic of Romania	Romania	23rd April 1973
Spain	Spain	13th May 1974
The Kingdom of Sweden	Sweden	1st July 1969
The Swiss Confederation	Switzerland	28th May 1970
The Socialist Federal Republic of Yugoslavia	Yugoslavia	2nd July 1961]

NOTES

Amendment Substituted by SI 1980/697.

[264]

BRITISH TRANSPORT (TRANSFERS FROM BRITISH WATERWAYS BOARD PENSION SCHEMES) ORDER 1968
SI 1968/825

Authority Made by the Minister of Transport under the Transport Act 1962, s 74.
Date made 20 May 1968.
Commencement 12 June 1968; however, this order has retroactive effect from 1 April 1965.
Summary This order provides for the payment of transfer values in respect of employees of the British Waterways Board who are members of specified pension schemes, namely: Cheshire County Council Superannuation Fund—Divided; Grand Union Canal Company Superannuation Fund; Nottingham Corporation Superannuation Fund—Divided; Caledonian and Crinan

Canals—Employees' Scheme; and Lee Conservancy Board—Employees' Scheme (being schemes in relation to which rights, liabilities and functions are vested in the British Waterways Board), and who, within 12 months (or such longer period as may be allowed) of leaving the Board's employment, enter other employment and become members of approved pension schemes in connection with that employment. The order also states how the transfer values are to be calculated and prescribes the conditions to be satisfied by the pension schemes to which the payments are to be made.

[265]

BRITISH TRANSPORT DOCKS BOARD (ALTERATION OF PENSION SCHEMES) ORDER 1968
SI 1968/1217

Authority Made by the Minister of Transport under the Transport Act 1962, s 74.
Date made 29 July 1968.
Commencement 1 September 1968.
Summary This order provides for the termination of membership of, and rights in, the British Transport Commission (Male Wages Grades) Pension Scheme (established by SI 1954/898) and certain other pension schemes, in the case of members in the service of the British Transport Docks Board (now Associated British Ports) who join the British Transport Docks Board (Wages Grades) Pension Scheme (established by the Board, with the consent of the Minister of Transport, under the terms of an Interim Trust Deed executed by the Board on 25 June 1968). Provision is also made for relieving new entrants to the service of the Board and certain other persons of any obligation to enter the British Transport Commission (Male Wages Grades) Pension Scheme; that scheme is modified accordingly. The order provides, in addition, for the ascertainment of transfer values and for certain other consequential matters.

[266]

BRITISH TRANSPORT POLICE (TRANSFERS FROM PENSION SCHEMES) ORDER 1968
SI 1968/1498

Authority Made by the Minister of Transport under the Transport Act 1962, s 74. S 74 has been repealed by the Railways Act 1993, s 134(2), (3) in so far as relating to the British Railways Board and its subsidiaries, but without prejudice to the continuing validity of any orders made under that section.
Date made 19 September 1968.
Commencement 30 September 1968.
Summary This order provides for termination of membership of, and rights in, specified pension schemes, in the case of members who join the British Transport Police Force Superannuation Fund and British Transport Police Force Retirement Benefit Fund (established by the British Railways Board under the terms of a trust deed executed by the Board on 1 September 1968). The pension schemes concerned are: Great Western Railway Superannuation Fund; London and North Eastern Railway Superannuation Fund; London Midland and Scottish Railway Superannuation Fund; London Transport (Administrative & Supervisory) Staff Superannuation Fund; Railway Clearing System Superannuation Fund; Southern Railway Superannuation Fund. The order also provides for the ascertainment of transfer values and for certain other consequential matters.

[267]

TRANSPORT ACT 1968 (COMMENCEMENT NO 1) ORDER 1968
SI 1968/1822

Authority Made by the Minister of Transport and the Secretary of State under the Transport Act 1968, s 166.
Date made 14 December 1968.
Summary This order brought various provisions of the Transport Act 1968 into force as follows:

(a) on 18 November 1968: ss 1, 2, 3(1)(b)–(d), 4(2), (5), 5 (except sub-s (3)(b)), 6–26, 27(1)(b)–(d), 28(4)–(6), 29(1), (5), (6), 30–33, 37, 39, 40, 41(8), 45–52, 56–58, 104–111, 112(1)–(6), 113–115, 119–125, 130 (part), 132–149, 151–155, 156 (part), 157–164, 165 (part), 166, Schs 1, 3, 4 (part), 5–8, 12, 13, 14 (part), 15, 16 (part), 17, 18 (part); and
(b) on 1 January 1969: ss 3(1)(a), (e), (2), (3), 4(1), (3), 5(3)(b), 27(1)(a), (e), (2), (3), 28(1)–(3), 29(2)–(4), 34–36, 38, 41 (except sub-s (8)), 42–44, 53–55, 112(7), 116 (part), 117 (part), 118, 150, 165 (part), Schs 2, 18 (part).

Further orders Other provisions of the 1968 Act were brought into force by the following orders made under s 166:

(a) by SI 1969/507, on 21 April 1969: ss 126–129, 130 (in so far as not already in force), 165 (part), Sch 14 (in so far as not already in force), Sch 18 (part);
(b) by SI 1969/1613, on 20 November 1969 and (in relation to specified persons) various later dates between 1 December 1969 and 1 December 1970 (both dates inclusive): those provisions of Pt V (s 59 et seq) relevant to operators' licensing; and on 20 November 1969: ss 95, 98, 101, 102, 103(1)–(7), (9);
(c) by SI 1970/41, on 22 January 1970: s 96(10), (12);
(d) by SI 1970/188, on 1 March 1970: s 131 (except sub-s (1)); and on 1 September 1970: ss 131(1), 165 (part), Sch 18 (part);

(e) by SI 1970/259, on 1 March 1970: ss 64(5), 71(8) (part), 82(6) (part), 82(7)–(9), 96(1)–(9), (11) (except as to passenger vehicles), 99(1)–(9) (part), 100, 103(8), 165 (part), Schs 11, 18 (part);
(f) by SI 1970/385, on 15 March 1970: ss 96(1)–(9), (11) in relation to passenger vehicles, 165 (part), Sch 18 (part);
(g) by SI 1970/1151, on 1 January 1971: ss 116, 117 in so far as not already in force;
(h) by SI 1970/1631, on 30 November 1970 (as to vehicles used by the Post Office) and 1 March 1971 (as to farmers' goods vehicles): those provisions of Pt V of the Act relevant to operators' licensing (in so far as not already in force); and on 1 December 1970: s 94(8), (9), (10);
(i) by SI 1970/1767, on 1 December 1970: s 165(d), Sch 10, Pt II, Sch 18, Pt IV;
(j) by SI 2003/1985, on 1 September 2003: s 99(1)–(9) (in so far as not already in force), (10).

Amendments and repeals of the 1968 Act are noted in Halsbury's Statutes, 4th edn Vol 36, title Roads, Railways and Transport.

[268]

BRITISH TRANSPORT (PENSIONS OF EMPLOYEES) (NO 1) ORDER 1968
SI 1968/2011

Authority Made by the Minister of Transport and the Secretary of State under the Transport Act 1962, s 74 (as read with the Transport Act 1968, s 136).
Date made 17 December 1968.
Commencement 31 December 1968; however, the order has effect (except for certain provisions thereof) from 18 November 1968.
Amendment Amended by SI 1969/1824, SI 1971/1128.
Summary This order makes provision for certain changes in connection with established pension schemes in the nationalised transport industry, consequent on the setting up of the National Freight Corporation (now dissolved), the National Bus Company (now dissolved) and the Scottish Transport Group by the Transport Act 1968, s 1 (repealed), s 24 (effectively repealed in so far as it related to the National Bus Company); see the Preliminary Note "Reorganisation of transport undertakings". The order extends to staff of the new authorities (and their subsidiaries) the same facility to join and re-enter pension schemes as is conferred on the staff of the existing nationalised transport bodies by SI 1964/1329 (that order being modified accordingly) and it modifies SI 1962/2758 to meet the new circumstances arising from the provisions of the 1968 Act and the present order. Provision is made to confer on staff of the new authorities additional eligibility to join pension schemes, and for the transfer to the new authorities of the property, rights and liabilities of the Transport Holding Company (now dissolved) in relation to certain established pension schemes.

[269]

BRITISH TRANSPORT (PENSIONS OF EMPLOYEES) (NO 2) ORDER 1968
SI 1968/2012

Authority As noted to SI 1968/2011.
Date made 17 December 1968.
Commencement 31 December 1968; however, the order has effect from 28 November 1968.
Amendment Amended by SI 2006/680.
Summary This order deals with the preservation of the pension rights of persons who, because of any of the various reorganisations in the nationalised transport industry provided for in the Transport Act 1968, either lose their employment or suffer diminution of emoluments or a change in the nature or terms of their employment.

In the case of a person who loses his employment, the pension accrued up to the date on which he was discharged is normally to be paid to him at the age of 65 or at such time as, by the terms of his employment or of his pension scheme, he would have been entitled to receive a pension. A discharged person may, however, elect within three months of his discharge to have a return of contributions if the rules of his pension scheme permit this; but, if he does so, he will have no rights under the order. The appropriate body may discharge its liability to preserve a discharged person's accrued pension rights by arranging for a life assurance company to make the payments at the appropriate time. In certain cases, where the new employment obtained by a discharged person is pensionable, the appropriate body may, with the prior agreement of the discharged person, pay or arrange for the payment to that person's new pension scheme of the sum representing the value of that person's rights in his former scheme.

A person who does not lose his employment but who suffers a reduction in pay may be allowed to continue to contribute to, and benefit from, his pension scheme on the basis of his former pay. Similarly, if such a person is transferred from a pensionable to a non-pensionable grade he can (within three months) choose to remain in his pension scheme.

The order also provides for contributions between the nationalised transport bodies concerned and for the settlement of disputes.

[270]

MERSEYSIDE PASSENGER TRANSPORT AREA (DESIGNATION) ORDER 1969
SI 1969/94

Title See the note "Change of name of passenger transport areas and authorities" below.

Authority Made by the Minister of Transport under the Transport Act 1968, ss 9, 10(1)(ii)(b), Sch 5. By virtue of the Transport Act 1985, s 57(4), in so far as this order makes, with respect to a Passenger Transport Executive, any provision relating to matters mentioned in Pt III of Sch 5 to the 1968 Act (as amended by ss 57(6), 139(3) of, and paras 2, 21 of Sch 3 and Sch 8 to, the 1985 Act), it now has effect as if made under s 9(3) of the 1968 Act, as substituted by s 57(1) of the 1985 Act. In so far as it was made under s 10(1)(ii)(b) of the 1968 Act, this order has lapsed on the amendment of that subsection by s 57(6) of, and para 4(a) of Sch 3 to, the 1985 Act. S 9 of the 1968 Act has been amended by the Local Transport Act 2008, s 77(5), Sch 4, Pt 1, paras 1, 2, in consequence of the renaming of passenger transport areas and passenger transport authorities in England as integrated transport areas and Integrated Transport Authorities respectively by s 77(1), (2) of the 2008 Act.
Date made 27 January 1969.
Commencement 10 February 1969.
Amendment Amended by SI 1973/1731.
Summary This order, as originally made, designated the passenger transport area for Merseyside and provided for the establishment of the Passenger Transport Authority and the Passenger Transport Executive for that area under the Transport Act 1968, Pt II; it also made various provisions with respect to the Authority and the Executive. Consequent on the amendments made by SI 1973/1731 and on the provisions of the Transport Act 1985, s 57(4) (see the note "Authority" above), this order now applies only in relation to the said Executive (which, under SI 1973/1731, became on 1 April 1974 the Passenger Transport Executive for the metropolitan county of Merseyside). Apart from providing for the establishment of the Executive, the order (as amended and as it now takes effect under s 9(3) of the 1968 Act, as substituted) makes provision as to proceedings thereof, applies to the Executive certain enactments relating to local authorities and enables persons employed by the Executive or its subsidiaries to participate in a local government superannuation fund. It also deals with the appointment of committees, the delegation of functions to the Director General of the Executive, the validity of acts of the Executive and the authentication of documents.
Change of name of passenger transport areas and authorities By the Local Transport Act 2008, s 77(1), passenger transport areas in England established under the Transport Act 1968 are to be known as integrated transport areas, and by s 77(2) of the 2008 Act passenger transport authorities for those areas are to be known as Integrated Transport Authorities, as from 9 February 2009 (see SI 2009/107). In consequence, any reference in any enactment (whenever passed or made) to a passenger transport area or a Passenger Transport Authority is to be read respectively as a reference to an integrated transport area (s 77(3)) or an Integrated Transport Authority (s 77(4)).

[271]

SOUTH EAST LANCASHIRE AND NORTH EAST CHESHIRE PASSENGER TRANSPORT AREA (DESIGNATION) ORDER 1969
SI 1969/95

Title See the note "Change of name of passenger transport areas and authorities" to SI 1969/94.
Authority Made by the Minister of Transport under the Transport Act 1968, s 9, Sch 5. By virtue of the Transport Act 1985, s 57(4), in so far as this order makes, with respect to a Passenger Transport Executive, any provision relating to matters mentioned in Pt III of Sch 5 to the 1968 Act (as amended by ss 57(6), 139(3) of, and paras 2, 21 of Sch 3 and Sch 8 to, the 1985 Act), it now has effect as if made under s 9(3) of the 1968 Act, as substituted by s 57(1) of the 1985 Act. S 9 of the 1968 Act has been amended by the Local Transport Act 2008, s 77(5), Sch 4, Pt 1, paras 1, 2, in consequence of the renaming of passenger transport areas and passenger transport authorities in England as integrated transport areas and Integrated Transport Authorities respectively by s 77(1), (2) of the 2008 Act.
Date made 27 January 1969.
Commencement 10 February 1969.
Amendment Amended by SI 1973/1727.
Summary This order, as originally made, designated the passenger transport area for South East Lancashire and North East Cheshire and provided for the establishment of the Passenger Transport Authority and the Passenger Transport Executive for that area under the Transport Act 1968, Pt II; it also made various provisions with respect to the Authority and the Executive. Consequent on the amendments made by SI 1973/1727 and on the provisions of the Transport Act 1985, s 57(4) (see the note "Authority" above), this order now applies only in relation to the said Executive (which, under SI 1973/1727, became on 1 April 1974 the Passenger Transport Executive for the metropolitan county of Greater Manchester). Apart from providing for the establishment of the Executive, the order (as amended and as it now takes effect under s 9(3) of the 1968 Act, as substituted) makes provision as to proceedings thereof, applies to the Executive certain enactments relating to local authorities and enables persons employed by the Executive or its subsidiaries to participate in the Manchester Corporation Pension Fund. It also deals with the appointment of committees, the delegation of functions to the Director General of the Executive, the validity of acts of the Executive and the authentication of documents.
Change of name of passenger transport areas and authorities See the corresponding note to SI 1969/94.

[272]

TYNESIDE PASSENGER TRANSPORT AREA (DESIGNATION) ORDER 1969
SI 1969/96

Title See the note "Change of name of passenger transport areas and authorities" to SI 1969/94.

Authority As noted to SI 1969/95.
Date made 27 January 1969.
Commencement 10 February 1969.
Amendment Amended by SI 1973/1732. Previously amended by SI 1973/153 (revoked).
Summary This order, as originally made, designated the passenger transport area for Tyneside and provided for the establishment of the Passenger Transport Authority and the Passenger Transport Executive for that area under the Transport Act 1968, Pt II; it also made various provisions with respect to the Authority and the Executive. (The designated area was later extended and the membership of the Authority increased by SI 1973/153 (now revoked.)) Consequent on the amendments made by SI 1973/1732 and on the provisions of the Transport Act 1985, s 57(4) (see the note "Authority" to SI 1969/95), this order now applies only in relation to the said Executive (which, under SI 1973/1732, became on 1 April 1974 the Passenger Transport Executive for the metropolitan county of Tyne and Wear). Apart from providing for the establishment of the Executive, the order (as so amended and as it now takes effect under s 9(3) of the 1968 Act, as substituted) makes provision as to proceedings of the Executive, applies to the Executive certain enactments relating to local authorities and enables persons employed by the Executive or its subsidiaries to participate in a local government superannuation fund. It also deals with the appointment of committees, the delegation of functions to the Director General of the Executive, the validity of acts of the Executive and the authentication of documents.
Change of name of passenger transport areas and authorities See the corresponding note to SI 1969/94.

[273]

WEST MIDLANDS PASSENGER TRANSPORT AREA (DESIGNATION) ORDER 1969
SI 1969/97

Title See the note "Change of name of passenger transport areas and authorities" to SI 1969/94.
Authority As noted to SI 1969/95.
Date made 27 January 1969.
Commencement 10 February 1969.
Amendment Amended by SI 1973/1730.
Summary This order, as originally made, designated the passenger transport area for the West Midlands and provided for the establishment of the Passenger Transport Authority and the Passenger Transport Executive for that area under the Transport Act 1968, Pt II; it also made various provisions with respect to the Authority and the Executive. Consequent on the amendments made by SI 1973/1730 and on the provisions of the Transport Act 1985, s 57(4) (see the note "Authority" to SI 1969/95), this order now applies only in relation to the said Executive (which, under SI 1973/1730, became on 1 April 1974 the Passenger Transport Executive for the metropolitan county of West Midlands). Apart from providing for the establishment of the Executive, the order (as amended and as it now takes effect under s 9(3) of the 1968 Act, as substituted) makes provision as to proceedings of the Executive, applies to the Executive certain enactments relating to local authorities and enables persons employed by the Executive or its subsidiaries to participate in a local government superannuation fund. It also deals with the appointment of committees, the delegation of functions to the Director General of the Executive, the validity of acts of the Executive and the authentication of documents.
Change of name of passenger transport areas and authorities See the corresponding note to SI 1969/94.

[274]

TRANSPORT (LONDON) ACT 1969 (COMMENCEMENT NO 1) ORDER 1969
SI 1969/1130

Authority Made by the Minister of Transport under the Transport (London) Act 1969, s 47.
Date made 6 August 1969.
Summary This order brought into force on 8 August 1969 the following provisions of the Transport (London) Act 1969: ss 43, 45, 46, 47(1), (2) (in part), (4), (5) and Sch 6 in so far as it repealed certain enactments. The order also brought into force certain other provisions which have subsequently been repealed.
Further orders Further provisions of the Transport (London) Act 1969 were brought into force by the following orders made under s 47 of that Act:

(a) SI 1969/1510 brought into force:
  (1) on 30 October 1969, s 42 (and other provisions all now repealed); and
  (2) on 1 January 1970, certain repeals made by s 47(2), Sch 6 (and other provisions all now repealed);

(b) SI 1974/407 brought into force on 1 April 1974 certain repeals made by s 47(2), Sch 6 (and other provisions all now repealed).

Further provisions of the 1969 Act, which have all been repealed, were brought into force by SI 1969/1588 and SI 1972/1097, both now spent.

[275]

BRITISH TRANSPORT (CLOSED RAILWAY PENSION SCHEME) ORDER 1969
SI 1969/1695

Authority Made by the Minister of Transport under the Transport Act 1962, s 74. S 74 has been repealed by the Railways Act 1993, s 134(2), (3) in so far as relating to the British Railways Board and its subsidiaries, but without prejudice to the continuing validity of any orders made under that section.
Date made 25 November 1969.
Commencement 10 December 1969.
Summary This order provides for the functions of the management committee of the London and North Western Railway Provident Society for Providing Pensions for Widows and Orphans of Salaried Staff to be transferred to and exercised by the British Railways Board. Existing provisions of the scheme relating to the election or appointment of members of the management committee are revoked and the audit of the funds of the scheme is to be carried out by auditors appointed by the British Railways Board. Provision is also made for the disposal of surplus funds on the winding up of the scheme. As to the winding down and abolition of the British Railways Board, see the Transport Act 2000 and the Preliminary Note "Privatisation of the railway system" (under the main head "Reorganisation of transport undertakings").

[276]

BRITISH TRANSPORT (PENSIONS OF EMPLOYEES) (NO 1) ORDER 1969
SI 1969/1824

Authority Made by the Minister of Transport and the Secretary of State under the Transport Act 1962, s 74 (as read with the Transport Act 1968, s 136 and the Transport (London) Act 1969, s 18 (repealed by the London Regional Transport Act 1984, s 71(3)(b), Sch 7)). This order continued in force notwithstanding the repeal of s 18 of the 1969 Act by virtue of para 6 of Sch 5 to the 1984 Act (repealed by the Greater London Authority Act 1999, s 423, Sch 34, Pt II). S 74 of the 1962 Act has been repealed by the Railways Act 1993, s 134(2), (3) in so far as relating to the British Railways Board and its subsidiaries, but without prejudice to the continuing validity of any orders made under that section.
Date made 17 December 1969.
Commencement 31 December 1969; however, the order (except for certain provisions) has effect from 30 October 1969.
Amendment Amended by SI 1980/1351.
Modification Modified by SI 1994/2005 so as to apply certain provisions of the order in relation to the Railways Pension Scheme established by SI 1994/1433 as if that scheme were an established scheme as defined in this order.
Application of order Applied by SI 1970/1298, SI 1970/1299, SI 1971/116, SI 1971/117, SI 1971/629, SI 1971/1780. By the British Railways (No 2) Act 1986, s 48(4), certain provisions of this order were applied in relation to "the new scheme" within the meaning of s 48(1) of that Act (i e the BR Pension Scheme constituted by the trust deed dated 25 November 1985 made by the British Railways Board and the British Rail Pension Trustee Company Limited).
Summary This order makes provision for certain changes in connection with established pension schemes in the public sector of the transport industry consequent upon the establishment of the London Transport Executive by the Transport (London) Act 1969 (generally repealed), and the establishment of a new subsidiary of the National Bus Company (now dissolved; see SI 1991/510) for the purposes of that Act. The order revokes and replaces, with amendments, provisions in SI 1962/2758 and SI 1964/1329 relating to obligations of employing bodies to deduct employees' pension contributions from their salaries and to pay such contributions, together with employers' pension contributions and contributions towards administrative expenses, to the bodies responsible for the pension schemes in question; and provisions relating to the preservation of pension rights of certain persons who become members or directors of publicly owned transport bodies. The provisions relating to contributions are also applied (by the amending SI 1980/1351) in the case of subsequent changes effected in the public transport sector by the Transport Acts 1978 and 1980.

The order enables employees of one national transport authority to participate in or re-enter pension schemes of another national transport authority, and amends SI 1968/2011 by making further provisions as to the transfer of rights and liabilities of the Transport Holding Company (now dissolved) under the Transport Act 1968. Provision is also made to confer on staff of the national transport authorities (and their subsidiaries) additional eligibility to join or to remain in pension schemes, and for the transfer to the London Transport Executive (subsequently London Regional Transport, now dissolved and replaced by Transport for London) and the new subsidiary of the National Bus Company (now dissolved) of the property, rights and liabilities of the London Transport Board in relation to certain established pension schemes. As to the transition from London Regional Transport to Transport for London and the dissolution of LRT, see the Greater London Authority Act 1999 and the Preliminary Note "Transport for London" (under the main head "London").

[277]

BRITISH TRANSPORT (PENSIONS OF EMPLOYEES) (NO 2) ORDER 1969
SI 1969/1825

Authority As noted to SI 1969/1824.

Date made 17 December 1969.
Commencement 31 December 1969; however, the order has effect from 30 October 1969.
Summary This order deals with the preservation of the pension rights of persons who, because of changes brought about as provided for in the Transport (London) Act 1969 (generally repealed), either lose their employment or suffer diminution or a change in the nature of terms of their employment. Its provisions are similar to those of SI 1968/2012.

[278]

BRITISH TRANSPORT (ALTERATION OF PENSION SCHEMES) ORDER 1969
SI 1969/1858

Authority Made by the Minister of Transport under the Transport Act 1962, s 74. S 74 has been repealed by the Railways Act 1993, s 134(2), (3) in so far as relating to the British Railways Board and its subsidiaries, but without prejudice to the continuing validity of any orders made under that section.
Date made 19 December 1969.
Commencement 31 December 1969.
Amendment Amended by SI 1988/962, SI 2001/3649.
Summary This order provided for:
(a) the widening of the powers of investment in respect of the London and North Eastern Railways Superannuation Fund (as to which see further SI 1970/477); and
(b) the payment by the British Railways Board of interest on money forming part of the Fund held by the Board.

The provision made by head (b) has been replaced by SI 1973/2019.

[279]

BRITISH TRANSPORT (SOUTHERN RAILWAY SUPERANNUATION FUND) ORDER 1970
SI 1970/22

Authority Made by the Minister of Transport under the Transport Act 1962, s 74 (as read with the Transport Act 1968, s 136). S 74 has been repealed by the Railways Act 1993, s 134(2), (3) in so far as relating to the British Railways Board and its subsidiaries, but without prejudice to the continuing validity of any orders made under that section.
Date made 8 January 1970.
Commencement 21 January 1970.
Summary This order enables the rules of the pension fund established under the Southern Railway (Superannuation Fund) Act 1927, as amended, to be altered from time to time so as to permit payment from the fund, with the agreement of the member and the British Railways Board, of annuities payable during the joint lives of the member and his wife or other dependant relative and during the life of the survivor of them, in lieu of any annuity or other benefit to which the member would otherwise be entitled under the rules. As to the winding down and abolition of the British Railways Board, see the Transport Act 2000 and the Preliminary Note "Privatisation of the railway system" (under the main head "Reorganisation of transport undertakings").

[280]

DRIVERS' HOURS (PASSENGER VEHICLES) (EXEMPTIONS) REGULATIONS 1970
SI 1970/145

Authority Made by the Minister of Transport under the Transport Act 1968, s 96(10).
Date made 3 February 1970.
Commencement 1 March 1970.
Amendment Amended by SI 1970/649, SI 2003/2155.
Summary These regulations provide exemptions, subject to conditions, from the requirements of the Transport Act 1968, s 96(1)–(6) (which relate to permitted driving times and periods of duty), to enable drivers of passenger vehicles to deal with certain cases of emergency and to meet certain special needs. The special needs are connected with the blood transfusion service and the carriage of handicapped persons for certain social and recreational purposes.

[281]

BRITISH TRANSPORT (COMPENSATION TO EMPLOYEES) REGULATIONS 1970
SI 1970/187

Authority Made by the Minister of Transport and the Secretary of State under the Transport Act 1968, s 135(1), (7).
Date made 9 February 1970.
Commencement 19 February 1970; however, the regulations have retrospective effect from 18 November 1968.

Summary These regulations provide for the payment of compensation by the appropriate compensation authority (listed in Sch 1 to the regulations) to or in respect of any person who suffers loss of employment, or loss or diminution of emoluments or pension rights, or worsening of his position, which is attributable to the happening of the relevant event specified in the Transport Act 1968, s 135(1) (and also set out in Sch 1 to the regulations). The compensation payable is:

(a) resettlement compensation for loss of employment;
(b) long-term compensation for loss of employment or loss or diminution of emoluments or worsening of position;
(c) retirement compensation for loss or diminution of pension rights; and
(d) payments in respect of a deceased pensionable officer to his widow, child or other dependant or to his personal representatives.

The regulations specify the qualifications and other conditions which persons must satisfy to be eligible for compensation, the method of calculating the amount of compensation and the procedure for making claims and notifying decisions. Provision is also made for appeals by aggrieved claimants; appeals lie to a tribunal established under the Employment Protection (Consolidation) Act 1978, s 128 (repealed); see now the Employment Tribunals Act 1996, s 1.

[282]

DRIVERS' HOURS (GOODS VEHICLES) (MODIFICATIONS) ORDER 1970
SI 1970/257

Authority Made by the Minister of Transport under the Transport Act 1968, s 96(12).
Date made 19 February 1970.
Commencement 1 March 1970.
Amendment Amended by SI 1971/818 (itself amended by SI 1986/1459), SI 1986/1459.
Summary This order modifies in relation to certain drivers of goods vehicles the effect of the Transport Act 1968, s 96 (which relates to permitted driving times and periods of duty). Art 3 of the order, which contained certain exemptions for drivers of light goods vehicles, was revoked by SI 1986/1459 and replaced by provisions thereof. By art 4 of the order, the exemption in s 96(9) of the Act for agriculture and forestry, under which the driving of a goods vehicle elsewhere than on a road in the course of those industries is not treated as driving, is extended to vehicles driven in the course of quarrying operations or of carrying out any building, construction or civil engineering work.

[283]

BRITISH TRANSPORT (AMALGAMATION OF RAILWAYS' PENSION FUNDS) (NO 1) ORDER 1970
SI 1970/477

Authority Made by the Minister of Transport under the Transport Act 1962, s 74. S 74 has been repealed by the Railways Act 1993, s 134(2), (3) in so far as relating to the British Railways Board and its subsidiaries, but without prejudice to the continuing validity of any orders made under that section.
Date made 20 March 1970.
Commencement 6 April 1970.
Amendment Amended by SI 1970/1298, SI 1973/2019.
Summary This order provides for the amalgamation of the London and North Eastern Railway, the Great Western Railway, the Southern Railway and the London Midland and Scottish Railway Superannuation Funds. The amalgamated fund, which is vested in the British Railways Board, is to be known as the British Railways Superannuation Fund and is to have four sections, each section corresponding to one of the existing funds. By the British Railways Act 1980, s 48, Sch 4, the British Railways Board may by deed cancel or modify all or any of the provisions of this order so far as they relate to the pension and superannuation funds defined in the said s 48.

As to the winding down and abolition of the British Railways Board, see the Transport Act 2000 and the Preliminary Note "Privatisation of the railway system" (under the main head "Reorganisation of transport undertakings").

[284]

PASSENGER TRANSPORT (COMPENSATION TO OFFICERS) REGULATIONS 1970
SI 1970/749

Authority Made by the Minister of Transport under the Water Officers Compensation Act 1960, s 1, as applied by the Transport Act 1968, s 17(3) (repealed by the Transport Act 1985, ss 57(6), 139(3), Sch 3, para 1, Sch 8). Regulations under s 17(3) of the 1968 Act are saved by s 139(1) of, and para 19 of Sch 6 to, the 1985 Act.
Date made 14 May 1970.
Commencement 30 May 1970; however, the regulations have retrospective effect from 2 September 1969.
Summary These regulations provide for the payment of compensation to or in respect of local authority officers who suffer loss of employment or loss or diminution of emoluments which was attributable to an order under the Transport Act 1968, s 17(1) (repealed), or to anything done in pursuance of any such order. Orders under s 17(1) have lapsed consequent on the repeal of that section

by the Transport Act 1985, ss 57(6), 139(3), Sch 3, para 1, Sch 8, subject to a saving in para 26 of Sch 6 to that Act. These regulations are similar to other compensation regulations included in this title; see, for example, SI 1970/187.

[285]

BRITISH TRANSPORT (AMALGAMATION OF RAILWAYS' PENSION FUNDS) (NO 2) ORDER 1970
SI 1970/1298

Authority Made by the Minister of Transport under the Transport Act 1962, s 74. S 74 has been repealed by the Railways Act 1993, s 134(2), (3) in so far as relating to the British Railways Board and its subsidiaries, but without prejudice to the continuing validity of any orders made under that section.
Date made 28 August 1970.
Commencement 14 September 1970.
Amendment Amended by SI 1973/1390.
Summary This order makes provision for co-ordinating the New Section of the British Railways Superannuation Fund (referred to in the order as "the New Fund") (established under the terms of a Trust Deed executed by the Board on 21 August 1970) with the existing sections of that fund which are regulated by SI 1970/477; it also makes certain amendments to that order. The order provides for the application of the inter-availability arrangements for pensions in the publicly owned transport industry (see SI 1964/1329, SI 1969/1824) to the New Fund. Provision is further made for regulating the position of persons who are members of the British Transport Commission (Male Wages Grades) Pension Scheme (established by SI 1954/898) or of certain other pension schemes (including insurance and ex-gratia schemes) and who become members of the New Fund, so as to avoid duplication of membership. The order also provides for the payment of transfer values to the New Fund, for certain consequential matters and for the determination of questions. SI 1954/898 is modified. By the British Railways Act 1980, s 48, Sch 4, the British Railways Board may by deed cancel or modify all or any of the provisions of this order so far as they relate to the pension and superannuation funds defined in the said s 48.

As to the winding down and abolition of the British Railways Board, see the Transport Act 2000 and the Preliminary Note "Privatisation of the railway system" (under the main head "Reorganisation of transport undertakings").

[286]

BRITISH TRANSPORT DOCKS BOARD (ALTERATION OF PENSION SCHEMES) ORDER 1970
SI 1970/1299

Authority As noted to SI 1970/1298.
Date made 28 August 1970.
Commencement 4 September 1970.
Summary This order relates to the British Transport Docks Board (Salaried Staff) Pension Scheme (referred to in the order as "the New Fund") (established by the Board under the terms of an Interim Trust executed on 19 August 1970), to the British Transport Commission (Male Wages Grades) Pension Scheme (established by SI 1954/898), and to certain other pension schemes (including insurance and ex-gratia schemes) mentioned in the order. The British Transport Docks Board has been reconstituted as Associated British Ports; see the Preliminary Note "Reorganisation of transport undertakings". The order provides for the application of the inter-availability arrangements for pensions in the publicly owned transport industry (see SI 1964/1329, SI 1969/1824) to the New Fund. It also regulates the position of members of the British Transport Commission (Male Wages Grades) Pension Scheme or of the other pension schemes referred to, who become members of the New Fund, so as to avoid duplication of membership. The order provides for the payment of transfer values, for certain consequential matters and for the determination of questions. SI 1954/898 is modified.

[287]

FUNCTIONS OF TRAFFIC WARDENS ORDER 1970
SI 1970/1958

Authority Made by the Home Secretary under the Road Traffic Regulation Act 1967, s 81(3), (4A), (4B), as inserted by the Transport Act 1968, s 131(6) (repealed). Now has effect (by virtue of the Interpretation Act 1978, s 17(2)(b), printed in the title Statutory Instruments (Pt 2), Vol 1 of this work) under the Road Traffic Regulation Act 1984, ss 95(5), 96.
Date made 16 December 1970.
Commencement 1 January 1971; see art 1(1).
Interpretation See arts 1(2), 2.
Amendment Printed as amended by SI 1986/1328, SI 1993/1334, SI 2002/2975.
General Under the Road Traffic Regulation Act 1984, s 95 (which replaced the Road Traffic Regulation Act 1967, s 81), police authorities may appoint traffic wardens to undertake such functions in connection with the control and regulation of, or the enforcement of the law relating to, traffic (including pedestrians) or stationary vehicles as may be prescribed as appropriate by order of the Home Secretary. This order accordingly prescribes certain functions as appropriate for discharge by traffic wardens.

[288]

1 (1) This Order may be cited as the Functions of Traffic Wardens Order 1970 and shall come into operation on 1st January 1971.

(2) The Interpretation Act 1889 applies to the interpretation of this Order as it applies to the interpretation of an Act of Parliament.

(3) The Functions of Traffic Wardens Order 1960 and the Functions of Traffic Wardens Order 1965 are hereby revoked.

(4) This Order shall not extend to Scotland.

NOTES

Interpretation Act 1889 Repealed and replaced by the Interpretation Act 1978, printed in the title Statutory Instruments (Pt 2), Vol 1 of this work.
Functions of Traffic Wardens Order 1960 SI 1960/1582.
Functions of Traffic Wardens Order 1965 SI 1965/1151.

[289]

2 In this Order—

"the Act of 1960" and "the Act of 1967" mean respectively the Road Traffic Act 1960 and the Road Traffic Regulation Act 1967;

"street parking place order" means an order made under the Act of 1967 relating to a street parking place;

"traffic order" means an order made under section 1, 5, 6, 9, 11 or 84A of the Act of 1967.

NOTES

Road Traffic Act 1960 Largely repealed and replaced by the Road Traffic Act 1972, which has itself been repealed by the Road Traffic (Consequential Provisions) Act 1988, s 3(1), Sch 1, Pt I, and replaced by the Road Traffic Act 1988.
Road Traffic Regulation Act 1967 Largely repealed and replaced by the Road Traffic Regulation Act 1984. Ss 1, 5, 6, 9, 11, 84A of the 1967 Act were replaced by, respectively, ss 1, 37, 6, 9, 12 of, and Pt I of Sch 9 to, the 1984 Act. S 12 of the 1984 Act has been repealed by the Greater London Authority Act 1999, ss 294(1)(a), 423, Sch 34, Pt VI.

[290]

3 (1) The functions set out in the Schedule to this Order are hereby prescribed as appropriate for discharge by traffic wardens.

(2) For the purposes of the discharge by traffic wardens of such functions, references to a constable or police constable in the following enactments shall include references to a traffic warden—

(a) section 52 of the Metropolitan Police Act 1839 so far as it relates to the giving by the commissioner of directions to constables for preventing obstruction;
(b) section 22 of the local Act of the second and third year of the reign of Queen Victoria, chapter 94, so far as it makes similar provision with respect to the City of London;
(c) sections 14 and 15 of the Act of 1960 (drivers and pedestrians to comply with traffic directions given by police constables);
(d) section 229 of the Act of 1960 (the power of constables to obtain the names and addresses of pedestrians failing to comply with traffic directions);
(e) section 242 of the Act of 1960 and section 89 of the Act of 1967 (the giving of evidence of an admission by certificate);
[(f) section 100(3) of the Road Traffic Regulation Act 1984 (the interim disposal of vehicles removed under section 99 of that Act);
(g) sections 104 and 105 of the Road Traffic Regulation Act 1984 (the immobilisation of illegally parked vehicles)];
[(h) section 67(3) of the Road Traffic Act 1988 (power to stop vehicles for testing);
(i) section 163 of the Road Traffic Act 1988 (power to stop vehicles).]

(3) For the purposes of the discharge by traffic wardens of the functions set out in the Schedule to this Order, references in section 226(1) of the Act of 1960 to a police constable shall, in so far as it applies to the furnishing of names and addresses, include references to a traffic warden if the traffic warden has reasonable cause to believe that there has been committed an offence—

(a) in respect of a vehicle by its being left or parked on a road during the hours of darkness (as defined by the Road Transport Lighting Act 1957) without the lights or reflectors required by law;
(b) in respect of a vehicle by its obstructing a road, or waiting, or being left or parked, or being loaded or unloaded, in a road;
(c) in contravention of section 14 of the Act of 1960;
(d) in contravention of a provision of the Vehicles (Excise) Act 1962;
(e) created by section 42 of the Act of 1967 (offences relating to parking places on highways where charges made).

[(4) References in section 164(1), (2) and (6) of the Road Traffic Act 1988 to a constable or police constable shall include references to a traffic warden only where—

(a) the traffic warden has reasonable cause to believe that there has been committed an offence by causing a vehicle, or any part of it, to stop in contravention of regulations made under section 25 of the Road Traffic Regulation Act 1984 or an offence in contravention of section 22 of the Road Traffic Act 1988 (leaving vehicles in dangerous positions); or
(b) the traffic warden is employed to perform functions in connection with the custody of vehicles removed from a road or land in the open air in pursuance of regulations made under section 99 of the Road Traffic Regulation Act 1984 or from a parking place in pursuance of a street parking place order, and he has reasonable cause to believe that there has been committed an offence in respect of a vehicle by its obstructing a road, or waiting, or being left or parked, or being loaded or unloaded, in a road.]

NOTES

Amendment Para (2)(f), (g): inserted by SI 1993/1334.
Para (2)(h), (i): inserted by SI 2002/2975.
Para (4): substituted by SI 1993/1334.

Road Traffic Act 1960, ss 14, 15, 226(1), 229, 242 These provisions of the 1960 Act, except s 242, were repealed and replaced by corresponding provisions in the Road Traffic Act 1972. The 1972 Act has itself been repealed by the Road Traffic (Consequential Provisions) Act 1988, s 3(1), Sch 1, Pt I, and replaced by corresponding provisions in the Road Traffic Act 1988. The provisions of the 1960 Act cited, except s 242, are now to be construed as referring, respectively, to the following provisions of the Road Traffic Act 1988: ss 35, 37, 165(1), (4), 169. The Road Traffic Act 1960, s 242 is now to be construed as referring also to the Road Traffic Offenders Act 1988, s 11, which replaced corresponding provisions in the Road Traffic Act 1972, s 181.

Road Traffic Act 1988, s 164(6) Note that there is now no reference in s 164(6) to a constable by virtue of the amendment of that subsection by the Road Traffic Act 1991, s 83, Sch 8.

Road Traffic Regulation Act 1967, ss 42, 89 Repealed and replaced by the Road Traffic Regulation Act 1984, ss 47, 113. S 113 of the 1984 Act has itself been repealed by the Road Traffic (Consequential Provisions) Act 1988, s 3(1), Sch 1, Pt I, and replaced by the Road Traffic Offenders Act 1988, s 11.

Road Transport Lighting Act 1957 Repealed. For the meaning of "hours of darkness", see now the Road Traffic Act 1972, s 82; that definition was repealed by the Road Traffic Act 1974, s 24(3), Sch 7, but saving provisions in s 9(4) thereof continued its application. S 9(4) has been repealed and replaced by corresponding provisions in the Road Traffic (Consequential Provisions) Act 1988, s 5(1), Sch 4, para 3.

Vehicles (Excise) Act 1962 Now the Vehicle Excise and Registration Act 1994.

Regulations made under the Road Traffic Regulation Act 1984, ss 25, 99
See SI 1986/183 (made partly under s 99 of the 1984 Act) and SI 1997/2400 (made partly under s 25 of that Act), both in the title Highways, Streets and Bridges.

[291]

SCHEDULE
FUNCTIONS OF TRAFFIC WARDENS

Article 3

1 (1) Traffic wardens may be employed to enforce the law with respect to an offence—

(a) committed in respect of a vehicle by its being left or parked on a road during the hours of darkness (as defined by the Road Transport Lighting Act 1957) without the lights or reflectors required by law; or
(b) committed in respect of a vehicle by its obstructing a road, or waiting, or being left or parked, or being loaded or unloaded, in a road or other public place; or
(c) committed in contravention of a provision of the Vehicles (Excise) Act 1962;
(d) created by section 42 of the Act of 1967 (offences relating to parking places on highways where charges made);

[(e) committed by causing a vehicle, or any part of it, to stop in contravention of regulations made under section 25 of the Road Traffic Regulation Act 1984.]

[(2) For the purposes of the enforcement of the law with respect to such of the offences described in sub-paragraph (1) of this paragraph as are fixed penalty offences within the meaning of section 27(5) of the Transport Act 1982, … traffic wardens may exercise the functions conferred on constables by Part III of the said Act of 1982.]

2 (1) Traffic wardens may, under arrangements made with the Secretary of State or a local authority, be employed to act as parking attendants at street parking places provided or controlled by the Secretary of State or local authority.

(2) A traffic warden may exercise functions conferred on a traffic warden by a traffic order or a street parking place order.

3 Without prejudice to the generality of paragraph 1 above, traffic wardens may be employed in connection with obtaining information under section 232 of the Act of 1960 or section 85 of the Act of 1967 (duty to give information as to identity of driver, etc in certain cases).

4 Traffic wardens may be employed to perform functions in connection with the custody of vehicles removed from a road or land in the open air in pursuance of regulations under section 20 of the Act of 1967 or from a parking place in pursuance of a street parking place order.

5 Where a police authority provides school crossing patrols under section 24 of the Act of 1967, whether as the appropriate authority or by agreement with the appropriate authority, traffic wardens appointed by that police authority may be employed to act as school crossing patrols.

[5A Traffic wardens may be employed to stop vehicles for the purposes of a test under subsection (1) of section 67 of the Road Traffic Act 1988 (testing of conditions of vehicles on roads).

5B Traffic wardens may be employed to escort vehicles or trailers carrying loads of exceptional dimensions the use of which is authorised by an order made by the Secretary of State under section 44(1)(d) of the Road Traffic Act 1988.]

6 (1) Subject to the foregoing paragraphs, traffic wardens may be employed in the control and regulation of traffic (including foot passengers) or vehicles whether on a highway or not and to discharge any other functions normally undertaken by the police in connection with the control and regulation of traffic (including foot passengers) or vehicles.

(2) …

NOTES

Amendment Para 1(1)(e): inserted by SI 1993/1334.
Para 1(2): substituted by SI 1986/1328; words omitted revoked by SI 1993/1334.
Paras 5A, 5B: inserted by SI 2002/2975.
Para 6(2): revoked by SI 2002/2975.

Road Traffic Act 1960, s 232 This is to be construed as referring also to the Road Traffic Act 1988, s 172.

Road Traffic Regulation Act 1967, ss 24, 42, 85 Repealed and replaced by the Road Traffic Regulation Act 1984, ss 26, 47, 112.

Road Transport Lighting Act 1957 As to this Act, and the meaning of "hours of darkness", see the notes to art 3.

Transport Act 1982, s 27(5), Pt III Repealed; as to corresponding provisions, see the Road Traffic Offenders Act 1988, s 51(1), Pt III.

Vehicles (Excise) Act 1962 See the notes to art 3.

Regulations under the Road Traffic Regulation Act 1967, s 20 See SI 1986/183, in the title Highways, Streets and Bridges, made partly under the Road Traffic Regulation Act 1984, s 99, which replaced s 20 of the 1967 Act.

Regulations made under the Road Traffic Regulation Act 1984, s 25
See the notes to art 3.

[292]

LONDON TRANSPORT (ALTERATION OF PENSION SCHEMES) ORDER 1970
SI 1970/1990

Authority Made by the Secretary of State for the Environment under the Transport Act 1962, s 74 (as read with the Transport (London) Act 1969, s 18 (repealed by the London Regional Transport Act 1984, s 71(3)(b), Sch 7)). This order continued in force notwithstanding the repeal of s 18 of the 1969 Act by virtue of para 6 of Sch 5 to the 1984 Act, itself repealed by the Greater London Authority Act 1999, s 423, Sch 34, Pt II. The order is retained in this title but is now of limited application.

Date made 16 December 1970.

Commencement 31 December 1970.

Amendment Amended by SI 1973/1390.

Summary This order relates to the London Transport 1970 Superannuation Fund (referred to in the order as the "New Fund") (established by the London Transport Executive under the terms of an Interim Deed executed on 1 December 1970) and to certain other pension schemes. It makes provision for avoiding duplication of membership in the case of persons who are, or may become, members of these other pension schemes but who become members of the New Fund. Transfer values may be paid from these other schemes to the New Fund. The order also provides for certain consequential matters and for the determination of questions, and safeguards existing rights. The London Transport Executive was reconstituted as London Regional Transport (dissolved); as to the transition from London Regional Transport to Transport for London and the dissolution of LRT, see the Greater London Authority Act 1999 and the Preliminary Note "Transport for London" (under the main head "London").

[293]

VEHICLE AND DRIVING LICENCES RECORDS (EVIDENCE) REGULATIONS 1970
SI 1970/1997

Authority Made by the Secretary of State for the Environment under the Vehicle and Driving Licences Act 1969, s 27(3) (repealed). Subsequently took effect under the Vehicles (Excise) Act 1971, s 31(3) (repealed) (by virtue of para 1 of Pt II of Sch 7 to that Act), and under the Road Traffic Offenders Act 1988, s 13(5) (by virtue of the Road Traffic (Consequential Provisions) Act 1988, s 2(2)). In so far as the regulations had effect under s 31(3) of the 1971 Act, they now take effect under the Vehicle Excise and Registration Act 1994, s 52(1), by virtue of s 64 of, and para 2 of Sch 4 to, that Act.
Date made 21 December 1970.
Commencement 1 February 1971; see reg 1.
Amendment Printed as amended by SI 2002/2742.
Interpretation See reg 2.
General The Vehicle Excise and Registration Act 1994, s 52 and the Road Traffic Offenders Act 1988, s 13 provide that a statement contained in certain documents duly authenticated and purporting to be, intèr alia, part of the records maintained by the Secretary of State in connection with his functions under or by virtue of the 1994 Act or by virtue of the Road Traffic Act 1988, Pt III, or any other records maintained by him with respect to vehicles, should be admissible in civil or criminal proceedings as evidence of any fact stated therein, to the same extent as oral evidence of that fact would be admissible. These regulations prescribe the matters in respect of which evidence may be given in this way.

[294]

Commencement and citation

1 These Regulations shall come into operation on the 1st February 1971 and may be cited as the Vehicle and Driving Licences Records (Evidence) Regulations 1970.

[295]

Interpretation

2 (1) In these Regulations, except where the context otherwise requires, the following expressions have the meanings hereby respectively assigned to them:—

"the Act" means the Vehicle and Driving Licences Act 1969;

. . .

"certificate of competence to drive" means a certificate issued in pursuance of Regulation 20(1) of the Motor Vehicles (Driving Licences) Regulations 1970;

"certificate of temporary exemption" means a certificate of temporary exemption issued by virtue of section 14(8)(c) of the Road Safety Act 1967, as amended by section 148(3) of the Transport Act 1968;

"driving licence" means a licence under Part II of the Road Traffic Act 1960 to drive a motor vehicle;

"Ministry plate" and "Ministry test date disc" have the same meanings respectively as they have in the Motor Vehicles (Construction and Use) Regulations 1969, as amended;

"plating certificate" and "goods vehicle test certificate" have the same meanings respectively as they have in section 9(1) of the Road Safety Act 1967 and "notification of the refusal of a goods vehicle test certificate" means a written notification given under section 9(1)(c) of that Act;

. . .

(2) Any reference in these Regulations to any enactment shall be construed as a reference to that enactment as amended by any subsequent enactment.

(3) The Interpretation Act 1889 shall apply for the interpretation of these Regulations as it applies for the interpretation of an Act of Parliament.

NOTES

Amendment Definitions "the 1962 Act", "registration book", "registration mark", "trade licence" and "vehicle licence" (omitted) revoked by SI 2002/2742.

Interpretation Act 1889 Repealed and replaced by the Interpretation Act 1978, printed in the title Statutory Instruments (Pt 2), Vol 1 of this work.

Road Traffic Act 1960, Pt II Now the Road Traffic Act 1988, Pt III.

Road Safety Act 1967, ss 9(1), 14(8)(c) Now the Road Traffic Act 1988, ss 49(1)–(3), 53(5)(b).

Vehicle and Driving Licences Act 1969 Largely repealed and replaced by the Vehicles (Excise) Act 1971 (repealed; see now the Vehicle Excise and Registration Act 1994), and the Road Traffic Act 1972 (repealed; see now the Road Traffic Act 1988).

Motor Vehicles (Construction and Use) Regulations 1969 SI 1969/321 (revoked). See now SI 1986/1078.

Motor Vehicles (Driving Licences) Regulations 1970, reg 20(1) SI 1970/170 (revoked). See now SI 1999/2864, regs 47, 48.

[296]

Matters prescribed for s 27(3) of the Act

3 The following matters are prescribed for the purposes of section 27(3) of the Act—

(1) In connection with the licensing of drivers under Part II of the Road Traffic Act 1960—

- (a) a document being, forming part of, or submitted in connection with, an application for a driving licence;
- (b) a driving licence;
- (c) a certificate of competence to drive;
- (d) the conviction of an offence specified in Part I or Part II of Schedule 1 to the Road Traffic Act 1962 or of an offence treated as so specified by virtue of section 5 of the Road Safety Act 1967 of any person or any order made by the Court as a result of any such conviction;

(2) …

(3) In connection with the examination of a goods vehicle under regulations under section 9 of the Road Safety Act 1967—

- (a) an application for an examination of a vehicle under the said regulations;
- (b) a notifiable alteration made to a vehicle and required by the said regulations to be notified to the Secretary of State;
- (c) a plating certificate, goods vehicle test certificate, notification of the refusal of a goods vehicle test certificate, Ministry plate, Ministry test date disc or certificate of temporary exemption.

NOTES

Amendment Para (2): revoked by SI 2002/2742.

S 27(3) of the Act Now the Vehicle Excise and Registration Act 1994, s 52(1) and the Road Traffic Offenders Act 1988, s 13(5).

Road Safety Act 1967, s 9 Now the Road Traffic Act 1988, s 49. For regulations under that section, see SI 1988/1478.

Road Traffic Act 1960, Pt II See the note to reg 2.

Road Traffic Act 1962, Sch 1, Pts I, II; Road Safety Act 1967, s 5 Now the corresponding provisions of the Road Traffic Act 1988.

[297]

LONDON TRANSPORT (COMPENSATION TO EMPLOYEES) REGULATIONS 1970

SI 1970/2019

Authority Made by the Secretary of State for the Environment under the Transport (London) Act 1969, s 37 (repealed by the London Regional Transport Act 1984, s 71(3)(b), Sch 7). These regulations continued in force notwithstanding the repeal of s 37 of the 1969 Act by virtue of para 13 of Sch 5 to the 1984 Act, itself repealed by the Greater London Authority Act 1999, s 423, Sch 34, Pt II. They are retained in this title but are now of limited application.

Date made 22 December 1970.

Commencement 29 December 1970; however, the regulations have retrospective effect from 22 October 1969.

Summary These regulations provide for the payment of compensation by the appropriate compensating authority (listed in Sch 1 to the regulations) to or in respect of any person who suffers loss of employment, or loss or diminution of emoluments or pension rights, or worsening of his position, which was attributable to the happening of the relevant event specified in the Transport (London) Act 1969, s 37(1) (repealed) (also set out in Sch 1 to the regulations). The compensation payable is:

(a) resettlement compensation for loss of employment;

(b) long-term compensation for loss of employment or loss or diminution of emoluments or worsening of position;
(c) retirement compensation for loss or diminution of pension rights; and
(d) payments in respect of a deceased pensionable officer to his widow, child or other dependant or to his personal representatives in specified circumstances.

The regulations specify the qualifying and other conditions for compensation, the method of calculating the amount of compensation and the procedure for making claims and notifying decisions. Provision is also made for appeals by aggrieved claimants; appeals lie to an employment tribunal (formerly known as an industrial tribunal) established under the Employment Protection (Consolidation) Act 1978, s 128 (repealed); see now the Employment Tribunals Act 1996, s 1.

[298]

NATIONAL FREIGHT CORPORATION (ALTERATION OF PENSION SCHEMES) (NO 1) ORDER 1971
SI 1971/116

Authority Made by the Secretary of State for the Environment under the Transport Act 1962, s 74 (as read with the Transport Act 1968, s 136).
Date made 25 January 1971.
Commencement 31 January 1971.
Summary This order relates to the National Freight Corporation (Wages Grades) Pension Fund (referred to in the order as "the New Fund") (established by the Corporation under the terms of an Interim Trust Deed executed on 12 January 1971), to the British Transport Commission (Male Wages Grades) Pension Scheme (established by SI 1954/898), and to certain other pension schemes mentioned in the order. The order provides for the application of the inter-availability arrangements for pensions in the publicly owned transport industry (see SI 1964/1329 and SI 1969/1824) to the New Fund. It also regulates the position of members of the British Transport Commission (Male Wages Grades) Pension Scheme or of the other pension schemes, who become members of the New Fund, so as to avoid duplication of membership. Provision is made for the payment of transfer values, for certain consequential matters, for the determination of questions and for safeguarding existing rights. SI 1954/898 is modified. (Cf SI 1971/117.)

As to the subsequent dissolution of the National Freight Corporation and transfer of its undertaking to a successor company, see the Preliminary Note "Reorganisation of transport undertakings"; and as to the transfer of Corporation schemes to a central trust, see SI 1978/1290.

[299]

NATIONAL FREIGHT CORPORATION (ALTERATION OF PENSION SCHEMES) (NO 2) ORDER 1971
SI 1971/117

Authority As noted to SI 1971/116.
Date made 25 January 1971
Commencement 31 January 1971.
Summary This order relates to the National Freight Corporation (Salaried Staff) Pension Fund (referred to in the order as "the New Fund") (established by the Corporation under the terms of an Interim Trust Deed executed on 12 January 1971), to the British Transport Commission (Male Wages Grades) Pension Scheme (established by SI 1954/898), and to certain other pension schemes mentioned in the order. It provides for the application of the inter-availability arrangements for pensions in the publicly owned transport industry (see SI 1964/1329 and SI 1969/1824) to the New Fund. It also regulates the position of members of the British Transport Commission (Male Wages Grades) Pension Scheme or of the other pension schemes referred to, who become members of the New Fund, so as to avoid duplication of membership. Provision is made for the payment of transfer values, for certain consequential matters, for the determination of questions and for safeguarding existing rights. SI 1954/898 is modified. (Cf SI 1971/116.)

As to the subsequent dissolution of the National Freight Corporation and transfer of its undertaking to a successor company, see the Preliminary Note "Reorganisation of transport undertakings"; and as to the transfer of Corporation schemes to a central trust, see SI 1978/1290.

[300]

BRITISH WATERWAYS BOARD (ALTERATION OF PENSION SCHEMES) ORDER 1971
SI 1971/629

Authority Made by the Secretary of State for the Environment under the Transport Act 1962, s 74.
Date made 8 April 1971.
Commencement 13 May 1971.
Summary This order relates to the British Waterways Board (Wages Grades) Pension Scheme (referred to in the order as "the New Fund") (established by the Board under the terms of an Interim Trust Deed executed on 1 April 1971), to the British Transport Commission (Male Wages Grades) Pension Scheme (established by SI 1954/898), and to certain other pension schemes (including insurance schemes) mentioned in the order. It provides for the application of the inter-availability arrangements for pensions in the publicly owned transport industry (see SI 1964/1329 and

SI 1969/1824) to the New Fund. It also regulates the position of members of the British Transport Commission (Male Wages Grades) Pension Scheme or of the other pension schemes referred to, who become members of the New Fund, so as to avoid duplication of membership. The order provides for the payment of transfer values, for certain consequential matters and for the determination of questions. SI 1954/898 is modified. (Cf SI 1971/1780.)

[301]

DRIVERS' HOURS (PASSENGER AND GOODS VEHICLES) (MODIFICATIONS) ORDER 1971
SI 1971/818

Authority Made by the Secretary of State for the Environment under the Transport Act 1968, ss 96(12), 101, 157.
Date made 17 May 1971.
Commencement 29 May 1971.
Amendment Amended by SI 1986/1459.
Summary This order modifies, in relation to drivers of passenger vehicles and good vehicles, the requirements of the Transport Act 1968, s 96, which relates to permitted driving times and periods of duty. Pt II of the order relates to drivers of passenger vehicles. It revokes the Drivers' Hours (Passenger Vehicles) (Modifications) Order 1970, SI 1970/356, and provides for modification of the requirements as to the intervals of rest and refreshment which a driver must have during a working day, the length of the working day, the intervals for rest between working days and the period off duty in a working week. It also provides that the requirements as to the maximum periods of duty of a driver in a working week are not to apply and that none of the requirements of s 96 will apply in the case of a driver who, in a working week, does not drive for a period or periods of more than four hours in more than two of the 24 hour periods beginning at midnight which make up that week if, in relation to any such 24 hour periods, certain conditions are complied with. Pt III of the order amends SI 1970/257, and is partially revoked by SI 1986/1459.
See also SI 1986/1458.

[302]

BRITISH TRANSPORT (PENSIONS OF EMPLOYEES) ORDER 1971
SI 1971/1128

Authority Made by the Secretary of State for the Environment under the Transport Act 1962, s 74 (as read with the Transport Act 1968, s 136).
Date made 9 July 1971.
Commencement 22 July 1971.
Summary This order revokes the provisions of SI 1962/2758 and SI 1968/2011 which required national transport authorities to obtain the consent of the Secretary of State before paying pensions or entering into obligations under pension schemes. The order also set aside specific provisions to the same effect appearing in existing pension schemes of national transport authorities.

[303]

BRITISH WATERWAYS BOARD (ALTERATION OF PENSION SCHEMES) (NO 2) ORDER 1971
SI 1971/1780

Authority Made by the Secretary of State for the Environment under the Transport Act 1962, s 74.
Date made 1 November 1971.
Commencement 12 November 1971.
Summary This order relates to the British Waterways (Salaried Staff) Pension Fund (referred to in the order as "the New Fund") (established by the Board under the terms of an Interim Trust Deed executed on 9 September 1971), to the British Transport Commission (Male Wages Grades) Pension Scheme (established by SI 1954/898), and to certain other pension schemes (including insurance schemes) mentioned in the order. It provides for the application of the inter-availability arrangements for pensions in the publicly owned public transport industry (see SI 1964/1329 and SI 1969/1824) to the New Fund. It also regulates the position of members of the British Transport Commission (Male Wages Grades) Pension Scheme or of the other pension schemes referred to, who become members of the New Fund, so as to avoid duplication of membership. The order provides for the payment of transfer values, for certain consequential matters and for the determination of questions. SI 1954/898 is modified. (Cf SI 1971/629.)

[304]

TRANSPORT HOLDING COMPANY (COMPENSATION TO EMPLOYEES) REGULATIONS 1972
SI 1972/632

Authority Made by the Secretary of State for the Environment under the Transport Holding Company Act 1972, s 2(4).
Date made 21 April 1972.

Commencement 19 May 1972; however, the regulations have retrospective effect from 23 March 1972.

Summary These regulations provided for the payment of compensation by the Transport Holding Company (or by the authority to which the responsibilities of the Company were transferred on its dissolution; see SI 1973/338) to or in respect of any person who suffered loss of employment, or loss or diminution of emoluments or pension rights, or worsening of his position, as a result of a body ceasing to be a subsidiary of the Company after the passing of the Transport Holding Company Act 1972. The compensation payable is:

(a) resettlement compensation for loss of employment;
(b) long-term compensation for loss of employment or loss or diminution of emoluments or worsening of position;
(c) retirement compensation for loss or diminution of pension rights; and
(d) payments in respect of a deceased pensionable officer to his widow, child, or other dependant or to his personal representatives.

The regulations specify the qualifying and other conditions for compensation, the method of calculating the amount of compensation and the procedure for making claims and notifying decisions. Provision is also made for appeals by aggrieved claimants; appeals lie to an employment tribunal (formerly known as an industrial tribunal) established under the Employment Protection (Consolidation) Act 1978, s 128 (repealed); see now the Employment Tribunals Act 1996, s 1.

[305]

LONDON CAB ORDER 1972
SI 1972/1047

Authority Made by the Secretary of State under the London Cab Act 1968, s 2.
Date made 12 July 1972.
Commencement 7 August 1972.
Summary This order provides that, in relation to hirings in respect of journeys which begin at Heathrow Airport, London, for the reference to the distance of six miles in the London Hackney Carriage Act 1853, ss 7, 17(2) (being the length of journey which a cab driver is by law obliged to undertake), there is to be substituted a reference to the distance of 20 miles.
Further orders See also SR & O 1934/1346, SI 1973/1671.

[306]

TRANSPORT HOLDING COMPANY (PENSIONS) ORDER 1973
SI 1973/337

Authority Made by the Secretary of State for the Environment under the Transport Holding Company Act 1972, s 2.
Date made 28 February 1973.
Commencement 28 March 1973; however, the order has retrospective effect from 26 June 1972.
Summary This order makes provision with respect to the pension rights of certain persons who are or have been employed by Thos Cook and Son Ltd or by a subsidiary of that company. The provision is made in consequence of the disposal by the Transport Holding Company (now dissolved; see SI 1973/338) of its shares in Thos Cook and Son Ltd on 26 June 1972.

[307]

TRANSPORT HOLDING COMPANY (DISSOLUTION) ORDER 1973
SI 1973/338

Authority Made by the Secretary of State for the Environment under the Transport Act 1968, s 53(1), as amended by the Transport Holding Company Act 1972, s 1(3), and under ss 1(6), 2(6) of the 1972 Act.
Date made 28 February 1973.
Commencement 29 March 1973.
Summary This order transferred to the National Freight Corporation on 30 March 1973 all outstanding property, rights and liabilities of the Transport Holding Company and dissolved that Company as from 31 March 1973. The order also provided:

(a) for conferring on the National Freight Corporation such additional powers as they need to deal with the transferred property and liabilities;
(b) for certain amendments to the Transport Holding Company Act 1972, s 2 and for repeals; and
(c) for the preparation and submission by the National Freight Corporation of the final accounts and report of the Transport Holding Company.

As to the subsequent dissolution of the National Freight Corporation and transfer of its undertaking to a successor company, see the Preliminary Note "Reorganisation of transport undertakings". See also, as to pensions, SI 1974/2001, SI 1980/1351.

[308]

TRANSPORT HOLDING COMPANY (COMMENCING CAPITAL DEBT) (EXTINGUISHMENT) ORDER 1973
SI 1973/366

Authority Made by the Secretary of State for the Environment, with the approval of the Treasury, under the Transport Act 1968, s 53(5), as extended by the Transport Holding Company Act 1972, s 1(4).
Date made 2 March 1973.
Commencement 30 March 1973.
Summary This order extinguishes the commencing capital debt of the Transport Holding Company (as to which debt, see SI 1964/448). This extinguishment is consequent on the sale by that Company of its interest in Thos Cook and Son Ltd and on the transfer of its residual assets to the National Freight Corporation. For the dissolution of the Transport Holding Company, see SI 1973/338.

[309]

LONDON CAB (NO 2) ORDER 1973
SI 1973/1671

Authority Made by the Secretary of State under the London Cab Act 1968, s 4A, as amended by the London Cab Act 1973. S 4A of the 1968 Act and the whole of the 1973 Act are repealed by the Private Hire Vehicles (London) Act 1998, s 39(2), Sch 2. By s 29 of the 1998 Act, that Act does not apply to any vehicle whose use as a private hire vehicle is limited to use in connection with funerals or weddings.
Date made 5 October 1973.
Commencement 5 November 1973.
Summary This order prohibits, within the metropolitan police district and the City of London, the display by private hire-cars of signs etc which include the word "taxi", "cab" or "hire", or a telephone number or address, or which suggest that the car carries passengers for reward. Statutory signs and certain signs displayed when a passenger is being met are excepted from this prohibition. This order now applies only to vehicles whose use as a private hire vehicle is limited to use in connection with funerals or weddings; see the note "Authority" above.
Further orders See also SR & O 1934/1346, SI 1972/1047.

[310]

GREATER MANCHESTER PASSENGER TRANSPORT AREA (ADAPTATION OF ENACTMENTS AND INSTRUMENTS) ORDER 1973
SI 1973/1727

Title Passenger transport areas in England are renamed integrated transport areas by the Local Transport Act 2008, s 77(1), as from 9 February 2009 (see SI 2009/107).
Authority Made by the Secretary of State for the Environment under the Local Government Act 1972, s 202(4), (5) (repealed by the Transport Act 1985, s 139(3), Sch 8). By virtue of s 57(4) of the 1985 Act, in so far as this order makes, with respect to a Passenger Transport Executive, any provision relating to matters mentioned in the Transport Act 1968, Sch 5, Pt III, it now has effect as if made under s 9(3) of the 1968 Act, as substituted by s 57(1) of the 1985 Act. S 9(3) of the 1968 Act has been amended by the Local Transport Act 2008, s 77(5), Sch 4, Pt 1, paras 1, 2, in consequence of the renaming of passenger transport areas in England as integrated transport areas by s 77(1) of the 2008 Act.
Date made 17 October 1973.
Commencement 19 November 1973.
Amendment Amended by SI 1990/1285.
Summary This order provided for the South East Lancashire and North East Cheshire Passenger Transport Executive to become on 1 April 1974 the Passenger Transport Executive for the metropolitan county of Greater Manchester, for the dissolution on that date of the existing South East Lancashire and North East Cheshire Passenger Transport Authority, and for the vesting of its property, rights and liabilities in the County Council of Greater Manchester. It also provided for the transfer to the Executive on 1 April 1974 of the powers and duties of Wigan County Borough Council in connection with its road passenger transport undertaking. The existing orders relating to the South East Lancashire and North East Cheshire Transport Area (of which only SI 1969/95 remains in force) were amended accordingly. This order is therefore now effective only to amend SI 1969/95.

[311]

SOUTH YORKSHIRE PASSENGER TRANSPORT AREA (ESTABLISHMENT OF EXECUTIVE) ORDER 1973
SI 1973/1728

Title Passenger transport areas in England are renamed integrated transport areas by the Local Transport Act 2008, s 77(1), as from 9 February 2009 (see SI 2009/107).
Authority Made by the Secretary of State for the Environment under the Local Government Act 1972, s 202(4) (repealed by the Transport Act 1985, s 139(3), Sch 8). By virtue of s 57(4) of the 1985 Act, in so far as this order makes, with respect to a Passenger Transport Executive, any provision

relating to matters mentioned in the Transport Act 1968, Sch 5, Pt III, it now has effect as if made under s 9(3) of the 1968 Act, as substituted by s 57(1) of the 1985 Act. S 9(3) of the 1968 Act has been amended by the Local Transport Act 2008, s 77(5), Sch 4, Pt 1, paras 1, 2, in consequence of the renaming of passenger transport areas in England as integrated transport areas by s 77(1) of the 2008 Act.
Date made 17 October 1973.
Commencement 19 November 1973.
Amendment Amended by SI 1990/1285.
Summary This order provided for the establishment of a Passenger Transport Executive for the metropolitan county of South Yorkshire. As it now takes effect under the Transport Act 1968, s 9(3), as substituted (see the note "Authority" above), it makes provision with respect to the proceedings of the Executive, for applying to the Executive certain enactments relating to local authorities, for enabling the Executive to appoint committees and to delegate functions to its Director General, and for securing the validity of acts of the Executive and the authentication of documents issued by it. In addition, provision was made for the transfer to the Executive, as from 1 April 1974, of the powers and duties of the existing local authorities in connection with the road passenger transport undertakings which they operated within the new county of South Yorkshire, for the modification of statutory provisions relating to those undertakings, and for enabling certain arrangements with respect to travel concessions on the services of those undertakings to be continued.

[312]

WEST YORKSHIRE PASSENGER TRANSPORT AREA (ESTABLISHMENT OF EXECUTIVE) ORDER 1973
SI 1973/1729

Title Passenger transport areas in England are renamed integrated transport areas by the Local Transport Act 2008, s 77(1), as from 9 February 2009 (see SI 2009/107).
Authority As noted to SI 1973/1728.
Date made 17 October 1973.
Commencement 19 November 1973.
Amendment Amended by SI 1990/1285.
Summary This order provided for the establishment of a Passenger Transport Executive for the metropolitan county of West Yorkshire; it also contains other provisions relating to the Executive which are similar to those contained in SI 1973/1728.

[313]

WEST MIDLANDS PASSENGER TRANSPORT AREA (ADAPTATION OF ENACTMENTS AND INSTRUMENTS) ORDER 1973
SI 1973/1730

Title Passenger transport areas in England are renamed integrated transport areas by the Local Transport Act 2008, s 77(1), as from 9 February 2009 (see SI 2009/107).
Authority As noted to SI 1973/1727.
Date made 17 October 1973.
Commencement 19 November 1973.
Amendment Amended by SI 1990/1285.
Summary This order provided for the West Midlands Passenger Transport Executive to become on 1 April 1974 the Passenger Transport Executive for the metropolitan county of West Midlands, for the dissolution on that date of the West Midlands Passenger Transport Authority, and for the vesting of its property, rights and liabilities in the County Council of West Midlands. It also provided for the transfer to the Executive, as from 1 April 1974, of the powers and duties of Coventry City Council in connection with their road passenger transport undertaking. The existing orders relating to the West Midlands Passenger Transport Area (of which only SI 1969/97 remains in force) were amended accordingly. This order is therefore now effective only to amend SI 1969/97.

[314]

MERSEYSIDE PASSENGER TRANSPORT AREA (ADAPTATION OF ENACTMENTS AND INSTRUMENTS) ORDER 1973
SI 1973/1731

Title Passenger transport areas in England are renamed integrated transport areas by the Local Transport Act 2008, s 77(1), as from 9 February 2009 (see SI 2009/107).
Authority As noted to SI 1973/1727.
Date made 17 October 1973.
Commencement 19 November 1973.
Summary This order provided for the Merseyside Passenger Transport Executive to become on 1 April 1974 the Passenger Transport Executive for the metropolitan county of Merseyside, for the dissolution on that date of the Merseyside Passenger Transport Authority, and for the vesting of its property, rights and liabilities in the County Council of Merseyside. It also provided for the transfer to the Executive, as from 1 April 1974, of the powers and duties of St Helens and Southport County

Borough Councils in connection with their road passenger transport undertakings. The existing orders relating to the Merseyside Passenger Transport Area (of which only SI 1969/94 remains in force) were amended accordingly. This order is therefore now effective only to amend SI 1969/94.

[315]

TYNE AND WEAR PASSENGER TRANSPORT AREA (ADAPTATION OF ENACTMENTS AND INSTRUMENTS) ORDER 1973
SI 1973/1732

Title Passenger transport areas in England are renamed integrated transport areas by the Local Transport Act 2008, s 77(1), as from 9 February 2009 (see SI 2009/107).
Authority As noted to SI 1973/1727.
Date made 17 October 1973.
Commencement 19 November 1973.
Summary This order provided for the Tyneside Passenger Transport Executive to become on 1 April 1974 the Passenger Transport Executive for the metropolitan county of Tyne and Wear, for the dissolution on that date of the Tyneside Passenger Transport Authority, and for the vesting of its property, rights and liabilities in the County Council of Tyne and Wear. The existing orders relating to the Tyneside Passenger Transport Area (of which only SI 1969/96 remains in force) were accordingly amended; and the Tyneside Passenger Transport (Designation of Additional Area) Order 1973, SI 1973/153 was revoked. This order is therefore now effective only to amend SI 1969/96.

[316]

BRITISH RAILWAYS BOARD (ALTERATION OF PENSION SCHEMES) ORDER 1973
SI 1973/2019

Authority Made by the Secretary of State for the Environment under the Transport Act 1962, s 74. S 74 has been repealed by the Railways Act 1993, s 134(2), (3) in so far as relating to the British Railways Board and its subsidiaries, but without prejudice to the continuing validity of any orders made under that section.
Date made 30 November 1973.
Commencement 2 January 1974.
Summary This order relates to certain railways pension funds of the British Railways Board and to the British Transport Docks Board (Salaried Staff) Pension Scheme. The order terminates the powers of the persons administering the railway pension funds to apply to the general purposes of the Board's undertaking, or to invest by way of deposit with the Board, money belonging to those funds. It also provides for the payment by the Board of interest at current rates on the existing deposits with the Board belonging to the railway pension funds and to the British Transport Docks Board (Salaried Staff) Pension Scheme, and for the redemption by the Board of the capital of those deposits in annual instalments spread over the years 1974 to 1978 (inclusive). Certain provisions of SI 1969/1858, SI 1970/477 relating to rates of interest on deposits are replaced.

As to the reconstitution of the British Transport Docks Board as Associated British Ports, under the control of a holding company, see the Preliminary Note "Reorganisation of transport undertakings". As to the winding down and abolition of the British Railways Board, see the Transport Act 2000 and the Preliminary Note "Privatisation of the railway system" (under the main head "Reorganisation of transport undertakings").

[317]

MOTORWAYS TRAFFIC (SPEED LIMIT) REGULATIONS 1974
SI 1974/502

Authority Made by the Secretary of State for the Environment and the Secretaries of State for Scotland and Wales under the Road Traffic Regulation Act 1967, s 13 (repealed). Now have effect (by virtue of the Interpretation Act 1978, s 17(2)(b), printed in the title Statutory Instruments (Pt 2), Vol 1 of this work) under the Road Traffic Regulation Act 1984, s 17(2).
Date made 21 March 1974.
Commencement 29 March 1974.
Amendment Amended by SI 2000/1811 (of local application only and accordingly outside the scope of this work).
Summary These regulations re-impose a maximum speed limit of 70 miles per hour (in place of the 50 miles per hour speed limit imposed by the Motorways Traffic (Speed Limit) Regulations 1973, SI 1973/2059, which are revoked) on the driving of motor vehicles on motorways, except on:

(a) specified lengths of motorway on which speed limits of 60 mph or 50 mph are re-imposed by these regulations, and
(b) other lengths of motorway which are for the time being subject to speed limits lower than 70 mph.

In relation to roads other than motorways, see the 70 miles per hour, 60 miles per hour and 50 miles per hour (Temporary Speed Limit) Order 1977.

[318]

PIPE-LINES ACT 1962 (REPEALS AND MODIFICATIONS) REGULATIONS 1974
SI 1974/1986

Authority Made by the Secretary of State under the Health and Safety at Work etc Act 1974, ss 15(1), (3)(a), 80(1), 82(3)(a).
Date made 24 November 1974.
Commencement 1 January 1975.
Summary These regulations contain repeals and modifications of provisions of the Pipe-lines Act 1962 in consequence of the establishment on 1 January 1975 of the Health and Safety Executive and the coming into operation on that date of the provisions of the Health and Safety at Work etc Act 1974 which supersede or affect provisions of the 1962 Act. The regulations therefore:
(a) transfer certain powers from the Secretary of State to the Health and Safety Executive;
(b) transfer the functions of inspectors appointed under the 1962 Act to inspectors appointed by the Health and Safety Executive under the 1974 Act;
(c) apply to certain offences under the 1962 Act committed on or after 1 January 1975 the penalties prescribed in the 1974 Act; and
(d) repeal or modify powers and provisions which are superseded or affected by powers and provisions contained in the 1974 Act.

The regulations also provide for inspectors appointed under the 1962 Act to have, in relation to their functions under that Act concerning matters other than the safety of pipe-lines, the powers of inspectors appointed under the 1974 Act.

[319]

BRITISH RAILWAYS BOARD (CENTRAL TRUST) ORDER 1974
SI 1974/2001

Authority Made by the Secretary of State for the Environment under the Transport Act 1962, s 74. S 74 has been repealed by the Railways Act 1993, s 134(2), (3) in so far as relating to the British Railways Board and its subsidiaries, but without prejudice to the continuing validity of any orders made under that section.
Date made 2 December 1974.
Commencement 1 January 1975.
Summary This order provided for the transfer of the assets and liabilities of certain railway pension schemes (listed in the Schedule to the order) to the trustees of a Central Trust established by the British Railways Board in connection with the funding of pension scheme obligations under the Railways Act 1974, s 5 (now repealed, consequent on the cancellation of remaining debts, by the Transport Act 1980, s 58(1)(a)). The order preserves the rights of the members of, and the beneficiaries from, the various pension schemes and provides protection against any possible worsening of their position. As to the winding down and abolition of the British Railways Board, see the Transport Act 2000 and the Preliminary Note "Privatisation of the railway system" (under the main head "Reorganisation of transport undertakings").

[320]

ROAD TRAFFIC ACT 1974 (COMMENCEMENT NO 1) ORDER 1974
SI 1974/2075

Authority Made by the Home Secretary, the Secretary of State for the Environment and the Secretaries of State for Scotland and Wales under the Road Traffic Act 1974, s 24(4).
Date made 10 December 1974.
Summary This order brought various provisions of the Road Traffic Act 1974 into force as follows:
(a) on 1 January 1975: ss 6, 9(1), 10(1)–(6), (7) (part), 11, 12, 13(1) (part), 14–19, 21–23, 24(1), (2) (part), (3) (part), (4), (5), Schs 2 (part), 3 (part), 4, 5, 6 (part), 7 (part); and
(b) on 1 March 1975: ss 8, 13(1) (part), (3), 20(1), (3) (in their application to Great Britain), 24(2) (part), Schs 3 (part), 6 (part).

Further orders Other provisions of the 1974 Act were brought into force by the following orders made under s 24(4):
(a) by SI 1975/489, on 1 April 1975: ss 13(1) (part), 24(2) (part), (3) (part), Schs 3 (part), 6 (part), 7 (part);
(b) by SI 1975/756, on 1 June 1975: s 13(1) (part), Sch 3 (part);
(c) by SI 1975/1154, on 1 September 1975: ss 1–5, 24(3) (part), Schs 1, 7 (part);
(d) by SI 1975/1479, on 1 October 1975: s 13(1) (part), Sch 3 (part); and on 1 January 1976: ss 13 (part), 24(3) (part), Schs 3 (part), 7 (part);
(e) by SI 1975/1653, on 31 October 1975: s 7(1) (part);
(f) by SI 1984/811, on 1 August 1984: ss 9(3)–(6), 24(3) (part), Sch 7 (part).

The 1974 Act has largely been repealed, and the commencement orders relating to it are now largely spent.

[321]

MOTOR VEHICLES (INTERNATIONAL CIRCULATION) ORDER 1975
SI 1975/1208

Authority Made under the Motor Vehicles (International Circulation) Act 1952, s 1(1), (4), as extended by SI 1973/2163, in the title Northern Ireland.

Date made 23 July 1975.

Commencement 2 August 1975.

Amendment Amended by SI 1980/1095, SI 1985/459 (both partially revoked by SI 1989/993), SI 1989/993, SI 1991/771, SI 1991/1727, SI 1996/1929, SI 1996/1974, SI 2004/1992. Note that SI 1989/993 is still to be brought fully into force pending the coming into force of the Convention on Road Traffic (Vienna 1968; Cmnd 4032) as respects the United Kingdom.

Summary This Order in Council revoked and replaced with amendments the Motor Vehicles (International Circulation) Order 1957, SI 1957/1074, and subsequent amending orders. It also revoked and replaced certain provisions having effect in Northern Ireland relating to vehicle excise duty and the registration of vehicles.

The order gives effect to certain provisions of the following international agreements: the Convention on Road Traffic of 1949 (Cmd 7997); the Convention on the Taxation of Road Vehicles for Private Use in International Traffic of 1956 (Cmnd 220); the Convention on the Taxation of Road Vehicles engaged in International Passenger Traffic of 1956 (Cmnd 320); the Convention on the Taxation of Road Vehicles engaged in International Goods Transport of 1956 (Cmnd 4206); the Convention on Motor Traffic of 1926 (Cmnd 3510); Article IV of the Agreement regarding the Status of Forces of Parties to the North Atlantic Treaty (Cmnd 8279); a Decision of the Council of the Organisation for European Economic Co-operation adopted on 28 June 1957, relating to identification marks for hired chauffeur-driven vehicles going abroad from the United Kingdom; and the Convention on Road Traffic of 1968 (Cmnd 4032) (see, however, the note "Amendment" above).

The Secretary of State (formerly the Minister of Transport) is empowered to issue to United Kingdom residents for use outside the United Kingdom an international driving permit in one of three forms in Sch 1 to the order, referred to below. The Secretary of State may also issue for use outside the United Kingdom an international certificate for motor vehicles registered under the Vehicle Excise and Registration Act 1994, and the form of this certificate is also set out in Sch 1. The fee for the issue of such a document is £5.50. The Secretary of State may delegate any of these functions to any body concerned with motor vehicles or to any Northern Ireland department.

Persons resident outside the United Kingdom who hold either a "Convention driving permit" or a "domestic driving permit" issued by a country outside the United Kingdom, as defined by the order may, during a period of 12 months from the date of their last entry into the United Kingdom, drive, or cause or permit such persons to drive, in Great Britain motor vehicles of the class which they are authorised by their permits to drive without holding driving licences issued under the Road Traffic Act 1988, Pt III. Holders of a Convention driving permit or a domestic driving permit issued in a country outside the United Kingdom may, during a period of 12 months from the date of their last entry into the United Kingdom, drive, or cause or permit such persons to drive:

(a) in the case of any such person who is resident in an EEA State, the Isle of Man, Jersey or Guernsey, a medium-sized goods vehicle, a large goods vehicle, a privately-operated passenger vehicle or a passenger-carrying vehicle; and

(b) in the case of any other such person, a medium-sized goods vehicle, a large goods vehicle, a privately-operated passenger vehicle or a passenger-carrying vehicle brought temporarily into Great Britain,

which he is authorised by that permit to drive, notwithstanding that he is not the holder of a medium-sized goods vehicle driver's licence, a large goods vehicle driver's licence, a privately-operated passenger vehicle driver's licence or a passenger-carrying vehicle driver's licence.

The previous provisions relating to visitors' driving permits do not authorise persons to drive, or to cause or permit persons to drive, motor vehicles while under age by virtue of the Road Traffic Act 1988, s 101, although further provision is made in relation to such disqualification. Nor do those provisions authorise driving while disqualified in consequence of a conviction or the order of a court. The Secretary of State may by order withdraw the rights mentioned in relation to holders of domestic driving permits.

Provision is made for members of a visiting force and their dependants and members of a civilian component of such a force and their dependants who hold foreign driving permits and who are not disqualified from driving by virtue of a conviction or the order of a court to drive in Great Britain motor vehicles of any class which they are authorised by their permits to drive without holding driving licences issued under Pt III of the 1988 Act.

Provision is made for the exemption from excise duty under the Vehicle Excise and Registration Act 1994, to the extent specified in the order, of vehicles brought temporarily into the United Kingdom by persons resident outside the United Kingdom; the exemption applies to vehicles entering the United Kingdom from other member states in conformity with specified EEC Council Directives and Regulations. The Secretary of State may by regulations provide for the furnishing to a registration authority by persons who import such vehicles of such particulars as may be prescribed, for the recording by a registration authority of any particulars which the Secretary of State may by the regulations direct to be recorded, for the manner of such recording, and for the making of such particulars available for use by such persons who may be specified on payment of a fee, for the production to a registration authority of prescribed documents and for the registration of vehicles which are exempt from excise duty and for the assignment of registration marks to, and for the issue of registration cards for, such vehicles.

The order also makes provision with respect to registration marks assigned under the Vehicle Excise and Registration Act 1994 to motor vehicles brought temporarily into Great Britain; and it enables regulations under the provisions of the Road Traffic Act 1988 relating to the lighting of vehicles to vary or grant exemptions from the requirements of those provisions in the case of motor vehicles or trailers brought temporarily into Great Britain.

The following forms are set out in Sch 1 to the order:

Form A	International Driving Permit under Convention of 1949
Form B	International Driving Permit under Convention of 1926
Form C	International Driving Permit under Convention of 1968
Form D	International Certificate for Motor Vehicles under Convention of 1926.

[322]

INTERNATIONAL CARRIAGE OF DANGEROUS GOODS (REAR MARKING OF MOTOR VEHICLES) REGULATIONS 1975
SI 1975/2111

Authority Made by the Secretary of State for the Environment under the Road Traffic Act 1972, ss 73(5), 78(5) (repealed). Those sections were repealed by the Road Traffic Act 1974, s 24(3), Sch 7, but, by virtue of s 9(4) thereof, these regulations continued to have effect as if made under the Road Traffic Act 1972, s 40 (repealed). By virtue of s 9(4) of the 1974 Act (repealed), the Road Traffic (Consequential Provisions) Act 1988, ss 2(2), 5(1), Sch 4, para 1(2), and the Interpretation Act 1978, s 17(2)(b), printed in the title Statutory Instruments (Pt 2), Vol 1 of this work, these regulations now have effect as if made under the Road Traffic Act 1988, s 41.
Date made 10 December 1975.
Commencement 12 January 1976.
Summary These regulations, which revoke and replace the Motor Vehicles (Rear Markings) Regulations 1975, SI 1975/29, apply to any vehicle when carrying dangerous goods (i e any substance in respect of the carriage of which special provision is made by Annex B, Chapter I, s 5, marginal 10 500 of the European Agreement concerning the International Carriage of Dangerous Goods by Road, signed at Geneva on 30 September 1957 (Cmnd 3769), as amended) by road on a journey some part of which has taken place, or will take place, outside the United Kingdom. The regulations prescribe the size, colour and type of rear markings which may be displayed by such vehicles (with special markings applicable to tank-vehicles carrying dangerous goods consisting of not more than one kind of substance) and make provision as to the position of the rear markings on the vehicles.

[323]

GOODS VEHICLES (ASCERTAINMENT OF MAXIMUM GROSS WEIGHTS) REGULATIONS 1976
SI 1976/555

Authority Made by the Secretary of State for the Environment under the Road Traffic Act 1972, ss 107, 110 (repealed); subsequently took effect (by virtue of the Interpretation Act 1978, s 17(2)(b), printed in the title Statutory Instruments (Pt 2), Vol 1 of this work, and the Road Traffic (Consequential Provisions) Act 1988, s 2(2)), under the Road Traffic Act 1988, ss 105, 108, 110. S 110 of the 1988 Act has been repealed, subject to savings, and re-enacted by the Road Traffic (Driver Licensing and Information Systems) Act 1989, ss 1(1), 2(1), 16, Schs 2, 6; these regulations have lapsed in so far as they were made under s 110 as originally enacted.
Date made 7 April 1976.
Commencement 5 May 1976, but with retrospective effect from 1 January 1976.
Summary These regulations prescribe for the purposes of the Road Traffic Act 1988, Pt III (which relates to the licensing of drivers) the multipliers which are to be used to ascertain, by reference to the unladen weight of the vehicle, the notional maximum gross weights of motor goods vehicles, goods trailers and articulated goods vehicle combinations in cases where the appropriate gross weight or train weight of the vehicle or vehicle combination is not marked on the vehicle itself in accordance with SI 1986/1078. The retrospective effect of the regulations was authorised by the Road Traffic (Drivers' Ages and Hours of Work) Act 1976, s 1(3) (now consolidated in the Road Traffic Act 1988).

[324]

CARRIAGE OF GOODS (PROHIBITION OF DISCRIMINATION) REGULATIONS 1977
SI 1977/276

Authority Made by the Secretary of State for Transport under the European Communities Act 1972, s 2(2).
Date made 21 February 1977.
Commencement 23 March 1977.
Amendment Amended by virtue of the Criminal Justice Act 1988, s 51 and the Road Traffic Act 1991, s 9(2).
Summary These regulations make provisions for Great Britain supplementary to the requirements of Council Regulation (EEC) 11 of 1960 (OJ L52, 16.08.1960, p 1121) concerning the abolition of discrimination in transport rates and conditions. The regulations make it an offence for persons carrying

on transport undertakings to fail to notify the Secretary of State of measures involving tariffs or agreements concerning transport rates or conditions which vary according to the country of origin or destination of the goods in question. They also make it an offence for a carrier of goods to fail to prepare or maintain prescribed transport documents. Transport documents must be produced for inspection by examiners and inspectors appointed by the Secretary of State, who are given powers of entry onto premises for the purpose of such inspection. Certain information relating to transport tariffs and agreements or arrangements on transport rates and conditions may be required to be furnished to the EC Commission or to the Secretary of State. Failure to supply required information, or the supply of false information, is an offence, as is a breach of confidentiality of information given.

[325]

BRITISH RAILWAYS BOARD (PENSION FUNDS INVESTMENT PROVISIONS) ORDER 1977
SI 1977/699

Authority Made by the Secretary of State for Transport under the Transport Act 1962, s 74. S 74 has been repealed by the Railways Act 1993, s 134(2), (3) in so far as relating to the British Railways Board and its subsidiaries, but without prejudice to the continuing validity of any orders made under that section.

Date made 18 April 1977.

Commencement 6 May 1977.

Summary This order confers additional powers on the British Railways Board as the trustees of certain of the Board's old pension funds to which new members are not now admitted. The Board is given power to act by its proper officers or to delegate functions to a Committee, to use a nominee company (being a wholly-owned subsidiary of the Board) to hold and manage investments, and to appoint a competent and responsible person to advise on investment. By the British Railways Act 1980, s 48, Sch 4, the British Railways Board may by deed cancel or modify all or any of the provisions of this order so far as they relate to the pensions and superannuation funds defined in the said s 48.

As to the winding down and abolition of the British Railways Board, see the Transport Act 2000 and the Preliminary Note "Privatisation of the railway system" (under the main head "Reorganisation of transport undertakings").

[326]

VEHICLE AND DRIVING LICENCES (COMPENSATION TO OFFICERS) REGULATIONS 1977
SI 1977/1316

Authority Made by the Secretary of State for Transport under the Vehicle and Driving Licences Act 1969, s 2(3).

Date made 28 July 1977.

Commencement 2 September 1977.

Summary These regulations, which revoke and replace the Vehicle and Driving Licences (Compensation to Officers) Regulations 1970, SI 1970/301, provide for the payment of compensation to or in respect of persons who suffered loss of employment or loss or diminution of emoluments which was attributable to the Vehicle and Driving Licences Act 1969, s 1 (repealed) (which provided for the transfer to the Ministry of Transport (now the Secretary of State) of local authorities' functions relating to vehicle and driving licences, etc). The compensation payable is:

(a) resettlement compensation for loss of employment;
(b) long-term compensation for loss of employment or loss or diminution of emoluments;
(c) retirement compensation; and
(d) compensation payable to the widow or dependants of a claimant.

The regulations specify the qualifications and other conditions which claimants must satisfy in order to be eligible for compensation, the methods of calculating the amount of compensation and the procedure for making claims and notifying decisions. There is a right of appeal from the decision of the Secretary of State to an employment tribunal (formerly known as an industrial tribunal) established under the Employment Protection (Consolidation) Act 1978, s 128 (repealed); see now the Employment Tribunals Act 1996, s 1.

[327]

70 MILES PER HOUR, 60 MILES PER HOUR AND 50 MILES PER HOUR (TEMPORARY SPEED LIMIT) ORDER 1977

Authority Made by the Secretary of State for Transport and the Secretaries of State for Scotland and Wales under the Road Traffic Regulation Act 1967, s 77(1), (2) (repealed). Now has effect (by virtue of the Interpretation Act 1978, s 17(2)(b), printed in the title Statutory Instruments (Pt 2), Vol 1 of this work) under the Road Traffic Regulation Act 1984, s 88.

Date made 25 May 1977.

Commencement 1 June 1977.

Amendment Amended by an order dated 16 August 1978 and by SI 1978/1548, which continued the operation of the order indefinitely.

Summary This order imposes speed limits of 50 mph on certain lengths of dual and single carriageway road; 60 mph on all other lengths of single carriageway road (not being a motorway) and on certain lengths of dual carriageway road; and 70 mph on all other lengths of dual carriageway road (not being a motorway). This order as originally made was to expire at midnight on 30 November 1978 but it has been continued in operation indefinitely by SI 1978/1548.

In relation to motorways, see SI 1974/502.

[328]

TRANSPORT ACT 1978 (COMMENCEMENT NO 1) ORDER 1978 SI 1978/1150

Authority Made by the Secretary of State for Transport under the Transport Act 1978, s 24(1).
Date made 3 August 1978.
Summary This order brought into force on 4 August 1978 the following provisions of the Transport Act 1978: ss 15, 17, 18, 21, 23, 24(1)–(3), (4) (part), Sch 4 (part).
Further orders The remaining provisions of the 1978 Act (with the exception of s 25) were brought into force as follows:

(a) by SI 1978/1187, on 1 September 1978: ss 1–4, 7, 8 (part), 10–14, 16, 22, 24(4) (part), Schs 1, 2 (part), 4 (part); and on 1 November 1978: ss 5, 6, 8 (part), 9, 24(4) (part), Schs 2 (part), 3, 4 (part); and

(b) by SI 1978/1289 (spent), on 1 October 1978: ss 19, 20.

SI 1978/1289 is spent following the repeal of ss 19, 20 of the 1978 Act by the Transport Act 1980, ss 58(1)(b), 69, Sch 9, Pt II. Repeals of the 1978 Act are noted in Halsbury's Statutes, 4th edn Vol 36, title Roads, Railways and Transport.

[329]

WEIGHING OF MOTOR VEHICLES (USE OF DYNAMIC AXLE WEIGHING MACHINES) REGULATIONS 1978 SI 1978/1180

Authority Made by the Secretary of State for Transport under the Road Traffic Act 1972, s 160(1), (1A), (5) (repealed), as amended by the Road Traffic Act 1974, s 14 (repealed). Now have effect under the Road Traffic Act 1988, s 78, by virtue of the Road Traffic (Consequential Provisions) Act 1988, s 2(2) and the Interpretation Act 1978, s 17(2)(b), printed in the title Statutory Instruments (Pt 2), Vol 1 of this work.
Date made 7 August 1978.
Commencement 15 September 1978.
Amendment Amended by virtue of the Road Traffic Act 1991, s 9(2).
Summary These regulations make provision for facilitating the use of dynamic axle weighing machines in order to ascertain the weights transmitted to the road surface by the wheels of each axle of a motor vehicle or trailer and in consequence, the gross weight of the motor vehicle or trailer. The regulations prescribe the manner in which the weighing should be carried out, and specify limits of presumed accuracy of plus or minus 150 kg for the wheels of each axle. They also prescribe a form of certificate of weight to be issued when a dynamic axle weighing machine is used.

[330]

NATIONAL FREIGHT CORPORATION (CENTRAL TRUST) ORDER 1978 SI 1978/1290

Authority Made by the Secretary of State for Transport under the Transport Act 1962, s 74.
Date made 1 September 1978.
Commencement 1 October 1978.
Summary This order provided for the transfer of the assets and liabilities of certain pension schemes of the National Freight Corporation (listed in the Schedule to the order) to the trustees of a Central Trust established by the Corporation in connection with the funding of pension scheme obligations under the Transport Act 1978, s 19 (now repealed, consequent on the cancellation of remaining debts, by the Transport Act 1980, s 58(1)(b)). The rights of the members of, and the beneficiaries from, the various pension schemes are preserved and provision is made to protect them against any possible worsening of their position. The Corporation has since been dissolved and its undertaking transferred to a successor company; see the Preliminary Note "Reorganisation of transport undertakings".
Further order SI 1980/657, which was also made under the Transport Act 1962, s 74, and came into force on 10 June 1980, transferred to the Central Trust responsibility for certain supplemental pensions previously payable by the National Freight Corporation out of revenue. It also deleted provisions in the Central Trust deed restricting pension schemes and arrangements which can be brought within the central Trust to those which could have been prescribed under the Transport Act 1978, s 19 (repealed).

[331]

BRITISH RAILWAYS BOARD (WINDING UP OF CLOSED PENSION FUNDS) ORDER 1978
SI 1978/1358

Authority Made by the Secretary of State for Transport under the Transport Act 1962, s 74. S 74 has been repealed by the Railways Act 1993, s 134(2), (3) in so far as relating to the British Railways Board and its subsidiaries, but without prejudice to the continuing validity of any orders made under that section.

Date made 17 September 1978.

Commencement 11 October 1978; however, the order has retrospective effect from 6 April 1978.

Amendment Amended by SI 2001/3649.

Modification Previously modified by SI 1994/1696 (revoked).

Summary This order amends the terms of the British Railways Superannuation Fund (Amalgamated Sections) and the Great Western Railway Supplemental Pensions Reserve Fund so as to permit the employment of any member of either fund to be contracted-out of the earnings-related component of the state pension scheme provided for in the Social Security Pensions Act 1975 (repealed; see now, generally, the Social Security Contributions and Benefits Act 1992). By the British Railways Act 1980, s 48, Sch 4, the British Railways Board may by deed cancel or modify all or any of the provisions of this order so far as they relate to the pension and superannuation funds defined in the said s 48.

As to the winding down and abolition of the British Railways Board, see the Transport Act 2000 and the Preliminary Note "Privatisation of the railway system" (under the main head "Reorganisation of transport undertakings").

[332]

CONTROL OF OFF-STREET PARKING (ENGLAND AND WALES) ORDER 1978
SI 1978/1535

Authority Made under the Transport Act 1978, s 11 (repealed). Now has effect under the Road Traffic Regulation Act 1984, s 44, by virtue of the Interpretation Act 1978, s 17(2)(b), printed in the title Statutory Instruments (Pt 2), Vol 1 of this work.

Date made 24 October 1978.

Commencement 1 December 1978.

Amendment Amended by SI 1996/1008.

Summary The Transport Act 1978, s 11 enabled an Order in Council to be made providing, in the remainder of England and Wales (and Scotland), controls over public off-street parking equivalent to those provided in relation to Greater London by the Transport (London) Act 1969, s 36, Sch 5. These provisions were repealed by the Road Traffic Regulation Act 1984, s 146, Sch 14 and replaced by provisions of that Act. S 44 of the 1984 Act provides that an Order in Council under that section may make such provision for the remainder of England and Wales as is made for Greater London by s 43 of the Act. This Order in Council takes effect as if made under the said s 44 and for the avoidance of doubt it is declared by SI 1986/225 that this order continues to have effect with respect to the regulation of off-street parking places in non-metropolitan counties in England and counties in Wales (now, by virtue of the Local Government (Wales) Act 1994, counties or county boroughs in Wales). Arts 3, 4 of the order enable county councils in England and county councils or, as the case may be, county borough councils in Wales by regulations to designate controlled areas in which under art 5 the provision of public off-street parking places will require a licence. The procedure for such designation is specified in Pt I of the Schedule; regulations which designate controlled areas are outside the scope of this work.

Arts 6, 7 provide for permanent or limited licences and for the terms and conditions of licences. Inspection of parking places is provided for in art 8. Local authorities are required to give reasons for their decisions by art 9. Art 10 and Pt II of the Schedule deal with the transfer, surrender, variation and revocation of licences. Provision for appeals against decisions with respect to licences and for compensation in certain cases is made in arts 11, 13 and in Pts III, IV of the Schedule. In particular, para 17 of the Schedule enables the Secretary of State to make regulations governing the procedure to be followed in connection with appeals; see further the note "Appeals procedure" below.

Contravention by the holder of a licence of its terms and conditions is an offence under art 12, as is the operation of a public off-street parking place without a licence. County councils and local authorities are required by art 15 to apply the principles of the control to their own public off-street parking places situated in a controlled area. Art 16 gives the Secretary of State power to suspend the control in an emergency. Pt V of the Schedule provides for permissible periods of unlicensed operation of public off-street parking places in certain cases.

Appeals procedure SI 1979/236, as amended by SI 1996/1008 (in force on 3 April 1979), was made under the powers provided by para 17 of the Schedule to the above order and now has effect as if made under the Road Traffic Regulation Act 1984, s 44. (SI 1979/236 has been modified by SI 1991/2684, in the title Courts and Legal Services, as to application to recognised bodies within the meaning of the Administration of Justice Act 1985, s 9.) For the avoidance of doubt it is declared by SI 1986/264, noted under the head "Appeals procedure" to SI 1986/225, that these regulations continue to have effect for prescribing the procedure for appeals against decisions of local authorities (other than metropolitan district councils) outside Greater London in connection with licences for the operation of public off-street parking places. They prescribe the procedure for appeals to the Secretary of State against decisions of local authorities in England (outside Greater London) and Wales in connection with licences for the operation of public off-street parking places in those areas where such operation is controlled under this order.

[333]

PUBLIC SERVICE VEHICLES (LOST PROPERTY) REGULATIONS 1978
SI 1978/1684

Authority Made by the Secretary of State for Transport under the Road Traffic Act 1960, s 160 (repealed); now have effect under the Public Passenger Vehicles Act 1981, s 60, by virtue of the Interpretation Act 1978, s 17(2)(b), printed in the title Statutory Instruments (Pt 2), Vol 1 of this work.
Date made 23 November 1978.
Commencement 1 January 1979.
Amendment Amended by SI 1995/185, SI 2003/1615. Previously amended by SI 1981/1623 (superseded by SI 1995/185).
Penalty Any person who contravenes or fails to comply with these regulations is liable on summary conviction to a fine not exceeding level 2 on the standard scale for each offence; see the Public Passenger Vehicles Act 1981, s 67.
Summary These regulations, which revoke and replace with amendments the Public Service Vehicles (Lost Property) Regulations 1934, SR & O 1934/1268, and the amending SI 1958/2262, SI 1960/2397, govern action to be taken where property is accidentally left in or on public service vehicles. A duty is placed on the finder to hand it over immediately to the conductor, or if this is impracticable, to deliver it to the operator's lost property office; the conductor is obliged to search the vehicle for lost property at the end of every journey. The conductor must deliver any property found to the operator or his representative within 24 hours, unless he has previously returned it to a person whom he is satisfied is the owner. The property must be kept in safe custody until it is returned to its owner, or disposed of, in pursuance of these regulations, except that official documents should wherever practicable be returned to the appropriate government body and, except in the case of such documents, where the name and address of a person who may be the owner is readily ascertainable, that person should be notified. If a person claims property while it is in the custody of the operator, and satisfies the operator of his ownership and gives his name and address, it must be returned to him upon payment of an amount not exceeding £2, if required. If, within one month of the property being delivered to an operator, the property is not claimed, no person satisfies the operator that he is the owner or a person satisfies the operator that he is the owner but refuses or omits to give his name and address or pay the charge, the property vests in the operator, who is entitled to dispose of it as he thinks fit.

Special provision enables perishable property to be disposed of within 48 hours of finding; other provisions relate to liability for the cost of packing and carriage, and examination of property. The regulations do not apply to property found in vehicles belonging to Transport for London or any of its subsidiaries (within the meaning of the Greater London Authority Act 1999) (see instead the London Transport Act 1982, s 19, Sch 2).

[334]

PASSENGER AND GOODS VEHICLES (RECORDING EQUIPMENT) REGULATIONS 1979
SI 1979/1746

Authority Made by the Minister of Transport under the European Communities Act 1972, s 2(2) and the Transport Act 1968, ss 95(1), (1A), 101(1), (2), (5), 157.
Date made 21 December 1979.
Commencement 14 January 1980.
Amendment Amended by SI 1984/144, SI 1986/1457, SI 1986/2076, SI 2006/3276. Previously amended by SI 1985/1801 (revoked by SI 1986/2076), SI 1991/381, SI 1994/1838 (both revoked by SI 1996/941), SI 1996/941 (revoked by SI 2006/3276).
Summary These regulations, which revoke the Passenger and Goods Vehicles (Recording Equipment) Regulations 1977, SI 1977/777, apply to passenger and goods vehicles to which the Transport Act 1968, Pt VI applies. They amend Pt VI of the 1968 Act by substituting new ss 97, 97A, 97B for the original s 97. The regulations, as amended, implement: Council Regulation (EEC) 3821/85 (OJ L370, 31.12.1985, p 8) (as it has effect in accordance with Commission Regulations (EEC) 3314/90 (OJ L318, 17.11.1990, p 20) and 3688/92 (OJ L374, 22.12.1992, p 12), Commission Regulations (EC) 2479/95 (OJ L256, 26.10.1995, p 8), 1056/97 (OJ L154, 12.06.1997, p 21), 1360/2002 (OJ L207, 05.08.2002, p 1), 432/2004 (OJ L071, 10.03.2004, p 3), Art 1 of Council Regulation (EC) 2135/98 (OJ L274, 09.10.1998, p 1), the Act concerning the conditions of accession of the Czech Republic, the Republic of Estonia, the Republic of Cyprus, the Republic of Latvia, the Republic of Lithuania, the Republic of Hungary, the Republic of Malta, the Republic of Poland, the Republic of Slovenia and the Slovak Republic and the adjustments to the Treaties on which the European Union is founded (OJ L236, 23.09.2003, p 33), and Regulations (EC) 1882/2003 (OJ L284, 31.10.2003, p 1) and 561/2006 (OJ L102, 11.04.2006, p 1) of the European Parliament and of the Council, and as read with SI 2007/1819).

The provisions inserted in the 1968 Act relate to the installation and use of recording equipment (tachographs) in road transport and the production of records produced by such equipment etc. The regulations provided a timetable for the coming into force of the requirements of ss 97, 97A relating to the installation of tachographs and their use, and the supplementary provisions of s 97A. The latest date specified in relation to any requirement was 31 December 1981.

The regulations also make consequential amendments to ss 98, 99 of the 1968 Act, and to the Road Traffic (Foreign Vehicles) Act 1972, Sch 1. Provision is made for the approval by the Minister of Transport (now the Secretary of State) of fitters and workshops for the installation and repair of tachographs in Great Britain. The period for which drivers of vehicles registered in Great Britain are required to retain record sheets is reduced from seven days to two days.

Further regulations The following regulations amending Pt VI of the Transport Act 1968 have been made under the European Communities Act 1972, s 2(2):

(a) SI 1984/144 (in force on 13 March 1984), as amended by SI 1986/1457, SI 1996/941 (revoked), SI 2006/3276, amends s 97 of the 1968 Act; also amends and partially revokes SI 1979/1746;
(b) SI 1986/1457 (in force on 29 September 1986) amends ss 96(11A), 97, 97A, 97B, 99, 103 of the 1968 Act; also amended the Road Traffic Act 1972, s 82, the effect of which amendment has been incorporated in the Road Traffic Act 1988, s 85; also amends SI 1979/1746, SI 1984/144 and partially revokes SI 1979/1746;
(c) SI 1989/2121 (in force on 23 November 1989) amends s 97 of the 1968 Act and inserts s 97AA thereof;
(d) SI 2005/1904, as amended by SI 2006/3276 (in force on 5 August 2005) amends ss 97, 97B, 98, 99, 99A, 103 of the 1968 Act and the Road Traffic (Foreign Vehicles) Act 1972, Sch 1;
(e) SI 2006/1117 (in force on 1 May 2006) amends s 97(7) of the 1968 Act; and
(f) SI 2006/3276 (in force on 3 January 2007) amends s 97(7) of the 1968 Act and the Road Traffic Act 1988, s 85; also amends SI 1979/1746, SI 1984/144, SI 2005/1140, SI 2006/1937; revokes SI 1996/941 and partially revokes SI 2005/1904 (also amended SI 1986/1456 (revoked)).

See also SI 1986/1458, SI 2007/1819.

Fees SI 1986/2128 (which was made under the Finance Act 1973, s 56(1), (2) and came into force on 30 January 1987) has been amended by SI 2009/866 (and was previously amended by SI 1988/2043, SI 1989/2016, SI 1991/457, SI 1993/3066, SI 1997/219, SI 2000/1465, SI 2001/1810, SI 2002/538, SI 2003/1812, SI 2004/1885, SI 2005/2458, SI 2007/606, SI 2008/1581 (all superseded)). The 1986 regulations, which revoke the Passenger and Goods Vehicles (Recording Equipment) (Approval of fitters and workshops) (Fees) Regulations 1977, SI 1977/1413, and the amending SI 1985/1802, provide that the fees which the Secretary of State may require to be paid in connection with the approval of a fitter or workshop for the installation or repair of recording equipment in accordance with Art 12 of Council Regulation (EEC) 3821/85 (OJ L370, 31.12.1985, p 8) are:

(a) a fee of £361 on the issue of an approval; and
(b) a fee of £148 on the renewal of an approval.

Tachograph cards As to regulations providing for the issuing and use of driver cards, company cards, workshop cards and control cards for use with digital tachographs, which are tachographs complying with Annexes IB and II to Council Regulation (EEC) 3821/85 (OJ L370, 31.12.1985, p 8), see SI 2005/1140, SI 2006/1937.

[335]

MOTORCYCLES (SOUND LEVEL MEASUREMENT CERTIFICATES) REGULATIONS 1980
SI 1980/765

Authority Made by the Minister of Transport under the European Communities Act 1972, s 2(2).
Date made 19 May 1980.
Commencement 3 July 1980.
Amendment Amended by SI 1988/1640, SI 1989/713, SI 1989/1591.
Summary These regulations make provision for the issue of sound level measurement certificates to signify whether or not certain types of motorcycles comply with the harmonised requirements specified in Council Directive (EEC) 78/1015 on the approximation of the laws of the member states on the permissible sound level and exhaust system of motorcycles (OJ L349, 13.12.1978, p 21) (repealed and replaced by Directive 97/24/EC of the European Parliament and of the Council on certain components and characteristics of two or three-wheel motor vehicles (OJ L226, 18.8.1997, p 1)). Reg 3 prescribes requirements as to applications for certificates, and reg 4 provides for the issue, cancellation and suspension of certificates. Reg 5 requires manufacturers to give notice of cessation of, or alteration in, the manufacture of type vehicles or alterations in the prescribed characteristics. Regs 6–8 contain further provisions as to cancellation, suspension or modification of certificates. Reg 9 provides for appeals by those aggrieved by a decision as to a certificate, and reg 10 contains provisions relating to the stations where examination of vehicles may be carried out for the purposes of these regulations. Reg 11 provides for the issue of duplicate certificates. For fees payable, see SI 1999/2149.

[336]

TRANSPORT ACT 1980 (COMMENCEMENT NO 1) ORDER 1980
SI 1980/913

Authority Made by the Minister of Transport under the Transport Act 1980, s 70(5), (6).
Date made 2 July 1980.
Amendment Amended by SI 1980/1353, SI 1981/256.
Summary This order brought the following provisions of the Transport Act 1980 into force on 31 July 1980: ss 1(3), (4) (as it relates to the following sections), 27, 36, 39, 43(1) (part), 64, 69 (part), Sch 5, Pt I, paras 4 (part), 5, 6, 12 (part), 14, 15, Sch 9, Pt I (part).

Further orders The remaining provisions of the Act were brought into force as follows:

(a) by SI 1980/1353 (as amended by SI 1981/256), on 6 October 1980: ss 1(3), (4) (as it relates to the following sections), 2–15, 28(1)–(5), (7)–(10) (as it relates to road service licences), 29 (as it relates to road service licences), 32, 33, 35, 37, 38 (part), 40, 41 (as it relates to road service licences), 42 (part), 43(1) (part), (2), 44 (part), 61, 62, 65, 69 (part), Sch 1, Pts I–III, Sch 4, Sch 5, Pt I, paras 4 (part), 7, 9, 11 (part), 13, Sch 5, Pt II (part), Sch 9, Pt I (part) (SI 1980/1353 also amends SI 1980/913);

(b) by SI 1980/1424 (spent), on 6 October 1980: Sch 1, Pt IV, Sch 2;

(c) by SI 1981/256, on 1 April 1981: ss 1(3), (4) (as it relates to the following sections), 16–26, 28(1)–(5), (9), (10) (as it relates to PSV operators' licences), 28(6), 29 (as it relates to PSV operators' licences and otherwise), 30, 31, 34, 38 (part), 41 (part), 42 (part), 43 (part), 44 (part), 63, 69 (part), Sch 5, Pt I, paras 1–3, 4 (part), 8, 10, 11 (part), 12 (part), Sch 5, Pt II (part), Sch 9, Pt I (part) (SI 1981/256 also amends SI 1980/913 and 1353).

The orders contain various transitional provisions, particularly relating to the use of public service vehicle licences during the period from 1 April 1981 to 1 October 1982 and statements on driving licences in the period up to 1 April 1983. SI 1980/1424 is spent following the repeal of Schs 1 and 2 to the 1980 Act by the Public Passenger Vehicles Act 1981, s 88(3), Sch 8. Repeals of the 1980 Act are noted in Halsbury's Statutes, 4th edn Vol 36, title Roads, Railways and Transport.

[337]

MOTOR VEHICLES (TYPE APPROVAL) REGULATIONS 1980 SI 1980/1182

Authority Made by the Minister of Transport under the European Communities Act 1972, s 2(2).
Date made 6 August 1980.
Commencement 9 September 1980.
Amendment Amended by SI 1982/7 (partially revoked by SI 1986/1501), SI 1986/1501, SI 1988/1103, SI 1989/2262, SI 1991/2830. Previously amended by SI 1982/1623, SI 1984/1927, SI 1985/1072 (all revoked by SI 1986/1501), SI 1987/524, SI 1988/1669, SI 1989/1578, SI 1991/820, SI 1991/2681, SI 1992/2154 (all revoked by SI 1992/3107), SI 1992/3107 (revoked by SI 1998/2051 in so far as amended these regulations).
Summary These regulations, which revoke and replace, with amendments, the Motor Vehicles (Type Approval) Regulations 1973, SI 1973/1199, and the amending SI 1974/763, SI 1978/1832, SI 1979/1089, originally provided (in accordance with Council Directive 70/156/EEC (OJ L42, 23.02.1970, p 1)) for the type approval of certain motor vehicles and trailers and their components. The vehicles in question are those manufactured on or after 1 July 1973 (other than land tractors), having four or more wheels and capable of exceeding a speed of 25 kph. In addition to being partially revoked by SI 1992/3107 (so as to delete Sch 2, Pt I, which specified EEC directives relating to the design, construction, equipment and marking of vehicles or vehicle components for the purposes of these regulations), these regulations have now been superseded by SI 1998/2051 (which largely revoked SI 1992/3107), except so far as they relate to the type approval of recording equipment in road transport (tachographs). (The said Council Directive 70/156/EEC has been repealed and replaced as from 29 April 2009 by Directive 2007/46/EC of the European Parliament and of the Council establishing a framework for the approval of motor vehicles and their trailers, and of systems, components and separate technical units intended for such vehicles (OJ L263, 09.10.2007, p 1), which is implemented by SI 2009/717.)

Pt II of the regulations (reg 5) provides that where the Secretary of State for Transport (formerly the minister) is satisfied, on application being made to him for type approval, that a vehicle or vehicle component conforms with the type approval requirements, he is required to approve the vehicle or component as a type vehicle or type vehicle component and issue a type approval certificate. The type approval requirements specified in Sch 2 to the regulations are now only those requirements contained in Council Regulation (EEC) 3821/85 (OJ L370, 31.12.1985, p 8) on recording equipment in road transport. Pt III of the regulations (regs 6–14) deals with procedure and related matters. Applications for type approval are to be made to the Secretary of State in writing by the manufacturer of the vehicle or component in question. A manufacturer of a type vehicle in respect of which a type vehicle certificate is in force may issue a certificate of conformity in respect of each vehicle manufactured by him which conforms to the type in the relevant aspects of design etc; similarly vehicle components conforming with a type vehicle component may be marked with the relevant approval mark (see SI 1979/1088, in the title Trade Marks and Trade Names). Provision is made as to the conditions of issue of type approval certificates and their cancellation or suspension for breach of condition; for notice to be given by manufacturers who cease to manufacture type vehicles or components or alter their manufacture or design etc and for the consequent cancellation, suspension or modification of the type approval certificate; and for the cancellation or suspension of type approval certificates where manufacture is not in conformity with type approval requirements. The Secretary of State is required to give notice of his decision to cancel, suspend or modify type approval certificates and there is a right of appeal to him against any such decision. Pt IV (regs 15, 16) contains supplementary provisions which authorise the Secretary of State to provide testing stations and require manufacturers to keep records relating to certificates of conformity.

As to the fees payable in respect of the issue of type approval certificates, see SI 1999/2149.

[338]

BRITISH TRANSPORT (PENSIONS OF EMPLOYEES) ORDER 1980
SI 1980/1351

Authority Made by the Minister of Transport under the Transport Act 1962, s 74. S 74 has been repealed by the Railways Act 1993, s 134(2), (3) in so far as relating to the British Railways Board and its subsidiaries, but without prejudice to the continuing validity of any orders made under that section.
Date made 8 September 1980.
Commencement 30 September 1980.
Summary This order makes certain changes in pension schemes in the nationalised transport sector in consequence of the transfer of the National Freight Corporation to a successor company under the Transport Act 1980, Pt II. Certain provisions of SI 1969/1824 relating to contributions are amended so as to be applicable in circumstances where employees are members of pension schemes which are not the responsibility of their employing body by virtue of transport legislation enacted subsequent to SI 1969/1824. Provision is also made to regulate the position of members of the Corporation's pension schemes who become members of pension schemes for which the British Railways Board is responsible, so as to avoid duplication of membership, and for payment of transfer values and determination of questions.

As to the winding down and abolition of the British Railways Board, see the Transport Act 2000 and the Preliminary Note "Privatisation of the railway system" (under the main head "Reorganisation of transport undertakings").

[339]

ROAD TRANSPORT (NORTHERN IRELAND PASSENGER SERVICES) REGULATIONS 1980
SI 1980/1460

Authority Made by the Minister of Transport under the Road Traffic Act 1960, ss 159(1), 160(1) (repealed); now have effect under the Public Passenger Vehicles Act 1981, ss 52(1), 60(1), by virtue of the Interpretation Act 1978, s 17(2)(b), printed in the title Statutory Instruments (Pt 2), Vol 1 of this work.
Date made 23 September 1980.
Commencement 3 November 1980.
Amendment Amended SI 1981/462.
Summary These regulations apply to public service vehicles authorised under the law of Northern Ireland to carry passengers for reward in Northern Ireland and used for the carriage of passengers on services between Northern Ireland and Great Britain. Such vehicles, when used on occasional services (as defined in Council Regulation (EEC) 684/92 on common rules for the international carriage of passengers by coach and bus (OJ L74, 20.03.1992, p 1) (which repealed and replaced Council Regulation 117/66/EEC)) are exempted from the provisions of the Public Passenger Vehicles Act 1981 (which replaced equivalent provisions in the Road Traffic Act 1960, Pt III and the Transport Act 1980, Pt I) relating to road service licences (now abolished by the Transport Act 1985) and licensing of vehicles and their drivers (these provisions as to licensing of drivers have been repealed; see now the Road Traffic Act 1988, Pt IV). That exemption also applies to vehicles used on regular and shuttle services, so long as they are used under an authorisation issued by the Secretary of State for Transport (formerly the minister). All such vehicles are also exempted from the requirements in SI 1981/257. Further provisions relate to applications and fees payable for authorisations.

[340]

CARRIAGE BY AIR AND ROAD ACT 1979 (COMMENCEMENT NO 1) ORDER 1980
SI 1980/1966

Authority Made under the Carriage by Air and Road Act 1979, s 7(2).
Date made 17 December 1980.
Summary This Order in Council brought the following provisions of the Carriage by Air and Road Act 1979 into force on 28 December 1980: ss 3(3), 4(2), (4) (in so far as it relates to the amendment made by s 4(2)), 5 (in so far as it relates to the amendment made by s 4(2)), 6(1)(b).
Further orders Other provisions of the 1979 Act were brought into force by the following orders made under s 7(2):

(a) by SI 1997/2565, on 1 December 1997: ss 4(1), (4) (in so far as it relates to the enactments amended by s 4(1)), 5 (in so far as it relates to the enactments amended by s 4(1)), 6(1)(a) (in so far as it relates to the Carriage by Air Act 1961, ss 9, 10), 6(3) (in so far as it relates to the provisions of the 1979 Act brought into force by this order); and
(b) by SI 2000/2768, on 12 October 2000: ss 3(2), 6(1)(a) (in so far as not already in force), 6(3) (in so far as it relates to the provisions of the 1979 Act brought into force by this order).

S 3(1) of the Act was brought into force on 22 October 1998 by SI 1998/2562, in the title Aviation.

[341]

PUBLIC SERVICE VEHICLES (CONDITIONS OF FITNESS, EQUIPMENT, USE AND CERTIFICATION) REGULATIONS 1981
SI 1981/257

Authority Made by the Minister of Transport under the Road Traffic Act 1960, ss 130, 159, 160(1), the Road Traffic Act 1972, s 40(1), (3) and the Transport Act 1980, ss 17(1), 28(9). In so far as made

under the 1960 and 1980 Acts, the regulations now have effect under the Public Passenger Vehicles Act 1981, ss 6, 10, 52, 60(1), by virtue of the Interpretation Act 1978, s 17(2)(b), printed in the title Statutory Instruments (Pt 2), Vol 1 of this work. In so far as made under the 1972 Act, they now have effect under the Road Traffic Act 1988, s 41, by virtue of s 17(2)(b) of the 1978 Act and the Road Traffic (Consequential Provisions) Act 1988, ss 2(2), 5(1), Sch 4, para 1(2).
Date made 23 February 1981.
Commencement 1 April 1981.
Amendment Amended by SI 1982/20, SI 1982/1058, SI 1984/1763, SI 1986/1812, SI 1988/340, SI 1989/2359, SI 1995/305, SI 1998/1670, SI 2002/335, SI 2005/1403, SI 2005/2986, SI 2005/3128, SI 2008/1458, SI 2009/141, SI 2009/877. Previously amended by SI 1982/1482, SI 1986/370, SI 1987/1150, SI 1989/322, SI 1990/450, SI 1991/456, SI 1992/565, SI 1993/3012, SI 1997/84, SI 2000/1431, SI 2001/1649, SI 2002/489, SI 2003/1817, SI 2004/1880, SI 2005/2342, SI 2007/502 (all superseded, except SI 1987/1150 (revoked by SI 1992/1285)).
Modification By:

(a) SI 1984/748, Pts II–V of these regulations do not have effect in relation to a vehicle to which Pt III of SI 1984/748 applies or to a vehicle registered in Northern Ireland to which Pt II of SI 1984/748 applies; and

(b) SI 1999/3413, Pts II–V of these regulations do not have effect in relation to a vehicle which is carrying out a cabotage transport operation in Great Britain in accordance with Council Regulation (EC) 12/98 (OJ L4, 08.01.1998, p 10).

Summary These regulations revoke and replace the Public Service Vehicles (Conditions of Fitness, Equipment and Use) Regulations 1972, SI 1972/751, and the amending SI 1976/726, SI 1980/141, SI 1980/1097, and those provisions in the Public Service Vehicles (Licences and Certificates) Regulations 1952, SI 1952/900 which related to certificates of fitness, type approval and conformity (SI 1952/900 was also partially revoked by SI 1980/1354 (revoked), and wholly revoked by SI 1981/258 (revoked)). The regulations have been amended by SI 2002/335 so as to provide for consistency between the requirements under these regulations and the provisions which now apply to and regulate new public service vehicles under SI 2000/1970 (which imposed new accessibility requirements for disabled persons to single-deck and double-deck buses and coaches). The regulations, as amended, consist of five parts, the provisions of which are described briefly below.

Pt I (regs 1–4) contains preliminary provisions and includes an exemption from Pt IV of the regulations for Crown and visiting force vehicles; an exemption from Pts III and IV for vehicles belonging to local education authorities being used to provide free school transport; an exemption from regs 6–33, 35–44, 45A for minibuses complying with, required to comply with or exempted from SI 1986/1078, regs 41–43; and an exemption from reg 43 for other motor vehicles used by local education authorities to provide free school transport where the only other fare paying passengers are school pupils.

Pt II (regs 4A–34 (revoked in part)) prescribes the conditions as to fitness of public service vehicles which must be fulfilled before a certificate of initial fitness can be granted in respect of a vehicle under the Public Passenger Vehicles Act 1981, s 6 (in place of the Transport Act 1980, s 17). The prescribed conditions contained in Pt II of these regulations may alternatively be met by a vehicle satisfying the alternative conditions set out in reg 4A. The prescribed conditions of fitness set out in regs 5–34 (which apply subject to specified exceptions for vehicles registered before certain dates, for articulated buses and for certain vehicles bearing a designated approval mark) relate to stability, guard rails, fuel tanks, carburettors, exhaust pipe, luggage racks, artificial lighting, electrical equipment, the body of a vehicle, height of sides of body, steps, platforms and stairs, entrances and exits, doors, emergency exits, gangways, seats, crew seats, passenger protection, ventilation, driver's accommodation, windscreens, passengers' communication with driver and general construction. The last condition requires that construction, weight and equipment requirements in regulations made under the Road Traffic Act 1988, s 41 (i e SI 1986/1078) be complied with, that vehicles be soundly and properly constructed and in good and serviceable condition, and be capable of complying with all lighting requirements in the 1988 Act or regulations made thereunder (see SI 1989/1796).

Pt III (regs 35, 36), together with Schs 4, 5, specifies the fire extinguishing apparatus to be carried by all public service vehicles and first aid equipment to be carried by vehicles being used as express carriages or contract carriages (as to the meaning of which see the Transport Act 1985, Sch 1, para 16). Such apparatus and equipment must be readily available for use, clearly marked and maintained in good condition.

Pt IV (regs 37–45B) contains prohibitions and requirements as to the use of public service vehicles. The provisions relate to obstruction of entrances, exits and gangways, obstruction of the driver, body maintenance, lamps, use of device for operating power-operated doors, filling of petrol tank, carriage of conductors, carriage of inflammable or dangerous substances, marking of vehicles, use of seats, and route and destination displays.

Pt V (regs 46–57) relates to certificates of initial fitness, approval as a type vehicle and conformity to an approved type vehicle. The manner of application for certificates, the fees payable, and the form of certificates are prescribed. Where a vehicle is registered after the issue of a certificate of initial fitness or a certificate of conformity, the Secretary of State (formerly the minister) must be notified immediately of the registration mark assigned.

Penalties Any person who contravenes or fails to comply with these regulations is liable to either a fine not exceeding level 2 on the standard scale or a fixed penalty; see the Public Passenger Vehicles Act 1981, s 67, the Road Traffic Act 1988, s 42 and the Road Traffic Offenders Act 1988, s 51(1), Sch 3.

Appeals A right of appeal to the Secretary of State exists where an examiner has refused to grant a certificate of initial fitness or a type approval certificate; see the Public Passenger Vehicles Act 1981, s 51 and the Public Passenger Vehicles (Exemptions and Appeals against Refusals to Issue Certificates or Remove Prohibitions) Regulations 1987, SI 1987/1150 (revoked, but see further the note "General" to SI 1992/1285).

[342]

BRITISH RAILWAYS PENSION SCHEMES (UNFUNDED PROPORTIONS) (NO 1) ORDER 1981
SI 1981/346

Authority Made by the Secretary of State for Transport under the Transport Act 1980, s 54.
Date made 6 March 1981.
Commencement 4 April 1981.
Summary This order applies to the British Railways (Wages Grades) Pension Fund and determines, for the purpose of the Transport Act 1980, s 54, that the unfunded proportion of the relevant pension obligations (as defined in s 53 of that Act) of that Scheme, is 0.1365. All previous determinations in relation to that scheme are varied.
Further orders The following orders have been made under the Transport Act 1980, s 54:
(a) SI 1981/347 (in force on 30 March 1981) determines, for the purpose of s 54, the unfunded proportions of the relevant pensions obligations of specified National Freight Corporation pension schemes as follows: NFC (Salaried Staff) Pension Fund, 0.6359; NFC (Wages Grades) Pension Fund, 0.7918; and NFC (1978) Pension Fund, 1.0000. All previous determinations in relation to those schemes are varied; and
(b) SI 1981/1646 (in force on 30 December 1981) determines, for the purposes of s 54, the unfunded proportion of the relevant pension obligations of the British Railways pension schemes and confirms or varies all previous determinations made in relation to those schemes.

[343]

MOTOR VEHICLES (TYPE APPROVAL) (EEC MANUFACTURERS) REGULATIONS 1981
SI 1981/493

Authority Made by the Secretary of State for Transport under the European Communities Act 1972, s 2(2).
Date made 27 March 1981.
Commencement 27 April 1981.
Summary These regulations extend to vehicles and vehicle parts manufactured in other member states the provisions of the Road Traffic Act 1988, ss 54–62 (which replaced the Road Traffic Act 1972, ss 47–50), and of certain regulations made thereunder, so far as relating to type approval certificates and certificates of conformity (see SI 1984/981, SI 1999/2149). However, the Secretary of State is not required to issue type approval certificates under those provisions as so applied before 27 April 1982.

[344]

TRANSPORT ACT 1981 (COMMENCEMENT NO 1) ORDER 1981
SI 1981/1331

Authority Made by the Home Secretary under the Transport Act 1981, ss 35(5), 40(4).
Date made 14 September 1981.
Summary This order brought into force on 12 October 1981 the Transport Act 1981, s 35 (except sub-ss (1), (2)) and in Sch 12, Pt III the entry relating to the Town Police Clauses Act 1847.
Further orders Other provisions of the 1981 Act were brought into force by further orders made under ss 18(3), 32(2), 35(5), 40(4) of the Act, and under s 31(1), (2) (repealed) thereof, as follows:
(a) by SI 1981/1617 (spent), on 1 December 1981: ss 21, 22, 26, 27, 30 (part), Sch 9, paras 14, 18 (part), 22;
(b) by SI 1982/300 (spent), on 29 March 1982: ss 23(6) (7), 30 (part);
(c) by SI 1982/310, on 1 April 1982: s 35(1), (2), Sch 12, Pt III (part);
(d) by SI 1982/866 (spent), on 1 October 1982: ss 23(1), (4), (5), 30 (part); and on 1 February 1983: ss 23 (part), 30 (part);
(e) by SI 1982/1451, on 1 November 1982: ss 19, 20, 30 (part), Sch 7, Sch 9, paras 2, 4, 5, 6, 7, 8, 9, 10, 11, 13, 15, Sch 12, Pt III (part);
(f) by SI 1982/1341 (spent), on 31 January 1983: ss 28, 30 (part);
(g) by SI 1982/1803 (spent), on 20 December 1982: Sch 9, para 12 (part);
(h) by SI 1983/576, on 6 May 1983: ss 24, 30 (part), Sch 8, Sch 9, paras 1, 3, 12 (part), 17, 18 (part), 19, 20, 21, 23, 24, 25, Sch 12 (part);
(i) by SI 1983/930, on 2 August 1983: Sch 6, para 10;
(j) by SI 1983/1089, on 25 August 1983: s 32, Sch 10, Sch 12, Pt II (part);
(k) by SI 1988/1037 (spent), on 13 July 1988: Sch 9, para 16; and
(l) by SI 1988/1170 (spent), on 13 July 1988: s 30(3) in so far as not already in force.

SI 1981/1617, SI 1982/300, SI 1982/866, SI 1982/1341, SI 1982/1803, SI 1988/1037, SI 1988/1170 became spent following the repeal of all the provisions brought into force by those orders. Repeals of the 1981 Act are noted in the relevant titles of Halsbury's Statutes.

[345]

MOTOR VEHICLES (TESTS) REGULATIONS 1981
SI 1981/1694

Authority Made by the Secretary of State for Transport under the Road Traffic Act 1972, ss 43(1), (2), (6), 44(4), (6), (7) (repealed). Now have effect under the Road Traffic Act 1988, ss 45–47, by virtue of the Road Traffic (Consequential Provisions) Act 1988, s 2(2) and the Interpretation Act 1978, s 17(2)(b), printed in the title Statutory Instruments (Pt 2), Vol 1 of this work.

Date made 25 November 1981.

Commencement 31 December 1981.

Amendment Amended by SI 1982/814, SI 1982/1477, SI 1982/1715, SI 1983/1434, SI 1984/1126, SI 1985/45, SI 1985/1923, SI 1988/989, SI 1988/1894, SI 1989/1694, SI 1991/253, SI 1991/455, SI 1991/1525, SI 1991/2229, SI 1991/2791, SI 1992/566, SI 1992/1217, SI 1992/1609, SI 1992/3160, SI 1993/3011, SI 1995/1457, SI 1995/2438, SI 1997/81, SI 1997/1679, SI 1998/1672, SI 2000/1432, SI 2001/3330, SI 2002/488, SI 2002/1698, SI 2003/1113, SI 2003/1698, SI 2003/1815, SI 2004/1879, SI 2005/1832, SI 2006/594, SI 2006/1998, SI 2007/506, SI 2007/1161, SI 2007/1898, SI 2009/643, SI 2009/802.

Previously amended by SI 1982/783, SI 1983/1147, SI 1984/401, SI 1984/727, SI 1984/815, SI 1985/834, SI 1986/372, SI 1986/904 (all superseded), SI 1986/1794 (superseded in so far as it amended these regulations), SI 1987/1144 (superseded), SI 1987/1228 (superseded in so far as it amended these regulations), SI 1988/339, SI 1989/321, SI 1989/920, SI 1990/449, SI 1990/628, SI 1994/2136, SI 1996/1751, SI 1999/2199, SI 2000/2322 (all superseded), SI 2001/1648 (partially superseded; remainder spent), SI 2004/1632, SI 2005/2341, SI 2006/2680, SI 2008/1402, SI 2008/1461 (all superseded).

Summary These regulations revoke and replace, with amendments, the Motor Vehicles (Tests) Regulations 1976, SI 1976/1977, and the amending SI 1976/2155, SI 1978/1574, SI 1979/439, SI 1979/1215, SI 1980/616, SI 1981/951. They make provision for the examination under the Road Traffic Act 1988, s 45 (formerly the Road Traffic Act 1972, s 43) of certain classes of motor vehicles for the purpose of ascertaining whether prescribed statutory requirements (as to which, see below) relating to motor vehicles, their accessories and equipment are complied with, and for the issue of a test certificate where those requirements are complied with, or the issue of a notification of refusal where they are not. Motor vehicles to which the regulations apply are classified as follows:

(a) Class I: light motor bicycles;
(b) Class II: motor bicycles;
(c) Class III: light motor vehicles other than motor bicycles;
(d) Class IV: motor cars and heavy motor cars not being vehicles within Classes III, IVA, V, VA, VI, VIA or VII;
(e) Class IVA: certain minibuses, not being vehicles within Classes III, V, VA, VI or VIA, in respect of which any forward-facing seat is fitted with a relevant seat belt;
(f) Class V: motor vehicles not being vehicles within Class VA which are:
    (1) large passenger-carrying vehicles;
    (2) public service vehicles of a specified type and constructed or adapted to carry more than 12 seated passengers; and
    (3) play buses;
(g) Class VA: certain motor vehicles which satisfy heads (1)–(3) of Class V and in respect of which any forward-facing seat is fitted with a relevant seatbelt;
(h) Class VI: certain public service vehicles not within Class VIA;
(i) Class VIA: certain public service vehicles, other than those of a specified type, in respect of which any forward facing seat is fitted with a relevant seat belt; and
(j) Class VII: goods vehicles with a design gross weight of more than 3000 kg but less than 3500 kg.

The regulations also exempt the following vehicles from the requirement for a test certificate under s 47 of the 1988 Act (formerly s 44 of the 1972 Act) (as to s 47, see the note "Obligatory test certificates" below): heavy locomotives; light locomotives; motor tractors; track laying vehicles; goods vehicles with a design gross weight of more than 3500 kg; articulated vehicles which are not articulated buses; vehicles used on a public road for distances not exceeding an aggregate of six miles a week; works trucks; pedestrian controlled vehicles; certain invalid vehicles; certain vehicles temporarily in Great Britain; vehicles proceeding to a port for export; vehicles in the service of a visiting force or headquarters; police vehicles; vehicles provided for the purposes of the Serious Organised Crime Agency; certain naval, military or air force vehicles; Northern Ireland licensed vehicles and vehicles with a Northern Ireland test certificate; electrically propelled goods vehicles with a design gross weight of not more than 3500 kg; licensed hackney carriages or cabs; licensed private hire cars; agricultural motor vehicles; certain motor vehicles constructed and not merely adapted for street cleansing or the collection or disposal of refuse; goods vehicles covered by certain transitional provisions; tramcars; and trolley vehicles which are not auxiliary trolley vehicles. Exemption from the requirement for a test certificate is also provided for the use of vehicles for various purposes, including:

(a) the purpose of submitting vehicles for examination, or delivering them for work to be done or for breaking up where a test certificate has been refused;
(b) the purpose of testing vehicles by a motor trader during the course of or after completion of repairs;
(c) any purpose for which vehicles are authorised to be used on roads under s 44 of the 1988 Act (formerly s 42 of the 1972 Act); and
(d) purposes connected with the delivery of imported vehicles, the removal of vehicles obstructing the road, and the detention or seizure of vehicles by the police or customs.

Exemption from the requirement for a test certificate is also provided for the use of vehicles on any island in any area mainly surrounded by water from which they cannot be conveniently driven to a road in any other part of Great Britain (subject to exceptions in the case of the Isle of Wight and certain of the larger islands off Scotland).

The statutory requirements which are prescribed for the purposes of examinations consist of specified provisions of SI 1981/257, SI 1986/1078, SI 1989/1796, SI 2001/561 and Council Regulation (EEC) 3821/85 (OJ L370, 31.12.1985, p 8) on recording equipment in road transport. S 45(3) of the 1988 Act (formerly s 43(3) of the 1972 Act) sets out the persons by whom examinations for the purposes of that section are to be carried out, i e authorised examiners appointed in accordance with these regulations; nominated testers (i e persons nominated by, and acting under the supervision of, authorised examiners); authorised inspectors; vehicle examiners appointed under s 66A of the 1988 Act; and inspectors who are appointed by any council designated by the Secretary of State for the purposes of ss 45, 46 of that Act and approved by the Secretary of State.

The scope and nature of the provisions contained in the regulations may be seen from the following arrangement:

ARRANGEMENT OF REGULATIONS

PART I
GENERAL

1 Commencement and citation
2 Revocation
3 Interpretation (*amended by SI 1982/1477, SI 1983/1434, SI 1985/45, SI 1991/253, SI 1991/1525, SI 1997/81, SI 1998/1672, SI 2000/1432, SI 2003/1113, SI 2003/1698*)
4 The prescribed statutory requirements (*amended by SI 1991/253, SI 1991/2229, SI 1998/1672*)
5 Classification of vehicles and application of regulations (*amended by SI 1982/814, SI 1984/1162, SI 1988/1894, SI 1991/253, SI 1998/1672*)
6 Exemptions (*amended by SI 1982/814, SI 1983/1434, SI 1985/45, SI 1991/253, SI 1992/1217, SI 1995/1457, SI 1998/1672, SI 2003/1113, SI 2006/594*)

PART II
APPLICATIONS FOR, AND CONDITIONS AND CESSATIONS OF, APPROVAL, AUTHORISATION AND DESIGNATION

(Substituted for Original Pt II (Regs 7–11) by SI 2003/1113)
7 Application for approval as nominated tester or inspector or authorisation as authorised examiner (*substituted by SI 2003/1113 as noted to Part heading*)
7A Application for designation (*substituted by SI 2003/1113 as noted to Part heading*)
8 Approvals, authorisations and designations (*substituted by SI 2003/1113 as noted to Part heading*)
8A The approval conditions (*substituted by SI 2003/1113 as noted to Part heading*)
8B The general authorisation conditions (*substituted by SI 2003/1113 as noted to Part heading*)
8C The corporate authorisation conditions (*substituted by SI 2003/1113 as noted to Part heading*)
8D The individual authorisation conditions (*substituted by SI 2003/1113 as noted to Part heading*)
8E The designation conditions (*substituted by SI 2003/1113 as noted to Part heading*)
8F Supplementary provision relating to vehicle testing station signs (*substituted by SI 2003/1113 as noted to Part heading*)
9 Cessations: general (*substituted by SI 2003/1113 as noted to Part heading; amended by SI 2007/1898*)
10 Cessations: action by Secretary of State (*substituted by SI 2003/1113 as noted to Part heading*)
11 Cessations: return of documents and apparatus (*substituted by SI 2003/1113 as noted to Part heading*)

PART III
EXAMINATIONS

12 Applications for examinations (*amended by SI 1989/1694, SI 1995/2438, SI 1998/1672, SI 2003/1113, SI 2003/1698*)
13 Requirements as to vehicles submitted for examinations (*substituted by SI 2003/1698*)
14 Conditions as to responsibility for damage to vehicles and third party liabilities (*amended by SI 1995/2438, SI 2003/1113*)
15 Notification of examinations and results (*substituted by SI 2003/1113*)
16 Refusal of a test certificate where braking test cannot be carried out (*amended by SI 1995/2438, SI 2003/1113*)
17 Removal of vehicles submitted for examination (*amended by SI 1995/2438, SI 2003/1113*)

PART IV
APPEALS

18 Appeal on refusal of a test certificate (*amended by SI 1995/2438, SI 2003/1113*)
19 Payments to examiners and designated councils at whose premises examinations on appeals are carried out (*amended by SI 2003/1113*)

PART V
FEES

20 Fees for examinations (*amended by SI 1984/1126, SI 1989/1694, SI 1991/1525, SI 1991/2229, SI 1992/1609, SI 1992/3160, SI 1995/2438, SI 1997/81, SI 1998/1672, SI 2001/3330, SI 2002/488, SI 2002/1698, SI 2003/1113, SI 2003/1815, SI 2004/1879, SI 2006/1998, SI 2007/506, SI 2007/1161, SI 2009/643, SI 2009/802*)

21 Fees on appeals (*amended by SI 2003/1113*)

PART VI
OTHER MATTERS

22 Other records to be kept and returns to be furnished (*substituted by SI 2003/1113*)

23 Duplicate test certificates (*substituted by SI 2003/1113; amended by SI 2005/1832*)

23A Correction of errors in records and test certificates (*inserted by SI 2003/1113*)

24 Inspection of premises, apparatus and records (*amended by SI 1991/253, SI 2003/1113*)

24A Return of apparatus and documents (*inserted by SI 2003/1113*)

25 Charges for entries in the electronic record and payments on account (*substituted, together with regs 25A, 25B, for reg 25, with savings, by SI 2003/1113; amended by SI 2009/643; amended, in so far as saved, by SI 2003/1698*)

25A Charges for apparatus, etc connected with the electronic record (*substituted as noted to reg 25; amended by SI 2003/1698*)

25B Refunds (*substituted as noted to reg 25*)

26 Notices

27 Computation of time

28 Certificates of temporary exemption (*inserted by SI 1982/1715; amended by SI 1983/1434*)

29 Access to particulars in the records (*inserted by SI 2003/1113*)

30 Sale of particulars in, and information derived from, the records (*inserted by SI 2003/1113*)

SCHEDULES

Sch 1 Sign to be displayed by authorised examiners (*Pt I (diagram of sign to be displayed by authorised examiners) revoked by SI 2003/1113*)

Sch 2 The prescribed statutory requirements (*substituted by SI 1991/2229; amended by SI 1992/3160, SI 1998/1672, SI 2002/488, SI 2003/1698, SI 2007/506, SI 2009/643*)

Sch 3 Charges for purposes of regulation 25A (*inserted by SI 2003/1113; original Sch 3 revoked by SI 1991/253*)

Sch 4 Regulations revoked

Obligatory test certificates Motor vehicles may be used on roads without a test certificate under the above regulations (ie SI 1981/1694) having been issued except where the Road Traffic Act 1988, s 47 applies. Subject to the exemptions granted by these regulations (see the note "Summary" above), that section makes it an offence to use on a road at any time a motor vehicle to which the section applies, and as respects which no test certificate has been issued within the appropriate period (ie 12 months or such shorter period as may be prescribed) before that time. By s 47(2) of the 1988 Act, that section applies at any time to the following vehicles (other than goods vehicles required by SI 1988/1478 to be submitted for a goods vehicle test):

(a) those first registered not less than three years previously, and
(b) those which, having been manufactured not less than three years previously, have been used on a road before being registered.

S 47(3) provides that s 47(2)(a) is to have effect as respects motor vehicles used for the carriage of passengers and with more than eight seats (excluding the driver's seat), taxis and ambulances, as if for the period mentioned in s 47(2)(a) there were substituted a period of one year. Under s 47(9), the Secretary of State may by order direct that s 47(2) is to have effect with the substitution for three years (in both places) of such other period (not being more than 10 years) as may be specified; as at the date of issue of this volume, no such order has been made.

SI 2004/1896 (made under the Road Traffic Act 1988, s 66(1), (2) and in force on 1 September 2004), revokes and replaces the Motor Vehicles (Production of Test Certificates) Regulations 1969, SI 1969/418. The regulations provide that where an application is made for an excise licence for a vehicle to which s 47 of the 1988 Act applies, the licence must not be granted unless:

(a) an effective test certificate is produced;
(b) records maintained under s 45(6B) of the 1988 Act provide evidence of the granting of an effective test certificate;
(c) the applicant makes a declaration in the form specified in the Schedule to the regulations (or a form to the like effect) that the vehicle is not intended to be used during the period for which the licence is to be in force except for a purpose or in an area prescribed by reg 6(2) or (3) of SI 1981/1694; or
(d) in the case of an application relating to a vehicle to which s 47 of the 1988 Act applies by virtue of sub-s (2)(b) of that section, the owner of the vehicle declares in writing the year in which the vehicle was manufactured, and the period of three years from the date of manufacture has not expired.

Cf SI 2004/2577, noted to SI 1988/1478.

Other testing provisions As to the testing of the condition of vehicles on roads, see now the Road Traffic Act 1988, s 67, and as to the testing of vehicles on premises, see SI 1986/1078, reg 74. Provision for the examination of certain classes of goods vehicles is made by regulations under s 49 of the 1988 Act; see SI 1988/1478.

[346]

MOTOR VEHICLES (TYPE APPROVAL FOR GOODS VEHICLES) (GREAT BRITAIN) REGULATIONS 1982
SI 1982/1271

Authority Made by the Secretary of State for Transport under the Road Traffic Act 1972, ss 47(1), (2), 48(2), (5), (6), (7), 49, 50(1), 52(2) (all repealed). Now have effect under the Road Traffic Act 1988, ss 54, 59, 60, 61, 66, by virtue of the Road Traffic (Consequential Provisions) Act 1988, s 2(2) and the Interpretation Act 1978, s 17(2)(b), printed in the title Statutory Instruments (Pt 2), Vol 1 of this work.
Date made 6 September 1982.
Commencement 1 October 1982.
Amendment Amended by SI 1984/697, SI 1984/1402, SI 1985/46, SI 1986/427, SI 1986/1089, SI 1987/1508, SI 1988/1523, SI 1989/1579, SI 1991/1021, SI 1991/1970, SI 1992/25, SI 1992/1342, SI 1992/3084, SI 1993/2200, SI 1994/2191, SI 1995/1323, SI 1996/2331, SI 1996/3014 (amended by SI 1997/1365 (superseded)), SI 1998/1006, SI 2003/582, SI 2003/1866, SI 2006/2565, SI 2007/361 (subject to transitional provisions), SI 2009/2084 (subject to savings). Previously amended by SI 1997/2936 (superseding the amendment by SI 1997/1365 to SI 1996/3014, and itself superseded by SI 1998/1006).
Modification Modified by SI 1998/3093.
Summary These regulations revoke and replace the Motor Vehicles (Type Approval for Goods Vehicles) (Great Britain) Regulations 1981, SI 1981/1340. They apply to every motor vehicle manufactured on or after 1 October 1982 and not first used before 1 April 1983 and which has four or more wheels and is either a goods vehicle, the tractive unit of an articulated vehicle or a bi-purpose vehicle (and parts of such vehicles), with specified exceptions. The regulations have effect with modifications in relation to light goods vehicles to which SI 2001/25 (formerly the Motor Vehicles (Approval) Regulations 1996, SI 1996/3013 (revoked)) applies.

The regulations require that all vehicles or vehicle parts to which they apply must be type approved to the prescribed type approval requirements, ie:

(a) the determination of plated weights which, in the Secretary of State's opinion, should not be exceeded by such vehicles; and
(b) the requirements with respect to the design, construction, equipment or marking of such vehicles or vehicle parts specified in Sch 1 to the regulations.

Excepted vehicles are: certain vehicles brought temporarily into Britain, export vehicles, vehicles in the service of a visiting force or headquarters, certain former Crown vehicles, test or trial vehicles or prototypes, publicity and demonstration vehicles, motor tractors and light and heavy locomotives, agricultural motor vehicles, engineering plant, pedestrian-controlled vehicles, straddle-carriers, works trucks, track-laying vehicles, special vehicles, tower wagons, fire engines, road rollers, steam vehicles, gritters or snow ploughs, two-wheeled motor cycles, electric vehicles, break-down vehicles, motor ambulances, motor caravans, recovery vehicles first used before 1 January 1988 and road sweepers.

Applications for type approval of a vehicle or vehicle part by a manufacturer must be made in writing to the Secretary of State, who must then notify the applicant of the time and place for an examination and of the prescribed fees (as to which, see SI 1999/2149). Application for a minister's approval certificate may also be made by any person in respect of a vehicle or vehicle part. The Secretary of State must be notified if certain alterations are made to a vehicle issued with a certificate of conformity or a minister's approval certificate before the vehicle is used on the road; certificates may consequently be suspended, amended or cancelled. There is a right of appeal against decisions of the Secretary of State with respect to certificates.

The Secretary of State may authorise persons to carry out examinations for type approval of vehicles or vehicle parts. Manufacturers are required to keep records relating to certificates of conformity issued by them. The regulations specify 1 July 1998 as the appointed day for the purposes of the Road Traffic Act 1988, s 63(1), from when the prescribed type approval requirements must be complied with in relation to vehicles to which the Motor Vehicles (Approval) Regulations 1996, SI 1996/3013 (revoked and replaced by SI 2001/25) applied. Licences for vehicles may not be issued under the Vehicle Excise and Registration Act 1994 unless the appropriate certificates are in force.

[347]

DRIVING LICENCES (COMMUNITY DRIVING LICENCE) REGULATIONS 1982
SI 1982/1555

Authority Made by the Secretary of State for Transport under the European Communities Act 1972, s 2(2).
Date made 29 October 1982.
Commencement 1 January 1983.
Amendment Partially revoked by the Road Traffic (Consequential Provisions) Act 1988, s 3, Sch 1, Pt II (and replaced by provisions now contained in the Road Traffic Act 1988), and by SI 1991/486. Previously amended by the Road Traffic (Driving Licences) Act 1983, s 2(3) (repealed by SI 1991/486).
Summary These regulations, as originally made, gave effect for Great Britain to Art 8 of Council Directive (EEC) 80/1263 by way of amendments made to certain provisions of the Road Traffic Act 1972 (repealed and replaced by the Road Traffic Act 1988). Council Directive (EEC) 80/1263 has been repealed by Council Directive 91/439/EEC on driving licences (OJ L237, 24.08.1991, p 1) (itself repealed and replaced as from 19 January 2013 by Directive 2006/126/EC of the European Parliament and of the Council on driving licences (OJ L403, 30.12.2006, p 18)).

The regulations have been entirely revoked except for reg 4, which provides for the recognition of the temporary validity of a community licence in the case of a person who becomes normally resident in Great Britain, Northern Ireland or Gibraltar, modifying s 84(5) of the 1972 Act (repealed; see now s 88(5), (6) of the 1988 Act) and SI 1981/952, reg 23(1) (revoked; see now SI 1999/2864, reg 80(1)).

[348]

TRANSPORT ACT 1982 (COMMENCEMENT NO 1) ORDER 1982 SI 1982/1561

Authority Made by the Secretary of State for Transport under the Transport Act 1982, s 76(2).
Date made 29 October 1982.
Summary This order brought the following provisions of the Transport Act 1982 into force on 1 November 1982: ss 16, 58, 60, 61, 68, 70, 72 (part), Sch 5, paras 25, 26 and Sch 6 in so far as it relates to the Road Traffic Regulation Act 1967, s 72(2), (4).
Further orders Other provisions of the 1982 Act were brought into force by the following orders made under s 76:

(a) by SI 1982/1804, on 20 December 1982: Pt I (ss 1–7), ss 64, 67, 71;
(b) by SI 1983/276, on 1 April 1983: Sch 5, para 10(b); and on 11 April 1983: ss 57, 63, 65;
(c) by SI 1983/577 (spent), on 6 May 1983: s 59, Sch 5, para 13;
(d) by SI 1984/175, on 1 June 1984: s 52, Sch 4, Sch 5, para 6 and Sch 6 in so far as it relates to the Transport Act 1968;
(e) by SI 1986/1326, on 1 October 1986: Pt III (ss 27–51) (except s 39), ss 73, 75, 76, Sch 1, Sch 3;
(f) by SI 1996/1943, on 1 August 1996: s 18 (subject to a transitional provision).

SI 1983/577 is now spent following the repeal of all the provisions brought into force by that order. Repeals of the 1982 Act are noted in the relevant titles of Halsbury's Statutes.

[349]

ROAD VEHICLES (MARKING OF SPECIAL WEIGHTS) REGULATIONS 1983 SI 1983/910

Authority Made by the Secretary of State for Transport under the Road Traffic Act 1972, s 172 (repealed). Now have effect under the Road Traffic Act 1988, s 64 by virtue of the Road Traffic (Consequential Provisions) Act 1988, s 2(2) and the Interpretation Act 1978, s 17(2)(b), printed in the title Statutory Instruments (Pt 2), Vol 1 of this work.
Date made 24 June 1983.
Commencement 29 July 1983.
Amendment Amended by SI 1987/1326.
Summary Under the Road Traffic Act 1988, s 64 (formerly the Road Traffic Act 1972, s 172), if a goods vehicle displays a plate containing plated weights determined for that vehicle, the vehicle must not, while it is used on a road, display any other weight markings, except other plated weights, other weights required or authorised to be marked on a vehicle by regulations under s 41 of the 1988 Act (formerly s 40 of the 1972 Act), or weights authorised for the purposes of the said s 64 by regulations and marked in the prescribed manner. These regulations authorise for those purposes certain weights which the manufacturer considers should not be exceeded when the vehicle is travelling at a speed of not more than 12, 20, 25, 30, 35 or 40 miles per hour. The prescribed manner in which such weights must be marked is that they must be clearly and indelibly marked on a plate securely affixed to the vehicle in a conspicuous and readily accessible position, and all letters and figures shown on the plate must be not less than 4 mm in height.

[350]

ELECTRICALLY ASSISTED PEDAL CYCLES REGULATIONS 1983 SI 1983/1168

Authority Made by the Secretary of State for Transport under the Road Traffic Regulation Act 1967, s 103(1) (repealed) and the Road Traffic Act 1972, s 193(1) (repealed). In so far as they were made under the 1967 Act, the regulations now have effect as if made under the Road Traffic Regulation Act 1984, s 140(1), by virtue of the Interpretation Act 1978, s 17(2)(b), printed in the title Statutory Instruments (Pt 2), Vol 1 of this work; in so far as they were made under the 1972 Act, they now have effect as if made under the Road Traffic Act 1988, s 189(1), by virtue of the Road Traffic (Consequential Provisions) Act 1988, s 2(2) and s 17(2)(b) of the 1978 Act.
Date made 1 July 1983.
Commencement 12 August 1983.
Summary By the Road Traffic Regulation Act 1984, s 140 (formerly the Road Traffic Regulation Act 1967, s 103), and the Road Traffic Act 1988, s 189 (formerly the Road Traffic Act 1972, s 193), certain vehicles are not treated as motor vehicles for the purposes of the 1984 Act and the Road Traffic Acts (ie the Road Traffic Act 1988, the Road Traffic Offenders Act 1988 and the Road Traffic (Consequential Provisions) Act 1988 (in so far as it reproduces the effect of provisions repealed by that Act)). Such vehicles include electrically assisted pedal cycles of such class as may be prescribed by regulations. By these regulations, the class of electrically assisted pedal cycles prescribed for these purposes consists of bicycles or tricycles complying with the requirements that the vehicle must:

(a) have a kerbside weight not exceeding, in the case of a bicycle, other than a tandem bicycle, 40 kg, and in the case of a tandem bicycle and a tricycle, 60 kg;

(b) be fitted with pedals by means of which it is capable of being propelled; and
(c) be fitted with no motor other than an electric motor which has a continuous rated output which, when installed in the vehicle with the nominal voltage supplied, does not exceed, in the case of a bicycle, other than a tandem bicycle, 0.2 kilowatts, and in the case of a tandem bicycle and a tricycle, 0.25 kilowatts; and cannot propel the vehicle when it is travelling at more than 15 mph.

Cases relating to these regulations *Winter v DPP* [2002] EWHC 2482 (Admin), [2003] RTR 210.

[351]

PEDAL CYCLES (CONSTRUCTION AND USE) REGULATIONS 1983
SI 1983/1176

Authority Made by the Secretary of State for Transport under the Road Traffic Act 1972, s 66(1), (3), (4) (repealed). Now have effect under the Road Traffic Act 1988, s 81 by virtue of the Road Traffic (Consequential Provisions) Act 1988, s 2(2) and the Interpretation Act 1978, s 17(2)(b), printed in the title Statutory Instruments (Pt 2), Vol 1 of this work.
Date made 1 August 1983.
Commencement 1 September 1983; see reg 1.
Interpretation See reg 3.
General These regulations, which revoke and replace the Brakes on Pedal Cycles Regulations 1954, SI 1954/966, exercise powers under the Road Traffic Act 1988, s 81 (formerly the Road Traffic Act 1972, s 66), relating to the construction and use of pedal cycles. For provisions as to lights and reflectors on pedal cycles, see SI 1989/1796.

[352]

Commencement and citation

1 These Regulations shall come into operation on 1st September 1983, and may be cited as the Pedal Cycles (Construction and Use) Regulations 1983.

[353]

2 (*Revokes the Brakes on Pedal Cycles Regulations 1954, SI 1954/966.*)

Interpretation

3 (1) In these Regulations:—

(a) a reference to the manufacturer of a vehicle means, in the case of a vehicle which has been altered so as to become an electrically assisted pedal cycle, the person who made that alteration;
(b) "pedal cycle" means a pedal cycle which is either—
  (i) not propelled by mechanical power, or
  (ii) an electrically assisted pedal cycle prescribed for the purposes of section 103 of the Road Traffic Regulation Act 1967 and section 193 of the Road Traffic Act 1972 by virtue of the Electrically Assisted Pedal Cycles Regulations 1983;
(c) "the 1971 British Standard" has the same meaning as in the Electrically Assisted Pedal Cycles Regulations 1983; and
(d) "the 1981 British Standard" means the Specification for safety requirements for bicycles published by the British Standard Institution under the reference BS 6102: Part I: 1981.

(2) In these Regulations, unless the context otherwise requires, a reference to a numbered Regulation is to the Regulation bearing that number in these Regulations, and a reference to a numbered paragraph is to the paragraph bearing that number in the Regulation in which the reference occurs.

NOTES
Erratum Para (1)(d): "British Standard Institution" should read "British Standards Institution".
Road Traffic Act 1972, s 193 Repealed; see now the Road Traffic Act 1988, s 189.
Road Traffic Regulation Act 1967, s 103 Repealed; see now Road Traffic Regulation Act 1984, s 140.
Electrically Assisted Pedal Cycles Regulations 1983 SI 1983/1168. "The 1971 British Standard" is defined in those regulations as the specification for motors for battery operated vehicles published by the British Standards Institution under the reference 1727:1971 as amended by Amendment Slip No 1 published on 31 January 1973, Amendment Slip No 2 published on 31 July 1974 and Amendment Slip No 3 published on 31 March 1978.

[354]

Requirements as to a pedal cycle to which the Electrically Assisted Pedal Cycles Regulations 1983 apply

4 No person shall ride, or cause or permit to be ridden, on a road a pedal cycle to which the Electrically Assisted Pedal Cycles Regulations 1983 apply unless it is fitted with—

(a) a plate securely fixed in a conspicuous and readily accessible position showing—
- (i) the name of the manufacturer of the vehicle,
- (ii) the nominal voltage of the battery (as defined in the 1971 British Standard) of the vehicle, and
- (iii) the continuous rated output (as defined in the 1971 British Standard) of the motor of the vehicle;

(b) braking systems which are so designed and constructed that—
- (i) in the case of a bicycle they comply with the standards specified in clause 6 of the 1981 British Standard, and
- (ii) in the case of a tricycle they comply with standards no less than the standards of braking systems fitted to a bicycle which comply with clause 6 of the 1981 British Standard;

(c) a battery which does not leak so as to be a source of danger; and

(d) a device biased to the off position which allows power to come from the motor only when the device is operated so as to achieve that result.

NOTES

Electrically Assisted Pedal Cycles Regulations 1983 SI 1983/1168.

[355]

5 No person shall ride, or cause or permit to be ridden, on a road a pedal cycle to which the Electrically Assisted Pedal Cycles Regulations 1983 apply unless the parts of the vehicle mentioned in—

(a) Regulation 4(b) and (c) of those Regulations, and

(b) Regulation 4(b), (c) and (d) of these Regulations,

are in efficient working order.

NOTES

Electrically Assisted Pedal Cycles Regulations 1983 SI 1983/1168.

[356]

Requirements as to a pedal cycle to which the Electrically Assisted Pedal Cycles Regulations 1983 do not apply

6 No person shall ride, or cause or permit to be ridden, on a road a pedal cycle to which the Electrically Assisted Pedal Cycles Regulations 1983 do not apply unless it complies with such of the requirements specified in Regulation 7 or 8 as apply to it.

NOTES

Electrically Assisted Pedal Cycles Regulations 1983 SI 1983/1168.

[357]

7 (1) Save as provided in Regulations 8 and 9—

(a) every pedal cycle shall be equipped with at least one braking system;

(b) every bicycle or tricycle the height of the saddle of which is 635 millimetres or more and every cycle with four or more wheels shall—
- (i) if it is so constructed that one or more of the wheels is incapable of rotating independently of the pedals, be equipped with a braking system operating on the front wheel or, if it has more than one front wheel, on at least two front wheels;
- (ii) if it is not so constructed that one or more of the wheels is incapable of rotating independently of the pedals, be equipped with two independent braking systems one of which operates on the front wheel, or if it has more than one front wheel, on at least two front wheels, and the other of which operates on the rear wheel, or if it has more than one rear wheel, on at least two rear wheels.

(2) The reference in paragraph (1)(b) to the height of the saddle is a reference to the height above the ground of the part of the seating area of the saddle which is furthest from the ground when the cycle to which the saddle is attached is vertical and the saddle is raised to the fullest extent compatible with safety and the tyres on the wheels of the cycle are fully inflated.

[358]

8 (1) The requirements of Regulation 7 do not apply to a pedal cycle manufactured before 1st August 1984 if, save as provided in Regulation 9 in the case where the cycle has any wheel of which the outside diameter (including any tyre when fully inflated) exceeds 460 millimetres—

(i) the cycle is so constructed that one or more of the wheels is incapable of rotating independently of the pedals, it is equipped with a braking system operating on the front wheel or both the front wheels if it has two front wheels;

(ii) the cycle is not so constructed, it is equipped with two independent braking systems one of which operates on the front wheel or both the front wheels if it has two front wheels, and the other of which operates on the rear wheel or one of the rear wheels if it has two rear wheels.

NOTES

Although numbered as para (1), this regulation does not contain further paragraphs.

[359]

9 (1) Nothing in Regulation 7 or 8 applies to—

(a) any pedal cycle so constructed that the pedals act on any wheel or on the axle of any wheel without the interposition of any gearing or chain; or

(b) any pedal cycle brought temporarily into Great Britain by a person resident abroad and intending to make only a temporary stay in Great Britain, while the cycle is being ridden by that person, provided that its brakes comply with the requirements of Article 26 of the International Convention on Road Traffic signed at Geneva on 19th September 1949 as amended.

(2) In the case of a tricycle not constructed or adapted for the carriage of goods it shall be a sufficient compliance with the requirements specified in Regulation 7(1)(b)(ii) and 8(1)(a)(ii) if the tricycle is equipped with two independent braking systems operating on the front wheel if it has two rear wheels, or on the rear wheel if it has two front wheels.

NOTES

International Convention on Road Traffic signed at Geneva on 19th September 1949 as amended Cmnd 7997 and 3152.

[360]

10 (1) No person shall ride, or cause or permit to be ridden, on a road a pedal cycle to which Regulation 6 applies unless the braking system or systems with which it is required to be fitted in accordance with Regulation 7 or, as the case may be, Regulation 8 are in efficient working order.

(2) For the purpose of this Regulation, except in the case of a cycle having four or more wheels, none of which has a diameter exceeding 250 millimetres (including any tyre when fully inflated), a braking system shall be deemed not to be in efficient working order if any brake operates directly on a pneumatic tyre on any wheel.

[361]

Testing and inspection

11 Any constable in uniform is hereby empowered to test and inspect a pedal cycle for the purpose of ascertaining whether any of the requirements specified in Regulation 4(b), or Regulation 7 or, as the case may be, Regulation 8, are satisfied provided he does so either—

(a) on any premises where the cycle is if the cycle has been involved in an accident, and the test and inspection are carried out within 48 hours of the accident and the owner of the premises consents; or

(b) on a road.

[362]

Requirements as to sale or supply etc of pedal cycles

12 No person shall sell or supply, or offer to sell or supply for delivery—

(a) a pedal cycle to which the Electrically Assisted Pedal Cycles Regulations 1983 apply unless it is equipped with braking systems as specified in Regulation 4(b); or

(b) on and after 1st August 1984, a pedal cycle to which those Regulations do not apply unless it is

(i) equipped with braking systems as specified in Regulation 7 or, as the case may be, Regulation 8; or

(ii) a pedal cycle which has no braking system and is specifically designed for off-road racing on enclosed tracks.

NOTES
Electrically Assisted Pedal Cycles Regulations 1983 SI 1983/1168.

[363]

DRIVING LICENCES (EXCHANGEABLE LICENCES) ORDER 1984 SI 1984/672

Authority Made by the Secretary of State for Transport under the Road Traffic Act 1972, s 110(2) (repealed); now has effect under the Road Traffic Act 1988, s 108(2), by virtue of the Road Traffic (Consequential Provisions) Act 1988, s 2(2) and the Interpretation Act 1978, s 17(2)(b), printed in the title Statutory Instruments (Pt 2), Vol 1 of this work.
Date made 14 May 1984.
Commencement 1 June 1984.
Amendment Amended by SI 2002/1593.
Summary This order designates the following countries within para (b) of the definition "exchangeable licence" in the Road Traffic Act 1988, s 108(1): Australia, New Zealand, Norway, Singapore, Spain, Sweden and Switzerland, and the territory of Hong Kong. (Kenya ceased to be a designated country under this order by the amending SI 2002/1593.) The effect of the order is that licences issued by the competent authorities of those countries and that territory will be exchangeable for an equivalent licence without a driving test under Pt III of the 1988 Act, if the holders satisfy the requirements of that Part of the Act for the grant of a licence in exchange.
Further orders The following orders have been made or have effect under the Road Traffic Act 1988, s 108(2) designating countries and territories for the purposes of the definition "exchangeable licence":

(a) SI 1985/65 (in force on 2 February 1985), designating Barbados, the Republic of Cyprus, Finland, Malta and Zimbabwe and the territory of the British Virgin Islands;
(b) SI 1985/1461 (in force on 1 November 1985), designating Austria and Japan;
(c) SI 1999/1641 (made under s 108(2)–(2B) of the 1988 Act), as amended by SI 2007/96 (in force on 2 July 1999), designating South Africa and the provinces and territories of Canada;
(d) SI 2002/2379 (made under s 108(2)(b), (2A), (2B) of the 1988 Act) (in force on 20 September 2002), designating the Republic of Korea and the Principality of Monaco;
(e) SI 2004/301 (made under s 108(2)(b), (2A), (2B) of the 1988 Act) (in force on 9 February 2004), designating the Falkland Islands; and
(f) SI 2007/95 (made under s 108(2)(b), (2A), (2B) of the 1988 Act) (in force on 31 January 2007), designating the Faroe Islands.

[364]

ROAD TRANSPORT (INTERNATIONAL PASSENGER SERVICES) REGULATIONS 1984 SI 1984/748

Authority Made by the Secretary of State for Transport under the European Communities Act 1972, s 2(2), the Road Traffic Act 1972, s 40(1) (repealed), the Public Passenger Vehicles Act 1981, s 60(1) and, with the consent of the Treasury, under the Finance Act 1973, s 56(1), (2). In so far as they were made under the Road Traffic Act 1972, these regulations now have effect as if made under the Road Traffic Act 1988, s 41, by virtue of the Interpretation Act 1978, s 17(2)(b), printed in the title Statutory Instruments (Pt 2), Vol 1 of this work, and the Road Traffic (Consequential Provisions) Act 1988, ss 2(2), 5(1), Sch 4, para 1(2).
Date made 25 May 1984.
Commencement 1 July 1984.
Amendment Amended by SI 1987/1755, SI 1988/1809, SI 1990/1103, SI 2003/1118, SI 2004/1882, SI 2008/1577, SI 2009/879, and by virtue of the Criminal Justice Act 1988, s 52 and the Road Traffic Act 1991, s 9(2).
Summary These regulations revoke and replace the Road Transport (International Passenger Services) Regulations 1980, SI 1980/1459, and the amending SI 1981/461, SI 1983/1025. They make

provision supplementary to EEC regulations which relate to the international carriage of passengers by coach and bus (i e Council Regulation (EEC) 684/92 (OJ L74, 20.03.1992, p 1), which repealed and replaced Council Regulations (EEC) 117/66, 516/72, 517/72, and Commission Regulation (EC) 2121/98 (OJ L268, 03.10.1998, p 10) (originally Commission Regulation (EEC) 1016/68 (repealed))). The regulations implement in relation to Great Britain the Agreement on the International Carriage of Passengers by Road by Means of Occasional Coach and Bus Services (ASOR), which requires EEC member states and other states party to that agreement to facilitate the operation of such services, and Council Regulation (EEC) 56/83 (OJ L10, 13.01.1983, p 1) concerning the implementation of that Agreement.

The regulations consist of five parts. Pt I contains general provisions. Pt II contains modifications of the Public Passenger Vehicles Act 1981 and the Transport Act 1985, Pts I, II in relation to vehicles registered in the United Kingdom when used for the international carriage of passengers. Pt III contains modifications of the 1981 Act in relation to vehicles registered outside the United Kingdom. Pt IV designates the Secretary of State as the competent authority for the purposes of ASOR, the Council Regulations and the Commission Regulation in relation to the international carriage of passengers to, from or through Great Britain and provides as to applications for issue of authorisations and other documents and fees in respect thereof. Pt V contains provisions relating to penalties and enforcement and makes consequential amendments to the Road Traffic (Foreign Vehicles) Act 1972. Pt V also disapplies requirements as to fitness, equipment type approval and certification of public service vehicles by providing that SI 1981/257, Pts II–V do not have effect in relation to a vehicle to which Pt III of these regulations applies or to a vehicle registered in Northern Ireland to which any provision of Pt II thereof applies.

Offences Certain offences under Pt V of these regulations are: (a) fixed penalty offences; see SI 2009/483, noted to SI 1990/335; (b) offences in respect of which a financial penalty deposit requirement may be imposed; see SI 2009/491 (and see also SI 2009/492).

[365]

MOTOR VEHICLES (TYPE APPROVAL) (GREAT BRITAIN) REGULATIONS 1984

SI 1984/981

Authority Made by the Secretary of State for Transport under the Road Traffic Act 1972, ss 47(1), 49, 50(1), 51(1), 52(2) (all repealed). Now have effect under the Road Traffic Act 1988, ss 54, 60, 61, 63, 66, by virtue of the Road Traffic (Consequential Provisions) Act 1988, s 2(2) and the Interpretation Act 1978, s 17(2)(b), printed in the title Statutory Instruments (Pt 2), Vol 1 of this work.

Date made 10 July 1984.

Commencement 21 August 1984.

Amendment Amended by SI 1984/1401, SI 1984/1761, SI 1985/1651, SI 1986/739, SI 1987/1509, SI 1988/1522, SI 1989/1580, SI 1990/94, SI 1990/1839, SI 1991/1022, SI 1991/1971, SI 1992/1341, SI 1992/2161, SI 1992/2908 (amended by SI 1992/3173), SI 1993/2201, SI 1994/2190, SI 1995/1322, SI 1996/2330, SI 1996/3015 (amended by SI 1997/1367 (superseded)), SI 1997/1502, SI 1998/1005. Previously amended by SI 1997/2933 (superseding the amendment by SI 1997/1367 to SI 1996/3015, and itself superseded by SI 1998/1005).

Summary These regulations revoke and replace, with amendments, the Motor Vehicles (Type Approval) (Great Britain) Regulations 1979, SI 1979/1092, and the amending SI 1980/879, SI 1980/1165, SI 1981/696, SI 1981/1619, SI 1982/8, SI 1983/328. They provide for a scheme of type approval of motor vehicles and motor vehicle parts in relation to certain classes of motor vehicle in Great Britain on a national basis. The regulations apply to every motor vehicle manufactured on or after 1 October 1977 and not first used before 1 August 1978 of a description specified in reg 3 of the regulations (which, generally, excludes goods vehicles, vehicles adapted to carry more than eight passengers and certain three-wheeled vehicles), subject to certain exceptions.

The following vehicles are excepted from the regulations: motor vehicles temporarily imported by persons resident abroad; vehicles of a visiting force or headquarters; tax exempt vehicles which are to be exported from Great Britain; prototypes not intended for general use on the road; pre-release vehicles; certain vehicles used in the public service of the Crown; vehicles first licensed under the Vehicles (Excise) Act (Northern Ireland) 1972 (repealed) on or after 2 December 1985 and before 1 October 1991; and vehicles in respect of which there exists a certificate issued in accordance with the Road Traffic (Northern Ireland) Order 1981, SI 1981/154 (NI 1) (outside the scope of this work), or parts of any such vehicle.

The regulations have effect with modifications in relation to passenger vehicles to which SI 2001/25 (formerly the Motor Vehicles (Approval) Regulations 1996, SI 1996/3013, Pt II (revoked)) applies.

Type approval requirements, i e requirements with respect to the design, construction, equipment or marking of vehicles or vehicle parts, are set out in Schs 1, 1A, 1B to the regulations; an application by the manufacturer of a vehicle or vehicle part for type approval and for the issue of a type approval certificate or a further type approval certificate must be made in writing to the Secretary of State for Transport, as should an application by any person in respect of a vehicle or vehicle part for a minister's approval certificate. As soon as reasonably practicable, the Secretary of State must send to the applicant notice of the place, date and time for examination of the vehicle or part, and of the prescribed fees payable in respect of application and examination (as to which, see SI 1999/2149). The Secretary of State is empowered to authorise persons to carry out examinations. A right of appeal lies under the Road Traffic Act 1988, s 60 (formerly the Road Traffic Act 1972, s 49), from a determination made on behalf of the Secretary of State with respect to a type approval certificate, certificate of conformity or minister's approval certificate.

Records relating to certificates of conformity must be kept by manufacturers and produced for inspection by an authorised person. The regulations specify 1 July 1998 as the appointed day for the purposes of the Road Traffic Act 1988, s 63(1) from when the prescribed type approval requirements must be complied with in relation to vehicles to which the Motor Vehicles (Approval) Regulations 1996, SI 1996/3013 (revoked and replaced by SI 2001/25) applied. Licences under the Vehicle Excise and Registration Act 1994 must not be granted unless the appropriate certificates are in force.

[366]

PUBLIC SERVICE VEHICLES (CARRYING CAPACITY) REGULATIONS 1984
SI 1984/1406

Authority Made by the Secretary of State for Transport under the Public Passenger Vehicles Act 1981, ss 26(1), 60(1).
Date made 30 August 1984.
Commencement 4 October 1984.
Amendment Amended by SI 1996/167 and by virtue of the Road Traffic Act 1991, s 9(2).
Summary These regulations, which revoke and replace the Public Service Vehicles and Trolley Vehicles (Carrying Capacity) Regulations 1954, SI 1954/1612, and the amending SI 1958/472, SI 1966/674, SI 1980/76, SI 1981/260, impose new provisions as to the carrying capacity of public service vehicles adapted to carry more than eight passengers. Reg 4 prescribes that the maximum seating capacity in respect of a vehicle for which a certificate of initial fitness or conformity has been issued is either the capacity stated on that certificate or a greater or lesser capacity authorised by an examiner and that the maximum seating capacity in respect of other vehicles is as calculated in accordance with SI 1971/450, reg 42 (revoked; see now SI 2002/2742, reg 44), or a greater or lesser capacity authorised by a certifying officer. Reg 5 provides that the number of seated passengers carried must not exceed the number for which the vehicle has capacity and makes special provision for children; a child under five years who is not occupying a seat does not count as a passenger, and three seated children under 14 count as two passengers if none of them is occupying a seat provided with a seat belt. Reg 6 provides that the maximum standing capacity in respect of a vehicle for which a certificate of initial fitness or conformity has been issued is either the capacity stated on that certificate or a greater or lesser capacity authorised by an examiner, and that the maximum standing capacity in respect of other vehicles is one-third of the seating capacity or eight, whichever is the less, or such other number as is authorised by an examiner. The standing capacity of vehicles with a seating capacity of less than 13, vehicles with a gangway height of less than 1.77 metres and of half-decked vehicles is nil. Reg 7 imposes restrictions on the carriage of standing passengers. Reg 8 requires a vehicle to be marked to show its seating and standing capacities. Reg 9 requires increases in capacities to be notified to the traffic commissioner. Reg 10 requires authorisations of increased capacity to be in writing. Reg 11 provides for exemptions as to certain international and Northern Irish passenger services. Reg 12 provides for appeals to the Secretary of State against certification by an examiner in certain circumstances.

[367]

MOTOR VEHICLES (INTERNATIONAL CIRCULATION) REGULATIONS 1985
SI 1985/610

Authority Made by the Secretary of State for Transport under the Vehicles (Excise) Act 1971, s 23(1)(d), (e), (f) (repealed), as modified by s 39(1) of, and Sch 7, Pt I, para 20 to, that Act (repealed), and SI 1975/1208, art 5(4)–(7). Now take effect under the Vehicle Excise and Registration Act 1994, ss 22(1), 23(4), by virtue of s 64 of, and para 2 of Sch 4 to, that Act.
Date made 15 April 1985.
Commencement 16 May 1985.
Summary These regulations revoke and replace the Motor Vehicles (International Circulation) Regulations 1971, SI 1971/937. They provide for the assignment, by registration authorities as defined in SI 1975/1208 (ie the Automobile Association, the Royal Automobile Club, the Royal Scottish Automobile Club or the Secretary of State), of registration marks in respect of motor vehicles brought temporarily into Great Britain by persons resident outside the United Kingdom (reg 5), for the issue in certain cases of registration cards to such persons (reg 6), and for the licensing of such vehicles under the Vehicle Excise and Registration Act 1994 (reg 7). Provision is also made for the production, when required, of registration and motor insurance documents to a registration authority, the police or a person acting on behalf of the Secretary of State (reg 4), for the form and exhibition of registration marks (reg 8) and as to the records to be kept by a registration authority (reg 9).

The regulations apply, with modifications, certain provisions of SI 1971/450 (revoked and replaced in part by SI 2001/561; see the note "Application of previous regulations to visiting vehicles" thereto, and in full by SI 2002/2742; see the note "Application of previous regulations to visitors' registration cards" thereto).

[368]

MOTOR VEHICLES (EXEMPTION FROM VEHICLES EXCISE DUTY) ORDER 1985
SI 1985/722

Authority Made by the Secretary of State for Transport under the Vehicles (Excise) Act 1971, s 7(2A), (2B) (repealed). Now takes effect under the Vehicle Excise and Registration Act 1994, Sch 2, para 19(5), by virtue of s 64 of, and para 2 of Sch 4 to, that Act.
Date made 8 May 1985.
Commencement With effect from 21 November 1983.
Summary This order specifies certain payments to former members of the armed forces disabled prior to 3 September 1939 as being of a similar nature to a mobility supplement, and thus brings those members of the armed forces within the scope of the exemption from vehicle excise duty contained in the Vehicle Excise and Registration Act 1994, Sch 2, para 19 (vehicles for disabled people).

[369]

TRANSPORT ACT 1985 (COMMENCEMENT NO 1) ORDER 1985
SI 1985/1887

Authority Made by the Secretary of State for Transport under the Transport Act 1985, s 140(2), (3).
Date made 5 December 1985.
Summary This order, and the further commencement orders made under the Transport Act 1985, s 140(2), (3) (ie SI 1986/80, SI 1986/414, SI 1986/1088, SI 1986/1450, SI 1986/1794 (as amended by SI 1988/2294 in relation to transitional provisions), SI 1987/1228), brought provisions of the 1985 Act into force on various dates. The table below sets out the provisions of the Act brought into force by these orders. SI 1986/1794, SI 1987/1228 also amended SI 1981/1694; those amendments have been superseded by subsequent provision.

Provision	*Date and extent (if any)*
s 1(1), (2)	26 October 1986 (SI 1986/1794)
s 1(3)	See Sch 1
ss 2, 3	6 January 1986 (SI 1985/1887)
s 4	6 January 1986 (to the extent necessary to replace Public Passenger Vehicles Act 1981, s 54 with sub-ss (1), (2) only of the new s 54) (SI 1985/1887) 26 October 1986 (otherwise) (SI 1986/1794)
s 5	6 January 1986 (SI 1985/1887)
s 6	26 October 1986 (SI 1986/1794)
ss 7–9	14 July 1986 (SI 1986/1088)
ss 10, 11	1 August 1986 (SI 1986/1088)
s 12(1), (2)	6 January 1986 (SI 1985/1887)
s 12(3)	Repealed
s 12(4)–(13)	6 January 1986 (SI 1985/1887)
s 13	6 January 1986 (to the extent that it supplements s 12 of this Act) (SI 1985/1887) 1 August 1986 (otherwise) (SI 1986/1088)
ss 14, 15	1 January 1987 (SI 1986/1794)
s 16	6 January 1986 (SI 1985/1887)
s 17	1 August 1986 (SI 1986/1088)
s 18	1 August 1986 (so far as it relates to the use of any vehicle under a permit granted under s 22 or the driving of any vehicle so used) (SI 1986/1088) 13 August 1987 (otherwise) (SI 1987/1228)
ss 19–21	13 August 1987 (SI 1987/1228)
ss 22, 23	1 August 1986 (SI 1986/1088)
s 24(1)	26 October 1986 (SI 1986/1794)
s 24(2)	Repealed
ss 25–28	26 October 1986 (SI 1986/1794)
ss 29, 30	6 January 1986 (SI 1985/1887)

Provision	*Date and extent (if any)*
s 31	15 September 1986 (SI 1986/1450)
s 32	6 January 1986 (to the extent that this section applies to Public Passenger Vehicles Act 1981, s 28) (SI 1985/1887) 26 October 1986 (otherwise) (SI 1986/1794)
s 33	1 August 1986 (SI 1986/1088)
s 34	6 January 1986 (SI 1985/1887) (repealed by Greater London Authority Act 1999, s 423, Sch 34, Pt II, as from a date to be appointed)
ss 35–46	26 October 1986 (SI 1986/1794) (repealed by Greater London Authority Act 1999, s 423, Sch 34, Pt II, as from a date to be appointed)
ss 47–53	Repealed
ss 54–56	6 January 1986 (SI 1985/1887)
s 57(1)–(5)	6 January 1986 (SI 1985/1887)
s 57(6)	See Sch 3
ss 59–84	6 January 1986 (SI 1985/1887)
ss 85, 86	13 August 1987 (SI 1987/1228)
ss 87–92	6 January 1986 (SI 1985/1887)
s 93(1)–(7)	14 February 1986 (SI 1986/80)
s 93(8)(a)	14 February 1986 (SI 1986/80)
s 93(8)(b)	1 April 1986 (SI 1986/414)
s 93(9), (10)	14 February 1986 (SI 1986/80)
ss 94–101	14 February 1986 (SI 1986/80)
s 102	1 April 1986 (SI 1986/414)
s 103	14 February 1986 (SI 1986/80)
s 104	15 September 1986 (SI 1986/1450)
s 105	14 February 1986 (SI 1986/80)
s 106	6 January 1986 (SI 1985/1887)
s 107	Repealed
s 108	1 April 1986 (SI 1986/414)
ss 109–111	Repealed
ss 112, 113	6 January 1986 (SI 1985/1887)
s 114	26 July 1986 (SI 1986/1088)
ss 115, 116	Repealed
s 117	15 September 1986 (SI 1986/1450)
ss 118–125	6 January 1986 (SI 1985/1887)
s 126(1), (2)	1 August 1986 (so far as they relate to fees chargeable in respect of applications for, and the grant of, permits under s 22) (SI 1986/1088) 26 October 1986 (otherwise, except so far as sub-s (1) relates to applications for, and the grant of, permits under s 19) (SI 1986/1794) 13 August 1987 (otherwise) (SI 1987/1228)
s 126(3)(a)	26 October 1986 (SI 1986/1794)
s 126(3)(b)	14 July 1986 (SI 1986/1088)
s 126(3)(c)	26 October 1986 (SI 1986/1794)
s 127(1), (2)	1 August 1986 (SI 1986/1088)
s 127(3)	6 January 1986 (SI 1985/1887)
s 127(4)	6 January 1986 (so far as it relates to s 30(2)) (SI 1985/1887) 1 August 1986 (so far as it relates to s 23(5)) (SI 1986/1088) 26 October 1986 (otherwise) (SI 1986/1794)

Provision	*Date and extent (if any)*
s 127(5)–(7)	6 January 1986 (SI 1985/1887)
ss 128–130	6 January 1986 (SI 1985/1887)
s 131(1)–(5)	Repealed
s 131(6), (7)	6 January 1986 (SI 1985/1887)
ss 132–138	6 January 1986 (SI 1985/1887)
s 139(1)–(3)	See Schs 6–8
s 139(4), (5)	6 January 1986 (SI 1985/1887)
Sch 1, paras 1, 2	6 January 1986 (SI 1985/1887)
Sch 1, para 3(1), (2)	6 January 1986 (SI 1985/1887)
Sch 1, para 3(3)	26 October 1986 (SI 1986/1794)
Sch 1, para 3(4)	6 January 1986 (except for the omission of the words "or Part III") (SI 1985/1887) 26 October 1986 (exception noted above) (SI 1986/1794)
Sch 1, para 3(5)	6 January 1986 (SI 1985/1887)
Sch 1, para 4	6 January 1986 (SI 1985/1887)
Sch 1, para 5	Repealed
Sch 1, para 6	6 January 1986 (SI 1985/1887)
Sch 1, paras 7–11	26 October 1986 (SI 1986/1794)
Sch 1, para 12	6 January 1986 (SI 1985/1887)
Sch 1, para 13	6 January 1986 (except for the omission of the definitions "excursion or tour", "road service licence" and "trial area") (SI 1985/1887) 26 October 1986 (exceptions noted above) (SI 1986/1794)
Sch 1, para 14	6 January 1986 (SI 1985/1887)
Sch 1, para 15(1)	6 January 1986 (SI 1985/1887)
Sch 1, para 15(2), (3)	26 October 1986 (SI 1986/1794)
Sch 1, para 15(4), (5)	6 January 1986 (SI 1985/1887)
Sch 1, para 16	6 January 1986 (SI 1985/1887)
Sch 2	6 January 1986 (SI 1985/1887)
Sch 3, paras 1–7	6 January 1986 (SI 1985/1887)
Sch 3, para 8	Repealed
Sch 3, paras 9–21	6 January 1986 (SI 1985/1887)
Sch 3, para 22	Repealed
Sch 3, para 23	6 January 1986 (SI 1985/1887)
Sch 3, para 24	6 January 1986 (to the extent that it relates to Local Government Act 1972, s 202(1), (4)–(7)) (SI 1985/1887) 1 April 1986 (otherwise) (SI 1986/414)
Sch 3, para 25	6 January 1986 (SI 1985/1887)
Sch 3, para 26	1 April 1986 (SI 1986/414)
Sch 3, paras 27, 28	6 January 1986 (SI 1985/1887)
Sch 3, para 29	Repealed
Sch 3, paras 30–33	6 January 1986 (SI 1985/1887)
Sch 4	15 September 1986 (SI 1986/1450)
Sch 5	6 January 1986 (SI 1985/1887)
Sch 6, paras 1–11	6 January 1986 (SI 1985/1887)
Sch 6, para 13	6 January 1986 (SI 1985/1887)
Sch 6, para 14	26 October 1986 (SI 1986/1794)
Sch 6, para 15	6 January 1986 (SI 1985/1887)

Provision	*Date and extent (if any)*
Sch 6, paras 16–18	26 October 1986 (SI 1986/1794)
Sch 6, para 19	6 January 1986 (SI 1985/1887)
Sch 6, para 20	Spent
Sch 6, para 21	6 January 1986 (SI 1985/1887)
Sch 6, paras 22, 23	14 February 1986 (SI 1986/80) (also purportedly brought into force, to the extent that they are not already in force, by SI 1986/414)
Sch 6, paras 24, 25	15 September 1986 (SI 1986/1450)
Sch 6, para 26	6 January 1986 (SI 1985/1887)
Sch 7, para 1	6 January 1986 (SI 1985/1887)
Sch 7, para 2	1 August 1986 (SI 1986/1088)
Sch 7, para 3	1 April 1986 (SI 1986/414)
Sch 7, para 4	6 January 1986 (SI 1985/1887)
Sch 7, para 5	26 October 1986 (SI 1986/1794)
Sch 7, para 6	6 January 1986 (SI 1985/1887)
Sch 7, paras 7, 8	15 September 1986 (SI 1986/1450)
Sch 7, para 9	1 April 1986 (SI 1986/414)
Sch 7, paras 10–12	6 January 1986 (SI 1985/1887)
Sch 7, para 13	Repealed
Sch 7, para 14	6 January 1986 (SI 1985/1887)
Sch 7, para 15	Repealed
Sch 7, para 16	26 October 1986 (SI 1986/1794)
Sch 7, para 17	1 April 1986 (SI 1986/414)
Sch 7, para 18	6 January 1986 (SI 1985/1887)
Sch 7, para 19	1 April 1986 (SI 1986/414)
Sch 7, para 20	6 January 1986 (SI 1985/1887)
Sch 7, para 21(1)	6 January 1986 (SI 1985/1887)
Sch 7, para 21(2), (3)	Repealed
Sch 7, para 21(4)	6 January 1986 (except that the words "sub-section (1A) below and" are omitted from the insertion) (SI 1985/1887) 26 October 1986 (exception noted above) (SI 1986/1794)
Sch 7, para 21(5)	26 October 1986 (SI 1986/1794)
Sch 7, para 21(6)	6 January 1986 (SI 1985/1887)
Sch 7, para 21(7)	Repealed
Sch 7, para 21(8)	6 January 1986 (SI 1985/1887)
Sch 7, para 21(9), (10)	26 October 1986 (SI 1986/1794)
Sch 7, para 21(11)	15 September 1986 (SI 1986/1450)
Sch 7, para 21(12)	6 January 1986 (SI 1985/1887)
Sch 7, para 22	Repealed
Sch 7, para 23	6 January 1986 (SI 1985/1887)
Sch 7, para 24	1 April 1986 (SI 1986/414)
Sch 7, paras 25, 26	26 October 1986 (SI 1986/1794)

Provision	*Date and extent (if any)*
Sch 8	6 January 1986 (repeals of or in Road Traffic Act 1930; Transport Act 1962, ss 4, 92; Finance Act 1965; Transport Act 1968, ss 9, 10(2), 11(1), 12(3)(d), 14(3), 15, 15(A)(1), 16(2), 17–19, 20, 21, 22, 24(3), 29(4), 34, 36, 54, 59(3), 90, 103(1), 159(1), Sch 5; Post Office Act 1969; Local Government Act 1972, ss 80(4), 202, Sch 24, Pt II; Local Government Act 1974; Energy Act 1976, Sch 1, para 1(2); Transport Act 1978; Transport Act 1980; Public Passenger Vehicles Act 1981, ss 1, 2, 28, 46, 53(1) (word "the" before words "traffic commissioners"), 56, 60, 61(2), 62, 81(2), 82(1) (definitions "contract carriage", "express carriage", "express carriage service", "stage carriage" and "stage carriage service"), 83, Sch 1, paras 3, 4; Transport Act 1982, s 73(4); Transport Act 1983, s 9(2); Road Traffic Regulation Act 1984, Sch 13, para 49; London Regional Transport Act 1984, s 28, Sch 6, paras 3, 6) (SI 1985/1887)
	1 April 1986 (repeals of or in Finance Act 1970; Local Government Act 1972, s 202(2), (3); Local Government (Scotland) Act 1973, s 150; Transport Act 1983, s 3; Local Government Act 1985) (SI 1986/414)
	26 July 1986 (repeal of London Regional Transport Act 1984, Sch 6, para 15(1)(a)) (SI 1986/1088)
	15 September 1986 (repeals of or in Transport Act 1962, s 57, Sch 10; Transport Act 1968, s 88, Sch 10) (SI 1986/1450)
	26 October 1986 (all other repeals, except those of or in Town Police Clauses Act 1847; Public Passenger Vehicles Act 1981, ss 42–44, 52, 67, 76 (words "except sections 42 to 44" and word "thereof")) (SI 1986/1794)
	13 August 1987 (all other repeals, except repeal of words "such number of" and "as they think fit" in Town Police Clauses Act 1847, s 37 (which repeal entry is now itself repealed)) (SI 1987/1228)

[370]

PUBLIC TRANSPORT COMPANIES (PERMITTED MAXIMUM AND REQUIRED MINIMUM NUMBER OF DIRECTORS) ORDER 1985

SI 1985/1901

Authority Made by the Secretary of State for Transport, the Secretary of State for Scotland and the Secretary of State for Wales under the Transport Act 1985, s 73(6).

Date made 5 December 1985.

Commencement 6 January 1986.

Summary This order prescribes seven as the permitted maximum number of persons who are not full-time employees of a public transport company as defined in the Transport Act 1985, s 72(1) who may be directors of such a company. The order also prescribes three as the required minimum number of persons who are full-time employees of the company, in positions of responsibility for the management of the company's business or any part of that business, who are to be directors of the company where the company owns 50 or more buses. In cases where the company owns fewer than 50 buses, the required minimum is two.

[371]

TRANSPORT ACT 1985 (EXCLUSION OF BUS OPERATING POWERS AND EXEMPTION FOR COUNCILS RUNNING SMALL BUS UNDERTAKINGS) ORDER 1985

SI 1985/1902

Authority Made by the Secretary of State for Transport, the Secretary of State for Scotland and the Secretary of State for Wales under the Transport Act 1985, ss 66(2), (3), (4), 71(1).

Date made 5 December 1985.

Commencement 6 January 1986.

Summary The Transport Act 1985, s 66(1) provides that, subject to s 71 of that Act, a non-metropolitan district council in England or a county council or county borough council in Wales does not have power to provide a service for the carriage of passengers by road which requires a PSV operator's licence. (S 66(1) of the 1985 Act is amended by the Local Transport Act 2008, s 40(3), as from a day to be appointed by order, so as to be subject also to the Transport Act 2000, s 132C (power of authorities to provide services in exceptional circumstances), inserted by s 40(1) of the 2008 Act.)

This order specified the period ending with 25 October 1986 as the period at the end of which s 66(1) has effect in relation to certain specified councils. In addition, the order specified a shorter period ending with 1 April 1986 as the period before the end of which those councils were to comply with such of the requirements of ss 67–69 of the Act as were applicable to them. The order also specifies ten as the maximum number of vehicles above which a council operating a bus undertaking may not be exempted from s 66(1) of the Act under s 71(1) thereof.

[372]

TRANSPORT ACT 1985 (MODIFICATIONS IN SCHEDULE 4 TO THE TRANSPORT ACT 1968) ORDER 1985
SI 1985/1903

Authority Made by the Secretary of State for Transport, the Secretary of State for Scotland and the Secretary of State for Wales under the Transport Act 1985, s 129(5).
Date made 5 December 1985.
Commencement 6 January 1986; see art 1.
Interpretation See art 2.
Amendment Printed as amended by SI 1987/337.
General This order makes modifications to the Transport Act 1968, Sch 4 for the purposes of its application to transfers of bus undertakings to companies under the Transport Act 1985, s 50(4) (repealed), 59(7), 61(11) or 68(7). For further modifications to Sch 4 to the 1968 Act for the purposes of its application to transfers under s 61(11) of the 1985 Act, see SI 1993/2797.

[373]

1 This Order may be cited as the Transport Act 1985 (Modifications in Schedule 4 to the Transport Act 1968) Order 1985 and shall come into operation on 6th January 1986.

[374]

2 In this Order—

"the Act" means the Transport Act 1985;
"Schedule 4" means Schedule 4 to the Transport Act 1968.

[375]

3 For the purposes of its application to transfers under section [50(4),] 59(7), 61(11) or 68(7) of the Act, Schedule 4 shall be modified in accordance with the provisions of the First Schedule to this Order.

NOTES
Amendment Number in square brackets inserted by SI 1987/337.
S 50(4) of the Act Repealed by SI 1991/510.

[376]

4 Schedule 4, as modified in accordance with the provisions of the First Schedule to this Order, and with consequential adjustments in the headings to and numbering of the paragraphs, is set out in the Second Schedule to this Order.

[377]

FIRST SCHEDULE
MODIFICATIONS TO SCHEDULE 4 FOR THE PURPOSES OF ITS APPLICATION TO TRANSFERS UNDER SECTION 59(7), 61(11) OR 68(7) OF THE ACT

Article 3

1 In paragraph 1—

(a) in sub-paragraph (1), for the words "an agreement for the rendering of personal services" there shall be substituted the words "a contract of employment";
(b) in sub-paragraph (4), the words from "or, if either" to the end shall be omitted;
(c) in sub-paragraph (7), the words from "(not being" to "wholly-owned subsidiary" in the second place where those words occur shall be omitted; and
(d) in sub-paragraphs (5) and (7), for the words "this Act" there shall be substituted the words "the Transport Act 1985".

2 Paragraph 2 shall be omitted.

3 In paragraph 3, a colon shall be substituted for the full stop at the end, and there shall be added the following—

"in Scotland, section 16(1) and (2) of the Land Registration (Scotland) Act 1979 shall apply as if the transfer had been effected by deed" and the words "unless specially qualified" were omitted from those subsections.".

4 In paragraph 4, for the words "this Act" there shall be substituted the words "the Transport Act 1985".

5 In paragraph 5—

- (a) for the words "Railways Board and the Scottish Group" there shall be substituted the words "transferor and the transferee";
- (b) for the words "this Act" there shall be substituted the words "the Transport Act 1985";
- (c) for the words "the certifying authorities" there shall be substituted the word "them";
- (d) for the words "one of those authorities" there shall be substituted the words "either of them"; and
- (e) for the words "the authorities concerned" there shall be substituted the word "they".

6 In paragraph 6—

- (a) for the words "Railways Board or the Scottish Group" there shall be substituted the words "transferor or the transferee";
- (b) for the words "that authority" there shall be substituted the words "one of them";
- (c) for the words "another of those authorities" there shall be substituted the words "the other of them";
- (d) for the words "none of those authorities or" there shall be substituted the words "neither the transferor nor the transferee nor";
- (e) for the words "one of those authorities" in sub-paragraph (b) there shall be substituted the words "either the transferor or the transferee";
- (f) for the words "any of those authorities" in both places where they occur there shall be substituted the words "either the transferor or the transferee";
- (g) in sub-paragraph (b)(ii), the words "authority or subsidiary" shall be omitted;
- (h) for the words "one of those authorities" in both places where they appear there shall be substituted the words "the transferor or the transferee"; and
- (i) for the words "those authorities" there shall be substituted the words "the transferor and the transferee".

7 In sub-paragraph (c) of paragraph 7—

- (a) for the words "any officer or any servant of the transferor" there shall be substituted the words "a person employed by, or engaged in the business of, the transferor and holding a specified office or serving in a specified capacity";
- (b) for the words "the officer or servant" there shall be substituted the words "a person employed by, or engaged in the business"; and
- (c) for the words "that officer or servant of the transferor" there shall be substituted the words "the first mentioned person".

8 In paragraph 8—

- (a) for the words "this Act" there shall be substituted the words "the Transport Act 1985";
- (b) after the words "the provision in question relates to" there shall be inserted "(a)";
- (c) after the words "transferred rights and liabilities" there shall be inserted "; or (b) any business or activity to which any of those rights and liabilities relates"; and
- (d) for the words "officers or servants" there shall be substituted the words "persons employed by, persons engaged in the business of, or agents".

9 Paragraph 9 shall be omitted.

10 In paragraph 10—

- (a) for the words "7 to 9" there shall be substituted the words "7 and 8";
- (b) for the words "this Act" in the first place where they appear there shall be substituted the words "the Transport Act 1985"; and
- (c) for the words "this Act" in the second place where they appear there shall be substituted the words "that Act".

11 Paragraph 11 and sub-paragraph (1) of paragraph 12 shall be omitted.

12 In sub-paragraph (2) of paragraph 12, for the words "7 to 11" there shall be substituted the words "7 to 10", and the words: "the said" shall be omitted.

13 In paragraph 13—

- (a) in sub-paragraph (1), for the words "7 to 12" there shall be substituted the words "7 to 10";
- (b) for the words "one of the Boards or new authorities" in the first place where they occur there shall be substituted the words "the transferor and the transferee", and for those words in the second and third places where they occur there shall be substituted the words "the transferor or the transferee"; and
- (c) in sub-paragraph (5) for the words "this Act" there shall be substituted the words "the Transport Act 1985".

14 There shall be added the following new paragraph—

"In this Schedule "statutory provision" means a provision, whether of a general or a special nature, contained in, or in a document made or issued under, the Transport Act 1985 or any Act (whether of a general or of a special nature) other than that Act.".

[378]

SECOND SCHEDULE

NOTES
This Schedule, which is referred to in art 4, contains the text of the Transport Act 1968, Sch 4, as modified by art 3 of, and Sch 1 to, this order.

[379]

TRAVEL CONCESSION SCHEMES REGULATIONS 1986
SI 1986/77

Authority Made by the Secretary of State for Transport and the Secretaries of State for Scotland and Wales under the Transport Act 1985, ss 93(4), 94(1), 96(1), (5), 97(6), 100(1), (6), 134(4), (5).
Date made 21 January 1986.
Commencement 14 February 1986.
Amendment Amended by SI 1996/2711.
Summary These regulations make provision for the arrangements between authorities administering travel concession schemes and operators of public passenger transport services participating in such schemes, and for certain other matters in connection with travel concession schemes.

Pt II of the regulations deals with arrangements between operators and authorities. Regs 4, 5 apply to reimbursement arrangements with respect to operators of all descriptions. They provide that it is an objective (but not a duty) of an authority when formulating reimbursement arrangements to provide that operators both individually and in the aggregate are financially no better and no worse off as a result of their participation in the scheme, and also provide that reimbursement arrangements adopted by an authority are to be so formulated that the costs to operators of providing concessions are met by the payments made by the authority to operators. Regs 7–12 apply to arrangements with respect to operators of eligible services and provide that it is an objective of an authority when formulating reimbursement arrangements for operators of eligible services to provide that such operators receive appropriate reimbursement for providing concessions to the persons eligible to receive those concessions. Provision is made for the inclusion in these arrangements of provisions for calculating the amount, and timing and frequency, of reimbursement payments. Regs 14–21 make further provision for the inclusion in reimbursement arrangements of provisions for the supply of information by operators. Regs 23–26 contain provisions relating to arrangements other than reimbursement arrangements.

Pt III of the regulations and the Schedules make provision for the content and manner of service of notices in connection with travel concession schemes. Pt IV prescribes the periods of notice which are to be given in the same connection. Pt V prescribes the procedure to be followed in connection with applications for the cancellation or variation of participation and certain other notices, and for release from compulsory participation in a travel concession scheme.

[380]

PUBLIC PASSENGER TRANSPORT POLICIES (ANTICIPATORY EXERCISE OF POWERS) ORDER 1986
SI 1986/81

Authority Made by the Secretary of State under the Local Government Act 1985, s 101.
Date made 22 January 1986.
Commencement 13 February 1986.
Summary This order enabled the metropolitan county passenger transport authorities (renamed integrated transport authorities as noted below) established pursuant to the Local Government Act 1985, ss 23, 28 (amended as noted below) to take at any time before 1 April 1986 the following steps:

(a) seeking and having regard to the advice of the relevant Passenger Transport Executive;
(b) consulting with every Passenger Transport Authority or county or regional council whose area might be affected by the proposed policies of the authority;
(c) consulting with persons operating public passenger transport services within the area of the authority or with organisations appearing to the authority to be representative of such persons;
(d) consulting with councils of districts in the area of the authority about the requirements for transport arising out of or in connection with the exercise and performance by those councils of their functions as local education authorities or of their social services functions; and
(e) having regard to the transport needs of members of the public who are elderly or disabled, which are required to be taken as a preliminary to the exercise of the powers necessary to perform the duties imposed by the Transport Act 1968, s 9A(1), (7) (s 9A(1) has been repealed in relation to England and Wales by the Transport Act 2000, ss 161, 274, Sch 11, paras 2, 3(1), (2), Sch 31, Pt II).

These duties relate to the formulation of policies for the provision of public passenger transport services, and on 1 April 1986 became duties of the above-mentioned authorities.

Change of name of passenger transport authorities By the Local Transport Act 2008, s 77(2), metropolitan county passenger transport authorities established under the Local Government Act 1985, s 28 are to be known as Integrated Transport Authorities, as from 9 February 2009 (see SI 2009/107). In consequence, any reference in any enactment (whenever passed or made) to a Passenger Transport Authority is to be read as a reference to an Integrated Transport Authority (s 77(4) of the 2008 Act). S 28 of the 1985 Act is amended by s 77(5) of, and para 53 of Pt 4 of Sch 4 to, the 2008 Act, as from 9 February 2009, so as to provide for the establishment of Integrated Transport Authorities.

[381]

CONTROL OF OFF-STREET PARKING (ENGLAND AND WALES) (METROPOLITAN DISTRICTS) ORDER 1986
SI 1986/225

Authority Made under the Road Traffic Regulation Act 1984, s 44(1)(a).
Date made 12 February 1986.
Commencement 1 April 1986.
Amendment Amended by virtue of the Criminal Justice Act 1988, s 52.
Summary This Order in Council applies the provisions of the Road Traffic Regulation Act 1984, s 43, Sch 4, with appropriate modifications, to metropolitan districts so as to deal with the control of public off-street parking. (Note that by virtue of the provisions of the Local Government (Wales) Act 1994 there are no longer any districts in Wales.) Arts 3 and 4 of the order enable metropolitan district councils by regulations to designate controlled areas in which under art 5 the provision of public off-street parking places will require a licence from the council. The procedure for such designation is set out in Pt I of the Schedule.

Arts 6, 7 provide for permanent or limited licences and for the terms and conditions of licences. Inspection of parking places is provided for in art 8. District councils are required to give reasons for their decisions by art 9. Art 10 and Pt II of the Schedule deal with the transfer, surrender, variation and revocation of licences. Provision for appeals against decisions with respect to licences and for compensation in certain cases is made in arts 11, 13 and in Pts III and IV of the Schedule. In particular, para 17 of the Schedule enables the Secretary of State to make regulations governing the procedure to be followed in connection with appeals (see further the note "Appeals procedure" below).

Contravention by the holder of a licence of its terms and conditions is an offence under art 12, as also is the operation of a public off-street parking place without a licence. District councils are required by art 15 to apply the principles of the control to their own public off-street parking places situated in a controlled area. Art 16 gives the Secretary of State power to suspend the control in an emergency. Pt V of the Schedule provides for permissible periods of unlicensed operation of public off-street parking places in certain cases.

Similar provision is made in respect of the control of public off-street parking in non-metropolitan counties in England and counties and county boroughs in Wales by SI 1978/1535.

Appeals procedure SI 1986/264 (in force on 1 April 1986), has been made under the powers provided by para 17 of the Schedule to the above order. (SI 1986/264 has been modified by SI 1991/2684, in the title Courts and Legal Services, as to application to recognised bodies within the meaning of the Administration of Justice Act 1985, s 9.) The 1986 regulations prescribe the procedure for appeals to the Secretary of State against decisions of metropolitan district councils in connection with licences for the operation of public off-street parking places in those areas where such operation is controlled under this order. Similar provision in respect of appeals against decisions of other local authorities outside Greater London in connection with licences for the operation of public off-street parking places is made by SI 1979/236, noted to SI 1978/1535.

[382]

CONTROL OF OFF-STREET PARKING IN GREATER LONDON (APPEALS PROCEDURE) REGULATIONS 1986
SI 1986/262

Authority Made by the Secretary of State for Transport under the Road Traffic Regulation Act 1984, Sch 4, Pt III, para 17.
Date made 17 February 1986.
Commencement 1 April 1986.
Modification Modified by SI 1991/2684, in the title Courts and Legal Services, so that references to solicitors in these regulations (see Sch 1) are to be construed as including references to recognised bodies within the meaning of the Administration of Justice Act 1985, s 9.
Summary These regulations prescribe the procedure for appeals to the Secretary of State against decisions of local authorities in Greater London in connection with licences for the operation of public off-street parking places in those areas where such operation is controlled under the provisions of the Road Traffic Regulation Act 1984, s 43, Sch 4. They revoke and replace the Control of Off-Street Parking in Greater London (Appeals Procedure) Regulations 1977, SI 1977/1317.

The requirements with respect to the notice of appeal and supporting documents are set out in reg 4 and Schs 1, 2. Regs 5, 6 provide for written representations, and for requests for a hearing of the appeal by a person appointed by the Secretary of State, and reg 7 deals with the case where an appeal is decided on written representations. Reg 8 lays down the procedure to be followed in cases where, by virtue of para 15 of Pt III of Sch 4 to the 1984 Act, the Secretary of State is entitled to refuse to entertain the appeal.

Provisions with respect to the hearing of appeals are contained in regs 9 (notification), 10 (statements to be served), 11 (appearances), 12 (procedure at the hearing), 13 (site inspections), 14 (procedure after the hearing). Reg 15 provides for the notification of the decision consequent on a hearing of an appeal and for the giving of reasons for the decision. Reg 17 adapts the provisions of the regulations for the cases where, in exercise of his power under para 16(2) of Pt III of Sch 4 to the 1984 Act, the Secretary of State decides to hold an inquiry in connection with an appeal, instead of a hearing by a person appointed by him. Reg 17 also makes provision for requiring public notice of the inquiry to be given.

[383]

LOCAL SERVICES (OPERATION BY TAXIS) (LONDON) REGULATIONS 1986
SI 1986/566

Authority Made by the Secretary of State for Transport under the Transport Act 1985, s 12(9), (10).
Date made 20 March 1986.
Commencement 16 April 1986.
Summary These regulations prescribe the provisions of the "taxi code", as defined in the Transport Act 1985, s 13(3), which apply in relation to a taxi licensed under the Metropolitan Public Carriage Act 1869, s 6 when it is being used to provide local services under s 12 of the 1985 Act. Provision is also made for the display of certain notices and of a fare table.

[384]

LOCAL SERVICES (OPERATION BY TAXIS) REGULATIONS 1986
SI 1986/567

Authority Made by the Secretary of State for Transport under the Transport Act 1985, s 12(9), (10).
Date made 20 March 1986.
Commencement 16 April 1986.
Summary These regulations prescribe the provisions of the "taxi code" which apply in relation to a taxi licensed under the Town Police Clauses Act 1847, s 37 when it is being used to provide local services under the Transport Act 1985, s 12. Provision is also made for the display of certain notices on the vehicle and the display of a fare table inside the vehicle.
London These regulations have no application to London taxis. In relation to the use of taxis to provide local services in London see instead SI 1986/566.

[385]

ROAD VEHICLES (CONSTRUCTION AND USE) REGULATIONS 1986
SI 1986/1078

Authority Made by the Secretary of State for Transport under the Road Traffic Act 1972, ss 34(5), 40(1), (2), (3), 172 (all repealed). Now have effect under the Road Traffic Act 1988, s 41, by virtue of the Road Traffic (Consequential Provisions) Act 1988, s 2(2) and the Interpretation Act 1978, s 17(2)(b), printed in the title Statutory Instruments (Pt 2), Vol 1 of this work.
Date made 25 June 1986.
Commencement 11 August 1986; see reg 1.
Amendment Amended by:

(a) SI 1986/1597;
(b) SI 1987/676, SI 1987/1133;
(c) SI 1988/271, SI 1988/1177, SI 1988/1178, SI 1988/1287, SI 1988/1524, SI 1988/1871;
(d) SI 1989/1478, SI 1989/1695, SI 1989/1865, SI 1989/2360;
(e) SI 1990/317, SI 1990/1131, SI 1990/1163, SI 1990/1981, SI 1990/2212;
(f) SI 1991/1526, SI 1991/1527, SI 1991/2003, SI 1991/2125, SI 1991/2710;
(g) SI 1992/352, SI 1992/422, SI 1992/646, SI 1992/1217, SI 1992/2016, SI 1992/2137, SI 1992/2909, SI 1992/3088, SI 1992/3285;
(h) SI 1993/1946, SI 1993/2199, SI 1993/3048;
(i) SI 1994/14, SI 1994/329, SI 1994/2192, SI 1994/2567, SI 1994/3270;
(j) SI 1995/551 (amended by SI 1995/737), SI 1995/1201, SI 1995/1458, SI 1995/2210, SI 1995/3051;
(k) SI 1996/16, SI 1996/163, SI 1996/252, SI 1996/2064, SI 1996/2085, SI 1996/2329, SI 1996/3017 (amended by SI 1997/1458), SI 1996/3033, SI 1996/3133;
(l) SI 1997/530, SI 1997/1096, SI 1997/1340, SI 1997/1544, SI 1997/2935;
(m) SI 1998/1, SI 1998/1000, SI 1998/1188, SI 1998/1281, SI 1998/1563, SI 1998/2429, SI 1998/3112;
(n) SI 2000/1434, SI 2000/1971, SI 2000/3197;
(o) SI 2001/306, SI 2001/1043, SI 2001/1149, SI 2001/1825, SI 2001/3208;
(p) SI 2002/227, SI 2002/1474, SI 2002/2126;
(q) SI 2003/182, SI 2003/1690, SI 2003/1946, SI 2003/2096, SI 2003/2155, SI 2003/2695, SI 2003/3145;
(r) SI 2004/2102, SI 2004/3168 (the latter in relation to England only);
(s) SI 2005/2560, SI 2005/2929 (the latter in relation to Wales only), SI 2005/2987, SI 2005/3165, SI 2005/3170;

(t) SI 2006/594, SI 2006/2565;
(u) SI 2007/361, SI 2007/1898, SI 2007/2544, SI 2007/3132;
(v) SI 2008/1277;
(w) SI 2009/142, SI 2009/1806, SI 2009/2196.

Also amended by the Road Traffic (Consequential Provisions) Act 1988, s 3, Sch 1, Pt II, and by virtue of the Road Traffic Act 1991, s 9(2), the Environment Act 1995, s 120(1), Sch 22, para 233, the Utilities Act 2000, s 76(7), and SI 1997/2971, SI 2001/2568, SI 2002/2626, all in the title Constitutional Law (Pt 2). Amended in relation to Scotland only by SSI 2005/344, SSI 2006/129 (outside the scope of this work).

Previously amended by SI 1988/1102, which was revoked by SI 1988/1177, which provides that these regulations have effect as if SI 1988/1102 had never been made. Also amended by SI 1999/1521 (itself amended by SI 1999/1959), SI 2004/1706, SI 2005/1641, SI 2006/1756, SI 2007/1817, SI 2008/1702 (all superseded).

Application Para 2(2) of Sch 7XA to these regulations applies to a light goods type approval end of series vehicle which was first used before 1 January 2008 as if, by virtue of Sch 1C to SI 1982/1078, the type approval requirements in items 2B, 2G in the Table in Pt I of Sch 1 to SI 1982/1078 applied to the vehicle on 1 January 2007; see reg 3 of SI 2007/361.

Interpretation See reg 3. See also the Road Traffic Act 1988, ss 185, 192.

Offences As to the contravention of these regulations, see the Road Traffic Act 1988, ss 41A, 41B, 41D, 42 (and s 41C of the 1988 Act, inserted by the Road Safety Act 2006, s 18(2), as from a day to be appointed by order). As to prosecution and punishment of offences, see the entries relating to those sections in the Road Traffic Offenders Act 1988, s 9, Sch 2, Pt I, together with s 28 of that Act and s 34 et seq thereof. An offence of using a vehicle in a dangerous condition is created by the Road Traffic Act 1988, s 40A. Under the Road Traffic Act 1988, s 75, it is an offence to sell or supply or offer to sell or supply or expose for sale a vehicle in an unroadworthy condition, ie in such a condition that its use on a road would be unlawful by virtue of any provision made by regulations under s 41 of that Act as respects:

(a) brakes, steering gear or tyres, or
(b) the construction, weight or equipment of vehicles,

or in such a condition that its use on a road would involve a danger of injury to any person.

S 75 also makes it an offence to alter a vehicle so as to render its condition such that its use on a road would be unlawful by virtue of any provision made as respects the construction, weight or equipment of vehicles by regulations under s 41 of the 1988 Act, or would involve a danger of injury to any person. By the Road Traffic Act 1988, s 76, it is an offence to fit a vehicle part to a vehicle in such circumstances that the use of the vehicle on a road would involve a danger of injury to any person or constitute a contravention of or failure to comply with any of the construction and use requirements imposed under s 41 of that Act.

General These regulations, which revoke and replace the Motor Vehicles (Construction and Use) (Track Laying Vehicles) Regulations 1955, SI 1955/990, as amended, and the Motor Vehicles (Construction and Use) Regulations 1978, SI 1978/1017, as amended, govern the construction, equipment and maintenance of vehicles (both wheeled and track-laying) and the conditions relating to their use. They also contain provisions relating to plates for goods vehicles and buses, markings on certain vehicles and testing and inspection of brakes, silencers, steering gear and tyres. The provisions relating to construction, equipment and maintenance of vehicles (Pt II) are not printed in this work.

For exemptions relating to special types of vehicles, see SI 2003/1998.

[386]

ARRANGEMENT OF REGULATIONS

PART I
PRELIMINARY

PART II
REGULATIONS GOVERNING THE CONSTRUCTION, EQUIPMENT AND MAINTENANCE OF VEHICLES

A—DIMENSIONS AND MANOEUVRABILITY

12 Minimum ground clearance
13 Turning circle—buses
13A Turning circle—articulated vehicles other than those incorporating a car transporter
13B Turning circle—articulated vehicles incorporating a car transporter
13C Turning circle—heavy motor car
14 Connecting sections and direction-holding of articulated buses.

B—BRAKES
15 Braking systems of certain vehicles first used on or after 1st April 1983
16 Braking systems of vehicles to which regulation 15 does not apply
17 Vacuum or pressure brake warning devices
17A Couplings on trailer pneumatic braking systems
18 Maintenance and efficiency of brakes
19 Application of brakes of trailers

C—WHEELS, SPRINGS TYRES AND TRACKS
20 General requirement as to wheels and tracks
21 (*Revoked*)
22 Springs and resilient material
23 Wheel loads
24 Tyres
25 Tyres for vehicles for which a plating certificate has been issued
26 Mixing of tyres
27 Condition and maintenance of tyres
28 Tracks

D—STEERING
29 Maintenance of steering gear

E—VISION
30 View to the front
31, 32 Glass
33 Mirrors and other devices for indirect vision
34 Windscreen wipers and washers

F—INSTRUMENTS AND EQUIPMENT
35 Speedometers
36 Maintenance of speedometers
36A, 36B Speed limiters
36C Speed limiters-authorised sealers
37 Audible warning instruments
38 Motor cycle sidestands

G—FUEL
39, 39A,
39B Petrol tanks
40 Gas propulsion systems and gas-fired appliances

H—MINIBUSES
41 Construction
41A Alternative means of compliance
42 Fire extinguishing apparatus
43 First aid equipment
44 Carriage of dangerous substances

I—POWER TO WEIGHT RATIO
45 (*Revoked*)

J—PROTECTIVE SYSTEMS
46 Seat belt anchorage points
47 Seat belts
48 Maintenance of seat belts and anchorage points
48A Minibuses and coaches to be fitted with additional seat belts when used in certain circumstances
49 Rear under-run protection
50 Maintenance of rear under-run protective device
51 Sideguards
52 Maintenance of sideguards
53 Mascots
53A Strength of superstructure
53B Additional exits from double-decked coaches
53C Alternative means of compliance

PART I
PRELIMINARY

Commencement and citation

1 These Regulations shall come into operation on 11th August 1986, and may be cited as the Road Vehicles (Construction and Use) Regulations 1986.

[387]

Revocation

2 The Regulations specified in Schedule 1 are hereby revoked.

[388]

Interpretation

3 (1) In these Regulations, unless the context otherwise requires—

(a) any reference to a numbered regulation or a numbered Schedule is a reference to the regulation or Schedule bearing that number in these Regulations,

(b) any reference to a numbered or lettered paragraph or sub-paragraph is a reference to the paragraph or sub-paragraph bearing that number or letter in the regulation or Schedule or (in the case of a sub-paragraph) paragraph in which the reference occurs, and

(c) any reference to a Table, or to a numbered Table, is a reference to the Table, or to the Table bearing that number, in the regulation or Schedule in which that reference occurs.

(2) In these Regulations, unless the context otherwise requires, the expressions specified in column 1 of the Table have the meaning, or are to be interpreted in accordance with the provisions, specified for them in column 2 of the Table.

TABLE

(Regulation 3(2))

1 *Expression*	2 *Meaning*
The 1971 Act	The Vehicles (Excise) Act 1971.
The 1972 Act	The Road Traffic Act 1972.
The 1981 Act	The Public Passenger Vehicles Act 1981.
The 1984 Act	The Road Traffic Regulation Act 1984.
[The 1988 Act	The Road Traffic Act 1988]
The Approval Marks Regulations	The Motor Vehicles (Designation of Approval Marks) Regulations 1979.
[The EC Whole Vehicle Type Approval Regulations	The Motor Vehicles (EC Type Approval) Regulations 1998]
The Lighting Regulations	The Road Vehicles Lighting Regulations 1984.
The Plating and Testing Regulations	The Goods Vehicles (Plating and Testing) Regulations 1982.
The Type Approval Regulations	The Motor Vehicles (Type Approval) Regulations 1980.
The Type Approval (Great Britain) Regulations	The Motor Vehicles (Type Approval) (Great Britain) Regulations 1984.
The Type Approval for Goods Vehicles Regulations	The Motor Vehicles (Type Approval for Goods Vehicles) (Great Britain) Regulations 1982.
The Type Approval for Agricultural Vehicles Regulations	The Agricultural or Forestry Tractors and Tractor Components (Type Approval) Regulations 1979.
[The Vehicle Approval Regulations	The Road Vehicles (Approval) Regulations 2009]
The Act of Accession	the Treaty concerning the Accession of the Kingdom of Denmark, Ireland, the Kingdom of Norway and the United Kingdom of Great Britain and Northern Ireland to the European Economic Community and the European Atomic Energy Community
[agricultural or forestry tractor	an agricultural or forestry tractor within the meaning of Community Directive 82/890]
agricultural motor vehicle	a motor vehicle which is constructed or adapted for use off roads for the purpose of agriculture, horticulture or forestry and which is primarily used for one or more of those purposes, not being a dual-purpose vehicle.
Agricultural trailer	a trailer which is constructed or adapted for the purpose of agriculture, horticulture or forestry and which is only used for one or more of those purposes, not being an agricultural trailed appliance.

1 *Expression*	2 *Meaning*
Agricultural trailed appliance	a trailer— (a) which is an implement constructed or adapted— (i) for use off roads for the purpose of agriculture, horticulture or forestry and which is only used for one or more of those purposes, and (ii) so that, save in the case of an appliance manufactured before 1st December 1985, or a towed roller, its maximum gross weight is not more than twice its unladen weight; but (b) which is not— (i) a vehicle which is used primarily as living accommodation by one or more persons, and which carries no goods or burden except those needed by such one or more persons for the purpose of their residence in the vehicle; or (ii) an agricultural, horticultural or forestry implement rigidly but not permanently mounted on any vehicle whether or not any of the weight of the implement is supported by one or more of its own wheels; so however that such an implement is an agricultural trailed appliance if —part of the weight of the implement is supported by one or more of its own wheels, and —the longitudinal axis of the greater part of the implement is capable of articulating in the horizontal plane in relation to the longitudinal axis of the rear portion of the vehicle on which it is mounted.
Agricultural trailed appliance conveyor	an agricultural trailer which— (a) has an unladen weight which does not exceed 510 kg; (b) is clearly and indelibly marked with its unladen weight; (c) has a pneumatic tyre fitted to each one of its wheels; (d) is designed and constructed for the purpose of conveying one agricultural trailed appliance or one agricultural, horticultural or forestry implement.
[anti-lock braking system ("ABS")	a part of a service braking system which automatically controls the degree of slip, in the direction of rotation of the wheel or wheels, on one or more wheels of the vehicle during braking.]
articulated bus	a bus so constructed that— (a) it can be divided into two parts, both of which are vehicles and one of which is a motor vehicle, but cannot be so divided without the use of facilities normally available only at a workshop; and (b) passengers carried by it can at all times pass from either part to the other.

1 *Expression*	2 *Meaning*
Articulated vehicle	a heavy motor car or motor car, not being an articulated bus, with a trailer so attached that part of the trailer is superimposed on the drawing vehicle and, when the trailer is uniformly loaded, not less than 20% of the weight of its load is borne by the drawing vehicle.
Axle	any reference to the number of axles of a vehicle is to be interpreted in accordance with paragraph (8).
axle weight	in relation to each axle of a vehicle, the sum of the weights transmitted to the road surface by all the wheels of that axle, having regard to the provisions of paragraph (8).
braking efficiency	the maximum braking force capable of being developed by the brakes of a vehicle, expressed as a percentage of the weight of the vehicle including any persons or load carried in the vehicle.
Braking system	is to be interpreted in accordance with paragraph (6).
bus	a motor vehicle which is constructed or adapted to carry more than eight seated passengers in addition to the driver.
[car transporter	a trailer which is constructed and normally used for the purpose of carrying at least two other wheeled vehicles.]
cc	cubic centimetre(s).
close-coupled	in relation to wheels on the same side of a trailer, fitted so that at all times while the trailer is in motion they remain parallel to the longitudinal axis of the trailer, and that the distance between the centres of their respective areas of contact with the road surface does not exceed 1 m.
. . .	. . .
cm	centimetre(s).
cm^2	square centimetre(s).
[coach	a large bus with a maximum gross weight of more than 7.5 tonnes and with a maximum speed exceeding 60 mph]
Community Directive, followed by a number	the Directive adopted by the Council or the Commission of the European Communities [or the European Parliament and the Council of the European Union] of which identifying particulars are given in the item in column 3 of Table I in Schedule 2 in which that number appears in column 2; where such a Directive amends a previous Directive mentioned in column 3(d) of the Table [the reference to the amending Directive includes a reference to] that previous Directive as so amended. Any reference to a Directive which has been amended by the Act of Accession is a reference to the Directive as so amended.
The Community Recording Equipment Regulation	[Council Regulation (EEC) 3821/85 of 20th December 1985 on recording equipment in road transport, as read with the Community Drivers' Hours and Recording Equipment (Exemptions and Supplementary Provisions) Regulations 1986.]
[combined transport operation	shall be construed in accordance with paragraph 9 of Schedule 11A.]

1 *Expression*	2 *Meaning*
composite trailer	a combination of a converter dolly and a semi-trailer.
Container	an article of equipment, not being a motor vehicle or trailer, having a volume of at least 8 cubic metres, constructed wholly or mostly of metal and intended for repeated use for the carriage of goods or burden.
Converter dolly	[(a) a trailer which is— (i) equipped with 2 or more wheels, (ii) designed to be used in combination with a semi-trailer without any part of the weight of the semi-trailer being borne by the drawing vehicle, and (iii) not itself a part either of the semi-trailer or the drawing vehicle when being so used; or (b) a trailer which is— (i) equipped with 2 or more wheels; (ii) designed to be used in combination with a semi-trailer with part of the weight of the semi-trailer being borne by the drawing vehicle; (iii) not itself a part either of the semi-trailer or the drawing vehicle when being so used; and (iv) used solely for the purposes of agriculture, horticulture or forestry, or for any two or for all of those purposes.]
Council Regulation (EEC), followed by a number	the Regulation adopted by the Council of the European Communities.
Deck	a floor or platform on which seats are provided for the accommodation of passengers.
Design weight	in relation to the gross weight, each axle weight or the train weight of a motor vehicle or trailer, the weight at or below which in the opinion of the Secretary of State or of a person authorised in that behalf by the Secretary of State the vehicle could safely be driven on roads.
Double-decked vehicle	a vehicle having two decks one of which is wholly or partly above the other and each of which is provided with a gangway serving seats on that deck only.
Dual-purpose vehicle	a vehicle constructed or adapted for the carriage both of passengers and of goods or burden of any description, being a vehicle of which the unladen weight does not exceed 2040 kg, and which either— (i) is so constructed or adapted that the driving power of the engine is, or by the appropriate use of the controls of the vehicle can be, transmitted to all the wheels of the vehicle; or (ii) satisfies the following conditions as to construction, namely— (a) the vehicle must be permanently fitted with a rigid roof, with or without a sliding panel;

1 *Expression*	2 *Meaning*
	(b) the area of the vehicle to the rear of the driver's seat must— (i) be permanently fitted with at least one row of transverse seats (fixed or folding) for two or more passengers and those seats must be properly sprung or cushioned and provided with upholstered back-rests, attached either to the seats or to a side or the floor of the vehicle; and (ii) be lit on each side and at the rear by a window or windows of glass or other transparent material having an area or aggregate area of not less than 1850 square centimetres on each side and not less than 770 square centimetres at the rear; and (c) the distance between the rearmost part of the steering wheel and the back-rests of the row of transverse seats satisfying the requirements specified in head (i) of sub-paragraph (b) (or, if there is more than one such row of seats, the distance between the rearmost part of the steering wheel and the back-rests of the rearmost such row) must, when the seats are ready for use, be not less than one-third of the distance between the rearmost part of the steering wheel and the rearmost part of the floor of the vehicle.
ECE Regulation, followed by a number	the Regulation, annexed to the Agreement concerning the adoption of uniform conditions of approval for Motor Vehicles Equipment and Parts and reciprocal recognition thereof concluded at Geneva on 20th March 1958 as amended, to which the United Kingdom is a party, of which identifying particulars are given in the item in column (3)(a), (b) and (c) of Table II in Schedule 2 in which that number appears in column (2); and where that number contains more than two digits, it refers to that Regulation with the amendments in force at the date specified in column (3)(d) in that item.
Engine power in kilowatts (kW)	the maximum net power ascertained in accordance with Community Directive 80/1269.
[engineering equipment	engineering plant and any other plant or equipment designed and constructed for the purpose of engineering operations.]

1 *Expression*	2 *Meaning*
engineering plant	(a) movable plant or equipment being a motor vehicle or trailer specially designed and constructed for the special purposes of engineering operations, and which cannot, owing to the requirements of those purposes, comply with all the requirements of these Regulations and which is not constructed primarily to carry a load other than a load being either excavated materials raised from the ground by apparatus on the motor vehicle or trailer or materials which the vehicle or trailer is specially designed to treat while carried thereon; or (b) a mobile crane which does not comply in all respects with the requirements of these Regulations.
Exhaust system	a complete set of components through which the exhaust gases escape from the engine unit of a motor vehicle including those which are necessary to limit the noise caused by the escape of those gases.
[Framework Directive	Council Directive 70/156/EEC as amended by Council Directive 87/403/EEC, Council Directive 92/53/EEC[, Commission Directive 93/81/EEC and Commission Directive 98/14/EC].]
first used	is to be interpreted in accordance with paragraph (3).
gangway	the space provided for obtaining access from any entrance to the passengers' seats or from any such seat to an exit other than an emergency exit, but excluding a staircase and any space in front of a seat which is required only for the use of passengers occupying that seat or a seat in the same row of seats.
Gas	any fuel which is wholly gaseous at 17.5°C under a pressure of 1.013 bar absolute.
Gas-fired appliance	a device carried on a motor vehicle or trailer when in use on a road, which consumes gas and which is neither— (a) a device owned or operated by or with the authority of the British Gas Corporation for the purpose of detecting gas, nor (b) an engine for the propulsion of a motor vehicle, nor (c) a lamp which consumes acetylene gas.
Goods vehicle	a motor vehicle or trailer constructed or adapted for use for the carriage or haulage of goods or burden of any description.
Gritting trailer	a trailer which is used on a road for the purpose of spreading grit or other matter so as to avoid or reduce the effect of ice or snow on the road.
Gross weight	(a) in relation to a motor vehicle, the sum of the weights transmitted to the road surface by all the wheels of the vehicle. (b) in relation to a trailer, the sum of the weights transmitted to the road surface by all the wheels of the trailer and of any weight of the trailer imposed on the drawing vehicle.

1 *Expression*	2 *Meaning*
Heavy motor car	a mechanically propelled vehicle, not being a locomotive, a motor tractor, or a motor car, which is constructed itself to carry a load or passengers and the weight of which unladen exceeds 2540 kg.
indivisible load	a load which cannot without undue expense or risk of damage be divided into two or more loads for the purpose of conveyance on a road.
Industrial tractor	a tractor, not being an agricultural motor vehicle, which— (a) has an unladen weight not exceeding 7370 kg, (b) is designed and used primarily for work off roads, or for work on roads in connection only with road construction or maintenance (including any such tractor when fitted with an implement or implements designed primarily for use in connection with such work, whether or not any such implement is of itself designed to carry a load), and (c) has a maximum speed not exceeding 20 mph.
invalid carriage	a mechanically propelled vehicle the weight of which unladen does not exceed 254 kg and which is specially designed and constructed, and not merely adapted, for the use of a person suffering from some physical defect or disability and is solely used by such a person.
[ISO	International Organisation for Standardisation.
ISO 7638 connector	an electrical connector which complies with standard ISO 7638: 1997–1 or ISO 7638: 1997–2 and is used to provide a dedicated power supply and a communication link between the tow vehicle and trailer.]
kerbside weight	the weight of a vehicle when it carries— (a) in the case of a motor vehicle, (i) no person; and (ii) a full supply of fuel in its tank, an adequate supply of other liquids incidental to its propulsion and no load other than the loose tools and equipment with which it is normally equipped; (b) in the case of a trailer, no person and is otherwise unladen.
Kg	kilogram(s).
km/h	kilometre(s) per hour.
kW	kilowatt(s).
[large bus	a vehicle constructed or adapted to carry more than 16 seated passengers in addition to the driver.]
[light trailer	a trailer with a maximum gross weight which does not exceed 3500 kg.]
living van	a vehicle used primarily as living accommodation by one or more persons, and which is not also used for the carriage of goods or burden which are not needed by such one or more persons for the purpose of their residence in the vehicle.

1 *Expression*	2 *Meaning*
Locomotive	a mechanically propelled vehicle which is not constructed itself to carry a load other than the following articles, that is to say, water, fuel, accumulators and other equipment used for the purpose of propulsion, loose tools and loose equipment, and the weight of which unladen exceeds 7370 kg.
longitudinal plane	a vertical plane parallel to the longitudinal axis of a vehicle.
[low loader	a semi-trailer which is constructed and normally used for the carriage of engineering equipment so constructed that the major part of the load platform does not extend over or between the wheels and the upper surface of which is below the height of the top most point of the tyres of those wheels, measured on level ground and when— (a) any adjustable suspension is at the normal travelling height, (b) all pneumatic tyres are suitably inflated for use when the vehicle is fully laden, and (c) the semi-trailer is unladen, (see also the definition of stepframe low loader).]
[low platform trailer	a trailer fitted with tyres with a rim diameter size code of less than 20 and displaying a rectangular plate which— (a) is at least 225 mm wide and at least 175 mm high; and (b) bears two black letters "L" on a white ground each at least 125 mm high and 90 mm wide with a stroke width of 12 mm.]
m	metre(s).
m^2	square metre(s).
m^3	cubic metre(s).
[maximum permitted axle weight	in relation to an axle— (a) in the case of a vehicle which is equipped with a Ministry plate in accordance with regulation 70, the axle weight shown in column (2) of that plate (where the plate is in the form required by [Schedule 10 or 10B]) or in column (2) of that plate (where the plate is in the form required by [Schedule 10A or 10C]) in relation to that axle; (b) in the case of a vehicle which is not equipped with a Ministry plate but which is equipped with a plate in accordance with regulation 66, the maximum axle weight shown for that axle on the plate in respect of item 9 of Part I of Schedule 8 in the case of a motor vehicle and item 7 of Part II of Schedule 8 in the case of a trailer; and (c) in any other case, the weight which the axle is designed or adapted not to exceed when the vehicle is travelling on a road.]

1 *Expression*	2 *Meaning*
maximum gross weight	(a) in the case of a vehicle equipped with a Ministry plate in accordance with regulation 70, the design gross weight shown in column (3) of that plate [(where the plate is in the form required by [Schedule 10 or 10B]) or in column (4) of that plate (where the plate is in the form required by [Schedule 10A or 10C])] or, if no such weight is shown, the gross weight shown in column (2) of that plate; (b) in the case of a vehicle not equipped with a Ministry plate, but which is equipped with a plate in accordance with regulation 66, the maximum gross weight shown on the plate in respect of item 7 of Part I of Schedule 8 in the case of a motor vehicle and item 6 of Part II of Schedule 8 in the case of a trailer; (c) in any other case, the weight which the vehicle is designed or adapted not to exceed when the vehicle is travelling on a road.
[maximum total design axle weight (an expression used only in relation to trailers)	(a) in the case of a trailer equipped with a Ministry plate in accordance with regulation 70, the sum of the relevant axle weights; (b) in the case of a trailer which is not equipped with a Ministry plate, but which is equipped with a plate in accordance with regulation 66, the sum of the maximum axle weights shown on the plate in respect of item 4 of Part II of Schedule 8; or (c) in the case of any other trailer, the sum of the axle weights which the trailer is designed or adapted not to exceed when the vehicle is travelling on a road; and for the purposes of sub-paragraph (a) the relevant axle weight, in respect to an axle, is the design axle weight shown in column (3) of the Ministry plate (where the plate is in the form required by [Schedule 10 or 10B]) or in column (4) of that plate (where the plate is in the form required by [Schedule 10A or 10C]) in relation to that axle or if no such weight is shown, the axle weight shown in column (2) of that plate in relation to that axle;]
maximum speed	the speed which a vehicle is incapable, by reason of its construction, of exceeding on the level under its own power when fully laden.
Minibus	a motor vehicle which is constructed or adapted to carry more than 8 but not more than 16 seated passengers in addition to the driver.
Ministry plate	[is to be interpreted in accordance with regulation 70].
mm	millimetre(s).
motor ambulance	a motor vehicle which is specially designed and constructed (and not merely adapted) for carrying, as equipment permanently fixed to the vehicle, equipment used for medical, dental, or other health purposes and is used primarily for the carriage of persons suffering from illness, injury or disability.

1 *Expression*	2 *Meaning*
Motor car	a mechanically propelled vehicle, not being a motor tractor, a motor cycle or an invalid carriage, which is constructed itself to carry a load of passengers and the weight of which unladen— (a) if it is constructed solely for the carriage of passengers and their effects and is adapted to carry not more than seven passengers exclusive of the driver does not exceed 3050 kg; (b) if it is constructed for use for the conveyance of goods or burden of any description, does not exceed 3050 kg; (c) does not exceed 2540 kg in a case falling within neither of the foregoing paragraphs.
[motor caravan	a motor vehicle which is constructed or adapted for the carriage of passengers and their effects and which contains, as permanently installed equipment, the facilities which are reasonably necessary for enabling the vehicle to provide mobile living accommodation for its users.]
motor cycle	a mechanically propelled vehicle, not being an invalid carriage, having less than four wheels and the weight of which unladen does not exceed 410 kg.
motor tractor	a mechanically propelled vehicle which is not constructed itself to carry a load, other than the following articles, that is to say, water, fuel, accumulators and other equipment used for the purpose of propulsion, loose tools and loose equipment, and the weight of which unladen does not exceed 7370 kg.
motor vehicle	a mechanically propelled vehicle intended or adapted for use on roads.
Mph	mile(s) per hour.
N/mm^2	newton(s) per square millimetre.
[off-road vehicle	an off-road vehicle as defined in Annex I to Council Directive 70/156/EEC of 6th February 1970 as read with Council Directive 87/403/EEC of 25th June 1987.]
overall height	the vertical distance between the ground and the point on the vehicle which is furthest from the ground, calculated when— (a) the tyres of the vehicle are suitably inflated for the use to which it is being put; (b) the vehicle is at its unladen weight; and (c) the surface of the ground under the vehicle is reasonably flat; but, in the case of a trolley bus, exclusive of the power collection equipment mounted on the roof of the vehicle.
Overall length	in relation to a vehicle, the distance between transverse planes passing through the extreme forward and rearward projecting points of the vehicle inclusive of all parts of the vehicle, of any receptacle which is of a permanent character and accordingly strong enough for repeated use, and any fitting on, or attached to, the vehicle except—

1 *Expression*	2 *Meaning*
	(i) for all purposes— (a) any driving mirror; (b) any expanding or extensible contrivance forming part of a turntable fire escape fixed to a vehicle; (c) any snow-plough fixed in front of a vehicle; (d) any receptacle specially designed to hold and keep secure a seal issued for the purposes of customs clearance; (e) any tailboard which is let down while the vehicle is stationary in order to facilitate its loading or unloading; (f) any tailboard which is let down in order to facilitate the carriage of, but which is not essential for the support of, loads which are in themselves so long as to extend at least as far as the tailboard when upright; (g) any fitting attached to a part of, or to a receptacle on, a vehicle which does not increase the carrying capacity of the part or receptacle but which enables it to be —transferred from a road vehicle to a railway vehicle or from a railway vehicle to a road vehicle, —secured to a railway vehicle by a locking device, and —carried on a railway vehicle by the use of stanchions: (h) any plate, whether rigid or movable, fitted to a trailer constructed for the purpose of carrying other vehicles and designed to bridge the gap between that trailer and a motor vehicle constructed for that purpose and to which the trailer is attached so that, while the trailer is attached to the motor vehicle, vehicles which are to be carried by the motor vehicle may be moved from the trailer to the motor vehicle before a journey begins, and vehicles which have been carried on the motor vehicle may be moved from it to the trailer after a journey ends; (i) any sheeting or other readily flexible means of covering or securing a load; (j) . . . (k) any empty receptacle which itself forms a load; (l) any receptacle which contains an indivisible load of exceptional length; (m) any receptacle manufactured before 30th October 1985, not being a maritime container (namely a container designed primarily for carriage on sea transport without an accompanying road vehicle); . . .

1 *Expression*	2 *Meaning*
	(n) any special appliance or apparatus as described in regulation 81(c) which does not itself increase the carrying capacity of the vehicle; [or (o) any rearward projecting buffer made of rubber or other resilient material.] (ii) for the purposes of [regulations 7, 13A, 13B and 13C]— (a) any part of a trailer (not being in the case of an agricultural trailed appliance a drawbar or other thing with which it is equipped for the purpose of being towed) designed primarily for use as a means of attaching it to another vehicle and any fitting designed for use in connection with any such part; (b) the thickness of any front or rear wall on a semi-trailer and of any part forward of such front wall or rearward of such rear wall which does not increase the vehicle's load-carrying space.
Overall width	the distance between longitudinal planes passing through the extreme lateral projecting points of the vehicle inclusive of all parts of the vehicle, of any receptacle which is of permanent character and accordingly strong enough for repeated use, and any fitting on, or attached to, the vehicle except— (a) any driving mirror; (b) any snow-plough fixed in front of the vehicle; (c) so much of the distortion of any tyre as is caused by the weight of the vehicle; (d) any receptacle specially designed to hold and keep secure a seal issued for the purposes of customs clearance; (e) any lamp or reflector fitted to the vehicle in accordance with the Lighting Regulations; (f) any sideboard which is let down while the vehicle is stationary in order to facilitate its loading or unloading; (g) any fitting attached to part of, or to a receptacle on, a vehicle which does not increase the carrying capacity of the part or receptacle but which enables it to be —transferred from a road vehicle to a railway vehicle or from a railway vehicle to a road vehicle; —secured to a railway vehicle by a locking device; and —carried on a railway vehicle by the use of stanchions; (h) any sheeting or other readily flexible means of covering or securing a load; (i) any receptacle with an external width, measured at right angles to the longitudinal axis of the vehicle, which does not exceed 2.5 m; (j) any empty receptacle which itself forms a load; (k) any receptacle which contains an indivisible load of exceptional width;

1 *Expression*	2 *Meaning*
	(l) any receptacle manufactured before 30th October 1985, not being a maritime container (namely a container designed primarily for carriage on sea transport without an accompanying road vehicle); ... (m) any special appliance or apparatus as described in regulation 81(c) which does not itself increase the carrying capacity of the vehicle [; or (n) any apparatus fitted to a bus which enables it to be guided wholly or mainly by means of wheels bearing outwards against fixed apparatus, provided that no part of the apparatus projects more than 75mm beyond the side of the bus when the wheels of the bus are parallel to its longitudinal axis; and the reference in paragraph (n) above to the side of a bus is a reference to the longitudinal plane passing through the extreme lateral projecting points of the vehicle inclusive of all parts of the vehicle, of any receptacle which is of permanent character and accordingly strong enough for repeated use, and any fitting on, or attached to, the vehicle except those items referred to in paragraphs (a) to (n).]
overhang	the distance measured horizontally and parallel to the longitudinal axis of a vehicle between two transverse planes passing through the following two points— (a) the rearmost point of the vehicle exclusive of— (i) any expanding or extensible contrivance forming part of a turntable fire escape fixed to a vehicle; (ii) in the case of a motor car constructed solely for the carriage of passengers and their effects and adapted to carry not more than eight passengers exclusive of the driver, any luggage carrier fitted to the vehicle; and (b) (i) in the case of a motor vehicle having not more than three axles of which only one is not a steering axle, the centre point of that axle; (ii) in the case of a motor vehicle having three axles of which the front axle is the only steering axle and of a motor vehicle having four axles of which the two foremost are the only steering axles, a point 110mm behind the centre of a straight line joining the centre points of the two rearmost axles; and (iii) in any other case a point situated on the longitudinal axis of the vehicle and such that a line drawn from it at right angles to that axis will pass through the centre of the minimum turning circle of the vehicle.
Passenger vehicle	a vehicle constructed solely for the carriage of passengers and their effects.
Pedestrian-controlled vehicle	a motor vehicle which is controlled by a pedestrian and not constructed or adapted for use or used for the carriage of a driver or passenger.

1 *Expression*	2 *Meaning*
Pneumatic tyre	a tyre which— (a) is provided with, or together with the wheel upon which it is mounted forms, a continuous closed chamber inflated to a pressure substantially exceeding atmospheric pressure when the tyre is in the condition in which it is normally used, but is not subjected to any load; (b) is capable of being inflated and deflated without removal from the wheel or vehicle; and (c) is such that, when it is deflated and is subjected to a normal load, the sides of the tyre collapse.
Public works vehicle	[a mechanically propelled vehicle which is used on a road by or on behalf of— (a) the Central Scotland Water Development Board; (b) a ferry undertaking; (c) a highway or roads authority; (d) a local authority; (e) a market undertaking; (f) the [Environment Agency]; (g) an operator of [an electronic communications code network]; (h) a police authority; (i) [a universal service provider (within the meaning of the Post Services Act 2000) in connection with the provision of a universal postal service (within the meaning of that Act)]; (j) a public electricity supplier within the meaning of Part I of the Electricity Act 1989; (k) [a [gas transporter] within the meaning of Part I of the Gas Act 1986]; (l) a statutory undertaker within the meaning of section 329(1) of the Highways Act 1980; (m) an undertaking for the supply of district heating; (n) a water authority within the meaning of the Water (Scotland) Act 1980; or (o) a water or sewerage undertaker within the meaning of the Water Act 1989; for the purpose of works which such a body has a duty or power to carry out, and which is used only for the carriage of— (i) the crew, and (ii) goods which are needed for works in respect of which the vehicle is used.]
recut pneumatic tyre	a pneumatic tyre in which all or part of its original tread pattern has been cut deeper or burnt deeper or a different tread pattern has been cut deeper or burnt deeper than the original tread pattern.

1 *Expression*	2 *Meaning*
Refuse vehicle	a vehicle designed for use and used solely in connection with street cleansing, the collection or disposal of refuse, or the collection or disposal of the contents of gullies or cesspools.
Registered	registered under any of the following enactments— (a) the Roads Act 1920, (b) the Vehicles (Excise) Act 1949, (c) the Vehicles (Excise) Act 1962, or (d) the 1971 Act and, in relation to the date on which a vehicle was registered, the date on which it was first registered under any of those enactments.
Relevant braking requirement	a requirement that the brakes of a motor vehicle (as assisted, where a trailer is being drawn, by the brakes on the trailer) comply— (i) in a case to which item 1 in Table 1 in regulation 18 applies, with the requirements specified in regulation 18(3) for vehicles falling in that item; (ii) in any other case, with the requirements specified in regulation 18(3) for vehicle classes (a) and (b) in item 2 of that Table (whatever the date of first use of the motor vehicle and the date of manufacture of any trailer drawn by it may be).
Resilient tyre	a tyre, not being a pneumatic tyre, which is of soft or elastic material, having regard to paragraph (5).
[restricted speed vehicle	a vehicle displaying at its rear a "50" plate in accordance with the requirements of Schedule 13.]
[retreaded tyre	a tyre which has been reconditioned to extend its useful life by replacement of the tread rubber or by replacement of the tread rubber and renovation of the sidewall rubber.]
rigid vehicle	a motor vehicle which is not constructed or adapted to form part of an articulated vehicle or articulated bus.
[rim diameter	is to be interpreted in accordance with the British Standard BS AU 50: Part 2: Section 1: 1980 entitled "British Standard Automobile Series: Specification for Tyres and Wheels Part 2. Wheels and rims Section 1. Rim profiles and dimensions (including openings for valves)" which came into effect on 28th November 1980.]
[rim diameter size code	is to be interpreted in accordance with the British Standard referred to in the meaning given in this Table to "rim diameter".]
secondary braking system	a braking system of a vehicle applied by a secondary means of operation independent of the service braking system or by one of the sections comprised in a split braking system.
Service braking system	the braking system of a vehicle which is designed and constructed to have the highest braking efficiency of any of the braking systems with which the vehicle is equipped.

1 *Expression*	2 *Meaning*
Semi-trailer	a trailer which is constructed or adapted to form part of an articulated vehicle [including (without prejudice to the generality of that) a vehicle which is not itself a motor vehicle but which has some or all of its wheels driven by the drawing vehicle].
Silencer	a contrivance suitable and sufficient for reducing as far as may be reasonable the noise caused by the escape of exhaust gases from the engine of a motor vehicle.
Single-decked vehicle	a vehicle upon which no part of a deck or gangway is vertically above another deck or gangway.
Split braking system	in relation to a motor vehicle, a braking system so designed and constructed that— (a) it comprises two independent sections of mechanism capable of developing braking force such that, excluding the means of operation, a failure of any part (other than a fixed member or a brake shoe anchor pin) of one of the said sections will not cause a decrease in the braking force capable of being developed by the other section; (b) the said two sections are operated by a means of operation which is common to both sections; (c) the braking efficiency of either of the said two sections can be readily checked.
[staircase	a staircase by means of which passengers on a double-decked vehicle may pass to and from the upper deck of the vehicle.]
[stepframe low loader	a semi-trailer (not being a low loader) which is constructed and normally used for the carriage of engineering equipment and is so constructed that the upper surface of the major part of the load platform is at a height of less than 1m above the ground when measured on level ground and when— (a) any adjustable suspension is at the normal travelling height, (b) all pneumatic tyres are suitably inflated for use when the vehicle is fully laden, and (c) the semi-trailer is unladen.]
stored energy	in relation to a braking system of a vehicle, energy (other than the muscular energy of the driver or the mechanical energy of a spring) stored in a reservoir for the purpose of applying the brakes under the control of the driver, either directly or as a supplement to his muscular energy.
Straddle carrier	a motor vehicle constructed to straddle and lift its load for the purpose of transportation.
Statutory power of removal	a power conferred by or under any enactment to remove or move a vehicle from any road or from any road or from any part of a road.
Temporary use spare tyre	a pneumatic tyre which is designed for use on a motor vehicle only—

1 *Expression*	2 *Meaning*
	(a) in the event of the failure of one of the tyres normally fitted to a wheel of the vehicle, and (b) at a speed lower than that for which such normally fitted tyres are designed.
Three-wheeled motor cycle	a motor cycle having three wheels, not including a two-wheeled motor cycle with a sidecar attached.
Towing implement	a device on wheels designed for the purpose of enabling a motor vehicle to draw another vehicle by the attachment of that device to that other vehicle in such a manner that part of that other vehicle is secured to and either rests on or is suspended from the device and some but not all of the wheels on which that other vehicle normally runs are raised off the ground.
Track-laying	in relation to a vehicle, so designed and constructed that the weight thereof is transmitted to the road surface either by means of continuous tracks or by a combination of wheels and continuous tracks in such circumstances that the weight transmitted to the road surface by the tracks is not less than half the weight of the vehicle.
Trailer	means a vehicle drawn by a motor vehicle and is to be interpreted in accordance with paragraphs (9) and (11).
train weight	in relation to a motor vehicle which may draw a trailer, the maximum laden weight for the motor vehicle together with any trailer which may be drawn by it.
Transverse plane	a vertical plane at right angles to the longitudinal axis of a vehicle.
Trolley bus	a bus adapted for use on roads without rails and moved by power transmitted thereto from some external source.
Unbraked trailer	any trailer other than one which, whether or not regulation 15 or 16 applies to it, is equipped with a braking system in accordance with one of those regulations.
Unladen weight	the weight of a vehicle or trailer inclusive of the body and all parts (the heavier being taken where alternative bodies or parts are used) which are necessary to or ordinarily used with the vehicle or trailer when working on a road, but exclusive of the weight of water, fuel or accumulators used for the purpose of the supply of power for the propulsion of the vehicle or, as the case may be, of any vehicle by which the trailer is drawn, and of loose tools and loose equipment.
Vehicle in the service of a visiting force or of a headquarters	a vehicle so described in Article 8(6) of the Visiting Forces and International Headquarters (Application of Law) Order 1965.
wheel	a wheel the tyre or rim of which when the vehicle is in motion on a road is in contact with the ground; two wheels are to be regarded as one wheel in the circumstances specified in paragraph (7).
wheeled	in relation to a vehicle, so constructed that the whole weight of the vehicle is transmitted to the road surface by means of wheels.

1 *Expression*	2 *Meaning*
Wide tyre	a pneumatic tyre of which the area of contact with the road surface is not less than 300 mm in width when measured at right angles to the longitudinal axis of the vehicle.
Works trailer	a trailer designed for use in private premises and used on a road only in delivering goods from or to such premises to or from a vehicle on a road in the immediate neighbourhood, or in passing from one part of any such premises to another or to other private premises in the immediate neighbourhood or in connection with road works while at or in the immediate neighbourhood of the site of such works.
Works truck	a motor vehicle (other than a straddle carrier) designed for use in private premises and used on a road only in delivering goods from or to such premises to or from a vehicle on a road in the immediate neighbourhood, or in passing from one part of any such premises to another or to other private premises in the immediate neighbourhood or in connection with road works while at or in the immediate neighbourhood of the site of such works.

[(2A) Without prejudice to section 17 of the Interpretation Act 1978 and subject to the context, a reference in these Regulations to any enactment comprised in subordinate legislation (within the meaning of that Act) is a reference to that enactment as from time to time amended or re-enacted with or without modification.]

(3) For the purpose of these Regulations, the date on which a motor vehicle is first used is—

(a) in the case of a vehicle not falling within sub-paragraph (b) and which is registered, the date on which it was registered;

(b) in each of the following cases—

(i) a vehicle which is being or has been used under a trade licence as defined in section 16 of the 1971 Act (otherwise than for the purposes of demonstration or testing or of being delivered from premises of the manufacturer by whom it was made or of a distributor of vehicles, or dealer in vehicles, to premises of a distributor of vehicles, dealer in vehicles or purchaser thereof or to premises of a person obtaining possession thereof under a hiring agreement or hire purchase agreement);

(ii) a vehicle belonging, or which has belonged, to the Crown and which is or was used or appropriated for use for naval, military or air force purposes;

(iii) a vehicle belonging, or which has belonged, to a visiting force or a headquarters or defence organisation to which in each case the Visiting Forces and International Headquarters (Application of Law) Order 1965 applies;

(iv) a vehicle which has been used on roads outside Great Britain before being imported into Great Britain; and

(v) a vehicle which has been used otherwise than on roads after being sold or supplied by retail and before being registered;

the date of manufacture of the vehicle.

In sub-paragraph (b)(v) of this paragraph "sold or supplied by retail" means sold or supplied otherwise than to a person acquiring it solely for the purpose of resale or re-supply for a valuable consideration.

(4) The date of manufacture of a vehicle to which the Type Approval for Goods Vehicles Regulations apply shall be the date of manufacture described in regulation 2(4)(a) of those Regulations.

(5) Save where otherwise provided in these Regulations a tyre shall not be deemed to be of soft or elastic material unless the said material is either—

(a) continuous round the circumference of the wheel; or

(b) fitted in sections so that so far as reasonably practicable no space is left between the ends thereof,

and is of such thickness and design as to minimise, so far as reasonably possible, vibration when the vehicle is in motion and so constructed as to be free from any defect which might in any way cause damage to the surface of a road.

(6) For the purpose of these Regulations a brake drum and a brake disc shall be deemed to form part of the wheel and not of the braking system.

(7) For the purpose of these Regulations other than regulations 26 and 27 any two wheels of a motor vehicle or trailer shall be regarded as one wheel if the distance between the centres of the areas of contact between such wheels and the road surface is less than 460 mm.

(8) For the purpose of these Regulations other than regulations 26 and 27 in counting the number of axles of, and in determining the sum of the weights transmitted to the road surface by any one axle of, a vehicle, all the wheels of which the centres of the areas of contact with the road surface can be included between any two transverse planes less than [0.5] m apart shall be treated as constituting one axle.

[(8A) For the purposes of these Regulations, a reference to axles being closely-spaced is a reference to—

(a) two axles (not being part of a group of axles falling within sub-paragraph (b) or (c)) which are spaced at a distance apart of not more than 2.5m;

(b) three axles (not being part of a group of axles falling within sub-paragraph (c)) the outermost of which are spaced at a distance apart of not more than 3.25m; or

(c) four or more axles the outermost of which are spaced at a distance apart of not more than 4.6m;

the number of axles for the purposes of these paragraphs being determined in accordance with paragraph (8); and a reference to any particular number of closely-spaced axles shall be construed accordingly.]

(9) The provisions of these Regulations relating to trailers do not apply to any part of an articulated bus.

(10) For the purpose of [paragraph (8A) above,] regulations 51, [76, 77 and 79] and [Schedules 11 and 11A] … , the distance between any two axles shall be obtained by measuring the shortest distance between the line joining the centres of the areas of contact with the road surface of the wheels of one axle and the line joining the centres of the areas of contact with the road surface of the wheels of the other axle.

(11) For the purpose of the following provisions only, a composite trailer shall be treated as one trailer (not being a semi-trailer or a converter dolly)—

(a) regulations 7, 76 and 83;

(b) paragraph (2) of, and items 3 and 10 in the Table in, regulation 75;

(c) item 2 in the Table in regulation 78.

NOTES

Amendment Para (2), Table:
definition "The 1988 Act" inserted by SI 2009/2196;
definition "The EC Whole Vehicle Type Approval Regulations" inserted by SI 2006/2565;
definition "The Vehicle Approval Regulations" inserted by SI 2009/2196;
definition "agricultural or forestry tractor" inserted by SI 1996/2329;
definition "anti-lock braking system ("ABS")" inserted by SI 2001/3208;
definition "car transporter" inserted by SI 1990/317;
definition "closely-spaced" revoked by SI 1992/2016;
definition "coach" inserted by SI 1987/1133;
definition "combined transport operation" inserted by SI 1994/329;
in definition "Community Directive, followed by a number", words in first pair of square brackets inserted by SI 2005/3165; words in second pair of square brackets substituted by SI 1989/1865;
definition "the Community Recording Equipment Regulation" substituted by SI 1989/1865;
definition "converter dolly" substituted by SI 1991/1526;
definition "engineering equipment" inserted by SI 1990/317;
definition "Framework Directive" inserted by SI 1996/2329; words in square brackets substituted by SI 2001/3208;

definitions "ISO" and "ISO 7638 connector" inserted by SI 2001/3208;
definition "large bus" inserted by SI 1987/1133;
definition "light trailer" inserted by SI 1990/1981;
definition "low loader" inserted by SI 1990/317;
definition "low platform trailer" inserted by SI 1990/1981;
definition "maximum permitted axle weight" inserted by SI 1990/1981 (in the place directed by SI 1990/1981, although out of alphabetical order); words in square brackets substituted by SI 1994/329;
in definition "maximum gross weight", words in first (outer) pair of square brackets inserted by SI 1990/1981 and words in the second (inner) pair substituted by SI 1994/329;
definition "maximum total design axle weight (an expression used only in relation to trailers)" inserted by SI 1990/1981 (in the place directed by SI 1990/1981, although out of alphabetical order); words in square brackets substituted by SI 1994/329;
definition "Ministry plate" substituted by SI 1998/3112;
definition "motor caravan" inserted by SI 1987/1133;
definition "off-road vehicle" inserted by SI 1990/1131;
definition "overall length": in para (i), sub-para (j) revoked by SI 2003/182; word omitted in sub-para (m) revoked, and sub-para (o) (and word "or" immediately preceding it), inserted by SI 1991/2125; in para (ii), words in square brackets substituted by SI 1998/1188;
in definition "overall width", word omitted revoked and words in square brackets inserted, by SI 1995/3051;
definition "public works vehicle" substituted by SI 1990/1981; words in square brackets in para (f) of that definition substituted by virtue of the Environment Act 1995, s 120(1), Sch 22, para 233; in para (g) words in square brackets substituted by SI 2003/2155; in para (i) words in square brackets substituted by SI 2001/1149 (it is thought that the reference to "the Post Services Act 2000" should be to "the Postal Services Act 2000"); para (k) substituted by SI 1996/252, and words in square brackets therein substituted by virtue of the Utilities Act 2000, s 76(7);
definitions "restricted speed vehicle", "retreaded tyre", "rim diameter" and "rim diameter size code" inserted by SI 1990/1981;
in definition "semi-trailer", words in square brackets inserted by SI 1987/676;
definition "staircase" inserted by SI 1987/1133; and
definition "stepframe low loader" inserted by SI 1990/317.
Para (2A): inserted by SI 1993/2199.
Para (8): number in square brackets substituted by SI 1992/2016.
Para (8A): inserted by SI 1992/2016.
Para (10): words in first pair of square brackets inserted, and words omitted revoked, by SI 1992/2016; words in second pair of square brackets substituted by SI 1988/1287; and words in third pair substituted by SI 1994/329.

British Gas Corporation As from 24 August 1986, the property, rights and liabilities of the British Gas Corporation were transferred by the Gas Act 1986, s 49 and SI 1986/1318, in the title Energy, to British Gas plc, i e the company nominated as the successor company for the purposes of s 49 by SI 1986/1317, in the same title. The Corporation was dissolved on 28 February 1990 by s 57 (repealed) of the 1986 Act and SI 1990/147 (lapsed).

British Standard British Standards publications may be obtained as detailed at www.bsi-global.com/Global/BuyStandards.xalter.

Environment Agency As to the constitution and functions of this body, see the Environment Act 1995, s 1 et seq.

Statutory power of removal See, in particular, the Road Traffic Regulation Act 1984, s 99 and SI 1986/183, in the title Highways, Streets and Bridges.

Universal service provider within the meaning of the Post Services Act 2000 It is thought this should be a reference to a universal service provider within the meaning of the Postal Services Act 2000, as to which see s 4(3) of that Act.

Agreement concerning the adoption of uniform conditions of approval for Motor Vehicles Equipment and Parts and reciprocal recognition thereof concluded at Geneva on 20th March 1958 Cmnd 2535, 3562.

Commission Directive 93/81 OJ L264, 23.10.1993, p 49.

Commission Directive 98/14/EC OJ L91, 25.03.1998, p 1.

Community Directive 80/1269 OJ L375, 31.12.1980, p 46.

Community Directive 82/890 OJ L378, 31.12.1982, p 45.

Council Directive 70/156/EEC OJ L42, 23.02.1970, p 1. Repealed and replaced by Directive 2007/46/EC of the European Parliament and of the Council establishing a framework for the approval of motor vehicles and their trailers, and of systems, components and separate technical units intended for such vehicles (OJ L263, 09.10.2007, p 1).

Council Directive 87/403/EEC OJ L220, 08.08.1987, p 44.

Council Directive 92/53 EEC OJ L225, 10.08.1992, p 1.

Council Regulation (EEC) 3821/85 OJ L370, 31.12.1985, p 8.

Act of Accession Cmnd 5179–1.

Electricity Act 1989, Pt I The meaning of "public electricity supplier" in Pt I of the 1989 Act was previously contained in s 6(9) thereof. S 6 has been substituted by the Utilities Act 2000, s 30, and s 6, as substituted, refers to "electricity supplier". By s 31(1) of the 2000 Act, references in any enactment to public electricity suppliers have effect after the commencement of that section as if they were references to:

(a) electricity suppliers;
(b) electricity distributors; or

(c) both electricity suppliers and electricity distributors, according to the nature of the activities carried on by the persons to whom they referred before that time.

Gas Act 1986, Pt I As to the meaning of "gas transporter" in Pt I of the 1986 Act, see s 7(1) thereof.

Interpretation Act 1978, s 17 Printed in the title Statutory Instruments (Pt 2), Vol 1 of this work.

Road Traffic Act 1972 Repealed by the Road Traffic (Consequential Provisions) Act 1988, s 3(1), Sch 1, Pt I and consolidated in the Road Traffic Act 1988 and the Road Traffic Offenders Act 1988.

Roads Act 1920 The relevant provisions of that Act were repealed and replaced by the Vehicles (Excise) Act 1949.

Vehicles (Excise) Act 1949 Repealed and replaced by the Vehicles (Excise) Act 1962.

Vehicles (Excise) Act 1962 Repealed and largely replaced by the Vehicles (Excise) Act 1971, itself now repealed and replaced by the Vehicle Excise and Registration Act 1994.

Vehicles (Excise) Act 1971 Repealed; see now the Vehicle Excise and Registration Act 1994.

Water Act 1989 Largely repealed by the Water Consolidation (Consequential Provisions) Act 1991, s 3(1), Sch 3, Pt I, and consolidated in the Water Industry Act 1991, the Water Resources Act 1991, and the Statutory Water Companies Act 1991. As to the meaning of a water or sewerage undertaker, see now the Water Industry Act 1991, s 6.

Agricultural or Forestry Tractors and Tractor Components (Type Approval) Regulations 1979 SI 1979/221 (revoked); see now SI 2005/390.

Community Drivers' Hours and Recording Equipment (Exemptions and Supplementary Provisions) Regulations 1986 SI 1986/1456. Revoked and replaced by SI 2007/1819.

Goods Vehicles (Plating and Testing) Regulations 1982 SI 1982/1478; revoked and replaced by SI 1988/1478.

Motor Vehicles (Designation of Approval Marks) Regulations 1979 SI 1979/1088, in the title Trade Marks and Trade Names.

Motor Vehicles (EC Type Approval) Regulations 1998 SI 1998/2051. Revoked and replaced by SI 2009/717.

Motor Vehicles (Type Approval) Regulations 1980 SI 1980/1182 (now largely superseded); see now SI 2009/717.

Motor Vehicles (Type Approval) (Great Britain) Regulations 1984 SI 1984/981.

Motor Vehicles (Type Approval for Goods Vehicles) (Great Britain) Regulations 1982 SI 1982/1271.

Road Vehicles (Approval) Regulations 2009 SI 2009/717.

Road Vehicles Lighting Regulations 1984 SI 1984/812; revoked and replaced by SI 1989/1796.

Visiting Forces and International Headquarters (Application of Law) Order 1965 SI 1965/1536; revoked and replaced by SI 1999/1736, in the title Armed Forces.

Cases relating to this regulation *Langton v Johnson* [1956] 3 All ER 474, [1956] 1 WLR 1322.

[389]

[Modification of Regulations in relation to vehicles for which a Minister's approval certificate has been issued under the Motor Vehicles (Approval) Regulations 1996

3A Schedule 2A shall have effect for the purpose of modifying these Regulations in relation to vehicles in respect of which a Minister's approval certificate has been issued by virtue of the Motor Vehicles (Approval) Regulations 1996.]

NOTES

Amendment Inserted by SI 1996/3017.

Motor Vehicles (Approval) Regulations 1996 SI 1996/3013 (revoked); see now SI 2001/25.

[390]

Application and Exemptions

4 (1) Save where the context otherwise requires, these Regulations apply to both wheeled vehicles and track-laying vehicles.

(2) Where a provision is applied by these Regulations to a motor vehicle first used on or after a specified date it does not apply to that vehicle if it was manufactured at least six months before that date.

(3) Where an exemption from, or relaxation of, a provision is applied by these Regulations to a motor vehicle first used before a specified date it shall also apply to a motor vehicle first used on or after that date if it was manufactured at least six months before that date.

(4) [Subject to paragraph (7),] the regulations specified in an item in column 3 of the Table do not apply in respect of a vehicle of a class specified in that item in column 2.

TABLE

(Regulation 4(4))

1 *Item*	2 *Class of Vehicle*	3 *Regulations which do not apply*
1	A vehicle proceeding to a port for export.	The regulations in Part II insofar as they relate to construction and equipment, except regulations 16 (insofar as it concerns parking brakes) 20, 30, 34, 37 [and 53] Regulations 66 to 69 and 71.
2	A vehicle brought temporarily into Great Britain by a person resident abroad, provided that the vehicle complies in every respect with the requirements relating to motor vehicles or trailers contained in— (a) article 21 and paragraph (1) of article 22 of the Convention on Road Traffic concluded at Geneva on 19th September 1949 and [Part I,] Part II (so far as it relates to direction indicators and stop lights) and Part III of Annex 6 to that Convention; or (b) paragraphs I, III and VIII of article 3 of the International Convention relative to Motor Traffic concluded at Paris on 24th April 1926	The regulations in Part II insofar as they relate to construction and equipment except regulations 7, 8, … 10, [10A,] 40 [and 53][; and (a) additionally, in respect of any passenger vehicle with a maximum gross weight exceeding 10 tonnes registered in one or more member States, regulations 36A(2), 36A(7) and 36A(9); (b) additionally, in respect of any goods vehicle with a maximum gross weight exceeding 12 tonnes registered in one or more member States, regulations 36(B)(2), 36B(9) and 36B(11)]. Regulations 66 to 69 and 71
3	A vehicle manufactured in Great Britain which complies with the requirements referred to in item 2 above and contained in the Convention of 1949, or, as the case may be, 1926 referred to in that item as if the vehicle had been brought temporarily into Great Britain, and either— (a) is exempt from car tax by virtue of [section 7(1), (2) and (3) of the Car Tax Act 1983], or (b) has been zero rated under [regulation 56 or 57 of the Value Added Tax (General) Regulations 1985].	The regulations in Part II insofar as they relate to construction and equipment, except regulations 7, 8, … 10, [10A,] 40 [and 53]. Regulations 66 to 69 and 71.
4	A vehicle in the service of a visiting force or of a headquarters.	The regulations in Part II insofar as they relate to construction and equipment, except regulations … 16 (insofar as it concerns parking brakes), 21, 53 … and 61. Regulations 66 to 69, [71, 75 to 79 and 93A].

1 *Item*	2 *Class of Vehicle*	3 *Regulations which do not apply*
5	A vehicle which has been submitted for an examination under section 43 or [section 45] of the 1972 Act while it is being used on a road in connection with the carrying out of that examination and is being so used by a person who is empowered under that section to carry out that examination, or by a person acting under the direction of a person so empowered.	The regulations in Part II … Regulations 75 to 79 and 100.
6	A motor car or a motor cycle in respect of which a certificate has been issued by the Officer in Charge of the National Collections of Road Transport, the Science Museum, London SW7, that it was designed before 1st January 1905 and constructed before 31st December 1905.	Regulations 16 (except insofar as it applies requirements 3 and 6 in Schedule 3), 21, 37(4), 63 and 99(4).
7	(a) A towing implement which is being drawn by a motor vehicle while it is not attached to any vehicle except the one drawing it if— (i) the towing implement is not being so drawn during the hours of darkness, and (ii) the vehicle by which it is being so drawn is not driven at a speed exceeding 20 mph; or (b) a vehicle which is being drawn by a motor vehicle in the exercise of a statutory power of removal.	The regulations in Part II insofar as they relate to the construction and equipment of trailers, except regulation 20.
[8	Tramcars	The regulations in Parts II, III and IV]
[9	A public works vehicle which has a maximum design weight of 7500kg and is specifically designed for use and used solely for the purpose of street cleansing.	Regulation 15(1E) and (5B) in respect of the requirements in Community Directive 98/12/EC and ECE Regulation 13.09 which require the fitting of ABS to goods vehicles over 3500kg in weight.
10	A vehicle being used by a Police Authority which has been authorised by a Chief Constable to perform accident reconstruction duties	Regulation 15(1E) and (5B) in respect of the requirements in Community Directive 98/12/EC and ECE Regulation 13.09 which prohibit the use of an isolation switch for the operation of ABS]
[11	A vehicle being used on a road by a vehicle examiner, who has been authorised in writing by the Secretary of State for the purpose of—	The regulations in Part 2. Regulations 67, 75 to 79 and 100.]

1 *Item*	2 *Class of Vehicle*	3 *Regulations which do not apply*
	(a) submitting the vehicle for an examination under section 45 of the Road Traffic Act 1988 in order to ascertain whether the examination is carried out in accordance with regulations made under that section; or (b) removing the vehicle following that examination.	

(5) Any reference to a broken down vehicle shall include a reference to any towing implement which is being used for the drawing of any such vehicle.

(6) The Secretary of State is satisfied that it is requisite that the provisions of regulation 40(2) should apply, as from the date on which these Regulations come into operation, to track-laying vehicles registered before the expiration of one year from the making of these Regulations; and that, notwithstanding that those provisions will then apply to these vehicles, no undue hardship or inconvenience will be caused thereby.

[(7) The exemption provided by item 11 in the Table in paragraph (4) shall only apply to the extent that the vehicle examiner using the vehicle in question reasonably believes that any defects in that vehicle do not give rise to a danger of injury to any person while it is being used by that person for a purpose mentioned in that item.

(8) In item 11 in the Table in paragraph (4) and paragraph (7), "vehicle examiner" means an examiner appointed under section 66A of the Road Traffic Act 1988.]

NOTES

Amendment Para (4): words in first pair of square brackets inserted by SI 2005/3165.
Para (4), Table:
item 1, column 3: words in square brackets substituted by SI 1994/14;
item 2, column 2: words in square brackets inserted by SI 1988/271;
item 2, column 3: words omitted revoked by SI 1995/1201; entry in first pair of square brackets inserted by SI 1997/530; entry in second pair substituted by SI 1994/14; paras (a), (b) and word "; and" immediately preceding them inserted by SI 2003/1946;
item 3, column 2: words in square brackets substituted by SI 1988/271;
item 3, column 3: words omitted revoked by SI 1995/1201; words in first pair of square brackets inserted by SI 1997/530; words in second pair substituted by SI 1994/14;
item 4, column 3: first words omitted revoked by SI 1995/1201; second words omitted revoked by SI 1994/14; words in square brackets substituted by SI 1996/3133;
item 5, column 2: words in square brackets substituted by SI 1988/271;
item 5, column 3: words omitted revoked by SI 1994/14;
item 8: inserted by SI 1992/1217;
items 9, 10: inserted by SI 2001/3208;
item 11: inserted by SI 2005/3165.
Paras (7), (8): inserted by SI 2005/3165.
Convention on Road Traffic concluded at Geneva on 19th September 1949
Cmnd 7997.
International Convention relative to Motor Traffic concluded at Paris on 24th April 1926
Treaty Series No 11 (1930).
Community Directive 98/12/EC OJ L81, 18.03.1998, p 1.
Car Tax Act 1983 Repealed by the Statute Law (Repeals) Act 2004, s 1(1), Sch 1, Pt 9, Group 5.
S 43 or 45 of the 1972 Act Repealed; see now the Road Traffic Act 1988, s 45 or 49.
Value Added Tax (General) Regulations 1985 SI 1985/886; revoked and replaced by SI 1995/2518, in the title Value Added Tax.

[391]

5 (*Revoked by SI 2008/1277.*)

Compliance with Community Directives and ECE Regulations

6 (1) For the purposes of any regulation which requires or permits a vehicle to comply with the requirements of a Community Directive or an ECE Regulation, a vehicle shall be deemed so to have complied at the date of its first use only if—

(a) one of the certificates referred to in paragraph (2) has been issued in relation to it; or

(b) the marking referred to in paragraph (3) has been applied; or

(c) it was, before it was used on a road, subject to a relevant type approval requirement as specified in paragraph (4).

(2) The certificates mentioned in paragraph (1) are—

(a) a type approval certificate issued by the Secretary of State under regulation 5 of the Type Approval Regulations or of the Type Approval for Agricultural Vehicles Regulations;

(b) a certificate of conformity issued by the manufacturer of the vehicle under regulation 6 of either of those Regulations; …

(c) a certificate issued under a provision of the law of any member state of the European Economic Community which corresponds to the said regulations 5 or 6[; or

(d) a sound level measurement certificate issued by the Secretary of State under regulation 4 of the Motorcycles (Sound Level Measurement Certificates) Regulations 1980;]

being in each case a certificate issued by reason of the vehicle's conforming to the requirements of the Community Directive in question.

(3) The marking mentioned in paragraph (1) is a marking designated as an approval mark by regulation 4 of the Approval Marks Regulations, being in each case a mark shown in column 2 of an item in Schedule 2 to those Regulations which refers, in column 5, to the ECE Regulation in question, applied as indicated in column 4 in that item.

(4) A relevant type approval requirement is a requirement of the Type Approval (Great Britain) Regulations or the Type Approval for Goods Vehicles Regulations which appears—

(a) in column 4 of Table I in Schedule 2 in the item in which the Community Directive in question appears in column 3, or

(b) in column 4 of Table II in Schedule 2 in the item in which the ECE Regulation in question appears in column 3.

NOTES

Amendment Para (2)(b): word omitted revoked by SI 1989/1865.

Para (2)(d): inserted (together with word "or" immediately preceding it) by SI 1989/1865.

Motorcycles (Sound Level Measurement Certificates) Regulations 1980

SI 1980/765.

[392]

PART II
REGULATIONS GOVERNING THE CONSTRUCTION, EQUIPMENT AND MAINTENANCE OF VEHICLES

NOTES

This Part of the regulations, which is not printed in this work, contains detailed requirements affecting the construction, equipment and maintenance of vehicles. The nature and scope of its provisions may be ascertained from the arrangement printed at the beginning of the regulations. The following regulations have been amended, substituted or inserted by the instruments mentioned in brackets:

reg 7	(SI 1990/317, SI 1990/1163, SI 1991/2125, SI 1998/1188, SI 1998/3112, SI 2003/182)
reg 8	(SI 1988/1871, SI 1995/3051)
reg 9	(SI 1994/329, SI 1995/1201)
reg 10	(SI 1990/317, SI 1997/530)
reg 10A	(SI 1997/530)
reg 10B	(SI 1997/530, SI 2004/3168 (in relation to England only), SI 2005/2929 (in relation to Wales only))
reg 10C	(SI 1997/530, SI 1998/1188, SI 2004/3168 (in relation to England only), SI 2005/2929 (in relation to Wales only))
reg 11	(SI 1998/1188)
reg 13	(SI 1990/317, SI 1998/1188, SI 2003/182)
reg 13A	(SI 2000/3197)
reg 13B	(SI 1990/317, SI 1998/1188)
reg 13C	(SI 1998/1188)
reg 15	(SI 1995/551 (amended by SI 1995/737), SI 1996/3033, SI 2001/3208, SI 2002/1474)

reg 16	(SI 1990/1981, SI 1992/352, SI 1995/551, SI 1996/3033, SI 1998/2429, SI 2001/3208)
reg 17	(SI 1987/676, SI 1990/1981, SI 1992/352, SI 1995/551, SI 1998/2429, SI 2001/3208)
reg 17A	(SI 1996/3033, SI 2001/3208)
reg 18	(SI 1990/1981, SI 1992/352, SI 1995/551, SI 2001/3208)
reg 19	(SI 1990/1981)
reg 21	(*Revoked by SI 1995/1201*)
reg 23	(SI 1998/3112)
reg 24	(SI 1992/3088)
reg 25	(SI 1990/1981, SI 1991/2710, SI 1992/3088, SI 1995/551)
reg 26	(SI 1990/1981)
reg 27	(SI 1990/1981, SI 1991/2710)
reg 30	(SI 1991/2003)
reg 31	(SI 1987/676, SI 1992/3088)
reg 32	(SI 1987/676, SI 1992/3088, SI 2003/3145)
reg 33	(SI 1988/1178, SI 1992/3088, SI 2005/3165, SI 2009/142)
reg 35	(SI 1998/1188)
reg 36A	(SI 1988/271, SI 1988/1524, SI 1992/422, SI 1993/1946, SI 1993/3048, SI 1997/1340, SI 2003/1946, SI 2004/2102, SI 2005/3170, SI 2009/142)
reg 36B	(SI 1991/1527, SI 1992/422, SI 1993/1946, SI 1993/3048, SI 1994/329, SI 1995/1458, SI 1996/2064, SI 2003/1946, SI 2004/2102, SI 2004/3168 (in relation to England only), SI 2005/2929 (in relation to Wales only), SI 2005/3170, SI 2009/142)
reg 36C	(SI 1992/422)
reg 37	(SI 1994/2567, SI 2000/1971, SI 2004/3168 (in relation to England only), SI 2005/2560, SI 2005/2929 (in relation to Wales only), SI 2006/594)
reg 39	(SI 1990/2212, SI 1992/3285)
regs 39A, 39B	(SI 1988/1524)
reg 40	(SI 2003/1690)
reg 41	(SI 2003/1690)
reg 41A	(SI 2005/2987, SI 2009/142)
reg 45	(*Revoked by SI 1995/1201*)
reg 46	(Substituted by SI 2001/1043)
reg 47	(SI 1987/1133, SI 1989/1478, SI 1991/2003, SI 1994/3270, SI 1996/163, SI 1998/2429, SI 2001/1043)
reg 48	(SI 1987/1133, SI 2001/1043)
reg 48A	(SI 1996/163, SI 2001/1043)
reg 49	(SI 1987/676, SI 1998/1188)
reg 51	(SI 1987/676, SI 1989/1695)
reg 53A	(SI 1987/1133, SI 1989/2360)
reg 53B	(SI 1987/1133)
reg 53C	(SI 2005/2987, SI 2009/142)
reg 54	(SI 1994/14, SI 1996/2329)
reg 55	(SI 1989/1865, SI 1994/14, SI 1996/2329)
reg 55A	(SI 1996/2329)
reg 57	(SI 1989/1865, SI 1994/14)
reg 57A	(SI 1994/14, SI 1996/16)
reg 57B	(SI 1994/14)
reg 58	(*Revoked by SI 1995/1201*)
reg 59	(SI 1989/1865, SI 1994/14, SI 1995/1201, SI 1996/2329)
reg 60	(SI 1996/2329, SI 2002/2126)
reg 61	(SI 1988/1524, SI 1990/1131, SI 1991/1526, SI 1992/2137, SI 1992/2909, SI 1992/3285, SI 1993/2199, SI 1994/2192, SI 1995/2210, SI 1996/2085, SI 1996/2329, SI 1996/3017 (amended by SI 1997/1458), SI 1997/1544, SI 1997/2935, SI 1998/1000, SI 1998/1563, SI 2000/3197, SI 2003/3145, SI 2007/3132)
reg 61A	(SI 2000/3197, SI 2001/306, SI 2001/1825, SI 2001/3208, SI 2002/1474, SI 2006/2565)
reg 61B	(SI 2009/2196)
reg 64	(SI 1986/1597, SI 1992/646)

Cases relating to these regulations *Andrews v H E Kershaw Ltd* [1952] 1 KB 70, [1951] 2 All ER 764;
Bason v Vipond [1962] 1 All ER 520, [1962] 1 WLR 271;
Claude Hughes & Co (Carlisle) Ltd v Hyde [1963] 2 QB 757, [1963] 1 All ER 598;

Guest Scottish Carriers Ltd v Trend [1967] 3 All ER 52, [1967] 1 WLR 1371;
Hawkins v Harold A Russett Ltd [1983] 1 All ER 215;
Langton v Johnson [1956] 3 All ER 474, [1956] 1 WLR 1322;
Patterson v Redpath Bros Ltd [1979] 2 All ER 108, [1979] 1 WLR 553;
Peak Trailer and Chassis Ltd v Jackson [1967] 1 All ER 172, [1967] 1 WLR 155;
Robinson v DPP [1991] RTR 315, 155 JP 223;
Saines v Woodhouse [1970] 2 All ER 388, [1970] 1 WLR 961;
Wilkinson v Barrett (1958) 122 JP 349;
William Gwennap (Agricultural) Ltd v Amphlett [1957] 2 All ER 605, [1957] 1 WLR 910.

[393]

PART III
PLATES, MARKINGS, TESTING AND INSPECTION

Plates for goods vehicles and buses

66 (1) This regulation applies to—

(a) a wheeled heavy motor car or motor car first used on or after 1st January 1968 not being—
  (i) a dual-purpose vehicle;
  (ii) an agricultural motor vehicle;
  (iii) a works truck;
  (iv) a pedestrian-controlled vehicle; …
  (v) save as provided in sub-paragraph (b) below, a passenger vehicle; [or
  (vi) a vehicle which is exempt from section 63(1) of the Road Traffic Act 1988 by virtue of regulation 14(6) of the Motor Vehicles (Approval) Regulations 1996.]

(b) a bus (whether or not it is an articulated bus) first used on or after 1st April 1982;

(c) a wheeled locomotive or motor tractor first used on or after 1st April 1973 not being—
  (i) an agricultural motor vehicle;
  (ii) an industrial tractor;
  (iii) a works truck;
  (iv) engineering plant; or
  (v) a pedestrian-controlled vehicle;

(d) a wheeled trailer manufactured on or after 1st January 1968 which exceeds 1020 kg in weight unladen not being—
  (i) a trailer not constructed or adapted to carry any load, other than plant or special appliances or apparatus which is a permanent or essentially permanent fixture, and not exceeding 2290 kg in total weight;
  (ii) a living van not exceeding 2040 kg in weight unladen and fitted with pneumatic tyres;
  (iii) a works trailer;
  (iv) a trailer mentioned in regulation 16(3)(b) to (g); or
  (v) a trailer which was manufactured and used outside Great Britain before it was first used in Great Britain; and

(e) a converter dolly manufactured on or after 1st January 1979.

(2) Every vehicle to which this regulation applies shall be equipped with a plate securely attached to the vehicle in a conspicuous and readily accessible position which either—

(a) contains the particulars required, in the case of a motor vehicle by Part I of Schedule 8 or, in the case of a trailer, by Part II of that Schedule, and complies with the provisions of Part III of that Schedule; or

(b) complies with the requirements specified in the Annex to Community Directive 78/507 or, in the case of a vehicle first used before 1st October 1982, in the Annex to Community Directive 76/114, such requirements being in any case modified as provided in paragraph (3).

(3) Instead of the particulars required by items 2.1.4 to 2.1.7 of that Annex, the plate required by paragraph (2)(b) shall show, for a vehicle of a class specified in column 2 of the Table against an item of that Annex so specified in column 1, the following particulars—

(a) the maximum permitted weight for that class, if any, shown in column 3 of the Table;
(b) where the maximum weight shown in column 4 of the Table exceeds the maximum permitted weight, the maximum weight in a column on the plate to the right of the maximum permitted weight; and
(c) if no weight is shown in column 3 of the Table, the maximum weight shown in column 4 of the Table, in the right hand column of the plate.

TABLE

(Regulation 66(3))

1 *Item in Annex to Directive*	2 *Class of vehicle*	3 *Maximum permitted weight*	4 *Maximum weight*
2.1.4 (Laden weight of vehicle)	(i) Motor vehicles	The maximum gross weight in Great Britain referred to in item 10 in Part I of Schedule 8.	The maximum gross weight referred to in item 7 in Part I of Schedule 8.
	(ii) Trailers, other than semi-trailers	The maximum gross weight in Great Britain referred to in item 8 in Part II of Schedule 8.	The maximum gross weight referred to in item 6 in Part II of Schedule 8.
	(iii) Semi-trailers		The maximum gross weight referred to in item 6 in Part II of Schedule 8.
2.1.5 (Train weight of motor vehicle)	Motor vehicles constructed to draw a trailer	The lower of— (a) the maximum train weight referred to in item 8 in Part I of Schedule 8; and (b) the maximum laden weight specified, in the case of vehicles constructed to form part of an articulated vehicle, in regulation 77, and, in other cases, in regulation 76.	The maximum train weight referred to in item 8 in Part I of Schedule 8.
2.1.6 (Axle weight of vehicle)	(i) Motor vehicles	The maximum weight in Great Britain for each axle referred to in item 9 in Part I of Schedule 8.	The maximum weight for each axle referred to in item 6 in Part I of Schedule 8.

1 *Item in Annex to Directive*	2 *Class of vehicle*	3 *Maximum permitted weight*	4 *Maximum weight*
	(ii) Trailers	The maximum weight in Great Britain for each axle referred to in item 7 in Part II of Schedule 8.	The maximum weight for each axle referred to in item 4 in Part II of Schedule 8.
2.1.7 (Load imposed by semi-trailer)	Semi-trailers		The maximum load imposed on the drawing vehicle referred to in item 5 in Part II of Schedule 8.

(4) Part III of Schedule 8 applies for determining the relevant weights to be shown on a plate in accordance with this regulation.

[(5) Where, in accordance with the provisions of this regulation and of Schedule 8, a motor vehicle first used, or a trailer manufactured, after 31st December 1998, is required to be equipped with a plate showing the maximum gross weight in Great Britain or the maximum weight in Great Britain for each axle of the vehicle, the plate may instead show particulars of the maximum authorised weight for the vehicle or, as the case may be, the maximum authorised weight for each axle of the vehicle.

(6) In paragraph (5) the references to the maximum authorised weight for a vehicle and maximum authorised for each axle of a vehicle mean those weights determined in accordance with the Motor Vehicles (Authorised Weight) Regulations 1998.

(7) The plate for a vehicle which falls within paragraph (1)(a) and which is a motor vehicle first used after 31st December 1998 need not include the particulars referred to in paragraph 9 or 10 of Part I of Schedule 8.]

NOTES

Erratum The reference in para (6) to the Motor Vehicles (Authorised Weight) Regulations 1998 should be to the Road Vehicles (Authorised Weight) Regulations 1998.

Amendment Para (1)(a)(iv): word omitted revoked by SI 1996/3017.

Para (1)(a)(vi): inserted (together with word "or" immediately preceding it) by SI 1996/3017.

Paras (5)–(7): inserted by SI 1998/3112.

Exemptions See reg 4(4).

Community Directive 76/114; Community Directive 78/507 OJ L24, 30.01.1976, p 1; OJ L155, 13.06.1978, p 31.

Motor Vehicles (Approval) Regulations 1996 SI 1996/3013 (revoked); see now SI 2001/25.

Motor Vehicles (Authorised Weight) Regulations 1998 SI 1998/3111 (see note "Erratum" above).

[394]

Vehicle identification numbers

67 (1) This regulation applies to a wheeled vehicle which is first used on or after 1st April 1980 and to which the Type Approval (Great Britain) Regulations apply.

(2) A vehicle to which this regulation applies shall be equipped with a plate which is in a conspicuous and readily accessible position, is affixed to a vehicle part which is not normally subject to replacement and shows clearly and indelibly—

- (a) the vehicle identification number in accordance with the requirements specified—
  - (i) in the case of a vehicle first used before 1st April 1987, in paragraphs 3.1.1 and 3.1.2 of the Annex to Community Directive 76/114/EEC; or
  - (ii) in any case, in sections 3 and 4 of the Annex to Community Directive 78/507/EEC;
- (b) the name of the manufacturer; and

(c) the approval reference number of either—

(i) the type approval certificate which relates to the vehicle model or the model variant of the vehicle model, as the case may be, issued in accordance with the provisions of regulation 9(1) of, and Part I of Schedule 3 to, the Type Approval (Great Britain) Regulations; or

(ii) the Minister's approval certificate which relates to the vehicle, issued in accordance with the provisions of regulation 9(2) of, and Part 1A of Schedule 4 to, the said Regulations.

Provided that the information required under sub-paragraph (c) above may be shown clearly and indelibly on an additional plate which is fitted in a conspicuous and readily accessible position and which is affixed to a vehicle part which is not normally subject to replacement.

(3) The vehicle identification number of every vehicle to which this regulation applies shall be marked on the chassis, frame or other similar structure, on the off side of the vehicle, in a clearly visible and accessible position, and by a method such as hammering or stamping, in such a way that it cannot be obliterated or deteriorate.

NOTES
Exemptions See reg 4(4).
Community Directive 76/114/EEC; Community Directive 78/507/EEC
See the corresponding notes to reg 66.

[395]

Plates—agricultural trailed appliances

68 (1) Save as provided in paragraph (3) below, every wheeled agricultural trailed appliance manufactured on or after 1st December 1985 shall be equipped with a plate affixed to the vehicle in a conspicuous and readily accessible position and which is clearly and indelibly marked with the particulars specified in paragraph (2) below.

(2) Those particulars are—

(a) the name of the manufacturer of the appliance;
(b) the year in which the appliance was manufactured;
(c) the maximum gross weight;
(d) the unladen weight; and
(e) the maximum load which would be imposed by the appliance on the drawing vehicle.

(3) In the case of a towed roller consisting of several separate rollers used in combination, a single plate shall satisfy the requirement specified in paragraph (2) above.

NOTES
Exemptions See reg 4(4).

[396]

Plates—motor cycles

69 (1) This regulation applies to every motor cycle first used on or after 1st August 1977 which is not—

(a) propelled by an internal combustion engine with a cylinder capacity exceeding 150 cc if the vehicle was first used before 1st January 1982 or 125 cc if it was first used on or after 1st January 1982;
(b) a mowing machine; or
(c) a pedestrian-controlled vehicle.

(2) Every vehicle to which this regulation applies shall be equipped with a plate which is securely affixed to the vehicle in a conspicuous and readily accessible position and which complies with the requirements of Schedule 9.

NOTES
Exemptions See reg 4(4).

[397]

Ministry plates

70 (1) Every goods vehicle to which the Plating and Testing Regulations apply and in respect of which a plating certificate has been issued shall, from the date specified in paragraph (2), be equipped with a Ministry plate securely affixed, so as to be legible at all times, in a conspicuous and readily accessible position, and in the cab of the vehicle if it has one.

(2) That date is in the case of—

(a) a vehicle to which the Type Approval for Goods Vehicles Regulations apply, the date of the fourteenth day after the plate was issued; or

(b) any other vehicle, the date by which it is required, by the said Regulations, to be submitted for examination for plating.

[(3) In these Regulations "Ministry plate" means a plate which—

(a) is issued by the Secretary of State following the issue or amendment of a plating certificate; and

(b) subject to paragraph (4), contains the particulars required by Schedule 10, 10A, 10B or 10C.

(4) Instead of particulars of the gross weight, train weight and axle weights of the vehicle to which it relates, a Ministry plate may contain particulars of the maximum authorised weight for the vehicle, maximum authorised weight for a combination of which the vehicle forms part and maximum authorised axle weights for the vehicle, determined in accordance with the Road Vehicles (Authorised Weight) Regulations 1998 and the form of the plate shall be amended accordingly.]

NOTES
Amendment Paras (3), (4): inserted by SI 1998/3112.
Road Vehicles (Authorised Weight) Regulations 1998 SI 1998/3111.

[398]

[Speed limiters—plates

70A (1) This regulation applies to every vehicle to which regulation 36A or 36B applies and which is fitted with a speed limiter.

(2) Every vehicle to which this regulation applies shall be equipped with a plate which meets the requirements specified in paragraph (3).

(3) […] The requirements are that the plate is in conspicuous position in the driving compartment of the vehicle and is clearly and indelibly marked with the speed at which the speed limiter has been set.]

NOTES
Erratum It is thought that para (3) should read "is in a conspicuous position" instead of "is in conspicuous position".
Amendment Substituted (together with reg 70B) by SI 1993/3048 (original reg 70A inserted by SI 1988/271).
Para (3): words omitted (inserted by SI 1996/2064) revoked by SI 2004/2102.

[399]

[70B] (*Inserted by SI 1988/271; substituted, together with original reg 70A, by new reg 70A, by SI 1993/1946.*)

[Plate relating to dimensions

70B (1) This regulation applies to a vehicle which is not a goods vehicle fitted in accordance with regulation 70 with a Ministry plate containing the particulars required by Schedule 10A or 10C and which is either—

(a) a bus or a heavy motor car and which was manufactured after 31st May 1998; or

(b) a trailer used in combination with a vehicle falling within paragraph (a) and manufactured after 31st May 1998.

(2) A vehicle to which this regulation applies shall not be used unless—

(a) the vehicle is equipped with a plate securely attached to the vehicle in a conspicuous and readily accessible position and containing the particulars as to the dimensions of the vehicle specified in Annex III of Community Directive 96/53/EC; or

(b) those particulars are included in the particulars shown on the plate with which the vehicle is equipped in accordance with regulation 66.]

NOTES
Amendment Inserted by SI 1998/1188.
Community Directive 96/53/EC OJ L235, 17.09.1996, p 59.

[400]

Marking of weights on certain vehicles

71 (1) This regulation applies to a vehicle (other than an agricultural motor vehicle which is either a track-laying vehicle not exceeding 3050 kg in unladen weight or a wheeled vehicle) which is—

- (a) a locomotive;
- (b) a motor tractor;
- (c) [a bus] which is registered under the 1971 Act (or any enactment repealed thereby) ... ; or
- (d) an unbraked wheeled trailer, other than one mentioned in [regulation 16(3)(b), (bb), (bc), (c), (d), (e), (f), or (g)].

(2) There shall be plainly marked in a conspicuous place on the outside of a vehicle to which this regulation applies, on its near side—

- (a) if it is a vehicle falling in paragraph (1)(a), (b) or (c), its unladen weight; and
- (b) if it is a vehicle falling in paragraph (1)(d), its maximum gross weight.

NOTES
Amendment Para (1)(c): words in square brackets substituted, and words omitted revoked, by SI 1994/329.
Para (1)(d): words in square brackets substituted by SI 1996/3033.
Exemptions See reg 14(4).

[401]

[Marking of date of manufacture of trailers

71A (1) This regulation applies to a trailer that—

- (a) is not a motor vehicle;
- (b) is manufactured on or after 1st January 1997; and
- (c) has a maximum total design axle weight not exceeding 750 kg.

(2) The year of manufacture of every trailer to which this regulation applies shall be marked on the chassis, frame or other similar structure on the nearside of the vehicle, in a clearly visible and accessible position, and by a method such as hammering or stamping, in such a way that it cannot be obliterated or deteriorate.]

NOTES
Amendment Inserted by SI 1996/3033.

[402]

Additional markings

72 (1) This regulation applies to every goods vehicle to which the Plating and Testing Regulations apply and for which a plating certificate has been issued.

(2) Without prejudice to the provisions of regulation 70, any weight which by virtue of regulation 80 may not be exceeded in the case of a goods vehicle to which this regulation applies may be marked on either side, or on both sides, of the vehicle.

(3) Where at any time by virtue of any provision contained in regulation 75 a goods vehicle to which this regulation applies may not be used in excess of a weight which is less than the gross weight which may not be exceeded by that vehicle by virtue of regulation 80, the first mentioned weight may be marked on either side, or on both sides, of the vehicle.

(4) Where at any time by virtue of any provision contained in regulation 76 and 77 a goods vehicle to which this regulation applies is drawing, or being drawn by, another vehicle and those vehicles may not be used together in excess of a laden weight applicable to those vehicles by virtue of any such provision, that weight may be marked on either side, or on both sides, of that goods vehicle.

[403]

Test date discs

73 (1) Every Ministry test date disc which is issued, following the issue of a goods vehicle test certificate, in respect of a trailer to which the Plating and Testing Regulations apply and for which a plating certificate has been issued shall be carried on the trailer in a legible condition and in a conspicuous and readily accessible position in which it is clearly visible by daylight from the near side of the road, from the date of its issue until but not beyond the date of expiry of that test certificate or the date of issue of a further test certificate for that trailer, whichever date is the earlier.

(2) In this regulation "Ministry test date disc" means a plate issued by the Secretary of State for a goods vehicle, being a trailer, following the issue of a goods vehicle test certificate for that trailer under the Plating and Testing Regulations and containing the following particulars—

(a) the identification mark allotted to that trailer and shown in that certificate;
(b) the date until which that certificate is valid; and
(c) the number of the vehicle testing station shown in that certificate.

[404]

Testing and inspection

74 (1) Subject to the conditions specified in paragraph (2), the following persons are hereby empowered to test and inspect the brakes, silencers, steering gear and tyres of any vehicle, on any premises where that vehicle is located—

(a) a police constable in uniform;
(b) a person appointed by the Commissioner of Police of the Metropolis to inspect public carriages for the purpose of the Metropolitan Public Carriage Act 1869;
(c) a person appointed by the police authority for a police area to act for the purposes of section 53 of the 1972 Act;
(d) a goods vehicle examiner as defined in section 56 of the 1972 Act;
(e) a certifying officer as defined in section 7(1) of the 1981 Act; and
(f) a public service vehicle examiner appointed as mentioned in section 7(2) of the 1981 Act.

(2) Those conditions are—

(a) any person empowered as there mentioned shall produce his authorisation if required to do so;
(b) no such person shall enter any premises unless the consent of the owner of those premises has first been obtained;
(c) no such person shall test or inspect any vehicle on any premises unless—
    (i) the owner of the vehicle consents thereto;
    (ii) notice has been given to that owner personally or left at his address not less than 48 hours before the time of the proposed test or inspection, or has been sent to him at least 72 hours before that time by the recorded delivery service to his address last known to the person giving the notice; or
    (iii) the test or inspection is made within 48 hours of an accident to which section 25 of the 1972 Act applies and in which the vehicle was involved.

(3) For the purposes of this regulation, the owner of the vehicle shall be deemed to be in the case of a vehicle—

(a) which is for the time being registered under the 1971 Act, and is not being used under a trade licence under that Act the person appearing as the owner of the vehicle in the register kept by the Secretary of State under that Act;
(b) used under a trade licence, the holder of the licence; or
(c) exempt from excise duty by virtue of the Motor Vehicles (International Circulation) Order 1975, the person resident outside the United Kingdom who has brought the vehicle into Great Britain;

and in cases (a) and (b) the address of the owner as shown on the said register or, as the case may be, on the licence may be treated as his address.

NOTES

S 53 of the 1972 Act Now the Road Traffic Act 1988, s 67.

Goods vehicle examiner as defined in s 56 of the 1972 Act; certifying officer as defined in s 7(1) of the 1981 Act; public service vehicle examiner appointed as mentioned in s 7(2) of the 1981 Act S 56 of the 1972 Act has been replaced by the Road Traffic Act 1988, s 68. S 7 of the 1981 Act has been repealed by the Road Traffic Act 1991, ss 9(1), 83, Sch 8; by s 9(2) of the 1991 Act, references in any Act, or in any instrument made under any Act, to a certifying officer or public service vehicle examiner appointed under the 1981 Act or to an examiner appointed under s 68(1) of the 1988 Act are to be construed, so far as may be appropriate, as references to an examiner appointed under s 66A of the 1988 Act.
S 25 of the 1972 Act Now the Road Traffic Act 1988, s 170.
Motor Vehicles (International Circulation) Order 1975 SI 1975/1208.

[405]

PART IV
CONDITIONS RELATING TO USE

A—Laden Weight

Maximum permitted laden weight of a vehicle

75 (1) Save as provided in paragraph (2), the laden weight of a vehicle of a class specified in an item in column 2 of the Table shall not exceed the maximum permitted laden weight specified in that item in column 3.

(2) The maximum permitted laden weight of a vehicle first used before 1st June 1973 which falls in item 1 or 2 shall not be less than would be the case if the vehicle fell in item 9.

TABLE

(Regulation 75(1))

1 *Item*	2 *Class of vehicle*	3 *Maximum permitted laden weight (kg)*
1	A wheeled heavy motor car or motor car which is not described in items [1A, 2,] 4 or 5 and which complies with the relevant braking requirement [(see regulation 78(3) to (6) in relation to buses)]	[The weight determined in accordance with Part I of Schedule 11]
[1A	A wheeled heavy motor car or motor car which is not described in item 2, 4, or 5, which complies with the relevant braking requirement and in which— (a) every driving axle not being a steering axle is fitted with twin tyres; and (b) either every driving axle is fitted with road friendly suspension or no axle has an axle weight exceeding 9,500kg	The weight determined in accordance with Part IA of Schedule 11]
2	A wheeled heavy motor car or motor car (not being an agricultural motor vehicle) which forms part of an articulated vehicle and which complies with the relevant braking requirement	The weight specified in column (5) in Part II of Schedule 11 in the item which is appropriate having regard to columns (2), (3) and (4) in that Part
3	A wheeled trailer, including a composite trailer, but not including a semi-trailer, which is drawn by a motor tractor, heavy motor car or motor car which complies with the relevant braking requirement, other than a trailer described in items 6, 7, 8 or 11	As for item 1

1 *Item*	2 *Class of vehicle*	3 *Maximum permitted laden weight (kg)*
[4	An articulated bus (see regulation 78(3) to (5))	27,000]
5	A wheeled agricultural motor vehicle	As for item 1, but subject to a maximum of 24,390
6	A balanced agricultural trailer, as defined in paragraph (4), which is not described in items 8, 11 or 16	As for item 1, but subject to a maximum of 18,290
7	An unbalanced agricultural trailer, as defined in paragraph (4) which is not described in items 8, 11 or 16	18,290 inclusive of the weight imposed by the trailer on the drawing vehicle
8	A wheeled trailer manufactured on or after 27th February 1977 and fitted with brakes which automatically come into operation on the overrun of the trailer (whether or not it is fitted with any other brake), except an agricultural trailer which is being drawn by an agricultural motor vehicle, which complies with the requirements specified in items 3, 14 and 17 of Schedule 3 and of which the brakes can be applied either by the driver of the drawing vehicle or by some other person on that vehicle or on the trailer	3,500
9	A wheeled heavy motor car or motor car not described in items 1, 2, 4 or 5—	
	(a) with not more than 4 wheels	14,230
	(b) with more than 4 but not more than 6 wheels	20,330
	(c) with more than 6 wheels	24,390
10	A wheeled trailer not described in items 3, 6, 7, 8 or 11 having less than 6 wheels, and not forming part of an articulated vehicle; and an agricultural trailed appliance	14,230
11	A trailer manufactured before 27th February 1977 and having no brakes other than—	
	(i) a parking brake and	
	(ii) brakes which come into operation on the overrun of the trailer	3,560
12	A wheeled locomotive, not described in item 5, which is equipped with suitable and sufficient springs between each wheel and the vehicle's frame and with a pneumatic tyre or a tyre of soft or elastic material fitted to each wheel—	
	(a) if having less than 6 wheels	22,360
	(b) if having 6 wheels	26,420
	(c) if having more than 6 wheels	30,490

1 *Item*	2 *Class of vehicle*	3 *Maximum permitted laden weight (kg)*
13	A track-laying locomotive with resilient material interposed between the rims of the weight-carrying rollers and the road so that the weight of the vehicle (other than that borne by any wheels and the portion of the track in contact with the road) is supported by the resilient material.	22,360
14	A locomotive not described in items 5, 12 or 13	20,830
15	A track-laying heavy motor car or motor car	22,360
16	A track-laying trailer	13,210

(3) The maximum total weight of all trailers, whether laden or unladen, drawn at any one time by a locomotive shall not exceed [44,000 kg].

[(3A) Nothing in item 1 or 1A of the Table shall prevent a vehicle being used on a road if—

(a) a plating certificate in respect of the vehicle was in force immediately before the 1st January 1993; and

(b) the laden weight of the vehicle does not exceed the weight shown in that certificate as being the weight not to be exceeded in Great Britain]

(4) [In this Part of these Regulations and in Schedule 11—]

["air spring" means a spring operated by means of air or other compressible fluid under pressure;

"air suspension" means a suspension system in which at least 75% of the spring effect is caused by an air spring.]

"balanced agricultural trailer" means an agricultural trailer the whole of the weight of which is borne by its own wheels; and

"unbalanced agricultural trailer" means an agricultural trailer of which some, but not more than 35%, of the weight is borne by the drawing vehicle and the rest of the weight is borne by its own wheels.

[(5) For the purposes of this Part of these Regulations and Schedule 11, an axle shall be regarded as fitted with a road friendly suspension if its suspension is—

(a) an air suspension, or

(b) a suspension, not being an air suspension, which is regarded as being equivalent to an air suspension for the purposes of Community Directive 92/7.

(6) For the purposes of this Part of these Regulations and Schedule 11, an axle shall be regarded as fitted with twin tyres if it would be regarded as fitted with twin tyres for the purposes of Community Directive 92/7.]

NOTES

Amendment Para (2), Table: item 1: in column 2, words in first pair of square brackets substituted, and words in second pair inserted, by SI 1992/2016; entry in square brackets in column 3 substituted by SI 1992/2016;
item 1A: inserted by SI 1992/2016;
item 4: substituted by SI 1992/2016.
Para (3): words in square brackets substituted by SI 1998/3112.
Para (3A): inserted by SI 1992/2016.
Para (4): words in first pair of square brackets substituted, and definitions "air spring" and "air suspension" inserted, by SI 1992/2016.
Paras (5), (6): inserted by SI 1992/2016.
Exemptions See reg 4(4). As to application, see also reg 80(3).
Tyre of soft or elastic material See reg 3(5).
Community Directive 92/7 OJ L57, 02.03.1992, p 29; repealed by Council Directive 96/53/EC (OJ L235, 17.09.1996, p 59).
Cases relating to this regulation *Grierson v Clark* [1958] SC (J) 22;
Prosser v Richings [1936] 2 All ER 1627.

[406]

Maximum permitted laden weight of a vehicle and trailer, other than an articulated vehicle

76 (1) The total laden weight of a motor vehicle and the trailer or trailers (other than semi-trailers) drawn by it shall not, in a case specified in an item in column 2 of the Table, exceed the maximum permitted train weight specified in that item in column 3.

[(1A) This regulation is subject to Schedule 11A (exemptions relating to combined transport operations).]

[(2) In this regulation, the expressions "road friendly suspension", "twin tyres" and "unbalanced agricultural trailer" shall be construed in accordance with regulation 75(4), (5) and (6).]

TABLE

(Regulation 76(1))

1 *Item*	2 *Vehicle Combination*	3 *Maximum permitted train weight (kg)*
[[1	A wheeled trailer which is drawn by a wheeled motor tractor, heavy motor car (not being in any case an agricultural motor vehicle), where— (a) the combination has a total of 4 axles and is being used for international transport; and (b) the drawing vehicle is a vehicle which was first used on or after 1st April 1973 and complies with the relevant braking requirement	35,000
1A	A wheeled trailer which is drawn by a wheeled motor tractor, heavy motor car or motor car (not being in any case an agricultural motor vehicle), where the combination has a total of 4 axles and the following conditions are satisfied in relation to the drawing vehicle, namely— (a) it was first used on or after 1st April 1973; (b) it complies with the relevant braking requirement; (c) every driving axle not being a steering axle is fitted with twin tyres; and (d) every driving axle is fitted with road friendly suspension	35,000
1AA	A wheeled trailer which is drawn by a wheeled motor tractor, heavy motor car or motor car (not being in any case an agricultural motor vehicle), where the combination has a total of 5 or more axles and the following conditions are satisfied in relation to the drawing vehicle, namely— (a) it was first used on or after 1st April 1973;	38,000

1 *Item*	2 *Vehicle Combination*	3 *Maximum permitted train weight (kg)*
	(b) it complies with the relevant braking requirement; (c) every driving axle not being a steering axle is fitted with twin tyres; and (d) either every driving axle is fitted with road friendly suspension or no axle has an axle weight exceeding 8,500kg	
1B	A wheeled trailer, not being part of a combination described in items 1, 1A or 1AA which is drawn by a wheeled motor tractor, heavy motor car or motor car (not being in any case an agricultural motor vehicle), where— (a) the trailer is fitted with power-assisted brakes which can be operated by the driver of the drawing vehicle and are not rendered ineffective by the non-rotation of its engine; and (b) the drawing vehicle is equipped with a warning device so placed as to be readily visible to the driver of the vehicle and which is capable of indicating any impending failure of, or deficiency in, the vacuum or pressure system	32,520]
1C	A wheeled trailer which is of a description specified in item 8 in the Table of regulation 75 drawn by a wheeled motor tractor, heavy motor car or motor car (not being in any case an agricultural motor vehicle), the drawing vehicle being a vehicle which— (a) was first used on or after 1st April 1973; and (b) complies with the relevant braking requirement	29,500]
2	A wheeled agricultural motor vehicle drawing a wheeled unbalanced agricultural trailer, if the distance between the rearmost axle of the trailer and the rearmost axle of the drawing vehicle does not exceed 2.9 m	20,000
3	A wheeled trailer or trailers drawn by a wheeled motor tractor, heavy motor car, motor car or agricultural motor vehicle, not being a combination of vehicles mentioned in items 1[, 1A, [1AA,] 1B, 1C] or 2	24,390

1 *Item*	2 *Vehicle Combination*	3 *Maximum permitted train weight (kg)*
4	A track-laying trailer drawn by a motor tractor, heavy motor car or motor car, whether wheeled or track-laying and a wheeled trailer, drawn by a track-laying vehicle being a motor tractor, heavy motor car or motor car	22,360

NOTES
Amendment Para (1A): inserted by SI 1994/329.
Para (2): substituted by SI 1992/2016.
Table: items 1, 1A, 1AA, 1B: substituted for items 1, 1A, 1B (previously substituted, together with item 1C, for item 1 by SI 1992/2016) by SI 1994/329;
item 1C: substituted (together with former items 1, 1A, 1B) for item 1 by SI 1992/2016;
item 3: figures in first (outer) pair of square brackets inserted by SI 1992/2016; figure in second (inner) pair inserted by SI 1994/329.
Exemptions See reg 4(4). As to application, see also reg 80(3).

[407]

Maximum permitted laden weight of an articulated vehicle

77 (1) Except as provided in paragraph (2), the laden weight of an articulated vehicle of a class specified in an item in column 2 of the Table shall not exceed the weight specified in column 3 in that item.

TABLE

(Regulation 77(1))

1 *Item*	2 *Class of vehicle*	3 *Maximum permitted laden weight (kg)*
1	An articulated vehicle which complies with the relevant braking requirement.	Whichever is the lower of— (a) the weight specified in column (3) of Part III of Schedule 11 in the item in which the spacing between the rearmost axles of the motor vehicle and the semi-trailer is specified in column (2), … ; and (b) if the vehicle is of a description specified in an item in column (2) of Part IV of Schedule 11, the weight specified in column (3) of that item
2	An articulated vehicle which does not comply with the relevant braking requirement if the trailer has—	
	(a) less than 4 wheels	20,330
	(b) 4 wheels or more	24,390

(2) This regulation does not apply to an agricultural motor vehicle, an agricultural trailer or an agricultural trailed appliance.

[(2A) This regulation is subject to Schedule 11A (exemptions relating to combined transport operations).]

[(3) In Part IV of Schedule 11, "road friendly suspension" and "twin tyres" shall be construed in accordance with regulation 75(5) and (6).]

NOTES

Amendment Para (1), Table: in item 1, words omitted revoked by SI 1994/329.
Para (2A): inserted by SI 1994/329.
Para (3): inserted by SI 1992/2016.
Exemptions See reg 4(4). As to application, see also reg 80(3).

[408]

Maximum permitted wheel and axle weights

78 (1) The weight transmitted to the road by one or more wheels of a vehicle as mentioned in an item in column 2 of the Table shall not exceed the maximum permitted weight specified in that item in column 3.

(2) The Parts of the Table have the following application—

(a) Part I applies to wheeled heavy motor cars, motor cars and trailers which comply with the relevant braking requirement and to wheeled agricultural motor vehicles, agricultural trailers and agricultural trailed appliances; items 1(b) and 2 also apply to buses;

(b) Part II applies to wheeled heavy motor cars, motor cars and trailers which do not fall in Part I;

(c) Part III applies to wheeled locomotives; and

(d) Part IV applies to track-laying vehicles.

TABLE

(Regulation 78(1))

PART I

(wheeled heavy motor cars, motor cars and trailers which comply with the relevant braking requirement and wheeled agricultural motor vehicles, agricultural trailers and agricultural trailed appliances; and, in respect of items 1(b) and 2, buses)

1 *Item*	2 *Wheel criteria*	3 *Maximum permitted weight (kg)*
1	Two wheels in line transversely each of which is fitted with a wide tyre or with two pneumatic tyres having the centres of their areas of contact with the road not less than 300 mm apart, measured at right angles to the longitudinal axis of the vehicle—	
	(a) if the wheels are on the sole driving axle of a motor vehicle [not being a bus].	10,500
	(b) if the vehicle is a bus which has 2 axles and of which the weight transmitted to the road surface by its wheels is calculated in accordance with regulation 78(5),	10,500
	(c) in any other case	10,170
2	Two wheels in line transversely otherwise than as mentioned in item 1	9,200
3	More than two wheels in line transversely—	
	(a) in the case of a vehicle manufactured before 1st May 1983 [where] the wheels are on one axle of a group of … closely spaced axles …	10,170

1 *Item*	2 *Wheel criteria*	3 *Maximum permitted weight (kg)*
	(b) in the case of a vehicle manufactured on or after 1st May 1983,	10,170
	(c) in any other case	11,180
4	One wheel not transversely in line with any other wheel—	
	(a) if the wheel is fitted as described in item 1,	5,090
	(b) in any other case	4,600

PART II

(wheeled heavy motor cars, motor cars and trailers not falling in Part I)

1 *Item*	2 *Wheel criteria*	3 *Maximum permitted weight (kg)*
5	More than two wheels transmitting weight to a strip of the road surface on which the vehicle rests contained between two parallel lines at right angles to the longitudinal axis of the vehicle—	
	(a) less than 1.02 m apart,	11,180
	(b) 1.02 m or more apart but less than 1.22 m apart,	16,260
	(c) 1.22 m or more apart but less than 2.13 m apart	18,300
6	Two wheels in line transversely	9,200
7	One wheel, where no other wheel is in the same line transversely.	4,600

PART III

(wheeled locomotives)

1 *Item*	2 *Wheel criteria*	3 *Maximum permitted weight (kg)*
8	Two wheels in line transversely (except in the case of a road roller, or a vehicle with not more than four wheels first used before 1st June 1955)	11,180
9	Any two wheels in the case of a wheeled locomotive having not more than four wheels first used before 1st June 1955 (not being a road roller or an agricultural motor vehicle which is not driven at more than 20 mph)	Three quarters of the total weight of the locomotive.

PART IV

(track-laying vehicles)

1 *Item*	2 *Wheel criteria*	3 *Maximum permitted weight (kg)*
10	The weight of a heavy motor car, motor car or trailer transmitted to any strip of the road surface on which the vehicle rests contained between two parallel lines 0.6 m apart at right angles to the longitudinal axis of the vehicle	10,170
11	Two wheels in line— (a) heavy motor cars or motor cars with 2 wheels, (b) heavy motor cars or motor cars with more than 2 wheels	 8,130 7,630
12	One wheel, where no other wheel is in the same line transversely, on a heavy motor car or a motor car	4,070

(3) In the case of an articulated bus, or, subject to paragraph (4), of a bus first used before 1st April 1988, the laden weight, for the purposes of ... regulation 75, and the weight transmitted to the road surface by wheels of the vehicle, for the purposes of items 1 and 2 of the Table in this regulation, shall be calculated with reference to the vehicle when it is complete and fully equipped for service with—

(a) a full supply of water, oil and fuel; and

(b) weights of 63.5 kg for each person (including crew)—

(i) for whom a seat is provided in the position in which he may be seated; and

(ii) who may by or under any enactment be carried standing, the total of such weights being reasonably distributed in the space in which such persons may be carried, save that in the case of a bus (not being an articulated bus) only the number of such persons exceeding 8 shall be taken into account.

(4) The weights for the purposes referred to in paragraph (3) may, in the case of a bus to which that paragraph applies, be calculated in accordance with paragraph (5) instead of paragraph (3).

(5) In the case of a bus first used on or after 1st April 1988, the weights for the purposes referred to in paragraph (3) shall be calculated with reference to the vehicle when it is complete and fully equipped for service with—

(a) a full supply of water, oil and fuel;

(b) a weight of 65 kg for each person (including crew)—

(i) for whom a seat is provided, in the position in which he may be seated; and

(ii) who may by or under any enactment be carried standing, the total of such weights being reasonably distributed in the space in which such persons may be so carried, save that in the case of a bus (not being an articulated bus) only the number of such persons exceeding 4 shall be taken into account;

(c) all luggage space within the vehicle but not within the passenger compartment loaded at the rate of 100 kg per m^2 or 10 kg per person mentioned in sub-paragraph (b) above, whichever is the less; and

(d) any area of the roof of the vehicle constructed or adapted for the storage of luggage loaded with a uniformly distributed load at the rate of 75 kg per m^2.

[(6) Regulation 75 shall not apply to a two axle bus if—

(a) its laden weight as calculated in accordance with paragraph (5) does not exceed 17,000 kg; and

(b) the distance between the two axles is at least 3.0 m.]

NOTES

Amendment Para (2), Table: item 1: words in square brackets substituted by SI 1987/676; item 3: word in square brackets substituted, and words omitted revoked, by SI 1992/2016.
Para (3): words omitted revoked by SI 1992/2016.
Para (6): inserted by SI 1992/2016.
Each person ... who may by or under any enactment be carried standing
See SI 1984/1406.
Exemptions See reg 4(4). As to application, see also reg 80(3).
Cases relating to this regulation Thomas v Galloway [1935] SC (J) 27.

[409]

Maximum permitted weights for certain closely-spaced axles etc

79 (1) This regulation applies to—

(a) a wheeled motor vehicle which complies with the relevant braking requirement;
(b) a wheeled trailer which is drawn by such a motor vehicle; and
(c) an agricultural motor vehicle, an agricultural trailer and an agricultural trailed appliance.

[(2) Save as provided in paragraph (5), where a vehicle to which this regulation applies is of a description specified in an item in column 2 of Part V of Schedule 11 and has two closely-spaced axles, the total weight transmitted to the road surface by all the wheels of those axles shall not exceed the maximum permitted weight specified in column 3 of that item.

(3) Save as provided in paragraph (5), where a vehicle to which this regulation applies is of a description specified in an item in column 2 of Part VI of Schedule 11 and has three closely-spaced axles, the total weight transmitted to the road surface by all the wheels of those axles shall not exceed the weight specified in column 3.

(4) Save as provided by paragraph (5), where a vehicle is fitted with four or more closely-spaced axles, the weight transmitted to the road surface by all the wheels of those axles shall not exceed 24,000kg.]

(5) Nothing in paragraphs (2), (3) or (4) of this regulation shall apply so as to prevent a vehicle first used before 1st June 1973 from being used on a road at a weight as respects those axles at which it could be used if it fell within item 5 in the Table in regulation 78 [and nothing in those paragraphs shall prevent a vehicle being used on a road if—

(a) a plating certificate in respect of the vehicle was in force immediately before the 1st January 1993; and
(b) no axle has an axle weight exceeding the weight shown in that certificate as being the weight not to be exceeded in Great Britain for that axle.]

[(6) In Parts V and VI of Schedule 11, "air-suspension" "road friendly suspension" and "twin tyres" shall be construed in accordance with regulation 75(4), (5) and (6).]

NOTES

Amendment Paras (2)–(4): substituted by SI 1992/2016.
Para (5): words in square brackets substituted by SI 1992/2016.
Para (6): substituted for paras (6)–(8) (inserted by SI 1988/1287) by SI 1992/2016.
Exemptions See reg 4(4). As to application, see also reg 80(3).

[410]

[Saving for the Road Vehicles (Authorised Weight) Regulations 1998

79A Nothing in regulations 75 to 79 shall be taken to prohibit the use of a vehicle in circumstances where the maximum authorised weight for the vehicle, for any vehicle combination of which the vehicle forms part and for any axle of the vehicle, as determined in accordance with the Road Vehicles (Authorised Weight) Regulations 1998, is not exceeded.]

NOTES

Amendment Inserted by SI 1998/3112.
Road Vehicles (Authorised Weight) Regulations 1998 SI 1998/3111.

[411]

Over-riding weight restrictions

80 (1) Subject to [paragraphs (2), (2A) and [(2B), (2C) and (4)]], no person shall use, or cause or permit to be used, on a road a vehicle—

- (a) fitted with a plate in accordance with regulation 66, but for which no plating certificate has been issued, if any of the weights shown on the plate is exceeded;
- (b) for which a plating certificate has been issued, if any of the weights shown in column (2) of the plating certificate is exceeded; or
- (c) required by regulation 68 to be fitted with a plate, if the maximum gross weight referred to in paragraph (2)(c) of that regulation is exceeded.

(2) Where any two or more axles are fitted with a compensating arrangement in accordance with regulation 23 the sum of the weights shown for them in the plating certificate shall not be exceeded. In a case where a plating certificate has not been issued the sum of the weights referred to shall be that shown for the said axles in the plate fitted in accordance with regulation 66.

[(2A) Paragraph (1) shall not apply to a vehicle for which a plating certificate has been issued in the form set out in Schedule 10A or 10C where—

- (a) the vehicle is being used for international transport; and
- (b) none of the weights shown in column (3) of the plating certificate is exceeded.

(2B) Where both a train weight and a maximum train weight are shown in column (2) of a plating certificate issued for a motor vehicle, paragraph (1)(b) in so far as it relates to train weights shall not apply to the motor vehicle if—

- (a) the motor vehicle is a wheeled heavy motor car drawing a wheeled trailer and the requirements set out in Part II of Schedule 11A are for the time being fulfilled; or
- (b) the motor vehicle is comprised in an articulated vehicle and the requirements set out in Part III of Schedule 11A are for the time being fulfilled,

and the train weight of the motor vehicle does not exceed the maximum train weight shown in column (2) of the certificate.]

(3) Nothing in regulations 75 to 79 [or in the Road Vehicles (Authorised Weight) Regulations 1998] shall permit any such weight as is mentioned in the preceding provisions of this regulation to be exceeded and nothing in this regulation shall permit any weight prescribed by regulations 75 to 79 [or in the Road Vehicles (Authorised Weight) Regulations 1998] in relation to the vehicle in question to be exceeded.

[(4) Paragraph (1) shall not apply where a vehicle is used on a road before 1st January 2000 if—

- (a) the vehicle is fitted with a plate in accordance with regulation 66(1)(b) and the maximum gross weight and the maximum weight for any axle of the vehicle are not exceeded; or
- (b) there is in force a plating certificate for the vehicle that was issued before 1st January 1999 and the design weight of the vehicle is not exceeded; and
- (c) in either case the maximum authorised weight for the vehicle, maximum authorised weight for a combination of which the vehicle forms part and maximum authorised weight for any axle of the vehicle, determined in accordance with the Road Vehicles (Authorised Weight) Regulations 1998, are not exceeded.]

NOTES

Amendment Para (1): words in first (outer) pair of square brackets substituted by SI 1997/1096; words in second (inner) pair substituted by SI 1998/3112 (but note that notwithstanding the reference to it in para (1), as amended, there is no para (2C) in this regulation).
Paras (2A), (2B): inserted by SI 1994/329.
Para (3): words in square brackets inserted by SI 1998/3112.
Para (4): inserted by SI 1998/3112.
Road Vehicles (Authorised Weight) Regulations 1998 SI 1998/3111.
Cases relating to this regulation *DPP v Marshall and Bell* [1990] RTR 384, (1989) 154 JP 508.

[412]

B—Dimensions of Laden Vehicles

Restrictions on use of vehicles carrying wide or long loads or having fixed appliances or apparatus

81 For the purposes of this regulation, regulation 82 and Schedule 12—

(a) "lateral projection", in relation to a load carried by a vehicle, means that part of the load which extends beyond a side of the vehicle;

(b) the width of any lateral projection shall be measured between longitudinal planes passing through the extreme projecting point of the vehicle on that side on which the projection lies and that part of the projection furthest from that point;

(c) references to a special appliance or apparatus, in relation to a vehicle, are references to any crane or other special appliance or apparatus fitted to the vehicle which is a permanent or essentially permanent fixture;

(d) "forward projection" and "rearward projection"—

(i) in relation to a load carried in such a manner that its weight [is borne by] only one vehicle, mean respectively that part of the load which extends beyond the foremost point of the vehicle and that part which extends beyond the rearmost point of the vehicle;

(ii) in relation to a load carried in such a manner that part of its weight [is borne by] more than one vehicle, mean respectively that part of the load which extends beyond the foremost point of the foremost vehicle by which the load is carried except where the context otherwise requires and that part of the load which extends beyond the rearmost point of the rearmost vehicle by which the load is carried; and

(iii) in relation to any special appliance or apparatus, mean respectively that part of the appliance or apparatus which, if it were deemed to be a load carried by the vehicle, would be a part of a load extending beyond the foremost point of the vehicle and that part which would be a part of a load extending beyond the rearmost point of the vehicle,

and references in regulation 82 and Schedule 12 to a forward projection or to a rearward projection in relation to a vehicle shall be construed accordingly;

(e) the length of any forward projection or of any rearward projection shall be measured between transverse planes passing—

(i) in the case of a forward projection, through the foremost point of the vehicle and that part of the projection furthest from that point; and

(ii) in the case of a rearward projection, through the rearmost point of the vehicle and that part of the projection furthest from that point.

In this and the foregoing sub-paragraph "vehicle" does not include any special appliance or apparatus or any part thereof which is a forward projection or a rearward projection;

(f) references to the distance between vehicles, in relation to vehicles carrying a load, are references to the distance between the nearest points of any two adjacent vehicles by which the load is carried, measured when the longitudinal axis of each vehicle lies in the same vertical plane.

For the purposes of this sub-paragraph, in determining the nearest point of two vehicles any part of either vehicle designed primarily for use as a means of attaching the one vehicle to the other and any fitting designed for use in connection with any such part shall be disregarded;

(g) references to a combination of vehicles, in relation to a motor vehicle which is drawing one or more trailers, are references to the motor vehicle and the trailer or trailers drawn thereby, including any other motor vehicle which is used for the purpose of assisting in the propulsion of the trailer or the trailers on the road;

(h) the overall length of a combination of vehicles shall be taken as the distance between the foremost point of the drawing vehicle comprised in the combination and the rearmost point of the rearmost vehicle comprised therein, measured when the longitudinal axis of each vehicle comprised in the combination lies in the same vertical plane;

(i) the extreme projecting point of a vehicle is the point from which the overall width of the vehicle is calculated in accordance with the definition of overall width contained in regulation 3(2);

(j) without prejudice to sub-paragraph (e) the foremost or, as the case may be, the rearmost point of a vehicle is the foremost or rearmost point from which the overall length of the vehicle is calculated in accordance with the definition of overall length contained in regulation 3(2); and

(k) an agricultural, horticultural or forestry implement rigidly but not permanently mounted on an agricultural motor vehicle, agricultural trailer or agricultural trailed appliance, whether or not part of its weight is supported by one or more of its own wheels, shall not be treated as a load, or special appliance, on that vehicle.

NOTES

Amendment Para (d): words in square brackets substituted by SI 1991/2125.

[413]

82 (1) No load shall be carried on a vehicle so that the overall width of the vehicle together with the width of any lateral projection or projections of its load exceeds 4.3m.

(2) Subject to the following provisions of this regulation, no load shall be carried on a vehicle so that—

(a) the load has a lateral projection or projections on either side exceeding 305mm; or

(b) the overall width of the vehicle and of any lateral projection or projections of its load exceeds 2.9m.

Provided that this paragraph does not apply to the carriage of—

(i) loose agricultural produce not baled or crated; or

(ii) an indivisible load if—

(A) it is not reasonably practicable to comply with this paragraph and the conditions specified in [paragraphs 1 and 5] of Schedule 12 are complied with; and

(B) where the overall width of the vehicle together with the width of any lateral projection or projections of its load exceeds 3.5m, the conditions specified in paragraph 2 of Schedule 12 are complied with.

(3) Where a load is carried so that its weight rests on a vehicle or vehicles, the length specified in paragraph (5) shall not exceed 27.4m.

[(4) A load shall not be carried so that its weight is borne by a vehicle or vehicles if either—

(a) the length specified in paragraph (5) exceeds 18.65m; or

(b) the load is borne by a trailer or trailers and the length specified in paragraph (6) exceeds 25.9m,

unless the conditions specified in paragraphs 1 and 2 of Part I of Schedule 12 are complied with.]

(5) The length referred to in paragraphs (3) and (4)(a) is—

(a) where the [weight of the load is borne by] a single vehicle, the overall length of the vehicle together with the length of any forward and rearward projection of the load;

(b) where the [weight of the load is borne by] a motor vehicle and one trailer, whether or not forming an articulated vehicle, the overall length of the trailer together with the length of any projection of the load in front of the foremost point of the trailer and of any rearward projection of the load; and

(c) in any other case, the overall length of all the vehicles [which bear the weight of the load], together with the length of any distance between them and of any forward or rearward projection of the load.

(6) The length referred to in paragraph (4)(b) is the overall length of the combination of vehicles, together with the length of any forward or rearward projection of the load.

(7) Subject to the following provisions of this regulation no person shall use, or cause or permit to be used, on a road a vehicle, not being a straddle carrier, carrying a load or fitted with a special appliance or apparatus if the load, appliance or apparatus has a forward projection of a length specified in an item in column 2 of the Table, or rearward projection of a length specified in an item in column 3, unless the conditions specified in that item in column 4 are complied with.

TABLE

(Regulation 82(7))

1 *Item*	2 *Length of forward projection*	3 *Length of rearward projection*	4 *Conditions to be complied with*	
			(a) if the load consists of a racing boat propelled solely by oars.	(b) in any other case
1	Exceeding 1 m but not exceeding 2 m	—	Para 4 of Schedule 12	—
2	Exceeding 2 m but not exceeding 3.05 m	—	Para 4 of Schedule 12	Paras 2 and 3 of Schedule 12
3	Exceeding 3.05 m	—	Paras 1 and 4 of Schedule 12	Paras 1, 2 and 3 of Schedule 12
4	—	Exceeding 1 m but not exceeding 2 m	Para 4 of Schedule 12	Para 4 of Schedule 12
5	—	Exceeding 2 m but not exceeding 3.05 m	Para 4 of Schedule 12	Para 3 of Schedule 12
6	—	Exceeding 3.05 m	Paras 1 and 4 of Schedule 12	Paras 1, 2 and 3 of Schedule 12

(8) Subject to the following provisions of this regulation, no person shall use, or cause or permit to be used, on a road a straddle carrier carrying a load if—

(a) the load has a rearward projection exceeding 1m unless the conditions specified in paragraph 4 of Schedule 12 are met;

(b) the load has a forward projection exceeding 2m or a rearward projection exceeding 3m; or

(c) the overall length of the vehicle together with the length of any forward projection and of any rearward projection of its load exceeds 12.2m

Provided that—

(i) sub-paragraph (a) does not apply to a vehicle being used in passing from one part of private premises to another part thereof or to other private premises in the immediate neighbourhood;

(ii) sub-paragraphs (b) and (c) do not apply to a vehicle being used as in proviso (i) above if—

(A) the vehicle is not being driven at a speed exceeding 12mph; and

(B) where the overall length of the vehicle together with the length of any forward projection and of any rearward projection of its load exceeds 12.2m, the conditions specified in paragraphs 1 and 2 of Schedule 12 are complied with.

(9) Where another vehicle is attached to that end of a vehicle from which a projection extends, then for the purposes of any requirement in this regulation to comply with paragraph 3 or 4 of Schedule 12, that projection shall be treated as a forward or rearward projection only if, and to the extent that it extends beyond the foremost point or, as the case may be, the rearmost point, of that other vehicle, measured when the longitudinal axis of each vehicle lies in the same vertical plane.

(10) In the case of a vehicle being used—

(a) for fire brigade [or, in England, fire and rescue authority], ambulance or police purposes or for defence purposes (including civil defence purposes); or

(b) in connection with the removal of any obstruction to traffic,

if compliance with any provision of this regulation would hinder or be likely to hinder the use of the vehicle for the purpose for which it is being used, that provision does not apply to that vehicle while it is being so used.

(11) No person shall use, or cause or permit to be used, on a road an agricultural, horticultural or forestry implement rigidly, but not permanently, mounted on a wheeled agricultural motor vehicle, agricultural trailer, or agricultural trailed appliance, whether or not part of its weight is supported by one or more of its own wheels if—

(a) the overall width of the vehicle together with the lateral projection of the implement exceeds [2.55]m; or

(b) the implement projects more than 1m forwards or rearwards of the vehicle,

so however, that this restriction shall not apply in a case where—

(i) part of the weight of the implement is supported by one or more of its own wheels; and

(ii) the longitudinal axis of the greater part of the implement is capable of articulating in the horizontal plane in relation to the longitudinal axis of the rear portion of the vehicle.

NOTES

Amendment Para (2): words in square brackets substituted by SI 1991/2125.
Para (4): substituted by SI 1991/2125.
Para (5): words in square brackets substituted by SI 1991/2125.
Para (10)(a): words in square brackets inserted by SI 2004/3168 (in relation to England only); in relation to Wales, words "or, in England or Wales, fire and rescue authority" inserted by SI 2005/2929.
Para (11)(a): figure in square brackets substituted by SI 1995/3051.

[414]

C—Trailers and Sidecars

Number of trailers

83 (1) No person shall use, or cause or permit to be used, on a road a wheeled vehicle of a class specified in an item in column 2 of the Table drawing a trailer, subject to any exceptions which may be specified in that item in column 3.

TABLE

(Regulation 83(1))

1 *Item*	2 *Class of vehicles*	3 *Exceptions*
1	A straddle carrier	—
2	An invalid carriage	—
3	An articulated bus	—

1 *Item*	2 *Class of vehicles*	3 *Exceptions*
4	A bus not being an articulated bus or a mini-bus	(a) 1 broken down bus where no person other than the driver is carried in either vehicle or [(b) 1 trailer]
5	A locomotive	3 trailers
6	A motor tractor	[1 trailer] 2 trailers if neither is laden
7	A heavy motor car or a motor car not described in item 1, 3 or 4	2 trailers if one of them is a towing implement and part of the other is secured to and either rests on or is suspended from that implement 1 trailer in any other case
5	A locomotive	3 trailers
6	A motor tractor	[1 trailer] 2 trailers if neither is laden
7	A heavy motor car or a motor car not described in item 1, 3 or 4	2 trailers if one of them is a towing implement and part of the other is secured to and either rests on or is suspended from that implement 1 trailer in any other case

(2) For the purposes of items 5, 6 and 7 of the Table—

(a) an unladen articulated vehicle, when being drawn by another motor vehicle because it has broken down, shall be treated as a single trailer; and

(b) a towed roller used for the purposes of agriculture, horticulture or forestry and consisting of several separate rollers shall be treated as one agricultural trailed appliance.

(3) No track-laying motor vehicle which exceeds 8 m in overall length shall draw a trailer other than a broken down vehicle which is being drawn in consequence of the breakdown.

[(4) For the purpose of this regulation, the word "trailer" does not include a vehicle which is drawn by a steam powered vehicle and which is used solely for carrying water for the purpose of the drawing vehicle.]

NOTES

Amendment Para (1), Table: in items 4 and 6, column 3, words in square brackets substituted by SI 1989/2360.

Para (4): inserted by SI 1987/676.

[415]

Trailers drawn by motor cycles

84 (1) Save as provided in paragraph (2), no person shall use, or cause or permit to be used, on a road a motor cycle—

(a) drawing behind it more than one trailer;

(b) drawing behind it any trailer carrying a passenger;

(c) drawing behind it a trailer with an unladen weight exceeding 254 kg;

(d) with not more than 2 wheels, without a sidecar, and with an engine capacity which does not exceed 125 cc, drawing behind it any trailer; or

(e) with not more than 2 wheels, without a sidecar and with an engine capacity exceeding 125 cc, drawing behind it any trailer unless—

(i) the trailer has an overall width not exceeding 1 m;

(ii) the distance between the rear axle of the motor cycle and the rearmost part of the trailer does not exceed 2.5 m;

- (iii) the motor cycle is clearly and indelibly marked in a conspicuous and readily accessible position with its kerbside weight;
- (iv) the trailer is clearly and indelibly marked in a conspicuous and readily accessible position with its unladen weight; and
- (v) the laden weight of the trailer does not exceed 150 kg or two thirds of the kerbside weight of the motor cycle, whichever is the less.

(2) The provisions of paragraph (1)(b), (d) and (e) do not apply if the trailer is a broken down motorcycle and one passenger is riding it.

[416]

Trailers drawn by agricultural motor vehicles

85 (1) No person shall use, or cause or permit to be used, on a road a wheeled agricultural motor vehicle drawing one or more wheeled trailers if the weight of the drawing vehicle is less than a quarter of the weight of the trailer or trailers, unless the brakes fitted to each trailer in compliance with regulation 15 or 16 are operated directly by the service braking system fitted to the motor vehicle.

(2) No person shall use, or cause or permit to be used, on a road, any motor vehicle drawing an agricultural trailer of which—

- (a) more than 35% of the weight is borne by the drawing vehicle; or
- (b) the gross weight exceeds 14,230 kg, unless it is fitted with brakes as mentioned in paragraph (1).

(3) No person shall use, or cause or permit to be used, on a road an agricultural trailer manufactured on or after 1st December 1985 which is drawn by a motor vehicle first used on or after 1st June 1986 unless the brakes fitted to the trailer—

- (a) in accordance with regulation 15 can be applied progressively by the driver of the drawing vehicle, from his normal driving position and while keeping proper control of that vehicle, using a means of operation mounted on the drawing vehicle; or
- (b) automatically come into operation on the over-run of the trailer.

[417]

Distance between motor vehicles and trailers

86 (1) Where a trailer is attached to the vehicle immediately in front of it solely by means of a rope or chain, the distance between the trailer and that vehicle shall not in any case exceed 4.5 m, and shall not exceed 1.5 m unless the rope or chain is made clearly visible to any other person using the road within a reasonable distance from either side.

(2) For the purpose of determining the said distance any part of either vehicle designed primarily for use as a means of attaching the one vehicle to the other and any fitting designed for use in connection with any such part shall be disregarded.

[418]

[Use of secondary coupling on trailers

86A (1) No person shall use or cause or permit to be used on a road a motor vehicle drawing one trailer if the trailer—

- (a) is a trailer to which regulation 15 applies; and
- (b) is not fitted with a device which is designed to stop the trailer automatically in the event of the separation of the main coupling while the trailer is in motion,

unless the requirements of paragraph (2) are met in relation to the motor vehicle and trailer.

(2) The requirements of this paragraph, in relation to a motor vehicle drawing a trailer, are that a secondary coupling is attached to the motor vehicle and trailer in such a way that, in the event of the separation of the main coupling while the trailer is in motion,—

- (a) the drawbar of the trailer would be prevented from touching the ground; and
- (b) there would be some residual steering of the trailer.

(3) No person shall use or cause or permit to be used on a road a motor vehicle drawing one trailer if—

(a) the trailer is a trailer to which regulation 15 applies;

(b) the trailer is fitted with a device which is designed to stop the trailer automatically in the event of the separation of the main coupling while the trailer is in motion;

(c) the operation of the device in those circumstances depends upon a secondary coupling linking the device to the motor vehicle; and

(d) the trailer is not also fitted with a device which is designed to stop the trailer automatically in those circumstances in the absence of such a secondary coupling,

unless the requirements of paragraph (4) are met in relation to the motor vehicle and trailer.

(4) The requirements of this paragraph, in relation to a motor vehicle drawing a trailer, are that the secondary coupling is attached to the motor vehicle and trailer in such a way that, in the event of the separation of the main coupling while the trailer is in motion, the device of the kind referred to in paragraph (3)(b) and (c) fitted to the trailer would stop the trailer.

(5) This regulation is without prejudice to any other provision in these Regulations.]

NOTES
Amendment Inserted by SI 1995/551.

[419]

[Use of mechanical coupling devices

86B (1) This regulation applies to every light passenger vehicle first used on or after 1st August 1998 in respect of which an EC certificate of conformity has effect.

(2) No person shall use or cause or permit to be used on a road any vehicle to which this regulation applies unless any mechanical coupling device which is attached to it complies with the relevant technical and installation requirements of Annexes I, V, VI and VII of Community Directive 94/20 and is marked in accordance with sub-paragraphs 3.3.4 to 3.3.5 of Annex I to that Directive.

(3) For the purposes of this regulation, in a case where a vehicle is drawing a trailer a mechanical coupling device shall not be regarded as being attached to that vehicle if it forms part of the trailer.

(4) In this regulation "mechanical coupling device" shall be construed in accordance with paragraph 2.1 of Annex I to Community Directive 94/20.]

NOTES
Amendment Inserted by SI 1998/1281.
Community Directive 94/20 OJ L195, 29.07.1994, p 1.

[420]

Unbraked trailers

87 (1) Save as provided in paragraph (2), no person shall use, or cause or permit to be used, on a road an unbraked wheeled trailer if—

(a) its laden weight exceeds its maximum gross weight; or

(b) it is drawn by a vehicle of which the kerbside weight is less than twice the sum of the unladen weight of the trailer and the weight of any load which the trailer is carrying.

(2) This regulation does not apply to—

(a) an agricultural trailer; or

(b) a trailer mentioned in [paragraph (b), (bb) (bc), (c), (d), (e), (f) or (g) of regulation 16(3)].

NOTES
Amendment Para (2)(b): words in square brackets substituted by SI 1996/3033.

[421]

88 *(Revoked by SI 1998/2429.)*

Leaving trailers at rest

89 No person in charge of a motor vehicle, or trailer drawn thereby, shall cause or permit such trailer to stand on a road when detached from the drawing vehicle unless one at least of the wheels of the trailer is (or, in the case of a track-laying trailer, its tracks are) prevented from revolving by the setting of [a parking brake] or the use of a chain, chock or other efficient device.

NOTES

Amendment Words in square brackets substituted by SI 1996/3033.

[422]

Passengers in trailers

90 (1) Save as provided in paragraph (2), no person shall use, or cause or permit to be used, on a road any trailer for the carriage of passengers for hire or reward.

(2) The provisions of paragraph (1) do not apply in respect of a wheeled trailer which is, or is carrying, a broken down motor vehicle if—

- (a) the trailer is drawn at a speed not exceeding 30mph; and
- (b) where the trailer is, or is carrying, a broken down bus, it is attached to the drawing vehicle by a rigid draw bar.

(3) Save as provided in paragraph (4), no person shall use, or cause or permit to be used, on a road a wheeled trailer in which any person is carried and which is a living van having either—

- (a) less than 4 wheels; or
- (b) 4 wheels consisting of two close-coupled wheels on each side.

(4) The provisions of paragraph (3) do not apply in respect of a trailer which is being tested by—

- (a) its manufacturer;
- (b) a person by whom it has been, or is being, repaired; or
- (c) a distributor of, or dealer in, trailers.

[423]

91 *(Revoked by the Road Traffic (Consequential Provisions) Act 1988, s 3, Sch 1, Pt II.)*

Attachment of sidecars

92 Every sidecar fitted to a motor cycle shall be so attached that the wheel thereof is not wholly outside the space between transverse planes passing through the extreme projecting points at the front and at the rear of the motor cycle.

[424]

Use of sidecars

93 No person shall use or cause or permit to be used on a road any two-wheeled motor cycle registered on or after 1st August 1981, not being a motor cycle brought temporarily into Great Britain by a person resident abroad, if there is a sidecar attached to the right (or off) side of the motor cycle.

[425]

[CA—Use of Motor Vehicles for the Carriage or Haulage of Dangerous Goods

Additional braking requirements for motor vehicles carrying or hauling dangerous goods

93A (1) Subject to paragraph (5), no person shall use or cause or permit to be used a motor vehicle for the carriage or haulage of dangerous goods on a road if it is a vehicle within the meaning of the Framework Directive and—

- (a) its maximum gross weight exceeds 16,000 kg; or
- (b) it is drawing a trailer which has a maximum total design axle weight exceeding 10,000 kg,

unless the vehicle meets the requirements of paragraph (2).

(2) Subject to paragraph (6), in order for a motor vehicle to meet the requirements of this paragraph—

(a) it must not be drawing more than one trailer;
(b) without prejudice to regulation 15, it must be fitted with an anti-lock braking system that meets the requirements of paragraph (1) of marginal 220 521 of Appendix B.2 to Annex B to the ADR;
(c) it must be fitted with an endurance braking system (which may consist of one device or a combination of several devices) that meets the requirements of sub-paragraphs (a) to (d) of paragraph (2) of marginal 220 522 of Appendix B.2 to Annex B to the ADR;
(d) if it is not drawing a trailer, it must meet the requirements of the 4th, 5th, 6th and 7th sub-paragraphs of paragraph (2) of marginal 10 221 of Annex B to the ADR;
(e) without prejudice to regulation 15, if it is drawing a trailer with a maximum total design axle weight exceeding 10,000 kg—
  (i) the trailer must be fitted with an anti-lock braking system that meets the requirements of paragraph (2) of marginal 220 521 of Appendix B.2 to Annex B to the ADR, and
  (ii) the electrical connections between the motor vehicle and the trailer must meet the requirements of paragraph (3) of marginal 220 521 of Appendix B.2 to Annex B to the ADR;
(f) if it is drawing a trailer, the combination of vehicles must meet the requirements of the 4th, 5th, 6th and 7th sub-paragraphs of paragraph (2) of marginal 10 221 of Annex B to the ADR;
(g) if it is drawing a trailer fitted with an endurance braking system, the trailer must meet the requirements of paragraph (3) of marginal 220 522 of Appendix B.2 to Annex B to the ADR; and
(h) if it is drawing a trailer, the requirements of either paragraph (3) or (4) must be met.

(3) The requirements of this paragraph are that the motor vehicle meets the requirements of paragraph (2)(e) of marginal 220 522 of Appendix B.2 to Annex B to the ADR.

(4) The requirements of this paragraph are that the motor vehicle—
(a) does not contravene the restriction mentioned in sub-paragraph (f) of paragraph (2) of marginal 220 522 of Appendix B.2 to Annex B to the ADR; and
(b) meets the requirements of the second sentence of that sub-paragraph in relation to the trailer.

(5) Paragraph (1) does not apply to a motor vehicle manufactured before 1st January 1997.

(6) Sub-paragraph (e) of paragraph (2) does not apply to a trailer manufactured before 1st January 1997.

(7) For the purposes of this regulation, Annex B to the ADR (including the Appendices to that Annex) shall have effect as if—
(a) references to ECE Regulation 13 (however expressed) were references to ECE Regulation 13.06 or 13.07;
(b) references to Directive 71/320/EEC were references to Community Directive 91/422;
(c) references to the corresponding EEC Directive, in relation to Annex 5 to ECE Regulation 13, were references to paragraph 1.5 of Annex II to Community Directive 91/422.

(8) Subject to paragraph (9), a reference in this regulation to dangerous goods is a reference to a load comprising explosives of such type and in such quantity that it could not be carried by road in a single transport unit of Type I and II without there being a contravention of the restrictions set out in marginal 11 401 of Annex B to the ADR as read with marginal 11 402 of that Annex.

(9) For the purposes of paragraph (8)—
(a) marginal 11 402 of Annex B to the ADR shall have effect with the omission of the words "in conformity with the prohibitions of mixed loading contained in 11 403"; and
(b) "transport unit of Type I or II" means a transport unit of Type I or a transport unit of Type II as defined in marginal 11 204 of that Annex.

(10) In this regulation, "ADR" means the 1995 edition of the "European Agreement concerning the International Carriage of Dangerous Goods by Road (ADR)" produced by [the Department for Transport] and published by Her Majesty's Stationery Office (ISBN 0-11-551265-9).]

NOTES

Amendment Inserted, together with immediately preceding cross-heading, by SI 1996/3133.
Para (10): words in square brackets substituted by virtue of SI 1997/2971, 2001/2568, 2002/2626.
ADR The 2007 ADR has now been published and is available in book form from The Stationery Office. The ISBN number is 9211391121 (9789211391121).
Exemptions See reg 4(4).
Directive 71/320/EEC; Community Directive 91/422 OJ L202, 06.09.1971, p 37; OJ L233, 22.08.1991, p 21.

[426]

D—Use of Gas Propulsion Systems and Gas-Fired Appliances

Use of gas propulsion systems

94 (1) No person shall use, or cause or permit to be used, on a road a vehicle with a gas propulsion system unless the whole of such system is in a safe condition.

(2) No person shall use, or cause or permit to be used, in any gas supply system for the propulsion of a vehicle when the vehicle is on a road any fuel except liquefied petroleum gas.

(3) No person shall use, or cause or permit to be used, on a road a vehicle which is propelled by gas unless the gas container in which such fuel is stored is on the motor vehicle, and not on any trailer, and in the case of an articulated vehicle on the portion of the vehicle to which the engine is fitted.

(4) In this regulation and in regulation 95 "liquefied petroleum gas" means—

- (a) butane gas in any phase which meets the requirements contained in the specification of commercial butane and propane issued by the British Standards Institution under the number BS 4250: 1975 and published on 29th August 1975; or
- (b) propane gas in any phase which meets the requirements contained in the said specification; or
- (c) any mixture of such butane gas and such propane gas.

[427]

Use of gas-fired appliances—general

95 (1) No person shall use, or cause or permit to be used, in or on a vehicle on a road any gas-fired appliance unless the whole of such appliance and the gas system attached thereto is in an efficient and safe condition.

(2) No person shall use, or cause or permit to be used, in any gas-fired appliance in or on a vehicle on a road any fuel except liquefied petroleum gas as defined in regulation 94(4).

(3) No person shall use, or cause or permit to be used, in or on a vehicle on a road any gas-fired appliance unless the vehicle is so ventilated that—

- (a) an ample supply of air is available for the operation of the appliance;
- (b) the use of the appliance does not adversely affect the health or comfort of any person using the vehicle; and
- (c) any unburnt gas is safely disposed of to the outside of the vehicle.

(4) No person shall use, or cause or permit to be used, on a road a vehicle in or on which there is—

- (a) one gas-fired appliance unless the gas-supply for such appliance is shut off at the point where it leaves the container or containers at all times when the appliance is not in use;
- (b) more than one gas-fired appliance each of which has the same supply of gas unless the gas supply for such appliances is shut off at the point where it leaves the container or containers at all times when none of such appliances is in use; or
- (c) more than one gas-fired appliance each of which does not have the same supply of gas unless each gas supply for such appliances is shut off at the

point where it leaves the container or containers at all times when none of such appliances which it supplies is in use.

[428]

Use of gas-fired appliances when a vehicle is in motion

96 (1) Subject to paragraph (2), this regulation applies to every motor vehicle and trailer.

(2) Paragraphs (3) and (4) do not apply to a vehicle constructed or adapted for the conveyance of goods under controlled temperatures.

(3) No person shall use, or cause or permit to be used, in any vehicle to which this paragraph applies, while the vehicle is in motion on a road, any gas-fired appliance except—

(a) a gas-fired appliance which is fitted to engineering plant while the plant is being used for the purposes of the engineering operations for which it was designed;

(b) a gas-fired appliance which is permanently attached to a bus, provided that any appliance for heating or cooling the interior of the bus for the comfort of the driver and any passengers does not expose a naked flame on the outside of the appliance; or

(c) in any other vehicle, a refrigerating appliance or an appliance which does not expose a naked flame on the outside of the appliance and which is permanently attached to the vehicle and designed for the purpose of heating any part of the interior of the vehicle for the comfort of the driver and any passengers.

(4) No person shall use, or cause or permit to be used, in any vehicle to which this paragraph applies, while the vehicle is in motion on a road, any gas-fired appliance to which—

(a) sub-paragraph (3)(a) refers, unless the appliance complies with the requirements specified in paragraphs 12 and 13 of Schedule 5 and the gas system to which it is attached complies with the requirements specified in paragraphs 2 to 9 and 15 of Schedule 5; or

(b) sub-paragraph (3)(b) refers, unless the appliance complies with the requirements specified in paragraphs 12, 13 and 14 of Schedule 5 and the gas system to which it is attached complies with the requirements specified in paragraphs 2 to 9, 11 and 15 of Schedule 5; or

(c) sub-paragraph (3)(c) refers, unless the appliance complies—

(i) if it is fitted to a motor vehicle, with the requirements specified in paragraphs 12, 13 and 14 of Schedule 5; and

(ii) in any other case, with the requirements specified in paragraphs 12 and 13 of Schedule 5;

and the gas system to which the appliance is attached complies with the requirements specified in paragraphs 2 to 9 and 15 of Schedule 5.

(5) No person shall use, or cause or permit to be used, in a vehicle to which this regulation applies which is in motion on a road any gas-fired appliance unless it is fitted with a valve which stops the supply of gas to the appliance if the appliance fails to perform its function and causes gas to be emitted.

[429]

E—Control of Noise

Avoidance of excessive noise

97 No motor vehicle shall be used on a road in such manner as to cause any excessive noise which could have been avoided by the exercise of reasonable care on the part of the driver.

[430]

Stopping of engine when stationary

98 (1) Save as provided in paragraph (2), the driver of a vehicle shall, when the vehicle is stationary, stop the action of any machinery attached to or forming part of the vehicle so far as may be necessary for the prevention of noise [or of exhaust emissions].

(2) The provisions of paragraph (1) do not apply—

(a) when the vehicle is stationary owing to the necessities of traffic;

(b) so as to prevent the examination or working of the machinery where the examination is necessitated by any failure or derangement of the machinery or where the machinery is required to be worked for a purpose other than driving the vehicle; or

(c) in respect of a vehicle propelled by gas produced in plant carried on the vehicle, to such plant.

NOTES

Amendment Para (1): words in square brackets inserted by SI 1998/1.

[431]

Use of audible warning instruments

99 (1) Subject to the following paragraphs, no person shall sound, or cause or permit to be sounded, any horn, gong, bell or siren fitted to or carried on a vehicle which is—

(a) stationary on a road, at any time, other than at times of danger due to another moving vehicle on or near the road; or

(b) in motion on a restricted road, between 23.30 hours and 07.00 hours in the following morning.

(2) The provisions of paragraph (1)(a) do not apply in respect of the sounding of a reversing alarm when the vehicle to which it is fitted is about to move backwards and its engine is running [or in respect of the sounding of a boarding aid alarm].

(3) No person shall sound, or cause or permit to be sounded, on a road any reversing alarm [or any boarding aid alarm] fitted to a vehicle—

(a) unless the vehicle is a goods vehicle which has a maximum gross weight not less than 2000 kg, a bus, engineering plant, [a refuse vehicle,] or a works truck; or

(b) if the sound of the alarm is likely to be confused with a sound emitted in the operation of a pedestrian crossing established, or having effect as if established, under Part III of the 1984 Act.

(4) Subject to the provisions of the following paragraphs, no person shall sound, or cause or permit to be sounded a gong, bell, siren or two-tone horn, fitted to or otherwise carried on a vehicle (whether it is stationary or not).

(5) Nothing in paragraph (1) or (4) shall prevent the sounding of—

(a) an instrument or apparatus fitted to, or otherwise carried on, a vehicle at a time when the vehicle is being used for one of the purposes specified in regulation 37(5) and it is necessary or desirable to do so either to indicate to other road users the urgency of the purposes for which the vehicle is being used, or to warn other road users of the presence of the vehicle on the road; or

(b) a horn (not being a two-tone horn), bell, gong or siren—

(i) to raise alarm as to the theft or attempted theft of the vehicle or its contents; or

(ii) in the case of a bus, to summon help for the driver, the conductor or an inspector.

(6) Subject to the provisions of section 62 of the Control of Pollution Act 1974 and notwithstanding the provisions of paragraphs (1) and (4) above, a person may, between 12.00 hours and 19.00 hours, sound or cause or permit to be sounded an instrument or apparatus, other than a two-tone horn, fitted to or otherwise carried on a vehicle, being an instrument or apparatus designed to emit a sound for the purpose of informing members of the public that the vehicle is conveying goods for sale, if, when the apparatus or instrument is sounded, it is sounded only for that purpose.

(7) For the purposes of this regulation the expressions which are referred to in regulation 37(10) have the meanings there given to them and the expression "restricted road" in paragraph (1) means a road which is a restricted road for the purpose of section 81 of the 1984 Act.

NOTES

Amendment Para (2): words in square brackets inserted by SI 2000/1971.
Para (3): words in square brackets inserted by SI 2000/1971.

Para (3)(a): words in square brackets inserted by SI 1987/676.
Exemptions See reg 4(4).

[432]

F—Avoidance of Danger

Maintenance and use of vehicle so as not to be a danger, etc

100 (1) A motor vehicle, every trailer drawn thereby and all parts and accessories of such vehicle and trailer shall at all times be in such condition, and the number of passengers carried by such vehicle or trailer, the manner in which any passengers are carried in or on such vehicle or trailer, and the weight, distribution, packing and adjustment of the load of such vehicle or trailer shall at all times be such, that no danger is caused or is likely to be caused to any person in or on the vehicle or trailer or on a road.

Provided that the provisions of this regulation with regard to the number of passengers carried shall not apply to a vehicle to which the Public Service Vehicles (Carrying Capacity) Regulations 1984 apply.

(2) The load carried by a motor vehicle or trailer shall at all times be so secured, if necessary by physical restraint other than its own weight, and be in such a position, that neither danger nor nuisance is likely to be caused to any person or property by reason of the load or any part thereof falling or being blown from the vehicle or by reason of any other movement of the load or any part thereof in relation to the vehicle.

(3) No motor vehicle or trailer shall be used for any purpose for which it is so unsuitable as to cause or be likely to cause danger or nuisance to any person in or on the vehicle or trailer or on a road.

NOTES
Exemptions See reg 4(4).
Public Service Vehicles (Carrying Capacity) Regulations 1984 SI 1984/1406.
Cases relating to this regulation *British Road Services Ltd v Owen* [1971] 2 All ER 999, [1971] RTR 372;
Dickson v Brown 1959 JC 19, 1959 SLT 207;
Gifford v Whittaker [1942] 1 KB 501, [1942] 1 All ER 604;
Madden v Quirk [1989] 1 WLR 702, [1989] RTR 304;
O'Neill v Brown [1961] 1 QB 420, [1961] 1 All ER 571;
Rushton v Martin [1952] WN 258, 96 Sol Jo 345;
Tan Chye Choo v Chong Kew Moi [1970] 1 All ER 266, [1970] 1 WLR 147.

[433]

[100A (1) No person shall use, or cause or permit to be used, on a road a vehicle displaying the rectangular plate described in the definition of "low platform trailer" in the Table in regulation 3(2) or anything resembling such a plate at a speed exceeding 40 mph.

(2) No person shall use, or cause or permit to be used on a road a vehicle displaying the rectangular plate described in Schedule 13 (Plate for restricted speed vehicle) or anything resembling such a plate at a speed exceeding 50 mph.]

NOTES
Amendment Inserted by SI 1990/1981.

[434]

Parking in darkness

101 (1) Save as provided in paragraph (2) no person shall, except with the permission of a police officer in a uniform, cause or permit any motor vehicle to stand on a road at any time between … sunset and … sunrise unless the near side of the vehicle is as close as may be to the edge of the carriageway.

(2) The provisions of paragraph (1) do not apply in respect of any motor vehicle—

(a) being used for fire brigade [or, in England, fire and rescue authority], ambulance or police purposes or for defence purposes (including civil defence purposes) if compliance with those provisions would hinder or be likely to hinder the use of the vehicle for the purpose for which it is being used on that occasion;

(b) being used in connection with—

(i) any building operation or demolition;
(ii) the repair of any other vehicle;
(iii) the removal of any obstruction to traffic;
(iv) the maintenance, repair or reconstruction of any road; or
(v) the laying, erection, alteration or repair in or near to any road of any sewer, main, pipe or apparatus for the supply of gas, water or electricity, of any [electronic communications apparatus] as defined in Schedule 2 to the Telecommunication Act 1984 or of the apparatus of any electric transport undertaking,

if, in any such case, compliance with those provisions would hinder or be likely to hinder the use of the vehicle for the purpose for which it is being used on that occasion;

(c) on any road in which vehicles are allowed to proceed in one direction only;
(d) standing on a part of a road set aside for the parking of vehicles or as a stand for hackney carriages or as a stand for buses or as a place at which such vehicles may stop for a longer time than is necessary for the taking up and setting down of passengers where compliance with those provisions would conflict with the provisions of any order, regulations or byelaws governing the use of such part of a road for that purpose; or
(e) waiting to set down or pick up passengers in accordance with regulations made or directions given by a chief officer of police in regard to such setting down or picking up.

NOTES

Amendment Para (1): words omitted revoked by SI 1991/2125.
Para (2)(a): words in square brackets inserted by SI 2004/3168 (in relation to England only); in relation to Wales, words "or, in England or Wales, fire and rescue authority" inserted by SI 2005/2929.
Para (2)(b)(v): words in square brackets substituted by SI 2003/2155.
Telecommunication Act 1984, Sch 2 It is thought that this is intended to be a reference to Sch 2 to the Telecommunications Act 1984. As to the definition "electronic communications apparatus", see para 1(1) of Sch 2 to the 1984 Act.

[435]

Passengers on motor cycles

102 If any person in addition to the driver is carried astride a two-wheeled motor cycle on a road (whether a sidecar is attached to it or not) suitable supports or rests for the feet shall be available on the motor cycle for that person.

[436]

Obstruction

103 No person in charge of a motor vehicle or trailer shall cause or permit the vehicle to stand on a road so as to cause any unnecessary obstruction of the road.

NOTES

Cases relating to this regulation *Bryant v Marx* [1932] All ER Rep 518, (1932) 48 TLR 624;
Dunn v Holt (1904) 2 LGR 502, 68 JP 271;
Ellis v Smith [1962] 3 All ER 954, [1962] 1 WLR 1486;
Gill v Carson and Nield [1917] 2 KB 674, 15 LGR 567;
Hinde v Evans (1906) 4 LGR 1152, 70 JP 548;
Solomon v Durbridge (1956) 120 JP 231;
Worth v Brooks [1959] Crim LR 855;
WR Anderson (Motors) Ltd v Hargreaves [1962] 1 QB 425, [1962] 1 All ER 129.

[437]

Driver's control

104 No person shall drive or cause or permit any other person to drive, a motor vehicle on a road if he is in such a position that he cannot have proper control of the vehicle or have a full view of the road and traffic ahead.

NOTES

Cases relating to this regulation *Wallace v Major* [1946] KB 473, [1946] 2 All ER 87.

[438]

Opening of doors

105 No person shall open, or cause or permit to be opened, any door of a vehicle on a road so as to injure or endanger any person.

[439]

Reversing

106 No person shall drive, or cause or permit to be driven, a motor vehicle backwards on a road further than may be requisite for the safety or reasonable convenience of the occupants of the vehicle or other traffic, unless it is a road roller or is engaged in the construction, maintenance or repair of the road.

[440]

Leaving motor vehicles unattended

107 (1) Save as provided in paragraph (2), no person shall leave, or cause or permit to be left, on a road a motor vehicle which is not attended by a person licensed to drive it unless the engine is stopped and any parking brake with which the vehicle is required to be equipped is effectively set.

(2) The requirement specified in paragraph (1) as to the stopping of the engine shall not apply in respect of a vehicle—

- (a) being used for ambulance, fire brigade [or, in England, fire and rescue authority] or police purposes; or
- (b) in such a position and condition as not to be likely to endanger any person or property and engaged in an operation which requires its engine to be used to—
  - (i) drive machinery forming part of, or mounted on, the vehicle and used for purposes other than driving the vehicle; or
  - (ii) maintain the electrical power of the batteries of the vehicle at a level required for driving that machinery or apparatus.

(3) In this regulation "parking brake" means a brake fitted to a vehicle in accordance with requirement 16 or 18 in Schedule 3.

NOTES

Amendment Para (2)(a): words in square brackets inserted by SI 2004/3168 (in relation to England only); in relation to Wales, words "or, in England or Wales, fire and rescue authority" inserted by SI 2005/2929.

[441]

Securing of suspended implements

108 Where a vehicle is fitted with any apparatus or appliance designed for lifting and part of the apparatus or appliance consists of a suspended implement, the implement shall at all times while the vehicle is in motion on a road and when the implement is not attached to any load supported by the appliance or apparatus be so secured either to the appliance or apparatus or to some part of the vehicle that no danger is caused or is likely to be caused to any person on the vehicle or on the road.

[442]

Television sets

109 (1) No person shall drive, or cause or permit to be driven, a motor vehicle on a road, if the driver is in such a position as to be able to see, whether directly or by reflection, a television receiving apparatus or other cinematographic apparatus used to display anything other than information—

- (a) about the state of the vehicle or its equipment;
- (b) about the location of the vehicle and the road on which it is located;
- (c) to assist the driver to see the road adjacent to the vehicle; or
- (d) to assist the driver to reach his destination.

(2) In this regulation "television receiving apparatus" means any cathode ray tube carried on a vehicle and on which there can be displayed an image derived from a television broadcast, a recording or a camera or computer.

[443]

[Mobile telephones

110 (1) No person shall drive a motor vehicle on a road if he is using—

(a) a hand-held mobile telephone; or

(b) a hand-held device of a kind specified in paragraph (4).

(2) No person shall cause or permit any other person to drive a motor vehicle on a road while that other person is using—

(a) a hand-held mobile telephone; or

(b) a hand-held device of a kind specified in paragraph (4).

(3) No person shall supervise a holder of a provisional licence if the person supervising is using—

(a) a hand-held mobile telephone; or

(b) a hand-held device of a kind specified in paragraph (4),

at a time when the provisional licence holder is driving a motor vehicle on a road.

(4) A device referred to in paragraphs (1)(b), (2)(b) and (3)(b) is a device, other than a two-way radio, which performs an interactive communication function by transmitting and receiving data.

(5) A person does not contravene a provision of this regulation if, at the time of the alleged contravention—

(a) he is using the telephone or other device to call the police, fire, ambulance or other emergency service on 112 or 999;

(b) he is acting in response to a genuine emergency; and

(c) it is unsafe or impracticable for him to cease driving in order to make the call (or, in the case of an alleged contravention of paragraph (3)(b), for the provisional licence holder to cease driving while the call was being made).

(6) For the purposes of this regulation—

(a) a mobile telephone or other device is to be treated as hand-held if it is, or must be, held at some point during the course of making or receiving a call or performing any other interactive communication function;

(b) a person supervises the holder of a provisional licence if he does so pursuant to a condition imposed on that licence holder prescribed under section 97(3)(a) of the Road Traffic Act 1988 (grant of provisional licence);

(c) "interactive communication function" includes the following:

(i) sending or receiving oral or written messages;

(ii) sending or receiving facsimile documents;

(iii) sending or receiving still or moving images; and

(iv) providing access to the internet;

(d) "two-way radio" means any wireless telegraphy apparatus which is designed or adapted—

(i) for the purpose of transmitting and receiving spoken messages; and

(ii) to operate on any frequency other than 880 MHz to 915 MHz, 925 MHz to 960 MHz, 1710 MHz to 1785 MHz, 1805 MHz to 1880 MHz, 1900 MHz to 1980 MHz or 2110 MHz to 2170 MHz; and

(e) "wireless telegraphy" has the same meaning as in section 19(1) of the Wireless Telegraphy Act 1949.]

NOTES

Amendment Inserted by SI 2003/2695.

Wireless Telegraphy Act 1949, s 19(1) Repealed by the Wireless Telegraphy Act 2006, s 125(1), Sch 9, Pt 1; for the meaning of "wireless telegraphy" in that Act, see s 116 thereof.

[444]

SCHEDULES 1–13

NOTES

The Schedules to these regulations are not printed in this work, but are as follows:

Sch 1 This Schedule specifies the following regulations revoked by reg 2: the Motor Vehicles (Construction and Use) (Track Laying Vehicles) Regulations 1955, SI 1955/990, and the amending SI 1957/439, SI 1957/972, SI 1959/2053, SI 1984/817, 1811; and the Motor Vehicles (Construction and Use) Regulations 1978, SI 1978/1017, and the amending SI 1978/1233, SI 1978/1235,

SI 1978/1263, SI 1978/1317, SI 1979/138, SI 1979/843, SI 1979/1062, SI 1980/139, SI 1980/140, SI 1980/289, SI 1980/610, SI 1980/880, SI 1980/1166, SI 1980/1789, SI 1981/261, SI 1981/697, SI 1981/915, SI 1981/1189, SI 1981/1580, SI 1981/1663, SI 1981/1688, SI 1982/1057, SI 1982/1132, SI 1982/1223, SI 1982/1272, SI 1982/1422, SI 1982/1480, SI 1982/1576, SI 1983/112, SI 1983/471, SI 1983/932, SI 1984/195, SI 1984/331, SI 1984/386, SI 1984/679, SI 1984/813, SI 1984/1543, SI 1984/1809, SI 1985/91, SI 1985/730, SI 1985/1363, SI 1985/2039, SI 1985/2051.

Sch 2 This Schedule gives particulars of the Community Directives and ECE Regulations referred to in these regulations (see the definitions "Community Directive" and "ECE Regulation" in reg 3) (amended by SI 1987/676, SI 1988/1178, SI 1988/1524, SI 1989/1478, SI 1989/1695, SI 1989/1865, SI 1990/1131, SI 1990/1981, SI 1991/2003, SI 1991/2710, SI 1992/352, SI 1992/646, SI 1992/2016, SI 1992/2137, SI 1992/3088, SI 1993/1946, SI 1993/2199, SI 1994/14, SI 1994/3270, SI 1995/551, SI 1995/2210, SI 1996/2064, SI 1996/2329, SI 1996/3033, SI 1996/3133, SI 1998/1188, SI 1998/1281, SI 1998/2429, SI 2000/3197, SI 2001/1043, SI 2001/1825, SI 2001/3208, SI 2002/1474, SI 2002/2126, SI 2003/1690, SI 2005/3165, SI 2006/2565, SI 2007/3132, SI 2009/142, SI 2009/2196).

Sch 2A This Schedule, mentioned in reg 3A, sets out modifications to these regulations in relation to vehicles in respect of which a minister's approval certificate has been issued by virtue of SI 2001/25 (formerly SI 1996/3013 (revoked)) (inserted by SI 1996/3017; amended by SI 2000/3197, SI 2009/2196).

Sch 3 This Schedule sets out the braking requirements referred to in reg 16(4) (amended by SI 1987/676, SI 1990/1981, SI 1992/352, SI 1995/551, SI 2001/3208).

Sch 3A This Schedule excludes certain vehicles from the application of reg 39A (inserted by SI 1988/1524; amended by SI 1990/1131).

Sch 3B This Schedule relates to authorised sealers, i e persons or bodies authorised to seal speed limiters for the purposes of reg 36A or 36B (see reg 36C) (inserted by SI 1992/422; amended by SI 2003/1946, SI 2003/2096, SI 2007/1898, SI 2007/3132).

Sch 4 This Schedule contains provisions to be complied with under reg 40 where vehicles or trailers are fitted with gas containers.

Sch 5 This Schedule contains provisions to be complied with under regs 40, 96 relating to gas systems for vehicles or trailers (amended by SI 2003/1690).

Sch 6 This Schedule sets out the requirements referred to in reg 41 for the construction of minibuses.

Sch 7 This Schedule specifies types of fire extinguishing apparatus to be carried on minibuses under reg 42, and lists the items of first aid equipment to be carried on minibuses under reg 43 (amended by SI 1989/2360).

Sch 7XA This Schedule sets out modifications to regs 55A, 61 in relation to end of series vehicles (inserted by SI 1996/2329; amended by SI 2000/3197, SI 2006/2565, SI 2007/361, SI 2007/2544, SI 2009/2196).

Sch 7A This Schedule sets out the requirements referred to in regs 57, 57A, 57B for the construction of motor cycles (inserted by SI 1994/14).

Sch 7B This Schedule sets out provisions relating to emissions from certain motor vehicles for the purposes of reg 61(10AA), (10AB), (10BA) (inserted by SI 1995/2210; amended by SI 1996/2085, SI 1997/1544, SI 1998/1563, SI 2000/1434, SI 2001/1825, SI 2002/227, SI 2002/1474, SI 2003/1690, SI 2003/3145, SI 2009/1806).

Sch 8 This Schedule specifies for the purpose of reg 66 particulars to be shown on plates for motor vehicles (including motor vehicles forming part of articulated vehicles) and for trailers (including trailers forming part of articulated vehicles), and contains further provisions relating to plates to be complied with (amended by SI 1990/1131, SI 1991/1526, SI 2001/306).

Sch 9 This Schedule specifies for the purpose of reg 69 provisions to be complied with relating to plates for motor cycles.

Sch 10 This Schedule sets out the form of Ministry plate (see reg 70) issued for a goods vehicle following the issue of a plating certificate.

Sch 10A This Schedule sets out an alternative form of Ministry plate (see reg 70) (inserted by SI 1987/676).

Sch 10B This Schedule sets out another alternative form of Ministry plate (see reg 70) (inserted by SI 1994/329).

Sch 10C This Schedule sets out another alternative form of Ministry plate (see reg 70) (inserted by SI 1994/329).

Sch 11 This Schedule specifies maximum permitted laden weights for trailers and heavy motor cars and motor cars not fitted with road friendly suspension, in each case not forming part of an articulated vehicle (see reg 75), maximum permitted gross weights for heavy cars and motor cars if the driving axles are fitted with road friendly suspension and in each case not forming part of an articulated vehicle (see reg 75), maximum permitted laden weights for heavy motor cars and motor cars forming part of articulated vehicles (see reg 75), maximum permitted laden weight of articulated vehicles (see reg 77), vehicles with two closely-spaced axles (see reg 79(2)), and vehicles with three closely-spaced axles (see reg 79(3)) (amended by SI 1987/676, SI 1988/1287, SI 1992/2016, SI 1994/329).

Sch 11A This Schedule provides for exemptions relating to combined transport operations (see regs 76(1A), 77(2A), 80(2C)) (inserted by SI 1994/329; amended by SI 1997/1096, SI 1998/3112).

Sch 12 This Schedule sets out conditions to be complied with in relation to the use of vehicles carrying wide or long loads or vehicles carrying loads or having fixed appliances or apparatus which project (see regs 81, 82) (amended by SI 1991/2125).

Sch 13 This Schedule sets out the plate for restricted speed vehicles (see reg 3(2)) (inserted by SI 1990/1981).

[445]

LONDON TAXIS (LICENSING APPEALS) REGULATIONS 1986 SI 1986/1188

Authority Made by the Secretary of State for Transport under the Transport Act 1985, s 17(2), (5). As to the amendment of s 17 of the 1985 Act, see the note "Summary" below.
Date made 10 July 1986.
Commencement 1 August 1986.
Summary These regulations provide that the prescribed period for the purposes of the Transport Act 1985, s 17(2), (5) in relation to reconsideration of, or appeals against, decisions relating to taxi licences, is 28 days from the date of the written notice of decision of the licensing authority. S 17(2), (5) of the 1985 Act have been amended by the Greater London Authority Act 1999, s 253, Sch 20, para 8(1), (3)(a) so as to refer to "designated period" instead of "prescribed period". By s 17(10) of the 1985 Act, as amended by para 8(1), (3)(b) of Sch 20 to the 1999 Act, "designated period" means such period as may be specified by London cab order made by Transport for London. However, para 17(2) of Sch 20 to the 1999 Act provides that any regulations prescribing a period for the purposes of s 17(2), (5) of the 1985 Act and in force immediately before para 8 of Sch 20 comes into force (3 July 2000; see SI 2000/801, in the title Local Government) are to continue in force until such time as a period is specified by London cab order and have effect as if the period prescribed were the period specified by London cab order.

[446]

FIXED PENALTY (PROCEDURE) REGULATIONS 1986 SI 1986/1330

Authority Made by the Home Secretary under the Transport Act 1982, ss 49(1), 73(5) (repealed). Now have effect under the Road Traffic Offenders Act 1988, s 84, by virtue of the Road Traffic (Consequential Provisions) Act 1988, s 2(2).
Date made 29 July 1986.
Commencement 1 October 1986; see reg 1(1).
Amendment Printed as amended by SI 2001/926, SI 2005/617, SI 2009/494.
Application of regulations These regulations are applied with modifications to Crown roads in the Royal Parks by SI 1987/363, in the title Open Spaces and National Heritage.
General See the Preliminary Note "Penalties" (under the main head "Road traffic"). These regulations do not apply to fixed penalty notices issued by a vehicle examiner (see reg 1(4)), as to which, see SI 2009/495.

[447]

1 (1) These Regulations may be cited as the Fixed Penalty (Procedure) Regulations 1986 and shall come into operation on 1st October 1986.

(2) In these Regulations any reference to a section is a reference to a section of the Transport Act 1982.

(3) These Regulations do not extend to Scotland.

[(4) These Regulations shall not apply if the fixed penalty notice is given or affixed by a vehicle examiner in accordance with the Road Traffic Offenders Act 1988.]

NOTES

Amendment Para (4): inserted by SI 2009/494.
Transport Act 1982 The relevant provisions of this Act have been repealed by the Road Traffic (Consequential Provisions) Act 1988, s 3(1), Sch 1, Pt I, and consolidated in the Road Traffic Offenders Act 1988, Pt III (ss 51–90, Schs 3, 4).

[448]

2 (1) Subject to paragraph (2) below, in the documents described in column 1 of the Schedule to these Regulations and referred to in the provisions of the Act specified in column 2 of the Schedule there shall be provided the information or, as the case may be, further information prescribed in column 3 of the Schedule.

(2) The information prescribed in the Schedule in relation to a fixed penalty notice need not be provided if the offender's driving licence [(if the offender holds a driving licence) or driving record (if the offender does not hold a driving licence)] would not be subject to endorsement on conviction of the offence in respect of which the notice was given.

NOTES

Amendment Para (2): words in square brackets inserted by SI 2009/494.

[449]

3 (1) A copy of any fixed penalty notice given or affixed under section 27 shall be forwarded by or on behalf of the constable or traffic warden giving or affixing the notice to the fixed penalty clerk unless the fixed penalty clerk has notified the chief officer of police that he does not wish to receive a copy of any such notice.

(2) Where a fixed penalty notice has been given to a person under section 27 and that person has surrendered his driving licence [(if held)] in accordance with that section the driving licence shall be forwarded by or on behalf of the constable to the fixed penalty clerk.

NOTES
Amendment Para (2): words in square brackets inserted by SI 2009/494.
S 27 Repealed; see now the Road Traffic Offenders Act 1988, ss 54, 62(1).

[450]

4 (1) Where a constable has issued a fixed penalty notice to a person under section 28(2), he shall send a notice indicating that fact to the chief officer of police together with that person's driving licence [(if that person is a holder of a licence which has been surrendered or delivered)].

(2) Subject to paragraph (3) below, on receipt of the documents referred to in paragraph (1) above the chief officer of police shall send the driving licence and a copy of the notice issued under section 28(1) to the fixed penalty clerk and notify him that a fixed penalty notice has been issued under section 28(2).

(3) The chief officer of police shall not send a copy of the notice issued under section 28(1) to the fixed penalty clerk under paragraph (2) above if the fixed penalty clerk has notified the chief officer of police that he does not wish to receive a copy of any such notice.

NOTES
Amendment Para (1): words in square brackets inserted by SI 2009/494.
S 28(1), (2) Repealed; see now the Road Traffic Offenders Act 1988, s 54.

[451]

5 (1) On receipt of the remittance in respect of a fixed penalty the fixed penalty clerk shall notify the chief officer of police that the remittance has been received.

(2) If payment of the fixed penalty is made by a person otherwise than as required by the fixed penalty notice the fixed penalty clerk shall return the remittance to that person.

(3) Where a remittance in respect of a fixed penalty is sent by a person to [the designated officer for a magistrates' court] who is not the fixed penalty clerk specified in the fixed penalty notice, the [designated officer] shall return the remittance to that person.

NOTES
Amendment Para (3): words in square brackets substituted by SI 2005/617.

[452]

6 Where—

(a) the suspended enforcement period has expired; and
(b) the fixed penalty has not been paid; and
(c) either the person to whom the fixed penalty notice was given has requested a hearing under section 30(2) or 31(3) or no registration certificate has been issued under section 36(2),

the chief officer of police shall notify the fixed penalty clerk accordingly and the fixed penalty clerk shall, where an endorsable offence is involved, return the driving licence to the person to whom the fixed penalty notice was given[, if that person holds a driving licence].

NOTES
Amendment Words in square brackets inserted by SI 2009/494.
Ss 30(2), 31(3), 36(2) Repealed; see now the Road Traffic Offenders Act 1988, ss 55(2), 63(3), 70(2) respectively.

[453]

7 Where—

(a) the suspended enforcement period has expired; and
(b) the fixed penalty has not been paid; and
(c) a registration certificate has been issued under section 36(2),

the chief officer of police shall notify the fixed penalty clerk accordingly.

NOTES

S 36(2) Repealed; see now the Road Traffic Offenders Act 1988, s 70(2).

[454]

8 Where in a case involving an endorsable offence any sum determined by reference to the fixed penalty is registered under section 36 for enforcement against the licence holder as a fine the [[designated officer] for] the court where the sum is registered shall notify the fixed penalty clerk … that the sum has been registered.

NOTES

Amendment Words in first (outer) pair of square brackets substituted by SI 2001/926; words in second (inner) pair substituted by SI 2005/617. Words omitted revoked by SI 2009/494.

S 36 Repealed; see now the Road Traffic Offenders Act 1988, s 71.

[455]

9 Where a fixed penalty notice is issued under section 27(1) or 28(2) the fixed penalty clerk shall not accept payment of the fixed penalty after the expiry of the suspended enforcement period.

NOTES

S 27(1) or 28(2) Repealed; see now the Road Traffic Offenders Act 1988, s 54(2) or 54(5).

[456]

10 Where a fixed penalty is paid within the suspended enforcement period the fixed penalty clerk shall send a receipt for the payment, if requested, to the payer.

[457]

11 For the purposes of section 35(3)(a) (which provides that a licence receipt issued by a constable is to cease to have effect on the expiration of the period of one month beginning with the date of issue) there shall be prescribed a longer period of two months beginning with the same date.

NOTES

S 35(3)(a) Repealed; see now the Road Traffic Offenders Act 1988, s 56(3)(a).

[458]

SCHEDULE
INFORMATION OR FURTHER INFORMATION TO BE PROVIDED IN CERTAIN DOCUMENTS MENTIONED IN PART III OF THE TRANSPORT ACT 1982

Regulation 2

Document	*Provision of Act*	*Information or further information to be provided*
1 Fixed penalty notice	Section 27(8)	(i) The name of the police force of which the constable giving the notice is a member.
		(ii) The serial number of the fixed penalty notice.
		(iii) Whether the notice relates to an endorsable offence.
		(iv) The name, date of birth and address of the person to whom the notice is given.
		(v) The date, time and place of the alleged offence.
		(vi) The details of the vehicle including the registration number.
		(vii) The documents, if any, to be produced at a police station and the period within which they must be produced.
		(viii) An explanation of the action to be taken by the driver where

Document	*Provision of Act*	*Information or further information to be provided*
		(a) he has not or (b) he has surrendered the licence[, if he holds such a licence]. (ix) The fact that the person to whom the notice is given may opt for trial. (x) The method of paying the fixed penalty. (xi) The name, rank and number of the constable issuing the fixed penalty notice. (xii) Guidance to the driver as to the legal consequences of a fixed penalty notice.
2 Receipt for driving licence	Section 35(1)	(i) Whether the driving licence [if the offender holds a driving licence] is full or provisional. (ii) The driver number as shown on the licence [if the offender holds a driving licence]. (iii) The groups of vehicles which the driver is entitled to drive. (iv) The expiry date of the licence [if the offender holds a driving licence]. (v) The duration of the validity of the licence [if the offender holds a driving licence] receipt. (vi) The method of obtaining a new receipt on the expiry of an old receipt. (vii) The name, rank and number of the constable issuing the fixed penalty notice.
3 Receipt for driving licence	Section 35(2)	(i) The date of issue of receipt. (ii) The code of the magistrates' court issuing receipt. (iii) The name, address and date of birth of driver. (iv) Whether the driving licence [if the offender holds a driving licence] is full or provisional. (v) The driver number as shown on the licence [if the offender holds a driving licence]. (vi) The groups of vehicles which the driver is entitled to drive. (vii) The expiry date of the licence [if the offender holds a driving licence]. (viii) The duration of the validity of the licence [if the offender holds a driving licence] receipt.
4 Registration certificate	Section 36	(i) The serial number and date, time and place of issue of the notice to owner, notice to hirer or fixed penalty notice (as case may be). (ii) The vehicle registration number. (iii) The driver number. (iv) The amount of the appropriate fixed penalty. (v) The sum to be registered in default of payment of the fixed penalty.
5 Notice requesting new statutory statement	Section 37(8)	(i) The particulars of the statutory declaration. (ii) The details of the alleged fixed penalty offence. (iii) A request to furnish a statutory statement of ownership.

Document	*Provision of Act*	*Information or further information to be provided*
		(iv) The period allowed for a response to the notice. (v) The consequence of providing, or, as the case may be, not providing the statutory statement of ownership
6 Statement of liability	Section 45(2)	(i) The name, date of birth and address of hirer. (ii) The duration of the hiring agreement.

NOTES

Amendment Item 1, column 3: in entry (viii), words in square brackets inserted by SI 2009/494; items 2, 3, column 3: words in square brackets inserted by SI 2009/494 (the Queen's Printer's copy of SI 2009/494 purports to amend column 1 of items 2 and 3, but that is understood to be a drafting error and the amendment should be to column 3 of those items.

Transport Act 1982, Pt III, ss 27(8), 35(1), (2), 36, 37(8), 45(2) Repealed; see now the Road Traffic Offenders Act 1988, Pt III, ss 52(1), 56(1), (2), 70, 73(4), 66(2) respectively.

[459]

TRANSPORT ACT 1985 (EXTENSION OF ELIGIBILITY FOR TRAVEL CONCESSIONS) ORDER 1986
SI 1986/1385

Authority Made by the Secretary of State for Transport and the Secretaries of State for Wales and Scotland under the Transport Act 1985, s 93(7)(f).

Date made 7 August 1986.

Commencement 1 September 1986.

Amendment Amended by SI 1989/2293 (itself partially revoked by the Transport Act 2000, s 274, Sch 31, Pt II) and partially revoked by s 274 of, and Pt II of Sch 31 to, the 2000 Act. Also amended and partially revoked in relation to Wales only by SI 2001/3765 (itself revoked by the Concessionary Bus Travel Act 2007, s 13(2), Sch 3).

Summary The Transport Act 1985, s 93 makes provision for travel concession schemes in relation to eligible services (local bus services). S 93(7) defines the classes of persons entitled to concessions under such schemes; these classes may be extended by order (see s 93(7)(f)). This order has largely been revoked, but in so far as it remains in force, art 3A(a) thereof (inserted in relation to Wales only by SI 2001/3765 (revoked)) specifies the following class of persons as eligible persons in Wales: persons to whom current statutory travel concession permits had been issued in accordance with the Transport Act 2000, s 145(2) by any travel concession authority in Wales, provided the permits were in such form as may be approved by the National Assembly for Wales (now the Welsh Ministers) for the purposes of s 145(1B) of that Act. The original s 145 of the 2000 Act has been replaced in relation to Wales by s 145B thereof (mandatory concessions), as inserted by the Concessionary Bus Travel Act 2007, s 13(1), Sch 2, paras 10, 11. In particular, the original s 145(1B), (2) of the 2000 Act have been replaced in relation to Wales by s 145B(2), (3) respectively of that Act.

It should be noted that art 3A(b) of this order (inserted by SI 2001/3765 (revoked)) specified as eligible persons in Wales, where a journey took place on or after 1 April 2003, persons over the age of 60 years other than those who already fell within s 93(7)(a) of the 1985 Act. However, SI 2001/3765 provided that art 3A(b) ceased to have effect and was revoked on the coming into force in relation to Wales of any amendment to the said s 93(7)(a) extending the classes of person eligible to receive travel concessions under a scheme under that section to anyone who had attained the age of 60 years. That amendment (by the Travel Concessions (Eligibility) Act 2002, s 1(1)) came into force on 1 April 2003 (see SI 2002/3014), on which date art 3A(b) of this order ceased to have effect.

[460]

LICENSED TAXIS (HIRING AT SEPARATE FARES) ORDER 1986
SI 1986/1386

Authority Made by the Secretary of State for Transport under the Transport Act 1985, s 13(1).

Date made 6 August 1986.

Commencement 3 September 1986.

Summary This order modifies the "taxi code", defined in the Transport Act 1985, s 13(3), in its application to taxis licensed under the Town Police Clauses Act 1847, s 37, while it is being used subject to the provisions of ss 10, 11 of the 1985 Act, which relate to the hiring of taxis at separate fares. The modifications are set out in art 4 and include the disapplication of certain provisions concerning oral touting, fares, byelaws and conditions attached to licences, obligatory hirings, the number of passengers to be carried and the hirer's consent to other passengers, the use of taxi meters and luggage required to be carried, and certain local matters.

London This order has no application to London taxis. In relation to the hiring of taxis at separate fares in London, see SI 1986/1387.

[461]

LICENSED TAXIS (HIRING AT SEPARATE FARES) (LONDON) ORDER 1986
SI 1986/1387

Authority Made by the Secretary of State for Transport under the Transport Act 1985, s 13(1).
Date made 6 August 1986.
Commencement 3 September 1986.
Summary This order modifies the "taxi code", defined in the Transport Act 1985, s 13(3), in its application to taxis licensed under the Metropolitan Public Carriage Act 1869, s 6 (London taxis) while being used subject to the provisions of ss 10, 11 of the 1985 Act, which relate to the hiring of taxis at separate fares. The modifications are the disapplication of:
(a) the London Hackney Carriage Act 1831, ss 35, 50;
(b) the London Hackney Carriage Act 1853, ss 7, 9, 10, 17(1), (2); and
(c) SR & O 1934/1346, arts 34, 38–50.

[462]

VEHICLE LICENCES (DURATION OF FIRST LICENCES AND RATE OF DUTY) ORDER 1986
SI 1986/1428

Authority Made by the Secretary of State for Transport under the Vehicles (Excise) Act 1971, s 2A (as set out in para 5 of Sch 7 thereto) (repealed). Now takes effect under the Vehicle Excise and Registration Act 1994, s 3(3), as read with s 4(4)–(6), by virtue of s 64 of, and para 2 of Sch 4 to, the 1994 Act.
Date made 20 August 1986.
Commencement 1 October 1986.
Amendment Amended by SI 1994/3095.
Summary This order makes provision for the first licences for mechanically propelled vehicles to run from specified dates during a month. Licences, other than temporary licences, may be taken out for any vehicle in respect of which duty is chargeable under the Vehicle Excise and Registration Act 1994, and such licences may run for a period of six or 12 months plus a further period commencing on the 10th, 17th or 24th day (as appropriate) of the months in which the licence first has effect. The rate of duty is the same as that for a licence for six or 12 months plus an additional amount in respect of the further period.

[463]

DRIVERS' HOURS (HARMONISATION WITH COMMUNITY RULES) REGULATIONS 1986
SI 1986/1458

Authority Made by the Secretary of State for Transport under the Transport Act 1968, s 95(1), (1A).
Date made 22 August 1986.
Commencement 29 September 1986.
Summary These regulations revoke and replace the Drivers' Hours (Harmonisation with Community Rules) Regulations 1978, SI 1978/1157, and modify the application of the Transport Act 1968, Pt VI, which relates to permitted driving hours and periods of duty, to take account of the operation of Regulation (EC) 561/2006 of the European Parliament and of the Council on the harmonisation of certain social legislation relating to road transport (OJ L102, 11.04.2006, p 1) (which repealed and replaced Council Regulation (EEC) 3820/85 (OJ L370, 31.12.1985, p 1)). The effect of the modification is to provide that, subject to certain conditions, the domestic driver's hours code (as defined in s 96(13) of the 1968 Act) does not apply in relation to any Community driving or work of a driver of a vehicle to which Pt VI of the 1968 Act applies.

[464]

DRIVERS' HOURS (GOODS VEHICLES) (MODIFICATIONS) ORDER 1986
SI 1986/1459

Authority Made by the Secretary of State for Transport under the Transport Act 1968, ss 96(12), 101(2), 157.
Date made 22 August 1986.
Commencement 29 September 1986.
Summary This order modifies, in relation to the drivers of goods vehicles, the provisions of the Transport Act 1968, s 96, which relates to permitted driving times and periods of duty. The order provides that drivers who drive goods vehicles for all or the greater part of their time spent driving vehicles to which Pt VI of the 1968 Act applies are exempt from all the provisions of s 96, except the daily driving limit in s 96(1) and the daily duty limit in s 96(3)(a). The order partially revokes SI 1970/257 and SI 1971/818 so as to take account of the modifications made to the 1968 Act by this order.

[465]

DRIVERS' HOURS (GOODS VEHICLES) (EXEMPTIONS) REGULATIONS 1986
SI 1986/1492

Authority Made by the Secretary of State for Transport under the Transport Act 1968, s 96(10).
Date made 28 August 1986.
Commencement 29 September 1986.
Amendment Amended by SI 2003/2155.
Summary These regulations revoke and replace the Drivers' Hours (Goods Vehicles) (Exemptions) Regulations 1978, SI 1978/1364, and the amending SI 1982/1554. The regulations provide exemptions, subject to certain conditions, from the requirements of the Transport Act 1968, s 96(1), (3)(a), which relate to permitted driving times and periods of duty, to enable drivers of goods vehicles to deal with certain cases of emergency, namely:

(a) events which cause or are likely to cause such:
  (1) danger to life of individuals, or animals; or
  (2) a serious interruption in the maintenance of public services for the supply of water, gas, electricity or drainage or of electronic communications or postal services; or
  (3) a serious interruption in the use of roads, railways, ports or airports, as to necessitate the taking of immediate preventive action; and

(b) events which are likely to cause such serious damage to property as to necessitate the taking of immediate preventive action.

[466]

OPERATION OF PUBLIC SERVICE VEHICLES (PARTNERSHIP) REGULATIONS 1986
SI 1986/1628

Authority Made by the Secretary of State for Transport under the Public Passenger Vehicles Act 1981, s 58.
Date made 22 September 1986.
Commencement 26 October 1986.
Amendment Amended by SI 1990/1850, SI 2007/1898.
Summary These regulations revoke and replace the Operation of Public Passenger Vehicles (Partnership) Regulations 1981, SI 1981/259, and the amending SI 1985/1906, so as to up-date certain statutory references and make provision in relation to London local service licences, which replaced road service licences in London (see the Transport Act 1985, s 1). The regulations provide that partnerships may hold public service vehicle operators' licences or London local service licences. They also make certain modifications to the Public Passenger Vehicles Act 1981, ss 12(3), 14(1), 17(1), 18(1), 19(1), (2), (3), 57(2), Sch 3, paras 1, 2, 3, 5, 8, and the Transport Act 1985, s 12(12), to provide for the cases of such licences being held by partnership firms.
London local service licences See the corresponding note SI 1986/1691.

[467]

PUBLIC SERVICE VEHICLES (TRAFFIC COMMISSIONERS: PUBLICATION AND INQUIRIES) REGULATIONS 1986
SI 1986/1629

Authority Made by the Secretary of State for Transport under the Public Passenger Vehicles Act 1981, ss 5(1), (2)(b), 54(3), (4), (5), (6), 56(1), 60(1).
Date made 22 September 1986.
Commencement 26 October 1986.
Amendment Amended by SI 1993/2754, SI 2004/2682, SI 2008/2683, SI 2009/443.
Summary These regulations make provision with respect to the publication of the statement known as "Notices and Proceedings" by traffic commissioners and with respect to inquiries. Reg 3 provides for the publication of "Notices and Proceedings", the contents of which should include specified details relating to: (a) registration of local services under the Transport Act 1985, s 6, (b) public service vehicle operators' licences, (c) determinations under s 111 of the 1985 Act (s 111 has been repealed by the Transport Act 2000, ss 154(6), 274, Sch 31, Pt II), and (d) notices of the dates and places at which inquiries are to be held.

Reg 4 contains a requirement that copies of "Notices and Proceedings" be available for inspection at the offices of the traffic commissioner, and provides that a fee of £3.50 is to be payable for supply of a copy of "Notices and Proceedings". Reg 5 relates to the records required to be kept by traffic commissioners. Reg 6 concerns the postponement or adjournment of inquiries. Reg 7 enables a traffic commissioner to restrict in such manner as he directs attendance of the public at any inquiry in so far as that inquiry relates to the financial position of any person. Reg 8 sets out the circumstances in which traffic commissioners may order a party to pay costs incurred by them or the Secretary of State in connection with an inquiry, and prescribes the maximum amount of such costs. Reg 9 has been revoked by SI 2004/2682 in so far as it amended the Public Service Vehicles (Traffic Regulation Conditions) Regulations 1986, SI 1986/1030 (revoked), and is spent in so far as it amended the Transport Tribunal Rules 1986, SI 1986/1547 (revoked).

[468]

TYNE AND WEAR PASSENGER TRANSPORT EXECUTIVE (EXCLUSION OF BUS OPERATING POWERS) ORDER 1986
SI 1986/1648

Authority Made by the Secretary of State under the Transport Act 1985, s 60(5).
Date made 23 September 1986.
Commencement 26 October 1986.
Amendment Amended by virtue of the Local Transport Act 2008, s 77(3), (4), in consequence of the renaming of passenger transport areas in England as integrated transport areas by s 77(1) of that Act, and the renaming of Passenger Transport Authorities for those areas as Integrated Transport Authorities by s 77(2) thereof, as from 9 February 2009 (see SI 2009/107).
Summary The Transport Act 1985, s 60 applies where in the case of any integrated transport area (formerly passenger transport area) a company ("the initial company") has been formed by the Passenger Transport Executive for that area in pursuance of s 59 of that Act. By s 60(5), at any time after the transfer required under s 59(8) of the 1985 Act of shares in or other securities of the initial company to the Integrated Transport Authority (formerly Passenger Transport Authority) for the Executive's area has taken place, the Secretary of State may by order provide that the Executive is to cease, on a day specified in the order, to have the powers under the Transport Act 1968, s 10(1)(i) (power to carry passengers by road), (viii) (power to let passenger vehicles on hire).

This order accordingly provided that on 4 November 1986 the Tyne and Wear Passenger Transport Executive was to cease to have the power under s 10(1)(i) of the 1968 Act to carry passengers by road; and that on 26 October 1988 the Executive was to cease to have the power under s 10(1)(viii) thereof to let passenger vehicles on hire with or without trailers for the carriage of goods. S 10(1)(i) of the 1968 Act has been repealed by the Local Transport Act 2008, ss 66(6)(a), 131, Sch 7, Pt 3, as from 9 February 2009 (see SI 2009/107).
Further orders The following additional orders have been made under the Transport Act 1985, s 60(5) specifying the above dates in relation to other Passenger Transport Executives:

(a) the Greater Manchester Passenger Transport Executive (SI 1986/1649);
(b) the Merseyside Passenger Transport Executive (SI 1986/1650);
(c) the South Yorkshire Passenger Transport Executive (SI 1986/1651);
(d) the West Midlands Passenger Transport Executive (SI 1986/1652); and
(e) the West Yorkshire Passenger Transport Executive (SI 1986/1653).

[469]

PUBLIC SERVICE VEHICLES (REGISTRATION OF LOCAL SERVICES) REGULATIONS 1986
SI 1986/1671

Authority Made by the Secretary of State for Transport under the Public Passenger Vehicles Act 1981, ss 52(1), 60(1)(f) and the Transport Act 1985, ss 6(2)(a), (3)(a), (8)(a), (9), 8(6).
Date made 26 September 1986.
Commencement 26 October 1986.
Amendment Amended by SI 1988/1879, SI 1989/1064, SI 1994/3271, SI 2002/182, SI 2004/10, SI 2009/443, SI 2009/878. Previously amended by SI 1993/2752, SI 2002/2536, SI 2004/2250, SI 2005/2355, SI 2007/690, SI 2008/1470 (all superseded). Revoked in relation to Scotland only by SSI 2001/219 (outside the scope of this work).
Summary The Transport Act 1985, s 6 requires particulars of local services to be registered with the traffic commissioner for any traffic area in which there is a stopping place for that service. The provisions made by these regulations relate to such registration. Reg 3 specifies the traffic commissioner to whom applications should be made when the service covers more than one traffic area and the authorities to which copies of applications should be sent. Reg 4 and the Schedule prescribe the particulars to be registered. Reg 5 sets out the period following registration or variation or cancellation of a registration before a new service or varied service may be provided or a service cancelled (subject to regs 7 and 8 of these regulations, and to reg 6 of SI 2009/443). Reg 8 prescribes the cases in which the requirement for such a period is excluded. Reg 9 makes provision for the variation of a registered service without variation of the registration. Reg 9A makes provision for the cancellation of registrations relating to discontinued services. Reg 10 provides for the exclusion from the operation of s 6 of the 1985 Act of excursions and tours other than of a class specified. Reg 11 sets out the period during which failure to operate a service in accordance with the registered particulars is disregarded in specified circumstances. Reg 12 relates to fees payable for an application to register or to vary the registration of particulars of a service. Where a vehicle is being used to provide a standard service, reg 13 makes provision in relation to the display of fare tables, timetables and destination and route notices; where a vehicle is being used to provide a flexible service, provision is made in relation to the display of information about fares and the name by which the service is known. Reg 14 requires the operator of a flexible service to make specified information about that service available, in any reasonably accessible form, to all persons who may wish to use the service. Reg 15 concerns the records to be kept by the operator of a flexible service.

As to the registration of local services where a quality partnership scheme containing registration restrictions has been made, see SI 2009/443.

[470]

PUBLIC SERVICE VEHICLES (LONDON LOCAL SERVICE LICENCES) REGULATIONS 1986
SI 1986/1691

Authority Made by the Secretary of State for Transport under the Public Passenger Vehicles Act 1981, ss 5, 52(1), 57(3), 59, 60(1) and the Transport Act 1985, s 42(10). S 42 of the 1985 Act (appeals to the Secretary of State) is repealed by the Greater London Authority Act 1999, s 423, Sch 34, Pt II, as from a day to be appointed by order under s 425(2) thereof. See further the note "London local service licences" below.
Date made 30 September 1986.
Commencement 26 October 1986.
Amendment Amended by SI 1988/408 and by virtue of the Road Traffic Act 1991, s 9(2).
Summary These regulations revoke the Public Service Vehicles (Road Service Licences and Express Services) Regulations 1980, SI 1980/1354, and the amending SI 1981/264, SI 1985/1907, and replace those regulations, with modifications, in London following the abolition of the system of road service licences by the Transport Act 1985, s 1, and its replacement in Greater London by a system of London local service licences (as to which, see the note below).

Reg 4 provides the information for insertion in the statement known as "Notices and Proceedings" (see further SI 1986/1629) to be included in applications for licences. Reg 5 relates to the inspection of applications for licences. Reg 6 prescribes the information to be included in "Notices and Proceedings". Regs 7, 8 set out the procedure on applications for licences and reg 9 sets out the procedure on the variation of conditions and attachment of new conditions to licences. Reg 10 makes provision for variations in the procedure in respect of licences granted for a short period. Reg 11 sets out the procedure as regards the revocation or suspension of licences. Reg 12 prescribes fees for applications and the grant of licences. Reg 13 lays down certain requirements for the display of fare tables, timetables and destination notices. Regs 14, 15 set out requirements for the surrender and return of licences. Reg 16 prescribes events on the occurrence of which the licences held by companies terminate. Reg 17 prescribes the procedure for the issue of duplicate licences. Reg 18 sets out certain requirements for the production of licences for examination. Reg 19 prescribes the procedure for appeals and applications to the Secretary of State. Reg 20 provides for the notification of decisions by the traffic commissioner for the Metropolitan Traffic Area and reg 21 makes provision for all notices, applications, appeals, objections and other representations to be made in writing and for the proper means of delivery of notices sent to holders of or applicants for licences by the commissioner.
London local service licences The Transport Act 1985, Pt II (ss 34–46), which provides for London local service licences, is repealed by the Greater London Authority Act 1999, s 423, Sch 34, Pt II, as from a day to be appointed by order under s 425(2) thereof. Bus services in Greater London are now regulated by Chapter V (ss 179–195) of Pt IV of the 1999 Act, which introduces a system of London service permits. S 180(1) of the 1999 Act provides that no London local service may be provided except in accordance with the provisions of Chapter V of Pt IV of the 1999 Act. However, s 180(1) is modified by SI 2000/1462 for the duration of the transitional period (ie the period beginning on 3 July 2000 and ending on the last day on which a London local service licence granted under the 1985 Act ceases to be in force), so as to allow holders of London local service licences to continue operating under those licences after the introduction of London service permits. SI 2000/1462 also provides that Pt II of the 1985 Act ceases to have effect immediately after the end of the transitional period.

[471]

TAXIS (SCHEMES FOR HIRE AT SEPARATE FARES) REGULATIONS 1986
SI 1986/1779

Authority Made by the Secretary of State for Transport under the Transport Act 1985, s 10(5)(c), (8).
Date made 15 October 1986.
Commencement 14 November 1986.
Summary The Transport Act 1985, s 10 provides for schemes to be made by the authorities in England and Wales which license taxis to regulate the immediate hiring of taxis at separate fares. These regulations apply to all schemes outside London and prescribe the description of the provisions which are required to be included, namely:

(a) a provision which permits any vehicle, which is licensed by the authority to ply for hire in an area where the scheme is in operation, to be used at the option of the holder of the licence for the carriage of passengers at separate fares under the terms of the scheme;
(b) a provision by which, when a vehicle is hired in accordance with the scheme, the provisions of the scheme applying to the journey for which it is hired are applied to any part of that journey outside the area in which the scheme is in operation as they apply to any part within that area; and
(c) a provision which requires any vehicle standing for hire under the terms of the scheme at an authorised place to display (in addition to any sign, mark or notice which it is required to display by the taxi code) a notice which indicates that the vehicle is available for hire at separate fares.

Procedural requirements relating to consents and consultations, publication of notices and making draft schemes available for inspection, and the making of the schemes are set out. Similar procedural requirements are made with respect to the variation of schemes.

[472]

SECTION 19 MINIBUS (DESIGNATED BODIES) ORDER 1987
SI 1987/1229

Authority Made by the Secretary of State for Transport under the Transport Act 1985, s 19(7).
Date made 14 July 1987.
Commencement 13 August 1987.
Amendment Amended by SI 1990/1708, SI 1995/1540, SI 1997/535.
Summary This order designates certain specified bodies which may grant permits in relation to the use of small buses under the Transport Act 1985, s 19. The order replaces the Minibus (Designated Bodies) Order 1980, SI 1980/1356, as amended, which lapsed on the repeal of the Public Passenger Vehicles Act 1981, s 42 by Sch 8 to the 1985 Act. Traffic commissioners may grant similar permits. A designated body may grant a permit to itself and to the bodies specified in relation to it. Each designated body is required to make returns in respect of permits granted by it.

[473]

DRIVERS' HOURS (GOODS VEHICLES) (KEEPING OF RECORDS) REGULATIONS 1987
SI 1987/1421

Authority Made by the Secretary of State for Transport under the Transport Act 1968, ss 98, 101(2).
Date made 5 August 1987.
Commencement 2 November 1987.
Summary These regulations revoke and replace the Drivers' Hours (Keeping of Records) Regulations 1976, SI 1976/1447, and the amending SI 1986/1493. They apply to the driving of goods vehicles which is not governed by Regulation (EC) 561/2006 of the European Parliament and of the Council on the harmonisation of certain social legislation relating to road transport (OJ L102, 11.04.2006, p 1) (which repealed and replaced Council Regulation (EEC) 3820/85 (OJ L370, 31.12.1985, p 1)) (in connection with Regulation (EC) 561/2006, see SI 2007/1819). In particular, reg 5 of, and the Schedule to, the regulations provide for the form of drivers' record books; regs 6–8 concern the issue of record books and the making of entries in them, and contain supplementary provisions as to the manner of keeping drivers' record books; reg 9 concerns the production of drivers' record books; reg 10 provides that drivers' record books should be carried by drivers when they are on duty; reg 11 makes provision for the preservation of drivers' record books and duplicates of weekly sheets; reg 12 contains exemptions; and reg 13 makes provision for cases where a driver drives passenger vehicles as well as goods vehicles.

[474]

LONDON TAXI SHARING SCHEME ORDER 1987
SI 1987/1535

Authority Made by the Secretary of State for Transport under the Transport Act 1985, s 10(4), (5), (6), (10). S 10(10) of the 1985 Act has been repealed by the Greater London Authority Act 1999, ss 253, 423, Sch 20, para 8(1), (2)(d), Sch 34, Pt V. See further the note "Summary" below.
Date made 1 September 1987.
Commencement 28 September 1987.
Summary This order contains in its Annex the London Taxi Sharing Scheme, which applies to taxis standing for hire or hired at any place at which a taxi may lawfully ply for hire (an "authorised place"). A taxi operating under the scheme must display a sign bearing the words "Shared Taxi". Provision is also made in relation to fares, fare and conversion tables, obligatory hiring, arrangements for a shared service, cessation of availability for hire, luggage and the route to be followed. The order also revokes the Heathrow Taxi Sharing Scheme Order 1987, SI 1987/784, and the London (British Rail) Taxi Sharing Scheme Order 1987, SI 1987/839.

The Transport Act 1985, s 10, which empowers taxi sharing schemes to be made, has been amended by the Greater London Authority Act 1999, ss 253, 423, Sch 20, para 8(1), (2), Sch 34, Pt V, so that schemes for the London taxi area are to be made by Transport for London instead of by the Secretary of State. However, para 17(1) of Sch 20 to the 1999 Act provides that any scheme made under s 10 of the 1985 Act by the Secretary of State and in force immediately before para 8(2)(a) of Sch 20 comes into force (3 July 2000; see SI 2000/801, in the title Local Government) has effect from that date as a scheme made by Transport for London.

Orders made under s 10 of the 1985 Act by Transport for London are not statutory instruments and are outside the scope of this work; however, they may be found at www.tfl.gov.uk. See, for example, the London Taxi Sharing (Fixed Fares) Scheme set out in the London Taxi Sharing Scheme Order 2005, as amended by the London Taxi Sharing Scheme Order 2006, which applies to specified journeys undertaken by taxis standing for hire or hired at specified authorised places designated in the scheme. A taxi operating under the scheme must display a sign containing the words "Fixed-Fare Shared Taxi".

[475]

INTERNATIONAL CARRIAGE OF DANGEROUS GOODS BY ROAD (FEES) REGULATIONS 1988
SI 1988/370

Authority Made by the Secretary of State for Transport, with the consent of the Treasury, under the Finance Act 1973, s 56(1), (2).

Date made 2 March 1988.
Commencement 1 April 1988.
Amendment Amended by SI 1991/458, SI 2003/1811, SI 2007/634, SI 2009/856. Previously amended by SI 1992/714, SI 1993/3067, SI 1997/158, SI 2001/1812, SI 2002/537, SI 2004/1884, SI 2005/2456, SI 2008/1578 (all superseded).
Summary These regulations revoke and replace the International Carriage of Dangerous Goods by Road (Fees) Regulations 1986, SI 1986/589, and prescribe the fees payable in connection with the issue by the Secretary of State for Transport of a special certificate of approval for a vehicle following inspection in pursuance of the European Agreement Concerning the International Carriage of Dangerous Goods by Road of 30 September 1957, as amended ("ADR certificate"), and the fee for issue of a copy of such a certificate. The fees are as follows:
(a) where a first inspection is carried out on the same day as an examination under SI 1988/1478, the fee is £99;
(b) the fee for first inspection in any other case is £99 plus the amount which would be payable in respect of an examination under those regulations;
(c) where an application is made for a first ADR certificate in respect of a tractor for a semi trailer, and an inspection of the tractor is waived, the fee is £28;
(d) where a vehicle fails to pass an inspection and arrangements are made for a further inspection to be carried out not more than 14 days after the first an additional fee of £50 is payable; and
(e) the fee for the issue of a copy of a certificate which has been lost or destroyed is £14.

Where a person has cancelled an appointment for an inspection and does not apply for another inspection, any sum paid by him in respect of the application for a certificate must be returned.

[476]

INTERNATIONAL TRANSPORT OF GOODS UNDER COVER OF TIR CARNETS (FEES) REGULATIONS 1988
SI 1988/371

Authority Made by the Secretary of State for Transport, with the consent of the Treasury, under the Finance Act 1973, s 56(1), (2).
Date made 2 March 1988.
Commencement 1 April 1988.
Amendment Amended by SI 1991/459, SI 2009/861. Previously amended by SI 1992/715, SI 1993/3068, SI 2000/1464, SI 2001/1811, SI 2002/539, SI 2003/1813, SI 2004/1911, SI 2005/2457, SI 2007/632, SI 2008/1580 (all superseded).
Summary These regulations prescribe the fees payable in connection with approval of a vehicle design-type and with the issue by the Secretary of State for Transport of a certificate of approval for a vehicle following inspection of the vehicle in pursuance of Annex 3 to the Customs Convention on the International Transport of Goods under cover of TIR Carnets of 14 November 1975 and the fee for the issue of a certificate for a vehicle which conforms to an approved design type. The fees prescribed are as follows:
(a) the fee for the inspection of a vehicle design-type for a TIR design-type approval in pursuance of the Customs Convention is £106 where the design-type is a variation of one for which a TIR design-type approval has been granted and £644 in any other case;
(b) the fee for the issue of a TIR vehicle approval certificate (or a duplicate thereof) is £14; and
(c) the fee for the inspection of a vehicle in connection with the issue of a TIR vehicle approval certificate is £70 where the inspection is carried out following refusal of such a certificate and £106 in any other case.

[477]

DEPARTMENT OF TRANSPORT (FEES) ORDER 1988
SI 1988/643

Authority Made by the Secretary of State for Transport under the Finance (No 2) Act 1987, s 102.
Date made 29 March 1988.
Commencement 1 April 1988.
Amendment Amended by SI 1991/811, SI 1995/1684, SI 1996/1961, SI 2003/1094, SI 2003/2994, SI 2009/711, SI 2009/1885, and by virtue of the Road Traffic Act 1991, s 9(2). Previously amended by SI 1993/1601 (superseded by SI 1995/1684), SI 1998/459 (spent).
Summary This order specifies functions and matters which are to be taken into account in the determination of fees to be fixed by the Secretary of State for Transport in respect of certain activities under the Finance Act 1973, the Road Traffic Act 1988 and the Public Passenger Vehicles Act 1981. The order has been partially revoked and replaced by SI 2009/711; see the note "Further orders" below.
Further orders The following orders have been made by the Secretary of State for Transport under the Finance (No 2) Act 1987, s 102:
(a) SI 2003/2994, as amended by SI 2008/908 (made under s 102 of the 1987 Act, and in force on 21 November 2003), specifies functions, the costs of which the Secretary of State may recover when setting fees relating to driver licensing and vehicle registration (in particular, it enables him to recover costs relating to vehicle licensing when setting driver licensing fees and vice versa). It also specifies matters which are to be taken into account in determining the cost of the specified functions, and amends SI 1988/643;

(b) SI 2009/711, as amended by SI 2009/1885 (made under s 102(3), (4) of the 1987 Act, and in force on 17 March 2009), specifies functions, the costs of which are to be taken into account in the determination of fees to be fixed by the Secretary of State in respect of certain activities concerning road vehicles, road transport, goods vehicle operators, public service vehicle operators and bus services under the International Carriage of Perishable Foodstuffs Act 1976, the Public Passenger Vehicles Act 1981, the Road Traffic Act 1988, the Vehicle Excise and Registration Act 1994, the Goods Vehicles (Licensing of Operators) Act 1995 and the Disability Discrimination Act 1995. SI 2009/711 also specifies matters which are to be taken into account in determining the cost of the specified functions, and partially revokes and replaces SI 1988/643.

[478]

GOODS VEHICLES (PLATING AND TESTING) REGULATIONS 1988

SI 1988/1478

Authority Made by the Secretary of State for Transport under the Road Traffic Act 1972, ss 45, 46(5), 51(5) (repealed). Now have effect under the Road Traffic Act 1988, ss 49, 53(5), 63(5), by virtue of the Road Traffic (Consequential Provisions) Act 1988, s 2(2) and the Interpretation Act 1978, s 17(2)(b), printed in the title Statutory Instruments (Pt 2), Vol 1 of this work.

Date made 22 August 1988.

Commencement 23 September 1988.

Amendment Amended by SI 1989/1693, SI 1990/448, SI 1991/252, SI 1993/2048, SI 1993/3013, SI 1994/328, SI 1995/1456, SI 1997/82, SI 1997/263, SI 1998/3113, SI 2000/1433, SI 2001/307, SI 2002/487, SI 2003/1816, SI 2004/1873, SI 2005/2343, SI 2008/1460, SI 2009/799, and by virtue of the Road Traffic Act 1991, s 9(2).

Previously amended by SI 1989/320, SI 1991/454, SI 1992/564, SI 1992/2447, SI 1998/1671, SI 2001/1650, SI 2007/503 (all superseded).

Summary These regulations revoke and replace with amendments the Goods Vehicles (Plating and Testing) Regulations 1982, SI 1982/1478, and the amending SI 1983/239, SI 1983/1800, SI 1984/178, SI 1984/402, SI 1984/816, SI 1984/1024, SI 1985/44, SI 1985/1525, SI 1986/371, SI 1986/1090, SI 1988/338. They make provision for the examination of specified classes of goods vehicles for the purpose of determining particulars applicable to those vehicles and ascertaining whether the vehicles comply with prescribed construction and use requirements.

The regulations consist of nine Parts. Pt I (regs 1–8) contains general provisions. Under reg 4, various classes of goods vehicles (specified in Sch 2) are excepted from these regulations, but subject to such exceptions the regulations apply to the following goods vehicles:

(a) heavy motor cars and motor cars constructed or adapted for the purpose of forming part of an articulated vehicle;
(b) other heavy motor cars;
(c) other motor cars having a design gross weight of more than 3500 kg;
(d) semi-trailers;
(e) converter dollies of any unladen weight manufactured on or after 1 January 1979; or
(f) other trailers (not being converter dollies or semi-trailers) with an unladen weight of more than 1020 kg.

By reg 5, every vehicle submitted for a goods vehicle test in accordance with these regulations must be examined for the purpose of ascertaining whether the prescribed construction and use requirements are complied with. These requirements are those specified in Pt I of Sch 3 (being various requirements of SI 1986/1078, SI 1989/1796 and Council Regulation (EEC) 3821/85 (OJ L370, 31.12.1985, p 8) (ie the Community Recording Equipment Regulation, as defined by the Road Traffic Act 1988, s 85(1))) and the requirements of Pt II of Sch 3, which are that the condition of the vehicle is such that its use on a road would not involve a danger of injury to any person having regard in particular to specified items.

Pt II (regs 9–16) relates to the timing and method of application for first examinations and periodical tests.

Pt III (regs 20–25 (regs 17–19 have been revoked)) governs examination for plating on a first examination, and requires a vehicle examiner to determine the plated weights of a vehicle having regard to certain matters. After an examination for plating has been carried out, a goods vehicle examiner must arrange for the vehicle to undergo a goods vehicle test (ie an examination for ascertaining whether the vehicle complies with the prescribed construction and use requirements). Provision is made for the issue of plating certificates and goods vehicle test certificates, for re-test procedures and for appeals against determinations made on a first examination or on a re-test.

Pt IV (regs 25A–29) provides for a vehicle in respect of which a goods vehicle test certificate has been issued on a first examination, or on a re-test or following an appeal, to be submitted for subsequent periodical tests (a periodical test includes a goods vehicle test).

Pt V (regs 30–37) requires certain alterations to a vehicle to be notified to the Secretary of State. This Part also provides in certain cases for the re-examination of a vehicle and for the issue of a new plating certificate, when a notifiable alteration has been made to the vehicle or when any particular contained in its plating certificate is or may not be applicable to that vehicle.

Pt VA (regs 37A–37D) provides for the alteration of the plated weights of a vehicle without an examination. Under this Part, plated weights may be determined without an examination if a plating certificate is in force for the vehicle and the alteration applied for would not affect the safety of the vehicle on the road. Provision is made for an application for the alteration of plated weights without an examination, for the disposal of applications and for appeals.

Pt VA (regs 37A–37D) provides for the alteration of the plated weights for a vehicle without an examination if a plating certificate is in force for the vehicle and the alteration applied for would not affect the safety of the vehicle on the road. Provision is made for applications for the alteration of plated weights without an examination, for the disposal of applications and for appeals.

Pt VI (regs 39–42, 42A (reg 38 has been revoked)) contains miscellaneous matters relating to, in particular, the fees payable in respect of examinations under the regulations.

Pt VII (reg 43) modifies the regulations in their application to Crown vehicles.

Pt VIII (regs 44–46) contains exemptions from certain provisions of the Road Traffic Act 1988. Vehicles used for specified purposes or in certain areas are exempt from s 53(1), (2), which provide that a goods vehicle required to be submitted for examination for plating and for a goods vehicle test must not be used on a road without a plating certificate and a goods vehicle test certificate. Vehicles other than those manufactured on or after 1 October 1982 and first used on or after 1 April 1983, not constructed or adapted to form part of an articulated vehicle are exempt from s 63(2), which provides that a goods vehicle for which a plating certificate has been issued must not draw a trailer unless a maximum laden weight for that vehicle and trailer is shown in that certificate. Provision is made for the issue of a certificate of temporary exemption from s 53(1) or (2) in certain circumstances.

Cf SI 1981/1694.

Evidence of test certificates The Road Traffic Act 1988, s 66 enables regulations to be made providing that where an application is made for an excise licence for a vehicle which is required under s 53(2) of the 1988 Act to have a goods vehicle test certificate, that licence must not be granted unless one of certain requirements is satisfied. SI 2004/2577, which was made under s 66(3) of the 1988 Act and came into force on 15 November 2004, revokes and replaces the Goods Vehicles (Production of Test Certificates) Regulations 1970, SI 1970/560. The 2004 regulations provide that the said excise licence may not be granted unless:

(a) evidence is produced that an effective goods vehicle test certificate is in force for the vehicle;
(b) the applicant makes a declaration in the form specified in the Schedule to the regulations (or a form to the like effect) that the vehicle is not intended to be used during the period covered by the application except for a purpose prescribed by SI 1988/1478, reg 44(1) or in an area prescribed by reg 44(2) thereof; or
(c) a certificate of temporary exemption issued by virtue of s 53(5)(b) of the 1988 Act, for a period which includes the date on which the licence is to come into force, is produced in respect of the vehicle.

Cf SI 2004/1896, noted to SI 1981/1694.

[479]

USE OF INVALID CARRIAGES ON HIGHWAYS REGULATIONS 1988
SI 1988/2268

Authority Made by the Secretary of State for Transport under the Chronically Sick and Disabled Persons Act 1970, s 20.

Date made 21 December 1988.

Commencement 30 January 1989.

Summary The Chronically Sick and Disabled Persons Act 1970, s 20(1) provides for the modification of certain statutory provisions relating to the use of vehicles on footways and roads in their application to invalid carriages which comply with prescribed requirements and are used in accordance with prescribed conditions. These regulations, which revoke and replace with savings the Use of Invalid Carriages on Highways Regulations 1970, SI 1970/1391, prescribe conditions and requirements for the purposes of the said s 20(1) in relation to the following classes of invalid carriage: class 1 (not mechanically propelled), class 2 (mechanically propelled but incapable of exceeding 4 mph), class 3 (mechanically propelled and capable of exceeding 4 mph but not 8 mph). The prescribed conditions as to use include provisions:

(a) specifying the persons who may use any class of invalid carriage, so as to include, in particular, persons suffering from some physical defect or disability;
(b) restricting the use of horns fitted to any class of invalid carriage; and
(c) prohibiting a class 3 invalid carriage from being used by a person under the age of 14 years or driven on a footway at a speed in excess of 4 mph.

The prescribed requirements to be complied with by any class of invalid carriage relate to the following matters: unladen weight, means of stopping, lighting, speed device and speed indicator, width, audible warning instruments, vision and rear view mirrors.

[480]

RECOVERY VEHICLES (NUMBER OF VEHICLES RECOVERED) ORDER 1989
SI 1989/1226

Authority Made by the Secretary of State for Transport under the Vehicles (Excise) Act 1971, Sch 3, Pt I, para 8(4) (repealed). Now takes effect under the Vehicle Excise and Registration Act 1994, Sch 1, Pt V, para 5(5), by virtue of s 64 of, and para 2 of Sch 4 to, that Act.

Date made 17 July 1989.

Commencement 27 July 1989.

Summary This order specifies two as the number of vehicles which "recovery vehicles", as defined in the Vehicle Excise and Registration Act 1994, Sch 1, Pt V, para 5(2), may recover at any time without ceasing to be recovery vehicles.

[481]

ROAD VEHICLES LIGHTING REGULATIONS 1989
SI 1989/1796

Authority Made by the Secretary of State for Transport under the Road Traffic Act 1988, s 81, in so far as these regulations revoke enactments having effect as if made under that section, and under s 41 of the 1988 Act, as read with s 43 thereof, as regards all other provisions.
Date made 28 September 1989.
Commencement 1 November 1989.
Amendment Amended by SI 1992/1217, SI 1994/2280, SI 1994/2567, SI 1996/3016, SI 2001/560, SI 2004/3168 (the latter in relation to England only), SI 2005/2559, SI 2005/2929 (the latter in relation to Wales only), SI 2005/3169, SI 2006/594, SI 2006/1914, SI 2008/1277. The amendments made by SI 2006/1914 came into force on 19 October 2007; see *London Gazette,* 20 July 2007. Also amended in relation to Scotland only by SSI 2005/344, SSI 2006/129 (outside the scope of this work).
Summary These regulations, which revoke and replace the Road Vehicles Lighting Regulations 1984, SI 1984/812, and the amending SI 1987/1315, contain provisions relating to the lighting of road vehicles.

Pt I (regs 1–9B) contains preliminary provisions (reg 10 has been revoked by SI 2008/1277). Exemptions from certain of the regulations are conferred by regs 4–9A; these include exemptions for vehicles being used on a road by vehicle examiners, temporarily imported vehicles and vehicles proceeding to a port for export, vehicles towing or being towed, military vehicles, invalid carriages, vehicles drawn or propelled by hand and tramcars. Reg 9B modifies the regulations in relation to certain passenger vehicles which are the subject of a minister's approval certificate given under SI 2001/25 (formerly the Motor Vehicles (Approval) Regulations 1996, SI 1996/3013 (revoked)).

Pt II (regs 11–22) contains regulations governing the fitting of lamps, reflectors, rear markings and devices; these provisions relate to the colour of light shown by lamps and reflectors; movement of lamps and reflectors; the requirement for lamps to show a steady light; filament lamps; general requirements for electrical connections; restrictions on fitting blue warning beacons, special warning lamps and similar devices; obligatory warning beacons; signs on buses carrying children; obligatory lamps, reflectors, rear markings and devices; restrictions on the obscuration of certain lamps and reflectors; optional lamps, reflectors, rear markings and devices; projecting trailers and vehicles carrying overhanging or projecting loads or equipment; and additional side marker lamps.

Pt III (regs 23–27) contains provisions governing the maintenance and use of lamps, reflectors, rear markings and devices; these provisions relate to the maintenance of lamps etc; requirements about the use of front and rear position lamps, rear registration plate lamps, side marker lamps and end-outline marker lamps; requirements about the use of headlamps, front fog lamps and warning beacons; and restrictions on the use of certain lamps.

Pt IV (reg 28) relates to the testing and inspection of lighting equipment and reflectors.

The regulations also contain 24 schedules relating to the following matters: obligatory lamps, reflectors, rear markings and devices; front position lamps; dim-dip devices and running lamps; dipped-beam headlamps; main-beam headlamps; front fog lamps; direction indicators; hazard warning signal devices; side marker lamps; rear position lamps; rear fog lamps; stop lamps; end-outline marker lamps; reversing lamps; rear registration plate lamps; warning beacons; side retro reflectors; rear markings; pedal retro reflectors; front retro reflectors; provision for a special sign indicating the presence of children on school buses; diagram showing where unlit parking is not permitted near a junction; and an example of a marking showing the vertical downwards inclination of the dipped-beam headlamps.
Offences As to offences to do with reflectors and tail lamps, see the Road Traffic Act 1988, s 83. Under s 75 of that Act, it is an offence to sell or supply or offer to sell or supply or expose for sale a vehicle in an unroadworthy condition (s 75(1), (2)). A motor vehicle is in an unroadworthy condition if: (a) its use on a road in that condition would be unlawful by virtue of any provision made by regulations under s 41 of that Act as respects brakes, steering gear or tyres, or construction, weight or equipment of vehicles, or (b) its use on a road would involve a danger of injury to any person (s 75(3)).

S 75 also makes it an offence to alter a vehicle so as to render its condition such that its use on a road would be unlawful by virtue of any provision made as respects the construction, weight or equipment of vehicles by regulations under s 41 of the 1988 Act, or would involve a danger of injury to any person (s 75(4)). By the Road Traffic Act 1988, s 76, it is an offence to fit a vehicle part to a vehicle in such circumstances that the use of the vehicle on a road would involve a danger of injury to any person or constitute a contravention of or failure to comply with any of the construction and use requirements imposed under s 41 of that Act. As to the prosecution and punishment of offences, see the Road Traffic Offenders Act 1988, s 9, Sch 2, Pt I.

[482]

ROAD TRAFFIC (DRIVER LICENSING AND INFORMATION SYSTEMS) ACT 1989 (COMMENCEMENT NO) 1) ORDER 1989
SI 1989/1843

Authority Made by the Secretary of State for Transport under the Road Traffic (Driver Licensing and Information Systems) Act 1989, s 17(2).

Date made 6 October 1989.

Summary This order, and the further commencement orders made under the Road Traffic (Driver Licensing and Information Systems) Act 1989, s 17(2) (ie SI 1990/802, SI 1990/2228, SI 1990/2610), brought provisions of the 1989 Act into force on various dates. The table below sets out the provisions of the Act brought into force by these orders.

Provision	*Date and extent (if any)*
s 1(1)	1 April 1991 (SI 1990/2610)
s 1(7)	1 June 1990 (so far as relates to definitions "the 1981 Act", "the 1988 Act") (SI 1990/802) 1 April 1991 (otherwise) (SI 1990/2610)
s 2	1 April 1991 (SI 1990/2610)
s 3	1 June 1990 (SI 1990/802)
s 4	1 April 1991 (SI 1990/2610)
s 5(1)	1 June 1990 (except so far as relates to s 5(5)) (SI 1990/802) 1 April 1991 (exception noted above) (SI 1990/2610)
s 5(2)	1 June 1990 (SI 1990/802)
s 5(4)	1 June 1990 (SI 1990/802)
s 5(5)	1 April 1991 (SI 1990/2610)
s 5(6)–(10)	1 June 1990 (SI 1990/802)
s 6	1 December 1990 (SI 1990/2228)
s 7	See Sch 3
ss 8–15	1 June 1990 (SI 1990/802)
s 16	See Sch 6
s 17	8 November 1989 (SI 1989/1843)
Sch 2	1 April 1991 (SI 1990/2610)
Sch 3, paras 2–5	1 April 1991 (SI 1990/2610)
Sch 3, para 6	1 December 1990 (SI 1990/2228)
Sch 3, para 8(a)	1 April 1991 (SI 1991/2610)
Sch 3, para 8(b)(i)	1 April 1991 (SI 1990/2610)
Sch 3, para 8(b)(ii), (iii)	1 June 1990 (SI 1990/802)
Sch 3, para 8(c)–(e)	1 April 1991 (SI 1990/2610)
Sch 3, para 9(a), (c)	1 April 1991 (SI 1990/2610)
Sch 3, para 9(b), (d)	1 June 1990 (SI 1990/802)
Sch 3, para 11(b)	1 June 1990 (SI 1990/802)
Sch 3, para 11(c)	1 December 1990 (SI 1990/2228)
Sch 3, para 11(d)	1 June 1990 (SI 1990/802)
Sch 3, para 12(a)	1 April 1991 (SI 1990/2610)
Sch 3, para 12(b), (c)	1 June 1990 (SI 1990/802)
Sch 3, para 14	1 June 1990 (SI 1990/802)

Provision	*Date and extent (if any)*
Sch 3, para 15(a)	1 June 1990 (SI 1990/802)
Sch 3, para 15(b)–(d)	1 April 1991 (SI 1990/2610)
Sch 3, para 15(e)	1 June 1990 (so far as relates to definitions "NI driving licence", "NI licence") (SI 1990/802) 1 April 1991 (so far as relates to definition "passenger carrying vehicle") (SI 1990/2610)
Sch 3, para 15(f)	1 June 1990 (SI 1990/802)
Sch 3, para 15(g)	1 December 1990 (SI 1990/2228)
Sch 3, para 16	1 June 1990 (SI 1990/802)
Sch 3, para 18(a)	1 April 1991 (SI 1990/2610)
Sch 3, para 18(b)–(d)	1 December 1990 (SI 1990/2228)
Sch 3, para 19	1 June 1990 (SI 1990/802)
Sch 3, para 20	1 April 1991 (SI 1990/2610)
Sch 3, para 22, 23	1 April 1991 (SI 1990/2610)
Sch 3, para 24	1 June 1990 (SI 1990/802)
Sch 3, para 26	8 November 1989 (SI 1989/1843)
Sch 3, para 27(e)	1 April 1991 (SI 1990/2610)
Sch 3, para 28(a), (b)	1 June 1990 (SI 1990/802)
Sch 3, para 28(c), (d)	1 April 1991 (SI 1990/2610)
Sch 3, para 30(a)	1 June 1990 (SI 1990/802)
Sch 3, para 30(b), (c)	1 April 1991 (SI 1990/2610)
Schs 4, 5	1 June 1990 (SI 1990/802)
Sch 6	1 June 1990 (repeals of or in Road Traffic Act 1988, s 97(1); Road Traffic Offenders Act 1988, s 45(3), Sch 2, Pt I (entry relating to s 45 of that Act)) (SI 1990/802) 1 December 1990 (repeals in Road Traffic Act 1988, s 97(3)) (SI 1990/2228) 1 April 1991 (otherwise, except repeal of Road Traffic (Driver Licensing and Information Systems) Act 1989, Sch 1, para 11 (repealed)) (SI 1990/2610)

[483]

DRIVING LICENCES (COMMUNITY DRIVING LICENCE) REGULATIONS 1990

SI 1990/144

Authority Made by the Secretary of State for Transport under the European Communities Act 1972, s 2(2).

Date made 29 January 1990.

Commencement 1 April 1990.

Amendment Partially revoked by SI 1998/1420, the Powers of Criminal Courts (Sentencing) Act 2000, s 165(4), Sch 12, Pt II and the Road Safety Act 2006, s 59, Sch 7(3).

Prospective amendment Partially revoked by the Road Safety Act 2006, s 59, Sch 7(4), as from a day to be appointed by order under s 61(1) thereof.

Summary These regulations (as partially revoked) amend various provisions so as to give further effect to Art 2 of Council Directive 80/1263/EEC on the introduction of a Community driving licence (repealed; see now Directive 2006/126/EC of the European Parliament and of the Council on driving licences (OJ L403, 30.12.2006, p 18)). The provisions amended are as follows: the Road Traffic

Act 1988, ss 88(6), 92(7C), 93, 97(1), 98, 99, 105(2), 108(1), 109, 118, 121, 122, 164, 167, 173, 176; the Road Traffic Offenders Act 1988, ss 7, 26, 27, 29(1), 30, 32, 36(4), 44(1), 45, 46(2), 47, 48, 54, 56, 57, 58, 61, 72, 75(7), 76(5), 77, 83(1), 98(1), Schs 1, 2, 5; the Road Traffic (Driver Licensing and Information Systems) Act 1989, s 5, Schs 2, 3; and the Criminal Justice Act 1972, s 24(3). Certain amendments made by these regulations to the Road Traffic Act 1988, the Road Traffic Offenders Act 1988 and the Road Traffic (Driver Licensing and Information Systems) Act 1989 are revoked by the Road Safety Act 2006, s 59, Sch 7(4), as from a day to be appointed under s 61(1) thereof.

The amendments made by these regulations are set out in full in the relevant titles of Halsbury's Statutes, which also notes any repealed provisions.

Further regulations See SI 1996/1974, SI 1998/1420.

[484]

FIXED PENALTY OFFENCES ORDER 1990
SI 1990/335

Authority Made by the Home Secretary under the Road Traffic Offenders Act 1988, s 51(3).

Date made 23 February 1990.

Commencement 1 April 1990.

Summary This order provides for certain offences relating to pedestrian crossings regulations to be fixed penalty offences for the purposes of the Road Traffic Offenders Act 1988, Pt III, and makes consequential amendments to Sch 3 to the 1988 Act, which specifies the offences which are fixed penalty offences for those purposes (the amendment to the said Sch 3 has been superseded by SI 1999/1851; see "Further orders" below). The pedestrian crossings offences concerned are:

(a) failing to accord precedence to a foot passenger on a "zebra" crossing in contravention of the "Zebra" Pedestrian Crossings Regulations 1971, SI 1971/1524, reg 8 (revoked and replaced by SI 1997/2400, reg 25, in the title Highways, Streets and Bridges);

(b) causing a vehicle to proceed across a "pelican" crossing in contravention of the "Pelican" Pedestrian Crossings Regulations and General Directions 1987, SI 1987/16, reg 16 (revoked and replaced by reg 23 of SI 1997/2400); and

(c) failing to accord precedence to a pedestrian on a "pelican" crossing in contravention of reg 17 of the said SI 1987/16 (revoked and replaced by reg 26 of SI 1997/2400).

As to the penalties for fixed penalty offences, see SI 2000/2792.

Further orders The following orders made under the Road Traffic Offenders Act 1988, s 51(3) provide for specified offences to be fixed penalty offences for the purposes of Pt III of that Act, and make consequential amendments to Sch 3 to that Act:

(a) SI 1992/345 (in force on 1 April 1992) specifies as a fixed penalty offence the offence under the Road Traffic Act 1988, s 15(4) of driving a motor vehicle in breach of the restriction in s 15(3) on carrying children under the age of 14 years not wearing seat belts in the rear of vehicles;

(b) SI 1999/1851 (in force on 1 August 1999) specifies the following as fixed penalty offences:

   (1) overtaking a moving or stationary vehicle on a zebra, pelican or puffin crossing contrary to SI 1997/2400, reg 24, in the title Highways, Streets and Bridges;

   (2) failure to fix a registration mark to a vehicle in accordance with the requirements of SI 1971/450, reg 17 (revoked and replaced by SI 2001/561);

   (3) driving on the footway contrary to the Highway Act 1835, s 72;

   (4) carrying more than one person on a pedal cycle contrary to the Road Traffic Act 1988, s 24; and

   (5) cycling on the footway contrary to s 72 of the 1835 Act;

(c) SI 2003/1253 (in force on 1 June 2003) specifies as fixed penalty offences any offence contrary to the Road Traffic Act 1988, ss 47 (using a motor vehicle without the required test certificate being in force), 143 (using a motor vehicle while uninsured or unsecured against third party risks) and 172 (failure of person keeping vehicle and others to give the police information as to the identity of the driver etc in the case of certain offences);

(d) SI 2004/2922 (in force on 1 December 2004) specifies as a fixed penalty offence the offence under the Road Traffic Act 1988, s 18 of driving or riding a motor cycle on a road while using eye protectors if the eye protectors are not of a type prescribed by regulations under that section (see SI 1999/535) or they are used in contravention of such regulations; and

(e) SI 2009/483 (in force on 31 March 2009) specifies offences under the following provisions as fixed penalty offences:

   (1) the Transport Act 1968, ss 96(11), (11A), 97(1), 98(4), 99C;

   (2) the Transport Act 1968, s 99(4), but only in so far as the offence relates to: (i) failing to comply with a requirement under s 99(1)(a), or (ii) obstructing an officer in the exercise of his powers under s 99(2)(a) or 99(3);

   (3) the Transport Act 1968, s 99ZD(1), except where that offence is committed by: (i) failing to sign a hard copy of downloaded data when required to do so under s 99ZC(1), or (ii) obstructing an officer in the exercise of powers under s 99ZF;

   (4) the Road Traffic (Foreign Vehicles) Act 1972, s 3(1);

   (5) the Public Passenger Vehicles Act 1981, s 12(5);

   (6) the Road Traffic Act 1988, s 71(1);

   (7) the Road Traffic Offenders Act 1988, s 90D;

   (8) the Vehicle Excise and Registration Act 1994, s 34;

(9) the Goods Vehicles (Licensing of Operators) Act 1995, s 2(5);
(10) SI 1984/748, reg 19(1), (2);
(11) SI 1992/3077, regs 3, 7;
(12) SI 1999/1322, regs 3, 7;
(13) SI 1999/3413, regs 3, 4, 7(1), (3); and
(14) SI 2007/605, reg 11(7).

[485]

DRIVER INFORMATION SYSTEMS (EXEMPTION) ORDER 1990
SI 1990/865

Authority Made by the Secretary of State for Transport and the Secretaries of State for Scotland and Wales under the Road Traffic (Driver Licensing and Information Systems) Act 1989, s 9(2)
Date made 4 April 1990.
Commencement 1 June 1990.
Summary This order specifies those descriptions of driver information systems to which the Road Traffic (Driver Licensing and Information Systems) Act 1989, Pt II does not apply. That Part does not apply to any such system other than a system which has the following characteristics:
(a) it is a system whose operation requires the installation in, upon, under, over, along or across a public road of system apparatus capable of transmitting data to, or collecting information from, motor vehicles or both; or, subject to certain exceptions; and
(b) it is a system which, when in operation, will have as its primary purpose (or one of them) the provision during the course of a journey of specific directions to the driver of a motor vehicle as to the precise route which that vehicle should follow for the purposes of that journey, in such manner that the directions may be revised as traffic conditions change during the course of that journey, will use equipment in motor vehicles which has been designed to give the specific directions referred to, and will be available for use by the public.

[486]

PUBLIC SERVICE VEHICLES (CONDUCT OF DRIVERS, INSPECTORS, CONDUCTORS AND PASSENGERS) REGULATIONS 1990
SI 1990/1020

Authority Made by the Secretary of State for Transport under the Public Passenger Vehicles Act 1981, ss 24(1), 25(1), (4), 60 and the Transport Act 1985, ss 23(2)(b), 134(1), 137(1).
Date made 2 May 1990.
Commencement 1 June 1990; see reg 1.
Amendment Printed as amended by SI 1995/186, SI 2002/1724.
Interpretation See regs 3, 11.
General These regulations revoke and replace the Public Service Vehicles (Conduct of Drivers, Conductors and Passengers) Regulations 1936, SR & O 1936/619, and the amending SR & O 1946/357, SI 1975/461, SI 1980/915. The regulations have been amended by SI 2002/1724 in consequence of the introduction by SI 2000/1970 of accessibility requirements for disabled persons (including those in wheelchairs) to single-deck and double-deck buses and coaches; the amendments made by SI 2002/1724 provide for the additional duties of the drivers and conductors of these vehicles towards such persons.
Penalties Under the Public Passenger Vehicles Act 1981, s 25(3), passengers who contravene or fail to comply with these regulations are liable to a fine not exceeding level 3 on the standard scale. Under s 24(2) of that Act (as amended by the Road Safety Act 2006, s 9(6), Sch 2, para 1(1), (2)), drivers, conductors and inspectors of public service vehicles and tramcars who contravene or fail to comply with these regulations are liable to a fine not exceeding level 2 on the standard scale; and in the case of a driver of a public service vehicle the court may cause particulars of a conviction to be endorsed on the counterpart of his licence or, if he is not the holder of a licence, on his driving record. By s 24(3) failure to produce a licence and its counterpart for endorsement is punishable by a fine not exceeding level 3 on the standard scale.

As from a day to be appointed by order, s 24(2) of the 1981 Act is amended by the Road Safety Act 2006, s 10(12), Sch 3, para 1(1), (2), so that in the case of a driver of a public service vehicle, the court may send notice of the particulars of the conviction to the Secretary of State requiring the Secretary of State to endorse them on the person's driving record; and s 24(3) of the 1981 Act is repealed by ss 10(12), 59 of, and para 1(1), (3) of Sch 3 and Sch 7(4) to, the 2006 Act.

[487]

PART I

1 These Regulations may be cited as the Public Service Vehicles (Conduct of Drivers, Inspectors, Conductors and Passengers) Regulations 1990 and shall come into force on 1st June 1990.

[488]

Revocation

2 The Regulations specified in the Schedule to these Regulations are hereby revoked.

[489]

PART II

Interpretation

3 (1) In this Part of the Regulations unless the context otherwise requires—

"the 1981 Act" means the Public Passenger Vehicles Act 1981;

"the 1985 Act" means the Transport Act 1985;

["the 1995 Act" means the Disability Discrimination Act 1995;

"the 1984 Regulations" means the Public Service Vehicles (Carrying Capacity) Regulations 1984;

"the 2000 Regulations" means the Public Service Vehicles Accessibility Regulations 2000;

"assistance dog" means a dog which—

(a) is trained by a specified charity to assist a disabled person with a physical impairment for the purpose of section 1 of the 1995 Act which—

(i) consists of epilepsy; or

(ii) otherwise affects his mobility, manual dexterity, physical coordination or ability to lift, carry or otherwise move everyday objects; and

(b) at the time it is providing assistance to a disabled person, is wearing a jacket inscribed with the name of one of the following charities, that is to say—

(i) "Dogs for the Disabled" registered with the Charity Commission under registration number 700454;

(ii) "Support Dogs" registered with the Charity Commission under registration number 1017237; or

(iii) "Canine Partners for Independence" registered with the Charity Commission under registration number 803680;

"boarding lift" means a lift fitted to a regulated public service vehicle for the purpose of allowing wheelchair users to board and alight from the vehicle;

"boarding ramp" means a ramp fitted to a regulated public service vehicle for the purpose of allowing wheelchair users to board and alight from the vehicle;

"disabled person" has the same meaning as in section 1 of the 1995 Act;

"guide dog" has the same meaning as in section 37(11) of the 1995 Act;

"hearing dog" has the same meaning as in section 37(11) of the 1995 Act;]

"licence" means a licence to drive a vehicle granted under section 22 of the 1981 Act;

["local service" has the same meaning as in section 2 of the 1985 Act;

"maximum seating capacity" has the same meaning as in regulation 4 of the 1984 Regulations;

"maximum standing capacity" has the same meaning as in regulation 6 of the 1984 Regulations;

"portable ramp" means a ramp which is carried on a regulated public service vehicle for the purpose of allowing wheelchair users to board or alight from the vehicle;

"regulated public service vehicle" means a public service vehicle to which the 2000 Regulations apply;

"scheduled service" means a service, using one or more public service vehicles, for the carriage of passengers at separate fares—

(a) along specified routes,

(b) at specified times, and

(c) with passengers being taken up and set down at pre-determined stopping points, but does not include a tour service (being a service where a public service vehicle is used for or in conjunction with the carriage of passengers to a particular location, or particular locations, and back to their point of departure);]

"ticket" means a document which, in accordance with the terms and conditions under which it has been issued, constitutes a valid authority to travel on a vehicle;

"vehicle" means any vehicle used as a public service vehicle as defined in the 1981 Act but excluding any vehicle used under a permit granted by virtue of section 19 of the 1985 Act.

["wheelchair restraint system" means a system which is designed to keep a wheelchair restrained within the wheelchair space;

"wheelchair space" means a space for a wheelchair with which a regulated public service vehicle is fitted in accordance with paragraph 2 of Schedule 1 to the 2000 Regulations;

"wheelchair user" means a disabled person using a wheelchair; and

"wheelchair user restraint" means a system which is designed to keep a wheelchair user restrained in the wheelchair].

(2) For the purposes of this Part of the Regulations, a sum payable by a passenger on the vehicle shall not be regarded as a fare unless—

(a) it is computed in accordance with a fare table available on the vehicle; and
(b) the fare table contains sufficient information to enable the passenger to ascertain the fare for his journey or the manner in which it is computed.

(3) In this Part of the Regulations, in relation to a vehicle—

"conductor" means a person, not being the driver, who is authorised by the operator to act as a conductor on the vehicle, but does not include an inspector; and

"driver" means a person who is the holder of a licence and who is for the time being responsible for driving the vehicle.

(4) In this Part of the Regulations, any reference to a numbered regulation is a reference to the regulation bearing that number in this Part of the Regulations.

(5) In this Part of the Regulations, any reference to a numbered or lettered paragraph or sub-paragraph is a reference to the paragraph or sub-paragraph bearing that number or letter in the regulation or (in the case of a sub-paragraph) paragraph in which the reference appears.

NOTES

Amendment Para (1): definitions "the 1995 Act", "the 1984 Regulations", "the 2000 Regulations", "assistance dog", "boarding lift", "boarding ramp", "disabled person", "guide dog", "hearing dog", "local service", "maximum seating capacity", "maximum standing capacity", "portable ramp", "regulated public service vehicle", "scheduled service", "wheelchair restraint system", "wheelchair space", "wheelchair user" and "wheelchair user restraint" inserted by SI 2002/1724.

Public Passenger Vehicles Act 1981, s 22 Repealed, subject to savings, by the Road Traffic (Driver Licensing and Information Systems) Act 1989, ss 1, 16, Sch 6. S 1(1) of the 1989 Act provides that the repeal of s 22 of the 1981 Act (which required a special licence to be held for driving a public service vehicle (PSV)) does not imply that that it is lawful to drive a PSV of any class on the authority of an existing licence under the Road Traffic Act 1988, Pt III (ordinary licences).

Public Service Vehicles Accessibility Regulations 2000 SI 2000/1970.

Public Service Vehicles (Carrying Capacity) Regulations 1984 SI 1984/1406.

[490]

The conduct of drivers, inspectors and conductors

4 (1) A driver shall not, when a vehicle is in motion, hold a microphone or any attachment thereto unless it is necessary for him, either in an emergency or on grounds of safety, to speak into the microphone.

(2) Subject to paragraph (3), a driver shall not, when a vehicle is in motion, speak to any person either directly or by means of a microphone.

(3) Nothing in paragraph (2) shall prevent—

(a) the driver of a vehicle from—

(i) speaking in circumstances when he is obliged to do so by reason of an emergency or on grounds of safety; or

(ii) speaking to a relevant person in relation to the operation of the vehicle provided that he can do so without being distracted from his driving of the vehicle; and

(b) the driver of a vehicle which is being used to provide a relevant service from making short statements from time to time limited to indicating the location of the vehicle or operational matters provided that he can do so without being distracted from his driving of the vehicle.

(4) In this regulation—

(a) "relevant person" is a person fulfilling one of the following descriptions—

(i) an employee of the operator;

(ii) when the operator is a firm, a partner of the firm;

(iii) if the operator is an individual, that individual; or

(iv) if the operator is a company, a director; and

(b) "relevant service" is a service for the carriage of passengers for hire or reward at separate fares which is neither—

(i) an excursion or tour within the meaning of section 137(1) of the 1985 Act; nor

(ii) a service the primary purpose of which is sightseeing, not falling within sub-paragraph (i).

[491]

5 (1) A driver and a conductor shall take all reasonable precautions to ensure the safety of passengers who are on, or who are entering or leaving, the vehicle.

(2) A driver, inspector and conductor shall take all reasonable steps to ensure that the provisions of these Regulations relating to the conduct of passengers are complied with.

(3) A driver, inspector or conductor—

(a) shall, if so requested by a constable or other person having reasonable cause, give his name, the person by whom he is employed and, in the case of a driver, particulars of the licence by virtue of which he drives the vehicle; and

(b) shall not smoke in or on a vehicle except in one of the circumstances specified in paragraph (4).

(4) The circumstances referred to in paragraph (3)(b) are that—

(a) the vehicle is not available for the carriage of passengers and the person concerned is in or on any part of the vehicle where smoking by passengers is not prohibited by regulation 6(1)(d); or

(b) the vehicle is hired as a whole and the person concerned has the permission of the operator and the hirer.

(5) A driver shall, when picking up or setting down passengers, stop the vehicle as close as is reasonably practicable to the left or near side of the road.

(6) A conductor shall not, while the vehicle is in motion and without reasonable cause, distract the driver's attention or obstruct his vision.

[(7) A driver, inspector and a conductor shall not, subject to there being a suitable space available, prevent a disabled person accompanied by an assistance dog, a guide dog or a hearing dog, being allowed to board and travel in the vehicle with his dog.]

NOTES

Amendment Para (7): inserted by SI 2002/1724.

Cases relating to this regulation *Dianbuca v Arriva London North Ltd* [2003] All ER (D) 161 (May);

Marshall v Clark [1957] SC (J) 68) (decided under the corresponding revoked regulation);

Nicholson v Goddard (1954) 118 JP 394 (decided under the corresponding revoked regulation);

Reid v MacNicol [1958] SLT 42 (decided under the corresponding revoked regulation).

[492]

The conduct of passengers

6 (1) No passenger on a vehicle shall—

(a) where the vehicle has a door which passengers are by a notice informed is for a particular purpose, use that door for any other purpose, unless otherwise directed or authorised by a driver, inspector or conductor;

(b) put at risk or unreasonably impede or cause discomfort to any person travelling on or entering or leaving the vehicle, or a driver, inspector, conductor or employee of the operator when doing his work on the vehicle;

(c) throw or trail any article from the vehicle;

(d) smoke or carry lighted tobacco or light a match or a cigarette lighter in or on any part of the vehicle where passengers are by a notice informed that smoking is prohibited, unless the vehicle has been hired as a whole and both the operator and the hirer have given their permission to the contrary;

(e) except with the permission of the operator, distribute any paper or other article for the purpose of giving or seeking information about or comment upon any matter;

(f) except with the permission of the operator, sell or offer for sale any article;

[(g) speak to the driver whilst the vehicle is in motion except—

(i) in an emergency;

(ii) for reasons of safety; or

(iii) to give directions as to the stopping of the vehicle;]

(h) without reasonable cause distract the driver's attention, obstruct his vision or give any signal which might reasonably be interpreted by the driver as a signal—

(i) to stop the vehicle in an emergency; or

(ii) to start the vehicle;

(j) travel on any part of the vehicle which is not provided for the carriage of passengers;

(k) remain on the vehicle, when directed to leave by the driver, inspector or conductor on the following grounds—

(i) that his remaining would result in the number of passengers exceeding the maximum seating capacity or the maximum standing capacity marked on the vehicle in accordance with the Public Service Vehicles (Carrying Capacity) Regulations 1984;

(ii) that he has been causing a nuisance; or

(iii) that his condition is such as would be likely to cause offence to a reasonable passenger or that the condition of his clothing is such that his remaining would be reasonably expected to soil the fittings of the vehicle or the clothing of other passengers;

(l) play or operate any musical instrument or sound reproducing equipment to the annoyance of any person on the vehicle or in a manner which is likely to cause annoyance to any person on the vehicle; or

(m) intentionally interfere with any equipment with which the vehicle is fitted.

[(1A) Paragraph (1)(k)(ii) and (iii) shall not apply to a direction given by a driver, inspector or conductor solely on the grounds that a person is a disabled person.]

(2) Subject to paragraph (3), a passenger on a vehicle who has with him any article or substance mentioned in paragraph (4) or any animal—

(a) if directed by the driver, inspector or conductor to put it in a particular place on the vehicle, shall put it where directed; and

(b) if requested to move it from the vehicle by the driver, inspector or conductor, shall remove it.

[(3) Paragraph (2)(b) does not require the removal of an animal where the passenger is a disabled person and the animal is an assistance dog, a guide dog or a hearing dog.]

[(3A) Without prejudice to regulation 5(7), a disabled person shall comply with any direction given by a driver, inspector or conductor to remove his assistance dog, guide dog or hearing dog from the gangway.]

(4) The article or substance referred to in paragraph (2) is—

(a) any bulky or cumbersome article;

(b) any article or substance which causes or is likely to cause annoyance to any person on the vehicle; or

(c) any article or substance which would be reasonably expected to constitute—

(i) a risk of injury to any person on the vehicle; or

(ii) a risk of damage to the property of any person on the vehicle or to the vehicle.

(5) …

NOTES

Amendment Para (1)(g): substituted by SI 1995/186.
Para (1A): inserted by SI 2002/1724.
Para (3): substituted by SI 2002/1724.
Para (3A): inserted by SI 2002/1724.
Para (5): revoked by SI 2002/1724.
Public Service Vehicles (Carrying Capacity) Regulations 1984 SI 1984/1406.

[493]

7 (1) No passenger on a vehicle being used for the carriage of passengers at separate fares shall use any ticket which has—

(a) been altered or defaced;

(b) been issued for use by another person on terms that it is not transferable; or

(c) expired.

(2) Save as provided in paragraph (3), every passenger on a vehicle being used for the carriage of passengers at separate fares shall—

(a) declare, if so requested by the driver, inspector or conductor, the journey which he intends to take, is taking or has taken in the vehicle;

(b) where the vehicle is being operated by the driver without a conductor—

(i) save as provided in (ii) below, immediately on boarding the vehicle, pay the fare for the journey he intends to take to the driver or, where appropriate, by inserting in any fare-collection equipment provided on the vehicle the money or token required to pay that fare; or

(ii) if otherwise directed by the driver, an inspector or a notice displayed on the vehicle, shall pay the fare for his journey in accordance with the direction;

(c) where the vehicle is being operated by the driver with a conductor, pay the fare for the journey which he intends to take, is taking, or has taken in the vehicle to the conductor immediately on being requested to do so by the conductor or an inspector;

(d) accept and retain for the rest of his journey any ticket which is provided on payment of a fare in accordance with sub-paragraph (b) or (c);

(e) produce during his journey any ticket which has been issued to him either under sub-paragraph (d) or before he started his journey for inspection by the driver, inspector or conductor on being requested to do so by the driver, inspector or conductor; and

(f) as soon as he has completed the journey for which he has a ticket, either—

(i) leave the vehicle; or

(ii) pay the fare for any further journey which he intends to take on the vehicle.

(3) Paragraph (2)(b) and (c) do not apply to a passenger who has with him a ticket which was issued to him before his journey in respect of that journey, provided he complies with all such directions in relation to the ticket as may be—

(a) printed on the ticket;

(b) displayed on the vehicle; or

(c) given by the driver, inspector or conductor.

(4) Any passenger who—

(a) fails to comply with paragraph 2(b) or (c); or

(b) does not have with him a ticket which was issued to him before his journey in respect of that journey;

shall pay the fare for his journey to the driver, inspector or conductor on request and in any case before he leaves the vehicle unless otherwise agreed by the driver, inspector or conductor.

(5) Any passenger on a vehicle being used for the carriage of passengers at separate fares who has with him a ticket which he is not entitled to retain for any reason including—

(a) the alteration or defacement of the ticket;
(b) the fact that the ticket, having been issued for use by another person, was not transferable to him;
(c) the expiry of the ticket; or
(d) a mistake in consequence of which the ticket was issued;

shall surrender the ticket to a driver, inspector or conductor on being required to do so.

[494]

8 (1) Any passenger on a vehicle who is reasonably suspected by the driver, inspector or conductor of the vehicle of contravening any provision of these Regulations shall give his name and address to the driver, inspector or conductor on demand.

(2) Any passenger on a vehicle who contravenes any provision of these Regulations may be removed from the vehicle by the driver, inspector or conductor of the vehicle or, on the request of the driver, inspector or conductor, by a police constable.

[495]

9 (*Relates to Scotland.*)

PART III

10 (*Amended SI 1986/1245; superseded by SI 1996/3087 in so far as amended those regulations.*)

[PART IV
THE CONDUCT OF DRIVERS AND CONDUCTORS OF REGULATED PUBLIC SERVICE VEHICLES WITH RESPECT TO WHEELCHAIR USERS AND OTHER DISABLED PERSONS

Interpretation of Part IV

11 In this Part—

"Schedule 1" means Schedule 1 (wheelchair accessibility requirements) to the 2000 Regulations;

"Schedule 2" means Schedule 2 (general accessibility requirements for single-deck and double-deck buses) to the 2000 Regulations;

"Schedule 3" means Schedule 3 (general accessibility requirements for single-deck and double-deck coaches) to the 2000 Regulations;

a "Schedule 1 vehicle" means a regulated public service vehicle which is required to comply with the provisions of Schedule 1; and

a "Schedule 2 or 3 vehicle" means a regulated public service vehicle which is required to comply (as the case may be) with the provisions of either Schedule 2 or Schedule 3.]

NOTES

Amendment Inserted, together with the preceding Part heading, by SI 2002/1724.

[496]

[Duties towards wheelchair users of Schedule 1 vehicles

12 (1) This regulation applies (subject to regulation 15(1) (duties requiring the proper functioning of equipment)) in relation to a driver and a conductor of a Schedule 1 vehicle.

(2) If there is an unoccupied wheelchair space on the vehicle, a driver and a conductor shall allow a wheelchair user to board if—

- (a) the wheelchair is of a type or size that can be correctly and safely located in that wheelchair space, and
- (b) in so doing, neither the maximum seating nor standing capacity of the vehicle would be exceeded.

(3) For the purpose of paragraph (2), a wheelchair space is occupied if—

- (a) there is a wheelchair user in that space; or
- (b) passengers or their effects are in that space and they or their effects cannot readily and reasonably vacate it by moving to another part of the vehicle.

(4) A driver and a conductor shall ensure—

- (a) where the carriage of a portable ramp is required by Schedule 1, that a portable ramp is carried on the vehicle where the vehicle is operating on a local service or on a scheduled service;
- (b) that any boarding lift, boarding ramp or portable ramp is in its normal position for vehicle travel and is securely stowed before the vehicle is driven;
- (c) where the vehicle is operating on a local or a scheduled service and it is fitted with a boarding lift or a boarding ramp which, in order to comply with Schedule 1, requires a means of control for it to be capable of being operated manually in the event of a power failure, that such a separate means of control is carried on the vehicle;
- (d) that wheelchair users can gain access into and can get out of a wheelchair space;
- (e) before the vehicle is driven, that any wheelchair user is correctly and safely positioned in a wheelchair space and that any retractable rail (being a rail fitted in accordance with the requirements of paragraph 4(3)(b) of Schedule 1) or any similar device is in a position to restrict the lateral movement of the wheelchair; and
- (f) where a wheelchair user using a wheelchair space faces the front of the vehicle, that the wheelchair restraint system is attached in accordance with the relevant instructions pursuant to paragraph 8(3) of Schedule 1.

(5) If the vehicle has a seat in a wheelchair space which is capable of being quickly dismantled or removed, a driver and a conductor shall ensure that any such seat—

- (a) when it is not in use and is stowed on the vehicle, is safely stowed; and
- (b) whenever it is in position for use within the wheelchair space, is secured.]

NOTES
Amendment Inserted by SI 2002/1724.

[497]

[Duties concerning kneeling systems etc towards disabled persons using Schedule 2 or 3 vehicles

13 (1) This regulation (subject to regulations 15 (effects of faulty or malfunctioning equipment) and 17 (extent of driver's and conductor's duty)) applies in relation to a driver and to a conductor of a Schedule 2 and 3 vehicle where that vehicle is equipped with—

- (a) a kneeling system, or
- (b) a folding or retractable step.

(2) A driver and a conductor shall operate the kneeling system or the folding or retractable step—

- (a) whenever they consider that a disabled person will need the system to be operated or the step to be deployed, or
- (b) if requested to do so,

for the purpose of enabling that person to board or to alight from the vehicle, and in such a manner that the distance between the vehicle and the ground or the vehicle and the kerb is the minimum that is reasonably practicable.

(3) "Kneeling system" means any system which enables the bodywork of the vehicle to be lowered relative to its normal height of travel and a "folding or retractable

step" means a step which can either fold or retract and which meets the requirements applicable to external steps pursuant to paragraph 4 of Schedule 2 or Schedule 3 (as the case may be).

(4) A driver and a conductor shall ensure that disabled persons who are not wheelchair users may, when boarding or alighting from the vehicle, use an entrance or an exit which is provided in compliance with (as the case may be) the provisions of either Schedule 2 or Schedule 3.]

NOTES
Amendment Inserted by SI 2002/1724.

[498]

[General duties towards wheelchair users and other disabled persons

14 (1) Where a wheelchair user wishes to board or to alight from a Schedule 1 vehicle, a driver and a conductor shall first safely deploy (subject to regulation 15(1) (duties requiring the proper functioning of equipment)) any boarding lift, boarding ramp or portable ramp in its correct operating position.

(2) Where a wheelchair user wishes to board or to alight from a Schedule 1 vehicle and requests assistance to do so, a driver and a conductor shall provide assistance to him.

(3) Where a disabled person who is not a wheelchair user wishes to board or to alight from a Schedule 2 or 3 vehicle and requests assistance to do so, a driver and a conductor shall provide assistance to him.

(4) Where a wheelchair user wishes to occupy a wheelchair space in a Schedule 1 vehicle which is fitted with a wheelchair user restraint, a driver and a conductor shall—

(a) offer to provide such assistance as may be required so as to enable the wheelchair user to wear that restraint, and

(b) in providing that assistance, apply (subject to regulation 15(1) (duties requiring the proper functioning of equipment)) the wheelchair user restraint only in accordance with the user instructions which are displayed pursuant to paragraph 8(3) of Schedule 1.]

NOTES
Amendment Inserted by SI 2002/1724.

[499]

[Effects of faulty or malfunctioning equipment

15 (1) Where the fulfilment of a duty owed by a driver or a conductor under—

(a) regulation 12 (duties towards wheelchair users of Schedule 1 vehicles),

(b) regulation 13 (duties concerning kneeling systems etc towards disabled persons using Schedule 2 or 3 vehicles) or

(c) regulation 14 (general duties towards wheelchair users and other disabled persons),

requires the use or operation of any equipment, kneeling system or folding or retractable step and there is a fault in, or a failure in the operation of, that equipment, system or step, the person owing the duty shall not permit a wheelchair user, or other disabled person or any other passenger to board or alight from the vehicle or (if already on board) to travel on the vehicle unless he is satisfied that such persons can do so in safety.

(2) A driver or a conductor shall not be considered to have failed to ensure fulfilment of the duty under either regulation 13(2) (duties concerning kneeling systems etc) or regulation 16 (display of route numbers etc) if, and to the extent that, the performance of that duty involves the proper functioning of equipment on the vehicle but there is a fault in, or a failure in the operation of, that equipment which prevents it being used.

(3) In this regulation—

"equipment" means any equipment fitted to a regulated public service vehicle in order to comply with Schedule 1, Schedule 2 or Schedule 3 and which a driver and a conductor must operate for the safe fulfilment of the relevant duty; and "kneeling system or folding or retractable step" has the same meaning as in regulation 13(3).]

NOTES
Amendment Inserted by SI 2002/1724.

[500]

[Route numbers etc

16 (1) Subject to regulation 15(2) (equipment failure preventing use), a driver and a conductor of a regulated public service vehicle shall ensure that—

(a) a route number (if any) and a destination is displayed in the positions provided for such displays with respect to the vehicle in accordance (as the case may be) with either paragraph 8 of Schedule 2 or paragraph 7 of Schedule 3;

(b) a route number and a destination displayed in accordance with sub-paragraph (a) which is required to be provided with a means of illumination shall have characters that are kept illuminated between sunset and sunrise; and

(c) the vehicle shall at all times display the correct route number and destination.

(2) Sub-paragraphs (a) and (b) of paragraph (1) shall not apply to an emergency replacement vehicle or to a temporary service vehicle until 21 days has elapsed from the day when the vehicle is first used as an emergency replacement vehicle or as a temporary service vehicle, provided that—

(a) the route number (if any) and a destination shall be displayed either on the front or on the nearside of the vehicle as close as practical to the foremost passenger entrance; and

(b) the requirement of sub-paragraph (c) of paragraph (1) is complied with.

(3) In this regulation, "destination" and "route number" have the same meanings as in paragraph 7(6) of Schedule 3 to the 2000 Regulations and—

"emergency replacement vehicle" means a public service vehicle which has been brought into service on the route in question to provide emergency cover; and

"temporary service vehicle" means a public service vehicle which is in service on a temporary route or service.]

NOTES
Amendment Inserted by SI 2002/1724.

[501]

[Extent of driver's and conductor's duty

17 (1) Where, in any of the preceding provisions of this Part, a duty is expressed to be owed by the driver and the conductor of a vehicle, but a function to be performed to fulfil that duty is, according to arrangements made by the operator of the vehicle, the responsibility of one only of them, then that one only, and not the other, owes that duty in relation to that function.

(2) The duties which a driver or a conductor owes under regulation 13 (duties concerning kneeling systems etc) and 14 (general duties towards wheelchair users and other disabled persons) are duties—

(a) to take such care as in all the circumstances of the case is reasonable to see that the wheelchair user or other disabled person will be reasonably safe in boarding or in alighting from the vehicle, and

(b) shall not oblige the person owing the duty to take any steps if, on reasonable grounds, he considers that—

(i) there will be a risk to his health, safety or security or to that of the wheelchair user or other disabled person or to that of any other passenger or member of the public; or

(ii) there will be a risk to the safety and security of the vehicle.

(3) The duties which a driver or a conductor owes under regulations 13 (duties concerning kneeling systems etc) and 14 (general duties towards wheelchair users and other disabled persons) are duties to operate the kneeling system or the folding or

retractable step, or to deploy the boarding lift, boarding ramp or portable ramp to the extent that it is practicable having regard to the construction of the vehicle and the condition of the road.]

NOTES
Amendment Inserted by SI 2002/1724.

[502]

SCHEDULE

NOTES
The Schedule specifies the regulations revoked by reg 2, i e the Public Service Vehicles (Conduct of Drivers, Conductors and Passengers) Regulations 1936, SR & O 1936/619, and the amending SR & O 1946/357, SI 1975/461, SI 1980/915.

[503]

GOODS VEHICLES (COMMUNITY CABOTAGE AUTHORISATIONS) (FEES) REGULATIONS 1990
SI 1990/1192

Authority Made by the Secretary of State for Transport, with the consent of the Treasury, under the Finance Act 1973, s 56(1), (2).
Date made 6 June 1990.
Commencement 1 July 1990.
Summary These regulations prescribe a fee of £5 payable on the issue of a Community cabotage authorisation granted pursuant to Council Regulation (EEC) 4059/89 laying down conditions under which non-resident carriers may operate national road haulage services within a member state (annulled; see now Council Regulation (EEC) 3118/93 (OJ L279, 12.11.1993, p 1) laying down the conditions under which non-resident carriers may operate national road haulage services within a member state).

[504]

SECRETARY OF STATE'S TRAFFIC ORDERS (PROCEDURE) (ENGLAND AND WALES) REGULATIONS 1990
SI 1990/1656

Authority Made by the Secretary of State for Transport and the Secretary of State for Wales under the Road Traffic Regulation Act 1984, s 124, Sch 9, Pt III.
Date made 6 August 1990.
Commencement 6 September 1990.
Amendment Amended by SI 2004/3168 (in relation to England only), SI 2005/2929 (in relation to Wales only).
Summary These regulations revoke and replace the Secretary of State's Traffic Orders (Procedure) (England and Wales) Regulations 1986, SI 1986/180. They lay down the procedure to be followed by the Secretary of State for Transport and the Secretary of State for Wales in connection with the making by them of the main types of traffic and parking place orders under the Road Traffic Regulation Act 1984. The regulations are divided into five Parts and there are four schedules.

Pt I (regs 1–3) contains general provisions. By virtue of reg 3, the regulations apply to orders made or proposed to be made:

(a) in respect of trunk roads under ss 1, 6, 9, 84 of the 1984 Act (i e traffic regulation orders, experimental traffic orders and speed limit orders); and
(b) in respect of non-trunk roads whether under s 22 of that Act, as read with s 132 thereof (countryside road orders), or under the reserve powers of the Secretaries of State by virtue of para 3 of Pt I of or under para 7 of Pt I of Sch 9 to the 1984 Act (reserve power orders).

Pt II (regs 4–11) lays down the procedure to be followed before an order is made. Provisions are made for preliminary consultations, publication of proposals, objections, public inquiries and modification of proposals. Pt III (regs 12–15) contains requirements about the commencement date of an order and notification thereof, and provides for the erection of traffic signs to convey information as to the effect of an order. Pt IV (regs 16–23) makes special procedural provisions for certain orders, including consolidation orders, minor orders, experimental traffic orders, reserve power orders, orders made in part, and revocation and replacement orders. Pt V (reg 24) makes transitional provisions. Schs 1–3 to the regulations contain:

(a) particulars to be included in the press notices of an order;
(b) requirements as to the display of notices of an order in the road; and
(c) requirements as to the availability for public inspection of documents relating to an order.

Sch 4 relates to minor orders.

As to the procedure to be followed by local authorities in England and Wales in connection with the making by them of the main types of traffic and parking place orders under the Road Traffic Regulation Act 1984, see SI 1996/2489.
Transfer of functions Functions of a minister of the Crown under provisions of the Road Traffic Regulation Act 1984 mentioned in these regulations, so far as exercisable in relation to Wales, were

transferred to the National Assembly for Wales by SI 1999/672, in the title Constitutional Law (Pt 3). As to the transfer of the functions of the Assembly to the Welsh Ministers, see the Government of Wales Act 2006, s 162(1), Sch 11, paras 30, 32.

[505]

TRAFFIC AREAS (REORGANISATION) ORDER 1990
SI 1991/288

Authority Made by the Secretary of State for Transport under the Public Passenger Vehicles Act 1981, ss 3(2), (3), 80(2).
Date made 19 December 1990.
Commencement Partly on 4 March 1991; fully on 1 June 1991.
Amendment Amended by SI 1991/634, SI 1999/1204.
Summary The Public Passenger Vehicles Act 1981, s 3(1) provided for the division of Great Britain into 11 traffic areas. The Traffic Areas (Reorganisation) (No 2) Order 1983, SI 1983/1714, which is revoked by this order, reduced the number of those areas to nine. This order, as amended, abolishes the Metropolitan Traffic Area, thereby further reducing the number to eight, namely: the Scottish Traffic Area; the North-Western Traffic Area; the North-Eastern Traffic Area; the West Midland Traffic Area; the Eastern Traffic Area; the Welsh Traffic Area; the Western Traffic Area; and the South-Eastern and Metropolitan Traffic Area. Provision is made for the greater part of the area formerly comprised in the Metropolitan Traffic Area to become part of the South-Eastern and Metropolitan Traffic Area, and the remainder to become part of the Eastern Traffic Area. The order also makes certain consequential and incidental provisions, particularly with regard to existing goods vehicle operators' licences, PSV operators' licences and pending proceedings, which are necessary or expedient in consequence of the reduction.
Wales SI 1999/1204 was made under the Public Passenger Vehicles Act 1981, ss 3(2), (3), 80(2), and came into force on 29 April 1999. It creates a new traffic area which covers Wales and is known as the Welsh Traffic Area. The area previously within the South-Wales Traffic Area (which is abolished) and the former counties of Clwyd and Gwynedd within the North-Western Traffic Area are transferred to the Welsh Traffic Area. Consequential amendments are made to SI 1991/288. The order also makes incidental provision relating to, in particular, existing goods vehicle operators' licences and PSV operators' licences and pending proceedings.

[506]

NATIONAL BUS COMPANY (DISSOLUTION) ORDER 1991
SI 1991/510

Authority Made by the Secretary of State for Transport under the Transport Act 1985, s 54(1)–(3).
Date made 7 March 1991.
Commencement 1 April 1991.
Amendment Amended by SI 1991/1997.
Summary This order provides for the dissolution and transfer of liabilities etc of the National Bus Company on 1 April 1991 as provided for, generally, in the Transport Act 1985, s 54 (see further the Preliminary Note "Reorganisation of transport undertakings"). The order makes consequential amendments to the Transport Act 1981, Sch 3, para 31(4) and the Transport Act 1982, Sch 5, para 5(1) (which, as amended, applied to Scotland only, and has now been repealed in relation to Scotland by SSI 2002/263 (outside the scope of this work)). It also makes repeals of or in the following enactments: Industrial Development Act 1966, Sch 2; Transport Act 1968, ss 24, 25, 27, 28, 29, 44, 47, 50, 159, Sch 1, para 2, Schs 7, 16; Transport (Grants) Act 1972, s 1(1); House of Commons Disqualification Act 1975, Sch 1, Pt II; Transport Act 1981, Sch 3; Transport (Finance) Act 1982, s 4; Transport Act 1982, Sch 5, para 5(2); Miscellaneous Financial Provisions Act 1983, Sch 2; National Audit Act 1983, Sch 4; London Regional Transport Act 1984, Sch 4, paras 10, 11; and Transport Act 1985, ss 47–53.

[507]

ROAD TRAFFIC ACT 1991 (COMMENCEMENT NO 1) ORDER 1991
SI 1991/2054

Authority Made by the Secretary of State for Transport under the Road Traffic Act 1991, s 84.
Date made 10 September 1991.
Summary This order, and the further commencement orders made under the Road Traffic Act 1991, s 84 (ie SI 1992/199, SI 1992/421, SI 1992/1286 (amended by SI 1992/1410), SI 1992/2010, SI 1993/1461 (amended by SI 1993/1686, SI 1993/2229 (amended by SI 1998/967), SI 1998/967), SI 1993/2229, SI 1993/2803 (amended by SI 1998/967), SI 1993/3238 (amended by SI 1994/81, SI 1998/967), SI 1994/81, SI 1994/1482, SI 1994/1484 (all amended by SI 1998/967), SI 1998/967), brought provisions of the 1991 Act into force on various dates. The amendments made to earlier commencement orders by SI 1998/967 relate to spent transitional provisions in those orders. Provisions relating to Scotland only have been brought into force by SI 1993/975, SI 1997/1580, SI 1997/2260, outside the scope of this work. The table below sets out the provisions of the Act brought into force by commencement order. Provisions of the 1991 Act which have subsequently been repealed are noted in Halsbury's Statutes, 4th edn Vol 38(1), title Roads, Railways and Transport.

Provision	*Date and extent (if any)*
ss 1–21	1 July 1992 (SI 1992/1286)
s 22	See Sch 1
ss 23–25	1 July 1992 (SI 1992/1286)
s 26	See Sch 2
ss 27–30	1 July 1992 (SI 1992/1286)
ss 32–34	1 July 1992 (SI 1992/1286)
s 35(1)	1 October 1991 (so far as relates to s 35(2), (5)) (SI 1991/2054) 2 March 1992 (otherwise) (SI 1992/199)
s 35(2)	1 October 1991 (SI 1991/2054)
s 35(3), (4)	2 March 1992 (SI 1992/199)
s 35(5)	1 October 1991 (SI 1991/2054)
s 35(6)	2 March 1992 (SI 1992/199)
ss 39, 40	1 July 1992 (SI 1992/1286)
ss 41, 42	5 July 1993 (SI 1993/1461, as amended by SI 1993/1686)
ss 43, 44	1 October 1991 (SI 1991/2054)
ss 45, 46	1 July 1992 (SI 1992/1286)
s 48	See Sch 4
s 64(1)	Ss 64(1), 65, 66(1)–(6), 67(4), (6), 68(2)(b), 69, 81 (so far as relates to Sch 7), Sch 7, para 5(2), (3), brought into force on various dates and in respect of various London boroughs as follows: 5 July 1993 (only in London borough of Wandsworth) (SI 1993/1461) 4 October 1993 (only in London boroughs of Bromley, Hammersmith and Fulham and Lewisham) (SI 1993/2229) 6 December 1993 (only in London boroughs of Camden, Hackney and Hounslow) (SI 1993/2803) 31 January 1994 (only in London borough of Richmond upon Thames) (SI 1993/3238, as amended by SI 1994/81) 5 April 1994 (only in London borough of Southwark) (SI 1994/81) 4 July 1994 (only in City of London and London boroughs of Barking and Dagenham, Barnet, Brent, Croydon, Ealing, Enfield, Greenwich, Haringey, Harrow, Havering, Hillingdon, Islington, Royal borough of Kensington and Chelsea, Royal borough of Kingston upon Thames, Lambeth, Merton, Newham, Redbridge, Sutton, Tower Hamlets, Waltham Forest, City of Westminster) (SI 1994/1482) 4 July 1994 (only in London borough of Bexley, and not in relation to ss 67(4), (6), 68(2)(b), 69) (SI 1994/1484) 10 April 1998 (in relation to ss 67(4), 68(2)(b), 69 (so far as those provisions are not already in force)) (SI 1998/967)
s 64(2)	1 October 1991 (SI 1991/2054)
s 65	See s 64(1)
s 66(1)–(6)	See s 64(1)
s 66(7)	See Sch 6
s 67(1)–(3)	5 July 1993 (SI 1993/1461)
s 67(4)	See s 64(1)
s 67(5)	5 July 1993 (SI 1993/1461)
s 67(6)	See s 64(1)
s 67(7)	5 July 1993 (SI 1993/1461)
s 68(1)	5 July 1993 (SI 1993/1461)
s 68(2)(a)	5 July 1993 (SI 1993/1461)
s 68(2)(b)	See s 64(1)

Provision	*Date and extent (if any)*
s 68(3), (4)	5 July 1993 (SI 1993/1461)
s 69	See s 64(1)
ss 70–72	5 July 1993 (SI 1993/1461)
ss 73–78	1 October 1991 (SI 1991/2054)
s 79	5 July 1993 (SI 1993/1461)
s 81	See Sch 7
s 82	1 October 1991 (SI 1991/2054)
s 83	See Sch 8
Schs 1, 2	1 July 1992 (SI 1992/1286)
Sch 3	1 October 1991 (SI 1991/2054)
Sch 4, paras 2, 3	1 July 1992 (SI 1992/1286)
Sch 4, paras 6–26	1 July 1992 (SI 1992/1286)
Sch 4, paras 27, 28	1 October 1991 (SI 1991/2054)
Sch 4, paras 29, 30	1 July 1992 (SI 1992/1286)
Sch 4, paras 31–35	1 October 1991 (SI 1991/2054)
Sch 4, para 36	1 April 1992 (SI 1992/421)
Sch 4, paras 37–49	1 July 1992 (SI 1992/1286)
Sch 4, para 50	1 April 1992 (SI 1992/421)
Sch 4, paras 51, 52	1 July 1992 (SI 1992/1286)
Sch 4, para 53	1 July 1992 (SI 1992/1286)
Sch 4, paras 54–72	1 July 1992 (SI 1992/1286)
Sch 4, para 73(1)	1 April 1992 (so far as relates to para 73(2), (3)) (SI 1992/421) 1 July 1992 (otherwise) (SI 1992/1286)
Sch 4, para 73(2), (3)	1 April 1992 (SI 1992/421)
Sch 4, para 73(4)–(6)	1 July 1992 (SI 1992/1286)
Sch 4, para 74	1 July 1992 (SI 1992/1286)
Sch 4, para 75	1 April 1992 (SI 1992/421)
Sch 4, paras 76–78	1 July 1992 (SI 1992/1286)
Sch 4, paras 80–84, 86–101	1 July 1992 (SI 1992/1286)
Sch 4, para 102	1 April 1992 (but does not apply to offence alleged to have been committed before 1 April 1992) (SI 1992/199)
Sch 4, paras 103–105	1 July 1992 (SI 1992/1286)
Sch 4, para 106	1 October 1991 (SI 1991/2054)
Sch 4, paras 107–114	1 July 1992 (SI 1992/1286)
Sch 6	5 July 1993 (SI 1993/1461)
Sch 7, para 2	1 July 1992 (SI 1992/1286)
Sch 7, paras 3, 4	1 October 1991 (SI 1991/2054)
Sch 7, para 5(1)	1 October 1991 (SI 1991/2054)
Sch 7, para 5(2), (3)	See s 64(1)
Sch 7, para 5(4)	1 October 1991 (SI 1991/2054)
Sch 7, para 6	10 April 1998 (SI 1998/967)
Sch 7, para 7	1 October 1991 (SI 1991/2054)
Sch 7, para 8	1 September 1992 (SI 1992/2010)
Sch 7, paras 9–11	1 October 1991 (SI 1991/2054)
Sch 7, para 12	10 April 1998 (SI 1998/967)

Provision	*Date and extent (if any)*
Sch 8	1 October 1991 (repeals of or in Chronically Sick and Disabled Persons Act 1970, s 21(5); Road Traffic Regulation Act 1984, ss 35(9), 51(5), 55(4)(c), 99(2), 104(10), 105(3)(b), 106(2)–(6), (9), (10), 117(3)) (SI 1991/2054) 1 April 1992 (repeal of Road Traffic Act 1988, s 41(3)(b), (c)) (SI 1992/421) 1 July 1992 (otherwise, except repeals in Public Passenger Vehicles Act 1981, s 66A; Road Traffic Regulation Act 1984, s 102) (SI 1992/1286) 5 July 1993 (repeals in Road Traffic Regulation Act 1984, s 102) (SI 1993/1461)

[508]

VEHICLES (CHARGES FOR RELEASE FROM IMMOBILISATION DEVICES) REGULATIONS 1992
SI 1992/386

Authority Made by the Home Secretary under the Road Traffic Regulation Act 1984, ss 104(4), 142(1).
Date made 25 February 1992.
Commencement 1 April 1992.
Summary These regulations, which revoke and replace the Vehicles (Charges for Release from Immobilisation Devices) Regulations 1991, SI 1991/338, provide for the payment of a fee of £38 for the release of a vehicle from an immobilisation device affixed to it in accordance with the Road Traffic Regulation Act 1984, s 104.

[509]

ROAD TRAFFIC OFFENDERS (PRESCRIBED DEVICES) ORDER 1992
SI 1992/1209

Authority Made by the Home Secretary under the Road Traffic Offenders Act 1988, s 20(9), (10).
Date made 21 May 1992.
Commencement 1 July 1992.
Summary This order provides that a device designed or adapted for measuring by radar the speed of motor vehicles is a prescribed device for the purposes of the Road Traffic Offenders Act 1988, s 20.
Further orders The following orders have been made under the Road Traffic Offenders Act 1988, s 20(9) prescribing devices for the purposes of s 20 of that Act (SI 1997/384, SI 2001/1814 were also made under s 20(3) thereof):

(a) SI 1992/2843 (in force on 1 January 1993) prescribes a device designed or adapted for recording the position of motor vehicles in relation to light signals by photographic or other image recording means (in connection with this order, see *The Pict v Crown Prosecution Service* [2009] All ER (D) 185 (Apr));
(b) SI 1993/1698 (in force on 9 August 1993) prescribes a device:
   (1) designed or adapted for recording a measurement of the speed of motor vehicles activated by means of sensors or cables on or near the surface of the highway; and
   (2) designed or adapted for recording a measurement of the speed of motor vehicles activated by means of a light beam or beams;
(c) SI 1997/384 (in force on 18 March 1997) prescribes a camera designed or adapted to record the presence of a vehicle on an area of road which is a bus lane or a route for use by buses only (and amends s 20(2) of the 1988 Act);
(d) SI 1999/162 (in force on 1 March 1999) prescribes a device designed or adapted for recording a measurement of the speed of motor vehicles by:
   (1) capturing by means of unattended cameras images of the motor vehicle at each of two pre-determined positions on the road;
   (2) digitally recording each image and the time when it is captured;
   (3) calculating the average speed of the motor vehicle over the distance between the two positions mentioned in head (1) by reference to the times mentioned in head (2);
(e) SI 2001/1814 (in force on 1 June 2001) prescribes a device designed or adapted to register:
   (1) an image of a vehicle and its registration mark; and
   (2) the time at which the image is registered,

and to record that information if, according to data stored by or otherwise accessible by the device, that vehicle is unlicensed (and amends s 20(2) of the 1988 Act); and

(f) SI 2008/1332 (in force on 16 June 2008) prescribes a manually activated device designed or adapted for recording the measurement of the speed of a motor vehicle ("vehicle A") from another motor vehicle ("vehicle B") by:

(1) measuring the time taken by vehicle A to pass two positions on the road either directly or by reference to the time taken by vehicle B to pass the same two positions on the road;

(2) recording the distance between the two positions by counting the odometer pulses (as defined) from vehicle B as it travels between the two positions; and

(3) calculating the average speed of vehicle A over the distance between the two positions by reference to the time recorded in head (a) and the distance either calculated in accordance with head (b) or measured manually.

[510]

ROAD TRAFFIC (TEMPORARY RESTRICTIONS) PROCEDURE REGULATIONS 1992
SI 1992/1215

Authority Made by the Secretary of State for Transport and the Secretary of State for Wales and for Scotland under the Road Traffic Regulation Act 1984, s 16(2), (2A).
Date made 8 June 1992.
Commencement 1 July 1992.
Amendment Amended by SI 2004/3168 (in relation to England only), SI 2005/2929 (in relation to Wales only), SI 2006/1177. Also amended in relation to Scotland only by SSI 2005/299, SSI 2005/344 (outside the scope of this work).
Summary These regulations set out the procedure to be followed in connection with the exercise of the powers in the Road Traffic Regulation Act 1984, ss 14, 15 to regulate traffic for temporary periods by order or notice. (As to the procedure for making permanent traffic orders, see SI 1996/2489.) They lay down in Pt II the general procedure to be followed before a temporary order is made. In particular, they provide for advance publication of proposals in local newspapers and notification to various bodies, including the chief officer of the fire and rescue authority where the traffic authority is not the fire and rescue authority, and any concessionaire (as defined in the New Roads and Street Works Act 1991, s 1(1)) affected, and for a subsequent notice of the making of the order; the posting of street notices is discretionary rather than mandatory, with certain exceptions, including in particular that the posting of such notices is obligatory in respect of orders relating to footpaths, bridleways, cycle tracks, byways open to all traffic or restricted byways. The regulations require the operator of a tramcar or trolley vehicle to be consulted by the traffic authority before any temporary order is made where it appears that the operation of the vehicle is likely to be affected. In the case of temporary orders to which s 15(2) of the 1984 Act applies, which may extend beyond a period of 18 months, the period of advance notice for publicity in local newspapers is extended from seven to 21 days, the chief officer of police and of the fire and rescue authority (where the traffic authority is not the fire and rescue authority) and organisations representing road users must be consulted, and prior notice of intention to make the order published in the *London* or *Edinburgh Gazettes*. Provision is made for cases where a temporary order is made for the purpose of continuing in force a prohibition or restriction imposed by a temporary notice under s 14 of the 1984 Act. The regulations make provision in respect of the revocation of orders and provide for circumstances where the Secretary of State directs the continuation of an order under s 15(3) or (5) of that Act, including a requirement to publish notice of the direction in local newspapers and give notice to specified persons or bodies.

These regulations also make provision in Pt III in connection with temporary notices issued by traffic authorities. Similar requirements are imposed with respect to notifying relevant bodies and posting street notices as in the case of temporary orders and there is a further requirement to consult tramcar or trolley vehicle operators before introducing temporary traffic regulation by notice which would be likely to affect the operation of any such vehicle, unless it appears to the authority that the notice needs to be issued without delay. Equivalent provision is made in connection with notices issued by concessionaires. Finally, provision is made for the display of street notices in the case of temporary regulation by order or by notice and the display of appropriate traffic signs for the duration of the restriction.
Transfer of functions Functions of a minister of the Crown under the provisions of the 1984 Act mentioned above, so far as exercisable in relation to Wales, were transferred to the National Assembly for Wales by SI 1999/672, in the title Constitutional Law (Pt 3). As to the transfer of the relevant functions of the Assembly to the Welsh Ministers, see the Government of Wales Act 2006, s 162(1), Sch 11, paras 30, 32. Functions of a minister of the Crown under those provisions of the 1984 Act and under SI 1992/1215, in relation to the imposition of speed limits, so far as exercisable in relation to Scotland, were transferred to the Scottish Ministers by SI 1999/1750, also in the title Constitutional Law (Pt 3).
Application of regulations to road tunnels in the trans-European road network
These regulations apply, subject to modifications, to an order made under reg 7(1) or (2) of SI 2007/1520 (suspension or restriction of use of a road tunnel) in relation to a road tunnel in Great Britain in the trans-European road network, as if it were an order made under the Road Traffic Regulation Act 1984, s 14(1); see reg 7(3) of SI 2007/1520.

[511]

TRAMCARS AND TROLLEY VEHICLES (MODIFICATION OF ENACTMENTS) REGULATIONS 1992
SI 1992/1217

Authority Made by the Secretary of State for Transport under the Road Traffic Regulation Act 1984, s 141A and the Road Traffic Act 1988, ss 41, 45, 46, 193A.

Date made 3 June 1992.
Commencement 1 July 1992.
Summary In consequence of the amendments made to the Road Traffic Regulation Act 1984 and the Road Traffic Act 1988 by the Road Traffic Act 1991, these regulations provide that certain sections of those Acts are not to apply to tramcars or trolley vehicles and that other sections of those Acts are to apply to tramcars and trolley vehicles with modifications. The sections of the 1984 Act which are disapplied or modified in relation to tramcars and/or trolley vehicles are ss 1, 6, 9, 14, 18; and the sections of the 1988 Act which are so disapplied or modified are ss 40A, 68, 69–73, 75, 76, 77, 78, 79, 83, 87, 190, 191. Saving provision is made so that the 1984 and 1988 Acts apply to "Duobuses" without modification. The regulations define a "Duobus" as a trolley vehicle which is able to operate either by means of overhead wires or by utilising a source of power on board. In order to come within the definition the vehicle has to meet specified minimum speed and range requirements when utilising the source of power on board. SI 1981/1694, SI 1986/1078, SI 1989/1796 are amended in consequence of the amendments made to the 1988 Act by the Road Traffic Act 1991. Transitional provision is also made.

[512]

ROAD VEHICLES (PROHIBITION) REGULATIONS 1992
SI 1992/1285

Authority Made by the Secretary of State for Transport under the Road Traffic Act 1988, ss 71(2), 72.
Date made 3 June 1992.
Commencement 1 July 1992; see reg 1.
Interpretation See reg 2.
Amendment Printed as amended by SI 1997/83.
General These regulations provide for exemptions from the offence under the Road Traffic Act 1988, s 71 of driving a vehicle in contravention of a prohibition, and prescribe the persons who can remove the prohibition which may be imposed under s 69A(3) of the 1988 Act on a vehicle which is subject to the MOT testing scheme making it irremovable until it has been inspected and an MOT test certificate issued, and the requirements which have to be complied with. They set out the requirements relating to the inspection of a vehicle which have to be complied with before a prohibition under s 69A(4) of that Act on a vehicle which is not subject to either the MOT testing scheme or the goods vehicle testing scheme can be removed; provide for appeals to the Secretary of State against a refusal to remove a prohibition; and prescribe fees for the inspection of a vehicle with a view to the removal of a prohibition. The regulations revoke SI 1987/1149, SI 1987/1150 (see reg 9), but it should be noted that they make no provision relating to appeals under the Public Passenger Vehicles Act 1981, s 51 to replace that formerly made by SI 1987/1150.

[513]

Preliminary

1 These Regulations may be cited as the Road Vehicles (Prohibition) Regulations 1992 and shall come into force on 1st July 1992.

[514]

Interpretation

2 (1) In these Regulations—

"the 1981 Regulations" means the Motor Vehicles (Tests) Regulations 1981 as from time to time amended;

"the 1988 Regulations" means the Goods Vehicles (Plating and Testing) Regulations 1988 as from time to time amended;

"the 1988 Act" means the Road Traffic Act 1988;

"authorised constable" means a constable authorised to act for the purpose of section 72 of the 1988 Act by or on behalf of a chief officer of police;

"vehicle examiner" has the meaning given by section 66A of the 1988 Act;

"prohibition" means a prohibition under section 69 of the 1988 Act; and

"relevant test certificate", in relation to a prohibition, means a test certificate issued in respect of the vehicle after the prohibition had been imposed.

(2) A reference to an inspection by a vehicle examiner shall be read as including a reference to an inspection under the direction of a vehicle examiner.

NOTES
Goods Vehicles (Plating and Testing) Regulations 1988 SI 1988/1478.
Motor Vehicles (Tests) Regulations 1981 SI 1981/1694.

[515]

Exemptions from section 71(1) of the 1988 Act

3 (1) The driving of a vehicle on a road—

(a) solely for the purpose of submitting it by previous arrangement for a specified time on a specified date for an inspection by a vehicle examiner or authorised constable with a view to the removal of the prohibition;

(b) solely for the purpose of submitting it by previous arrangement for a specified time on a specified date for an inspection by a vehicle examiner with a view to the removal of the prohibition and the issue of either a test certificate or a goods vehicle test certificate;

(c) in the course of an inspection with a view to the removal of a prohibition; or

(d) within 3 miles from where it is being, or has been, repaired solely for the purpose of its test or trial with a view to the removal of a prohibition,

is exempted from section 71(1)(a) and (b) of the 1988 Act.

(2) Where a prohibition has been imposed with a direction under section 69A(3) of the 1988 Act, the driving of the vehicle on a road solely for the purpose of submitting it by previous arrangement at a specified time for an examination under section 45(3) of the 1988 Act with a view to obtaining a test certificate or bringing it away from such an examination is exempted from section 71(1)(a) and (b) of that Act.

(3) Where—

(a) a prohibition has been imposed with a direction under section 69A(3) of the 1988 Act, and

(b) a relevant test certificate has been issued,

the driving of the vehicle on a road to a police station with a view to the prohibition being removed under regulation 4(3) of these Regulations is exempted from section 71(1)(a) and (b) of that Act.

[516]

Removal of prohibitions imposed with a direction under section 69A(3) of the 1988 Act

4 (1) This regulation applies where a prohibition has been imposed with a direction under section 69A(3) of the 1988 Act.

(2) Where a vehicle examiner has issued a relevant test certificate, the prohibition may be removed by—

(a) the vehicle examiner who issued the certificate, or

(b) a person who has been authorised for the purpose by or on behalf of the Secretary of State and to whom the certificate has been produced.

(3) The prohibition may also be removed by a person who has been authorised for the purpose by or on behalf of a chief officer of police and to whom a relevant test certificate has been produced at a police station.

[517]

Removal of prohibitions imposed with a direction under section 69A(4)

5 (1) This regulation applies where a prohibition has been imposed under section 69A(4) of the 1988 Act.

(2) The requirements relating to the inspection of the vehicle which have to be complied with before the prohibition can be removed are that the vehicle must have been inspected by a vehicle examiner or an authorised constable.

[518]

Appeals relating to prohibitions

6 (1) This regulation applies to appeals to the Secretary of State under section 72(5) of the 1988 Act (appeals against the refusal of a vehicle examiner or authorised constable to remove a prohibition).

(2) Every appeal to which the section applies shall be made within 14 days of the date on which the vehicle examiner or authorised constable refused to remove the prohibition in question.

(3) Every such appeal shall—

(a) be in writing; and
(b) contain a statement of the grounds on which it is made,

and shall be delivered to the Secretary of State.

(4) Every such appeal relating to a goods vehicle shall be accompanied by such fee as is payable in respect of the vehicle under regulation 25 of the 1988 Regulations on an appeal to the Secretary of State under those Regulations.

(5) Every such appeal relating to a vehicle other than a goods vehicle shall be accompanied by such fee as is payable in respect of the vehicle under regulation 21 of the 1981 Regulations on an appeal under those Regulations.

[519]

Fees relating to inspection of goods vehicles

7 (1) This regulation shall have effect for the purpose of prescribing the scales and rates of fees for the inspection of a vehicle which is of a class to which regulations under section 49 of the 1988 Act apply with a view to the removal of a prohibition.

(2) Subject to paragraph (3) below, the fee shall be such fee as is payable in respect of the vehicle under regulation 12 of the 1988 Regulations on an application for a periodical test.

(3) If after an inspection of a vehicle a vehicle examiner refuses to remove the prohibition, the fee for a further inspection shall be such fee (if any) as would be payable in like circumstances under regulation 16 of the 1988 Regulations for a re-test of the vehicle after a notification of a refusal of a goods vehicle test certificate.

[(4) Regulations 12(4) and (4A), and 16(4), (4A), (5) and (5A) of the 1988 Regulations shall apply with appropriate modification to an inspection or further inspection after a vehicle has failed an inspection.]

NOTES
Amendment Para (4): substituted by SI 1997/83.
Regulations under s 49 of the 1988 Act See SI 1988/1478.

[520]

Fees relating to the inspection of vehicles other than goods vehicles

8 (1) This regulation shall have effect for the purpose of prescribing the scales and rates of fees for the inspection of a vehicle, not being a vehicle to which regulation 7 applies, with a view to the removal of a prohibition.

(2) Subject to paragraph (3) below, the fee shall be such fee as is payable under regulation 20 of the 1981 Regulations for an examination pursuant to an application made under regulation 12 of those Regulations.

(3) [Regulation 20(2A), (2B), (3), (3A) and (4) of the 1981 Regulations] shall apply with appropriate modification to an inspection or further inspection after a vehicle has failed an inspection.

NOTES
Amendment Para (3): words in square brackets substituted by SI 1997/83.

[521]

9 (*Revokes the Goods Vehicles (Prohibitions) (Exemptions and Appeals) Regulations 1987, SI 1987/1149, and the Public Passenger Vehicles (Exemptions, and Appeals Against Refusals to Issue Certificates or Remove Prohibitions) Regulations 1987, SI 1987/1150.*)

TRANSPORT AND WORKS ACT 1992 (COMMENCEMENT NO 1) ORDER 1992

SI 1992/1347

Authority Made by the Secretary of State for Transport under the Transport and Works Act 1992, s 70(1), (2).
Date made 8 June 1992.
Summary This order brought the following provisions of the Transport and Works Act 1992 into force, subject to transitional provisions, on 15 July 1992: ss 45, 46, 49, 57–60, 63, 65(1)(a), (e), (2), 66, 67, 68(1) (in so far as it relates to the specified entries in Sch 4), 69, Sch 3, Sch 4, Pt I (in so far as it relates to the repeals of or in the British Railways Act 1965, the London Transport Act 1965, the Criminal Justice Act 1967, the London Transport Act 1977 and the British Railways Act 1977) and Sch 4, Pt II.

Further orders Other provisions of the 1992 Act were brought into force by the following orders made under s 70(1), (2) (except for SI 1992/2043, SI 1998/274, which were made under s 70(1) only):

(a) by SI 1992/2043, on 7 December 1992: Pt II, Chapter I (ss 26–39), s 68(1) (in so far as it relates to the specified entries in Sch 4), Sch 4, Pt I (in so far as it relates to the repeal in the Railway Regulation Act 1842);

(b) by SI 1992/2784, on 1 January 1993, subject to transitional provisions: Pt I (ss 1–25), ss 65(1)(b) (part), (c), (d), (f), 68(1) (in so far as it relates to the specified entries in Sch 4), Sch 1, Sch 4 (in so far as it relates to the repeals in the Tramways Act 1870, except s 48 and the words "and shall not be opened" onwards in s 25; the Municipal Corporations Act 1882; the Military Tramways Act 1887; the Light Railways Act 1896; the Railways (Electrical Power) Act 1903; the Light Railways Act 1912; the Railways Act 1921; the Transport Act 1962; the Administration of Justice Act 1965; the Transport Act 1968, except ss 124, 125(4); the Local Government Act 1972; the Supply Powers Act 1975; the Administration of Justice Act 1982; the Telecommunications Act 1984 and the Insolvency Act 1986);

(c) by SI 1992/3144:

  (1) on 22 December 1992, so much of s 47(1) and Sch 2 as is necessary for the purpose of conferring on the Secretary of State the power to make regulations as to the making, submission, confirmation or validity of, or otherwise in relation to, rail crossing extinguishment orders or rail crossing diversion orders; and

  (2) on 31 January 1993, ss 41, 42, 47(1) (in so far as it is not already in force), 47(2), 48, 51, 61, 64, 68(1) (in so far as it relates to the specified entries in Sch 4), Sch 2 (in so far as it is not already in force), Sch 4, Pt I (in so far as it relates to the repeals in the Regulation of Railways Act 1871, s 3 and the Highways Act 1980;

(d) by SI 1994/718, on 5 April 1994, subject to transitional provisions: s 65(1)(b) (the words "in section 25, the words "and shall not be opened" onwards" only), s 68(1) (in so far as it relates to the specified entries in Sch 4), Sch 4, Pt I (in so far as it relates to the repeals of or in the Tramways Act 1870 (the words "In section 25, the words "and shall not be opened" onwards" only), the Road and Rail Traffic Act 1933, s 41, and the Transport Act 1968, s 125(4));

(e) by SI 1996/1609, on 8 July 1996, subject to a saving: ss 50, 52–56, 62, s 65(1)(b) (the words "section 48," only), s 68(1) (in so far as it relates to the specified entries in Sch 4), Sch 4, Pt I (in so far as it relates to the repeals of the Tramways Act 1870, s 48 and the Transport Act 1968, s 124 (except as it applies to Scotland)); and

(f) by SI 1998/274, on 26 February 1998: s 68(1) (in so far as it relates to the specified entries in Sch 4), Sch 4, Pt I (in so far as it relates to the Town Police Clauses Act 1889, the Notice of Accidents Act 1894, the Notice of Accidents Act 1906, the Road and Rail Traffic Act 1933, s 43, the Transport Charges &c (Miscellaneous Provisions) Act 1954, the Public Service Vehicles (Arrest of Offenders) Act 1975, and the Channel Tunnel Act 1987).

Provisions of the 1992 Act which have subsequently been repealed are noted in Halsbury's Statutes, 4th edn Vol 38(1), title Roads, Railways and Transport.

[522]

TRANSPORT (GUIDED SYSTEMS) ORDER 1992
SI 1992/2044

Authority Made by the Secretary of State for Transport under the Transport and Works Act 1992, s 26(3).
Date made 27 August 1992.
Commencement 7 December 1992.
Amendment Amended by SI 2005/2290 (in relation to England only).
Summary This order specifies certain systems using modes of guided transport (namely monorail and track-based with side guidance) for the purposes of the Transport and Works Act 1992, Pt II, Chapter I, and has the effect of applying to these systems the provisions of that Act which introduce new offences involving drink and drugs.

[523]

TRANSPORT LEVYING BODIES REGULATIONS 1992
SI 1992/2789

Authority Made by the Secretary of State for Transport under the Local Government Finance Act 1988, ss 74, 143(1), (2).
Date made 9 November 1992.
Commencement 1 December 1992.
Modification Modified by SI 1997/165 (made under the Local Government Act 1992, ss 19(1), (2), 26(4) and in force on 26 February 1997) in consequence of a reorganisation order made under Pt II of the 1992 Act giving effect to recommendations for local government changes in England. The effect of SI 1997/165 is to enable the levying powers under these regulations to be exercised in relation to:

(a) authorities which succeed to or acquire all or part of the area of a relevant local authority under a reorganisation order; and

(b) county councils which do not have the functions of district councils and certain billing authorities in advance of the reorganisation date.

Summary The Local Government Finance Act 1988, s 117 provides that specified levying bodies no longer have a statutory power, in respect of any chargeable financial year, to issue a precept to, make a levy on, or have its expenses paid by, a county council or charging authority. However, by s 74 of that

Act, the Secretary of State (or, in relation to Wales, the Welsh Ministers; see SI 1999/672, in the title Constitutional Law (Pt 3), and the Government of Wales Act 2006, s 162(1), Sch 11, paras 30, 32), may by regulations confer on levying bodies the power to issue to the council concerned a levy in respect of any chargeable year. These regulations, which revoke and replace the Transport Levying Bodies Regulations 1990, SI 1990/71, subject to a transitional provision, confer a general power on certain transport bodies (including metropolitan county passenger transport authorities and certain local Act levying bodies) to issue levies to local authorities for the purpose of meeting their liabilities and expenses in respect of financial years beginning in or after 1993 where, but for s 117 of the 1988 Act, they would have a statutory power to require the authorities to pay those expenses. In particular, provision is made as to:

(a) when levies are to be issued;
(b) the maximum amount of certain levies;
(c) the issue of substituted levies; and
(d) the payment of levies and the interest which is payable on unpaid levies.

The method of apportionment of levies in cases where a body may issue levies to more than one authority is prescribed, and billing authorities are required to supply information as to the council tax base in cases where this is a factor determining the proportion of levy to be paid. Provision is also made for local authorities to anticipate a levy which may be issued to them when estimating their expenditure. Different provision is made for different bodies according to the terms of the Act or instrument conferring the specific power.

[524]

ROAD TRAFFIC (COURSES FOR DRINK-DRIVE OFFENDERS) REGULATIONS 1992
SI 1992/3013

Authority Made by the Secretary of State for Transport under the Road Traffic Offenders Act 1988, ss 34B(3), (8), 34C(3). Ss 34B, 34C are substituted by the Road Safety Act 2006, s 35, as from a day to be appointed by order under s 61(1) thereof.

Date made 2 December 1992.

Commencement 24 December 1992.

Summary These regulations make provision with regard to the Road Traffic Offenders Act 1988, ss 34A, 34B (which are substituted by the Road Safety Act 2006, s 35, as from a day to be appointed by order under s 61(1) thereof), which give courts power to order that the period of disqualification imposed on a person convicted of a drink-drive offence is to be reduced if he completes a course approved by the Secretary of State. The regulations:

(a) provide that the form and content of the certificate to be given to an offender when he satisfactorily completes a course is to be such as may from time to time be determined by the Secretary of State;
(b) provide that the person responsible for giving such certificates is to be the person for the time being nominated for that purpose by the manager of the course; and
(c) prescribe the circumstances in which a notice of non-completion of a course is to be treated as given to the offender.

Transfer of functions Functions of a minister of the Crown under the Road Traffic Offenders Act 1988, ss 34A, 34B (except sub-s (9)) so far as exercisable in relation to Wales, were transferred to the National Assembly for Wales by SI 1999/672, in the title Constitutional Law (Pt 3). As to the transfer of the functions of the Assembly to the Welsh Ministers, see the Government of Wales Act 2006, s 162(1), Sch 11, paras 30, 32.

[525]

GOODS VEHICLES (COMMUNITY AUTHORISATIONS) REGULATIONS 1992
SI 1992/3077

Authority Made by the Secretary of State for Transport under the European Communities Act 1972, s 2.

Date made 8 December 1992.

Commencement 1 January 1993.

Amendment Amended by SI 1995/1290, SI 1996/2186, SI 2009/1885, and the Goods Vehicles (Licensing of Operators) Act 1995, s 60(2), Sch 8, Pt II.

Summary These regulations implement Council Regulation (EEC) 881/92 (OJ L95, 09.04.1992, p 1), which prohibits the carriage of goods by road between member states without Community authorisation. They enforce the prohibition by imposing a penalty for breach and designating competent authorities for the purposes of the Regulation. Entitlement to Community authorisation is conferred on the basis of the issue of a standard operator's licence covering both international and national transport operations under the Goods Vehicles (Licensing of Operators) Act 1995, s 2, and rights of appeal to the Upper Tribunal (previously the Transport Tribunal) against refusal or withdrawal of authorisation are conferred (as to the establishment of the Upper Tribunal, see the Tribunals, Courts and Enforcement Act 2007, s 3 and the title Courts and Legal Services). A person who uses a vehicle under a Community authorisation and without reasonable excuse fails to comply with any of the conditions governing its use is guilty of an offence. Authorised inspecting officers are designated by these regulations to inspect the Community authorisation documents. Provision is also made requiring a holder to return the authorisation and all certified true copies if it is withdrawn, and to return

certified true copies if they are suspended or if the number of vehicles is reduced, and for the supply of information by the holder of a Community authorisation to the competent authority. The regulations provide for the automatic transfer of an authorisation in certain circumstances following the death, bankruptcy or incapacity of the holder. Provision is also made concerning offences by bodies corporate.
Offences Certain offences under these regulations are: (a) fixed penalty offences; see SI 2009/483, noted to SI 1990/335; (b) offences in respect of which a financial penalty deposit requirement may be imposed; see SI 2009/491 (and see also SI 2009/492).

[526]

TRANSPORT AND WORKS APPLICATIONS (LISTED BUILDINGS, CONSERVATION AREAS AND ANCIENT MONUMENTS PROCEDURE) REGULATIONS 1992
SI 1992/3138

Authority Made by the Secretary of State for Transport under the Transport and Works Act 1992, s 15.
Date made 9 December 1992.
Commencement 1 January 1993.
Summary These regulations make provision for the assimilation of the procedures for making applications and holding inquiries where proposals contained in an application made under the Transport and Works Act 1992, s 6 give rise to a requirement for listed building consent or conservation area consent under the Planning (Listed Buildings and Conservation Areas) Act 1990, or scheduled monument consent under the Ancient Monuments and Archaeological Areas Act 1979. The regulations apply when either:
(a) the application for a relevant consent is made not later than 10 weeks after the application under s 6 of the 1992 Act is made; or
(b) the application for the relevant consent is made later but the Secretary of State considers it to be appropriate that the procedural changes made by these regulations should nevertheless apply and gives a direction to that effect.

SI 1981/1301, in the title Open Spaces and National Heritage, and SI 1990/1519, in the title Town and Country Planning, are modified in relation to the documentation which must be submitted with an application for a relevant consent and the publishing of notices in local newspapers, and consequential modifications are also made to the 1979 and 1990 Acts. Provision is also made for the holding of concurrent inquiries and for the application thereto of SI 2004/2018).
Transfer of functions As to the transfer to the National Assembly for Wales of certain functions of the Secretary of State under the Transport and Works Act 1992 (and instruments made thereunder), so far as exercisable in relation to Wales, see SI 1999/672, in the title Constitutional Law (Pt 3). As to the transfer of the functions of the Assembly to the Welsh Ministers, see the Government of Wales Act 2006, s 162(1), Sch 11, paras 30, 32.

[527]

TRANSPORT AND WORKS (DESCRIPTIONS OF WORKS INTERFERING WITH NAVIGATION) ORDER 1992
SI 1992/3230

Authority Made by the Secretary of State for Transport under the Transport and Works Act 1992, s 4(1), (2).
Date made 16 December 1992.
Commencement 1 January 1993.
Amendment Amended by SI 1997/2906.
Summary This order applies the provisions of the Transport and Works Act 1992, Pt I (orders authorising works etc) to works of a prescribed description which interfere with rights of navigation. The prescribed works are as follows: barrages, bridges, cables, fountains, land reclamation, navigational aids, observation structures, offshore installations, piers, pipe-lines, tunnels and utilities structures. Authority for the carrying out of some of these works may be secured under other enactments and s 13(2) of the 1992 Act provides that in such circumstances the Secretary of State may determine not to make an order applied for under that Act in respect of those works. The scope of this order is further constrained by s 3(2) of the Act, which prevents the Secretary of State from making an order under the Act if the primary object of the order could be achieved by means of an order under the Harbours Act 1964.
Transfer of functions As to the transfer to the National Assembly for Wales of the functions of a minister of the Crown under the relevant provisions of the 1992 Act, so far as exercisable in relation to Wales, see SI 1999/672, in the title Constitutional Law (Pt 3). As to the transfer of the functions of the Assembly to the Welsh Ministers, see the Government of Wales Act 2006, s 162(1), Sch 11, paras 30, 32.

[528]

TRANSPORT AND WORKS (GUIDED TRANSPORT MODES) ORDER 1992
SI 1992/3231

Authority Made by the Secretary of State for Transport under the Transport and Works Act 1992, s 2(1), (2).

Date made 16 December 1992.
Commencement 1 January 1993.
Amendment Amended by SI 1997/1951.
Summary The Transport and Works Act 1992, s 1 enables orders to be made relating to, or to matters ancillary to, the construction or operation of certain kinds of transport system, including a system using a mode of guided transport prescribed by order made under s 2 of that Act. This order, made under s 2, prescribes the following modes for these purposes (all as defined by the order): aerial cableway; lift; magnetic levitation; monorail; road-based with cable guidance; road-based with rail guidance; road-based with side guidance; and track-based with side guidance. The application of the order is limited to a mode of guided transport which employs vehicles used for the carriage of passengers or goods.

[529]

MOTOR VEHICLES (WEARING OF SEAT BELTS BY CHILDREN IN FRONT SEATS) REGULATIONS 1993
SI 1993/31

Authority Made by the Secretary of State for Transport under the Road Traffic Act 1988, s 15(1), (5), (5A), (6).
Date made 11 January 1993.
Commencement 2 February 1993; see reg 1(1).
Amendment Printed as amended by SI 2006/2213.
Interpretation See regs 2, 4, 7(4), Schs 1, 2.
General These regulations revoke and replace the Motor Vehicles (Wearing of Seat Belts by Children) Regulations 1982, SI 1982/1342, and partially implement Council Directive 91/671/EEC on the approximation of the laws of the member states relating to compulsory use of safety belts in vehicles of less than 3,5 tonnes (OJ L373, 31.12.1991, p 26). They make provision as to the wearing of seat belts and other restraints in the front of motor vehicles by children under the age of 14 years. The amendments made by SI 2006/2213 implement requirements of Council Directive 2003/20/EC of the European Parliament and of the Council (OJ L115, 09.05. 2003, p 63). For the purposes of the regulations children are divided into two categories according to size.

As to regulations relating to the wearing of seat belts in the front or rear of motor vehicles by adults and to the wearing of seat belts and other restraints by children in the rear of motor vehicles, see SI 1993/176.

[530]

Citation, commencement and revocations

1 (1) These Regulations may be cited as the Motor Vehicles (Wearing of Seat Belts by Children in Front Seats) Regulations 1993 and shall come into force on 2nd February 1993.

(2) *(Revokes the Motor Vehicles (Wearing of Seat Belts by Children) Regulations 1982, SI 1982/1342.)*

[531]

General interpretation

2 (1) In these Regulations—

"the Act" means the Road Traffic Act 1988;

"Construction and Use Regulations" means the Road Vehicles (Construction and Use) Regulations 1986;

"front seat", in relation to a vehicle, means a seat which is wholly or partially in the front of the vehicle and "rear seat", in relation to a vehicle, means any seat which is not a front seat (see also regulation 4);

"maximum laden weight" has the meaning given by Part IV of Schedule 6 to the Road Traffic Regulation Act 1984;

"medical certificate" has the meaning given in Schedule 1 to these Regulations;

["operator", in relation to a bus, means—

(a) the owner of the bus, or

(b) if the bus is in the possession of any other person under an agreement for hire, hire-purchase, conditional sale, loan or otherwise, that person;]

"restraint system" means a system combining a seat fixed to the structure of the vehicle by appropriate means and a seat belt for which at least one anchorage point is located on the seat structure;

"seat belt", except in this Regulation, includes a child restraint and references to wearing a seat belt shall be construed accordingly;

"disabled person's belt", "lap belt", "seat", and "three point belt" have the meanings given by regulation 47(8) of the Construction and Use Regulations.

(2) Without prejudice to section 17 of the Interpretation Act 1978, a reference to a provision of the Construction and Use Regulations is a reference to that provision as from time to time amended or as from time to time re-enacted with or without modification.

(3) In these Regulations—

"child" means a person under the age of 14 years;

"large child" means a child who is not a small child; and "small child" means a child who is—

(a) aged under 12 years; and
(b) under [135] centimetres in height.

(4) In these Regulations, "adult belt" means a seat belt in respect of which one or more of the following requirements is satisfied, namely that—

(a) it is a three-point belt which has been marked in accordance with regulation 47(7) of the Construction and Use Regulations;
(b) it is a lap belt which has been so marked;
(c) it is a seat belt that falls within regulation 47(4)(c)(i) or (ii) of those Regulations;
(d) it is a seat belt fitted [in a vehicle] and comprised in a restraint system—
  (i) of a type which has been approved by an authority of another member State for use by all persons who are either aged 13 years or more or of 150 centimetres or more in height, and
  (ii) in respect of which, by virtue of such approval, the requirements of the law of another member State corresponding to these Regulations would be met were it to be worn by persons who are either aged 13 years or more or of 150 centimetres or more in height when travelling [in that vehicle in that State].

(5) In these Regulations, "child restraint" means a seat belt or other device in respect of which the following requirements are satisfied, namely that—

(a) it is a seat belt or any other description of restraining device for the use of a child which is—
  (i) designed either to be fitted directly to a suitable anchorage or to be used in conjunction with an adult belt and held in place by the restraining action of that belt, and
  (ii) marked in accordance with regulation 47(7) of the Construction and Use Regulations; or
(b) it is a seat belt consisting of or comprised in a restraint system fitted [in a vehicle], being a restraint system—
  (i) of a type which has been approved by an authority of another member State for use by a child, and
  (ii) in respect of which, by virtue of such approval, the requirements of the law of that State corresponding to these Regulations would be met were it to be worn by a child when travelling [in that vehicle in that State].

(6) Subject to paragraph (7), for the purposes of these Regulations, a seat shall be regarded as provided with an adult belt if an adult belt is fixed in such a position that it can be worn by an occupier of that seat.

(7) A seat shall not be regarded as provided with an adult belt if the belt—

(a) has an inertia reel mechanism which is locked as a result of the vehicle being, or having been, on a steep incline, or
(b) does not comply with the requirements of regulation 48 of the Construction and Use Regulations.

(8) For the purposes of these Regulations, a seat shall be regarded as provided with a child restraint if a child restraint is—

(a) fixed in such a position that it can be worn by an occupier of that seat, or
(b) elsewhere in or on the vehicle but—

(i) could readily be fixed in such a position without the aid of tools, and
(ii) is not being worn by a child for whom it is appropriate and who is occupying another seat.

[(9) For the purposes of these Regulations, a seat belt is appropriate—

(a) in relation to a small child, if it is a child restraint of a description prescribed for a child of his height and weight by regulation 5;
(b) in relation to a large child, if it is a child restraint of a description prescribed for a child of his height and weight by regulation 5 or an adult belt; or
(c) in relation to a person aged 14 years or more, if it is an adult belt.]

[(9A) For the purposes of these Regulations, references to a bus being used to provide a service in a "built-up area" shall be construed in the same way as in section 15B(6) of the Act.]

(10) Unless the context otherwise requires, in these Regulations—

(a) any reference to a numbered regulation is a reference to the regulation bearing that number in these Regulations; and
(b) a numbered paragraph is a reference to the paragraph bearing that number in the regulation or Schedule in which the reference appears.

NOTES

Amendment Para (1): definition "operator" inserted by SI 2006/2213.
Para (3): in definition "small child" in para (b) reference to "135" in square brackets substituted by SI 2006/2213.
Paras (4)(d), (5)(b): words in square brackets substituted by SI 2006/2213.
Para (9): substituted by SI 2006/2213.
Para (9A): inserted by SI 2006/2213.
Interpretation Act 1978, s 17 Printed in the title Statutory Instruments (Pt 2), Vol 1 of this work.
Road Vehicles (Construction and Use) Regulations 1986 SI 1986/1078.

[532]

3 *(Revoked by SI 2006/2213.)*

Interpretation of references to the front of a vehicle

4 (1) This regulation has effect for the purpose of defining in relation to a vehicle what part of the vehicle is to be regarded as the front of the vehicle for the purposes of section 15(1) of the Act and these Regulations.

(2) Subject to paragraph (3), every part of the vehicle forward of the transverse vertical plane passing through the rearmost part of the driver's seat shall be regarded as the front of the vehicle; and accordingly no part of the vehicle to the rear of that plane shall be regarded as being in the front of the vehicle.

(3) Where a vehicle has a deck which is above the level of the driver's head when he is in the normal driving position, no part of the vehicle above that level shall be regarded as being in the front of the vehicle.

[533]

Description of seat belts to be worn by children

5 (1) For a child of any particular height and weight travelling in a particular vehicle, the description of seat belt prescribed for the purposes of section 15(1) of the Act to be worn by him is—

(a) if he is a small child … , a child restraint of a description specified in sub-paragraph (a) or (b) of paragraph (2);
(b) …
(c) if he is a large child, a child restraint of a description specified in sub-paragraph (a) of paragraph (2) or an adult belt.

(2) The descriptions of seat belt referred to in paragraph (1) are—

(a) a child restraint with the marking required under regulation 47(7) of the Construction and Use Regulations if the marking indicates that it is suitable for his weight and either indicates that it is suitable for his height or contains no indication as respects height;

(b) a child restraint which would meet the requirements of the law of another member State corresponding to these Regulations were it to be worn by that child when travelling in that vehicle in that State.

NOTES
Amendment Para (1)(a): words omitted revoked by SI 2006/2213.
Para (1)(b): revoked by SI 2006/2213.

[534]

Vehicles to which section 15(1) of the Act does not apply

6 Two-wheeled motor cycles with or without sidecars are exempt from the prohibition in section 15(1) of the Act.

[535]

Exemptions

7 [(1) The prohibition in section 15(1) of the Act shall not apply in relation to—

(a) a small child aged 3 years or more who is riding in a bus and is wearing an adult belt if an appropriate seat belt is not available for him in the front or rear of the vehicle;
(b) a child for whom there is a medical certificate; or
(c) a disabled child who is wearing a disabled person's belt.

(2) The prohibition in section 15(1) of the Act shall not apply in relation to a child riding in a bus—

(a) which is being used to provide a local service (within the meaning of the Transport Act 1985) in a built-up area, or
(b) which is constructed or adapted for the carriage of standing passengers and on which the operator permits standing.]

(3) The prohibition in section 15(1) of the Act shall not apply in relation to a large child if no appropriate seat belt is available for him in the front of the vehicle.

(4) For the purposes of this regulation, a reference to a seat belt being available shall be construed in accordance with Schedule 2.

NOTES
Amendment Paras (1), (2): substituted by SI 2006/2213.
Transport Act 1985 For the meaning of "local service" in the 1985 Act, see s 2 thereof.

[536]

SCHEDULE 1
MEANING OF "MEDICAL CERTIFICATE"

Regulation 2(1)

PART I

1 Subject to paragraph 2, in these Regulations, "medical certificate", in relation to a person driving or riding in a vehicle, means—

(a) a valid certificate signed by a medical practitioner to the effect that it is inadvisable on medical grounds for him to wear a seat belt, or
(b) a valid certificate to such effect issued by the authority having power to issue such a certificate under the law of another member State corresponding to these Regulations.

2 A certificate shall not be regarded as a medical certificate in relation to a person driving or riding in a vehicle for the purposes of these Regulations unless—

(a) it specifies its period of validity and bears the symbol shown in Part II of this Schedule; or
(b) the person is aged under 14 years …

3 Paragraph 2 does not apply in relation to a certificate issued before 1st January 1995.

NOTES
Amendment Para (2)(b): words omitted revoked by SI 2006/2213.
Certificate … to the effect that it is inadvisable on medical grounds … to wear a seat belt As to payments by the Secretary of State in respect of the examination of certain applicants for medical certificates required as a condition of the exemption prescribed by reg 7(1)(b), see the Transport Act 1982, s 70.

[537]

PART II

NOTES
Pt II of this Schedule sets out the symbol referred to in Pt I, para 2(a).

[538]

SCHEDULE 2
INTERPRETATION OF REFERENCE TO AVAILABILITY OF SEAT BELTS

Regulation 7(4)

1 For the purposes of these Regulations, in relation to a child riding in a vehicle,—

(a) if any front seat in the vehicle (other than the driver's seat) is provided with an [appropriate seat belt], that belt shall be regarded as being available for him in the front of the vehicle unless the requirements of paragraph 2 are satisfied in relation to [that child], that seat and that belt; and

(b) if any rear seat in the vehicle is provided with an [appropriate seat belt], that belt shall be regarded as being available for him in the rear of the vehicle unless the requirements of paragraph 2 are satisfied in relation to [that child], that seat and that belt.

2 The requirements of this paragraph are satisfied in relation to a particular child ("the child in question") and a particular seat ("the relevant seat") provided with a particular seat belt ("the relevant belt") if—

(a) another person is wearing the relevant belt;

(b) another child is occupying the relevant seat and wearing a child restraint which is an appropriate child restraint for that child;

(c) another person, being a person holding a medical certificate, is occupying the relevant seat;

(d) a disabled person (not being the child in question) is occupying the relevant seat and wearing a disabled person's belt;

(e) by reason of his disability, it would not be practicable for the child in question to wear the relevant belt;

(f) . . .

(g) the child in question is prevented from occupying the relevant seat by the presence of a child restraint which could not readily be removed without the aid of tools; or

(h) the relevant seat is specially designed so that—

  (i) its configuration can be adjusted in order to increase the space in the vehicle available for goods or personal effects, and

  (ii) when it is so adjusted the seat cannot be used as such,

and the configuration is adjusted in the manner described in sub-paragraph (i) above and it would not be reasonably practicable for the goods and personal effects being carried in the vehicle to be so carried were the configuration not so adjusted.

3 Paragraphs 2(b) and (d) shall not apply unless the presence of the other person renders it impracticable for the child in question to wear the relevant belt.

4 . . .

5 Paragraph 2(g) shall not apply if the child restraint is appropriate for the child in question.

NOTES
Amendment Para 1: words in square brackets substituted by SI 2006/2213.
Para 2(f): revoked by SI 2006/2213.
Para 4: revoked by SI 2006/2213.

[539]

MOTOR VEHICLES (WEARING OF SEAT BELTS) REGULATIONS 1993

SI 1993/176

Authority Made by the Secretary of State for Transport under the Road Traffic Act 1988, ss 14(1), (2), 15(3), (3A), (5), (6).
Date made 1 February 1993.
Commencement 2 February 1993; see reg 1(1).
Amendment Printed as amended by SI 2004/3168 (in relation to England only), SI 2005/27, SI 2005/2929 (in relation to Wales only), SI 2006/594, SI 2006/1892. Also amended in relation to Scotland only by SSI 2005/344, SSI 2006/129 (outside the scope of this work).
Interpretation See reg 2, Schs 1, 2.
General These regulations revoke and replace the Motor Vehicles (Wearing of Seat Belts) Regulations 1982, SI 1982/1203, the Motor Vehicles (Wearing of Seat Belts by Children in Rear Seats) Regulations 1989, SI 1989/1219, and the Motor Vehicles (Wearing of Seat Belts in Rear Seats by Adults) Regulations 1991, SI 1991/1255, and partially implement Council Directive 91/671/EEC on

the approximation of the laws of the member states relating to compulsory use of safety belts in vehicles of less than 3,5 tonnes (OJ L373, 31.12.1991, p 26). They make provision as to the wearing of seat belts in the front or rear of motor vehicles by adults and to the wearing of seat belts and other restraints by children in the rear of motor vehicles. The amendments made by SI 2006/1892 (which also amends provisions of the Road Traffic Act 1988 and the Road Traffic Offenders Act 1988) implement requirements of Council Directive 2003/20/EC of the European Parliament and of the Council (OJ L115, 09.05. 2003, p 63). For the purposes of the regulations children are divided into two categories according to size.

As to regulations relating to the wearing of seat belts and other restraints by children in the front of motor vehicles, see SI 1993/31.

[540]

PART I
INTRODUCTION

Citation, commencement and revocations

1 (1) These Regulations may be cited as the Motor Vehicles (Wearing of Seat Belts) Regulations 1993 and shall come into force on 2nd February 1993.

(2) The Regulations set out in Schedule 3 to these Regulations are hereby revoked.

[541]

General interpretation

2 (1) In these Regulations—

"the Act" means the Road Traffic Act 1988;

"the Construction and Use Regulations" means the Road Vehicles (Construction and Use) Regulations 1986;

["large bus" means a motor vehicle which—

(a) is constructed or adapted for use for the carriage of passengers,
(b) has more than eight seats in addition to the driver's seat,
(c) has four or more wheels,
(d) has a maximum design speed exceeding 25 kilometres per hour, and
(e) has a maximum laden weight exceeding 3.5 tonnes;]

"licensed hire car" has the meaning given by section 13(3) of the Transport Act 1985;

"licensed taxi" has the meaning given by section 13(3) of the Transport Act 1985;

["light goods vehicle" means a motor vehicle which—

(a) has four or more wheels,
(b) has a maximum design speed exceeding 25 kilometres per hour, and
(c) has a maximum laden weight not exceeding 3.5 tonnes;]

"maximum laden weight" has the meaning given by Part IV of Schedule 6 to the Road Traffic Regulation Act 1984;

"medical certificate" has the meaning given in Schedule 1 to these Regulations;

["operator", in relation to a small or large bus, means—

(a) the owner of the bus, or
(b) if the bus is in the possession of any other person under an agreement for hire, hire-purchase, conditional sale, loan or otherwise, that person;]

"passenger car" has the same meaning as in section 15 of the Act;

"private hire vehicle" means a motor vehicle which has no more than 8 seats in addition to the driver's seat, other than a licensed taxi or a public service vehicle (within the meaning of the Public Passenger Vehicles Act 1981), which is provided for hire with the services of a driver for the purpose of carrying passengers and which displays a sign pursuant to either section 21 of the Vehicles (Excise) Act 1971 or section 48(2) of the Local Government (Miscellaneous Provisions) Act 1976 or any similar enactment;

"rear seat" in relation to a vehicle means a seat not being the driver's seat, a seat alongside the driver's seat or a specified passenger seat;

"restraint system" means a system combining a seat fixed to the structure of the vehicle by appropriate means and a seat belt for which at least one anchorage point is located on the seat structure;

"seat belt" except in this regulation, includes a child restraint and references to wearing a seat belt shall be construed accordingly;

["small bus" means a motor vehicle which—

(a) is constructed or adapted for use for the carriage of passengers,
(b) has more than eight seats in addition to the driver's seat,
(c) has four or more wheels,
(d) has a maximum design speed exceeding 25 kilometres per hour, and
(e) has a maximum laden weight not exceeding 3.5 tonnes;]

"trade licence" has the meaning given by section 38(1) of the Vehicles (Excise) Act 1971;

"disabled person's belt", "lap belt", "seat", "specified passenger seat" and "three point belt" have the meanings given by regulation 47(8) of the Construction and Use Regulations.

(2) Without prejudice to section 17 of the Interpretation Act 1978, a reference to a provision in any subordinate legislation (within the meaning of that Act) is a reference to that provision as from time to time amended or as from time to time re-enacted with or without modification.

(3) In these Regulations—

"child" means a person under the age of 14 years;
"large child" means a child who is not a small child; and
"small child" means a child who is—

(a) aged under 12 years, and
(b) under [135] centimetres in height.

(4) In these Regulations, "adult belt" means a seat belt in respect of which one or more of the following requirements is satisfied, namely that—

(a) it is a three-point belt which has been marked in accordance with regulation 47(7) of the Construction and Use Regulations,
(b) it is a lap belt which has been so marked,
(c) it is a seat belt that falls within regulation 47(4)(c)(i) or (ii) of those Regulations;
(d) it is a seat belt fitted [in a vehicle] and comprised in a restraint system—
    (i) of a type which has been approved by an authority of another member State for use by all persons who are either aged 13 years or more or of 150 centimetres or more in height, and
    (ii) in respect of which, by virtue of such approval, the requirements of the law of another member State corresponding to these Regulations would be met were it to be worn by persons who are either aged 13 years or more or of 150 centimetres or more in height when travelling [in that vehicle in that State].

(5) In these Regulations, "child restraint" means a seat belt or other device in respect of which the following requirements are satisfied, namely that—

(a) it is a seat belt or any other description of restraining device for the use of a child which is—
    (i) designed either to be fitted directly to a suitable anchorage or to be used in conjunction with an adult seat belt and held in place by the restraining action of that belt, and
    (ii) marked in accordance with regulation 47(7) of the Construction and Use Regulations; or
(b) it is a seat belt consisting of or comprised in a restraint system fitted [in a vehicle], being a restraint system—
    (i) of a type which has been approved by an authority of another member State for use by a child, and
    (ii) in respect of which, by virtue of such approval, the requirements of the law of that State corresponding to these Regulations would be met were it to be worn by a child when travelling [in that vehicle in that State].

(6) Subject to paragraph (7), for the purposes of these Regulations, a seat shall be regarded as provided with an adult seat belt if it is fixed in such a position that it can be worn by an occupier of that seat.

(7) A seat shall not be regarded as provided with an adult seat belt if the seat belt—

(a) has an inertia reel mechanism which is locked as a result of the vehicle being, or having been, on a steep incline, or

(b) does not comply with the requirements of regulation 48 of the Construction and Use Regulations.

[(8) For the purposes of these Regulations, a seat belt is appropriate—

(a) in relation to a small child, if it is a child restraint of a description prescribed for a child of his height and weight by regulation 8;

(b) in relation to a large child, if it is a child restraint of a description prescribed for a child of his height and weight by regulation 8 or an adult belt; or

(c) in relation to a person aged 14 years or more, if it is an adult belt.]

(9) For the purposes of these Regulations, any reference to a seat belt being available shall be construed in accordance with Schedule 2 to these Regulations.

[(9A) For the purposes of these Regulations, references to a bus being used to provide a service in a "built-up area" shall be construed in the same way as in section 15B(6) of the Act.]

(10) Unless the context otherwise requires, in these Regulations—

(a) any reference to a numbered regulation is a reference to the regulation bearing that number in these Regulations; and

(b) a numbered paragraph is a reference to the paragraph bearing that number in the regulation or Schedule in which the reference appears.

NOTES

Amendment Para (1): definitions "large bus", "light goods vehicle", "operator", "small bus" inserted by SI 2006/1892.
Para (3): in definition "small child" in para (b) reference to "135" in square brackets substituted by SI 2006/1892.
Paras (4)(d), (5)(b): words in square brackets substituted by SI 2006/1892.
Para (8): substituted by SI 2006/1892.
Para (9A): inserted by SI 2006/1892.
Interpretation Act 1978, s 17 Printed in the title Statutory Instruments (Pt 2), Vol 1 of this work.
Public Passenger Vehicles Act 1981 For the meaning of "public service vehicle" in the 1981 Act, see s 1 thereof.
Vehicles (Excise) Act 1971, ss 21, 38(1) S 21 of the 1971 Act was repealed by the Finance Act 1994, ss 5, 258, Sch 2, para 9, Sch 26, Pt I(3). The 1971 Act was entirely repealed and replaced by the Vehicle Excise and Registration Act 1994; for the meaning of "trade licence", see s 11(1) of the 1994 Act.
Road Vehicles (Construction and Use) Regulations 1986 SI 1986/1078.

[542]

3 (*Revoked by SI 2006/1892.*)

PART II
ADULTS IN THE FRONT OR REAR OF A VEHICLE

General

4 This Part of these Regulations shall have effect for the purpose of section 14 of the Act.

[543]

Requirement for adults to wear adult belts

5 [(1) Subject to the following provisions of these Regulations, every person—

(a) driving a motor vehicle (other than a two-wheeled motor cycle with or without a sidecar), or

(b) riding in a front or rear seat of a motor vehicle (other than a two-wheeled motor cycle with or without a sidecar),

shall wear an adult belt.]

(2) Paragraph (1) does not apply to a person under the age of 14 years.

NOTES
Amendment Para (1): substituted by SI 2006/1892.

[544]

Exemptions

6 (1) The requirements of regulation 5 do not apply to—

(a) a person holding a medical certificate;

[(b) the driver of or a passenger in a motor vehicle constructed or adapted for carrying goods, while on a journey which does not exceed 50 metres and which is undertaken for the purpose of delivering or collecting any thing;]

(c) a person driving a vehicle while performing a manoeuvre which includes reversing;

(d) a qualified driver (within the meaning given by [regulation 17 of the Motor Vehicles (Driving Licences) Regulations 1999]) who is supervising the holder of a provisional licence (within the meaning of Part III of the Act) while that holder is performing a manoeuvre which includes reversing;

(e) a person by whom, as provided in [the Motor Vehicles (Driving Licences) Regulations 1999], a test of competence to drive is being conducted and his wearing a seat belt would endanger himself or any other person;

(f) a person driving or riding in a vehicle while it is being used for fire brigade [or, in England, fire and rescue authority] or police purposes or for carrying a person in lawful custody (a person who is being so carried being included in this exemption);

[(fa) as regards England and Wales, and so far as relating to the functions of the Serious Organised Crime Agency which are exercisable in or as regards Scotland and which relate to reserved matters (within the meaning of the Scotland Act 1998), a person driving or riding in a vehicle while it is being used for Serious Organised Crime Agency purposes;]

(g) the driver of—

(i) a licensed taxi while it is being used for seeking hire, or answering a call for hire, or carrying a passenger for hire, or

(ii) a private hire vehicle while it is being used to carry a passenger for hire;

(h) a person riding in a vehicle, being used under a trade licence, for the purpose of investigating or remedying a mechanical fault in the vehicle;

(j) a disabled person who is wearing a disabled person's belt; or

(k) a person riding in a vehicle while it is taking part in a procession organised by or on behalf of the Crown.

(2) Without prejudice to paragraph (1)(k), the requirements of regulation 5 do not apply to a person riding in a vehicle which is taking part in a procession held to mark or commemorate an event if either—

(a) the procession is one commonly or customarily held in the police area or areas in which it is being held, or

(b) notice in respect of the procession was given in accordance with section 11 of the Public Order Act 1986.

(3) The requirements of regulation 5 do not apply to—

(a) a person driving a vehicle if the driver's seat is not provided with an adult belt;

(b) a person riding in the front of a vehicle if no adult belt is available for him in the front of the vehicle;

(c) a person riding in the rear of a vehicle if no adult belt is available for him in the rear of the vehicle.

[(4) The requirements of regulation 5(1)(b) do not apply to a person riding in a small or large bus—

(a) which is being used to provide a local service (within the meaning of the Transport Act 1985) in a built-up area, or

(b) which is constructed or adapted for the carriage of standing passengers and on which the operator permits standing.]

NOTES
Amendment Para (1)(b): substituted by SI 2005/27.
Para (1)(d), (e): words in square brackets substituted by SI 2005/27.

Para (1)(f): words in square brackets inserted by SI 2004/3168 (in relation to England only); words "or, in England or Wales, fire and rescue authority" inserted by SI 2005/2929 (in relation to Wales only).
Para (1)(fa): inserted by SI 2006/594.
Para (4): inserted by SI 2006/1892.
Transport Act 1985 For the meaning of "local service" in the 1985 Act, see s 2 thereof.
Motor Vehicles (Driving Licences) Regulations 1999 SI 1999/2864.

[545]

PART III
CHILDREN IN THE REAR OF A VEHICLE

General

7 This Part of these Regulations has effect for the purposes of section 15(3) and (3A) of the Act.

[546]

Description of seat belts to be worn by children

8 (1) For a child of any particular height and weight travelling in a particular vehicle, the description of seat belt prescribed for the purposes of section 15(3) of the Act to be worn by him is—

- (a) if he is a small child … , a child restraint of a description specified in sub-paragraph (a) or (b) of paragraph (2);
- (b) …
- (c) if he is a large child, a child restraint of a description specified in sub-paragraph (a) of paragraph (2) or an adult belt.

(2) The descriptions of seat belt referred to in paragraph (1) are—

- (a) a child restraint with the marking required under regulation 47(7) of the Construction and Use Regulations if the marking indicates that it is suitable for his weight and either indicates that it is suitable for his height or contains no indication as respects height;
- (b) a child restraint which would meet the requirements of the law of another member State corresponding to these Regulations were it to be worn by that child when travelling in that vehicle in that State.

NOTES
Amendment Para (1)(a): words omitted revoked by SI 2006/1892.
Para (1)(b): revoked by SI 2006/1892.

[547]

Vehicles to which section 15(3) and (3A) of the Act do not apply

9 The following classes of vehicles are exempt from the prohibition in section 15(3) and (3A) of the Act, that is to say—

- [(a) large buses;]
- (b) licensed taxis and licensed hire cars in which (in each case) the rear seats are separated from the driver by a fixed partition.

NOTES
Amendment Para (a): substituted by SI 2006/1892.

[548]

Exemptions

10 [(1) The prohibitions in section 15(3) and (3A) of the Act do not apply in relation to—

- (a) a child for whom there is a medical certificate;
- (b) a small child aged under 3 years who is riding in a licensed taxi or licensed hire car, if no appropriate seat belt is available for him in the front or rear of the vehicle;
- (c) a small child aged 3 years or more who is riding in a licensed taxi, a licensed hire car or a small bus and wearing an adult belt if an appropriate seat belt is not available for him in the front or rear of the vehicle;
- (d) a small child aged 3 years or more who is wearing an adult belt and riding in a passenger car or light goods vehicle where the use of child restraints

by the child occupants of two seats in the rear of the vehicle prevents the use of an appropriate seat belt for that child and no appropriate seat belt is available for him in the front of the vehicle;

(e) a small child who is riding in a vehicle being used for the purposes of the police, security or emergency services to enable the proper performance of their duty;

(f) a small child aged 3 years or more who is wearing an adult belt and who, because of an unexpected necessity, is travelling a short distance in a passenger car or light goods vehicle in which no appropriate seat belt is available for him; or

(g) a disabled child who is wearing a disabled person's belt or whose disability makes it impracticable to wear a seat belt where a disabled person's belt is unavailable to him.]

[(2) The prohibition in section 15(3) of the Act does not apply in relation to a child aged under 3 years riding in a rear seat of a small bus.]

[(3) The prohibition in section 15(3) of the Act does not apply to a small child aged 3 years or more riding in a rear seat of a small bus if neither an appropriate seat belt nor an adult belt is available for him in the front or rear of the vehicle.

(3A) For the purposes of paragraph (3) of this regulation, a reference to an appropriate seat belt in paragraphs 2 and 3 of Schedule 2 shall be read as including reference to an adult belt.]

(4) The prohibition in section 15(3) of the Act does not apply in relation to a large child in any vehicle if no appropriate seat belt is available for him in the rear of the vehicle.

[(4A) The prohibition in section 15(3) of the Act does not apply to a child riding in a small bus—

(a) which is being used to provide a local service (within the meaning of the Transport Act 1985) in a built-up area, or

(b) which is constructed or adapted for the carriage of standing passengers and on which the operator permits standing.]

(5) The prohibition in section 15(3A) of the Act does not apply in relation to a child if no appropriate seat belt is available for him in the front of the vehicle.

NOTES

Amendment Paras (1), (2): substituted by SI 2006/1892.
Paras (3), (3A): substituted for para (3) by SI 2006/1892.
Para (4A): inserted by SI 2006/1892.
Transport Act 1985 For the meaning of "local service" in the 1985 Act, see s 2 thereof.

[549]

SCHEDULE 1
MEANING OF "MEDICAL CERTIFICATE"

Regulation 2(1)

PART I

1 Subject to paragraph 2, in these Regulations, "medical certificate", in relation to a person driving or riding in a vehicle, means—

(a) a valid certificate signed by a medical practitioner to the effect that it is inadvisable on medical grounds for him to wear a seat belt, or

(b) a valid certificate to such effect issued by the authority having power to issue such a certificate under the law of another member State corresponding to these Regulations.

2 A certificate shall not be regarded as a medical certificate in relation to a person driving or riding in a vehicle for the purposes of these Regulations unless—

(a) it specifies its period of validity and bears the symbol shown in Part II of this Schedule;
. . .

(b) . . .

3 Paragraph 2 does not apply in relation to a certificate issued before 1st January 1995.

NOTES

Amendment Para 2(b): revoked (with word omitted immediately preceding it) by SI 2006/1892.

Certificate ... to the effect that it is inadvisable on medical grounds ... to wear a seat belt
As to payments by the Secretary of State in respect of the examination of certain applicants for medical certificates required as a condition of the exemption prescribed by regs 6(1)(a), 10(1)(a), see the Transport Act 1982, s 70.

[550]

PART II

NOTES
Pt II of this Schedule sets out the symbol referred to in para 2(a) of Pt I.

[551]

SCHEDULE 2
INTERPRETATION OF REFERENCES TO AVAILABILITY OF SEAT BELTS

Regulation 2(9)

1 For the purposes of these Regulations, in relation to a person aged 14 years or more riding in a vehicle,—

(a) if any front seat in the vehicle (other than the driver's seat) is provided with an adult belt, that belt shall be regarded as being available for him in the front of the vehicle unless the requirements of paragraph 3 are satisfied in relation to that person, that seat and that belt; and
(b) if any rear seat in the vehicle is provided with an adult belt, that belt shall be regarded as being available for him in the rear of the vehicle unless the requirements of paragraph 3 are satisfied in relation to that person, that seat and that belt.

2 For the purposes of these Regulations, in relation to a child riding in a vehicle,—

(a) if any front seat in the vehicle (other than the driver's seat) is provided with an appropriate seat belt, that belt shall be regarded as an appropriate seat belt available for him in the front of the vehicle unless the requirements of paragraph 3 are satisfied in relation to that child, that seat and that belt; and
(b) if any rear seat in a vehicle is provided with an appropriate seat belt, that belt shall be regarded as an appropriate seat belt available for him in the rear of the vehicle unless the requirements of paragraph 3 are satisfied in relation to that child, that seat and that belt.

3 The requirements of this paragraph are satisfied in relation to a particular person ("the person in question") and a particular seat ("the relevant seat") provided with a particular seat belt ("the relevant belt") if—

(a) another person is wearing the relevant belt;
(b) a child is occupying the relevant seat and wearing a child restraint which is an appropriate child restraint for that child;
(c) another person, being a person holding a medical certificate, is occupying the relevant seat;
(d) a disabled person (not being the person in question) is occupying the relevant seat and wearing a disabled person's belt;
(e) by reason of his disability, it would not be practicable for the person in question to wear the relevant belt;
(f) ...
(g) the person in question is prevented from occupying the relevant seat by the presence of a child restraint which could not readily be removed without the aid of tools; or
(h) the relevant seat is specially designed so that—
    (i) its configuration can be adjusted in order to increase the space in the vehicle available for goods or personal effects, and
    (ii) when it is so adjusted the seat cannot be used as such,

    and the configuration is adjusted in the manner described in sub-paragraph (i) and it would not be reasonably practicable for the goods and personal effects being carried in the vehicle to be so carried were the configuration not so adjusted.

4 Paragraph 3 shall have effect in relation to regulation 10(5) as if sub-paragraphs (a) to (d) of that paragraph were omitted.

5 Paragraph 3(b) and (d) shall not apply unless the presence of the other person renders it impracticable for the person in question to wear the relevant belt.

6 ...

7 Paragraph 3(g) shall not apply if—

(a) the person in question is a child; and
(b) the child restraint is appropriate for him.

8 A child restraint shall be regarded as provided for a seat for the purposes of this Schedule if—

(a) it is fixed in such a position that it can be worn by an occupier of that seat, or

(b) it is elsewhere in or on the vehicle but—

(i) it could readily be fixed in such a position without the aid of tools, and

(ii) it is not being worn by a child for whom it is appropriate and who is occupying another seat.

NOTES

Amendment Para 3(f): revoked by SI 2006/1892.
Para 6: revoked by SI 2006/1892.

[552]

SCHEDULE 3

NOTES

This Schedule specifies the instruments revoked by reg 1(2), namely the Motor Vehicles (Wearing of Seat Belts) Regulations 1982, SI 1982/1203, the Motor Vehicles (Wearing of Seat Belts by Children in Rear Seats) Regulations 1989, SI 1989/1219 and the Motor Vehicles (Wearing of Seat Belts in Rear Seats by Adults) Regulations 1991, SI 1991/1255.

[553]

RETENTION OF REGISTRATION MARKS REGULATIONS 1993 SI 1993/987

Authority Made by the Secretary of State for Transport under the Finance Act 1989, s 11 (repealed). Now take effect under the Vehicle Excise and Registration Act 1994, s 26, by virtue of s 64 of, and para 2 of Sch 4 to, that Act.

Date made 1 April 1993.

Commencement 1 May 1993.

Amendment Amended by SI 1994/2976, SI 2008/2850.

Summary These regulations, which generally replace SI 1992/510 (see the note "Previous regulations" below), provide that the Secretary of State may, in respect of the registration mark assigned to a vehicle, grant a right of retention to the person in whose name the vehicle is registered under the Vehicle Excise and Registration Act 1994 or, if that person so requests, to another person (reg 3(a)). A right of retention is exercisable only during the retention period (i e a period of 12 months, 24 months or 36 months) for which application is made, or any extension of that period granted under reg 5 (reg 3(b)). Reg 4 sets out the manner in which an application for the grant of a right of retention must be made to the Secretary of State. Reg 4A relates to the nomination of a nominated person for certain purposes under the regulations. Reg 5 (extensions) provides that the relevant period (i e the period during which a right of retention is exercisable) may be extended on one or more occasions, and that any such extension may be for a period of 12 months, 24 months or 36 months, beginning on the day after that on which the relevant period would otherwise have ended.

Under reg 6, the Secretary of State may refuse an application for the grant of a right of retention, or for an extension of the period in which a right of retention may be exercised, or for the assignment of a registration mark under a right of retention, if it appears to him that there are special reasons for doing so. Reg 7 sets out the fees payable on an application for a right of retention, and reg 8 sets out the fees payable in respect of the grant of an extension or further extension of the period in which a right of retention may be exercised. If the Secretary of State decides to grant a right of retention he must issue a retention document to the grantee, containing specified information (reg 9). Reg 10 deals with the exercise of a right of retention in respect of a registration mark. Reg 11 provides that a registration mark may not be assigned to a vehicle in pursuance of a right of retention unless specified conditions are satisfied. A right of retention is not transferable, but without prejudice to the vesting of any such right in a person by operation of law (reg 13). The Secretary of State may revoke a right of retention, whether or not the period in which the right is exercisable has been extended, if it appears to him that there are special reasons for doing so (reg 14).

Previous regulations SI 1992/510 was made under the Finance Act 1989, s 11 (repealed) and now takes effect under the Vehicle Excise and Registration Act 1994, s 26, by virtue of s 64 of, and para 2 of Sch 4 to, that Act. The regulations came into force on 1 April 1992 and have been amended by SI 1993/988, SI 1994/2976. They provide for persons in whose names vehicles are registered to be granted rights (by the Secretary of State) exercisable within a year (or such further period as the Secretary of State thinks fit) to have the marks for the time being assigned to the vehicles assigned to other vehicles registered in their names or the names of their nominees. Specific provision is made with regard to applications for such grant, for the issue of retention documents, refusal of applications, nominations, the exercise of rights of retention (and their revocation), the conditions for the assignment of a registration mark and the payment of a charge upon an assignment. By the amending SI 1993/988, these regulations apply only where an application for the grant of a right of retention is made before 1 May 1993; where such an application is made on or after that date, see SI 1993/987 above.

Cases relating to these regulations Regs 4*(1)*, 13: *Goel v Pick* [2006] EWHC 833 (Ch), [2007] 1 All ER 982.

[554]

TRANSPORT AND WORKS APPLICATIONS (INLAND WATERWAYS PROCEDURE) REGULATIONS 1993
SI 1993/1119

Authority Made by the Secretary of State for Transport under the Transport and Works Act 1992, s 15.
Date made 21 April 1993.
Commencement 1 June 1993.
Summary These regulations make provision for the assimilation of the procedures for the making of applications for orders under the Transport and Works Act 1992, s 6, and proposals for orders under s 7 of that Act, and the making of orders under the Transport Act 1968, s 104(3), 105(3) or 112, and the holding of inquiries in respect thereof when an order under the 1968 Act is required in consequence of proposals contained in an application under, or made by virtue of, the 1992 Act. The principal modifications made to the procedures are that a person making an application for an order under s 6 of the 1992 Act must submit with his application a draft of the proposed order under the 1968 Act (by means of a modification to the Transport and Works (Applications and Objections Procedure) Rules 1992, SI 1992/2902 (revoked; see now SI 2006/1466)), and in such a case the procedures laid down by the 1968 Act for publicity and for the notification of and consultation with interested bodies are altered. The rules applying to inquiries held under the 1992 Act into applications for, or proposals by the Secretary of State to make, orders under that Act (ie SI 2004/2018) are applied to concurrent inquiries held under s 11 of the 1992 Act and s 158(1) of the 1968 Act.
Transfer of functions As to the transfer to the National Assembly for Wales of certain functions of the Secretary of State under the Transport and Works Act 1992 (and instruments made thereunder), so far as exercisable in relation to Wales, see SI 1999/672, in the title Constitutional Law (Pt 3). As to the transfer of the functions of the Assembly to the Welsh Ministers, see the Government of Wales Act 2006, s 162(1), Sch 11, paras 30, 32.

[555]

ROAD TRAFFIC (PARKING ADJUDICATORS) (LONDON) REGULATIONS 1993
SI 1993/1202

Authority Made by the Secretary of State for Transport under the Road Traffic Act 1991, s 73(11), (12). S 73 of the 1991 Act has been repealed by the Traffic Management Act 2004, s 98, Sch 12, Pt 1, as from 31 March 2008 (see SI 2007/2053). Notwithstanding the repeal of the said s 73(11), (12), these regulations continue in force for the purpose of applying in relation to:

(a) proceedings before traffic adjudicators under the London Local Authorities Act 1996, and for that purpose s 73(11)–(13) of the 1991 Act continue to have effect; see s 6(2) of the 1996 Act, as substituted during the transitional period (see below) by SI 2007/2053;
(b) proceedings before traffic adjudicators under the London Local Authorities and Transport for London Act 2003, and for that purpose s 73(11)–(13) of the 1991 Act continue to have effect; see para 10(2) of Sch 1 to the 2003 Act, as substituted during the transitional period by SI 2007/2053.

By art 1(2) of SI 2007/2053, "the transitional period", in relation to a provision modified by that order, means the period beginning with 31 March 2008 and ending on the day on which the repeal of that provision comes into force. S 6 of the 1996 Act is repealed by the Transport Act 2000, s 274, Sch 31, Pt II, and Sch 1 to the 2003 Act is repealed by the Traffic Management Act 2004, s 98, Sch 12, Pt 1, as from a day to be appointed by order in both cases.
Date made 4 May 1993.
Commencement 1 July 1993.
Amendment Amended by SI 1999/1205, SI 2000/1547, SI 2008/2683.
Summary These regulations now apply for a transitional period so as to prescribe the procedure to be followed in relation to proceedings before traffic adjudicators under the London Local Authorities Act 1996 and the London Local Authorities and Transport for London Act 2003, in relation to parking in London; see the note "Authority" above.

Pt I of the regulations relates to preliminary matters. Pt II sets out the procedure relating to appeals and provides for: initiating an appeal; action upon receipt of notice of appeal and copy of such notice; further representations; power to require attendance of witnesses; disposing of an appeal without a hearing; notice of time and place of hearing; procedure at a hearing; decisions on appeals; review of adjudicator's decision; costs; consolidation of proceedings; miscellaneous powers of the adjudicator; clerical errors; service of documents; and delivery of documents to the proper officer. Pt IV relates to the keeping and inspection of a register of appeals and decisions. (Pt III of the regulations concerned the procedure on references to the adjudicator under the Road Traffic Act 1991, Sch 6, para 8(7), which has been repealed by the Traffic Management Act 2004, s 98, Sch 12, Pt 1.)

[556]

PARKING ATTENDANTS (WEARING OF UNIFORMS) (LONDON) REGULATIONS 1993
SI 1993/1450

Authority Made by the Secretary of State for Transport under the Road Traffic Regulation Act 1984, s 63A.
Date made 8 June 1993.
Commencement 5 July 1993.

Summary These regulations prescribe functions for the purposes of the Road Traffic Regulation Act 1984, s 63A(4), as originally enacted, under which parking attendants in Greater London were required to wear uniform when exercising prescribed functions, and could not exercise any of those functions when not in uniform. The functions prescribed are those conferred by or under:

(a) s 99 of the 1984 Act, relating to removing vehicles, and

(b) the Road Traffic Act 1991, ss 66(1), 69, 77(4) (fixing and giving of penalty charge notices and the immobilisation of vehicles) (repealed by the Traffic Management Act 2004, s 98, Sch 12, Pt 1; as to the fixing and giving of penalty charge notices and the immobilisation of vehicles under the 2004 Act, see ss 78, 79 thereof).

S 63A(4) (requirement to wear uniform) of the 1984 Act has been substituted by the Traffic Management Act 2004, s 91, Sch 11, para 2, so as to apply to parking attendants in an area that is a civil enforcement area for parking contraventions. As to the status of Greater London as a civil enforcement area, see s 74 of, and Pt 1 of Sch 8 to, the 2004 Act.

[557]

TRANSPORT ACT 1985 (MODIFICATIONS IN SCHEDULE 4 TO THE TRANSPORT ACT 1968) (FURTHER MODIFICATION) ORDER 1993

SI 1993/2797

Authority Made by the Secretary of State for Transport under the Transport Act 1985, s 129(5).
Date made 11 November 1993.
Commencement 6 December 1993; see art 1.
Amendment Printed as amended by SI 1993/2909.
Interpretation See art 2.
General This order makes a further modification to the Transport Act 1968, Sch 4, as modified in its application to transfers of bus undertakings to companies under the Transport Act 1985, s 50(4) (repealed), 59(7), 61(11) or 68(7) by SI 1985/1903.

[558]

1 This Order may be cited as the Transport Act 1985 (Modifications in Schedule 4 to the Transport Act 1968) (Further Modification) Order 1993 and shall come into force on [6th December 1993].

NOTES
Amendment Words in square brackets substituted by SI 1993/2909.

[559]

2 In this Order—

"the Act" means the Transport Act 1985; and

"Schedule 4 as modified" means Schedule 4 to the Transport Act 1968 as modified for the purposes of its application to transfers under section 50(4), 59(7), 61(11) or 68(7) of the Act by the Transport Act 1985 (Modifications in Schedule 4 to the Transport Act 1968) Order 1985.

NOTES
S 50(4) ... of the Act Repealed by SI 1991/510.
Transport Act 1985 (Modifications in Schedule 4 to the Transport Act 1968) Order 1985 SI 1985/1903.

[560]

3 Schedule 4 as modified is further modified for the purposes of its application to transfers under section 61(11) of the Act by the insertion after paragraph 10 of that Schedule of paragraph 10A as set out in the Schedule to this Order.

[561]

SCHEDULE
PARAGRAPH TO BE INSERTED IN SCHEDULE 4 AS MODIFIED

Article 3

"TRANSFERS UNDER SECTION 61 OF THE TRANSPORT ACT 1985

10A (1) This paragraph applies to a transfer which is made pursuant to a scheme under section 61 of the Transport Act 1985 whereby the property, rights and liabilities of an initial company (within the meaning of section 60 of that Act) are transferred to two or more companies.

(2) In relation to a transfer to which this paragraph applies, the preceding provisions of this Schedule have effect subject to the following modifications:—

(a) for paragraph 1(2) substitute—

"(2)

(a) Any property, rights or liabilities (whether contractual or otherwise) held or subsisting partly for the purpose of or in connection with a part of the transferor's undertaking which is transferred to one transferee and partly for the purpose or in connection with a part of the undertaking which is transferred to another transferee shall be divided or apportioned between the transferees in such manner and in such proportions as may be specified in the scheme under section 61 of the Transport Act 1985 or, if not so specified and where the nature of the property, rights and liabilities permits, in such proportions and in such manner as may be appropriate.

(b) Where any estate or interest in land falls to be divided pursuant to paragraph (a) of this sub-paragraph, any rent payable under a lease in respect of that estate or interest, and any rent charged on that estate or interest, shall be correspondingly apportioned or divided so that each part is payable in respect of, or charged on, only a specified part of the estate or interest.";

(b) in paragraph 1(4) for the words "the transferee or retained by the transferor" substitute "one or other of the transferees";

(c) for paragraph 1(5) substitute—

"(5) It shall be the duty of the transferees, whether before or after the transfer date, so far as practicable to arrive at such written agreements, and to execute such other instruments, as are necessary or expedient to identify or define the property, rights and liabilities transferred to each transferee and as will—

(a) afford to each of the transferees as against one another such rights and safeguards as they may reasonably require for the carrying on of their respective businesses; and

(b) make as from such date, not being earlier than the transfer date, as may be specified in that agreement or instrument such clarifications or modifications of the division of the transferor's undertaking as will best enable the transferees to carry on their respective businesses.";

(d) in paragraph 1(7)—

(i) for the words "the transferor or the transferee" substitute "any transferee";

(ii) for the words "the transferor and the transferee" substitute "the transferees"; and

(iii) for the word "transferee" in the last two places where it occurs substitute "transferees";

(e) for paragraph 2 substitute—

"2 Where on any transfer to which this Schedule applies a transferee is entitled to retain possession of any document relating to the title to, or to the management of, any land or other property part of which is transferred to that transferee and another part of which is transferred to another transferee, the first mentioned transferee shall be deemed to have given to the other transferee an acknowledgement in writing of the other's right to production of that document and to delivery of copies thereof and section 64 of the Law of Property Act 1925 shall have effect accordingly and on the basis that the acknowledgement did not contain any such expression of contrary intention as is mentioned in that section.";

(f) in paragraph 4, for the words "the transferor and the transferee" substitute "both, or as the case may be, all the transferees";

(g) for paragraph 5 substitute—

"5 If the Secretary of State is satisfied on the representation of a transferee that, in consequence of a transfer to which this Schedule applies, different interests in land, whether the same or different land, are held by, or by a wholly owned subsidiary of, one transferee and by, or by a wholly owned subsidiary of, another transferee and that the circumstances are such that this paragraph should have effect, the Secretary of State may direct that this paragraph shall apply to such land as may be specified in the direction, and while that direction remains in force—

(a) no transferee or subsidiary of a transferee entitled to any interest in any of the specified land shall dispose of that interest except with the consent of the Secretary of State; and

(b) if in connection with any proposal to dispose of an interest of a transferee or a subsidiary of a transferee in any of the specified land it appears to the Secretary of State to be necessary or expedient for the protection of any one of them, the Secretary of State may—

(i) require a transferee or a subsidiary of a transferee entitled to an interest in any of the specified land to dispose of that interest to such person and in such manner as may be specified in the requirement; or

(ii) require a transferee or a subsidiary of a transferee to acquire from any other of them any interest in any of the specified land to which the other is entitled; or

(iii) consent to the proposed disposal subject to compliance with such conditions as the Secretary of State may see fit to impose;

but a person other than a transferee or subsidiary of a transferee dealing with, or with a person claiming under, a transferee or a subsidiary shall not be concerned to see or inquire whether this paragraph applies or has applied in relation to any land to which the dealing relates or as to whether the provisions of this paragraph have been complied with in connection with that or any other dealing with that land, and no transaction between person other than the transferees or subsidiaries shall be invalid by reason of any failure to comply with these provisions.";

(h) for paragraph 6(d) substitute—

"(d) where the agreement refers or relates to property, rights or liabilities which fall to be apportioned or divided (whether pursuant to paragraph 1(2) above or otherwise) between two or more transferees, the agreement constituted separate agreements separately enforceable by and against each transferee as regards the part of the property, rights and liabilities vested in the transferee but not as regards any other part thereof;";

(i) in paragraph 10(1) for the words "a transferor and a transferee" substitute "transferees";

(j) in paragraph 10(2)—

(i) for the words "the transferor and transferee" substitute "the transferees";

(ii) for the words "the transferor and as to part by and against the transferee" substitute "one transferee and as to part by or against another transferee";

(iii) for the words "the transferor and the transferee" substitute "the transferees";

(k) for paragraph 10(3) substitute—

"(3) If, in consequence of a transfer to which this Schedule applies or of anything done in pursuance of the provisions of this Schedule, the rights and liabilities of any person other than the transferor or a transferee or a wholly owned subsidiary thereof which were enforceable against or by the transferor become enforceable as to different parts against or by different transferees, and the value of any property or interest of that person is thereby diminished, such compensation as shall be just shall be paid to that person by one or more of the transferees, and any dispute as to compensation shall be referred to and determined by an arbitrator appointed by the Lord Chancellor.";

(l) in paragraph 10(5)—

(i) for the words "the transferor or transferee under a transfer to which this Schedule applies", substitute "a transferee under a transfer to which this Schedule applies";

(ii) for the words "the transferor and the transferee" wherever those words occur, substitute "the transferees";

(iii) for the words "the other of them" substitute "the other transferees"; and

(iv) omit the word "both".

(m) for paragraph 10(6) substitute—

"(6) It shall be the duty of the transferees under any transfer to which this Schedule applies to keep one another informed of any case where one of them may be prejudiced by sub-paragraphs (4) or (5) of this paragraph, and if a transferee claims that he has been so prejudiced and that another transferee ought to indemnify or make a payment to him on that account and has unreasonably failed to meet the claim, he may refer the matter to the Secretary of State for determination by the Secretary of State."."

NOTES

Erratum It is thought that para 5, as substituted by para 10A(2)(g), should read "transaction between persons other than" instead of "transaction between person other than".

[562]

RAILWAYS ACT 1993 (COMMENCEMENT NO 1) ORDER 1993 SI 1993/3237

Authority Made by the Secretary of State for Transport under the Railways Act 1993, s 154(2).

Date made 23 December 1993.

Summary This order, and the further commencement orders SI 1994/202, SI 1994/447, SI 1994/571, SI 1994/1648, SI 1994/2142, brought provisions of the Railways Act 1993 into force on various dates. All the further commencement orders were made under s 154(2) of the 1993 Act; SI 1994/571, SI 1994/1648 (which made transitional provision) were also made under s 143(3). The table below sets out the provisions of the Act brought into force by commencement order.

Provision	*Date/ Extent (if any)*
ss 2, 3	1 April 1994 (SI 1994/571)
s 4(1)	24 December 1993 (for purposes of functions of Secretary of State under s 33) (SI 1993/3237) 22 February 1994 (for purpose of functions of Regulator under s 70) (SI 1994/447) 21 March 1994 (otherwise) (SI 1994/571)
s 4(2)	22 February 1994 (for purpose of functions of Regulator under s 70) (SI 1994/447) 21 March 1994 (otherwise) (SI 1994/571)

Provision	*Date/ Extent (if any)*
s 4(3)	24 December 1993 (for purposes of functions of Secretary of State under s 33) (SI 1993/3237) 22 February 1994 (for purpose of functions of Regulator under s 70) (SI 1994/447) 21 March 1994 (otherwise) (SI 1994/571)
s 4(4)	21 March 1994 (SI 1994/571)
s 4(5), (6)	22 February 1994 (for purpose of functions of Regulator under s 70) (SI 1994/447) 21 March 1994 (otherwise) (SI 1994/571)
s 4(7)	24 December 1993 (for purposes of functions of Secretary of State under s 33) (SI 1993/3237) 21 March 1994 (otherwise) (SI 1994/571)
s 4(8)	21 March 1994 (SI 1994/571)
s 4(9)	24 December 1993 (for purposes of definitions "environment" and "through ticket") (SI 1993/3237) 21 March 1994 (otherwise) (SI 1994/571)
s 5	21 March 1994 (SI 1994/571)
s 6(1)	1 April 1994 (SI 1994/571)
s 6(2)	6 January 1994 (SI 1993/3237)
s 6(3), (4)	1 April 1994 (SI 1994/571)
ss 7–16	1 April 1994 (SI 1994/571)
ss 17–22	2 April 1994 (SI 1994/571)
s 23(1), (2)	1 April 1994 (SI 1994/571)
s 23(3), (4)	6 January 1994 (SI 1993/3237)
s 24	1 April 1994 (SI 1994/571)
s 25(1), (2)	6 January 1994 (for purpose of providing definition "public sector operator") (SI 1993/3237) 1 April 1994 (otherwise) (SI 1994/571)
s 25(3)–(9)	1 April 1994 (SI 1994/571)
ss 26–28	1 April 1994 (SI 1994/571)
s 29(1)–(7)	1 April 1994 (SI 1994/571)
s 29(8)	6 January 1994 (SI 1993/3237)
ss 30, 31	1 April 1994 (SI 1994/571)
ss 32, 33	24 December 1993 (SI 1993/3237)
ss 34–51	1 April 1994 (SI 1994/571)
s 52	21 March 1994 (SI 1994/571)
s 53	1 April 1994 (SI 1994/571)
s 54(1)	1 April 1994 (SI 1994/571)
s 54(2)	21 March 1994 (SI 1994/571)
s 54(3)	21 March 1994 (for purpose of definitions "franchising functions", in relation to the Franchising Director, and "railway investment") (SI 1994/571) 1 April 1994 (otherwise) (SI 1994/571)
ss 55–69	1 April 1994 (SI 1994/571)
s 70	22 February 1994 (SI 1994/447)
ss 71–80	1 April 1994 (SI 1994/571)
ss 81, 82	24 December 1993 (SI 1993/3237)

Provision	*Date/ Extent (if any)*
s 83(1)	24 December 1993 (for purposes of definitions "goods", "light maintenance services", "locomotive", "network", "network services", "premises", "passenger service operator", "railway", "railway services", "railway vehicle", "rolling stock", "station", "station services", "track", "train" and "vehicle") (SI 1993/3237) 6 January 1994 (for purposes of definitions "additional railway asset", "the Director", "franchise agreement", "franchise operator", "franchise term", "franchised services", "franchisee", "information", "licence" and "licence holder", "light maintenance depot", "operator", "passenger licence", "private sector operator", "public sector operator", "railway asset", "railway passenger service", "records" and "station licence") (SI 1993/3237) 22 February 1994 (for purposes of definitions "network licence" and "railway facility") (SI 1994/447) 1 April 1994 (otherwise) (SI 1994/571)
s 83(2)	24 December 1993 (SI 1993/3237)
ss 84, 85	6 January 1994 (SI 1993/3237)
s 86	1 April 1994 (SI 1994/571)
s 87(1)	6 January 1994 (for purpose of enabling Secretary of State to transfer functions to himself) (SI 1993/3237) 1 April 1994 (otherwise) (SI 1994/571)
s 87(2)	6 January 1994 (SI 1993/3237)
s 87(3), (4)	1 April 1994 (SI 1994/571)
s 87(5)	6 January 1994 (SI 1993/3237)
ss 88–92	6 January 1994 (SI 1993/3237)
s 93(1), (2)	6 January 1994 (SI 1993/3237)
s 93(3)(a)	6 January 1994 (SI 1993/3237)
s 93(3)(b)	1 April 1994 (SI 1994/571)
s 93(4)–(13)	6 January 1994 (SI 1993/3237)
ss 94–116	6 January 1994 (SI 1993/3237)
s 117	2 February 1994 (SI 1994/202)
ss 118–121	8 March 1994 (SI 1994/571)
ss 122–125	1 April 1994 (SI 1994/571)
ss 126–128	6 January 1994 (SI 1993/3237)
s 129	1 April 1994 (SI 1994/571)
ss 130, 131	6 January 1994 (SI 1993/3237)
s 132(1)–(7)	8 March 1994 (SI 1994/571)
s 132(8)	See Sch 10 below
s 132(9), (10)	8 March 1994 (SI 1994/571)
s 133	8 March 1994 (SI 1994/571)
s 134(1)	See Sch 11 below
s 134(2), (3)	6 January 1994 (SI 1993/3237)
ss 135–137	1 April 1994 (SI 1994/571)
s 138	21 March 1994 (SI 1994/571)
ss 139, 140	15 July 1994 (subject to transitional provisions) (SI 1994/1648)
s 141(1) (except para (a))	6 January 1994 (SI 1993/3237)
s 141(1)(a)	1 April 1994 (SI 1994/571)
s 141(2)–(5)	6 January 1994 (SI 1993/3237)
ss 142–144	24 December 1993 (SI 1993/3237)

Provision	*Date/ Extent (if any)*
s 145(1)–(6)	24 December 1993 (except for purposes of sub-s (5)(a), (b)(i)) (SI 1993/3237) 1 April 1994 (exceptions noted above) (SI 1994/571)
s 145(7)	1 April 1994 (SI 1994/571)
ss 146–149	24 December 1993 (SI 1993/3237)
s 150(1)–(3)	24 December 1993 (SI 1993/3237)
s 150(4)	1 April 1994 (SI 1994/571)
s 151(1)	24 December 1993 (for purposes of definitions "the Board", "body corporate", "company", "contravention", "the Franchising Director", "functions", "local authority", "the Monopolies Commission", "notice", "the Regulator", "subsidiary" and "wholly owned subsidiary") (SI 1993/3237) 6 January 1994 (otherwise) (SI 1993/3237)
s 151(2)–(4)	6 January 1994 (SI 1993/3237)
s 151(5)	24 December 1993 (SI 1993/3237)
s 151(6)–(9)	6 January 1994 (SI 1993/3237)
s 152(1)	See Sch 12 below
s 152(2)	See Sch 13 below
s 152(3)	See Sch 14 below
s 153	6 January 1994 (SI 1993/3237)
s 154	24 December 1993 (SI 1993/3237)
Schs 2, 3	1 April 1994 (SI 1994/571)
Sch 4	2 April 1994 (SI 1994/571)
Schs 5–7	1 April 1994 (SI 1994/571)
Schs 8, 9	6 January 1994 (SI 1993/3237)
Sch 10, paras 1, 2	8 March 1994 (subject to transitional provisions) (SI 1994/571)
Sch 10, para 3(1)	8 March 1994 (so far as repeals Transport Act 1962, ss 69, 71) (SI 1994/571)
Sch 10, para 3(2), (3)	8 March 1994 (SI 1994/571)
Sch 11, paras 1–8	6 January 1994 (SI 1993/3237)
Sch 11, para 9(1), (2)	6 January 1994 (SI 1993/3237)
Sch 11, para 9(3)	6 January 1994 (for purpose of inserting Transport Act 1980, s 52D(6)–(8)) (SI 1993/3237) 16 August 1994 (otherwise) (SI 1994/2142)
Sch 11, para 9(4)	6 January 1994 (SI 1993/3237)
Sch 11, para 10	6 January 1994 (SI 1993/3237)
Sch 11, para 11	16 August 1994 (SI 1994/2142)
Sch 11, paras 12–14	6 January 1994 (SI 1993/3237)
Sch 12, paras 1–3	1 April 1994 (SI 1994/571)
Sch 12, paras 4, 5	6 January 1994 (SI 1993/3237)
Sch 12, para 6(1)–(5)	6 January 1994 (SI 1993/3237)
Sch 12, para 6(6)	1 April 1994 (SI 1994/571)
Sch 12, para 6(7)	6 January 1994 (SI 1993/3237)
Sch 12, paras 7, 8	6 January 1994 (SI 1993/3237)
Sch 12, para 9	1 April 1994 (SI 1994/571)
Sch 12, paras 10–13	6 January 1994 (SI 1993/3237)
Sch 12, para 14(1)–(3)	6 January 1994 (SI 1993/3237)
Sch 12, para 14(4)–(6)	1 April 1994 (SI 1994/571)

Provision	*Date/ Extent (if any)*
Sch 12, paras 15–22	1 April 1994 (SI 1994/571)
Sch 12, paras 23, 24	6 January 1994 (SI 1993/3237)
Sch 12, para 25	1 April 1994 (SI 1994/571)
Sch 12, para 26	6 January 1994 (SI 1993/3237)
Sch 12, para 27	1 April 1994 (SI 1994/571)
Sch 12, para 28	6 January 1994 (SI 1993/3237)
Sch 12, para 29	1 April 1994 (SI 1994/571)
Sch 12, paras 30, 31	6 January 1994 (SI 1993/3237)
Sch 13	1 April 1994 (SI 1994/571)
Sch 14	6 January 1994 (repeals of or in British Transport Commission Act 1950, s 43; Transport Act 1962, ss 4, 5, 13, 53; Transport Act 1968, ss 42, 45, 50, 137) (SI 1993/3237) 8 March 1994 (repeals of Transport Act 1962, ss 54(1)(b), (2), 69, 71) (SI 1994/571) 31 March 1994 (repeal of Transport Act 1981, Pt I, Sch 1) (SI 1994/571) 1 April 1994 (all repeals so far as not already in force except repeals of Transport Act 1962, s 70, Railways Act 1974, s 8, Transport Act 1981, s 36) (SI 1994/571) 15 July 1994 (repeals of Railways Act 1974, s 8, Transport Act 1981, s 36) (subject to transitional provisions) (SI 1994/1648)

[563]

RAILWAYS (LICENCE APPLICATION) REGULATIONS 1994 SI 1994/572

Authority Made by the Secretary of State for Transport under the Railways Act 1993, ss 8(3), 143(3).
Date made 7 March 1994.
Commencement 1 April 1994; see reg 1.
Amendment By the Railways and Transport Safety Act 2003, s 16(5), Sch 3, para 4, a reference in any instrument to the Rail Regulator is to be treated, so far as necessary or appropriate in consequence of s 16 of that Act, as a reference to the Office of Rail Regulation. S 16 of the 2003 Act abolished the office of the Rail Regulator as from 5 July 2004 (see SI 2004/827) and transferred his functions to the Office of Rail Regulation.
Interpretation See reg 2.
General These regulations prescribe the manner in which applications for a licence to operate a railway asset under the Railways Act 1993, s 8 are to be made, including the documents which are to be submitted and the manner in which applications are to be published, if required by the Secretary of State under s 8(3)(c) of that Act.

[564]

Citation and commencement

1 These Regulations may be cited as the Railways (Licence Application) Regulations 1994 and shall come into force on 1st April 1994.

[565]

Interpretation

2 (1) In these Regulations,

"application" means an application for a licence;

"the Act" means the Railways Act 1993.

(2) In these Regulations, any reference to a numbered regulation shall mean the regulation bearing that number in these Regulations and any reference in a regulation to a numbered paragraph is a reference to the paragraph bearing that number in that regulation.

[566]

Manner of making licence applications

3 (1) Every application—

(a) shall be in writing;
(b) shall specify in full the name of the applicant and his address (being, in the case of a company, the address of its registered or principal office);
(c) shall specify the railway assets, or class or description of railways assets, of which the applicant wishes to be authorised to be the operator;
(d) shall describe the activities which the applicant wishes to carry out pursuant to the licence;
(e) shall specify every licence held, and every licence applied for, by the applicant;
(f) shall be signed by or on behalf of the applicant.

(2) Every application shall specify any bankruptcy order, as defined in section 381(1) of the Insolvency Act 1986, which has at any time been made against the applicant, or, where the applicant is a company, against the directors for the time being of that company.

(3) Every application made by a company shall specify—

(a) the amount of any issued share capital of that company and the full name and address of every person owning more than 3% of that issued share capital; and
(b) the full name and address of every director of that company;

and, where any such person or any such director is a company, the address shall be that of the registered or principal office of that company.

[567]

Lodgement of applications

4 Every application shall be addressed to the Regulator and shall be delivered to or sent by pre-paid post to the principal office of the Regulator.

NOTES

The Regulator Now the Office of Rail Regulation; see the note "Amendment" at the beginning of these regulations.

[568]

Fee payable with applications

5 The fee to accompany an application shall be £250.

[569]

Documents to accompany applications

6 (1) Subject to paragraph (2), every application shall include the following documents—

(a) the most recent audited financial statements of the applicant (in this regulation referred to as the "audited accounts");
(b) the audited financial statements of the applicant for the two financial years preceding that to which the audited accounts relate;
(c) an interim financial statement whether audited or not for the period or any part of the period from the end of the financial year in respect of which the audited accounts relate, up to the date of the application.

(2) Where the applicant is a subsidiary undertaking, the application shall include the following documents—

(a) the most recent audited group accounts (in this regulation referred to as "the latest audited group accounts") in respect of the group of which the subsidiary undertaking forms part;
(b) the audited group accounts in respect of that group for the two financial years preceding that to which the latest audited group accounts relate;
(c) an interim financial statement for that group, whether audited or not, for the period or any part of the period from the end of the financial year in respect of which the audited group accounts relate to the date of the application.

(3) The audited accounts, the latest audited group accounts, the audited financial statements referred to in paragraph (1)(b) and the audited group accounts referred to in paragraph (2)(b) shall include any audited consolidated financial statements or accounts for the relevant periods.

(4) In this regulation—

"the 1985 Act" means the Companies Act 1985;

"group" has the meaning given by section 262 of the 1985 Act;

the expression "group accounts" has the same meaning as it has in section 227 of the 1985 Act;

"subsidiary undertaking" has the meaning given by section 258 of the 1985 Act.

NOTES

Companies Act 1985, ss 227, 258, 262 Repealed by the Companies Act 2006, s 1295, Sch 16; see now ss 399, 1162, 474(1) respectively of the 2006 Act.

[570]

Manner of publishing applications

7 (1) If the Secretary of State requires that an application be published by the applicant pursuant to section 8(3)(c) of the Act, the manner of publication shall be in accordance with paragraph (2).

(2) There shall be published at least once in the London Gazette, the Edinburgh Gazette and in one or more newspapers whose circulation (together) covers the whole of Great Britain a notice containing the following particulars—

(a) a statement that the applicant has made an application for a licence under the Act;

(b) the information referred to in regulation 3(1)(b) and (e), and a summary of the information referred to in regulation 3(1)(c) and (d), contained in the application;

(c) a statement that the application has been sent to the Regulator and the address of the principal office of the Regulator.

NOTES

The Regulator Now the Office of Rail Regulation; see the note "Amendment" at the beginning of these regulations.

[571]

RAILWAYS (LONDON REGIONAL TRANSPORT) (EXEMPTIONS) ORDER 1994

SI 1994/573

Title As to the transition from London Regional Transport to Transport for London and the dissolution of LRT, see the Greater London Authority Act 1999 and the Preliminary Note "Transport for London" (under the main head "London").

Authority Made by the Secretary of State for Transport under the Railways Act 1993, ss 7(1), (2), (10), 20(1), (2), (9), (12), 24(1), (2), (11), 49(2), (4), (5), 143(4), 151(5). Ss 7(10), 20(9), (12) of the 1993 Act have been repealed by the Transport Act 2000, ss 252, 274, Sch 27, paras 17, 18, Sch 31, Pt IV. S 49(2), (4), (5) of the 1993 Act have been repealed by the Railways Act 2005, s 59(6), Sch 13, Pt 1. S 38(4) of the 2005 Act provides that where any order under s 49(2), (4) or (5) of the 1993 Act (exclusions from closure procedures under the 1993 Act) is in force immediately before the commencement of s 38 of the 2005 Act (1 December 2006; see SI 2006/2911), that order has effect after the commencement:

(a) in the case of an order under s 49(2), as an order under s 38 of the 2005 Act excluding the services to which it applies from ss 22–24 of the 2005 Act;

(b) in the case of an order under s 49(4), as an order under s 38 excluding the networks, or parts of networks, to which it applies from ss 26–28 of the 2005 Act; and

(c) in the case of an order under s 49(5), as an order under s 38 excluding any stations, or parts of stations, to which it applies from ss 29–31 of the 2005 Act.

Date made 7 March 1994.

Commencement Partly on 1 April 1994; fully on 2 April 1994.

Amendment Amended by SI 2003/1615 and the Greater London Authority Act 1999, s 198.

Interpretation In this order, "TfL company" means:

(a) Transport for London or any of its subsidiaries; or

(b) a PPP company, so far as carrying out qualifying activities.

"PPP company" is defined by reference to the provisions of the Greater London Authority Act 1999, Pt IV, Chapter VII relating to public-private partnership agreements. "Qualifying activities", in relation to a PPP company, means light maintenance services, network services or station services carried out by the PPP company in fulfilment of obligations imposed on the company by a PPP agreement.

Summary This order provides for the grant of exemptions from the provisions of the Railways Act 1993 relating to licensing (s 6), access (ss 17, 18), franchising (s 23(1)) and closure (ss 37, 39, 41) to every TfL company (formerly LRT company). (Ss 37, 39, 41 of the 1993 Act have been repealed by the Railways Act 2005, s 59(6), Sch 13, Pt 1. S 34(11) of the 2005 Act provides that any conditions agreed to under s 37(1), 39(1) or 41(1) of the 1993 Act in connection with any determination under the section in question that a closure is a minor closure have effect after the commencement of s 34 of the 2005 Act (1 December 2006; see SI 2006/2911) as if agreed to for the purposes of s 34(5).)

This order:

(a) exempts every TfL company from the requirement to hold a licence to be the operator of:

(1) any network, station or light maintenance depot which is used solely in connection with services provided by a TfL company, and

(2) any train being used for purposes associated with the operation of any such network, or the provision of light maintenance services at any such depot;

(b) grants an exemption from ss 17, 18 of the 1993 Act (access to railway facilities) to every TfL company in respect of track comprised in the network referred to in the order, together with the stations and light maintenance depots also referred to, and applies the facility exemption to parts of TfL stations which are used solely in connection with services provided by a TfL company;

(c) provides that services provided by any TfL company are to be exempt from s 23(1) of the 1993 Act (designation of passenger services as eligible for franchising); and

(d) provides that the closure provisions in ss 37, 39, 41 of the 1993 Act (repealed as noted above) are not to apply to services provided by, or networks, stations or light maintenance depots operated by, any TfL company.

Further exemptions The following orders provide further exemptions from provisions of the Railways Act 1993:

(a) SI 1994/574 (as amended by SI 2002/2703) was made under ss 7(1), (2), (9), (10), 20(1), (2), (8), (9), (12), 24(1), (2), (8), (11), 49(4), (5), 143(4), 151(5) of the 1993 Act (as to the repeal of ss 7(10), 20(9), (12), 49(4), (5), see the note "Authority" above) and came into force partly on 1 April 1994 and fully on 2 April 1994. The order provides for the grant of exemptions from the licensing, access, franchising and closure provisions of the Railways Act 1993 in respect of the proposed new railway between the Great Western Main Line and Heathrow Airport, and associated stations and light maintenance depots at Heathrow. It provides:

(1) for the grant of a licence exemption in respect of the proposed networks, stations and light maintenance depots, and any train being used on the networks;

(2) for the grant of an exemption from ss 17, 18 of the 1993 Act in respect of track comprised in the proposed networks and in respect of the stations and light maintenance depots;

(3) for the grant of an exemption from s 23(1) of the 1993 Act in respect of any service provided on any line comprised in the exempt networks;

(4) for the above exemptions to continue in force until 30 years after the commencement of the first service between Paddington Station and the new stations at Heathrow; and

(5) that s 37 of the 1993 Act (proposals to discontinue non-franchised passenger services) is not to apply to railway passenger services provided on any extension to the Heathrow Express Railway to any part of Heathrow Airport; and that ss 39, 41 (closure of operational passenger networks and facilities) are not to apply in relation to the proposed networks, stations or light maintenance depots (as to the repeal of ss 37, 39, 41, see the note "Summary" above).

(b) SI 1994/606 was made under ss 7(1), (2), (9), (10), 20(1), (2), (8), (9), (11), (12), 24(1), (2), (8), (11), 49(2), (4), (5), 143(4), 151(5) of the 1993 Act (as to the repeal of ss 7(10), 20(9), (12), 49(2), (4), (5), see the note "Authority" above) and came into force partly on 1 April 1994 and fully on 2 April 1994. It provides for the grant of class and miscellaneous exemptions from the licensing, access, franchising and closure provisions of the Railways Act 1993. The order:

(1) provides for any person to be exempt from the requirement to hold a licence to be the operator of:

(a) any network, station or light maintenance depot operated otherwise than by the British Railways Board ("the Board"), London Regional Transport ("LRT" (now dissolved and replaced by Transport for London ("TfL"))), or any subsidiary of the Board or LRT, immediately before 1 April 1994,

(b) the network consisting of the railway line between Poplar and Beckton Stations in London, together with stations along that line and the light maintenance depot at Beckton,

(c) the network consisting of a stretch of line running from Altrincham Station in Greater Manchester and used only by Manchester Metrolink,

(d) the network consisting of the Old Dalby test track in Leicestershire and any light maintenance depot associated with that network,

(e) West Hoathly and Kingscote Stations in West Sussex, together with the network consisting of the line between them,

(f) the network consisting of a stretch of line running from Greet Tunnel in Gloucestershire,

(g) any network, station or light maintenance depot comprised in the Channel Tunnel system;

(h) certain goods light maintenance depots listed in the order,

(i) certain railway goods terminals listed in the order,

(j) any network, station or light maintenance depot situated on premises used for certain industrial and similar purposes,

(k) any network situated on premises used for certain recreational purposes, or in the grounds of a dwelling house, and any station or light maintenance depot situated on such premises or in such grounds and used only for passenger services provided there,

(l) networks used only for the conveyance of filming equipment,

(m) any network, station or light maintenance depot where none of the track is of standard gauge (1435 millimetres, or 4' 8½"),

(n) any train being used on a network which is the subject of any of the preceding exemptions, any train being used on any other network for certain purposes ancillary to being used on such exempt network, or to the provision of light maintenance services at an exempt depot, and any train being used on a network situated within a harbour or harbour area;

(2) grants an exemption from ss 17, 18 of the 1993 Act in respect of track comprised in any network, and any station or light maintenance depot, which is the subject of the licence exemption granted by the order (the exemption is only granted to any private sector operator in the case of light maintenance depots listed in the order); the exemption does not apply to any part of a light maintenance depot listed in the order which consists of a locomotive fuelling point, or to any track or part of light maintenance depots to which access is required in order to use any such fuelling point, nor to track comprised in the railway goods terminals listed in the order;

(3) grants a facility exemption in respect of Waterloo International and Ashford International Stations, and the light maintenance depots at Longsight and North Pole, and a facility exemption in respect of parts of stations used only by operators other than the Board, LRT (now dissolved and replaced by TfL) and their subsidiaries;

(4) grants an exemption from s 23(1) of the 1993 Act in respect of all services provided immediately before 1 April 1994 other than by the Board, LRT (now dissolved and replaced by TfL) and their subsidiaries, all services provided wholly on network which is the subject of the licence exemption granted by the order, and all services which involve travel through the Channel Tunnel;

(5) provides that the above exemptions can be revoked by agreement between the Secretary of State and the person having the benefit of the exemption, and the exemption for certain facilities used for international services can also be revoked by the Secretary of State if any of the facilities is used other than for such services;

(6) provides that s 37 of the 1993 Act is not to apply to railway passenger services provided on any of the networks referred to in the order (as to the repeal of s 37, see the note "Summary" above); and

(7) provides that ss 39, 41 of the 1993 Act are not to apply to those networks, stations and light maintenance depots referred to in the order, or to the stations and light maintenance depots mentioned therein (as to the repeal of ss 39, 41, see the note "Summary" above).

(c) SI 1996/1356 was made under ss 49(2), (4), (5), 143(4), 151(5) of the 1993 Act and came into force on 24 May 1996. It provides for the grant of exemptions from the closure provisions of the Railways Act 1993 in respect of the proposed Croydon Tramlink light rail system; it also provides that ss 37, 39, 41 of the Act are not to apply in relation to the proposed railway passenger services, networks and stations. (As to the repeal of ss 37, 39, 41, 49(2), (4), (5) of the 1993 Act, see above.)

(d) SI 1999/3111 was made under ss 49(4), (5), 143(4) of the 1993 Act and came into force on 13 December 1999. It exempts certain stretches of railway line and Pudding Mill Lane Station, which form part of the Docklands Light Railway, from the closure provisions contained in ss 39, 41 of the Act. (As to the repeal of ss 39, 41, 49(4), (5) of the 1993 Act, see above.)

(e) SI 1999/3112 was made under ss 24(1), (2), (11), 49(2), (4), (5), 143(4), 151(5) of the 1993 Act and came into force on 13 December 1999. It exempts services provided by Docklands Light Railway Ltd on the Lewisham Extension from the franchising provisions of s 23(1) of the Act. It also provides that ss 37, 39, 41 are not to apply in relation to railway passenger services, networks and stations. (As to the repeal of ss 37, 39, 41, 49(2), (4), (5) of the 1993 Act, see above.)

(f) SI 2001/218 was made under ss 7(1), 143 of the 1993 Act and came into force on 1 March 2001. It exempted the Strategic Rail Authority and every wholly owned subsidiary of the Authority from the licensing requirements of s 6 of the Act. S 7(1) of the 1993 Act has been amended by the Railways Act 2005, ss 1(1), 59(6), Sch 1, para 1, Sch 13, Pt 1, so as to transfer railway licensing functions from the Strategic Rail Authority to the Office of Rail Regulation.

(g) SI 2005/2628 was made under s 16B of the 1993 Act and came into force on 15 October 2005. It exempts certain operators and railway facilities from the provisions of s 16A(1), (2) of the 1993 Act (which empowers the Office of Rail Regulation to direct the owner or operator of a railway facility to provide new railway facilities or to improve or develop an existing facility).

(h) SI 2007/1790 was made under s 24(1), (2) of the 1993 Act and came into force on 11 November 2007. It exempts from the franchising provisions of s 23(1) of the Act railway passenger services operated by a TfL concessionaire on specified routes (ie Gospel Oak station to Barking station; Willesden Junction (High Level) station to Clapham Junction station via Kensington Olympia station and West Brompton station; London Euston station to Watford Junction station via Watford High Street station; and Stratford Low Level station to Richmond station via Kensal Rise).

As to the transition from London Regional Transport (referred to in SI 1994/606 above) to Transport for London and the dissolution of LRT, see the Greater London Authority Act 1999 and the Preliminary Note "Transport for London" (under the main head "London"). As to the winding down and abolition of the British Railways Board, see the Transport Act 2000 and the Preliminary Note "Privatisation of the railway system" (under the main head "Reorganisation of transport undertakings").

[572]

RAILWAYS (REGISTERS) ORDER 1994
SI 1994/575

Authority Made by the Secretary of State for Transport under the Railways Act 1993, ss 72(7), (8), 73(5), (6). S 73(5), (6) have been repealed by the Railways Act 2005, ss 1(1), 59(6), Sch 1, para 30(6), Sch 13, Pt 1; see further "Summary" below.
Date made 7 March 1994.
Commencement 1 April 1994.
Amendment Amended by virtue of the Transport Act 2000, s 215(6).
Summary This order prescribes the hours during which the register maintained by the Office of Rail Regulation (formerly the Rail Regulator) under the Railways Act 1993, s 72 is to be available for public inspection, i e between 10am and 4pm on each working day, except when the premises are closed due to an emergency. It has lapsed in so far as it prescribed the hours during which the register maintained by the Strategic Rail Authority (now the Secretary of State) under s 73 of the 1993 Act is to be available for public inspection; see "Authority" above. The order also prescribes £2, together with 10p for each page supplied, as the fee to be paid for the supply of a copy of, or extract from, the register.

[573]

RAILWAYS (PENALTY FARES) REGULATIONS 1994
SI 1994/576

Authority Made by the Secretary of State for Transport under the Railways Act 1993, ss 130, 143(3), (4). S 130 of the 1993 Act is amended by the Railways Act 2005, ss 1(1), 47, 59(6), Sch 1, para 34, Sch 13, Pt 1, so as to abolish the functions of the Strategic Rail Authority relating to penalty fares.
Date made 7 March 1994.
Commencement 1 April 1994; see reg 1(2).
Amendment Printed as amended by SI 2005/1095.
Interpretation See reg 2.
General These regulations make provision for the charging of penalty fares for failure to produce, when required to do so, a ticket or other authority authorising a person to travel by train or to be present in a compulsory ticket area at a station. They also empowered the Strategic Rail Authority (originally the Rail Regulator) to make rules governing the charging and imposition of penalty fares (see reg 11); as to the abolition of the Strategic Rail Authority's functions relating to penalty fares, see the note "Authority" above.

[574]

Citation and commencement

1 (1) These Regulations may be cited as the Railways (Penalty Fares) Regulations 1994.

(2) These Regulations shall come into force on 1st April 1994.

[575]

Interpretation

2 (1) In these Regulations—

"authorised collector" means a person authorised to be a collector by or under rules;

"compulsory ticket area" means any area at a station identified by a notice which indicates that persons may not enter that area without being able to produce a ticket or other authority authorising travel on a train arriving at or departing from that area or otherwise authorising entry into that area;

"operator", in relation to any train, means the person having the management of that train for the time being and, in relation to any station, means the person having the management of that station for the time being, and "operated" shall be construed accordingly;

"preceding train" means a train

(a) by which a person travelled before changing to the train by which he is travelling, on which he is present or which he is leaving for the purposes of these Regulations; and

(b) which was operated by the operator of the train to which that person changed;

"rules" means rules made by the Regulator under regulation 11;

"section 130" means section 130 of the Railways Act 1993.

(2) In these Regulations any reference to a person leaving a train includes a person present in or leaving a compulsory ticket area having left a train arriving at that compulsory ticket area.

(3) Where the terms on which a ticket or other authority is issued require the holder to produce on request any other document when using that ticket or other authority, any reference in these Regulations to a ticket or other authority includes such a document.

(4) In these Regulations, where the context so admits, any reference to a ticket or other authority includes a ticket or other authority valid for the class of travel used or being used by the holder of that ticket or other authority.

(5) In these Regulations, any reference to a numbered regulation shall mean the regulation bearing that number in these Regulations and any reference in a regulation to a numbered paragraph is a reference to the paragraph bearing that number in that regulation.

NOTES

Rules made by the Regulator under reg 11 The power to make rules conferred by these regulations was subsequently conferred on the Strategic Rail Authority instead of the Rail Regulator; see the Railways Act 1993, s 130(5), (6), (10), as amended by the Transport Act 2000, s 216, Sch 17, Pt II, paras 17, 30. S 130(5), (6), (10) of the 1993 Act were repealed by the Railways Act 2005, ss 1(1), 59(6), Sch 1, para 34, Sch 13, Pt 1, so as to abolish the functions of the Strategic Rail Authority relating to penalty fares (reg 11 has accordingly lapsed).

[576]

Requirement to produce a ticket

3 (1) Subject to the provisions of these Regulations and to rules, any person present travelling by, present on or leaving a train shall, if required to do so by or on behalf of the operator of that train in accordance with these Regulations and with rules, produce a ticket or other authority authorising his travelling by or his being present on that train, as the case may be.

(2) Subject to the provisions of these Regulations and to rules, any person present in or leaving a compulsory ticket area, other than a person leaving a train, shall, if required to do so by or on behalf of the operator of a train in accordance with these Regulations and with rules, produce a ticket or other authority authorising him to be present in or leave that compulsory ticket area.

(3) Any requirement imposed pursuant to this regulation shall be imposed by an authorised collector in the manner specified in rules.

[577]

Charge to a penalty fare

4 (1) Subject to the provisions of these Regulations and to rules, where a person fails to produce a ticket or other authority when required to do so by or on behalf of an operator pursuant to regulation 3, that operator, or any person acting on behalf of that operator, may charge that person a penalty fare.

(2) Nothing in these Regulations or in rules shall authorise the operator of a train or a person acting on behalf of him to charge a penalty fare in respect of:

- (a) travel by, presence on or leaving a train other than a train operated by that operator; or
- (b) presence in or leaving a compulsory ticket area unless it is a compulsory ticket area at which a train operated by that operator has arrived or from which such a train will depart.

(3) Any charge made pursuant to this regulation shall be imposed by an authorised collector in the manner specified in rules.

(4) The amount of any penalty fare charged in accordance with these Regulations shall be paid in the manner and within the period specified in rules.

[578]

Amount of a penalty fare

5 (1) Subject to paragraph (5), the amount of any penalty fare which may be charged under regulation 4 is [£20.00] or twice the amount of the full single fare applicable in the case, whichever is the greater.

(2) The full single fare applicable in the case of a person charged a penalty fare while travelling by, being present on or leaving a train, having travelled on or having been present on a preceding train, is the full single fare in respect of a journey from the station (in this regulation referred to as "the first boarding station"), at which that person boarded the preceding train, to the next station at which the train by which he is travelling or on which he is present is scheduled to stop, or, where that person is leaving the train at a station, that station.

(3) The full single fare applicable in the case of a person, other than a person referred to in paragraph (2), charged a penalty fare while travelling by, being present on or leaving a train is the full single fare in respect of a journey from the station (in this regulation referred to as "the boarding station"), at which that person boarded the train, to the next station at which the train by which he is travelling or on which he is present is scheduled to stop, or, where that person is leaving the train at a station, that station.

(4) Where the first boarding station or, as the case may be, the boarding station is not known to the authorised collector, the full single fare applicable in the case of a person charged a penalty fare while travelling by, being present on or leaving a train is the full single fare in respect of a journey from the station at which the train last made a scheduled stop, to the next station at which the train by which he is travelling or on which he is present is scheduled to stop, or, where that person is leaving the train at a station, that station.

(5) The amount of any penalty fare which may be charged under regulation 4 to a person present in or leaving a compulsory ticket area, other than a person leaving a train, is [£20.00].

NOTES
Amendment Paras (1), (5): figure in square brackets substituted by SI 2005/1095.

[579]

Circumstances in which a penalty fare is not to be charged where a person is travelling on a train

6 (1) Subject to the provisions of paragraph (3), in the case of a person travelling by, being present on or leaving a train (in this regulation referred to as "the relevant train"), no person shall be charged a penalty fare in the circumstances to which this regulation applies.

(2) The circumstances to which this regulation applies are that, at the time when and at the station where the person in question boarded the relevant train, or, in the case where a person has boarded the relevant train after travelling on a preceding train, that, at the time when and at the station where the person in question boarded that preceding train,

- (a) there were no facilities in operation for the sale of the appropriate ticket or other authority to make the journey being or having been made by that person;
- (b) the requirements of rules in respect of the display of notices were not satisfied;
- (c) a notice was displayed indicating that the person in question was, or persons generally were, permitted to travel by or be present on the relevant train or, as the case may be, the preceding train without having a ticket or other authority; or
- (d) a person acting or purporting to act on behalf of
  - (i) the operator of the relevant train, or
  - (ii) the operator of the station in question,

  indicated that the person in question was, or persons generally were, permitted to travel by or be present on the relevant train or, as the case may be, any preceding train without having a ticket or other authority.

(3) Paragraphs (1) and (2) of this regulation shall not prevent a person from being charged a penalty fare where he had been invited by anybody acting on behalf of the operator of the relevant train or any preceding train to obtain a ticket or other authority while travelling on or present on the relevant train or that preceding train.

[580]

Circumstances in which a penalty fare is not to be charged where a person is in a compulsory ticket area

7 (1) No person present in or leaving a compulsory ticket area, but who is not leaving a train, shall be charged a penalty fare in the circumstances to which this regulation applies.

(2) The circumstances to which this regulation applies are that

(a) there were no facilities in operation at the station (in this regulation referred to as "the relevant station") of which the compulsory ticket area formed part for the sale of the appropriate ticket or other authority to be present in that compulsory ticket area;

(b) the requirements of rules with respect to the display of notices were not satisfied in relation to that compulsory ticket area;

(c) a notice was displayed at the relevant station indicating that the person in question was, or persons generally were, permitted to be present in that compulsory ticket area without having a ticket or other authority; or

(d) a person acting or purporting to act on behalf of

(i) the operator of any train departing from that compulsory ticket area, or

(ii) the operator of the relevant station

indicated that the person in question was, or persons in general were, permitted to be present in that compulsory ticket area without having a ticket or other authority.

[581]

Recovery of a penalty fare as a civil debt

8 The amount of any penalty fare charged in accordance with these Regulations and rules and not paid within the period specified in rules in accordance with regulation 4(4) may be recovered from the person charged as a civil debt.

[582]

Relevant statement

9 (1) Where a person charged a penalty fare has in due time provided the operator by or on whose behalf the penalty fare was charged with a relevant statement, in any proceedings for the recovery of that penalty fare, it shall be for that operator to show that any of the facts described in the relevant statement is not true.

(2) A relevant statement is a statement in writing informing the operator in question—

(a) in the case of a person charged a penalty fare in circumstances where he was travelling by, present on or leaving a train—

(i) of the train and of any preceding train by which he was travelling or had travelled or on which he was present or had been present;

(ii) of the station and the time at which he boarded that train and any preceding train and, other than in the case of his leaving a train at a station, the station at which he intended to leave that train;

(iii) whether any of the circumstances described in regulation 6(2) arose in relation to the station at which he boarded the train and any preceding train, and, if so, which;

(b) in the case of a person charged a penalty fare in circumstances where he was present in or leaving a compulsory ticket area but was not leaving a train—

(i) whether he was proposing to travel by train, and if so, by which train and to which station, and if not so proposing to travel, the reason for his presence in the compulsory ticket area;

(ii) whether any of the circumstances described in regulation 7(2) arose in relation to the station of which the compulsory ticket area formed part and, if so, which.

(3) For the purpose of paragraph (1) a relevant statement is provided in due time if it is provided at any time within the period of 21 days commencing with the day on which the person was charged a penalty fare.

[583]

Exclusion of double liability

10 (1) Where a person has been charged a penalty fare in respect of his failure to produce a ticket or other authority when required to do so pursuant to regulation 3, and, arising from that failure, proceedings are brought against that person in respect of any of the offences specified in paragraph (2), that person shall cease to be liable to pay the penalty fare which he has been charged, and, if he has paid it, the operator by or on whose behalf the penalty fare was charged shall be liable to repay to him an amount equal to the amount of that penalty fare.

(2) The offences mentioned in paragraph (1) are an offence under section 5(3)(a) or (b) of the Regulation of Railways Act 1889, or an offence under any byelaw made under section 67 of the Transport Act 1962 [section 129 of the Railways Act 1993 or section 219 of the Transport Act 2000] in respect of:

(a) his travelling by, or his presence on, a train without having previously paid his fare, or, having paid his fare for a certain distance, his travelling beyond that distance without previously paying the additional fare for the additional distance;

(b) his travelling by, or his presence on, a train without a ticket or other authority entitling him to travel by or be present on a train;

(c) his presence in part of a station without a ticket or other authority authorising him to be present there.

NOTES

Amendment Para (2): words in square brackets substituted by SI 2005/1095.

Railways Act 1993, s 129 Repealed by the Transport Act 2000, s 274, Sch 31, Pt IV.

Transport Act 1962, s 67 Repealed, subject to transitional and saving provisions, by the Transport Act 2000, ss 253, 274, Sch 28, para 5, Sch 31, Pt IV, as from a day to be appointed by order under s 275(1) thereof.

Transport Act 2000, s 219 Repealed, subject to savings, by the Railways Act 2005, ss 1(1), 59(6), (7), Sch 1, para 36(c), Sch 13, Pts 1, 2.

[584]

11 (*Reg 11, which conferred power on the Rail Regulator, and subsequently on the Strategic Rail Authority, to make rules relating to penalty fares, has lapsed; see the notes to reg 2.*)

Requirement for a person to give his name and address

12 (1) A person charged a penalty fare pursuant to regulation 4 shall give his name and address to the authorised collector when so required.

(2) Any person who fails to give his name and address in accordance with paragraph (1) shall be guilty of an offence and liable on summary conviction to a fine not exceeding level 2 on the standard scale.

[585]

RAILWAYS (ALTERNATIVE CLOSURE PROCEDURE) ORDER 1994

SI 1994/607

Authority Made by the Secretary of State under the Railways Act 1993, ss 49(3), 143(4). S 49(3) of the 1993 Act has been repealed by the Railways Act 2005, s 59(6), Sch 13, Pt 1. S 25(10) of the 2005 Act provides that where any order under s 49(3) of the 1993 Act is in force immediately before the commencement of s 25 of the 2005 Act (1 December 2006; see SI 2006/2911), that order has effect after commencement as an order under s 25 designating any services, or descriptions of service, to which it applies as special procedure services.

Date made 8 March 1994.

Commencement 1 April 1994.

Amendment Amended by SI 1999/3113, SI 2003/1615.

Summary This order designates the railway passenger services provided or operated under a number of local Acts in relation to which the Railways Act 1993, Sch 5 (discontinuance of railway passenger services) is to have effect, being services in relation to which s 37 of the 1993 Act does not have effect by virtue of SI 1994/573 and certain of the orders noted thereto.

S 37 of, and Sch 5 to, the 1993 Act have been repealed by the Railways Act 2005, s 59(6), Sch 13, Pt 1; as to the continued operation of this order, see the note "Authority" above.

[586]

RAILWAYS ACT 1993 (CONSEQUENTIAL MODIFICATIONS) ORDER 1994

SI 1994/857

Authority Made by the Secretary of State for Transport under the Railways Act 1993, s 153.

Date made 22 March 1994.
Commencement 1 April 1994.
Amendment Amended by SI 1994/2229 (so as to revoke certain amendments of the Regulation of Railways Act 1871, which are superseded by amendments made by SI 1994/2229), SI 2007/1819.
Summary This order amends certain statutory provisions in consequence of the provisions of the Railways Act 1993 and instruments made under or by virtue of that Act. The order amends the Railways Clauses Consolidation Act 1845, ss 115–120; the Regulation of Railways Act 1868, s 2; the Regulation of Railways Act 1871, ss 3, 4; the Regulation of Railways Act 1889, s 5; and the Transport Act 1968, s 125 (the order has been revoked by SI 2007/1819 in so far as it amended SI 1986/1456 (revoked)). Other provisions of the order relate to Scotland only. The amendments made by this order (and those made by the orders noted under "Further orders" below) are set out in full in Halsbury's Statutes, which also notes any repealed provisions.
Further orders The following orders amend certain statutory provisions in consequence of the provisions of the Railways Act 1993 and instruments made under or by virtue of that Act (the orders were all made under the Railways Act 1993, s 153, and SI 1999/1443, SI 1999/1998 were also made under s 143 thereof):

(a) SI 1994/1649 (in force on 14 July 1994) amends the Railways Act 1974, s 8(3) and the Transport Act 1985, ss 6(1), 35(2) (SI 1994/1649 is revoked by the Transport Act 2000, s 274, Sch 31, Pt IV, as from a day to be appointed by order under s 275(1) thereof);
(b) SI 1994/2229 (in force on 1 October 1994) makes further amendments to the Regulation of Railways Act 1871, ss 2, 6 in substitution for certain amendments made by SI 1994/857;
(c) SI 1994/2520 (in force on 1 October 1994) amends certain provisions of the British Railways (Pension Schemes) Act 1981 (1981 c xv);
(d) SI 1996/420 amends the Transport Act 1968, ss 116, 117, 118, 119, 122, 123, 124 and SI 1972/1705, in the title Highways, Streets and Bridges;
(e) SI 1999/1443 (in force on 16 June 1999) amends the Environmental Protection Act 1990, s 98, Sch 4 and SI 1991/1043, in the title Environment; and
(f) SI 1999/1998, as amended by the Transport Act 2000, s 252, Sch 27, para 63 (in force on 13 August 1999) modifies the British Transport Commission Act 1949, ss 54, 55, 56, 57 and amends the Police and Criminal Evidence Act 1984, s 6.

[587]

CHANNEL TUNNEL (APPLICATION OF ROAD TRAFFIC ENACTMENTS) ORDER 1994
SI 1994/970

Authority Made by the Secretary of State for Transport under the Channel Tunnel Act 1987, s 23.
Date made 29 March 1994.
Commencement 5 April 1994.
Amendment Amended by SI 1994/1667.
Summary This order has largely been revoked by SI 1994/1667 (see the note "Further order" below). In so far as it remains in force, the order specifies 5 April 1994 as the date upon which the enactments relating to road traffic start to apply to roads in the Channel Tunnel system.
Further order SI 1994/1667 was made under the Channel Tunnel Act 1987, s 23 and came into force on 22 July 1994. It partially revokes SI 1994/970 above and:

(a) confers on the Concessionaires (ie the persons with the function of constructing and operating the Channel Tunnel) functions which are exercisable by a local authority under the Road Traffic Regulation Act 1984, and subordinate legislation thereunder; and
(b) provides that the road traffic enactments are not to apply to certain roads in the tunnel system.

[588]

RAILWAY PENSIONS (PROTECTION AND DESIGNATION OF SCHEMES) ORDER 1994
SI 1994/1432

Authority Made by the Secretary of State for Transport under the Railways Act 1993, s 143(3), (4), Sch 11, paras 1(1), 5(b)(iii), 6(1), (2), (4)(b), (6), (8), (9), 7(1), (3), 8(1), (2)(b)(iii), (6)–(11).
Date made 27 May 1994.
Commencement 31 May 1994.
Amendment Amended by SI 1994/2005 and the Transport Act 2000, ss 245(2)–(8), 274, Sch 31, Pt IV.
Modification Certain provisions of this order are modified by SI 1994/2005 where pension rights are transferred by that order; and by SI 2007/2205 where certain pension rights or liabilities are transferred by that order.
Summary This order makes provision for the protection of the relevant pension rights of protected persons for the purposes of the Railways Act 1993, Sch 11.

Pt II (arts 2–10) of the order relates to protected persons. It sets out the conditions which a person who was not participating in an occupational pension scheme as a British Rail employee immediately before 5 November 1993 must satisfy in order to qualify as a protected person under para 5(b) of Sch 11 to the 1993 Act. It provides that the protected period for a person who satisfies the conditions set out in the order is to begin when, as an employee in the railway industry, he re-joins an occupational pension scheme. The employer of a protected employee is required to provide an occupational pension scheme in which that employee may acquire relevant pension rights which are no less favourable than the relevant pension rights which were provided under his designated scheme. None of the persons mentioned in para 7(2) of Sch 11 to the Act nor any servant or agent of any such person nor, where such person is a body corporate, any person who controls that body corporate is to prevent a protected employee from joining an occupational pension scheme provided by his employer. Any amendment of an occupational pension scheme which would make the relevant pension rights of protected persons (both pensioners and participants) less favourable to them, and any transfer of such rights which would make them less favourable to the persons transferred, are to have no effect. An occupational pension scheme in which a protected person is participating may not be wound up unless replacement arrangements are made which are no less favourable than the provision made by the scheme which is to be wound up. The employer's contribution to an occupational pension scheme of which a protected person is a member must be sufficient, in the opinion of the scheme actuary, to meet the cost of providing pensions to the members of that scheme, having taken into account the resources of the scheme, including employee contributions. Subject to exceptions, this order will cease to apply where the continuity of the period of employment of a protected employee is broken, a protected person voluntarily withdraws from an occupational pension scheme or a protected person requests that his relevant pension rights be transferred from an occupational pension scheme; provision is made for disregarding certain breaks in the continuity of employment so that, for example, the right to protection would not be lost because of a break in that continuity where a person has the right to return to employment in the railway industry. Provision is made for disregarding voluntary withdrawal from an occupational pension scheme in certain circumstances.

Pt III (art 11) relates to participation in the joint industry scheme; the right to participate in the scheme is conferred on certain persons whose employers are engaged in the railway industry. Pt IV (art 12) relates to election (arts 13, 14, relating to arbitration and enforcement, were revoked by the Transport Act 2000, ss 245(7), 274, Sch 31, Pt IV). A person may elect that this order is not to apply to him. Provision is made for disputes which arise under the order to be referred to arbitration, and for the enforcement of the order by the courts. In Pt V (art 15, Schedule), the order designates as "existing schemes" for the purposes of Sch 11 to the Act certain occupational pension schemes which provide pensions for, or in respect of, persons with service in the railway industry.

[589]

RAILWAYS PENSION SCHEME ORDER 1994
SI 1994/1433

Authority Made by the Secretary of State for Transport under the Railways Act 1993, s 143(3), (4), Sch 11, paras 1(1), 2.

Date made 27 May 1994.

Commencement 31 May 1994.

Amendment Amended by SI 1994/2005 and by virtue of the Transport Act 2000, s 215(6), so as to refer to the Strategic Rail Authority instead of the Franchising Director. As to the transfer of functions and abolition of the Strategic Rail Authority, see the Railways Act 2005, s 1, Sch 1 and the Preliminary Note "Privatisation of the railway system" (under the main head "Reorganisation of transport undertakings").

Summary This order provides for the establishment of the Railways Pension Scheme and the appointment of the Railways Pension Trustee Company Limited as the first trustee in relation to that Scheme, and for the designation of that Scheme as the "joint industry scheme" for the purposes of the Railways Act 1993, Sch 11. The Scheme is a centralised occupational pension scheme for employers which are not associated (as defined in the Income and Corporation Taxes Act 1988, s 590A(3), (4) (repealed, as from 6 April 2006, by the Finance Act 2004, s 326, Sch 42, Pt 3; for transitional provisions and savings see s 283(1) of, and Sch 36 to, the 2004 Act)). Employers who wish to participate in the Scheme may, in appropriate circumstances, adhere to already existing Sections of the Scheme or may alternatively establish their own Sections. A participating employer which establishes its own Section must adopt the Rules of one of the three specified Arrangements. The Pension Trust governing the Scheme is set out in the Schedule to the order and contains provisions which apply to the whole of the Scheme, including those which relate to:

(a) the appointment of trustees;

(b) participation in the Scheme and the establishment of Sections;

(c) contribution, investment and contracting-out;

(d) amendment of the Scheme and its winding-up (either in whole or in part).

The principal appendices to the Pension Trust contain:

(a) the Rules of the 1994 Pensioners "A" and "B" Sections into which assets and liabilities of the BR Pension Scheme in relation to pensioners and deferred pensioners are to be transferred;

(b) the Rules of the Arrangements which may be adopted by participating employers who wish to establish new Sections of the Scheme, of the following types:

   (1) shared cost arrangement,

   (2) defined benefit arrangement, and

   (3) defined contribution arrangement; and

(c) a Deed of Establishment and Participation which must be entered into by participating employers who wish to establish new Sections of the Scheme.

[590]

RAILWAY PENSIONS (TRANSFER AND MISCELLANEOUS PROVISIONS) ORDER 1994

SI 1994/2005

Authority Made by the Secretary of State for Transport under the Railways Act 1993, s 143(3), (4), Sch 11, paras 2–4, 6–8, 10, 12.

Date made 28 July 1994.

Commencement Partly on 1 August 1994; partly on 1 October 1994; fully on 2 October 1994.

Modification Modified by SI 2003/1633.

Summary This order makes provision for the transfer of the pension rights of the members of the BR Pension Scheme to the Railways Pension Scheme established by SI 1994/1433, together with the related assets and liabilities, and amends SI 1994/1433. The trust deed of the BR (1974) Pension Fund is amended to allow for the amendment by the trustees of that Fund, with the consent of the British Railways Board, of schemes included in that Fund and to enable such schemes to be wound up; and a number of existing schemes are amended to provide an indemnity for the trustees. Sections of the Railways Pension Scheme are designated for the purpose of enabling or requiring the Secretary of State to make payments under the Transport Act 1980, Pt III. The British Railways (No 2) Act 1986, s 48 is amended and SI 1964/1329, SI 1969/1824 are modified. Minor amendments and modifications are also made to SI 1994/1432. As to the winding down and abolition of the British Railways Board, see the Transport Act 2000 and the Preliminary Note "Privatisation of the railway system" (under the main head "Reorganisation of transport undertakings").

[591]

RAILWAYS PENSIONS GUARANTEE (PRESCRIBED PERSONS) ORDER 1994

SI 1994/2150

Authority Made by the Secretary of State for Transport under the Railways Act 1993, Sch 11, para 11(5).

Date made 16 August 1994.

Commencement 18 August 1994.

Summary This order prescribes classes of persons whose membership of the 1994 Pensioners "A" Section of the Railways Pension Scheme is to be disregarded for the purpose of determining whether that section satisfies the conditions set out in the Railways Act 1993, Sch 11, para 11(3). The following classes of persons are prescribed:

(a) persons whose pension rights are transferred to the 1994 Pensioners "A" Section under rule 17 of the rules of the 1994 Pensioners "B" Section; and

(b) persons who are admitted under the second paragraph of rule 2 of the rules of the 1994 Pensioners "A" Section.

Further order SI 2007/1595 (made under the Railways Act 1993, Sch 11, para 11(5) and in force on 1 August 2007) prescribes classes of persons whose membership of the 1994 Pensioners' Section of the Railways Pension Scheme is to be disregarded for the purpose of determining whether that section satisfies the conditions set out in para 11(3) of Sch 11 to the 1993 Act. The prescribed persons are those admitted to membership of that section with effect from 30 December 2000 who were formerly members of the BR Section of the Railways Pension Scheme.

[592]

RAILWAY PENSIONS (SUBSTITUTION) ORDER 1994

SI 1994/2388

Authority Made by the Secretary of State for Transport under the Transport Act 1980, ss 52B, 52D(4), (5).

Date made 12 September 1994.

Commencement 13 September 1994.

Amendment Amended by SI 1995/430 (itself amended by SI 2001/2264), SI 2001/2264; see the note "Further orders" below.

Summary This order terminates, on 13 October 1994, the liability of the Secretary of State to make payments under the Transport Act 1980, s 52(1) in respect of two sections of the Railways Pension Scheme established by SI 1994/1433, and makes provision for payments to be made in substitution for that liability. The order specifies the capital value of the unfunded obligations (as defined in s 52B of the 1980 Act) in respect of each of the sections as at the termination date. It requires the Secretary of State to make payments in respect of the capital values of the unfunded obligations, and provides for the accrual and payment of interest on the outstanding balances of those capital values. Sch 1 to the order makes such provision in respect of one half of the total of the capital values and Sch 2 in respect of the other half. The order also provides for the liability of the Secretary of State to make payments under Schs 1, 2 to be discharged in the event of the winding up of both sections.

This order should be read in conjunction with SI 1995/430, SI 2001/2264 below.

Further orders The following orders have been made under the Transport Act 1980, ss 52B, 52D(4), (5) (SI 2001/2264 was also made under the Railways Act 1993, Sch 11, para 10):

(a) SI 1995/430, as amended by SI 2001/2264 (in force on 12 March 1995), terminates, on 13 April 1995, the liability of the Secretary of State to make payments under the Transport Act 1980, s 52(1) in respect of two further sections of the Railways Pension Scheme established by

SI 1994/1433, and makes provision for payments to be made in substitution for that liability. The provisions made by SI 1995/430 are broadly similar to those made by SI 1994/2388 above (which is amended by SI 1995/430); and

(b) SI 2001/2264 (in force on 13 July 2001), terminates, on 13 August 2001, the liability of the Secretary of State to make payments under the Transport Act 1980, s 52(1) in respect of two sections of the Railways Pension Scheme established by SI 1994/1433, and makes provision for payments to be made in substitution for that liability. The provisions made by SI 2001/2264 are broadly similar to those made by SI 1994/2388, SI 1995/430 above (both of which are amended by SI 2001/2264).

[593]

PIPE-LINES (INQUIRIES PROCEDURE) RULES 1995
SI 1995/1239

Authority Made by the Lord Chancellor under the Tribunals and Inquiries Act 1992, s 9(1), (2), (3).
Date made 5 May 1995.
Commencement 1 June 1995; see r 1.
Amendment Printed as amended by SI 1996/1008, SI 1997/712, SI 2008/2831.
Interpretation See r 2.
General These rules revoke and replace the Pipe-lines (Inquiries Procedure) Rules 1967, SI 1967/1769, subject to savings. The rules prescribe the new procedure to be followed at public inquiries in connection with applications in England and Wales under the Pipe-lines Act 1962, Sch 1, Pt I, paras 4, 6A, Sch 2, Pt I, para 4; see further the Preliminary Note "Public inquiries and hearings" (under the main head "Pipe-lines").

[594]

Citation and commencement

1 These rules may be cited as the Pipe-lines (Inquiries Procedure) Rules 1995 and shall come into force on 1st June 1995.

[595]

Interpretation

2 (1) In these Rules, unless the context otherwise requires,

"the Act" means the Pipe-lines Act 1962;

"application" means an application for the grant of an authorisation or an order and "applicant" means the person who makes the application;

"assessor" means a person appointed by the Secretary of State to sit with an inspector at an inquiry or a re-opened inquiry to advise the inspector on such matters as the Secretary of State may specify;

"authorisation" means a pipe-line construction authorisation for which an application has been made to the Secretary of State under section 1 of the Act or a pipe-line diversion authorisation for which an application has been made to the Secretary of State under section 3 of the Act;

"document" includes a photograph, map or plan;

"inquiry" means any inquiry to which these Rules apply;

"inspector" means a person appointed by the Secretary of State to hold an inquiry or a re-opened inquiry;

"order" means a compulsory purchase order under section 11 of the Act or a compulsory rights order under section 12 of the Act for which an application has been made to the Secretary of State;

"outline statement" means a written statement of the principal submissions which a person proposes to put forward at an inquiry;

"person entitled to appear at an inquiry" means a person described in rule 10 and cognate expressions shall be construed accordingly;

"pre-inquiry meeting" means a meeting held before an inquiry to consider what may be done with a view to securing that it is conducted efficiently and expeditiously, and where two or more such meetings are held references to the conclusion of a pre-inquiry meeting are references to the conclusion of the final meeting;

"relevant date" means the date of the Secretary of State's written notice to the applicant, the relevant planning authority and statutory objectors of his intention to cause an inquiry to be held and "relevant notice" means that notice;

"relevant planning authority" means a local planning authority within the meaning of the Town and Country Planning Act 1990;

"statement of case" means a written statement which contains full particulars of the case which a person proposes to put forward at an inquiry and a list of any documents which that person intends to refer to or put in evidence;

"statutory objector" means, where the Secretary of State has caused an inquiry to be held—

(a) under paragraph 4(1) of Schedule 1 to the Act, any person who has duly made an objection to the authorisation in accordance with the said Schedule and whose objection has not been withdrawn; or

(b) under paragraph 4(1) of Schedule 2 to the Act, any owner, lessee or occupier (except a tenant for a month or any period less than a month) of any land proposed to be comprised in the order who has duly made an objection to the application in accordance with the said Schedule, and whose objection has not been withdrawn or disregarded under paragraph 4(3) of the said Schedule.

["Welsh new towns residuary body" means the Welsh Ministers so far as exercising functions in relation to anything transferred (or to be transferred) to them as mentioned in section 36(1)(a)(i) to (iii) of the New Towns Act 1981.]

(2) In these Rules, unless the context otherwise requires—

(a) any reference to a numbered section or Schedule is a reference to that section of, or that Schedule to, the Act; and

(b) any reference in a rule to a paragraph is a reference to a paragraph of that rule.

NOTES

Amendment Para (1): definition "Welsh new towns residuary body" inserted by SI 2008/2831.

Pipe-line diversion authorisation for which an application has been made ... under s 3 of the Act The Pipe-lines Act, 1962, s 3 has been repealed by SI 1999/742. See now s 1(1A) of the 1962 Act, as inserted by SI 1999/742, which provides that the construction of a diversion to a pipe-line is to be treated as the construction of a separate pipe-line for the purposes of s 1 of that Act.

[596]

Application of the Rules

3 (1) These rules apply in relation to any inquiry caused by the Secretary of State to be held in England or Wales under the provisions of paragraphs 4 and 6A of Schedule 1 to the Act for the purpose of an application, or under the provisions of paragraph 4 of Schedule 2 to the Act for the purpose of an Order.

(2) The provisions of subsections (1) and (3) of section 47 of the Act, which apply the provisions of subsections (2) to (5) of section 250 of the Local Government Act 1972, apply to these rules.

[597]

Procedure before inquiry

4 (1) The Secretary of State shall, as soon as possible, notify the applicant of the substance of each objection received by him from a statutory objector and, so far as possible, of the substance of other objections.

(2) The Secretary of State may cause a pre-inquiry meeting to be held if it appears to him desirable and where he does so the following provisions shall apply.

(3) The Secretary of State shall serve with the relevant notice a notification of his intention to cause a pre-inquiry meeting to be held and a statement of the matters about which he particularly wishes to be informed for the purposes of his consideration of the application in question; and where another Minister of the Crown or a government department has expressed in writing to the Secretary of State a view that the application should not be granted either wholly or in part, or should be granted only subject to conditions, the Secretary of State shall set this out in his statement and shall supply a copy of the statement to the Minister or government department concerned.

(4) In respect of each locality through which the proposed pipeline is to pass, the applicant shall cause to be published in one or more newspapers circulating in that locality, a notice of the Secretary of State's intention to cause a pre-inquiry meeting to be held and of the statement served in accordance with paragraph (3).

(5) The notice published pursuant to paragraph (4) shall refer to and include the text of any statement served in accordance with paragraph (3).

(6) The applicant and any statutory objector shall, not later than 8 weeks after the relevant date, serve an outline statement on each other and on the Secretary of State.

(7) The Secretary of State may in writing require any person who has notified him of an intention or a wish to appear at an inquiry to serve, within 4 weeks of being so required, an outline statement on the Secretary of State, on any statutory objector and on the applicant.

(8) The pre-inquiry meeting shall be held not later than 16 weeks after the relevant date.

(9) The Secretary of State shall give not less than 3 weeks' written notice of the pre-inquiry meeting to any statutory objector, the applicant, any person known at the date of the notice to a be a person entitled to appear at the inquiry and any other person whose presence at the pre-inquiry meeting seems to him to be desirable; and he may require the applicant to take, in relation to notification of the pre-inquiry meeting, one or more steps which he may under rule 9 require him to take in relation to notification of the inquiry.

(10) The inspector shall preside at the pre-inquiry meeting and shall determine the matters to be discussed and the procedure to be followed, and he may require any person present at the meeting who, in his opinion, is behaving in a disruptive manner to leave it, and he may refuse to permit that person to return or to attend any further pre-inquiry meeting, or may permit him to return or to attend only on such conditions as he may specify.

NOTES

Erratum It is thought that para (9) should read "to be a person" instead of "to a be a person".

[598]

Inspector's power to hold pre-inquiry meetings

5 (1) An inspector may hold a pre-inquiry meeting where he considers it desirable (whether or not one was held pursuant to rule 4(2)), and shall arrange for not less than 3 weeks' written notice of any such meeting to be given to the applicant, any statutory objector, any person known at the date of the notice to be a person entitled to appear at the inquiry and any other person whose presence at the meeting appears to him to be desirable.

(2) Rule 4(10) shall apply to a pre-inquiry meeting held in accordance with this rule.

[599]

Inquiry time-table

6 Where a pre-inquiry meeting is held, an inspector shall (so far as is reasonably practicable) and, in any other case may, arrange a time-table for the proceedings at, or at any part of, an inquiry and may at any time vary the time-table.

[600]

Service of statement of case, etc

7 (1) Subject to paragraphs (4) and (7), each of—

(a) the applicant;

(b) any person who, having notified the Secretary of State of his intention or wish to appear at the inquiry, has been required in writing by the Secretary of State to comply with the requirements of this paragraph; and

(c) any statutory objector,

shall serve a statement of case on each of the others and on the Secretary of State.

(2) A statement of case required to be served by the applicant and any statutory objector shall be served not later than—

(a) 6 weeks after the relevant date, or

(b) in any case where the Secretary of State or the inspector causes a pre-inquiry meeting to be held pursuant to rule 4(2) or rule 5(1), 4 weeks after the conclusion of that meeting.

(3) Any other statement of case shall be served not later than 4 weeks after the date of the Secretary of State's notice requiring it to be served.

(4) The statement of case mentioned in paragraph (1) or, as the case may be, paragraph (3), shall be served no later than the day which is 4 weeks before the date fixed for the holding of the inquiry, where that day falls within whichever of the periods mentioned in either of those paragraphs is applicable to the case.

(5) The Secretary of State shall inform any person from whom he requires a statement of case in accordance with paragraph (1)(b) of the name and address of every person on whom the statement of case is required to be served.

(6) The Secretary of State or the inspector may require any person who has served a statement of case in accordance with this rule to provide each of those on whom a statement of case has been served, the Secretary of State and the inspector with such further information about the matters contained in the statement as he may specify.

(7) Any further information served pursuant to paragraph (6), shall be served not later than 4 weeks after the date of the Secretary of State's notice requiring it to be served.

(8) Any person serving a statement of case shall serve with it a copy of any document, or the relevant part of any document, referred to in it.

(9) Where the Secretary of State considers it expedient, having regard to the number of statutory objectors and the length of a statement of case, he may authorise any person required to serve a statement of case under paragraph (1)(b) to serve it only on the applicant and himself; and where the Secretary of State so authorises he shall make arrangements for notice to be given to the other parties referred to in paragraph (1), stating the times and places at which they may examine the statement of case and, where practicable, take copies of it.

[601]

Notification of appointment of assessor

8 Where the Secretary of State appoints an assessor to sit at an inquiry, he shall notify every person entitled to appear at the inquiry of the name of the assessor and of the matters on which he is to advise the inspector.

[602]

Date and notification of inquiry

9 (1) The date fixed by the Secretary of State for the holding of an inquiry shall be not later than—

- (a) 22 weeks after the relevant date; or
- (b) in a case where the Secretary of State or the inspector causes a pre-inquiry meeting to be held pursuant to rule 4(2) or rule 5(1), 8 weeks after the conclusion of that meeting.

(2) Where the Secretary of State considers it impracticable to fix a date in accordance with paragraph (1) the date fixed shall be the earliest date after the end of the period mentioned in that paragraph which he considers to be practicable.

(3) Unless the Secretary of State agrees a lesser period of notice with the applicant and statutory objectors, he shall give to every person entitled to appear at the inquiry not less than 4 weeks' written notice of the date, time and place fixed by him for the holding of an inquiry.

(4) The Secretary of State may vary the date fixed for the holding of an inquiry, whether or not the date so varied is within the period mentioned in paragraph (1), and paragraph (3) shall apply to a date so varied as it applied to the date originally fixed.

(5) The Secretary of State may also vary the time or place for the holding of an inquiry and shall give such notice of any such variation as appears to him to be reasonable.

(6) The Secretary of State may require the applicant to take one or more of the following steps—

- (a) to cause to be published not less than 14 days before the date fixed for holding the inquiry a notice of the inquiry in one or more newspapers circulating in each of the localities through which the proposed pipe-line is to run;

(b) to serve within such period as he may specify notice of the inquiry on such persons or classes of persons as he may specify; and

(c) within such period as he may specify, to post a notice of the inquiry in conspicuous places near to the route of the proposed pipe-line.

(7) Any notice of the inquiry published, served or posted pursuant to paragraph (6) shall specify the date and time of the inquiry and the full address of where it is to be held, shall clearly identify the route of the pipe-line and shall specify the powers enabling the Secretary of State to determine the application.

[603]

Appearances at inquiry

10 (1) The persons entitled to appear at an inquiry are—

(a) the applicant;

(b) any statutory objector;

(c) the relevant planning authority;

(d) any of the following bodies if the route of the proposed pipe-line runs through land situated in their area and they are not the relevant planning authority—

(i) a county[, county borough] or district council (including the council of the Isles of Scilly);

(ii) . . .

(iii) a joint planning board constituted under section 2(1) [or 2(1B)] of the Town and Country Planning Act 1990; . . .

(iv) an urban development corporation established under section 135 of the Local Government, Planning and Land Act 1980;

(e) where land along the route of the proposed pipe-line is an area designated as a new town, the development corporation for the new town [or, as its successor—

(i) in England, the Homes and Communities Agency;

(ii) in Wales, the Welsh new towns residuary body.]

(f) any other person who has served a statement of case in accordance with rule 7(1)(b) or who has served an outline statement in accordance with rule 4(7).

(2) Nothing in paragraph (1) shall prevent the inspector from permitting any other person to appear at an inquiry, and such permission shall not unreasonably be withheld.

(3) Any person entitled or permitted to appear may do so on his own behalf or be represented by counsel, solicitor or any other person.

(4) An inspector may allow one or more persons to appear for the benefit of some or all of any persons having a similar interest in the matter under inquiry.

NOTES

Amendment Para (1)(d)(i): words in square brackets inserted by SI 1996/1008.
Para (1)(d)(ii): revoked by SI 1997/712.
Para (1)(d)(iii): words in square brackets inserted, and words omitted revoked, by SI 1997/712.
Para (1)(e): words in square brackets substituted by SI 2008/2831.

New town; development corporation As to the designation of an area as a new town, see the New Towns Act 1981, s 1; and as to the establishment of a development corporation for a new town, see s 3 of that Act.

[604]

Representatives of government departments at inquiry

11 (1) Where a government department has expressed a view such as is mentioned in rule 4(3) and the Secretary of State has included its terms in a statement served in accordance with that rule or rule 7(5), a representative of the government department concerned shall be made available to attend the inquiry.

(2) A person attending an inquiry as a representative in pursuance of this rule shall state the reasons for the expression of the view in question and shall give evidence and be subject to cross-examination to the same extent as any other witness.

(3) Nothing in paragraph (2) shall require a representative of a government department to answer any question which in the opinion of the inspector is directed to the merits of government policy.

[605]

Proofs of evidence

12 (1) Where a person entitled to appear at an inquiry proposes to give, or to call another person to give, evidence at the inquiry by reading a proof of evidence, he shall send a copy of the proof to the inspector together with, subject to paragraph (2), a written summary.

(2) No written summary shall be required where the proof of evidence proposed to be read contains no more than 1,500 words.

(3) The proof and any summary shall be sent to the inspector not later than—

(a) 3 weeks before the date fixed for the holding of the inquiry; or

(b) where a time-table has been arranged pursuant to rule 6 which specifies a date by which the proof and any summary shall be sent to the inspector, that date.

(4) Where the applicant or any statutory objector sends a copy of a proof to the inspector in accordance with paragraph (1), with or without a summary, he shall at the same time send a copy of that proof and any summary to the other parties set out in rule 7(1) and rule 10(1); and where any other party listed in rule 7(1) and rule 10(1) so sends a copy of such documents he shall at the same time send a copy to the applicant and any (or any other) statutory objector.

(5) Where a written summary is provided in accordance with paragraph (1), only that summary shall be read at the inquiry, unless the inspector permits or requires otherwise.

(6) Any person required by this rule to send a copy of a proof to any other person shall send with it a copy of the whole, or the relevant part, of any documents referred to in it, unless a copy of the document or part of the document in question is already available for inspection pursuant to rule 7(9).

(7) The applicant and the relevant planning authority shall afford to any person who so requests a reasonable opportunity to inspect and, where practicable, take copies of any document sent to or by them in accordance with this rule.

[606]

Procedure at inquiry

13 (1) Except as otherwise provided in these rules, the inspector shall determine the procedure at the inquiry.

(2) Unless in any particular case the inspector with the consent of the applicant otherwise determines, the applicant shall begin and have the right of final reply; and other persons entitled or permitted to appear shall be heard in such order as the inspector may determine.

(3) A person entitled to appear at an inquiry shall be entitled to call evidence and the applicant, the relevant planning authority and any statutory objector shall be entitled to cross-examine any person giving evidence but, subject to paragraphs (4) and (5), the calling of evidence and the cross-examination of persons giving evidence shall otherwise be at the inspector's discretion.

(4) The inspector may refuse to permit—

(a) the giving or production of evidence;

(b) the cross-examination of persons giving evidence; or

(c) the presentation of any other matter,

which he considers to be irrelevant or repetitious; but where he so refuses to permit the giving of oral evidence, the person wishing to give the evidence may submit to him any written evidence or other matter in writing before the close of the inquiry.

(5) Where a person gives evidence at an inquiry by reading a summary of his evidence in accordance with rule 12(5), the proof of evidence referred to in rule 12(1) shall, unless the person required to supply the summary notifies the inspector that he now wishes to rely on the contents of that summary only, be treated as tendered in

evidence, and the person whose evidence the proof contains shall then be subject to cross-examination on it to the same extent as if it were evidence he had given orally.

(6) The inspector may direct that facilities shall be afforded to any person appearing at the inquiry to take or obtain copies of documentary evidence open to public inspection.

(7) The inspector may require any person appearing or present at the inquiry who, in his opinion, is behaving in a disruptive manner to leave it and may refuse to permit that person to return, or may permit him to return only on such conditions as he may specify; but any such person may submit to him any written evidence or other matter in writing before the close of the inquiry.

(8) The inspector may allow any person to alter or add to a statement of case served under rule 7 so far as may be necessary for the purposes of the inquiry; but he shall (if necessary by adjourning the inquiry) give every other person entitled to appear who is appearing at the inquiry an adequate opportunity of considering any fresh matter or document.

(9) The inspector may proceed with an inquiry in the absence of any person entitled to appear at it.

(10) The inspector may take into account any written representation or evidence or any other document received by him from any person before an inquiry opens or during the inquiry provided he discloses it at the inquiry.

(11) The inspector may from time to time adjourn an inquiry and, if the date, time and place of the adjourned inquiry are announced at the inquiry before the adjournment, no further notice shall be required.

[607]

Site inspections

14 (1) The inspector may make an unaccompanied inspection of the route of the proposed pipe-line before or during an inquiry without giving notice of his intention to the persons entitled to appear at the inquiry.

(2) The inspector may, during an inquiry or after its close, inspect the route of the proposed pipe-line in the presence of the applicant, the relevant planning authority and, subject to paragraph (3), any statutory objector; and he shall make such an inspection if he is so requested by the applicant or the relevant planning authority before or during an inquiry.

(3) Where the inspector inspects the proposed route of the pipe-line after the close of an inquiry, a statutory objector shall only be entitled to accompany him on that inspection if the objector appeared at the inquiry.

(4) In all cases where the inspector intends to make an inspection of the kind referred to in paragraph (2) he shall announce during the inquiry the date and time at which he proposes to make it.

(5) The inspector shall not be bound to defer an inspection of the kind referred to in paragraph (2) where any person mentioned in that paragraph is not present at the time appointed.

[608]

Procedure after inquiry

15 (1) After the close of an inquiry, the inspector shall make a report in writing to the Secretary of State which shall include his conclusions and recommendations or his reasons for not making any recommendation.

(2) Where an assessor has been appointed, he may, after the close of an inquiry, make a report in writing to the inspector in respect of the matters on which he was appointed to advise.

(3) Where an assessor makes a report in accordance with paragraph (2), the inspector shall append it to his own report and shall state in his own report how far he agrees or disagrees with the assessor's report and, where he disagrees with the assessor, his reasons for that disagreement.

(4) If, after the close of the inquiry, the Secretary of State—

(a) differs from the inspector on any matter of fact mentioned in, or appearing to him to be material to, a conclusion reached by the inspector; or

(b) takes into consideration any new evidence or new matter of fact (not being a matter of government policy),

and is by reason thereof disposed to disagree with a recommendation made by the inspector, he shall not come to a decision which is at variance with that recommendation without first notifying the persons entitled to appear at the inquiry who appeared at it of his disagreement and the reasons for it; and affording them an opportunity of making written representations to him within 3 weeks of the date of notification, or (if the Secretary of State has taken into consideration any new evidence or new matter of fact, not being a matter of government policy) an opportunity of asking within that period for the re-opening of the inquiry.

(5) The Secretary of State may, as he thinks fit, cause an inquiry to be re-opened to afford an opportunity for persons to be heard on such matters relating to an application as he may specify, and he shall do so if asked to do so by the applicant, the relevant planning authority, any statutory objector or any other person mentioned in paragraph (1) of rule 10 pursuant to paragraph (4) and in the circumstances and within the period mentioned in that paragraph; and where an inquiry is re-opened (whether by the same or a different inspector)—

(a) the Secretary of State shall send to the persons entitled to appear at the inquiry who appeared at it a written statement of the matters specified pursuant to paragraph (5); and

(b) rules 9(3) to 9(7) shall apply as if the references to an inquiry were references to a re-opened inquiry.

[609]

Notification of decision

16 (1) The Secretary of State shall notify his decision on an application and his reasons for it in writing to all persons entitled to appear at the inquiry who did appear at it and any other person who, having appeared at the inquiry, has asked to be notified of the decision.

(2) Where a copy of the inspector's report is not sent with the notification of the decision, the notification shall be accompanied by a statement of his conclusions and of any recommendations made by him; and if a person entitled to be notified of the decision has not received a copy of that report, he shall be supplied with a copy of it on written application made to the Secretary of State within 4 weeks from the date of the decision.

(3) In this rule "report" includes any assessor's report appended to the inspector's report but does not include any other documents so appended; but any person who has received a copy of the report may apply to the Secretary of State in writing, within 6 weeks of the date of the Secretary of State's decision, for an opportunity of inspecting any such documents and the Secretary of State shall afford him that opportunity.

[610]

Procedure following quashing of decision

17 (1) Where a decision of the Secretary of State on an application in respect of which an inquiry has been held is quashed in proceedings before any court, the Secretary of State—

(a) shall send to the persons entitled to appear at the inquiry who appeared at it a written statement of the matters which appear to him to be relevant to his further consideration of the application; and

(b) shall afford to those persons an opportunity of making, within 3 weeks of the date of such written statement, written representations to him in respect of such matters or of asking for the re-opening of the inquiry; and

(c) may, as he thinks fit, cause the inquiry to be re-opened (whether by the same or a different inspector), and, if he does so, rules 9(3) to 9(7) shall apply as if the references to an inquiry were references to a re-opened inquiry.

NOTES
Although numbered as para (1), this rule does not contain further paragraphs.

[611]

Allowing further time

18 The Secretary of State may at any time in any particular case allow further time for the taking of any step which is required or enabled to be done by virtue of these Rules, and references in these Rules to a day by which or a period within which any step is required or enabled to be taken shall be construed accordingly.

[612]

Service of notices

19 Notices or documents required or authorised to be served or sent under any of the provisions of these rules may be sent by post.

[613]

Revocation and savings

20 (1) Subject to paragraph (2), the Pipe-lines (Inquiries Procedure) Rules 1967 ("the 1967 Rules") are hereby revoked.

(2) The 1967 Rules shall continue to apply both to any inquiry which commenced before the date on which these Rules come into force and to any inquiry re-opened under rule 9(4) of the 1967 Rules, and for the purposes of this rule an inquiry shall be taken to have commenced on the day on which the Secretary of State issued the relevant notice under the 1967 Rules of his intention to cause the inquiry to be held.

NOTES
Pipe-lines (Inquiries Procedure) Rules 1967 SI 1967/1769.

[614]

MOTOR VEHICLES (OFF ROAD EVENTS) REGULATIONS 1995 SI 1995/1371

Authority Made by the Secretary of State for Transport and the Secretary of State for Wales and for Scotland under the Road Traffic Act 1988, s 13A.
Date made 24 May 1995.
Commencement 15 June 1995.
Summary The Road Traffic Act 1988, s 13A(1) provides that a person is not guilty of an offence under s 1, 2 or 3 of that Act by virtue of driving a vehicle in a public place other than a road if he shows that he was driving in accordance with an authorisation for a motoring event given under regulations made by the Secretary of State. These regulations, which revoke and replace the Motor Vehicles (Off Road Events) Regulations 1992, SI 1992/1370, and the amending SI 1992/1523:
(a) prescribe as the bodies which may grant an authorisation for a motoring event for the purposes of s 13A of the 1988 Act the following: Amateur Motor Cycle Association Ltd, Association of Rover Clubs Ltd, the Auto-Cycle Union, the British Schoolboy Motorcycle Association, the International Organisation of Professional Drivers Ltd, the National Autograss Sport Association Ltd, NORA 92 Ltd, National Traction Engine Trust, the Royal Automobile Club, Scottish Auto Cycle Union Ltd, and Youth Motorcycle Sport Association (YMSA) Ltd; and
(b) require a person applying for an authorisation to pay a fee specified by the body concerned.
Transfer of functions Functions of a minister of the Crown under the Road Traffic Act 1988, s 13A, so far as exercisable in relation to Wales, were transferred to the National Assembly for Wales by SI 1999/672, in the title Constitutional Law (Pt 3). As to the transfer of the functions of the Assembly to the Welsh Ministers, see the Government of Wales Act 2006, s 162(1), Sch 11, paras 30, 32. Functions under the said s 13A, so far as exercisable in relation to Scotland, were transferred to the Scottish Ministers by SI 1999/1750, also in the title Constitutional Law (Pt 3).

[615]

VEHICLE EXCISE DUTY (DESIGNATION OF SMALL ISLANDS) ORDER 1995
SI 1995/1397

Authority Made by the Secretary of State for Transport under the Vehicle Excise and Registration Act 1994, Sch 1, Pt VIII, para 18(4).
Date made 30 May 1995.
Commencement 1 July 1995.
Amendment Amended by SI 2002/1072.

Summary This order designates certain islands in the Inner Hebrides, the Orkney Islands, the Outer Hebrides, the Scilly Isles and the Shetland Islands, and other islands, as small islands for the purposes of the Vehicle Excise and Registration Act 1994, Sch 1, Pt VIII, para 18, which defines the expression "island goods vehicle" for the purposes of Pt VIII of that Schedule (annual rates of duty for goods vehicles).

[616]

VEHICLE EXCISE (DESIGN WEIGHT CERTIFICATE) REGULATIONS 1995

SI 1995/1455

Authority Made by the Secretary of State for Transport under the Vehicle Excise and Registration Act 1994, ss 57, 61A.

Date made 8 June 1995.

Commencement 1 July 1995.

Amendment Amended by SI 2009/881.

Summary These regulations make provision for the issue of design weight certificates and related matters for the purposes of the Vehicle Excise and Registration Act 1994. The regulations make provision for applications for a design weight certificate and for the issue of such a certificate following an examination; provision is made for appeals to the Secretary of State by persons aggrieved by a determination. They provide that a design weight certificate is to be conclusive evidence of the design weight of a vehicle at the time of the examination and specify circumstances in which the Secretary of State can require a design weight certificate to be produced before he makes a determination for the purposes of s 7(5) of the 1994 Act (under which the Secretary of State can refuse to issue a vehicle excise licence if he is not satisfied that the licence applied for is the appropriate licence for the vehicle in question). The regulations also provide that an adaptation reducing the design weight of a vehicle is to be treated as permanent for the purposes of s 60A(5) of the 1994 Act if and only if it is an adaptation in respect of which a design weight certificate has been issued.

[617]

MOTOR CYCLE SILENCER AND EXHAUST SYSTEMS REGULATIONS 1995

SI 1995/2370

Authority Made by the Secretary of State for Transport under the Motor Cycle Noise Act 1987, s 1 and the European Communities Act 1972, s 2(2).

Date made 30 August 1995.

Commencement 1 August 1996.

Amendment Amended by SI 2008/1277.

Summary These regulations prescribe requirements to be met by motorcycle silencers and exhaust systems supplied in the course of carrying on a business. In general, it will be an offence under the Motor Cycle Noise Act 1987, s 1 for a person to supply, offer or agree to supply, or expose or possess for supply a silencer or exhaust system comprising a silencer for a motor cycle, motor scooter or moped unless specified conditions are fulfilled relating to the marking of the silencer or exhaust system. The regulations also impose requirements as to the packaging and labelling of silencers and exhaust systems and the provision of accompanying instructions. Certain exemptions from s 1 of the 1987 Act are provided and provision is made for corresponding EEA standards.

[618]

GOODS VEHICLES (LICENSING OF OPERATORS) REGULATIONS 1995

SI 1995/2869

Authority Made by the Secretary of State for Transport under the Goods Vehicles (Licensing of Operators) Act 1995, ss 2, 5(3), (8), 8(3), (4), (5), 10, 11(2), 12(2), (3), (6), (7), 14(5), 17(2), 18(3), 19(9), (10), 23(2), 30(1), (4), 31(5), 33, 34(1), 35(3), 36(2), (3), 46(1), (2), 47, 48(2), (3), (4), 57(1)–(5), (7)–(9), Sch 4, paras 1, 3 and the European Communities Act 1972, s 2(2).

Date made 6 November 1995.

Commencement 1 January 1996; see reg 1.

Amendment Printed as amended by SI 2003/2096, SI 2004/3168 (the latter in relation to England only), SI 2005/2060, SI 2005/2929 (the latter in relation to Wales only), SI 2006/594, SI 2007/1898, SI 2009/1307.

Modification Modified by SI 1996/2186, in relation to foreign goods vehicles.

Interpretation See reg 3.

General These regulations revoke and partially replace the Goods Vehicles (Operators' Licences, Qualifications and Fees) Regulations 1984, SI 1984/176, as amended, which made provision in respect of the licensing of goods vehicle operators. Provisions of SI 1994/176 dealing with the qualification requirements of operators were revoked by the Goods Vehicles (Licensing of Operators) Act 1995, s 60(2), Sch 8, Pt II and are consolidated in that Act; provisions dealing with fees are now contained in SI 1995/3000.

[619]

PART I
GENERAL

Commencement and citation

1 These Regulations may be cited as the Goods Vehicles (Licensing of Operators) Regulations 1995, and shall come into force on 1st January 1996.

[620]

Revocation

2 The Regulations set out in Schedule 5 are hereby revoked.

[621]

Interpretation

3 (1) In these Regulations, unless the context otherwise requires, any reference to—

(a) a numbered section is a reference to the section bearing that number in the Goods Vehicles (Licensing of Operators) Act 1995;
(b) a numbered regulation or Schedule is a reference to the regulation or, as the case may be, the Schedule bearing that number in these Regulations; and
(c) a numbered paragraph is a reference to the paragraph bearing that number in the regulation in which the reference appears.

(2) In these Regulations, unless the context otherwise requires—

"the 1995 Act" means the Goods Vehicles (Licensing of Operators) Act 1995;
"application for a licence" means an application for an operator's licence for which publication is required by section 10(1);
"application for the variation of a licence" means an application for the variation of an operator's licence for which publication is required by section 17(3) and, "application" when used otherwise than as part of those expressions means—

(a) an application for a licence, or
(b) an application for the variation of a licence;

"Applications and Decisions" means a statement issued by a traffic commissioner under regulation 21;
"company" shall be construed as provided in section 735 of the Companies Act 1985;
"disc" means a disc issued in accordance with regulation 23(1) and (2) or 27(2);
"dual purpose vehicle" has the meaning given in column 2 of the Table in regulation 3(2) of the Road Vehicles (Construction and Use) Regulations 1986;
"farm" includes a market garden;
"firm" has the same meaning as in section 4 of the Partnership Act 1890;
"goods vehicle" has the same meaning as in section 58(1) but excludes a small goods vehicle as described in Schedule 1 to the 1995 Act;
"keeper", in relation to a goods vehicle, is the person in whose name the vehicle is registered under the Vehicle Excise and Registration Act 1994;
"licence" means an operator's licence (whether standard or restricted) as defined in section 2(1) and, where the context so requires, includes the documentation which evidences the grant of an application;
"licence-holder", and "holder" in relation to a licence, mean the person to whom the licence was issued;
"motor vehicle" means a mechanically propelled vehicle intended or adapted for use on roads;
"maintenance" in relation to a goods vehicle includes inspection, repair and fuelling;
"officer" has the meaning given in section 42;
"recovery vehicle" has the same meaning as in Part V of Schedule 1 to the Vehicle Excise and Registration Act 1994;

"relevant conviction" means any conviction mentioned in paragraph 5 of Schedule 2 to the 1995 Act or any conviction of contravening any provision of the law of Northern Ireland or of a country or territory outside the United Kingdom corresponding to any such conviction, not being in either case a spent conviction within the meaning of section 1(1) of the Rehabilitation of Offenders Act 1974;

"showman's goods vehicle" has the same meaning as in section 62 of the Vehicle Excise and Registration Act 1994;

"tower wagon" has the same meaning as in paragraph 17(2) of Schedule 2 to the Vehicle Excise and Registration Act 1994 (as originally enacted);

"trade licence" is a licence granted under section 11 of the Vehicle Excise and Registration Act 1994;

"visiting force", "headquarters" and "vehicle in the service of a visiting force or a headquarters" have the same meanings as in the Visiting Forces and International Headquarters (Application of Law) Order 1965.

NOTES

"Company" shall be construed as provided in the Companies Act 1985, s 735
S 735 of the 1985 Act has been repealed by the Companies Act 2006, s 1295, Sch 16; as to the general meaning of "company" in the 2006 Act, see s 1 thereof.

Road Vehicles (Construction and Use) Regulations 1986 SI 1986/1078.

Visiting Forces and International Headquarters (Application of Law) Order 1965
SI 1965/1536; revoked and replaced by SI 1999/1736, in the title Armed Forces.

[622]

PART II
APPLICATIONS

Manner of making applications

4 Every application shall—

(a) be made on a form supplied by the traffic commissioner to whom the application is made and contain the information required by that form;

(b) be signed—

- (i) if made by an individual, by that person,
- (ii) if made by a firm, by all of the partners of that firm or by one of them with the authority of the others, and
- (iii) if made by any other body or group of persons, by one or more individual persons authorised for that purpose by the body or group;

(c) if made for the issue of a licence, state whether it relates to a standard licence or to a restricted licence and, if it relates to a standard licence, state whether the licence is to cover—

- (i) both national and international transport operations, or
- (ii) national transport operations only.

[623]

Time of applications

5 Every application shall be sent to the traffic commissioner so as to reach him not less than 9 weeks before the time at which the applicant desires the licence or variation applied for to take effect.

[624]

Dispensations as to applications

6 The traffic commissioner may consider an application notwithstanding that the requirement specified in regulation 5 has not been complied with.

[625]

Notice of applications

7 (1) The prescribed manner in which a notice of any application for a licence as mentioned in section 10 or for a variation as mentioned in section 17 is published by the traffic commissioner is that a summary of the application which adequately specifies the subject-matter of the application shall be published in Applications and Decisions as mentioned in regulation 21.

(2) The notice of an application to be published in accordance with section 11 or section 18 shall give the information specified in Schedule 1.

[626]

Restrictions on applications

8 (1) The traffic commissioner may decline to proceed with an application for a licence if it appears to him that the grant of that application would lead to a contravention of section 8(2).

(2) The traffic commissioner may decline to proceed with an application if and so long as it appears to him that the application relates to any motor vehicle which is specified in an existing licence, and the grant of that application would lead to a contravention of section 5(8).

[627]

Inspection of applications

9 (1) The traffic commissioner by whom an application is received shall, until the application has been determined, make available for inspection—

(a) to any person authorised to make the inspection by a local authority, a planning authority, chief officer of police or trade union or association specified in regulation 10, such part of the application (or the whole of it) as any such person in writing requests to see; and

(b) to any person who is, by virtue of section 12(4) or 19(2)(b) entitled to make representations in respect of the application, or a person authorised by such a person to make the inspection on his behalf, such part of the application as is, in the opinion of the traffic commissioner, relevant to the representation.

(2) A traffic commissioner by whom a licence is issued shall, during the currency of the licence, make a copy of it available for inspection by any person who appears to the traffic commissioner to have reasonable grounds for making such an inspection.

(3) A traffic commissioner shall satisfy his obligation under paragraph (1) by—

(a) making the application or, as the case may be, part of it, available for inspection at the office of his traffic area; or

(b) on prior receipt of his expenses in that behalf, by posting a copy of the application or, as the case may be, part of it, to the address given for that purpose by the person wanting to make the inspection.

(4) A traffic commissioner shall satisfy his obligation under paragraph (2) by—

(a) making a copy of the licence or, as the case may require, part of it, available for inspection at the office of his traffic area; or

(b) on prior receipt of his expenses in that behalf, by posting a copy of the licence or, as the case may require, part of it, to the address given for that purpose by the person requesting to make the inspection.

[628]

PART III

OBJECTIONS AND REPRESENTATIONS

Prescribed trade unions and associations

10 (1) The trade unions and associations specified in paragraph (2), being trade unions or associations whose members consist of or include persons holding licences or employees of any such persons, are hereby prescribed as persons who may object as provided in section 12(2), either as applied by section 19(2)(a) or not.

(2) Those trade unions and associations are—

The British Association of Removers;
The Freight Transport Association;
The General and Municipal Workers' Union;
The National Union of Rail, Maritime and Transport Workers;

The Road Haulage Association;
The Transport and General Workers' Union;
The Union of Shop, Distributive and Allied Workers; and
The United Road Transport Union.

[629]

Manner of making objections and representations

11 (1) For the purposes of sections 12(6)(b), 12(7)(b) and 19(10), the prescribed manner of making an objection to, or representation against, an application is by delivering a document to the traffic commissioner at the office of his traffic area—

(a) setting out the objection or representation as the case may be; and
(b) signed—
 (i) if made by an individual, by that person,
 (ii) if made by a firm, by all of the partners of that firm or by one of them with the authority of the others,
 (iii) if made by any other body or group of persons, by one or more individual persons authorised for that purpose by the body or group,

or, in any of the above cases, by a solicitor acting on behalf of (as the case may be) the person, firm, body or group.

(2) A copy of the document delivered under paragraph (1) shall be sent by the objector, or the person making the representation, to the applicant on the same day as, or the next working day after, the delivery to the traffic commissioner.

[630]

Time of making objections and representations

12 (1) The prescribed time within which an objection under section 12(1)(a) or (b) to an application for a licence must be made is the period commencing immediately after notice of the application is published under section 11(2) and ending 21 days after the date on which notice of the application is published in Applications and Decisions.

(2) The prescribed time within which a representation under section 12(4) in respect of an application for a licence must be made is the period of 21 days beginning with the date on which notice of the application is published under section 11(2).

(3) The prescribed time within which an objection under section 12(1)(a) as applied by section 17(5) or section 19(2) to or in respect of an application for a variation of a licence must be made is the period commencing immediately after notice of the application is published under section 18(3) (or, if none, the making of the application to which the objection relates) and ending 21 days after the date on which the notice of the application is published in Applications and Decisions.

(4) The prescribed time within which a representation under section 19(2) in respect of an application for a variation of a licence must be made is the period of 21 days beginning with the date on which the notice of the application is published under section 18(3).

[631]

Consideration of objections and representations

13 (1) The traffic commissioner shall consider every objection duly made in considering whether or not to hold an inquiry as provided in section 35.

(2) The traffic commissioner shall consider every representation duly made in considering whether or not to hold an inquiry as provided in section 35.

[632]

PART IV
OPERATING CENTRES

Conditions which may be attached to a licence

14 The conditions which may be attached under section 23 to a licence are conditions regulating—

(a) the number, type and size of authorised motor vehicles or trailers which may at any one time be at any operating centre of the licence-holder in the area of the traffic commissioner for the purposes of maintenance and parking;

(b) the parking arrangements to be provided for authorised motor vehicles or trailers at or in the vicinity of every such operating centre;

(c) the times between which there may be carried out at every such operating centre any maintenance or movement of any authorised motor vehicle or trailer and the times at which any equipment may be used for any such maintenance or movement; and

(d) the means of ingress to and egress from every such operating centre for any authorised motor vehicle or trailer.

[633]

Considerations relevant to determinations

15 (1) The considerations prescribed as relevant to any determination of a kind specified in section 34(2) are—

(a) the nature and the use of any other land in the vicinity of the land used or proposed to be used as an operating centre, and any effect which the use of the land as an operating centre has, or would be likely to have, on the environment of that vicinity;

(b) in a case where the land proposed to be used as an operating centre is, or has previously been, used as an operating centre, the extent to which the grant of the application would result in any material change as regards that operating centre, or its use, which would adversely affect the environment of the vicinity of that land;

(c) in the case of an application which, if granted, would result in land which has not previously been used as an operating centre being used as one, any information known to the traffic commissioner to whom the application is made about any planning permission or application for planning permission relating to the land or any other land in the vicinity of that land;

(d) the number, type and size of motor vehicles or trailers;

(e) the arrangements for the parking of motor vehicles or trailers or the proposed or likely arrangements for such parking;

(f) the nature and the times of the use of the land for the purpose of an operating centre or the proposed nature and times of the use of the land proposed to be used for that purpose;

(g) the nature and the times of the use of any equipment installed on the land used as an operating centre for the purpose of the use of that land as an operating centre or of any equipment proposed or likely to be installed on the land proposed to be used as an operating centre for that purpose; and

(h) the means and frequency of vehicular ingress to, and egress from, the land used as an operating centre or the proposed means and frequency of such ingress to, and egress from, the land proposed to be used as an operating centre.

(2) In this regulation—

"operating centre" includes part of an operating centre and the place which would be the operating centre if the application were granted; and

"planning permission" has the same meaning, as regards England and Wales, as in section 336(1) of the Town and Country Planning Act 1990, and, as regards Scotland, as in section 274(1) of the Town and Country Planning (Scotland) Act 1972.

[634]

Conditions to be satisfied in relation to specified operating centres

16 The prescribed condition under sections 14(5)(c), 19(9)(c) and paragraphs 1(7)(b) and 3(7)(b) of Schedule 4 to the 1995 Act is that either—

(a) proceedings on any appeal (including any proceedings on or in consequence of an appeal) have been determined and any time for appealing or further appealing has expired; or

(b) any review under section 36 has been determined or the time for giving notice of intention to review under section 36(2) has expired and no such notice of review has been served,

and if any appeal or notice of intention is withdrawn or abandoned the date of such withdrawal or abandonment shall be taken to be the time of expiry.

[635]

Period for service of notice on review of an operating centre

17 The period prescribed for the purpose of section 30(1) is two months.

[636]

Manner of service of notice on review of an operating centre

18 Paragraph 6 of Schedule 4 shall have effect in relation to serving of notices by the traffic commissioner on a licence-holder for the purposes of section 30(1), as if "section 30" were substituted for "the Schedule" in sub-paragraph (1) of that paragraph.

[637]

Manner of making representations in relation to a review

19 Without prejudice to section 31(5), the prescribed manner of making representations in relation to a review is by delivering a document to the traffic commissioner at the office of his traffic area—

(a) setting out the representations;

(b) clearly identifying—

(i) the person making the representations,

(ii) the place specified in the operator's licence to which the representations relate,

(iii) land or property in the vicinity which is owned or occupied by the person making the representations; and

(c) signed—

(i) if made by an individual, by that person,

(ii) if made by a firm, by all of the partners of that firm or by one of them with the authority of the others,

(iii) if made by any other body or group of persons, by one or more individual persons authorised for that purpose by the body or group,

or, in any of the above cases, by a solicitor acting on behalf of (as the case may be) the person, firm, body or group.

[638]

PART V
INQUIRIES

Provisions about inquiries

20 Schedule 4 shall have effect in relation to any inquiry held by a traffic commissioner.

[639]

PART VI
APPLICATIONS AND DECISIONS

Statement to be issued by the traffic commissioner

21 (1) The traffic commissioner shall publish as occasion may require a statement known as "Applications and Decisions" which shall contain (unless previously notified)—

(a) as regards applications—

(i) notices of the applications,

(ii) the dates on which and the places at which he proposes to hold inquiries and the applications which he proposes to consider at those inquiries, and

(iii) the traffic commissioner's decisions on applications, other than his decisions to issue an interim licence under section 24, or to make an interim direction under section 25;

(b) any direction to revoke, suspend or curtail a licence given under section 26 or section 27;

(c) the dates on which and the places at which he proposes to hold any inquiries other than those mentioned in sub-paragraph (a)(ii) above; and

(d) any decision of his following a review under section 30.

(2) The publication of the date of any inquiry in Applications and Decisions shall not prevent the traffic commissioner from adjourning, cancelling or postponing the consideration of any application and in particular any inquiry held or proposed to be held in connection with the application.

(3) Copies of Applications and Decisions may be inspected at the office of the traffic area of the traffic commissioner by whom it was issued and at such other places (if any) as he may determine and copies of the whole or the relevant parts thereof shall be supplied to any person requiring them on payment of such sum as the traffic commissioner may require to cover the cost of supplying the copy.

[640]

Notification of decisions

22 (1) Subject to paragraph (2), where a traffic commissioner grants or refuses an application, he shall send a written statement of his reasons to—

(a) the applicant;

(b) every objector; and

(c) every person who has made a representation in accordance with sections 12(4), 19(2) or 19(4) and asked the traffic commissioner for such a statement.

(2) Paragraph (1) does not apply where—

(a) the traffic commissioner grants an application in the terms applied for; and

(b) no objection or representation has been made in accordance with sections 12(1), 12(4), 19(2) or 19(4).

(3) Where a traffic commissioner makes a direction under section 31 or 32, he shall send a written statement of his reasons to the licence-holder.

[641]

PART VII
OTHER MATTERS

Identification of motor vehicles

23 (1) The traffic commissioner shall, when any motor vehicle to be used under a licence is specified in the licence, issue to the licence-holder a disc in respect of the vehicle.

(2) The disc shall clearly indicate (by colour or other means)—

(a) whether a vehicle is being used under a standard licence or under a restricted licence; and

(b) in the case of a vehicle being used under a standard licence, whether the vehicle covers both international and national transport operations or national transport operations only.

(3) The licence-holder shall, during such time as any motor vehicle is specified in the licence and whether or not for the time being the vehicle is being used for the purpose for which a licence is required, cause a disc appropriate to the vehicle to be fixed to, and exhibited in a legible condition on, that vehicle in a waterproof container—

(a) in the case of a vehicle fitted with a front windscreen, on the near side and near the lower edge of the windscreen with the obverse side facing forwards;

(b) in the case of a vehicle not fitted with a front windscreen, in a conspicuous position on the front or near side of the vehicle.

(4) At no time shall any person except the traffic commissioner, or a person authorised to do so on his behalf, write on or make any other alteration to a disc.

[642]

Temporary addition of a motor vehicle

24 Where—

(a) a motor vehicle specified in an operator's licence ("the specified vehicle") has been rendered unfit for service, or withdrawn from service for overhaul or repair, and the licence-holder informs the traffic commissioner of his desire to have a variation of the licence specifying another motor vehicle in its place ("the additional vehicle"); or

(b) the specified vehicle has been rendered fit for service again, and the licence-holder informs the traffic commissioner of his desire to have a variation of the licence whereby the additional vehicle will cease to be specified on the licence,

the provisions of regulations 4 and 5 shall not apply.

[643]

Notification of change of address

25 If during the currency of a licence the address for correspondence as notified in the licence-holder's application or as subsequently notified under this regulation ceases to be an effective address for correspondence the licence-holder shall within 28 days from the date of such event notify the traffic commissioner by whom the licence was granted of an effective address for correspondence.

[644]

Production of licence for examination

26 (1) The licence-holder shall produce the licence for inspection by an officer or a police constable on being required by such a person to do so, and the licence-holder may do so at any operating centre covered by the licence or at his head or principal place of business within the traffic area in which any such operating centre lies or, if the requirement is made by a police constable, at a police station chosen by the licence-holder.

(2) The licence-holder shall comply with any requirement mentioned in paragraph (1) within 14 days of the day on which the requirement is made.

[645]

Issue of copies of licences and discs

27 (1) If a licence or disc has been lost, destroyed or defaced, the person to whom it was issued shall forthwith notify in writing the traffic commissioner by whom the licence or disc was issued.

(2) If—

(a) the traffic commissioner is satisfied that a licence or disc has been lost, destroyed or defaced; and

(b) in the case of a licence or disc which has been defaced, it is surrendered to the traffic commissioner,

the traffic commissioner shall issue a copy (so marked) which shall have effect as the original licence or disc.

(3) Where a licence or disc has been lost and after a copy has been issued the lost licence or disc is found by or comes into the possession of the licence-holder he shall forthwith return the original licence or disc to the traffic commissioner.

[646]

Return of licences and discs

28 (1) If the licence-holder ceases to use under the licence any motor vehicle specified in the licence he shall within 21 days beginning with the date of ceasing to use the vehicle or vehicles notify the traffic commissioner by whom the licence was issued and return to that traffic commissioner the licence for variation and the disc relating to the vehicle.

(2) If a licence is varied under section 17, 31, 32 or 36 its holder shall, when required by the traffic commissioner so to do, return to the traffic commissioner—

(a) the licence; and

(b) if the number of motor vehicles specified in the licence has been reduced, the disc relating to any vehicle no longer specified in the licence.

(3) If a licence is revoked, surrendered, suspended, curtailed or terminated for any other reason, or if a traffic commissioner has given a direction in respect of a licence under section 26(2), the licence-holder shall on or before the date specified in a notice to that effect, send or deliver to the office of the traffic area of the traffic commissioner by whom the licence was issued—

(a) the licence; and

(b) the disc relating to any motor vehicle which the traffic commissioner may specify,

for cancellation, retention during the time of suspension, or alteration as the case may be.

(4) The notice referred to in paragraph (3) shall be delivered personally to the licence-holder or sent to him by recorded delivery service at the address shown in his application or last notified in accordance with regulation 25.

(5) In the event of the traffic commissioner deciding to make a variation under paragraph 9 of the Schedule to the Goods Vehicles (Licensing of Operators) Act 1995 (Commencement and Transitional Provisions) Order 1995 the licence-holder shall return the licence to the traffic commissioner for him to amend the licence so that it conforms to the variation before returning it to the holder.

NOTES

Goods Vehicles (Licensing of Operators) Act 1995 (Commencement and Transitional Provisions) Order 1995 SI 1995/2181.

[647]

Partnerships

29 (1) The provision in section 8(2) that a person shall not at the same time hold more than one operator's licence in respect of the same area shall apply so that a firm shall be treated as a person separate from any partner of that firm or an individual in any other partnership.

(2) For the purposes of authorising goods vehicles to be used under section 5(1) when the licence-holder is a firm, any vehicle in the lawful possession of any partner of a firm shall be regarded as in the lawful possession of the firm.

(3) The provisions of section 13(3) shall apply in any case where an applicant for a standard licence is a firm so that the traffic commissioner is required to satisfy himself that—

(a) every one of the partners of that firm is of good repute;

(b) the firm satisfies the requirement of appropriate financial standing; and

(c) either—

(i) if one of the firm's partners manage the road transport business carried on by the firm, he, or if more than one each of them, is professionally competent, or

(ii) the firm employs a transport manager or transport managers who, or if more than one each of whom, is of good repute and professionally competent.

(4) The provisions of section 13(4) shall apply in any case where an applicant for a restricted licence is a firm so that the traffic commissioner is required to satisfy himself that everyone of the partners of that firm is not unfit to hold an operator's licence by reason of any activities or convictions covered by section 34(a) or (b).

(5) The provisions of section 13(6) shall apply in any case where an applicant is a firm and in such case the financial resources referred to in that subsection shall be those of the firm.

(6) The provisions of section 26 shall apply in any case where the licence-holder is a firm and in such a case any act, omission or conviction of a partner of that firm shall be regarded as the act, omission or conviction of the firm.

(7) The provisions of section 27(1) shall apply in any case where the licence-holder is a firm if—

(a) any one or more of the partners of that firm cease to satisfy the requirement to be of good repute; or

(b) the firm ceases to satisfy the requirement to be of appropriate financial standing; or

(c) when the requirement as to professional competence is satisfied by one or more of the firm's partners who manage the road transport business carried on by the firm, he, or if more than one each of them, ceases to do so, or when the firm employs a transport manager or transport managers such manager, or if more than one any of them, ceases to be of good repute, or when the firm relies upon the employment of a single transport manager to satisfy the requirement as to professional competence, that transport manager ceases to be employed by the firm.

(8) The provisions of section 28 shall apply to the revocation of an operator's licence held by a firm and in such a case the powers conferred by subsections (1) and (4) shall be exercisable in respect of each and every partner of that firm.

(9) Except in a case falling within paragraph (9) any requirement, obligation or prohibition (however expressed) placed on a person making an application or on the licence-holder by, or in pursuance of, a provision in the 1995 Act or these Regulations, shall apply where the licence-holder is a firm and the duty to meet the requirement or obligation or to comply with the prohibition, shall apply to the partners of that firm severally as well as jointly.

(10) Where an application is made by, or the licence-holder is a firm a requirement or obligation placed on the applicant or licence-holder by virtue of sections 8(4), 9(1) or 17(2) of the 1995 Act to inform the traffic commissioner of a notifiable conviction within the meaning given in paragraph 4 of Schedule 2 to the 1995 Act shall apply in relation to the notifiable conviction of each partner of that firm, and the duty to meet the requirement shall apply to the person convicted.

(11) The provisions in section 16(5) as to the events on which an operator's licence held by an individual terminates apply in a case where such a licence is held by a firm, if—

(a) the partnership is dissolved; or

(b) one or more of the persons dies or becomes a [person who lacks capacity (within the meaning of the Mental Capacity Act 2005) to carry on the activities covered by the licence], or if (in Scotland) a curator bonis is appointed in respect of him, with the result that only one other of such persons who is not such a *patient* or so incapable remains in the partnership.

(12) In Schedule 3 to the 1995 Act—

(a) the provisions in paragraph 1 as regards determining whether an individual is of good repute apply, in a case of a firm in respect of each of the partners of that firm as they apply to an individual;

(b) the provision in paragraph 6 as regards determining whether the applicant for, or the holder of, a licence is of appropriate financial standing shall apply, in the case of a firm, to the financial standing of the firm;

(c) the provision in paragraph 8(2) that a company satisfies the requirement as to professional competence if, and so long as, it has a transport manager or transport managers of its road transport business who, or if more than one each of whom, is of good repute and professionally competent shall apply in the case of a firm so that the firm satisfies the said requirement if, and so long as, each of its partners is of good repute, and either—

(i) if one or more of the firm's partners manage the road transport business carried on by the firm, he, or if more than one each of them, is professionally competent, or

(ii) the firm employs a transport manager or transport managers of its road transport business who, or if more than one each of whom, if of good repute and professionally competent; and

(d) in a case where one or more partners of a firm manage the road transport business carried on by that firm or the firm employs a transport manager or transport managers the provision in paragraphs 10 and 11 shall apply—

(i) as regards one such person or a single transport manager employed by the firm as it applies as regards a single transport manager employed by a company, and

(ii) as regards two or more such persons or two or more transport managers employed by the firm as it applies as regards two or more transport managers employed by a company.

NOTES

Erratum Para (4): it is thought that the reference to activities or convictions covered by s 34(a) or (b) should be a reference to activities or convictions covered by s 13(4)(a) or (b).

Para (11)(b): it is thought that, in consequence of the amendment made by SI 2007/1898 noted below, the reference to "patient" should read "person who lacks capacity".

Amendment Para (11)(b): words in square brackets substituted by SI 2007/1898 (see also the note "Erratum" above).

[648]

Holding companies and subsidiaries

30 (1) A holding company may apply to the traffic commissioner for any traffic area—

(a) if it does not already hold a licence in respect of that area, for the issue of a licence; or

(b) if it already holds a licence in respect of that area, for a variation of its licence by a direction under section 17(1)(a),

which would have the effect, if the application were granted, of including in the licence to be issued to, or already held by, the holding company, goods vehicles in the lawful possession of a subsidiary of that company specified in the application.

(2) An application by a holding company under paragraph (1) shall, unless

(a) the subsidiary is not the licence-holder; or

(b) the licence or variation applied for by the holding company will not take effect until any licence held by the subsidiary has been surrendered or has otherwise terminated,

be accompanied by an application by the subsidiary for the variation of the licence held by the subsidiary by a direction under section 17(1)(b) for the removal therefrom of all or some of the goods vehicles authorised to be used thereunder, being the vehicles to which the application of the holding company relates.

(3) Where a holding company, on an application under paragraph (1) signifies to the traffic commissioner its desire that the provisions of this regulation should have effect as respects a subsidiary of that company, then, in relation to the application and to any licence granted to the holding company, or held by the holding company and varied, on that application, and to the use of any goods vehicles authorised to be used under any such licence, the 1995 Act and these Regulations shall have effect subject to the modifications specified in Schedule 2.

(4) The provisions of this regulation shall cease to have effect as respects a holding company and its subsidiary—

(a) if the holding company gives notice to the traffic commissioner who issued or varied its licence that it desires that this regulation should, as from any date, cease to apply to the holding company and that subsidiary, as from that date; or

(b) as from the date on which that subsidiary ceases to be a subsidiary of that holding company.

(5) Where by virtue of the provisions of paragraphs (1) to (3) a holding company holds a licence which includes goods vehicles in the lawful possession of a subsidiary of that company, and the holding company gives notice under paragraph (4)(a), then, in relation to any application by the subsidiary for the issue of a licence in respect of all or any of those vehicles, section 10 shall have effect as if for sub-section (1) there were substituted the following sub-section—

> "(1) The traffic commissioner may publish in the prescribed manner notice of any application to him for an operator's licence made by a company or other body corporate in pursuance of Regulations made under section 46 of this Act.".

(6) Where the provisions of this regulation cease to have effect as respects a holding company and its subsidiary by virtue of paragraph (4)(b) the company which

was the holding company shall within 21 days of the event which caused the subsidiary to cease to be a subsidiary of that company—

(a) notify the traffic commissioner by whom the licence was issued, and
(b) supply all material details of the event, and
(c) return to the traffic commissioner the licence and the discs relating to the motor vehicles authorised to be used thereunder,

and in so far as the holding company fails to satisfy those requirements the company which was the subsidiary company shall, on being so directed by the traffic commissioner, within 7 days of that direction supply the details, or return the licence and the discs, as the case may require.

(7) In a case where the applicant for, or the holder of, a standard licence is a holding company and the goods vehicles used, or to be used, under the licence belong to, or are in the possession of, a subsidiary of that holding company, the provisions of these Regulations apply as if—

(a) the road transport undertaking and any operating centre of the subsidiary were the road transport undertaking and an operating centre of the holding company;
(b) for purposes of, or relating to, the reputation and financial standing of the holding company, the activities, relevant convictions and financial resources of the subsidiary were activities, convictions and resources of the holding company; and
(c) in relation to a transport manager, his employment by the subsidiary were employment by the holding company.

[649]

Continuance of licence on death, bankruptcy etc

31 (1) In this regulation, "actual holder" in relation to a licence means the person to whom the licence was issued.

(2) This regulation applies in the event—

(a) of the death of the actual holder of a licence;
(b) of the actual holder of a licence becoming a [person who lacks capacity (within the meaning of the Mental Capacity Act 2005) to carry on the activities covered by the licence], or in Scotland a curator bonis being appointed in respect of him on the ground that he is incapable, by reason of mental disorder, of adequately managing his property and affairs;
(c) of the bankruptcy of the actual holder of a licence;
(d) in the case of a company, of the actual holder of a licence going into liquidation or [entering administration]; or
(e) of the appointment of a receiver or manager of the trade or business of the actual holder of a licence.

(3) After the happening of either of the events mentioned in paragraphs (2)(a) or (b) the traffic commissioner may direct that the licence shall not be treated as terminated when the actual holder died or became a *patient* but suspended until the date when a direction under paragraph (4) comes into force.

(4) After the happening of any of the events mentioned in paragraph (2) the traffic commissioner may direct that a person carrying on the trade or business of the actual holder of the licence is to be treated for the purposes of the 1995 Act as if he were the holder thereof for such purpose and to such extent as is specified in the direction for a period not exceeding—

(a) if it appears to the traffic commissioner that there are special circumstances, 18 months;
(b) in any other case, 12 months,

from the date of the coming into force of that direction.

(5) The powers under paragraph (4) shall be exercisable in relation to a standard licence whether or not the person carrying on the trade or business of the actual holder of the licence satisfies the requirement of professional competence.

(6) Where a person is treated as if he were the licence-holder by virtue of a direction under this regulation—

(a) any goods vehicle which had been in the lawful possession of the actual holder of the licence shall for the purposes of the 1995 Act be treated as if it was in the lawful possession of that person; and

(b) if the licence is a standard licence, nothing in section 27 shall oblige the traffic commissioner to revoke the licence by reason only of that person not satisfying the requirement of professional competence.

NOTES
Erratum Para (3): in consequence of the amendment to para (2)(b) by SI 2007/1898, it is thought that the reference in para (3) to "patient" should read "person who lacks capacity".
Amendment Para (2)(b): words in square brackets substituted by SI 2007/1898.
Para (2)(d): words in square brackets substituted by SI 2003/2096.

[650]

Offences

32 Any contravention of, or failure to comply with, a provision in regulations 23(3), 23(4), 25, 26, 27(1), 27(3), 28(1), 28(2), 28(3), 28(4) or 30(6), is hereby declared to be an offence and for the purposes of section 57(9) any provision mentioned above shall be regarded as made under the 1995 Act.

[651]

Classes of vehicle for which a licence is not required

33 (1) The classes of vehicle specified under section 2(2)(d) as those to which section 2(1) does not apply are the classes mentioned in Part I of Schedule 3.

(2) The relevant plated weight of a goods vehicle, for the purposes of Schedule 1 to the 1995 Act (meaning of "small goods vehicle") is the gross weight not to be exceeded in Great Britain of the vehicle as shown on a Ministry plate as defined in column 2 of the Table in regulation 3(2) of the Road Vehicles (Construction and Use) Regulations 1986 or, if no such plate has been issued in respect of that vehicle, the maximum gross weight of the vehicle as shown on a plate affixed to the vehicle by virtue of regulation 66 of those Regulations.

NOTES
Road Vehicles (Construction and Use) Regulations 1986 SI 1986/1078.

[652]

Period for service of notice of review on ground of procedural irregularity

34 The period prescribed for the purposes of section 36(2) is two months.

[653]

Manner of service of notice of review on ground of procedural irregularity

35 Paragraph 6 of Schedule 4 shall have effect in relation to the serving of notices by the traffic commissioner on the applicant or (as the case may be) the licence-holder which state his intention to review a decision referred to in section 36(1), and in such a case "section 36(2)(a)" shall be substituted for "this Schedule" in sub-paragraph (1) of that paragraph.

[654]

Meaning of "relevant weight"

36 (1) A motor vehicle or trailer of any prescribed class referred to in section 5(3) means any vehicle described in section 2(1) as needing an operator's licence, and the relevant weight of such a vehicle is its revenue weight.

(2) For purposes of this regulation "revenue weight" shall have the meaning given in section 60A of the Vehicle Excise and Registration Act 1994.

(3) In its application to this regulation, section 60A of that Act shall have effect as if—

(a) subsection (6) of that section were omitted; and
(b) no provision had been made under section 61A(2) of that Act.

[655]

SCHEDULE 1
NOTICE OF APPLICATION FOR A LICENCE OR A VARIATION OF A LICENCE

Regulation 7(2)

1 Information to be given in Notice of Application—

(a) Name of applicant.
(b) Trading name, if any.
(c) Address for receipt of correspondence.
(d) Whether the application is in respect of a new licence, or the variation of a licence.
(e) The place or places proposed to be used as an operating centre or centres (including, if available, the postal address or addresses).
(f) The number of motor vehicles and trailers proposed to be kept at each operating centre or centres.
(g) The number of motor vehicles and trailers now kept, if different.
(h) In respect of an existing licence, details of any proposed changes to or removal of existing conditions or undertakings affecting an operating centre.

2 Every notice shall contain the following wording:

"Owners or occupiers of land (including buildings) near the operating centre(s) who believe that their use or enjoyment of that land would be affected, should make written representations to the Traffic Commissioner at [address of Traffic Area Office] stating their reasons, within 21 days of this notice. Representors must at the same time send a copy of their representations to the applicant at the address given at the top of this notice. A Guide to making representations is available from the Traffic Commissioner's office."

[656]

SCHEDULE 2
MODIFICATIONS IN RELATION TO HOLDING COMPANIES AND SUBSIDIARIES

Regulation 30(3)

1 The 1995 Act and these Regulations have effect as if any reference (except in this Schedule) to a provision which is modified by this Schedule were a reference to that provision as so modified.

2 The 1995 Act has effect as if—

(a) goods vehicles in the lawful possession of the subsidiary were in the lawful possession of the holding company;
(b) where a goods vehicle is used in circumstances in which, but for the provisions of regulation 30 the subsidiary would be deemed to be the user, the holding company were the user;
(c) a trade or business carried on by the subsidiary were carried on by the holding company;
(d) the subsidiary were an applicant for the grant or variation of the licence;
(e) any operating centre of the subsidiary were an operating centre of the holding company;
(f) any person who is a director of the subsidiary were a director of the holding company;
(g) any person who is an employee of the subsidiary were an employee of the holding company;
(h) for section 10(1) there were substituted the following sub-section—

"(1) The traffic commissioner may publish in the prescribed manner notice of any application to him for an operator's licence made by a company or other body corporate in pursuance of Regulations made under section 46 of this Act";

(i) in section 22(1) the reference in paragraph (b) to persons holding shares in the company included a reference to persons holding shares in the subsidiary, and the reference in paragraph (c) to the licence-holder included a reference to the subsidiary;
(j) in section 17(3) for the words "Except in the case mentioned in subsection (4), the traffic commissioner shall publish" there were substituted "In the case of an application for a direction under subsection (1)(a) of this section made by a company or other body corporate in pursuance of Regulations made under section 46 of this Act, the traffic commissioner may publish";
(k) in section 26(1) the references in paragraphs (a), (b), (d), (e), (g) and (h) to the licence-holder included references to the subsidiary;
(l) in section 26(5) the reference to the licence-holder included a reference to the subsidiary;
(m) in section 26(1)(c) the references to the licence-holder or any servant or agent of his included references to the subsidiary or any servant or agent of it, and as if the reference in sub-paragraph (iii) to a vehicle of which the licence-holder was the owner included a reference to a vehicle of which the subsidiary was the owner;
(n) in section 28(1) the reference to the licence-holder included a reference to the subsidiary;
(o) in section 28(4)(a) after sub-paragraph (ii) there were inserted the following sub-paragraph—

"(iii) a company which is a subsidiary of such a company; or";

(p) in section 28(5) there were substituted for paragraph (a) "where that person is a company or other body corporate which is the licence-holder in respect of a subsidiary of that company or other body corporate in pursuance of Regulations made under section 46 of this Act, in relation to any director of that company or other body corporate or of that subsidiary.".

3 These Regulations shall have effect as if—

(a) in section 8 the reference to an operating centre of the applicant included a reference to an operating centre of the subsidiary;

(b) in regulation 26 the reference to the licence-holder included a reference to the subsidiary.

[657]

SCHEDULE 3
CLASSES OF VEHICLES FOR WHICH A LICENCE IS NOT REQUIRED

Regulation 33

PART I

1 Any tractor as defined in paragraph 4(3) of Part IV of Schedule 1 to the Vehicle Excise and Registration Act 1994 (as originally enacted) while being used for one or more of the purposes specified in Part II of this Schedule.

2 A dual-purpose vehicle and any trailer drawn by it.

3 A vehicle used on a road only in passing from private premises to other private premises in the immediate neighbourhood belonging (except in the case of a vehicle so used only in connection with excavation or demolition) to the same person, provided that the distance travelled on a road by any such vehicle does not exceed in the aggregate 9.654 kilometres, (6 miles), in any one week.

4 A motor vehicle constructed or adapted primarily for the carriage of passengers and their effects, and any trailer drawn by it, while being so used.

5 A vehicle which is being used for funerals.

6 A vehicle which is being used for police, [relevant authority (as defined in section 6 of the Fire (Scotland) Act 2005)] [or, in England, fire and rescue authority] or ambulance [or Serious Organised Crime Agency] purposes.

7 A vehicle which is being used for fire-fighting or rescue operations at mines.

8 A vehicle on which no permanent body has been constructed, which is being used only for carrying burden which either is carried solely for the purpose of test or trial, or consists of articles and equipment which will form part of the completed vehicle when the body is constructed.

9 A vehicle which is being used under a trade licence.

10 A vehicle in the service of a visiting force or of a headquarters.

11 A vehicle used by or under the control of Her Majesty's United Kingdom forces.

12 A trailer not constructed primarily for the carriage of goods but which is being used incidentally for that purpose in connection with the construction, maintenance or repair of roads.

13 A road roller and any trailer drawn by it.

14 A vehicle while being used under the direction of HM Coastguard or of the Royal National Lifeboat Institution for the carriage of life-boats, life-saving appliances or crew.

15 A vehicle fitted with a machine, appliance, apparatus or other contrivance which is a permanent or essentially permanent fixture, provided that the only goods carried on the vehicle are—

(a) required for use in connection with the machine, appliance, apparatus or contrivance or the running of the vehicle;

(b) to be mixed by the machine, appliance, apparatus or contrivance with other goods not carried on the vehicle on a road in order to thresh, grade, clean or chemically treat grain;

(c) to be mixed by the machine, appliance, apparatus or contrivance with other goods not carried on the vehicle in order to make fodder for animals; or

(d) mud or other matter swept up from the surface of a road by the use of the machine, appliance, apparatus or other contrivance.

16 A vehicle while being used by a local authority for the purposes of the enactments relating to weights and measures or the sale of food and drugs.

17 A vehicle while being used by a local authority in the discharge of any function conferred on or exercisable by that authority under Regulations made under the Civil Defence Act 1948.

18 A steam-propelled vehicle.

19 A tower wagon or trailer drawn thereby, provided that the only goods carried on the trailer are goods required for use in connection with the work on which the tower wagon is ordinarily used as such.

20 A vehicle while being used for the carriage of goods within an aerodrome within the meaning of section 105(1) of the Civil Aviation Act 1982.

21 An electrically propelled vehicle.

22 A showman's goods vehicle and any trailer drawn thereby.

23 A vehicle permitted to carry out cabotage in the United Kingdom under Community Council Regulation (EEC) No 3118/93 dated 25 October 1993 laying down conditions under which non-resident carriers may operate national road haulage services within a Member State.

24 A goods vehicle first used before 1 January 1977 which has an unladen weight not exceeding 1525 kilograms and for which the maximum gross weight, as shown on a plate affixed to the vehicle by virtue of regulation 66 of the Motor Vehicles (Construction and Use) Regulations 1986 or any provision which that regulation replaced, exceeds 3500 kilograms but does not exceed 3556.21 kilograms (3 1/2 tons).

25 A vehicle while being used by a highway authority for the purposes of section 196 of the Road Traffic Act 1988.

26 A vehicle being held ready for use in an emergency by an undertaking for the supply of water, electricity, gas or telephone services.

27 A recovery vehicle.

28 A vehicle which is being used for snow clearing, or for the distribution of grit, salt or other materials on frosted, icebound or snow-covered roads or for going to or from the place where it is to be used for the said purposes or for any other purpose directly connected with those purposes.

29 A vehicle proceeding to or from a station provided by the Secretary of State under section 45 of the Road Traffic Act 1988 for the purposes of an examination of that vehicle under that section provided that—

(a) the only load being carried is a load required for the purposes of the examination; and
(b) it is being carried at the request of the Secretary of State.

NOTES
Amendment Para 6: words in first pair of square brackets substituted, in relation to Scotland only, by SI 2005/2060; words in second pair of square brackets inserted by SI 2004/3168 (in relation to England only) (words "or, in England or Wales, fire and rescue authority" inserted by SI 2005/2929 (in relation to Wales only)); words in third pair of square brackets inserted by SI 2006/594.
Council Regulation (EEC) 3118/93 OJ L279, 12.11.1993, p 1.
Civil Defence Act 1948 Repealed by the Civil Contingencies Act 2004, s 32, Sch 2, Pt 1, para 3, Sch 3.
Motor Vehicles (Construction and Use) Regulations 1986 SI 1986/1078.
Cases relating to this Schedule Sch 3, Pt I, para 15: *Vehicle Operator Services Agency v Law Fertilisers Ltd* [2004] EWHC 3000 (Admin), [2004] All ER (D) 50 (Dec).

[658]

PART II
PURPOSES REFERRED TO IN PARAGRAPH 1 OF PART I OF THIS SCHEDULE

1 Hauling—

(a) threshing appliances;
(b) farming implements;
(c) a living van for the accommodation of persons employed to drive the tractor; or
(d) supplies of water or fuel required for the tractor.

2 Hauling articles for a farm required by the keeper, being either the occupier of the farm or a contractor employed to do agricultural work on the farm by the occupier of the farm.

3 Hauling articles for a forestry estate required by the keeper where the keeper is the occupier of that estate or employed to do forestry work on the estate by the occupier or a contractor employed to do forestry work on the estate by the occupier.

4 Hauling within 24.135 kilometres, (15 miles), of a farm or a forestry estate occupied by the keeper, agricultural or woodland produce of that farm or estate.

5 Hauling within 24.135 kilometres, (15 miles), of a farm or a forestry estate occupied by the keeper, material to be spread on roads to deal with frost, ice or snow.

6 Hauling a snow plough or a similar contrivance for the purpose of clearing snow; and

7 Hauling—

(a) soil for landscaping or similar works; or
(b) a mowing machine,

where the keeper is a local authority.

[659]

SCHEDULE 4
INQUIRIES

Regulation 20

Notification of an inquiry

1 (1) The traffic commissioner shall send to every person entitled to appear in accordance with paragraph 3 of this Schedule at an inquiry written notice of the date, time and place fixed for the holding of the inquiry.

Such notice shall be sent at least 21 days before the date so fixed.

(2) The traffic commissioner may vary the date, time or place for the holding of the inquiry; and when he varies the date he shall send to every person so entitled to appear at the inquiry, written notice of the date, time and place of the holding of the inquiry as varied.

Such notice shall be sent at least 21 days before the date as varied.

(3) The periods referred to in sub-paragraph (1) and (2) may be abridged with the consent of every person so entitled to appear at the inquiry.

(4) Where the traffic commissioner varies the time or place for the holding of an inquiry without varying the date, he shall give such notice of the variation as appears to him to be reasonable.

(5) Nothing in this paragraph shall authorise the traffic commissioner to hold an inquiry before the date published in Applications and Decisions pursuant to regulation 21.

(6) The foregoing provisions of this paragraph shall apply to an adjourned inquiry save that—

(a) if the date, time and place of the adjourned inquiry are announced at the inquiry before the adjournment, no further notice of that date, time and place shall be required; and
(b) sub-paragraphs (1) and (2) shall have effect in relation to an adjourned inquiry as if for "21 days" there were substituted "7 days".

Admission to an inquiry

2 (1) Subject to the provisions of this paragraph, an inquiry shall be held in public.

(2) The traffic commissioner may direct that the whole or any part of an inquiry be held in private if he is satisfied that by reason of—

(a) the likelihood of disclosure of intimate personal or financial circumstances;
(b) the likelihood of disclosure of commercially sensitive information or information obtained in confidence; or
(c) exceptional circumstances not falling within sub-paragraphs (a) or (b),

it is just and reasonable for him so to do.

(3) Where the hearing is in private the traffic commissioner may admit such persons as he considers appropriate.

(4) Without prejudice to sub-paragraph (2), where any question relating to the appropriate financial resources of any persons is to be or is being considered during an inquiry, the traffic commissioner may exclude such persons as he thinks fit from the part of the inquiry during which that question is considered.

(5) …

Appearances at an inquiry

3 (1) The following persons shall be entitled to appear at an inquiry relating to an application namely—

(a) the applicant;

(b) a person who has duly made an objection to the application; and
(c) a person who has duly made representations in respect of the application.

(2) Where a traffic commissioner holds an inquiry with a view to exercising his powers under section 26 or 30, in respect of a licence, the licence-holder shall be entitled to appear at the inquiry.

(3) Without prejudice to sub-paragraph (2), where a person has requested an inquiry under section 29(1), that person shall be entitled to appear at any inquiry held at his request.

(4) If, in relation to any proceedings,

(a) a transport manager has been given notice under paragraph 15 of Schedule 3 to the 1995 Act that an issue in the proceedings is whether he is of good repute or professionally competent;
(b) the transport manager has duly made a representation under that paragraph; and
(c) the issue is to be considered at an inquiry,

the transport manager shall be entitled to appear at the inquiry.

(5) Any other person may appear at an inquiry at the discretion of the traffic commissioner.

(6) Any person entitled or permitted to appear at an inquiry may do so on his own behalf or be represented by counsel, solicitor or, at the discretion of the traffic commissioner, by any other person.

Inquiries relating to more than one application

4 Without prejudice to section 35(2), where a traffic commissioner decides that two or more applications should be the subject of an inquiry, he may hold a single inquiry in relation to those applications if it appears to him that it would be just and convenient so to do.

Procedure at inquiry

5 (1) Except as otherwise provided in this Schedule, the traffic commissioner shall determine the procedure at an inquiry.

(2) Subject to sub-paragraph (5), a person entitled to appear at an inquiry in accordance with paragraph 3 of this Schedule shall be entitled to give evidence, call witnesses, to cross examine witnesses and to address the traffic commissioner both on the evidence and generally on the subject matter of the proceedings.

(3) The giving of evidence, the calling of witnesses, the cross examination of witnesses and the making of such addresses by other persons appearing at an inquiry shall be at the traffic commissioner's discretion.

(4) Subject to sub-paragraph (5), any person present at an inquiry may submit any written evidence or other matter in writing before the close of the inquiry.

(5) Without prejudice to sub-paragraph (3), the traffic commissioner may refuse to permit—

(a) the giving or calling of evidence;
(b) cross examination of persons giving evidence; or
(c) the presentation of any other matter,

which he considers to be irrelevant, repetitious, frivolous or vexatious.

(6) The traffic commissioner may require any person appearing or present at an inquiry who, in his opinion, is behaving in a disruptive manner to leave and may refuse to permit that person to return.

(7) The traffic commissioner may proceed with an inquiry in the absence of any person entitled to appear, but if he was required to give such a person notice of the inquiry under paragraph 1 of this Schedule he shall not so proceed in the person's absence unless—

(a) he is satisfied that such notice had been duly given; or
(b) he decides to proceed with the inquiry under paragraph 7 of this Schedule on the basis that no injustice would be caused to the person as a result of such notice not having been duly given to him.

(8) The traffic commissioner shall not take into account any written evidence or other matter in writing received by him from any person before an inquiry opens or during any inquiry unless he discloses it at the inquiry.

(9) The traffic commissioner may from time to time adjourn an inquiry.

Giving of notices

6 (1) A notice required or authorised to be sent to a person under this Schedule may be effected by—

(a) delivering it to him at an address which is his proper address; or
(b) sending it to him by post to an address which is his proper address; or
(c) transmitting to him a facsimile copy of it by means of electronic signals.

(2) A notice sent under paragraph (1) shall, for the purposes of this Schedule, be deemed to have been sent when it would have been delivered in the ordinary course of post notwithstanding that—

(a) the notice was returned as undelivered or was for any reason not received; or
(b) was in fact delivered or received at some other time.

(3) Any such document may—

(a) in the case of a body corporate, be sent to the secretary or clerk of that body;
(b) in the case of a partnership, be sent to any partner;

(c) in the case of an unincorporated association other than a partnership, be sent to any member of the governing body of the association.

(4) For the purposes of this paragraph and section 7 of the Interpretation Act 1978, the proper address of any person is his last known address (whether of his residence or a place where he carries on business or is employed) and also any address applicable in his case under the following provisions—

(a) in the case of a body corporate, its secretary or its clerk, the address of its registered or principal office in the United Kingdom;

(b) in the case of an unincorporated association (other than a partnership) or member of its governing body, its principal office in the United Kingdom.

(5) Where a person has in the licence-holder's application notified the traffic commissioner of an address, or, subsequently notified a new address under regulation 25, at which documents may be given to him for the purposes of correspondence that address shall also be his proper address for service for the purposes mentioned in sub-paragraph (3) or, as the case may be, his proper address for those purposes in substitution for that previously notified.

Irregularities in the giving of notices

7 Where a notice of the date, time and place fixed for the holding of an inquiry is not given in accordance with this Schedule, the traffic commissioner may nevertheless proceed with the inquiry as if notice had been duly given provided he is satisfied that no injustice or inconvenience would be caused.

Interpretation

8 In this Schedule "inquiry" means an inquiry held for the purposes of the Goods Vehicles (Licensing of Operators) Act 1995.

NOTES

Amendment Para 2(5): revoked by SI 2009/1307.

Interpretation Act 1978 Printed in the title Statutory Instruments (Pt 2), Vol 1 of this work.

[660]

SCHEDULE 5

NOTES

This Schedule specifies the regulations revoked by reg 2, namely the Goods Vehicles (Operators' Licences, Qualifications and Fees) Regulations 1984, SI 1984/176, and the amending SI 1986/666, SI 1986/1391, SI 1987/841, SI 1987/2170, SI 1988/2128, SI 1990/1849, SI 1990/2640, SI 1991/1969, SI 1991/2239, SI 1991/2319, SI 1993/301, SI 1994/1209, SI 1995/1488.

[661]

SALE OF REGISTRATION MARKS REGULATIONS 1995
SI 1995/2880

Authority Made by the Secretary of State for Transport under the Vehicle Excise and Registration Act 1994, ss 27, 57(2).

Date made 7 November 1995.

Commencement 18 December 1995.

Amendment Amended by SI 2008/2372.

Summary These regulations revoke and replace, subject to transitional provisions, the Sale of Registration Marks Regulations 1989, SI 1989/1938 and the amending SI 1993/986, SI 1994/2977. They give effect to the Sale of Registration Marks Scheme 1995, which provides for registration marks to which the Vehicle Excise and Registration Act 1994, s 27 applies to be assigned to vehicles registered in the names of, or of the nominees of, persons who have acquired rights under the scheme to have marks so assigned. The scheme also makes provision in relation to:

(a) the issue of replacement certificates of entitlement;
(b) the exercise of rights acquired under the scheme;
(c) the non-transferability of such a right;
(d) the revocation of such rights;
(e) the conditions for the assignment of a registration mark under the scheme;
(f) the payment of a charge upon an assignment; and
(g) arrangements by the Secretary of State authorising other persons for the purpose of enabling them to act on his behalf in certain circumstances.

[662]

PUBLIC SERVICE VEHICLES (OPERATORS' LICENCES) REGULATIONS 1995
SI 1995/2908

Authority Made by the Secretary of State for Transport under the Public Passenger Vehicles Act 1981, ss 14A(2), 16(1A), (3), (4), 18(1), (3), 49A(2), (3), 57(3), 59, 60, 81(1), 82(1) and the Transport Act 1985, s 27(1), (3).

Date made 11 November 1995.

Commencement 1 January 1996.

Amendment Amended by SI 2001/1149, SI 2009/786.
Summary These regulations revoke and replace, subject to savings, the Public Service Vehicles (Operators' Licences) Regulations 1986, SI 1986/1668, and the amending SI 1990/1852, SI 1993/2753, SI 1995/689. The regulations make provision concerning: the inspection of applications for public service vehicle licences by persons authorised by any chief officer of police or local authority (reg 4); the time and manner in which objections to an application for a PSV operator's licence are to be made (reg 5); the determination of applications, providing that an application for a PSV operator's licence may not be refused without the applicant being given an opportunity to state his case (reg 6); the description of conditions which may be attached to a licence so as to restrict or regulate the use of a vehicle (reg 7); the requirements of notice and the consideration of representations, providing for the traffic commissioner, before carrying out specified functions (including attaching or altering conditions on a licence or suspending or revoking a licence), to notify the licence holder of his right to make written representations (regs 8, 9); the form of and particulars to be contained on discs (reg 10); the coming into force and expiry of discs (reg 11); the manner in which discs are to be fixed and exhibited (reg 12); the issue of duplicate licences and discs and the prohibition on the unauthorised alteration of a disc, prescribing the procedure for obtaining a duplicate licence or disc and for notifying the traffic commissioner if the original is lost or destroyed (reg 13); the compulsory return of licences and discs, requiring the licence holder to return the licence and discs in specified circumstances (including suspension, surrender, attachment or alteration of conditions on a licence) (reg 14); the voluntary return of discs (reg 15); the production of licences and discs for examination by a police officer, vehicle examiner or other authorised person, when so required (reg 16); the notification by the traffic commissioner of his decisions (reg 17); the review of decisions, prescribing the time limit for the traffic commissioner to take decisions on review (reg 18); prescribing the manner in which notices from the traffic commissioner are to be delivered, the address to which they are to be sent and the circumstances whereby a notice that a decision has been reviewed will be deemed to have been delivered (reg 19); the notification by the licence holder to the traffic commissioner of a change of address (reg 20); relevant convictions for the purposes of meeting the requirements under the Public Passenger Vehicles Act 1981 of repute and competence (reg 21); operators under hiring arrangements, prescribing circumstances in which the person from whom a vehicle is hired is to be regarded as the operator (reg 22); the termination of licences held by companies (reg 23); the computation of time (reg 24); and an exemption for a universal service provider (within the meaning of the Postal Services Act 2000) for any purposes in connection with the provision of a universal postal service from the limit imposed by the Public Passenger Vehicles Act 1981, s 16(1A) on the number of vehicles to be used under a restricted licence (reg 25).

Provision concerning fees for operators' licences and discs and refunds of fees is made by SI 1995/2909.

[663]

PUBLIC SERVICE VEHICLES (OPERATORS' LICENCES) (FEES) REGULATIONS 1995
SI 1995/2909

Authority Made by the Secretary of State for Transport under the Public Passenger Vehicles Act 1981, ss 52, 60(1)(e).
Date made 11 November 1995.
Commencement 1 January 1996.
Amendment Amended by SI 2002/2535, SI 2009/787 (subject to transitional provisions). Previously amended by SI 2004/1876, SI 2005/2346, SI 2007/689, SI 2008/1473 (all superseded).
Prospective amendment Partially revoked by SI 2009/787, as from 1 April 2010 (see the note "Summary" below).
Summary These regulations introduce a new fee structure in respect of public service vehicles operators' licences and replace the provisions relating to fees in the Public Service Vehicles (Operators' Licences) Regulations 1986, SI 1986/1668, which have been revoked by SI 1995/2908. The regulations set out the fees for operators' licences and discs and when they are payable, and make provision for fees to be refunded, in specified circumstances, for discs which are unused.

The amending SI 2009/787 increases fees on 20 April 2009; it also abolishes certain fees (i e fees for the grant or continuation of operators' licences and the issue of discs) on 1 April 2010.

[664]

GOODS VEHICLES (LICENSING OF OPERATORS) (FEES) REGULATIONS 1995
SI 1995/3000

Authority Made by the Secretary of State for Transport under the Goods Vehicles (Licensing of Operators) Act 1995, ss 45(1), 57(1), 58(1).
Date made 17 November 1995.
Commencement 1 January 1996.
Amendment Amended by SI 2009/804 (subject to transitional provisions). Previously amended by SI 2002/2778, SI 2004/1878, SI 2005/2345, SI 2007/687, SI 2008/1474 (all superseded).
Prospective amendment Partially revoked by SI 2009/804, as from 1 April 2010 (see the note "Summary" below).
Summary These regulations make provision for the fees payable in respect of the licensing of goods vehicle operators. They replace provisions in the Goods Vehicles (Operators' Licences, Qualifications and Fees) Regulations 1984, SI 1984/176, reg 35 (revoked by SI 1995/2869). The regulations:

(a) set out what fees are payable and when those fees become due;
(b) enable charges to be made by the traffic commissioner in accordance with an administrative arrangement made by the licence holder;
(c) provide for unused vehicle fees covering 12 month periods to be refunded in specified circumstances (no refunds are payable in the case of: (i) vehicles specified on a licence where the decision to grant the application for its issue is made on or after 20 April 2009, or (ii) additional vehicles specified on a licence, on or after that date); and
(d) provide for a licence holder to transfer vehicle fees paid from a vehicle which is removed from the licence to one which is added to it.

The fees prescribed by the Schedule to these regulations are as follows:
(a) fee with an application for a licence, £250;
(b) fee for the issue of a licence, £391;
(c) fee for the issue of a publishable variation, £250;
(d) fee for the issue of an interim licence, £66;
(e) fee for continuation in force of a licence, £391;
(f) fee for motor vehicles specified on a licence, fee for additional motor vehicles specified on a licence which is varied, and fee for motor vehicles specified on a licence which is continued in force, £2 per month or part thereof, for each vehicle; and
(g) additional fee for motor vehicles specified on an interim licence, £6 for each vehicle.

The fees for vehicles specified on a licence (heads (f), (g) above) are abolished on 1 April 2010 by SI 2009/804.

Note that by SI 1996/2186, these regulations do not have effect in relation to any foreign goods vehicles.

[665]

RAILWAYS ACT 1993 (EXTINGUISHMENT OF RELEVANT LOANS) (RAILTRACK PLC) ORDER 1996
SI 1996/664

Authority Made by the Secretary of State for Transport, with the consent of the Treasury, under the Railways Act 1993, s 106(1). S 106 is repealed by the Transport Act 2000, s 274, Sch 31, Pt IV, as from a day to be appointed by order under s 275(1) thereof.

Date made 7 March 1996.

Commencement 29 March 1996.

Summary This order extinguishes all of Railtrack plc's liabilities in respect of the principal of the loans set out in the order. The sum of the liabilities so extinguished amounts to £1,229,418,952.48. The loans in question were made to the British Railways Board under the Transport Act 1962, s 20 and were paid out of the National Loans Fund. The Board's liability to repay these loans was transferred to, and vested in, Railtrack plc on 1 April 1994 by a transfer scheme made under the Railways Act 1993, s 85 (repealed by the Transport Act 2000, s 274, Sch 31, Pt IV, as from a day to be appointed by order under s 275(1) thereof). As to the winding down and abolition of the British Railways Board, see the Transport Act 2000 and the Preliminary Note "Privatisation of the railway system" (under the main head "Reorganisation of transport undertakings").

Target investment limit SI 1996/2551 (in force on 4 November 1996) was made under the Railways Act 1993, s 101(1). The order fixes the target investment limit for the government shareholding in Railtrack Group plc as 1.25 per cent of the voting rights which are exercisable in all circumstances at general meetings of the company. S 101 of the 1993 Act is repealed by the Transport Act 2000, s 274, Sch 31, Pt IV, as from a day to be appointed by order under s 275(1) thereof.

[666]

PRIVATE CROSSINGS (SIGNS AND BARRIERS) REGULATIONS 1996
SI 1996/1786

Authority Made by the Secretary of State for Transport under the Transport and Works Act 1992, s 52.

Date made 9 July 1996.

Commencement 1 August 1996.

Summary These regulations prescribe signs and barriers for the purposes of the Transport and Works Act 1992, s 52(1), which authorises the operator of a railway or tramway that is crossed by a private road or path to cause or permit the placement near the crossing of signs or barriers that are prescribed in regulations made by the Secretary of State or otherwise authorised by him. Signs are generally to be of a size, colour and type described and shown in diagrams in these regulations or in the Traffic Signs Regulations and General Directions 1994, SI 1994/1519 (revoked and replaced by SI 2002/3113). In connection with the signs shown in these regulations, provision is made relating to colours of the backs of signs, variations in dimensions, permitted variants, illumination of signs and miniature stop lights. In connection with the signs shown in SI 1994/1519 (revoked and replaced by 2002/3113), provision is made relating to proportions and significance of signs. Barriers are to be of the character described in these regulations. Special provision is made concerning the placement of signs relating to telephones.

[667]

DRIVING LICENCES (COMMUNITY DRIVING LICENCE) REGULATIONS 1996

SI 1996/1974

Authority Made by the Secretary of State for Transport under the European Communities Act 1972, s 2(2).
Date made 22 July 1996.
Commencement Partly on 23 July 1996; fully on 1 January 1997.
Amendment Partially revoked by SI 1998/1420 and the Powers of Criminal Courts (Sentencing) Act 2000, s 165(4), Sch 12, Pt II.
Prospective amendment Partially revoked by the Road Safety Act 2006, s 59, Sch 7(4), (14), as from a day to be appointed by order under s 61(1) thereof.
Summary These regulations (as partially revoked) amend various provisions so as to give effect to Council Directive 91/439/EEC (repealed); see now Directive 2006/126/EC of the European Parliament and of the Council on driving licences (OJ L403, 30.12.2006, p 18).

The Acts amended are as follows: the Road Traffic Act 1988, ss 88, 89, 92, 93, 94A, 97, 98, 99, 99A, 99B, 99C, 99D, 99E, 100, 101, 103, 105, 107, 108, 110, 111, 114, 115, 115A, 116, 117A, 119, 121, 141A, 164, 167, 173, 176, 183, 193A; the Road Traffic Offenders Act 1988, ss 3, 26, 36, 91A, 91B, 98, Schs 1, 2; the Transport Act 1985, ss 18, 23; the Local Government (Miscellaneous Provisions) Act 1976, ss 51, 59; the Energy Act 1976, Sch 1; the Public Passenger Vehicles Act 1981, s 24; and the Road Traffic (New Drivers) Act 1995, ss 1, 9. The regulations also amend SI 1975/1208.

Note that certain amendments made by these regulations to the Road Traffic Act 1988, ss 92, 98 have been revoked by SI 1998/1420. Certain other amendments to the Road Traffic Act 1988, the Road Traffic Offenders Act 1988 and the Public Passenger Vehicles Act 1981, s 24, are revoked by the Road Safety Act 2006, s 59, Sch 7(4), (14), as from a day to be appointed by order under s 61(1) thereof.

The amendments made by these regulations are set out in full in the relevant titles of Halsbury's Statutes, which also notes any repealed provisions.
Further regulations See SI 1990/144, SI 1998/1420.

[668]

GOODS VEHICLES (LICENSING OF OPERATORS) (TEMPORARY USE IN GREAT BRITAIN) REGULATIONS 1996

SI 1996/2186

Authority Made by the Secretary of State for Transport under the Goods Vehicles (Licensing of Operators) Act 1995, s 57(1), (2), (6), (7), (8).
Date made 22 August 1996.
Commencement 26 September 1996.
Amendment Amended by SI 2001/1149, SI 2004/462.
Summary These regulations revoke and replace the Goods Vehicles (Operators' Licences) (Temporary Use in Great Britain) Regulations 1980, SI 1980/637, and the amending SI 1981/37, SI 1981/527, SI 1982/1713, SI 1983/1832, SI 1984/179, SI 1984/1835, SI 1985/30, SI 1988/1811, SI 1989/2183, SI 1990/1191, SI 1991/2696, SI 1993/1416, SI 1993/2120, and revoke SI 1992/3077 in so far as it amended those regulations.

The regulations modify in relation to Northern Ireland goods vehicles and certain foreign goods vehicles brought temporarily into Great Britain the requirements of the Goods Vehicles (Licensing of Operators) Act 1995 as to operators' licences. They exempt operators of foreign vehicles from the requirements of s 2(1) of that Act to obtain an operator's licence when the vehicles are used in Great Britain only for the carriage of certain types of goods, i e luggage being carried to or from an airport, goods being carried to or from an airport in a case where an air service has been diverted, postal packets, damaged vehicles, animal corpses (other than those intended for human consumption) for the purpose of disposal, bees or fish stock or the body of a deceased person, and further exempt from s 2(1) the use in Great Britain of a foreign goods vehicle with a Community cabotage authorisation under Council Regulation (EEC) 3118/93 (OJ L279, 12.11.1993, p 1) and the use in Great Britain of a Northern Ireland goods vehicle for the carriage of goods between places of loading or unloading in Great Britain or between one such place in Northern Ireland and another such place in Great Britain.

The regulations also exempt from s 2(1):

(a) the operators of Northern Ireland or foreign goods vehicles used in Great Britain for the carriage of goods between member states of the European Communities:

  (1) where the vehicle is loaded or unloaded at a place not more than 25 km from the coast of Great Britain and unloaded or loaded at a place not more than 25 km from the coast of another member state and the distance between the place where the goods are loaded and the place where they are off-loaded does not exceed 100 km, where the vehicle is a motor vehicle, or trailer drawn by a foreign goods vehicle, having a permissible laden weight or a permissible pay load not exceeding specified amounts, or the vehicle is a relief vehicle;

  (2) where the goods so carried are goods for medical or surgical care in emergency relief (and in particular for relief in natural disasters), spare parts and provisions for ocean-going ships and aircraft, goods which by reason of their value are carried in vehicles constructed or adapted for the carriage of goods requiring special security precautions and which are accompanied by guards, works of art, goods carried exclusively for publicity or educational purposes, properties, equipment or animals being carried to or from theatrical, musical, cinematographic or circus performances or sporting events, exhibitions or fairs, or to or from the making of radio or television broadcasts or films, refuse or sewage;

(3) where the vehicle is being used on a journey for combined transport as defined in Art 1 of Council Directive 92/106/EEC (OJ L368, 17.12.1992, p 38) and the appropriate document is carried; or

(4) where the goods are being carried for or in connection with any trade or business carried on by the carrier and specified conditions are fulfilled; and

(b) the use in Great Britain of a Northern Ireland or foreign goods vehicle for the carriage of goods for hire or reward if it is being used by virtue of a licence issued pursuant to the scheme adopted by Resolution of the Council of Ministers of Transport on 14 June 1973 and the licence is carried.

Further exemptions from s 2(1) are granted in respect of the operators of goods vehicles of the following countries and territories when used temporarily in Great Britain: Albania, Austria, Bulgaria, the Channel Islands, Croatia, Cyprus, the Czech Republic, Estonia, the Faroe Islands, Georgia, Hungary, Jordan, Latvia, Lithuania, Macedonia, the Isle of Man, Moldova, Morocco, Northern Ireland, Poland, Romania, the Slovak Republic, Slovenia, Republics of the former Soviet Union, Switzerland, Tunisia, Turkey and the Ukraine. Different ranges of goods are specified in respect of the exemption of goods vehicles from each country or territory, and in some cases s 2(1) is applied with modifications so as to allow the use of vehicles without an operator's licence if specified permits or other documents are carried.

The regulations also make certain other modifications to the Goods Vehicles (Licensing of Operators) Act 1995 in relation to foreign goods vehicles, and modify SI 1995/2869. These modifications simplify the procedure for the grant etc of operators' licences in respect of foreign goods vehicles temporarily in Great Britain. The regulations also provide that SI 1995/2181, SI 1995/3000 do not have effect in relation to any foreign goods vehicles.

[669]

LOCAL AUTHORITIES' TRAFFIC ORDERS (PROCEDURE) (ENGLAND AND WALES) REGULATIONS 1996
SI 1996/2489

Authority Made by the Secretary of state for Transport and the Secretary of State for Wales under the Road Traffic Regulation Act 1984, ss 35C(3), (4), 46A(3), (4), 124(1), Sch 9, Pt III and the Local Government Act 1985, Sch 5, paras 6(3), 7(1).

Date made 26 September 1996.

Commencement 1 December 1996.

Amendment Amended by SI 2000/1547, SI 2004/696, SI 2004/3168 (in relation to England only), SI 2005/2929 (in relation to Wales only), SI 2009/1116 (in relation to England only).

Summary These regulations revoke and replace the Local Authorities' Traffic Orders (Procedure) (England and Wales) Regulations 1989, SI 1989/1120, and the amending SI 1993/1500, subject to savings. They prescribe the procedure to be followed by local authorities in England and Wales for making the main types of traffic and parking orders under the Road Traffic Regulation Act 1984. The regulations specify the orders to which they apply, lay down the procedure which is to be followed before making an order, deal with the making of an order and make special procedural provision for certain orders.

[670]

DRIVING LICENCES (DESIGNATION OF RELEVANT EXTERNAL LAW) ORDER 1996
SI 1996/3206

Authority Made by the Secretary of State for Transport under the Road Traffic Act 1988, ss 88(8), 89(2)(c).

Date made 18 December 1996.

Commencement 1 January 1997.

Summary This order revokes and replaces the Driving Licences (Designation of Relevant External Law) Order 1992, SI 1992/3281, and the Driving Licences (Designation of Relevant External Law) Order 1994, SI 1994/116. It designates the laws of the Isle of Man and Jersey which correspond to the Road Traffic Act 1988, Pt III as laws which make satisfactory provision for the granting of licences to drive all classes of goods vehicles and passenger-carrying vehicles.

[671]

ROAD TRAFFIC (NEW DRIVERS) ACT 1995 (COMMENCEMENT) ORDER 1997
SI 1997/267

Authority Made by the Secretary of State for Transport under the Road Traffic (New Drivers) Act 1995, s 10(2).

Date made 5 February 1997.

Summary This order brought the Road Traffic (New Drivers) Act 1995 into force as follows:

(a) on 1 March 1997, ss 5(1), (2), (8), (9), (10), 10(1), (5), Sch 1, para 11 (and s 6 in so far as it relates thereto); and

(b) on 1 June 1997, the remaining provisions.

[672]

LEVEL CROSSINGS REGULATIONS 1997
SI 1997/487

Authority Made by the Secretary of State for Transport under the Health and Safety at Work etc Act 1974, ss 15(1), (2), (3)(a), (6)(a), (b), 82(3)(a).

Date made 25 February 1997.

Commencement Partly on 1 April 1997; fully on 1 October 1997.

Summary These regulations:

(a) repeal, subject to savings, the British Transport Commission Act 1957, s 66 and the Transport Act 1968, s 124 (in so far as it applies to Scotland), and repeal the British Transport Commission Act 1954, s 40; and

(b) amend the Level Crossings Act 1983, s 1.

The regulations also provide that it is an offence for the operator of a level crossing, in relation to which an order has been made under s 1 of the 1983 Act (relating to safety arrangements at level crossings), not to comply with that order. A defence is provided for the person charged to prove that the contravention of the order was due to the act or default of another person not being one of his employees and that he took all reasonable precautions and exercised all due diligence to avoid the contravention.

[673]

RAILWAY SAFETY (MISCELLANEOUS PROVISIONS) REGULATIONS 1997
SI 1997/553

Authority Made by the Secretary of State for Transport and the Secretary of State for the Environment under the Health and Safety at Work etc Act 1974, ss 15(1), (2), (3)(a), (6)(a), (b), 18, 47(2), 82(3)(a), Sch 3, paras 1(1)(c), 18(a).

Date made 28 February 1997.

Commencement 10 May 1997; see reg 1.

Amendment Printed as amended by SI 1998/494, SI 1999/2024, SI 2006/557, SI 2006/599.

Interpretation See reg 2.

General These regulations revoke the Prevention of Accidents Rules 1902, 1907 and 1911, SR & O 1902/616, SR & O 1907/696, SR & O 1911/1058, and partially revoke a number of regulations (see the notes to the Schedule). They also repeal the Regulation of Railways Act 1871 and the Railway Employment (Prevention of Accidents) Act 1900, and partially repeal various other enactments (see the notes to the Schedule). The regulations make provision with regard to the safe operation of transport systems, defined as meaning, subject to exceptions, railways, tramways, trolley vehicles and other systems using guided transport.

[674]

Citation and commencement

1 These Regulations may be cited as the Railway Safety (Miscellaneous Provisions) Regulations 1997 and shall come into force on 10th May 1997.

[675]

Interpretation

2 (1) In these Regulations, unless the context otherwise requires—

"1992 Act" means the Transport and Works Act 1992;

"1994 Regulations" means the Railways and Other Transport Systems (Approval of Works, Plant and Equipment) Regulations 1994;

"construction work" has the meaning assigned to it by regulation 2(1) of the Construction (Design and Management) Regulations 1994;

"factory" means a factory within the meaning of section 175 of the Factories Act 1961 and premises to which section 123(1) or (2) or 125(1) of that Act applies;

["guided bus system" and "guided transport" have the meanings assigned to them by regulation 2(1) of the Railways and Other Guided Transport Systems (Safety) Regulations 2006;]

"harbour" and "harbour area" have the meanings assigned to them by regulation 2(1) of the Dangerous Substances in Harbour Areas Regulations 1987;

["mine" has the meaning assigned to it by section 180 of the Mines and Quarries Act 1954;]

. . .

["quarry" has the meaning assigned to it by regulation 3 of the Quarries Regulations 1999;]

"railway" has the meaning assigned to it by section 67(1) of the 1992 Act;

["relevant authority" means—

- (a) the Office of Rail Regulation where it is made the enforcing authority in relation to the operation of a transport system by regulation 3(1) of the Health and Safety (Enforcing Authority for Railways and Other Guided Transport Systems) Regulations 2006; and
- (b) the Health and Safety Executive in any other case;]

"station" means a passenger station or terminal of a transport system but does not include any permanent way or plant used for signalling or exclusively for supplying electricity for operational purposes to the transport system;

"street" has the meaning assigned to it by section 67(1) of the 1992 Act;

"train of vehicles" means two or more vehicles attached to each other;

["tramway" has the meaning assigned to it by regulation 2(1) of the Railways and Other Guided Transport Systems (Safety) Regulations 2006;]

["transport system" means a railway, a tramway, a trolley vehicle system or any other system using guided transport except that it does not include a guided bus system or any part of any of those systems which—]

- (a) employs parallel rails forming a track of a gauge of less than 920 millimetres and is—
  - (i) part of a factory;
  - (ii) within a maintenance or goods depot;
- (b) employs parallel rails forming a track of a gauge of less than 1.432 metres and is above ground at a mine or quarry;
- (c) is below ground at a mine;
- (d) runs along and at the same level as a street or in any other place to which the public has access (including a place to which the public has access only on making a payment);
- (e) is used solely for the purpose of carrying out construction work;

["trolley vehicle system" has the meaning assigned to it by regulation 2(1) of Railways and Other Guided Transport Systems (Safety) Regulations 2006;]

"vehicle" means a vehicle which is being used on a transport system and includes a mobile traction unit.

(2) Any reference in these Regulations to the infrastructure of a transport system is a reference to the fixed assets used for the operation of the transport system including its permanent way and plant used for signalling or exclusively supplying electricity for operational purposes to the transport system, but does not include a station.

(3) Any reference in these Regulations to a person in control of any infrastructure of a transport system is a reference to a person who, in the course of a business or other undertaking carried on by him (whether for profit or not), is in operational control of that infrastructure, except that where such control is for the time being exercised by a person undertaking maintenance, repair or alteration work on the infrastructure, it is a reference to a person who would be in operational control of the infrastructure if such work were not being undertaken.

(4) Any reference in these Regulations to a person operating a vehicle is a reference to the person operating the vehicle for the time being in the course of a business or other undertaking carried on by him (whether for profit or not), but it does not include a self-employed person by reason only that he himself drives or otherwise controls the movement of a vehicle.

(5) Any reference in these Regulations to the maintenance of any equipment is a reference to—

- (a) the maintenance of that equipment in an efficient state, in efficient working order and in good repair; and
- (b) where appropriate, subjecting that equipment to a suitable system of maintenance.

NOTES

Amendment Para (1): definition ""guided bus system" and "guided transport"" inserted by SI 2006/599;
definitions "mine" and "quarry" substituted by SI 1999/2024;
definition "prescribed system of guided transport" (omitted) revoked by SI 2006/599;

definition "relevant authority" inserted by SI 2006/557;
definition "tramway" substituted by SI 2006/599;
in definition "transport system" words in square brackets substituted by SI 2006/599;
definition "trolley vehicle system" inserted by SI 2006/599.
Construction (Design and Management) Regulations 1994 SI 1994/3140. Revoked and replaced by SI 2007/320, in the title Health and Safety at Work.
Dangerous Substances in Harbour Areas Regulations 1987 SI 1987/37, in the title Health and Safety at Work.
Health and Safety (Enforcing Authority for Railways and Other Guided Transport Systems) Regulations 2006 SI 2006/557, in the title Health and Safety at Work.
Quarries Regulations 1999 SI 1999/2024, in the title Mines, Minerals and Quarries.
Railways and Other Guided Transport Systems (Safety) Regulations 2006 SI 2006/599.
Railways and Other Transport Systems (Approval of Works, Plant and Equipment) Regulations 1994 SI 1994/157; revoked and replaced by SI 2006/599.

[676]

Unauthorised access

3 (1) So far as is reasonably practicable, a person in control of any infrastructure of a transport system to which this regulation applies shall ensure, where and to the extent necessary for safety, that unauthorised access to that infrastructure is prevented.

(2) In paragraph (1) "access" means access by any person not at work on the transport system or by any animal.

(3) This regulation applies to any transport system except that it does not apply to any part of such a system which—

(a) is within a harbour, harbour area, maintenance or goods depot; or
(b) is part of a factory, mine or quarry,

where access to the harbour, harbour area, maintenance or goods depot, factory, mine or quarry is adequately controlled.

(4) Breach of a duty imposed by this regulation shall not confer a right of action in any civil proceedings.

[677]

Means of communication

4 The operator of a vehicle which is being used for the carriage of fare paying passengers shall ensure that there is provided and maintained on such a vehicle suitable and sufficient means whereby passengers can communicate with a person who is in a position to take appropriate action in the event of an emergency.

[678]

Measures to prevent collisions and derailments

5 (1) A person in control of any infrastructure of a transport system shall ensure, so far as is reasonably practicable, that—

(a) appropriate procedures are in place;
(b) where appropriate, equipment which is suitable and sufficient is provided and maintained,

for the purpose of preventing any of the events referred to in paragraph (2).

(2) The events referred to in paragraph (1) are—

(a) collisions between vehicles;
(b) collisions between vehicles and buffer-stops;
(c) the derailment of vehicles on account of excessive speed or incorrectly set points.

[679]

Brakes

6 The operator of a vehicle shall ensure that a suitable and sufficient braking system is provided and maintained for that vehicle and, where the vehicle is part of a train of vehicles, for that train of vehicles.

[680]

Accidents to persons at work from moving vehicles

7 (1) A person to whom this regulation applies shall ensure, so far as is reasonably practicable and insofar as they are matters within his control, that—

(a) appropriate procedures are in place;
(b) where appropriate, equipment which is suitable and sufficient is provided and maintained,

for the purpose of preventing any person at work on a transport system from being struck by, or falling from, a moving vehicle.

(2) This regulation applies to—

(a) a person in control of any infrastructure of a transport system;
(b) an operator of a vehicle;
(c) an employer of a person at work on a transport system;
(d) a self-employed person as it applies to an employer and a person at work on a transport system as if that self-employed person were both the employer and the person at work.

[681]

Exemptions

8 (1) Subject to paragraph (2) and to any Community obligation of the United Kingdom the [relevant authority] may, by a certificate in writing, exempt any person or class of persons from any requirement imposed by these Regulations and any such exemption may be granted subject to conditions and to a limit of time and may be revoked by a further certificate in writing at any time.

(2) The [relevant authority] shall not grant any such exemption unless, having regard to the circumstances of the case, and in particular to—

(a) the conditions, if any, which it proposes to attach to the exemption; and
(b) any other requirements imposed by or under any enactment which apply to the case,

it is satisfied that the health and safety of persons who are likely to be affected by the exemption will not be prejudiced in consequence of it.

(3) Subject to any Community obligation of the United Kingdom, the Secretary of State for Defence may, in the interests of national security, by a certificate in writing exempt any person or class of persons from the requirements of these Regulations and any such exemption may be granted subject to conditions and to a limit of time and may be revoked by the said Secretary of State by a further certificate in writing at any time.

NOTES

Amendment Paras (1), (2): words in square brackets substituted by SI 2006/557.

[682]

Defence

9 (1) In any proceedings for an offence for a contravention of any of the provisions of these Regulations it shall be a defence for the person charged to prove—

(a) that the contravention was due to the act or default of another person not being one of his employees (hereinafter called "the other person"); and
(b) that he took all reasonable precautions and exercised all due diligence to avoid the contravention.

(2) The person charged shall not, without leave of the court, be entitled to rely on the defence referred to in paragraph (1) above unless, within a period ending seven clear days—

(a) before the hearing to determine mode of trial, where the proceedings are in England or Wales; or
(b) before the trial, where the proceedings are in Scotland,

he has served on the prosecutor a notice in writing giving such information identifying or assisting in the identification of the other person as was then in his possession.

(3) Where a contravention of any of the provisions of these Regulations by any person is due to the act or default of some other person, that other person shall be

guilty of the offence which would, but for any defence under this regulation available to the first-mentioned person, be constituted by the act or default.

[683]

Transfer of functions from the Secretary of State to the Health and Safety Executive

10 (1) …

(2) Any approval, dispensation, notice or written consent granted or given under the 1994 Regulations or direction given under section 45 of the 1992 Act, by the Secretary of State, prior to the coming into force of these Regulations, shall have effect as if it had been granted or given, as the case may be, by the Health and Safety Executive.

NOTES

Amendment Para (1): revoked by SI 2006/557.

[684]

11 (*Revoked by SI 1998/494.*)

Repeals and revocations

12 (1) The enactments specified in column 1 of Part I of the Schedule shall be repealed to the extent specified in the corresponding entries in column 2.

(2) The instruments specified in column 1 of Part II of the Schedule shall be revoked to the extent specified in the corresponding entries in column 2.

[685]

SCHEDULE

NOTES

This Schedule specifies the enactments repealed and the instruments revoked in whole or in part by reg 12. Pt I of the Schedule provides for the repeal of: the Highway (Railway Crossings) Act 1839, ss 1 (in part), 2; the Railway Regulation Act 1842, s 10; the Regulation of Railways Act 1868, s 22; the Regulation of Railways Act 1871; the Regulation of Railways Act 1889, ss 1, 4; the Railway Employment (Prevention of Accidents) Act 1900; the Transport Act 1968, s 125; and the Transport and Works Act 1992, s 42.

Pt II of the Schedule provides for the revocation of: the Prevention of Accidents Rules 1902, SR & O 1902/616; the Locomotives and Wagons (Used in Lines and Sidings) Regulations 1906, SR & O 1906/679, regs 1, 2, 5–7, 9–19; the Prevention of Accidents Rules 1907, SR & O 1907/696; the Prevention of Accidents Rules 1911, SR & O 1911/1058; the Coal and Other Mines (Sidings) Regulations 1956, SI 1956/1773, regs 2(2)–5, 7–20; and the Quarries (General) Regulations 1956, SI 1956/1780, regs 24–26, 27(2)–(5), 28–35.

[686]

NEW DRIVERS (APPEALS PROCEDURE) REGULATIONS 1997
SI 1997/1098

Authority Made by the Secretary of State for Transport under the Road Traffic (New Drivers) Act 1995, s 5, Sch 1, Pt V, para 11.

Date made 26 March 1997.

Commencement 1 June 1997.

Summary These regulations provide for the procedure to be followed when a person whose licence or test certificate has been revoked by the Secretary of State under the Road Traffic (New Drivers) Act 1995 appeals against his conviction or the terms of the licence endorsement order made by the court. The regulations specify the nature and duration of a licence granted by the Secretary of State pending determination of the appeal and prescribe which court must give to the Secretary of State notice of the appeal and of any subsequent abandonment thereof.

[687]

VEHICLE EXCISE DUTY (IMMOBILISATION, REMOVAL AND DISPOSAL OF VEHICLES) REGULATIONS 1997
SI 1997/2439

Authority Made by the Secretary of State for the Environment, Transport and the Regions under the Vehicle Excise and Registration Act 1994, s 57(1), (2), (3), Sch 2A.

Date made 9 October 1997.

Commencement 3 November 1997.

Amendment Amended by SI 1997/3063, SI 1998/1217, SI 2001/936, SI 2001/1149, SI 2002/745, SI 2008/2266. Previously amended by SI 1999/35 (superseded).

Summary The Vehicle Excise and Registration Act 1994, s 29(1) makes it an offence to use or keep on a public road a vehicle (other than an exempt vehicle) which is unlicensed. These regulations, which revoke the Vehicle Excise Duty (Immobilisation, Removal and Disposal of Vehicles) Regulations 1996, SI 1996/107, and the amending SI 1997/565, provide for the immobilisation and removal of unlicensed mechanically propelled vehicles which are stationary in a relevant place. "Relevant place" is defined by the regulations as a place to which Sch 2A to the 1994 Act applies. By para 1(1A) of Sch 2A, that Schedule does *not* apply to: (a) any place which is within the curtilage of, or in the vicinity of, a dwelling-house, mobile home or houseboat and which is normally enjoyed with it, or (b) a place which is within the curtilage of, or in the vicinity of, a building consisting entirely (apart from common parts) of two or more dwellings and which is normally enjoyed only by the occupiers of one or more of those dwellings.

Reg 3 specifies the authorised persons for the purposes of the regulations. Reg 4 sets out the circumstances in which the regulations do not apply. Reg 5 enables an authorised person to fix an immobilisation device to an unlicensed vehicle in a relevant place, and reg 6 sets out the conditions to be fulfilled (including the payment of prescribed charges) for the release of a vehicle from a device. Offences in connection with immobilisation are created by regs 7, 8. Detailed provision is made by regs 9–14 relating to, inter alia, the removal and disposal of vehicles, the retention of a removed vehicle until prescribed charges are paid and the conditions under which a removed vehicle can be recovered. Reg 15 provides for the issue of a voucher on the making of a surety payment where a vehicle is released after immobilisation or removal but a licence for the vehicle is not produced, and for obtaining a refund of the surety payment when the vehicle is licensed. Reg 16 creates offences relating to vouchers. Provision for the resolution of disputes under the regulations is made by reg 17.

[688]

TEMPORARY TRAFFIC SIGNS (PRESCRIBED BODIES) (ENGLAND AND WALES) REGULATIONS 1998
SI 1998/111

Authority Made by the Secretary of State for the Environment, Transport and the Regions and the Secretary of State for Wales under the Road Traffic Regulation Act 1984, s 65(3A).

Date made 22 January 1998.

Commencement 1 March 1998.

Summary The Road Traffic Regulation Act 1984, s 65(3A) prohibits a local highway authority from making a charge for permission to erect a temporary traffic sign if the sign is placed by a body prescribed as being a body appearing to the Secretary of State to be representative of the interests of road users or any class of road users. These regulations prescribe the following bodies for the purposes of s 65(3A): the Automobile Association, the Cyclists' Touring Club and the Royal Automobile Club.

Transfer of functions The relevant functions of the Secretary of State under the Road Traffic Regulation Act 1984, s 65, so far as exercisable in relation to Wales, are transferred to the National Assembly for Wales by SI 1999/672, in the title Constitutional Law (Pt 3). As to the transfer of the functions of the Assembly to the Welsh Ministers, see the Government of Wales Act 2006, s 162(1), Sch 11, paras 30, 32.

[689]

LOCAL AUTHORITIES (TRANSPORT CHARGES) REGULATIONS 1998
SI 1998/948

Authority Made by the Secretary of State for the Environment, Transport and the Regions and the Secretary of State for Wales under the Local Government and Housing Act 1989, ss 150, 152(5).

Date made 31 March 1998.

Commencement 28 April 1998.

Amendment Amended by SI 2003/1615.

Summary These regulations authorise local authorities to impose charges on persons dealing with the local authority in connection with specified matters relating to highways, road traffic regulation and travel concessions. Under the regulations, "travel concession":

(a) in relation to a London borough council or the Common Council of the City of London, has the meaning given by the Greater London Authority Act 1999, s 240(8); and in relation to any other authority has the meaning given by the Transport Act 1985, s 112(1)(f); and

(b) "travel concession permit" has the same meaning as in Chapter VII of Pt IV of the 1999 Act (see s 243(5) thereof).

The amount of any charge is to be at the discretion of the local authority imposing it, but the authority must have regard to the cost of dealing with matters of the description in question. A charge for the issue of a travel concession permit or a replacement permit is only to be imposed by a London borough council or the Common Council of the City of London if all the borough councils and the Common Council have agreed to the imposition of the charge and its amount.

[690]

DRIVING LICENCES (COMMUNITY DRIVING LICENCE) REGULATIONS 1998
SI 1998/1420

Authority Made by the Secretary of State for the Environment, Transport and the Regions under the European Communities Act 1972, s 2(2).
Date made 6 June 1998.
Commencement 1 July 1998.
Summary These regulations amend various provisions so as to give effect to amendments to Council Directive 91/439/EEC (repealed); see now Directive 2006/126/EC of the European Parliament and of the Council on driving licences (OJ L403, 30.12.2006, p 18). The Acts amended are as follows: the Road Traffic Act 1988, ss 88, 92, 93, 97, 98, 99, 99A, 105, 108, 117A, 118, 164, 183; the Road Traffic Offenders Act 1988, Schs 1, 2; and the Road Traffic (Driver Licensing and Information Systems) Act 1989, s 5, Sch 3. The regulations also partially revoke SI 1990/144, SI 1996/1974. The amendments made by these regulations are set out in full in Halsbury's Statutes, 4th edn Vols 37, 38(1), title Roads, Railways and Transport, which also notes any repealed provisions.
Further regulations See SI 1990/144, SI 1996/1974.

[691]

MOTOR CYCLES (PROTECTIVE HELMETS) REGULATIONS 1998
SI 1998/1807

Authority Made by the Secretary of State for the Environment, Transport and the Regions under the Road Traffic Act 1988, ss 16, 17.
Date made 22 July 1998.
Commencement 21 August 1998.
Amendment Amended by SI 2000/1488, SI 2008/1207.
Summary These regulations revoke and replace the Motor Cycles (Protective Helmets) Regulations 1980, SI 1980/1279, and the amending SI 1981/374, SI 1986/472. They require every person driving or riding (otherwise than in a side-car) on a motor cycle on a road to wear protective headgear, as defined. This requirement does not extend to a mowing machine or a vehicle being propelled by a person on foot. In addition, by virtue of the Road Traffic Act 1988, s 16(2), it does not extend to a follower of the Sikh religion while he is wearing a turban.

The regulations prescribe certain types of helmet recommended as affording protection to persons on or in motor cycles from injury in the event of an accident. The prescribed types are those conforming with:

(a) British Standard 6658:1985, as amended;
(b) any other standard accepted by a European Economic Area state which offers in use equivalent levels of safety, suitability and fitness for purpose; or
(c) ECE Regulation 22.05 (as defined), including the approval, marking and conformity of production requirements of that Regulation.

In the case of heads (a), (b), helmets must be marked with an approved certification mark of an approved body (whether or not they are required to be so marked by the relevant standard).

Nothing in these regulations authorises any person to apply any number or mark in contravention of the Consumer Protection Act 1987.

As to eye protectors authorised for use by persons on a motor cycle, see SI 1999/535.

[692]

RAIL VEHICLE ACCESSIBILITY REGULATIONS 1998
SI 1998/2456

Authority Made by the Secretary of State for the Environment, Transport and the Regions under the Disability Discrimination Act 1995, s 46(1), (2), (5).
Date made 5 October 1998.
Commencement 1 November 1998.
Amendment Amended by SI 2000/3215, SI 2008/1746.
Summary These regulations apply to rail vehicles used on railways, tramways, monorail systems, magnetic levitation systems or systems which are track-based with side guidance ("regulated rail vehicles") which are first brought into use, or belong to a class of vehicle first brought into use, after 31 December 1998 (see the Disability Discrimination Act 1995, s 46(6); note that the definition "rail vehicle" in that subsection is substituted by the Disability Discrimination Act 2005, s 6(2), as from a day to be appointed by order under s 20(3) thereof). The regulations do not apply to rail vehicles used in the provision of a service for the carriage of passengers on the high-speed rail system or the conventional TEN rail system (as defined by reg 2(3) of SI 2006/397).

Regs 4–14 concern facilities for disabled persons. Requirements are specified in relation to doors; door controls; steps; floors; seats; tramcar request stop controls; interior transparent surfaces; handrails and handholds; door handles; passenger information; and toilets.

Regs 15–24 concern facilities for disabled persons in wheelchairs. Requirements are specified in relation to wheelchair spaces; wheelchair space specifications; sleeping accommodation; tables; wheelchair compatible doorways; toilets for disabled persons in wheelchairs; telephones; internal doorways; boarding devices; and catering services.

As to regulations providing for the accessibility of public service vehicles, see SI 2000/1970.

(Note that s 46(4A) of the 1995 Act, as inserted by the Disability Discrimination Act 2005, s 6(1) as from a day to be appointed by order under s 20(3) thereof, provides that the Secretary of State must exercise the power to make rail vehicle accessibility regulations so as to secure that on and after 1 January 2020 every rail vehicle is a regulated rail vehicle, but not so as to affect the powers conferred by s 46(5), 47(1) or 67(2) of the 1995 Act.)

Exemption from rail vehicle accessibility regulations Under the Disability Discrimination Act 1995, s 47(1), (1A), as substituted for sub-s (1) by the Disability Discrimination Act 2005, s 6(3), the Secretary of State may by order (an "exemption order") authorise the use for carriage of a regulated rail vehicle even though the vehicle does not conform with the provisions of rail vehicle accessibility regulations with which it is required to conform, or authorise a regulated rail vehicle to be used for carriage otherwise than in conformity with the provisions of rail vehicle accessibility regulations with which use of the vehicle is required to conform (see SI 1998/2456 above). The following current exemption orders have been made under s 47 as originally enacted or as amended as noted above relating to the vehicles specified in brackets (note that in certain cases the authorisation conferred by the exemption order expires on a specified date):

SI 1999/2932 (Serco Metrolink T68A);
SI 2000/524 (North Western Trains Class 175/0 and Class 175/1);
SI 2000/1349 (Chiltern Railway Co Ltd Class 168/1);
SI 2000/1441 (Central Trains Class 170/5 and Class 170/6);
SI 2000/1770 (Anglia Railways Class 170/2);
SI 2000/2050, as amended by SI 2001/250 (Connex South Eastern Class 375);
SI 2000/2397, as amended by SI 2000/3218 (Chiltern Railway Co Ltd Class 168/1);
SI 2000/2953, as amended by SI 2000/3217 (South West Trains Class 170/3);
SI 2001/277 (ScotRail Class 334);
SI 2001/499 (Midland Mainline Class 170/1);
SI 2001/785 (revokes SI 1999/520, SI 1999/586, SI 1999/1256) (Midland Metro T69);
SI 2001/847, as amended by SI 2001/3954, SI 2004/2150 (revokes SI 2000/770, SI 2000/2327, SI 2000/3187) (Gatwick Express Class 460);
SI 2001/1747 (Great Western Trains Company Class 180);
SI 2001/3434 (North Western Trains Class 175/0 and Class 175/1);
SI 2001/3952, as amended by SI 2002/3001 (superseded), SI 2005/395 (revokes SI 2000/6) (Croydon Tramlink Class CR4000);
SI 2001/3953 (revokes SI 2000/1769) (ScotRail Class 170/4);
SI 2001/3955, as amended by SI 2002/3002 (revokes SI 2000/182) (C2C Class 357/0);
SI 2002/656, as amended by SI 2002/1762, SI 2004/2149 (revokes SI 2001/848) (South West Trains Class 458);
SI 2002/1617 (South Central Class 375/3);
SI 2002/1694 (Isle of Wight Railway LCDR No 2515);
SI 2002/2873 (Summerlee Tramcar No 392);
SI 2003/1436 (Furness Railway Trust North London Coach);
SI 2003/1562 (Great Eastern Railway Class 360);
SI 2003/1687 (Festiniog Railway Company Vehicle Number 122);
SI 2003/1704, as amended by SI 2004/3139 (South West Trains Class 444 and Class 450);
SI 2003/2408 (Bristol Harbour Railway Vehicle Number DB978121);
SI 2004/954 (Midland Mainline Class 222);
SI 2004/955 (CrossCountry Trains Class 220 and Class 221);
SI 2004/1205 (Seaton Tramway Tramcars 9, 10 and 11);
SI 2004/1302 (South Eastern Trains Class 376);
SI 2004/1410 (Hull Trains Class 170/3);
SI 2004/2180 (Hull Trains Class 222);
SI 2004/3198 (South Central Class 377/4);
SI 2005/86, as amended by SI 2005/1404 (Heathrow Express Class 360/2);
SI 2005/329 (revokes SI 2002/1699) (Virgin West Coast Class 390);
SI 2006/933 (Gatwick Express Class 458);
SI 2008/925 (B2007 Vehicles);
SI 2008/2969 (London Underground Victoria Line 09TS Vehicles).

As to parliamentary procedures in connection with the making of rail vehicle accessibility exemption orders, see SI 2008/2975.

Applications for exemption SI 1998/2457 (in force on 1 November 1998) was made under the Disability Discrimination Act 1995, s 47. The regulations specify the manner in which applications are to be made to the Secretary of State for exemption under s 47 from any requirement of SI 1998/2456 with which a rail vehicle is required to conform. They also specify the information which must be supplied with any such application and provide for the period and revocation of exemptions.

[693]

MOTOR VEHICLES (TYPE APPROVAL OF REDUCED POLLUTION ADAPTATIONS) REGULATIONS 1998
SI 1998/3093

Authority Made by the Secretary of State for the Environment, Transport and the Regions under the Road Traffic Act 1988, ss 54(1), 61.
Date made 9 December 1998.
Commencement 1 January 1999.

Amendment Amended by SI 2000/3275.
Summary These regulations prescribe type approval and marking requirements for reduced pollution devices (ie a device fitted to the engine of a motor vehicle so as to adapt it to meet the reduced pollution requirements prescribed by SI 2002/2742 (which revoked and replaced the Vehicle Excise Duty (Reduced Pollution) Regulations 1998, SI 1998/3094)). A vehicle must be adapted so that, when tested in accordance with the regulations, the rate and content of its particulate emissions do not exceed a specified number of grams per kilowatt-hour, according to the instrument setting the standard to which the vehicle was first used. A reduced pollution device must be uniquely marked so as to identify its type. The regulations also apply specified provisions of SI 1982/1271 to the type approval of reduced pollution devices, subject to modification.

[694]

ROAD VEHICLES (AUTHORISED WEIGHT) REGULATIONS 1998
SI 1998/3111

Authority Made by the Secretary of State for the Environment, Transport and the Regions under the Road Traffic Act 1988, s 41.
Date made 11 December 1998.
Commencement 1 January 1999.
Amendment Amended by SI 2000/3224 (itself amended by SI 2001/1125), SI 2001/1125.
Summary These regulations provide for the weights of wheeled motor vehicles and trailers which fall within category M_2, M_3, N_2, N_3, O_3 or O_4 of the vehicle categories defined in Annex II of Council Directive 70/156/EEC (OJ L42, 23.02.1970, p 1), as substituted by Council Directive 92/53/EC (OJ L225, 10.08.1992, p 1), except vehicle combinations fulfilling the requirements of SI 1986/1078, Sch 11A, Pt II, III or IIIA. Council Directive 70/156/EEC has been repealed and replaced as from 29 April 2009 by Directive 2007/46/EC of the European Parliament and of the Council establishing a framework for the approval of motor vehicles and their trailers, and of systems, components and separate technical units intended for such vehicles (OJ L263, 09.10.2007, p 1).

The regulations lay down maximum authorised weights for individual vehicles (Sch 1), for vehicle combinations (Sch 2) and for axle weights (Sch 3), and prohibit the use of a vehicle on a road if any of these weights are exceeded. A vehicle which complies with regs 75–79 of SI 1986/1078 is taken to comply with these regulations except, in the case of a vehicle fitted with one or more retractable or loadable axles, for the provisions of Sch 3, paras 3, 4 (the exception applies as from 1 January 2002). The new weight limits are subject to the overriding limit in reg 80 of SI 1986/1078. However, as from 1 January 2002, reg 80 is not contravened when a vehicle to which Sch 3, para 3 of these regulations applies is operated in accordance with para 3(3) thereof.

[695]

MOTOR CYCLES (EYE PROTECTORS) REGULATIONS 1999
SI 1999/535

Authority Made by the Secretary of State for the Environment, Transport and the Regions under the Road Traffic Act 1988, s 18.
Date made 3 March 1999.
Commencement 1 April 1999.
Amendment Amended by SI 2000/1489.
Summary These regulations, which revoke and replace the Motor Cycles (Eye Protectors) Regulations 1985, SI 1985/1593, and the amending SI 1987/675, SI 1988/1031, prescribe certain types of eye protectors as authorised for use by persons driving or riding (otherwise than in a side-car) on a motor bicycle. The eye protectors are so prescribed by reference to:

(a) conformity with certain grades within specified British Standards (and must be marked with an approved certification mark of an approved body);
(b) conformity with any other standard accepted by a European Economic Area state which offers in use equivalent levels of safety, suitability and fitness for purpose (and must be marked with an approved certification mark of an approved body);
(c) conformity with ECE Regulation 22.05 (as defined), including the approval, marking and conformity of production requirements of that Regulation;
(d) compliance with Council Directive 89/686/EEC relating to personal protective equipment (OJ L399, 30.12.1989, p 18); or
(e) in the case of eye protectors first used before 1 April 1989, compliance with certain other requirements.

The types of eye protector prescribed by heads (a)–(e) are not prescribed for use by persons driving or riding on a motor bicycle if the vehicle is a mowing machine, is propelled by a person on foot, or is brought temporarily into Great Britain, or if that person is in the armed forces of the Crown and is wearing an eye protector supplied to him as part of his service equipment.

As to protective helmets to be worn by persons on a motor cycle, see SI 1998/1807.

[696]

DEREGULATION (PIPE-LINES) ORDER 1999
SI 1999/742

Authority Made by the Secretary of State for Trade and Industry under the Deregulation and Contracting Out Act 1994, s 1 (repealed by the Regulatory Reform Act 2001, s 12(1)–(3), with a

saving in s 12(4) of the 2001 Act for existing orders made under s 1 of the 1994 Act. S 12 of the 2001 Act has been repealed by the Legislative and Regulatory Reform Act 2006, s 30(1), Schedule, with a saving in s 30(5) thereof for existing orders made under s 1 of the 1994 Act continued in force by virtue of s 12(4) of the 2001 Act.
Date made 6 March 1999.
Commencement 3 April 1999.
Summary This order makes the following amendments to provisions of the Pipe-lines Act 1962:
(a) ss 2, 3, 7, 8, Sch 1, Pt II are repealed;
(b) ss 1, 4, 5, 6, 9, 10, 12, 16, 35, 36, 43, 46, 47, 58, 59, 64, 66, Sch 1, Pt I are amended; and
(c) ss 9A, 10A are inserted.

See further the Preliminary Note "Pipe-lines" and "Control of construction".

[697]

ROAD TRAFFIC (NHS CHARGES) (REVIEWS AND APPEALS) REGULATIONS 1999
SI 1999/786

Authority Made by the Secretary of State for Health under the Road Traffic (NHS Charges) Act 1999, ss 6(1), 7(4), 9, 16(2). The whole of the 1999 Act has been repealed by the Health and Social Care (Community Health and Standards) Act 2003, ss 169(1), 196, Sch 14, Pt 3, as from 29 January 2007 (see SI 2006/3397, in the title National Health Service). However, by saving provisions in SI 2006/3397, the 1999 Act continues to have effect in relation to injuries to which it applied which occurred before 29 January 2007. These regulations are retained in this title in the light of that saving.
Date made 15 March 1999.
Commencement 5 April 1999.
Amendment Amended and partially revoked by SI 2008/2683 (and amended by SI 2006/3398, in the title National Health Service, which is spent in so far as it amended these regulations). Also wholly revoked in relation to Scotland by SI 1999/1843 (S 111) (outside the scope of this work).
Summary These regulations, as originally enacted, made provision for the purposes of the Road Traffic (NHS Charges) Act 1999, which provided for the recovery from insurers and certain other persons of charges in connection with the treatment of road traffic casualties by the national health service. The regulations provided for:
(a) the circumstances in which a certificate of NHS charges could be reviewed;
(b) the procedure for appeals against a certificate before a tribunal specified in s 8(6) of the 1999 Act (i e an appeal tribunal constituted under the Social Security Act 1998, Pt I, Chapter I (largely repealed by SI 2008/2833, in the title Courts and Legal Services)); and
(c) appeals to the High Court on a point of law.

The 1999 Act has been repealed as from 29 January 2007, subject to savings, by the Health and Social Care (Community Health and Standards) Act 2003, ss 169(1), 196, Sch 14, Pt 3, and these regulations accordingly lapsed, but are retained in the light of the savings in SI 2006/3397 (see the note "Authority" above). With the exception of regs 1–3, the regulations have been revoked by SI 2008/2683, in the title Courts and Legal Services, as a consequence of the transfer of relevant tribunal functions to the First-tier Tribunal, established under the Tribunals, Courts and Enforcement Act 2007, s 3.

In so far as the regulations remain in force, reg 1 (as amended by SI 2008/2683) provides for commencement and interpretation. Reg 2 (review of certificates) provides that a certificate of NHS charges, issued under s 2 of the 1999 Act (repealed), may be reviewed under s 6 of that Act where the Secretary of State is satisfied that:
(a) a mistake (whether in computation of the amount specified or otherwise) occurred in the preparation of the certificate;
(b) the amount specified in the certificate is in excess of the amount due to the Secretary of State;
(c) incorrect or insufficient information was supplied to the Secretary of State by the person who applied for the certificate and in consequence the amount specified in the certificate was less than it would have been had the information supplied been correct or sufficient; or
(d) it appears to the Secretary of State that, under s 7 of the 1999 Act (repealed), a ground for appeal to the First-tier Tribunal is satisfied.

Reg 3 (as amended by SI 2008/2683) (manner of making appeals and time limits) provides that an appeal to the First-tier Tribunal against a certificate made in accordance with Tribunal Procedure Rules must be made on a form approved by the Secretary of State and sent to the Compensation Recovery Unit of the Department for Work and Pensions (formerly the Department of Social Security) (reg 3(1)). Where an appeal is not made on the approved form, but is made in writing and contains all the particulars required by Tribunal Procedure Rules, the Secretary of State may treat that appeal as duly made (reg 3(10)). Where it appears to the Secretary of State that an appeal or application does not contain the particulars required by those rules, he may direct the person making the appeal or application to provide such particulars or such document (reg 3(11)). In such a case, the Secretary of State may extend the time specified by Tribunal Procedure Rules for making the application by a period of not more than 14 days (reg 3(12)). Where further particulars of a document are required under reg 3(11), they must be sent or delivered to the Compensation Recovery Unit within such period as the Secretary of State may direct (reg 3(13)). The date of an appeal is the date on which all the required particulars are received by the Compensation Recovery Unit (reg 3(14)). By reg 3(17), the Secretary of State may treat any appeal as an application for review under s 6 of the 1999 Act.

[698]

PUBLIC SERVICE VEHICLES (COMMUNITY LICENCES) REGULATIONS 1999
SI 1999/1322

Authority Made by the Secretary of State for the Environment, Transport and the Regions under the European Communities Act 1972, s 2(2).
Date made 10 May 1999.
Commencement Partly on 1 June 1999; fully on 11 June 1999.
Amendment Amended by SI 2009/1885.
Summary These regulations give effect in Great Britain to Art 3a of Council Regulation (EEC) 684/92 on common rules for the international carriage of passengers by coach and bus (OJ L74, 20.03.1992, p 1) ("the Council Regulation"), as amended by Council Regulation (EC) 11/98 (OJ L4, 08.01.1998, p 1). The Council Regulation prohibits the carriage of passengers in public service vehicles between member states without a Community licence.

These regulations provide that a person who uses a vehicle in Great Britain in contravention of this prohibition is guilty of an offence and designates the competent authority for the purposes of the Council Regulation. A person is entitled to be issued with a Community licence by the competent authority if he holds a standard licence which authorises use on both national and international operations, or a restricted licence (as to definitions, see the Public Passenger Vehicles Act 1981, s 82(1)). A person aggrieved by the refusal of the competent authority to issue a Community licence or by the decision of the competent authority to withdraw it, may appeal to the Upper Tribunal (formerly to the Transport Tribunal). Further provisions are made relating to: a failure to comply with any condition governing the use of a Community licence; authorised inspecting officers for the purposes of the Council Regulation; the return to the competent authority of a Community licence if it is withdrawn; the supply of information by the holder of a Community licence; the death, bankruptcy etc of the holder of a Community licence; and bodies corporate. The regulations also amend the Road Traffic (Foreign Vehicles) Act 1972, s 1(1)(a), Schs 1, 2.
Offences Certain offences under these regulations are: (a) fixed penalty offences; see SI 2009/483, noted to SI 1990/335; (b) offences in respect of which a financial penalty deposit requirement may be imposed; see SI 2009/491 (and see also SI 2009/492).

[699]

ROAD TRAFFIC REGULATION ACT 1984 (AMENDMENT) ORDER 1999
SI 1999/1608

Authority Made by the Secretary of State for the Environment, Transport and the Regions and the Secretary of State for Wales and for Scotland under the Road Traffic Regulation Act 1984, s 124, Sch 9, Pt II, para 15.
Date made 6 June 1999.
Commencement 16 June 1999.
Summary This order removes from the orders for which the consent of the Secretary of State would otherwise be required by the Road Traffic Regulation Act 1984, Sch 9, Pt II, para 13 or 14 any order made by a local authority under s 84(1) of that Act which contains a provision applying to any road a speed limit of 20 miles per hour.

[700]

MOTOR VEHICLES (TYPE APPROVAL AND APPROVAL MARKS) (FEES) REGULATIONS 1999
SI 1999/2149

Authority Made by the Secretary of State for the Environment, Transport and the Regions under the Road Traffic Act 1988, s 61(1), (2), the Finance Act 1973, s 56(1), (2) (with the consent of the Treasury), SI 1988/643 and the Finance Act 1990, s 128.
Date made 26 July 1999.
Commencement 1 September 1999.
Amendment Amended by SI 2006/1638, SI 2009/719, and in relation to the transfer of ministerial functions by virtue of SI 1997/2971, SI 2001/2568, SI 2002/2626, all in the title Constitutional Law (Pt 2). Previously amended by SI 2003/2258, SI 2004/2106 (both spent).
Summary These regulations revoke and replace the Motor Vehicles (Type Approval and Approval Marks) (Fees) Regulations 1997, SI 1997/564. They prescribe the fees payable for:

(a) the examination of vehicles and vehicle parts (reg 4);
(b) the examination of complete vehicles under the national type approval scheme (see SI 1982/1271, SI 1984/981) (reg 5);
(c) the examination of vehicles under the national small series type approval scheme (see SI 2009/717) (reg 5A);
(d) the examination of vehicles with a view to the issue of an EC vehicle type approval certificate (issued under reg 13 of SI 2009/717) (reg 6).

The fee for the inspection of data by an officer of the Department for Transport with a view to the issue of certain certificates in circumstances where an examination is unnecessary is determined by the amount of work involved charged at an hourly rate (reg 7).

Provision is made by reg 8 to avoid duplication of examination fees. Fees are prescribed for the issue of documents (reg 9), with additional fees payable for the issue of documents under the national scheme (reg 10), and for visits outside the United Kingdom by certain persons in connection with the examination of vehicles or vehicle parts (reg 11). In addition, a fee is prescribed by reg 9(5) for the issue of a sound level measurement certificate for the purposes of SI 1980/765.

Provision is made as to the time of payment of fees (reg 12), for fees payable on withdrawals and cancellations (reg 13) or when an alternative vehicle or vehicle part is submitted for examination (reg 14) and for fees to be paid in relation to notifiable alterations to a vehicle (reg 15). The regulations also prescribe the fees payable for:

(a) the examination of premises with a view to their being approved for the purposes of carrying out examinations in accordance with a type approval scheme, a Community instrument or an ECE Regulation (reg 16); and

(b) advising a manufacturer whether his arrangements for securing conformity of production are likely to be accepted by the Secretary of State (reg 17).

In addition, different fees are prescribed for work carried out in the United States of America, Canada or Mexico or in Japan, China, South Korea, Malaysia or Taiwan (regs 19, 20).

[701]

RAILWAY SAFETY REGULATIONS 1999
SI 1999/2244

Authority Made by the Secretary of State for the Environment, Transport and the Regions under the Health and Safety at Work etc Act 1974, ss 15(1), (2), (4)(a), (5)(b), (6)(b), 82(3)(a), Sch 3, para 1(1)(a), (c).

Date made 30 July 1999.

Commencement Partly on 30 January 2000, 1 April 2000 and 1 January 2003, and fully on 1 January 2005; see reg 1.

Amendment Printed as amended by SI 2001/3291, SI 2006/557, SI 2006/599. Previously amended by SI 2000/2688 (revoked by SI 2006/599).

General These regulations contain provisions with respect to the use of a train protection system, Mark I rolling stock and rolling stock with hinged doors.

[702]

Citation and commencement

1 These Regulations may be cited as the Railway Safety Regulations 1999 and shall come into force on 30th January 2000, except regulation 4 which shall come into force on 1st January 2003, regulation 5 which shall come into force on 1st January 2005, and regulation 7 which shall come into force on 1st April 2000.

[703]

Interpretation

2 (1) In these Regulations, unless the context otherwise requires—

"approved" means approved for the time being in writing;

"buffer stop" means a buffer stop at the end of a passenger platform;

"emergency crossover" means a connection between two railway tracks to enable trains to change tracks and which is used—

(a) in an emergency, or

(b) to enable engineering work to be carried out,

in accordance with special procedures established by the infrastructure controller;

"excessive speed" in relation to—

(a) an approach to a stop signal or buffer stop, means such speed as would prevent the train from stopping at that signal or buffer stop,

(b) an approach to part of the railway where there is a speed restriction, means such speed as would prevent the restriction from being complied with when the train enters that part, and for the purposes of this sub-paragraph a speed restriction shall be treated as being complied with if the speed of the train does not exceed the total of the permitted speed and such additional speed as may be approved by the [relevant authority] for the purpose of this sub-paragraph;

["infrastructure controller" means a person who controls railway infrastructure;]

"line speed" means the highest of the permitted speeds on the railway concerned;

"Mark I rolling stock" means rolling stock which has a structural underframe which provides its own longitudinal strength and has a passenger compartment created on the underframe which relies mainly on the underframe for its longitudinal strength;

"permitted speed" means the maximum speed permitted on the part of the railway concerned;

"railway" has the meaning assigned to it by the Schedule to these Regulations;

["railway infrastructure" means fixed assets used for the operation of a railway including its permanent way and plant used for signalling or exclusively for supplying electricity for operational purposes to the railway, but it does not include a station;]

"relevant approach" means—

- (a) an approach to a stop signal referred to in sub-paragraph (a)(i) of the definition of "train protection system" in this regulation except where a train travelling at the maximum speed it could attain on that approach would be stopped within the distance between the signal and the point where it could collide with another train by reason of the train protection system installed at the stop signal;
- (b) an approach to part of the railway where there is a speed restriction if—
  - (i) the permitted speed on that approach is 60 miles per hour or more; and
  - (ii) in order to comply with the restriction, a train travelling at the permitted speed on that approach would need to have its speed reduced by one third or more;
- (c) an approach to a buffer stop;

["relevant authority" means—

- (a) the Office of Rail Regulation where it is made the enforcing authority in relation to the operation of a railway by regulation 3(1) of the Health and Safety (Enforcing Authority for Railways and Other Guided Transport Systems) Regulations 2006; and
- (b) the Health and Safety Executive in any other case;]

"speed restriction" means a permitted speed other than the line speed;

["station" means a railway passenger station or terminal, but does not include any permanent way or plant used for signalling or exclusively for supplying electricity for operational purposes to the railway;]

"stop signal" means a signal conveying to the driver of the train an instruction that he should stop the train except that it does not include—

- (a) a signal provided for shunting purposes only;
- (b) a hand signal; or
- (c) a buffer stop;

"temporary speed restriction" means a speed restriction which is in place for no longer than 3 months and used in accordance with special procedures established by the infrastructure controller;

"train" has the same meaning as in section 83(1) of the Railways Act 1993;

"train protection system" means equipment which—

- (a) causes the brakes of the train to apply automatically if the train—
  - (i) passes without authority a stop signal such passing of which could cause the train to collide with another train, or
  - (ii) travels at excessive speed on a relevant approach;
- (b) is installed so as to operate at every stop signal referred to in sub-paragraph (a), except a stop signal on the approach to an emergency crossover, and at an appropriate place on every relevant approach;

  except that where it is reasonably practicable to install it, it means equipment which automatically controls the speed of the train to ensure, so far as possible, that a signal is not passed without authority and that the permitted speed is not exceeded at any time throughout its journey.

(2) Nothing in these Regulations shall require equipment referred to in sub-paragraphs (a) and (b) of the definition of a train protection system to function in relation to a temporary speed restriction, and accordingly any reference in these Regulations to the permitted speed in relation to such equipment is, in a case where a temporary speed restriction is in place, a reference to the permitted speed which normally applies on that part of the line concerned.

(3) Any reference in these Regulations to a person operating a train or rolling stock is a reference to the person operating a train or rolling stock for the time being in the course of a business or other undertaking carried on by him (whether for profit or not), but it does not include a self-employed person by reason only that he himself drives or otherwise controls the movement of a train.

(4) Any reference in these Regulations, except regulation 4, to a train colliding with another train does not include a reference to a train colliding with the rear of another train travelling in the same direction on the same track.

[(4A) Any reference in these Regulations to a person who controls railway infrastructure is a reference to a person who—

(a) in the course of a business or other undertaking carried on by him (whether for profit or not);

(b) is in operational control of that infrastructure,

except that where such control is for the time being exercised by a person undertaking maintenance, repair or alteration work on the infrastructure, it is a reference to a person who would be in operational control of the infrastructure if such work were not being undertaken.]

(5) Any reference in these Regulations to—

(a) a numbered regulation is a reference to the regulation in these Regulations so numbered, and

(b) a numbered paragraph is a reference to the paragraph so numbered in the regulation in which the reference appears.

NOTES

Amendment Para (1): in definition "excessive speed" in para (b) words in square brackets substituted by SI 2006/557;
definition "infrastructure controller" substituted by SI 2006/599;
definition "railway infrastructure" inserted by SI 2006/599;
definition "relevant authority" inserted by SI 2006/557;
definition "station" inserted by SI 2006/599.
Para (4A): inserted by SI 2006/599.
Health and Safety (Enforcing Authority for Railways and Other Guided Transport Systems) Regulations 2006 SI 2006/557, in the title Health and Safety at Work.

[704]

Use of a train protection system

3 (1) No person shall operate, and no infrastructure controller shall permit the operation of, a train on a railway unless a train protection system is in service in relation to that train and railway.

(2) Until 1st January 2004 it shall be sufficient compliance with paragraph (1) if—

(a) a programme for the installation and bringing into service of a train protection system in relation to that train and railway has been approved by the Executive and is being implemented; and

(b) each part of the system which has been brought into service under that programme is maintained in service.

(3) It shall be sufficient compliance with paragraph (1) if the train is being operated on a railway—

(a) which immediately before the coming into force of this regulation was used (exclusively or not) by London Underground Limited, Tyne and Wear Passenger Transport Executive, Strathclyde Passenger Transport Executive, or Serco Metrolink Limited; and

(b) in relation to which there is in service equipment which causes the brakes of the train to apply automatically if the train passes a stop signal without authority.

(4) In any proceedings against a person for an offence for contravening paragraph (1) it shall be a defence for that person to prove that—

(a) at the relevant time the train protection system (or, where paragraph (3) is relied on, the equipment referred to therein) or a relevant part had failed, or had been taken out of service, because of a fault;

(b) in the case where the fault is in equipment on the train, the train had commenced its journey before the discovery of the fault or is being driven without passengers to a place for the purpose of repair;

(c) it was not reasonably practicable to remedy the fault sooner; and
(d) suitable measures had been taken after the discovery of the fault to mitigate the risk of trains colliding or derailing.

(5) In any proceedings against a person for an offence of contravening paragraph (1) in so far as that paragraph relates to having in service in relation to a train on a railway the equipment referred to in the exception in the definition of "train protection system" in regulation 2(1), it shall be a defence for that person to prove that—

(a) at the relevant time the equipment or a relevant part of it had failed, or had been taken out of service, because of a fault;
(b) it was not reasonably practicable to remedy the fault sooner; and
(c) equipment referred to in sub-paragraphs (a) and (b) of that definition was at the relevant time in service in relation to that train and railway.

[705]

Prohibition of Mark I rolling stock

4 (1) No person shall operate, and no infrastructure controller shall permit the operation of, any Mark I rolling stock on a railway.

(2) Paragraph (1) shall not apply to rolling stock which at the relevant time is being exclusively operated other than for the carriage of fare paying passengers or by London Underground Limited, Tyne and Wear Passenger Transport Executive, Strathclyde Passenger Transport Executive or Serco Metrolink Limited.

(3) Until 1st January 2005 paragraph (1) shall not apply to Mark I rolling stock which has been modified so as to ensure that in the event of a collision—

(a) the underframe of one vehicle will not ride over the underframe of another vehicle so modified (whether or not the other vehicle is part of the same train);
(b) where sub-paragraph (a) is not practicable, the extent of any such riding over is as small as can practicably be achieved by a modification to the rolling stock.

(4) In this regulation "modified" means modified by the installation of interlocking devices on vehicles and "modification" shall be construed accordingly.

[706]

Prohibition of hinged doors

5 (1) No person shall operate, and no infrastructure controller shall permit the operation of any rolling stock on a railway if the rolling stock has hinged doors for use by passengers for boarding and alighting from the train (other than doors which have a means of centrally locking them in a closed position).

(2) Paragraph (1) shall not apply to rolling stock which at the relevant time is being exclusively operated other than for the carriage of fare paying passengers.

[707]

Exemption certificates

6 (1) The [relevant authority] may, by certificate in writing, exempt any person or class of persons, railway, part of a railway or class of railways, train or rolling stock, or class of train or rolling stock from any prohibition imposed by these Regulations and any such exemption may be granted subject to conditions and to a limit of time and may be revoked by a certificate in writing at any time.

(2) Before granting an exemption the [relevant authority] shall consult such persons as it considers appropriate.

(3) In deciding whether to grant any such exemption the [relevant authority] shall have regard to—

(a) the conditions, if any which it proposes to attach to the exemption;
(b) any other requirements imposed by or under any enactment which apply to the case;
(c) all other circumstances of the case.

NOTES

Amendment Paras (1)–(3): words in square brackets substituted by SI 2006/557.

[708]

7 (*Amends SI 1995/3163, in the title Health and Safety at Work.*)

SCHEDULE
THE MEANING OF RAILWAY

Regulation 2(1)

1 "Railway" means a system of transport employing parallel rails which provide support and guidance for vehicles carried on flanged wheels and form a track which either is of a gauge of at least 350 millimetres or crosses a carriageway (whether or not on the same level), except that it does not include—

(a) a tramway;
(b) any part which runs along and at the same level as a street or in any other place to which the public has access (including a place to which the public has access only on making a payment);
(c) any part where the permitted speed is such as to enable the driver to stop the train in the distance he can see ahead in clear weather conditions;
(d) any part normally used other than for the carriage of fare paying passengers; or
(e) such a system if on no part of it there is a line speed exceeding [40 kilometres per hour].

2 In this Schedule—

"carriageway" has the same meaning as in the Highways Act 1980 or in Scotland, the Roads (Scotland) Act 1984;

"street" means—

(a) in England and Wales, a street within the meaning of section 48 of the New Roads and Street Works Act 1991, together with land on the verge of a street or between two carriageways;
(b) in Scotland, a road within the meaning of section 107 of the New Roads and Street Works Act 1991, together with land on the verge of a road or between two carriageways;

["tramway" means a system of transport used wholly or mainly for the carriage of passengers—

(a) which employs parallel rails which—
    (i) provide support and guidance for vehicles carried on flanged wheels; and
    (ii) are laid wholly or partly along a road or in any other place to which the public has access (including a place to which the public only has access on making payment); and
(b) on any part of which the permitted speed is such as to enable the driver to stop a vehicle in the distance he can see to be clear ahead;]

"vehicle" includes a mobile traction unit.

NOTES

Amendment Para 1(e): words in square brackets substituted by SI 2001/3291.
Para 2: definition "tramway" substituted by SI 2006/599.

[709]

MOTOR VEHICLES (DRIVING LICENCES) REGULATIONS 1999 SI 1999/2864

Authority Made by the Secretary of State for the Environment, Transport and the Regions under the Road Traffic Act 1988, ss 88(5), (6), 89(1A), (2A), (3), (4), (5), (5A), (6), (7), (9), (10), 89A(3), (5), 91, 92(2), (4), 94(4), (5), 97(1), (1A), (3), (3A), (3B), (4), 98(2), (4), 99(1), (1A), 99A(3), (4), (6), 101(2), (3), 105(1), (2), (3), (4), 108(1), 114(1), 115(1), (3), 115A(1), 117(2A), 118(4), 120, 121, 122, 164(2), 183(6), 192(1), with the approval of the Treasury in the case of regs 14, 30, 35.

In relation to the above provisions of the 1988 Act, note:

(a) s 89A(3) has been repealed by the Road Safety Act 2006, s 59, Sch 7;
(b) ss 89(2A), (5A), 97(3A), (3B) are repealed by the Transport Act 2000, s 274, Sch 31, Pt V(1), as from a day to be appointed by order; and
(c) s 99A(6) is repealed by the Road Safety Act 2006, ss 10(12), 59, Sch 3, paras 2, 10, Sch 7, as from a day to be appointed by order.

Date made 19 October 1999.

Commencement 12 November 1999.

Amendment Amended by SI 2000/2766, SI 2000/3157, SI 2001/53 (itself amended by SI 2001/236), SI 2001/236, SI 2001/937, SI 2003/166, SI 2003/222, SI 2003/636, SI 2003/2003 (itself partially (transitional provisions) revoked by SI 2007/698), SI 2003/3313, SI 2004/265, SI 2004/696, SI 2004/1519, SI 2004/3028, SI 2004/3168 (the latter in relation to England only), SI 2005/1975, SI 2005/2717, SI 2005/2929 (the latter in relation to Wales only), SI 2006/524,

SI 2007/605, SI 2007/698, SI 2008/508, SI 2008/1312, SI 2008/1435 (subject to savings and transitional provisions), SI 2008/2508, SI 2009/788 (subject to savings and transitional provisions), SI 2009/2362.

Amended in relation to Scotland only by SSI 2005/344 (outside the scope of this work). Also amended by SI 2001/2779 (superseded), SI 2001/3486, SI 2002/2641 (both spent), SI 2008/1038 (revoked).

Summary These regulations, which revoke and replace the Motor Vehicles (Driving Licences) Regulations 1996, SI 1996/2824, and the amending SI 1997/256, SI 1997/669, SI 1997/846, SI 1997/2070, SI 1997/2915, SI 1998/20, SI 1998/528, SI 1998/1229, SI 1998/2038, SI 1999/72, SI 1999/617, make detailed provision for the licensing of drivers of vehicles. The text of the regulations is not printed in this work, but the scope and nature of their provisions may be seen from the following arrangement (references therein to "the Traffic Act" are to the Road Traffic Act 1988).

ARRANGEMENT OF REGULATIONS

PART I
PRELIMINARY

24 Persons by whom practical and unitary tests may be conducted (*amended by SI 2000/3157, SI 2003/2003, SI 2004/3168 (England only), SI 2005/2929 (Wales only), SI 2007/698, SI 2008/508, SI 2008/1435, SI 2009/788*)
25 Revocation of authority to conduct tests (*amended by SI 2009/788*)

Applications for tests

26 Applicants for theory tests: applicants in person (*amended by SI 2006/524*)
27 Applicants for theory tests: motor bicycle instructors (*amended by SI 2005/2717, SI 2008/1435*)
28 Applicants for theory tests: large vehicle instructors (*amended by SI 2005/2717, SI 2008/1435*)
28A Applications for theory tests: motor car instructors (*inserted by SI 2006/524*)
29 Eligibility to apply for further theory test
30 Fees for theory tests (*substituted by SI 2007/698; amended by SI 2008/508, SI 2008/1435, SI 2009/788*)
31 Applicants for practical and unitary tests: applicants in person (*amended by SI 2009/788*)
32 Applications for practical tests: motor bicycle instructors (*amended by SI 2005/2717, SI 2009/788*)
33 Applications for practical tests: large vehicle instructors (*amended by SI 2005/2717*)
34 Eligibility to apply for further practical or unitary test (*amended by SI 2007/698, SI 2009/788*)
35 Fees in respect of practical or unitary tests (*amended by SI 2003/2003, SI 2004/3028, SI 2005/1975, SI 2006/524, SI 2007/698, SI 2008/508, SI 2008/1435, SI 2009/788*)
36 Cancellation of tests (*amended by SI 2005/2717, SI 2009/788*)

Requirements at tests

37 Test vehicles (*amended by SI 2003/2003, SI 2006/524, SI 2009/788*)
38 Further requirements at test (*amended by SI 2005/2717, SI 2007/698, SI 2008/1435, SI 2009/788*)
39 Examiner's right to refuse to conduct test (*amended by SI 2009/788*)

Nature and conduct of test

40, 40A Nature of tests other than extended tests (*reg 40 substituted by SI 2008/1435, and amended by SI 2009/788; reg 40A inserted by SI 2008/1435, and amended by SI 2009/788*)
40B Content of the tests (*inserted by SI 2008/1435; amended by SI 2008/2508, SI 2009/788, SI 2009/2362*)
40C Passing the test (*inserted by SI 2008/1435; amended by SI 2008/2508, SI 2009/788*)
41 Nature of extended driving tests (*amended by SI 2008/1435*)
42 Exemption from theory test (*amended by SI 2001/53, SI 2003/166*)

Entitlements upon passing test

43 Entitlement upon passing a test other than an appropriate driving test (*amended by SI 2001/53 (itself amended by SI 2001/236), SI 2001/236, SI 2009/788*)
44 Entitlement upon passing a test other than an appropriate driving test: category A (*amended by SI 2009/788*)
44A Entitlement upon passing a test other than an appropriate driving test: category P (*inserted by SI 2001/53*)
45 Upgrading of entitlements by virtue of passing second test
46 Entitlement upon passing an appropriate driving test (*amended by SI 2009/788*)

Test results

47 Evidence of result of theory test: vehicles other than category C or D (*amended by SI 2003/2003, SI 2005/1975, SI 2007/698, SI 2008/508, SI 2008/1435, SI 2009/788*)
47A Evidence of result of theory test: category C and D (*inserted by SI 2008/1435*)
47B Large vehicle theory test pass certificates (*inserted by SI 2008/1435; amended by SI 2009/788*)
48 Evidence of result of practical or unitary test (*amended by SI 2003/2003, SI 2008/508, SI 2008/1435, SI 2009/788*)

PART IV
GOODS AND PASSENGER-CARRYING VEHICLES

General

49 Part III of the Traffic Act: prescribed classes of goods and passenger-carrying vehicle
50 Part IV of the Traffic Act: prescribed classes of goods and passenger-carrying vehicle
51 Exempted goods and military vehicles (*amended by SI 2003/166*)
52 Correspondences
53 Part IV of the Traffic Act: dual purpose vehicles

Persons under the age of 21

54 Large goods vehicle drivers' licences granted to persons under the age of 21 (*substituted by SI 2003/636; amended by SI 2004/1519*)

Drivers' conduct

Sch 10D Forms of certificate and statement (*inserted by SI 2009/788*)
Sch 11 Forms of certificate and statement of practical and unitary test result
Sch 12 Elements of an approved training course (*amended by SI 2001/53, SI 2003/166*)
Sch 13 Approved motor bicycle training courses: forms of certificate (*amended by SI 2001/53*)

[710]

MOTOR CYCLES ETC (EC TYPE APPROVAL) REGULATIONS 1999
SI 1999/2920

Authority Made by the Secretary of State for the Environment, Transport and the Regions under the European Communities Act 1972, s 2(2).
Date made 25 October 1999.
Commencement 30 November 1999.
Amendment Amended by SI 2001/368, SI 2001/1547, SI 2003/1099, SI 2004/1948, SI 2004/2539, SI 2006/2935, SI 2007/2656.
Summary These regulations revoke and replace the Motor Cycles (EC Type Approval) Regulations 1995, SI 1995/1513, and the amending SI 1997/2282, subject to transitional provisions. They implement Directive 2002/24/EC of the European Parliament and of the Council relating to the type approval of two or three-wheel motor vehicles and repealing Council Directive 92/61/EEC (OJ L124, 09.05.2002, p 1), as amended from time to time ("the Framework Directive"), which requires member states to set up a system for granting EC type approval for two- or three-wheel motor vehicles (mopeds, motor cycles and motor tricycles) and certain four-wheel vehicles (quadricycles). Decisions about granting EC type approval must be made in accordance with the Framework Directive and the separate Directives listed in the regulations.

Pt II (regs 5–15) of the regulations relates to EC type approval granted by the Secretary of State. Where the Secretary of State decides, on application being made to him for EC type approval, to grant or amend an EC type approval, he must issue an EC type approval certificate or an amended EC type approval certificate. EC component type approval may be granted for separate technical units or components. The holder of an EC type approval granted by the Secretary of State must issue an EC certificate of conformity with each vehicle and affix an approval mark to each component that conforms with the approved type; he must also comply with provisions of the Framework Directive relating to checking the conformity of production. A duty is imposed on the holder of an EC type approval to co-operate with the Secretary of State in carrying out his obligations in relation to the approval. The holder of an EC type approval granted by the Secretary of State must also comply with certain requirements of Art 9 of the Framework Directive. The Secretary of State may withdraw or suspend an EC type approval in specified circumstances. Where the Secretary of State considers that vehicles, components or separate technical units of a particular type in respect of which an EC type approval has effect are a serious risk to road safety, he may direct that for a specified period not exceeding six months all EC certificates of conformity issued under that EC type approval are invalid for the purposes of the Road Traffic Act 1988, Pt II and any regulations made thereunder, and reg 16 (grant of first licence or nil licence) of these regulations.

Pt III (regs 16–18) relates to the licensing of vehicles. Where a person applies for a first licence or nil licence under the Vehicle Excise and Registration Act 1994 for a vehicle to which these regulations apply, the Secretary of State may not grant the licence or nil licence unless:

(a) there is in respect of that vehicle an EC certificate of conformity or a minister's approval certificate issued under s 58(1) or (4) of the 1988 Act; or
(b) the application is made before 17 June 2003 and the vehicle belongs to the same type as a vehicle used before 17 June 1999.

The previous provision does not apply to vehicles used for the purposes of the Crown, the police or civil defence, or prototypes. Provision is made in relation to end of series vehicles (as defined by the regulations) applying where an EC type approval has been granted by the Secretary of State or under any provision of the law of an EEA State other than the United Kingdom giving effect to Art 4 of the Framework Directive, and the Secretary of State is satisfied that it is going to cease to have effect in consequence of the provisions of the Framework Directive or a separate Directive. In such circumstances and subject to conditions, the Secretary of State may direct that every relevant EC certificate of conformity is to continue to have effect for the period of 12 months from the date on which the EC type approval lost its validity.

Pt IV (regs 19–21) relates to offences. Amendments are made to the Road Traffic Act 1988, ss 64A, 65A, 85, the Road Traffic Offenders Act 1988, Sch 2, Pt I, the Road Traffic (Northern Ireland) Order 1981, SI 1981/154 (NI 1) and the Road Traffic Offenders (Northern Ireland) Order 1996, SI 1996/1320 (NI 10) (both outside the scope of this work). Offences are created relating to EC type approval, such as forging an EC type approval certificate or an EC certificate of conformity, and making false statements

Pt V (regs 22–26) contains miscellaneous provisions relating to, inter alia, the review of decisions and the provision of testing stations by the Secretary of State. Transitional provision is also made.

As to the fees payable in respect of the issue of type approval certificates, see SI 1999/2149.

[711]

ROAD TRANSPORT (PASSENGER VEHICLES CABOTAGE) REGULATIONS 1999
SI 1999/3413

Authority Made by the Secretary of State for the Environment, Transport and the Regions under the European Communities Act 1972, s 2(2).
Date made 20 December 1999.
Commencement 28 January 2000.
Amendment Amended by SI 2000/3114, SI 2009/1885.
Summary These regulations implement in Great Britain Council Regulation (EC) 12/98 (OJ L4, 08.01.1998, p 10) laying down the conditions under which non-resident carriers may operate national road passenger transport services within a member state. Under the regulations, a person is guilty of an offence if he uses a vehicle on a road, or causes or permits a vehicle to be so used, for the purpose of UK cabotage operations which:

(a) are carried out by a Community carrier without a valid Community licence; or
(b) take the form of occasional services in Great Britain or between Great Britain and Northern Ireland and are carried out in contravention of Art 6(1) of the Council Regulation, which requires such services to be carried out under the cover of a control document.

The regulations specify the competent authorities in Great Britain for the purposes of the Council Regulation. A carrier who is aggrieved by an administrative penalty imposed on him:

(a) by the Secretary of State, may request him to review that decision; or
(b) by the appropriate traffic commissioner, may appeal to the Upper Tribunal (established by the Tribunals, Courts and Enforcement Act 2007, s 3; see further the title Courts and Legal Services).

The driver of a vehicle which is required by the Council Regulation to have on board a Community licence or a control document commits an offence if he fails, without reasonable cause, to produce the Community licence (or a certified copy) or the control document when requested to do so by an authorised inspecting officer. The regulations also specify authorised inspecting officers for the purposes of the Council Regulation. The following provisions are amended: the Road Traffic (Foreign Vehicles) Act 1972, Schs 1, 2; the Public Passenger Vehicles Act 1981, ss 65(1), 66; and the Transport Act 1985, Sch 4, para 9. Modifications are made to the 1981 Act. The regulations also provide that none of the provisions of SI 1981/257, Pts II, III, IV, V has effect in relation to a vehicle which is carrying out a cabotage transport operation in Great Britain in accordance with the Council Regulation.
Offences Certain offences under these regulations are: (a) fixed penalty offences; see SI 2009/483, noted to SI 1990/335; (b) offences in respect of which a financial penalty deposit requirement may be imposed; see SI 2009/491 (and see also SI 2009/492).

[712]

GREATER LONDON AUTHORITY ACT 1999 (HACKNEY CARRIAGES AND PRIVATE HIRE VEHICLES) (TRANSITIONAL AND CONSEQUENTIAL PROVISIONS) ORDER 2000
SI 2000/412

Authority Made by the Secretary of State for the Environment, Transport and the Regions under the Greater London Authority Act 1999, ss 255, 405(2), 406, 415(9), 420.
Date made 21 February 2000.
Commencement 13 March 2000.
Summary The Greater London Authority Act 1999, s 323, which came into force on 1 April 2000 ("the appointed day"; see SI 1999/3271, in the title Local Government), amends the London Government Act 1963, s 76, so as to change the boundary of the metropolitan police district, excluding all parts of that district lying outside Greater London. S 255 of the 1999 Act provides that on the appointed day the licensing of hackney carriages and private hire vehicles to operate in those areas becomes the responsibility of the relevant district councils in accordance with the Town Police Clauses Act 1847 and the Local Government (Miscellaneous Provisions) Act 1976. This order makes transitional and consequential provisions in relation to the licensing of taxis and private hire vehicles in the affected areas.

The order refers to wholly and partially excluded districts (determined by reference to whether the whole or a part only of a district ceases to be within the metropolitan police district on the appointed day); references to excluded districts are to wholly or partially excluded districts. Where a council of a partially excluded district has byelaws in force under the Town Police Clauses Act 1847 in part of its district, those byelaws are to apply to the whole district from the appointed day. Provision is made for the anticipatory powers of excluded district councils, enabling such councils generally to do anything appropriate for the purpose of securing that hackney carriages and private hire vehicles may operate lawfully in their district on the appointed day (this includes power to grant licences in anticipation of the appointed day). Hackney carriage or hackney carriage driver licences granted in the metropolitan police district before the appointed day cease to have effect on that day in any excluded district. Standings for hackney carriages appointed in the excluded part of a partially excluded district under the legislation applying to the metropolitan police district continue to have effect from the appointed day under the corresponding provisions of the Local Government (Miscellaneous Provisions) Act 1976. Consequential amendments are made to ss 74, 80(1) of that Act.

[713]

DISABLED PERSONS (BADGES FOR MOTOR VEHICLES) (ENGLAND) REGULATIONS 2000
SI 2000/682

Authority Made by the Secretary of State for the Environment, Transport and the Regions under the Chronically Sick and Disabled Persons Act 1970, s 21.
Date made 9 March 2000.
Commencement 1 April 2000.
Amendment Amended by SI 2000/1507, SI 2005/617, SI 2007/2531 (itself amended by SI 2007/2600).
Summary These regulations, as originally enacted, amended the Disabled Persons (Badges for Motor Vehicles) Regulations 1982, SI 1982/1740, so as to disapply them in relation to England (SI 1982/1740 is wholly revoked by SI 2000/1786; see below). The regulations, which replace SI 1982/1740 in England, prescribe various matters in connection with the issue of badges to disabled persons under the Chronically Sick and Disabled Persons Act 1970, s 21, entitling them to special local parking facilities. Detailed provisions are made in relation to the issue, duration and revocation of badges and the form and display of badges.
Wales SI 2000/1786 was made under the Chronically Sick and Disabled Persons Act 1970, s 21, and came into force on 1 July 2000. The regulations, which revoke SI 1982/1740 mentioned above, subject to transitional provisions, make similar provision in relation to Wales as is made in relation to England by SI 2000/682.

[714]

LOCAL AUTHORITIES' TRAFFIC ORDERS (EXEMPTIONS FOR DISABLED PERSONS) (ENGLAND) REGULATIONS 2000
SI 2000/683

Authority Made by the Secretary of State for the Environment, Transport and the Regions under the Road Traffic Regulation Act 1984, Sch 9, Pt III, para 23, as extended by the Chronically Sick and Disabled Persons Act 1970, s 21(1)(b).
Date made 9 March 2000.
Commencement 1 April 2000.
Summary These regulations amended the Local Authorities' Traffic Orders (Exemptions for Disabled Persons) (England and Wales) Regulations 1986, SI 1986/178, so as to disapply them in relation to England (SI 1986/178 is wholly revoked by SI 2000/1785; see below). The regulations, which replace SI 1986/178 in England, concern orders made by local authorities under the Road Traffic Regulation Act 1984 which, inter alia, prohibit vehicles from waiting at all times or during specified periods on roads marked by yellow lines, or prohibit beyond a certain period the waiting of vehicles in roads or in street parking places, whether a charge is made or not. The regulations require the orders to which they relate to include exemptions in favour of a vehicle displaying a disabled person's badge (ie a badge issued under SI 2000/682 or SI 2000/1786 or under corresponding regulations having effect in Scotland). Provision is made in relation to an exemption from prohibitions on waiting beyond a specified time, from prohibitions on waiting at all times or during specified periods, and from other provisions of orders under s 45 or 46 of the 1984 Act.
Wales SI 2000/1785 was made under the same provisions as SI 2000/683 and came into force on 5 July 2000. The regulations, which revoke SI 1986/178, mentioned above, make similar provision in relation to Wales as is made in relation to England by SI 2000/683.

[715]

TRANSPORT FOR LONDON (PRELIMINARY ARRANGEMENTS) ORDER 2000
SI 2000/1045

Authority Made by the Secretary of State for the Environment, Transport and the Regions under the Greater London Authority Act 1999, ss 406, 420(1).
Date made 13 April 2000.
Commencement 8 May 2000.
Summary Transport for London was established by the Greater London Authority Act 1999, s 154(1) on 8 May 2000 (see SI 2000/801, in the title Local Government), and assumed its principal functions on 3 July 2000 (see generally ss 154(2), (3), 156–158 of the 1999 Act). This order provides for arrangements for the exercise of Transport for London's functions in connection with the matters set out in Schs 1 (standing orders as to conduct of business) and 2 (financial arrangements) to the order to have effect from 8 May 2000 until varied or replaced by Transport for London under any provision of Sch 10 to the 1999 Act.

[716]

REGULATION OF BUS SERVICES IN GREATER LONDON (TRANSITIONAL PROVISIONS) ORDER 2000
SI 2000/1462

Authority Made by the Secretary of State for the Environment, Transport and the Regions under the Greater London Authority Act 1999, ss 405(2), 406.

Date made 5 June 2000.
Commencement 28 June 2000.
Summary This order makes provision for the transition from London local service licensing of bus services under the Transport Act 1985, Pt II (ss 34–46) to London service permits under the Greater London Authority Act 1999, Pt IV, Chapter V (ss 179–195). Pt II of the 1985 Act is repealed by s 423 of, and Pt II of Sch 34 to, the 1999 Act, as from a day to be appointed by order under s 425(2) thereof.

Modifications are made to the 1985 and 1999 Acts during the transitional period (i e the period beginning on 3 July 2000 and ending on the last day on which a London local service licence granted under the 1985 Act ceases to be in force). Pt II of the 1985 Act remains in force so as to enable all subsisting licences to continue in force and to enable the traffic commissioner to deal with applications for London local service licences received before 3 July 2000. Pt II of the 1985 Act ceases to have effect immediately after the end of the transitional period. During that period, the 1999 Act is modified so as to allow holders of London local service licences to continue operating under those licences after the introduction of London service permits.

Provision is made for the interim continuation of London local service licences granted under the 1985 Act where the holder has applied for a London service permit under the 1999 Act. Agreements entered into by London Regional Transport (dissolved by SI 2003/1913 on 16 July 2003) under the London Regional Transport Act 1984, s 3 (repealed by s 423 of, and Pt II of Sch 34 to, the 1999 Act) are to be treated as entered into by Transport for London under s 156 of the 1999 Act. The Secretary of State may issue an interim guidance document on the criteria to be applied by Transport for London in considering applications for London service permits until such time as the Mayor of London adopts his own guidance document in accordance with s 185(2) of the 1999 Act.

[717]

LONDON TRANSPORT USERS' COMMITTEE (TRANSITIONAL PROVISIONS) ORDER 2000
SI 2000/1484

Authority Made by the Secretary of State for the Environment, Transport and the Regions under the Greater London Authority Act 1999, ss 405(2), 406, 408, 410(1), 411(1), (3)(c), 420(1).
Date made 5 June 2000.
Commencement 28 June 2000.
Summary This order makes transitional provision in connection with the abolition of the London Regional Passengers' Committee (LRPC) by the Greater London Authority Act 1999, s 246, and its replacement by the London Transport Users' Committee, established under s 247 of that Act. Provision is made in relation to the final report and accounts of LRPC; superannuation of LRPC staff; property, rights and liabilities; continuity in the exercise of functions; and London Regional Transport services during the transitional period (i e the period beginning on 3 July 2000 and ending on the day on which London Regional Transport ceases to provide or secure the provision of public passenger transport services). London Regional Transport was dissolved on 16 July 2003 by SI 2003/1913.

[718]

GREATER LONDON HIGHWAYS AND ROAD TRAFFIC (VARIOUS PROVISIONS) ORDER 2000
SI 2000/1547

Authority Made by the Secretary of State for the Environment, Transport and the Regions under the Greater London Authority Act 1999, ss 405(2), 406 and the Road Traffic Act 1991, s 76A(3)(a). S 76A of the 1991 Act has been repealed by the Traffic Management Act 2004, s 98, Sch 12, Pt 1.
Date made 9 June 2000.
Commencement 3 July 2000.
Summary This order makes provision for various highways and road traffic matters arising out of the Greater London Authority Act 1999. Sch 22 to the 1999 Act amends the Town and Country Planning Act 1990, Pt X, so as to enable London borough councils and the Common Council of the City of London, instead of the Secretary of State, to make orders authorising the stopping up of highways. This order makes transitional provision enabling the Secretary of State to continue to deal with applications for such orders received by him before 3 July 2000. Areas in the City of Westminster were specified for the purposes of the Road Traffic Act 1991, s 76A(3)(a) as areas which, on grounds of national security, were not to be brought within a special parking area (s 76A of the 1991 Act has been repealed by the Traffic Management Act 2004, s 98, Sch 12, Pt 1). The order also amends the Road Traffic Regulation Act 1984, Sch 9, and SI 1993/1202, SI 1996/2489.

[719]

TRANSPORT FOR LONDON (SPECIFIED ACTIVITIES) ORDER 2000
SI 2000/1548

Authority Made by the Secretary of State for the Environment, Transport and the Regions, with the consent of the Treasury, under the Greater London Authority Act 1999, s 157(1).
Date made 8 June 2000.
Commencement 3 July 2000.

Summary This order provides that Transport for London may not carry on any activity specified in the Schedule to the order, except through a company limited by shares and registered under the Companies Act 1985 (now replaced by the Companies Act 2006) which is:
(a) a subsidiary of Transport for London; or
(b) a company which Transport for London formed, or joined with others in forming, by virtue of s 156(1) of the 1999 Act and which does not fall within head (a).

[720]

PUBLIC SERVICE VEHICLES ACCESSIBILITY REGULATIONS 2000 SI 2000/1970

Authority Made by the Secretary of State for the Environment, Transport and the Regions under the Disability Discrimination Act 1995, ss 40(1), (2), (6), 41(2), 42(3), (4), (5), 44(1)(b), (2)(b), (4), 45(1), 67.
Date made 20 July 2000.
Commencement 30 August 2000.
Amendment Amended by SI 2000/3318, SI 2002/2981, SI 2005/2988, SI 2009/143, SI 2009/876. Previously amended by SI 2003/1818, SI 2004/1881, SI 2007/500, SI 2008/1459 (all superseded).
Summary These regulations apply to single-deck and double-deck buses and coaches with a capacity of more than 22 passengers, which are used to provide local and scheduled services ("regulated public service vehicles"). The regulations are framed so as to ensure that disabled persons can get on and off a regulated public service vehicle in safety and without reasonable difficulty and, in the case of wheelchair users, whilst remaining in their wheelchairs. They are also framed to ensure that disabled persons are carried in regulated public service vehicles in safety and reasonable comfort. The regulations provide for phased implementation of their requirements and certain vehicles do not require accessibility certificates until 2020.

Pt I of the regulations contains preliminary provisions, including interpretation. Pt II concerns the application of the regulations to regulated public service vehicles; exemptions from the requirements of the regulations; and the recognition of compliance with EC and EEA equivalent requirements. It sets out detailed wheelchair accessibility requirements and general accessibility requirements for single-deck and double-deck buses and coaches. Pt III relates to accessibility certificates, and provides for applications and fees for such certificates, and the information to be contained therein.

Pt IV concerns the approval by the Secretary of State under the Disability Discrimination Act 1995, s 42(1) of a particular regulated public service vehicle as satisfying the provisions of these regulations ("type vehicle approval"). Provision is made relating to applications for type vehicle approval, copies of drawings and specifications, and fees for approval as a type vehicle. Pt V concerns the declaration by an authorised person under s 42 of the 1995 Act that a particular regulated public service vehicle conforms in design, construction and equipment with a type vehicle. The form of a declaration of conformity is prescribed. Pt VI concerns the issue by a vehicle examiner of a certificate under s 42(4) of that Act that a declaration of conformity has been issued in respect of a regulated public service vehicle. The form of a conformity certificate and the fee payable for it are prescribed.

Pt VII contains miscellaneous provisions relating to the issue of duplicate documentation, reviews and appeals.

As to regulations providing for the accessibility of rail vehicles, see SI 1998/2456.

[721]

ROAD TRAFFIC (OWNER LIABILITY) REGULATIONS 2000 SI 2000/2546

Authority Made by the Home Secretary under the Road Traffic Offenders Act 1988, s 84.
Date made 16 September 2000.
Commencement 16 October 2000.
Amendment Amended by SI 2001/1222. Also amended by SI 2001/925 (revoked by SI 2001/1222 before being published).
Summary These regulations revoke and replace the Road Traffic (Owner Liability) Regulations 1975, SI 1975/324, and the Road Traffic (Owner Liability) (Scotland) Regulations 1975, SI 1975/706 (outside the scope of this work). They prescribe forms for use in connection with the Road Traffic Offenders Act 1988, ss 62–68 (notices fixed to vehicles). The regulations also prescribe particulars for the purposes of s 66(8) of that Act; these particulars must be contained in a hiring agreement in order for it to comply with s 66.

The forms set out are as follows:

FIXED PENALTIES

1	Notice to owner of vehicle (FP1) (*amended by SI 2001/1222*)
2	Statutory statement of ownership and statement by vehicle-hire firm in lieu (FP2)
3	Statutory statement of facts (owner) (FP3)
4	Notice to hirer of vehicle (FP4) (*amended by SI 2001/1222*)
5	Statutory statement of hiring (FP5)
6	Statutory statement of facts (hirer) (FP6)

EXCESS CHARGES

7	Notice to owner of vehicle (EC1)
8	Statutory statement of ownership and statement by vehicle-hire firm in lieu (EC2)

9 Statutory statement of facts (owner) (EC3)
10 Notice to hirer of vehicle (EC4)
11 Statutory statement of hiring (EC5)
12 Statutory statement of facts (hirer) (EC6)
VEHICLE HIRE
13 Statement of liability (H).

[722]

FIXED PENALTY ORDER 2000
SI 2000/2792

Authority Made by the Home Secretary under the Road Traffic Offenders Act 1988, s 53. As to the prospective amendment of the said s 53, see the Preliminary Note "Penalties" under the main head "Road Traffic".

Date made 10 October 2000.

Commencement 1 November 2000.

Amendment Amended by SI 2003/1254, SI 2009/488, SI 2009/1487.

Summary This order, which revokes and replaces the Fixed Penalty Order 1992, SI 1992/346 and the Fixed Penalty (Increase) (Scotland) Order 1992, SI 1992/435 (outside the scope of this work), prescribes fixed penalties and graduated fixed penalties under the Road Traffic Offenders Act 1988, s 53.

The prescribed fixed penalties are as follows:

for a fixed penalty offence under the Road Traffic Act 1988, s 143, £200;
for a fixed penalty offence under s 172 of that Act, £120;
for any other fixed penalty offence involving obligatory endorsement, £60.00;
for a fixed penalty parking offence (as defined in the order) committed in Greater London on a red route, £60.00;
for any other fixed penalty parking offence committed in Greater London, £40.00;
for a fixed penalty offence under the Road Traffic Act 1988, ss 14, 15(2), (4), 47, £60;
for a fixed penalty offence under the Vehicle Excise and Registration Act 1994, ss 33, 59, £60;
for a fixed penalty offence under the Transport Act 1968, ss 98(4), 99(4), 99ZD(1), 99C, £200;
for a fixed penalty offence under the Road Traffic (Foreign Vehicles) Act 1972, s 3(1), £200;
for a fixed penalty offence under the Public Passenger Vehicles Act 1981, s 12(5), £200;
for a fixed penalty offence under the Road Traffic Act 1988, s 71(1), £200;
for a fixed penalty offence under the Road Traffic Offenders Act 1988, s 90D(6), £200;
for a fixed penalty offence under the Goods Vehicles (Licensing of Operators) Act 1995, s 2(5), £200;
for a fixed penalty offence under SI 1992/3077, reg 3, SI 1999/1322, reg 3, and SI 1999/3413, regs 3(1), 4(1), £60; and
for any other fixed penalty offence, £30.00.

The order also prescribes graduated fixed penalties (determined according to the nature of the contravention or failure constituting the offence and, in specified cases, its seriousness) for offences under the Transport Act 1968, ss 96(11), (11A), 97(1) and the Road Traffic Act 1988, ss 41A, 41B, 42.

[723]

DISABILITY DISCRIMINATION ACT 1995 (TAXIS) (CARRYING OF GUIDE DOGS ETC) (ENGLAND AND WALES) REGULATIONS 2000
SI 2000/2990

Authority Made by the Secretary of State for the Environment, Transport and the Regions under the Disability Discrimination Act 1995, ss 37(8)(b), (9), 67(2).

Date made 8 November 2000.

Commencement Partly on 1 December 2000; fully on 31 March 2001.

Amendment Amended by SI 2006/1616.

Summary The Disability Discrimination Act 1995, s 37 imposes a duty on the driver of a taxi to carry, without additional charge, a guide dog, hearing dog and any other prescribed category of dog when it accompanies the hirer of the taxi. A person may be exempted from this duty if the licensing authority is satisfied that it is appropriate on medical grounds and issues him with a certificate of exemption. The prescribed notice of his exemption must be exhibited on the taxi in the prescribed manner. These regulations prescribe the form of notice of exemption and the manner of exhibiting it. The regulations also prescribe as a category of dog to which s 37 applies an assistance dog (i e a dog which is trained by a specified charity to assist a disabled person with a physical impairment which consists of epilepsy or otherwise affects his mobility, manual dexterity, physical co-ordination or ability to lift, carry or otherwise move everyday objects).

[724]

PRIVATE HIRE VEHICLES (LONDON) ACT 1998 (COMMENCEMENT NO 1) ORDER 2000
SI 2000/3144

Authority Made by the Secretary of State for the Environment, Transport and the Regions under the Private Hire Vehicles (London) Act 1998, s 40(2).

Date made 28 November 2000.
Summary This order and SI 2003/580, SI 2004/241 (also made under the Private Hire Vehicles (London) Act 1998, s 40(2)) brought provisions of the 1998 Act into force as noted in the table below.

Provision	*Date and extent (if any)*
s 1	22 January 2001 (SI 2000/3144)
s 2	22 October 2001 (SI 2000/3144)
s 3	22 January 2001 (SI 2000/3144)
s 4(1)	22 January 2001 (SI 2000/3144)
s 4(2)	8 June 2004 (SI 2004/241)
s 4(3), (4)	22 January 2001 (SI 2000/3144)
s 4(5), (6)	22 October 2001 (SI 2000/3144)
s 5(1)–(4)	22 October 2001 (SI 2000/3144)
s 5(5)	22 January 2001 (SI 2000/3144)
s 6	8 June 2004 (SI 2004/241)
ss 7–11	8 March 2004 (for the purposes of existing private hire vehicles as defined by SI 2004/242, reg 2) (SI 2004/241) 8 April 2004 (for all other purposes) (SI 2004/241)
s 12(1)–(6)	1 June 2003 (SI 2003/580)
s 12(7)	8 June 2004 (SI 2004/241)
s 13(1), (2)(a)	1 April 2003 (SI 2003/580)
s 13(2)(b)	1 April 2003 (except so far as relates to the requirement mentioned in s 13(3)) (SI 2003/580) 1 April 2006 (so far as not already in force) (in relation to applications for London PHV drivers' licences received by Transport for London on or after that day) (SI 2003/580)
s 13(3)	1 April 2006 (in relation to applications for London PHV drivers' licences received by Transport for London on or after that day) (SI 2003/580)
s 13(4)–(7)	1 April 2003 (SI 2003/580)
s 14(1), (2)	1 April 2003 (SI 2003/580)
s 14(3)	1 June 2003 (SI 2003/580)
s 14(4)	1 April 2003 (SI 2003/580)
s 14(5)	1 June 2003 (SI 2003/580)
s 15(1)–(3)	22 January 2001 (SI 2000/3144)
s 15(4)	1 April 2003 (SI 2003/580)
s 15(5)	22 January 2001 (SI 2000/3144)
s 16(1), (2)	22 January 2001 (SI 2000/3144)
s 16(3)	8 June 2004 (SI 2004/241)
s 16(4)	1 April 2003 (SI 2003/580)
ss 17–20	22 January 2001 (SI 2000/3144)
s 21(1)	22 January 2001 (SI 2000/3144)
s 21(2)	8 June 2004 (SI 2004/241)
s 21(3)	22 January 2001 (SI 2000/3144)
s 21(4)	22 October 2001 (SI 2000/3144)
s 22(1)	22 January 2001 (SI 2000/3144)
s 22(2)	8 March 2004 (for the purposes of existing private hire vehicles as defined by SI 2004/242, reg 2) (SI 2004/241) 8 April 2004 (for all other purposes) (SI 2004/241)
s 22(3)	1 April 2003 (SI 2003/580)
s 22(4)	22 January 2001 (SI 2000/3144)

Provision	*Date and extent (if any)*
s 22(5), (6)	22 October 2001 (SI 2000/3144)
s 22(7)	8 June 2004 (SI 2004/241)
ss 23–29	22 January 2001 (SI 2000/3144)
s 30	8 June 2004 (SI 2004/241)
s 31	1 June 2003 (SI 2003/580)
ss 32, 33	22 January 2001 (SI 2000/3144)
s 34(1), (2)	22 January 2001 (SI 2000/3144)
s 34(3)	8 March 2004 (for the purposes of existing private hire vehicles as defined by SI 2004/242, reg 2) (SI 2004/241) 8 April 2004 (for all other purposes) (SI 2004/241)
s 35	8 March 2004 (for the purposes of existing private hire vehicles as defined by SI 2004/242, reg 2) (SI 2004/241) 8 April 2004 (for all other purposes) (SI 2004/241)
ss 36–38	22 January 2001 (SI 2000/3144)
s 39(2)	See Sch 2 below
Sch 1	8 June 2004 (SI 2004/241)
Sch 2	1 June 2003 (repeals of or in London Cab Act 1968, s 4; Broadcasting Act 1990; Transport and Works Act 1992) (SI 2003/580) 8 June 2004 (so far as not already in force) (SI 2004/241)

[725]

PRIVATE HIRE VEHICLES (LONDON) (OPERATORS' LICENCES) REGULATIONS 2000
SI 2000/3146

Authority Made by the Secretary of State for the Environment, Transport and the Regions under the Private Hire Vehicles (London) Act 1998, ss 3(4), 4(3), (4), 20(1), (2), 23(1), 32, 37. The functions of the Secretary of State under those provisions of the 1998 Act, except s 37, have been transferred to Transport for London by the Greater London Authority Act 1999, s 254(1), (2), and consequential amendments have been made to those provisions of the 1998 Act by s 254(3) of, and Sch 21 to, the 1999 Act. S 254(4) of the 1999 Act provides that any regulations made, licence issued, authorisation granted, or other thing done under the 1998 Act (other than, inter alia, s 37), by or in relation to the Secretary of State before the coming into force of s 254 has effect as from the commencement of that section as made, issued, granted or done by or in relation to Transport for London (as to the commencement of the said s 254, see SI 2000/3145, SI 2001/3603, noted to SI 1999/3271, in the title Local Government).
Date made 28 November 2000.
Commencement 22 January 2001.
Amendment Amended by the Private Hire Vehicles (London) (Operators' Licences) (Amendment) Regulations 2003, the Private Hire Vehicles (London) (Operators' Licences) (Amendment) Regulations 2004 and the Private Hire Vehicles (London) (Operators' Licences) (Amendment) Regulations 2006. These regulations, which were made by Transport for London, were not made by statutory instrument and are therefore outside the scope of this work.
Summary These regulations make provision for the licensing of private hire vehicle operators in London. Pt I contains general provisions, including interpretation. Pt II prescribes matters relating to applications for the grant or variation of a private hire vehicle operator's licence. Pt III relates to the grant and variation of licences, fees and the conditions to be attached to a licence. Pt IV concerns the keeping and preservation of records. Pt V deals with other matters concerning licences, including the register of licences and replacement licences.

[726]

TRANSPORT TRIBUNAL RULES 2000
SI 2000/3226

Authority Made by the Lord Chancellor under the Transport Act 1985, Sch 4, para 11(1).
Date made 7 December 2000.
Commencement 1 January 2001.
Amendment Amended by SI 2001/4041, SI 2002/643, SI 2008/2142.
Summary These rules, which revoke the Transport Tribunal Rules 1986, SI 1986/1547, subject to savings, made provision concerning:

(a) applications to the Transport Tribunal under the Public Passenger Vehicles Act 1981, s 50(8) and the Goods Vehicles (Licensing of Operators) Act 1995, s 29(3);
(b) appeals to the Tribunal under s 50 of the 1981 Act and s 37 of the 1995 Act;
(c) applications in relation to a stay in driving instructor appeals, and driving instructor appeals, under the Road Traffic Act 1988, s 131;
(d) applications under the Postal Services Act 2000, s 94;
(e) appeals under the Vehicle Drivers (Certificates of Professional Competence) Regulations 2007, SI 2007/605, reg 6A;
(f) general matters relating to the procedure of the Tribunal; and
(g) costs in relation to Tribunal matters.

Following the creation of a new two tier tribunal structure by the Tribunals, Courts and Enforcement Act 2007, Pt 1, specified functions of the Transport Tribunal were transferred on 1 September 2009 to the First-tier Tribunal and the Upper Tribunal, established under s 3 of the 2007 Act; see the Transfer of Functions (Transport Tribunal and Appeal Panel) Order 2009, SI 2009/1885, in the title Courts and Legal Services. The provisions of the enactments in heads (a), (b) above have been amended by SI 2009/1885 so as to transfer the relevant functions of the Transport Tribunal to the Upper Tribunal; and the provisions of the enactments in heads (c)–(e) have been amended by SI 2009/1885 so as to transfer the relevant functions of the Transport Tribunal to the First-tier Tribunal.

As a consequence of the transfer of the relevant functions of the Transport Tribunal to the First-tier Tribunal or the Upper Tribunal, it is thought that these rules are now spent.

It should be noted that SI 2009/1885 does not abolish the Transport Tribunal, which retains jurisdiction to deal with appeals in relation to matters devolved to Scotland. It also retains jurisdiction for appeals relating to quality contracts schemes under the Transport Act 2000, ss 127A, 131E, 131F, 132, 132A, 132B (all inserted by the Local Transport Act 2008, ss 27(1), 35, 36, 38, 39, as from a day to be appointed by order, except s 132, which is amended by s 37 of the 2008 Act, as from a day to be appointed by order).

[727]

TRANSPORT ACT 2000 (COMMENCEMENT NO 1 AND TRANSITIONAL PROVISIONS) ORDER 2000
SI 2000/3229

Authority Made by the Secretary of State for the Environment, Transport and the Regions under the Transport Act 2000, ss 275(1), (2), (3), 276. S 275(3) of the 2000 Act has been repealed by the Statute Law (Repeals) Act 2004, s 1(1), Sch 1, Pt 14.
Date made 7 December 2000.
Summary This order brought various provisions of the Transport Act 2000 into force as set out in the table below. Transitional provision is also made; see the note at the end of the table.
Further orders Further provisions of the Transport Act 2000 were brought into force by SI 2000/3376, SI 2001/57 (as amended by SI 2001/115), SI 2001/242, SI 2001/869, SI 2001/1498, SI 2001/2788 (Wales only), SI 2001/3342 (England only), SI 2002/658 (as amended by SI 2002/846), SI 2002/1014, SI 2002/2024 (Wales only), SI 2003/1694, SI 2005/2862, SI 2006/1933, as set out in the table below. SI 2001/57, SI 2002/658, SI 2002/1014 also make transitional provision; see the note at the end of the table.

Provision	*Date and extent (if any)*
ss 1, 2	1 February 2001 (SI 2001/57)
s 3	1 May 2001 (SI 2001/1498)
ss 4–35	1 February 2001 (SI 2001/57)
ss 36, 37	1 April 2001 (SI 2001/869)
ss 38–96	1 February 2001 (SI 2001/57)
s 97	See Sch 8
ss 98–107	1 February 2001 (SI 2001/57)
ss 108–113	1 February 2001 (England) (SI 2001/57) 1 August 2001 (Wales) (SI 2001/2788)
ss 114–118	1 August 2001 (Wales) (SI 2001/2788) 26 October 2001 (England) (SI 2001/3342)
s 119	1 February 2001 (England) (SI 2001/57) 1 August 2001 (Wales) (SI 2001/2788)
ss 120–123	1 August 2001 (Wales) (SI 2001/2788) 26 October 2001 (England) (SI 2001/3342)
ss 124–127	1 August 2001 (in relation to the powers to make regulations under specified provisions[1]) (Wales) (SI 2001/2788)

Provision	*Date and extent (if any)*
	26 October 2001 (England) (SI 2001/3342)
s 128(1)–(3)	1 August 2001 (in relation to the powers to make regulations under specified provisions[1]) (Wales) (SI 2001/2788) 26 October 2001 (England) (SI 2001/3342)
s 128(4)	1 August 2001 (Wales) (SI 2001/2788) 26 October 2001 (England) (SI 2001/3342)
s 128(5)	1 August 2001 (in relation to the powers to make regulations under specified provisions[1]) (Wales) (SI 2001/2788) 26 October 2001 (England) (SI 2001/3342)
s 129	1 August 2001 (in relation to the powers to make regulations under specified provisions[1]) (Wales) (SI 2001/2788) 26 October 2001 (England) (SI 2001/3342)
s 130(1)–(7)	1 August 2001 (in relation to the powers to make regulations under specified provisions[1]) (Wales) (SI 2001/2788) 26 October 2001 (England) (SI 2001/3342)
s 130(8)	1 August 2001 (Wales) (SI 2001/2788) 26 October 2001 (England) (SI 2001/3342)
s 131(1)	1 August 2001 (in relation to the powers to make regulations under specified provisions[1]) (Wales) (SI 2001/2788) 26 October 2001 (England) (SI 2001/3342)
s 131(2), (3), (4)	1 August 2001 (Wales) (SI 2001/2788) 26 October 2001 (England) (SI 2001/3342)
s 131(5)	1 August 2001 (in relation to the powers to make regulations under specified provisions[1]) (Wales) (SI 2001/2788) 26 October 2001 (England) (SI 2001/3342)
s 132(1)–(5)	1 August 2001 (in relation to the powers to make regulations under specified provisions[1]) (Wales) (SI 2001/2788) 26 October 2001 (England) (SI 2001/3342)
s 132(6)	1 August 2001 (Wales) (SI 2001/2788) 26 October 2001 (England) (SI 2001/3342)
ss 133, 134	1 August 2001 (Wales) (SI 2001/2788) 26 October 2001 (England) (SI 2001/3342)
ss 135–143	1 February 2001 (England) (SI 2001/57) 1 August 2001 (Wales) (SI 2001/2788)
s 144	1 February 2001 (except for the purposes of enabling regulations to be made as respects civil penalties for bus lane contraventions in relation to roads in Greater London) (England) (SI 2001/57) 1 August 2001 (Wales) (SI 2001/2788) 1 April 2002 (in so far as not already in force) (England) (SI 2002/658)
s 145(1)–(3)	1 January 2001 (for the purposes of s 150) (England) (SI 2000/3229) 1 February 2001 (for the purposes of s 145(4), (5), (7), (8)) (England) (SI 2000/3229) 1 June 2001 (in so far as not already in force) (England) (SI 2000/3229) 1 April 2002 (Wales) (SI 2001/2788)
s 145(4), (5)	1 February 2001 (England) (SI 2000/3229) 1 August 2001 (Wales) (SI 2001/2788)

Provision	*Date and extent (if any)*
s 145(6)	1 February 2001 (for the purposes of s 145(4), (5), (7), (8)) (England) (SI 2000/3229) 1 June 2001 (in so far as not already in force) (England) (SI 2000/3229) 1 August 2001 (Wales) (SI 2001/2788)
s 145(7), (8)	1 February 2001 (England) (SI 2000/3229) 1 August 2001 (Wales) (SI 2001/2788)
s 146	1 January 2001 (definition of "travel concession authority", and the remainder thereof, for the purposes of s 150) (England) (SI 2000/3229) 1 February 2001 (definition of "disabled person") (England) (SI 2000/3229) 1 June 2001 (in so far as not already in force) (England) (SI 2000/3229) 1 August 2001 (Wales) (SI 2001/2788)
s 147, 148	1 June 2001 (England) (SI 2000/3229) 1 August 2001 (Wales) (SI 2001/2788)
s 149(1), (2)	1 January 2001 (for the purposes of s 150) (England) (SI 2000/3229) 1 June 2001 (in so far as not already in force) (England) (SI 2000/3229) 1 August 2001 (Wales) (SI 2001/2788)
s 149(3)	1 January 2001 (England) (SI 2000/3229) 1 August 2001 (Wales) (SI 2001/2788)
s 150	1 January 2001 (England) (SI 2000/3229) 1 August 2001 (Wales) (SI 2001/2788)
s 151	1 April 2001 (SI 2000/3229)
s 152	1 February 2001 (England) (SI 2001/57) 1 August 2001 (Wales) (SI 2001/2788)
s 153	See Sch 10
s 154(1)–(5)	1 February 2001 (England) (SI 2001/57) 1 August 2001 (Wales) (SI 2001/2788)
s 154(6)	1 May 2002 (England) (SI 2002/1014) 14 August 2002 (Wales) (SI 2002/2024)
s 155	1 August 2001 (Wales) (SI 2001/2788) 1 May 2002 (England) (SI 2002/1014)
ss 156–160	1 February 2001 (England) (SI 2001/57) 1 August 2001 (Wales) (SI 2001/2788)
s 161	See Sch 11
s 162(1)	1 January 2001 (definition of "travel concession authority") (England) (SI 2000/3229) 1 February 2001 (definition of "disabled person") (England) (SI 2000/3229) 1 June 2001 (definitions of "elderly person", "eligible service", "half-price travel concession" and "relevant time") (England) (SI 2000/3229) 1 February 2001 (except in so far as already brought into force by SI 2000/3229) (England) (SI 2001/57) 1 August 2001 (Wales) (SI 2001/2788)

Provision	*Date and extent (if any)*
s 162(2)	1 June 2001 (in so far as it relates to the meaning of "fares") (England) (SI 2000/3229) 1 February 2001 (except in so far as already brought into force by SI 2000/3229) (England) (SI 2001/57) 1 August 2001 (Wales) (SI 2001/2788)
s 162(3)	1 January 2001 (in so far as it relates to the meaning of "local service") (England) (SI 2000/3229) 1 June 2001 (in so far as it relates to the meaning of "public passenger transport services") (England) (SI 2000/3229) 1 February 2001 (except in so far as already brought into force by SI 2000/3229) (England) (SI 2001/57) 1 August 2001 (Wales) (SI 2001/2788)
s 162(4)	1 February 2001 (England) (SI 2001/57) 1 August 2001 (Wales) (SI 2001/2788)
s 162(5)	1 January 2001 (England) (SI 2000/3229) 1 August 2001 (Wales) (SI 2001/2788)
s 162(6), (7)	1 February 2001 (England) (SI 2001/57) 1 August 2001 (Wales) (SI 2001/2788)
s 163(1)	1 February 2001 (England) (SI 2001/57) 1 August 2001 (in relation to the powers to make regulations under specified provisions[2]) (Wales) (SI 2001/2788)
s 163(2)(a)	1 February 2001 (England) (SI 2001/57) 1 August 2001 (in relation to the powers to make regulations under specified provisions[2]) (Wales) (SI 2001/2788)
s 163(2)(b)	1 February 2001 (England) (SI 2001/57) 1 August 2001 (Wales) (SI 2001/2788)
s 163(3)–(6)	1 February 2001 (England) (SI 2001/57) 1 August 2001 (in relation to the powers to make regulations under specified provisions[2]) (Wales) (SI 2001/2788)
ss 164, 165	1 February 2001 (England) (SI 2001/57) 1 August 2001 (in relation to the powers to make regulations under specified provisions[2]) (Wales) (SI 2001/2788)
s 166	1 February 2001 (England) (SI 2001/57)
s 167	1 February 2001 (England) (SI 2001/57) 1 August 2001 (in relation to the powers to make regulations under specified provisions[2]) (Wales) (SI 2001/2788)
s 168(1), (2)	1 February 2001 (England) (SI 2001/57) 1 August 2001 (in relation to the powers to make regulations under specified provisions[2]) (Wales) (SI 2001/2788)
s 168(3)	1 February 2001 (England) (SI 2001/57) 1 August 2001 (Wales) (SI 2001/2788)
s 168(4)	1 February 2001 (England) (SI 2001/57) 1 August 2001 (in relation to the powers to make regulations under specified provisions[2]) (Wales) (SI 2001/2788)
ss 169–171	1 February 2001 (England) (SI 2001/57) 1 August 2001 (in relation to the powers to make regulations under specified provisions[2]) (Wales) (SI 2001/2788)
s 172(1)	1 February 2001 (England) (SI 2001/57)1 August 2001 (Wales) (SI 2001/2788)
s 172(2)–(4)	1 February 2001 (England) (SI 2001/57)

Provision	*Date and extent (if any)*
	1 August 2001 (in relation to the powers to make regulations under specified provisions[2]) (Wales) (SI 2001/2788)
s 173(1)–(4)	1 February 2001 (England) (SI 2001/57) 1 August 2001 (Wales) (SI 2001/2788)
s 173(5)–(9)	1 February 2001 (England) (SI 2001/57) 1 August 2001 (in relation to the powers to make regulations under specified provisions[2]) (Wales) (SI 2001/2788)
s 174(1), (2)	1 February 2001 (England) (SI 2001/57) 1 August 2001 (Wales) (SI 2001/2788)
s 174(3), (4)	1 February 2001 (England) (SI 2001/57) 1 August 2001 (in relation to the powers to make regulations under specified provisions[2]) (Wales) (SI 2001/2788)
s 174(5)	1 February 2001 (England) (SI 2001/57) 1 August 2001 (Wales) (SI 2001/2788)
s 174(6)	1 February 2001 (England) (SI 2001/57) 1 August 2001 (in relation to the powers to make regulations under specified provisions[2]) (Wales) (SI 2001/2788)
s 175(1)	1 February 2001 (England) (SI 2001/57) 1 August 2001 (Wales) (SI 2001/2788)
s 175(2)–(8)	1 February 2001 (England) (SI 2001/57) 1 August 2001 (in relation to the powers to make regulations under specified provisions[2]) (Wales) (SI 2001/2788)
s 176(1)	1 February 2001 (England) (SI 2001/57) 1 August 2001 (in relation to the powers to make regulations under specified provisions[2]) (Wales) (SI 2001/2788)
s 176(2)	1 February 2001 (England) (SI 2001/57) 1 August 2001 (Wales) (SI 2001/2788)
s 176(3)	1 February 2001 (England) (SI 2001/57) 1 August 2001 (in relation to the powers to make regulations under specified provisions[2]) (Wales) (SI 2001/2788)
s 177	1 February 2001 (England) (SI 2001/57) 1 August 2001 (in relation to the powers to make regulations under specified provisions[2]) (Wales) (SI 2001/2788)
s 178(1)	1 February 2001 (England) (SI 2001/57) 1 August 2001 (in relation to the powers to make regulations under specified provisions[3]) (Wales) (SI 2001/2788)
s 178(2)(a)	1 February 2001 (England) (SI 2001/57) 1 August 2001 (in relation to the powers to make regulations under specified provisions[3]) (Wales) (SI 2001/2788)
s 178(2)(b)	1 February 2001 (England) (SI 2001/57) 1 August 2001 (Wales) (SI 2001/2788)
s 178(3)–(7)	1 February 2001 (England) (SI 2001/57) 1 August 2001 (in relation to the powers to make regulations under specified provisions[3]) (Wales) (SI 2001/2788)
ss 179, 180	1 February 2001 (England) (SI 2001/57) 1 August 2001 (in relation to the powers to make regulations under specified provisions[3]) (Wales) (SI 2001/2788)
s 181	1 February 2001 (England) (SI 2001/57)
s 182(1)–(4)	1 February 2001 (England) (SI 2001/57)

Provision	*Date and extent (if any)*
	1 August 2001 (in relation to the powers to make regulations under specified provisions[3]) (Wales) (SI 2001/2788)
s 182(5)	1 February 2001 (England) (SI 2001/57) 1 August 2001 (Wales) (SI 2001/2788)
s 183(1), (2)	1 February 2001 (England) (SI 2001/57) 1 August 2001 (in relation to the powers to make regulations under specified provisions[3]) (Wales) (SI 2001/2788)
s 183(3)	1 February 2001 (England) (SI 2001/57) 1 August 2001 (Wales) (SI 2001/2788)
s 183(4)	1 February 2001 (England) (SI 2001/57) 1 August 2001 (in relation to the powers to make regulations under specified provisions[3]) (Wales) (SI 2001/2788)
ss 184–186	1 February 2001 (England) (SI 2001/57) 1 August 2001 (in relation to the powers to make regulations under specified provisions[3]) (Wales) (SI 2001/2788)
s 187(1)	1 February 2001 (England) (SI 2001/57) 1 August 2001 (Wales) (SI 2001/2788)
s 187(2)–(4)	1 February 2001 (England) (SI 2001/57) 1 August 2001 (in relation to the powers to make regulations under specified provisions[3]) (Wales) (SI 2001/2788)
s 188	1 February 2001 (England) (SI 2001/57) 1 August 2001 (in relation to the powers to make regulations under specified provisions[3]) (Wales) (SI 2001/2788)
s 189(1), (2)	1 February 2001 (England) (SI 2001/57) 1 August 2001 (Wales) (SI 2001/2788)
s 189(3)(a)	1 February 2001 (England) (SI 2001/57) 1 August 2001 (in relation to the powers to make regulations under specified provisions[3]) (Wales) (SI 2001/2788)
s 189(3)(b)	1 February 2001 (England) (SI 2001/57) 1 August 2001 (Wales) (SI 2001/2788)
s 189(4)	1 February 2001 (England) (SI 2001/57) 1 August 2001 (Wales) (SI 2001/2788)
s 190	1 February 2001 (England) (SI 2001/57) 1 August 2001 (in relation to the powers to make regulations under specified provisions[3]) (Wales) (SI 2001/2788)
s 191	See Sch 12 below
ss 192–198	1 February 2001 (SI 2001/57) 1 August 2001 (Wales) (SI 2001/2788)
s 199	See Sch 13 below
s 200	1 February 2001 (SI 2001/57) 1 August 2001 (Wales) (SI 2001/2788)
ss 201–210	15 January 2001 (SI 2000/3376)
s 211	30 January 2001 (SI 2001/57)
ss 212–215	1 February 2001 (SI 2001/57)
s 216	See Sch 17
s 217	1 February 2001 (SI 2001/57)
s 218	30 January 2001 (SI 2001/57)
ss 219–221	1 February 2001 (SI 2001/57)

Provision	*Date and extent (if any)*
s 222	15 January 2001 (SI 2000/3376)
s 223	15 October 2005 (SI 2005/2862)
ss 224–227	1 February 2001 (SI 2001/57)
s 228	29 July 2003 (SI 2003/1694)
ss 229, 230	1 February 2001 (SI 2001/57)
ss 232–240	1 February 2001 (SI 2001/57)
s 241	15 January 2001 (SI 2000/3376)
ss 242–244	1 February 2001 (SI 2001/57)
s 245(2)	1 February 2001 (except in so far as brought into force by s 275(5)) (SI 2001/57)
s 245(6), (7)	1 February 2001 (SI 2001/57)
s 245(8)	1 February 2001 (except in so far as brought into force by s 275(5)) (SI 2001/57)
ss 246, 247	1 February 2001 (SI 2001/57)
s 248	1 October 2006 (SI 2006/1933)
s 249	1 February 2001 (SI 2001/57)
s 250	15 January 2001 (SI 2000/3376)
s 251	1 February 2001 (SI 2001/57)
s 252	See Sch 27
s 254	30 January 2001 (SI 2001/57)
ss 255, 256	1 February 2001 (SI 2001/57) (amended by SI 2001/115)
s 257	1 May 2002 (SI 2002/1014)
ss 258, 259	1 April 2002 (SI 2002/658)
s 260	See Sch 29
ss 261, 262	1 February 2001 (SI 2001/57) (amended by SI 2001/115)
s 264	1 February 2001 (SI 2001/57) (amended by SI 2001/115)
s 265	1 May 2001 (SI 2001/1498)
s 266	1 February 2001 (SI 2001/57) (amended by SI 2001/115)
s 267(1)	See sub-ss (2)–(8)
s 267(2)	1 April 2002 (SI 2002/658)
s 267(3)	1 February 2001 (for the purposes of making regulations with regard to appeals under Greater London Authority Act 1999, s 189 made after the date on which s 267 of the 2000 Act is fully in force) (England) (SI 2001/57) 1 April 2002 (in so far as not already in force) (SI 2002/658)
s 267(4)	1 April 2002 (SI 2002/658)
s 267(5)	1 February 2001 (for the purposes of making regulations with regard to appeals under Greater London Authority Act 1999, s 189 made after the date on which s 267 of the 2000 Act is fully in force) (England) (SI 2001/57) 1 April 2002 (in so far as not already in force) (SI 2002/658)
s 267(6), (7)	1 April 2002 (SI 2002/658)
s 267(8)	1 February 2001 (for the purposes of making regulations with regard to appeals under Greater London Authority Act 1999, s 189 made after the date on which s 267 of the 2000 Act is fully in force) (England) (SI 2001/57) 1 April 2002 (in so far as not already in force) (SI 2002/658)
s 268	1 February 2001 (SI 2001/57) (amended by SI 2001/115)
s 270	30 January 2001 (SI 2001/57)

Provision	*Date and extent (if any)*
ss 271–273	1 February 2001 (SI 2001/57)
s 274	See Sch 31
Schs 1–3	1 February 2001 (SI 2001/57)
Schs 4, 5	1 April 2001 (SI 2001/869)
Schs 6, 7	1 February 2001 (SI 2001/57)
Sch 8, paras 1, 2	1 February 2001 (SI 2001/57)
Sch 8, paras 3–10	1 April 2001 (SI 2001/869)
Sch 8, paras 11–17	1 February 2001 (SI 2001/57)
Sch 8, para 18	1 April 2001 (SI 2001/869)
Sch 8, para 19	1 February 2001 (SI 2001/57)
Sch 9	1 February 2001 (SI 2001/57)
Sch 10, para 1(1)(a)	26 October 2001 (England) (SI 2001/3342)
Sch 10, para 1(1)(b), (c)	1 February 2001 (England) (SI 2001/57)
	1 August 2001 (Wales) (SI 2001/2788)
Sch 10, para 1(2)(a)	26 October 2001 (England) (SI 2001/3342)
Sch 10, para 1(2)(b), (c)	1 February 2001 (England) (SI 2001/57) 1 August 2001 (Wales) (SI 2001/2788)
Sch 10, paras 2–11	1 February 2001 (England) (SI 2001/57) 1 August 2001 (Wales) (SI 2001/2788)
Sch 10, para 12(1)	1 February 2001 (England) (SI 2001/57) 1 August 2001 (Wales) (SI 2001/2788)
Sch 10, para 12(2)	1 February 2001 (except words "a quality partnership scheme or") (England) (SI 2001/57) 1 August 2001 (except words "a quality partnership scheme or") (Wales) (SI 2001/2788) 26 October 2001 (exception noted above) (England) (SI 2001/3342)
Sch 10, para 12(3)–(5)	1 February 2001 (England) (SI 2001/57) 1 August 2001 (Wales) (SI 2001/2788)
Sch 10, paras 13–16	1 February 2001 (England) (SI 2001/57) 1 August 2001 (Wales) (SI 2001/2788)
Sch 11, para 1	1 August 2001 (Wales) (SI 2001/2788) 26 October 2001 (England) (SI 2001/3342)
Sch 11, paras 2–5	1 February 2001 (England) (SI 2001/57) 1 August 2001 (Wales) (SI 2001/2788)
Sch 11, paras 6–8	1 August 2001 (Wales) (SI 2001/2788) 26 October 2001 (England) (SI 2001/3342)
Sch 11, para 9	1 February 2001 (England) (SI 2001/57) 1 August 2001 (Wales) (SI 2001/2788)
Sch 11, para 10(1)	1 February 2001 (England) (SI 2001/57) 1 August 2001 (Wales) (SI 2001/2788)
Sch 11, para 10(2)	1 August 2001 (Wales) (SI 2001/2788) 26 October 2001 (England) (SI 2001/3342)
Sch 11, para 10(3)	1 February 2001 (England) (SI 2001/57) 1 August 2001 (Wales) (SI 2001/2788)
Sch 11, paras 11–13	1 February 2001 (England) (SI 2001/57) 1 August 2001 (Wales) (SI 2001/2788)

Provision	*Date and extent (if any)*
Sch 11, para 14	1 August 2001 (Wales) (SI 2001/2788) 26 October 2001 (England) (SI 2001/3342)
Sch 11, paras 15–19	1 June 2001 (England) (SI 2000/3229) 1 April 2002 (Wales) (SI 2001/2788)
Sch 11, para 20	1 April 2002 (Wales) (SI 2001/2788)
Sch 11, para 21	1 August 2001 (Wales) (SI 2001/2788) 26 October 2001 (England) (SI 2001/3342)
Sch 11, para 22	1 February 2001 (except for Transport Act 1985, s 111(1)(b), as substituted by para 22) (England) (SI 2001/57) 20 February 2001 (in so far as it relates to the words "operated a local service in contravention of that section" in Transport Act 1985, s 111(1)(b), as substituted by para 22(2)) (England) (SI 2001/242) 1 August 2001 (Wales) (SI 2001/2788) 26 October 2001 (in so far as not already in force) (England) (SI 2001/3342)
Sch 11, para 23	1 April 2001(SI 2000/3229) 1 August 2001 (Wales) (SI 2001/2788)
Schs 12, 13	1 February 2001 (England) (SI 2001/57)
Sch 14	15 January 2001 (SI 2000/3376)
Sch 15	30 January 2001 (SI 2001/57)
Sch 16	1 February 2001 (SI 2001/57) (amended by SI 2001/115)
Sch 17, Pts I, II	1 February 2001 (SI 2001/57)
Sch 17, Pt III	30 January 2001 (SI 2001/57)
Sch 18	1 February 2001 (SI 2001/57)
Sch 19	30 January 2001 (SI 2001/57)
Schs 20–23	1 February 2001 (SI 2001/57)
Sch 25	1 February 2001 (SI 2001/57) (amended by SI 2001/115)
Sch 26	15 January 2001 (SI 2000/3376)
Sch 27, paras 1–15	1 February 2001 (SI 2001/57)
Sch 27, paras 17–49	1 February 2001 (SI 2001/57)
Sch 27, para 50	15 January 2001 (SI 2000/3376)
Sch 27, paras 51–63	1 February 2001 (SI 2001/57)
Sch 29, paras 7–12	1 April 2002 (SI 2002/658)
Sch 30	1 February 2001 (SI 2001/57) (amended by SI 2001/115)
Sch 31, Pt I	1 April 2001 (SI 2001/869)
Sch 31, Pt II	1 February 2001 (entries relating to Transport Act 1968; Transport Act 1983; Local Government Act 1985; Transport Act 1985, except for entries relating to ss 94(4), 104(2), 108(1), 110, 111, 112(2) of that Act) (England) (SI 2001/57) 1 April 2001 (entries relating to Greater London Authority Act 1999) (SI 2000/3229) 1 June 2001 (entries relating to SI 1986/1385, 1989/2293) (England) (SI 2000/3229) 26 October 2001 (entry relating to Transport Act 1985, s 104(2)) (England) (SI 2001/3342) 1 May 2002 (entries relating to Finance Act 1965; Finance Act 1974; Excise Duties (Surcharges or Rebates) Act 1979; Magistrates' Courts Act 1980; Finance Act 1981; Transport Act 1985, ss 94(4), 110, 111, 112(2); Transport Act 2000) (England) (SI 2002/1014)

Provision	*Date and extent (if any)*
	14 August 2002 (Wales) (SI 2002/2024)
Sch 31, Pt III	1 February 2001 (England) (SI 2001/57)
Sch 31, Pt IV	15 January 2001 (entries relating to Railways Act 1993, ss 7(10), 113) (SI 2000/3376) 1 February 2001 (entries relating to British Transport Commission Act 1949; Transport Act 1962, s 1(3); British Transport Commission Act 1962; Harbours Act 1964; Docks and Harbours Act 1966; Parliamentary Commissioner Act 1967; Transport (Grants) Act 1972; House of Commons Disqualification Act 1975, except for entry in Sch 1, Pt II to that Act relating to the British Railways Board; Channel Tunnel Act 1987, ss 40, 42; Transport and Works Act 1992; Railways Act 1993, except for entries relating to ss 7(10), 84–116, 129, Schs 7–9, Sch 12, paras 5, 6(2)–(5), 32; SI 1994/1432; Competition Act 1998; Greater London Authority Act 1999; SI 1999/277, in the title Constitutional Law (Pt 2); and SI 1999/1750, in Pt 3 of that title) (England) (SI 2001/57) 15 October 2005 (entry relating to Railways Act 1993, s 129) (SI 2005/2862)
Sch 31, Pt V	1 April 2002 (entries relating to Road Traffic Act 1988, ss 130, 131(5), Sch 3) (SI 2002/658) (amended by SI 2002/846)

1 The specified provisions are ss 128(4), 130(8), 131(2), (3), (4), 132(6), 133, 134 of the 2000 Act (see paras 2, 3 of Sch 1 to SI 2001/2788)
2 The specified provisions are ss 163(2)(b), 168(3), 172(1), 173(1), (2), (3), (4), 174(1), (2), (5), 175(1), 176(2) of the 2000 Act (see paras 13, 14 of Sch 1 to SI 2001/2788)
3 The specified provisions are ss 178(2)(b), 182(5), 183(3), 187(1), 189(1), (2), (3)(b), (4) of the 2000 Act (see paras 15, 16 of Sch 1 to SI 2001/2788)

Transitional provisions Transitional provisions and savings have been made by the following instruments:

SI 2000/3229 makes the following transitional provision about concessionary travel:

(a) In relation to concessionary travel outside Greater London, a document ("a current permit") which:
   (1) is a document issued by a travel concession authority pursuant to a travel concession scheme made by that authority under the Transport Act 1985, s 93 for the purpose of providing evidence that a person is eligible to receive travel concessions under that scheme,
   (2) has been issued before 1 June 2001, and
   (3) is held on 1 June 2001 by a person who is an elderly or disabled person,

   is to be treated for the purposes of the Transport Act 2000, s 145 as a statutory travel concession permit.
(b) A current permit ceases to be treated as a statutory travel concession permit from the date upon which:
   (1) it ceases to be valid for the purposes of the scheme made by the authority under s 93 of the 1985 Act, or
   (2) the authority issues a statutory travel concession permit to that elderly or disabled person upon an application made under s 145(2) of the 2000 Act, whichever date first occurs.

Notwithstanding that a current permit is treated as a statutory travel concession permit, s 145(2) is not to be construed so as to require the authority which issued it to refund any payment made in respect of the issue of the permit; in relation to concessionary travel in Greater London, SI 2000/3229 provides that for the purposes of the determination to be made by Transport for London under the Greater London Authority Act 1999, s 241(1) immediately before 1 January 2001, the requirements of ss 242 and 243 of that Act referred to in s 241(1)(a), (b) are the requirements imposed by those enactments as amended by s 151 of the 2000 Act.

SI 2001/57 makes the following transitional provision and saving in relation to provisions coming into force on 1 February 2001:

(a) the rights, powers and privileges of any general or local lighthouse authority are not to be prejudiced by, or by any instrument, directions or specifications under, the Transport Act 2000, ss 73–80, 93 or 94;
(b) notwithstanding the amendments made by Sch 27, para 1 to the 2000 Act to the Transport Act 1962, s 43, that section continues to apply to any undertaking of the British Railways Board which commenced before 1 February 2001 or which commences after 1 February 2001 in consequence of any liability incurred before that date.

SI 2001/57, as amended by SI 2001/115, contains the following savings in relation to provisions coming into force on 1 February 2001 as respects England:

(a) notwithstanding the coming into force of s 267(5) of the 2000 Act, the Greater London Authority Act 1999, s 189(7) continues to apply as respects appeals made before the date on which s 267 is fully in force;

(b) the Transport Act 1985, s 111 continues to apply as respects any proceedings under the Public Passenger Vehicles Act 1981, s 54 instigated by a traffic commissioner before 1 February 2001, in respect of the operation of a local service, as if s 158 of, and Sch 11, para 22 to, the 2000 Act had not come into force; and

(c) notwithstanding their repeal under Sch 31, Pt II to the 2000 Act, the Transport Act 1985, ss 89, 90 and 92 continue to apply as respects invitations to tender issued before 1 February 2001.

SI 2002/658 makes the following transitional provision concerning driving instructors:

(a) where, on or before 31 March 2002, the Registrar (i e the person appointed to compile and maintain the register of approved instructors established under the Road Traffic Act 1962, s 23 (and continued by virtue of the Road Traffic Act 1988, s 125) has made any of the following decisions, namely:

  (1) a decision to refuse an application for the retention of a person's name in the register under s 127 of the 1988 Act,

  (2) a decision to remove a person's name from the register under s 128 of the 1988 Act, or

  (3) a decision to revoke a licence under s 130 of the 1988 Act,

and that decision has not (by virtue of the enactments then in force) taken effect by that date, the decision takes effect at the time specified in s 127, 128 or 130 of the 1988 Act, as the case may be, as if those enactments had not been amended by the 2000 Act;

(b) the Road Traffic Act 1988, s 131, Sch 3 as originally enacted continue to apply in respect of an appeal against:

  (1) a decision to which head (a) above applies, and

  (2) a decision made by the Registrar on or before 31 March 2002 to refuse the entry of a person's name in the register under s 125, 125A or 125B of the 1988 Act;

(c) the Transport Act 2000, s 260, in so far as it relates to para 11 of Sch 29, does not come into force in respect of any test of continued ability and fitness to give instruction in the driving of motor cars (or appropriate motor cars), or emergency control assessment, which takes place on or before 31 March 2002.

SI 2002/1014 makes the following transitional provision concerning penalties for unreliable bus services etc:

(1) where, following an inquiry under the Public Passenger Vehicles Act 1981, s 54, a traffic commissioner makes a determination after 30 April 2002 in respect of relevant breaches (see below) occurring wholly before 1 May 2002, the Transport Act 1985, s 111 continues to apply (and the Transport Act 2000, s 155 does not apply) but as if in sub-s (2) for "the day on which the determination under subsection (1) above is made" there were substituted "30th April 2002";

(2) where, following an inquiry under s 54 of the 1981 Act, a traffic commissioner makes a decision after 30 April 2002 to impose a penalty under s 155 of the 2000 Act in respect of relevant breaches (see below) occurring both before 1 May 2002 and on or after that date, the penalty is not to exceed the maximum amount which would have been due from the operator under s 111 of the 1985 Act if the decision in respect of that inquiry had been made on 30 April 2002.

(A reference to a relevant breach is a reference to an operator of a local service, without reasonable excuse, failing to operate a local service registered under the Transport Act 1985, s 6; operating such a service in contravention of that section or the Transport Act 2000, s 118(4) or 129(1)(b); or failing to comply with s 138 or 140(3) of the 2000 Act.)

[728]

LONDON TRANSPORT PENSION ARRANGEMENTS ORDER 2000 SI 2000/3386

Authority Made by the Secretary of State for the Environment, Transport and the Regions under the Greater London Authority Act 1999, ss 405(2), 406(1)(a), (b), 411, Sch 32, paras 3, 6.

Date made 22 December 2000.

Commencement Partly on 29 January 2001; fully on 30 January 2001.

Summary This order provides for the protection of the pension arrangements of persons who are protected persons for the purposes of the Greater London Authority Act 1999, Sch 32, para 3. Under para 3, protected persons are persons who, having been employed by London Regional Transport (dissolved on 16 July 2003 by SI 2003/1913) or one of its subsidiaries, become employees of private sector companies as a result of prescribed relevant transactions.

The order supplements the definition "protected person" by prescribing the transactions as a result of which a person may become a protected person. Provision is made as to the scope of protected rights, by prescribing the LRT Pension Fund as the only pension scheme where membership immediately before the transfer of employment to a private sector company may be protected. Employers of protected persons whose continuity of employment is not broken must provide an occupational pension scheme in which they may participate as contributing members. The scheme must provide benefits which are overall materially at least as good as benefits provided by the LRT Pension Fund in respect of the person's service immediately before he joined the private sector company. Trustees of schemes from which a protected person's pension rights are transferred must pay a transfer value reflecting the value of his protected rights in the old scheme. Employers of protected persons must make contributions to their pension schemes which are adequate to fund their pension rights under this order. This order ceases to have effect as respects a protected person if he voluntarily withdraws from a pension scheme in which he has a right to participate under the order or transfers his pension rights out of it.

The order also provides for the amendment and winding up of the London Transport (Male Wages Grades) Pension Scheme and the amendment of the LRT Pension Fund.

[729]

MOTOR VEHICLES (APPROVAL) REGULATIONS 2001
SI 2001/25

Authority Made by the Secretary of State for the Environment, Transport and the Regions under the Road Traffic Act 1988, ss 54, 61, 63, 66.
Date made 9 January 2001.
Commencement 1 February 2001.
Amendment Amended by SI 2004/623, SI 2009/815.
Summary These regulations revoke and replace the Motor Vehicles (Approval) Regulations 1996, SI 1996/3013, and the amending SI 1997/1366, SI 1997/2934, SI 1998/1008, SI 1999/2082, SI 1999/3226, SI 2000/1972. They establish a revised system for approving the construction of single vehicles before they enter into service. The regulations apply to passenger vehicles and dual-purpose vehicles constructed to carry no more than eight passengers excluding the driver, certain three wheeled vehicles having a maximum unladen weight of more than 410 kg (ie not motor cycles), light goods vehicles (maximum gross weight not exceeding 3,500 kg) and certain other goods vehicles with a design gross weight not exceeding 5,500 kg.

Pt II of the regulations concerns the approval requirements. By reg 4(1), the regulations apply to:

(a) every motor vehicle within category M1 which is a special purpose vehicle within the meaning of Annex II to the Framework Directive (Directive 2007/46/EC of the European Parliament and of the Council establishing a framework for the approval of motor vehicles and their trailers, and of systems, components and separate technical units intended for such vehicles (OJ L263, 09.10.2007, p 1)), and

(b) every motor vehicle to which SI 1982/1271 applies which has a design gross weight not exceeding 3,500 kg or complies with the requirements of reg 4(2).

The requirements of reg 4(2) are that the vehicle:

(a) has a design gross weight exceeding 3,500 kg but not exceeding 5,500 kg;

(b) has a kerbside weight not exceeding 3,425 kg; and

(c) belongs to the same family of types as at least one vehicle to which these regulations apply by virtue of reg 4(1) and which has been granted a minister's approval certificate on the basis that it complies with the approval requirements by virtue of these regulations or the said SI 1996/3013 (revoked).

Reg 5 specifies two sets of approval requirements, namely basic requirements (Sch 3) and enhanced requirements (Sch 4). However, vehicles which do not fall within the special classes specified in Sch 2 and which have complied with the enhanced requirements in Sch 4 do not have to comply with the basic requirements in Sch 3 (with an exception for disabled person's vehicles and certain adapted vehicles, which must comply with requirements relating to seat belt anchorages). In addition, certain basic and enhanced requirements do not apply to goods vehicles.

Pt III deals with miscellaneous administrative arrangements. Reg 6 relates to applications to the Secretary of State for a minister's approval certificate. Reg 7 provides for the assignment of vehicle identification numbers to vehicles not having a number which meets the requirements specified in reg 7(1). Criteria for determining design weights are specified by reg 8. Reg 9 sets out the procedure for appeals under the Road Traffic Act 1988, s 60 by persons aggrieved by a determination made by the Secretary of State following an application under reg 6. Reg 10 provides for an application or appeal to be refused without an examination of the vehicle to which the application relates in specified circumstances. Reg 11 and Sch 5 prescribe the form of minister's approval certificate. Reg 12 relates to replacement certificates. Provision concerning notices under the regulations is made by reg 13. Reg 14 appoints 1 February 2001 for the purposes of s 63(1) of the 1988 Act, on or after which it is an offence to use a vehicle of a prescribed class without the appropriate certificate in force under ss 54–58 thereof. This applies for all vehicles to which these regulations apply which are not of a class for which a day had previously been appointed. The requirement imposed by reg 14 is disapplied in respect of specified types of vehicle or types of use. Reg 15 provides that a licence under the Vehicle Excise and Registration Act 1994 is not to be granted in respect of a vehicle to which reg 14 applies unless, in the first application made for it after the relevant appointed day, evidence is produced that a certificate (or certificates) is in force for the vehicle under ss 54–58 of the 1988 Act from which it appears that the vehicle complies with the approval requirements.
Fees SI 2001/2486 (as amended by SI 2007/495, SI 2008/1443, SI 2009/863), was made under the Road Traffic Act 1988, s 61(1), (2), SI 1988/643 and the Finance Act 1990, s 128, and came into force on 1 August 2001. These regulations, which revoke and replace the Motor Vehicles (Approval) (Fees) Regulations 1997, SI 1997/1459, prescribe the fees payable in connection with applications and appeals made in accordance with SI 2001/25. They also prescribe the fee payable for the replacement of a minister's approval certificate which has been lost or defaced and make provision for the repayment of fees in certain circumstances.

[730]

GRADUATED VEHICLE EXCISE DUTY (PRESCRIBED TYPES OF FUEL) REGULATIONS 2001
SI 2001/93

Authority Made by the Secretary of State for the Environment, Transport and the Regions, with the consent of the Treasury, under the Vehicle Excise and Registration Act 1994, Sch 1, Pt 1A, paras 1C(2), 1F. Para 1C(2) has been substituted by the Finance Act 2006, s 13(1), (4)(a), but not so as to affect these regulations.

Date made 18 January 2001.

Commencement 15 February 2001.

Summary These regulations prescribe the types of fuel by which vehicles must be propelled in order to qualify for the reduced rate of vehicle excise duty prescribed for certain light passenger vehicles first registered on or after 1 March 2001 by the Vehicle Excise and Registration Act 1994, Sch 1, Pt 1A, para 1C. Under the regulations, vehicles propelled solely by road fuel gas, and those capable of being propelled both by petrol and road fuel gas or by electricity and either petrol or diesel, qualify for the reduced rate.

[731]

STRATEGIC RAIL AUTHORITY (CAPITAL ALLOWANCES) ORDER 2001
SI 2001/262

Authority Made by the Secretary of State for the Environment, Transport and the Regions under the Transport Act 2000, Sch 26, Pt II, para 5, Pt III, para 13.

Date made 26 January 2001.

Commencement 1 February 2001.

Summary This order makes provision relating to the expenditure which the Strategic Rail Authority (see below), for the purposes of capital allowances under the Corporation Tax Acts, is to be taken as having incurred on certain plant and machinery which is transferred to it under provisions in the Transport Act 2000, Pt IV (which are repealed as noted below). The order prescribes £470,600 as the amount of capital expenditure which the Authority is to be taken as having incurred on certain plant and machinery which is transferred to it from the Franchising Director by virtue of s 215 of the 2000 Act. The order also provides a mechanism for the determination of the amount of expenditure which the Strategic Rail Authority is, for capital allowances purposes, to be taken as having incurred on the plant and machinery which was transferred to it from the British Railways Board by virtue of para 11 of Pt II of Sch 18 to the 2000 Act (transfer of property etc relating to the British Transport Police) (repealed). The amount is that determined by the Secretary of State to be equivalent to the plant and machinery capital allowances "pool" attributable to the British Transport Police activities (calculated on the notional basis that these had at all times been treated separately from the remainder of the Board's activities) in the British Railways Board immediately prior to the transfer.

The Railways and Transport Safety Act 2003, Pt 3 creates an independent police authority for the British Transport Police Force and transfers responsibility for that Force from the Strategic Rail Authority to the new British Transport Police Authority; see further the Preliminary Note "British Transport Police" (under the main head "Railways, tramways and inland waterways").

Strategic Rail Authority Provision for the transfer of functions and abolition of the Strategic Rail Authority is made by the Railways Act 2005, s 1, Sch 1. The Transport Act 2000, Pt IV, Chapter I (ss 201–222 and Schs 14–21) related specifically to the Strategic Rail Authority; the said Chapter I is largely repealed by ss 1(1), 59(6) of, and para 36 of Sch 1 and Pt 1 of Sch 13 to, the 2005 Act. See further the Preliminary Note "Privatisation of the railway system" (under main head "Reorganisation of transport undertakings").

[732]

ROAD VEHICLES (DISPLAY OF REGISTRATION MARKS) REGULATIONS 2001
SI 2001/561

Authority Made by the Secretary of State for the Environment, Transport and the Regions under the Vehicle Excise and Registration Act 1994, ss 23(3), (4), 57.

Date made 26 February 2001.

Commencement Partly on 21 March 2001 and fully on 1 September 2001; see reg 1(1).

Amendment Printed as amended by SI 2001/1079, SI 2002/2687, SI 2009/811.

Interpretation See reg 2.

General Under the Vehicle Excise and Registration Act 1994, s 23, where the Secretary of State registers a vehicle under s 21(1) of that Act he must assign a registration mark to the vehicle indicating the registered number of the vehicle. These regulations, which revoke and replace the Road Vehicles (Registration and Licensing) Regulations 1971, SI 1971/450, regs 17–22, Schs 2, 3, and reg 6 of the amending SI 1972/1865 (both wholly revoked by SI 2002/2742), and wholly revoke and replace the amending SI 1975/1089, SI 1984/814, make new provision in respect of the fixing and lighting of registration plates on vehicles and for the format of registration marks.

Application of previous regulations to visiting vehicles By SI 1985/610, reg 8(1), (3), which relates to visiting vehicles (ie vehicles brought temporarily into Great Britain by a person resident outside the United Kingdom), the Road Vehicles (Registration and Licensing) Regulations 1971, SI 1971/450, regs 17, 20, 22, Schs 2, 3 (revoked and replaced by SI 2001/561) were applied, with modifications, to a vehicle exempt from excise duty by virtue of SI 1975/1208. The said reg 17, Sch 2 concerned the size, shape and character of registration marks required to be fitted on a vehicle; reg 20, Sch 3 related to the exhibition of registration marks on certain vehicles registered before 1 October 1938; and reg 22 concerned the registration mark to be fixed to a trailer or rearmost trailer attached to a mechanically propelled vehicle.

[733]

PART I
PRELIMINARY

Citation, commencement and revocation

1 (1) These Regulations may be cited as the Road Vehicles (Display of Registration Marks) Regulations 2001 and shall come into force—

(a) for the purposes of this paragraph and regulation 17, on 21st March 2001, and

(b) for all other purposes, on 1st September 2001.

(2) The regulations specified in Schedule 1 are hereby revoked.

[734]

Interpretation: general

2 (1) In these Regulations the following expressions shall have the following meanings—

"the Act" means the Vehicle Excise and Registration Act 1994;

"agricultural machine" means a vehicle which is—

(a) an agricultural tractor, as defined in paragraph 4B(2) of Schedule 1 to the Act, or

(b) an off-road tractor, as defined in paragraph 4B(4) of that Schedule, or

(c) a light agricultural vehicle, as defined in paragraph 4C(2) of that Schedule, or

(d) an agricultural engine, or

(e) a mowing machine;

...

"EEA State" means a state which is a contracting party to the Agreement on the European Economic Area signed at Oporto on 2nd May 1992 as adjusted by the Protocol signed at Brussels on 17th March 1993;

"motor cycle" means a vehicle having 2 wheels and includes a vehicle of that description in combination with a sidecar;

"motor tricycle" means a vehicle having 3 wheels symmetrically arranged;

"quadricycle" means a vehicle having four wheels, a maximum net engine power not exceeding 15 kilowatts and an unladen mass (excluding the mass of batteries in the case of an electrically-powered vehicle) not exceeding—

(a) 550 kilograms in the case of a goods vehicle, and

(b) 400 kilograms in any other case;

"registration plate" means a plate or other device displaying the registration mark of the vehicle[, but does not include such part of a plate or device as is intended for the display of material specified in regulation 16(3) and (4)];

"prescribed font" means the style shown in Schedule 4 for a character of the height specified in that Schedule;

"relevant date" means—

(a) in Great Britain, 1st October 1938, and

(b) in Northern Ireland, 1st January 1948;

"works truck" means a vehicle which is—

(a) designed for use in private premises, and

(b) used on public roads only—

(i) for carrying goods between private premises and a vehicle on a road in the immediate vicinity, or

(ii) in passing from one part of private premises to another or between private premises and other private premises in the immediate vicinity, or

(iii) in connection with road works at or in the immediate vicinity of the site of the works.

(2) Unless the context otherwise requires, a reference in these Regulations to—

(a) a registration plate fixed or to be fixed to a vehicle, or

(b) a registration mark displayed or to be displayed on a plate,

is to be construed, where the vehicle is towing a trailer, so as to include a reference to the registration plate which is required under these Regulations to be fixed to the trailer or a reference to the mark displayed on the plate fixed to that trailer.

NOTES

Amendment Para (1): definitions "the Council Regulation" and "dual purpose plate" (omitted) revoked by SI 2009/811;
in definition "registration plate" words in square brackets substituted by SI 2009/811.

Agreement on the European Economic Area signed at Oporto on 2nd May 1992 Cm 2073; OJ L1, 03.01.1994, p 1.

Protocol signed at Brussels on 17th March 1993 Cm 2183; OJ L1, 03.01.1994, p 572.

Paras 4B, 4C of Sch 1 to the Act Repealed by the Finance Act 2001, ss 13(3), 110, Sch 33, Pt 1(3). "Agricultural tractor", "off-road tractor" and "light agricultural vehicle" are now defined by the Vehicle Excise and Registration Act 1994, Sch 2, paras 20B(2), (4), 20C(2) respectively.

[735]

Exempt vehicles

3 Nothing in these Regulations applies to—

(a) an invalid vehicle, that is a vehicle the unladen weight of which does not exceed 254 kilograms and which is specially designed and constructed, and not merely adapted, for the use of a person suffering from a physical disability and solely used by that person; or

(b) a pedestrian-controlled vehicle, that is a vehicle the unladen weight of which does not exceed 450 kilograms which is neither constructed nor adapted for the carriage of a driver or passenger.

[736]

PART II
REGISTRATION PLATES

NOTES

Application of previous regulations to visiting vehicles See the note at the beginning of these regulations.

Interpretation of Part II

4 In this Part the following expressions shall have the following meanings—

"diagonal length", in relation to a relevant area, means the length of a line drawn diagonally across the square enclosing the area (so that the extent of the relevant area is thereby delimited);

"relevant area", in relation to a registration plate, means the area contained in a square described on the ground—

(a) in front of the vehicle in the case of a plate fixed on the front of the vehicle, and

(b) behind the vehicle in the case of a plate fixed on the rear of the vehicle,

where one corner of the square is immediately below the middle of the plate and the diagonal of the square from that corner is parallel to the longitudinal axis of the vehicle;

"relevant type-approval directive" means—

(a) in the case of a motor cycle, motor tricycle or quadricycle—

(i) Council Directive 93/94/EEC (as amended by Commission Directive 99/26/EC) as regards the space to be provided for fixing of the rear registration plate, and

(ii) Council Directive 93/92/EEC as regards the rear registration plate lamp;

(b) in the case of any other vehicle or a trailer—

(i) Council Directive 70/222/EEC as regards the space to be provided for fixing of the rear registration plate, and

(ii) Council Directive 76/760/EEC (as amended by Commission Directive 97/31/EC) as regards the rear registration plate lamp.

NOTES

Council Directive 70/222/EEC OJ L76, 06.04.1970, p 25.

Council Directive 76/760/EEC (as amended by Commission Directive 97/31/EC) OJ L262, 27.09.1976, p 85; OJ L171, 30.06.1997, p 49.

Council Directive 93/92/EEC OJ L311, 14.12.1993, p 1.

Council Directive 93/94/EEC (as amended by Commission Directive 99/26/EC) OJ L311, 14.12.1993, p 83; OJ L118, 06.05.1999, p 32.

[737]

Fixing of rear registration plates: vehicles registered on or after the relevant date

5 (1) This regulation applies to vehicles, other than works trucks, road rollers and agricultural machines, first registered on or after the relevant date.

(2) A registration plate must be fixed on the rear of—

(a) the vehicle, or

(b) where the vehicle is towing a trailer, the trailer, or

(c) where the vehicle is towing more than one trailer, the rearmost trailer.

(3) Where a vehicle (or, in a case where the plate is required to be fixed on a trailer, that trailer) has been constructed so as to satisfy the requirements of the relevant type-approval directive, whether or not it is required by law to satisfy them, the plate may be fixed in the space provided in accordance with those requirements but if it is not so fixed it must be fixed in the manner required by paragraph (5).

(4) Except as provided in paragraph (3) the plate must be fixed in the manner required by paragraph (5).

(5) This paragraph requires the plate to be fixed—

(a) vertically or, where that is not reasonably practicable, in a position as close to the vertical as is reasonably practicable, and

(b) in such a position that in normal daylight the characters of the registration mark are easily distinguishable from every part of a relevant area having the diagonal length specified in paragraph (6).

(6) The diagonal length of the relevant area is—

(a) in the case of a mark having characters the width of which is at least 57 millimetres, 22 metres,

(b) in the case of a mark having characters the width of which is 50 millimetres, 21.5 metres,

(c) in the case of a mark having characters the width of which is 44 millimetres, 18 metres.

[738]

Fixing of front registration plates: vehicles registered on or after the relevant date

6 (1) This regulation applies to vehicles, other than works trucks, road rollers and agricultural machines, first registered on or after the relevant date.

(2) Except as provided in paragraph (5), a registration plate must be fixed on the front of the vehicle in the manner required by paragraph (3).

(3) This paragraph requires the plate to be fixed—

(a) vertically or, where that is not reasonably practicable, in a position as close to the vertical as is reasonably practicable,

(b) in such a position that in normal daylight the characters of the registration mark are easily distinguishable from every part of a relevant area having the diagonal length specified in paragraph (4).

(4) The diagonal length of the relevant area is—

(a) in the case of a mark having characters the width of which is at least 57 millimetres, 22 metres,

(b) in the case of a mark having characters the width of which is 50 millimetres, 21.5 metres,

(c) in the case of a mark having characters the width of which is 44 millimetres, 18 metres.

(5) In the case of a motor cycle or a motor tricycle which does not have a body of a type which is characteristic of the body of a four-wheeled vehicle—

(a) a registration plate must not be fixed on the front of a vehicle if it was first registered on or after 1st September 2001,

(b) a plate need not be fixed on the front of the vehicle if it was first registered before 1st September 2001.

[739]

Fixing of registration plates: vehicles registered before the relevant date

7 (1) This regulation applies to vehicles, other than works trucks, road rollers and agricultural machines, first registered before the relevant date.

(2) Except as provided in paragraph (4), a registration plate must be fixed in the manner required by paragraph (3) on—

(a) the front of the vehicle, and

(b) the rear of—

(i) the vehicle or,

(ii) where the vehicle is towing a trailer, the trailer or,

(iii) where the vehicle is towing more than one trailer, the rearmost trailer.

(3) This paragraph requires each plate to be fixed—

(a) in a vertical position or, where that is not possible, in a position as close to the vertical as is reasonably practicable, and

(b) in such a position that in normal daylight the characters of the registration mark are easily distinguishable, in the case of a plate fixed on the front of the vehicle, from in front of the vehicle and, in the case of a plate fixed on the rear of the vehicle or trailer, from behind the vehicle or trailer.

(4) In the case of a motor cycle and a motor tricycle which does not have a body of a type which is characteristic of the body of a four-wheeled vehicle, a registration plate need not be fixed on the front of the vehicle.

[740]

Fixing of registration plates: works trucks, road rollers and agricultural machines

8 (1) This regulation applies to works trucks, road rollers and agricultural machines.

(2) A registration plate must be fixed on the vehicle in a vertical position or, where that is not possible, in a position as close to the vertical as is reasonably practicable—

(a) on both sides of the vehicles, so that the characters of the mark are easily distinguishable from both sides of the vehicle, or

(b) on the rear of the vehicle, so that the characters of the mark are easily distinguishable from behind the vehicle, or

(c) where the vehicle is towing a trailer or trailers and the plate is not fixed on the sides of the vehicle, on the trailer or the rearmost trailer (as the case may be) so that the characters of the mark are easily distinguishable from behind the trailer.

(3) Where the towing vehicle is an agricultural machine, a plate fixed on the trailer may, instead of displaying the registration mark of the towing vehicle, display the mark of any other agricultural machine kept by the keeper of the towing vehicle.

[741]

Lighting of rear registration plates

9 (1) This regulation applies to vehicles other than—

(a) works trucks,

(b) road rollers,
(c) agricultural machines, and
(d) vehicles first registered before the relevant date.

(2) Where the vehicle is being used on a road between sunset and sunrise the registration plate fixed on the rear of—

(a) the vehicle, or
(b) where the vehicle is towing a trailer, the trailer or,
(c) where the vehicle is towing more than one trailer, the rearmost trailer,

must be lit in accordance with this regulation.

(3) Where a vehicle (or, in a case where the plate is required to be fixed on a trailer, that trailer) has been constructed so as to satisfy the requirements of the relevant type-approval directive, whether or not it is required by law to satisfy them, that plate may be lit by a lamp which complies with those requirements but if it is not so lit it must be lit in the manner required by paragraph (5).

(4) Except as provided in paragraph (3) that plate must be lit in the manner required by paragraph (5).

(5) This paragraph requires the plate to be lit so that it is easily distinguishable from every part of a relevant area having a diagonal length—

(a) in the case of a plate displaying a mark having characters with a width of 44 millimetres, of 15 metres, and
(b) in any other case, of 18 metres.

[742]

Specifications for registration plates

10 (1) A registration mark must be displayed on a registration plate conforming to the requirements prescribed by this regulation.

(2) In the case of a vehicle first registered on or after 1st September 2001 the registration plate must conform to the requirements set out in Part 1 of Schedule 2.

(3) Subject to paragraph (4), in the case of a vehicle first registered on or after 1st January 1973 but before 1st September 2001 the registration plate must conform either to the requirements set out in Part 2 of Schedule 2 or to the requirements set out in Part 1 of that Schedule.

(4) Where on or after 1st September 2001 a new registration plate is fixed to a vehicle to which paragraph (3) applies to replace a plate previously fixed thereto, the plate must conform to the requirements set out in Part 1 of Schedule 2.

(5) In the case of a vehicle first registered before 1st January 1973, the registration plate must conform either to one of the requirements set out in Part 3 of Schedule 2 or to the requirements set out in Part 2 of that Schedule or to the requirements set out in Part 1 of that Schedule.

(6) The corners of a registration plate may be rounded off provided that the requirements of regulation 14(9) (margins around registration marks) are not thereby infringed.

[743]

Further requirements for registration plates

11 (1) No reflex-reflecting material may be applied to any part of a registration plate and the plate must not be treated in such a way that the characters of the registration mark become, or are caused to act as, retroreflective characters.

[(1A) The surface of a registration plate must not comprise or incorporate any design, pattern or texture, or be treated in any way which gives to any part of the plate the appearance of a design, pattern or texture.]

(2) A registration plate must not be treated in any other way which renders the characters of the registration mark less easily distinguishable to the eye or which would prevent or impair the making of a true photographic image of the plate through the medium of camera and film or any other device.

(3) A registration plate must not be fixed to a vehicle—

(a) by means of a screw, bolt or other fixing device of any type or colour,
(b) by the placing of a screw, bolt or other fixing device in any position, or

(c) in any other manner,

which has the effect of changing the appearance or legibility of any of the characters of the registration mark, which renders the characters of the registration mark less easily distinguishable to the eye or which prevents or impairs the making of a true photographic image of the plate through the medium of camera and film or any other device.

(4) Section 59(2)(a) of the Act (regulations the contravention of which attracts a level 3 fine) applies to paragraphs (1), (2) and (3) of this regulation.

NOTES

Amendment Para (1A): inserted by SI 2002/2687.

[744]

PART III
REGISTRATION MARKS

NOTES

Application of previous regulations to visiting vehicles See the note at the beginning of these regulations.

Interpretation of Part III

12 (1) In this Part and in Schedule 3, the following expressions shall have the following meanings—

(a) "diagram" means a diagram shown in Part 2 of Schedule 3 and a reference to a numbered diagram is a reference to the diagram identified by that number in that part of that Schedule,

(b) "Table A" means the table in Part 1 of Schedule 3,

(c) "Table B" means the table in Part 3 of Schedule 3,

(d) a reference to "relevant character height"[, except in relation to a vehicle to which regulation 14A applies,] is a reference to the height of the characters in the registration mark shown at the head of column (2), (3) or (4) of Table B as the case may be.

(2) Any provision as to measurement contained in this Part or in Schedule 3 shall be taken to be complied with—

(a) in the case of a provision prescribing character height, if the height of the character is not more than 1 millimetre more or less than the measurement prescribed herein, and

(b) in the case of a provision prescribing any other dimension, if the dimension of the character or the space in question is not more than 0.5 millimetres more or less than the measurement prescribed herein.

(3) For the purpose of any provision contained in this Part or in Schedule 3 as to the spacing between characters or between groups of characters or as to the width of a margin the measurement shall be made—

(a) in the case of a horizontal spacing requirement, between vertical lines passing through the extreme edges of each character or group of characters or between a vertical line passing through the extreme edge of a character and the lateral edge of the plate (as the case may be), and

(b) in the case of a vertical spacing requirement, between horizontal lines passing through the extreme edges of each group of characters or between a horizontal line passing through the extreme edge of a group of characters and the top or bottom edge of the plate (as the case may be).

NOTES

Amendment Para (1)(d): words in square brackets inserted by SI 2002/2687.

[745]

Layout of marks

13 (1) Subject to paragraphs (2) and (3), a registration mark of a description specified in column (1) of Table A must be laid out on the registration plate in conformity with one of the diagrams specified in relation to that description in column (2) of Table A.

(2) A mark displayed on a motor cycle may not be laid out in conformity with diagram 1a, 2a, 3a, 4a, 5a, 6a, 7a, 8a or 9a.

(3) A mark may not be laid out in conformity with diagram 2c, 3c, 4b or 7b if it is displayed on—

(a) a registration plate fixed to a vehicle first registered on or after 1st September 2001, or

(b) a new registration plate fixed to a vehicle on or after 1st September 2001 to replace a plate previously fixed thereto (except where the vehicle was first registered before 1st January 1973).

[746]

Size and spacing of characters

14 (1) Except in the cases mentioned in paragraphs (2) and (3) [and regulation 14A], each character in a registration mark must be 79 millimetres high.

(2) In the case of a registration mark displayed on a vehicle first registered before 1st September 2001, a character in a registration mark may be 89 millimetres high unless—

(a) the vehicle was first registered on or after 1st January 1973 and the mark is displayed on a new registration plate fixed to the vehicle to replace a plate previously fixed thereto, or

(b) the vehicle is a motor cycle, motor tricycle, quadricycle, agricultural machine, works truck or road roller.

(3) In the case of a registration mark fixed on a motor cycle, motor tricycle, quadricycle, agricultural machine, works truck or road roller, each character of the mark may be 64 millimetres high.

(4) [Subject to regulation 14A, the] width of each character of a mark other than the letter "I" and the figure "1" must be—

(a) in the case of a mark displayed—

(i) on a registration plate fixed to a vehicle first registered on or after 1st September 2001, or

(ii) on a new registration plate fixed to a vehicle on or after 1st September 2001 to replace a plate previously fixed thereto (except where the vehicle was first registered before 1st January 1973),

that shown in line 1 ofTable B in relation to the relevant character height,

(b) in any other case, that shown in line 2 of Table B in relation to the relevant character height.

(5) [Subject to regulation 14A, the] width of every part of the stroke forming a character in a mark must be that shown in line 3 ofTable B in relation to the relevant character height.

(6) Except in a case to which paragraph (11) [or regulation 14A] applies, the spacing between any two characters within a group must be that shown in line 4 of Table B in relation to the relevant character height.

(7) [Subject to regulation 14A, the] horizontal spacing between groups of characters in a mark must be that shown in line 5 ofTable B in relation to the relevant character height.

(8) [Subject to regulation 14A, the] vertical spacing between groups of characters must be that shown in line 6 of Table B in relation to the relevant character height.

(9) [Subject to regulation 14A, the] width of a margin between the mark and the top, bottom and lateral edges of the registration plate must be not less than that shown in line 7 of Table B in relation to the relevant character height.

(10) Paragraph (11) applies where—

(a) one or both of the characters is "I" or "1",

(b) those characters are either 79 millimetres or 89 millimetres high,

(c) the mark is displayed on a vehicle first registered before 1st September 2001,

(d) the registration plate displaying the mark was fixed to the vehicle before 1st September 2001 or, if that is not the case, the vehicle was first registered before 1st January 1973 and,

(e) the plate is made of cast or pressed metal with raised characters.

(11) Where this paragraph applies the spacing between—

[(a)] two characters one of which is "I" or "1" must be within the limits shown in line 8 of Table B in relation to the relevant character height, and

[(b)] two characters both of which are "I" or "1" must be within the limits shown in line 9 of Table B in relation to the relevant character height,

but where one or more characters in a group is "I" or "1" all the characters within that group must be evenly spaced.

NOTES

Amendment Para (1): words in square brackets inserted by SI 2002/2687.
Paras (4), (5): words in square brackets substituted by SI 2002/2687.
Para (6): words in square brackets inserted by SI 2002/2687.
Paras (7)–(9): words in square brackets substituted by SI 2002/2687.
Para (11): letters "(a)" and "(b)" in square brackets substituted by SI 2001/1079.

[747]

[Size and spacing of characters: special cases

14A (1) This regulation applies in relation to any vehicle imported into the United Kingdom which—

(a) does not have European Community Whole Vehicle Type Approval; and

(b) is so constructed that the area available for the fixing of the registration plate precludes the display on the plate of a registration mark in conformity with the requirements of regulation 14.

(2) In relation to a vehicle to which this regulation applies—

(a) each character in the registration mark must be 64 millimetres high;

(b) the width of each character of the mark, other than the letter "I" and the figure "1", must be 44 millimetres;

(c) the width of every part of the stroke forming a character in a mark must be 10 millimetres;

(d) the spacing between any two characters within a group must be 10 millimetres;

(e) the vertical spacing between groups of characters must be 5 millimetres;

(f) the width of a margin between the mark and the top and lateral sides of the registration plate must be not less than 5 millimetres;

(g) the space between the bottom of the mark and the bottom of the registration plate must be not less than 13 millimetres; but, within that space, the space between the bottom of the mark and the top of the name and postcode of the person by whom the plate was supplied must be not less than 5 millimetres.]

NOTES

Amendment Inserted by SI 2002/2687.

[748]

Style of characters

15 (1) In the case of a registration mark displayed—

(a) on a registration plate fixed to a vehicle first registered on or after 1st September 2001, or

(b) on a new registration plate fixed to a vehicle on or after 1st September 2001 to replace a plate previously fixed thereto (except where the vehicle was first registered before 1st January 1973),

each of the characters of the mark must be in the prescribed font.

(2) Except in a case to which paragraph (1) applies, each of the characters of the registration mark must either be in the prescribed font or in a style which is substantially similar to the prescribed font so that the character is easily distinguishable and in particular, but without prejudice to the generality of those requirements, characters must not be formed in any way described in paragraph (4) or in a manner which is similar to any of those ways.

(3) For the purposes of paragraph (2), a character shall not be treated as being in a style which is not substantially similar to the prescribed font merely by virtue of the fact that it has, or does not have, serifs.

(4) The ways of forming characters referred to in paragraph (2) are their formation—

(a) in italic script,
(b) using a font, other than italic script, in which the characters are not vertical,
(c) using a font in which the curvature or alignment of the lines of the stroke is substantially different from the prescribed font,
(d) using multiple strokes,
(e) using a broken stroke,
(f) in such a way as to make a character or more than one character appear like a different character or characters.

[749]

PART IV
MISCELLANEOUS

[International distinguishing signs and other material

16 (1) No material other than a registration mark and material complying with the requirements of any of the relevant standards mentioned in Schedule 2 may be displayed on a registration plate.

(2) Subject to the following paragraphs of this regulation, a registration plate may not be combined with any other plate or a device of any kind.

(3) The letters "GB" may be displayed on a plate or other device in accordance with the Annex to Council Regulation (EC) No 2411/98 on the recognition in intra-Community traffic of the distinguishing sign of the Member State in which motor vehicles and their trailers are registered.

(4) Subject to paragraphs (5) to (8), there may be displayed on a plate or other device an arrangement of letters corresponding with one of the sub-paragraphs of paragraph (9) and an emblem corresponding with one of the sub-paragraphs of paragraph (10).

(5) The arrangement of letters and emblem referred to in paragraph (4)—

(a) must be displayed to the left of the registration plate;
(b) must not encroach into the margin,

and for this purpose the expression "margin" is to have the same meaning as in regulations 14(9) and 14A(2)(f).

(6) The emblem referred to in paragraph (4) must be positioned above the arrangement of letters referred to in that paragraph.

(7) Neither the arrangement of letters referred to in paragraph (4), nor the emblem referred to in that paragraph, must be more than fifty millimetres wide.

(8) Paragraph (4) does not apply—

(a) if the letters "GB" are displayed in accordance with paragraph (3); or
(b) if the relevant vehicle is recorded in the part of the register relating to Northern Ireland.

(9) The arrangements of letters referred to in paragraph (4) are—

(a) "United Kingdom" or "UNITED KINGDOM";
(b) "UK";
(c) "Great Britain" or "GREAT BRITAIN";
(d) "GB";
(e) "England" or "ENGLAND";
(f) "Eng" or "ENG";
(g) "Scotland" or "SCOTLAND";
(h) "Sco" or "SCO";
(i) "Wales" or "WALES";
(j) "Cymru" or "CYMRU";
(k) "Cym" or "CYM".

(10) The emblems referred to in paragraph (4) are—

(a) an image of the Union flag;
(b) an image of the Cross of Saint George, as depicted on the flag of England;

(c) an image of the Cross of Saint Andrew (the Saltire), as depicted on the flag of Scotland;

(d) an image of the Red Dragon of Wales, as depicted on the flag of Wales.]

NOTES
Amendment Substituted by SI 2009/811.
Council Regulation (EC) 2411/98 OJ L299, 10.11.1998, p 1.

[750]

Optional early use of new-specification plates and prescribed font

17 (1) This regulation applies in a case where, on or after 21st March and before 1st September 2001 a registration mark on a vehicle—

(a) is displayed on a registration plate which conforms to the specification set out in Part 1 of Schedule 2 and is otherwise fixed on the vehicle and lit in accordance with the requirements of Part II of these Regulations,

(b) conforms to the requirements of regulations 13 and 14 as to layout and spacing of characters in so far as they apply to vehicles first registered on or after 1st September 2001, and

(c) is comprised of characters each of which is in the prescribed font.

(2) Where this regulation applies—

(a) regulations 17 to 22 of the Road Vehicles (Registration and Licensing) Regulations 1971 or, as the case may be,

(b) regulations 18 to 23 of the Road Vehicles (Registration and Licensing) Regulations (Northern Ireland) 1973,

(which provide for the format and means of display of registration plates and marks) shall cease to apply in respect of that vehicle and any trailer being towed by it and the provisions of these Regulations shall apply instead.

NOTES
Road Vehicles (Registration and Licensing) Regulations 1971, regs 17–22; Road Vehicles (Registration and Licensing) Regulations (Northern Ireland) 1973, regs 18–23
SI 1971/450, SR & O (NI) 1973/490; both partially revoked by reg 1(2), Sch 1.

[751]

Saving for vehicles constructed before 1st January 1973

18 For the purposes of these Regulations a vehicle which was first registered on or after 1st January 1973 shall be treated as if it was first registered before that date if—

(a) it is an exempt vehicle for the purposes of paragraph 1A(1) of Schedule 2 to the Act, or

(b) not being such a vehicle, it was constructed before 1st January 1973.

[752]

Offences under section 59 of the Act

19 (1) For the purposes of section 59(1) of the Act (regulations: offences), the person responsible for complying with these Regulations is the person driving the vehicle or, where it is not being driven, the person keeping it.

(2) Paragraph (1) does not apply to a regulation the breach of which would constitute an offence under section 42(1) of the Act (not fixing a registration mark as required by virtue of section 23).

[753]

SCHEDULE 1

NOTES
This Schedule specifies the following regulations revoked by reg 1(2): the Road Vehicles (Registration and Licensing) Regulations 1971, SI 1971/450, regs 17–22, Schs 2, 3 (now wholly revoked by SI 2002/2742); the Road Vehicles (Registration and Licensing) (Amendment) Regulations 1972, SI 1972/1865, reg 6 (now wholly revoked by SI 2002/2742); the Road Vehicles (Registration and Licensing) (Amendment) Regulations 1975 and 1984, SI 1975/1089, SI 1984/814; and the Road Vehicles (Registration and Licensing) Regulations (Northern Ireland) 1973, SR & O (NI) 1973/490, regs 18–23, Schs 2, 3 and the amending SI 1976/2180, reg 2(6), (8), (9) (outside the scope of this work).

[754]

SCHEDULE 2
REQUIREMENTS FOR REGISTRATION PLATES

Regulation 10

PART 1
VEHICLES REGISTERED AND NEW REGISTRATION PLATES FITTED ON OR AFTER 1ST SEPTEMBER 2001 (MANDATORY SPECIFICATION)

1 The plate must be made of retroreflecting material which, as regards its construction, colour and other qualities, complies with the requirements of—

(a) the British Standard specification for retroreflecting number plates published on 15 January 1998 under number BS AU 145d, or

(b) any other relevant standard or specification recognised for use in an EEA State and which, when in use, offers a performance equivalent to that offered by a plate complying with the British Standard specification,

and which, in either case, is marked with the number (or such other information as is necessary to permit identification) of that standard or specification.

2 Where the registration mark is displayed on the front of the vehicle, it must have black characters on a white background.

3 Where the registration mark is displayed on the back of the vehicle, it must have black characters on a yellow background.

[755]

PART 2
VEHICLES REGISTERED ON OR AFTER 1ST JANUARY 1973 AND BEFORE 1ST SEPTEMBER 2001 (OPTIONAL SPECIFICATION)

1 The plate must be made of reflex-reflecting material which, as regards its construction, colour and other qualities, complies with the requirements of—

(a) the British Standard Specification for reflex-reflecting number plates, published on 11 September 1972 under the number BS AU 145a, or

(b) any other relevant standard or specification recognised for use in an EEA State and which, when in use, offers a performance equivalent to that offered by a plate complying with the British Standard specification,

and which, in either case, is marked with the number (or such other information as is necessary to permit identification) of that standard or specification.

2 Where the registration mark is displayed on the front of the vehicle, it must have black characters on a white background.

3 Where the registration mark is displayed on the back of the vehicle, it must have black characters on a yellow background.

[756]

PART 3
VEHICLES REGISTERED BEFORE 1ST JANUARY 1973 (OPTIONAL SPECIFICATIONS)

A Requirements where the vehicle carries a registration plate which is constructed so that the mark may be illuminated from behind by virtue of the translucency of its characters.

1 The registration mark must be formed of white translucent characters on a black background on the surface of that plate.

2 When the registration mark is illuminated during the hours of darkness, the characters on that plate must appear white against a black background.

B Requirements where the vehicle carries a registration plate which is not so constructed.

Either of the following is permitted—

1 A plate made of reflex-reflecting material complying with the requirements of the British Standard Specification for reflex-reflecting number plates published on 31 October 1967 under the number BS AU 145 and which displays black characters on a white background where it is fixed on the front of the vehicle and black characters on a yellow background where it is fixed on the rear of the vehicle.

2 A plate displaying white, silver or light grey letters and numbers on a black surface having every character indelibly inscribed on the surface or so attached to the surface that it cannot readily be detached from it, which may either—

(a) be made of cast or pressed metal with raised characters, or
(b) consist of a plate to which separate characters are attached, or
(c) consist of a plastic plate having either reverse engraved characters or characters of a foil type, or
(d) consist of an unbroken rectangular area on the surface of the vehicle which is either flat or, if there is no flat area where the mark is required to be displayed, an area which is almost flat.

[757]

SCHEDULES 3, 4

NOTES
Sch 3 (mentioned in regs 12, 13, 14), which is not printed in this work, is divided into three Parts; Pt I sets out in Table A the permitted layouts for registration marks; Pt 2 sets out diagrams showing permitted layouts; and Pt 3 sets out in Table B stroke and character width, spacing and margins.
Sch 4 (mentioned in reg 15(1)), which is not printed in this work, sets out the prescribed font.

[758]

BRITISH WATERWAYS BOARD (LIMIT FOR BORROWING) ORDER 2001
SI 2001/1054

Authority Made by the Secretary of State for the Environment, Transport and the Regions under the Transport Act 1962, s 19(3)(iv).
Date made 19 March 2001.
Commencement 20 March 2001.
Summary This order specifies a new limit of £35m for the purposes of the Transport Act 1962, s 19(3)(iv), on the outstanding debt on the British Waterways Board at any one time in respect of the principal of any money it has borrowed under s 19 and in respect of its commencing capital debt. The British Waterways Board (Limit for Borrowing) Order 1983, SI 1983/1957, is revoked.

[759]

ROAD TRAFFIC (VEHICLE TESTING) ACT 1999 (COMMENCEMENT NO 1) ORDER 2001
SI 2001/1896

Authority Made by the Secretary of State for the Environment, Transport and the Regions under the Road Traffic (Vehicle Testing) Act 1999, s 9.
Date made 10 May 2001.
Summary This order, and the further commencement order SI 2003/1095, brought into force provisions of the Road Traffic (Vehicle Testing) Act 1999, as noted in the table below.

Provision	*Date and extent (if any)*
s 1(1), (2)	11 April 2003 (SI 2003/1095)
s 1(3)	1 June 2001 (in so far as it relates to the insertion of Road Traffic Act 1988, s 45(6B)) (SI 2001/1896) 11 April 2003 (in so far as not already in force) (SI 2003/1095)
s 2	11 April 2003 (SI 2003/1095)
s 3	1 June 2001 (SI 2001/1896)
ss 4, 5	11 April 2003 (SI 2003/1095)
s 7(1)	See Schedule below
Schedule, para 3	11 April 2003 (SI 2003/1095)

[760]

ROAD USER CHARGING (CHARGES AND PENALTY CHARGES) (LONDON) REGULATIONS 2001
SI 2001/2285

Authority Made by the Secretary of State for Transport, Local Government and the Regions under the Greater London Authority Act 1999, Sch 23, paras 12(1), (2), 13(b), 26, 27.
Date made 22 June 2001.
Commencement 16 July 2001.
Amendment Amended by SI 2003/109.
Summary These regulations deal with procedures relating to the imposition of charges and penalty charges by road user charging schemes in Greater London under the Greater London Authority Act 1999, Sch 23. In particular the regulations make provision relating to:

(a) the imposition, setting and liability for charges and penalty charges;
(b) the power for an authorised person to examine vehicles, enter vehicles and seize items in accordance with prescribed conditions; and
(c) the immobilisation of vehicles; the release of immobilised vehicles; the removal and disposal of removed vehicles; the recovery of penalty charges in relation to removed vehicles; the taking possession of a vehicle; and claims by owners of vehicles after their disposal.

Enforcement and adjudication As to the procedure for the enforcement and adjudication of road user charging schemes in Greater London, see SI 2001/2313.

[761]

TRUNK ROAD CHARGING SCHEMES (BRIDGES AND TUNNELS) (ENGLAND) PROCEDURE REGULATIONS 2001
SI 2001/2303

Authority Made by the Secretary of State for Transport, Local Government and the Regions under the Transport Act 2000, s 168(3).
Date made 25 June 2001.
Commencement 20 July 2001.
Amendment Amended by SI 2004/3168.
Summary These regulations, which relate only to England, prescribe the procedure for the making, variation and revocation of orders under the Transport Act 2000, s 168(3), for trunk road charging schemes under that Act in respect of roads carried by a bridge or passing through a tunnel of at least 600 metres in length (see s 167(1)(a), (2)(a)). Provision is made relating to: consultation; publication of proposals; objections and representations; making an order, commencement of an order and notice of the making an order; and the variation and revocation of an order.

[762]

ROAD USER CHARGING (ENFORCEMENT AND ADJUDICATION) (LONDON) REGULATIONS 2001
SI 2001/2313

Authority Made by the Lord Chancellor under the Greater London Authority Act 1999, s 420(1), Sch 23, paras 12(3), 28, 30.
Date made 26 June 2001.
Commencement 30 July 2001.
Amendment Amended by SI 2003/108, SI 2008/1956, SI 2008/2683.
Summary These regulations set out the procedure for the enforcement and adjudication of road user charging schemes in Greater London under the Greater London Authority Act 1999, Sch 23 (and are to be read in conjunction with SI 2001/2285). In particular the regulations make provision for:
(a) adjudicators (including provision concerning their appointment and administrative support; the procedure to be followed by adjudicators; the recovery of amounts payable under an adjudication; and reports by adjudicators);
(b) representations and appeals in relation to the removal or immobilisation of vehicles; and
(c) the recovery of penalty charges by a charging authority.

[763]

ROAD USER CHARGING AND WORKPLACE PARKING LEVY (CLASSES OF MOTOR VEHICLES) (ENGLAND) REGULATIONS 2001
SI 2001/2793

Authority Made by the Secretary of State for Transport, Local Government and the Regions under the Transport Act 2000, ss 197(1), 198(3).
Date made 2 August 2001.
Commencement 28 August 2001.
Summary These regulations, which extend to England only, relate to the provisions of the Transport Act 2000, Pt III, which enable road user charging schemes ("charging schemes") or workplace parking levy schemes ("licensing schemes") to be made by certain bodies. S 171(1)(c) of the 2000 Act requires a charging scheme to specify the classes of motor vehicles in respect of which charges are imposed; and s 186(3)(d) provides that the charges that may be imposed by a licensing scheme include different charges for different cases, including different classes of motor vehicles. These regulations specify classes of motor vehicles for the purposes of Pt III of the 2000 Act.

As to regulations making provision in relation to licensing schemes under Pt III of the 2000 Act, see SI 2009/2085.

[764]

VEHICLES (CRIME) ACT 2001 (COMMENCEMENT NO 1) ORDER 2001
SI 2001/3215

Authority Made by the Home Secretary under the Vehicles (Crime) Act 2001, s 44.

Date made 23 September 2001.
Summary This order brought provisions of the Vehicles (Crime) Act 2001 into force, as noted in the table below.
Further orders SI 2001/4059, SI 2002/1914, SI 2002/2377, SI 2002/2957 (all made under s 44 of the 2001 Act) brought further provisions of the 2001 Act into force, as noted in the table below.

Provision	*Date/extent (if any)*
ss 1–7, 9–16	21 October 2002 (SI 2002/1914)
s 17(1)	1 December 2002 (to the extent necessary to enable the Secretary of State to make regulations) (SI 2002/2957) 1 March 2003 (so far as not already in force) (SI 2002/2957)
s 17(2)–(4)	1 December 2002 (to the extent necessary to enable the Secretary of State to make regulations) (SI 2002/2957) 1 January 2003 (so far as not already in force) (SI 2002/2957)
ss 18–23	1 December 2002 (to the extent necessary to enable the Secretary of State to make regulations) (SI 2002/2957) 1 January 2003 (so far as not already in force) (SI 2002/2957)
s 24(1)–(3)	1 December 2002 (to the extent necessary to enable the Secretary of State to make regulations) (SI 2002/2957) 1 January 2003 (so far as not already in force) (SI 2002/2957)
s 24(4), (5)	1 December 2002 (to the extent necessary to enable the Secretary of State to make regulations) (SI 2002/2957) 1 March 2003 (so far as not already in force) (SI 2002/2957)
s 25(1), (2)	1 December 2002 (to the extent necessary to enable the Secretary of State to make regulations) (SI 2002/2957) 1 January 2003 (so far as not already in force) (SI 2002/2957)
s 25(3), (4)	1 December 2002 (to the extent necessary to enable the Secretary of State to make regulations) (SI 2002/2957) 1 March 2003 (so far as not already in force) (SI 2002/2957)
s 26	1 December 2002 (to the extent necessary to enable the Secretary of State to make regulations) (SI 2002/2957) 1 March 2003 (so far as not already in force) (SI 2002/2957)
ss 27, 28	1 December 2002 (to the extent necessary to enable the Secretary of State to make regulations) (SI 2002/2957) 1 January 2003 (so far as not already in force) (SI 2002/2957)
s 29	1 December 2002 (to the extent necessary to enable the Secretary of State to make regulations) (SI 2002/2957) 1 March 2003 (so far as not already in force) (SI 2002/2957)
ss 30, 31	1 December 2002 (to the extent necessary to enable the Secretary of State to make regulations) (SI 2002/2957) 1 January 2003 (so far as not already in force) (SI 2002/2957)
ss 32, 33	17 September 2002 (SI 2002/2377)
s 37	1 October 2001 (SI 2001/3215)
s 38	2 January 2002 (SI 2001/4059)
s 43	See Schedule below
Schedule, paras 3–6	17 September 2002 (SI 2002/2377)
Schedule, paras 7–10	2 January 2002 (SI 2001/4059)

[765]

QUALITY PARTNERSHIP SCHEMES (EXISTING FACILITIES) REGULATIONS 2001
SI 2001/3317

Authority Made by the Secretary of State for Transport, Local Government and the Regions under the Transport Act 2000, s 119.
Date made 3 October 2001.

Commencement 26 October 2001.
Summary The Transport Act 2000, ss 114–123 empower a local transport authority, or two or more such authorities acting jointly, to make a quality partnership scheme if they are satisfied that the scheme will to any extent implement the policies set out in their bus strategy or strategies. Under s 119, regulations may make provision about the specifying in quality partnership schemes of facilities which are already being provided before the schemes are proposed ("existing facilities").

These regulations, which extend to England only, make provision for existing facilities which may form part of a quality partnership scheme ("scheme"). An existing facility may not be specified in a scheme if that facility was first provided more than ten years before notice of the proposed scheme is given under s 115(1) of the 2000 Act. An existing facility which was first provided more than five years but fewer than ten years before notice of the proposed scheme is given may not be specified in a scheme if a person who relies on that facility in the provision of local services has objected to it being specified and that objection has not been withdrawn. Provision is made as to the making of objections. S 115 of the 2000 Act is modified in its application to proposed schemes which specify existing facilities.
Wales SI 2002/3017 (made by the National Assembly for Wales under the Transport Act 2000, s 119, and in force on 20 December 2002) makes similar provision in relation to Wales for existing facilities which may form part of a quality partnership scheme as SI 2001/3317 above makes in relation to England.

[766]

MOTOR VEHICLES (ACCESS TO DRIVER LICENSING RECORDS) REGULATIONS 2001
SI 2001/3343

Authority Made by the Secretary of State for Transport, Local Government and the Regions under the Criminal Justice and Court Services Act 2000, s 71(2).
Date made 5 October 2001.
Commencement 29 October 2001.
Amendment Amended by SI 2008/1965.
Summary These regulations set out the purposes for which constables and members of the staff of the Serious Organised Crime Agency may be given access to information contained in the Driver Licensing Register and made available to the National Policing Improvement Agency.

The purposes referred to above include:

(a) the prevention, investigation or prosecution of a contravention of any provision of the Road Traffic Act 1988, the Road Traffic Offenders Act 1988 and the Vehicle Drivers (Certificates of Professional Competence) Regulations 2007, SI 2007/605; and
(b) ascertaining whether a person has had an order made in relation to him under the Child Support Act 1991, s 40B(1) or (5), or the Crime (Sentences) Act 1997, s 39(1) or 40(2) (s 39 of the 1997 Act has been repealed by the Powers of Criminal Courts (Sentencing) Act 2000, s 165(4), Sch 12, Pt I, and replaced by s 146 of the 2000 Act; s 40 of the 1997 Act is repealed by the Criminal Justice Act 2003, ss 303(b)(iii), 332, Sch 37, Pt 7, as from a day to be appointed by order under s 336(3) thereof, and replaced by s 301 of the 2003 Act).

The regulations also provide for such information to be further disclosed by constables to civilian employees of police authorities to facilitate the use of the information by constables.

[767]

GOODS VEHICLES (AUTHORISATION OF INTERNATIONAL JOURNEYS) (FEES) REGULATIONS 2001
SI 2001/3606

Authority Made by the Secretary of State for Transport, Local Government and the Regions, with the consent of the Treasury, under the Finance Act 1973, s 56(1), (2).
Date made 5 November 2001.
Commencement 1 December 2001.
Amendment Amended by SI 2008/1576, SI 2009/855. Previously amended by SI 2004/1883 (superseded).
Summary These regulations revoke and replace the Goods Vehicles (Authorisation of International Journeys) (Fees) Regulations 2000, SI 2000/3207, and the amending SI 2001/309. They prescribe the fees to be paid to the Department for Transport for the issue of documents authorising the operation of goods vehicles on journeys:

(a) between the United Kingdom and other member countries of the European Conference of Ministers of Transport (ECMT);
(b) between the United Kingdom and certain states with which bilateral agreements or arrangements have been concluded.

In particular, the regulations specify the fees payable on the issue of:

(a) an ECMT licence (ie a licence granted pursuant to the scheme adopted by Resolution No 26 of the ECMT Council of 14 June 1973);
(b) a journey permit issued pursuant to an agreement or arrangement concluded with a particular state (specified in the Schedule to the regulations);
(c) an authorisation for removals carriage carried out by undertakings having special staff and equipment for the purpose granted in accordance with Resolution No 53 of the ECMT Council

of 29 and 30 May 1985 amending Resolution No 44 of that Council of 1 June 1978 concerning the regulations governing international transport by road and the liberalisation of certain types of such transport.

[768]

MANDATORY TRAVEL CONCESSIONS (REIMBURSEMENT ARRANGEMENTS) (WALES) REGULATIONS 2001 (W 312)
SI 2001/3764

Authority Made by the National Assembly for Wales under the Transport Act 2000, ss 149(3), 150(6).
Date made 22 November 2001.
Commencement 30 November 2001.
Summary The Transport Act 2000, s 145, as originally enacted, provided for mandatory travel concessions to be provided outside Greater London by operators of eligible services (local bus services) to certain classes of passenger, including the elderly or disabled. S 145 has been replaced by two new sections by the Concessionary Bus Travel Act 2007. S 145A of the 2000 Act (substituted for the original s 145 by s 1 of the 2007 Act) replaces s 145 in England for journeys not beginning on the London bus network. S 145B of the 2000 Act (inserted by s 13(1) of, and paras 10, 11 of Sch 2 to, the 2007 Act) replaces the original s 145 in Wales. S 149 of the 2000 Act requires travel concession authorities to reimburse operators for providing concessions in accordance with arrangements agreed with the operators or, in the absence of agreement, determined by the authorities. S 150 provides for the procedure for reimbursement arrangements determined by the travel concession authorities.

These regulations, made under ss 149, 150, make provision with respect to arrangements between operators and travel concession authorities in Wales; the manner of making reimbursement payments to operators; and applications to the Welsh Ministers (previously the National Assembly for Wales) by operators who consider that they may be prejudicially affected by proposed reimbursement arrangements.

[769]

GOODS VEHICLES (ENFORCEMENT POWERS) REGULATIONS 2001
SI 2001/3981

Authority Made by the Secretary of State for Transport, Local Government and the Regions under the Goods Vehicles (Licensing of Operators) Act 1995, Sch 1A.
Date made 11 December 2001.
Commencement 4 January 2002.
Amendment Amended by SI 2005/617, SI 2008/2683, SI 2009/1885, SI 2009/1965.
Summary These regulations empower an authorised person to detain a heavy goods vehicle and its contents, in accordance with the Goods Vehicles (Licensing of Operators) Act 1995, Sch 1A, where he has reason to believe it is being operated without a licence, in contravention of s 2 of the 1995 Act. Provision is made for:

(a) the release of a detained vehicle to an owner, without the need for an application to a traffic commissioner (see head (d) below), in circumstances where one or more of the following grounds is or are made out:
    (1) at the time the vehicle was detained, the person using the vehicle held a valid operator's licence (whether or not authorising the use of the vehicle);
    (2) at the time the vehicle was detained, the vehicle was not being, and had not been, used in contravention of s 2 of the 1995 Act;
    (3) although at the time the vehicle was detained it was being, or had been, used in contravention of s 2 of the 1995 Act, the owner did not know that it was being, or had been, so used;
    (4) although knowing at the time the vehicle was detained that it was being, or had been, used in contravention of s 2 of the 1995 Act, the owner had taken steps with a view to preventing that use and has taken steps with a view to preventing any further such use;

(b) the immobilisation of vehicles, criminal offences arising from the unlawful removal of, or interference with, immobilisation notices or devices, and the release of immobilised vehicles;
(c) the removal and delivery of vehicles and contents detained and the giving of notice of detention;
(d) an application by the owner of a vehicle to a traffic commissioner for the return of a vehicle;
(e) appeals from a traffic commissioner to the Upper Tribunal (previously to the Transport Tribunal);
(f) the return of a vehicle detained where a traffic commissioner determines that one or more of the grounds specified in head (a) above is or are made out;
(g) the disposal of vehicles;
(h) the return of the contents of detained vehicles and the disposal of such contents;
(i) the application of the proceeds of sale of any property sold by an authorised person;
(j) disputes in relation to the return or disposal of the contents of a vehicle, or the application of the proceeds of sale of a vehicle or its contents;
(k) the offence of obstructing an authorised person in the exercise of his powers, and of making a false or misleading declaration with a view to securing the return of a vehicle; and
(l) the service of notices.

As to the detention of a vehicle adapted to carry more than eight passengers which is being, or has been, used on a road in contravention of public service vehicle operator licensing requirements in the Public Passenger Vehicles Act 1981, s 12, see SI 2009/1964.

[770]

DRIVING LICENCES (DISQUALIFICATION UNTIL TEST PASSED) (PRESCRIBED OFFENCE) ORDER 2001
SI 2001/4051

Authority Made by the Secretary of State for Transport, Local Government and the Regions under the Road Traffic Offenders Act 1988, s 36(3). S 36(3) is amended by the Road Safety Act 2006, s 37(1), (2), as from a day to be appointed by order under s 61(1) thereof; see further the note "Summary" below.

Date made 20 December 2001.

Commencement 31 January 2002.

Summary The Road Traffic Offenders Act 1988, s 36(1) requires the court, where that subsection applies to a person, to order him to be disqualified until he passes the appropriate driving test. S 36(1) applies to a person who has been disqualified under s 34 of that Act on conviction of manslaughter, causing death by dangerous driving or dangerous driving (see s 36(2)). S 36(3)(b) enables the Secretary of State by order to prescribe other offences involving obligatory endorsement to which s 36(1) is to apply. (S 36(3) is amended by the Road Safety Act 2006, s 37(1), (2), as from a day to be appointed by order under s 61(1) thereof, so as to enable the Secretary of State by order to specify offences involving obligatory endorsement.) This order prescribes an offence under the Road Traffic Act 1988, s 3A of causing death by careless driving when under the influence of drink or drugs.

[771]

BUS SERVICE OPERATORS GRANT (ENGLAND) REGULATIONS 2002
SI 2002/1015

Authority Made by the Secretary of State for Transport, Local Government and the Regions under the Transport Act 2000, s 154(5).

Date made 9 April 2002.

Commencement 1 May 2002.

Amendment Amended by SI 2003/1036, SI 2004/9, SI 2008/1879.

Summary Under the Transport Act 2000, s 154, grants may be made to operators of eligible bus services towards their costs in operating those services. These regulations, which extend to England only, re-enact the previous eligibility rules for fuel duty rebates under the Finance Act 1965, s 92 (repealed), which has been superseded by s 154 of the 2000 Act. The regulations provide that a bus service is an eligible bus service for the purposes of the said s 154 if it is of one of the following classes:

(a) a local service provided or secured:

  (1) by a local education authority pursuant to arrangements made under what is now (in relation to England) the Education Act 1996, s 508B et seq (in relation to Wales, see the Learner Travel (Wales) Measure 2008), or

  (2) for persons who have attained the age of 60 years or disabled persons,

  and in respect of which specified conditions are satisfied;

(b) a local service, other than a service described in head (a) above, in respect of which specified conditions are satisfied;

(c) a bus service being provided by an operator to whom a permit under the Transport Act 1985, s 19 has been issued and remains in force, and in respect of which specified conditions are satisfied; or

(d) a domestic coach service, to the extent of its travel in England, and in respect of which specified conditions are satisfied.

Wales SI 2002/2022, as amended by SI 2003/943, SI 2004/1827, SI 2008/1879, was made by the National Assembly for Wales under the Transport Act 2000, s 154(5), and came into force on 14 August 2002. The regulations, which apply to Wales only, make similar provision as to eligible bus services for the purposes of s 154 of the 2000 Act as SI 2002/1015 above makes in relation to England.

[772]

TRAVEL CONCESSIONS (ELIGIBLE SERVICES) ORDER 2002
SI 2002/1016

Authority Made by the Secretary of State for Transport, Local Government and the Regions under the Transport Act 1985, s 94(4) and the Transport Act 2000, s 146.

Date made 9 April 2002.

Commencement 1 May 2002.

Amendment Amended by SI 2009/575.

Summary This order, which extends to England only, prescribes bus services which are eligible for the purposes of the provisions of the Transport Act 1985, Pt IV (local passenger transport services) relating to participation in travel concession schemes, and reimbursement arrangements and the mandatory travel concession under what is now (in relation to England) the Transport Act 2000, s 145A (in relation to Wales, see s 145B of the 2000 Act).

Subject to the provision below, a service is an eligible service under s 94 of the 1985 Act and under s 146 of the 2000 Act if it is of one of the following classes:

(a) a local service provided or secured:

(1) by a local education authority pursuant to arrangements made under what is now (in relation to England) the Education Act 1996, s 508B et seq (in relation to Wales, see the Learner Travel (Wales) Measure 2008), or

(2) for elderly persons or disabled persons,

and in respect of which specified conditions are satisfied; or

(b) a local service, other than a service described in head (a) above, which is provided by means of a vehicle adapted to carry more than eight passengers (or by a smaller vehicle, but only if the services are operated in accordance with a time table), and in respect of which specified conditions are satisfied.

A service is not an eligible service under s 146 of the 2000 Act if:

(a) more than half of the accommodation on the vehicle by means of which the service is provided can be reserved by members of the general public in advance of travel;

(b) it is intended to operate for less than six consecutive weeks;

(c) it is operated primarily for the purposes of tourism or because of the historical interest of the vehicle;

(d) it is a bus substitution service (ie a service for the carriage of passengers by road provided temporarily in place of the whole or part of any service for the carriage of passengers by railway that has been temporarily discontinued, reduced or modified); or

(e) the fare for the service includes a special amenity element (a fare includes a special amenity element if it is significantly high in relation to the general level of fares for comparable journeys).

Wales SI 2002/2023 was made by the National Assembly for Wales under the Transport Act 1985, s 94(4) and the Transport Act 2000, s 146, and came into force on 14 August 2002. The order, which applies to Wales only, makes similar provision as to eligible bus services for the purposes of: (a) the provisions of Pt IV of the 1985 Act relating to participation in travel concession schemes, and reimbursement arrangements; and (b) the mandatory travel concession under s 145 of the 2000 Act, as SI 2002/1016 above makes in relation to England.

[773]

ROAD TRAFFIC (VEHICLE EMISSIONS) (FIXED PENALTY) (ENGLAND) REGULATIONS 2002
SI 2002/1808

Authority Made by the Secretary of State for Transport under the Environment Act 1995, s 87(1), (2), (5), Sch 11, para 5.

Date made 11 July 2002.

Commencement 18 July 2002.

Summary These regulations, which apply to England only, revoke and replace the Road Traffic (Vehicle Emissions) (Fixed Penalty) Regulations 1997, SI 1997/3058 (revoked in relation to Wales by SI 2003/300 (see below)). The regulations enable a local authority in England to apply to the Secretary of State for designation under these regulations where any part of its area is designated as an air quality management area in accordance with the Environment Act 1995, s 83. A local authority so designated may issue fixed penalty notices to enforce offences under SI 1986/1078, regs 61, 61A (emissions of smoke, vapour, gases, oily substances etc) ("emission offences") in its area, and under so much of reg 98 (stopping of engine when stationary) of SI 1986/1078 as relates to the prevention of exhaust emissions ("stationary idling offences").

Pt 2 of the regulations specifies the circumstances in which an application for designation can be made; sets out the criteria for designation; and provides for the revocation of designation. Pt 3 relates to the authorisation of persons to carry out emission tests on vehicles and to issue fixed penalty notices. Pt 4 prescribes emission offences and stationary idling offences as fixed penalty offences and prescribes the amount of the penalty. Pt 5 confers power on an authorised person to conduct emission tests and to issue a fixed penalty notice where an emissions offence has been committed. Pt 6 enables an authorised person to stop the running of the engine of a stationary vehicle and to issue a fixed penalty notice where a stationary idling offence has been committed. Pt 7 relates to fixed penalty notices, including provision for the time for issue and contents of a notice; the effect of the issue of a notice; the request by a person to whom a notice has been issued for a hearing in respect of the offence to which the notice relates; applications for the reduction or waiver of a fixed penalty for an emissions offence; and the withdrawal of a notice. Pt 8 contains miscellaneous provisions, including provision relating to the recovery of unpaid fixed penalties.

Wales SI 2003/300 (made by the National Assembly for Wales under the Environment Act 1995, s 87(1), (2), (5), Sch 11, para 5, and in force on 1 May 2003) revokes the Road Traffic (Vehicle Emissions) (Fixed Penalty) Regulations 1997, SI 1997/3058, in relation to Wales. SI 2003/300 makes similar provision to enable local authorities in Wales to carry out emission tests on vehicles and to issue fixed penalty notices as SI 2002/1808 above makes in relation to local authorities in England.

[774]

SERVICE SUBSIDY AGREEMENTS (TENDERING) (ENGLAND) REGULATIONS 2002
SI 2002/2090

Authority Made by the Secretary of State for Transport under the Transport Act 1985, ss 90(2), (3), 91(1), (7), 134(5).

Date made 6 August 2002.
Commencement 2 September 2002.
Amendment Amended by SI 2004/609.
Summary These regulations, which extend to England only, revoke and replace the Service Subsidy Agreement (Tendering) Regulations 1985, SI 1985/1921, and the amending SI 1989/464, SI 1994/1227, SI 1998/2197, which accordingly now apply in relation to Wales only (see below). The Transport Act 1985, s 89 provides that an authority responsible for expenditure on public passenger transport services may not enter into an agreement providing for service subsidies under which a local service is to be provided except by accepting a tender invited in pursuance of that section. These regulations specify certain descriptions of agreements providing for service subsidies which are excepted from these tendering requirements (according to whether an authority's forecast expenditure for the financial year does not exceed £600,000 or exceeds that amount); prescribe the information which is to be published with respect to tenders submitted in response to invitations to tender under s 89; and prescribe the manner in which that information and certain other matters relating to tenders is to be published.
Wales Similar provision exempting service subsidy agreements from the tendering requirements of the Transport Act 1985, s 89 in relation to Wales is now made by SI 1985/1921, as amended by SI 1989/464, SI 1994/1227 (both now superseded), SI 1998/2197, SI 2002/520 (made under the Transport Act 1985, ss 90(2), (3), 91(1), (7)). The 1985 regulations, as amended by SI 1989/464, SI 1994/1227, SI 1998/2197, which originally applied to England and Wales, were revoked by SI 2002/2090 above in so far as they applied to England (the amending SI 2002/520 applies to Wales only).

[775]

ROAD VEHICLES (TESTING) (DISCLOSURE OF INFORMATION) (GREAT BRITAIN) REGULATIONS 2002
SI 2002/2426

Authority Made by the Secretary of State for Transport under the European Communities Act 1972, s 2(2).
Date made 23 September 2002.
Commencement 15 October 2002.
Summary These regulations provide that the Secretary of State may give information about vehicles or persons obtained from tests and inspections carried out under the Road Traffic Act 1988, s 67 or 68 or under the Road Traffic (Foreign Vehicles) Act 1972, s 1, to the competent authorities in other member states, and in Northern Ireland and Gibraltar, in compliance with Directive 2000/30/EC of the European Parliament and of the Council on the technical roadside inspection of the roadworthiness of commercial vehicles circulating in the Community (OJ L203, 10.08.2000, p 1).

[776]

DRIVING LICENCES (DESIGNATION OF RELEVANT EXTERNAL LAW) ORDER 2002
SI 2002/2590

Authority Made by the Secretary of State for Transport under the Road Traffic Act 1988, s 89(2)(c).
Date made 14 October 2002.
Commencement 1 November 2002.
Summary Under the Road Traffic Act 1988, s 89(1), a licence authorising the driving of motor vehicles of any class may not be granted to any person unless he meets the relevant residence requirement and satisfies the Secretary of State of any of certain conditions, including (see s 89(1)(d)) that at some time not earlier than the appointed day (as defined) he has held a full British external licence to drive vehicles of that or a corresponding class. By s 89(2)(c), a British external licence to drive any class of goods or passenger-carrying vehicle is to be disregarded for the purposes of s 89(1)(d) unless the Secretary of State designates the relevant external law under which it is granted as one which makes satisfactory provision for the granting of such licences. This order designates the law in force in Guernsey which corresponds to Pt III of the 1988 Act as one which makes satisfactory provision for the granting of licences to drive all classes of goods and passenger-carrying vehicles.

[777]

ROAD VEHICLES (REGISTRATION AND LICENSING) REGULATIONS 2002
SI 2002/2742

Authority Made by the Secretary of State for Transport under the Vehicle Excise and Registration Act 1994, ss 7(6), 10(1), 11(1), (1A), 12(2), (3), (4), 14(3)(b), (4), 21(3), 22(1), (1A), (1B), (1C), (1D), (1E), (1G), (2), (2A), (2B), (2C), (4), 22A, 23(5), 25, 33(1)(b), (1A)(c), (3)(a), (4), (5), 52(1), 57(1), (2), (3), 59(2)(a), 61A, 61B, 62(1), Sch 1, paras 1(2B), 3(5), 5(3)(e), (4)(c), Sch 2, paras 2A, 24.
Date made 4 November 2002.
Commencement Partly on 30 November 2002 and fully on 7 April 2003; see reg 1(2), (3).
Interpretation See reg 3.
Amendment Printed as amended by SI 2003/2154, SI 2003/2635, SI 2003/2981, SI 2003/3073, SI 2004/238, SI 2004/1773, SI 2004/3298, SI 2005/2713, SI 2006/2320, SI 2007/1018,

SI 2007/2553, SI 2008/642, SI 2008/1444, SI 2008/2849, SI 2009/880. Also amended by virtue of the Commissioners for Revenue and Customs Act 2005, s 50(2), (7). Previously amended by SI 2003/2335 (superseded by SI 2004/1872 in so far as it amended these regulations), SI 2003/3110, SI 2004/1872, SI 2004/2099, SI 2005/2344, SI 2007/498 (all superseded).

General These regulations revoke and replace a number of regulations (specified in Sch 1), including the Road Vehicles (Registration and Licensing) Regulations 1971, SI 1971/450, as amended, and corresponding Northern Ireland regulations, so as to provide a single set of regulations for the registration and licensing of vehicles for the whole of the United Kingdom.

Application of previous regulations to visitors' registration cards SI 1985/610, reg 6 makes provision as to registration cards issued to a person bringing a visiting vehicle into Great Britain. By reg 6(2) of SI 1985/610, the Road Vehicles (Registration and Licensing) Regulations 1971, SI 1971/450, regs 6, 8(2), (4) (revoked by SI 2002/2742) were applied, with modifications, to a visitor's registration card as they applied to a registration book. Reg 6 of SI 1971/450 related to duplicate registration books, and reg 8 related to the production of registration books and their defacement or mutilation.

[778]

PART I
PRELIMINARY

Citation and commencement

1 (1) These regulations may be cited as the Road Vehicles (Registration and Licensing) Regulations 2002.

(2) These regulations except regulations 15(3) and 20(4) and (5) and Schedule 3 shall come into force on 30th November 2002.

(3) Regulations 15(3) and 20(4) and (5) and Schedule 3 shall come into force on 7th April 2003.

[779]

Revocation

2 (1) The regulations specified in column (1), whose numbers are specified in column (2), of the tables in Parts I and III of Schedule 1 are hereby revoked in their entirety.

(2) The Regulations specified in column (1), whose number is specified in column (2), of the table in Part II of Schedule 1 are hereby revoked to the extent specified in column (3).

[780]

Interpretation

3 (1) In these regulations—

"the 1988 Act" means the Road Traffic Act 1988;

"the 1994 Act" means the Vehicle Excise and Registration Act 1994 and a reference to the "predecessor legislation" of the 1994 Act is a reference to any of the following Acts—

(a) the Roads Act 1920;
(b) the Vehicles (Excise) Act 1949;
(c) the Vehicles (Excise) Act (Northern Ireland) 1954;
(d) the Vehicles (Excise) Act 1962;
(e) the Vehicles (Excise) Act 1971;
(f) the Vehicles (Excise) Act (Northern Ireland) 1972;

"bicycle" means a mechanically propelled bicycle (including a motor scooter, a bicycle with an attachment for propelling it by mechanical power and a mechanically propelled bicycle used for drawing a trailer or sidecar) not exceeding 450 kgs in weight unladen;

["the Directive" means Council Directive 1999/37/EC of 29 April 1999 on the registration documents for vehicles as amended by Commission Directive 2003/127/EC of 23 December 2003;]

"GB records" means the part of the register which is maintained on behalf of the Secretary of State by the Driver and Vehicle Licensing Agency;

"insurer" means an authorised insurer as defined by section 145 of the 1988 Act;

"invalid vehicle" means a vehicle (including a cycle with an attachment for propelling it by mechanical power) which does not exceed 508 kgs in weight unladen and is adapted and used or kept on a public road for an invalid;

"keeper" in relation to a vehicle means the person by whom that vehicle is kept;

"kgs" means kilograms;

"local authority" has, in relation to each part of the United Kingdom, the meaning given in the following table—

England	County council, district council, London borough council, Council of the Isles of Scilly, Common Council of the City of London
Northern Ireland	District Council as defined in the Local Government Act (Northern Ireland) 1972
Scotland	Council constituted under section 2 of the Local Government etc (Scotland) Act 1994
Wales	County council, county borough council

"mm" means millimetres;

"NI records" means the part of the register which is maintained on behalf of the Secretary of State by Driver and Vehicle Licensing Northern Ireland;

"reduced pollution certificate" means a certificate issued with respect to a vehicle by virtue of Schedule 2;

"register" means the record kept by or on behalf of the Secretary of State of the vehicles registered by him, in Great Britain or in Northern Ireland, under section 21 of the 1994 Act;

"registered keeper" in relation to a vehicle means the person for the time being shown in the register as the keeper of that vehicle;

"trade plates" means plates issued in accordance with regulation 40 or 41;

"tricycle" means a mechanically propelled tricycle (including a motor scooter and a tricycle with an attachment for propelling it by mechanical power) not exceeding 450 kgs in weight unladen and not being a pedestrian controlled vehicle as defined by regulation 4(3)(b); and

"valeting" means the thorough cleaning of a vehicle before its registration by the Secretary of State under section 21 of the 1994 Act or in order to prepare it for sale and includes removing wax and grease from the exterior, engine and interior, and "valeted" shall be construed accordingly.

[(1A) For the purposes of these Regulations "the registration document fee exemption" applies in relation to the issue of a new registration document for a vehicle if the following conditions are satisfied—

(a) the vehicle has sustained damage to its bodywork;

(b) the insurer of the vehicle has notified the Secretary of State that the vehicle was capable of being repaired but that the cost to the insurer of having it repaired would exceed the value of the vehicle in the condition in which it was immediately before it sustained the damage; and

(c) the last registration document to be issued for the vehicle was destroyed by the insurer in accordance with regulation 20(5).]

(2) In regulations 21 to 25 "vehicle trader" has the meaning given by regulation 20(6) and in Schedule 4 "relevant vehicle trader" has the meaning given by paragraph 1(4) of that Schedule.

(3) Any application, notification, notice, information, particulars, appeal, declaration or other document or thing given or made in pursuance of these Regulations shall, except where it is expressly provided otherwise, be in writing.

NOTES

Amendment Para (1): definition "the Directive" inserted by SI 2004/3298.
Para (1A): inserted by SI 2004/1773.

Council Directive 1999/37/EC; Commission Directive 2003/127/EC
OJ L138, 01.06.1999, p 57; OJ L10, 16.01.2004, p 29.

[781]

Electrically assisted pedal cycles and pedestrian controlled vehicles

4 (1) The requirements specified in regulation 4 of the Electrically Assisted Pedal Cycles Regulations 1983 are hereby prescribed as requirements for the purposes of paragraph 2A of Schedule 2 to the 1994 Act (electrically assisted pedal cycles exempt vehicles if of a class complying with prescribed requirements).

(2) Nothing in the following provisions of these Regulations applies to a vehicle which is an electrically assisted pedal cycle or pedestrian controlled vehicle.

(3) In this regulation—

(a) "electrically assisted pedal cycle" means a vehicle which, by virtue of paragraph (1), is an electrically assisted pedal cycle for the purposes of paragraph 2A of Schedule 2 to the 1994 Act; and

(b) "pedestrian controlled vehicle" means a vehicle with three or more wheels which does not exceed 450 kgs in weight unladen and which is neither constructed nor adapted for use nor used for the carriage of a driver or passenger.

NOTES

Electrically Assisted Pedal Cycles Regulations 1983 SI 1983/1168.

[782]

PART II
LICENCES

Application for a vehicle licence on the basis that the reduced pollution requirements are satisfied

5 (1) Where an application is made for a vehicle licence on the basis that the rate of vehicle excise duty applicable is a rate specified in one of the provisions of Schedule 1 to the 1994 Act specified in paragraph (2), the Secretary of State may require the applicant to furnish a reduced pollution certificate before he determines the rate at which vehicle excise duty is payable on the licence.

(2) The provisions of Schedule 1 to the 1994 Act referred to in paragraph (1) are—

(a) paragraph 3(1A) (buses);
(b) paragraph 6(2A)(b) (vehicles used to carry exceptional loads);
(c) paragraph 7(3A)(b) (haulage vehicles);
(d) paragraph 9A (rigid goods vehicles); and
(e) paragraph 11A (tractive units).

(3) Schedule 2 shall have effect with respect to reduced pollution certificates and the reduced pollution requirements.

[783]

Exhibition of vehicle and nil licences

6 (1) When a vehicle licence or nil licence has been delivered to the Secretary of State with an application for a replacement licence, no licence need be fixed to and exhibited on the vehicle to which the licence relates until the replacement licence is obtained.

(2) Except where paragraph (1) applies, the manner in which any vehicle licence or nil licence in force for a vehicle is to be fixed to and exhibited on the vehicle in accordance with the provisions of section 33(1) or (1A) of the 1994 Act, when it is used or kept on a public road, is that specified in the following provisions of this regulation.

(3) Each such licence shall be fixed to the vehicle in a holder sufficient to protect the licence from the weather to which it would otherwise be exposed.

(4) The licence shall be exhibited on the vehicle—

(a) in the case of an invalid vehicle, tricycle or bicycle, other than in a case specified in sub-paragraph (b) or (c) of this paragraph, on the near side of the vehicle;

(b) in the case of a bicycle drawing a side-car or to which a side-car is attached, on the near side of the handlebars of the bicycle or on the near side of the side-car;

(c) in the case of any vehicle fitted with a glass windscreen in front of the driver extending across the vehicle to its near side, on or adjacent to the near side of the windscreen;

(d) in the case of any other vehicle—

(i) if the vehicle is fitted with a driver's cab containing a near side window, on that window; or

(ii) on the near side of the vehicle in front of the driver's seat and not less than 760 mm and not more than 1.8 metres above the surface of the road.

(5) In each case referred to in paragraph (4), the licence shall be so exhibited that all the particulars on the licence are clearly visible in daylight from the near side of the road.

[784]

Prohibition against exhibiting anything resembling a vehicle, trade or nil licence

7 No person shall exhibit on a vehicle which is kept or used on a public road anything—

(a) which is intended to be, or

(b) which could reasonably be,

mistaken for a vehicle licence, a nil licence or a trade licence which is for the time being in force for, or in respect of, the vehicle.

[785]

Issue of duplicate vehicle, trade and nil licences

8 (1) Where a vehicle licence, trade licence or nil licence—

(a) has been, or may have been, lost, stolen, destroyed or damaged; or

(b) contains any particulars which have become illegible,

the holder of the licence shall apply to the Secretary of State for the issue of a duplicate.

(2) An application under paragraph (1) shall be accompanied by—

(a) the registration document issued in respect of the vehicle or, if the applicant is unable to comply with this requirement, by an application to the Secretary of State for the issue of a replacement registration document in accordance with regulation 13;

(b) a fee of £7, if the licence to be replaced is a vehicle or trade licence; and

(c) the licence to be replaced, if the reason for replacement is that it has been damaged or contains any particulars which have become illegible.

(3) No fee is payable under paragraph (2)(b) if the Secretary of State is satisfied that the loss of the licence occurred in the course of the transmission of the licence by the office issuing it to the keeper of the vehicle.

(4) On receiving an application under paragraph (1) made in accordance with this regulation, the Secretary of State shall issue a replacement licence if he is satisfied that the licence has been, or may have been, lost, stolen, destroyed or damaged.

(5) If a replacement licence has been issued on the ground that the original has been, or may have been, lost, stolen or destroyed, and the original licence is subsequently found or recovered, the keeper of the vehicle—

(a) if the original is in his possession, shall forthwith return it to the Secretary of State, or

(b) if it is not in his possession but he becomes aware that it is found or recovered, shall take all reasonable steps to obtain possession of it and return it to the Secretary of State.

[786]

Surrender of vehicle and trade licences

9 (1) The holder of a vehicle licence or trade licence who wishes to surrender his licence and to claim a rebate in respect of the unexpired term, in accordance with section 19(1) of the 1994 Act, shall make an application, signed by him, to the Secretary of State.

(2) The application shall be accompanied by the licence and, in the case of a trade licence, any trade plates held by the holder in connection with the licence.

[787]

[Supplement payable on late renewal of vehicle licence

9A (1) Where paragraph (2) applies a supplement of the amount prescribed in paragraph (3) shall be payable.

(2) This paragraph applies where—

(a) a vehicle licence taken out for a vehicle expires,

(b) no vehicle licence was issued for the vehicle before the end of a period of one month beginning with the date of that expiry, and]

[(c) the registered keeper has failed to comply with requirements contained in Schedule 4.

(3) The supplement shall be £80, except when it is paid to the Secretary of State before the expiry of 28 days beginning with the date on which the registered keeper is notified that a supplement may or has become payable, when it shall be £40.

(4) The supplement shall be payable by the person in whose name the vehicle is registered under the 1994 Act at the date of the expiry of the licence by reason of whose late renewal the supplement becomes payable.

[(5) The Secretary of State shall notify the person referred to in paragraph (4) that the supplement is payable and that notification shall—

(a) state the amount of the supplement payable; and

(b) be sent to the address of the person as given in the register.]]

NOTES

Amendment Inserted by SI 2003/2981.
Para (5): inserted by SI 2003/3073.

[788]

PART III
REGISTRATION AND REGISTRATION DOCUMENTS

Registration and issue of registration document

10 (1) A vehicle shall not be registered under section 21 of the 1994 Act unless a fee of [£55] has been paid to the Secretary of State.

(2) Paragraph (1) does not apply to a vehicle which is an exempt vehicle by virtue of paragraph 18 or 19 of Schedule 2 to the 1994 Act.

(3) The Secretary of State may register a vehicle in either the GB records or the NI records as he considers appropriate and may, if he thinks fit, remove the particulars of a vehicle included in one of those parts of the register and include them in the other.

(4) On registering a vehicle the Secretary of State shall issue a registration document to the keeper of the vehicle.

(5) Subject to paragraph (6) and regulation 11, the Secretary of State shall issue the registration document forthwith, except where the vehicle is registered in consequence of an application for a vehicle licence by a person applying as mentioned in section 7(3A) of the 1994 Act, in which case the registration document shall be issued when that person asks for it to be issued.

(6) Before issuing a registration document to the keeper of a vehicle, the Secretary of State may require him to produce the vehicle for inspection or to produce other evidence that the vehicle accords with the particulars furnished when a vehicle or nil licence was applied for in respect of it.

(7) The Secretary of State may refuse to issue a registration document or replacement registration document for a vehicle if he is not satisfied that the vehicle accords with those particulars.

NOTES

Amendment Para (1): sum in square brackets substituted by SI 2008/642.

[789]

[Registration document

10A (1) [Subject to paragraph (1A),] this regulation applies to vehicles falling within the definition of "vehicle" in Article 2 of Council Directive 70/156/EEC on the approximation of the laws of the Member States relating to the type approval of motor vehicles and their trailers and in Article 2 of Council Directive 92/61/EEC relating to the type-approval of two or three-wheeled motor vehicles.

[(1A) Paragraph (3A) applies to any vehicle registered under the 1994 Act or its predecessor legislation.]

(2) The Secretary of State shall not issue a new registration document on or after 31st January 2004 unless it complies with Annex I of [the Directive] as regards—

- (a) dimensions;
- (b) composition; and
- (c) information contained within it;

except that in relation to a new registration document, the information contained may be limited to that available to the Secretary of State.

(3) Any registration document which does not comply with [the Directive] shall cease to have effect on the earlier of—

- (a) the date on which the Secretary of State issues a new registration document under these Regulations; or
- (b) 1st July 2005.

[(3A) Notwithstanding any other provision of these Regulations, the Secretary of State may, without charge and on surrender by the registered keeper of a registration document issued before 31st January 2004, issue to the registered keeper a registration document which is in a form provided for by the Directive in respect of the same vehicle if it appears proper and reasonable to him to do so.]

(4) In registering for the first time on or after 1st June 2004 a vehicle, which has been registered in another member State or Gibraltar, the Secretary of State shall recognise as a registration document a document which has been issued in respect of that vehicle by that other member State or Gibraltar if it complies with Annex I or Annexes I and II of [the Directive].

(5) Where the Secretary of State registers a vehicle in accordance with paragraph (4) he shall—

- (a) retain the former registration document for not less than 6 months; and
- (b) within 2 months of registration in the United Kingdom, notify the authorities in the member State or in Gibraltar where the vehicle was previously registered of his act of registration.]

NOTES

Amendment Inserted by SI 2003/3073.

Para (1): words in square brackets inserted by SI 2004/3298.

Para (1A): inserted by SI 2004/3298.

Paras (2), (3): words in square brackets substituted by SI 2004/3298.

Para (3A): inserted by SI 2004/3298.

Para (4): words in square brackets substituted by SI 2004/3298.

Council Directive 70/156/EEC OJ L42, 23.02.1970, p 1. Repealed and replaced by Directive 2007/46/EC of the European Parliament and of the Council establishing a framework for the approval of motor vehicles and their trailers, and of systems, components and separate technical units intended for such vehicles (OJ L263, 09.10.2007, p 1).

Council Directive 92/61/EEC OJ L225, 10.08.1992, p 72. Repealed and replaced by Directive 2002/24/EC of the European Parliament and of the Council relating to the type-approval of two or three-wheel motor vehicles (OJ L124, 09.05.2002, p 1).

[790]

Production of vehicle for inspection before assignment of registration mark

11 Where at the request of the keeper of a vehicle a particular registration mark is to be assigned to it, having previously been assigned to another vehicle, that other vehicle shall be made available for inspection by the Secretary of State at a place designated by him, and the keeper of the first mentioned vehicle shall, before the registration mark is so assigned, pay to the Secretary of State a charge of £80 for the assignment.

[791]

Production of registration document for inspection

12 The keeper of a vehicle in respect of which a registration document has been issued shall produce the document for inspection if he is required to do so at any reasonable time by a constable or by a person acting on behalf of the Secretary of State.

[792]

Issue of replacement registration document

13 (1) Where a registration document has been, or may have been, lost, stolen, destroyed or damaged, or it contains any particulars that have become illegible, the registered keeper shall apply to the Secretary of State for the issue of a replacement document.

(2) In a case where the registration document has been damaged or contains any particulars which have become illegible, an application under paragraph (1) shall be accompanied by the document and, in any other case, the Secretary of State may, if he thinks fit, accept an application made orally by telephone.

[(2A) An application for the issue of a replacement registration document under this regulation shall[, unless the registration document fee exemption applies,] be accompanied by a fee of [£25].]

(3) If the Secretary of State—

(a) receives an application made in accordance with this regulation; and

(b) he is satisfied that a registration document has been, or may have been, lost, stolen, destroyed or damaged, or that it contains any particulars that have become illegible,

he shall, subject to regulation 15, issue a replacement registration document to the registered keeper.

(4) If a replacement registration document has been issued on the ground that the original has been, or may have been, lost, stolen or destroyed, and the original is subsequently found or recovered, the keeper of the vehicle—

(a) if the original is in his possession, shall forthwith return it to the Secretary of State, or

(b) if it is not in his possession but he becomes aware that it is found or recovered, shall take all reasonable steps to obtain possession of it and return it to the Secretary of State.

NOTES

Amendment Para (2A): inserted by SI 2004/238; words in square brackets inserted by SI 2004/1773; sum in square brackets substituted by SI 2007/1018.

[793]

Correction of registration document

14 (1) Where the keeper of a vehicle believes that the particulars in the registration document issued in respect of that vehicle are, or have become, inaccurate, he shall forthwith notify the Secretary of State of the inaccuracy.

(2) Notification under paragraph (1) shall be accompanied by the registration document, unless it has been, or may have been, lost stolen or destroyed.

[(2A) Where the registration document has been, or may have been, lost, stolen or destroyed, notification under paragraph (1) shall be accompanied by an application for the issue of a new registration document and[, except where the registration document fee exemption applies, by] a fee of [£25].]

(3) Where the Secretary of State believes that the particulars in the registration document issued in respect of a vehicle are inaccurate—

(a) if the document has not been sent to him … , he may require the registered keeper of the vehicle to send it to him;

(b) whether or not he has received the document, he may correct the particulars in the register; and

[(c) after correcting the particulars in the register, he shall, provided that paragraphs (2) or (2A) have been complied with, and subject to regulation 15, issue a new registration document containing the correct particulars to the registered keeper].

NOTES

Amendment Para (2A): inserted by SI 2004/238; words in square brackets inserted by SI 2004/1773; sum in square brackets substituted by SI 2007/1018.

Para (3)(a): words omitted revoked by SI 2004/238.

Para (3)(c): substituted by SI 2004/238.

[794]

Issue of new registration document

15 (1) Before issuing a new registration document in respect of a vehicle under any provision of these Regulations, the Secretary of State may require the keeper of the vehicle to satisfy him by the production of the vehicle or other sufficient evidence that the vehicle—

- (a) accords with the particulars furnished when a vehicle or nil licence was last applied for in respect of it; or
- (b) is the registered vehicle.

[(1A) Before issuing a new registration document the Secretary of State may take actions to satisfy himself that the identity and address of the person seeking to be the registered keeper accords with the information given to him.]

(2) The Secretary of State may refuse to issue a new registration document in respect of a vehicle if he is not satisfied as mentioned in [paragraphs (1) and (1A)].

(3) The provisions of Schedule 3 shall have effect in relation to the issue of a new registration document in respect of a vehicle (in this regulation and in Schedule 3 called "the relevant vehicle") where—

- (a) the relevant vehicle falls within category M1 of Annex II to Council Directive 70/156/EEC, and
- (b) either an insurer has informed the Secretary of State that it has decided to pay the value of the relevant vehicle to the owner in preference to paying for the cost of repairing it or the registration document has been surrendered to the Secretary of State under regulation 20(5).

(4) For the purposes of paragraph (3) and Schedule 3 the return of a registration document for a vehicle registered in the NI records in accordance with regulation 18(2)(b) shall be taken to be the issue of a new registration document.

NOTES

Amendment Para (1A): inserted by SI 2003/3073.

Para (2): words in square brackets substituted by SI 2003/3073.

Council Directive 70/156/EEC OJ L42, 23.02.1970, p 1. Repealed and replaced as from 29 April 2009 by Directive 2007/46/EC of the European Parliament and of the Council establishing a framework for the approval of motor vehicles and their trailers, and of systems, components and separate technical units intended for such vehicles (OJ L263, 09.10.2007, p 1).

[795]

PART IV
NOTIFICATION AND CHANGES

Notification of an alteration to a vehicle

16 (1) Where any alteration is made to a vehicle so as to make any of the particulars set out in the registration document incorrect, the registered keeper shall deliver to the Secretary of State—

- (a) notification of the alteration;
- (b) except where the registration document [has been, or may have been,] lost, stolen or destroyed, the registration document.

[(1A) Where the registration document has been, or may have been, lost, stolen or destroyed, notification under paragraph (1) shall be accompanied by an application for the issue of a new registration document and[, except where the registration document fee exemption applies, by] a fee of [£25].]

(2) If the alteration makes any of the particulars shown on the vehicle licence or nil licence incorrect, the registered keeper shall also deliver to the Secretary of State the appropriate licence, unless it is lost, stolen or destroyed.

(3) The Secretary of State may require the registered keeper to furnish such evidence as he may reasonably require to show that the alteration has taken place.

(4) On receiving notification under this regulation the Secretary of State shall, subject to regulation 15, if he is satisfied that the vehicle has been altered in the way notified to him,—

- (a) record the alteration in the register;
- (b) send to the registered keeper a new registration document showing the correct particulars; and
- (c) in a case falling within paragraph (2), [issue] to the registered keeper a new vehicle [licence] or nil licence showing the correct particulars.

NOTES

Amendment Para (1)(b): words in square brackets substituted by SI 2004/238.

Para (1A): inserted by SI 2004/238; words in square brackets inserted by SI 2004/1773; sum in square brackets substituted by SI 2007/1018.

Para (4)(c): word in first pair of square brackets substituted, and word in second pair inserted, by SI 2004/238.

[796]

Notification of destruction or permanent export of a vehicle

17 Where a vehicle is … sent permanently out of—

- (a) Great Britain; or
- (b) Northern Ireland,

the registered keeper shall immediately notify the Secretary of State of the fact …

NOTES

Amendment Words omitted in first place revoked by SI 2003/2635; words omitted at end revoked by SI 2004/3298.

[797]

[Vehicles to which the End-of-Life Vehicles Directive applies

17A (1) This regulation applies to a vehicle to which Directive 2000/53 of the European Parliament and of the Council on end-of-life vehicles applies and which is—

- (a) registered in the GB or NI records; or
- (b) designed or adapted for use on a road and would be registered but for the fact that it falls within the exemption in regulation 29(2).

(2) Where a vehicle to which this regulation applies is transferred to an authorised treatment facility—

- (a) if that facility is in the United Kingdom, the owner or operator thereof shall notify the Secretary of State of the issue of a certificate of destruction pursuant to regulation 27 of the End-of-Life Vehicles Regulations and at the same time shall surrender the registration document to him, except where the registration document has been lost, stolen or destroyed; and
- (b) if that facility is in an EEA State other than the United Kingdom, the registered keeper of the vehicle shall notify the Secretary of State of the issue in that other EEA State of a certificate of destruction and at the same time the registered keeper shall surrender the registration document to him except where the registration document has been lost, stolen or destroyed.

(3) Where the Secretary of State has been notified of the issue of a certificate of destruction he shall not as respects the vehicle to which it relates—

- (a) record in the GB records or, in the case of a vehicle registered in Northern Ireland, in the NI records any further change of keeper;
- (b) accept the required declaration in paragraph 1(1) of Schedule 4.

(4) In this regulation "authorised treatment facility", "certificate of destruction" and "EEA State" have the meanings that those expressions have in the End-of-Life Vehicles Regulations 2003.]

NOTES

Amendment Inserted by SI 2003/2635.

Directive 2000/53 OJ L269, 21.10.2000, p 34.

End-of-Life Vehicles Regulations 2003 SI 2003/2635, in the title Environment.

[798]

Notification of a change of the keeper's name or address

18 (1) If the registered keeper of a vehicle changes his name or his address, he shall forthwith notify the new name or address to the Secretary of State and, except where the registration document has been[, or may have been,] lost, stolen or destroyed, shall deliver the registration document to him.

[(1A) Where the registration document has been, or may have been, lost, stolen or destroyed, notification under paragraph (1) shall be accompanied by an application for the issue of a new registration document and[, except where the registration document fee exemption applies, by] a fee of [£25].]

(2) On receiving notification in accordance with [this regulation] the Secretary of State shall, subject to regulation 15,—

- (a) record the alteration in the register, and
- [(b) send to the registered keeper a new registration document showing the new name or address.]

NOTES

Amendment Para (1): words in square brackets inserted by SI 2004/238.
Para (1A): inserted by SI 2004/238; words in square brackets inserted by SI 2004/1773; sum in square brackets substituted by SI 2007/1018.
Para (2): words in first pair of square brackets substituted by SI 2004/238.
Para (2)(b): substituted by SI 2003/3073.

[799]

Notification of a change of the name or address of the holder of a trade licence

19 (1) If the holder of a trade licence changes the name of his business or his business address, he shall notify the Secretary of State of this fact and of the new name or address forthwith and shall at the same time deliver up the licence to the Secretary of State.

(2) On receiving notification in accordance with paragraph (1) the Secretary of State shall—

- (a) record the alteration in the register of trade licences; and
- (b) send to the holder a new trade licence showing the correct particulars.

[800]

Change of keeper: general provisions

20 (1) Regulations 21 to 25 have effect subject to the provisions of this regulation.

(2) On a change in the keeper of a vehicle, any current vehicle licence for the vehicle may be delivered to the new keeper.

(3) So far as they provide for the issue of a new registration document, regulations 21 to 25 have effect subject to the provisions of regulation 15.

(4) Paragraph (5) shall apply and regulations 21 to 25 shall not apply where—

- (a) a vehicle has sustained damage to its bodywork such that the cost of commercial repair would exceed the value of the vehicle when repaired; and
- (b) either the keeper of the vehicle does not have the benefit of a policy of insurance or cover note which covers the damage or the keeper is an insurer.

(5) On a change of keeper to which this paragraph applies the keeper shall forthwith surrender the registration document to the Secretary of State or, if an insurer, destroy it.

(6) In regulations 21 to 25 "vehicle trader" means any person who—

- (a) is the holder of a trade licence;
- (b) carries on business as a dealer in motor vehicles;
- (c) carries on business as an auctioneer of motor vehicles;
- (d) carries on business as a dismantler of motor vehicles; or
- (e) in relation to a particular vehicle, is—
    - (i) a finance company which has acquired that vehicle under an order for repossession; or

(ii) an insurer which has acquired that vehicle in satisfaction of a total loss claim.

[801]

21 (*Revoked as from 1 July 2005 by SI 2003/3073.*)

Change of keeper: registration document issued in Great Britain on or after 24th March 1997 and the new keeper not a vehicle trader

22 (1) This regulation applies where—

(a) there is a change in the keeper of a vehicle;

(b) a vehicle registration document has been issued in respect of the vehicle … ; and

(c) the new keeper is not a vehicle trader.

(2) The registered keeper of the vehicle—

(a) if the registration document issued in respect of the vehicle is in his possession, shall deliver to the new keeper that part of the document marked as the part which is to be given to the new keeper; and

(b) shall forthwith deliver [to the Secretary of State on the remainder of the registration document, or otherwise in writing, the following information]—

(i) the name and address of the new keeper;

(ii) the date on which the vehicle was sold or transferred to the new keeper;

(iii) a declaration signed by the registered keeper that the details given in accordance with paragraph (i) are correct to the best of his knowledge and that the details given in accordance with paragraph (ii) are correct; and

(iv) a declaration signed by the new keeper that the details given in accordance with paragraphs (i) and (ii) are correct.

[(3) Where all parts of the registration document have been, or may have been, lost, stolen or destroyed, the new keeper shall submit an application to the Secretary of State for the issue of a new registration document [and, except where the registration document fee exemption applies, that application shall be] accompanied by a fee of [£25].

(4) Where the new keeper can produce to the Secretary of State that part of the document marked as the part which is to be given to the new keeper, the new keeper may submit an application to the Secretary of State for the issue of a new registration document accompanied by that part.

(5) On receiving notification of a change in keeper in accordance with paragraphs (2), (3) or (4), the Secretary of State shall, subject to regulation 15—

(a) record the change in the register, and

(b) issue to the new registered keeper a new registration document.]

NOTES

Amendment Para (1)(b): words omitted revoked by SI 2003/3073.

Para (2)(b): words in square brackets substituted by SI 2003/2154.

Para (3): inserted (together with paras (4), (5)) by SI 2004/238; words in square brackets inserted by SI 2004/1773; sum in square brackets substituted by SI 2007/1018.

Paras (4), (5): inserted (together with para (3)) by SI 2004/238.

[802]

Change of keeper: obligations of registered keeper where vehicle registration document issued in Great Britain on or after 24th March 1997 and the new keeper a vehicle trader

23 (1) Subject to regulation 24, this regulation applies where—

(a) there is a change in the keeper of a vehicle;

(b) the person disposing of the vehicle is the registered keeper;

(c) a vehicle registration document has been issued in respect of the vehicle … ; and

(d) the new keeper is a vehicle trader.

(2) The registered keeper shall forthwith notify the Secretary of State, on that part of the registration document which relates to the transfer to a vehicle trader, or otherwise in writing, of the following—

(a) the name and address of the vehicle trader;
(b) the date on which the vehicle was transferred to the vehicle trader;
(c) a declaration signed by the registered keeper that he transferred the vehicle to the vehicle trader on the date specified in accordance with sub-paragraph (b); and
(d) a declaration signed by the vehicle trader that the vehicle was transferred to him on the date specified in accordance with sub-paragraph (b).

(3) If the registration document issued in respect of the vehicle is in his possession, the registered keeper shall deliver to the vehicle trader those parts of it not required to be sent to the Secretary of State under paragraph (2).

NOTES
Amendment Para (1)(c): words omitted revoked by SI 2003/3073.

[803]

Change of keeper: obligations of vehicle traders where registration document issued in Great Britain on or after 24 March 1997

24 (1) This regulation applies where a vehicle trader becomes the keeper of a vehicle in respect of which a vehicle registration document has been issued …

(2) Where this regulation applies the vehicle trader shall, on or before the appropriate date and on that part of the registration document which relates to a change of keeper … , notify the Secretary of State as to—

(a) the transfer of the vehicle to him; and
(b) the date on which he became the keeper of the vehicle.

[(2A) Where the registration document has been, or may have been, lost, stolen or destroyed, notification in accordance with paragraph (2) shall be effected by an application to the Secretary of State for the issue of a new registration document [and, except where the registration document fee exemption applies, that application shall be] accompanied by a fee of [£25].]

(3) For the purposes of paragraph (2) the appropriate date is whichever is the earliest of—

(a) the day on which the vehicle trader first uses, or permits the use of, the vehicle on a public road otherwise than under a trade licence;
(b) the day on which he first keeps the vehicle on such a road;
(c) the day immediately following the expiration of the period of three months ("the three months period of grace") beginning with the day after the date on which the vehicle was last kept by a person who was not a vehicle trader.

(4) Where this regulation applies and the vehicle trader transfers the vehicle to another vehicle trader before the expiration of the three months period of grace, he shall give to the new keeper any part of the registration document in his possession.

(5) Where the vehicle trader transfers the vehicle to another person in a case not falling within paragraph (4), he shall—

(a) forthwith deliver to the Secretary of State, on that part of the registration document which relates to the change of keeper or otherwise in writing, the following—
    (i) the name and address of the new keeper;
    (ii) the date on which the vehicle was transferred to the new keeper;
    (iii) a declaration signed by the [vehicle trader] that the details given in accordance with paragraph (i) are correct to the best of his knowledge and that the details given in accordance with paragraph (ii) are correct; and
    (iv) a declaration signed by the new keeper that the details given in accordance with paragraphs (i) and (ii) are correct; and
(b) if the registration document issued in respect of the vehicle is in his possession, deliver to the new keeper those parts of it not required to be sent to the Secretary of State under sub-paragraph (a).

[(6) Where all parts of the registration document have been, or may have been, lost, stolen or destroyed, the new keeper shall submit an application to the Secretary of State for the issue of a new registration document [and, except where the registration document fee exemption applies, that application shall be] accompanied by a fee of [£25].

(7) Where the new keeper can produce to the Secretary of State that part of the document marked as the part which is to be given to the new keeper, the new keeper may submit an application to the Secretary of State for the issue of a new registration document accompanied by that part.

(8) On receiving notification of a change in keeper in accordance with paragraphs (2), (2A), (5), (6) or (7), the Secretary of State shall, subject to regulation 15—

- (a) record the change in the register, and
- (b) issue to the new registered keeper a new registration document.]

NOTES

Amendment Para (1): words omitted revoked by SI 2003/3073.
Para (2): words omitted revoked by SI 2004/238.
Para (2A): inserted by SI 2004/238; words in square brackets inserted by SI 2004/1773; sum in square brackets substituted by SI 2007/1018.
Para (5)(a)(iii): words in square brackets substituted by SI 2003/2154.
Para (6): inserted (together with paras (7), (8)) by SI 2004/238; words in square brackets inserted by SI 2004/1773; sum in square brackets substituted by SI 2007/1018.
Paras (7), (8): inserted (together with para (6)) by SI 2004/238.

[804]

25 (*Revoked as from 1 July 2005 by SI 2003/3073.*)

Statutory off-road notification

26 Schedule 4 shall have effect for the purpose of prescribing, the particulars to be furnished and the declarations to be made, and the times at which and the circumstances and manner in which they are to be made, by a person who—

- (a) surrenders a vehicle licence;
- (b) does not renew a vehicle licence on its expiration; or
- (c) keeps an unlicensed vehicle.

[805]

[Exceptions to section 31A

26A (1) The requirements prescribed for the purposes of the first condition in section 31B of the 1994 Act are whichever are applicable in the circumstances of the requirements specified in—

- (a) regulation 20(5) (surrender or destruction of registration document for damaged vehicle), in so far as it requires surrender of the registration document,
- (b) . . .
- (c) regulation 22(2)(b) (delivery of remainder of registration document to the Secretary of State),
- (d) regulation 23(2) (notifying the Secretary of State when the transfer is to a vehicle trader),
- (e) regulation 24(5) (vehicle trader notifying the Secretary of State of a transfer), and
- (f) regulation 25(1)(a) (delivery of registration document and notification to the Secretary of State where the registration document was issued in Northern Ireland).

(2) The requirement prescribed for the purposes of the second condition in section 31B is the making of the required declaration and the furnishing of the prescribed particulars to the Secretary of State in accordance with Schedule 4.

(3) The requirement prescribed under subsection (6) of section 31B for the purposes of subsection (4)(c) (the third condition) is that before the expiry of 14 days beginning with the date on which the theft came to the knowledge of the registered keeper notification of the theft was given to—

(a) a member of a police force maintained for any police area in England and Wales or Scotland,
(b) a member of the Police Service of Northern Ireland, or
(c) a person employed to assist such a police force or that Police Service.

(4) The prescribed length of the period for the purpose of the fourth condition shall be 14 days.]

NOTES
Amendment Inserted by SI 2003/3073.
Para (1)(b): revoked by SI 2003/3073.

[806]

PART V
DISCLOSURE OF INFORMATION

Disclosure of registration and licensing particulars

27 (1) The Secretary of State may make any particulars contained in the register available for use—

[(a)
(i) by a local authority for any purpose connected with the investigation of an offence,
(ii) by a local authority in Scotland, for any purpose connected with the investigation of a decriminalised parking contravention, or
(iii) by a local authority in England and Wales, for any purpose connected with its activities as an enforcement authority within the meaning of Part 6 of the Traffic Management Act 2004;]

(b) by a chief officer of police;
(c) by a member of the Police Service of Northern Ireland;
(d) by an officer of [Revenue and Customs] ... ; or
(e) by any person who can show to the satisfaction of the Secretary of State that he has reasonable cause for wanting the particulars to be made available to him.

(2) Particulars may be provided to such a person as is mentioned in paragraph (1)(e) on payment of such fee, if any, of such amount as appears to the Secretary of State reasonable in the circumstances of the case.

(3) In this regulation—

(a) "a decriminalised parking contravention" means any act or omission which would have been an offence but for any of the following provisions of the Road Traffic Act 1991, that is to say—
(i), (ii)..
(iii) paragraph 1(4) of Schedule 3 (contravention of certain orders relating to parking places outside London not to be a criminal offence); and
(iv) paragraph 2(4) of Schedule 3 (provisions creating certain stationary vehicle offences to cease to apply in special parking areas outside London); and

(b) "an officer of [Revenue and Customs]" means an officer as defined in section 1(1) of the Customs and Excise Management Act 1979 and includes any person engaged as mentioned in section 8(2) of that Act.

NOTES
Amendment Para (1)(a): substituted by SI 2008/2849.
Para (1)(d): words in square brackets substituted by virtue of the Commissioners for Revenue and Customs Act 2005, s 50(2), (7); words omitted revoked by SI 2003/2154.
Para (3)(a)(i), (ii): revoked by SI 2008/2849.
Para (3)(b): words in square brackets substituted by virtue of the Commissioners for Revenue and Customs Act 2005, s 50(2), (7).
Road Traffic Act 1991, Sch 3 Repealed by the Traffic Management Act 2004, s 98, Sch 12, Pt 1. Pt 6 (ss 72–93) of the 2004 Act provides a single framework to make regulations for the civil enforcement by local authorities of road traffic contraventions.

[807]

[Exchange of information

27A The Secretary of State may disclose such information, contained in the register, that he is required to disclose to comply with Article 9 of [the Directive].]

NOTES

Amendment Inserted by SI 2003/3073; words in square brackets substituted by SI 2004/3298.

[808]

Sale of information derived from particulars contained in the register

28 The Secretary of State may sell information derived from particulars contained in the register—

(a) to such persons as the Secretary of State thinks fit;
(b) for such price and on such other terms, and subject to such restrictions, as the Secretary of State thinks fit,

if the information does not identify any person or contain anything enabling any person to be identified.

[809]

PART VI
CROWN VEHICLES AND EXEMPT VEHICLES

Application of Regulations to Crown vehicles

29 (1) Except as provided by this Part of these Regulations, nothing in these Regulations applies to a vehicle kept by the Crown.

(2) Nothing in these Regulations or this Part of these Regulations applies to a vehicle kept by the Crown which is used or appropriated for use for naval, military or air force purposes.

[810]

Registration of Crown vehicles

30 (1) A Government Department which uses or keeps or, intends to use or keep, a vehicle on a public road shall—

(a) make to the Secretary of State such declaration and furnish him with such particulars as would be required by section 7 of the 1994 Act if the Department desired to take out a vehicle licence for the vehicle; and
(b) make to the Secretary of State a declaration that the vehicle is only to be used for the purposes of the Crown.

(2) Upon receipt of the declaration and particulars the Secretary of State shall—

(a) register the vehicle in the name of the Government Department;
(b) if there is no registration mark for the time being assigned to the vehicle, assign a registration mark to it; and
(c) issue a registration document for the vehicle.

(3) Any registration mark assigned under paragraph (2) shall be deemed to be assigned under section 23 of the 1994 Act for the purposes of subsection (2) of that section and of these Regulations.

(4) No vehicle licence or nil licence shall be issued by the Secretary of State in respect of the vehicle so registered.

[(5) Where a Government department is the registered keeper of a vehicle—

(a) regulations 13, 14, 15, 16 and 18 shall apply;
(b) regulations 20, 21, 22, 23, 24 and 25 shall apply on a change in the keeper of a vehicle; and
(c) regulations 20, 21, 22 and 25 shall apply on a change in the keeper of a vehicle from one Government department to another.]

NOTES

Amendment Para (5): substituted by SI 2004/238.

[811]

Certificates of Crown exemption

31 (1) Subject to regulation 29(2), for the purposes of identification, a certificate of Crown exemption shall be displayed on every vehicle belonging to the Crown which is used or kept on a public road.

(2) A certificate of Crown exemption is a certificate—

(a) marked with the registration mark of the vehicle to which it relates;

(b) stating that the vehicle is exempt from vehicle excise duty as a Crown vehicle;

(c) signed by a duly authorised officer of the Government Department by which the vehicle is kept.

(3) Regulation 7 (exhibition of vehicle and nil licences) of these Regulations shall apply as if references to a vehicle licence included a reference to a certificate of Crown exemption.

[812]

Application of Regulations to exempt vehicles

32 Subject to the provisions of these Regulations, these Regulations shall apply to exempt vehicles so far as they are capable of being applied to such vehicles.

[813]

Nil licences

33 (1) In this regulation "nil licensable vehicle" means a vehicle which is an exempt vehicle otherwise [than] by virtue of paragraph 2, 2A, 3, 22 or 23 of Schedule 2 to the 1994 Act.

(2) A nil licence is required to be in force in respect of a nil licensable vehicle which is used or kept on a public road.

(3) A nil licence shall—

(a) be granted for a period of 12 months beginning with the first day of the month in which the application for the licence is received by the Secretary of State; and

(b) be in the same form as a vehicle licence with the word "NIL" marked in the space provided for indicating the amount of vehicle excise duty payable.

(4) The keeper of a nil licensable vehicle may apply to the Secretary of State for a nil licence by making to him such a declaration and furnishing him with such particulars and such documentary or other evidence as might be specified under section 7 of the 1994 Act if the keeper desired to take out a vehicle licence for the vehicle.

(5) The Secretary of State may accept a declaration given, and particulars furnished, orally by telephone.

(6) In the case of a vehicle which is an exempt vehicle by virtue of—

(a) paragraph 19 of Schedule 2 to the 1994 Act, or

(b) paragraph 7 of Schedule 4 to that Act,

the Secretary of State shall require the keeper to furnish him with a certificate that paragraph 19 of Schedule 2 or, as the case may be, paragraph 7 of Schedule 4 applies, unless the Secretary of State satisfies himself by other means that one of those paragraphs applies.

(7) The certificate shall be obtained by the keeper of the vehicle from the Secretary of State for Work and Pensions, the Secretary of State for Defence or the Department for Social Development for Northern Ireland, whichever is appropriate.

(8) Paragraphs (4) to (7) do not apply where the person applying for a nil licence agrees to comply with such conditions as may be specified in relation to him by the Secretary of State.

[(8A) Section 22ZA of the 1994 Act shall apply to information of the following descriptions—

(a) the name of any person to whom—

(i) disability living allowance or mobility supplement is payable; or

(ii) disability living allowance has ceased to be payable and who would be entitled to receive the mobility component at the higher rate but for his failure to satisfy a condition referred to in paragraph 19(2A)(b) of Schedule 2 to the 1994 Act;

(b) that person's date of birth and National Insurance number; and

(c) if applicable, the date on which the allowance or supplement, as appropriate, will cease to be payable.

(8B) For the purposes of paragraph (8A)—

"disability living allowance" means a disability living allowance for the purposes of section 71 of the Social Security Contributions and Benefits Act 1992 (disability living allowance);

"mobility component" means the mobility component of a disability living allowance and "higher rate" means the higher rate of the mobility component for the time being prescribed under section 73 of that Act (the mobility component); and

"mobility supplement" has the meaning which that expression bears in paragraph 19 of Schedule 2 to the 1994 Act.]

(9) If, following an application made in accordance with this regulation, the Secretary of State is satisfied that a vehicle is a nil licensable vehicle, he shall issue a nil licence to the keeper of the vehicle.

(10) If at any time vehicle excise duty becomes chargeable under the 1994 Act in respect of a vehicle which immediately before that time was a nil licensable vehicle, the keeper of the vehicle shall forthwith return to the Secretary of State—

(a) any nil licence issued in respect of the vehicle; and

(b) any certificate obtained by him for the purposes of paragraph (6) in relation to the vehicle.

NOTES

Amendment Para (1): word in square brackets inserted by SI 2003/2154.
Paras (8A), (8B): inserted by SI 2005/2713.

[814]

Exemptions from vehicle excise duty: vehicles imported by members of foreign armed forces and others

34 Schedule 5, which provides for the exemption from vehicle excise duty of vehicles imported into Great Britain by members of foreign armed forces and other persons, shall have effect.

[815]

PART VII
TRADE LICENCES

Definition of "motor trader": descriptions of businesses

35 The following descriptions of business are hereby prescribed for the purposes of sub-paragraph (b) of the definition of "motor trader" in section 62(1) of the 1994 Act—

(a) the business of modifying vehicles, whether by the fitting of accessories or otherwise;

(b) the business of valeting vehicles.

[816]

Period for review of decision refusing an application for a trade licence

36 For the purposes of section 14(3)(b) of the 1994 Act (which relates to the review by the Secretary of State of his decision refusing an application for a trade licence by a person entitled to make such an application) the period within which such an applicant may request the Secretary of State for such a review shall be 28 days beginning with the day after the day on which the decision was given.

[817]

Conditions subject to which trade licences are to be issued

37 The conditions subject to which trade licences are to be issued, and with which every holder of a trade licence shall comply, shall be those specified in Part I of Schedule 6.

[818]

Purposes for which the holder of a trade licence may use a vehicle by virtue of the licence

38 Part II of Schedule 6 shall have effect for prescribing the purposes for which a vehicle may be used by virtue of a trade licence.

[819]

Assignment of general registration marks

39 On issuing a trade licence the Secretary of State shall assign to the holder of the licence a general registration mark in respect of that licence.

[820]

Issue of trade plates

40 (1) Subject to paragraphs (3) and (4), the Secretary of State shall issue to every holder of a trade licence, as respects each licence held by him, a set of trade plates appropriate to the class of vehicles for which the licence is to be used.

(2) Each trade plate shall show the general registration mark assigned to the holder of the licence in respect of the licence, and one of the trade plates shall include a means whereby the licence may be fixed to it.

(3) Where the holder of a trade licence satisfies the Secretary of State that the vehicles which he will use by virtue of the licence include vehicles which would otherwise be liable to vehicle excise duty under paragraph 2 of Schedule 1 to the 1994 Act (motorcycles) and other vehicles, the Secretary of State shall issue to the holder an additional trade plate in respect of the vehicles otherwise liable to vehicle excise duty under that paragraph.

(4) Where the licence is to be used only in respect of vehicles to which paragraph 2 of Schedule 1 to the 1994 Act applies (motorcycles), the Secretary of State shall issue only one trade plate to the holder of the licence and that plate shall include a means whereby the licence may be fixed to it.

(5) Each trade plate shall remain the property of the Secretary of State and shall be returned forthwith to the Secretary of State by the person to whom it was issued if that person ceases to be—

- (a) the holder of the trade licence in respect of which the trade plate was issued; or
- (b) a motor trader or a vehicle tester.

[821]

Issue of replacement trade plates

41 (1) If any trade plate issued by the Secretary of State to the holder of a trade licence is lost, stolen, destroyed or materially damaged, the holder of the licence shall apply to the Secretary of State for the issue to him of a replacement set of trade plates.

(2) On receipt of an application under paragraph (1) the Secretary of State shall so issue a replacement set if—

- (a) he has received all those trade plates in the set which are still in the possession of the holder of the licence;
- (b) except where paragraph (3) applies, the fee prescribed by paragraph (4) has been paid; and
- (c) he is satisfied that any plate has been lost, stolen, destroyed or materially damaged.

(3) If only that part of a trade plate which consists of a means whereby the trade licence may be fixed to it is lost, stolen, destroyed or materially damaged, the holder of the licence shall apply to the Secretary of State for the issue to him of a replacement means of fixing the licence and, upon payment of the fee prescribed by paragraph (4)(c), the Secretary of State shall issue such a replacement.

(4) The fees payable under paragraphs (2) and (3) shall be—

(a) for a replacement set of trade plates comprising two plates, £13.50;

(b) for a replacement set of trade plates comprising three plates, £18;

(c) for a replacement of a single trade plate issued under regulation 40(4), £7; and

(d) for a replacement means of fixing a trade licence to a trade plate, £2.

(5) No fee shall be payable under paragraph (4)(a) or (b) on account of the replacement of a trade plate, if the Secretary of State is satisfied that the plate has become illegible or the colour of the plate has been altered (whether by fading or by other means) otherwise than by reason of any act or omission of the licence holder.

(6) If a replacement set of trade plates has been issued on the ground that any of the original trade plates has been lost, stolen or destroyed, and the original plate is subsequently found or recovered, the holder of the licence—

(a) if the original plate is in his possession, shall forthwith return it to the Secretary of State, or

(b) if it is not in his possession but he becomes aware that it is found or recovered, shall take all reasonable steps to obtain possession of it and return it to the Secretary of State.

[822]

Display of general registration mark of holder of a trade licence and exhibition of licence

42 (1) Where a vehicle is in use under a trade licence the general registration mark assigned to the holder of a trade licence shall be displayed on the vehicle in the manner specified in paragraph (2).

(2) The trade plates issued by the Secretary of State shall be fixed to and displayed on the vehicle in such a manner that, if the general registration mark assigned to the holder were a registration mark assigned to the vehicle, the provisions of regulations 5 and 6 of the Road Vehicles (Display of Registration Marks) Regulations 2001 (the "2001 Regulations") would be complied with, notwithstanding the vehicle may not have been first registered on or after the relevant date, as defined in regulation 2(1) of the 2001 Regulations, or it is a works truck (as defined by paragraph 4(6) of Schedule 1 to the 1994 Act) or an agricultural machine (as defined by regulation 2(1) of the 2001 Regulations) or a road roller.

(3) The prescribed manner of exhibiting a trade licence on a vehicle for the purposes of section 33(1)(b) of the 1994 Act is that specified in paragraph (4).

(4) The trade licence shall be—

(a) exhibited on the front of the vehicle so as to be clearly visible at all times in daylight; and

(b) fixed by means of the trade plate issued to the licence holder which contains a means for fixing the licence to it.

NOTES

Road Vehicles (Display of Registration Marks) Regulations 2001 SI 2001/561.

[823]

PART VIII
MISCELLANEOUS

Cylinder capacity

43 (1) For the purposes of Schedule 1 to the 1994 Act (annual rates of vehicle excise duty) the cylinder capacity of an internal combustion engine shall be taken to be—

(a) in the case of a single-cylinder engine, the cylinder capacity attributable to the cylinder of the engine; and

(b) in the case of an engine having two or more cylinders, the sum of the cylinder capacities attributable to the separate cylinders.

(2) The cylinder capacity attributable to any cylinder of an internal combustion engine shall be deemed to be equal to—

(a) in the case of a cylinder having a single piston, the product expressed in cubic centimetres of the square of the internal diameter of the cylinder measured in centimetres, and the distance through which the piston associated with the cylinder moves during one half of a revolution of the engine measured in centimetres multiplied by 0.7854; and

(b) in the case of a cylinder having more than one piston, the sum of the products expressed in cubic centimetres of the square of the internal diameter of each part of the cylinder in which a piston moves measured in centimetres, and the distance through which the piston associated with that part of the cylinder moves during one half of a revolution of the engine measured in centimetres multiplied by 0.7854.

(3) In measuring cylinders for the purpose of calculating cylinder capacity, and in calculating cylinder capacity, fractions of centimetres are to be taken into account.

[824]

Seating capacity of buses

44 (1) For the purpose of Part III of Schedule 1 to the 1994 Act (annual rates of vehicle excise duty applicable to buses), the seating capacity of a bus shall be taken to be the number of persons that may be seated in the bus at any one time, as determined in accordance with the principles specified in paragraph (2).

(2) Those principles are—

(a) where separate seats for each person are provided one person shall be counted for each separate seat provided;

(b) where the vehicle is fitted with continuous seats one person shall be counted for each complete length of 410 mm measured in a straight line lengthwise on the front of each seat;

(c) where any continuous seat is fitted with arms in order to separate the seating spaces and the arms can be folded back or otherwise put out of use, the arms shall be ignored in measuring the seat;

(d) no account shall be taken of—

(i) the driver's seat; or

(ii) any seats alongside the driver's seat, whether separate from or continuous with it, if the Secretary of State is satisfied that the use of those seats by members of the public will not be permitted during the currency of the licence applied for.

(3) In paragraph (2) "driver's seat" means—

(a) any separate seat occupied by the driver; or

(b) where no such seat is provided and the driver occupies a portion of a continuous seat, so much of that seat as extends from the right edge of the seat if the vehicle is steered from the right-hand side, or from the left edge of the seat if the vehicle is steered from the left-hand side, to a point 460 mm left or right, as the case may be, of the point on the seat directly behind the centre of the steering column.

[825]

Recovery vehicles: prescribed purposes

45 (1) The purposes specified in Part I of Schedule 7 are hereby prescribed for the purposes of paragraph 5(3)(e) of Schedule 1 to the 1994 Act (purposes for which a recovery vehicle may be used).

(2) The purposes specified in Part II of Schedule 7 are hereby prescribed for the purposes of paragraph 5(4) of Schedule 1 to the 1994 Act (purposes to be disregarded in determining whether a vehicle is a recovery vehicle).

[826]

Admissibility of evidence from records

46 (1) The matters specified in paragraph (2) are hereby prescribed for the purposes of section 52(1) of the 1994 Act (matters with respect to which statements in documents are admissible in evidence).

(2) The matters are anything relating to—

(a) an application for—
   (i) a vehicle licence;
   (ii) a trade licence;
   (iii) a repayment of vehicle excise duty under section 19 of the 1994 Act (surrender of licences); or
   (iv) the recovery of overpaid vehicle excise duty;
(b) a vehicle licence, trade licence, nil licence, registration document or registration mark;
(c) a trade plate;
(d) the recovery of underpaid vehicle excise duty;
(e) the conviction of any person for an offence under the 1994 Act or its predecessor legislation;
(f) the exemption of a vehicle from vehicle excise duty;
(g) the liability of the person by whom a vehicle is kept to pay any sum in accordance with section 30 of the 1994 Act;
(h) the immobilisation, removal or disposal of a vehicle pursuant to regulations made under Schedule 2A to the 1994 Act.

NOTES
Regulations made under Sch 2A to the 1994 Act See SI 1997/2439.

[827]

Regulations prescribed under section 59(2) of the 1994 Act

47 The regulations specified in column (1), whose subject matter is referred to in column (2), of the table in Schedule 8 are hereby prescribed as regulations to which section 59(2)(a) of the 1994 Act [(fines not to exceed level 3 on the standard scale) applies].

NOTES
Amendment Words in square brackets substituted by SI 2003/2154.

[828]

SCHEDULE 1

NOTES
Pt I of this Schedule specifies the following regulations revoked by reg 2:

Road Vehicles (Registration and Licensing) Regulations 1971, SI 1971/450, and the amending SI 1972/1865, SI 1973/870, SI 1975/1342, SI 1976/1680, SI 1976/2089, SI 1977/230, SI 1978/1536, SI 1981/366, SI 1982/1802, SI 1983/1248, SI 1986/607, SI 1986/1177, SI 1986/2101, SI 1987/2123, SI 1990/2185, SI 1993/1760, SI 1994/1364, SI 1994/1911, SI 1994/3296, SI 1995/1470, SI 1997/401, SI 2002/2382;

Road Vehicles (Excise) (Prescribed Particulars) Regulations 1981, SI 1981/931, and the amending SI 1986/2100, SI 1987/2122, SI 1988/847;

Road Vehicles (Exemptions from Duty) Regulations 1986, SI 1986/1467;

Road Vehicles (Prescribed Regulations for the Purposes of Increased Penalties) Regulations 1987, SI 1987/2085;

Recovery Vehicles (Prescribed Purposes) Regulations 1989, SI 1989/1376;

Vehicle Registration (Sale of Information) Regulations 1996, SI 1996/2800;

Road Vehicles (Statutory Off-Road Notification) Regulations 1997, SI 1997/3025, and the amending SI 1999/713;

Road Vehicles Registration Fee Regulations 1998, SI 1998/572, and the amending SI 1998/995; and

Vehicle Excise Duty (Reduced Pollution) Regulations 1998, SI 1998/3094, and the amending SI 2000/3274.

Pt II of the Schedule partially revokes SI 1970/1997; and Pt III wholly revokes numerous Northern Ireland regulations, which are outside the scope of this work.

[829]

SCHEDULE 2
REDUCED POLLUTION CERTIFICATES AND THE REDUCED POLLUTION REQUIREMENTS

Regulation 5

Interpretation of Schedule

1 (1) In this Schedule—

"authorised examiner" means—

(a) a vehicle examiner appointed by the Secretary of State pursuant to section 66A of the 1988 Act;
(b) a vehicle examiner appointed by the Department of the Environment for Northern Ireland pursuant to Article 74 of the Road Traffic (Northern Ireland) Order 1995; or
(c) a person authorised by the Secretary of State to conduct reduced pollution examinations;

["diesel engine" has the same meaning as that expression bears in section 2.1 of Annex I to Directive 2005/55/EC;]

"Directive 1999/96" means Directive 1999/96/EC of the European Parliament and of the Council of 13th December 1999 on the approximation of the laws of the Member States relating to measures to be taken against the emission of gaseous and particulate pollutants from compression ignition engines for use in vehicles, and against the emission of gaseous and particulate pollutants from positive ignition engines fuelled with natural gas or liquefied petroleum gas for use in vehicles and amending Council Directive 88/77/EEC;

["Directive 2005/55/EC" means Directive 2005/55/EC of the European Parliament and of the Council of 28th September 2005 on the approximation of the laws of the Member States relating to the measures to be taken against the emission of gaseous and particulate pollutants from compression-ignition engines for use in vehicles, and the emission of gaseous pollutants from positive-ignition engines fuelled with natural gas or liquefied petroleum gas for use in vehicles;

"Directive 2005/78/EC" means Commission Directive 2005/78/EC of 14th November 2005 of the European Parliament and of the Council on the approximation of the laws of the Member States relating to the measures to be taken against the emission of gaseous and particulate pollutants from compression ignition engines for use in vehicles and the emission of gaseous pollutants from positive ignition engines fuelled with natural gas or liquefied petroleum gas for use in vehicles and amending Annexes I, II, III, IV and VI thereto;]

"eligible vehicle" means a vehicle which is an eligible vehicle as defined by section 61B(4) of the 1994 Act;

["gas engine" has the same meaning as that expression bears in section 2.1 of Annex I to Directive 2005/55/EC;

"limit value" has the same meaning as in Directive 2005/55/EC;]

["prescribed adaptation" means an adaptation of a description specified in paragraph 4(2) or 4A(b)(ii);]

"prescribed fee" means the fee prescribed by paragraph 13;

"rectification notice" has the meaning given by paragraph 9(1);

"reduced pollution examination" means an examination of an eligible vehicle for the purpose of determining whether a reduced pollution certificate should be issued for that vehicle";

["registered" in relation to an eligible vehicle means registered under section 21 of the 1994 Act;]

"vehicle identification number" has the same meaning as in regulation 67 of the Road Vehicles (Construction and Use) Regulations 1986 or in regulation 80 of the Motor Vehicles (Construction and Use) Regulations (Northern Ireland) 1999; and

a reference, in whatever terms, to an eligible vehicle which satisfies or does not satisfy the reduced pollution requirements is to an eligible vehicle with respect to which the reduced pollution requirements are, or are not, satisfied.

(2) For the purposes of this Schedule and of regulation 5, a reduced pollution certificate shall be deemed to be issued, and a notice or notification shall be deemed to be given, by an authorised examiner if it is signed by that examiner or on behalf of that examiner by a person authorised by him to sign it on his behalf.

Applications for reduced pollution certificates

2 (1) An application for a reduced pollution certificate shall be made to the Secretary of State.

(2) The Secretary of State shall fix the time when and the place where a reduced pollution examination is to be carried out and shall inform the applicant accordingly.

(3) The Secretary of State may by notice to the applicant alter the time or place fixed for the examination, but shall not alter the time to an earlier time without the consent of the applicant.

Reduced pollution examinations

3 (1) A reduced pollution examination shall be carried out by an authorised examiner.

(2) An authorised examiner may refuse to examine an eligible vehicle if—

(a) the vehicle is not presented at the time and place appointed for the examination;
(b) the prescribed fee has not been paid;
(c) the information specified in sub-paragraph (3) has not been provided;
[(cc) a reduced pollution certificate has previously been issued in respect of the vehicle and the last such certificate issued is not surrendered;]
(d) the person presenting the vehicle is not willing, to the extent necessary for the purpose of properly carrying out the examination,—

- (i) to give the examiner access to the engine and the fuel and exhaust systems,
- (ii) to operate the controls of the vehicle, or
- (iii) generally to co-operate with the examiner;

(e) the vehicle is in so dangerous or dirty a condition that the examination cannot be carried out properly;

(f) the vehicle has insufficient fuel or oil in it for the examination to be carried out; or

(g) the vehicle's engine has failed electrically or mechanically.

(3) The information referred to in sub-paragraph (2)(c) is—

(a) the name and address (including post code) of the applicant;

(b) the registration mark of the vehicle (if the vehicle has been registered);

(c) the make and model of the vehicle;

(d) the vehicle identification number of the vehicle;

(e) the date of manufacture of the vehicle; and

(f) particulars of [any prescribed adaptation] made to the vehicle, whereby it is claimed that the vehicle satisfies the reduced pollution requirements.

[The reduced pollution requirements

3A An eligible vehicle satisfies the reduced pollution requirements for the purposes of the 1994 Act at any time if paragraph 4 or 4A applies to it.]

...

4 [(1) This paragraph applies to an eligible vehicle where, as a result of an adaptation of a description specified in paragraph (2) having been made to it after 17th March 1998, it satisfies the reduced pollution requirements in accordance with sub-paragraph (3) or (4).]

(2) [The adaptation referred to in sub-paragraph (1) is—]

(a) the fitting of a new engine to an eligible vehicle; or

(b) the fitting to the engine of an eligible vehicle of a device, for which there is in force a certificate of conformity issued by the manufacturer of the vehicle under section 57 of the 1988 Act on the basis that the device complies with approval requirements prescribed for the purpose of these Regulations by the Secretary of State in regulations made by him under section 54 of that Act.

(3) An eligible vehicle—

[(za) which is registered before 1st October 2006;]

(a) for which a reduced pollution certificate was not in force on 4th January 2001; and

(b) which at the time that it was [registered] was required to comply or did comply, as to the rate and content of its emissions, with the requirements specified in an instrument referred to in column (2) of an item in Table 1 below,

satisfies the reduced pollution requirements if it is so adapted that the rate and content of its particulate emissions do not exceed the number of grams per kilowatt-hour specified in column (3) of the item.

TABLE 1

(1) Item	*(2)* Instrument setting the standard to which the eligible vehicle was [registered]	*(3)* Rate and content of particulate emissions after adaptation (grams per kilowatt-hour)
1	Directive 88/77/EEC	0.16
2	Directive 91/542/EEC (limits A)	0.16
3	Directive 91/542/EEC (limits B)	0.03
4	Directive 1999/96 Annex I, paragraph 6.2.1, Table 1 Row A and Table 2 Row A	0.03

(4) An eligible vehicle—

[(za) which is registered before 1st October 2006;]

(a) for which a reduced pollution certificate was in force on 4th January 2001; and

(b) which at the time that it was [registered] was required to comply or did comply, as to the rate and content of its emissions, with the requirements specified in an instrument referred to in column (2) of an item in Table 2 below,

satisfies the reduced pollution requirements if it is so adapted that the rate and content of its particulate emissions do not exceed the number of grams per kilowatt-hour specified in column (3) of the item.

TABLE 2

(1) *Item*	*(2)* *Instrument setting the standard to which the eligible vehicle was [registered]*	*(3)* *Rate and content of particulate emissions after adaptation (grams per kilowatt-hour)*
1	Directive 88/77/EEC	0.16
2	Directive 91/542/EEC (limits A)	0.16
3	Directive 91/542/EEC (limits B)	0.08
4	European Commission Proposal Com (97) 627 for a European and Council Directive amending Council Directive 88/77	0.04

(5) An eligible vehicle which was [registered] before 1st April 1991 shall be taken—

(a) if it is a vehicle such as is referred to in paragraph (3), to be a vehicle to which item 1 of Table 1 applies; or

(b) if it is a vehicle such as is referred to in paragraph (4), to be a vehicle to which item 1 of Table 2 applies.

(6) …

[4A This paragraph applies to an eligible vehicle which—

(a) is registered before 1st October 2009; and

(b) complies with the requirements of paragraph 4B as a result of—

(i) its design, construction or equipment as manufactured; or

(ii) an adaptation made to the vehicle after 30th September 2006 which—

(aa) affects the durability or in-service conformity of the engine control system,

(bb) affects or introduces an on-board diagnostic system,

(cc) affects or introduces a sensor for the detection of oxides of nitrogen, or

(dd) otherwise concerns the system for controlling or managing the emissions of the vehicle.

4B The requirements of this paragraph, in relation to an eligible vehicle, are that—

(a) the vehicle complies with the limit values in section 6.2.1 of Annex I to Directive 2005/55/EC in accordance with that Directive and as set out—

(i) in the case of a vehicle propelled by a diesel engine, in row B2 of table 1 and row B2 of table 2 of the Directive; and

(ii) in the case of a vehicle propelled by a gas engine, in row B2 of table 2 of the Directive;

(b) an on-board diagnostic system as described in Article 4(2) of Directive 2005/55/EC is fitted to the vehicle in accordance with the requirements of Annex IV to Directive 2005/78/EC; and

(c) the vehicle meets the requirements of section 6.5 of Annex 1 to Directive 2005/55/EC.]

Determination of applications and issue of certificates or notification of refusal

5 (1) An authorised examiner who has carried out a reduced pollution examination shall issue a reduced pollution certificate to the applicant if and only if he is satisfied that the eligible vehicle satisfies the reduced pollution requirements.

(2) A reduced pollution certificate shall be granted for such period as the Secretary of State may determine.

(3) If an authorised examiner is not satisfied that an eligible vehicle that he has examined satisfies the reduced pollution requirements, he shall notify the applicant of his refusal of the application and of the reasons for it.

Contents of a reduced pollution certificate

6 A reduced pollution certificate shall contain the following information—

(a) the registration mark of the eligible vehicle;

(b) the date on which the certificate expires;

(c) the make and model of the vehicle;

(d) the vehicle identification number;

(e) particulars of [any prescribed adaptation] that has been made to the vehicle;

[(f) the emission standard with which the vehicle complies;]

(g) the vehicle testing station or other place at which the reduced pollution examination was conducted.

Reduced pollution certificate to be conclusive

7 (1) If at any time a reduced pollution certificate is in force for an eligible vehicle [which is registered,] that certificate shall be conclusive evidence that the vehicle satisfies the reduced pollution requirements at that time.

(2) If at any time no reduced pollution certificate is in force for an eligible vehicle, that fact shall be conclusive evidence that the vehicle does not satisfy the reduced pollution requirements at that time.

Re-examination of an eligible vehicle for which a reduced pollution certificate is in force

8 (1) An authorised examiner may at any time by notice require the registered keeper of an eligible vehicle for which a reduced pollution certificate is in force to submit it, at a place and within a period specified in the notice (or at such other place or within such longer period as may be agreed by the Secretary of State), for a re-examination for the purpose of determining whether it still satisfies the reduced pollution requirements.

(2) Paragraphs 2(3) and 3(2) (except paragraph 3(2)(b)) apply to a re-examination under this paragraph.

(3) If an eligible vehicle for which a reduced pollution certificate is in force is found after a re-examination under this paragraph to satisfy the reduced pollution requirements, the authorised examiner who carried out the re-examination shall give notice to that effect to the registered keeper or to the person who brought the vehicle to the re-examination and to the Secretary of State.

Rectification notice

9 (1) If, after an examination under paragraph 8 or otherwise, an eligible vehicle for which a reduced pollution certificate is in force is found no longer to satisfy the reduced pollution requirements, the authorised examiner who carried out the examination shall give notice ("a rectification notice") to that effect to the registered keeper or the person who brought the vehicle to the examination.

(2) A rectification notice shall state in what respect the vehicle was found not to satisfy the reduced pollution requirements.

(3) A rectification notice shall state that, unless the vehicle is submitted for a further examination, at the place and within the period specified in the notice (or at such other place) or within longer period as may be agreed by the Secretary of State), and is found at that further examination to satisfy the reduced pollution requirements, the Secretary of State will at the expiration of that period revoke the reduced pollution certificate for the vehicle.

(4) Paragraphs 2(3) and 3(2) apply to an examination under sub-paragraph (3).

Revocation, surrender and cancellation of a reduced pollution certificate

10 (1) [Subject to paragraph 10A,] the Secretary of State may by notice given to the registered keeper revoke a reduced pollution certificate—

(a) if he is satisfied, in consequence of a re-examination under paragraph 9(3) that an eligible vehicle for which the reduced pollution certificate is in force no longer satisfies the reduced pollution requirements; or

(b) if the registered keeper of an eligible vehicle who has been required to submit it for re-examination under paragraph 8 or following a rectification notice has failed to do so in accordance with this Schedule.

(2) A reduced pollution certificate which has been revoked by notice under paragraph (1) shall cease to have effect on the date specified for that purpose in the notice.

(3) Where a notice has been given in respect of the eligible vehicle under paragraph 8(1) or 9(3), the notice under paragraph (1) shall not be given before the end of the period for submitting the vehicle for a further examination specified in the notice under paragraph 8(1) or, as the case may be, 9(3).

(4) The registered keeper of a vehicle for which a reduced pollution certificate is in force may at any time surrender the certificate to the Secretary of State for cancellation, whereupon the certificate shall cease to have effect.

(5) Where a certificate is revoked in accordance with paragraph (1) the registered keeper shall surrender the certificate to the Secretary of State for cancellation within the period specified for this purpose in the notice given under paragraph (1).

[10A (1) Where pursuant to regulation 5(1) an applicant furnishes a reduced pollution certificate in respect of a vehicle which is not registered, the Secretary of State shall revoke that certificate if he is satisfied that it relates to an eligible vehicle which does not fall within paragraph 4(3) or (4).

(2) Where the Secretary of State revokes a reduced pollution certificate under sub-paragraph (1) he shall cancel that certificate, whereupon it shall cease to have effect.]

Replacement certificates

11 At any time when a reduced pollution is in force in respect of a vehicle the Secretary of State may, on surrender of the certificate or its identifiable remains, issue a replacement certificate for the remainder of the period for which the surrendered certificate was in force.

Appeal against refusal or revocation of a certificate

12 (1) A person aggrieved by a refusal to issue a reduced pollution certificate following a reduced pollution examination, or by the revocation of a reduced pollution certificate, may appeal to the Secretary of State.

(2) An appeal shall—

(a) be made before the expiration of the period of 14 days beginning with the day on which an authorised examiner gives notice under paragraph 5(3) or the Secretary of State gave notice under paragraph 10(1);

(b) state the grounds on which it is made; and

(c) be sent by post or facsimile transmission to the Secretary of State—

(i) at [such office of the Vehicle and Operator Services Agency as he may direct], in the case of a vehicle which was examined in Great Britain; or

(ii) at the Driver and Vehicle Testing Agency, Headquarters, Balmoral Road, Belfast BT12 6QL, in the case of a vehicle which was examined in Northern Ireland.

(3) As soon as reasonably practicable after the receipt of an appeal made in accordance with sub-paragraph (2) the Secretary of State shall notify the appellant of—

(a) the place at which the examination for the purposes of the appeal will take place; and

(b) the time when it will start.

(4) The examination shall be carried by a person who has not previously examined the vehicle and who is—

(a) in the case of an examination carried out in Great Britain, authorised by the Secretary of State to carry out examinations for the purposes of this paragraph; or

(b) in the case of an examination carried out in Northern Ireland, an authorised examiner.

(5) At the conclusion of an examination under this paragraph the Secretary of State shall either issue a reduced pollution certificate or give the appellant notice that the appeal is dismissed and the grounds of dismissal.

(6) Paragraphs 2(3) and 3(2) apply to an examination under this paragraph.

Prescribed fees

13 (1) Subject to sub-paragraphs (1) and (3) the prescribed fee for carrying out any examination of an eligible vehicle under this Schedule (except an examination under paragraph 8, for which no fee shall be payable) shall be—

(a) [£32], except in a case falling within paragraph (b);

(b) [£19], if it is carried out at the same time as an examination of the vehicle—

(i) for the purposes of determining whether a certificate of initial fitness should be issued under section 6 of the Public Passenger Vehicles Act 1981 or a public service vehicle licence should be granted under Article 61 of the Road Traffic (Northern Ireland) Order 1981;

(ii) for the purposes of an examination carried out for the purposes of section 45 of the 1988 Act, Article 61(1) of the Road Traffic (Northern Ireland) Order 1995 (test certificates); or

(iii) for one or more of the purposes mentioned in section 49(1) of the 1988 Act or Article 65 of the Road Traffic (Northern Ireland) Order 1995 (plating and testing of goods vehicles).

(2) If, at the request of the applicant, the time appointed for an examination is out of hours, the fee payable under sub-paragraph (1) shall be increased by [£12].

(3) If, at the request of the applicant, an examination is carried out otherwise than at premises provided and maintained by the Secretary of State under section 52 of the 1988 Act or Article 73, of the Road Traffic (Northern Ireland) Order 1995 the fee payable under the preceding provisions of this paragraph shall be increased by [£3].

(4) In sub-paragraph (2) "out of hours" means—

(a) at any time on Saturday, Sunday, Christmas Day, a Bank Holiday (as defined by the Banking and Financial Dealings Act 1971) or (in relation to Great Britain) Good Friday or (in relation to Northern Ireland) Easter Tuesday or any other day on which tests are not normally conducted at vehicle testing stations;

(b) or on any other day except—

(i) in Great Britain, between 8.00 am and 5.00 pm on Monday to Thursday inclusive or between 8.00 am and 4.30 on a Friday; or

(ii) in Northern Ireland, between 8.45 am and 4.55 pm on Monday to Friday inclusive.

NOTES

Amendment Para 1(1): definitions "diesel engine", "Directive 2005/55/EC", "Directive 2005/78/EC", "gas engine" and "limit value" inserted, and definition "prescribed adaptation" substituted, by SI 2007/2553;
definition "registered" inserted by SI 2006/2320.
Para 3(2)(cc): inserted by SI 2007/2553.
Para 3(3)(f): words in square brackets substituted by SI 2007/2553.
Para 3A: inserted by SI 2007/2553.
Para 4: heading (omitted) revoked by SI 2007/2553.

Para 4(1): substituted by SI 2007/2553.
Para 4(2): words in square brackets substituted by SI 2007/2553.
Para 4(3)(za): inserted by SI 2006/2320.
Para 4(3)(b): word in square brackets substituted by SI 2006/2320.
Para 4(3): in Table 1 in heading to column 2 word in square brackets substituted by SI 2006/2320.
Para 4(4)(za): inserted by SI 2006/2320.
Para 4(4)(b): word in square brackets substituted by SI 2006/2320.
Para 4(4): in Table 2 in heading to column 2 word in square brackets substituted by SI 2006/2320.
Para 4(5): word in square brackets substituted by SI 2006/2320.
Para 4(6): revoked by SI 2006/2320.
Paras 4A, 4B: inserted by SI 2007/2553.
Para 6(e): words in square brackets substituted by SI 2007/2553.
Para 6(f): substituted by SI 2007/2553.
Para 7(1): words in square brackets inserted by SI 2006/2320.
Para 10(1): words in square brackets inserted by SI 2006/2320.
Para 10A: inserted by SI 2006/2320.
Para 12(2)(c)(i): words in square brackets substituted by SI 2008/1444.
Para 13(1)(a), (b): sum in square brackets substituted by SI 2009/880.
Para 13(2), (3): sum in square brackets substituted by SI 2009/880.
Directive 88/77/EEC; Directive 91/542/EEC; Directive 1999/96/EC
OJ L36, 09.02.1988, p 33; OJ L295, 25.10.1991, p 1; OJ L44, 16.02.2000, p 1 respectively. All repealed by Directive 2005/55/EC of the European Parliament and of the Council on the approximation of the laws of the Member States relating to the measures to be taken against the emission of gaseous and particulate pollutants from compression-ignition engines for use in vehicles, and the emission of gaseous pollutants from positive-ignition engines fuelled with natural gas or liquefied petroleum gas for use in vehicles (OJ L275, 20.10.2005, p 1).
Directive 2005/55/EC OJ L275, 20.10.2005, p 1.
Commission Directive 2005/78/EC OJ L313, 29.11.2005, p 1.
European Commission Proposal Com (97) 627 for a European and Council Directive amending Council Directive 88/77 OJ 98C 173/1, 08.06.1998, p 18.
Road Vehicles (Construction and Use) Regulations 1986 SI 1986/1078.
Motor Vehicles (Construction and Use) Regulations (Northern Ireland) 1999
SR 1999/454 (outside the scope of this work).
Road Traffic (Northern Ireland) Order 1981 SI 1981/154 (NI 1) (outside the scope of this work).
Road Traffic (Northern Ireland) Order 1995 SI 1995/2994 (NI 18) (outside the scope of this work).

[830]

SCHEDULE 3
ISSUE OF NEW REGISTRATION DOCUMENT

Regulation 15(3)

Duty of the Secretary of State

1 Where this Schedule has effect, before issuing a new registration document for the relevant vehicle, the Secretary of State—

(a) shall require the keeper of the relevant vehicle to produce the vehicle for examination by a person authorised by the Secretary of State at a time and place fixed by the Secretary of State and notified to the keeper; and
(b) may require the keeper to provide such other evidence as he may specify,

for the purpose of ascertaining whether the relevant vehicle is the registered vehicle concerned.

Examination of vehicle

2 A person authorised by the Secretary of State to conduct an examination under paragraph 1(a) may refuse to conduct the examination if—

(a) the Secretary of State has not received an application form completed and signed by or on behalf of the keeper and containing such information as the Secretary of State may specify;
(b) the vehicle is not presented at the time and place appointed for the examination;
(c) the prescribed fee has not been paid;
(d) the person presenting the vehicle is not willing, to the extent necessary for the purpose of properly carrying out the examination,—
    (i) to give the person authorised to conduct the examination access to the engine and the fuel and exhaust systems,
    (ii) to operate the controls of the vehicle, or
    (iii) generally to co-operate with that person;
(e) the vehicle is obviously unroadworthy;
(f) the vehicle is in so dangerous or dirty a condition that the examination cannot be carried out safely and properly;
(g) the vehicle has insufficient fuel or oil in it for the examination to be carried out; or
(h) the vehicle's engine has failed electrically or mechanically.

Determination of the Secretary of State

3 (1) The Secretary of State, having considered the report of the person who conducted any examination under paragraph 1(a) and the evidence (if any) provided under paragraph 1(b), shall give notice of his decision as to whether or not he is satisfied that the vehicle is the relevant vehicle.

(2) The Secretary of State's notification of a decision that he is not so satisfied shall state—

- (a) the reasons for his decision;
- (b) that the keeper of the vehicle may appeal against the decision on the ground that the reasons given are insufficient or that there has been an error in the conduct of the examination or the consideration of evidence;
- (c) the name and address of the person to whom an appeal against the decision may be made; and
- (d) that notice of the appeal stating the grounds on which it is made must be received by that person before the last day of the period of 28 days beginning with the day on which notification of the decision is sent or such later date as the Secretary of State may determine.

Appeals

4 (1) Where an appeal is received in accordance with paragraph 3(2)(d), the Secretary of State shall authorise a person ("the appeal officer") to determine the appeal on his behalf.

(2) The appeal officer shall be an individual who has not previously examined the relevant vehicle or been involved in any other way in the taking of the decision appealed against.

(3) The appeal officer shall require the appellant to produce the relevant vehicle for re-examination by him at a specified time and place and may also require him—

- (a) to produce the evidence provided under paragraph 1(b) for re-consideration; or
- (b) to provide such other evidence as the appeal officer may specify.

(4) Paragraph 2 applies to a re-examination of the relevant vehicle on appeal.

(5) The appeal officer, having examined the relevant vehicle and considered the evidence (if any) provided to him, shall notify the appellant of his decision as to whether or not he is satisfied that the relevant vehicle is the registered vehicle.

Certificates

5 Where the Secretary of State is satisfied, whether on appeal or otherwise, that the relevant vehicle is the registered vehicle he shall issue a certificate to that effect and may at any time issue a replacement certificate to correct an error in a certificate.

Giving of notices and certificates

6 A notice or certificate under this Schedule may be given or issued by—

- (a) handing it over to the person producing the relevant vehicle for examination or re-examination; or
- (b) by sending it by pre-paid ordinary post addressed to the person who signed the application referred to in paragraph 2(a), and

shall be taken to have been given or issued at the time it was handed over or, as the case may be, put in the post.

The prescribed fee

7 (1) Subject to sub-paragraphs (2) and (3), the prescribed fee for an examination, whether under paragraph 1 or under paragraph 4, shall be [£41].

(2) If, at the request of the person submitting the vehicle for examination, the examination is conducted otherwise than at premises such as are mentioned in paragraph 13(3) of Schedule 2 the fee shall be increased by [£4].

(3) If, at the request of that person the examination is conducted out of hours the fee shall be increased by [£9].

(4) In sub-paragraph (3) "out of hours" has the meaning given by paragraph 13(4) of Schedule 2.

Refund of the prescribed fee

8 (1) Where a certificate under paragraph 5 is issued following a re-examination on appeal, the fee for the re-examination shall be refunded to the person who paid it.

(2) No fee shall be refunded in the event of an examination not being carried out in consequence of any act or omission on the part of the person who paid the fee.

NOTES

Amendment Para 7(1)–(3): sums in square brackets substituted by SI 2009/880.

[831]

SCHEDULE 4
STATUTORY OFF-ROAD NOTIFICATION

Regulation 26

PART I
GENERAL

Interpretation of Schedule

1 (1) In this Schedule—

"authorised insurer" has the meaning given in section 145(5) of the 1988 Act;

"personal credit agreement" has the meaning given in section 8(1) of the Consumer Credit Act 1974;

"relevant vehicle" means a vehicle which is either a relevant GB vehicle or a relevant NI vehicle;

"the required declaration" means a declaration made to the Secretary of State by a person surrendering a vehicle licence or the keeper of a relevant vehicle to the effect that (except for use under a trade licence) he does not for the time being intend to use or keep the vehicle on a public road and will not use or keep the vehicle on a public road without first taking out a vehicle licence (or if appropriate a nil licence) for the vehicle;

"the required particulars" in relation to a relevant vehicle are particulars of—

(a) the registration mark of the vehicle;
(b) the make and model of the vehicle; and
(c) the address of the premises at which the vehicle is kept; and

"unlicensed vehicle" means a relevant vehicle for which no vehicle licence is for the time being in force and "unlicensed" shall be construed accordingly.

(2) In this Schedule, subject to sub-paragraph (3),—

(a) a "relevant GB vehicle" means a vehicle which is registered in the GB records and kept in Great Britain, but does not include a vehicle in relation to which each of the following conditions is satisfied—

(i) neither a vehicle licence nor a nil licence was in force for the vehicle on 31st January 1998;
(ii) such a licence has not been taken out for the vehicle for a period starting after that date; and
(iii) the vehicle has not been used or kept on a public road on or after that date; and

(b) a "relevant NI vehicle" means a vehicle which is registered in the NI records and kept in Northern Ireland, but does not include a vehicle in relation to which each of the following conditions is satisfied—

(i) neither a vehicle licence nor a nil licence was in force for the vehicle on 30th November 2002;
(ii) such a licence has not been taken out for the vehicle for a period starting after that date; and
(iii) the vehicle has not been used or kept on a public road on or after that date.

(3) A vehicle which is an exempt vehicle falling within a description specified in paragraph 2, 2A, 3, 23 or 24 of Schedule 2 to the 1994 Act is neither a relevant GB nor a relevant NI vehicle.

(4) For the purposes of this Schedule a person is a "relevant vehicle trader" in relation to a vehicle if he falls within a description mentioned in column (2) of an item in the Table below and the vehicle falls within a description mentioned in column (3) of that item.

TABLE

(1) *Item*	*(2)* *Descriptions of person*	*(3)* *Descriptions of vehicle*
1	The holder of a trade licence	A vehicle temporarily in his possession in the course of the business by virtue of which he is a person eligible to hold such a licence
2	An auctioneer of vehicles	A vehicle temporarily in his possession in the course of his business as such an auctioneer
3	A motor dealer	A vehicle temporarily in his possession in the course of his business as a motor dealer
4	A person who carries on business as a dismantler of vehicles	A vehicle temporarily in his possession in the course of that business
5	An authorised insurer	A vehicle temporarily in his possession in consequence of settling a claim under a policy of insurance which related to the vehicle

(1) Item	(2) Descriptions of person	(3) Descriptions of vehicle
6	The holder of a licence under Part II of the Consumer Credit Act 1974	A vehicle temporarily in his possession under an order for the repossession of the vehicle made in pursuance of a personal credit agreement relating to the vehicle

Manner in which declaration is to be made and particulars furnished

2 (1) For the purposes of this Schedule the required declaration may be made and the required particulars furnished in such way as the Secretary of State may accept including—

(a) in writing on a form specified by the Secretary of State;
(b) orally by telephone to a person authorised by the Secretary of State; or
(c) by electronic means in a form specified by the Secretary of State.

(2) A person furnishing the required particulars need not provide particulars of the address at which the vehicle is kept unless required to do so—

(a) in a case falling within sub-paragraph (1)(a) or (c), by the form on which those particulars are furnished; or
(b) in a case falling within sub-paragraph (1)(b) , by the person to whom they are furnished.

NOTES

"Personal credit agreement" has the meaning given in s 8(1) of the Consumer Credit Act 1974 S 8(1) has been amended by the Consumer Credit Act 2006, s 2(1)(a), so as to refer to a "consumer credit agreement" instead of a "personal credit agreement".

[832]

PART II
VEHICLES REGISTERED IN THE GB RECORDS AND KEPT IN GREAT BRITAIN

Surrender of a vehicle licence—relevant GB vehicle

3 (1) When the holder of a vehicle licence for a relevant GB vehicle surrenders it under section 10(2) of the 1994 Act, he shall deliver to the Secretary of State the required declaration and the required particulars in relation to that vehicle.

(2) Paragraph (1) does not apply where a relevant GB vehicle is no longer kept by the holder of the licence or the holder is a relevant vehicle trader in relation to that vehicle.

Expiry of vehicle licence or nil licence—relevant GB vehicle

4 Where a vehicle licence or nil licence ceases to be in force for a relevant GB vehicle by reason of the expiration of the period for which the licence was granted and a vehicle licence or nil licence for the vehicle is not taken out so as to run from the expiration of that period, the keeper of the vehicle shall deliver to the Secretary of State the required declaration and the required particulars in relation to the vehicle—

(a) if he is a relevant vehicle trader, not later than the end of the period of three months starting with the day following the expired period; or
(b) in any other case, not later than that day.

Person keeping an unlicensed vehicle—relevant GB vehicle

5 (1) Subject to sub-paragraph (2) this paragraph applies to a person who is the keeper of a relevant GB vehicle which is unlicensed and as respects which there has elapsed a period of 12 months ("the unlicensed period")—

(a) throughout which the vehicle has been kept in Great Britain unlicensed; and
(b) within which neither the required declaration nor the required particulars have been delivered to the Secretary of State in relation to the vehicle.

(2) For the purposes of sub-paragraph (1)(a), where a vehicle licence has been surrendered under section 10(2) of the 1994 Act, the vehicle to which it relates shall be taken to be unlicensed from the first day of the month in which the licence was surrendered.

(3) A person to whom this paragraph applies shall, unless a vehicle licence or a nil licence has been taken out so as to run from the end of the unlicensed period, deliver the required declaration and the required particulars to the Secretary of State in relation to the relevant GB vehicle not later than the day following the end of that period.

Change of keeper of unlicensed vehicle—relevant GB vehicle

6 On a change in the keeper of a relevant GB vehicle which is unlicensed, unless a vehicle licence or nil licence is taken out for the vehicle, the new keeper shall deliver to the Secretary of State the required declaration and the required particulars in relation to the vehicle—

(a) if he is a relevant vehicle trader, not later than the end of the period of three months beginning with the day following the day on which the change of keeper occurs; or

(b) in any other case, not later than the day following the day on which the change of keeper occurs.

[833]

PART III
VEHICLES REGISTERED IN THE NI RECORDS AND KEPT IN NORTHERN IRELAND

Surrender of a vehicle licence—relevant NI vehicle

7 (1) When after 30th November 2002 the holder of a vehicle licence for a relevant NI vehicle surrenders it under section 10(2) of the 1994 Act, he shall deliver to the Secretary of State the required declaration and the required particulars in relation to that vehicle.

(2) Paragraph (1) does not apply where a relevant NI vehicle is no longer kept by the holder of the licence or the holder is a relevant trader in relation to that vehicle.

Expiry of vehicle licence or nil licence—relevant NI vehicle

8 Where, on or after 30th November 2002, a vehicle licence or nil licence ceases to be in force for a relevant NI vehicle by reason of the expiration of the period for which the licence was granted and a vehicle licence or nil licence for the vehicle is not taken out so as to run from the expiration of that period, the keeper of the vehicle shall deliver to the Secretary of State the required declaration and the required particulars in relation to the vehicle—

(a) if he is a relevant vehicle trader, not later than the end of the period of three months starting with the day following the expired period; or
(b) in any other case, not later than that day.

Person keeping an unlicensed vehicle—relevant NI vehicle

9 (1) Subject to sub-paragraph (2), this paragraph applies to a person who, at any time after 30th November 2003, is the keeper of a relevant NI vehicle which is unlicensed and as respects which there has elapsed a period of 12 months ("the unlicensed period")—

(a) throughout which the vehicle has been kept in Northern Ireland unlicensed; and
(b) within which neither the required declaration nor the required particulars have been delivered to the Secretary of State in relation to the vehicle.

(2) For the purposes of sub-paragraph (1(a), where a vehicle licence has been surrendered under section 10(2) of the 1994 Act, the vehicle to which it relates shall be taken to be unlicensed from the first day of the month on which the licence was surrendered.

(3) A person to whom this paragraph applies shall, unless a vehicle licence or a nil licence has been taken out so as to run from the end of the unlicensed period, deliver the required declaration and the required particulars to the Secretary of State in relation to the NI relevant vehicle not later than the day following the end of that period.

Change of keeper of unlicensed vehicle—relevant NI vehicle

10 On a change occurring after 30th November 2002 in the keeper of a relevant NI vehicle which is unlicensed, unless a vehicle licence or nil licence is taken out for the vehicle, the new keeper shall deliver to the Secretary of State the required declaration and the required particulars in relation to the vehicle—

(a) if he is a relevant vehicle trader, not later than the end of the period of three months beginning with the day following the day on which the change of keeper occurs; or
(b) in any other case, not later than the day following the day on which the change of keeper occurs.

[834]

SCHEDULE 5
EXEMPT VEHICLES: VEHICLES IMPORTED BY MEMBERS OF FOREIGN ARMED FORCES AND OTHERS

Regulation 34

Scope of exemption

1 (1) A vehicle is an exempt vehicle for the period specified in paragraph 2 if it was imported into Great Britain by or on behalf of—

(a) a member of a visiting force;
(b) a member of a headquarters or organisation; or
(c) a dependant of a person falling within paragraph (a) or (b),

and there is produced to the Secretary of State evidence that the person importing the vehicle has not been required to pay any tax or duty chargeable in respect of its importation.

(2) In sub-paragraph (1)—

(a) "dependant" means a member of the household of a person falling within sub-paragraph (1)(a) or (b) who is his spouse or any other person wholly or mainly maintained by him or in his custody, charge or care;

(b) "member of a visiting force" means a person for the time being appointed to serve with, or a member of the civilian component of, any body, contingent or detachment of the forces of any country specified in paragraph 3, which is for the time being present in the United Kingdom on the invitation of her Majesty's Government;

(c) "member of a headquarters or organisation" means a member of the military forces of any country, except the United Kingdom, who is for the time being appointed to serve in the United Kingdom under the orders of any headquarters or organisation specified in paragraph 4 and includes a person for the time being recognised by the Secretary of State as a civilian member of such a headquarters or organisation.

Period of exemption

2 (1) The period during which a vehicle is an exempt vehicle by virtue of this Schedule shall be the period of 12 months beginning with the day on which a nil licence is issued in respect of that vehicle.

(2) The exemption shall however cease to apply if, at any time during the period prescribed by sub-paragraph (1), the importer of the vehicle becomes liable to pay any duty or tax chargeable in respect of its importation.

[List of countries

3 The countries referred to in paragraph 1(2)(b) are—

Albania
Antigua and Barbuda
Armenia
Australia
Austria
Azerbaijan
The Bahamas
Bangladesh
Barbados
Belarus
Belgium
Belize
Botswana
Brunei
Bulgaria
Canada
The Republic of Cyprus
The Czech Republic
Denmark
Dominica
Estonia
Fiji
Finland
France
The Gambia
Georgia
Germany
Ghana
Greece
Grenada
Guyana
Hungary
India
Italy
Jamaica
Kazakhstan
Kenya
Kiribati
Kyrgyzstan
Latvia
Lesotho
Lithuania
Luxembourg
The Former Yugoslav Republic of Macedonia
Malawi
Malaysia
Maldives
Malta
Mauritius
Moldova
Namibia
Nauru
The Netherlands
New Zealand
Nigeria
Norway
Pakistan
Papua New Guinea
Poland
Portugal
Romania
Russia
Saint Christopher and Nevis
Saint Lucia
Saint Vincent and the Grenadines
Samoa
Seychelles
Sierra Leone
Singapore
Slovakia
Slovenia
Solomon Islands
South Africa
Spain
Sri Lanka
Swaziland
Sweden
Switzerland
Tanzania
Tonga
Trinidad and Tobago
Turkey

Turkmenistan
Tuvalu
Uganda
Ukraine
United States of America
Uzbekistan
Vanuatu
Zambia
Zimbabwe

List of headquarters and organisations

4 The headquarters and organisations referred to in paragraph 1(2)(c) are—

The Headquarters of the Supreme Allied Commander Atlantic (SACLANT)
The Supreme Headquarters Allied Powers Europe (SHAPE)
Headquarters Allied Forces North Western Europe (AFNORTHWEST)
Headquarters Allied Air Forces North Western Europe (AIRNORTHWEST)
Headquarters Allied Naval Forces North Western Europe (NAVNORTHWEST)
Headquarters Maritime Air Forces North West (MARAIRNORTHWEST)
Headquarters Submarine Forces North West (SUBNORTHWEST)
Headquarters Allied Forces Eastern Atlantic Area (EASTLANT)
Headquarters Maritime Air Forces Eastern Atlantic Area (MARAIREASTLANT)
Headquarters Submarine Forces Eastern Atlantic Area (SUBEASTLANT)
Headquarters United Kingdom—Netherlands Amphibious Force (UKNLAF)
Headquarters United Kingdom—Netherlands Landing Force (UKNLLF)
The NATO Airborne Early Warning Force Headquarters and the NATO E-3A Component]

NOTES

Amendment Paras 3, 4: substituted by SI 2003/2154.

[835]

SCHEDULE 6
TRADE LICENCES

Regulations 37 and 38

PART I
CONDITIONS SUBJECT TO WHICH TRADE LICENCES ARE TO BE ISSUED

1 If the holder of a trade licence changes his name, the name of his business or his business address he shall forthwith—

(a) notify the change and the new name or address to the Secretary of State; and
(b) send the licence to the Secretary of State for any necessary amendment.

2 The holder of the licence shall not, and shall not permit any person to, alter, deface, mutilate or add anything to a trade plate.

3 The holder of the licence shall not, and shall not permit any person to, exhibit on any vehicle any trade licence or trade plate—

(a) which has been altered, defaced mutilated or added to;
(b) upon which the figures or particulars have become illegible; or
(c) the colour of which has altered whether by fading or otherwise.

4 The holder of the licence shall not, and shall not permit any person to, exhibit on any vehicle anything which could be mistaken for a trade plate.

5 The holder of the licence shall not permit any person to display the trade licence or any trade plates on a vehicle except a vehicle which that person is using for the purposes of the holder under the licence.

6 The holder of the licence shall not, and shall not permit any person, to display the trade licence or any trade plates on any vehicle unless—

(a) that vehicle is within the classes of vehicle specified in section 11(2) of the 1994 Act (if the holder is a motor trader who is a manufacturer of vehicles), 11(3) (if the holder is any other motor trader) or 11(4) (if the holder is a vehicle tester); and
(b) the vehicle is being used for one or more of the prescribed purposes for which the holder may use the vehicle in accordance with regulation 36 and this Schedule.

7 The holder of the licence shall not display any trade plate on a vehicle used under the licence unless that trade plate shows the general registration mark assigned to the holder in respect of that licence.

[836]

PART II
PURPOSES FOR WHICH THE HOLDER OF A TRADE LICENCE MAY USE A VEHICLE BY VIRTUE OF THE LICENCE

General

Interpretation

8 Where a vehicle is so constructed that a semi-trailer may by partial superimposition be attached to it in such a manner as to cause a substantial part of the weight of the semi-trailer to be borne by the vehicle, the vehicle and the semi-trailer shall be taken, for the purposes of this Part of this Schedule to constitute a single vehicle.

9 The purposes prescribed by this Part of this Schedule as purposes for which the holder of a trade licence may use a vehicle on a public road by virtue of that licence—

(a) do not include the carrying of any person on the vehicle or any trailer drawn by it except a person carried in connection with such purposes; and
(b) are without prejudice to the provisions of subsections (4) to (6) of section 11 of the 1994 Act which specify the classes of vehicle which a trade licence is for, in the relation respectively to a motor trader who is a manufacturer of vehicles, any other motor trader and a vehicle tester.

Motor traders

Purposes for which a motor trader may use a vehicle by virtue of a trade licence

10 The purposes for which the holder of a trade licence who is a motor trader may use a vehicle (other than a vehicle to which paragraph 14 applies) on a public road by virtue of that licence are purposes which meet each of the following requirements—

(a) they are business purposes;
(b) they are paragraph 12 purposes; and
(c) they are purposes that do not include the conveyance of goods or burden of any description except specified loads.

Business purposes

11 A vehicle is used for "business purposes" if it is used for purposes connected with the motor trader's business—

(a) as a manufacturer or repairer of or dealer in vehicles,
(b) as a manufacturer or repairer of or dealer in trailers carried on in conjunction with his business as a motor trader,
(c) of modifying vehicles (whether by the fitting of accessories or otherwise); or
(d) of valeting vehicles.

Paragraph 12 purposes

12 A vehicle is used for "paragraph 12 purposes" if it is used for any of the following purposes—

(a) for its test or trial or the test or trial of its accessories or equipment, in either case in the ordinary course of construction, modification or repair or after completion;
(b) for proceeding to or from a public weighbridge for ascertaining its weight or to or from any place for its registration or inspection by a person acting on behalf of the Secretary of State;
(c) for its test or trial for the benefit of a prospective purchaser, for proceeding at the instance of a prospective purchaser to any place for the purpose of such test or trial, or for returning after such test or trial;
(d) for its test or trial for the benefit of a person interested in promoting publicity in regard to it, for proceeding at the instance of such a person to any place for the purpose of such test or trial, or for returning after such test or trial;
(e) for delivering it to the place where the purchaser intends to keep it;
(f) for demonstrating its operation or the operation of its accessories or equipment when it is being handed over to the purchaser;
(g) for delivering it from one part of the licence holder's premises to another part of his premises, or for delivering it from his premises to premises of, or between parts of premises of, another manufacturer or repairer of or dealer in vehicles or removing it from the premises of another manufacturer or repairer of or dealer in vehicles direct to his own premises;
(h) for proceeding to or returning from a workshop in which a body or a special type of equipment or accessory is to be or has been fitted to it or in which it is to be or has been painted, valeted or repaired;
(i) for proceeding from the premises of a manufacturer or repairer of or dealer in vehicles to a place from which it is to be transported by train, ship or aircraft or for proceeding to the premises of such a manufacturer, repairer or dealer from a place to which it has been so transported;

(j) for proceeding to or returning from any garage, auction room or other place at which vehicles are usually stored or usually or periodically offered for sale and at which it is to be or has been stored or is to be or has been offered for sale as the case may be;

(k) for proceeding to or returning from a place where it is to be or has been inspected or tested; or

(l) for proceeding to a place where it is to be broken up or otherwise dismantled.

Specified loads

13 (1) A specified load is one of the following kinds of load—

(a) a test load;

(b) in the case of a vehicle which is being delivered or collected and is being used for a purpose falling within paragraph 12(f) to (k), a load which consists of another vehicle used or to be used for travel from or to the place of delivery or collection;

(c) a load which is built in as part of the vehicle or permanently attached to it;

(d) in the case of a vehicle which is being used for a purpose falling within paragraph 12(h), (i) or (j), a load which consists of a trailer or of parts, accessories or equipment designed to be fitted to the vehicle and of tools for fitting them.

(2) In paragraph (1) a "test load" means a load which—

(a) is carried by a vehicle being used for a purpose falling within paragraph 12(b), (d), (e) or (g);

(b) is carried solely for the purpose of testing or demonstrating the vehicle or any of its accessories or equipment; and

(c) is returned to the place of loading without its having been removed from the vehicle except—

(i) for the purpose of testing or demonstrating the vehicle or any of its accessories or equipment,

(ii) in the case of accident, or

(iii) where the load consists of water, fertiliser or refuse.

Manufacturers keeping vehicles for research and development

Vehicle kept by a motor trader for research and development in the course of his business as a manufacturer

14 (1) This paragraph applies to a vehicle—

(a) kept by a motor trader, being the holder of a trade licence who is a manufacturer of vehicles; and

(b) kept solely for the purposes of conducting research and development in the course of his business as such a manufacturer.

(2) The purposes for which such a person may, by virtue of the trade licence, use a vehicle to which this paragraph applies on a public road are the purposes of conducting research and development in the course of his business as a manufacturer of vehicles.

(3) Those purposes shall not be taken to include the conveyance of goods or burden of any description except—

(a) a load which is carried solely for the purpose of testing the vehicle or any of its accessories or equipment and which is returned to the place of loading without having been removed from the vehicle except for such purpose or in the case of accident; or

(b) any load built in as part of the vehicle or permanently attached to it.

Vehicle testers

Purposes for which a vehicle tester may use a vehicle by virtue of a trade licence

15 (1) Subject to sub-paragraph (2) the purposes for which the holder of a trade licence who is a vehicle tester may use a vehicle on a public road by virtue of that licence are the purposes of testing it or any trailer drawn by it or any of the accessories or equipment on the vehicle or trailer in the course of the business of the holder of the trade licence as a vehicle tester.

(2) The purposes prescribed by sub-paragraph (1) do not include the conveyance of goods or any other burden of any description on the vehicle except—

(a) a load which is carried solely for the purpose of testing or demonstrating the vehicle or any of its accessories or equipment and is returned to the place of loading without having been removed from the vehicle except for that purpose or in the case of accident, or

(b) a load which is built in as part of the vehicle or permanently attached to it.

[837]

SCHEDULE 7
RECOVERY VEHICLES: PRESCRIBED PURPOSES

Regulation 45

PART I
PURPOSES PRESCRIBED FOR THE PURPOSES OF PARAGRAPH 5(3)(E) OF SCHEDULE 1 TO THE 1994 ACT

1 Carrying any person who, immediately before the vehicle became disabled was the driver of, or a passenger in that vehicle, together with his personal effects, from the premises at which the vehicle is to be repaired or scrapped to his original intended destination.

2 (1) At the request of a constable or a local authority empowered by or under statute to remove a vehicle from a road, removing such a vehicle to a place nominated by the constable or local authority.

(2) In sub-paragraph (1) "road" has the meaning given—

(a) in relation to England, Scotland or Wales by section 192 of the 1988 Act; and
(b) in relation to Northern Ireland by Article 2 of the Road Traffic (Northern Ireland) Order 1995.

3 Proceeding to a place at which the vehicle will be available for use for a purpose specified in paragraph 5(3)(a) or (b) of Schedule 1 to the 1994 Act and remaining temporarily at such a place so as to be available for such use.

4 Proceeding from—

(a) a place where the vehicle has remained temporarily so as to be available for such use;
(b) a place where the vehicle has recovered a disabled vehicle; or
(c) such premises as are mentioned in paragraph 5(3)(b) or (c) of Schedule 1 to the 1994 Act.

[838]

PART II
PURPOSES PRESCRIBED FOR THE PURPOSES OF PARAGRAPH 5(4)(C) OF SCHEDULE 1 TO THE 1994 ACT

5 Repairing a disabled vehicle at the place where it became disabled or to which it has been moved in the interests of safety after becoming disabled.

6 Drawing or carrying a single trailer if another vehicle had become disabled whilst drawing or carrying it.

NOTES
Road Traffic (Northern Ireland) Order 1995 SI 1995/2994 (NI 18) (outside the scope of this work).

[839]

SCHEDULE 8
REGULATIONS TO WHICH SECTION 59(2)(A) OF THE 1994 ACT APPLIES

Regulation 47

(1) *Regulation*	*(2)* *Subject matter of regulation*
16(1)	Notification of an alteration to a vehicle
17	Notification of destruction or permanent export of a vehicle
[17A	Notification of the issue of a certificate of destruction: vehicle to which the End-of-Life Vehicles Directive applies]
18(1)	Notification of change of keeper's name or address
19(1)	Notification of a change of the name or address of the holder of a trade licence
21	Notification of change of keeper: registration document issued in Great Britain before 24th March 1997
22	Notification of change of keeper: registration document issued in Great Britain on or after 24th March 1997 and the new keeper not a vehicle trader
23	Notification of change of keeper: registration document issued in Great Britain on or after 24th March 1997 and the new keeper a vehicle trader
24	Notification of change of keeper: obligations of vehicle traders where registration document issued in Great Britain on or after 24th March 1997
25	Notification of change of keeper: registration document issued in Northern Ireland
26 (including Schedule 4)	Statutory off-road notification
40(5)	Return of trade plates

(1) Regulation	(2) Subject matter of regulation
42	Exhibition of trade plates and licences

NOTES
Amendment Entry in square brackets relating to reg 17A inserted by SI 2003/2635.

[840]

TRAFFIC SIGNS REGULATIONS AND GENERAL DIRECTIONS 2002
SI 2002/3113

Authority Made by the Secretary of State for Transport under the Road Traffic Regulation Act 1984, ss 64, 65, 85(2) and the Road Traffic Act 1988, s 36(5).
Date made 16 December 2002.
Commencement 31 January 2003.
Amendment Amended by SI 2003/393, SI 2003/2155, SI 2004/1275, SI 2004/3168 (in relation to England only), SI 2005/1670, SI 2005/2929 (in relation to Wales only), SI 2005/3225, SI 2006/594, SI 2006/2083, SI 2008/2177. Also amended in relation to Scotland only by SSI 2005/344, SSI 2006/129 (outside the scope of this work).
Summary This instrument revokes and replaces, subject to savings and with amendments, the Traffic Signs Regulations and General Directions 1994, SI 1994/1519, and the amending SI 1995/2769, SI 1995/3107, SI 1999/1723.

Under the Road Traffic Act 1988, s 36(1), where a traffic sign of the prescribed size, colour and type or of another character authorised by the Secretary of State has been lawfully placed on or near a road, a person driving or propelling a vehicle who fails to comply with the indication given by the sign is guilty of an offence. Under s 36(2) of the 1988 Act, a traffic sign is not to be treated for the purposes of s 36 as having been lawfully placed unless either:

(a) the indication given by the sign is an indication of a statutory prohibition, restriction or requirement, or
(b) it is expressly provided by or under any provision of the Traffic Acts (ie the Road Traffic Regulation Act 1984, the Road Traffic Offenders Act 1988, the Road Traffic Act 1988 and the Road Traffic (Consequential Provisions) Act 1988 (so far as it reproduces the effect of provisions repealed by that Act)) that the Road Traffic Act 1988, s 36 is to apply to the sign or to signs of a type of which the sign is one.

Pt I of this instrument (ie the Traffic Signs Regulations 2002):

(a) prescribes certain traffic signs to be complied with in accordance with the Road Traffic Act 1988, s 36, and specifies those signs which involve discretionary disqualification for offences committed under that section;
(b) prescribes the size, colour and type of traffic signs which convey information or a warning, requirement, restriction, prohibition or speed limit;
(c) makes provision as to the extent to which it is permissible to vary the dimensions for signs;
(d) makes provision as to the proportions and form of letters, numerals, symbols and other characters;
(e) prescribes signs that can be attached to vehicles; and
(f) makes provision for warning, regulatory and informatory traffic signs; road markings; light signals and warning lights; and miscellaneous traffic signs.

The provisions of Pt I of this instrument do not limit the powers of the Secretary of State and the Welsh Ministers (formerly the National Assembly for Wales) under the Road Traffic Regulation Act 1984, s 64 to authorise the erection or retention of traffic signs of a character not prescribed by Pt I. Provision is made by Pt I of this instrument allowing certain signs prescribed by the Traffic Signs Regulations 1994 (Pt I of SI 1994/1519 (revoked)) or by earlier regulations, but not by the Traffic Signs Regulations 2002, to be treated as prescribed by the 2002 regulations until specified dates in 2005, 2007, 2010 and 2015.

Pt II of this instrument (ie the Traffic Signs General Directions 2002) contains general directions subject to which certain traffic signs, lights or road markings may be placed or mounted on or near a road. It also contains a saving for traffic signs placed in conformity with the Traffic Signs General Directions 1994 (Pt II of SI 1994/1519 (revoked)) or to be treated as placed in conformity with those Directions.

Welsh versions SI 1985/713 was made under the Road Traffic Regulation Act 1984, ss 28(4), 64(1), 65(1), under the provision in the Road Traffic Act 1972, Sch 4, Pt I, col 5 (repealed) which related to s 22 (repealed) of the 1972 Act, and under the Welsh Language Act 1967, s 2(2), (3) (repealed) (and came into force on 11 June 1985). In so far as it was made under the 1972 Act, this instrument now takes effect under the Road Traffic Act 1988, s 36(5); and in so far as it was made under the 1967 Act, it now takes effect under the Welsh Language Act 1993, s 26. This instrument:

(a) enables equivalent signs and permitted variants to be used in Wales in place of the English language signs set out in the Traffic Signs Regulations 1994 (now the Traffic Signs Regulations 2002; see above);
(b) provides that with minor amendments the provisions of the Traffic Signs Regulations and General Directions 1994 (now the Traffic Signs Regulations and General Directions 2002; see above) are to apply to the signs and permitted variants set out in the instrument; and

(c) applies the provisions of the Traffic Signs Regulations 1994 (now the Traffic Signs Regulations 2002; see above) to the characters specified in the instrument which are characters used in the Welsh language.

Other traffic signs The following regulations prescribing traffic signs have been made under provisions of the Road Traffic Regulation Act 1984:

(a) SI 1997/3053 was made under ss 64(1), (2), (3), (5), 67(3) of the 1984 Act and came into force on 1 March 1998. The regulations revoke the Traffic Signs (Temporary Obstructions) Regulations 1985, SI 1985/463, and make provision as to keep right signs, flat traffic delineators, traffic cones, road vehicle signs, traffic pyramids, traffic triangles and warning lamps which warn traffic of a temporary obstruction on any part of a road other than road works in a road. The regulations contain technical specifications and make provision for the placing and use of traffic signs; and

(b) SI 2006/2215 was made under s 28(4) of the 1984 Act and came into force on 4 September 2006. The regulations make provision as respects the size, colour and type of the sign which, in accordance with s 28 of that Act, a school crossing patrol may exhibit so as to require traffic to stop when approaching a place where a person is crossing or seeking to cross a road. The School Crossing Patrol Sign (England and Wales) Regulations 2002, SI 2002/3020, are revoked.

The size, colour and type of certain other traffic signs are prescribed by SI 1997/2400, in the title Highways, Streets and Bridges.

[841]

ROAD USER CHARGING AND WORKPLACE PARKING LEVY (NET PROCEEDS) (ENGLAND) REGULATIONS 2003
SI 2003/110

Authority Made by the Secretary of State for Transport under the Greater London Authority Act 1999, s 420(1), Sch 23, para 1(2), Sch 24, para 1(2) and the Transport Act 2000, s 197(1), Sch 12, para 2(2).

Date made 24 January 2003.

Commencement 17 February 2003.

Summary These regulations, which apply to England only, make provision for the determination by charging and licensing authorities of the net proceeds of road user charging schemes and workplace parking levy schemes ("relevant schemes") for the purposes of the Greater London Authority Act 1999, Sch 23, para 1(2), Sch 24, para 1(2) and the Transport Act 2000, Sch 12, para 2(2). The regulations specify the basis for determining the amounts received and expenses incurred in respect of a relevant scheme, and the extent to which such amounts or expenses are attributable to any financial year. Provision is made for interest to be earned on credit balances and payable on debit balances, and for the calculation of such balances.

[842]

TRUNK ROAD CHARGING SCHEMES (BRIDGES AND TUNNELS) (KEEPING OF ACCOUNTS) (ENGLAND) REGULATIONS 2003
SI 2003/298

Authority Made by the Secretary of State for Transport under the Transport Act 2000, s 197(1), Sch 12, paras 2(2), (3), 5.

Date made 9 February 2003.

Commencement 7 March 2003.

Summary These regulations, which apply to England only, require a charging authority for a trunk road charging scheme made under the Transport Act 2000 to keep proper accounts for that scheme showing how the net proceeds of the scheme are calculated, and to prepare an annual statement of accounts for the scheme. The regulations also specify which items of income and expenditure may be taken into account in calculating the annual net proceeds of a scheme for the purposes of para 2 of Sch 12 to the 2000 Act.

[843]

PRIVATE HIRE VEHICLES (LONDON) (TRANSITIONAL AND SAVING PROVISIONS) REGULATIONS 2003
SI 2003/655

Authority Made by the Secretary of State for Transport under the Private Hire Vehicles (London) Act 1998, s 37.

Date made 10 March 2003.

Commencement 1 April 2003.

Amendment Amended by SI 2003/3028, SI 2006/584.

Summary These regulations contain transitional provisions in connection with the introduction of private hire vehicle driver licensing under the Private Hire Vehicles (London) Act 1998. In particular, the regulations:

(a) enable an individual to be registered by Transport for London (TfL) as an "existing driver" if he has at any time before 1 April 2003 driven a private hire vehicle under a booking made through an operator licensed under the 1998 Act;

(b) require TfL to give each existing driver an application deadline by which that driver is invited to submit an application for a London PHV driver's licence;
(c) provide for the issue by TfL of a temporary permit to an existing driver or to an applicant who, at any time before 1 January 2007, applies for a London PHV driver's licence and pays the application fee;
(d) provide for the duration of a temporary permit;
(e) modify the application of s 13 of the 1998 Act in relation to an application for a London PHV driver's licence by an existing driver who is the holder of a temporary permit or is renewing a licence; and
(f) save rights in relation to private hire vehicles, in respect of which licences have been granted under the Plymouth City Council Act 1975, to carry passengers in certain circumstances within London.

Further regulations See SI 2004/242.

[844]

TRANSPORT FOR LONDON (RESERVED SERVICES) (LONDON UNDERGROUND LIMITED) EXCEPTION ORDER 2003
SI 2003/1613

Authority Made by the Secretary of State for Transport under the Greater London Authority Act 1999, s 207(5), (9).
Date made 20 June 2003.
Commencement 15 July 2003.
Summary The Greater London Authority Act 1999, s 207(2) provides that Transport for London (TfL) must not, without the consent of the Secretary of State, enter into or carry out any agreement under which an outside contractor is to provide or secure the provision of a reserved service (defined by s 207(1)) for TfL or a subsidiary of TfL. This order exempts from s 207(2) any agreement:
(a) under which an outside contractor is to provide, or secure the provision of, reserved services in respect of any public service for the carriage of passengers by railway which is under the control of London Underground Limited; and
(b) to which London Underground Limited was a party immediately before the date on which this order was made.

The order also amends the definition "station operating function" in s 207(7) of the 1999 Act.

[845]

TRANSPORT FOR LONDON (CONSEQUENTIAL PROVISIONS) ORDER 2003
SI 2003/1615

Authority Made by the Secretary of State for Transport under the Greater London Authority Act 1999, ss 405(2), 406, 420.
Date made 20 June 2003.
Commencement 15 July 2003.
Amendment Amended by SI 2006/5.
Summary This order makes provision consequential upon the completion of the transfer of the undertaking of London Regional Transport (LRT) to Transport for London (TfL) and the abolition of LRT (dissolved on 16 July 2003 by SI 2003/1913).

Art 2 introduces Sch 1, which amends legislation referring to LRT and its subsidiaries. Pt I of Sch 1 amends the following public general Acts: London Passenger Transport Act 1933; Transport Act 1962; London Cab Act 1968; Transport Act 1968; Local Government Act 1974; Competition Act 1980; Highways Act 1980; Public Passenger Vehicles Act 1981; Animal Health Act 1981; Transport Act 1981; Local Government (Miscellaneous Provisions) Act 1982; Transport Act 1985; Agricultural Holdings Act 1986; Town and Country Planning Act 1990; Water Industry Act 1991; Water Resources Act 1991; Land Drainage Act 1991; Transport and Works Act 1992; and Railways Act 1993.

Pt 2 of Sch 1 to the order amends the following local Acts: London Passenger Transport Act 1935; British Transport Commission Acts 1951 and 1953; London County Council (General Powers) Act 1963; City of London (Various Powers) Acts 1965 and 1967; Lee Valley Regional Park Act 1966; London Transport Acts 1969, 1971, 1975 and 1982; Greater London Council (General Powers) Acts 1969, 1970 and 1974; and London Local Authorities Acts 1990, 1994 and 1995.

Pt 3 of Sch 1 to the order revokes the London Regional Transport (Transitional Modifications) Order 2000, SI 2000/1504, and amends the following statutory instruments (instruments of local application only are not noted as they are outside the scope of this work):

SI 1978/1684, SI 1994/573, SI 1994/607, SI 1998/948, all in this title (SI 1998/948 is also in the title Highways, Streets and Bridges);
SI 1972/1705, in the title Highways, Streets and Bridges;
SI 1986/2194, SI 1992/1703, in the title Housing;
SI 1991/1043, in the title Environment; and
SI 1998/2573, in the title Insurance.

Pt 3 of Sch 1 to the order also amended the following statutory instruments which are no longer in force:

Banking Act 1987 (Exempt Transactions) Regulations 1987, SI 1987/817 (lapsed);
British Transport Police Force Scheme 1963 approved by SI 1964/1456 (revoked);

Community Drivers' Hours and Recording Equipment (Exemptions and Supplementary Provisions) Regulations 1986, SI 1986/1456 (revoked);
Heather and Grass etc (Burning) Regulations 1986, SI 1986/428 (revoked) and the amending SI 1987/1208 (revoked);
Motor Vehicles (Authorisation of Special Types) General Order 1979, SI 1979/1198 (revoked);
Transport and Works (Applications and Objections Procedure) (England and Wales) Rules 2000, SI 2000/2190 (revoked).

Art 3 of this order provides that any byelaws made or having effect as if made by LRT under any provision repealed or revoked by the Greater London Authority Act 1999 or by any provision of Sch 1 to this order, and in force immediately before the coming into force of this order, continue to have effect, but as if made by TfL under para 26 of Sch 11 to the 1999 Act. In any such byelaws, a reference to LRT or its subsidiaries is to be treated as a reference to TfL or its subsidiaries. Art 4 provides for the enactments set out in Sch 2 to this order (which confer works and maintenance powers on LRT and protection on third parties) to apply to TfL or its subsidiaries as they applied to LRT or its subsidiaries immediately before the coming into force of this order. Art 5 provides that in any order made by the Traffic Director for London under the Road Traffic Regulation Act 1984, s 6 or 9, in accordance with a direction given to him by the Secretary of State under the Road Traffic Act 1991, s 58(1) (repealed), references to bus services provided under an agreement with LRT are to be treated as references to bus services provided under an agreement with TfL or a subsidiary of TfL.

[846]

RAILWAYS (RAIL PASSENGERS' COUNCIL AND RAIL PASSENGERS' COMMITTEES) (EXEMPTIONS) ORDER 2003
SI 2003/1695

Authority Made by the Secretary of State for Transport under the Railways Act 1993, ss 76(7C), 77(9C). S 77 (Rail Passengers' Committees) of the 1993 Act has been repealed by the Railways Act 2005, s 59(6), Sch 13, Pt 1, and this order has been revoked by SI 2005/1737 in so far as it related to Rail Passengers' Committees.
Date made 7 July 2003.
Commencement 29 July 2003.
Amendment Amended by SI 2005/1737.
Summary This order relates to the obligations of the Rail Passengers' Council (see below) under the Railways Act 1993, s 76 to investigate any matter which relates to the provision of railway passenger services. The order has been revoked by SI 2005/1737 in so far as it related to Rail Passengers' Committees (abolished as from 24 July 2005 (see SI 2005/1909) by the Railways Act 2005, s 21(1)). The order provides that, in relation to the services to which it applies, the duties of the Rail Passengers' Council under s 76 are limited to the duties imposed by s 76(7A) relating to the review of railway passenger services and station services. The services to which the order applies are:
(a) railway passenger services which are provided by a passenger service operator which is not required under the terms of its passenger licence to provide through ticketing facilities; and
(b) railway passenger services in respect of which the passenger service operator is exempted under s 7 of the 1993 Act from the requirement under s 6 thereof to be authorised by licence to operate the railway assets used in the provision of those services.

Certain railway passenger services are excluded from the order (including services provided by or on behalf of London Underground Limited and international railway passenger services).

Rail Passengers' Council The Railways Act 2005, s 19(1) established on 24 July 2005 (see SI 2005/1909) a body corporate to be known as the Rail Passengers' Council, which replaces the Rail Passengers' Council which was established by the Railways Act 1993, s 3(2) (repealed by s 59(6) of, and Pt 1 of Sch 13 to, the 2005 Act); see s 19(6) of the 2005 Act.

[847]

MOTOR CYCLES ETC (SINGLE VEHICLE APPROVAL) REGULATIONS 2003
SI 2003/1959

Authority Made by the Secretary of State for Transport under the Road Traffic Act 1988, ss 54, 60, 61, 63, 66.
Date made 31 July 2003.
Commencement 8 August 2003.
Summary These regulations introduce a scheme for approving the design, construction, equipment and marking of the vehicles to which they apply and provide for such vehicles to be examined for the purposes of obtaining a Minister's approval certificate. By reg 3, the regulations apply to diesel mopeds, electric mopeds, 48 km/h mopeds, mopeds, motor cycles, motor tricycles, quadricycles and 350kg quadricycles ("relevant vehicles"). They do not apply to:
(a) any diesel moped, electric moped or 350kg quadricycle which is manufactured before 9 November 2003;
(b) any 48 km/h moped; or
(c) vehicles of a description referred to in the second paragraph of Art 1(1) of Directive 2002/24/EC of the European Parliament and of the Council relating to the type approval of two or three-wheel motor vehicles (OJ L124, 09.05.2002, p 1) as being those to which the Directive does not apply.

Reg 4 and Sch 2 set out the requirements to be met for approval. Reg 5 deals with an application to the Secretary of State for a Minister's approval certificate and the examination to be carried out for the purposes of an application. When an application is made under reg 5, the Secretary of State must assign a vehicle identification number to the vehicle in specified circumstances (reg 6). Reg 7 sets out the criteria to be used by the Secretary of State for determining design weights. Provision for an appeal against a determination made by the Secretary of State following an application under reg 5 is made by reg 8. In specified circumstances, the Secretary of State may refuse an application or an appeal even though an examination has not been carried out (reg 9). Regs 10–12 concern the form of a Minister's approval certificate, the replacement of lost or defaced certificates, and the giving of notices under the regulations. Reg 13 appoints 8 August 2003 for the purposes of the Road Traffic Act 1988, s 63(1), on or after which it is an offence to use a vehicle of a prescribed class without the appropriate certificate in force under ss 54–58 of that Act. All relevant vehicles are vehicles of the prescribed class, other than excepted vehicles (as defined). The use of a relevant vehicle other than an excepted vehicle may be exempted from the said s 63(1). Reg 14 provides that upon first application for a licence under the Vehicle Excise and Registration Act 1994 for a vehicle to which s 63(1) of the 1988 Act applies, a licence must not be granted unless there is a certificate in force under ss 54–58 of the 1988 Act to the effect that the vehicle complies with the approval requirements.

Fees SI 2003/1960 (as amended by SI 2009/865, and by SI 2007/507, SI 2008/1462 (both superseded)) was made by the Secretary of State for Transport under the Road Traffic Act 1988, s 61(1), (2), SI 1988/643 and the Finance Act 1990, s 128, and came into force on 8 August 2003. The regulations prescribe the fees payable in connection with applications for a Minister's approval certificate and appeals made under SI 2003/1959. They also require fees to be repaid in specified circumstances, prescribe the fee for replacing a lost or defaced certificate, and provide for the service of notices.

[848]

ROAD VEHICLES (AUTHORISATION OF SPECIAL TYPES) (GENERAL) ORDER 2003
SI 2003/1998

Authority Made by the Secretary of State for Transport under the Road Traffic Act 1988, s 44.
Date made 4 August 2003.
Commencement Partly on 25 August 2003 and fully on 1 December 2004.
Summary This order revokes and replaces the Motor Vehicles (Authorisation of Special Types) General Order 1979, SI 1979/1198, and the amending SI 1984/1810, SI 1986/313, SI 1987/1327, SI 1987/2161, SI 1989/1662, SI 1995/3052, SI 1998/2249, SI 1998/2884. The order applies only to motor vehicles or trailers: (a) which do not comply in all respects with the standard construction and use requirements (i e the requirements of such of the regulations made under the Road Traffic Act 1988, s 41 as would apply to a motor vehicle or trailer, apart from this order); and (b) which fall within a recognised category of special vehicles. A vehicle which falls within a recognised category of special vehicles is authorised to be used on roads by virtue of this order if it complies with the authorisation requirements applicable to vehicles in that category. "Authorisation requirements" in relation to a recognised category of special vehicles: (a) means all the requirements specified in this order as being applicable to vehicles in that category; and (b) includes such of the requirements of regulations made under s 41 of the 1988 Act as are specified in the order as being applicable to vehicles in that category (subject to any specified modifications or exceptions).

The order specifies the following as recognised categories of special vehicles (together with their authorisation requirements):

(a) vehicles for haulage, lifting, engineering and vehicle recovery (i e abnormal indivisible load vehicles, mobile cranes, engineering plant and road recovery vehicles);
(b) vehicles for agriculture (i e agricultural motor vehicles, agricultural trailers and agricultural trailed appliances);
(c) motor vehicles or trailers carrying loads of exceptional width (i e where the overall width of the vehicle carrying a load, together with the width of any lateral projection or projections of the load, exceeds 4.3 metres);
(d) local excavation vehicles;
(e) vehicles or trailers constructed for use outside the United Kingdom; any new or improved type of motor vehicle or trailer which is constructed for tests or trials; any motor vehicle or trailer which is equipped with new or improved equipment;
(f) track-laying motor vehicles or trailers;
(g) straddle carriers;
(h) vehicles fitted with a moveable platform;
(i) pedestrian-controlled road maintenance vehicles that are not constructed or used to carry a driver or passenger;
(j) motor vehicles used for cutting grass or trimming hedges;
(k) trailers used for cutting grass or trimming hedges;
(l) operational military vehicles;
(m) track-laying vehicles belonging to the Royal National Lifeboat Institution;
(n) highway testing vehicles; and
(o) vehicles propelled by compressed natural gas.

Cases relating to this order The following cases were decided by reference to the Motor Vehicles (Authorisation of Special Types) General Order 1979, SI 1979/1198 (revoked and replaced by this order):

George Cohen 600 Group Ltd v Hird [1970] 2 All ER 650, [1970] 1 WLR 1226;
Patterson v Redpath Bros Ltd [1979] 2 All ER 108, [1979] 1 WLR 553;
Siddle C Cook Ltd v Arlidge [1962] 1 WLR 203n, 60 LGR 121;
Siddle C Cook Ltd v Holden [1963] 1 QB 248, [1962] 3 All ER 984;
Sunter Bros Ltd v Arlidge [1962] 1 All ER 510, [1962] 1 WLR 199.

[849]

RAILWAYS AND TRANSPORT SAFETY ACT 2003 (COMMENCEMENT NO 1) ORDER 2003
SI 2003/2681

Authority Made by the Secretary of State for Transport under the Railways and Transport Safety Act 2003, s 120(1).

Date made 13 October 2003.

Summary This order, together with the further commencement orders SI 2004/827, SI 2004/1572, SI 2004/2759, SI 2005/1991 (all made under the Railways and Transport Safety Act 2003, s 120(1)) brought into force provisions of the 2003 Act, as noted in the table below.

Provision	*Date and extent (if any)*
ss 1–14	17 October 2005 (SI 2005/1991)
ss 15–17	5 July 2004 (SI 2004/827)
ss 18–33	1 July 2004 (SI 2004/1572)
s 34(1)	19 June 2004 (SI 2004/1572)
s 34(2), (3), (4)	1 July 2004 (SI 2004/1572)
s 34(5)	31 October 2004 (SI 2004/2759)
ss 35–73	1 July 2004 (SI 2004/1572)
s 74	19 June 2004 (SI 2004/1572)
ss 75–77	1 July 2004 (SI 2004/1572)
ss 78, 79, 80(4), (5), 81, 82	30 March 2004 (SI 2004/827)
s 83	29 March 2004 (for the purposes of bringing into force that part of para 1 of Sch 7 relating to Road Traffic Act 1988, s 6A(1), for the purpose of enabling the Secretary of State to approve a device for indicating whether the proportion of alcohol in a person's breath or blood is likely to exceed the limits prescribed in ss 81(1), 93(2), (3) of the 2003 Act) (SI 2004/827) 30 March 2004 (so far as not already in force) (SI 2004/827)
ss 84–95	30 March 2004 (SI 2004/827)
s 96	29 March 2004 (for the purposes of bringing into force that part of para 1 of Sch 7 relating to Road Traffic Act 1988, s 6A(1), for the purpose of enabling the Secretary of State to approve a device for indicating whether the proportion of alcohol in a person's breath or blood is likely to exceed the limits prescribed in ss 81(1), 93(2), (3) of the 2003 Act) (SI 2004/827) 30 March 2004 (so far as not already in force) (SI 2004/827)
ss 97–103, 106	30 March 2004 (SI 2004/827)
s 107	See Sch 7 below
s 109	30 March 2004 (SI 2004/827)
s 110	1 March 2005 (SI 2004/2759)
s 111	31 October 2003 (SI 2003/2681)
s 113	30 March 2004 (SI 2004/827)
s 115	31 October 2003 (SI 2003/2681)
s 116	5 July 2004 (for the purposes relating to a person becoming liable to dismissal under para 2(d) of Sch 1) (SI 2004/827) 31 October 2004 (so far as not already in force) (SI 2004/2759)
s 117	30 March 2004 (SI 2004/827)
s 118	See Sch 8 below

Provision	Date and extent (if any)
s 119	30 March 2004 (SI 2004/827)
Schs 1, 2, 3	5 July 2004 (SI 2004/827)
Schs 4, 5	1 July 2004 (SI 2004/1572)
Sch 6	30 March 2004 (SI 2004/827)
Sch 7, para 1	29 March 2004 (in so far as it relates to Road Traffic Act 1988, s 6A(1), for the purpose of enabling the Secretary of State to approve a device for indicating whether the proportion of alcohol in a person's breath or blood is likely to exceed the limits prescribed in ss 81(1), 93(2), (3) of the 2003 Act) (SI 2004/827) 30 March 2004 (so far as not already in force) (SI 2004/827)
Sch 7, paras 2–13	30 March 2004 (so far as not already in force) (SI 2004/827)
Sch 8	30 March 2004 (entries relating to Road Traffic Act 1988, s 11(2); Road Traffic Offenders Act 1988, s 76(2)(a); Merchant Shipping Act 1995, s 117) (SI 2004/827) 5 July 2004 (entries relating to House of Commons Disqualification Act 1975; Railways Act 1993, ss 15(4A), 15C(3), 21(5), 57B, 74(8), 151(1), Sch 1; Transport Act 2000, s 251(2), Sch 27, para 45) (SI 2004/827) 1 July 2004 (entries relating to British Transport Commission Act 1949; Railways Act 1993, ss 132, 133, Sch 10; Transport Act 2000, Sch 18, paras 7–10; Anti-terrorism, Crime and Security Act 2001) (SI 2004/1572) 5 July 2004 (entry relating to Railways Act 1993, s 1) (SI 2004/1572)

[850]

DISABILITY DISCRIMINATION ACT 1995 (PRIVATE HIRE VEHICLES) (CARRIAGE OF GUIDE DOGS ETC) (ENGLAND AND WALES) REGULATIONS 2003
SI 2003/3122

Authority Made by the Secretary of State for Transport under the Disability Discrimination Act 1995, ss 37A(8)(b), (9), 67(2).
Date made 3 December 2003.
Commencement Partly on 31 December 2003; fully on 31 March 2004.
Amendment Amended by SI 2006/1617.
Summary The Disability Discrimination Act 1995, s 37A imposes a duty on the operator and driver of a private hire vehicle to carry, without additional charge, an assistance dog which is accompanying a disabled person. This duty does not apply to the driver of a private hire vehicle if a certificate of exemption on medical grounds issued to him by the licensing authority is in force with respect to the vehicle and the prescribed notice is exhibited on the vehicle in the prescribed manner (s 37A(8)). These regulations prescribe the form of notice of exemption and the manner of exhibiting the notice on the vehicle (it must be affixed to the windscreen, facing outwards). Under s 37A(9), "assistance dog" includes a dog which has been trained by a prescribed charity to assist a disabled person who has a disability which consists of epilepsy or otherwise affects his mobility, manual dexterity, physical co-ordination or ability to lift, carry or otherwise move everyday objects. The regulations provide that each of the following is a prescribed charity for the purposes of s 37A(9): "Dogs for the Disabled", "Support Dogs" and "Canine Partners for Independence", all registered with the Charity Commission under specified registration numbers.

[851]

PRIVATE HIRE VEHICLES (CARRIAGE OF GUIDE DOGS ETC) ACT 2002 (COMMENCEMENT NO 1) ORDER 2003
SI 2003/3123

Authority Made by the Secretary of State for Transport under the Private Hire Vehicles (Carriage of Guide Dogs etc) Act 2002, s 6(2).
Date made 2 December 2003.
Summary This order brought the Private Hire Vehicles (Carriage of Guide Dogs etc) Act 2002 into force, in so far as applying to a private hire vehicle licensed by a licensing authority in England or Wales, as follows:

(a) on 31 December 2003, s 1(1) in so far as it relates to:
   (1) the Disability Discrimination Act 1995, s 37A(5), (6), (7), (9);
   (2) the power to make regulations under s 37A(8); and

(3) ss 3, 4, 5; and
(b) on 31 March 2004, s 1(1) for all other purposes.

Provisions of the Act relating to Scotland only have been brought into force by SSI 2004/57 (outside the scope of this work), and provisions relating to private hire vehicle licensed in Northern Ireland have been brought into force by SI 2007/3477 (outside the scope of this work).

[852]

CABLEWAY INSTALLATIONS REGULATIONS 2004
SI 2004/129

Authority Made by the Secretary of State for Transport under the European Communities Act 1972, s 2(2).

Date made 28 January 2004.

Commencement 3 May 2004.

Amendment Amended by SI 2004/1230, SI 2006/599, SI 2008/960.

Summary These regulations implement Directive 2000/9/EC of the European Parliament and of the Council relating to cableway installations designed to carry persons (OJ L106, 03.05.2000, p 21). Pt I (regs 1–3) of the regulations deals with preliminary matters, including interpretation and application. By reg 3, subject to exceptions, the regulations apply to any cableway installation put into service or modified after 3 May 2004, and to any subsystem or safety component placed on the market after that date. The regulations do not apply to: lifts; cableway installations used wholly or mainly for agricultural purposes; cableway installations (on-site or mobile) in fairgrounds or amusement parks which are designed for leisure purposes and not as a means for transporting persons; mining installations or on-site cableway installations used wholly or mainly for industrial purposes; cable operated ferries; rack railways; cableway installations that are chain driven; cable-operated tramways of a traditional construction; and subsystems and safety components for the installations previously referred to. In addition (and subject to exception), the regulations do not apply to a cableway installation constructed or put into service, or both, or a safety component or subsystem placed on the market in the United Kingdom before 3 May 2004 which complies with all the provisions by or under any enactment with which it was required to comply on 3 May 2000 before it could be put into service, or placed on the market.

Pt II (regs 4–12) sets out the main requirements of the regulations. Reg 4 prohibits the main contractor from carrying out works for the construction or modification of a cableway installation without a stage 1 authorisation from the Secretary of State under reg 13. Before applying for a stage 1 authorisation, the main contractor must ensure that a safety analysis is undertaken and a safety report is prepared. Reg 5 prohibits a cableway installation from being put into service without a stage 2 authorisation from the Secretary of State under reg 13. Reg 6 requires the operator of an authorised cableway installation to compile and maintain a log book in relation to the installation, and to comply with specified measures and conditions. Regs 7, 8 prohibit a responsible person from placing on the market any safety component or subsystem unless specified requirements (including the essential requirements set out in Sch 2 to the regulations) are met. Reg 9 deals with the conformity assessment procedures for safety components and subsystems. Where any of the requirements of reg 7 or 8 have not been met by the responsible person, reg 10 specifies other persons who must meet those requirements. Reg 11 exempts safety components and subsystems from regs 7, 8 if they are to be used or exported outside the Community. Reg 12 describes the circumstances under which safety components, subsystems and cableway installations are to be taken to meet the requirements of the regulations.

Pt III (regs 13–22) deals with authorisation procedures and notified bodies. Reg 13 provides for the Secretary of State to issue a stage 1 authorisation for the construction or modification of cableway installations and a stage 2 authorisation for the putting into service of cableway installations. Reg 14 concerns the bodies which have been appointed to carry out one or more of the conformity assessment procedures ("notified bodies"). Reg 15 provides for the appointment and termination of appointment of notified bodies. Fees may be charged by notified bodies and the Secretary of State (reg 16). Regs 17, 18 set out the procedure for applying for stage 1 and stage 2 authorisations. Reg 19 provides that a stage 1 authorisation may only be given if the Secretary of State is satisfied that when constructed or modified the cableway installation is likely to comply with the essential requirements and to be safe. A stage 2 authorisation may only be given in respect of the putting into service of a cableway installation if the Secretary of State is satisfied of certain matters, including that the installation complies with the essential requirements, is safe, the technical file is complete and any specified safety measures are complied with. Regs 20, 21 set out the procedure to be followed where the Secretary of State refuses to give a stage 1 or stage 2 authorisation or a notified body refuses to confirm that a safety component or subsystem conforms with the regulations. Reg 22 requires notified bodies to carry out their functions under the regulations.

Pt IV (regs 23–30) relates to enforcement. Regs 23, 24 provide for the enforcement of the regulations in Great Britain (by the Health and Safety Executive ("the Executive")) and in Northern Ireland. Regs 25, 27 enable the Executive to serve notice on an operator if a safety component bearing a CE conformity marking, a subsystem with a declaration of conformity or an authorised cableway installation is not safe. The Executive is required by reg 26 to notify the Commission of the European Communities, and where appropriate other member States, of a safety component or subsystem which has been put into service and is not safe. Reg 28 enables the Executive to serve notice on the responsible person where the CE conformity marking has not been properly affixed to a safety component, or to a label inseparably attached to a safety component. A defence of due diligence is provided by reg 29 in any proceedings for an offence under the regulations. Reg 30 deals with the liability of persons other than the principal offender under the regulations.

Pt V (reg 32) amends SI 1998/2306, in the title Health and Safety at Work, and regulations relating to Northern Ireland only (outside the scope of this work). Reg 31, which amended SI 1994/157 (revoked), has been revoked by SI 2006/599.

[853]

PRIVATE HIRE VEHICLES (LONDON) (TRANSITIONAL PROVISIONS) REGULATIONS 2004
SI 2004/242

Authority Made by the Secretary of State for Transport under the Private Hire Vehicles (London) Act 1998, s 37.
Date made 12 February 2004.
Commencement 8 March 2004.
Amendment Amended by SI 2007/3453.
Summary These regulations contain the transitional provisions necessary to commence those provisions of the Private Hire Vehicles (London) Act 1998 brought into force on 8 March 2004 by SI 2004/241. In particular, the regulations:
(a) enable the holder of a London PHV Operator's licence to apply to Transport for London (TfL) for a vehicle to be registered as an existing private hire vehicle;
(b) provide that the owner of an existing private hire vehicle is to be treated for the purposes of the Private Hire Vehicles (London) Act 1998 as if he had made an application for a London PHV licence, unless and until he notifies TfL that he does not wish to proceed with the application, in which case any temporary permit issued in respect of the vehicle is treated as having been surrendered;
(c) enable TfL to issue to the owner a temporary permit with respect to any existing private hire vehicle, which generally has effect for the purposes of the 1998 Act as if it were a London PHV licence; and
(d) provide for the duration of a temporary permit.
Further regulations See SI 2003/655.

[854]

RAILWAY SAFETY ACCREDITATION SCHEME REGULATIONS 2004
SI 2004/915

Authority Made by the Home Secretary under the Police Reform Act 2002, ss 43, 105(4).
Date made 24 March 2004.
Commencement 26 April 2004.
Amendment Amended by SI 2004/1573.
Summary These regulations enable the chief constable of the British Transport Police Force ("the Police Force") to establish and maintain a railway safety accreditation scheme in England and Wales. Reg 3 permits the chief constable to establish and maintain a scheme for the purposes of contributing to railway safety and security, and assisting the Police Force in combating crime and disorder, public nuisance and other forms of anti-social behaviour. Regs 4–6 set out requirements associated with the accreditation scheme including consultation, information to be included in any railways policing plan and the arrangements to be made with appropriate employers. Reg 7 permits the chief constable to grant an accreditation to certain persons, sets out the procedure for granting an accreditation and specifies the circumstances where such an accreditation is to cease to have effect. The Schedule sets out the powers which may be made available to an accredited person. Reg 8 sets out supplementary provisions, including requirements with regard to the identification of accredited persons, and provides that an accreditation may be modified or withdrawn. Reg 9 sets out various offences relating to assaulting, obstructing or impersonating accredited persons, and the maximum penalties for such offences.

[855]

BRITISH TRANSPORT POLICE (POLICE SERVICES AGREEMENT) ORDER 2004
SI 2004/1522

Authority Made by the Secretary of State for Transport under the Railways and Transport Safety Act 2003, ss 34(1), 74(1).
Date made 21 June 2004.
Commencement 1 July 2004.
Amendment Amended by SI 2005/3050.
Summary The Railways and Transport Safety Act 2003, s 34 provides that the Secretary of State may by order require a person, or each member of a class of persons, providing railway services to enter into a police services agreement. "A police services agreement" is defined by s 33 of the 2003 Act as an agreement between the British Transport Police Authority and any person ("the customer") which provides for:
(a) the British Transport Police Force to police a railway or railway property in connection with which the customer provides railways services, in accordance with the objectives, plans, targets and directions set under ss 50–55 of the Act;

(b) the Police Force to provide such additional policing services as may be specified in the agreement; and
(c) such incidental or ancillary matters as the parties think appropriate.

This order requires the following persons to enter into a police services agreement:
(a) a person who provides railway services in respect of:
  (1) a train used on a network for the purpose of carrying passengers;
  (2) a train used on a network for the purpose of carrying goods;
  (3) a light maintenance depot; or
  (4) a station, and
(b) a person who has been granted a licence pursuant to the Railways Act 1993, s 8 authorising him to be the operator of the train, light maintenance depot or station in question or who has been granted a European licence pursuant to SI 2005/3050 or pursuant to any action taken by an EEA State for the purpose of implementing Council Directive 1995/18/EC on the licensing of railway undertakings (OJ L143, 27.06.1995, p 70), as amended by Directive 2001/13/EC of the European Parliament and of the Council (OJ L75, 15.03.2001, p 26) and Directive 2004/49/EC of the European Parliament and of the Council (OJ L164, 30.04.2004, p 44), in connection with the railway services in question; and
(c) Network Rail Infrastructure Limited, being a body which provides railway services in respect of a network.

[856]

BRITISH TRANSPORT POLICE (TRANSITIONAL AND CONSEQUENTIAL PROVISIONS) ORDER 2004
SI 2004/1573

Authority Made by the Secretary of State for Transport under the Railways and Transport Safety Act 2003, ss 73(2), (3), (4), 74(1), Sch 4, Pt 3, para 24. S 73(3) of the 2003 Act has been amended by the Railways Act 2005, s 59(6), Sch 13, Pt 1, so as to omit references to the Strategic Rail Authority.
Date made 21 June 2004.
Commencement 1 July 2004.
Summary This order makes transitional and consequential provisions in relation to the Railways and Transport Safety Act 2003, Pt 3 (ss 18–77 and Schs 4, 5), which creates an independent police authority for the British Transport Police Force and transfers responsibility for the Force from the Strategic Rail Authority (see below) to the new British Transport Police Authority. The order concerns:
(a) the first meeting of the British Transport Police Authority;
(b) transitional provision about budget requirements and planning;
(c) transitional provision about the Chief Constable, the Deputy Chief Constable and Assistant Chief Constables of the British Transport Police Force;
(d) the transfer of constables, special constables and civilian employees from the Strategic Rail Authority to the British Transport Police Authority;
(e) the transfer of property, rights and liabilities from the Strategic Rail Authority to the British Transport Police Authority;
(f) the determination of disputes relating to the transfer of staff or of property, rights and liabilities;
(g) the transfer to the British Transport Police Authority of the Strategic Rail Authority's obligations in relation to the British Transport Police Force Superannuation Fund;
(h) transitional provision about police services agreements; and
(i) transitional provision about police regulations.

The order makes consequential amendments to the following enactments (and to enactments relating to Scotland only which are outside the scope of this work): the Firearms Act 1968, s 54, the Police and Criminal Evidence Act 1984, s 6, the Channel Tunnel Act 1987, s 14, the Criminal Justice and Public Order Act 1994, s 60, the Police Act 1996, ss 23, 24, 25, the Crime and Disorder Act 1998, ss 1, 16, the Terrorism Act 2000, ss 34, 44, 121, and the Police Reform Act 2002, s 43. The amendments made by this order are set out in full in the relevant titles of Halsbury's Statutes, which also notes any repealed provisions. The order revokes the British Transport Police Force Scheme 1963 (Approval) Order 1964, SI 1964/1456 (as amended by SI 1992/364, SI 1994/609) and amends SI 2004/672, in the title Police, and SI 2004/915, in this title.

Strategic Rail Authority Provision for the abolition of the Strategic Rail Authority is made by the Railways Act 2005, s 1(10), as from 1 August 2006 (see SI 2006/1951, SI 2006/2925). The Railways and Transport Safety Act 2003, s 73(3) (under which this order was partly made) has been amended by s 59(6) of, and Pt 1 of Sch 13 to, the 2005 Act, so as to omit references to the Strategic Rail Authority (see heads (d), (e) and (g) of the summary above).

[857]

TRANSPORT AND WORKS (INQUIRIES PROCEDURE) RULES 2004
SI 2004/2018

Authority Made by the Lord Chancellor under the Tribunals and Inquiries Act 1992, s 9.
Date made 25 July 2004.
Commencement 23 August 2004; see r 1.
Interpretation See r 2.

Modification The Transport and Works (Inquiries Procedure) Rules 1992, SI 1992/2817 (revoked and replaced by these rules) were modified by SI 2000/253, in the title Constitutional Law (Pt 3), so that:

(a) in relation to any inquiry to which the 1992 rules related, references to "government policy" had effect as if they included references to policy adopted or formulated by the National Assembly for Wales (now the Welsh Ministers); and

(b) in relation to any such inquiry which was held other than by the Assembly (now the Welsh Ministers), references to a government department had effect as if they included references to the Assembly (now the Welsh Ministers).

Head (b) does not include an inquiry held by an inspector where jurisdiction to determine the appeal to which that inquiry relates has been transferred to the inspector by the Assembly. As to references in the current rules (SI 2004/2018) to "government policy", see rr 15(3), 20(5).

General These rules, which revoke, subject to transitional provisions, and replace the Transport and Works (Inquiries Procedure) Rules 1992, SI 1992/2817, prescribe the procedure to be followed in connection with public local inquiries held under the Transport and Works Act 1992, s 11. These inquiries relate to applications for orders under Pt I of the 1992 Act authorising:

(a) the construction or operation of railways, tramways, trolley vehicle systems and other systems of guided transport (as prescribed under s 2 of the 1992 Act) and matters ancillary thereto;

(b) the construction and operation of inland waterways and matters ancillary thereto; and

(c) the carrying out of certain works which interfere with navigation and have been prescribed pursuant to s 4 of the 1992 Act.

These rules are applied to concurrent inquiries under s 11 of the 1992 Act and under other enactments by SI 1992/3138, SI 1993/1119.

[858]

Citation and commencement

1 These Rules may be cited as the Transport and Works (Inquiries Procedure) Rules 2004 and shall come into force on 23rd August 2004.

[859]

Interpretation

2 (1) In these Rules references to sections are references to sections of the Transport and Works Act 1992, and—

"address" includes any number or address used for the purposes of electronic transmission;

"applicant" means any person who has submitted an application to the Secretary of State in accordance with rules made under section 6; or, in the case where the Secretary of State has made a proposal for an order under section 7, the Secretary of State;

"application" means an application under section 6 for an order under section 1 or 3 or the publication of a notice by the Secretary of State of a proposal to make such an order by virtue of section 7;

"assessor" means a person appointed by the Secretary of State to sit with an inspector at an inquiry or re-opened inquiry to advise the inspector on such matters arising as the Secretary of State may specify;

"by local advertisement" means, in relation to the publication of a notice, by publication of the notice in at least one newspaper circulating in the locality, or each of the localities, in which the land to which an application relates is situated;

"document" includes a photograph, map or plan;

"electronic transmission" means a communication transmitted—

(a) by means of an electronic communications network; or

(b) by other means but while in electronic form;

"inquiry" means a public local inquiry to which these Rules apply by virtue of rule 3;

"inspector" means a person appointed by the Secretary of State to hold an inquiry or a re-opened inquiry;

"mediator" means a person appearing to the Secretary of State to have been trained in mediation techniques by an independent mediation organisation and who is appointed by the Secretary of State to undertake mediation under rule 12;

"official body" means a Minister of the Crown or a government department;

"official case" means a written statement by an official body setting out full particulars of its evidence in regard to an application;

"official representation" means a written objection or representation made by an official body in regard to an application;

"order" means an order under section 1 or 3;

"outline statement" means a written statement of the principal submissions which a person proposes to put forward at an inquiry;

"pre-inquiry meeting" means a meeting held before an inquiry to consider what may be done with a view to securing that the inquiry is conducted efficiently and expeditiously, and where more than one such meeting is held references to the conclusion of the pre-inquiry meeting are references to the conclusion of the final meeting;

"registration form" means a form for completion by interested parties who wish to participate in an inquiry to which rule 6 applies;

"relevant notice" means the Secretary of State's written notice under rule 4 that an inquiry is to be held;

"starting date" means the date of the relevant notice;

"statement of case" means a written statement containing full particulars of the case which a person proposes to put forward at an inquiry (including, where that person is the applicant, the reasons for submitting the application), together with a list of any documents which that person intends to refer to or put in evidence;

"statement of common ground" means a written statement prepared jointly by the applicant and any other party who wishes to participate in the inquiry, which contains factual information agreed between those persons about any proposal which is the subject of the application in question;

"statement of matters" means a statement by the Secretary of State of the matters about which he particularly wishes to be informed for the purposes of his consideration of the order in question;

"statutory body" means a body, not being an official body, which has been given by a public general Act functions relevant to the subject matter of the application;

"statutory objector" means a person within section 11(4);

"technical adviser" means a person appearing to the Secretary of State to have such qualifications and experience as are sufficient to enable him to conduct an expert assessment of scientific or technical evidence to be given to the inquiry and who is appointed by the Secretary of State for that purpose under rule 11.

(2) Where the Secretary of State is the applicant these Rules shall be construed so as not to require that—

(a) the Secretary of State shall serve a document upon himself, or
(b) he shall consult or agree with himself upon any matter, or
(c) any other person shall serve a document upon the Secretary of State more than once.

[860]

Application of Rules

3 (1) These Rules shall apply in relation to any inquiry which is caused to be held pursuant to section 11—

(a) by the National Assembly for Wales for the purposes of an application relating solely to Wales; or
(b) by the Secretary of State for the purposes of all other applications relating to England and Wales.

(2) In these Rules, references to the Secretary of State shall mean the National Assembly for Wales where an inquiry is to be held in relation to an application made to that Assembly.

NOTES

National Assembly for Wales Functions exercisable by the Assembly were transferred to the Welsh Ministers by the Government of Wales Act 2006, s 162(1), Sch 11, para 30, subject to any Order in Council made under para 31 of that Schedule. As to the consequential construction of references to the Assembly, see para 32 of Sch 11 to that Act.

[861]

Preliminary action to be taken by the Secretary of State

4 (1) Where the Secretary of State intends to cause an inquiry to be held, he shall, not later than 4 weeks after the date specified in paragraph (2), give written notice of that intention to the applicant, to each statutory objector, to any statutory body which has submitted an objection (unless such objection has been withdrawn) and to any official body which has made an official representation.

(2) The date referred to in paragraph (1) is—

- (a) in the case of an application to which section 9 applies, the date on which each House of Parliament passes a resolution under section 9(4) (or, if there are two such dates, the later of them); and
- (b) in every other case, the date of expiry of the period within which an objection to the application may be made.

[862]

Preliminary action to be taken by official bodies

5 Where an official body has made an official representation it shall (unless it has already done so) serve upon the Secretary of State, the applicant and any statutory objector an official case within 6 weeks of the starting date.

[863]

Special procedure for major inquiries where Secretary of State causes a pre-inquiry meeting to be held

6 (1) The Secretary of State may cause a pre-inquiry meeting to be held where it appears to him that this would be desirable because of the extent of interest in the inquiry and where he does so this rule applies.

(2) The Secretary of State shall serve with the relevant notice a notification of his intention to cause a pre-inquiry meeting to be held, a statement of matters and a registration form, which form shall include the address to which, and date by which, completed forms are to be returned and which shall request the following information—

- (a) the name, address and telephone number of the person registering;
- (b) the name, address and telephone number of any agent, or, in the case of an organisation, of the contact person;
- (c) whether or not the person registering has an interest in any land which will be affected by the application;
- (d) whether or not the person or organisation registering is likely to want to be represented formally and to play a major part in the inquiry;
- (e) if not, whether or not the person registering will wish to give oral evidence at the inquiry or will wish only to submit representations in writing.

(3) The applicant shall, not later than 3 weeks after the starting date, publish by local advertisement a notice of the Secretary of State's intention to cause a pre-inquiry meeting to be held.

(4) The notice published pursuant to paragraph (3) shall include the text of the statement of matters and shall state that persons interested in participating in the inquiry should obtain from the Secretary of State a copy of the registration form.

(5) The applicant shall, not later than 8 weeks after the starting date, serve on the Secretary of State and on each statutory objector an outline statement.

(6) The applicant shall include in the outline statement the text of any official case supplied under rule 5 upon which he wishes to rely, and shall, not later than 8 weeks after the starting date, serve a copy of that statement on the official body concerned.

(7) When required to do so by notice in writing from the Secretary of State—

- (a) any statutory objector; and
- (b) any other person who has notified him of any intention or wish to appear at the inquiry,

shall within 8 weeks from the date of such notice serve upon the Secretary of State, on the applicant and on any other person specified in such notice, an outline statement.

(8) The pre-inquiry meeting (or, where there is more than one, the first pre-inquiry meeting) shall be held not later than 16 weeks after the starting date.

(9) The Secretary of State shall give not less than 3 weeks' written notice of the date, time and location of the pre-inquiry meeting to the applicant, each statutory objector and any other person whose presence at the pre-inquiry meeting seems to him to be desirable.

(10) The Secretary of State may require the applicant to take, in relation to notification of the pre-inquiry meeting, one or more of the steps mentioned in rule 13(6).

(11) The inspector shall preside at the pre-inquiry meeting and shall determine the matters to be discussed and the procedure to be followed; and he may require any person present at the pre-inquiry meeting who, in his opinion, is behaving in a disruptive manner to leave and may refuse to permit that person to return or to attend any further pre-inquiry meeting, or may permit him to return or attend only on such conditions as he may specify.

(12) The inspector may at any time hold such other meetings (including pre-inquiry meetings) as he considers necessary for the efficient and expeditious conduct of the inquiry and he shall arrange for such notice to be given of such meetings as appears to him necessary; and paragraph (11) shall apply to such meetings.
[864]

Service of statements of case, etc

7 (1) The applicant shall not later than—

(a) 6 weeks after the starting date; or
(b) where a pre-inquiry meeting is held pursuant to rule 6, 4 weeks after the conclusion of that meeting,

serve a statement of case on the Secretary of State and on each statutory objector and each person who is required to serve a statement of case under paragraph (3).

(2) In addition to the statement of case served under paragraph (1), the applicant shall serve—

(a) upon the Secretary of State a copy of every document or the relevant part of any document which he intends to refer to or put in evidence and of the notice mentioned in sub-paragraph (b), and
(b) upon each statutory objector and each person who is required to serve a statement of case under paragraph (3) a notice giving the names of all places, within each area in which the proposals contained in the application are to have effect (or as close as reasonably possible to any such area), where a copy of every document or the relevant part of any document which the applicant intends to refer to or put in evidence may be inspected free of charge at all reasonable hours until the date of commencement of the inquiry.

(3) When required by notice in writing from the Secretary of State to do so—

(a) a statutory objector; or
(b) any other person who has notified him of an intention or wish to appear at the inquiry,

shall within 6 weeks from the date of such notice or, where a pre-inquiry meeting is held pursuant to rule 6, no later than 4 weeks after the conclusion of that meeting, serve a statement of case on the Secretary of State, on the applicant and on any other person specified in such notice and the Secretary of State shall notify the applicant forthwith of the name and address of each person required to serve a statement of case.

(4) In addition to the statement of case served under paragraph (3), every person mentioned in paragraph (3)(a) and (b) shall serve upon the Secretary of State and the applicant a copy of every document or the relevant part of any document which such person intends to refer to or put in evidence unless copies of the document or part of the document are available for inspection pursuant to paragraph (9).

(5) Any person who has served a statement of case in accordance with this rule shall—

(a) when required by notice in writing from the Secretary of State or the inspector provide such further information about the matters contained in the statement as the Secretary of State or the inspector may specify; and

(b) at the same time send a copy of such further information to any other person on whom the statement of case has been served.

(6) Unless a statement of matters has already been served pursuant to rule 6(2), the Secretary of State shall, within 12 weeks from the starting date, serve such a statement on the applicant, each statutory objector and any person from whom he has required a statement of case.

(7) The Secretary of State may amend a statement of matters served under paragraph (6) or rule 6(2) at any time up to 6 weeks before the commencement of the inquiry.

(8) Any person who has served a statement of case in accordance with this rule and who wishes to comment on another person's statement of case shall, not later than 6 weeks before the date fixed for the commencement of the inquiry, send further comments in writing to the Secretary of State, the applicant and the person whose statement of case is the subject of the comment if that person is not the applicant.

(9) The applicant shall afford to any person who so requests a reasonable opportunity to inspect and, where practicable and subject to payment by that person of a reasonable charge, take copies of any statement or document which, or a copy of which, has been served on or by him in accordance with any of the preceding paragraphs of this rule; and shall specify in his statement of case the time and place at which the opportunity will be afforded.

[865]

Further power of inspector to hold pre-inquiry meetings

8 (1) Where no pre-inquiry meeting is held pursuant to rule 6, the inspector may hold one if he thinks it desirable.

(2) The inspector shall arrange for not less than 2 weeks' written notice of a meeting pursuant to paragraph (1) to be given to the applicant, each statutory objector, any other person known at the date of the notice to be entitled to appear at the inquiry, and any other person whose presence at the meeting appears to him to be desirable.

(3) Rule 6(11) shall apply to a meeting held under this rule.

[866]

Inquiry timetable

9 (1) Where a pre-inquiry meeting is held pursuant to rule 6, the inspector shall at that meeting—

(a) propose a timetable for the proceedings at, or at part of, the inquiry, and
(b) specify the date by which any proof of evidence and summary sent in accordance with rule 16(1) shall be received by him,

and shall arrange for written notice to be given of the date so specified to every person entitled to appear at the inquiry.

(2) The inspector shall arrange—

(a) after the conclusion of a pre-inquiry meeting held pursuant to rule 6 for a copy of the timetable for the proceedings to be sent to the Secretary of State for approval; and
(b) following such approval for a copy of the timetable for the proceedings to be sent to every person entitled to appear at the inquiry.

(3) The inspector may subsequently vary the timetable mentioned in paragraph (2) but he shall not do so before the start of the inquiry without the approval of the Secretary of State.

(4) Where a pre-inquiry meeting is held pursuant to rule 8 the inspector may arrange a timetable for the proceedings at, or at part of, the inquiry and may at any time vary the timetable.

(5) An inspector may specify in a timetable arranged under paragraph (4) a date by which any proof of evidence and summary required by rule 16(1) to be sent to him shall be so sent.

[867]

Notification of appointment of assessor

10 (1) Where the Secretary of State appoints an assessor, he shall notify the persons specified in rule 14(1) of the assessor's name and of the matters on which he is to advise the inspector.

NOTES

Although numbered as para (1), this rule does not contain further paragraphs.

[868]

Appointment of technical adviser

11 (1) This rule applies where the Secretary of State has caused a pre-inquiry meeting to be held in pursuance of rule 6.

(2) If it appears to the Secretary of State that evidence to be given to the inquiry is, or is likely to be, of such a technical or scientific nature that the inquiry would be conducted more efficiently and expeditiously if an expert assessment of that evidence were to be made, he may at any time appoint a technical adviser for that purpose.

(3) Where the Secretary of State appoints a technical adviser he may in writing require the applicant to publish by local advertisement and within such period as he may specify a notice stating the name of the person so appointed and specifying the evidence to be assessed.

(4) The technical adviser shall assess the evidence so specified and shall report his assessment in writing to the inspector, identifying any areas of disagreement between the parties and stating his view of the significance of such disagreement.

(5) The inspector shall within 7 days of receipt of the technical adviser's report arrange for a copy to be sent to every person entitled to appear at the inquiry.

(6) The technical adviser shall give evidence on his report to the inquiry and shall be subject to cross-examination to the same extent as any other witness.

(7) The inspector may allow the technical adviser to alter or add to his report so far as may be necessary for the purposes of the inquiry; but he shall (if necessary by adjourning the inquiry) give every other person entitled to appear who is appearing at the inquiry an adequate opportunity of considering any such alteration or addition.

[869]

Mediation

12 (1) This rule applies where the Secretary of State has caused a pre-inquiry meeting to be held in pursuance of rule 6.

(2) If it appears to the Secretary of State that—

(a) there is an absence of agreement between persons entitled to appear at the inquiry on a matter which is relevant to the inquiry;

(b) the inquiry would be conducted more efficiently and expeditiously if agreement could be reached in relation to that matter or any disagreement in relation to it could be defined and narrowed; and

(c) such a result is capable of being achieved by mediation,

then he may, after consulting such persons entitled to appear at the inquiry as he considers appropriate, appoint a mediator for that purpose.

(3) Where the Secretary of State appoints a mediator he may in writing require the applicant to publish by local advertisement and within such period as he may specify a notice stating the name of the person so appointed and the matter in relation to which he is to mediate.

(4) The mediator shall determine the procedure for the mediation.

(5) Within 7 days from the conclusion of the mediation, the mediator shall give to the inspector a report describing the mediation procedure and its outcome and the inspector shall upon receipt of that report arrange for a copy to be sent to every person entitled to appear at the inquiry.

(6) The inspector shall permit any person entitled to appear at the inquiry to address him on the report referred to in paragraph (5), but the mediator shall not give evidence at the inquiry.

[870]

Date and notification of inquiry

13 (1) The date fixed by the Secretary of State for the commencement of an inquiry shall be determined in consultation with the applicant but shall be—

- (a) not later than 22 weeks after the starting date; or
- (b) in a case where a pre-inquiry meeting is held pursuant to rule 6, not later than 8 weeks after the conclusion of the meeting; or
- (c) where the Secretary of State is satisfied that in all the circumstances of the case it is impracticable to hold the inquiry within the applicable period mentioned in sub-paragraph (a) or (b), the earliest practicable date after the end of that period.

(2) The place at which the inquiry is to be held shall be determined by the Secretary of State in consultation with the applicant and where the Secretary of State is satisfied, having regard to the nature of the application, that it is reasonable to do so he may direct that it shall be held at more than one place.

(3) Unless the Secretary of State agrees to a lesser period of notice with the applicant and each statutory objector, he shall give not less than 6 weeks' notice of the date, time and place fixed by him for the holding of an inquiry to every person specified in rule 14(1).

(4) The Secretary of State may—

- (a) vary the date fixed for the commencement of an inquiry whether or not the revised date is within the applicable period mentioned in paragraph (1), and
- (b) where a direction has been given under paragraph (2) vary the date of the holding of the inquiry at any place,

and paragraph (3) shall apply to a variation of a date as it applied to the date originally fixed.

(5) The Secretary of State may vary the time or place for the holding of an inquiry and shall give such notice of any such variation as appears to him to be reasonable.

(6) Unless the Secretary of State otherwise directs, and subject to paragraph (7), the applicant shall not later than 2 weeks before the date fixed for the commencement of an inquiry—

- (a) post a notice of the inquiry in a conspicuous place or (in the case of an application for an order making provision for land based linear works more than 5 kilometres in length) at intervals of not more than 5 kilometres on, or as close as reasonably practicable to, the land to which the powers sought in the application relate;
- (b) post a notice of the inquiry in one or more places where public notices are usually posted in the area in which the proposals contained in the application relate;
- (c) publish a notice of the inquiry by local advertisement in the area in which the proposals contained in the application are to have effect.

(7) Where a direction has been given under paragraph (2), paragraph (6) shall have effect with the substitution—

- (a) for references to the inquiry, of references to the part of the inquiry which is to be held at a place specified in the direction; and
- (b) for references to the application, of references to that part of the application which is to be the subject of that part of the inquiry.

(8) Any notice posted pursuant to paragraph (6) (a) or (b) shall be readily visible to and legible by members of the public provided that where the notice is, without any fault or intention of the applicant, removed, obscured or defaced before the commencement of the inquiry, he shall be treated as having complied with the requirements of those sub-paragraphs if he has taken reasonable steps for the protection of the notice and, if need be, its replacement.

(9) Any notice of inquiry posted or published pursuant to paragraph (6) shall contain a statement of the date, time and place of the inquiry, and of the relevant section under which the application has been made, together with a sufficient description of the proposals in the application to identify their location with or without reference to a specified map.

[871]

Appearances at inquiry

14 (1) The persons entitled to appear at an inquiry are—

(a) the applicant;

(b) any statutory objector;

(c) any other person who has served an outline statement under rule 6 or a statement of case under rule 7.

(2) Nothing in paragraph (1) shall prevent the inspector from permitting any other person to appear at an inquiry, and such permission shall not be unreasonably withheld.

(3) Any person entitled or permitted to appear may do so on his own behalf or be represented by any other person.

[872]

Representation of official bodies at inquiry

15 (1) An official body which has provided an official case shall arrange for its representative to attend the inquiry if the official body has received, not later than 4 weeks before the date fixed for the holding of any inquiry, a written request for such attendance from the Secretary of State, the applicant or a statutory objector.

(2) A person attending an inquiry as a representative in pursuance of this rule shall give evidence and be subject to cross-examination to the same extent as any other witness.

(3) Nothing in paragraph (2) shall require a representative of an official body to answer any question which in the opinion of the inspector is directed to the merits of government policy or, in the case of any inquiry into an application to which section 9 applies, the merits of a resolution passed pursuant to section 9(4).

NOTES

Government policy See the note "Modification" at the beginning of these rules.

[873]

Proofs of evidence

16 (1) A person entitled to appear at an inquiry who proposes to give, or to call another person to give, evidence at the inquiry by reading a proof of evidence shall send to the inspector a copy of the proof and (subject to paragraph (2)) a written summary of it.

(2) No written summary shall be required where the proof which it is proposed to read contains no more than 1500 words.

(3) The proof and summary shall be sent to the inspector not later than—

(a) 4 weeks before the date fixed for the commencement of the inquiry; or

(b) where a timetable has been arranged pursuant to rule 9, which specifies a date by which the proof and summary shall be sent to the inspector, that date.

(4) Where the applicant sends a proof and a summary to an inspector in accordance with paragraph (1), he shall at the same time send a copy to every other person specified in rule 14(1); and where any other person so sends such a proof and summary he shall at the same time send a copy to the applicant.

(5) Unless paragraph (2) applies, only the summary shall be read at the inquiry unless the inspector permits or requires otherwise.

(6) Subject to paragraph (7), any person required by this rule to send a proof to any other person shall send with it a copy of the whole, or the relevant part, of any document referred to in it, unless copies of the document or part of the document in question are already available for inspection pursuant to rule 7(9).

(7) Where any person has confirmed to the applicant in writing that he does not wish to be sent a copy of, or a copy of part of, a proof, summary or other document that the applicant is required to send, the applicant shall not be required to send him that document or the relevant part of it.

(8) The applicant shall afford to any person who so requests a reasonable opportunity to inspect and, where practicable and on payment of a reasonable charge, take copies of any document sent to or by him in accordance with any of the preceding paragraphs of this rule.

[874]

Statement of common ground

17 (1) Where practicable, the applicant and any other party who wishes to participate in the inquiry may together prepare an agreed statement of common ground, and where this is done the applicant shall send a copy of such statement to the inspector no later than 4 weeks before the date fixed for the commencement of the inquiry.

(2) The applicant shall afford to any person who so requests a reasonable opportunity to inspect and, where practicable and on payment of a reasonable charge, take copies of any statement of common ground prepared under paragraph (1).

[875]

Procedure at inquiry

18 (1) Except as otherwise provided in these Rules, the inspector shall determine the procedure at an inquiry.

(2) Unless in any particular case the inspector with the consent of the applicant otherwise determines, the applicant shall begin and shall have the right of final reply and other persons entitled or permitted to appear shall be heard in such order as the inspector may determine.

(3) Persons specified in rule 14(1) shall be entitled to call evidence, and the applicant and the statutory objectors shall be entitled to cross-examine persons giving evidence, but, subject to paragraphs (2), (4), (5) and (6), the calling of evidence and the cross-examination of persons giving evidence shall otherwise be at the inspector's discretion.

(4) The inspector may refuse to permit—

(a) the giving or production of evidence,
(b) the cross-examination of persons giving evidence, or
(c) the presentation of any other matter

which he considers to be irrelevant or repetitious but, where he refuses to permit the giving of oral evidence for these reasons, the person wishing to give evidence may submit to him in writing any such evidence or other matter before the close of the inquiry.

(5) Where a person gives evidence at an inquiry by reading a summary in accordance with rule 16(5), the proof referred to in rule 16(1) and the documents referred to in rule 16(6) shall, unless the person required to provide the summary notifies the inspector that he now wishes to rely on the contents of that summary only, be treated as tendered in evidence, and the person whose evidence the proof contains shall then be subject to cross-examination on it to the same extent as if it were evidence he had given orally.

(6) The inspector may direct the applicant to provide facilities so that any person appearing at an inquiry may take or obtain copies of documentary evidence open to public inspection, subject to such a person paying to the applicant a reasonable charge for the use of the facilities.

(7) The inspector may require any person appearing or present at an inquiry who, in his opinion, is behaving in a disruptive manner to leave and may refuse to permit that person to return, or may permit him to return only on such conditions as he may specify; but any such person may submit to him in writing any evidence or other matter before the close of the inquiry.

(8) The inspector may refuse to permit the cross-examination of persons giving evidence, or may require such cross-examination to cease, if it appears to him that permitting such cross-examination or allowing it to continue (as the case may be) would have the effect that the timetable referred to in rule 9 could not be met.

(9) The inspector may allow any person to alter or add to a statement of case served under rule 7 so far as may be necessary for the purpose of the inquiry; but he shall (if necessary by adjourning the inquiry) give every other person specified in rule 14(1) an adequate opportunity of considering any fresh matter or document.

(10) The inspector may proceed with an inquiry in the absence of any person specified in rule 14(1).

(11) The inspector may take into account any written representation or evidence or any other document received by him from any person before an inquiry opens or during the inquiry provided that he discloses it at the inquiry.

(12) The inspector may from time to time adjourn an inquiry and

- (a) if at the inquiry he announces the date, time and place for reconvening the adjourned inquiry no further notice shall be required, but
- (b) if he makes no such announcement he shall give such notice as he considers reasonable and appropriate.

(13) Any person who appears at an inquiry and makes a closing submission shall by the close of the inquiry provide the inspector with a copy of his closing submission in writing.

[876]

Site inspections

19 (1) The inspector may make an unaccompanied inspection of any site to which the application relates before or during an inquiry without giving notice of his intention to the persons specified in rule 14(1).

(2) The inspector may, during an inquiry or after its close, inspect such a site in the company of a representative of the applicant and any statutory objector; and he shall make such an inspection if so requested by the applicant or by any statutory objector before or during an inquiry.

(3) In all cases where the inspector intends to make an inspection of the kind referred to in paragraph (2) he shall announce during the inquiry the date and time at which he proposes to make it.

(4) The inspector shall not be bound to defer an inspection of the kind referred to in paragraph (2) where any person mentioned in that paragraph is not present at the time appointed.

[877]

Procedure after inquiry

20 (1) After the close of an inquiry, the inspector shall make a report in writing to the Secretary of State, which shall include his conclusions and his recommendations or his reasons for not making any recommendations.

(2) Where an assessor has been appointed, he may, after the close of the inquiry, make a report in writing to the inspector in respect of the matters on which he was appointed to advise.

(3) Where an assessor makes a report in accordance with paragraph (2), the inspector shall append it to his own report and shall state in his own report how far he agrees or disagrees with the assessor's report and, where he disagrees with the assessor, his reasons for that disagreement.

(4) When making his decision the Secretary of State may disregard any written representations, evidence or any other document received after the close of the inquiry.

(5) If, after the close of an inquiry, the Secretary of State—

- (a) differs from the inspector on any matter of fact mentioned in, or appearing to him to be material to, a conclusion reached by the inspector, or
- (b) takes into consideration any new evidence or new matter of fact (not being a matter of government policy),

and is for that reason disposed to disagree with a recommendation made by the inspector, he shall not come to a decision which is at variance with that recommendation without first notifying such of the persons specified in rule 14(1) who appear to him to be likely to be affected thereby, and who have appeared at the inquiry, of his disagreement and the reasons for it; and affording them an opportunity either of making written representations to him within 3 weeks of the date of the notification, or (if the Secretary of State has taken into consideration any new evidence or new matter of fact, not being a matter of government policy) of asking within that period for the re-opening of the inquiry.

(6) If, after the close of an inquiry relating to an application in respect of which the appropriate resolutions have been passed under section 9(4), the Secretary of State is disposed to seek the approval of each House of Parliament to modified proposals by means of a resolution in accordance with section 9(5), he shall not do so without first—

(a) notifying any person who appears to him to be likely to be affected by the modification;

(b) giving that person an opportunity of making written representations to him about the modifications within such period (which shall not be less than 3 weeks) as he may specify in the notice; and

(c) considering any representation duly made to him.

(7) The Secretary of State may, as he thinks fit, cause an inquiry to be re-opened, and he shall do so if asked by the applicant or a statutory objector in the circumstances and within the period mentioned in paragraph (5); and where an inquiry is re-opened (whether by the same or a different inspector)—

(a) the Secretary of State shall send to the persons specified in rule 14(1) who appeared at the inquiry a written statement of the matters in respect to which further evidence is invited; and

(b) paragraphs (2) to (9) of rule 13 shall apply,

(i) as if references to an inquiry were references to a re-opened inquiry, but with the substitution in paragraph (3) of "4 weeks" for "6 weeks"; and

(ii) as if the words "whether or not the revised date is within the applicable period mentioned in paragraph (1)" were omitted from paragraph (4)(a).

NOTES

Government policy See the note "Modification" at the beginning of these rules.

[878]

Notification of decision

21 (1) Where the Secretary of State has published and given notice of his decision under section 14 and a copy of the inspector's report is not sent with the notification of the decision, the notification shall be accompanied by a copy of the inspector's conclusions and any recommendations made by him.

(2) Subject to paragraph (3) if a person entitled to be notified of the decision under section 14 has not received a copy of the inspector's report, he shall be supplied with a copy of it on written application to the Secretary of State.

(3) Any person applying to the Secretary of State under paragraph (2) shall send his application to the Secretary of State within 4 weeks of the date of the Secretary of State's decision.

(4) In this rule "inspector's report" includes any assessor's report appended to it but does not include any other documents so appended, but any person who has received a copy of the inspector's report may apply to the Secretary of State in writing, within 6 weeks of the date of the Secretary of State's decision, for an opportunity of inspecting any such documents and the Secretary of State shall afford him that opportunity.

[879]

Procedure following quashing of decision

22 (1) Where a decision of the Secretary of State on an application in respect of which an inquiry has been held is quashed in proceedings before any court, the Secretary of State—

(a) shall send to the persons entitled to appear at the inquiry who appeared at it a written statement of the matters with respect to which further representations are invited for the purpose of his further consideration of the application;

(b) shall afford to those persons the opportunity of making written representations to him in respect of those matters or of asking for the re-opening of the inquiry; and

(c) may, as he thinks fit, cause the inquiry to be re-opened (whether by the same or a different inspector) and if he does so paragraphs (2) to (9) of rule 13 shall apply,

(i) as if references to any inquiry were references to a re-opened inquiry, but with the substitution in paragraph (3) of "4 weeks" for "6 weeks"; and

(ii) as if the words "whether or not the revised date is within the applicable period mentioned in paragraph (1)" were omitted from paragraph (4)(a).

(2) Any persons making representations or asking for the inquiry to be re-opened under paragraph (1)(b) shall submit such representations or requests to the Secretary of State within 3 weeks of the date of the written statement sent under paragraph (1)(a).

[880]

Allowing further time

23 The Secretary of State may at any time in any particular case allow further time for the taking of any step which is required or enabled to be taken by virtue of these Rules, and references in these Rules to a day by which, or a period within which, any step is required or enabled to be taken shall be construed accordingly.

[881]

Service of notices

24 (1) Notices or documents required or authorised to be served or sent under any of the provisions of these Rules may be sent—

(a) by post; or
(b) subject to paragraphs (2) to (5), by electronic transmission.

(2) Where a notice or other document required to be served or sent for the purposes of these Rules is served or sent by electronic transmission the requirement shall be taken to be fulfilled where the recipient of the notice or other document to be transmitted has given his consent to the use of electronic transmission either in writing or by electronic transmission.

(3) Where the recipient of a notice or other document served or sent by electronic transmission notifies the sender within 7 days of receipt that he requires a paper copy of all or any part of that notice or other document the sender shall provide such a copy as soon as reasonably practicable.

(4) A person may revoke his consent to the use of electronic transmission in accordance with paragraph (5).

(5) Where a person is no longer willing to accept the use of electronic transmission for any of the purposes of these Rules he shall—

(a) give notice in writing or by electronic transmission revoking any consent given by him for that purpose; and
(b) such revocation shall be final and shall take effect on a date specified by the person in the notice but that date shall not be less than 7 days after the date on which the notice is given.

[882]

Revocation, savings and transitional provisions

25 (1) Subject to paragraph (2), the Transport and Works (Inquiries Procedure) Rules 1992 ("the 1992 Rules") are hereby revoked.

(2) Subject to paragraph (3), any application to which the 1992 Rules applied which has not been determined on the date when these Rules came into force shall continue to be subject to the 1992 Rules.

(3) Where a decision of the Secretary of State on an application to which the 1992 Rules applied is subsequently quashed in proceedings before any court, the decision shall be re-determined in accordance with these Rules.

NOTES

Transport and Works (Inquiries Procedure) Rules 1992 SI 1992/2817.

[883]

TRAFFIC MANAGEMENT ACT 2004 (COMMENCEMENT NO 1 AND TRANSITIONAL PROVISION) (ENGLAND) ORDER 2004 SI 2004/2380

Authority Made by the Secretary of State for Transport under the Traffic Management Act 2004, s 99.

Date made 13 September 2004.

Summary This order brought provisions of the Traffic Management Act 2004 into force in relation to England only, as noted in the table below.

Further commencement orders Provisions of the Traffic Management Act 2004 have been brought into force by further orders (made under s 99 of the Act) listed below, as noted in the following table:

(a) SI 2004/3110, SI 2006/1736, SI 2007/1890, SI 2007/2053 (as amended by SI 2008/757), SI 2007/3184, brought provisions of the Act into force in relation to England only;

(b) SI 2006/2826, SI 2007/3174, SI 2009/1095 brought provisions of the Act into force in relation to Wales only.

Transitional provisions made by SI 2007/1890, SI 2007/2053 (as amended by SI 2008/757), SI 2007/3174 are set out in full at the end of the table.

Provision	*Date and extent (if any)*
ss 1–4	4 October 2004 (England only) (SI 2004/2380) 1 May 2009 (Wales only) (SI 2009/1095)
s 5(1)–(3)	4 October 2004 (England only) (SI 2004/2380) 1 May 2009 (Wales only) (SI 2009/1095)
s 5(4), (5)	4 October 2004 (England only) (SI 2004/2380) 26 October 2006 (Wales only) (SI 2006/2826)
s 5(6)	4 October 2004 (England only) (SI 2004/2380) 1 May 2009 (Wales only) (SI 2009/1095)
ss 6–9	4 October 2004 (England only) (SI 2004/2380) 1 May 2009 (Wales only) (SI 2009/1095)
s 10	4 October 2004 (England only) (SI 2004/2380) 26 October 2006 (Wales only) (SI 2006/2826)
ss 11–15	4 October 2004 (England only) (SI 2004/2380) 1 May 2009 (Wales only) (SI 2009/1095)
ss 16–31	4 January 2005 (England only) (SI 2004/3110) 26 October 2006 (Wales only) (SI 2006/2826)
s 32	1 December 2007 (England only) (SI 2007/3184) 31 March 2008 (Wales only) (SI 2007/3174)
ss 33–36	31 March 2008 (Wales only) (SI 2007/3174) 1 April 2008 (England only) (SI 2007/3184)
s 37	1 December 2007 (England only) (SI 2007/3184) 31 March 2008 (Wales only) (SI 2007/3174)
s 38	31 March 2008 (Wales only) (SI 2007/3174) 1 April 2008 (England only) (SI 2007/3184)
s 39	1 December 2007 (England only) (SI 2007/3184) 31 March 2008 (Wales only) (SI 2007/3174)
s 40(1), (2)	4 October 2004 (England only) (SI 2004/2380) 26 November 2007 (Wales only) (SI 2007/3174)
s 40(3)	4 October 2004 (England only) (except words "or (4A)" in the substituted New Roads and Street Works Act 1991, s 70(6)(a)) (SI 2004/2380) 26 November 2007 (Wales only) (except words "or (4A)" in the substituted New Roads and Street Works Act 1991, s 70(6)(a)) (SI 2007/3174) 1 April 2008 (England only) (in so far as not already in force) (SI 2007/1890) 1 April 2008 (Wales only) (in so far as not already in force) (SI 2007/3174)
s 40(4), (5)	4 October 2004 (England only) (SI 2004/2380) 26 November 2007 (Wales only) (SI 2007/3174)

Provision	*Date and extent (if any)*
s 41(1)	29 June 2007 (England only) (in so far as confers power to make orders) (SI 2007/1890) 26 November 2007 (Wales only) (in so far as confers power to make orders) (SI 2007/3174) 12 May 2008 (England only) (in so far as not already in force) (SI 2007/1890) 12 May 2008 (Wales only) (in so far as not already in force) (SI 2007/3174)
s 41(2)	12 May 2008 (England only) (SI 2007/1890) 12 May 2008 (Wales only) (SI 2007/3174)
s 41(3)	See Schs 2, 3 below
s 42	29 June 2007 (England only) (in so far as confers power to make regulations) (SI 2007/1890) 26 November 2007 (Wales only) (in so far as confers power to make regulations) (SI 2007/3174)
s 43(1)	4 January 2005 (England only) (SI 2004/3110) 26 November 2007 (Wales only) (SI 2007/3174)
s 43(2)	4 January 2005 (England only) (SI 2004/3110) 1 April 2008 (Wales only) (SI 2007/3174)
s 43(3)	1 April 2008 (England only) (SI 2007/1890) 1 April 2008 (Wales only) (SI 2007/3174)
s 43(4)	4 January 2005 (England only) (SI 2004/3110) 1 April 2008 (Wales only) (SI 2007/3174)
s 44	29 June 2007 (England only) (in so far as confers power to: (a) make regulations, and (b) issue or approve a code of practice under the New Roads and Street Works Act 1991, s 56A(8) for the purposes of s 56A thereof) (SI 2007/1890) 26 November 2007 (Wales only) (in so far as confers power to: (a) make regulations, and (b) issue or approve a code of practice under the New Roads and Street Works Act 1991, s 56A(8) for the purposes of s 56A thereof) (SI 2007/3174) 1 April 2008 (England only) (in so far as not already in force) (SI 2007/1890) 1 April 2008 (Wales only) (in so far as not already in force) (SI 2007/3174)
s 49	29 June 2007 (England only) (in so far as confers power to make regulations) (SI 2007/1890) 26 November 2007 (Wales only) (in so far as confers power to make regulations) (SI 2007/3174) 1 April 2008 (England only) (in so far as not already in force) (SI 2007/1890) 1 April 2008 (Wales only) (in so far as not already in force) (SI 2007/3174)
s 51(1)–(3)	29 June 2007 (England only) (in so far as confer power to make regulations) (SI 2007/1890) 26 November 2007 (Wales only) (in so far as confer power to make regulations) (SI 2007/3174) 1 April 2008 (England only) (in so far as not already in force) (SI 2007/1890) 1 April 2008 (Wales only) (in so far as not already in force) (SI 2007/3174)
s 51(4)	29 June 2007 (England only) (SI 2007/1890) 26 November 2007 (Wales only) (SI 2007/3174)

Provision	*Date and extent (if any)*
s 51(5)	29 June 2007 (England only) (in so far as confers power to make regulations) (SI 2007/1890) 26 November 2007 (Wales only) (in so far as confers power to make regulations) (SI 2007/3174) 1 April 2008 (England only) (in so far as not already in force) (SI 2007/1890) 1 April 2008 (Wales only) (in so far as not already in force) (SI 2007/3174)
s 51(6)	1 April 2008 (England only) (SI 2007/1890) 1 April 2008 (Wales only) (SI 2007/3174)
s 51(7)–(9)	29 June 2007 (England only) (in so far as confer power to make regulations) (SI 2007/1890) 26 November 2007 (Wales only) (in so far as confer power to make regulations) (SI 2007/3174) 1 April 2008 (England only) (in so far as not already in force) (SI 2007/1890) 1 April 2008 (Wales only) (in so far as not already in force) (SI 2007/3174)
s 52(1)	29 June 2007 (England only) (in so far as confers power to make regulations) (SI 2007/1890) 26 November 2007 (Wales only) (in so far as confers power to make regulations) (SI 2007/3174) 1 April 2008 (England only) (in so far as not already in force) (SI 2007/1890) 1 April 2008 (Wales only) (in so far as not already in force) (SI 2007/3174)
s 52(2)	See Sch 4 below
s 52(3)	1 April 2008 (England only) (SI 2007/1890) 1 April 2008 (Wales only) (SI 2007/3174)
s 52(4), (5)	29 June 2007 (England only) (in so far as confer power to make regulations) (SI 2007/1890) 26 November 2007 (Wales only) (in so far as confer power to make regulations) (SI 2007/3174) 1 April 2008 (England only) (in so far as not already in force) (SI 2007/1890) 1 April 2008 (Wales only) (in so far as not already in force) (SI 2007/3174)
s 52(6), (7)	1 April 2008 (England only) (SI 2007/1890) 1 April 2008 (Wales only) (SI 2007/3174)
s 54	29 June 2007 (England only) (in so far as confers power to make regulations) (SI 2007/1890) 26 November 2007 (Wales only) (in so far as confers power to make regulations) (SI 2007/3174) 1 April 2008 (England only) (in so far as not already in force) (SI 2007/1890) 1 April 2008 (Wales only) (in so far as not already in force) (SI 2007/3174)
ss 60–63	4 October 2004 (England only) (SI 2004/2380)
s 71	26 November 2007 (Wales only) (SI 2007/3174)
ss 72, 73	26 October 2006 (Wales only) (SI 2006/2826) 23 July 2007 (England only) (SI 2007/2053)
s 74	See Sch 8 below
s 75	26 October 2006 (Wales only) (SI 2006/2826)

Provision	*Date and extent (if any)*
	31 March 2008 (England only) (SI 2007/2053, as amended by SI 2008/757)
s 76	26 October 2006 (Wales only) (SI 2006/2826) 23 July 2007 (England only) (SI 2007/2053)
s 77	See Sch 9 below
ss 78–83	26 October 2006 (Wales only) (SI 2006/2826) 23 July 2007 (England only) (SI 2007/2053)
s 84	See Sch 10 below
ss 85, 86	26 October 2006 (Wales only) (SI 2006/2826) 31 March 2008 (England only) (SI 2007/2053, as amended by SI 2008/757)
ss 87–90	26 October 2006 (Wales only) (SI 2006/2826) 23 July 2007 (England only) (SI 2007/2053)
s 91	See Sch 11 below
ss 92, 93	26 October 2006 (Wales only) (SI 2006/2826) 23 July 2007 (England only) (SI 2007/2053)
s 94	29 September 2006 (England only) (SI 2006/1736) 26 October 2006 (Wales only) (SI 2006/2826)
s 95	4 October 2004 (England only) (SI 2004/2380) 26 October 2006 (Wales only) (SI 2006/2826)
s 96	26 October 2006 (Wales only) (SI 2006/2826) 29 June 2007 (England only) (SI 2007/1890)
s 97	4 October 2004 (England only) (SI 2004/2380)
s 98	See Sch 12 below
Sch 1	4 October 2004 (England only) (SI 2004/2380) 26 November 2007 (Wales only) (SI 2007/3174)
Sch 2	12 May 2008 (England only) (SI 2007/1890) 12 May 2008 (Wales only) (SI 2007/3174)
Sch 3	29 June 2007 (England only) (in so far as confers power to make regulations) (SI 2007/1890) 26 November 2007 (Wales only) (in so far as confers power to make regulations) (SI 2007/3174) 12 May 2008 (England only) (in so far as not already in force) (SI 2007/1890) 12 May 2008 (Wales only) (in so far as not already in force) (SI 2007/3174)
Sch 4	29 June 2007 (England only) (in so far as confers power to make regulations) (SI 2007/1890) 26 November 2007 (Wales only) (in so far as confers power to make regulations) (SI 2007/3174) 1 April 2008 (England only) (in so far as not already in force) (SI 2007/1890) 1 April 2008 (Wales only) (in so far as not already in force) (SI 2007/3174)
Sch 7, para 1[1]	23 July 2007 (England only) (SI 2007/2053) 31 March 2008 (Wales only) (SI 2007/3174)
Sch 7, paras 2, 3[1]	23 July 2007 (England only) (SI 2007/2053)
Sch 7, paras 4, 5(1)[1]	23 July 2007 (England only) (SI 2007/2053) 31 March 2008 (Wales only) (SI 2007/3174)

Provision	*Date and extent (if any)*
Sch 7, para 5(2)[1]	23 July 2007 (England only) (SI 2007/2053)
Sch 7, paras 5(3), 6[1]	23 July 2007 (England only) (SI 2007/2053) 31 March 2008 (Wales only) (SI 2007/3174)
Sch 7, para 7[1]	23 July 2007 (England only) (SI 2007/2053)
Sch 7, para 8(1), (2)[1]	23 July 2007 (England only) (SI 2007/2053) 31 March 2008 (Wales only) (SI 2007/3174)
Sch 7, para 8(3)[1]	23 July 2007 (England only) (SI 2007/2053)
Sch 7, paras 8(4), 9, 10[1]	23 July 2007 (England only) (SI 2007/2053) 31 March 2008 (Wales only) (SI 2007/3174)
Sch 8, paras 1–3[1]	31 March 2008 (England only) (SI 2007/2053, as amended by SI 2008/757)
Sch 8, para 8(1)[1]	31 March 2008 (England only) (SI 2007/2053, as amended by SI 2008/757) 31 March 2008 (Wales only) (SI 2007/3174)
Sch 8, para 8(2)(a)[1]	31 March 2008 (England only) (SI 2007/2053, as amended by SI 2008/757)
Sch 8, para 8(2)(b)[1]	31 March 2008 (England only) (SI 2007/2053, as amended by SI 2008/757) 31 March 2008 (Wales only) (SI 2007/3174)
Sch 8, para 8(2)(c)–(e)[1]	31 March 2008 (England only) (SI 2007/2053, as amended by SI 2008/757)
Sch 8, para 8(3)–(5)[1]	31 March 2008 (England only) (SI 2007/2053, as amended by SI 2008/757) 31 March 2008 (Wales only) (SI 2007/3174)
Sch 8, paras 9, 10(1), (2)[1]	31 March 2008 (Wales only) (SI 2007/3174)
Sch 8, para 10(3)(b)[1]	31 March 2008 (Wales only) (SI 2007/3174)
Sch 8, para 10(4), (5)[1]	31 March 2008 (Wales only) (SI 2007/3174)
Sch 9, para 1[1]	23 July 2007 (England only) (SI 2007/2053) 26 November 2007 (Wales only) (SI 2007/3174)
Sch 9, paras 2–6[1]	23 July 2007 (England only) (SI 2007/2053)
Sch 9, paras 7–9[1]	23 July 2007 (England only) (SI 2007/2053) 26 November 2007 (Wales only) (SI 2007/3174)
Sch 10, paras 1, 2[1]	31 March 2008 (England only) (SI 2007/2053, as amended by SI 2008/757)
Sch 10, para 3(1), (2)[1]	31 March 2008 (England only) (SI 2007/2053, as amended by SI 2008/757) 31 March 2008 (Wales only) (SI 2007/3174)
Sch 10, para 3(3)(a)[1]	31 March 2008 (England only) (SI 2007/2053, as amended by SI 2008/757)
Sch 10, para 3(3)(b)[1]	31 March 2008 (England only) (SI 2007/2053, as amended by SI 2008/757) 31 March 2008 (Wales only) (SI 2007/3174)
Sch 10, para 3(3)(c)–(e)[1]	31 March 2008 (England only) (SI 2007/2053, as amended by SI 2008/757)
Sch 10, para 3(4), (5)[1]	31 March 2008 (England only) (SI 2007/2053, as amended by SI 2008/757) 31 March 2008 (Wales only) (SI 2007/3174)
Sch 11, paras 1, 2[1]	31 March 2008 (England only) (SI 2007/2053, as amended by SI 2008/757) 31 March 2008 (Wales only) (SI 2007/3174)

Provision	*Date and extent (if any)*
Sch 11, para 3[1]	23 July 2007 (England only) (to the extent that it inserts the Road Traffic Regulation Act 1984, s 101B) (SI 2007/2053) 31 March 2008 (England only) (in so far as not already in force) (SI 2007/2053, as amended by SI 2008/757) 31 March 2008 (Wales only) (SI 2007/3174)
Sch 11, paras 4, 5[1]	31 March 2008 (England only) (SI 2007/2053, as amended by SI 2008/757) 31 March 2008 (Wales only) (SI 2007/3174)
Sch 11, paras 6, 7[1]	31 March 2008 (England only) (SI 2007/2053, as amended by SI 2008/757)
Sch 12, Pt 1	31 March 2008 (England only) (repeals of or in Road Traffic Regulation Act 1984, ss 8(1A), 11(2), 47(1), 101(4)–(6), 102(8); Road Traffic Act 1991, ss 43, 65–67, 69–74A, 76–79, Schs 3, 6; Local Government (Wales) Act 1994, Sch 7, para 43(b); London Local Authorities Act 1995, ss 4, 7, 8; Greater London Authority Act 1999, ss 283(2), (4), 284, 286; London Local Authorities Act 2000, ss 4, 5, 7, 8; London Local Authorities and Transport for London Act 2003, s 15) (SI 2007/2053, as amended by SI 2008/757) 31 March 2008 (Wales only) (SI 2007/3174)
Sch 12, Pt 2	4 October 2004 (England only) (SI 2004/2380) 26 October 2006 (Wales only) (SI 2006/2826)

1 Note that SI 2006/2826 brought the sections which introduce Sch 7–11 into force on 26 October 2006, however these Schedules were not intended to be brought into force on that date

Transitional provisions

(a): SI 2007/1890 Arts 3–8 of SI 2007/1890 (which applies in England only) contain transitional provisions set out in full below.

Fixed penalty offences

3 Section 95A(1) of, and Schedule 4A to, the 1991 Act (fixed penalties under Part 3) shall not apply in relation to offences committed before 12th May 2008.

Directions as to timing of street works and placing of apparatus

4 Section 56(1A) of the 1991 Act (power to give directions as to timing of street works) and section 56A(1) of that Act (power to give directions as to placing of apparatus) shall not apply to street works in respect of which notice has been given under section 54(1) (advance notice of certain works) or section 55(1) of that Act (notice of starting date of works) before 1st April 2008.

Notices of street works

5 (1) The amendment to section 54(3) of the 1991 Act by section 49(1)(a) of the 2004 Act (notices of street works) shall not apply to notices given under section 54(1) of the 1991 Act before 1st April 2008.

(2) Section 54(4A) of the 1991 Act shall not apply in relation to street works in respect of which advance notice has been given under section 54(1) of that Act before 1st April 2008.

(3) Where an advance notice is given under section 54(1) of the 1991 Act specifying a starting date for the proposed works which is before 1st April 2008, section 54(4B) of that Act shall not apply but, if those works are not substantially begun before 22nd April 2008, the notice shall cease to have effect in relation to the proposed works so that section 54(1) applies again in relation to them.

(4) Section 55(8) and (9) of the 1991 Act shall not apply in relation to street works in respect of which notice has been given under either section 54(1) or section 55(1) of that Act before 1st April 2008.

(5) If an advance notice under section 54(1) of the 1991 Act given before 1st April 2008 specifies a starting date which is later than 30th June 2008, that notice shall cease to have effect on 1st April 2008 and section 54(1) shall apply again in relation to the proposed works.

Restriction on works following substantial road works

6 The amendments to section 58 of the 1991 Act (restriction on works following substantial road works) by section 51 of the 2004 Act shall not apply in relation to any notice given under section 58(1) of the 1991 Act before 1st April 2008.

Restriction on works following substantial street works

7 Section 58A of, and Schedule 3A to, the 1991 Act (restriction on works following substantial street works) shall only apply where a street authority receive a notice under section 54 or 55 of that Act, on or after 1st April 2008, that an undertaker is proposing to execute substantial street works in a highway.

Duty to notify street authority of reinstatement

8 The amendments to section 70 of the 1991 Act (duty of undertaker to reinstate) by section 54 of the 2004 Act (duty to notify street authority of reinstatement) shall not apply in relation to street works in respect of which notice has been given under section 54(1), 55(1) or 57 (notice of emergency works) of the 1991 Act before 1st April 2008.

(b): SI 2007/2053 Arts 4–8 of SI 2007/2053, as amended by SI 2008/757, contain transitional provisions (which apply in England only) set out in full below. In arts 5–8, "the transitional period" in relation to a provision modified by those provisions means the period beginning with 31 March 2008 and ending on the day on which the repeal of that provision comes into force (see art 1(2) of SI 2007/2053).

Transitional provisions

4 (1) None of the provisions of Part 6 of the Traffic Management Act 2004 or of any regulations or orders made thereunder shall have effect in relation to a parking contravention which occurred before the second appointed day and action may be taken, or if begun continued, by an enforcement authority, an adjudicator or a county court in relation to such a contravention as if none of the provisions of Part 6 had been brought into force.

(2) This article is without prejudice to section 16(1) of the Interpretation Act 1978.

[Transitional modifications of the London Local Authorities Act 1996

5 (1) The London Local Authorities Act 1996 shall, during the transitional period, apply as if it were subject to the following modifications.

(2) In section 3(1)—

(a) the definition of "the Act of 1991" is omitted;

(b) for "established under section 73 of the Act of 1991" in the definition of "Joint Committee" there is substituted "appointed pursuant to regulation 15 of the Civil Enforcement of Parking Contraventions (England) General Regulations 2007" .

(3) In section 6—

(a) in subsection (1) for "parking adjudicators under section 73 of the Act of 1991" there is substituted "adjudicators under regulation 17 of the Civil Enforcement of Parking Contraventions (England) General Regulations 2007";

(b) for subsection (2) there is substituted—

"(2) The Road Traffic (Parking Adjudicators) (London) Regulations 1993 shall (despite the repeal of section 73(11) and (12) of the Road Traffic Act 1991 under which the Regulations were made) continue in force for the purpose of applying in relation to proceedings before traffic adjudicators under this Act, and for that purpose section 73(11) to (13) shall continue to have effect.";

(c) for subsection (3) there is substituted—

"(3) Regulations 12(6) and (7) (reports by adjudicators and joint committee), 19 (power to require attendance and production of documents) and 25 (recovery of amount payable under an adjudication) of the Bus Lane Contraventions (Penalty Charges, Adjudication and Enforcement) (England) Regulations 2005 shall apply—

(a) to traffic adjudicators as they apply to adjudicators appointed under those Regulations; and

(b) to the Joint Committee as they apply to the Joint Committee appointed under those Regulations,

but regulation 25 of those Regulations shall not apply to a penalty charge under this Part of this Act which remains payable following an adjudication under paragraph 6 of Schedule 1 to this Act."

(4) For section 8 there is substituted—

"Setting the levels of penalty charges

8 Part 2 of Schedule 9 (except paragraph 6) to the Traffic Management Act 2004 and regulation 24 of the Civil Enforcement of Parking Contraventions (England) General Regulations 2007 shall apply to the levels of charges under this Act as they apply to the levels of charges relating to parking contraventions under the 2004 Act."

(5) In Schedule 1 for paragraph 9(3) there is substituted—

"(3) Sections 82 and 83 of the Traffic Management Act 2004 shall have effect as though an increased penalty charge recoverable under sub-paragraph (1) above were a traffic contravention debt for the purposes of those sections."

Transitional modification of the Transport Act 2000

6 (1) The Transport Act 2000 shall, during the transitional period, apply as if it were subject to the following modification.

(2) In section 144(3) for paragraph (a) there is substituted—

"(a) an order designating the whole or any part of its area as a civil enforcement area for parking contraventions has been made under paragraph 8(1) of Schedule 8 to the Traffic Management Act 2004;".

Transitional modifications of the London Local Authorities Act 2000

7 (1) The London Local Authorities Act 2000 shall, during the transitional period, apply as if it were subject to the following modifications.

(2) In section 3(1)—

(a) the definition of "the Act of 1991" is omitted;

(b) the following definitions are inserted at the appropriate places—

""the 2004 Act" means the Traffic Management Act 2004;"

""the Parking General Regulations" means the Civil Enforcement of Parking Contraventions (England) General Regulations 2007;"

""the Parking Representations and Appeals Regulations" means the Civil Enforcement of Parking Contraventions (England) Representations and Appeals Regulations 2007;"; and

(c) for the definitions of "parking adjudicator", "parking attendant" and "special parking area" there are substituted—

""parking adjudicator" means an adjudicator appointed under regulation 17 of the Parking General Regulations by the London authorities as defined by section 92(1) of the 2004 Act;"

""parking attendant" means a person who is a civil enforcement officer in accordance with section 76 of the 2004 Act;"

""special parking area" means an area which is a civil enforcement area for parking contraventions in accordance with Schedule 8 to the 2004 Act."

(3) In section 9—

(a) for "section 69 or 77 of the Act of 1991" there is substituted "regulation 12(1) of the Parking General Regulations"; and

(b) for paragraphs (b) and (c) there is substituted—

"(b) regulation 14(2)(a) or (b) of the Parking General Regulations."

(4) For section 11(1) there is substituted—

"(1) The relevant person may make representations to the participating council—

(a) in the case of a vehicle to which an immobilisation device has been fixed, on one or more of the grounds specified in regulation 8(5) of the Parking Representations and Appeals Regulations; or

(b) in the case of a vehicle which has been removed, on one or more of the grounds specified in regulation 11(5) of those Regulations."

(5) In section 11(7) for "Schedule 6 to the Act of 1991" there is substituted "regulation 4 of the Parking Representations and Appeals Regulations".

(6) In section 14(1) for "Schedule 6 to the Act of 1991 (which provides, among other things, for parking penalties) shall not" there is substituted "Neither Part 5 of the Parking General Regulations nor Part 2 of the Parking Representations and Appeals Regulations shall apply".

Transitional modifications of the London Local Authorities and Transport for London Act 2003

8 (1) The London Local Authorities and Transport for London Act 2003 shall, during the transitional period, apply as if it were subject to the following modifications.

(2) In section 4—

(a) in subsection (6)(b) for "section 77 of the Road Traffic Act 1991" there is substituted "regulation 4(b) of the Civil Enforcement of Parking Contraventions (England) General Regulations 2007";

(b) in subsection (12), for the words from "sections 74" to the end there is substituted "Part 2 of Schedule 9 to the Traffic Management Act 2004 (c 18) as it applies in relation to the levels of penalty charges under that Part of that Schedule";

(c) in subsection (13) for "section 74" there is substituted "Part 2 of Schedule 9"; and

(d) in subsection (16) for "established under section 73 of the Road Traffic Act 1991" in the definition of "Joint Committee" there is substituted "appointed pursuant to regulation 15 of the Civil Enforcement of Parking Contraventions (England) General Regulations 2007".

(3) In section 14(8) for the definition of "special parking area" there is substituted—

"“special parking area” means an area which is a civil enforcement area for parking contraventions in accordance with Schedule 8 to the Traffic Management Act 2004 (c 18);"

(4) In Schedule 1—

(a) in paragraph 6 for sub-paragraph (3) there is substituted—

"(3) Sections 82 and 83 of the Traffic Management Act 2004 shall have effect as though an increased penalty charge recoverable under sub-paragraph (1) were a traffic contravention debt for the purposes of those sections."

(b) in paragraph 10—

(i) in sub-paragraph (1) for "parking adjudicators under section 73 of the Road Traffic Act 1991 (c 40)" there is substituted "adjudicators under regulation 17 of the Civil Enforcement of Parking Contraventions (England) General Regulations 2007 (SI 2007/3483)";

(ii) for sub-paragraphs (2) and (3) there is substituted—

"(2) The Road Traffic (Parking Adjudicators) (London) Regulations 1993 shall (despite the repeal of section 73(11) and (12) of the Road Traffic Act 1991, under which the Regulations were made) continue in force for the purpose of applying to proceedings before traffic adjudicators under this Act, and for that purpose section 73(11) to (13) shall continue to have effect.

(3) Regulations 12(6) and (7) (reports by adjudicators and joint committee), 19 (power to require attendance and production of documents) and 25 (recovery of amount payable under an adjudication) of the Bus Lane Contraventions (Penalty Charges, Adjudication and Enforcement) (England) Regulations 2005 shall apply—

(a) to traffic adjudicators as they apply to adjudicators appointed under those Regulations; and

(b) to the Joint Committee as they apply to the Joint Committee appointed pursuant to those Regulations,

but regulation 25 of those Regulations shall not apply to a penalty charge under section 4 of this Act which remains payable following an adjudication under this Schedule."]

NOTES

Amendment Arts 5–8: inserted by SI 2008/757.

Bus Lane Contraventions (Penalty Charges, Adjudication and Enforcement) (England) Regulations 2005 SI 2005/2757.

Civil Enforcement of Parking Contraventions (England) General Regulations 2007 SI 2007/3483.

Civil Enforcement of Parking Contraventions (England) Representations and Appeals Regulations 2007 SI 2007/3482.

Road Traffic (Parking Adjudicators) (London) Regulations 1993 SI 1993/1202.

(c): SI 2007/3174 Arts 3–9 of SI 2007/3174 (which applies in Wales only) contain transitional provisions set out in full below.

Fixed penalty offences

3 Section 95A(1) of, and Schedule 4A to, the 1991 Act (fixed penalties under Part 3) will not apply in relation to offences committed before 12th May 2008.

Increase in maximum fines for certain summary offences

4 The increase in penalties effected by the coming into force of section 40 of, and Schedule 1 to, the 2004 Act will not apply in relation to offences committed before 26th November 2007.

Directions as to timing of street works and placing of apparatus

5 Section 56(1A) of the 1991 Act (power to give directions as to timing of street works) and section 56A(1) of that Act (power to give directions as to placing of apparatus) do not apply to street works in respect of which notice has been given under section 54(1) (advance notice of certain works) or section 55(1) of that Act (notice of starting date of works) before 1st April 2008.

Notices of street works

6 (1) The amendment to section 54(3) of the 1991 Act by section 49(1)(a) of the 2004 Act (notices of street works) does not apply to notices given under section 54(1) of the 1991 Act before 1st April 2008.

(2) Section 54(4A) of the 1991 Act does not apply in relation to street works in respect of which advance notice has been given under section 54(1) of that Act before 1st April 2008.

(3) Where an advance notice is given under section 54(1) of the 1991 Act specifying a starting date for the proposed works which is before 1st April 2008, section 54(4B) of that Act does not apply but, if those works are not substantially begun before 22nd April 2008, the notice will cease to have effect in relation to the proposed works so that section 54(1) applies again in relation to them.

(4) Section 55(8) and (9) of the 1991 Act do not apply in relation to street works in respect of which notice has been given under either section 54(1) or section 55(1) of that Act before 1st April 2008.

(5) If an advance notice under section 54(1) of the 1991 Act given before 1st April 2008 specifies a starting date which is later than 30th June 2008, that notice will cease to have effect on 1st April 2008 and section 54(1) will apply again in relation to the proposed works.

Restriction on works following substantial road works

7 The amendments to section 58 of the 1991 Act (restriction on works following substantial road works) by section 51 of the 2004 Act does not apply in relation to any notice given under section 58(1) of the 1991 Act before 1st April 2008.

Restriction on works following substantial street works

8 Section 58A of, and Schedule 3A to, the 1991 Act (restriction on works following substantial street works) will only apply where a street authority receive a notice under section 54 or 55 of that Act, on or after 1st April 2008, that an undertaker is proposing to execute substantial street works in a highway.

Duty to notify street authority of reinstatement

9 The amendments to section 70 of the 1991 Act (duty of undertaker to reinstate) by section 54 of the 2004 Act (duty to notify street authority of reinstatement) do not apply in relation to street works in respect of which notice has been given under section 54(1), 55(1) or 57 (notice of emergency works) of the 1991 Act before 1st April 2008.

[884]

PUBLIC SERVICE VEHICLES (TRAFFIC REGULATION CONDITIONS) (ENGLAND AND WALES) REGULATIONS 2004 SI 2004/2682

Authority Made by the Secretary of State for Transport under the Public Passenger Vehicles Act 1981, ss 5(1), 60(1) and the Transport Act 1985, ss 7(6), (9), (11), 9(3). S 9(3) of the 1985 Act has been repealed by the Local Transport Act 2008, ss 51(1), (3), 131, Sch 7, Pt 3; see the note "Summary" below.

Date made 13 October 2004.

Commencement 19 November 2004.

Summary The Transport Act 1985, ss 7–9 provide for the determination and application of traffic regulation conditions to local services subject to registration under the Act (see s 6 thereof). The provisions made by these regulations relate to: purposes, additional to those set out in s 7(6) of the Act, for which such conditions may be determined (reg 4); the publication of notices regarding conditions by the traffic commissioners (reg 5); the period in which requests for inquiries must be made to traffic commissioners (reg 6); and supplementary provision regarding requirements for writing and delivery and the computation of periods of time (regs 8, 9). The regulations also revoke the Public Service Vehicles (Traffic Regulation Conditions) Regulations 1986, SI 1986/1030, and the amending SI 1994/3272, and revoke SI 1986/1629 in so far as it amended SI 1986/1030.

S 9(3) of the 1985 Act, which enabled regulations to be made in connection with appeals to the Transport Tribunal against traffic regulation conditions under s 9, has been repealed by the Local Transport Act 2008, ss 51(1), (3), 131, Sch 7, Pt 3. Reg 7 of these regulations, which made provision for such appeals, has accordingly lapsed. S 9(1) of the 1985 Act, as amended by SI 2009/1885, in the title Courts and Legal Services, now provides for appeals under s 9 of the 1985 Act to be made to the Upper Tribunal.

[885]

TRACTOR ETC (EC TYPE-APPROVAL) REGULATIONS 2005 SI 2005/390

Authority Made by the Secretary of State for Transport under the European Communities Act 1972, s 2(2).

Date made 24 February 2005.

Commencement 1 July 2005.

Amendment Amended by SI 2006/2533, SI 2008/1980.

Interpretation In these regulations "vehicle" means any tractor, trailer or interchangeable towed machinery whether complete, incomplete or completed, which is constructed or adapted for the use of agriculture, horticulture or forestry and which has a maximum design speed of not less than 6 kilometres per hour.

Summary These regulations implement Directive 2003/37/EC of the European Parliament and of the Council (OJ L171, 09.07.2003, p 1) ("the Tractor Type Approval Directive"), as amended, which requires member states to set up a scheme for granting EC type-approval for agricultural or forestry tractors, their trailers and interchangeable towed machinery, together with their systems, components and separate technical units.

Reg 3 of the regulations provides that the regulations apply to any vehicle or component, with certain exceptions. An application for EC type-approval for a vehicle, system, component or separate technical unit to which the regulations apply must be made to the UK type-approval authority (the Secretary of State) by the manufacturer, in accordance with the applicable requirements of the Tractor Type Approval Directive (reg 4). Reg 5 provides for the grant or refusal of EC type-approval and the issue of the appropriate EC type-approval certificate. The holder of an EC type-approval certificate must issue a certificate of conformity in respect of each vehicle for which he has responsibility for conformity of production as manufacturer or assembler (reg 6). In the case of a vehicle which comes within the category T1, T2 and T3 (as defined in the Tractor Type Approval Directive), a certificate of conformity of production is necessary for a licence to be granted for that vehicle under the Vehicle Excise and Registration Act 1994 (reg 7), subject to certain exceptions (reg 8). Provision is made for the withdrawal of EC type-approval in specified circumstances by reg 9. Regs 10, 11 create offences under the regulations in the case of forgery, deception, the making of false statements and the production of false documents. Reg 12 concerns the review of decisions under the regulations and reg 13 relates to the giving of notices. Reg 14 amends the Road Traffic Act 1988, s 64A(1).

As to the fees payable in respect of EC type-approval, see SI 1999/2149.

[886]

ROAD TRANSPORT (WORKING TIME) REGULATIONS 2005 SI 2005/639

Authority Made by the Secretary of State for Transport under the European Communities Act 1972, s 2(2).

Date made 10 March 2005.

Commencement 4 April 2005; see reg 1(1).

Amendment Printed as amended by SI 2007/853.

Interpretation See reg 2.

General These regulations implement the provisions of Directive 2002/15/EC of the European Parliament and of the Council on the organisation of the working time of persons performing mobile road transport activities (OJ L80, 23.03.2002, p 35). They prescribe the maximum weekly working time and maximum average weekly working time of mobile workers who, in the course of their work, drive or travel in goods or passenger vehicles which are covered by Regulation (EC) 561/2006 of the European Parliament and of the Council on the harmonisation of certain social legislation relating to road transport (OJ L102, 11.04.2006, p 1) (the Community Drivers' Hours Regulation), and prescribe the reference periods over which such time is to be calculated. They also regulate periods of availability, breaks, rest periods and night work; require employers to keep records of time worked; and make failure to comply with the regulations an offence and provide for enforcement.

[887]

Citation, commencement and extent

1 (1) These Regulations may be cited as the Road Transport (Working Time) Regulations 2005 and shall come into force on 4th April 2005.

(2) These Regulations extend to Great Britain only.

[888]

Interpretation

2 In these Regulations—

"AETR" means the European agreement concerning the work of crews of vehicles engaged in international road transport of 1st July 1970;

"collective agreement" means a collective agreement within the meaning of section 178 of the Trade Union and Labour Relations (Consolidation) Act 1992, the trade union parties to which are independent trade unions within the meaning of section 5 of that Act;

["the Community Drivers' Hours Regulation" means Regulation (EC) No 561/2006 of the European Parliament and of the Council of 15 March 2006 on the harmonisation of certain social legislation relating to road transport (and amending and repealing certain Council Regulations)]

"employer" in relation to a worker, means the person by whom the worker is (or, where the employment has ceased, was) employed;

"employment" in relation to a worker, means employment under his contract, and "employed" shall be construed accordingly;

"goods" includes goods or burden of any description;

"goods vehicle" means a motor vehicle constructed or adapted for use for the carriage of goods, or a trailer so constructed or adapted;

"inspector" means a person appointed under paragraph 1 of Schedule 2;

"mobile worker" means any worker forming part of the travelling staff, including trainees and apprentices, who is in the service of an undertaking which operates transport services for passengers or goods by road for hire or reward or on its own account;

"night time" means in respect of goods vehicles the period between midnight and 4 a.m. and in respect of passenger vehicles the period between 1am and 5am;

"motor vehicle" means a mechanically propelled vehicle intended or adapted for use on roads;

"night work" means any work performed during night time;

"passenger vehicle" means a motor vehicle which is constructed or adapted to carry more than eight seated passengers in addition to the driver;

"period of availability" means a period during which the mobile worker is not required to remain at his workstation, but is required to be available to answer any calls to start or resume driving or to carry out other work , including periods during which the mobile worker is accompanying a vehicle being transported by a ferry or by a train as well as periods of waiting at frontiers and those due to traffic prohibitions;

"reference period" means the period for calculation of the average maximum weekly working time;

"relevant requirements" means regulations 4(8), 7(5), 8(2), 9(4), 10, 11 and 12;

"self-employed driver" means anyone whose main occupation is to transport passengers or goods by road for hire or reward within the meaning of Community legislation under cover of a Community licence or any other professional authorisation to carry out such transport, who is entitled to work for himself and who is not tied to an employer by an employment contract or by any other type of working hierarchical relationship, who is free to organise the relevant working activities, whose income depends directly on the profits made and who has the freedom, individually or through a co-operation between self-employed drivers, to have commercial relations with several customers;

"vehicle" means a goods vehicle or a passenger vehicle;

"week" means a period of seven days beginning at midnight between Sunday and Monday;

"worker" means an individual who has entered into or works under (or, where employment has ceased, worked under)—

(a) a contract of employment; or

(b) any other contract, whether express or implied and (if it is express) whether oral or in writing, whereby the individual undertakes to do or perform personally any work or services for another party to the contract;

and any reference to a worker's contract shall be construed accordingly;

"workforce agreement" means an agreement between an employer and mobile workers employed by him or their representatives in respect of which the conditions set out in Schedule 1 to these Regulations are satisfied;

"working time" means the time from the beginning to the end of work during which the mobile worker is at his workstation, at the disposal of his employer and exercising his functions or activities, being

(a) time devoted to all road transport activities, including, in particular—

(i) driving;

(ii) loading and unloading;

(iii) assisting passengers boarding and disembarking from the vehicle;

(iv) cleaning and technical maintenance;

(v) all other work intended to ensure the safety of the vehicle, its cargo and passengers or to fulfil the legal or regulatory obligations directly linked to the specific transport operation under way, including monitoring of loading and unloading and dealing with administrative formalities with police, customs, immigration officers and others; or

(b) time during which the mobile worker cannot dispose freely of his time and is required to be at his workstation, ready to take up normal work, with certain tasks associated with being on duty, in particular during periods awaiting loading or unloading where their foreseeable duration is not known in advance, that is to say either before departure or just before the actual start of the period in question, or under collective agreements or workforce agreements;

"workstation" means

(a) the location of the main place of business of the undertaking for which the person performing mobile transport activities carries out duties, together with its various subsidiary places of business, regardless of whether they are located in the same place as its head office or its main place of business;

(b) the vehicle which the person performing mobile road transport activities uses when he carries out duties; or

(c) any other place in which activities connected with transport are carried out.

NOTES

Amendment Definition "the Community Drivers' Hours Regulation": substituted by SI 2007/853.

Regulation (EC) 561/2006 of the European Parliament and of the Council

OJ L102, 11.04.2006, p 1.

[889]

Application

3 (1) These Regulations apply to mobile workers who are employed by, or who do work for, undertakings established in a Member State of the European Union, and to whom paragraph (2) or paragraph (3) applies.

[(2) This paragraph applies to mobile workers who, in the course of that employment or work, drive or travel in or on vehicles—

(a) which are vehicles within the meaning of Article 4(b) of the Community Drivers' Hours Regulation,

(b) which are not vehicles described in Article 3 of that Regulation, and

(c) which are not vehicles exempted from the provisions of that Regulation under regulation 2 of the Community Drivers' Hours and Recording Equipment (Exemptions and Supplementary Provisions) Regulations 1986.]

(3) This paragraph applies to mobile workers, to whom paragraph (2) does not apply, who in the course of that employment or work drive, or travel in, vehicles

(a) which fall within the meaning of a "vehicle" in Article 1 of the AETR;

(b) which are not referred to in Article 2(2)(b) of the AETR; and

(c) which are performing international transport.

(4) These Regulations do not apply to—

(a) self-employed drivers, or

(b) any worker who does work which is included in the calculation of working time—

(i) where the reference period is shorter than 26 weeks, on fewer than 11 days in a reference period applicable to that worker, or

(ii) in any other case on fewer than 16 days in a reference period applicable to that worker.

NOTES

Amendment Para (2): substituted by SI 2007/853.

Community Drivers' Hours and Recording Equipment (Exemptions and Supplementary Provisions) Regulations 1986 SI 1986/1456. Revoked and replaced by SI 2007/1819.

[890]

Working time

4 (1) Subject to paragraph (2) below, the working time, including overtime, of a mobile worker shall not exceed 60 hours in a week.

(2) In any reference period which is applicable to his case, a mobile worker's working time shall not exceed an average of 48 hours for each week.

(3) The reference periods which apply in the case of a mobile worker shall be—

(a) where a collective agreement or a workforce agreement provides for the application of this regulation in relation to successive periods of 17 weeks, each such period,

(b) in a case where—

(i) there is no such provision, and

(ii) the employer gives written notice to the mobile worker in writing that he intends to apply this subparagraph,

any period of 17 weeks in the course of the worker's employment, or

(c) in any other case, the period ending at midnight between Sunday 31st July 2005 and Monday 1st August 2005 and thereafter, in each year, the successive periods beginning at midnight at the beginning of the Monday which falls on, or is the first Monday after, a date in column 1 below and ending at midnight at the beginning of the Monday which falls on, or is the first Monday after, the date on the same line in column 2 below.

Column 1 (beginning)	Column 2 (end)
1st December	1st April
1st April	1st August
1st August	1st December

(4) The reference period may be extended in relation to particular mobile workers or groups of mobile workers for objective or technical reasons or reasons concerning the organisation of work, by a collective agreement or a workforce agreement, by the substitution for 17 weeks of a period not exceeding 26 weeks in the application of paragraphs (2) and (3)(a) above.

(5) A mobile worker's average weekly working time during a reference period shall be determined according to the formula—

$$(\mathbf{A} + \mathbf{B}) \div \mathbf{C}$$

where—

A is the aggregate number of hours comprised in the mobile worker's working time during the course of the reference period;

B is the number of excluded hours during the reference period; and

C is the number of weeks in the reference period.

(6) In paragraph (5), "excluded hours" means hours comprised in—

(a) any period of annual leave taken by the mobile worker in exercise of entitlement under regulation 13 of the Working Time Regulations 1998;

(b) any period of sick leave taken by the mobile worker;

(c) any period of maternity, paternity, adoption or parental leave taken by the mobile worker;

(7) For the purposes of paragraph (5), the number of hours in a whole day shall be eight and the number of hours in a whole week shall be forty-eight.

(8) An employer shall take all reasonable steps, in keeping with the need to protect the health and safety of the mobile worker, to ensure that the limits specified above are complied with in the case of each mobile worker employed by him.

[891]

5 The times of breaks, rests and periods of availability shall not be included in the calculation of working time.

[892]

Periods of availability

6 (1) A period shall not be treated as a period of availability unless the mobile worker knows before the start of the relevant period about that period of availability and its reasonably foreseeable duration.

(2) The time spent by a mobile worker, who is working as part of a team, travelling in, but not driving, a moving vehicle as part of that team shall be a period of availability for that mobile worker.

(3) Subject to paragraph (4) a period of availability shall not include a period of rest or a break.

(4) A period of availability may include a break taken by a mobile worker during waiting time or time which is not devoted to driving by the mobile worker and is spent in a moving vehicle, a ferry or a train.

[893]

Breaks

7 (1) No mobile worker shall work for more than six hours without a break.

(2) Where a mobile worker's working time exceeds six hours but does not exceed nine hours, the worker shall be entitled to a break lasting at least 30 minutes and interrupting that time.

(3) Where a mobile worker's working time exceeds nine hours, the worker shall be entitled to a break lasting at least 45 minutes and interrupting that period.

(4) Each break may be made up of separate periods of not less than 15 minutes each.

(5) An employer shall take all reasonable steps, in keeping with the need to protect the health and safety of the mobile worker, to ensure that the limits specified above are complied with in the case of each mobile worker employed by him.

[894]

Rest periods

8 (1) In the application of these Regulations, the provisions of the Community Drivers' Hours Regulation relating to daily and weekly rest shall apply to all mobile workers to whom they do not apply under that Regulation as they apply to other mobile workers under that Regulation.

(2) An employer shall take all reasonable steps, in keeping with the need to protect the health and safety of the mobile worker, to ensure that those provisions are complied with in the case of each mobile worker employed by him, to whom they are applied by paragraph (1).

[895]

Night work

9 (1) The working time of a mobile worker, who performs night work in any period of 24 hours, shall not exceed 10 hours during that period.

(2) The period of 10 hours may be extended in relation to particular mobile workers or groups of mobile workers for objective or technical reasons or reasons concerning the organisation of work, by a collective agreement or a workforce agreement.

(3) Compensation for night work shall not be given to a mobile worker in any manner which is liable to endanger road safety.

(4) An employer shall take all reasonable steps in keeping with the need to protect the health and safety of mobile workers to ensure that the limit specified in paragraph (1), or extended in accordance with paragraph (2), is complied with in the case of each mobile worker employed by him.

[896]

Information and records

10 An employer of mobile workers shall notify each worker of the provisions of these Regulations and the provisions of any collective or workforce agreement which is capable of application to that worker.

[897]

11 An employer of a mobile worker shall

- (a) request from each mobile worker details of any time worked by that worker for another employer;
- (b) include time worked for another employer in the calculation of the mobile worker's working time;
- (c) keep records which are adequate to show whether the requirements of these Regulations are being complied with in the case of each mobile worker employed by him to whom they apply;

(d) retain such records for at least two years after the end of the period covered by those records;
(e) provide, at the request of a mobile worker, a copy of the record of hours worked by that worker;
(f) provide to an enforcement officer copies of such records relating to mobile workers as the officer may require;
(g) provide to a mobile worker or enforcement officer copies of such documentary evidence in the employer's possession as may be requested by the worker or officer in relation to records provided to him in accordance with paragraph (e) or (f) above.

[898]

12 A mobile worker shall, at the request of his employer under regulation 11(a), notify his employer in writing of time worked by the worker for another employer for inclusion in the calculation of the mobile worker's working time.

[899]

13 (1) The Secretary of State shall arrange for the publication, in such form and manner as he considers appropriate, of information and advice concerning the operation of these Regulations.

(2) The information and advice shall be such as appear to him best calculated to enable employers and workers affected by these Regulations to understand their respective rights and obligations.

[900]

Agency workers not otherwise mobile workers

14 (1) This regulation applies in any case where an individual ("the agency worker")—

(a) is supplied by a person ("the agent") to do the work of a mobile worker for another ("the principal") under a contract or other arrangements made between the agent and the principal; but
(b) is not, as respects that work, a worker, because of the absence of a worker's contract between the individual and the agent or the principal; and
(c) is not a party to a contract under which he undertakes to do the work for another party to the contract whose status is, by virtue of the contract, that of a client or customer or any profession or business undertaking carried on by the individual.

(2) In a case where this regulation applies, the other provisions of these Regulations shall have effect as if there were a contract for the doing of the work by the agency worker made between the agency worker and—

(a) whichever of the agent and the principal is responsible for paying the agency worker in respect of the work; or
(b) if neither the agent nor the principal is so responsible, whichever of them pays the agency worker in respect of the work,
(c) and as if that person were the agency worker's employer.

[901]

[Individual carrying on own trade or business

15 (1) This regulation applies to an individual who—

(a) for the purpose of a trade or business carried on by him, drives a vehicle described in paragraph (2) or (3) of regulation 3, and
(b) is neither—
    (i) a self-employed driver, nor
    (ii) an agency worker within the meaning of regulation 14.

(2) Where this regulation applies, these Regulations shall have effect as if—

(a) the individual were both a mobile worker and the employer of that mobile worker, and
(b) regulations 10, 11(a) and (e) and 12 were omitted.]

NOTES
Amendment Substituted by SI 2007/853.

[902]

Enforcement

16 (1) It shall be the duty of the Secretary of State to enforce the requirements of these Regulations.

(2) Schedule 2 shall apply in relation to the enforcement of the relevant requirements.

[903]

17 (1) Any person who fails to comply with any of the relevant requirements shall be guilty of an offence.

(2) The provisions of paragraph (3) shall apply where an inspector is exercising or has exercised any power conferred by Schedule 2.

(3) It is an offence for a person—

- (a) to contravene any requirement imposed by an inspector under paragraph 2 of Schedule 2;
- (b) to prevent or attempt to prevent any other person from appearing before an inspector or from answering any question to which an inspector may by virtue of paragraph 2(2)(e) of Schedule 2 require an answer;
- (c) to contravene any requirement or prohibition imposed by an improvement notice or a prohibition notice referred to in paragraphs 3 and 4 of Schedule 2 (including any such notice as is modified on appeal);
- (d) intentionally to obstruct an inspector in the exercise or performance of his powers;
- (e) to use or disclose any information in contravention of paragraph 7 of Schedule 2;
- (f) to make a statement which he knows to be false or recklessly to make a statement which is false where the statement is made in purported compliance with a requirement to furnish any information imposed by or under these Regulations.

(4) Any person guilty of an offence under paragraph (1) shall be liable—

- (a) on summary conviction, to a fine not exceeding the statutory maximum;
- (b) on conviction on indictment, to a fine.

(5) A person guilty of an offence under paragraph (3)(b) or (d) shall be liable on summary conviction to a fine not exceeding level 5 on the standard scale.

(6) A person guilty of an offence under paragraph (3)(c) shall be liable—

- (a) on summary conviction, to imprisonment for a term not exceeding three months, or a fine not exceeding the statutory maximum;
- (b) on conviction on indictment, to imprisonment for a term not exceeding two years, or a fine or both.

(7) A person guilty of an offence under paragraph (3)(a), (e) or (f) shall be liable—

- (a) on summary conviction, to a fine not exceeding the statutory maximum;
- (b) on conviction on indictment—
  - (i) if the offence is under paragraph (3)(e), to imprisonment for a term not exceeding two years or a fine or both,
  - (ii) if the offence is under paragraph (3)(a) or (f), to a fine.

(8) The provisions set out in regulations 18 to 22 shall apply in relation to the offences provided for in paragraphs (1) and (3).

[904]

Offences due to fault of other person

18 Where the commission by any person of an offence is due to the act or default of some other person, that other person shall be guilty of the offence, and a person may be charged with the conviction of the offence by virtue of this regulation whether or not proceedings are taken against the first-mentioned person.

[905]

Offences by bodies corporate

19 (1) Where an offence committed by a body corporate is proved to have been committed with the consent or connivance of, or to have been attributable to any neglect on the part of, any director, manager, secretary or other similar officer of the body corporate or a person who was purporting to act in any such capacity, he as well as the body corporate shall be guilty of that offence and shall be liable to be proceeded against and punished accordingly.

(2) Where the affairs of a body corporate are managed by its members, the preceding paragraph shall apply in relation to the acts and defaults of a member in connection with his functions of management as if he were a director of the body corporate.

[906]

Restriction on institution of proceedings in England and Wales

20 Proceedings for an offence shall not be instituted in England or Wales except by an inspector or by, or with the consent of, the Director of Public Prosecutions.

[907]

Prosecution by inspectors

21 (1) If authorised in that behalf by the Secretary of State an inspector may prosecute proceedings for an offence before a magistrates court even though the inspector is not of counsel or a solicitor.

(2) This regulation shall not apply in Scotland.

[908]

Power of court to order cause of offence to be remedied

22 (1) This regulation applies where a person is convicted of an offence in respect of any matter which appears to the court to be a matter which it is in his power to remedy.

(2) In addition to or instead of imposing any punishment, the court may order the person in question to take such steps as may be specified in the order for remedying the said matters within such time as may be fixed by the order.

(3) The time fixed by an order under paragraph (2) may be extended or further extended by order of the court on an application made before the end of that time as originally fixed or as extended under this paragraph, as the case may be.

(4) Where a person is ordered under paragraph (2) to remedy any matters, that person shall not be liable under these Regulations in respect of that matter in so far as it continues during the time fixed by the order or any further time allowed under paragraph (3).

[909]

SCHEDULE 1
WORKFORCE AGREEMENTS

Regulation 2

1 An agreement is a workforce agreement for the purposes of these Regulations if the following conditions are satisfied—

- (a) the agreement is in writing;
- (b) it has effect for a specified period not exceeding five years;
- (c) it applies either—
  - (i) to all of the relevant members of the workforce, or
  - (ii) to all of the relevant members of the workforce who belong to a particular group;
- (d) the agreement is signed—
  - (i) in the case of an agreement of the kind referred to in sub-paragraph (c)(i), by the representatives of the workforce, and in the case of an agreement of the kind referred to in sub-paragraph (c)(ii), by the representatives of the group to which the agreement applies (excluding, in either case, any representative not a relevant member of the workforce on the date on which the agreement was first made available for signature), or
  - (ii) if the employer employed 20 or fewer workers on the date referred to in sub-paragraph (d)(i), either by the appropriate representatives in accordance with that sub-paragraph or by the majority of the workers employed by him; and

(e) before the agreement was made available for signature, the employer provided all the workers to whom it was intended to apply on the date on which it came into effect with copies of the text of the agreement and such guidance as those employees might reasonably require in order to understand it in full.

2 For the purposes of this Schedule—

"a particular group" is a group of the relevant members of a workforce who undertake a particular function, work at a particular workplace or belong to a particular department or unit within their employer's business;

"relevant members of the workforce" are all of the workers employed by a particular employer, excluding any worker whose terms and conditions of employment are provided for, wholly or in part, in a collective agreement;

"representatives of the group" are workers duly elected to represent the members of a particular group;

"representatives of the workforce" are workers duly elected to represent the relevant members of the workforce;

and representatives are "duly elected" if the election at which they were elected satisfied the requirements of paragraph 3.

3 The requirements concerning elections referred to in paragraph 2 are that—

(a) the number of representatives to be elected is determined by the employer;

(b) the candidates for election as representatives of the workforce are relevant members of the workforce, and candidates for election as representatives of the group are members of the group;

(c) no worker who is eligible to be a candidate is unreasonably excluded from standing for election;

(d) all the relevant members of the workforce are entitled to vote for representatives of the workforce, and all the members of a particular group are entitled to vote for representatives of the group;

(e) the workers entitled to vote may vote for as many candidates as there are representatives to be elected; and

(f) the election is conducted so as to secure that—

(i) so far as is reasonably practicable, those voting do so in secret, and

(ii) the votes given at the election are fairly and accurately counted.

[910]

SCHEDULE 2
ENFORCEMENT

Regulation 16(2)

Appointment of inspectors

1 (1) The Secretary of State may appoint as inspectors (under whatever title he may from time to time determine) such persons having suitable qualifications as he thinks necessary for carrying into effect these Regulations, and may terminate any appointment made under this paragraph.

(2) Every appointment of a person as an inspector under this paragraph shall be made by an instrument in writing specifying which of the powers conferred on inspectors by these Regulations are to be exercisable by the person appointed; and an inspector shall in right of his appointment under this paragraph be entitled to exercise only such of those powers as are so specified.

(3) So much of an inspector's instrument of appointment as specifies the powers which he is entitled to exercise may be varied by the Secretary of State.

(4) An inspector shall, if so required when exercising or seeking to exercise any power conferred on him by these Regulations, produce his instrument of appointment or a duly authenticated copy thereof.

Powers of inspectors

2 (1) Subject to the provisions of paragraph 1 and this paragraph, an inspector may for the purpose of carrying into effect these Regulations exercise the powers set out in sub-paragraph (2).

(2) The powers of an inspector are the following, namely—

(a) at any reasonable time (or in a situation which in his opinion may be dangerous, at any time) to enter any premises which he has reason to believe it is necessary for him to enter for the purposes mentioned in sub-paragraph (1);

(b) to take with him a constable if he has reasonable cause to apprehend any serious obstruction in the execution of his duty;

(c) without prejudice to paragraph (b), on entering any premises by virtue of paragraph (a) to take with him—

(i) any other person duly authorised by the Secretary of State; and

(ii) any equipment or material required for any purpose for which the power of entry is being exercised;

(d) to make such examination and investigation as may in any circumstances be necessary for the purpose mentioned in sub-paragraph (1);

(e) to require any person whom he has reasonable cause to believe to be able to give any information relevant to any examination or investigation under paragraph (d) to answer (in the absence of persons other than a person nominated by him to be present and any persons whom the inspector may allow to be present) such questions as the inspector thinks fit to ask and to sign a declaration of the truth of his answers;

(f) to require the production of, inspect, and take copies of, or of any entry in—

(i) any records which by virtue of these Regulations are required to be kept, and

(ii) any other books, records or documents which it is necessary for him to see for the purposes of any examination or investigation under paragraph (d);

(g) to require any person to afford him such facilities and assistance with respect to any matters or things within that person's control or in relation to which that person has responsibilities as are necessary to enable the inspector to exercise any of the powers conferred on him by this sub-paragraph;

(h) any other power which is necessary for the purpose mentioned in sub-paragraph (1).

(3) No answer given by a person in pursuance of a requirement imposed under sub-paragraph (2)(e) shall be admissible in evidence against that person or the husband or wife of that person in any proceedings.

(4) Nothing in this paragraph shall be taken to compel the production by any person of a document of which he would on grounds of legal professional privilege be entitled to withhold production on an order for discovery in an action in the High Court or, as the case may be, an order for the production of documents in an action in the Court of Session.

Improvement notices

3 If an inspector is of the opinion that a person—

(a) is contravening one or more of these Regulations; or

(b) has contravened one or more of these Regulations in circumstances that make it likely that the contravention will continue or be repeated,

he may serve on him a notice (in this Schedule referred to as "an improvement notice") stating that he is of that opinion, specifying the provision or provisions as to which he is of that opinion, giving particulars of the reasons why he is of that opinion, and requiring that person to remedy the contravention or, as the case may be, the matter occasioning it within such period (ending not earlier than the period within which an appeal against the notice can be brought under paragraph (6)) as may be specified in the notice.

Prohibition notices

4 (1) This paragraph applies to any activities which are being, or are likely to be, carried on by or under the control of any person, being activities to or in relation to which any of these Regulations apply or will, if the activities are so carried on, apply.

(2) If as regards any activities to which this paragraph applies an inspector is of the opinion that, as carried on by or under the control of the person in question, the activities involve or, as the case may be, will involve a risk of serious personal injury, the inspector may serve on that person a notice (in this Schedule referred to as "a prohibition notice").

(3) A prohibition notice shall—

(a) state that the inspector is of the said opinion;

(b) specify the matters which in his opinion give or, as the case may be, will give rise to the said risk;

(c) where in his opinion any of those matters involves or, as the case may be, will involve a contravention of any of these Regulations, state that he is of that opinion, specify the regulation or regulations as to which he is of that opinion, and give particulars of the reasons why he is of that opinion; and

(d) direct that the activities to which the notice relates shall not be carried on by or under the control of the person on whom the notice is served unless the matters specified in the notice in pursuance of paragraph (b) and any associated contraventions of provisions so specified in pursuance of paragraph (c) have been remedied.

(4) A direction contained in a prohibition notice in pursuance of sub-paragraph (3)(d) shall take effect—

(a) at the end of the period specified in the notice; or

(b) if the notice so declares, immediately.

Provisions supplementary to paragraphs 3 and 4

5 (1) In this paragraph "a notice" means an improvement notice or a prohibition notice.

(2) A notice may (but need not) include directions as to the measures to be taken to remedy any contravention or matter to which the notice relates; and any such directions—

(a) may be framed to any extent by reference to any approved code of practice; and

(b) may be framed so as to afford the person on whom the notice is served a choice between different ways of remedying the contravention or matter.

(3) Where an improvement notice or prohibition notice which is not to take immediate effect has been served—

(a) the notice may be withdrawn by an inspector at any time before the end of the period specified therein in pursuance of paragraph 3 or paragraph 4(4) as the case may be; and

(b) the period so specified may be extended or further extended by an inspector at any time when an appeal against the notice is not pending.

Appeal against improvement or prohibition notice

6 (1) In this paragraph "a notice" means an improvement or prohibition notice.

(2) A person on whom a notice is served may within 21 days from the date of its service appeal to an employment tribunal; and on such an appeal the tribunal may either cancel or affirm the notice and, if it affirms it, may do so either in its original form or with such modifications as the tribunal may in the circumstances think fit.

(3) Where an appeal under this paragraph is brought against a notice within the period allowed under the preceding sub-paragraph, then—

(a) in the case of an improvement notice, the bringing of the appeal shall have the effect of suspending the operation of the notice until the appeal is finally disposed of or, if the appeal is withdrawn, until the withdrawal of the appeal;

(b) in the case of a prohibition notice, the bringing of the appeal shall have the like effect if, but only if, on the application of the appellant the tribunal so directs (and then only from the giving of the direction).

(4) One or more assessors may be appointed for the purposes of any proceedings brought before an employment tribunal under this paragraph.

Restrictions on disclosure of information

7 (1) In this paragraph—

"relevant information" means information obtained by an inspector in pursuance of a requirement imposed under paragraph 2;

"relevant statutory provisions" means the provisions of Part 6 of the Transport Act 1968 and of any orders or regulations made under powers contained in that Part; and

"the recipient", in relation to any relevant information, means the person by whom that information was so obtained or to whom that information was so furnished, as the case may be.

(2) Subject to the following sub-paragraph, no relevant information shall be disclosed without the consent of the person by whom it was furnished.

(3) The preceding sub-paragraph shall not apply to—

(a) disclosure of information to a government department;

(b) without prejudice to paragraph (a), disclosure by the recipient of information to any person for the purpose of any function conferred on the recipient by or under any of the relevant statutory provisions or under these Regulations;

(c) without prejudice to paragraph (a), disclosure by the recipient of information to—

(i) an officer of a local authority who is authorised by that authority to receive it: or

(ii) a constable authorised by a chief officer of police to receive it; or

(d) disclosure by the recipient of information in a form calculated to prevent it from being identified as relating to a particular person or case.

(4) A person to whom information is disclosed in pursuance of sub-paragraph (3) shall not use the information for a purpose other than—

(a) in a case falling within sub-paragraph (3)(a), a purpose of a government department or local authority in connection with these Regulations or with the relevant statutory provisions, or any enactment whatsoever relating to working time;

(b) in the case of information given to a constable, the purposes of the police in connection with these Regulations, the relevant statutory provisions or any enactment relating to working time.

(5) A person shall not disclose any information obtained by him as a result of the exercise of any power conferred by paragraph 2 (including in particular any information with respect to any trade secret obtained by him in any premises entered by him by virtue of any such power) except—

(a) for the purposes of his functions; or

(b) for the purposes of any legal proceedings; or

(c) with the relevant consent.

In this sub-paragraph "the relevant consent" means, in the case of information furnished in pursuance of a requirement imposed under paragraph 2, the consent of the person who furnished it, and, in any other case, the consent of a person having responsibilities in relation to the premises where the information was obtained.

(6) Notwithstanding anything in sub-paragraph (5) an inspector shall, in circumstances in which it is necessary to do so for the purpose of assisting in keeping persons (or the representatives of persons) adequately informed about matters affecting their health, safety and welfare or working time, give to such persons or their representatives the following descriptions of information, that is to say—

(a) factual information obtained by him as mentioned in that sub-paragraph which relates to their working environment; and

(b) information with respect to any action which he has taken or proposes to take in or in connection with the performance of his functions in relation to their working environment;

and, where an inspector does as aforesaid, he shall give the like information to the employer of the first-mentioned persons.

(7) Notwithstanding anything in sub-paragraph (5), a person who has obtained such information as is referred to in that sub-paragraph may furnish to a person who appears to him to be likely to be a party to any civil proceedings arising out of any accident, occurrence, situation or other matter, a written statement of the relevant facts observed by him in the course of exercising any of the powers referred to in that sub-paragraph.

[911]

PASSENGER AND GOODS VEHICLES (RECORDING EQUIPMENT) (TACHOGRAPH CARD FEES) REGULATIONS 2005 SI 2005/1140

Authority Made by the Secretary of State for Transport under the European Communities Act 1972, s 2(2).
Date made 8 April 2005.
Commencement 1 June 2005.
Amendment Amended by SI 2006/3276.
Summary These regulations make provision for the issuing of driver cards, company cards, workshop cards and control cards ("tachograph cards") for use with digital tachographs, which are tachographs complying with Annexes IB and II to Council Regulation (EEC) 3821/85 on recording equipment in road transport (OJ L370, 31.12.1985, p 8) ("the Community Recording Equipment Regulation") (as it has effect in accordance with Commission Regulations (EEC) 3314/90 (OJ L318, 17.11.1990, p 20) and 3688/92 (OJ L374, 22.12.1992, p 12), Commission Regulations (EC) 2479/95 (OJ L256, 26.10.1995, p 8), 1056/97 (OJ L154, 12.06.1997, p 21), 1360/2002 (OJ L207, 05.08.2002, p 1), 432/2004 (OJ L71, 10.03.2004, p 3), Art 1 of Council Regulation (EC) 2135/98 (OJ L274, 09.10.1998, p 1), the Act concerning the conditions of accession of the Czech Republic, the Republic of Estonia, the Republic of Cyprus, the Republic of Latvia, the Republic of Lithuania, the Republic of Hungary, the Republic of Malta, the Republic of Poland, the Republic of Slovenia and the Slovak Republic and the adjustments to the Treaties on which the European Union is founded (OJ L236, 23.09.2003, p 33), and Regulations (EC) 1882/2003 (OJ L284, 31.10.2003, p 1) and 561/2006 (OJ L102, 11.2004.2006, p 1) of the European Parliament and of the Council, and as read with SI 1986/1456 (revoked and replaced by SI 2007/1819)).

Regs 3, 4 of the regulations relate to driver cards. The Secretary of State must issue a driver card to a person: (a) who is a driver subject to the provisions of what is now Regulation (EC) 561/2006 of the European Parliament and of the Council on the harmonisation of certain social legislation relating to road transport (OJ L102, 11.04.2006, p 1) (which repealed and replaced Council Regulation (EEC) 3820/85 on the harmonization of certain social legislation relating to road transport (OJ L370, 31.12.1985, p 1)) and the Community Recording Equipment Regulation; and (b) who complies with the prescribed requirements. The holder of a driver card may exchange his driver card in certain circumstances. Reg 5 provides that the Secretary of State must issue a company card to a person: (a) who is the owner or holder of a vehicle in which there is equipment for recording information as to the use of that vehicle which has been installed in accordance with the Community Recording Equipment Regulation and complies with Annexes IB and II to that Regulation; and (b) who complies with the prescribed requirements. By reg 6, the Secretary of State must not issue a workshop card to a person to whom an approval has not been issued in accordance with SI 1979/1746, reg 4, or a control card to a person who is not a constable or a vehicle examiner appointed under the Road Traffic Act 1988, s 66A. Reg 7 provides for the replacement of a tachograph card which is damaged, malfunctions, or is lost or stolen. Reg 8 sets out fees payable in respect of driver cards and company cards. No fees are payable in respect of workshop cards, which may be held by approved workshops only, or control cards, which may be held by the police and officers of the Vehicle and Operator Services Agency (an agency of the Department for Transport) only.

See further SI 2006/1937.

[912]

RAILWAYS ACT 2005 (COMMENCEMENT NO 1) ORDER 2005 SI 2005/1444

Authority Made by the Secretary of State for Transport under the Railways Act 2005, s 60(2).
Date made 27 May 2005.
Summary This order, and the further commencement orders SI 2005/1909, SI 2005/2252, SI 2005/2812, SI 2006/266, SI 2006/1951, SI 2006/2911, SI 2007/62, SI 2007/1993 (all made under the Railways Act 2005, s 60(2), except SI 2006/2911, which was made under s 60(2), (3)) brought provisions of the 2005 Act into force on specified dates, as noted in the table below. Transitional and savings provisions made by SI 2006/2911 are noted at the end of the table.

Provision	*Date and extent (if any)*
s 1(1)	See Sch 1 below
s 1(2), (3)(a)–(d)	8 June 2005 (SI 2005/1444)
s 1(3)(e)	24 July 2005 (SI 2005/1909)
s 1(3)(f), (4), (5)	8 June 2005 (SI 2005/1444)
s 1(6)	See Sch 2 below
s 1(7)–(9)	8 June 2005 (SI 2005/1444)
s 1(10)	1 August 2006 (SI 2006/1951)
s 2	See Sch 3 below
s 3(1)	See sub-ss (2)–(11) below
s 3(2)	8 June 2005 (except in so far as it inserts the words "that are not safety functions") (SI 2005/1444) 1 April 2006 (for remaining purposes) (SI 2006/266)
s 3(3)	26 June 2005 (SI 2005/1444)
s 3(4)	1 April 2006 (SI 2006/266)
s 3(5)	1 December 2006 (SI 2006/2911)
s 3(6)	16 October 2005 (in so far as the inserted Railways Act 1993, s 4(3B) relates to functions transferred or assigned to the Scottish Ministers under or by virtue of Pt 1 of that Act) (SI 2005/2812) 1 December 2006 (for remaining purposes) (SI 2006/2911)
s 3(7)	26 June 2005 (SI 2005/1444)
s 3(8)(a)	8 June 2005 (except in so far as it inserts the words "that are not safety functions") (SI 2005/1444) 1 April 2006 (for remaining purposes) (SI 2006/266)
s 3(8)(b)	16 October 2005 (SI 2005/2812)
s 3(8)(c)	8 June 2005 (SI 2005/1444)
s 3(8)(d)	24 July 2005 (SI 2005/1909)
s 3(9)	8 June 2005 (to the extent that it inserts Railways Act 1993, s 4(5A)) (SI 2005/1444) 1 April 2006 (to the extent that it inserts Railways Act 1993, s 4(5B)) (SI 2006/266) 29 January 2007 (for remaining purposes) (SI 2007/62)
s 3(10)	16 October 2005 (except for the words "or (5B)" in the substituted Railways Act 1993, s 4(7ZA)) (SI 2005/2812) 1 April 2006 (for remaining purposes) (SI 2006/266)
s 3(11)(a)	24 July 2005 (SI 2005/1909)
s 3(11)(b)	26 June 2005 (in so far as it relates to the definition of "railway service performance") (SI 2005/1444) 1 April 2006 (for remaining purposes) (SI 2006/266)
s 4	See Sch 4 below
s 5	21 August 2005 (SI 2005/2252)
s 6(1)–(3)	8 June 2005 (SI 2005/1444)
s 6(4)	8 June 2005 (except para (a) and the words "9 or" in the final line) (SI 2005/1444) 16 October 2005 (for remaining purposes) (SI 2005/2812)
ss 6(5)–(8), 7	8 June 2005 (SI 2005/1444)
ss 8, 9	16 October 2005 (SI 2005/2812)
s 10(1)–(5)	8 June 2005 (SI 2005/1444)
s 10(6)	24 July 2005 (except the words "or the Scottish Ministers" and "or their") (SI 2005/1909)

Provision	*Date and extent (if any)*
	16 October 2005 (for remaining purposes) (SI 2005/2812)
ss 10(7)–(12), 11	8 June 2005 (SI 2005/1444)
s 12(1)–(7)	24 July 2005 (SI 2005/1909)
s 12(8)	24 July 2005 (except para (b) in the definition "appropriate national authority" and the word "and" immediately preceding it) (SI 2005/1909) 16 October 2005 (for remaining purposes) (SI 2005/2812)
ss 13–16	24 July 2005 (SI 2005/1909)
s 17	8 August 2007 (SI 2007/1993)
ss 18–21	24 July 2005 (SI 2005/1909)
ss 22–39	1 December 2006 (SI 2006/2911)
s 40(1)–(3), (4)(a)	24 July 2005 (SI 2005/1909)
s 40(4)(b)	16 October 2005 (SI 2005/2812)
s 40(4)(c)	24 July 2005 (SI 2005/1909)
s 40(5)	16 October 2005 (SI 2005/2812)
s 40(6), (7)	24 July 2005 (SI 2005/1909)
s 41	1 December 2006 (SI 2006/2911)
ss 42, 43	1 August 2006 (SI 2006/1951)
s 44	1 December 2006 (SI 2006/2911)
s 45(1)	1 August 2006 (in so far as it relates to the definitions of "closure", "closures guidance" and "railway funding authority") (SI 2006/1951) 1 December 2006 (for remaining purposes) (SI 2006/2911)
s 45(2)	1 August 2006 (SI 2006/1951)
s 45(3)–(9)	1 December 2006 (SI 2006/2911)
s 46(1), (2)	24 July 2005 (SI 2005/1909)
s 46(3)	See Sch 9 below
s 46(4)–(6)	16 October 2005 (SI 2005/2812)
s 46(7), (8)	24 July 2005 (SI 2005/1909)
ss 47–50	16 October 2005 (SI 2005/2812)
s 51(1)(a)	8 June 2005 (SI 2005/1444)
s 51(1)(b)	1 April 2006 (SI 2006/266)
s 51(1)(c)	8 June 2005 (SI 2005/1444)
s 51(2)	16 October 2005 (SI 2005/2812)
s 51(3), (4)	8 June 2005 (SI 2005/1444)
s 51(5)	1 April 2006 (SI 2006/266)
s 52	24 July 2005 (SI 2005/1909)
s 53	See Sch 10 below
s 54(1)–(3)	8 June 2005 (SI 2005/1444)
s 54(4)	See Sch 11 below
s 55	8 June 2005 (SI 2005/1444)
s 56(1)	1 August 2006 (SI 2006/1951)
s 56(2)	8 June 2005 (except the words "or of the Scottish Parliament in para (b)) (SI 2005/1444) 1 August 2006 (for remaining purposes) (SI 2006/1951)
s 56(3)(a)	8 June 2005 (SI 2005/1444)
s 56(3)(b), (c)	1 August 2006 (SI 2006/1951)
s 56(4)	8 June 2005 (SI 2005/1444)

Provision	Date and extent (if any)
s 56(5)	8 June 2005 (except the words "or Scottish Ministers") (SI 2005/1444) 16 October 2005 (for remaining purposes) (SI 2005/2812)
ss 56(6), 57, 58	8 June 2005 (SI 2005/1444)
s 59(1)	See Sch 12 below
s 59(2)–(5)	8 June 2005 (SI 2005/1444)
s 59(6), (7)	See Sch 13 below
Sch 1, paras 1–10	24 July 2005 (SI 2005/1909)
Sch 1, para 11	16 October 2005 (SI 2005/2812)
Sch 1, para 12	1 December 2006 (SI 2006/2911)
Sch 1, para 13(1)	24 July 2005 (SI 2005/1909)
Sch 1, para 13(2)	16 October 2005 (SI 2005/2812)
Sch 1, para 13(3)	24 July 2005 (SI 2005/1909)
Sch 1, para 13(4)(a)	24 July 2005 (in so far as it relates to the Secretary of State) (SI 2005/1909) 16 October 2005 (for remaining purposes) (SI 2005/2812)
Sch 1, para 13(4)(b)	24 July 2005 (in so far as it relates to an agreement to which either the Secretary of State is party or the Secretary of State and the National Assembly for Wales are jointly party) (SI 2005/1909) 16 October 2005 (for remaining purposes) (SI 2005/2812)
Sch 1, para 13(5)	24 July 2005 (in so far as it relates to a designation which is to have effect as a designation by the Secretary of State) (SI 2005/1909) 16 October 2005 (for remaining purposes) (SI 2005/2812)
Sch 1, para 14	16 October 2005 (SI 2005/2812)
Sch 1, paras 15–19	24 July 2005 (in so far as they relate to the Secretary of State) (SI 2005/1909) 16 October 2005 (for remaining purposes) (SI 2005/2812)
Sch 1, para 20(1)	24 July 2005 (in so far as it relates to services for which the Secretary of State is the relevant franchising authority) (SI 2005/1909) 16 October 2005 (for remaining purposes) (SI 2005/2812)
Sch 1, para 20(2), (3)	24 July 2005 (SI 2005/1909)
Sch 1, para 20(4)	24 July 2005 (except in so far as the inserted Railways Act 1993, s 30(3A) relates to the Scottish Ministers) (SI 2005/1909) 16 October 2005 (for remaining purposes) (SI 2005/2812)
Sch 1, para 20(5)	24 July 2005 (in so far as it relates to services for which the Secretary of State is to be treated as the relevant franchising authority) (SI 2005/1909) 16 October 2005 (for remaining purposes) (SI 2005/2812)
Sch 1, para 21(1)	See para 21(2)–(8) below
Sch 1, para 21(2)	24 July 2005 (SI 2005/1909)
Sch 1, para 21(4)–(8)	24 July 2005 (except in so far as relating to: (a) the transfer of functions relating to the enforcement of relevant conditions or requirements which are closure restrictions or closure conditions from the Strategic Rail Authority to the Secretary of State and to the Scottish Ministers; and (b) the transfer of functions relating to the enforcement of relevant conditions or requirements which are terms of franchise agreements from the Strategic Rail Authority to the Scottish Ministers) (SI 2005/1909) 16 October 2005 (in so far as relates to the transfer of functions specified in (b) above) (SI 2005/2812) 1 December 2006 (for remaining purposes) (SI 2006/2911)

Provision	*Date and extent (if any)*
Sch 1, para 22	24 July 2005 (except in so far as relating to: (a) the transfer of functions relating to the enforcement of relevant conditions or requirements which are closure restrictions or closure conditions from the Strategic Rail Authority to the Secretary of State and to the Scottish Ministers; and (b) the transfer of functions relating to the enforcement of relevant conditions or requirements which are terms of franchise agreements from the Strategic Rail Authority to the Scottish Ministers) (SI 2005/1909) 16 October 2005 (in so far as relates to the transfer of functions specified in (b) above) (SI 2005/2812) 1 December 2006 (for remaining purposes) (SI 2006/2911)
Sch 1, para 23(1)	See para 23(2), (3) below
Sch 1, para 23(2), (3)	24 July 2005 (except in so far as relating to: (a) the transfer of functions relating to the enforcement of relevant conditions or requirements which are closure restrictions or closure conditions from the Strategic Rail Authority to the Secretary of State and to the Scottish Ministers; and (b) the transfer of functions relating to the enforcement of relevant conditions or requirements which are terms of franchise agreements from the Strategic Rail Authority to the Scottish Ministers) (SI 2005/1909) 16 October 2005 (in so far as relates to the transfer of functions specified in (b) above) (SI 2005/2812) 1 December 2006 (for remaining purposes) (SI 2006/2911)
Sch 1, para 24(1)	24 July 2005 (except in so far as relating to: (a) the transfer of functions relating to the enforcement of relevant conditions or requirements which are closure restrictions or closure conditions from the Strategic Rail Authority to the Secretary of State and to the Scottish Ministers; and (b) the transfer of functions relating to the enforcement of relevant conditions or requirements which are terms of franchise agreements from the Strategic Rail Authority to the Scottish Ministers) (SI 2005/1909) 16 October 2005 (in so far as relates to the transfer of functions specified in (b) above) (SI 2005/2812) 1 December 2006 (for remaining purposes) (SI 2006/2911)
Sch 1, para 24(2)	24 July 2005 (except the words ", by the Scottish Ministers") (SI 2005/1909) 16 October 2005 (for remaining purposes) (SI 2005/2812)
Sch 1, paras 25, 26	24 July 2005 (except in so far as relating to: (a) the transfer of functions relating to the enforcement of relevant conditions or requirements which are closure restrictions or closure conditions from the Strategic Rail Authority to the Secretary of State and to the Scottish Ministers; and (b) the transfer of functions relating to the enforcement of relevant conditions or requirements which are terms of franchise agreements from the Strategic Rail Authority to the Scottish Ministers) (SI 2005/1909) 16 October 2005 (in so far as relates to the transfer of functions specified in (b) above) (SI 2005/2812) 1 December 2006 (for remaining purposes) (SI 2006/2911)
Sch 1, paras 27, 28	24 July 2005 (SI 2005/1909)
Sch 1, para 29	26 June 2005 (SI 2005/1444)
Sch 1, para 30(1), (2), (3)(a)	24 July 2005 (SI 2005/1909)
Sch 1, para 30(3)(b)	16 October 2005 (SI 2005/2812)
Sch 1, para 30(3)(c), (d), (4)–(7)	24 July 2005 (SI 2005/1909)
Sch 1, para 31	16 October 2005 (SI 2005/2812)
Sch 1, para 32(1)	24 July 2005 (SI 2005/1909)

Provision	*Date and extent (if any)*
Sch 1, para 32(2)	1 December 2006 (in so far as it relates to Railways Act 1993, s 76(4)(b)) (SI 2006/2911)
Sch 1, paras 32(3)–(5), 33	24 July 2005 (SI 2005/1909)
Sch 1, para 34	1 December 2006 (SI 2006/2911)
Sch 1, para 35	24 July 2005 (except in so far as it relates to a transfer of functions from the Strategic Rail Authority to the Scottish Ministers) (SI 2005/1909) 16 October 2005 (for remaining purposes) (SI 2005/2812)
Sch 1, para 36(a)	24 July 2005 (SI 2005/1909)
Sch 1, para 36(b)	1 December 2006 (SI 2006/2911)
Sch 1, para 36(c)	16 October 2005 (SI 2005/2812)
Sch 1, para 37	8 June 2005 (SI 2005/1444)
Sch 2	8 June 2005 (in so far as it makes provision in relation to transfer schemes made under s 1(2)) (SI 2005/1444) 24 July 2005 (in so far as not already in force) (SI 2005/1909)
Sch 3, para 1	7 February 2006 (SI 2006/266)
Sch 3, paras 2–11	1 April 2006 (SI 2006/266)
Sch 3, para 12	7 February 2006 (SI 2006/266)
Sch 3, paras 13–15	1 April 2006 (SI 2006/266)
Sch 4	29 January 2007 (SI 2007/62)
Schs 5, 6	24 July 2005 (SI 2005/1909)
Schs 7, 8	1 December 2006 (SI 2006/2911)
Sch 9	24 July 2005 (in so far as it relates to bye-laws in relation to which the Secretary of State acting alone is the appropriate national authority by virtue of para 1(1)) (SI 2005/1909) 16 October 2005 (for remaining purposes) (SI 2005/2812)
Sch 10, Pts 1, 2	8 June 2005 (SI 2005/1444) 24 July 2005 (in so far as not already in force) (SI 2005/1909)
Sch 10, Pt 3	24 July 2005 (SI 2005/1909)
Sch 10, Pts 4, 5	8 June 2005 (in so far as they make provision in relation to transfer schemes made under s 1(2)) (SI 2005/1444) 24 July 2005 (in so far as not already in force) (SI 2005/1909)
Sch 11, para 1	See paras 2–16 below
Sch 11, paras 2–5	1 December 2006 (SI 2006/2911)
Sch 11, para 6	24 July 2005 (except in so far as it relates to: (a) the transfer of functions from the Strategic Rail Authority to the Scottish Ministers; and (b) the repeal of functions of Passenger Transport Authorities and Executives in Scotland) (SI 2005/1909) 16 October 2005 (in so far as relates to the transfer of functions from the Strategic Rail Authority to the Scottish Ministers) (SI 2005/2812)
Sch 11, para 7(1)	1 December 2006 (SI 2006/2911)
Sch 11, para 7(2)	24 July 2005 (SI 2005/1909)
Sch 11, para 7(3)–(6)	1 December 2006 (SI 2006/2911)
Sch 11, paras 8, 9	24 July 2005 (SI 2005/1909)
Sch 11, paras 10, 11	1 December 2006 (SI 2006/2911)
Sch 11, para 12	24 July 2005 (SI 2005/1909)
Sch 11, para 13	1 December 2006 (SI 2006/2911)
Sch 11, para 14(1)–(5)	8 June 2005 (SI 2005/1444)
Sch 11, para 14(6), (7)	24 July 2005 (SI 2005/1909)

Provision	*Date and extent (if any)*
Sch 11, para 15	24 July 2005 (except in so far as sub-paras (a)–(c) insert the words "or the Scottish Ministers") (SI 2005/1909) 16 October 2005 (for remaining purposes) (SI 2005/2812)
Sch 11, para 16(1)	8 June 2005 (SI 2005/1444)
Sch 11, para 16(2)	24 July 2005 (SI 2005/1909)
Sch 12, para 1(1)	See para 1(2), (3) below
Sch 12, para 1(2)	1 December 2006 (SI 2006/2911)
Sch 12, para 1(3)	24 July 2005 (SI 2005/1909)
Sch 12, para 2(1)	See para 2(2)–(4) below
Sch 12, para 2(2), (3), (4)(a)	24 July 2005 (SI 2005/1909)
Sch 12, para 2(4)(b)	24 July 2005 (except words ", the Scottish Ministers") (SI 2005/1909) 16 October 2005 (for remaining purposes) (SI 2005/2812)
Sch 12, para 3	24 July 2005 (SI 2005/1909)
Sch 12, para 4	1 April 2006 (SI 2006/266)
Sch 12, para 5	24 July 2005 (SI 2005/1909)
Sch 12, para 6	1 April 2006 (SI 2006/266)
Sch 12, para 7	8 June 2005 (SI 2005/1444)
Sch 12, para 8	24 July 2005 (except in so far as it relates to the transfer of functions from the Strategic Rail Authority to the Scottish Ministers) (SI 2005/1909) 16 October 2005 (for remaining purposes) (SI 2005/2812)
Sch 12, paras 9–11	8 June 2005 (SI 2005/1444)
Sch 12, para 12	1 April 2006 (SI 2006/266)
Sch 12, para 13	21 November 2005 (SI 2005/2812)
Sch 12, para 14(1)	See para 14(2)–(9) below
Sch 12, para 14(2)	1 December 2006 (SI 2006/2911)
Sch 12, para 14(3), (4)	24 July 2005 (SI 2005/1909)
Sch 12, para 14(5)(a)	1 December 2006 (SI 2006/2911)
Sch 12, para 14(5)(b)	8 June 2005 (SI 2005/1444)
Sch 12, para 14(6)–(9)	24 July 2005 (SI 2005/1909)
Sch 12, paras 15, 16	8 June 2005 (SI 2005/1444)
Sch 12, para 17(1)	See para 17(2)–(9) below
Sch 12, para 17(2), (3)	24 July 2005 (SI 2005/1909)
Sch 12, para 17(4)–(6)	1 August 2006 (SI 2006/1951)
Sch 12, para 17(7)	8 June 2005 (SI 2005/1444)
Sch 12, para 17(8), (9)	24 July 2005 (SI 2005/1909)
Sch 12, para 18(1)	See para 18(2)–(4) below
Sch 12, para 18(2)(a), (b)	24 July 2005 (SI 2005/1909)
Sch 12, para 18(2)(c), (3)	24 July 2005 (except in so far as relating to the transfer of functions from the Strategic Rail Authority to the Scottish Ministers) (SI 2005/1909) 16 October 2005 (for remaining purposes) (SI 2005/2812)
Sch 12, para 18(4)	8 June 2005 (SI 2005/1444)

Provision	*Date and extent (if any)*
Sch 13, Pt 1	8 June 2005 (entries relating to Ministry of Transport Act 1919, s 17(1)(a); Health and Safety at Work etc Act 1974, s 18(5); Railways Act 1993, s 4(5)(d) (words "London Regional Transport"); Transport Act 2000, Sch 27, para 41(2)) (SI 2005/1444)
	26 June 2005 (entries relating to Railways Act 1993, s 4(3A)(a); Transport Act 2000, s 206, Sch 28, para 15) (SI 2005/1444)
	24 July 2005 (entries relating to Transport Act 1962, s 56(4), (5), (6ZA), (20); Parliamentary Commissioner Act 1967, Sch 2, in so far as relating to Rail Passengers' Committees; Transport Act 1968; House of Commons Disqualification Act 1975, Sch 1, in so far as relating to a member of a Rail Passengers' Committee in receipt of remuneration; Transport Act 1985; Channel Tunnel Act 1987; Railways Act 1993, ss 2, 3, 7, 7A, 8 (except the repeal of the words "and to the Health and Safety Executive" in s 8(7)(a), (b)), 10(4), 11, 12, 13(1A)–(1C), 14(5A), 15, 15A(1), 15B (except the repeal of the words "and the Health and Safety Executive" in s 15B(5)), 15C(3), 16(3) (except the repeal of the words "and to the Health and Safety Executive"), 30(1), 34, 35, 43(4), 47(6), 54(3), 55(10)(a), 61, 62, 63(2), 68(1)(a), 71A, 72(1), 73, 76(3), (6)(a), (8), 77, 79, 83(3), 144(1), 145(7), Schs 2, 3, 6; Channel Tunnel Rail Link Act 1996, s 19(2), (5), (6); Greater London Authority Act 1999, ss 175(1), 197, 199(1), 201, 252(1), Sch 19, para 5; Freedom of Information Act 2000, Sch 1, Pt 6, in so far as relating to any Rail Passengers' Committee established under the Railways Act 1993, s 2(2); Transport Act 2000, ss 212(4), 213, 224(2)(b), 226(1)(c) (and the word "and" immediately preceding it), 227(1), (3), 228(2), (3)(b) (and the word "and" immediately preceding it), (5), 251, Sch 16 (paras 2–7, 9, 10, 40, 41, 44, 47, 48, 59, 62, 64), Sch 17 (paras 2(2)–(5), (7), (8), 3, 4(2)(a), (5)(a), 6(2), (3)(a), (4), (5), 7(2)–(4), (5)(a), (6)(a), (7), (8)(a), 8(2), (3)(a), (4), (5), 9(4)(b), (6)–(8), 10, 11(3), 13, 14, 16(b) (and the word "and" immediately preceding it), 18, 19, 20(2), (5), 21–24), Sch 22 (paras 2, 3, 7, 8(4)(b), (10), 9–13, 15(2)(c)–(e), (3), (4)(a), (5), (6), 18, 22, 23(a)), Sch 23 (paras 1–9), Sch 27 (paras 30(2), 39(5)), Sch 28 (paras 5(2), 14); Enterprise Act 2002, s 168(4)(h), (i); Scottish Public Services Ombudsman Act 2002, Sch 2, Pt 2, para 82; Railways and Transport Safety Act 2003, s 104, Sch 2, paras 3 (in so far as the entries in the table in para 3 relate to ss 7A, 77, 79, Schs 2, 3), 16) (SI 2005/1909)
	16 October 2005 (entries relating to Railways Act 1993, ss 23(2B), 24(3), 26(4), 59(6)(a); Transport Act 2000, s 219, Sch 16, paras 14(2), (3)(a), (4), 15, 16(2), (3)(a), 17(2)(a), (3), (4)(a), (5)(a), 18(2)(a), (3), 19, 39, 50, 51(4), (5), Sch 20, Sch 28, para 4; Enterprise Act 2002, s 168(5)) (SI 2005/2812)
	21 November 2005 (entries relating to Railway Heritage Act 1996, ss 1(a), (b), 2(2)(a); Transport Act 2000, Sch 31) (SI 2005/2812)
	1 April 2006 (entries relating to Health and Safety at Work etc Act 1974, s 78(7)(c); Railways Act 1993, s 4(3)(a); ss 8, 15B, 16(3) (for remaining purposes); and Sch 4A, para 7(4)(b); Railways and Transport Safety Act 2003, s 62(1)(m), (n)) (SI 2006/266)
	1 August 2006 (entry relating to Transport Act 2000, s 248(3)) (SI 2006/1951)

Provision	*Date and extent (if any)*
	1 December 2006 (entries relating to Transport Act 1962, s 43; Parliamentary Commissioner Act 1967 (for remaining purposes); Superannuation Act 1972; House of Commons Disqualification Act 1975, Sch 1, Pt 2; Northern Ireland Assembly Disqualification Act 1975; Race Relations Act 1976; Railways Act 1993, ss 4(3A) (for remaining purposes), 37–42, 43 (for remaining purposes), 44–46B, 47 (for remaining purposes), 47A–49, 50(1)(a), (2), 55(5), (10) (so far as it relates to the definition of "relevant condition or requirement"), 67(6), 69(4), 75, 83(1), 118, 130, 136, 145 (for remaining purposes), 151, Sch 4A, para 7(4)(b) (for remaining purposes), Schs 5, 11; Channel Tunnel Rail Link Act 1996 (for remaining purposes); Greater London Authority Act 1999 (for remaining purposes); Freedom of Information Act 2000 (for remaining purposes); Transport Act 2000, ss 201–205, 207–211, 214, 217(2), 218, 220–222, 234–239, 249, 278, Schs 14, 15, Sch 16, paras 11–13, 22–33, 35, 42, 45, 46, 49, 51(2), 52, 53, 61, 66, Sch 17, paras 25–27, 29, 30, Pt 3, Schs 18, 19, 21, Sch 22 (for remaining purposes), Sch 25, para 15, Sch 27 (for remaining purposes), Sch 28 (for remaining purposes, but excluding para 11); Railways and Transport Safety Act 2003, ss 62(1)(j), 73(3), Sch 2 (for remaining purposes), Sch 4) (SI 2006/2911) 29 January 2007 (entries relating to Railways Act 1993, Sch 4A (for remaining purposes); Transport Act 2000, Sch 28, para 11) (SI 2007/62)
Sch 13, Pt 2, para 1	1 December 2006 (SI 2006/2911)
Sch 13, Pt 2, para 2	16 October 2005 (SI 2005/2812)
Sch 13, Pt 2, paras 3, 4	1 December 2006 (SI 2006/2911)

Transitional provisions and savings SI 2006/2911 makes the following transitional and savings provisions relating to closures other than minor closures; minor closures; conditions; orders for securing compliance; and liability for breach of statutory duty.

Art 3 of SI 2006/2911 (closures other than minor closures) applies to a closure proposal which is made before 1 December 2006 and is not determined before that date. Despite the repeal of the Railways Act 1993, ss 37–45 (closures), those provisions have effect in relation to that proposal subject to specified modifications.

Under art 4 of SI 2006/2911 (minor closures), where before 1 December 2006 the Strategic Rail Authority:

(a) has been considering whether a closure is a minor closure as mentioned in s 37(1), 39(1) or 41(1) of the 1993 Act, and
(b) has not determined that question by that date,

the Secretary of State is to determine that question and the definition of "minor closure" in that section is to continue to have effect for the purposes of that determination. Where:

(a) the Authority has, before 1 December 2006, made a determination under s 37(1), 38(2), 39(1), 40(2), 41(1) or 42(2) of the 1993 Act that a closure is a minor closure but such closure has not taken effect before that date, or
(b) the Secretary of State has made a determination that a closure is a minor closure,

the closure may take effect at any time as a minor closure and Pt 4 of the 2005 Act does not apply in such a case. S 46B of the 1993 Act (notification of minor closures to the Office of Rail Regulation) is modified.

Under art 5 of SI 2006/2911 (conditions), where before 1 December 2006 the Secretary of State has imposed conditions pursuant to s 43(9) of the 1993 Act, those conditions are to continue to have effect on and after that date and s 46 of that Act is to continue to have effect in relation to those conditions. Where the Secretary of State:

(a) has made a determination under art 4 that a closure is a minor closure; and
(b) has imposed conditions as mentioned in s 37(1), 39(1) or 41(1) of the 1993 Act as applied by art 4,

the conditions are to have effect despite the repeal of that section and such conditions are to have effect as if agreed to for the purposes of s 34(5) of the 2005 Act. Where, on or after 1 December 2006, the Secretary of State allows a closure to take effect in accordance with s 43(9) of the 1993 Act subject to compliance with conditions, the conditions are to have effect despite the repeal of that section and s 46 of that Act is to have effect in relation to the conditions.

Under art 6 of SI 2006/2911 (orders for securing compliance), s 55 of the 1993 Act is to continue to have effect as it had effect immediately before 1 December 2006 for the purpose of ensuring that:

(a) a person who is required to comply with closure conditions; or
(b) a person under closure restrictions,

complies with those closure conditions or closure restrictions as the case may be but subject to specified modifications.

By art 7, the obligations of the Secretary of State imposed by or by virtue of SI 2006/2911:

(a) to comply with any closure conditions,
(b) to secure the provision of any railway services, or

(c) to secure the provision of any additional railway asset,
do not give rise to any form of duty or liability enforceable by civil proceedings for breach of statutory duty.

[913]

RAILWAYS ACT 2005 (TRANSITIONAL PROVISIONS AND SAVINGS) ORDER 2005
SI 2005/1738

Authority Made by the Secretary of State for Transport under the Railways Act 2005, s 60(3)(a), (c).
Date made 29 June 2005.
Commencement 24 July 2005.
Summary This order makes transitional provisions and savings in connection with the bringing into force on 24 July 2005 (see SI 2005/1909) of the Railways Act 2005, s 21(1), which abolishes the Rail Passengers' Committees, and the repeal of the Railways Act 1993, ss 43(4), 47(6) by s 59(6) of, and Pt 1 of Sch 13 to, the 2005 Act.

The transitional provisions in art 3 of the order had effect until the day appointed for the commencement of the repeal of ss 43 (other than sub-s (4)), 46, 47 (other than sub-s (6)), 47A, 48 of, and Sch 5 to, the 1993 Act. Following the commencement of these repeals (see the table to SI 2005/1444 above), art 3 of this order is spent.

Art 4 of the order provides that anything which has been done by a Rail Passengers' Committee under ss 43, 46, 47, 47A, 48 of, and Sch 5 to, the 1993 Act before 24 July 2005 is to be treated as from that date as if it had been done by the Rail Passengers' Council, so far as is necessary to give it continuing validity or effect. By art 5, nothing in s 145(1) of the 1993 Act (general restrictions on disclosure of information) is to be construed as limiting the matters which may be included in, or made public as part of, a report of the London Transport Users' Committee under any provision of Pt I of the 1993 Act, nor as applying to any information which has been made public as part of such a report, or which has otherwise been made available to the public by virtue of being disclosed in any circumstances in which, or for any purpose for which, disclosure is not precluded by s 145 of the 1993 Act.

[914]

MOTOR CARS (DRIVING INSTRUCTION) REGULATIONS 2005
SI 2005/1902

Authority Made by the Secretary of State for Transport under the Road Traffic Act 1988, ss 123(2), 125(3), (5), 125A(5)–(7), 125B(2), (6), 127(2), 129(5), 132, 133B, 134, 135(1). As from a day to be appointed by order, these provisions of the 1988 Act are amended by the Road Safety Act 2006 as follows:

(a) s 123 is substituted by new ss 123, 123A by the Road Safety Act 2006, s 42, Sch 6, paras 1, 2;
(b) s 125 is substituted by the Road Safety Act 2006, s 42, Sch 6, paras 1, 4;
(c) s 125A(5)–(7) are substituted by new s 125A(5)–(7), (7A)–(7E) by the Road Safety Act 2006, s 42, Sch 6, paras 1, 6(1), (3);
(d) s 125B(6) is repealed by the Road Safety Act 2006, ss 42, 59, Sch 6, paras 1, 7(1), (5), Sch 7;
(e) s 127(2) is substituted (together with original sub-ss (1), (3), (3A), (4)) by new s 127(1)–(4) by the Road Safety Act 2006, s 42, Sch 6, paras 1, 9(1), (2);
(f) s 129 is repealed by the Road Safety Act 2006, ss 42, 59, Sch 6, paras 1, 12, Sch 7;
(g) s 132 is substituted (together with original s 133) by new ss 132, 133, 133ZA, by the Road Safety Act 2006, s 42, Sch 6, paras 1, 14;
(h) ss 134, 135 are substituted by new ss 134, 135 by the Road Safety Act 2006, s 42, Sch 6, paras 1, 19, 20.

Date made 6 July 2005.
Commencement Partly on 10 August 2005; fully on 1 January 2007.
Amendment Amended by SI 2005/2716, SI 2006/525, SI 2007/697, SI 2008/419, SI 2009/844.
Summary These regulations, which revoke the Motor Cars (Driving Instruction) Regulations 1989, SI 1989/2057, and the amending SI 1990/1113, SI 1992/1621, SI 1994/554, SI 1995/1218, SI 1996/1938, SI 1997/650, SI 1998/2247, SI 2000/1805, SI 2002/2640, SI 2003/3027, SI 2004/2871, SI 2004/3159, and SI 1991/1129 in so far as it amended SI 1989/2057, make provision for the registration of driving instructors in the register of approved driving instructors and for the granting of licences to give driving instruction.

Pt 2 (regs 3–8A and Sch 1) makes provision regarding the examination of the ability to give instruction, which consists of the written examination, the driving ability and fitness test and the instructional ability and fitness test. Both the written examination and the element of the driving ability and fitness test that tests hazard perception must be passed on the same day; the remaining elements of the driving ability and fitness test must be passed on the first, second or third attempt after passing the written examination and the element of the driving ability and fitness test that tests hazard perception. Time limits are imposed on applying to take and passing the instructional ability and fitness test. A person who has passed the written examination before 14 November 2002 is not required to undertake the test of hazard perception as part of the driving ability and fitness test. Candidates for parts of the examination are required to produce evidence of identity and entitlement to drive to the examiner before undertaking each part of the examination. A candidate for the test of driving technique (part of the driving ability and fitness test) must satisfy the examiner of his ability to carry out vehicle safety checks. A candidate is required to provide a motor car for the practical part of the examination. Motor cars provided by candidates for the purpose of a driving ability and fitness test, the instructional ability and fitness test and the test of continued ability and fitness to give instruction must have a seat belt, head restraint and (where appropriate) an additional rear view mirror available for use by the examiner. A candidate for the driving ability and fitness test or the instructional ability and fitness test must, during the test, allow to travel in the motor car provided for the test any person authorised by the Secretary of State for the purpose of supervising the test or otherwise.

Pt 3 (regs 9–11) specifies conditions to be satisfied for the registration of a person in the register of approved driving instructors, in addition to the conditions under the Road Traffic Act 1988, s 125 or 125A (the latter relates to the registration of disabled persons). It also specifies, as from 1 January 2007: (a) a condition to be satisfied for the removal of a person's name from the register of approved driving instructors, in addition to the conditions under s 128 of the 1988 Act, and: (b) a condition to be satisfied for the retention of a person's name in the register, in addition to the conditions under s 127 of that Act.

Pt 4 (regs 12, 12A) provides for tests of continued ability and fitness to give instruction.

Pt 5 (regs 13–16 and Schs 2–4) provides for licences under s 129 of the 1988 Act (licences for giving instruction so as to obtain practical experience). Provision is made for additional conditions to be satisfied for the grant of a licence under s 129; the duration of licences; the conditions subject to which licences are granted; and the form of licences. (S 129 is repealed by the Road Safety Act 2006, ss 42, 59, Sch 6, paras 1, 12, Sch 7, as from a day to be appointed by order.)

Pt 6 (regs 17–22 and Schs 5–7) makes supplementary provision including provision for examination, test, licence and registration fees; official title as "Driving Standards Agency Approved Driving Instructor (Car)" and the form of certificate of registration; the form of badge for use by persons whose names are in the register of approved driving instructors; and the prescribed manner of exhibiting a certificate of registration or a licence.

[915]

RAILWAYS (ACCIDENT INVESTIGATION AND REPORTING) REGULATIONS 2005

SI 2005/1992

Authority Made by the Secretary of State for Transport under the European Communities Act 1972, s 2(2), and the Railways and Transport Safety Act 2003, ss 2, 6, 7(1), 9, 11, 13(1).

Date made 19 July 2005.

Commencement These regulations come into force: (a) in relation to the whole of the United Kingdom except the Channel Tunnel system, in so far as it forms part of the United Kingdom, on 17 October 2005; and (b) in relation to the Channel Tunnel System, in so far as it forms part of the United Kingdom, on 31 January 2006; see reg 1(2).

Amendment Printed as amended by SI 2005/3261, SI 2006/557. Also amended by SI 2007/1573 (revoked).

Interpretation See reg 2.

General These regulations, which implement in part Directive 2004/49/EC of the European Parliament and Council on safety on the Community's railways (OJ L164, 30.04.2004, p 44), set out the procedures for dealing with specified accidents and incidents, including notification requirements, dealing with evidence and publishing reports and recommendations.

[916]

Citation and commencement

1 (1) These Regulations may be cited as the Railways (Accident Investigation and Reporting) Regulations 2005.

(2) These Regulations shall come into force—

(a) on 17th October 2005 in relation to the whole of the United Kingdom except the Channel Tunnel system, in so far as it forms part of the United Kingdom; and

(b) on 31st January 2006 in relation to the Channel Tunnel system, in so far as it forms part of the United Kingdom.

[917]

Interpretation

2 (1) In these Regulations—

"the 2003 Act" means the Railways and Transport Safety Act 2003;

"accident" means a railway accident;

"the Branch" means the Rail Accident Investigation Branch;

"carriageway" means a way over which there is a public right of passage for motor vehicles;

"Channel Tunnel system" has the meaning given by section 1(7) of the Channel Tunnel Act 1987 to the words "the tunnel system";

"Chief Inspector" means the Chief Inspector of Rail Accidents appointed under section 3(2) of the 2003 Act;

"constable" means any person who is—

(a) a member or special constable of any police force who has been attested as a constable under section 29 of the Police Act 1996 or declared a constable under section 16 of the Police (Scotland) Act 1967; or

(b) a member of the Police Service of Northern Ireland or the Police Service of Northern Ireland Reserve;

"dangerous goods" has the meaning given by regulation 2(1) of the Carriage of Dangerous Goods and Use of Transportable Pressure Equipment Regulations [2007];

"European Railway Agency" means the agency for railway safety and interoperability established by Regulation (EC) No 881/2004 of the European Parliament and the Council of 29th April 2004 establishing a European Railway Agency;

"evidence" means anything involved in or relating to an accident or incident, whether at the site of the accident or incident or remote from it, including—

(a) written, electronic, photographic or other records;

(b) electronic or recording equipment;

(c) rolling stock, infrastructure, equipment and signalling systems;

(d) any personal, personnel, medical or other similar record or document; and

(e) anything else that an inspector identifies to—

(i) an owner of railway property;

(ii) a railway industry body; or

(iii) a manufacturer or supplier of equipment, components or services to an owner of railway property or to a railway industry body,

as being relevant to the accident or incident;

"extensive damage" means damage that can immediately be assessed by the Branch to cost at least 2 million Euros in total;

"incident" means a railway incident;

"infrastructure" means railway infrastructure;

"infrastructure manager" means any person who is responsible for establishing and maintaining infrastructure or a part thereof, which may also include the management of infrastructure control and safety systems, but does not include a maintainer;

"inspector" means a person appointed as an inspector of rail accidents under section 3(1) of the 2003 Act;

"Intergovernmental Commission" has the meaning given to those words by section 49 of the Channel Tunnel Act 1987;

"level crossing" means any place where a railway crosses on a level a highway or other road or passageway, whether or not there is public access to such land;

"maintainer" means a person who maintains, repairs or renews railway property or constructs new works in relation to railway property;

"motor vehicle" has the meaning given by section 185 of the Road Traffic Act 1988;

"railway" means a railway or tramway within the meaning given by section 67 of the Transport and Works Act 1992;

"railway accident" and "railway incident" have the meanings given in section 2(1) of the 2003 Act;

"railway industry body" means a person who is an infrastructure manager, a railway undertaking, a maintainer or an operator of rolling stock or railway assets;

"railway property" has the meaning given in section 1(1) of the 2003 Act;

"running line" means a railway line which is not a siding and is ordinarily used for the passage of trains or tramcars;

"safety authority"—

- (a) in relation to Great Britain, excluding the Channel Tunnel system, means the [Office of Rail Regulation];
- (b) in relation to Northern Ireland, means the Department for Regional Development; and
- (c) in relation to the Channel Tunnel system, means the Intergovernmental Commission; and

"Safety Directive" means Directive 2004/49/EC of the European Parliament and the Council of 29th April 2004 on safety on the Community's railways and amending Council Directive 95/18/EC on the licensing of railway undertakings and Directive 2001/14/EC on the allocation of railway infrastructure capacity and the levying of charges for the use of railway infrastructure and safety certification;

["working days" shall be taken to exclude Saturdays, Sundays, Christmas Day, Good Friday and, in relation to an accident or incident that occurs in England and Wales, any day which, under the Banking and Financial Dealings Act 1971, is a bank holiday in England and Wales, in relation to an accident or incident that occurs in Scotland, any other day which, under that Act, is a bank holiday in Scotland and, in relation to an accident or incident that occurs in Northern Ireland, any day which, under that Act, is a bank holiday in Northern Ireland].

(2) The following words have the meaning given to them in section 83 of the Railways Act 1993 or the meaning which would be given to them by an equivalent definition in relation to a tramway—

- (a) operator;
- (b) railway asset;
- (c) railway services;
- (d) rolling stock;
- (e) station;
- (f) track; and
- (g) train.

(3) "Serious accident" means an accident involving a derailment or collision of rolling stock which has an obvious impact on railway safety regulation or management of safety and includes such an accident that results in—

- (a) the death of at least one person;
- (b) serious injuries to five or more persons; or
- (c) extensive damage to rolling stock, the infrastructure or the environment.

(4) "Serious injury" includes—

- (a) a fracture other than to fingers, thumbs or toes;
- (b) amputation;
- (c) dislocation of the shoulder, hip, knee or spine;
- (d) loss of sight, whether temporary or permanent, in one or both eyes;
- (e) a chemical or hot metal burn or any penetrating injury to one or both eyes;
- (f) an injury leading to hypothermia or heat-induced illness;
- (g) an injury requiring resuscitation of the injured person;
- (h) an injury requiring admittance to hospital for more than 24 hours;
- (i) an injury directly leading to loss of consciousness; or
- (j) an injury resulting from the absorption of a substance by inhalation, ingestion or through the skin that causes acute illness requiring medical treatment.

(5) Any expression used both in these Regulations and the Safety Directive and not otherwise defined in these Regulations has the same meaning for the purposes of these Regulations as it has for the purposes of the Safety Directive.

NOTES

Amendment Para (1): in definition "dangerous goods" year "2007" in square brackets substituted by SI 2007/1573 (revoked);
in definition "safety authority" in para (a) words in square brackets substituted by SI 2006/557;
definition "working days" inserted by SI 2005/3261.

Directive 2004/49/EC OJ L164, 30.04.2004, p 44.

Regulation (EC) 881/2004 OJ L164, 30.04.2004, p 1.

Carriage of Dangerous Goods and Use of Transportable Pressure Equipment Regulations 2007 SI 2007/1573. Revoked and replaced by SI 2009/1348, in the title Health and Safety at Work.

[918]

Accidents and incidents excluded from the application of Part 1 of the Railways and Transport Safety Act 2003

3 (1) An accident or incident that occurs within an industrial curtilage shall not be treated as an accident or incident for the purposes of Part 1 of the 2003 Act except where the accident or incident—

- (a) involves a train being used within an industrial curtilage for the purpose of carrying passengers for reward; or
- (b) occurs on track that—
  - (i) is not used for any purpose connected with the industrial activity within that curtilage other than to facilitate the entry to or exit from that curtilage; or
  - (ii) is directly controlled or operated by the person who controls or operates the railway outside the industrial curtilage to which the track within the curtilage is connected.

(2) An accident or incident that occurs on a railway which is operated by a cable haulage system and has a track of a length not exceeding 1 kilometre shall not be treated as an accident or incident for the purposes of Part 1 of the 2003 Act.

(3) Subject to paragraph (4), an accident or incident that occurs on a railway, no part of which crosses a carriageway (whether or not at the same level), shall not be treated as an accident or incident for the purposes of Part 1 of the 2003 Act.

(4) Paragraph (3) shall not apply to an accident or incident occurring on a railway operated by a cable haulage system that is not excluded under paragraph (2).

(5) In this regulation—

- (a) "factory" means a factory within the meaning of section 175 of the Factories Act 1961 and premises to which section 123(1) or (2) or 125(1) of that Act apply unless such premises are used for the purposes of inspection, servicing, maintenance or repair (excluding construction or re-construction) of railway property;
- (b) "industrial curtilage" means a curtilage of a harbour, freight terminal, mine, quarry or factory;
- (c) "mine" has the same meaning as in section 180 of the Mines and Quarries Act 1954; and
- (d) "quarry" has the same meaning as in regulation 3 of the Quarries Regulations 1999.

NOTES

Quarries Regulations 1999 SI 1999/2024, in the title Mines, Minerals and Quarries.

[919]

Duty to notify the Rail Accident Investigation Branch of accidents and incidents

4 (1) Subject to paragraph (6), a railway industry body whose property or staff have been involved in an accident or incident of a type listed in Schedule 1 on a railway or on railway property other than within the Channel Tunnel system shall notify the Branch of its occurrence immediately it learns of the occurrence and by the quickest means available.

(2) Subject to paragraph (6), a railway industry body whose property or staff have been involved in an accident or incident of a type listed in Schedule 2 on a railway or railway property other than within the Channel Tunnel system shall notify the Branch of its occurrence as soon as is reasonably practicable and in any event within three working days of its occurrence.

(3) Where staff or property of a railway industry body have in any month been involved in an accident or incident of a type listed in Schedule 3 on a railway or railway property other than within the Channel Tunnel System, the body shall notify the Branch of every such occurrence during that month no later than 10 days after the end of the month and in accordance with paragraph (9).

(4) Subject to paragraph (6), a railway industry body whose property or staff have been involved in an accident or incident of a type listed in Schedule 4 within the Channel Tunnel system shall notify the Branch of its occurrence immediately it learns of the occurrence and by the quickest means available.

(5) Subject to paragraph (6), a railway industry body whose property or staff have been involved in an accident or incident of a type listed in Schedule 5 within the Channel Tunnel system shall notify the Branch of its occurrence as soon as is reasonably practicable and in any event within three working days of its occurrence.

(6) The duty in paragraphs (1), (2), (4) and (5) to notify the Branch of an accident or incident involving the death or serious injury of a person in circumstances described in Schedules 1, 2, 4 or 5, respectively, shall not arise where the railway industry body reasonably believes that—

- (a) the death or serious injury of that person was a result of natural causes, assault, suicide or attempted suicide;
- (b) the accident or incident—
  - (i) caused the death of or serious injury to a member of staff; and
  - (ii) did not involve the movement of rolling stock; or
- (c) the accident or incident caused the death or serious injury of a person who at the time of the accident or incident was on railway property involved in the accident or incident without lawful authority.

(7) A notification given under paragraph (1), (2), (4) or (5) shall contain as much of the following information relating to the accident or incident as the railway industry body is reasonably able to provide at the time of the notification—

- (a) the geographical position of the accident or incident and the nearest point of access to that position;
- (b) the date and time of the accident or incident;
- (c) the point of departure and intended destination of any rolling stock involved in the accident or incident;
- (d) brief details of the accident or incident and the sequence of events leading to it;
- (e) in the case of an accident, an estimate of the number of people seriously or fatally injured;
- (f) an estimate of the number of passengers on board any rolling stock involved at the time of the accident or incident;
- (g) the extent of damage caused to any railway, railway property or the environment by the accident or incident;
- (h) the weather conditions at the time of the accident or incident;
- (i) the type, and an estimate of the quantity, of any dangerous goods on board the rolling stock involved at the time of the accident or incident;
- (j) the number of crew on board the rolling stock involved at the time of the accident or incident;
- (k) the name of the railway industry body whose property is involved in the accident or incident;
- (l) the names and roles of staff with responsibility for the movement of rolling stock involved in the accident or incident;
- (m) the vehicle numbers and type of any rolling stock involved;
- (n) details of any emergency service attending the site of the accident or incident; and
- (o) contact details of the person in command or control of the accident or incident site.

(8) The railway industry body that notifies the Branch in accordance with paragraph (1), (2), (4) or (5) shall provide—

- (a) as soon as reasonably practicable after the notification, such of the information referred to in paragraph (7) that it has not supplied with it; and
- (b) within such time as the Branch specifies, such further information about the accident or incident as the Branch may reasonably require.

(9) A notification referred to in paragraph (3) shall contain a list of every occurrence during the month in question and shall specify the date, time and place of each occurrence.

(10) Where the railway industry body does not know the extent of a person's injuries, it shall regard that person as having suffered a serious injury if—

(a) the person has been removed from the site of the accident or incident to a hospital; and

(b) the railway industry body suspects that the person has sustained a serious injury.

(11) In this regulation "staff" means a person engaged in work for the railway industry body where such work was connected with the operation of the railway or railway property involved in the accident or incident at the time of its occurrence.

(12) A railway industry body that fails to notify the Branch of an accident or incident in accordance with paragraphs (1) to (5) and (7) to (9) shall be guilty of an offence.

[920]

Conduct of investigations by the Rail Accident Investigation Branch

5 (1) The Branch shall conduct every investigation of an accident or incident in a manner that will not undermine its independence from—

(a) an infrastructure manager;
(b) a railway undertaking;
(c) a charging body;
(d) an allocation body;
(e) a notified body; or
(f) any other party whose interests might conflict with the tasks of the Branch.

(2) The Branch shall not investigate occurrences other than accidents or incidents if such investigation could undermine its independence from any of the parties referred to in paragraph (1).

(3) The Branch shall make the necessary arrangements to commence an investigation of an accident or incident—

(a) where the accident is a serious accident; or
(b) where it is not a serious accident but is an accident or incident which, under slightly different conditions, might have led to a serious accident and the Branch has determined that it will conduct an investigation,

within seven days of being notified of the accident or incident.

(4) In making a determination under paragraph (3)(b) the Branch shall take into account—

(a) the seriousness of the accident or incident;
(b) whether it forms part of a series of accidents or incidents;
(c) its impact on railway safety;
(d) requests from railway industry bodies, the safety authority, or other member States;
(e) the extent to which an investigation will improve the safety of railways and prevent accidents and incidents; and
(f) any other matter that the Chief Inspector considers to be reasonable in the circumstances.

(5) The Branch may undertake a preliminary examination of the circumstances surrounding an accident or incident to determine—

(a) whether it is a serious accident; or
(b) where it is not a serious accident, whether an investigation is to be conducted.

(6) Within seven days of its determination to investigate an accident or incident the Branch shall provide the European Railway Agency with details of the date, time, place and type of the accident or incident, the number of persons injured or killed and the damage caused as a result of the accident or incident.

(7) Where an accident or incident of a type described in paragraph (3) occurs on or close to a border installation between the United Kingdom and another member State, the Branch—

(a) shall use its best endeavours to agree with the investigating body of the other member State which accident investigating body will conduct the investigation;

(b) shall permit the investigating body of the other member State to participate in an investigation of such accident or incident conducted by the Branch;

(c) shall share the results of the investigation of such accident or incident by the Branch with the investigating body of the other member State; and

(d) may agree to carry out the investigation of the accident or incident in co-operation with the investigating body of the other member State.

(8) Where an accident or incident of a type described in paragraph (3) involves a railway undertaking established and licensed in another member State, the Branch shall invite the investigating body in the other member State to participate in an investigation of that accident or incident.

(9) Where the accident or incident occurs within the part of the Channel Tunnel system which forms part of the United Kingdom and is either a serious accident or one which the Branch has determined it will investigate, the Branch shall invite and permit the rail accident investigating body in France to participate in the investigation of such accident or incident.

(10) During the course of its investigation, the Branch shall—

(a) keep the persons referred to in regulation 13(2)(b) informed of its progress; and

(b) so far as is reasonably practicable, take account of opinions relating to the investigation expressed by such persons.

(11) The Chief Inspector shall determine the extent of, and the procedure to be followed in carrying out, an investigation conducted by the Branch or by a person appointed pursuant to regulation 6(1); and in making this determination he shall take into account the principles and the objectives of articles 20 and 22 of the Safety Directive.

(12) The Branch shall conclude its examination at the site of an accident or incident in the shortest possible time in order to enable the infrastructure that is closed as a result of the accident or incident to be restored and opened to railway services as soon as possible.

(13) The Chief Inspector may discontinue an investigation conducted by the Branch at any time and shall publish his reasons for doing so.

(14) The Branch may undertake an investigation into the circumstances of an accident or incident where it has previously determined that no investigation will be conducted.

[921]

Persons conducting, participating in or assisting with an investigation by the Rail Accident Investigation Branch

6 (1) The Chief Inspector may appoint a person who is not an inspector to conduct or participate in an investigation by the Branch.

(2) A person appointed under paragraph (1) may exercise such powers of an inspector as are necessary to enable him to perform his functions under the terms of his appointment.

(3) In relation to an investigation of an accident or incident that the Branch is conducting, the Chief Inspector may—

(a) request assistance from a constable, the safety authority, any public body or any other person acting under a power conferred on him by an enactment, or a constable, a procurator fiscal or the Lord Advocate acting under a power conferred on him at common law in Scotland, or from an accident investigating body of another member State or the European Railway Agency; or

(b) request assistance (including assistance with the retrieval, delivery, storage, disposal or destruction of evidence) from a person other than a person mentioned in sub-paragraph (a),

at such times and in such manner as the Chief Inspector may reasonably determine.

(4) Where the Chief Inspector reasonably requests assistance from a person referred to in sub-paragraph (3)(b), that person shall assist him.

(5) Subject to paragraph (6) the Secretary of State may pay reasonable compensation to a person who assists the Chief Inspector pursuant to paragraph (3).

(6) Where a person who assists the Chief Inspector pursuant to paragraph (3) is—

(a) an owner of railway property, a railway industry body, or a manufacturer or supplier of equipment, components or services to an owner of railway property or to a railway industry body, whose property or staff have been involved in the accident or incident being investigated; and

(b) under a statutory duty or other legally enforceable requirement to investigate the causes of the accident or incident, including any duty or other legally enforceable requirement arising by virtue of his being authorised to control infrastructure or operate trains or stations,

in determining whether or not to pay compensation, the Secretary of State shall take account of whether the assistance concerned any matter to which the duty or other legally enforceable requirement to investigate referred to in sub-paragraph (b) relates.

(7) A person who fails to assist an inspector when required to do so in accordance with paragraph (4) shall be guilty of an offence.

[922]

Access to the site of an accident or incident

7 (1) Subject to paragraph (2), no person other than an inspector or a person appointed under regulation 6(1) shall—

(a) have access to the site of an accident or incident of a type described in Schedules 1 or 4, including the rolling stock, infrastructure or traffic control and signalling systems involved in such accident or incident; or

(b) remove from or interfere with, or cause to be removed from or interfered with, anything at the site of an accident or incident of a type described in Schedules 1 or 4,

without the consent of an inspector until such time as the Branch has concluded its examination or removal of evidence at the site or determined that it will not conduct an investigation.

(2) A person may have access to, or remove anything described in paragraph (1), only in so far as may be necessary for the purpose of—

(a) saving life or preventing further injury or suffering;

(b) preventing further damage or destruction;

(c) preventing danger, including from dangerous goods;

(d) protecting the site; or

(e) exercising a power conferred on that person by an enactment, or a power conferred on a constable, a procurator fiscal or the Lord Advocate at common law in Scotland.

(3) Subject to regulation 17 where a constable, the safety authority or any other person intends to enter a site referred to in paragraph (1) in exercise of a power conferred on him by an enactment—

(a) he shall, where practicable, notify an inspector of his intention to do so, together with details of any action he proposes to take while on the site; and

(b) where it is not practicable to notify an inspector in accordance with sub-paragraph (a), he shall inform an inspector as soon as practicable after he has entered the site and provide details of any action he has taken while on the site.

(4) In determining whether it is practicable to notify an inspector under paragraph (3)(a) a person intending to enter a site referred to in paragraph (1) shall have regard to whether the delay that would occur by giving such notification would, or would be likely to, affect adversely the result sought to be obtained from the exercise of his power.

(5) Where an inspector receives notification under paragraph (3)(a) of action proposed by a person referred to in paragraph (3) and a question arises as to the desirability of the proposed action to be taken, the inspector shall refer the question without delay to the Chief Inspector or an inspector acting on behalf of the Chief Inspector for determination pursuant to section 8(6) of the 2003 Act.

(6) A person who fails to comply with the requirements of paragraph (1) shall be guilty of an offence.

[923]

Preservation of evidence

8 (1) For the purpose of enabling him to carry out an investigation into an accident or incident in the most efficient way and within the shortest time, an inspector may, where appropriate in cooperation with the authorities responsible for the judicial inquiry, require a person to supply a list of all evidence relating to the accident or incident which is in his possession or control.

(2) Subject to paragraph (3) and regulation 17, a constable, the safety authority or any other person acting in exercise of a power conferred on him by an enactment, who is investigating an accident or incident shall—

- (a) preserve any evidence that he obtains in the course of his investigation into an accident or incident;
- (b) where practicable, notify an inspector of his intention to collect, examine or analyse evidence, or interview a witness, for his investigation;
- (c) where it is not practicable to notify an inspector in accordance with sub-paragraph (b), inform an inspector as soon as practicable after he has taken that action;
- (d) provide to the Branch details of the action he has taken under this paragraph; and
- (e) upon request by the Branch, provide the Branch with access to or copies of any evidence he has taken or information he has obtained under this paragraph.

(3) Paragraph (2) shall apply until such time as the Branch has concluded its investigation, no longer requires the evidence referred to in paragraph (2) or has determined that it will not conduct an investigation.

(4) In determining whether it is practicable to notify an inspector under paragraph (2)(b) a person intending to collect, examine or analyse evidence or interview a witness for his investigation pursuant to paragraph (2)(b) shall have regard to whether the delay that would occur by giving such notification would, or would be likely to, adversely affect the result sought to be obtained from the exercise of his power.

(5) Where an inspector receives notification under paragraph (2)(b) of action proposed by a person referred to in paragraph (2) and a question arises as to the desirability of the proposed action the inspector shall refer the question without delay to the Chief Inspector or an inspector acting on behalf of the Chief Inspector for determination pursuant to section 8(6) of the 2003 Act.

(6) An owner of railway property, a railway industry body, or a manufacturer or supplier of equipment, components or services to an owner of railway property or to a railway industry body, shall preserve all evidence over which he has control and—

- (a) which is, or which he reasonably considers may be, relevant to an investigation of an accident or incident of a type described in Schedules 1 or 4 by the Branch; or
- (b) that the Branch directs him to preserve,

until the Branch has concluded its investigation, no longer requires the evidence or has determined that it will not conduct an investigation.

(7) A person who contravenes paragraph (6) shall be guilty of an offence.

[924]

Use of evidence

9 (1) Except in so far as paragraph (2) or (3) applies, an owner of railway property, a railway industry body, or a manufacturer or supplier of equipment, components or services to an owner of railway property or to a railway industry body, shall not move or use any evidence that is, or may become, relevant to an investigation by the Branch except where it is necessary to do so for the purpose of—

- (a) saving life or preventing further injury or suffering;
- (b) preventing further damage or destruction;
- (c) preventing danger, including from dangerous goods; or

(d) protecting the site,

until the Branch has concluded its investigation, no longer requires the evidence or has determined that it will not conduct an investigation.

(2) An owner of railway property, a railway industry body, or a manufacturer or supplier of equipment, components or services to an owner of railway property or a railway industry body, may—

(a) with the consent of the Branch, move or use evidence relating to an accident or incident of a type described in Schedules 1 or 4; and

(b) unless the Branch gives notice to the contrary, move or use evidence relevant to an accident or incident of a type described in Schedules 2, 3 or 5 provided that there is no practicable alternative to the movement or use of that evidence and such movement or use is essential for the safe operation of the railway.

(3) An owner of railway property, a railway industry body, or a manufacturer or supplier of equipment, components or services to an owner of railway property or a railway industry body who moves or uses evidence pursuant to paragraph (2) shall make and retain a record of the condition, position and location of the evidence before it was moved or used and shall supply that record on demand to the Branch.

(4) Subject to paragraph (5), in the course of an investigation into an accident or incident, an inspector or a person appointed under regulation 6(1) may, for the purpose of examining or analysing an article, dismantle or alter the composition of it, whether or not such dismantling or altering has the effect of destroying it

(5) Where an inspector or a person appointed under regulation 6(1) decides to dismantle or alter the composition of an article under paragraph (4), and the inspector or person appointed under regulation 6(1) has reason to believe that a constable, the safety authority or any other person exercising a power conferred on him by an enactment, or a constable, a procurator fiscal or the Lord Advocate exercising a power conferred on him at common law in Scotland, would be entitled to analyse or examine that article for the purpose of his own investigation into that accident or incident, the inspector or person appointed under regulation 6(1) shall—

(a) before commencing such dismantling or alteration, give notice to those persons of his intention to do so;

(b) permit those persons to be present during such examination or analysis;

(c) consider any reasonable representations those persons may make as to the impact such dismantling or alteration may have on their own investigation; and

(d) provide those persons with access to all records and reports relating to the examination or analysis.

(6) Where an inspector or a person appointed under regulation 6(1) considers that it would not be detrimental to an investigation he may—

(a) inform a person of his intention to analyse or examine an article; or

(b) permit a person to be present during the analysis or examination.

(7) A person other than a person referred to in paragraph (5) whom the Branch allows to be present during an analysis or examination shall not disclose to anyone except a constable, the safety authority or any other person acting under a power conferred on him by an enactment, or to a constable, a procurator fiscal or the Lord Advocate acting under a power conferred on him at common law in Scotland, any information he obtains in connection with that analysis or examination without the consent of the Chief Inspector.

(8) The Branch may retain any evidence that it no longer requires for the purposes of the investigation for which it was obtained if that evidence may be required for the purposes of another investigation being conducted by the Branch.

(9) The Branch shall release to a constable, the safety authority or any other person exercising a power conferred on him by an enactment, or to a constable, a procurator fiscal or the Lord Advocate acting under a power conferred on him at common law in Scotland, any evidence that it no longer requires, where—

(a) the Branch has reason to believe that person would be entitled to collect that evidence for the purpose of his own investigation; and

(b) that evidence—

(i) is not prohibited from being disclosed by regulation 10(2) or any other enactment; or

(ii) is not evidence to which regulation 10(3) applies.

(10) The Branch shall release to its owner evidence that it no longer requires for the purposes of the investigation for which it was obtained or which it is not retaining under paragraph (8) and which the Branch is not required to release to a person referred to in paragraph (9) provided that before it does so the Branch shall consult with any person known to it to be leading an investigation under statutory or common law powers into the accident or incident in respect of which the evidence was obtained by the Branch.

(11) Where evidence is released to the owner pursuant to paragraph (10), the owner shall be responsible for the storage, destruction or disposal of it from the date of its release.

(12) Before releasing evidence under paragraphs (9) or (10) the Branch shall give seven days notice of its intention to do so to the intended recipient of such evidence.

(13) An owner of railway property, a railway industry body, or a manufacturer or supplier of equipment, components or services to an owner of railway property or to a railway industry body, that moves or uses evidence relating to an accident or incident other than for a purpose specified in paragraph (1) shall be guilty of an offence unless the movement or use of the evidence by that body is in compliance with paragraph (2).

(14) An owner of railway property, a railway industry body, or a manufacturer or supplier of equipment, components or services to an owner of railway property or to a railway industry body, that—

(a) moves or uses evidence that is relevant to an accident or incident of a type described in Schedule 1 or 4 without the consent of the Branch under paragraph (2)(a); or

(b) moves or uses evidence that is relevant to an accident or incident of a type described in Schedule 2, 3 or 5 where the Branch has given notice to the contrary under paragraph (2)(b),

shall be guilty of an offence unless that movement or use of such evidence is for a purpose specified in paragraph (1).

(15) An owner of railway property, a railway industry body, or a manufacturer or supplier of equipment, components or services to an owner of railway property or a railway industry body, that fails to make and retain a record as required by paragraph (3) shall be guilty of an offence.

(16) A person who discloses information that he obtains during an analysis or examination in contravention of paragraph (7) shall be guilty of an offence.

[925]

Disclosure of evidence

10 (1) Except as provided in paragraphs (2) and (3) the Branch—

(a) may publish or make available for inspection any evidence or information it may acquire during the course of an investigation where such disclosure would not obstruct it in its general aims contained in section 4 of the 2003 Act; and

(b) shall provide to a constable or the safety authority investigating an accident or incident, or any other person exercising a power conferred on him by an enactment, or to a constable, a procurator fiscal or the Lord Advocate exercising a power conferred on him at common law in Scotland to investigate an accident or incident, access to and copies of any evidence obtained by the Branch in the course of an investigation of that accident or incident, but only where the recipient would be entitled by an enactment, or in Scotland at common law, to collect that evidence for the purpose of his own investigation.

(2) Except by order of a relevant court and subject to paragraph (7) the Branch shall not disclose to anyone—

(a) a statement or declaration provided to the Branch or any recording or other note or record relating to such statement or declaration unless the person who has provided such statement, declaration, recording note or record consents to its disclosure;

(b) the name, address or other information relating to a person—

(i) who has provided to the Branch a statement or declaration or other note or record relating to such statement or declaration; or

(ii) who has indicated to an inspector or person appointed under regulation 6(1) that he intends to provide a statement or declaration or other note or record to the Branch,

unless that person consents to such disclosure; or

(c) a medical record relating to a person involved in the accident or incident.

(3) Except by order of a relevant court and subject to paragraph (7), the Branch shall not be required to disclose to anyone—

(a) personal information relating to a person involved in the accident or incident or with the investigation of that accident or incident (other than personal information protected by paragraph (2));

(b) the opinion of an inspector or a person appointed under regulation 6(1) which is unsubstantiated by evidence;

(c) the notes made by an inspector or person appointed under regulation 6(1), whether written or held electronically;

(d) any trade secret or other information, the release of which, in the opinion of the Chief Inspector would, or would be likely to, prejudice the commercial interests of the person holding it; or

(e) working documents of the Branch.

(4) Except by order of a relevant court a person who assists the Branch under regulation 6(1), 6(3)(b) or 15(2)(b) shall not disclose to anyone any of the evidence or information described in paragraphs (2) or (3) which the Branch is precluded from disclosing save by order of a relevant court. This paragraph shall similarly apply to evidence or information provided to such a person if it is such that, if provided to the Branch, would be subject to paragraphs (2) or (3).

(5) No order may be made under paragraphs (2), (3) or (4) unless the court is satisfied that disclosure is in the public interest, having regard in particular to any adverse impact such disclosure may have on the investigation by the Branch to which the evidence or information relates, upon any future investigation and upon public safety.

(6) Paragraphs (2)(a) and (b) shall not be construed as placing a duty on the Branch to seek consent to disclose from a person referred to in those sub-paragraphs or compelling the Branch to disclose where the Branch has not sought consent at the time of the making of the statement.

(7) Nothing in paragraphs (2) or (3) shall preclude the Branch from—

(a) publishing the opinion of a person in a report of the accident or incident in so far as it is relevant to the conclusions in the report;

(b) publishing in a report of the accident or incident information based on matters contained in a statement, declaration, recording or other note referred to in paragraph (2)(a) or in a medical record referred to in paragraph (2)(c);

(c) providing a person who makes a statement or declaration with a copy of such statement or declaration;

(d) sharing the results of the investigation of an accident or incident with an investigating body in another member State;

(e) disclosing or discussing information based on a matter contained in a statement, declaration, recording, or other note it has obtained during the course of an investigation with a person providing assistance, evidence or information to the Branch; or

(f) disclosing the name or address of a person to a person providing assistance, evidence or information to the Branch but only in so far as is necessary for the purpose of obtaining evidence or information in furtherance of the Branch's investigation.

(8) A person who assists the Branch under regulation 6(1), 6(3)(b) or 15(2)(b) shall not disclose to anyone other than a constable, the safety authority or any other person exercising a power conferred on him by an enactment, or a constable, a procurator fiscal or the Lord Advocate exercising a power conferred on him at common law in Scotland, evidence or any other information, to which paragraph (4) does not apply,

that he acquires about an investigation through the giving of such assistance without the consent of the Chief Inspector or an inspector acting on behalf of the Chief Inspector.

(9) A person who discloses evidence or information in contravention of paragraph (2), (4) or (8) shall be guilty of an offence.

(10) In this regulation "relevant court" means—

- (a) the Crown Court or High Court in England and Wales or Northern Ireland; or
- (b) the Court of Session or the High Court of Justiciary in Scotland.

[926]

Reports etc of accidents and incidents investigated by the Rail Accident Investigation Branch

11 (1) Subject to the requirements in the following paragraphs the Branch may at any time provide a report (including an interim report), advice, recommendations or information relating to an accident or incident to such persons, and in such form and in such manner, as the Chief Inspector considers appropriate in the circumstances, taking account of—

- (a) the nature and seriousness of the accident or incident;
- (b) the speed at which the report, advice, recommendations or information needs to be given or acted upon;
- (c) the stage which the investigation has reached; and
- (d) the relevance or importance of the examination or investigation findings.

(2) Upon the conclusion of an investigation conducted by the Branch into a serious accident, or an accident or incident which under slightly different conditions might have led to a serious accident, the Branch shall report to the Secretary of State and publish a final report—

- (a) in the shortest time possible and normally not later than twelve months after the date of the occurrence; and
- (b) shall include in it such of the information described in Schedule 6 as is relevant to the accident or incident.

(3) Upon the conclusion of an investigation conducted by the Branch, other than one to which paragraph (2) applies, the Branch shall report to the Secretary of State and publish a report in such form as may be determined by the Chief Inspector.

(4) A report published under this regulation may relate to more than one accident or incident.

(5) In relation to a report referred to in paragraph (2), the Branch shall provide a copy of the report to the European Railway Agency and to every person referred to in regulation 13(2).

[927]

Recommendations of the Rail Accident Investigation Branch

12 (1) The Branch shall address a recommendation contained in a report prepared under regulation 11(2) or (3)—

- (a) to the safety authority; and
- (b) to such other member State, public body or authority as it considers it appropriate to do so by reason of the character of the recommendation.

(2) A public body or authority to whom a recommendation is addressed under paragraph (1) shall, in relation to that recommendation—

- (a) ensure that the recommendation is duly taken into consideration and where appropriate acted upon;
- (b) report to the Branch without undue delay or within such other period, not exceeding twelve months, as may be agreed with the Chief Inspector—
  - (i) giving full details of any measure taken to implement the recommendation;
  - (ii) giving full details of any proposed measure to implement the recommendation and the proposed timetable for securing that implementation; or

(iii) giving a full explanation as to why the recommendation is not to be the subject of measures to be taken to implement it; and

(c) give notice to the Branch if at any time the information provided to the Branch pursuant to sub-paragraph (b) is rendered inaccurate.

(3) The requirement to report under paragraph (2)(b) or to give notice under paragraph (2)(c) shall only apply to the extent that it is reasonably practicable for the authority that is required to report to have the specified information or for it to become aware that the information has been rendered inaccurate.

(4) Having regard to the nature of a recommendation addressed to it, the safety authority may require any person, within such period as the safety authority may [reasonably] determine, to—

(a) take that recommendation into consideration and where appropriate act upon it;

(b) send to the safety authority—

(i) full details of any measure that body has taken to implement the recommendation;

(ii) full details of any measure proposed by that body to implement the recommendation and the proposed timetable for securing that implementation; and

(iii) a full explanation as to why the recommendation is not to be the subject of a measure to be taken by that body to implement the recommendation; and

(c) give notice to the safety authority if at any time any information provided to the safety authority under sub-paragraph (b)(ii) above is rendered inaccurate.

(5) A person who fails to comply with a requirement imposed on him by the safety authority in accordance with paragraph (4) shall be guilty of an offence.

NOTES

Amendment Para (4): word in square brackets inserted by SI 2005/3261.

[928]

Duty of the Rail Accident Investigation Branch to consider representations

13 (1) Before publishing a report under regulations 11(2) or (3) the Branch shall serve a notice in writing on every person referred to in paragraph (2) of its intention to publish the report, supply a copy of the report or the relevant part of the report to each person and invite each person to make representations to the Branch in response to its contents.

(2) The persons referred to in paragraph (1) are—

(a) any person whose reputation the Branch considers may be adversely affected by a report, or, if that person is deceased, such person as appears to the Chief Inspector, at the time he proposes to serve notice pursuant to paragraph (1), as best able to represent the interest and reputation of the deceased in the matter; and

(b) any of the following persons whom the Branch considers to be relevant—

(i) the owner of railway property;

(ii) a railway industry body, or a manufacturer or supplier of equipment, components or services to an owner of railway property or a railway industry body;

(iii) the safety authority;

(iv) victims and their relatives;

(v) owners of damaged property;

(vi) the emergency services involved;

(vii) representatives of staff and users of the railways; and

(viii) a person falling within the descriptions in sub-paragraphs (b)(i) to (vii) in other member States.

(3) A person upon whom notice is served under paragraph (1) may make representations in response to the report within fourteen days from service of the notice or within such longer period as may be determined by the Chief Inspector.

(4) The Branch shall consider any representations it receives under paragraph (3) and may amend the report in consequence of any such representation.

(5) A person to whom a report or part of a report has been supplied under paragraph (1) shall not disclose its contents without the permission of the Branch.

(6) A person who discloses the contents of a report in contravention of paragraph (5) shall be guilty of an offence.

[929]

Annual report of the Chief Inspector

14 (1) The Chief Inspector shall publish a report on the activities of the Branch—

(a) on or before 30th September 2006 in respect of the period from the coming into force of these Regulations to 31st December 2005; and

(b) thereafter on or before 30th September each year in respect of the previous calendar year.

(2) Every report under paragraph (1) shall contain in respect of the period to which it relates—

(a) a summary of the investigations conducted by the Branch;

(b) a list of the recommendations issued; and

(c) details of the measures that have been reported to the Branch as having been taken in response to its recommendations.

(3) A report may contain such other information relating to the activities and aims of the Branch specified in section 4 of the 2003 Act as the Chief Inspector may determine.

(4) The Branch shall send to the European Railway Agency a copy of each report published under paragraph (1).

[930]

Miscellaneous functions

15 (1) The Branch may conduct studies into, monitor and analyse any matter it considers may be relevant to the effective investigation of accidents or incidents including—

(a) the responses of those persons to whom the recommendations of the Branch are addressed;

(b) technological and other developments; and

(c) statistics and trends relating to the railway industry including those relating to accidents and incidents.

(2) In order to assist the Branch in carrying out the activities described in paragraph (1), the Chief Inspector may request assistance or information from—

(a) a constable, the safety authority, any public body or any other person exercising a power conferred on him by an enactment, or a constable, a procurator fiscal or the Lord Advocate exercising a power conferred on him at common law in Scotland, an accident investigating body of another member State or the European Railway Agency; or

(b) any other person,

at times and in a manner the Chief Inspector may reasonably determine.

(3) The Secretary of State may pay reasonable compensation to a person who assists the Chief Inspector pursuant to paragraph (2).

(4) The Chief Inspector may arrange for the publication, in such form and in such manner as he considers appropriate, of such information and advice as is relevant to the general aims of the Branch referred to in section 4 of the 2003 Act.

(5) The Branch shall use its best endeavours to conduct an active exchange of information and views with the investigation bodies established in other member States under the Safety Directive for the purpose of—

(a) developing common investigation methods;

(b) drawing up common principles for the follow-up of safety recommendations; or

(c) adapting to the development of technical and scientific progress.

[931]

Offences

16 (1) A person guilty of an offence under regulation 4(12), 7(6), 8(7) and 9(13) to 9(16) shall be liable—

(a) on summary conviction to imprisonment for a term not exceeding six months, or to a fine not exceeding £20,000, or both; and
(b) on conviction on indictment, to imprisonment for a term not exceeding six months, or a fine, or both.

(2) A person guilty of an offence under regulation 6(7) shall be liable—

(a) on summary conviction to a fine not exceeding £20,000; and
(b) on conviction on indictment to a fine.

(3) A person guilty of an offence under regulation 10(9), 12(5) or 13(6) shall be liable on summary conviction to a fine not exceeding level 5 on the standard scale.

[932]

17 (*Applies to Scotland only.*)

SCHEDULE 1
TYPES OF ACCIDENTS AND INCIDENTS OTHER THAN ANY OCCURRING WITHIN THE CHANNEL TUNNEL SYSTEM WHICH MUST BE NOTIFIED TO THE RAIL ACCIDENT INVESTIGATION BRANCH IMMEDIATELY AND BY THE QUICKEST MEANS AVAILABLE

Regulation 4(1)

1 An accident resulting in the death of a person or the serious injury of two or more persons.

2 An accident on a level crossing involving rolling stock, resulting in the death of a person or serious injury to a person.

3 A collision between rolling stock on a running line which causes damage or blocks a running line that was open to railway traffic at the time of the collision.

4 A derailment of rolling stock on a running line that was open to railway traffic at the time of the derailment, or which blocks a running line that was open to railway traffic at the time of the derailment.

5 A collision of rolling stock with an arrestor mechanism or buffer stop, other than in a siding, that causes damage to the rolling stock.

6 An accident involving the release or combustion of dangerous goods being carried on rolling stock that necessitates the evacuation of the area.

7 An accident or incident that is likely to result in suspension of a railway service for a period in excess of 6 hours.

8 An accident that causes extensive damage to rolling stock, the infrastructure or the environment.

9 An accident or incident which under slightly different conditions might have led to a death, serious injury or extensive damage to rolling stock, the infrastructure or the environment.

[933]

SCHEDULE 2
TYPES OF ACCIDENTS AND INCIDENTS OTHER THAN ANY OCCURRING WITHIN THE CHANNEL TUNNEL SYSTEM WHICH MUST BE NOTIFIED TO THE RAIL ACCIDENT INVESTIGATION BRANCH AS SOON AS REASONABLY PRACTICABLE AND IN ANY EVENT WITHIN THREE WORKING DAYS OF OCCURRENCE

Regulation 4(2)

1 A collision of rolling stock with an object on or adjacent to a running line which under slightly different conditions might have caused a derailment, except—

(a) if it is notifiable under regulation 4(1);
(b) if the object was an animal; or
(c) where the obstruction was caused by an obvious act of vandalism.

2 An accident resulting in the serious injury of one person only except if it is notifiable under regulation 4(1).

3 An obstruction of, or damage to, track, caused by a road vehicle encroaching onto a running line, except when the obstruction or damage occurs on a part of a tramway track laid along a carriageway.

4 Any unintended division of a train or a tramcar.

5 The failure of rolling stock on the track caused by—

(a) the failure of an axle;
(b) the failure of a wheel or tyre, including a tyre loose on its wheel; or
(c) a fire or severe electrical arcing or fusing, whether or not extinguished by a fire-fighting service.

6 The failure of a cable or the fastening thereof of the winding plant or other equipment involved in working a railway operated by a cable haulage system.

[934]

SCHEDULE 3
TYPES OF ACCIDENTS AND INCIDENTS OTHER THAN ANY OCCURRING WITHIN THE CHANNEL TUNNEL SYSTEM WHICH MUST BE NOTIFIED TO THE RAIL ACCIDENT INVESTIGATION BRANCH NO LATER THAN TEN DAYS AFTER THE END OF THE MONTH IN WHICH THE ACCIDENT OR INCIDENT OCCURRED

Regulation 4(3)

1 The failure of equipment at a level crossing which reduces the level of safety on the railway.

2 The failure of a rail, including a rack rail, on a running line whether by a complete fracture through its cross section, or by the buckling or detachment of a piece of rail and which necessitates an immediate closure of that running line or speed reduction on that running line.

3 The failure of a structure on railway property, including a tunnel, bridge, viaduct, culvert, railway cutting, embankment, station, signal or fixed electrical equipment which under slightly different circumstances may have led to a serious accident or which otherwise reduces the level of railway safety.

4 A failure in the signalling system which reduces the level of railway safety.

5 Rolling stock passing a railway signal displaying a stop aspect, unless either the driver had been given authority to pass the signal or the signal did not display in sufficient time to enable the driver to stop safely at the signal.

6 A collision between a tramcar and a road vehicle on a part of a tramway laid along a carriageway.

[935]

SCHEDULE 4
TYPES OF ACCIDENTS AND INCIDENTS OCCURRING WITHIN THE CHANNEL TUNNEL SYSTEM THAT MUST BE NOTIFIED TO THE RAIL ACCIDENT INVESTIGATION BRANCH IMMEDIATELY AND BY THE QUICKEST MEANS AVAILABLE

Regulation 4(4)

1 An accident resulting in death or serious injury to a person.

2 A derailment of rolling stock which causes damage to or blocks a running line.

3 A collision that occurs on any line other than a siding, between rolling stock and—

(a) other rolling stock;
(b) an object capable of causing damage to or derailment of the rolling stock; or
(c) a buffer stop.

4 An accident that causes extensive damage to rolling stock, the infrastructure or environment.

5 A collision on a level crossing involving a vehicle or pedestrian and rolling stock, whether or not a person suffers death or injury.

6 An accident involving the release or combustion of dangerous goods that necessitates the evacuation of a tunnel or part of the terminal.

7 Fire necessitating evacuation of passengers from one part of a train to another part of the same train or intervention of the fire brigade.

8 An accident or incident leading to the evacuation of passengers from a train.

9 Unauthorised passing of a closed marker or signal.

10 Runaway train on a line.

11 An accident or incident which, under slightly different conditions might have led to serious injuries or extensive damage to rolling stock, the infrastructure or the environment.

[936]

SCHEDULE 5
TYPES OF ACCIDENTS AND INCIDENTS OCCURRING WITHIN THE CHANNEL TUNNEL SYSTEM THAT MUST BE NOTIFIED TO THE RAIL ACCIDENT INVESTIGATION BRANCH AS SOON AS PRACTICABLE AND IN ANY EVENT WITHIN THREE WORKING DAYS OF OCCURRENCE

Regulation 4(5)

1 A fire, arcing or fusing which adversely affects the functioning of signalling, catenary or rolling stock control equipment.

2 A fire that results in the suspension of railway services or closure of a part of railway property affecting the track, for a period of more than 1 hour.

3 Any unintended division of a train, or breakage of coupling.

4 The failure of rolling stock on the track caused by—

(a) the failure or seizing of an axle;
(b) the failure of a wheel or tyre, including a tyre loose on its wheel;
(c) the failure of brakes on a train; or
(d) a fire or severe electrical arcing or fusing on rolling stock, whether or not extinguished by a fire-fighting service.

5 A broken rail, major failure of track equipment (weld, fastenings, etc) or track deformation.

6 Any significant safety related breakdown or any serious destruction or collapse of equipment, installations or structures.

7 Any failure in the signalling system, or any other safety system, which endangers or potentially endangers the safe operation of the railway.

8 Submersion of track that necessitates its closure.

9 Unscheduled stopping of a train in a tunnel for more than 30 minutes.

10 Damage to track caused by rolling stock or a dragging object.

11 Spillage of fuel from a road vehicle being carried on a shuttle train.

12 A breach of the requirements for the transport of dangerous goods contained or referred to in the Carriage of Dangerous Goods and Use of Transportable Pressure Equipment Regulations [2007].

13 Any incident during which installations, equipment or rolling stock come into unintended contact with live overhead power lines with a voltage in excess of 200 volts.

NOTES
Amendment Para 12: year "2007" in square brackets substituted by SI 2007/1573 (revoked).
Carriage of Dangerous Goods and Use of Transportable Pressure Equipment Regulations 2007 SI 2007/1573. Revoked and replaced by SI 2009/1348, in the title Health and Safety at Work.

[937]

SCHEDULE 6
PRINCIPAL CONTENT OF AN ACCIDENT AND INCIDENT INVESTIGATION REPORT

Regulation 11(2)

Summary

1 The summary shall contain a short description of the occurrence, when and where it took place and its consequences. It shall state the direct causes as well as contributing factors and underlying causes established by the investigation. The main recommendations shall be quoted and information shall be given on the addressees.

Immediate facts of the occurrence

2 (1) The occurrence—

date, exact time and location of the occurrence;
description of the events and the accident site including the efforts of the rescue and emergency services;
the decision to establish an investigation, the composition of the team of investigators and the conduct of the investigation.

(2) The background to the occurrence—

staff and contractors involved and other parties and witnesses;
the trains and their composition including the registration numbers of the items of rolling stock involved;
the description of the infrastructure and signalling system – track types, switches, interlocking, signals, train protection;
means of communication;
works carried out at or in the vicinity of the site;
trigger of the railway emergency plan and its chain of events;
trigger of the emergency plan of the public rescue services, the police and the medical services and its chain of events.

(3) Fatalities, injuries and material damage—

passengers and third parties, staff, including contractors;
cargo, luggage and other property;
rolling stock, infrastructure and the environment.

(4) External circumstances—

weather conditions and geographical references.

Record of investigations and inquiries

3 (1) Summary of testimonies (subject to the protection of identity of the persons)—

railway staff, including contractors;
other witnesses.

(2) The safety management system—

the framework organisation and how orders are given and carried out;
requirements on staff and how they are enforced;
routines for internal checks and audits and their results;
interface between different actors involved with the infrastructure.

(3) Rules and regulations—

relevant Community and national rules and regulations;
other rules such as operating rules, local instructions, staff requirements, maintenance prescriptions and applicable standards.

(4) Functioning of rolling stock and technical installations—

signalling and control command system, including registration from automatic data recorders;
infrastructure;
communications equipment;
rolling stock, including registration from automatic data recorders.

(5) Documentation on the operating system—

measures taken by staff for traffic control and signalling;
exchange of verbal messages in connection with the occurrence, including documentation from recordings;
measures taken to protect and safeguard the site of the occurrence.

(6) Man-machine-organisation interface—

working time applied to the staff involved;
medical and personal circumstances with influence on the occurrence, including existence of physical or psychological stress;
design of equipment with impact on man-machine interface.

(7) Previous occurrences of a similar character.

Analysis and conclusions

4 (1) Final account of the event chain—

establishing the conclusions on the occurrence, based on the facts established in paragraph 3.

(2) Discussion—

analysis of the facts established in paragraph 3 with the aim of drawing conclusions as to the causes of the occurrence and the performance of the rescue services.

(3) Conclusions—

direct and immediate causes of the occurrence including contributory factors relating to actions taken by persons involved or the condition of rolling stock or technical installations;
underlying causes relating to skills, procedures and maintenance;
root causes relating to the regulatory framework conditions and application of the safety management system.

(4) Additional observations—

deficiencies and shortcomings established during the investigation, but without relevance to the conclusions on causes.

(5) Measures that have been taken—

Record of measures already taken or adopted as a consequence of the occurrence.

(6) Recommendations.

[938]

RAILWAYS (CONVENTION ON INTERNATIONAL CARRIAGE BY RAIL) REGULATIONS 2005
SI 2005/2092

Authority Made by the Secretary of State for Transport under the Railways and Transport Safety Act 2003, s 103, Sch 6, paras 2(a)–(f), (o), (p), 3(1), (2)(a), (b), 4(a)–(d), 7(1), (2)(a), (b), 8(1), (2), 9(1), (2)(a).
Date made 26 July 2005.
Commencement 1 July 2006, being the date on which the Protocol signed at Vilnius on 3 June 1999 to modify the Convention concerning International Carriage by Rail (COTIF) of 9 May 1980 entered into force in respect of the United Kingdom; see the *London, Edinburgh* and *Belfast Gazettes*, 3 July 2006.
Summary These regulations provide that the Protocol signed at Vilnius on 3 June 1999 to modify the Convention concerning International Carriage by Rail (COTIF) of 9 May 1980 is to have the force of law following its ratification by, and entry into force for, the United Kingdom.

The regulations repeal and largely replace the International Transport Conventions Act 1983, ss 1–8, 11(3), (4), Sch 1. They amend the Civil Jurisdiction and Judgments Act 1982, ss 31(3), 32(4), the Contracts (Rights of Third Parties) Act 1999, s 6(8)(a), and other enactments relating to Scotland only. They also revoke the International Transport Conventions Act 1983 (Certification of Commencement of Convention) Order 1985, SI 1985/612, the International Transport Conventions Act 1983 (Amendment) Order 1992, SI 1992/237, and the International Transport Conventions Act 1983 (Amendment) Order 1994, SI 1994/1907, and amend SI 2000/128, in the title Health and Safety at Work (and amended SI 2002/1689 (revoked)).

[939]

BUS LANE CONTRAVENTIONS (PENALTY CHARGES, ADJUDICATION AND ENFORCEMENT) (ENGLAND) REGULATIONS 2005
SI 2005/2757

Authority Made by the Secretary of State for Transport under the Transport Act 2000, ss 144(1), (2), (8)–(10), 160, and by the Lord Chancellor under ss 144(11), (12), 160 of the 2000 Act, in so far as the regulations relate to the notification, adjudication and enforcement of penalty charges. S 144 of the 2000 Act is repealed in relation to England by the Traffic Management Act 2004, s 98, Sch 12, Pt 1, as from a day to be appointed by order under s 99(1) thereof.
Date made 6 October 2005.
Commencement 1 November 2005; see reg 1(1).
Amendment Printed as amended by SI 2008/2683.
Interpretation See reg 2. See also the Transport Act 2000, s 144(14).
General These regulations, which apply only to England exclusive of Greater London, make provision for the enforcement of bus lane contraventions by local authorities which are approved local authorities for the purposes of the Transport Act 2000, s 144. They authorise the imposition of a penalty charge in respect of a bus lane contravention only on the basis of a record produced by an approved device. Orders under s 144 specifying the names of local authorities which are approved local authorities are treated as local and outside the scope of this work. (S 144 of the 2000 Act is repealed in relation to England by the Traffic Management Act 2004, s 98, Sch 12, Pt 1, as from a day to be appointed by order under s 99(1) thereof.)
Approved devices SI 2005/2756 (made under the Transport Act 2000, ss 144(14), 160(1) and in force on 1 November 2005) provides that a device which is of a description specified in the order is an approved device in England for the purposes of regulations under the Transport Act 2000, s 144.

[940]

PART 1
PRELIMINARY

Citation, commencement and application

1 (1) These Regulations may be cited as the Bus Lane Contraventions (Penalty Charges, Adjudication and Enforcement) (England) Regulations 2005 and shall come into force on 1st November 2005.

(2) These Regulations apply only to England exclusive of Greater London.

[941]

Interpretation

2 (1) In these Regulations—

"the 2000 Act" means the Transport Act 2000;

"adjudicator", except in the expression "parking adjudicator", means a bus lane adjudicator appointed under regulation 11(1)(a);

"appeal" means an appeal against the imposition of a penalty charge;

"appeal period" means the period of 28 days specified in regulation 14(4);

"contravention" means a bus lane contravention in which a vehicle is involved;

"enforcing authority" in relation to a penalty charge means the approved local authority which imposed the penalty charge;

"notice of rejection" means a notice served under regulation 10(3);

"penalty charge notice" has the meaning given by regulation 8(1);

"proper officer" means a person appointed under regulation 11(1)(c);

"register" means the register of appeals and decisions kept in accordance with regulation 31;

"statutory grounds of appeal" means the grounds, as specified in regulation 9(2), on which—

(a) representations against a penalty charge notice may be made under regulation 9 to an approved authority; or

(b) an appeal made to an adjudicator under regulation 14;

"vehicle" means motor vehicle; and

"working day" means any day which is not a Saturday, a Sunday, Good Friday, Christmas Day, or a bank holiday in England and Wales by virtue of section 1 of the Banking and Financial Dealings Act 1971.

(2) Subject to regulation 10(2), for the purposes of these Regulations, the owner of a vehicle shall be taken to be the person by whom the vehicle is kept.

(3) In determining, for the purposes of these Regulations, who was the owner of a vehicle at any time, it shall, subject to regulation 10(2), be presumed that the owner was the person in whose name the vehicle was registered under the Vehicle Excise and Registration Act 1994 at that time.

(4) In determining, for the purposes of these Regulations, whether and when a penalty charge has been paid, it shall be taken to have been paid when the whole of the amount of the penalty charge applicable in the circumstances of the case is received by the approved local authority concerned.

(5) References to the service of a document include service by post and, in determining for the purposes of these Regulations the date on which a notice or other document is served by post, it shall be presumed that service of a notice sent by first class post was effected on the person to whom it was addressed on the second working day after the day on which it was posted.

[942]

PART 2
PENALTY CHARGES

Penalty charges

3 (1) Subject to paragraph (2) and regulation 4, an approved local authority may impose a penalty charge in respect of a contravention relating to any road within their area, except a road which is a special road in accordance with section 16 of the Highways Act 1980.

(2) A penalty charge may be imposed only on the basis of a record produced by an approved device.

[943]

Level of penalty charges

4 (1) An approved local authority shall not impose a penalty charge in accordance with these Regulations unless—

(a) it has first set the level of penalty charge that is to apply within its area;

(b) the Secretary of State has approved that level; and

(c) it has published in at least one local newspaper circulating in its area a notice specifying—
   (i) the circumstances in which a penalty charge may be imposed;
   (ii) the level of the penalty charge; and
   (iii) the date, being a day which falls after the end of the period of 15 days beginning with the day on which the notice is published, on which the authority will start to impose penalty charges at that level,

and no charge shall be imposed before the date so specified.

(2) In setting the level of penalty charge an approved local authority shall have regard to any guidance for the time being issued by the Secretary of State.

(3) Each approved local authority shall make available, at all reasonable times, free of charge and in a form which is readily accessible to any member of the public, information about the level of the penalty charge for the time being in force in its area.

(4) In the circumstances described in regulation 8(5)(f), an authority must accept a sum equivalent to one half of the level of charge approved by the Secretary of State, in full payment of a penalty charge.

(5) In the circumstances described in regulation 8(5)(j), an authority may increase a penalty charge to a sum equivalent to one and a half times the level of charge approved by the Secretary of State.

[944]

Person by whom penalty charge is to be paid

5 (1) Subject to paragraphs (2) and (3), a penalty charge shall be paid by the owner of the vehicle involved in the contravention.

(2) Where the vehicle involved in the contravention—

(a) was at the material time the subject of a hiring agreement; and
(b) the person hiring it, or an individual authorised to sign on his behalf, has signed a statement of liability acknowledging his liability in respect of any penalty charge incurred during the currency of the hiring agreement,

the penalty charge shall be paid by the person who has hired the vehicle under the agreement.

(3) Where—

(a) the vehicle involved in the contravention is kept by a vehicle trader; and
(b) at the time of the contravention, a person other than the vehicle trader is the registered keeper of the vehicle,

the penalty charge shall be paid by the vehicle trader.

(4) In this regulation—

"hiring agreement" means an agreement for the hire of a vehicle—
   (i) under the terms of which the vehicle is let to the hirer for a fixed period of any duration (whether or not that period is capable of extension by agreement between the parties or otherwise);
   (ii) which contains such particulars as may for the time being be prescribed for the purpose of section 66(8) (offences relating to hired vehicles) of the Road Traffic Offenders Act 1988; and
   (iii) which is not a hire purchase agreement within the meaning of the Consumer Credit Act 1974; and

"vehicle trader" has the same meaning as in regulation 20(6) (change of keeper: general provisions) of the Road Vehicle (Registration and Licensing) Regulations 2002.

NOTES

Consumer Credit Act 1974 For the meaning of "hire purchase agreement" in that Act, see s 189(1) thereof.

Road Vehicle (Registration and Licensing) Regulations 2002 The correct citation is the Road Vehicles (Registration and Licensing) Regulations 2002 (SI 2002/2742).

[945]

Circumstances in which penalty charge need not be paid or is to be refunded

6 (1) A penalty charge shall not be payable under these Regulations where—

(a) the conduct constituting the contravention is the subject of criminal proceedings; or

(b) a fixed penalty notice, as defined by section 52 of the Road Traffic Offenders Act 1988, has been given in respect of that conduct.

(2) Where, notwithstanding the provisions of paragraph (1)—

(a) a penalty charge has been paid in respect of a contravention; and

(b) the circumstances are as mentioned in paragraph (1)(a) or (b),

the authority shall, as soon as reasonably practicable after those circumstances come to their notice, refund the amount of the penalty charge.

[946]

PART 3
NOTIFICATION OF, AND REPRESENTATIONS ABOUT, PENALTY CHARGES

Interpretation of Part 3

7 In this Part—

"the detection date", in relation to a contravention, means the date on which, according to a record produced by an approved device, the contravention occurred;

"the recipient", in relation to a penalty charge notice, means the person on whom the penalty charge notice is served; and

"the 28 day period", in relation to a penalty charge notice, means the period of 28 days beginning with the date of service of the notice.

[947]

Penalty charge notices

8 (1) Where an approved local authority have reason to believe that a penalty charge is payable under Part 2 with respect to a vehicle, they may, in accordance with paragraphs (2) and (5) below, serve a notice ("penalty charge notice") on the person appearing to them to be the owner of the vehicle or on the person appearing to them to be the person liable to pay the charge.

(2) Subject to paragraph (3), a penalty charge notice shall be served before the end of the period of 28 days beginning with the detection date.

(3) Where—

(a) within 14 days of the detection date an approved local authority have made a request to the Secretary of State for the supply of relevant particulars; and

(b) those particulars have not been supplied before the date after which the authority would not be entitled to serve a penalty charge notice by virtue of paragraph (2),

the authority shall continue to be entitled to serve a penalty charge notice for a further period of six months beginning with the date mentioned in sub-paragraph (b).

(4) In paragraph (3) "relevant particulars" means particulars relating to the identity of the keeper of the vehicle contained in the register of mechanically propelled vehicles maintained by the Secretary of State under the Vehicle Excise and Registration Act 1994.

(5) A penalty charge notice must state—

(a) the registration mark of the vehicle involved in the alleged contravention;

(b) the detection date and the time at which the alleged contravention occurred;

(c) the reasons why the authority believe that a penalty charge is payable;

(d) the amount of the penalty charge;

(e) that the penalty charge must be paid before the end of the 28 day period;

(f) that if the penalty charge is paid before the end of the period of 14 days beginning with the date of service of the notice, the penalty charge will be reduced by one half;

(g) that representations may be made, on any of the statutory grounds of appeal, to the authority against the imposition of the penalty charge but that representations made outside the 28 day period may be disregarded;
(h) what are the statutory grounds of appeal;
(i) the postal address to which representations are to be sent;
(j) any electronic mail address or FAX number to which representations may be sent as an alternative to the postal address;
(k) that if at the end of the 28 day period—
   (i) no representations have been made; and
   (ii) the penalty charge has not been paid,

   the authority may increase the penalty charge by a half and take steps to enforce payment of the charge as so increased;
(l) the manner in which the penalty charge may be paid;
(m) that if the representations are rejected an appeal may be made on any of the statutory grounds of appeal may be made to an adjudicator in respect of a penalty charge; and
(n) that the recipient may, by notice in writing to the authority, request them—
   (i) to make available at an office of theirs specified by him, free of charge and at a time during normal office hours so specified, for viewing by him and by his representative (if any), the record of the contravention produced by the approved device pursuant to which the penalty charge was imposed; or
   (ii) to provide him, free of charge, with such still images from that record as, in the authority's opinion, establish the contravention.

(6) Where the recipient of the notice makes a request under paragraph (5)(m), the authority shall comply with the request within a reasonable time.

[948]

Representations in respect of penalty charges

9 (1) The recipient may make written representations on any of the statutory grounds of appeal to the authority against the imposition of the penalty charge; but the authority may disregard any such representations which are received by them after the end of the 28 day period.

(2) The grounds are—
(a) that the alleged contravention did not occur;
(b) that regulation 6(1) (other proceedings pursued) applies;
(c) in a case where the penalty charge notice has been served on the recipient on the basis that he was the owner of the vehicle concerned, that the recipient—
   (i) never was the owner of the vehicle in question;
   (ii) had ceased to be its owner before the detection date; or
   (iii) became its owner after the detection date;
(d) in a case where the penalty charge notice has been served on the recipient on the basis that he was the hirer of the vehicle concerned, that he was not liable to pay the penalty charge under regulation 5(2);
(e) that the recipient was the registered keeper of the vehicle in question on the detection date, but on that date—
   (i) the circumstances were as mentioned in regulation 5(2) (vehicle subject to hiring agreement);
   (ii) the circumstances were as mentioned in regulation 5(3) (vehicle kept by a vehicle trader), and the recipient was either not a vehicle trader or was a vehicle trader but not the vehicle trader keeping the vehicle; or
   (iii) the vehicle was in the control of a person who had assumed control of it without the recipient's consent; and
(f) that the penalty charge exceeded the amount applicable in the circumstances of the case.

(3) Where the ground mentioned in paragraph (2)(c)(ii) is relied on in any representations made under paragraph (1), those representations must include a

statement of the name and address of the person to whom the vehicle was disposed of by the recipient (if that information is in his possession).

(4) Where the ground mentioned in paragraph (2)(c)(iii) is relied on in any representations made under paragraph (1), those representations must include a statement of the name and address of the person from whom the vehicle was acquired by the recipient (if that information is in his possession).

[949]

Response to representations

10 (1) Where representations are duly made to an authority under regulation 9 and they are made within the 28 day period, it shall be the duty of the authority—

- (a) to consider them and any supporting evidence provided;
- (b) in relation to each ground on which representations are made, to serve on the person by whom the representations are made notice of their decision as to whether or not they accept that the ground has been established.

(2) Where an authority accept that at least one ground on which representations are made is established, they shall—

- (a) cancel the penalty charge notice; and
- (b) serve notice on the recipient stating that the penalty charge notice has been cancelled,

and where the ground that is accepted is that mentioned in regulation 9(2)(e)(ii), the person hiring the vehicle shall be deemed to be its owner for the purposes of these Regulations.

(3) Where an authority is not satisfied that any of the statutory grounds of appeal is established, the notice served in accordance with paragraph (1)(b) must be a notice stating that they do not accept that the ground has been established ("a notice of rejection").

(4) A notice of rejection shall—

- (a) state the reasons for the authority's decision;
- (b) state that an appeal against the imposition of the penalty charge may be made to an adjudicator within the appeal period;
- (c) specify the statutory grounds of appeal;
- (d) describe in general terms the procedure for making an appeal;
- (e) state that an adjudicator has power to make an award of costs;
- (f) indicate the circumstances in which the power may be exercised; and
- (g) state that unless, before the end of the appeal period—
  - (i) the penalty charge is paid; or
  - (ii) an appeal is made to an adjudicator against the imposition of the penalty charge,

  the authority may increase the penalty charge by 50 per cent and take steps to enforce payment.

(5) Where a penalty charge notice is cancelled under paragraph (2), the authority may serve on any person other than the person on whom the original penalty charge notice was served a fresh penalty charge notice in relation to the alleged contravention that was the subject of the cancelled notice.

(6) Regulation 8 shall apply in relation to a fresh notice served under paragraph (5) as if—

- (a) in paragraph (2), for "the detection date", there were substituted "the date on which the penalty charge notice is cancelled"; and
- (b) in paragraph (3)—
  - (i) in sub-paragraph (a), for "the detection date", there were substituted "the date on which the penalty charge notice is cancelled"; and
  - (ii) in sub-paragraph (b), the reference to paragraph (2) were a reference to that paragraph as modified by sub-paragraph (a) of this paragraph.

[950]

PART 4
BUS LANE ADJUDICATORS

Appointment of, and provision of facilities for, bus lane adjudicators

11 (1) Those approved local authorities which have resolved to impose penalty charges under regulation 3(1) shall—

- (a) with the consent of the Lord Chancellor, appoint at least one person to act as a bus lane adjudicator for the purposes of these Regulations;
- (b) provide, or make arrangements for the provision of, accommodation and administrative staff and facilities for adjudicators;
- (c) appoint a person to fulfil the functions of the proper officer under these Regulations and one or more persons to act as his deputy when the proper officer is unable to act; and
- (d) determine the places at which adjudicators are to sit.

(2) The Schedule to these Regulations, which makes provision relating to the appointment of bus lane adjudicators, shall have effect.

[951]

Discharge of functions under regulation 11

12 (1) Where two or more approved local authorities ("the participating authorities") have resolved to impose penalty charges pursuant to regulation 3(1), the functions conferred on them by regulation 11 shall be discharged through a joint committee ("the joint committee") set up in pursuance of arrangements entered into under section 101(5) of the Local Government Act 1972.

(2) All the participating authorities must be constituent authorities of the joint committee.

(3) The expenses of the joint committee incurred in the discharge of functions conferred on the participating authorities by this regulation shall be defrayed by them in such proportions as they may decide or, in default of a decision by them, as may be determined by an arbitrator nominated by the Chartered Institute of Arbitrators on the application of the joint committee.

(4) The costs of any reference to arbitration under paragraph (3) shall be borne by the participating authorities in equal shares.

(5) Where the Secretary of State is satisfied that there has been, or is likely to be, a failure on the part of the participating authorities to agree on the proportions in which the expenses of the joint committee are to be defrayed by them under paragraph (3), he may give the joint committee such directions as he considers appropriate in order to require it to refer the matter to arbitration under that paragraph.

(6) In accordance with such requirements as may be imposed by the joint committee, each bus lane adjudicator shall make an annual report to the joint committee on the discharge of his functions.

(7) The joint committee shall make and publish an annual report in writing to the Secretary of State on the discharge by the bus lane adjudicators of their functions.

[952]

PART 5
APPEALS AGAINST PENALTY CHARGES

Interpretation of Part 5

13 In this Part, in relation to an appeal or any process connected with an appeal—

"appellant" means the person making the appeal;

"authority" means the approved local authority which made the decision to impose the penalty charge;

"charge notice concerned" means the penalty charge notice conveying the authority's decision to impose the charge;

"hearing" means an oral hearing; and

"party" means the appellant or the authority.

[953]

Initiating an appeal

14 (1) A person on whom a penalty charge notice has been served may appeal against the imposition of the penalty charge if—

- (a) he has made representations to the authority under regulation 9; and
- (b) he has received from the authority a notice of rejection.

(2) An appeal shall be made by delivering a notice of appeal to the proper officer.

(3) A notice of appeal—

- (a) must be in writing and signed by the appellant or his duly authorised agent;
- (b) must state the name and address of the appellant;
- (c) may specify some other address as being the address to which he wishes documents to be sent to him in connection with the appeal;
- (d) must state the name of the authority by which the decision to impose the charge was made and the date and reference number of the charge notice concerned; and
- (e) may include any additional representations on any of the statutory grounds of appeal which the appellant desires to make.

(4) The notice of appeal shall be delivered to the proper officer within the period of 28 days beginning with the date of service of the notice of rejection ("the appeal period").

(5) If the notice of appeal is delivered to the proper officer outside the appeal period, the appellant must include in the notice a statement of the reasons on which he relies for justifying the delay.

(6) The adjudicator shall treat any such statement as a request to extend the appeal period and, if he thinks fit, may direct that the period be extended accordingly.

[954]

Action on receipt of notice of appeal

15 (1) On receiving a notice of appeal the proper officer shall send an acknowledgement of its receipt to the appellant.

(2) If he is satisfied that the notice is in accordance with regulation 14, the proper officer shall—

- (a) enter particulars of the appeal in the register; and
- (b) send to the authority a copy of the notice of appeal; and
- (c) notify both the appellant and the authority of any direction given by the adjudicator under regulation 14(6).

(3) Within seven days of the receipt of a copy of a notice of appeal, the authority shall deliver to the proper officer a copy of—

- (a) the charge notice concerned;
- (b) any representations made to the authority in respect of the decision to impose the charge; and
- (c) the notice of rejection.

(4) If a notice of appeal—

- (a) is received by the proper officer and he considers that it is not in accordance with regulation 14; or
- (b) is delivered outside the appeal period with a request to extend the appeal period and the adjudicator declines to direct that the period be extended,

the proper officer shall inform the appellant of the reasons why he considers that the notice does not accord with regulation 14 or, as the case may be, that adjudicator has declined the request for an extension and shall record the action taken in the register.

[955]

Further representations

16 (1) A party may, at any time before the determination of the appeal, deliver further representations on any of the statutory grounds of appeal to the proper officer.

(2) The adjudicator may invite a party to deliver to the proper officer representations dealing with such matters relating to the appeal as may be specified and any such representations shall be so delivered within the time and in the manner specified.

(3) Where a party fails to respond to an invitation under paragraph (2), the adjudicator may draw such inferences as appear to him proper.

(4) Any representations delivered under this regulation shall be signed by the party in question or his authorised representative.

(5) The proper officer shall send to the authority a copy of any representations delivered by the appellant under paragraph (1) or (2).

(6) Where the authority delivers representations to the proper officer under either of those paragraphs, it shall at the same time send a copy to the appellant.

[956]

Disposing of an appeal without a hearing

17 (1) Subject to the provisions of this Part of these Regulations, the adjudicator may decide the general procedure to be followed in connection with appeals and may dispose of an appeal without a hearing, unless in his opinion the appeal raises issues of public importance such as to require that a hearing be held.

(2) If either party has requested a hearing, the adjudicator shall not dispose of an appeal without a hearing unless—

(a) the request is withdrawn before notice of a hearing has been sent to the other party; or

(b) both parties have subsequently consented to the appeal being disposed of without a hearing.

(3) Where the adjudicator is minded to dispose of an appeal without a hearing, he—

(a) shall inform the parties of that intention; and

(b) shall not dispose of the appeal without a hearing unless and until either—

(i) there has elapsed a period of four weeks beginning with the date on which an acknowledgement is sent in accordance with regulation 15(1) during which neither party has requested a hearing; or

(ii) both parties have consented to its disposal without a hearing.

[957]

Notice of time and place of hearing

18 (1) This regulation shall have effect where a hearing is to be held for the purpose of disposing of an appeal.

(2) The proper officer shall—

(a) fix the time and place of the hearing; and

(b) not less than 21 days before the time so fixed, or such shorter time as the parties agree—

(i) send to each party a notice that the hearing is to be at that time and place; or

(ii) inform them of those matters in such other manner as he thinks fit.

(3) The adjudicator may alter the time and place of any hearing, and the proper officer shall, not less than seven days before the date on which the hearing is then to be held, or such shorter time as the parties agree—

(a) send to each party notice of the new time and place of the hearing; or

(b) inform them of those matters in such other manner as he thinks fit.

(4) This regulation applies to an adjourned hearing but, if, before the adjournment, the time and place of the adjourned hearing are notified to all persons expected to attend, no further notice shall be required.

[958]

Power to require attendance and production of documents

19 (1) The adjudicator may, by notice in writing sent to any person, require that person—

(a) to attend, at a time and place specified by the adjudicator, to give evidence at the hearing of an appeal; and

(b) to produce any documents in his custody or under his control, relating to any matter in the proceedings,

and any such notice shall contain a statement of the effect of paragraphs (2) to (5) below.

(2) A person in respect of whom a requirement has been made under paragraph (1) may apply to the adjudicator to vary or set aside the requirement.

(3) A person shall not be bound to comply with a requirement under paragraph (1) unless—

(a) he has been given at least seven days' notice of the hearing; or

(b) if less than seven days' notice has been given, he has informed the adjudicator that he accepts such notice as he has been given.

(4) No person shall be required under paragraph (1) to give any evidence or produce any document which he could not be required to give or produce on the trial of an action in a court of law.

(5) If any person who is required under paragraph (1) to attend a hearing held by an adjudicator, or to produce any document to an adjudicator, fails without reasonable excuse to do so, he shall be guilty of an offence and liable on summary conviction to a fine not exceeding level 2 on the standard scale.

[959]

Procedure at a hearing

20 (1) At the beginning of the hearing of an appeal the adjudicator shall explain the order of proceeding which he proposes to adopt.

(2) Subject to the provisions of this regulation, the adjudicator shall conduct the hearing of an appeal in such manner as he considers most suitable to the clarification of the issues before him and generally to the just handling of the proceedings and he shall, so far as appears to him appropriate, seek to avoid formality in the proceedings.

(3) Any hearing of an appeal by the adjudicator shall be in public except where the adjudicator is satisfied that, by reason of exceptional circumstances, it is just and reasonable for the hearing, or part of it, to be in private.

[(4) Any other adjudicator shall be entitled to attend the hearing of an appeal whether or not it is in private.]

(5) The adjudicator, with the consent of the parties, may permit any other person to attend the hearing of an appeal which is held in private or, where part of it is so held, that part.

(6) The adjudicator may exclude from the hearing of an appeal, or part of it, any person whose conduct has disrupted or is likely, in the opinion of the adjudicator, to disrupt the hearing.

(7) At the hearing the authority may be represented by a solicitor, counsel or any other person.

(8) At the hearing of an appeal, the appellant may conduct his case himself (with assistance from any person if he wishes) or may be represented, by a solicitor, counsel or any other person.

(9) If in any particular case the adjudicator is satisfied that there are good and sufficient reasons for doing so, he may refuse to permit a particular person to assist or represent either party at the hearing.

(10) At the hearing of an appeal—

(a) the parties shall be entitled to give evidence, to call witnesses, to question any witness and to address the adjudicator both on the evidence and generally on the subject matter of the appeal; and

(b) the adjudicator may receive evidence of any fact which appears to him to be relevant notwithstanding that such evidence would be inadmissible in proceedings before a court of law.

(11) Where a party who has been sent notice of the hearing of an appeal, or otherwise informed of the hearing in accordance with regulation 18, fails to attend or be represented at the hearing, the adjudicator may dispose of the appeal in his absence.

NOTES

Amendment Para (4): substituted by SI 2008/2683.

[960]

Evidence by production of record

21 (1) The adjudicator may permit evidence of the fact of a contravention to be given by the production of—

(a) a record produced by an approved device; and
(b) in the same or another document, a certificate as to the circumstances in which the record was produced, signed by a person authorised in that behalf by the authority.

(2) A document stated in evidence to be such a record as is mentioned in paragraph (1)(a), or such a certificate as is mentioned in paragraph (1)(b), shall be treated as such a record or certificate, unless the contrary is proved.

[961]

Decisions on appeals

22 (1) The adjudicator shall determine the appeal after considering all the evidence and all representations made by or on behalf of the parties.

(2) The adjudicator must state the reasons for his decision.

(3) Where an appeal is disposed of at a hearing, the adjudicator may give his decision and the reasons orally at the end of the hearing, or may reserve his decision and give it and his reasons subsequently in writing.

(4) If the adjudicator decides to allow the appeal he shall give the authority such directions as he considers appropriate.

(5) It shall be the duty of an authority to whom a direction is given under paragraph (4) to comply with it forthwith.

(6) Upon the decision being given (whether at a hearing or otherwise), the proper officer shall—

(a) forthwith record in the register the decision, the adjudicator's reasons and any directions given; and
(b) send a copy of the register entry to each party.

[962]

Review of adjudicator's or proper officer's decision

23 (1) The adjudicator may, on the application of a party, review and revoke or vary any decision to reject a notice of appeal or to dismiss or allow an appeal, or any decision as to costs, on the grounds (in each case) that—

(a) the decision was wrongly made as the result of an administrative error;
(b) the proper officer was wrong to reject the notice of appeal;
(c) a party who failed to appear or be represented at a hearing had good and sufficient reason for his failure to appear;
(d) where the decision was made after a hearing, new evidence has become available since the conclusion of the hearing, the existence of which could not reasonably have been known or foreseen;
(e) where the decision was made without a hearing, new evidence has become available since the decision was made, the existence of which could not reasonably have been known or foreseen; or
(f) the interests of justice require such a review.

(2) The adjudicator may, on the application of a party, review and revoke or vary any interlocutory decision.

(3) An application under paragraph (1) or (2) must—

(a) be delivered to the proper officer within the period of 14 days beginning with the date on which the copy of the register entry is served on the parties; and
(b) state the grounds in full.

(4) The parties shall have the opportunity to be heard on any application for review under paragraph (1) or (2).

(5) If, having reviewed the decision, the adjudicator directs that it be set aside, he shall substitute such decision as he thinks fit or order a re-determination by either himself or a different adjudicator.

(6) Regulation 22 shall apply to a confirmation, revocation or variation of a decision under this regulation as it applies to a decision made on the disposal of an appeal.

[963]

Costs

24 (1) The adjudicator shall not normally make an order awarding costs and expenses, but may, subject to paragraph (2), make such an order—

- (a) against a party (including an appellant who has withdrawn his appeal or an authority that has consented to an appeal being allowed) if he is of the opinion that the party has acted frivolously or vexatiously or that his conduct in making, pursuing or resisting an appeal was wholly unreasonable; or
- (b) against the authority, where he considers that the decision appealed against was wholly unreasonable.

(2) An order shall not be made under paragraph (1) against a party unless that party has been given an opportunity to make representations against the making of the order.

(3) An order under paragraph (1) shall require the party against whom it is made to pay the other party a specified sum in respect of the costs and expenses incurred by that other party in connection with the proceedings.

[964]

Recovery of amount payable under an adjudication

25 Any amount which is payable under an adjudication of an adjudicator shall, if a county court so orders, be recoverable by the person to whom the amount is payable, as if it were payable under a county court order.

[965]

Consolidation of proceedings

26 (1) Where two or more appeals are pending and it appears to the adjudicator—

- (a) that a question of law or fact common to both or all the appeals arises; or
- (b) for some other reason it is desirable to make an order under this regulation,

the adjudicator may order that all the appeals, or such of the appeals as he may specify, shall be conducted together, and may give such consequential directions as appear to him to be necessary.

(2) An order shall not be made under this regulation unless all parties concerned have been given an opportunity to make representations against the making of such an order.

[966]

Miscellaneous powers of the adjudicator

27 (1) The adjudicator may, if he thinks fit—

- (a) extend the time appointed by or under this Part for doing any act notwithstanding that the time appointed may have expired;
- (b) if the appellant at any time delivers to the proper officer notice of the withdrawal of his appeal, dismiss the proceedings;
- (c) if the authority consents to an appeal being allowed, allow the appeal;
- (d) if the parties agree in writing on the terms of a decision to be made by an adjudicator, decide accordingly; or
- (e) adjourn a hearing.

(2) The powers of the adjudicator conferred by these Regulations, other than regulation 23, may be exercised on his own initiative or on the application of a party.

[967]

Correction of clerical mistakes and errors

28 Clerical mistakes in any document recording a direction or decision of the adjudicator, or errors in such a document arising from an accidental slip or omission, may be corrected by the proper officer on the direction of the adjudicator.

[968]

Service of documents on the parties

29 (1) This regulation has effect in relation to any notice or other document required or authorised by these Regulations to be sent to a party to an appeal.

(2) Any document shall be regarded as having been sent to that party if it is—

(a) delivered to him;

(b) left at his proper address;

(c) sent by first class post to him at that address; or

(d) transmitted to him by fax or other means of electronic data transmission in accordance with paragraph (3).

(3) A document may be transmitted to a party by fax or by other means of electronic data transmission where—

(a) the party has indicated in writing that he is willing to regard a document as having been duly sent to him if it is transmitted to a specified fax telephone number or, as the case may be, a specified electronic address; and

(b) the document is transmitted to that number or address.

(4) In the case of an authority, an indication under paragraph (3)(a) may be expressed to apply in relation to any appeal to which they are the respondent.

(5) Where the proper address includes a box number at a document exchange the delivery of such a document may be effected by leaving the document addressed to that box number—

(a) at that document exchange; or

(b) at a document exchange which transmits documents every working day to that exchange,

and any such document so left shall be taken to have been delivered on the second working day after the day on which it was left.

(6) For the purposes of these Regulations, and of section 7 (references to service by post) of the Interpretation Act 1978 ("the 1978 Act") in its application to this regulation,—

(a) the proper address of the appellant is the address for service specified pursuant to regulation 14(3)(c) or, if no address is so specified, the address specified pursuant to regulation 14(3)(b), and

(b) the proper address of an authority in proceedings in which it is the respondent is such address as the authority from time to time specify in a notice delivered to the proper officer as being the authority's address for service in all such proceedings.

(7) If no address for service has been specified, the proper address for the purposes of this Part, and section 7 of the 1978 Act, shall be—

(a) in the case of an individual, his usual or last known address;

(b) in the case of a partnership, the principal or last known place of business of the firm within the United Kingdom;

(c) in the case of an incorporated or unincorporated body, the registered or principal office of the body.

(8) A party may at any time, by notice in writing delivered to the proper officer, change his proper address for the purposes of this Part and section 7 of the 1978 Act.

(9) A party may, by notice in writing delivered to the proper officer, vary or revoke any indication given under paragraph (3)(a).

(10) A notice or document—

(a) left at the proper address of a party shall be taken to have been delivered on the first working day after the day on which it was left;

(b) sent by fax or other means of electronic transmission shall be taken to have been delivered on the first working day after the day on which it was transmitted.

NOTES

Interpretation Act 1978, s 17 Printed in the title Statutory Instruments (Pt 2), Vol 1 of this work.

[969]

Delivery of notices or documents to the proper officer

30 (1) This regulation has effect in relation to any notice or other document required or authorised by or under this Part to be delivered to the proper officer.

(2) Any such notice or document may be delivered to the proper officer by being transmitted to the proper officer by fax or other means of electronic data transmission, but only to a telephone number or, as the case may be, electronic address for the time being published by the proper officer for the purpose of receiving such notices or documents.

(3) Any notice or document so transmitted shall be taken to have been delivered on the first working day after the day on which it was transmitted.

(4) Where the address of the proper officer includes a box number at a document exchange the delivery of such a document may be effected by leaving the document addressed to that box number—

(a) at that document exchange; or

(b) at a document exchange which transmits documents every working day to that exchange,

and any such document so left shall be taken to have been delivered on the second working day after the day on which it was left.

(5) Regulations 14(3)(a) and 16(4)—

(a) shall, in the case of a document transmitted by fax, be satisfied if a copy of the signature of the relevant person appears on the transmitted copy; and

(b) shall not apply in relation to a document transmitted by other means of electronic data transmission.

[970]

The register

31 (1) The joint committee set up pursuant to regulation 12(1) shall establish and maintain the register for the purposes of recording proceedings conducted under this Part of these Regulations.

(2) The register shall be kept open for inspection by any person without charge at all reasonable hours at the accommodation provided for adjudicators.

(3) The register may be kept in electronic form.

(4) If the register is kept in electronic form, the duty to allow inspection is to be treated as a duty to allow inspection of a reproduction in legible form of the recording of the entry the inspection of which is being sought.

(5) A document purporting to be certified by the proper officer to be a true copy of any entry of a decision in the register shall be evidence of the entry and of the matters contained in it.

[971]

PART 6
ENFORCEMENT OF PENALTY CHARGES

Charge certificates

32 (1) Where—

(a) a penalty charge notice is served on any person; and

(b) the penalty charge to which it relates is not paid before the end of the relevant period,

the enforcing authority may serve on that person a statement (a "charge certificate") to the effect that the penalty charge in question is increased by 50 per cent.

(2) The "relevant period" for the purposes of paragraph (1) means—

(a) where a notice of rejection is served but no appeal is made, the period of 28 days beginning with the date of service of the notice of rejection;

(b) where there has been an unsuccessful appeal against the imposition of the penalty charge, the period of 28 days beginning with the date on which the adjudicator's decision is sent to the appellant pursuant to regulation 22(6);

(c) where an appeal is withdrawn, the period of 14 days beginning with the date on which it is withdrawn; and

(d) where no representations are made, the period of 28 days beginning with the date on which the penalty charge notice is served.

[972]

Enforcement of penalty charges

33 Where, in relation to a penalty charge notice—

(a) the relevant period for the purposes of regulation 32(1) has expired; and

(b) the increased penalty charge for which the charge certificate provides is not paid before the end of the period of 14 days beginning with the date on which the certificate is served,

the authority concerned may, if the county court so orders, recover the charge as if it were payable under a county court order.

[973]

Cancellation of charge certificates, etc

34 (1) This regulation applies where—

(a) a county court makes an order under regulation 33;

(b) the person against whom it is made makes a statutory declaration complying with paragraph (2); and

(c) subject to paragraph (3), the declaration is, before the end of the period of 21 days beginning with the date on which notice of the county court's order is served on him, served on the county court which made the order.

(2) The statutory declaration must state (as the case may be) that the person making it—

(a) did not receive the penalty charge notice in question;

(b) made representations under regulation 9 but had no response to those representations; or

(c) appealed to the adjudicator under regulation 14 but had no response to the appeal.

(3) Where it appears to the court, on the application of a person on whom a charge certificate has been served, that it would be unreasonable in the circumstances of his case to insist on his serving his statutory declaration within the period mentioned in paragraph (1)(c), the court may allow such longer period for service of the statutory declaration as it considers appropriate.

(4) Where a statutory declaration is served pursuant to paragraph (1)(c) or within such longer period as may be allowed under paragraph (3)—

(a) the order of the court shall be treated as revoked;

(b) the charge certificate shall be treated as cancelled;

(c) where the declaration contains such a statement as is mentioned in paragraph (2)(a), the penalty charge notice shall be treated as cancelled; and

(d) the court shall serve written notice of the effect of service of the declaration on the person making it and on the enforcing authority concerned.

(5) Where a declaration contains such a statement as is mentioned in paragraph (2)(a), nothing in regulation 8(2) shall prevent the enforcing authority serving a fresh penalty charge notice on the person making the declaration or any other person.

(6) Where a declaration contains such a statement as is mentioned in paragraph (2)(b) or (c), the enforcing authority shall refer the case to the adjudicator, who may give such directions as he considers appropriate.

[974]

Enforcement by execution

35 (1) Subject to paragraph (2), a sum of money—

(a) representing an increased penalty charge recoverable in accordance with regulation 33; and

(b) payable by a person (other than the enforcing authority) under an adjudication of an adjudicator which is recoverable in accordance with regulation 25,

as if it were payable under a county court order shall be treated for the purposes of enforcement by execution as if it were a specified debt in article 2 of the Enforcement of Road Traffic Debts Order 1993 ("the 1993 Order").

(2) For the purposes of enforcement of payment of a sum referred to in paragraph (1)—

(a) any reference in the 1993 Order to the authority shall be a reference to the enforcing authority; and

(b) the reference in article 3(1) of the 1993 Order to the time for serving a statutory declaration shall be a reference to (as the case may be)—

(i) the period of 21 days allowed by regulation 34(1)(c); or

(ii) where a longer period has been allowed pursuant to regulation 34(3), that period.

NOTES

Enforcement of Road Traffic Debts Order 1993 SI 1993/2073, in the title Distress.

[975]

PART 7
FINANCIAL PROVISIONS

Accounts and application of sums paid by way of penalty charges

36 (1) Each approved local authority shall keep an account—

(a) of the sums paid to them by way of penalty charges under these Regulations; and

(b) of the expenditure incurred by them in relation to the enforcement of contraventions.

(2) As soon as reasonably practicable after the end of each financial year, the authority shall forward to the Secretary of State a copy of the account for that year.

(3) At the end of each financial year, any deficit in the account shall be made good out of that authority's general fund.

(4) Subject to paragraph (5), any surplus shall be applied for all or any of the purposes specified in paragraph (6) and, in so far as it is not so applied, shall be appropriated to the carrying out of some specific project falling within those purposes and carried forward until applied to that project.

(5) If the authority so determine, any amount not applied in any financial year, instead of being or remaining so appropriated, may be carried forward in the account kept under paragraph (1) to the next financial year.

(6) The purposes referred to in paragraph (4) are—

(a) the making good to the general fund of any amount charged to that fund under paragraph (3) in the four years immediately preceding the financial year in question;

(b) meeting costs incurred, whether by the authority or by some other person, in the provision or operation of, or of facilities for, public passenger transport services; and

(c) the purposes of a highway improvement project in the authority's area.

(7) For the purposes of paragraph (6)(c), a highway improvement project means a project connected with the carrying out by the appropriate highway authority (whether the approved local authority or not) of any operation which constitutes the improvement (within the meaning of the Highways Act 1980) of a highway.

NOTES

Highways Act 1980 For the meaning of "improvement" in that Act, see s 329(1) thereof.

[976]

SCHEDULE
BUS LANE ADJUDICATORS

Regulation 11

1 To be qualified for appointment as a bus lane adjudicator, a person must have a 5 year general qualification (within the meaning of section 71 of the Courts and Legal Services Act 1990).

2 A person may be appointed as a bus lane adjudicator notwithstanding that he is appointed to act as a parking adjudicator for the purposes of Part 2 of the Road Traffic Act 1991.

3 A bus lane adjudicator shall be appointed for such term, not exceeding five years, as may be specified in the instrument of appointment.

4 On the expiry of his term of appointment, a bus lane adjudicator shall be eligible for re-appointment.

5 A bus lane adjudicator may be removed from office only for misconduct or on the ground that he is unable or unfit to discharge his functions but shall otherwise hold and vacate office in accordance with the terms of his appointment.

NOTES

Parking adjudicator for the purposes of Pt 2 of the Road Traffic Act 1991
Parking adjudicators were appointed under s 73 of the 1991 Act, which has been repealed by the Traffic Management Act 2004, s 98, Sch 12, Pt 1. As to the appointment of adjudicators in England for the purposes of Pt 6 (civil enforcement of traffic contraventions) of the 2004 Act, see reg 17 of SI 2007/3483 (which also provides for parking adjudicators appointed under s 73 of the 1991 Act to be treated as having been appointed under that regulation).

[977]

DISCLOSURE OF VEHICLE INSURANCE INFORMATION REGULATIONS 2005
SI 2005/2833

Authority Made by the Secretary of State for Transport under the Serious Organised Crime and Police Act 2005, ss 153, 172. S 153 of the 2005 Act has been amended by the Police and Justice Act 2006, s 1(3), Sch 1, Pt 7, para 92, so as to refer to the National Policing Improvement Agency instead of the Police Information Technology Organisation (abolished by s 1(2)(b) of the 2006 Act).
Date made 11 October 2005.
Commencement 4 November 2005.
Summary These regulations make provision for the Motor Insurers' Information Centre ("MIIC") to provide information relating to the uninsured use of motor vehicles to the National Policing Improvement Agency ("NPIA") (formerly the Police Information Technology Organisation, which has been abolished; see the note "Authority" above).

MIIC is required to provide to NPIA a list of vehicles, the use of which was covered by a policy of insurance on the reference date, as defined, but is not covered under such a policy when the list is generated. The information must be provided at intervals specified by NPIA. Information which must be provided is the vehicle registration mark, the make and model of the vehicle (where this is available to MIIC) and the date on which the vehicle ceased to have a record of insurance on the database. NPIA is permitted to process information provided by MIIC so that it is available in a form that may assist a constable to determine if a vehicle has been used by a person who is not insured, contrary to the Road Traffic Act 1988, s 143. A chief officer of police may arrange for information received by him from NPIA to be further processed into a form in which it may be used by a constable. A constable may use the processed information provided by NPIA to assist him in deciding whether to use his powers under s 165 of the 1988 Act to require a person who is, or may have been, driving a vehicle to produce evidence that use of the vehicle is insured. The information provided to a constable by NPIA may not be further disclosed by him except where the disclosure is made in respect of the contravention of the 1988 Act or of legislation made under it.

[978]

RAILWAY HERITAGE SCHEME ORDER 2005
SI 2005/2905

Authority Made by the Secretary of State for Transport under the Railway Heritage Act 1996, s 2.
Date made 12 October 2005.
Commencement 21 November 2005.
Summary This order, which revokes and replaces the Railway Heritage Scheme Order 1997, SI 1997/39, gives effect to the Railway Heritage Scheme set out in the Schedule to the order. The Scheme provides for the continued establishment and membership of the Railway Heritage Committee and sub-committees; proceedings of the Committee; functions and proceedings of sub-committees; quorums; administration and expenses; and records and minutes.

[979]

RAILWAYS INFRASTRUCTURE (ACCESS AND MANAGEMENT) REGULATIONS 2005
SI 2005/3049

Authority Made by the Secretary of State for Transport under the European Communities Act 1972, s 2(2).

Date made 1 November 2005.
Commencement 28 November 2005; see reg 1(1).
Amendment Printed as amended by SI 2009/1122 (partly as from 1 January 2010; see the notes to regs 3, 5, 6, 33, 34, 35).
Interpretation See generally reg 3.
General These regulations revoke and replace the Railways Regulations 1998, SI 1998/1340, subject to transitional provisions. They implement Council Directive 91/440/EEC on the development of the Community's railways (OJ L237, 24.08.1991, p 25), as amended, and Directive 2001/14/EC of the European Parliament and of the Council on the allocation of railway infrastructure capacity and the levying of charges for the use of railway infrastructure (OJ L75, 15.03.2001, p 29), as amended.

The regulations:

(a) grant access rights to the entire rail network in Great Britain to railway undertakings for the purpose of the operation of any type of rail freight service or international passenger service (including access to terminals and ports linked to the rail network);
(b) impose certain separation requirements between the bodies responsible for management of the railway infrastructure and railway undertakings;
(c) set out the structure for the charging of fees for the use of railway infrastructure;
(d) set out the framework and timetable for the process of allocating infrastructure capacity; and
(e) allocate certain regulatory functions to the Office of Rail Regulation.

Disclosure of information SI 1998/1340 (revoked and replaced by these regulations) has been specified by SI 2003/1400, in the title Trade and Industry, for the purposes of the Enterprise Act 2002, s 241(3). By s 241(3) of the 2002 Act, a public authority may disclose specified information to any other person for the purpose of facilitating the exercise by that person of any function he has under or by virtue of such subordinate legislation as is specified by order.

[980]

PART 1
PRELIMINARY

Citation, commencement and extent

1 (1) These Regulations may be cited as the Railways Infrastructure (Access and Management) Regulations 2005 and shall come into force on 28th November 2005.

(2) With the exception of paragraphs 1 to 3 of Schedule 1, these Regulations do not extend to Northern Ireland.

[981]

Amendments, repeals, revocations and transitional provisions

2 (1) Subject to the transitional provisions in paragraphs (2) and (3), the Railways Regulations 1998, in so far as they continue to have effect, are revoked.

(2) The transitional provisions are that the Railways Regulations 1998 shall continue to have effect in relation to any—

(a) application for transit, or access and transit rights under regulation 11; or
(b) appeal brought under regulation 14,

of those regulations made, but not concluded, prior to their revocation by virtue of paragraph (1).

(3) In the case of an application or appeal to which paragraph (2) applies, references in regulations 11 and 14 of the Railways Regulations 1998 to the International Rail Regulator shall be taken to be a reference to the Office of Rail Regulation.

(4) Schedule 1 (amendments and repeals) shall have effect.

NOTES
Railways Regulations 1998 SI 1998/1340.

[982]

Interpretation

3 (1) In these Regulations—

["access rights" means rights of access to railway infrastructure for the purpose of operating a service for the transport of goods or passengers;]

"the Act" means the Railways Act 1993;

"access charges review" means a review of access charges carried out in accordance with Schedule 4A to the Act;

"the 1996 Act" means the Channel Tunnel Rail Link Act 1996;

"*ad hoc* request" means a request for individual train paths made other than in accordance with the timetable for the capacity allocation process as set out in Schedule 4;

"allocation body" means a body or undertaking, other than the infrastructure manager, which is responsible, by virtue of regulation 16(3), for the functions and obligations of the infrastructure manager under Part 5 and Schedule 4;

"applicant" means—

(a) a railway undertaking licensed in accordance with the provisions of Council Directive 95/18/EC dated 19th June 1995 on the licensing of railway undertakings, as amended by Directive 2001/13/EC dated 26th February 2001 and Directive 2004/49/EC dated 29th April 2004, both of the European Parliament and of the Council; [or]

(b) ...

(c) a body or undertaking with public service or commercial interest in procuring infrastructure capacity ...;

"charging body" means a body or undertaking, other than the infrastructure manager, which is responsible, by virtue of regulation 12(7), for the functions and obligations of the infrastructure manager under Part 4 and Schedule 3;

"charging scheme" means the specific charging rules established in accordance with regulation 12 by the Office of Rail Regulation or, as the case may be, the infrastructure manager;

["competent authority" has the same meaning as in Article 2 of Regulation (EC) No 1370/2007, as amended from time to time;]

"charging system" means the system established by an infrastructure manager to determine access charges;

"the Concessionaires", "the tunnel system" and "shuttle service" have the same meanings as in the Channel Tunnel Act 1987;

"the Council Directives" means—

(a) Council Directive No 91/440/EEC dated 29th July 1991 on the development of the Community's railways, as amended by Directive 2001/12/EC dated 26th February 2001[, Directive 2004/51/EC dated 29th April 2004 and Directive 2007/58/EC dated 23rd October 2007, all of the European Parliament and of the Council; and]

(b) Directive No 2001/14 dated 26th February 2001 on the allocation of railway infrastructure capacity and the levying of charges for the use of railway infrastructure, as amended by Directive 2004/49/EC dated 29th April 2004 [and Directive 2007/58/EC dated 23rd October 2007, all of the European Parliament and of the Council;]

"development agreement" and "rail link facility" have the same meanings as in the 1996 Act, except that the definition of "rail link facility" shall also include any rail maintenance depot which provides maintenance services primarily for rail vehicles providing services on the rail link, as defined in section 56 of that Act, and to which the rail access is via that rail link;

"EEA state" means a Member State, Norway, Iceland or Liechtenstein;

"electrical plant" has the same meaning as in the Electricity Act 1989;

"factory" has the same meaning as in the Factories Act 1961;

"framework agreement" means either—

(a) an access contract described in section 18(2)(a) of the Act which satisfies one of the conditions in sub-section (1) of that section; or

(b) a legally binding agreement made other than in pursuance of sections 17 or 18 of the Act setting out the rights and obligations of an applicant and the infrastructure manager or, as the case may be, allocation body in relation to the infrastructure capacity to be allocated and the charges to be levied over a period in excess of one working timetable period;

"infrastructure manager" means any body or undertaking that is responsible in particular for—

(a) the establishment and maintenance of railway infrastructure; and

(b) the provision with respect to that infrastructure of network services as defined in section 82 of the Act, but, notwithstanding that some or all of the functions of the infrastructure manager on a network or part of a network may be allocated to different bodies or undertakings, the obligations in respect of those functions remain with the infrastructure manager except where the functions and obligations pass to an allocation or charging body by virtue of regulations 16(3) and 12(7) respectively;

"military establishment" means an establishment intended for use for naval, military or air force purposes or for the purposes of the Department of the Secretary of State responsible for defence;

"mine" has the same meaning as in the Mines and Quarries Act 1954;

"nuclear site" has the same meaning as in the Radioactive Substances Act 1993;

["public passenger transport" has the same meaning as in Article 2 of Regulation (EC) No 1370/2007, as amended from time to time;

"public service contract" has the same meaning as in Article 2 of Regulation (EC) No 1370/2007, as amended from time to time;

"public service operator" has the same meaning as in Article 2 of Regulation (EC) No 1370/2007, as amended from time to time;]

"quarry" has the same meaning as in the Quarries Regulations 1999;

"the Office of Rail Regulation" means the body established under section 15 of the Railways and Transport Safety Act 2003;

"railway infrastructure" consists of the items described as "network", "station" and "track", in section 83 of the Act, but excludes such items—

(a) which consist of, or are situated on, branch lines and sidings whose main operation is not directly connected to the provision of train paths;

(b) within a maintenance or goods depot, or a marshalling yard;

(c) within a railway terminal, port, factory, mine, quarry, nuclear site or site housing electrical plant;

(d) which consist of, or are situated on, networks reserved mainly for local, historical or touristic use; and

(e) within a military establishment;

["Regulation (EC) No 1370/2007" means Regulation (EC) No 1370/2007 of the European Parliament and of the Council of 23rd October 2007 on public passenger transport services by rail and by road and repealing Council Regulations (EEC) No 1191/69 and 1107/70;

"relevant public service contract" means a public service contract under which a relevant public service operator provides public passenger transport, the route or routes of which overlap with the route of the international passenger service notified to the Office of Rail Regulation under regulation 16(4A);

"relevant public service operator" means a public service operator providing public passenger transport, the route or routes of which overlap with the route of the international passenger service notified to the Office of Rail Regulation under regulation 16(4A);]

"service provider" means a body or undertaking that supplies any of the services—

(a) to which access is granted by virtue of regulations 6 or 7; or

(b) listed in paragraphs 2, 3 or 4 of Schedule 2,

whether or not that body or undertaking is also an infrastructure manager;

. . .

"the Treaty" means the consolidated versions of the Treaty on European Union and of the Treaty establishing the European Community;

"working day" means any day which is not a Saturday, Sunday, Good Friday, Christmas Day or a bank holiday in England and Wales by virtue of section 1 of the Banking and Financial Dealings Act 1971; and

"working timetable period" means the calendar year commencing at midnight on the second Saturday in December.

(2) Except where a definition in paragraph (1) applies, expressions used in these Regulations and in the Council Directives shall have the same meaning as in the Council Directives.

NOTES

Prospective amendment Certain amendments to reg 3(1) by SI 2009/1122 come into force on 1 January 2010, as noted below.

Amendment Para (1): definition "access rights" substituted for definition "access and transit rights" by SI 2009/1122, as from 1 January 2010;
in definition "applicant", in sub-para (a) word "or" in square brackets inserted, sub-para (b) revoked, and in sub-para (c) words omitted revoked, by SI 2009/1122, as from 1 January 2010;
definition "competent authority" inserted by SI 2009/1122, as from 1 January 2010;
in definition "the Council Directives", in sub-paras (a), (b), words in square brackets substituted by SI 2009/1122;
definitions "public passenger transport", "public service contract" and "public service operator" inserted by SI 2009/1122;
definitions "Regulation (EC) No 1370/2007", "relevant public service contract" and "relevant public service operator" inserted by SI 2009/1122, as from 1 January 2010;
definition "transit rights" (omitted) revoked by SI 2009/1122, as from 1 January 2010.
Council Directive 95/18/EC OJ L143, 27.06.1995, p 70.
Directive 2001/13/EC OJ L75, 15.03.2001, p 26.
Directive 2004/49/EC OJ L164, 30.04.2004, p 44.
Council Directive 91/440/EEC OJ L237, 24.08.1991, p 25.
Directive 2001/12/EC OJ L75, 15.03.2001, p 1.
Directive 2004/51/EC OJ L164, 30.04.2004, p 164.
Directive 2007/58/EC OJ L315, 03.12.2007, p 44.
Directive 2001/14/EC OJ L75, 15.03.2001, p 29.
Regulation (EC) 1370/2007 OJ L315, 03.12.2007, p 1.
"Development agreement" and "rail link facility" have the same meanings as in the 1996 Act See the Channel Tunnel Rail Link Act 1996, ss 56, 17 respectively.
Channel Tunnel Act 1987 For the meaning of "the Concessionaires", "the tunnel system" and "shuttle service" in that Act, see s 49 thereof.
Electricity Act 1989 For the meaning of "electrical plant" in that Act, see s 64 thereof.
Factories Act 1961 For the meaning of "factory" in that Act, see s 175 thereof.
Mines and Quarries Act 1954 For the meaning of "mine" in that Act, see s 180 thereof.
Radioactive Substances Act 1993 For the meaning of "nuclear site" in that Act, see s 47(1) thereof.
Quarries Regulations 1999 SI 1999/2024, in the title Mines, Minerals and Quarries.

[983]

Scope

4 (1) Subject to paragraph (2), regulations 5, 6, 8 to 10, 12(5) and (6) and paragraph 1(2) of Schedule 3 apply to—

(a) the management of railway infrastructure; and
(b) the rail transport activities of the railway undertakings established or to be established in an EEA State.

(2) Paragraph (1) does not apply to railway undertakings whose activity is limited to the provision of solely urban, suburban or regional services.

(3) Subject to paragraphs (4) and (5), Parts 2 to 5 and Schedules 2 to 4, with the exception of the provisions referred to in paragraph (1), apply to the use of—

(a) railway infrastructure; and
(b) to the extent stated to apply, the services described in regulation 7 and Schedule 2,

for domestic and international rail traffic.

(4) Paragraph (3) does not apply—

(a) to stand-alone local and regional networks for passenger services on railway infrastructure;
(b) to networks intended only for the operation of urban or suburban passenger services;
(c) until such time as capacity is requested by another applicant, to regional networks used for regional freight services solely by a railway undertaking referred to in paragraph (2); or
(d) to networks—
    (i) situated within a factory, nuclear site, or site housing electrical plant;
    (ii) within a mine or quarry;
    (iii) used solely in connection with the carrying out of any building works; or
    (iv) within a military establishment,

    that are used only by the person responsible for that network for the purposes of freight operations connected with the premises or building works referred to in this subparagraph.

(5) Part 5 and Schedule 4 do not apply to the services referred to in regulation 6.

(6) Parts 6 and 7 and Schedule 1 apply to all matters within any part of the scope of Parts 2 to 5 and Schedules 2 to 4.

(7) These Regulations do not apply to the management of the tunnel system and the rail transport activity of the Concessionaires in respect of any shuttle service.

[984]

PART 2
ACCESS TO RAILWAY INFRASTRUCTURE AND SERVICES

[Access rights

5 (1) A railway undertaking is entitled on equitable conditions to such access as may be necessary for the purpose of the operation of any type of rail freight service or international passenger service.

(2) Subject to paragraph (3), the access rights of a railway undertaking for the purpose of the operation of an international passenger service include the right to pick up passengers at any station located on the international route and set them down at another, including stations located in the same Member State.

(3) The rights conferred by paragraphs (1) and (2) are exercisable subject to the provisions of regulation 29A.

(4) It is the duty of the infrastructure manager to ensure that the entitlements conferred by this regulation are honoured.

(5) Without prejudice to the generality of regulation 29, if a railway undertaking is denied the entitlements conferred on it by this regulation other than pursuant to a decision of the Office of Rail Regulation under regulation 29A, that railway undertaking has a right of appeal to the Office of Rail Regulation in accordance with regulation 29.]

NOTES

Amendment Substituted by SI 2009/1122, as from 1 January 2010.

[985]

Access to terminals and ports

6 (1) Subject to paragraph (2), [a] railway undertaking is entitled, for the purposes of the rail activities referred to in regulation 5, to track access to and the supply of services in terminals and ports linked to the rail network which serve, or potentially serve, more than one final customer.

(2) Requests by … railway undertakings, in accordance with the entitlements conferred by paragraph (1), may be subject to restrictions only if viable alternatives by rail under market conditions exist.

(3) The infrastructure manager or, as the case may be, service provider must ensure that the entitlements conferred by this regulation are honoured, and that access to, and the supply of, services is granted in a transparent and non-discriminatory manner.

(4) Without prejudice to the generality of regulation 29, if [a] railway undertaking is denied the entitlements conferred on it by this regulation, or if the entitlements are made subject to restrictions other than in accordance with paragraph (2), that … railway undertaking has a right of appeal to the Office of Rail Regulation in accordance with regulation 29.

NOTES

Amendment Para (1): word in square brackets substituted by SI 2009/1122, as from 1 January 2010.
Para (2): words omitted revoked by SI 2009/1122, as from 1 January 2010.
Para (4): word in square brackets substituted, and words omitted revoked, by SI 2009/1122, as from 1 January 2010.

[986]

Access to services

7 (1) Subject to paragraph (2), applicants are entitled to services comprising—

(a) the minimum access package; and
(b) the track access to service facilities and the supply of services,

described in paragraphs 1 and 2 of Schedule 2.

(2) If the infrastructure manager or service provider to whom a request has been made for the supply of a service referred to in paragraph (1) does not supply such a service, the infrastructure manager must, if he is the provider of the main infrastructure, use all reasonable endeavours to facilitate the supply of that service through the appropriate service provider.

(3) The infrastructure manager or, as the case may be, service provider must ensure that the entitlements granted by this regulation are honoured, and access to the services referred to in paragraph (1) must be provided in a non-discriminatory manner.

(4) Where the infrastructure manager or service provider supplies any of the services described in paragraph 2 of Schedule 2, requests for the supply of such services may only be refused if a viable alternative means of the service being provided under market conditions exists.

(5) Where the infrastructure manager or service provider offers to supply any of the services described in paragraph 3 of Schedule 2 he must, in response to a request from an applicant, supply the services to that applicant.

(6) An applicant may request the supply of any of the services described in paragraph 4 of Schedule 2 from an infrastructure manager or service provider but that infrastructure manager or service provider is under no obligation to supply the services requested.

(7) Without prejudice to the generality of regulation 29, if an applicant is denied the entitlements conferred on it by this regulation, that applicant has a right of appeal to the Office of Rail Regulation in accordance with regulation 29.

[987]

PART 3
INFRASTRUCTURE MANAGEMENT

Management independence

8 (1) Railway undertakings must, in their management, administration and internal control over administrative, economic and accounting matters, maintain the status of an independent operator and hold, in particular, assets, budgets and accounts which are separate from those of the State.

(2) Subject to the requirements set out in Parts 4 and 5 and Schedules 3 and 4 about the determination of infrastructure charges and the allocation of infrastructure capacity an infrastructure manager must be responsible for its own management, administration and internal control.

(3) Railway undertakings must keep and publish profit and loss accounts and either balance sheets or annual statements of assets and liabilities for business relating to the provision of rail-freight transport services.

(4) Funds paid for activities relating to the provision of passenger-transport services as public-service remits must be shown separately in the relevant accounts and may not be transferred to activities relating to the provision of other transport services or any other business.

[988]

Separation between infrastructure management and transport operations

9 (1) Any body which incorporates the functions of both infrastructure manager and railway undertaking must—

- (a) prepare and publish separate profit and loss accounts and balance sheets in respect of business relating to the—
  - (i) provision of transport services as a railway undertaking; and
  - (ii) management of railway infrastructure; and
- (b) ensure that public funds granted to such a body are not transferred between that part of the body responsible for the provision of transport services and that responsible for the management of railway infrastructure.

(2) Accounts for the two areas of activity described in paragraph (1) must be kept in such a way as to reflect the prohibition set out in that paragraph.

(3) The monitoring of the observance of public service obligations, where stipulated in the terms of a contract required by regulation 16(10), must be carried out by bodies or undertakings which do not provide rail transport services.

[989]

Business Plans

10 (1) The infrastructure manager must draw up a business plan which is designed for the purpose of ensuring—

(a) optimal and efficient use and development of the infrastructure; and
(b) financial balance.

(2) The plan referred to in paragraph (1) must include details of investment and financial programmes, and provide the means by which the objectives set out in that paragraph are to be achieved.

(3) Each railway undertaking must draw up a business plan, which must include their investment and financing programmes, and which is designed for the purpose of ensuring—

(a) financial equilibrium; and
(b) other technical, commercial and financial management objectives.

(4) The plan referred to in paragraph (3) must provide the means by which the objectives set out in that paragraph are to be achieved.

(5) The Office of Rail Regulation shall, at least once a year, request confirmation that a business plan has been produced in accordance with paragraphs (1) and (3) and each infrastructure manager or, as the case may be, railway undertaking, to whom such a request is made shall be under an obligation to comply with that request.

(6) For the purposes of regulation 31, a request by the Office of Rail Regulation in accordance with paragraph (5) shall be treated as a request for information.

[990]

Network Statement

11 (1) The infrastructure manager must, following consultation with all interested parties, develop and publish a network statement containing the information described in paragraph (4).

(2) Where, by virtue of regulations 12(7) or 16(3) a charging body or, as the case may be, allocation body is responsible for the functions of the infrastructure manager in Parts 4 or 5, that charging body or allocation body must provide the infrastructure manager with such information as is necessary to enable that infrastructure manager to—

(a) include the information described in paragraph (4) in the network statement; and
(b) keep the network statement up to date in accordance with paragraph (5).

(3) A service provider who is not the infrastructure manager must provide the infrastructure manager with such information as is necessary to enable that infrastructure manager to—

(a) include the information described in paragraph (4)(b) and, where applicable, (d) in the network statement; and
(b) keep the network statement up to date in accordance with paragraph (5).

(4) The information referred to in paragraph (1) is—

(a) a section setting out the nature of the railway infrastructure which is available to applicants and the conditions of access to it;
(b) details as to where further information may be obtained about the nature of the track access to, and supply of services in, any of the terminals, ports and service facilities to which access may be obtained pursuant to regulations 6 and 7;
(c) a description of the charging principles and tariffs, including details of the charging methodology, exceptions to the charging principles, and discounts;
(d) details of charges for the supply of those services listed in Schedule 2 which are provided by only one supplier;

(e) a description of the principles and criteria for the allocation of infrastructure capacity, setting out the general capacity characteristics of the infrastructure available and the restrictions on its use, including likely capacity requirements for maintenance;

(f) the procedures and deadlines in the capacity allocation process and specific criteria employed in that process, in particular—

(i) the procedures according to which applicants can request infrastructure capacity from the infrastructure manager;

(ii) the information to be provided by applicants;

(iii) the timetable for the application and allocation process;

(iv) the principles governing the co-ordination process, in particular the arrangement of international train paths, and the effect that modification of such paths might have on other infrastructure managers;

(v) information about the procedures established in accordance with regulation 17(4) for the allocation of infrastructure capacity at an international level, including information about the membership and methods of operation of any representative groups, and all relevant criteria used to assess and allocate infrastructure capacity which crosses more than one network;

(vi) the dispute resolution procedure established in accordance with regulation 20(5);

(vii) details of any section of railway infrastructure which has been designated for use by specified types of rail services in accordance with regulation 22;

(viii) the procedures to be followed for congested infrastructure, and any priority criteria for the allocation of congested infrastructure set in accordance with regulation 23(5) and (6);

(ix) the findings of any capacity enhancement plan completed in accordance with regulation 25;

(x) details of restrictions on the use of infrastructure;

(xi) the threshold quota to be applied by the infrastructure manager in requiring a train path to be surrendered under regulation 26(1); and

(xii) the conditions relating to previous levels of utilisation of capacity to be taken into account by the infrastructure manager in determining priorities in accordance with regulation 26(3); and

(g) the measures taken by the infrastructure manager to ensure fair treatment of freight services and international services, and in responding to *ad hoc* requests for infrastructure capacity.

(5) The infrastructure manager must keep the network statement up to date and modify it as necessary.

(6) The infrastructure manager must publish the network statement not less than four months before the deadline for applications for infrastructure capacity as described under paragraph (4)(f)(iii).

(7) Any fee charged by the infrastructure manager for the provision, on request, of a copy of the network statement must not exceed the cost of producing that copy.

(8) If the information required under paragraphs (2) or (3) is not provided to the satisfaction of the infrastructure manager, he may refer the matter to the Office of Rail Regulation for a determination as to whether additional information must be supplied.

(9) Where a matter is referred to the Office of Rail Regulation in accordance with paragraph (8), it is the duty of that Office to make the determination within such period as is reasonable in all the circumstances, and any such determination shall be binding on all parties.

[991]

PART 4
INFRASTRUCTURE CHARGES

Establishing, determining and collecting charges

12 (1) Subject to paragraph (3), the Office of Rail Regulation must establish the charging framework and the specific charging rules governing the determination of the fees to be charged in accordance with paragraph (5).

(2) Subject to paragraphs (3) and (7), the infrastructure manager must—

(a) determine the fees to be charged for use of the infrastructure in accordance with the charging framework, the specific charging rules, and the principles and exceptions set out in Schedule 3; and

(b) collect those fees.

(3) Paragraphs (1) and (2) do not apply where the infrastructure to which the charge relates is a rail link facility.

(4) Where paragraph (3) applies, the Secretary of State must establish the charging framework through the development agreement, and the infrastructure manager must, subject to paragraph (7)—

(a) establish the specific charging rules governing the determination of the fees to be charged in accordance with paragraph (5);

(b) determine the fees to be charged for the use of the infrastructure in accordance with the charging framework, the specific charging rules and the principles and exceptions set out in Schedule 3; and

(c) collect those fees.

(5) Subject to the provisions in paragraphs (1) to (4), the infrastructure manager must—

(a) charge fees for use of the railway infrastructure for which he is responsible; and

(b) utilise such fees as are received to fund his business.

(6) Applicants must, subject to the right of appeal to the Office of Rail Regulation provided in regulation 29, pay such fees as are charged by the infrastructure manager for use of the railway infrastructure.

(7) Subject to paragraph (8), an infrastructure manager responsible for any of the functions of the infrastructure manager described in this Part and Schedule 3 must, in its legal form, organisation or decision-making functions, be independent of any railway undertaking and, where he is not so independent, that infrastructure manager must ensure that the functions described in this Part and Schedule 3 are performed by a charging body that is so independent.

(8) The separation required by paragraph (7) does not apply to the function of the collection of fees charged in accordance with paragraph (2)(b) and (4)(c).

(9) The infrastructure manager must be able to justify that the charges invoiced to each railway undertaking for access to the infrastructure comply with the methodology, rules and, where applicable, scales laid down in the network statement and, where information about the charges imposed is requested by either the Secretary of State or the Office of Rail Regulation, the infrastructure manager must supply the information requested.

(10) Infrastructure managers must co-operate to achieve the efficient operation of train services which cross more than one infrastructure network and must, in particular, aim to guarantee the optimum competitiveness of international rail freight.

(11) Infrastructure managers may establish such joint organisations as may be appropriate to enable the co-operation referred to in paragraph (10) to be achieved and any such co-operation or joint organisations shall be bound by the rules set out in these Regulations.

(12) The infrastructure manager must respect the commercial confidentiality of information provided to it by applicants for infrastructure capacity.

[992]

Infrastructure costs and accounts

13 (1) The Office of Rail Regulation through the access charges review or, in the case of a rail link facility, the Secretary of State through the development agreement, must lay down conditions, including where appropriate advance payments, to ensure that, under normal business conditions and over a reasonable time period, the accounts of an infrastructure manager shall at least balance—

(a) income from infrastructure charges;

(b) surpluses from other commercial activities; and

(c) public funds,

with infrastructure expenditure.

(2) The infrastructure manager must, with due regard to safety and to maintaining and improving the quality of the infrastructure service, be provided with incentives to reduce the costs of provision of infrastructure and the level of access charges.

[(3) The Office of Rail Regulation must—

(a) in the case of a rail link facility, exercise its rights and responsibilities under or by virtue of the relevant development agreement; and

(b) in any other case, exercise its functions under the Act

in order to ensure that the requirements set out in paragraph (2) are complied with.]

NOTES

Amendment Para (3): substituted by SI 2009/1122.

[993]

Performance scheme

14 (1) The infrastructure manager must establish a performance scheme as part of the charging system to encourage railway undertakings and the infrastructure manager to minimise disruption and improve the performance of the railway network.

(2) The performance scheme referred to in paragraph (1) may include—

(a) penalties for actions which disrupt the operation of the rail network;

(b) compensation for undertakings which suffer from disruption; and

(c) bonuses that reward better than planned performance.

(3) The basic principles of the performance scheme must apply in a non-discriminatory manner throughout the network to which that scheme relates.

[994]

Reservation charges

15 (1) The infrastructure manager may levy an appropriate charge for capacity that is requested but not used, and the imposition of this charge must provide incentives for efficient use of capacity.

(2) The infrastructure manager must provide, to any interested party, information about the infrastructure capacity allocated to applicants.

[995]

PART 5

ALLOCATION OF INFRASTRUCTURE CAPACITY

Capacity allocation

16 (1) Whilst respecting the requirements for management independence stipulated in regulation 8, the Office of Rail Regulation or, in the case of a rail link facility, the Secretary of State, may establish a framework for the allocation of infrastructure capacity.

(2) The infrastructure manager shall, subject to paragraph (3), be responsible for the establishment of specific capacity allocation rules and for the process of allocating infrastructure capacity in respect of the infrastructure for which he has responsibility.

(3) An infrastructure manager responsible for any of the functions of the infrastructure manager described in this Part and Schedule 4 must, in its legal form, organisation or decision-making functions, be independent of any railway undertaking and, where he is not so independent, that infrastructure manager must ensure that the functions of the infrastructure manager described in this Part are performed by an allocation body that is so independent.

(4) Subject to paragraph (7), any applicant may apply to the infrastructure manager for the allocation of infrastructure capacity.

[(4A) An applicant applying for infrastructure capacity with a view to operating an international passenger service must give notice of that fact to the infrastructure manager concerned and to the Office of Rail Regulation and provide them with such information as the Office of Rail Regulation may reasonably require or prescribe.

(4B) When the Office of Rail Regulation receives a notice from an applicant under paragraph (4A), it must provide any competent authority that has awarded a rail passenger service defined in a relevant public service contract, any railway undertaking which is a relevant public service operator and any other competent authority with a right to limit access along the route of the international passenger service notified under paragraph (4A) with a copy of the information in relation to that service provided to it in accordance with that paragraph.]

(5) The infrastructure manager must ensure that the allocation process is conducted in accordance with the timetable set out in Schedule 4.

(6) Subject to paragraph (8), an applicant who has been granted capacity by the infrastructure manager, whether that capacity is in the form of—

(a) a framework agreement made in accordance with regulation 18 specifying the characteristics of the infrastructure granted; or

(b) specific infrastructure capacity in the form of a train path,

must not trade that capacity with another applicant or transfer it to another undertaking or service.

(7) Any person who trades in capacity contrary to the provisions of paragraph (6) shall not be entitled to apply for capacity under paragraph (4) for the period of the working timetable period to which the allocation of capacity transferred related.

(8) The use of capacity by a railway undertaking on behalf of an applicant who is not a railway undertaking, in order to further the business of that applicant, is not a transfer for the purposes of paragraph (6).

(9) The infrastructure manager must not allocate capacity in the form of specific train paths for any period in excess of one working timetable period.

(10) A contract, either in the form of a framework agreement or any other type of contract, setting out the rights and obligations of the parties, must be concluded between the infrastructure manager and any applicant to whom infrastructure capacity is allocated before that infrastructure capacity is utilised.

(11) The infrastructure manager must—

(a) ensure that infrastructure capacity is allocated on a fair and non-discriminatory basis;

(b) ensure that the contracts referred to in paragraph (10) are non-discriminatory, transparent, and in accordance with the requirements of these Regulations; and

(c) respect the confidentiality of information supplied to him as part of the capacity allocation process.

(12) In reserving infrastructure capacity for the purposes of scheduled track maintenance, as requested under regulation 19(5), the infrastructure manager must take into account the effect of that reservation on applicants.

NOTES
Amendment Paras (4A), (4B): inserted by SI 2009/1122.

[996]

Co-operation in the allocation of infrastructure capacity crossing more than one network

17 (1) This regulation applies to an application for infrastructure capacity crossing more than one network.

(2) The infrastructure managers must—

(a) co-operate to enable the efficient creation and allocation of infrastructure capacity pursuant to a request for capacity crossing more than one network; and

(b) before consulting on the draft working timetable agree with the other relevant infrastructure managers which international train paths are to be included in that draft working timetable.

(3) The international train paths referred to in paragraph 2(b) may only be adjusted if absolutely necessary.

(4) The infrastructure managers must establish such procedures as are appropriate, in accordance with the requirements set out in these Regulations, to enable the co-operation referred to in paragraph 2(a) to take place, and such procedures must include representatives of the infrastructure managers whose allocation decisions have an impact on one or more infrastructure managers.

(5) Subject to paragraph (6), the procedures established by virtue of paragraph (4) may permit appropriate representatives of infrastructure managers outside the European Community to be associated with these procedures.

(6) Where paragraph (5) applies, the infrastructure managers must inform the European Commission and invite representatives to attend appropriate meetings as an observer.

(7) At any meeting or other activity undertaken to facilitate the allocation of infrastructure capacity across more than one network, decisions may only be taken by representatives of the relevant infrastructure managers.

(8) In acting in accordance with paragraph (2) the infrastructure managers must assess the need for and, where necessary, propose and organise international train paths in such a way as to enable *ad hoc* capacity for freight services to be granted in accordance with regulation 21.

(9) The prearranged train paths referred to in paragraph (8) must be made available to applicants through any infrastructure manager who participates in the international co-ordination of train paths referred to in this regulation.

[997]

Framework agreements

18 (1) Subject to the requirements of this regulation, and without prejudice to articles 81, 82 and 86 of the Treaty, an infrastructure manager may enter into a framework agreement with an applicant for the purpose of specifying the characteristics of the infrastructure capacity required by and offered to the applicant over a period of time exceeding one working timetable period.

(2) An applicant who is a party to a framework agreement may apply for the allocation of capacity in accordance with the terms of that agreement

(3) Whilst seeking to meet the legitimate commercial needs of the applicant [and without prejudice to paragraph (9B)], a framework agreement must not specify any train path in detail.

(4) The effect of a framework agreement must not be such as to preclude the use of the railway infrastructure subject to that framework agreement by other applicants or services.

(5) A framework agreement must contain terms permitting the amendment or limitation of any condition contained in that framework agreement if such amendment or limitation would enable better use to be made of the railway infrastructure.

(6) A framework agreement may contain penalties applicable on modification or termination of the agreement by any party.

(7) Other than in circumstances described in paragraphs (8)[, (9) and (9A)], a framework agreement made in accordance with paragraph (1) shall in principle be for a period of up to five years[, renewable for periods equal to its original duration; provided that the infrastructure manager may agree to a shorter or longer period in specific cases.]

(8) [Subject to paragraphs 9 and (9A),] a framework agreement for a period [longer than five years] must be justified by the existence of commercial contracts, specialised investments or risks.

[(9) Subject to paragraph (9A), a framework agreement in relation to infrastructure which has been designated in accordance with regulation 22(2) ("a designated infrastructure framework agreement") may be for a period of up to fifteen years where there is a substantial and long-term investment justified by the applicant.]

[(9A) A designated infrastructure framework agreement may be for a period in excess of fifteen years in exceptional circumstances, in particular where there is large-scale and long-term investment and particularly where such investment is covered by contractual commitments including a multi-annual amortisation plan.

(9B) An application for a designated infrastructure framework agreement to which paragraph (9) or (9A) applies may specify the capacity characteristics, including the frequency, volume and quality of the train paths, to be provided to the applicant for the duration of the framework agreement in sufficient detail to ensure that these are clearly established.

(9C) The infrastructure manager may reduce capacity reserved under the terms of a designated infrastructure framework agreement to which paragraph (9) or (9A) applies where, over a continuous period of at least one month, that capacity has been used less than the threshold quota stipulated in the network statement.]

(10) Whilst respecting commercial confidentiality, the general nature of each framework agreement must be made available by the infrastructure manager to any interested party.

(11) This regulation is without prejudice to section 18 of the Act in the case of a framework agreement which is an access contract to which that section applies.

[(12) Before entering into a framework agreement in relation to a rail link facility, and before amending any such agreement, the infrastructure manager and the applicant must obtain the approval of the Office of Rail Regulation.

(13) Nothing in these Regulations has the effect of applying any of sections 17 to 22C of the Act to a rail link facility.]

NOTES

Amendment Para (3): words in square brackets inserted by SI 2009/1122.

Para (7): words in first pair of square brackets substituted, and words in second pair of square brackets inserted, by SI 2009/1122.

Para (8): words in first pair of square brackets inserted, and words in second pair of square brackets substituted, by SI 2009/1122.

Para (9): substituted by SI 2009/1122.

Paras (9A)–(9C): inserted by SI 2009/1122.

Paras (12), (13): substituted for original para (12) by SI 2009/1122.

[998]

Application for infrastructure capacity

19 (1) Applicants may submit a request to the infrastructure manager for an agreement granting rights to use railway infrastructure against a charge as provided for in Part 4.

(2) An applicant wishing to apply for infrastructure capacity must submit an application to the infrastructure manager in accordance with the timetable for the allocation process set out in Schedule 4.

(3) Applicants may submit a request to a single infrastructure manager for infrastructure capacity crossing more than one network and, where such an application is made, that infrastructure manager is permitted to act on behalf of that applicant in seeking from other infrastructure managers the infrastructure capacity requested.

(4) The infrastructure manager must ensure that, for infrastructure capacity crossing more than one network, applicants may apply direct to any joint body established by the infrastructure managers.

(5) Requests for infrastructure capacity to enable maintenance of the network to be carried out must be submitted in accordance with the timetable set out in Schedule 4.

[999]

Scheduling and co-ordination

20 (1) The infrastructure manager must, so far as possible—

(a) meet all requests for infrastructure capacity, including those requests for train paths which cross more than one network; and

(b) in so doing, take account of all constraints on applicants, including the economic effect on their business.

(2) The infrastructure manager may give priority to specific services within the scheduling and co-ordination process, but only in accordance with the provisions in regulations 22 and 23.

(3) The infrastructure manager must consult interested parties about the draft working timetable, and must allow such interested parties a period of at least one calendar month to submit their comments.

(4) In the event of conflict between different requests for infrastructure capacity, the infrastructure manager must use all best endeavours, in consultation with the appropriate applicants, and through co-ordination of the requests, to ensure the best

possible matching of all requirements and, in so far as it is reasonable to do so, may propose alternative infrastructure capacity from that requested in order to resolve the conflict.

(5) The infrastructure manager must facilitate the establishment and operation of a dispute resolution system to resolve disputes about the allocation of infrastructure capacity and, where that system is applied, a decision on the matters in dispute must be reached no later than ten working days after the final submission of all relevant information in accordance with that system.

(6) The infrastructure manager must take such measures as are appropriate to deal with any concerns about the allocation process raised by interested parties.

(7) For the purposes of this regulation "interested parties" includes—

(a) all applicants for infrastructure capacity as part of the specific allocation process to which the draft working timetable relates; and

(b) other parties who have indicated to the Office of Rail Regulation, in such form or manner as that Office may from time to time prescribe, that they wish to have the opportunity to comment as to the effect that the working timetable might have on their ability to procure rail services during the working timetable period to which the draft working timetable relates.

[1000]

Ad hoc requests

21 (1) In addition to making an application for capacity in accordance with the annual timetable process described in regulation 19, an applicant may submit *ad hoc* requests for infrastructure capacity in the form of individual train paths to the infrastructure manager.

(2) The infrastructure manager must respond to a request described in paragraph (1) as quickly as possible and, in any event, no later than five working days from receipt of the request.

(3) The infrastructure manager must make available, to all potential applicants for such individual train paths, information about available spare capacity on the network for which he is responsible.

(4) The infrastructure manager must, including in the case of congested infrastructure, undertake an evaluation of the need for reserve capacity to be kept available within the final working timetable to enable him to respond rapidly to foreseeable *ad hoc* requests for infrastructure capacity.

[1001]

Declaration of specialised infrastructure

22 (1) Subject to paragraph (2), all infrastructure capacity must be available for the use of all types of rail transport service which conform to the characteristics necessary for use of that infrastructure, as defined in the infrastructure manager's network statement.

(2) Subject to the provisions set out in paragraph (3), the infrastructure manager may designate particular sections of the infrastructure for use by specified types of rail service without prejudice to articles 81, 82 and 86 of the Treaty and, once the infrastructure is so designated, may give priority to that specified type of rail service in the allocation of infrastructure capacity.

(3) Those provisions are that—

(a) suitable alternative routes for other types of rail transport service must exist and be available;

(b) before making such a designation the infrastructure manager must consult—

(i) the Secretary of State;

(ii) where an element of the infrastructure which it is proposed to designate is in Scotland, Scottish Ministers;

(iii) the Office of Rail Regulation; and

(iv) all other interested parties; and

(c) such designation must not prevent the use of that designated infrastructure by other types of rail transport service when capacity is available and an application for that capacity is submitted by an applicant wishing to operate a service using rolling stock which conforms to the technical characteristics necessary for operation on that infrastructure.

[1002]

Congested infrastructure

23 (1) Where, after the co-ordination of requests for capacity and consultation with the applicants in accordance with regulation 20(4), it is not possible for the infrastructure manager to satisfy requests for infrastructure adequately, the infrastructure manager must declare that element of the infrastructure on which such requests cannot be satisfied to be congested.

(2) Where, during the preparation of the working timetable for the next timetable period, the infrastructure manager considers that an element of the infrastructure is likely to become congested during the period to which that working timetable relates, he must declare that element of the infrastructure to be congested.

(3) When infrastructure has been declared to be congested under the provisions of this regulation the infrastructure manager must inform—

(a) existing users of that infrastructure;
(b) new applicants for infrastructure capacity which includes that element of the infrastructure which has been declared to be congested;
(c) the Office of Rail Regulation;
(d) the Secretary of State; and
(e) where any element of the infrastructure which has been declared to be congested is in Scotland, Scottish Ministers.

(4) When infrastructure has been declared to be congested in accordance with paragraphs (1) or (2) the infrastructure manager must undertake a capacity analysis of the congested infrastructure, as described in regulation 24, unless a capacity enhancement plan, as described in regulation 25, is in the process of being implemented.

(5) When an element of the infrastructure has been declared to be congested in accordance with paragraphs (1) or (2) and either—

(a) a charge as described in paragraph 1(8) of Schedule 3 has not been levied; or
(b) the charge described in paragraph (a) has been levied but has not achieved a satisfactory result,

the infrastructure manager may set priority criteria for the allocation of infrastructure capacity which includes that congested element of the infrastructure.

(6) The priority criteria referred to in paragraph (5) must—

(a) take account of the importance of a service to society, relative to any other service which will consequently be excluded; and
(b) ensure that freight services, and in particular international freight services, are given adequate consideration in the determination of those criteria.

(7) If during the course of the working timetable period to which the declaration of congested infrastructure relates, but before the completion of the capacity analysis, the congestion is resolved, the infrastructure manager may revoke the declaration made in accordance with paragraph (1).

(8) Where paragraph (7) applies, the infrastructure manager must inform the persons referred to in paragraph (3) that the declaration has been revoked.

[1003]

Capacity analysis

24 (1) Where required in accordance with regulation 23(4), the infrastructure manager must carry out a capacity analysis of the congested infrastructure in order to identify the reasons for the congestion and the measures which might be taken in the short and medium term to ease that congestion.

(2) In conducting the capacity analysis, and in order to identify the reasons for the congestion, the infrastructure manager must consider the—

(a) characteristics of the congested infrastructure;
(b) operating procedures used on that infrastructure; and
(c) characteristics of the different rail services which have been allocated capacity to operate on that infrastructure.

(3) In seeking to determine measures to alleviate congestion the infrastructure manager must consider, in particular—

(a) re-routing of services;
(b) re-timing of services;
(c) alterations to the line-speed; and
(d) infrastructure improvements.

(4) The infrastructure manager must consult the Secretary of State or, where any part of the capacity analysis relates to railway infrastructure in Scotland, Scottish Ministers, during the preparation of the capacity analysis.

(5) The infrastructure manager must complete the capacity analysis within six months from the date on which the infrastructure is declared to be congested in accordance with regulation 23(1) or (2) and make the findings of the analysis available to the parties described in regulation 23(3).

[1004]

Capacity enhancement plan

25 (1) The infrastructure manager must, within six months of the publication of a capacity analysis in accordance with regulation 24, produce a capacity enhancement plan.

(2) In producing the capacity enhancement plan, the infrastructure manager must—

(a) consult such interested parties as he considers necessary, including those described in regulation 23(3); and
(b) at least one month before the deadline for completion of the plan seek the prior approval of the Secretary of State or, if any part of the capacity enhancement plan relates to infrastructure in Scotland, Scottish Ministers, to the capacity enhancement plan.

(3) The capacity enhancement plan must identify the—

(a) reasons for the congestion;
(b) likely future development of traffic;
(c) constraints on infrastructure development; and
(d) options for and costs of enhancing the capacity, including the potential effect on access charges.

(4) On the basis of a cost benefit analysis of the potential measures for action identified in the capacity enhancement plan, that plan must include—

(a) details of the action to be taken to enhance the capacity of the congested infrastructure; and
(b) a timetable for the completion of the detailed measures identified in accordance with sub-paragraph (a).

(5) Subject to paragraph (6), if the utilisation of capacity on that element of the infrastructure which is the subject of the capacity enhancement plan attracts a scarcity charge, in accordance with paragraph 1(8) of Schedule 3, the infrastructure manager must cease the levying of such charge in situations where—

(a) paragraph (1) applies but he does not produce a capacity enhancement plan for that part of the infrastructure which is subject to the scarcity charge, as required by this regulation; or
(b) he fails to make progress with implementation of those areas of the action plan produced in accordance with paragraph (4).

(6) Paragraph (5) does not apply where—

(a) the action plan produced in accordance with paragraph (4) cannot be implemented for reasons beyond the immediate control of the infrastructure manager; or
(b) the options identified in that action plan are not economical or financially viable,

provided that prior approval to continue to levy the scarcity charge is obtained from the Office of Rail Regulation or, in the case of a rail link facility, the Secretary of State.

(7) At the end of the six month period starting with the publication of the capacity analysis in accordance with regulation 24, whether or not the approval sought under paragraph (2)(b) has been received, the infrastructure manager must provide the parties consulted under paragraph (2)(a) with a copy of the plan and the timetable for completion of the measures identified to resolve the congestion.

[1005]

Use of train paths

26 (1) Subject to paragraph (2) the infrastructure manager must, in particular where infrastructure has been declared to be congested in accordance with regulation 23, require an applicant who has, over a period of at least one month, used a train path less often than the threshold quota stipulated in the network statement, to surrender that train path.

(2) Paragraph (1) does not apply if, in the view of the infrastructure manager, the failure to use the train path in accordance with the threshold quota stipulated in the network statement arose as a result of non-economic reasons outside the control of the applicant.

(3) The infrastructure manager may in the network statement specify conditions under which previous levels of capacity utilisation will be taken into account in determining the priorities to be used in making decisions on the allocation of capacity.

[1006]

Special measures to be taken in the event of disruption

27 (1) In the event of disruption to train movements caused by technical failure or accident, the infrastructure manager must take all such steps as are necessary to restore the normal operation of the network.

(2) The infrastructure manager must have in place a contingency plan listing the public bodies who are required to be informed in the event of a serious incident or serious disruption to train movements.

(3) The infrastructure manager may, in the event of an emergency and where absolutely necessary on account of a breakdown which renders a part of the infrastructure temporarily unusable, withdraw allocated train paths without warning and with immediate effect for such period as is necessary to repair the affected infrastructure.

(4) Subject to paragraph (5), the infrastructure manager may, if he deems it to be necessary, require applicants to make available to him such resources as he considers appropriate to restore the normal operation of the network as quickly as possible.

(5) Where a contract or framework agreement between an applicant and the infrastructure manager incorporates conditions as to the special measures to be taken in the event of disruption, the resources required by the infrastructure manager under paragraph (4) must be in accordance with those conditions.

[1007]

PART 6
REGULATION AND APPEALS

Regulatory body

28 (1) Section 4 of the Act has effect, to the extent relevant and consistent with the Council Directives, as if the reference to the functions assigned or transferred to the Office of Rail Regulation under or by virtue of Part 1 of the Act included the functions assigned to it under or by virtue of these Regulations.

(2) The Office of Rail Regulation … must ensure that charges for the use of railway infrastructure imposed by the infrastructure manager comply with the requirements of Part 4 and Schedule 3.

(3) … negotiations between an applicant and the infrastructure manager about the level of infrastructure charges shall only be permitted if these are carried out under the

supervision of the Office of Rail Regulation and, if such negotiations are likely to contravene the requirements of these Regulations, it shall be the duty of the Office of Rail Regulation to intervene.

(4) …

(5) The Office of Rail Regulation must exchange information about its—

(a) work;
(b) decision making principles; and
(c) practice,

with other national regulatory bodies for the purpose of co-ordinating decision making principles across the Community.

(6) Where the Office of Rail Regulation, by virtue of regulations 20(7)(b), 29(4) or 30(2), prescribes the manner and form of any notification, appeal or complaint to be lodged in accordance with those regulations, that Office must make that prescription and details of such manner and form publicly available.

NOTES
Amendment Paras (2), (3): words omitted revoked by SI 2009/1122.
Para (4): revoked by SI 2009/1122.

[1008]

Appeals to the regulatory body

29 (1) An applicant has a right of appeal to the Office of Rail Regulation if it believes that it has been unfairly treated, discriminated against or is in any other way aggrieved, and in particular against decisions adopted by the infrastructure manager, an allocation body, a charging body, a service provider or, as the case may be, a railway undertaking, concerning any of the matters described in paragraph (2).

(2) Those matters are—

(a) the network statement produced in accordance with regulation 11;
(b) the information which, by virtue of regulation 11(4), must be included in that network statement;
(c) the allocation process and its result as prescribed in Part 5 and Schedule 4;
(d) the charging scheme and charging system established in accordance with regulation 12;
(e) the level or structure of infrastructure fees, the principles of which are prescribed in Part 4 and Schedule 3, which it is, or may be, required to pay; and
(f) the arrangements in connection with the entitlements to access granted under Part 2 and Schedule 2.

(3) Where the matter of an appeal under this regulation is one in relation to which directions may be sought from the Office of Rail Regulation under sections 17 or 22A of the Act, the applicant must lodge the appeal by way of an application under the relevant section and, subject to any applicable provisions of these Regulations, the appropriate provisions of that Act shall apply to the consideration of that application.

(4) Where the matter of an appeal under this regulation is one to which paragraph (3) does not apply because—

(a) the railway facility to which the appeal relates is, by virtue of section 20 of the Act, an exempt facility;
(b) the appeal relates to a rail link facility; or
(c) the subject matter of the appeal is not within the scope of directions which may be sought under sections 17 or 22A of the Act,

the applicant must lodge the appeal by way of an application under this regulation, in such form and manner as the Office of Rail Regulation may from time to time prescribe.

(5) When considering an appeal in respect of circumstances described in paragraph (6), the Office of Rail Regulation is under a duty to determine whether, in respect of the access to which the appeal relates, viable alternatives under market conditions exist.

(6) Those circumstances are when the appeal contests that—

(a) viable alternatives by rail under market conditions do not exist so as to justify a request under regulation 6(2) being subject to restrictions; or

(b) viable alternative means of the service being provided under market conditions do not exist so as to justify the refusal of a request for the supply of services under regulation 7(4).

(7) Subject to paragraph (8), the Office of Rail Regulation must, within two months of the date of receipt of all relevant information (including information provided pursuant to regulation 31)—

(a) make a decision on; and

(b) where appropriate, issue a direction to the infrastructure manager, allocation body, charging body, service provider or, as the case may be, railway undertaking, to remedy the situation arising out of,

an appeal brought under this regulation.

(8) Where a decision or direction under paragraph (7) would affect a rail link facility or, as the case may be, the operation of the development agreement, the Office of Rail Regulation must consult and, subject to paragraph (9), take into account any representations made by, the Secretary of State before making or issuing such a decision or direction.

(9) Where paragraph (8) applies and, following consultation, the Secretary of State submits representations, the Office of Rail Regulation must, before making or issuing a decision or direction, consult such interested parties as it considers appropriate on the representations submitted by the Secretary of State.

(10) In making a decision on an appeal brought under this regulation against refusal by an infrastructure manager or allocation body to allocate infrastructure capacity, or against the terms of an offer of infrastructure capacity, the Office of Rail Regulation must either—

(a) confirm that no modification of the infrastructure manager or allocation body's decision is required; or

(b) require modification of that decision in accordance with directions issued by that Office.

(11) Without prejudice to the right of any person to make an application to the court under Part 54 of the Civil Procedure Rules 1998—

(a) a decision by the Office of Rail Regulation on an appeal brought under this regulation is binding on all parties affected by that decision; and

(b) it is the duty of any person to whom a direction is given under this regulation to comply with and give effect to that direction.

(12) Where the subject matter of an appeal relates to the allocation of capacity crossing more than one network and, in particular, the procedures described in regulation 17, the Office of Rail Regulation may, where the decision of an infrastructure manager in another Member State is a material fact, refer that appeal to the Commission for a decision.

NOTES

Civil Procedure Rules 1998 SI 1998/3132, in the title Courts and Legal Services (Vol 5(3)).

[1009]

[Regulatory decisions concerning international passenger services

29A (1) The Office of Rail Regulation must at the request of a relevant competent authorities or an interested railway undertaking or other party, or may on its own initiative, determine whether a service for the transport of passengers by train is an international passenger service.

(2) The Office of Rail Regulation-

(a) must at the request of a relevant party, or may on its own initiative, determine whether the exercise of the right conferred under regulation 5 by an applicant for infrastructure capacity notified under regulation 16(4A) would compromise the economic equilibrium of a relevant public service contract; and

(b) must make the determination on the basis of an objective economic analysis and in accordance with pre-determined criteria published by it.

(3) For the purposes of paragraph (2) relevant parties are the competent authority that awarded a relevant public service contract, any other competent authority with a right to limit access along the route of the international passenger service notified

under regulation 16(4A), any railway undertaking which is a relevant public service operator and the infrastructure manager concerned.

(4) Subject to paragraph (7), the Office of Rail Regulation must, within two months of the date of receipt of all relevant information (including information provided pursuant to regulation 31) and having consulted the relevant parties, as appropriate—

- (a) make a decision on a request made or following a decision to consider on its own initiative under paragraph (2);
- (b) where appropriate, issue a direction to the infrastructure manager, allocation body, charging body, service provider or, as the case may be, railway undertaking, limiting the access rights conferred in a framework agreement if the exercise of the rights would compromise the economic equilibrium of a relevant public service contract;
- (c) provide the relevant parties and any railway undertaking seeking access rights to infrastructure for the purpose of operating an international passenger service with the grounds for its decision; and
- (d) specify a reasonable time period within which, and the conditions under which, any competent authority that has awarded a relevant public service contract, any railway undertaking which is a relevant public service operator, the infrastructure manager concerned and any railway undertaking seeking access rights to infrastructure for the purpose of operating an international passenger service may request a reconsideration of the decision or direction or both.

(5) Where the Office of Rail Regulation has received a properly made request for a reconsideration of its decision or direction in accordance with paragraph (4)(d), any direction it has made under paragraph (4)(b) will not take effect pending reconsideration.

(6) Subject to paragraph (7), where the Office of Rail Regulation has received a properly made request for a reconsideration of its decision or direction under paragraph (2) in accordance with paragraph (4)(d), it must, within two months of the date of receipt of all relevant information (including information provided pursuant to regulation 31)—

- (a) make a reconsidered decision on a request; and
- (b) where appropriate, issue or reissue a direction or directions to the infrastructure manager, allocation body, charging body, service provider or, as the case may be, railway undertaking.

(7) Where a decision or direction under paragraphs (4) or (6) would affect a rail link facility or, as the case may be, the operation of the development agreement, the Office of Rail Regulation must consult and, subject to paragraph (8), take into account any representations made by, the Secretary of State before making or issuing such a decision or direction.

(8) Where paragraph (7) applies and, following consultation, the Secretary of State submits representations, the Office of Rail Regulation must, before making or issuing a decision or direction, or reconsidered decision or direction, consult such interested parties as it considers appropriate on the representations submitted by the Secretary of State.

(9) In making a decision on a request made or following a decision to consider on its own initiative under paragraph (2), or a request for a reconsideration of its decision under paragraph (5), the Office of Rail Regulation must either—

- (a) confirm that no modification of the infrastructure manager or allocation body's decision to award access rights is required; or
- (b) require modification of that decision in accordance with directions issued by that Office.

(10) Without prejudice to the right of any person to make an application to the court under Part 54 of the Civil Procedure Rules 1998—

- (a) a decision by the Office of Rail Regulation on a request made or following a decision to consider on its own initiative under paragraph (2) is binding on all parties affected by that decision; and
- (b) it is the duty of any person to whom a direction is given under this regulation to comply with and give effect to that direction.]

NOTES

Amendment Inserted by SI 2009/1122.

Civil Procedure Rules 1998 SI 1998/3132, in the title Courts and Legal Services (Vol 5(3)).

[1010]

Competition in the rail services markets

30 (1) The Office of Rail Regulation shall be responsible for—

(a) monitoring; and

(b) determining complaints lodged under paragraph (2) relating to,

competition in the rail services markets, including the rail freight transport market.

(2) Any applicant or interested party may submit a complaint to the Office of Rail Regulation, in such form and manner as that Office may from time to time prescribe, if it believes that it has been treated unjustly, been the subject of discrimination or has been injured in any other way.

(3) Subject to paragraph (4) where, following receipt of—

(a) a complaint lodged under paragraph (2); or

(b) information gathered on its own initiative,

the Office of Rail Regulation identifies undesirable developments in relation to competition in the rail services markets it must, at the earliest possible opportunity, determine measures and take appropriate action to correct those developments.

(4) Paragraph (3) is without prejudice to the rights of any person to make an application to the court under Part 54 of the Civil Procedure Rules 1998.

NOTES

Civil Procedure Rules 1998 SI 1998/3132, in the title Courts and Legal Services (Vol 5(3)).

[1011]

Provision of information to the regulatory body

31 If the Office of Rail Regulation requests information in connection with its functions under regulations 10, [13, 29, 29A or 30], section 80 of the Act (duty of certain persons to furnish information on request) shall apply as if—

(a) in subsection (1)—

(i) for "Licence holders" there were substituted "An infrastructure manager, allocation body, charging body, applicant, service provider or any other party";

(ii) for "he, they or it" in both places there were substituted "it"; and

(iii) for "functions of the Secretary of State, the Scottish Ministers or (as the case may be) that Office under this Part, the Transport Act 2000 or the Railways Act 2005 or any other function or activity of his, theirs or its in relation to railway services" there were substituted "of its functions under subordinate legislation made for the purpose of implementing Council Directive 91/440/EEC dated 29 July 1991 on the development of the Community's railways, as amended by Directive 2001/12/EC dated 26 February 2001[, Directive 2004/51/EC dated 29 April 2004 and Directive 2007/58/EC dated 23 October 2007, all] of the European Parliament and of the Council, and Directive 2001/14/EC dated 26 February 2001 on the allocation of railway infrastructure capacity and the levying of charges for the use of railway infrastructure, as amended by Directive 2004/49/EC dated 29 April 2004 [and Directive 2007/58/EC dated 23 October 2007, all] of the European Parliament and of the Council"; and

(b) for "Secretary of State, the Scottish Ministers or the Office of Rail Regulation" in each place there were substituted "Office of Rail Regulation".

NOTES

Amendment Words in first pair of square brackets substituted by SI 2009/1122.

Para (a)(iii): words in square brackets substituted by SI 2009/1122.

Council Directive 91/440/EEC OJ L237, 24.08.1991, p 25.

Directive 2001/12/EC OJ L75, 15.03.2001, p 1.

Directive 2004/51/EC OJ L164, 30.04.2004, p 164.

Directive 2007/58/EC OJ L315, 03.12.2007, p 44.
Directive 2001/14/EC OJ L75, 15.03.2001, p 29.
Directive 2004/49/EC OJ L164, 30.04.2004, p 44.

[1012]

The International Rail Regulator

32 (1) Subject to the transitional provisions set out in regulation 2, the office of "International Rail Regulator", as provided for in the Railways Regulations 1998, is abolished.

(2) All property, rights and liabilities to which the International Rail Regulator is entitled or subject at the coming into force of this regulation (including rights and liabilities relating to staff) are transferred to the Office of Rail Regulation.

NOTES
Railways Regulations 1998 SI 1998/1340; revoked by reg 2(1).

[1013]

PART 7
MISCELLANEOUS

Statutory authority to run trains

33 Any applicant granted [access] rights under these Regulations shall, if and to the extent that it would not, apart from this regulation, have statutory authority to run trains over any track in exercise of such rights, be taken to have statutory authority to do so.

NOTES
Amendment Word in square brackets substituted by SI 2009/1122, as from 1 January 2010.

[1014]

Application of enactments concerning railways

34 Paragraphs 2 (disapplication of enactments in the case of Concessionaires and through service operators), 3 (extension of enactments in relation to through service operators) and 4 (modification of enactments applying to Concessionaires and through service operators) of Schedule 6 to the Channel Tunnel Act 1987 shall apply to … railway undertakings, other than the Concessionaires and the British Railways Board, in relation to the provision of international services in exercise of access … rights under these Regulations who are not through service operators within the meaning of that Schedule as they apply to those who are.

NOTES
Amendment Words omitted revoked by SI 2009/1122, as from 1 January 2010.
British Railways Board As to the winding down and abolition of the British Railways Board, see the Transport Act 2000 and the Preliminary Note "Privatisation of the railway system" (under the main head "Reorganisation of transport undertakings").

[1015]

35 (*Revoked by SI 2009/1122, as from 1 January 2010.*)

Civil proceedings

36 (1) The obligation to comply with—

- (a) regulation 8;
- (b) regulation 9;
- (c) paragraphs (7) and (12) of regulation 12;
- (d) paragraphs (3), (10), and (11)(c) of regulation 16; …
- (e) paragraph (11) of regulation 29[; or
- (f) paragraph (10) of regulation 29A,]

shall be a duty owed to any person who may be affected by a breach of that duty and shall be actionable by any such person who sustains loss, damage or injury caused by the breach at the suit or instance of that person.

(2) In any proceedings brought against an infrastructure manager, … railway undertaking, allocation body, charging body or applicant under paragraph (1), it shall be a defence for it to prove that it took all reasonable steps and exercised all due diligence to avoid the breach of duty.

(3) Without prejudice to the right which any person may have by virtue of paragraph (1) to bring civil proceedings in respect of any breach of duty, the obligation to comply shall be enforceable by civil proceedings by the Office of Rail Regulation for an injunction or for interdict or any other relief.

NOTES

Amendment Para (1)(d): word omitted revoked by SI 2009/1122.
Para (1)(f): inserted, together with preceding word "; or", by SI 2009/1122.
Para (2): words omitted revoked by SI 2009/1122.

[1016]

Making of false statements etc

37 (1) If any person, in giving any information or making any application under or for the purposes of any provision of these Regulations, makes any statement which he knows to be false in a material particular, or recklessly makes any statement which is false in a material particular, he is guilty of an offence and shall be liable—

(a) on summary conviction, to a fine not exceeding the statutory maximum;
(b) on conviction on indictment, to a fine.

(2) No proceedings shall be instituted in England or Wales in respect of an offence under this regulation except by or with the consent of the Secretary of State or the Director of Public Prosecutions.

NOTES

Statutory maximum By virtue of the Interpretation Act 1978, ss 5, 23, Sch 1, printed in the title Statutory Instruments (Pt 2), Vol 1 of this work, this means the prescribed sum within the meaning of the Magistrates' Courts Act 1980, s 32(9).

[1017]

Offences by bodies corporate and Scottish partnerships

38 (1) Where an offence under these Regulations has been committed by a body corporate and it is proved to have been committed with the consent or connivance of, or to be attributable to any neglect on the part of, any director, manager, secretary or other similar officer of the body corporate or any person who was purporting to act in any such capacity, he as well as the body corporate shall be guilty of that offence and be liable to be proceeded against and punished accordingly.

(2) Where the affairs of a body corporate are managed by its members, paragraph (1) shall apply in relation to the acts and defaults of a member in connection with his functions of management as if he were a director of the body corporate.

(3) Where a Scottish partnership is guilty of an offence under these Regulations in Scotland and that offence is proved to have been committed with the consent or connivance of, or to be attributable to any neglect on the part of, a partner, he as well as the partnership shall be guilty of that offence and shall be liable to be proceeded against and punished accordingly.

[1018]

Restriction on disclosure of information

39 Section 145 of the Act (restriction on disclosure of information) shall have effect in relation to information which has been obtained under or by virtue of any provision of these Regulations and which relates to the affairs of any individual or to any particular business as it has effect in relation to such information obtained under or by virtue of any of the provisions of that Act.

[1019]

Offences outside the United Kingdom

40 (1) For the purpose of determining whether a breach of the duty imposed by regulation 9 has occurred, it is immaterial that the relevant acts or omissions occurred outside the United Kingdom if, when they occurred, the person—

(a) was a United Kingdom national, or

(b) was a body incorporated under the law of any part of the United Kingdom, or
(c) was a person (other than a United Kingdom national or such a body) maintaining a place of business in the United Kingdom.

(2) In this regulation "United Kingdom national" means an individual who is—
(a) a British citizen, a British Dependent Territories citizen, a British National (Overseas) or a British Overseas citizen;
(b) a person who under the British Nationality Act 1981 is a British subject; or
(c) a British protected person (within the meaning of that Act).

[1020]

SCHEDULE 1

(*Pt 1: para 1 amends the Parliamentary Commissioner Act 1967, Sch 2; para 2 amends the House of Commons Disqualification Act 1975, Sch 1, Pt 3; para 3 amends the Northern Ireland Assembly Disqualification Act 1975, Sch 1, Pt 3; para 4 amends the Railways Act 1993, ss 17, 18, 22A, 145; para 5 amends the Greater London Authority Act 1999, s 235; para 6 repeals the Channel Tunnel Rail Link Act 1996, s 22; para 7 repeals the Railways and Transport Safety Act 2003, Sch 3, para 6.*)

(*Pt 2: para 8 amended SI 2003/409 (revoked).*)

SCHEDULE 2
SERVICES TO BE SUPPLIED TO APPLICANTS

Regulation 7

1 The minimum access package referred to in regulation 7(1) shall comprise—
(a) handling of requests for infrastructure capacity; and
(b) the right to utilise such capacity as is granted and, in particular—
(i) the right to use such running track points and junctions as are necessary to utilise that capacity;
(ii) train control, including signalling, train regulation, dispatching and the communication and provision of information on train movements; and
(iii) all other information as is necessary to implement or to operate the service for which capacity has been granted.

2 Track access to services facilities and the supply of services referred to in regulation 7(1) and (4) shall comprise—
(a) where available, the use of electrical supply equipment for traction current;
(b) refuelling facilities;
(c) passenger stations, including buildings and other facilities;
(d) freight terminals;
(e) marshalling yards;
(f) train formation facilities;
(g) storage sidings; and
(h) maintenance and other technical facilities.

3 The additional services referred to in regulation 7(5) may comprise—
(a) traction current;
(b) pre-heating of passenger trains;
(c) the supply of fuel, shunting and all other services provided at the access services facilities referred to in paragraph (2); and
(d) tailor-made contracts for—
(i) control of the transport of dangerous goods; and
(ii) assistance in running abnormal trains.

4 The ancillary services referred to in regulation 7(6) may comprise—
(a) access to the telecommunication network;
(b) the provision of supplementary information; and
(c) technical inspection of rolling stock.

[1021]

SCHEDULE 3
ACCESS CHARGING

Regulation 12

Principles of access charging

1 (1) The infrastructure manager must ensure that the application of the charging scheme—

(a) complies with the rules set out in the network statement produced in accordance with regulation 11; and

(b) results in equivalent and non-discriminatory charges for different railway undertakings that perform services of an equivalent nature in a similar part of the market.

(2) The calculation of the fee may in particular take into account the mileage, composition of the train and any specific requirements in terms of such factors as speed, axle load and the degree or period of utilisation of the infrastructure.

(3) Except where specific arrangements are made in accordance with paragraph 3, the infrastructure manager must ensure that the charging system in use is based on the same principles over the whole of his network.

(4) The charges for the minimum access package and track access to service facilities referred to in paragraphs 1 and 2 of Schedule 2 shall be set at the cost that is directly incurred as a result of operating the train service.

(5) With the exception of sub-paragraphs (6) and (9), the supply of services referred to in paragraph 2 of Schedule 2 shall not be subject to the principles set out in this paragraph.

(6) In setting the charge for the supply of services referred to in sub-paragraph (5), account must be taken of the competitive situation of rail transport.

(7) If the additional or ancillary services referred to in paragraphs 3 and 4 of Schedule 2 are offered by only one supplier the charge imposed for the supply of those services must relate to the cost of providing the service, calculated on the basis of the actual level of use.

(8) The infrastructure charge may include a charge to reflect the scarcity of capacity of the identifiable segment of the infrastructure during periods of congestion.

(9) The charges referred to in sub-paragraphs (4) and (8) may be averaged over a reasonable spread of train services and times, but the relative magnitudes of the infrastructure charges must be related to the costs attributable to the services.

Exceptions to the charging principles

2 (1) In order to obtain full recovery of the costs incurred the infrastructure manager, with the approval of the Office of Rail Regulation under the access charges review or, in the case of a rail link facility, the Secretary of State through the development agreement, may levy mark-ups on the basis of efficient, transparent and non-discriminatory principles, whilst guaranteeing optimum competitiveness, in particular in respect of international rail freight.

(2) The effect of sub-paragraph (1) must not be to exclude the use of infrastructure by market segments which can pay at least the cost that is directly incurred as a result of operating the railway service, plus a rate of return which the market can bear.

(3) The charging system shall respect the productivity increases achieved by applicants.

3 (1) Subject to sub-paragraph (2), for specific investment projects completed—

(a) since 15th March 1988; or

(b) following the coming into force of these Regulations,

the infrastructure manager may set or continue to set higher charges on the basis of the long-term costs of the project.

(2) For sub-paragraph (1) to apply—

[(a) the project must increase efficiency or cost-effectiveness; and]

(b) the project could not otherwise have been undertaken without the prospect of such higher charges.

(3) A charging arrangement to which sub-paragraph (1) applies may incorporate agreements on the sharing of the risk associated with new investments.

4 (1) An infrastructure manager's average and marginal charges for equivalent uses of his infrastructure must be comparable and comparable services in the same market segment must be subject to the same charges.

(2) The network statement produced by the infrastructure manager in accordance with regulation 11 must demonstrate that the charging system meets the requirements in paragraph (1) in so far as this can be done without the disclosure of commercially confidential information.

5 If an infrastructure manager intends to modify the essential elements of the charging system referred to in paragraph 2 that infrastructure manager must make such modifications public at least three months in advance of the modification taking effect.

Discounts

6 (1) Subject to the provisions of articles 81, 82, 86 and 87 of the Treaty, and [notwithstanding] paragraph 1(4) of this Schedule, any discount on the charges levied on a user of railway infrastructure by the infrastructure manager, for any service, must comply with the principles set out in this paragraph.

(2) Except where sub-paragraph (3) applies, discounts shall be limited to the actual saving of the administrative cost to the infrastructure manager and, in determining the level of discount to be applied, no account may be taken of cost savings already incorporated in the charge levied.

(3) The infrastructure manager may introduce schemes available to all users of the infrastructure, with reference to specified traffic flows, granting time limited discounts to encourage the development of new rail services, or [discounts] encouraging the use of considerably under-utilised lines.

(4) The discounts available must be in accordance with the access charges review or, in the case of a rail link facility, the development agreement.

(5) Discounts may relate only to charges levied for a specified infrastructure section.

(6) Similar discount schemes must be applied to similar services.

NOTES

Amendment Para 3(2)(a): substituted by SI 2009/1122.
Para 6(1), (3): word in square brackets inserted by SI 2009/1122.

[1022]

SCHEDULE 4
TIMETABLE FOR THE ALLOCATION PROCESS

Regulations 16(5) and 19(2)

Date of timetable change

1 (1) Subject to sub-paragraph (2) the working timetable must be established once per calendar year, and the change of working timetable must take place at midnight on the second Saturday in December.

(2) Where a change or adjustment to the working timetable is carried out after the winter, in particular to take account, where appropriate, of changes in regional passenger traffic timetables, it must take place at midnight on the second Saturday in June.

(3) Further changes to the working timetable may be made at such other intervals as are required.

(4) The infrastructure manager may agree different dates to those stipulated in sub-paragraphs (1) and (2) and, in this case, must inform the European Commission if international traffic may be affected.

Timetable for the production of the working timetable

2 (1) The final date for receipt of requests for capacity to be incorporated into the working timetable must be no more than 12 months in advance of the entry into force of the working timetable described in paragraph 1.

(2) No later than 11 months before the working timetable comes into force, the infrastructure managers must ensure that provisional international train paths have been established in co-operation with other relevant infrastructure managers or, as the case may be, allocation bodies, in accordance with regulation 17.

(3) Infrastructure managers must ensure that, so far as possible, provisional international train paths established in accordance with sub-paragraph (2) are adhered to during the subsequent allocation process.

(4) No later than four months after the deadline for submission of bids by applicants, the infrastructure manager must prepare a draft working timetable.

[1023]

RAILWAY (LICENSING OF RAILWAY UNDERTAKINGS) REGULATIONS 2005
SI 2005/3050

Authority Made by the Secretary of State for Transport under the European Communities Act 1972, s 2(2).

Date made 1 November 2005.

Commencement 28 November 2005.

Amendment Amended by SI 2009/2054.

Summary These regulations implement Council Directive 95/18/EC on the licensing of railway undertakings (OJ L143, 27.06.1995, p 70), as amended by Directive 2001/13/EC of the European Parliament and of the Council (OJ L75, 15.03.2001, p 26) and Directive 2004/49/EC of the European Parliament and of the Council (OJ L164, 30.04.2004, p 44). They apply, subject to specified exceptions, in relation to the licensing of railway undertakings which provide train services and are established or to be established in an EEA State (reg 4).

The provision of train services without being authorised to do so by a European licence is a criminal offence (reg 5). The Office of Rail Regulation ("ORR") is designated as the body responsible for granting European licences (reg 6). Applicants for such licences must satisfy requirements as to good repute, financial fitness, professional competence and insurance cover for civil liabilities (reg 6 and Sch 2). Such licences continue in force as long as the ORR is satisfied that the licence holder continues to comply with the requirements referred to in Sch 2 and the requirements to submit the licence for review or approval when so required (reg 7). The licence is subject to monitoring and review by the ORR, which may suspend or revoke such licences in certain circumstances (reg 8).

Certain provisions of the Railways Act 1993 and of other legislation are amended so as to include references to European licences (Sch 1). The enactments concerned are: Railway Fires Act 1905, s 4; Insolvency Act 1986, Sch 2A; Railways Act 1993, ss 6, 59, 72, 80, 83, 145, Sch 7; Civil Contingencies Act 2004, Sch 1; Railways Act 2005, ss 46, 59. The regulations also amend the following instruments:

SI 1992/666, in the title Town and Country Planning; SI 2004/1522, in this title; SI 2005/422, SI 2005/551, both in the title Local Government, and a number of local instruments. SI 1998/1519 is revoked.

The licensing regime established by the Railways Act 1993 is amended to take account of the new licensing regime established by these regulations (regs 9–14). In addition to being authorised by a European licence, railway undertakings providing train services in Great Britain require a statement of national regulatory provisions (a "SNRP") (regs 9, 10). One or more conditions are to be included in a SNRP by the ORR; such conditions must be compatible with Community law and must not be applied in a discriminatory manner (reg 11). SNRPs may be modified by consent (reg 13). Specified statutory provisions are to have effect in relation to SNRPs and SNRP holders, subject to modifications (reg 14 and Sch 3).

Provision is made for the offence of making false statements (reg 15) and for offences by bodies corporate (reg 16). The Railways Act 1993, s 76(5) and the Greater London Authority Act 1999, s 252C(3), relating to the investigation by the Rail Passengers' Council or the London Transport Users' Committee of possible contraventions of conditions, are to have effect in relation to holders of European licences and possible contraventions of SNRPs held by them (regs 17, 19).

Transitional provisions are made in relation to existing licences and licence exemptions (reg 20 and Sch 4).

[1024]

DISABILITY DISCRIMINATION (TRANSPORT VEHICLES) REGULATIONS 2005
SI 2005/3190

Authority Made by the Secretary of State for Transport under the Disability Discrimination Act 1995, ss 21(5)(e), (f), (h), 21ZA(3).

Date made 15 November 2005.

Commencement 4 December 2005.

Summary These regulations disapply certain vehicles from the exemptions provided by the Disability Discrimination Act 1995, s 21ZA (application of ss 19–21 to transport vehicles). Specified transport services providers must now comply with certain provisions of ss 19 (discrimination in relation to goods, facilities and services) and 21 (duty of providers of services to make adjustments) of the 1995 Act.

[1025]

TRANSPORT FOR LONDON (BEST VALUE) (CONTRACTING OUT OF INVESTMENT AND HIGHWAY FUNCTIONS) ORDER 2006
SI 2006/91

Authority Made by the First Secretary of State under the Deregulation and Contracting Out Act 1994, s 70, as applied in relation to functions of a best value authority by the Local Government Act 1999, s 18.

Date made 19 January 2006.

Commencement 20 January 2006.

Amendment Partially revoked by SI 2009/721.

Summary This order enables Transport for London to contract out the same investment functions local authorities are authorised to contract out by virtue of SI 1996/1883, in the title Local Government. The order has been revoked and replaced by SI 2009/721, in the title Highways, Streets and Bridges, in so far as it enabled Transport for London to contract out certain highway functions local authorities were authorised to contract out.

[1026]

RAILWAYS (INTEROPERABILITY) REGULATIONS 2006
SI 2006/397

Authority Made by the Secretary of State for Transport under the European Communities Act 1972, s 2(2) and the Transport Act 2000, s 247.

Date made 16 February 2006.

Commencement Partly on 20 March 2006; fully on 2 April 2006.

Amendment Amended by SI 2007/3386, SI 2008/1746.

Summary These regulations revoke and replace the Railways (Interoperability) (High-Speed) Regulations 2002, SI 2002/1166, subject to savings and transitional provisions for projects on the high-speed rail system. They implement:

(a) Council Directive 96/48/EC on the interoperability of the trans-European high-speed rail system (OJ L235, 17.09.1996, p 6), as amended by Regulation (EC) 1882/2003 of the European Parliament and of the Council (OJ L284, 31.10.2003, p 1) and by Directive 2004/50/EC of the European Parliament and of the Council (OJ L164, 30.04.2004, p 114) ("High-Speed Directive"); and

(b) Directive 2001/16/EC of the European Parliament and of the Council on the interoperability of the trans-European conventional rail system (OJ L110, 20.04.2001, p 1), as amended by Directive 2004/50/EC of the European Parliament and of the Council ("Conventional Directive").

Annexes to both the High-Speed Directive and the Conventional Directive are reproduced in Schs 1–7, 10 to these regulations.

Reg 3 deals with the application of the regulations. Subject to reg 3(2), the regulations apply to the high-speed rail system (i e that part of the trans-European high-speed rail system located within the territory of the United Kingdom and identified by reference to the lines specified in Sch 11 to the regulations), the conventional TEN rail system (i e that part of the trans-European conventional rail system located within the territory of the United Kingdom), their subsystems (as defined) and to interoperability constituents (as defined). Reg 3(2) provides that (apart from reg 4B) the regulations do not apply to:

(a) a structural subsystem (as defined) placed in service on the conventional TEN rail system;

(b) an interoperability constituent placed on the market with a view to its use on the conventional TEN rail system; or

(c) a structural subsystem renewed and placed in service on the high-speed rail system,

before 1 August 2006. Notwithstanding reg 3(2):

(a) the placing in service of a structural subsystem on the high-speed rail system or the conventional TEN rail system before 1 August 2006 does not affect the application of these regulations to that subsystem for any upgrading or renewal where having been upgraded or renewed that subsystem is placed in service on the high-speed rail system or the conventional TEN rail system on or after 1 August 2006;

(b) the regulations apply to rolling stock to which reg 4A(2) (deemed authorisation) applies (reg 3(3)).

Pt 2 (regs 4–15) restricts the placing in service on the high-speed rail system or the conventional TEN rail system of structural subsystems which are new or have undergone major renewal or upgrade, to those authorised by the Safety Authority or ruled by the Competent Authority as not requiring authorisation (see generally reg 4). In the case of major upgrade or renewal works a decision must first be made by the Competent Authority as to whether an authorisation is needed for the subsystem to be placed in service and provision is made for application to the Competent Authority for this decision (see generally reg 5). "Safety Authority" means the Office of Rail Regulation except in relation to Northern Ireland, where it means the Department for Regional Development, and in relation to the Channel Tunnel system, where it means the Intergovernmental Commission (as defined in the Channel Tunnel Act 1987, s 49(1)). "Competent Authority" means in Great Britain, the Secretary of State, except in relation to the Channel Tunnel system, where it means the Intergovernmental Commission, and in Northern Ireland, where it means the Department for Regional Development. The Safety Authority and the Competent Authority are permitted to charge fees for certain work under the regulations.

Provision is made by reg 4A for deemed authorisation. Subject to certain exceptions, reg 4A applies to a unit of rolling stock which is constructed or adapted to transport passengers, was first brought into use after 31 December 1998 and before 1 August 2006, and is used in the provision of a service for the carriage of passengers on the high-speed rail system or the conventional TEN rail system (reg 4A(1)). In such cases, a unit of rolling stock is deemed: (a) to have been authorised under reg 4 to be placed in service on both the high-speed rail system and the conventional TEN rail system; and (b) to have been assessed against the Rail Vehicle Accessibility Regulations 1998, SI 1998/2456, as notified national technical rules, for that authorisation. Reg 4B provides that all passenger vehicles operating on the high-speed rail system or the conventional TEN rail system must comply with accessibility standards by 1 January 2020. These standards are the relevant European accessibility standards, or the standards required by the said SI 1998/2456 (or a prescribed combination of both).

Pt 3 (regs 16–23) contains requirements in relation to interoperability constituents. An EC declaration of conformity or of suitability for use indicates that the interoperability constituent satisfies the requirements which are comprised in European specifications and technical specifications for interoperability. This Part prohibits an interoperability constituent being placed on the market with a view to its use on the trans-European high-speed rail system or trans-European conventional rail system, as the case may be, unless the interoperability constituent meets the essential requirements which are relevant to an interoperability constituent of that type, the appropriate procedure for assessment of the conformity or suitability for use of the interoperability constituent has been carried out and an EC declaration of conformity or suitability for use in relation to that interoperability constituent has been drawn up. Duties are imposed on operators in relation to any interoperability constituent which is in use on, or is part of, the high-speed rail system or the conventional TEN rail system.

Pt 4 (regs 24–30) makes provision in respect of the bodies responsible for assessing conformity of subsystems and interoperability constituents to the relevant standards ("notified bodies"). The regulations set out the procedure to be followed where a notified body declines to draw up a certificate of verification or an intermediate statement of verification in relation to a project subsystem, or declines to confirm that an EC declaration of conformity or suitability for use can be drawn up in respect of an interoperability constituent. A notified body is defined as a body appointed by the Strategic Rail Authority (see below), by the Secretary of State or by a member state other than the United Kingdom in accordance with the Conventional Directive or the High-Speed Directive. The Secretary of State may appoint such persons as he thinks fit to be a notified body, provided he is satisfied that such persons are capable of meeting the minimum criteria specified in the regulations. Duties are imposed on the notified bodies and fees may be charged by notified bodies in connection with carrying out their functions under the regulations. Fees may be charged by the Secretary of State in connection with his functions under this Part.

Pt 5 (regs 31–33) contains provisions as to the keeping of registers of authorised infrastructure and rolling stock and a National Vehicle Register. Authorised rolling stock vehicles are issued with a vehicle identification code.

Pt 6 (regs 34–39) deals with enforcement. The regulations are to be enforced by the Office of Rail Regulation in Great Britain and specified provisions of the Health and Safety at Work etc Act 1974 apply for the purposes of the enforcement in Great Britain of these regulations as if they were health and safety regulations for the purposes of that Act. A defence of due diligence is provided and liabilities on persons other than the principal offender are imposed.

Strategic Rail Authority Provision for the transfer of functions and abolition of the Strategic Rail Authority is made by the Railways Act 2005, s 1, Sch 1. See further the Preliminary Note "Privatisation of the railway system" (under main head "Reorganisation of transport undertakings").

[1027]

RAILWAYS (ACCESS TO TRAINING SERVICES) REGULATIONS 2006
SI 2006/598

Authority Made by the Secretary of State for Transport under the European Communities Act 1972, s 2(2).

Date made 9 March 2006.

Commencement 10 April 2006.

Summary These regulations implement in part Directive 2004/49/EC of the European Parliament and of the Council on safety on the Community's railways (OJ L164, 30.04.2004, p 44). They do not apply to training services provided: (a) in relation to metros, trams and other light rail systems; networks which are functionally separate from the rest of the railway system and intended only for the operation of local, urban or suburban passenger services; or privately owned railway infrastructure which exists solely for use by the infrastructure owner for its own freight operations; or (b) by the operators of such systems.

The regulations provide that a railway undertaking applying for a safety certificate in accordance with Pt 2 of SI 2006/599 is entitled to fair and non-discriminatory access to training services for train drivers and staff accompanying the trains, whenever such training is necessary for the fulfilment of requirements to obtain that safety certificate. An infrastructure manager is, and those of his staff performing safety critical tasks are, entitled to fair and non-discriminatory access to training services. If the training services to which access is granted are available only through the services of one single railway undertaking or infrastructure manager, that railway undertaking or infrastructure manager must make those services available to other railway undertakings or, as the case may be, infrastructure managers, at a reasonable and non-discriminatory price, which is cost-related and may include a profit margin. The regulations also allow railway undertakings, infrastructure managers, staff of infrastructure managers performing safety critical tasks and employees of any railway undertaking a right of appeal to the Office of Rail Regulation where they are denied access to training services, or where the price charged for such access is contrary to the provisions in these regulations.

[1028]

RAILWAYS AND OTHER GUIDED TRANSPORT SYSTEMS (SAFETY) REGULATIONS 2006
SI 2006/599

Authority Made by the Secretary of State for Transport under the Health and Safety at Work etc Act 1974, ss 15(1), (2), (3)(a), (c), (4), (5), (6), 18(2), 43(2)–(6), 47(2), 80, 82(3)(a), Sch 3, paras 1(1)(a), (c), (2), 4(1), 6, 7, 8(1), 9, 14, 15(1), 16, 18(a), 20.

Date made 9 March 2006.

Commencement Partly on 10 April 2006; fully on 1 October 2006; see reg 1.

Interpretation See regs 2, 23.

Amendment Printed as amended by SI 2006/1057, SI 2007/3531 (as from 4 July 2008; see the *London Gazette*, 14 July 2008).

General These regulations implement in part Directive 2004/49/EC of the European Parliament and of the Council on safety on the Community's railways (OJ L164, 30.04.2004, p 44). They impose prohibitions in relation to the operation of trains or vehicles on railways and other guided transport systems and the management and use of infrastructure unless a person has established and is maintaining a safety management system and in specified cases has a safety certificate in relation to the operation of vehicles or a safety authorisation in relation to the management and use of infrastructure. They also impose requirements for a safety management system and the issuing of safety certificates and authorisations. The regulations revoke the Railways and Other Transport Systems (Approval of Works, Plant and Equipment) Regulations 1994, SI 1994/157; the Railways (Safety Critical Work) Regulations 1994, SI 1994/299; the Railways (Safety Case) Regulations 2000, SI 2000/2688, and the amending SI 2003/579; SI 2001/3291, in so far it as amended SI 1998/1340, SI 2000/2688; and SI 2004/129, in so far it as amended SI 1994/157. They also amend SI 1995/3163, in the title Health and Safety at Work, SI 1997/553, SI 1999/2244, both in this title, and SI 2003/1400, in the title Trade and Industry. SI 1994/157 was also amended prior to its revocation.

See further SI 2006/598.

Disclosure of information Pts 2, 3 of these regulations have been specified by SI 2003/1400, in the title Trade and Industry, for the purposes of the Enterprise Act 2002, s 241(3). By s 241(3) of the 2002 Act, a public authority may disclose specified information to any other person for the purpose of facilitating the exercise by that person of any function he has under or by virtue of such subordinate legislation as is specified by order.

[1029]

PART 1
INTRODUCTION

Citation and commencement

1 These Regulations may be cited as the Railways and Other Guided Transport Systems (Safety) Regulations 2006 and shall come into force—

(a) as respects all regulations except for regulations 19, 23 to 26, 29, and 34 on 10th April 2006; and

(b) as respects regulations 19, 23 to 26, 29 and 34 on 1st October 2006.

[1030]

Interpretation and application

2 (1) In these Regulations—

"building operation" means the—

(a) construction, structural alteration, repair or maintenance of a building and "maintenance" shall include repointing, redecoration and external cleaning of the structure;

(b) demolition of a building; or

(c) preparation for and laying the foundation of an intended building,

but does not include any operation which is a work of engineering construction;

"bus" means a motor vehicle which is designed or adapted to travel along roads and to carry more than eight passengers but which is not a tramcar;

"cableway installation" means an installation made up of several components that—

(a) is used or intended to be used for the purpose of providing an operational system for carrying persons in vehicles, on chairs or by towing devices;

(b) uses cables positioned along the line of travel to provide suspension or traction or both; and

(c) is one of the following—

(i) cable car (including a gondola and chair lift) where the cabins or chairs are lifted or displaced by one or more carrier cables;

(ii) drag lift, where users with appropriate equipment are dragged by means of a cable; or

(iii) funicular railway or other installation with vehicles mounted on wheels or on other suspension devices where traction is provided by one or more cables;

but does not include cable operated tramways, rack railways or lifts;

"carriageway" has the same meaning as in the Highways Act 1980, or in Scotland the Roads (Scotland) Act 1984;

"common safety methods" ("CSMs") means the methods, developed pursuant to article 6 of the Directive, to describe how—

(a) safety levels;

(b) achievement of safety targets; and

(c) compliance with other safety requirements,

are assessed, as revised and reissued from time to time;

"common safety targets" ("CSTs") means the safety levels, developed pursuant to article 7 of the Directive, that must be reached by—

(a) different parts of the mainline railway system; and

(b) that system as a whole,

expressed in risk acceptance criteria, as revised and reissued from time to time;

"competent person" means, except for the purposes of Part 4, a person who—

(a) has sufficient skills, knowledge, experience and resources to undertake the safety verification in relation to which he is appointed;

(b) has not borne such responsibility in relation to any of the matters he has to consider in undertaking that safety verification that might compromise his objectivity; and

(c) is sufficiently independent of a management system, or a part thereof, which has borne responsibility for any of the matters he has to consider in undertaking the safety verification, to ensure that he will be objective in carrying out the safety verification for which he is appointed;

"conventional Directive" means Council Directive 2001/16 of the European Parliament and of the Council on the interoperability of the conventional rail system;

"deemed safety authorisation" shall be construed in accordance with paragraph 1(b) of Schedule 5;

"deemed safety certificate" shall be construed in accordance with paragraph 1(a) of Schedule 5;

"the Directive" means Directive 2004/49/EC of the European Parliament and of the Council on safety on the Community's railways and amending Council Directive 95/18/EC on the licensing of railway undertakings and Directive 2001/14/EC on the allocation of infrastructure capacity and the levying of charges for the use of infrastructure and safety certification;

"engineering possession" means a section of track which is closed to normal traffic and where the closure is for the purpose of carrying out maintenance which shall include any repair alteration, reconditioning, examination or testing of infrastructure;

"European Railway Agency" means the Community agency for railway safety and interoperability established by Regulation (EC) No 881/2004 of the European Parliament and of the Council establishing a European Railway Agency;

"factory" means a factory within the meaning of section 175 of the Factories Act 1961 and premises to which section 123(1) or (2) or 125(1) of that Act applies;

"guided bus system" means a system of transport, used wholly or mainly for the carriage of passengers, that employs buses which for some or all of the time when they are in operation—

(a) travel along roads; and

(b) are guided (whether while on the road or at other times) by means of—

(i) apparatus, a structure or other device which is fixed and not part of the bus; or

(ii) a guidance system which is automatic;

"guided transport" means a system of transport, used wholly or mainly for the carriage of passengers, employing vehicles which for some or all of the time when they are in operation are guided by means of—

(a) rails, beams, slots, guides or other apparatus, structures or devices which are fixed and not part of the vehicle; or

(b) a guidance system which is automatic;

"harbour" and "harbour area" have the meanings assigned to them by regulation 2(1) of the Dangerous Substances in Harbour Areas Regulations 1987;

"heritage railway" means a railway which is operated to—

(a) preserve, re-create or simulate railways of the past; or

(b) demonstrate or operate historical or special types of motive power or rolling stock;

and is exclusively or primarily used for tourist, educational or recreational purposes;

"high-speed Directive" means Council Directive 96/48/EC on the interoperability of the trans-European high-speed rail system;

"infrastructure" means fixed assets used for the operation of a transport system which shall include, without prejudice to the generality of the foregoing—

(a) its permanent way or other means of guiding or supporting vehicles;

(b) any station; and

(c) plant used for signalling or exclusively for supplying electricity for operational purposes to the transport system;

"infrastructure manager" means the person who—

(a) in relation to infrastructure other than a station, is responsible for developing and maintaining that infrastructure or, in relation to a station, the person who is responsible for managing and operating that station, except that it shall not include any person solely on the basis that he carries out the construction of that infrastructure or station or its maintenance, repair or alteration; and

(b) manages and uses that infrastructure or station, or permits it to be used, for the operation of a vehicle;

"Interoperability Regulations" means the Railways (Interoperability) Regulations 2006;

"mainline application" means an application for—

(a) a safety certificate or an amended safety certificate; or

(b) a safety authorisation or an amended safety authorisation,

made in relation to an operation on the mainline railway;

"mainline railway" means any railway except for any railway or part of a railway—

(a) the infrastructure and rolling stock of which are reserved strictly for—

(i) a local use; or

(ii) the operating of a heritage railway; or

(iii) the purposes of tourism; or

(b) the infrastructure of which is functionally separate from any other railway which does not fall within sub-paragraph (a);

"mainline railway system" means the mainline railway and the management and operation of the mainline railway as a whole;

"material" includes plant;

"military establishment" means an establishment intended for use for naval, military or air force purposes or for the purposes of the Department of the Secretary of State responsible for defence;

"mine" has the meaning assigned to it by section 180 of the Mines and Quarries Act 1954;

"national safety rules" means any legislation and other requirements—

(a) applicable to the whole of Great Britain; and

(b) which contain requirements (including common operating rules) relating to railway safety which are imposed on more than one railway undertaking,

except that where the requirements in sub-paragraph (b) consist of common operating rules of the mainline railway it shall not include such rules which regulate matters which are covered by a TSI;

"new" in relation to regulations 5 and 6 means new to the transport system in question;

"non-mainline application" means an application for—

(a) a safety certificate or an amended safety certificate; or

(b) a safety authorisation or an amended safety authorisation,

made in relation to an operation on a transport system other than the mainline railway;

"operator of last resort" means a transport operator appointed by the Secretary of State to provide transport services in accordance with section 30 of the Railways Act 1993;

"Part A of a safety certificate" means that part of a safety certificate certifying the matters set out in regulation 7(4)(b)(i) and related expressions shall be construed accordingly;

"Part B of a safety certificate" means that part of a safety certificate certifying the matters set out in regulation 7(4)(b)(ii) and related expressions shall be construed accordingly;

"quarry" has the meaning assigned to it by regulation 3 of the Quarries Regulations 1999;

"railway" means a system of transport employing parallel rails which—

(a) provide support and guidance for vehicles carried on flanged wheels; and

(b) form a track which either is of a gauge of at least 350 millimetres or crosses a carriageway (whether or not on the same level),

but does not include a tramway;

"relevant infrastructure manager" means the infrastructure manager for any infrastructure used in relation to the operation in question;

"relevant infrastructure or vehicle" means any new or altered—

(a) infrastructure; or

(b) vehicle,

falling within regulation 5(4) or 6(4) and related expressions shall be construed accordingly;

"responsible person" means in relation to any relevant infrastructure or vehicle, any person who—

(a) has contracted with another person for the manufacture or construction by that other person of that infrastructure or vehicle; or

(b) manufactures or constructs that infrastructure or vehicle for his own use, or for sale to, or use by, another person but not where he is contracted to do so by a person falling under sub-paragraph (a),

and includes an authorised representative established in Great Britain of such a person.

"risk" means in Parts 1 and 2 a risk to the safety of a person;

"road" means in the definition of "guided bus system" and "tramway"–

(a) in England and Wales, any length of highway or of any other road to which the public has access, and includes bridges over which a road passes; and

(b) in Scotland, has the same meaning as in the Roads (Scotland) Act 1984;

"rolling stock" has the meaning in section 83(1) of the Railways Act 1993;

"ROTS" means the Railways and Other Transport Systems (Approval of Works, Plant and Equipment) Regulations 1994;

"safety authorisation" means a safety authorisation issued by the Office of Rail Regulation in accordance with regulation 10 or 12;

"safety authority" means—

(a) as regards a member State other than the United Kingdom, the authority established in that State in accordance with article 16.1 of the Directive;

(b) as regards Great Britain, the Office of Rail Regulation; or

(c) as regards Northern Ireland, the Department for Regional Development established by article 3(1) of the Departments (Northern Ireland) Order 1999;

"safety certificate" means a safety certificate issued by the Office of Rail Regulation in accordance with regulation 7 or 9;

"safety management system" means the organisation and arrangements established by a transport operator to ensure the safe management of its operation;

"significant safety risk" means, in relation to new or altered infrastructure or a new or altered vehicle the design or construction of which incorporates significant changes compared to any infrastructure or vehicle already in use on the transport system, the capability of significantly increasing an existing safety risk or creating a significant safety risk to—

(a) passengers on the transport system in question; or

(b) members of the public on roads and any other location where the transport system in question operates and to which the public have access (including a place to which the public has access only on making a payment), except a location which is a crossing subject to an Order made under section 1 of the Level Crossings Act 1983;

"station" means a passenger stop, station or terminal on a transport system but does not include any permanent way or other means of guiding or supporting vehicles or plant used for signalling or exclusively for supplying electricity for operational purposes to a transport system;

"technical specifications for interoperability" ("TSIs") means technical specifications for interoperability which are published in the Official Journal of the European Communities pursuant to—

(a) Article 6.1 of the high-speed Directive; or
(b) Article 6.1 of the conventional Directive,

and in force;

"train" includes any rolling stock;

"tramway" means a system of transport used wholly or mainly for the carriage of passengers—

(a) which employs parallel rails which—
   (i) provide support and guidance for vehicles carried on flanged wheels;
   (ii) are laid wholly or partly along a road or in any other place to which the public has access (including a place to which the public has access only on making a payment); and
(b) on any part of which the permitted maximum speed is such as to enable the driver to stop a vehicle in the distance he can see to be clear ahead;

"transport operator" means any transport undertaking or infrastructure manager;

"transport system" means a railway, a tramway, or any other system using guided transport where that other system is used wholly or mainly for the carriage of passengers but a transport system does not include—

(a) a guided bus system;
(b) a trolley vehicle system;
(c) any part of a transport system—
   (i) within a harbour or harbour area or which is part of a factory, mine or quarry;
   (ii) used solely for the purpose of carrying out a building operation or work of engineering construction;
   (iii) within a maintenance or goods depot;
   (iv) within a siding except where Part 4 applies; or
   (v) which is within a military establishment;
(d) any fairground equipment;
(e) any cableway installation; or
(f) any transport system where the track forms a gauge of less than 350mm except where such a track crosses a carriageway (whether or not on the same level),

except where the transport system in question forms part of the mainline railway;

"transport undertaking" means any person who operates a vehicle in relation to any infrastructure but shall not include a person who operates a vehicle solely within an engineering possession;

"trolley vehicle system" means a system of transport by vehicles constructed or adapted for use on roads without rails under electric power transmitted to them by overhead wires (whether or not there is in addition a source of power on board the vehicles);

"vehicle" includes a mobile traction unit;

"work of engineering construction" means the—

(a) construction of any line or siding otherwise than on an existing transport system; and
(b) construction, structural alteration, repair (including repointing and repainting) or demolition of any tunnel, bridge or viaduct except where carried on upon a transport system; and

"writing" apart from its usual meaning includes any text transmitted using electronic communications that is received, or accessible by the person to whom it is sent, in legible form.

(2) Any reference in these Regulations to a person who operates a train or a vehicle is a reference to the person operating the train or vehicle for the time being in

the course of a business or other undertaking carried on by him, whether for profit or not, but it does not include a self-employed person by reason only that he drives or otherwise controls the movement of a train or vehicle.

(3) Parts 2 and 3 of these Regulations shall not apply to or in relation to the operation of a train or the management or use of infrastructure in the tunnel system within the meaning of section 1(7) of the Channel Tunnel Act 1987.

NOTES

Council Directive 96/48/EC OJ L235, 17.09.1996, p 6.
Directive 2001/16/EC OJ L110, 20.04.2001, p 1.
Directive 2004/49/EC OJ L164, 30.04.2004, p 44.
Regulation (EC) 881/2004 OJ L164, 30.04.2004, p 1.
Highways Act 1980 For the meaning of "carriageway" in that Act, see s 329(1) thereof.
Dangerous Substances in Harbour Areas Regulations 1987 SI 1987/37, in the title Health and Safety at Work.
Departments (Northern Ireland) Order 1999 SI 1999/283 (NI 1) (outside the scope of this work).
Quarries Regulations 1999 SI 1999/2024, in the title Mines, Minerals and Quarries.
Railways and Other Transport Systems (Approval of Works, Plant and Equipment) Regulations 1994 SI 1994/157 (revoked by reg 34, Sch 7).
Railways (Interoperability) Regulations 2006 SI 2006/397.

[1031]

PART 2
SAFETY MANAGEMENT, CERTIFICATION AND AUTHORISATION

Use of infrastructure on the mainline railway

3 (1) After 30th September 2006 no person shall operate a train in relation to any infrastructure on the mainline railway unless—

- (a) he has established and is maintaining a safety management system which meets the requirements set out in regulation 5(1) to (4); and
- (b) he holds a current safety certificate in relation to the operation in question,

except to the extent that he is doing so within an engineering possession.

(2) After 30th September 2006 no person who is responsible for developing and maintaining infrastructure other than a station or who is responsible for managing and operating a station on the mainline railway shall manage and use it, or permit it to be used, for the operation of trains unless—

- (a) he has established and is maintaining a safety management system which meets the requirements referred to in regulation 5(7);
- (b) he holds a current safety authorisation in relation to the infrastructure in question; and
- (c) where he is using it or permitting such use, the person who is to use the infrastructure has complied with paragraph (1)(b).

[1032]

Use of infrastructure on other transport systems

4 (1) After 30th September 2006 no person shall operate a vehicle in relation to any infrastructure on a transport system other than the mainline railway unless—

- (a) he has established and is maintaining a safety management system which meets the requirements set out in regulation 6; and
- (b) subject to paragraph (3), he holds a current safety certificate in relation to the operation in question,

except to the extent that he is doing so within an engineering possession.

(2) After 30th September 2006 no person who is responsible for developing and maintaining infrastructure, other than a station, or who is responsible for managing and operating a station on a transport system other than the mainline railway shall manage and use it, or permit it to be used, for the operation of a vehicle unless—

- (a) he has established and is maintaining a safety management system which meets the requirements set out in regulation 6; and
- (b) subject to paragraph (3)—

(i) he holds a current safety authorisation in relation to the infrastructure in question; and

(ii) where he is using it or permitting such use, the person who is to use the infrastructure has complied with paragraph (1)(b).

(3) Paragraphs (1)(b) and (2)(b) shall not apply to the extent that the operation in question is only carried out—

(a) on a tramway; or

(b) on a transport system on no part of which there is a permitted maximum speed exceeding 40 kilometres per hour.

(4) Where the operation in question falls within paragraph (3)(a) or (b), the requirement in paragraphs (1)(a) and (2)(a) shall be read as if the date was, in each case, after 31st March 2007.

[1033]

Safety management system for the mainline railway

5 (1) The requirements for a safety management system referred to in regulation 3(1)(a) are that—

(a) subject to paragraph (2), it is established to ensure that the mainline railway system—

(i) can achieve the CSTs; and

(ii) is in conformity with relevant national safety rules and relevant safety requirements laid down in TSIs;

(b) it applies the relevant parts of CSMs;

(c) it meets the requirements and contains the elements set out in Schedule 1, adapted to the character, extent and other characteristics of the operation in question;

(d) subject to paragraph (2), it ensures the control of all categories of risk including new or existing risks associated with the operation in question which, without prejudice to the generality of the foregoing, shall include such risks relating to the—

(i) supply of maintenance and material;

(ii) use of contractors; and

(iii) placing in service of new or altered vehicles the design or construction of which incorporates significant changes compared to any vehicle already in use on the transport system and which changes would be capable of significantly increasing an existing risk or creating a significant safety risk;

(e) it takes into account, where appropriate and reasonable, the risks arising as a result of activities carried on by other persons; and

(f) all parts of it are documented.

(2) The requirements in paragraphs (1)(a) and (d) shall be met where the safety management system of a transport operator or of an applicant for a safety certificate or a safety authorisation ("the first operator") taken with that of any relevant transport operator is capable of meeting the requirements of the paragraph in question.

(3) In paragraph (2), "relevant transport operator" means another transport operator whose operation is capable of materially affecting the safety of the operation carried on by the first operator.

(4) In paragraph (1)(d)(iii) where such new or altered vehicles are intended to be placed in service, then before that placing in service the transport operator shall ensure that he has—

(a) an established written safety verification scheme which meets the requirements and contains the elements set out in Schedule 4; and

(b) appointed a competent person to undertake that safety verification, and the competent person has undertaken that safety verification in relation to the new or altered vehicles.

(5) Where a new or altered vehicle has been authorised under regulation 4(1)(a) of the Interoperability Regulations for the placing in service on the mainline railway, that authorisation shall be treated as satisfying the requirements of paragraph (4).

(6) In this regulation placing in service shall mean first placed in service for the provision of a transport service, and in ascertaining when this takes place no regard shall be had to any trials or testing that takes place to the relevant vehicle.

(7) The requirements for a safety management system referred to in regulation 3(2)(a) are the requirements in paragraphs (1) to (6) save that any reference to new or altered vehicles in those paragraphs shall be replaced with a reference to new or altered infrastructure and that—

- (a) it ensures the control of all categories of risk associated with the placing in service of new or altered infrastructure the design or construction of which incorporates significant changes compared to any infrastructure already in use on the transport system and which changes would be capable of significantly increasing an existing risk or creating a significant safety risk;
- (b) it takes into account the effects of operations of transport undertakings; and
- (c) it contains provisions to ensure that the way in which the infrastructure manager carries out his operation makes it possible for any transport undertaking to operate in accordance with—
  - (i) relevant TSIs and national safety rules; and
  - (ii) the means adopted by the transport undertaking to meet the requirements referred to in regulation 7(4), of which the Office of Rail Regulation accepted that there was sufficient evidence upon issue or amendment of its safety certificate pursuant to these Regulations; and
- (d) it aims to co-ordinate the emergency procedures of the infrastructure manager or of the applicant for a safety authorisation with those of transport undertakings,

and in each case the requirements in sub-paragraphs (a) to (d) shall only apply in relation to transport undertakings that operate or will operate a train in relation to the infrastructure of the infrastructure manager or of the applicant for a safety authorisation in question.

[1034]

Safety management system for other transport systems

6 (1) The requirements for a safety management system referred to in regulation 4(1)(a) and 4(2)(a) are that—

- (a) it is adequate to ensure that the relevant statutory provisions which make provision in relation to safety will be complied with in relation to the operation in question;
- (b) subject to paragraph (7), it meets the requirements and contains the elements set out in Schedule 1, adapted to the character, extent and other characteristics of the operation in question;
- (c) subject to paragraph (2), it ensures the control of all categories of risk associated with the operation in question which, without prejudice to the generality of the foregoing, shall include such risks relating to the—
  - (i) supply of maintenance and material;
  - (ii) use of contractors; and
  - (iii) placing in service of new or altered vehicles or infrastructure the design or construction of which incorporates significant changes compared to any vehicles or infrastructure already in use on the transport system and which changes would be capable of significantly increasing an existing risk or creating a significant safety risk;
- (d) it takes into account, where appropriate and reasonable, the risks arising as a result of activities carried on by other persons; and
- (e) all parts of it are documented.

(2) The requirement in paragraph (1)(c) shall be met where the safety management system of a transport operator or an applicant for a safety certificate or a safety authorisation ("the first operator") taken with that of any relevant transport operator is capable of meeting the requirements of the paragraph in question.

(3) In paragraph (2), "relevant transport operator" means another transport operator whose operation is capable of materially affecting the safety of the operation carried on by the first operator.

(4) In paragraph (1)(c)(iii) where such new or altered vehicles or infrastructure are intended to be placed in service, then before that placing in service the transport operator shall ensure that he—

(a) has an established written safety verification scheme which meets the requirements and contains the elements set out in Schedule 4; and

(b) has appointed a competent person to undertake that safety verification and the competent person has undertaken that safety verification in relation to the new or altered vehicle or infrastructure.

(5) In this regulation placed in service shall mean first placed in service for the provision of a transport service, and in ascertaining when this takes place no regard shall be had to any trials or testing that takes place to the relevant vehicle or infrastructure.

(6) In this regulation the requirements of paragraph (4) shall apply in the absence of a transport operator to a responsible person as they would apply to a transport operator.

(7) Paragraph 2(c) of Schedule 1 shall apply in relation to transport systems other than the mainline railway as if it read as follows—

"(c) procedures—

(i) to meet relevant technical specifications; and

(ii) relating to operations or maintenance,

insofar as they relate to the safety of persons, and procedures for ensuring that the procedures in sub-paragraphs (i) and (ii) are followed throughout the life-cycle of any relevant equipment or operation;".

[1035]

Safety certificate

7 (1) An application for a first safety certificate in respect of an operation shall—

(a) be made to the Office of Rail Regulation;

(b) subject to regulation 17(1) and (2), include the information set out in—

(i) Part 1 of Schedule 2 in respect of a mainline application; and

(ii) Part 2 of Schedule 2 in respect of a non-mainline application; and

(c) if it is a mainline application, clearly indicate in respect of which part of the safety certificate any information is provided.

(2) Where—

(a) an applicant sends to the Office of Rail Regulation in relation to a mainline application the matters specified in paragraphs 1(a) and 1(b)(i) of Schedule 2; and

(b) the Office of Rail Regulation is satisfied that the certificate in question is for an equivalent operation to that in respect of which the application is made,

then that certificate shall be deemed to be Part A of the safety certificate for the operation in respect of which the application is made.

(3) Subject to regulation 17(7), within four months of the date of receipt of the application, the Office of Rail Regulation shall—

(a) issue a safety certificate for the operation in question; or

(b) notify the applicant that it has refused the application,

and in either case shall give reasons for its decision.

(4) A safety certificate shall—

(a) specify the type and extent of the operation in respect of which it is issued; and

(b) certify acceptance by the Office of Rail Regulation that the applicant has provided sufficient evidence—

(i) subject to paragraph (2), to demonstrate that the safety management system of the applicant meets the requirements set out in regulations 5(1) to (4) in respect of a mainline application or regulation 6 in respect of a non-mainline application; and

(ii) of the provisions adopted by the applicant to meet the requirements that are necessary to ensure safe operation on the transport system in question,

and reference the information on which such acceptance is based; and

(c) be valid for no longer than five years from the date of issue and the period of validity shall be indicated in the safety certificate and where Part A of the certificate is deemed to be such a Part A in accordance with regulation 7(2) that period shall expire on or before the date of expiry of the certificate which is deemed to be the Part A.

(5) In paragraph (4)(b)(ii) "requirements" means in relation to—

(a) a mainline application, the TSIs, national safety rules and other safety requirements referred to in paragraph 2(a) of Schedule 2; and

(b) a non-mainline application, the relevant statutory provisions, technical specifications and procedures referred to in paragraph 5 of Schedule 2.

[1036]

Amended safety certificate

8 (1) Where it is proposed that the type or extent of an operation in respect of which a safety certificate has been issued is to be substantially changed then the holder of the safety certificate shall apply to the Office of Rail Regulation for the safety certificate to be amended accordingly and the substantial change shall not be made until the safety certificate is so amended.

(2) An application for an amended safety certificate under this regulation shall—

(a) provide details of the change proposed;

(b) provide details of any consequential changes to any information sent to the Office of Rail Regulation in respect of the operation in question which remains relevant to that operation; and

(c) if it is a mainline application, clearly indicate in respect of which part of the safety certificate any information is provided.

(3) Where Part A of a safety certificate in respect of which an application is made is deemed to be such a Part A in accordance with regulation 7(2) then the Office of Rail Regulation shall—

(a) consider whether the Part A in question would still be for an equivalent operation if the change were made; and

(b) if it considers that it would not be equivalent, notify the applicant in accordance with paragraph (4) that it has refused the application and that he should apply for a new safety certificate under regulation 7 if he wants to make the proposed change,

except that, in relation to Part B of the safety certificate, he only need provide the details set out in paragraph (2) above.

(4) Subject to regulation 17(7), within four months of the date of receipt of the application the Office of Rail Regulation shall—

(a) issue a notice making any necessary amendments to the matters set out in the safety certificate; or

(b) notify the applicant that it has refused the application,

and in either case shall give reasons for its decision.

[1037]

Further safety certificate

9 (1) Before the expiry of a safety certificate the holder of that safety certificate may apply to the Office of Rail Regulation for a further safety certificate to be issued for the operation in question.

(2) An application for a further safety certificate shall set out particulars of any changes to any information sent to the Office of Rail Regulation in respect of the operation in question which remains relevant to that operation.

(3) Regulations 7(1)(c) and 7(2) to (4) shall apply to an application for and the issuing of a further safety certificate as they apply to an application for and the issuing of a first safety certificate under regulation 7.

[1038]

Safety authorisation

10 (1) An application for a first safety authorisation in respect of infrastructure shall—

(a) be made to the Office of Rail Regulation;
(b) subject to regulation 17(1) and (2), set out particulars of—
  (i) the infrastructure in question;
  (ii) how the safety management system of the applicant meets the requirements in regulation 5(7) in relation to a mainline application or in regulation 6 in relation to a non-mainline application; and
  (iii) how the provisions adopted by the applicant meet any requirements which are necessary for the safe design, maintenance and operation of the infrastructure in question.

(2) Subject to regulation 17(7), within four months of the date of receipt of the application the Office of Rail Regulation shall—

(a) issue a safety authorisation in relation to the infrastructure in question; or
(b) notify the applicant that it has refused the application; and
(c) in either case shall give reasons for its decision.

(3) A safety authorisation shall—

(a) specify the infrastructure in respect of which the authorisation is issued;
(b) accept that the applicant has provided sufficient evidence to demonstrate that the safety management system of the applicant meets the requirements—
  (i) referred to in regulation 5(7) in relation to a mainline application; or
  (ii) in regulation 6 in relation to a non-mainline application;
(c) accept that the applicant has provided sufficient evidence of the provisions adopted by the applicant to meet any requirements that are necessary for the safe design, maintenance and operation of the infrastructure in question;
(d) reference the information on which the acceptance referred to in sub-paragraphs (b) and (c) is based; and
(e) be valid for no longer than five years from the date of issue and the period of validity shall be indicated in the safety authorisation.

[1039]

Amended safety authorisation

11 (1) Where it is proposed that a substantial change is to be made to—

(a) the infrastructure in respect of which a safety authorisation has been issued;
(b) any energy supply, not falling within sub-paragraph (a), which is used in connection with the infrastructure in question; or
(c) the principles of operation and maintenance of such infrastructure or energy supply,

then the holder of the safety authorisation shall apply to the Office of Rail Regulation for the safety authorisation to be amended accordingly and the substantial change shall not be made until the safety authorisation is so amended.

(2) An application for an amended safety authorisation under this regulation shall provide details of—

(a) the substantial changes proposed; and
(b) any consequential changes to any information sent to the Office of Rail Regulation in respect of the operation in question which remains relevant to that operation.

(3) Subject to regulation 17(7), within four months of the date of receipt of the application the Office of Rail Regulation shall—

(a) issue a notice making any necessary amendments to the matters set out in the safety authorisation; or

(b) notify the applicant that it has refused the application,

and in either case shall give reasons for its decision.

[1040]

Further safety authorisation

12 (1) Before the expiry of a safety authorisation the holder of that safety authorisation may apply to the Office of Rail Regulation for a further safety authorisation to be issued for the infrastructure in question.

(2) An application for a further safety authorisation shall set out particulars of any changes to any information sent to the Office of Rail Regulation in respect of the operation in question which remains relevant to that operation.

(3) Regulations 10(2) and 10(3) shall apply to an application for and the issuing of a further safety authorisation as they apply to an application for and the issuing of a first safety authorisation under regulation 10.

[1041]

Notice of changes by holder of a safety certificate or a safety authorisation

13 The holder of a safety certificate or a safety authorisation shall, without delay, notify the Office of Rail Regulation—

(a) of any major changes—

(i) to the means by which he meets the requirements relating to the safety management system as set out in—

(aa) regulation 5(1) to (4) in relation to an operation of a transport undertaking on the mainline railway;

(bb) regulation 5(7) in relation to an operation of an infrastructure manager on the mainline railway; or

(cc) regulation 6 in relation to an operation which is not carried out on the mainline railway;

(ii) in the case of a transport undertaking, to the provisions adopted by him to meet any requirements necessary to ensure safe operation on the transport system in relation to the operation in question; or

(iii) in the case of an infrastructure manager, to the provisions adopted by him to meet any requirements that are necessary for the safe design, maintenance and operation of the infrastructure in question;

(b) when persons first commence work directly relating to the operation which is of a type which has not previously been carried out in relation to that operation; or

(c) when types of vehicle which are new to the operation in question are first introduced.

[1042]

Direction to apply for an amended safety certificate or safety authorisation

14 (1) Where there is a substantial change to any of the relevant statutory provisions which make provision in relation to the safety of the transport system in question, then the Office of Rail Regulation may direct the holder of a safety certificate or a safety authorisation to apply to the Office of Rail Regulation for an amendment to its safety certificate or safety authorisation.

(2) A direction issued under paragraph (1) shall—

(a) state the reasons why the Office of Rail Regulation considers that it is necessary for the transport operator to apply for an amended safety certificate or safety authorisation;

(b) identify the information—

(i) on the basis of which the Office of Rail Regulation's acceptance referred to in regulation 7(4) or 10(3) was made upon issue or amendment of the safety certificate or safety authorisation; or

(ii) notified to the Office of Rail Regulation under regulation 13,

which it considers will have to be changed; and

(c) specify the period, being not less than 28 days from the date of issue of the direction, within which the application shall be sent to the Office of Rail Regulation.

(3) An application for an amended safety certificate or safety authorisation pursuant to this regulation shall provide details of any changes to any information—

(a) sent to the Office of Rail Regulation in respect of the operation in question which remains relevant to that operation; and

(b) which is consequential upon the relevant change to the relevant statutory provisions.

(4) Regulations 8(2)(c) and 8(4) shall apply to an application for and the issuing of a notice of amendment to a safety certificate under this regulation as they apply to an application for and issuing of an amendment to a safety certificate under regulation 8.

(5) Regulation 11(3) shall apply to an application for and the issuing of a notice of amendment to a safety authorisation under this regulation as it applies to an application for and issuing of an amendment to a safety authorisation under regulation 11.

[1043]

Revocation of safety certificate

15 (1) The Office of Rail Regulation shall revoke—

(a) either Part A or Part B of a safety certificate if it is satisfied that the holder is no longer satisfying the conditions of that part of the safety certificate and that there is a significant risk arising as a result;

(b) a safety certificate if it is satisfied that the holder—

(i) is no longer satisfying the conditions of that safety certificate and that there is a significant risk arising as a result; or

(ii) is not operating a vehicle in relation to any infrastructure on a transport system as intended pursuant to that safety certificate and has not done so throughout the period of one year commencing with the date of issue of the safety certificate by the Office of Rail Regulation,

except that this paragraph shall not apply in relation to Part A of a safety certificate where it is deemed to be such a Part A in accordance with regulation 7(2).

(2) In this regulation, "conditions" means in relation to—

(a) Part A of a safety certificate, any part of the requirements relating to the safety management system set out in—

(i) regulation 5(1) to (4) in relation to an operation carried out on the mainline railway; or

(ii) regulation 6 in relation to an operation carried out on a transport system other than the mainline railway;

(b) Part B of a safety certificate, that the provisions adopted by the applicant are sufficient to meet any requirements that are necessary to ensure safe operation on the transport system in question in relation to the operation in question; or

(c) a safety certificate, the matters referred to in sub-paragraphs (a) and (b).

(3) Before revoking any safety certificate or Part A or B of it, the Office of Rail Regulation shall—

(a) notify the holder that—

(i) it is considering revoking that safety certificate or Part A or B of it and the reasons why;

(ii) within a period specified in the notice, which shall be not less than 28 days, the holder may make representations in writing to the Office of Rail Regulation or, if the holder so requests, may make oral representations to the Office of Rail Regulation; and

(b) consider any representations which are duly made and not withdrawn.

(4) Where the Office of Rail Regulation revokes a safety certificate or Part A or B of it, it shall send to the holder with the notice of revocation a statement of the reasons why.

(5) Where—

(a) the Office of Rail Regulation revokes Part B of a safety certificate; and
(b) Part A of that safety certificate is deemed to be Part A of a safety certificate pursuant to regulation 7(2) and was issued by the safety authority in another member State or in Northern Ireland,

then the Office of Rail Regulation shall notify that safety authority as soon as reasonably possible of that revocation.

[1044]

Revocation of safety authorisation

16 (1) The Office of Rail Regulation shall revoke a safety authorisation if it is satisfied that the holder is no longer satisfying the conditions of that safety authorisation and there is a significant risk arising as a result.

(2) In this regulation, "conditions" means—

(a) any part of the requirements relating to the safety management system—
  (i) referred to in regulation 5(7) in relation to an operation carried out on the mainline railway; or
  (ii) in regulation 6 in relation to an operation carried out on a transport system other than the mainline railway; or
(b) that the provisions adopted by the applicant are sufficient to meet any requirements that are necessary for the safe design, maintenance and operation of the infrastructure in question.

(3) Before revoking any safety authorisation, the Office of Rail Regulation shall—

(a) notify the holder that—
  (i) it is considering revoking that safety authorisation and the reasons why;
  (ii) within a period specified in the notice, which shall be not less than 28 days, the holder may make representations in writing to the Office of Rail Regulation or, if the holder so requests, may make oral representations to the Office of Rail Regulation; and
(b) consider any representations which are duly made and not withdrawn.

(4) Where the Office of Rail Regulation revokes a safety authorisation, it shall send to the holder with the notice of revocation a statement of the reasons why.

[1045]

General provisions relating to safety certificates and safety authorisations

17 (1) Where an application is made under these Regulations for a safety certificate or safety authorisation or for an amended safety certificate or safety authorisation which relates to an operation on the mainline railway and on a transport system other than the mainline railway then—

(a) one application may be made for that operation but it shall be split into separate parts for the mainline railway and the other transport system; and
(b) these Regulations shall apply to those parts as if they were a mainline application and a non-mainline application,

except that where the same information is required it need not be stated twice.

(2) A transport operator may make one application for an operation in relation to which he requires both a safety certificate and a safety authorisation or an amended safety certificate and an amended safety authorisation but—

(a) such application shall be split into separate parts relating to the safety authorisation and the safety certificate; and
(b) these Regulations shall apply to those parts as if they were an application for a safety authorisation and a safety certificate or an amended safety authorisation and an amended safety certificate,

except that where the same information is required it need not be stated twice.

(3) Where—

(a) an applicant sends—
  (i) an application for a safety certificate or safety authorisation, an amended safety certificate or safety authorisation; or

(ii) further information to the Office of Rail Regulation pursuant to paragraph (5); or

(b) the holder of a safety certificate or a safety authorisation sends a notice pursuant to regulation 13 or paragraph 9 of Schedule 5,

then he shall at the same time either copy it to any affected party or notify any affected party without delay that the application or further information has been sent and of the address of the website where those documents may be accessed and how they may be accessed and, in either case, shall notify such a party, where the document in question is an application, of the time for making representations to the Office of Rail Regulation pursuant to paragraph (6).

(4) Where the Office of Rail Regulation issues a—

(a) safety certificate or safety authorisation, other than to an operator of last resort;
(b) notice amending a safety certificate or safety authorisation;
(c) notice refusing an application for a safety certificate or a safety authorisation or an amended safety certificate or safety authorisation;
(d) direction to apply for an amended safety certificate or safety authorisation;
(e) notice that it is considering revoking a safety certificate or a safety authorisation; or
(f) notice revoking a safety certificate or a safety authorisation,

then the Office of Rail Regulation shall at the same time either copy it and the reasons given for the Office of Rail Regulation's decision to any affected party or notify any affected party that the relevant document has been issued and of the address of the website where those documents and the reasons given for the decision may be accessed and how they may be accessed and, in either case, shall notify such a party, where the document in question is a notice that it is considering revocation as mentioned in sub-paragraph (e), of the time for making representations to the Office of Rail Regulation pursuant to paragraph (6).

(5) The Office of Rail Regulation may upon receipt of—

(a) an application for a safety certificate or safety authorisation;
(b) an application for an amended safety certificate or safety authorisation;
(c) any further information requested under this paragraph,

request as soon as reasonably possible such further information as it may reasonably require and the applicant shall provide such information as soon as reasonably possible except that in a case falling within paragraph (7)(c) the Office of Rail Regulation may request such information as soon as reasonably possible after the date at which the 4 month period starts to run as specified in that paragraph.

(6) Where an affected party receives a copy of an application or a notice relating to revocation pursuant to paragraph (3)(a) or (4)(e) then—

(a) he may make any representations in writing to the Office of Rail Regulation, which are relevant to the application or notice, within 28 days of the date of issue of the application or notice in question; and
(b) the Office of Rail Regulation shall consider any such representations in making its decision.

(7) The period of 4 months for the Office of Rail Regulation to make a decision referred to in regulations 7(3), 8(4), 10(2) and 11(3) shall not start to run—

(a) until the expiry of the 28 day period referred to in paragraph (6);
(b) until the date of receipt of the last information requested pursuant to paragraph (5); or
(c) where the application is made in respect of an operation for which the applicant holds a deemed safety certificate or deemed safety authorisation, until the date which falls 9 months before the date of expiry of that certificate or authorisation in accordance with paragraph 5 of Schedule 5 which shall apply as if paragraph 5(a) of that Schedule were omitted,

whichever is the later and in any event shall not start to run until 30th June 2006.

(8) Paragraph (7)(c) shall apply to an application in relation to a safety certificate or a safety authorisation made before 1st October 2006 in respect of which the applicant has an accepted safety case pursuant to the Railways (Safety Case) Regulations 2000 as if Schedule 5 were already in force.

(9) An employer who makes an application for a safety certificate or safety authorisation, an amended safety certificate or safety authorisation or sends a notice to the Office of Rail Regulation under regulation 13 or paragraph 9 of Schedule 5 shall, in relation to its preparation, consult—

(a) safety representatives within the meaning of regulation 2(1) of the Safety Representatives and Safety Committees Regulations 1977; and

(b) such other employees as he is required to consult by virtue of regulation 3 of the Health and Safety (Consultation with Employees) Regulations 1996.

(10) In this regulation, "affected party" means for a document sent or issued in relation to—

(a) a safety certificate or an application for a safety certificate—

  (i) any relevant infrastructure manager;

  (ii) a trade union which is a recognised trade union within the meaning of regulation 2(1) of the Safety Representatives and Safety Committees Regulations 1977 in relation to employees of the operator or applicant employed in relation to the operation in question; and

  (iii) the Rail Passengers' Council and the London Transport Users' Committee where, in each case, it represents passengers' interests in relation to the operation in question; and

(b) a safety authorisation or an application for a safety authorisation—

  (i) any transport undertaking who is or will be operating on the infrastructure of the applicant or infrastructure manager in question;

  (ii) any infrastructure manager who manages infrastructure which interfaces or will interface with the infrastructure of the infrastructure manager in question; and

  (iii) any person falling within paragraph (10)(a)(ii) or (iii).

NOTES

Railways (Safety Case) Regulations 2000 SI 2000/2688 (revoked by reg 34, Sch 7).

Safety Representatives and Safety Committees Regulations 1977; Health and Safety (Consultation with Employees) Regulations 1996 SI 1977/500 and SI 1996/1513, in the title Health and Safety at Work.

[1046]

Notification to the European Railway Agency regarding safety certificates and safety authorisations relating to the mainline railway

18 (1) The Office of Rail Regulation shall notify the European Railway Agency of the issuing, amendment or revocation of—

(a) Part A of a safety certificate; or

(b) a safety authorisation,

pursuant to these Regulations in relation to an operation on the mainline railway within one month of such issue, amendment or revocation.

(2) A notice under paragraph (1) shall include the following information in relation to the safety certificate or safety authorisation—

(a) the name and address of the holder;

(b) its date of issue and period of validity;

(c) the operation or infrastructure in relation to which it was issued; and

(d) where it relates to a revocation, the reasons for that decision.

[1047]

PART 3
GENERAL DUTIES

Risk assessment

19 (1) A transport operator shall—

(a) make a suitable and sufficient assessment of the risks to the safety of any persons for the purpose of identifying the measures he needs to take to ensure safe operation of the transport system in question insofar as this is affected by his operation; and

(b) implement the measures referred to in sub-paragraph (a).

(2) When carrying out an assessment or a review under paragraph (1) or (3), a transport operator shall apply the CSMs to the extent that the operation is carried out on the mainline railway.

(3) Any assessment under paragraph (1) shall be reviewed by the transport operator who made it if—

(a) there is a reason to suspect that it is no longer valid; or
(b) there has been a significant change in the matters to which it relates and where as a result of any such review changes to an assessment are required,

the transport operator concerned shall make them, and implement any changes to the measures identified pursuant to paragraph (1) as a result of the review.

(4) The transport operator shall record in relation to any assessment or review under this regulation—

(a) the assessment process undertaken, the methods of any calculation used and any assumptions made; and
(b) the significant findings of the risk assessment including the measures in place and any further measures the transport operator intends to take to ensure safe operation of the transport system in relation to his operation.

(5) Every transport operator shall make and give effect to such arrangements as are appropriate, having regard to the nature of his activities and the extent of the undertaking, for the effective planning, organisation, control, monitoring and review of the measures identified pursuant to paragraph (1) or (3) and shall record such arrangements.

[1048]

Annual safety reports

20 (1) Subject to paragraph (2), any transport operator who is subject to the prohibition in regulations 3(1)(b), 3(2)(b), 4(1)(b) or 4(2)(b) shall send to the Office of Rail Regulation an annual safety report relating to the previous calendar year which shall contain—

(a) information on how the transport operator's safety targets, referred to in paragraph 2(b) of Schedule 1, are met;
(b) the results achieved through putting the transport operator's safety plans, referred to in paragraph 2(b) of Schedule 1, into effect;
(c) statistics for the common safety indicators listed in Schedule 3 insofar as they are relevant to the operation in question except, to the extent the operation is carried out on a transport system other than the mainline railway, no statistics are required in relation to the indicators in paragraphs 1(1)(a)(vii), 1(1)(b)(v) and 3 of that Schedule;
(d) the findings of safety auditing carried out pursuant to the procedures referred to in paragraph 2(k) of Schedule 1; and
(e) comments on any deficiencies or malfunctions relating to the running of vehicles or the management of infrastructure relating to the operation in question that may be relevant to the safety of that transport system,

and where an operation is carried out in part on the mainline railway and in part on another transport system the report shall clearly indicate the information which relates to the part carried out on the mainline railway.

(2) The first annual report required under paragraph (1) shall be sent by 30th June 2007 and subsequent reports by 30th June in each subsequent calendar year.

(3) Subject to paragraph (4), the Office of Rail Regulation shall publish and send to the European Railway Agency an annual report relating to the previous calendar year which shall contain information on the following in relation to the mainline railway—

(a) the development of railway safety including an aggregation of all the statistics reported to the Office of Rail Regulation for the relevant calendar year pursuant to paragraph (1)(c) which relate to an operation or part of an operation which is carried out on the mainline railway;
(b) any important changes in relation to the regulation of railway safety;
(c) the development of the system for safety certification and authorisation; and

(d) the results of and experience relating to the supervision of transport operators,

in Great Britain.

(4) The first annual report required under paragraph (3) shall be sent to the European Railway Agency by 30th September 2007 and subsequent reports by 30th September in each subsequent calendar year.

(5) Where the Office of Rail Regulation discovers, after sending an annual report, that there were errors or omissions in it then it shall send a corrected report for that year to the European Railway Agency at the first convenient opportunity and in any event by no later than the time the next annual report is due to be sent.

[1049]

Sending, issuing, and keeping of documents and making them available for public inspection

21 (1) Any application, notice, report or any other information sent to the Office of Rail Regulation or records made pursuant to these Regulations shall be in writing and in English.

(2) Any certificate, authorisation, notice, direction, request for information, statement or report issued by the Office of Rail Regulation pursuant to these Regulations shall be in writing and in English.

(3) An applicant who makes an application in respect of a safety certificate or a safety authorisation pursuant to regulations 7, 9, 10 or 12 shall when sending the application, notify the Office of Rail Regulation of an address in Great Britain for the purposes of this regulation ("notified address").

(4) Subject to paragraphs (5) and (6), a transport operator shall keep at the notified address in relation to the operation in question—

(a) the safety certificate or safety authorisation issued in response to his application for such certificate or authorisation and the documentation referenced in that safety certificate or safety authorisation;

(b) any notice of amendment issued pursuant to Part 2 of these Regulations or any revision made pursuant to paragraph 8 of Schedule 5 in relation to his safety certificate or safety authorisation;

(c) any records he is required to make pursuant to regulation 19(4) and (5);

(d) any annual safety report sent to the Office of Rail Regulation under regulation 20(1);

(e) any notification of changes or of a revision notified to the Office of Rail Regulation under regulation 13 or paragraph 9 of Schedule 5; and

(f) a record of any findings of internal safety auditing carried out pursuant to the procedures referred to in paragraph 2(k) of Schedule 1 and of any action taken in consequence of such auditing,

or a hard or electronic copy of such documents.

(5) The documents referred to in paragraph (4) shall be kept as long as they—

(a) are or are a copy of the current safety certificate or safety authorisation or a notice of amendment thereof;

(b) are or are a copy of a notification of a major change or a revision which is relevant to the current operation of the transport undertaking;

(c) relate to the information on the basis of which the Office of Rail Regulation's acceptance referred to in regulation 7(4) or 10(3), as the case may be, was made in relation to a current safety certificate or safety authorisation; or

(d) relate to a risk assessment, as reviewed from time to time, carried out pursuant to regulation 19.

(6) The documents kept pursuant to paragraph (4)(d) or (4)(f) shall be kept for 5 years and the documents kept pursuant to sub-paragraphs (a), (b), (d) and (e) of paragraph (4) shall, subject to paragraph (7), be made available for public inspection at the notified address at reasonable times and on reasonable notice.

(7) Nothing in paragraph (6) shall require the disclosure of any information—

(a) relating to a named individual;

(b) which is commercially confidential; or

(c) which is detrimental to national security or to the security of the transport system in question.

(8) A person who has a notified address may subsequently notify the Office of Rail Regulation of a different address in Great Britain and in this case references in this regulation to the notified address shall be construed as a reference to the last address notified under this paragraph.

[1050]

Co-operation

22 (1) Every person to whom this paragraph applies shall co-operate as far as is necessary with a transport operator to enable him to comply with the provisions of these Regulations.

(2) Paragraph (1) applies to—

(a) any transport operator whose operations may affect or may be affected by operations carried out by the duty holder; and

(b) an employer of persons or a self-employed person carrying out work on or in relation to premises or plant owned or controlled by the duty holder.

(3) Every transport operator shall co-operate, insofar as is reasonable, with any other transport operator who operates on the same transport system where that other transport operator is taking action to achieve the safe operation of that transport system.

(4) In paragraph (2) "duty holder" means a transport operator referred to in paragraph (1).

[1051]

PART 4
SAFETY CRITICAL WORK

Interpretation and application of Part 4

23 (1) In this Part—

"assessor" means any person who is competent to make an impartial and objective assessment of another person's competence or fitness to carry out safety critical work, and related expressions shall be construed accordingly;

"controller of safety critical work" means any person controlling the carrying out of safety critical work on a transport system or in relation to a vehicle used on a transport system;

"fitness" means physical and mental fitness, and related expressions shall be construed accordingly;

"installation" includes the installation, examination or testing of components;

"maintenance" includes repair work, reconditioning, examination, testing or alteration;

"operator" means any person carrying on an undertaking which includes a transport system or any part of it or the provision of transport services on such a system;

"safety critical task" means—

(a) in relation to a vehicle used on a transport system—

(i) driving, dispatching or any other activity which is capable of controlling or affecting the movement of that vehicle;

(ii) signalling, and signalling operations, the operation of level crossing equipment, receiving and relaying of communications or any other activity which is capable of controlling or affecting the movement of that vehicle;

(iii) coupling or uncoupling;

(iv) installation of components, other than where the installation of those components is subject to supervision and checking by a safety critical worker or a controller of safety critical work;

(v) maintenance, other than where the carrying out of that maintenance is subject to supervision and checking by a safety critical worker or a controller of safety critical work; or

(vi) checking that that vehicle is working properly and, where carrying goods, is correctly loaded before being used;

(b) in relation to a transport system—

(i) installation or maintenance of any part of it or of the telecommunications system relating to it or used in connection with it, or of the means of supplying electricity directly to that transport system or to any vehicles using it or to the telecommunications system other than where the carrying out of that task is subject to supervision and checking by a safety critical worker or a controller of safety critical work;

(ii) controlling the supply of electricity directly to it or to any vehicles used on it;

(iii) receiving and relaying of communications; or

(iv) any person ensuring the safety of any persons working on or near to the track, whether or not the persons working on or near to the track are carrying out safety critical work;

(c) in relation to training, any practical training or the supervision of any such training in any of the tasks set out in sub-paragraphs (a) to (b),

which could significantly affect the health or safety of persons on a transport system;

"safety critical work" means any safety critical task carried out by any person in the course of their work or voluntary work on or in relation to a transport system and related expressions shall be construed accordingly; and

"telecommunications system" means any telecommunications system provided by a transport operator or its associated equipment, which is capable of controlling or affecting the movement of a vehicle, or which is provided by a transport operator for purposes which include calling the emergency services.

(2) Any reference in this Part to a safety critical worker or a controller of safety critical work supervising and checking the work of another person is to a safety critical worker or a controller of safety critical work who has been assessed as competent in the tasks to which that supervision and checking relates.

(3) Any reference in this Part to a person controlling the carrying out of safety critical work is a reference to a person managing, supervising or controlling that work in connection with the carrying on by him of a trade, business or other undertaking (whether or not for profit).

(4) This Part shall not apply to or in relation to—

(a) the police, ambulance or fire service when they are carrying out their emergency functions on or in relation to a transport system; and

(b) any voluntary worker for a period of twelve months from the date of the coming into force of this Part.

[1052]

Competence and fitness

24 (1) Every controller of safety critical work shall, so far as is reasonably practicable, ensure that a person under his management, supervision or control, with the exception of where that person is receiving practical training in a safety critical task, only carries out safety critical work where—

(a) that person has been assessed as being competent and fit to carry out that work following an assessment by an assessor;

(b) there is an accurate and up to date record in writing of that person's competence and fitness which references any criteria for determining competence and fitness against which that assessment of competence was made;

(c) the record, or an accurate summary of the record referred to in sub-paragraph (b) is available for inspection, on reasonable request, by any other controller of safety critical work or any operator who may be affected by any safety critical work carried out or to be carried out by that person, for the purposes of establishing that person's competence and fitness to carry out safety critical work; and

(d) there are in place arrangements for monitoring the competence and fitness of that person.

(2) Every controller of safety critical work shall without unreasonable delay review any person's competence or fitness assessment where—

(a) they have reason to doubt the competence or fitness of a person to carry out that safety critical work; or

(b) there has been a significant change in the matters to which the assessment relates,

and where, as a result of any such review a reassessment of competence or fitness is required, that reassessment of competence or fitness shall be carried out to ensure that the requirements of paragraph (1) are met.

(3) Where a reassessment of competence or fitness under paragraph (2) is required, the controller of safety critical work shall, so far as is reasonably practicable ensure that, as a result, the health and safety of persons on a transport system is not prejudiced.

[1053]

Fatigue

25 (1) Every controller of safety critical work shall have in place arrangements to ensure, so far as is reasonably practicable, that a safety critical worker under his management, supervision or control does not carry out safety critical work in circumstances where he is so fatigued or where he would be liable to become so fatigued that his health or safety or the health or safety of other persons on a transport system could be significantly affected.

(2) The arrangements in paragraph (1) shall be reviewed by the controller of safety critical work where he has reason to doubt the effectiveness of those arrangements.

[1054]

Co-operation requirements for safety critical work

26 (1) Every controller of safety critical work to whom this Part applies shall co-operate as far as is necessary with any other controller of safety critical work or any operator to enable that other controller of safety critical work to comply with the provisions of this Part.

(2) Every person carrying out safety critical work shall, as regards any requirement imposed on any controller of safety critical work under this Part, co-operate with that controller of safety critical work so far as is necessary to enable that requirement to be performed or complied with.

[1055]

PART 5
MISCELLANEOUS

Appeals

27 (1) A person who is aggrieved by a—

(a) decision of the Office of Rail Regulation to refuse his application for—

(i) a safety certificate or safety authorisation;

(ii) an amended safety certificate or safety authorisation;

(b) direction of the Office of Rail Regulation to make an application to amend his safety certificate or safety authorisation; or

(c) decision of the Office of Rail Regulation to revoke his—

(i) safety certificate or part of it; or

(ii) safety authorisation,

may appeal to the Secretary of State.

(2) For the purposes of paragraph (1) the Secretary of State may, in such cases as he considers it appropriate to do so, having regard to the nature of the questions which appear to him to arise, direct that an appeal under that paragraph shall be determined on his behalf by a person appointed by him for that purpose.

(3) Before the determination of an appeal the Secretary of State shall ask the appellant and the Office of Rail Regulation whether they wish to appear and be heard on the appeal and—

(a) The appeal may be determined without a hearing of the parties if both of them express a wish not to appear and be heard as aforesaid;

(b) The Secretary of State shall, if either of the parties expresses a wish to appear and be heard, afford to both of them an opportunity of doing so.

(4) The Tribunals and Inquiries Act 1992 shall apply to a hearing held by a person appointed in pursuance of paragraph (2) to determine an appeal as it applies to a statutory inquiry held by the Secretary of State, but as if in section 10(1) of that Act (statement of reasons for decisions) the reference to any decision taken by the Secretary of State included a reference to a decision taken on his behalf by that person.

(5) A person who determines an appeal under this regulation on behalf of the Secretary of State and the Secretary of State, if he determines such an appeal, may give such directions as he considers appropriate to give effect to his determination.

(6) The Secretary of State may pay to any person appointed to hear or determine an appeal under paragraph (2) on his behalf such remuneration and allowances as the Secretary of State may with the approval of the Minister for the Civil Service determine.

(7) For the purposes of paragraph (1)(a), a failure by the Office of Rail Regulation to make a decision on whether or not to issue or amend a safety certificate or safety authorisation within the four month period for making a decision calculated in accordance with regulation 17(7) shall be treated as a refusal of the application.

(8) The Health and Safety Licensing Appeals (Hearing Procedure) Rules 1974, as respects England and Wales, and the Health and Safety Licensing Appeals (Hearing Procedure) (Scotland) Rules 1974, as respects Scotland, shall apply to an appeal under paragraph (1) as they apply to an appeal under sub-section (1) of the said section 44, but with the modification that references to a licensing authority are to be read as references to the Office of Rail Regulation.

(9) Where an appeal is made under paragraphs (1)(a) or (1)(c), the decision in question shall be suspended pending the final determination of the appeal.

NOTES

Health and Safety Licensing Appeals (Hearing Procedure) Rules 1974
SI 1974/2040, in the title Health and Safety at Work.

Health and Safety Licensing Appeals (Hearing Procedure) (Scotland) Rules 1974
SI 1974/2068 (outside the scope of this work).

[1056]

Offences

28 A failure to discharge a duty placed on the Office of Rail Regulation by these Regulations shall not be an offence under section 33(1)(c) of the Health and Safety at Work etc Act 1974.

[1057]

Transitional provisions and savings

29 (1) Any competence and fitness assessments made pursuant to regulation 3 of the Railways (Safety Critical Work) Regulations 1994 shall have effect as if they were made under Part 4, provided that the assessment would, at the time it was made, have met the requirements for impartiality and objectivity in that Part.

(2) Notwithstanding the revocation of ROTS pursuant to regulation 34, and subject to paragraph (6) ROTS shall, up to and including 1st October 2008, continue in force as they had effect on 30th September 2006 for the purposes of—

(a) determining applications for approval made;

(b) issuing a written consent for the purposes set out in regulation 4(4)(b) of ROTS in relation to new or altered works, plant or equipment for which an application for approval has been made;

(c) making notices dispensing with or requiring compliance with certain provisions of ROTS under regulation 10(1)(a) or 11(1)(a) of ROTS in relation to new or altered works, plant or equipment, for which an application for approval has been made, to the Office of Rail Regulation in relation to a relevant transport system before 1st October 2006.

(3) Where an approval is issued by the Office of Rail Regulation in response to an application for approval made in relation to a transport system—

- (a) before 1st October 2006 but where the new or altered works, plant or equipment are placed in service within the meaning of regulation 5(6) and 6(5) on or after that date; or
- (b) on or before 1st October 2008 pursuant to paragraph (2),

in relation to new or altered works, plant or equipment that is relevant infrastructure or a vehicle then such works, plant or equipment shall be deemed to satisfy the requirements of regulations 5(4) and 6(4).

(4) Where a written consent is issued by the Office of Rail Regulation in relation to new or altered works, plant or equipment which is relevant infrastructure or a vehicle in relation to a transport system—

- (a) under regulation 4(4)(b)(i) of ROTS on or before 1st October 2008 pursuant to paragraph (2) then such relevant infrastructure or vehicle shall be deemed to satisfy the requirements of regulations 5(4) and 6(4); or
- (b) under regulation 4(4)(b)(ii) of ROTS on or before 1st October 2008 pursuant to paragraph (2) then no regard shall be taken of the use of such relevant infrastructure or vehicle for the purposes for which the written consent relates when determining whether the relevant infrastructure or vehicle has been placed in service in accordance with regulations 5(6) and 6(5).

(5) In this regulation—

- (a) "application for approval" means an application for approval made under regulation 5, 6 or 7 of ROTS;
- (b) "altered works, plant or equipment" shall have the meaning in regulation 2(a) of ROTS; and
- (c) "relevant transport system" shall have the meaning in regulation 2(a) of ROTS.

(6) For the purposes of heritage railways and tramways, all references in this regulation to 1st October 2006 shall be read as if those references were in each case to 1st October 2008, and all references to 1st October 2008 shall be read as if those references were in each case to 1st October 2010.

(7) Schedule 5 shall have effect.

NOTES

Railways (Safety Critical Work) Regulations 1994 SI 1994/299 (revoked by reg 34, Sch 7).

[1058]

Exemptions

30 (1) Subject to paragraphs (2) and (3), the Office of Rail Regulation may, by certificate in writing, exempt any person or class of persons or any transport system or part of a transport system from any requirement or prohibition imposed by these Regulations.

(2) The Office of Rail Regulation shall not grant any such exemption in relation to any requirement or prohibition imposed by Part 2 or 3 in relation to an operation carried out on the mainline railway other than an exemption to an operator of last resort from the requirement to copy the documents referred to in regulation 17(3)(a)(i) and (ii) to an affected party or to notify an affected party as the case may be.

(3) The Office of Rail Regulation shall not grant any such exemption unless, having regard to the circumstances of the case, and in particular to—

- (a) the conditions, if any, which it proposes to attach to the exemption; and
- (b) any other requirements imposed by or under any enactment which applies to the case,

it is satisfied that the health and safety of persons who are likely to be affected by the exemption will not be prejudiced in consequence of it.

(4) The Secretary of State for Defence may, in the interests of national security, by a certificate in writing exempt any person or class of persons from any requirement or prohibition imposed by these Regulations.

(5) An exemption granted pursuant to paragraph (1), (2) or (4) may be granted subject to conditions and to a limit of time.

(6) An exemption granted pursuant to—

(a) paragraph (1) or (2) may be revoked by the Office of Rail Regulation; and

(b) paragraph (4) may be revoked by the Secretary of State for Defence,

at any time by a further certificate in writing.

[1059]

Defence of due diligence

31 (1) Subject to the following provisions of this regulation, in any proceedings against any person for an offence under regulation 5(4) or 6(4) it shall be a defence for that person to show that he took all reasonable steps and exercised all due diligence to avoid committing the offence.

(2) Where in any proceedings against any person for such an offence the defence provided in paragraph (1) involves an allegation that the commission of the offence was due to—

(a) the act or default of another; or

(b) reliance on information given by another,

that person shall not, without the leave of the court, be entitled to rely on the defence unless, within a period ending seven clear days before the hearing of the proceedings (or in Scotland, the trial diet), he has served a notice under paragraph (3) on the person bringing the proceedings.

(3) A notice under this paragraph shall give such information identifying, or assisting in the identification of, the person who committed the act or default or gave the information as is in the possession of the person serving the notice at the time he serves it.

(4) A person shall not be entitled to rely on the defence provided by paragraph (1) by reason of his reliance on information supplied by another, unless he shows that it was reasonable in all the circumstances for him to have relied upon the information, having regard in particular—

(a) to the steps which he took, and those which might reasonably have been taken, for the purpose of verifying the information; and

(b) to whether he had any reason to disbelieve the information.

[1060]

32 (*Amends the Railways and Other Transport Systems (Approval of Works, Plant and Equipment) Regulations 1994, SI 1994/157 (revoked by reg 34, Sch 7.)*

Consequential amendments

33 The Regulations referred to in Schedule 6 shall be amended as set out in that Schedule.

[1061]

Revocation

34 The Regulations referred to in column (1) of Schedule 7 are revoked to the extent specified in column (3) of that Schedule.

[1062]

SCHEDULE 1
SAFETY MANAGEMENT SYSTEM

Regulations 5(1)(c), and 6(1)(b)

(This Schedule substantially reproduces the provisions of Annex III to the Directive)

Requirements on the safety management system

1 The safety management system shall—

(a) describe the distribution of responsibilities, within the operation, for the safety management system;

(b) show how control of the safety management system by the management on different levels is secured;

(c) show how persons carrying out work or voluntary work directly in relation to the operation and their representatives on all levels are involved with the safety management system; and

(d) show how continuous improvement of the safety management system is ensured.

Basic elements of the safety management system

2 The basic elements of a safety management system are—

(a) a statement of the safety policy which has been approved by the chief executive and communicated to all persons carrying out work or voluntary work directly in relation to the operation;

(b) qualitative and quantitative targets for the maintenance and enhancement of safety and plans and procedures for reaching those targets;

(c) procedures to meet relevant technical and operational standards or other requirements as set out in—

(i) TSIs;

(ii) national safety rules;

(iii) other relevant safety requirements; and

(iv) decisions of the Office of Rail Regulation addressed to the transport operator in question,

and procedures to ensure compliance with the requirements listed in this paragraph throughout the life-cycle of any relevant equipment or operation which is subject to the requirement in question.

(d) procedures and methods for carrying out risk evaluation and implementing risk control measures when—

(i) there is a change in the way in which the operation in question is carried out; or

(ii) new material is used in the operation in question,

which gives rise to new risks in relation to any infrastructure or the operation being carried out;

(e) provision of programmes for training of persons carrying out work or voluntary work directly in relation to the operation and systems to ensure that the competence of such persons is maintained and that they carry out tasks accordingly;

(f) arrangements for the provision of sufficient information relevant to safety—

(i) within the operation in question; and

(ii) between the operator in question and any other transport operator or an applicant for a safety certificate or a safety authorisation who carries out or who intends to carry out operations on the same infrastructure;

(g) procedures and formats for the documentation of safety information;

(h) procedures to control the lay out of, and changes to, vital safety information;

(i) procedures to ensure that accidents, incidents, near misses and other dangerous occurrences are reported, investigated and analysed and that necessary preventative measures are taken;

(j) provision of plans for action, alerts and information in the case of an emergency which are to be agreed with any public body, including the emergency services, that may be involved in such an emergency; and

(k) provisions for recurrent internal auditing of the safety management system.

[1063]

SCHEDULE 2
APPLICATION FOR A SAFETY CERTIFICATE

Regulation 7(1)(b)

PART 1
INFORMATION TO BE INCLUDED FOR A MAINLINE APPLICATION

1 The following information shall be included in relation to Part A of a safety certificate—

(a) particulars of the type and extent of the operation in respect of which the application is made; and

(b) either—

[(i) a copy of a current certificate issued to the applicant by—

(aa) the Office of Rail Regulation, other than a deemed safety certificate;

(bb) a safety authority in another member State;

(cc) a safety authority in Northern Ireland; or

(dd) the safety authority for the tunnel system within the meaning of section 1(7) of the Channel Tunnel Act 1987,

under provisions giving effect to article 10(2)(a) of the Directive which relates to an equivalent railway operation; or]

(ii) particulars of how the safety management system of the applicant meets the requirements set out in regulation 5(1) to (4).

2 The following information shall be included in relation to Part B of a safety certificate—

(a) information on the TSIs, national safety rules and other safety requirements relevant to the applicant's operation including those relevant to persons carrying out work in relation to the operation and the applicant's vehicles and an explanation of how compliance with these requirements is ensured by the safety management system;

(b) information on the different types of work being carried out by persons directly in relation to the operation including evidence of how the applicant ensures that when such persons are carrying out such work that they are doing so in accordance with the requirements of any relevant TSIs and national safety rules; and

(c) information on the different types of rolling stock used for the operation in question including evidence that they meet any relevant TSIs and national safety rules,

and where information is submitted concerning an interoperability constituent or a subsystem which is subject to and complies with the requirements of the Railways (Interoperability) (High-Speed) Regulations 2002 ("2002 Regulations") then only brief details need be supplied concerning compliance of such constituents or subsystems with relevant TSIs and other requirements of those Regulations and in this paragraph "interoperability constituent" and "subsystem" shall have the same meaning as in the 2002 Regulations.

NOTES

Amendment Para 1(b)(i): substituted by SI 2007/3531.

Railways (Interoperability) (High-Speed) Regulations 2002 SI 2002/1166; revoked and replaced by SI 2006/397.

[1064]

PART 2
INFORMATION TO BE INCLUDED FOR A NON-MAINLINE APPLICATION

3 Particulars of the type and extent of the operation in respect of which the application is made.

4 Particulars of how the safety management system of the applicant meets the requirements set out in regulation 6.

5 Information on the—

(a) relevant statutory provisions which make provision in relation to safety which are applicable to the operation; and

(b) technical specifications and procedures relating to operations and maintenance that are relevant to the safety of the transport system which the applicant proposes to follow,

and an explanation of how compliance with these requirements is ensured by the safety management system.

6 Information on the different types of work or voluntary work being carried out by persons directly in relation to the operation including evidence of how the applicant ensures that when such persons are carrying out work or voluntary work in relation to the operation that they are doing so in accordance with relevant requirements of the relevant statutory provisions referred to in paragraph 5(a).

7 Information on the different types of rolling stock used for the operation including evidence that they meet relevant requirements of the relevant statutory provisions referred to in paragraph 5(a).

[1065]

SCHEDULE 3
COMMON SAFETY INDICATORS

Regulation 20(1)(c)

(This Schedule substantially reproduces the provisions of Annex I to the Directive)

Indicators relating to accidents

1 (1) Total and relative, to vehicle kilometres, number of—

(a) accidents and a break-down of the following types of accidents—

(i) collisions of vehicles, including collisions with obstacles within the loading gauge;
(ii) derailments of vehicles;
(iii) level-crossing accidents which shall include accidents involving persons at level-crossings;
(iv) accidents to persons caused by vehicles in motion except for suicides;
(v) suicides;
(vi) fires in vehicles; and
(vii) any other types of accidents,

and each such accident shall be reported under the heading of the primary accident even where the consequences of any secondary accident are more severe such as where a fire follows a derailment.

(b) persons seriously injured or killed by type of accident divided into the following categories—

 (i) passengers;
 (ii) persons carrying out work or voluntary work directly in relation to the operation;
 (iii) level crossing users;
 (iv) unauthorised persons on premises of the transport system; and
 (v) any other types of person,

and the number of passengers seriously injured or killed shall also be indicated in relation to the total number of passenger kilometres.

(2) The provisions of Regulation 91/2003 of the European Parliament and the Council on rail transport statistics shall be applied to any information provided under this paragraph.

Indicators relating to incidents and near-misses

2 Total and relative, to vehicle kilometres, number of—

(a) broken rails;
(b) buckled rails;
(c) wrong-side signalling failures;
(d) signals passed at danger; and
(e) broken wheels and axles on vehicles in service.

Indicators relating to consequences of accidents

3 (1) Total and relative—

(a) to train kilometres, cost in Euros of all accidents, which shall include, where it is possible to provide such figures, the cost of the following—

 (i) deaths and injuries of persons;
 (ii) compensation for loss of or damage to the property of passengers, persons carrying out work directly in relation to the operation or to third parties including damage caused to the environment;
 (iii) replacement or repair of damaged rolling stock and railway installations; and
 (iv) delays, disturbances and re-routing of traffic including any additional costs to persons carrying out work directly in relation to the operation and the loss of future revenue;

(b) to number of hours worked, number of working hours of persons carrying out work directly in relation to the operation which have been lost as a consequence of accidents.

(2) In calculating the costs under sub-paragraph (1)(a), the amount of any indemnity or compensation recovered or expected to be recovered from third parties shall be deducted except for any relevant compensation recovered under insurance policies held by transport operators.

Indicators relating to technical safety of infrastructure and its implementation

4 The—

(a) percentage of tracks with a train protection system, within the meaning of regulation 2(1) of the Railway Safety Regulations 1999, in operation;
(b) percentage of train kilometres with a train protection system falling within paragraph (a) in operation;
(c) number of level crossings (total and total per kilometre of line); and
(d) percentage of level crossings with automatic or manual protection.

Indicators relating to the management of safety

5 Internal audits carried out by transport operators pursuant to the procedures referred to in paragraph 2(k) of Schedule 1 and the number of such audits which have been carried out and that number expressed as a percentage of the audits which were planned for that year.

NOTES
Regulation 91/2003 OJ L14, 21.01.2003, p 1.
Railway Safety Regulations 1999 SI 1999/2244.

[1066]

SCHEDULE 4
WRITTEN SAFETY VERIFICATION SCHEME REQUIREMENTS

Regulation 5(4)(a) and 6(4)(a)

Information to be Included in a Safety Verification Scheme

1 (1) The arrangements for the selection, appointment and retention of the competent person, which arrangements should at least provide for:

(a) the appointment of the competent person at an early stage in the design selection process;
(b) the involvement of the competent person in the establishing of the criteria to be applied in the verification process and the design selection process; and

(c) the communication to the competent person of information necessary for the proper implementation, or revision, of the verification scheme and which information is necessary in order for the competent person to undertake the verification.

(2) The arrangements for the examination and testing of new or altered vehicles or infrastructure, which arrangements should at least provide for:

(a) the means of controlling risks that arise during the carrying out of any testing or trials prior to placing in service; and

(b) the standards and criteria to be applied in the verification process.

(3) The arrangements for the review and revision of the verification scheme.

(4) The arrangements for the making and preservation of records showing—

(a) the examination and testing carried out to the new or altered vehicles or infrastructure prior to its being placed in service;

(b) the findings of that examination and testing;

(c) any remedial action recommended as a result of that examination and testing; and

(d) any remedial action performed.

(5) The arrangements for communicating the matters contained in sub-paragraphs (1) to (4) of this Schedule to an appropriate level in the management system of the transport operator or responsible person as the case may be.

[1067]

SCHEDULE 5
TRANSITIONAL PROVISIONS AND SAVINGS-SAFETY CERTIFICATES AND SAFETY AUTHORISATIONS

Regulation 29(7)

1 Subject to the following paragraphs of this Schedule—

(a) a notification of acceptance by the Office of Rail Regulation of a safety case in relation to the operation of trains pursuant to regulation 5(7)(a) of the 2000 Regulations in relation to a safety case—

(i) which is current immediately before 1st October 2006; or

(ii) which is issued pursuant to paragraph 3,

shall be deemed to be a safety certificate for that operation;

(b) a notification of acceptance by the Office of Rail Regulation of a safety case in relation to the use of railway infrastructure pursuant to regulation 4(4), or the operation of a station pursuant to regulation 5(7)(a), of the 2000 Regulations in relation to a safety case—

(i) which is current immediately before 1st October 2006; or

(ii) which is issued pursuant to paragraph 3,

shall be deemed to be a safety authorisation for the infrastructure in question, and the holder of a deemed safety certificate shall also be deemed to have met the applicable requirements of regulations 3(1)(a) and 4(1)(a) and the holder of a deemed safety authorisation shall also be deemed to have met the applicable requirements of regulations 3(2)(a) and 4(2)(a).

2 In paragraph 1 a notification of acceptance shall be construed as including the original notification referred to in paragraph 1(a) or 1(b) together with any notification of acceptance of a revision of the safety case in question by the Office of Rail Regulation pursuant to regulation 7(7) of the 2000 Regulations or that regulation as saved by paragraph 3 in relation to the operation in question.

3 Notwithstanding their revocation the 2000 Regulations shall continue in force as they had effect on 30th September 2006 for the purposes of—

(a) the consideration, acceptance or refusal of acceptance of safety cases and revisions to safety cases submitted to the Office of Rail Regulation for acceptance before 1st October 2006 under regulations 4, 5, 7 or 8 of the 2000 Regulations;

(b) the making and determination of appeals under regulation 15 of the 2000 Regulations in relation to—

(i) the determination of any such appeals made before but not determined on 30th September 2006; and

(ii) the making and determination of any such appeals in relation to decisions on submissions falling within paragraph (a).

4 A deemed safety certificate or safety authorisation shall—

(a) in the case of a deemed safety certificate or safety authorisation falling within paragraph 1(a)(i) or 1(b)(i), be deemed to be issued on 1st October 2006;

(b) in the case of a deemed safety certificate or safety authorisation falling within paragraph 1(a)(ii) or 1(b)(ii), be deemed to be issued on the date of the notification of acceptance in question; and

(c) be deemed to be held by the person to whom the notification of acceptance in question was addressed or, in the case of a deemed safety certificate or authorisation falling within paragraph 1(a)(i) or 1(b)(i), the person who is a successor of that person or a previous successor pursuant to regulation 2(7) of the 2000 Regulations on 30th September 2006.

5 A deemed safety certificate or safety authorisation shall be valid until—

(a) in the case of a deemed—

(i) safety certificate, the holder has applied for a safety certificate under regulation 7 for the operation in question and the Office of Rail Regulation has issued a safety certificate in response to that application; or

(ii) safety authorisation, the holder has applied for a safety authorisation for the operation in question under regulation 10 and the Office of Rail Regulation has issued a safety authorisation in response to that application;

(b) subject to paragraph 6, the date by which the periodic review of the safety case to which the deemed safety certificate or deemed safety authorisation relates would have been required under regulation 6 of the 2000 Regulations had it still been in force; or

(c) 1st October 2008,

whichever is the first to occur.

6 Where the date of the periodic review referred to in paragraph 5(b) would fall on or before 1st April 2007 then a deemed safety certificate or safety authorisation shall be valid up to and including 1st April 2007.

7 Where a transport operator—

(a) holds a deemed safety certificate or deemed safety authorisation; and

(b) the control of the operation in question is transferred to another person after 1st October 2006 so that regulation 2(7) of the 2000 Regulations would have operated to treat that other person as a successor had it still been in force,

then that other person may rely upon the deemed safety certificate or safety authorisation and if he does so rely shall comply with the provisions of these Regulations as though he were the holder of that deemed safety certificate or safety authorisation for a period of 6 months from the date he becomes a successor and may do so notwithstanding the prior expiry of such a certificate or authorisation in accordance with paragraph 5.

8 The holder of a deemed safety certificate or safety authorisation shall revise the contents of the safety case to which the deemed safety certificate or safety authorisation relates whenever it is appropriate to do so.

9 Where the revision referred to in paragraph 8 renders the safety case materially different from that accepted in the deemed safety certificate or safety authorisation then the holder of the deemed safety certificate or authorisation shall, without delay, notify the Office of Rail Regulation of such revision.

10 Where a holder of a deemed safety certificate or safety authorisation proposes a change to the operation to which a deemed safety certificate or safety authorisation relates which would have been a change falling within regulation 8(1) or 11(1) if those regulations had applied, then he shall not make such a change until he has applied for and the Office of Rail Regulation has issued a new safety certificate or safety authorisation for that operation pursuant to regulation 7 or 10 as the case may be.

11 Where a person—

(a) was granted an exemption, which has not been revoked, from the prohibition relating to the holding of an accepted safety case in regulation 4(1) or 5(1) of the 2000 Regulations; or

(b) was not subject to the requirements of the 2000 Regulations immediately before 1st October 2006 by virtue of their operation falling wholly within sub-paragraphs (a) to (c) of the definition of "railway" in the 2000 Regulations or because they were carrying out an operation on a transport system other than a railway,

then notwithstanding the revocation of the 2000 Regulations, that person shall not be required to comply with the provisions of Part 2 of these Regulations until 1st April 2007.

12 The 2000 Regulations shall apply in relation to—

(a) a deemed safety certificate as if regulations 8, 9 and 15 did not apply; and

(b) a deemed safety authorisation as if regulation 11, 12 and 16 did not apply;

(c) a deemed safety certificate or a deemed safety authorisation as if—

(i) regulations 13, 14 and 18 did not apply;

(ii) sub-paragraphs (a) and (b) of regulation 20(1) did not apply;

(iii) regulation 20(1)(d) referred to "the findings of an audit carried out pursuant to the arrangements referred to in paragraph 5(d) of Schedule 1 to the 2000 Regulations;"; and

(iv) regulation 21(4)(a) and 21(5)(a) referred to a deemed safety certificate or a deemed safety authorisation and the safety case to which it relates and as if the notified address referred to in regulation 21(3) were that notified in relation to the safety case in question under regulation 14 of the 2000 Regulations.

13 Notwithstanding the revocation of the 2000 Regulations, regulation 10 of the 2000 Regulations shall continue in effect in relation to the safety case to which a deemed safety certificate or deemed safety authorisation relates as it had effect on 30th September 2006 except that for the purposes of this Schedule the references in that regulation to—

(a) "any revision" shall be construed to include a revision pursuant to paragraph 8; and
(b) regulations 7 and 11 shall be construed as a reference to paragraph 8 of this Schedule and regulation 22(1) respectively.

14 For the purposes of this Schedule "the 2000 Regulations" means the Railways (Safety Case) Regulations 2000.

NOTES
Railways (Safety Case) Regulations 2000 SI 2000/2688 (revoked by reg 34, Sch 7).

[1068]

SCHEDULE 6

NOTES
This Schedule, mentioned in reg 33, has been amended by SI 2006/1057. It sets out amendments to the following instruments: SI 1995/3163, in the title Health and Safety at Work, SI 1997/553, SI 1999/2244, both in this title, and SI 2003/1400, in the title Trade and Industry.

[1069]

SCHEDULE 7

NOTES
This Schedule specifies the instruments revoked or partly revoked by reg 34. The revoked instruments are: the Railways and Other Transport Systems (Approval of Works, Plant and Equipment) Regulations 1994, SI 1994/157, the Railways (Safety Critical Work) Regulations 1994, SI 1994/299, the Railways (Safety Case) Regulations 2000, SI 2000/2688, and the amending SI 2003/579. The instruments which are partly revoked are SI 2001/3291 (in so far it as amended SI 1998/1340, SI 2000/2688) and SI 2004/129 (in so far it as amended SI 1994/157).

[1070]

RAILWAY SAFETY LEVY REGULATIONS 2006
SI 2006/1010

Authority Made by the Secretary of State for Transport under the Health and Safety at Work etc Act 1974, ss 43A(1), (5)–(8), 82(3)(a).
Date made 30 March 2006.
Commencement 1 April 2006.
Summary These regulations require railway service providers to pay a levy to the Office of Rail Regulation ("ORR") to meet the expenses it incurs in performing activities relating to railway safety. They enable the ORR to determine, in respect of each financial year, the total amount of the levy, the railway service providers who are liable to pay the levy, when the levy is to be paid and the criteria for determining the proportion of the levy to be paid by each railway service provider. The ORR may revise the determination of any of these matters, whether before, during or after the financial year to which the determination relates. In respect of each financial year, the ORR may calculate the amount of railway safety levy payable by each railway service provider by whom a levy is to be paid. As soon as reasonably practicable, it must publish each determination and revision of a determination in any manner which it considers appropriate. Provision is also made in respect of the provision of information, including financial information, by railway service providers. Where a railway service provider receives a request for information and fails to provide the information requested by the date specified in that request, the ORR may make such assumptions concerning the information as are reasonable in all the circumstances. Each railway service provider must, on receipt of a request in writing, pay to the ORR the amount of railway safety levy calculated in relation to that provider. The regulations also allow the ORR to refund levy paid to it where due to an error in its calculation or change in circumstances, a railway service provider has paid a greater amount of railway safety levy than the amount due by way of a correct calculation, or where the original determination is revised, the railway service provider has paid the railway safety levy and the amount of railway safety levy that railway service provider is liable to pay under the revised determination is less than the amount that it paid in accordance with the original determination.

[1071]

TRANSPORT AND WORKS (APPLICATIONS AND OBJECTIONS PROCEDURE) (ENGLAND AND WALES) RULES 2006
SI 2006/1466

Authority Made by the Secretary of State for Transport under the Transport and Works Act 1992, ss 6, 6A, 7(3)(b), (c), (4), 10, and, in so far as they relate to Wales, with the agreement of the National Assembly for Wales.

Date made 3 June 2006.
Commencement 11 September 2006.
Modification SI 1992/2902, which was revoked (by SI 2000/2190, itself revoked) and is now replaced by these rules, was modified in certain circumstances by SI 1993/1119 in relation to the documents to accompany an application.
Summary These rules, which revoke and replace, subject to transitional provisions, the Transport and Works (Applications and Objections Procedure) (England and Wales) Rules 2000, SI 2000/2190, prescribe the procedures for the following:
(a) the making of applications for orders under the Transport and Works Act 1992, Pt I;
(b) proposals for orders to be made by the Secretary of State otherwise than on application;
(c) the making of objections and representations relating to such applications and proposals; and
(d) the handling of objections where the Secretary of State decides not to hold a public inquiry or hearing under s 11 of the 1992 Act.

The rules implement Council Directive 85/337/EEC (OJ L175, 05.07.1985, p 40) on the assessment of the effects of certain public and private projects on the environment, as amended by Council Directive 97/11/EC (OJ L173, 14.03.1997, p 5) and Directive 2003/35/EC of the European Parliament and of the Council (OJ L156, 25.06.2003, p 17).

A requirement is imposed on the prospective applicant to send the Secretary of State, at least 28 days before an application is made, a draft of the proposed order and explanatory memorandum explaining the purpose and effect of the order provisions. Provision is made for the provision of environmental information to the prospective applicant by certain bodies having statutory responsibilities in particular areas. The form of the application and the documentation which must be submitted in support of it are prescribed; in particular, a statement of environmental information may be required in respect of certain works. In the case of certain other works, the Secretary of State may notify the applicant that an environmental impact assessment is not required, in which case he does not have to submit a statement of environmental information. Before making an application, an applicant may make a request to the Secretary of State for a decision as to whether or not an environmental impact assessment of the proposed works covered by the application is required ("a screening decision"). Before submitting an application in relation to works for which an environmental impact assessment is or may be required, the applicant may make a request to the Secretary of State to state his opinion as to the information to be provided in the environmental statement (a "scoping opinion").

Provision is made for, inter alia, the information to be included in an environmental statement; the service by the applicant of copies of an application and certain supporting documents on certain interested persons and bodies; the publication of notice of an application; and the service of notices on owners, occupiers etc who may be affected by the application. Where work is likely to have significant effects on the environment in another part of the United Kingdom or another member state, in the case of in another part of the United Kingdom, the applicant is required to publish, if so directed by the Secretary of State, specified information in such newspapers circulating in the place in question as the Secretary of State may specify and in the case of another member state, the Secretary of State is required to notify and consult that state and to enable it, if it wishes, to participate in the environmental assessment procedure. Where, in the opinion of the Secretary of State, the applicant's statement of environmental information should contain any additional information in order to constitute an environmental statement for the purposes of the application in question, the Secretary of State must direct the applicant to supply that information.

Provision is made for the Secretary of State to waive certain requirements in relation to applications. The fees payable on making an application are prescribed. Provision is made for the special circumstances occurring when the Secretary of State makes proposals for an order under s 7 of the 1992 Act. The rules provide for general matters relating to objections and other representations and for determining when objections are to be dealt with by the written representations procedure. The procedure by written representations is specified. Provision is also made as to the procedure to be followed where the Secretary of State causes a public local inquiry to be held or gives an objector an opportunity of being heard before a person appointed by the Secretary of State. The Secretary of State may in a particular case allow further time for the taking of such steps (including a step which he is required or enabled to take himself) which may or must be taken pursuant to these rules. Special provisions are made for applications relating solely to Wales.

[1072]

RAILWAYS (SUBSTITUTE ROAD SERVICES) (EXEMPTIONS) ORDER 2006
SI 2006/1935

Authority Made by the Secretary of State for Transport under the Transport Act 2000, s 248(4).
Date made 17 July 2006.
Commencement 1 October 2006.
Summary This order relates to the obligations of operators of railway passenger services pursuant to the Transport Act 2000, s 248 (substitute services to be suitable for disabled passengers). S 248(2) requires such operators, so far as is reasonably practicable, to ensure that any substitute road services allow disabled passengers to travel safely and in reasonable comfort. The order:
(a) exempts relevant operators from their obligations under the Transport Act, s 248(2), in respect of all substitute road services other than those relating to the railway passenger services listed in the Schedule to the order; and
(b) defines the relevant operators who are exempted from s 248(2).

[1073]

PASSENGER AND GOODS VEHICLES (RECORDING EQUIPMENT) (TACHOGRAPH CARD) REGULATIONS 2006
SI 2006/1937

Authority Made by the Secretary of State for Transport under the European Communities Act 1972, s 2(2).
Date made 18 July 2006.
Commencement 21 August 2006.
Amendment Amended by SI 2006/3276.
Summary These regulations make provision in relation to company cards, control cards, driver cards and workshop cards used with digital tachographs, which are tachographs complying with Annex IB to Council Regulation (EEC) 3821/85 on recording equipment in road transport (OJ L370, 31.12.1985, p 8) ("the Community Recording Equipment Regulation") (as it has effect in accordance with Commission Regulations (EEC) 3314/90 (OJ L318, 17.11.1990, p 20) and 3688/92 (OJ L374, 22.12.1992, p 12), Commission Regulations (EC) 2479/95 (OJ L256, 26.10.1995, p 8), 1056/97 (OJ L154, 12.06.1997, p 21), 1360/2002 (OJ L207, 05.08.2002, p 1), 432/2004 (OJ L71, 10.03.2004, p 3), Art 1 of Council Regulation (EC) 2135/98 (OJ L274, 09.10.1998, p 1), the Act concerning the conditions of accession of the Czech Republic, the Republic of Estonia, the Republic of Cyprus, the Republic of Latvia, the Republic of Lithuania, the Republic of Hungary, the Republic of Malta, the Republic of Poland, the Republic of Slovenia and the Slovak Republic and the adjustments to the Treaties on which the European Union is founded (OJ L236, 23.09.2003, p 33), and Regulations (EC) 1882/2003 (OJ L284, 31.10.2003, p 1) and 561/2006 (OJ L102, 11.04.2006, p 1) of the European Parliament and of the Council, and as read with SI 1986/1456 (revoked and replaced by SI 2007/1819)). "Company card", "control card", "driver card" and "workshop card" have the meanings given by Annex IB to the Community Recording Equipment Regulation.

The regulations prohibit the use by a person of more than one driver card, of a driver card of which he is not the holder, of a forged or altered card and of a card issued as a result of an incorrect application. Making a false statement in an application for a card is also prohibited. Breach of these requirements is an offence, the penalty for which is specified. The regulations also prohibit the use by a person of more than one workshop card, or personal identification number for use in connection with a workshop card ("PIN"), for each workshop in which he works, of a workshop card or PIN of which he is not the holder or in a place which is not his workplace, of a forged or altered card and of a card issued as a result of an incorrect application. They also prohibit the divulging of a PIN. Breach of these requirements is an offence, the penalty for which is specified.

Written notification of lost or stolen tachograph cards (i e a company card, control card, driver card or workshop card) is to be given and damaged or malfunctioning cards are to be returned to the Secretary of State. Failure to comply with these provisions is an offence punishable by a fine not exceeding level 5 on the standard scale. A tachograph card holder is required to notify the Secretary of State of any details on a card requiring correction and to return it for correction. The Secretary of State may also require the return of tachograph cards issued erroneously for correction. Failure to comply with these provisions is an offence punishable by a fine not exceeding level 5 on the standard scale. A tachograph card which identifies another person as the holder, which has been falsified or which has been issued as a result of a false application must be surrendered or may be confiscated by a constable or a vehicle examiner appointed under the Road Traffic Act 1988, s 66A. Failure to comply with any of these requirements is an offence punishable by a fine not exceeding level 5 on the standard scale.

See also SI 2005/1140.

[1074]

TRANSPORT AND WORKS (MODEL CLAUSES FOR RAILWAYS AND TRAMWAYS) ORDER 2006
SI 2006/1954

Authority Made by the Secretary of State for Transport under the Transport and Works Act 1992, s 8.
Date made 18 July 2006.
Commencement 8 August 2006.
Amendment Amended by SI 2008/2831.
Modification SI 1992/3270 (revoked and replaced by this order) was modified by SI 1995/2803, in the title Open Spaces and National Heritage, so as to provide for references to sewers or drains in the model clauses prescribed by this order to include references to sewers or drains belonging to National Park authorities in Wales.
Summary This order, which revokes and replaces the Transport and Works (Model Clauses for Railways and Tramways) Order 1992, SI 1992/3270, prescribes model clauses for inclusion in orders made under the Transport and Works Act 1992, s 1, which authorise the construction and operation of certain systems of transport, and ancillary matters. The use of the prescribed clauses is not mandatory and they may therefore be omitted entirely from orders if not appropriate or adapted to meet special requirements.

The model clauses relate to:

(a) railways, which term includes mainline, underground and mountain railways, mineral lines, pier lines, funiculars and railways operated by bodies concerned with the preservation of the railway heritage; and
(b) tramways.

The model clauses for railways, which provide for the incorporation of the Railways Clauses Acts, are divided into:

(a) works provisions, including powers to construct and maintain works and to deviate, power to execute street works, the permanent and temporary stopping up of streets, access to works, construction and maintenance of new or altered streets and construction of bridges and tunnels, the discharge of water, protective works to buildings and power to survey and investigate land;

(b) acquisition and possession of land, including the power to acquire land, the application of the Compulsory Purchase Act 1965, Pt I, and the Compulsory Purchase (Vesting Declarations) Act 1981, powers to acquire new rights, to acquire subsoil only and to acquire land limited to subsoil lying more than 9 metres beneath the surface, rights under or over streets, temporary use of land for the construction or maintenance of works, compensation, acquisition of part of certain properties, extinction or suspension of private rights of way and time limit for exercise of powers of acquisition; and

(c) miscellaneous provisions relating to, inter alia, planning permission, power to lop trees overhanging authorised works, power to operate and use railways, power to transfer undertakings, power to charge fares, obstruction of the construction of authorised works, trespass, disclosure of confidential information, arbitration etc.

The model clauses for tramways, which provide for the application of enactments relating to railways, are divided into:

(a) works provisions, including powers to construct and maintain works and to deviate, powers to alter the layout of streets, to keep apparatus in streets and to execute street works, the permanent and temporary stopping up of streets, access to works, construction and maintenance of new or altered streets and construction of bridges and tunnels, agreements with street authorities, the restoration of streets if a tramway is discontinued, level crossings, the attachment of equipment to buildings for the purposes of a tramway, the discharge of water, protective works to buildings, power to construct temporary tramways and power to survey and investigate land;

(b) acquisition and possession of land, including the power to acquire land, the application of the Compulsory Purchase Act 1965, Pt I, and the Compulsory Purchase (Vesting Declarations) Act 1981, powers to acquire new rights, to acquire subsoil only and to acquire land limited to subsoil lying more than 9 metres beneath the surface, rights under or over streets, temporary use of land for the construction or maintenance of works, compensation, acquisition of part of certain properties, extinction or suspension of private rights of way and time limit for exercise of powers of acquisition;

(c) the operation of the tramway system, including power to operate and use the system, power to charge fares, obstruction of the tramway and interference with the tramway, traffic control and regulation, power to lop trees overhanging the tramway, obstruction of the construction of authorised works, trespass on tramroads, power to make byelaws and power to contract for police services; and

(d) miscellaneous provisions relating to, inter alia, planning permission, power to transfer undertakings, disclosure of confidential information, arbitration etc.

[1075]

QUIET LANES AND HOME ZONES (ENGLAND) REGULATIONS 2006
SI 2006/2082

Authority Made by the Secretary of State for Transport under the Transport Act 2000, s 268.
Date made 26 July 2006.
Commencement 21 August 2006.
Summary These regulations make provision in respect of the making, variation and revocation of designations of roads as quiet lanes or home zones under the Transport Act 2000, s 268, and of use orders and speed orders in respect of those roads. They require the local traffic authority to give persons in the area of the relevant road an opportunity to make representations before a proposal for designation is developed. At least one public meeting must be held (reg 3). Regs 4–7 and Schs 1, 2 require an authority, before designating a road, to consult prescribed persons, to publish notice of the designation proposals and to consider objections. Regs 8, 9 provide for the making of use orders and speed orders in respect of designated roads. A use order permits the road to be used, for as long as may be specified, for a purpose which is communal, social, cultural, spiritual, educational, entertainment or recreational. A speed order describes in general terms the measures to be taken to reduce the speed of motor vehicles and/or cycles below the speed specified in the order. An authority is required, before making such an order, to consult prescribed persons, to publish notice of the order proposals and to consider objections (regs 10–13 and Schs 1, 2). Reg 14 permits the modification of proposed designations and of use orders and speed orders, subject to persons likely to be affected by substantial changes being given an opportunity to object. The regulations require notices to be given by an authority after it has made a designation or use or speed order (reg 15 and Sch 2) and provide for the variation and revocation of a designation or order subject to similar procedures as those for designation or making an order (reg 16). An authority must prepare and keep a map in connection with a designation, use order or speed order (reg 17 and Sch 3). Traffic signs informing road users of a designation are to be placed appropriately (reg 18).

[1076]

REGIONAL TRANSPORT PLANNING (WALES) ORDER 2006 (W 280)
SI 2006/2993

Authority Made by the National Assembly for Wales under the Transport Act 2000, ss 108, 109C, 113A.
Date made 15 November 2006.
Commencement 23 November 2006.
Amendment Amended by SI 2009/109. Previously amended by SI 2008/1286 (superseded).
Summary This order, which applies in relation to Wales only, modifies the Transport Act 2000, ss 108–109B, which require local transport authorities to develop policies for the promotion and encouragement of safe, integrated, efficient and economic transport to, from and within their area, so as to permit local transport plans to be made on a regional rather than individual authority basis.

The 22 Welsh local authorities are to be assembled into four groups for the purpose of preparing a single transport plan for each group. The groups are based upon four regional areas: South East Wales, South West Wales, Mid Wales and North Wales. The local transport authority of Gwynedd is to contribute to two separate local transport plans covering or including the district of Meirionnydd and the remainder of the county of Gwynedd respectively. In accordance with s 109C(2) of the 2000 Act, all qualifying local transport plans are required to be replaced no later than 31 December 2009.

[1077]

ROAD TOLLING (INTEROPERABILITY OF ELECTRONIC ROAD USER CHARGING AND ROAD TOLLING SYSTEMS) REGULATIONS 2007
SI 2007/58

Authority Made by the Secretary of State for Transport under the European Communities Act 1972, s 2(2).
Date made 13 January 2007.
Commencement 12 February 2007.
Summary These regulations implement the provisions of Directive 2004/52/EC of the European Parliament and of the Council (OJ L200, 07.06.2004, p 50, incorporating changes made by the corrigendum to the original version of the Directive published in OJ L166, 30.04.2004, p 124) which require the use of certain technical standards for the interoperability of electronic road toll systems in the Community.

"Electronic toll systems" are systems with certain electronic features which operate for the purpose of charging and collecting tolls or fares in respect of the use by a motor vehicle of a road (including any bridge or tunnel) or a ferry. The regulations apply to new electronic toll systems brought into service on or after 12 February 2007. The circumstances in which a new electronic toll system is to be regarded as being brought into service are set out; this includes certain significant upgrades. Specified technological requirements apply to all new electronic toll systems other than those which have been exempted. Provision is made for the issue by the appropriate national authority (the Secretary of State as respects England and the Welsh Ministers (formerly the National Assembly for Wales) as respects Wales) of an exemption certificate on specified grounds. The operator of a toll system may apply for an exemption certificate in accordance with the regulations and the procedure which must be followed where the appropriate national authority refuses an application or revokes an exemption certificate is set out. The appropriate national authority may require certain information and documents for the purpose of determining whether a system is an electronic toll system to which the regulations apply, whether the system is using the required technologies or whether to revoke an exemption certificate. If the appropriate national authority considers that the technological requirements of the regulations are not met, it may issue a stop notice requiring the operator of the system to cease charging and collecting tolls or fares by use of non-compliant electronic devices.

[1078]

ROAD SAFETY ACT 2006 (COMMENCEMENT NO 1) ORDER 2007
SI 2007/237

Authority Made by the Secretary of State for Transport under the Road Safety Act 2006, s 61.
Date made 1 February 2007.
Summary This order brought into force provisions of the Road Safety Act 2006, as noted in the table below.
Further commencement orders SI 2007/466, SI 2007/2472, SI 2007/3492, SI 2008/1862, SI 2008/1864, SI 2008/1918, SI 2008/3164 (all made under the Road Safety Act 2006, s 61) brought into force further provisions of the 2006 Act, as noted in the table below.

Provision	*Date and extent (if any)*
s 3	5 January 2009 (SI 2008/3164)
s 4	31 March 2009 (SI 2008/3164)
s 5	See Sch 1 below

Provision	*Date and extent (if any)*
ss 6, 7	31 March 2009 (SI 2008/3164)
s 8	1 April 2009 (SI 2008/3164)
s 9	See Sch 2 below
s 11	See Sch 4 below
s 12	5 January 2009 (SI 2008/3164)
s 14	24 September 2007 (SI 2007/2472)
ss 20, 21	18 August 2008 (SI 2008/1918)
ss 23–25	24 September 2007 (SI 2007/2472)
s 26	27 February 2007 (SI 2007/237)
ss 27–29	24 September 2007 (SI 2007/2472)
s 30	24 September 2007 (in so far as the Road Traffic Act 1988, s 3ZA has effect for the purposes of ss 3, 3A of that Act) (SI 2007/2472) 18 August 2008 (in so far as not already in force) (SI 2008/1918)
ss 31–33	24 September 2007 (SI 2007/2472)
ss 36, 40	27 February 2007 (SI 2007/237)
s 41	24 September 2007 (SI 2007/2472)
s 43	24 September 2007 (SI 2007/2472)
s 44	16 March 2007 (SI 2007/466)
s 45	30 July 2008 (SI 2008/1862)[1]
s 46	31 July 2008 (SI 2008/1864)
s 50	27 February 2007 (SI 2007/237)
s 52	16 March 2007 (SI 2007/466)
s 53	28 January 2008 (SI 2007/3492)
s 54	31 March 2008 (SI 2007/3492)
s 55	28 January 2008 (SI 2007/3492)
s 59	See Sch 7 below
Sch 1	31 March 2009 (SI 2008/3164)
Sch 2	1 April 2009 (SI 2008/3164)
Sch 4	5 January 2009 (SI 2008/3164)
Sch 7, para 1	5 January 2009 (SI 2008/3164)
Sch 7, para 2	31 March 2009 (SI 2008/3164)
Sch 7, para 3	1 April 2009 (SI 2008/3164)
Sch 7, para 5	24 September 2007 (SI 2007/2472)
Sch 7, paras 9, 12	27 February 2007 (SI 2007/237)
Sch 7, para 13	24 September 2007 (SI 2007/2472)
Sch 7, para 16	27 February 2007 (SI 2007/237)

1 Art 3 (transitional provisions) of SI 2008/1862 provides that: (a) s 45(2) of the 2006 Act does not have effect for the purposes of the Vehicles (Crime) Act 2001, s 28(1) until 1 November 2008; and (b) s 45(3)–(7) of the 2006 Act do not have effect until 1 November 2008

[1079]

VEHICLE DRIVERS (CERTIFICATES OF PROFESSIONAL COMPETENCE) REGULATIONS 2007
SI 2007/605

Authority Made by the Secretary of State for Transport under the European Communities Act 1972, s 2(2), the Road Traffic Act 1988, s 101(2), (3) and, with the consent of the Treasury, the Finance Act 1973, s 56(1), (2).

Date made 28 February 2007.

Commencement Partly on 27 March 2007, partly on 10 September 2008 and fully on 10 September 2009.

Amendment Amended by SI 2008/506, SI 2008/1965, SI 2009/1885.

Summary These regulations implement Directive 2003/59/EC of the European Parliament and of the Council on the initial qualification and periodic training of drivers of certain road vehicles for the carriage of goods or passengers (OJ L226, 10.09.2003, p 4).

Reg 3(1) prescribes the persons to whom the regulations apply, i e any person who drives a relevant vehicle on a road and is a national of a member state or a national of a third country employed or used by an undertaking established in a member state. Broadly, these are professional bus and lorry drivers. The main exceptions are for persons driving emergency vehicles, vehicles used by the police or armed forces and vehicles used for training or testing purposes (reg 3(2)). Reg 4 prohibits any new driver from driving a bus on or after 10 September 2008 or a lorry on or after 10 September 2009 on a public road unless he has passed a theoretical and practical driving test, referred to as an "initial CPC" test. Drivers undergoing a vocational training course may be exempted by the competent authority (the Secretary of State) for up to 12 months from taking that test, on the issue by the competent authority of an NVT certificate. Drivers who hold a bus or lorry driving licence before 10 September 2008 or 10 September 2009, as appropriate, are also exempt from taking the initial CPC test.

Reg 5 permits the competent authority or a person approved by it to organise provision of initial CPC tests; the fees payable by applicants are prescribed. Reg 5A requires a person submitting himself for either the theoretical test or the practical test to produce to the person conducting the test an appropriate licence authorising him to drive the vehicle and, except where he has produced an appropriate licence containing his photograph, evidence of his identity.

Reg 6 permits the competent authority to approve persons to provide periodic training courses; the fees payable to the authority by such persons are prescribed and approval is valid for five years. In addition, a fee is payable for approval for each course which such persons propose to provide, and such approval is valid for one year. Reg 6A provides for appeals to be made to the First-tier Tribunal (formerly to the Transport Tribunal) against certain decisions of the competent authority under the regulations. Reg 7 requires a person approved to provide periodic training to notify the competent authority each time a person to whom he has provided training has completed a periodic training course. The competent authority must keep a record of such courses notified to it.

Reg 8 requires the competent authority to issue a driver qualification card to a person to whom that regulation applies if it is satisfied that he has passed the initial CPC test in accordance with reg 5 or has completed 35 hours of periodic training entitling him to a periodic CPC. Reg 8 applies to a person who: (a) is a national of a member state and normally resident in the United Kingdom, a national of a member state and works in the United Kingdom, or a national of a third country and authorised to work in the United Kingdom; and (b) holds a driving licence in the form of a photocard. No fee is payable under reg 8. Reg 8A enables certain other persons (to whom reg 8 does not apply) to apply to the competent authority for a driver qualification card; a fee is payable under reg 8A.

Reg 8B sets out the procedure to be followed where certain documents, including driver qualification cards, are damaged, lost or stolen. Reg 9 prohibits anyone from driving a bus or lorry on a road unless that person has passed the initial CPC test within the previous five years or has completed 35 hours of periodic training within the previous five years. Drivers who held a bus or lorry driving licence before 10 September 2008 or 10 September 2009, as appropriate, who are not required to take the initial CPC test must complete 35 hours of periodic training by 10 September 2013 in respect of bus drivers and by 10 September 2014 in respect of lorry drivers.

Reg 10 makes it an offence punishable with a fine not exceeding level 3 on the standard scale for a person to drive without a CPC as required by the regulations. Subject to certain exceptions, reg 11 requires a person who is required to hold a CPC by virtue of reg 9, or who is exempt because he is undergoing a national vocational training course, to carry specified evidence of that CPC or an NVT certificate while driving the relevant vehicle. The evidence or document must be produced on demand by a police constable or vehicle examiner; failure to do so is an offence punishable by a fine not exceeding level 3 on the standard scale. Reg 12 sets out the procedure to be followed where an NVT certificate or a driver qualification card was granted in error, or with an error or omission in the particulars specified in it. Failure to surrender a card or document with errors is an offence punishable by a fine not exceeding level 3 on the standard scale. Reg 13 makes it an offence for a person to forge or make false statements with respect to any document which is evidence of entitlement to a CPC or an NVT certificate. Reg 14 permits constables and vehicle examiners to seize any documents in respect of which an offence may have been committed under the regulations.

SI 1999/2864 is amended.

Offences An offence under reg 11 of these regulations is a fixed penalty offence; see SI 2009/483, noted to SI 1990/335. Certain offences under regs 10, 11, 13 are offences in respect of which a financial penalty deposit requirement may be imposed; see SI 2009/491 (and see also SI 2009/492).

[1080]

ROAD TUNNEL SAFETY REGULATIONS 2007

SI 2007/1520

Authority Made by the Secretary of State for Transport under the European Communities Act 1972, s 2(2).

Date made 22 May 2007.

Commencement 22 June 2007; see reg 1.

Amendment Printed as amended by SI 2009/64.

Interpretation See reg 2.

General These regulations implement Directive 2004/54/EC of the European Parliament and of the Council on the minimum safety requirements for tunnels in the Trans-European Road Network (OJ L167, 30.04.2004, p 39), which ensures a minimum level of safety for road users in tunnels in the trans-European road network. The regulations apply in relation to a road tunnel in the United Kingdom that is over 500 metres in length and forms part of the trans-European road network, whether it is in operation or at the construction or design stage.

[1081]

PART 1
PRELIMINARY

Citation and commencement

1 These Regulations may be cited as the Road Tunnel Safety Regulations 2007 and shall come into force on 22nd June 2007.

[1082]

Interpretation etc

2 (1) In these Regulations "the Road Tunnel Directive" means Directive No 2004/54/EC of the European Parliament and of the Council of 29th April 2004 on the minimum safety requirements for tunnels in the Trans-European Road Network, and any reference in the Schedule to "the Directive" shall be construed accordingly.

(2) In these Regulations references to "Annex I" and "Annex II" are references to those Annexes as set out in the Road Tunnel Directive, and the reference in paragraph 2.12 of Annex I to "Annex III" should be read as a reference to the Schedule, which sets out Annex III of the Road Tunnel Directive ... in a modified form.

(3) In these Regulations—

"administrative authority" means a body designated in relation to a road tunnel pursuant to regulation 4;

"commissioning procedure" means the procedure for authorising the opening of a road tunnel to public traffic set out in paragraph 3 of Annex II;

"construction stage" means the period after the design stage has been completed but before that tunnel is open to traffic;

"design stage" means the stage after a feasibility study has been conducted in relation to a tunnel but before any construction of that tunnel has commenced;

"emergency services" means all local services, whether public or private or any of the road tunnel staff, which intervene in the event of an accident or incident in a road tunnel, including police services, fire brigades, highway authority traffic officers and rescue teams;

"inspection entity" means an entity appointed pursuant to regulation 12;

"modification" means a substantial change in the structure, construction, equipment or operation of a road tunnel which significantly alters any of the constituent components of the safety documentation, and cognate expressions shall be construed accordingly;

"operational schemes" means the schemes relating to a road tunnel drawn up pursuant to regulation 5(3);

"risk analysis" means an analysis prepared pursuant to regulation 18;

"risk reduction measure" means a measure to be used instead of adoption of a structural requirement set out in the safety requirements;

"road tunnel" means a tunnel to which these Regulations apply;

"safety documentation" means the documentation compiled pursuant to regulation 9;

"Safety Officer" means an officer designated pursuant to regulation 10;

"safety requirements" means the safety measures specified in Annex I and the Schedule;

"significant incident" has the same meaning as "emergency" in section 1 of the Civil Contingencies Act 2004;

"technical approval authority" means the person appointed pursuant to regulation 14;

"trans-European road network" means the road network identified in Section 2 of Annex I to Decision No 1692/96/EC of the European Parliament and of the Council of 23 July 1996 on Community guidelines for the development of the trans-European transport network and illustrated by maps and described in Annex II to that Decision; and

"Tunnel Manager" means a person designated pursuant to regulation 8.

NOTES

Amendment Para (2): words omitted revoked by SI 2009/64.
Directive 2004/54/EC OJ L167, 30.04.2004, p 39.
Decision 1692/96/EC OJ L228, 09.09.1996, p 1.

[1083]

Application of the Regulations

3 These Regulations apply in relation to a road tunnel in the United Kingdom that is—

- (a) over 500 metres in length and that forms part of the trans-European road network, and for the purpose of these Regulations a road tunnel is over 500 metres in length if the longest traffic lane on the fully enclosed part of that tunnel is over 500 metres in length; and
- (b) whether it is in operation or at the construction stage or the design stage.

[1084]

PART 2
GENERAL REQUIREMENTS

Designation of administrative authority

4 (1) For each road tunnel in England, Scotland or Wales, the national authority for the jurisdiction in which the road tunnel is situated, shall designate a traffic authority as the administrative authority.

(2) The Department for Regional Development is the administrative authority for each road tunnel in Northern Ireland.

(3) Where a road tunnel is situated in more than one jurisdiction, the national authorities for those jurisdictions shall jointly appoint a traffic authority as the administrative authority for that road tunnel.

(4) A designation made under paragraph (1) or (3)—

- (a) shall be in writing;
- (b) may provide that it is to remain in force (unless it is withdrawn or otherwise ceases to have effect) for a specified period; and
- (c) shall be made—
  - (i) in relation to a road tunnel that is at the design stage, construction stage or in the operation stage at the time these Regulations come into force, as soon as is practicable after that time; and
  - (ii) in any other case, at the beginning of the design stage.

(5) In this regulation—

- (a) "national authority" means in relation to—
  - (i) England, the Secretary of State,
  - (ii) Wales, the National Assembly for Wales, and
  - (iii) Scotland, the Scottish Ministers; and
- (b) "traffic authority" in relation to England, Wales and Scotland has the meaning given by section 121A of the Road Traffic Regulation Act 1984.

[1085]

Duties of administrative authority

5 (1) The administrative authority shall ensure that a road tunnel for which it is the administrative authority is subject to the commissioning procedure before it is opened to traffic—

- (a) for the first time; or
- (b) after any modification has been carried out in relation to it.

(2) The administrative authority in relation to a road tunnel for which it is the administrative authority shall—

(a) ensure that the tests and inspections required by regulation 13 are carried out;
(b) following an inspection pursuant to regulation 13, draw up such additional safety requirements it considers appropriate;
(c) ...
(d) ensure the procedure for that tunnel's immediate closure in the event of an emergency is established; and
(e) ensure the risk reduction measures permitted pursuant to regulation 17 are implemented within the timetable specified pursuant to that regulation.

(3) The administrative authority shall ensure that such operational and organisational schemes (including emergency response plans) are drawn up as are necessary for the training and equipping of the emergency services in the event of an emergency in relation to a road tunnel for which it is the administrative authority, and it shall ensure that—

(a) the schemes are in writing;
(b) a copy of the schemes is held as part of the safety documentation;
(c) the schemes are sent to the relevant emergency services; and
(d) the schemes are updated from time to time.

(4) If the administrative authority finds that a road tunnel for which it is the administrative authority is not in compliance with the provisions of these Regulations, it shall—

(a) notify the Tunnel Manager and the Safety Officer of the measures to increase tunnel safety that must be adopted; and
(b) define the conditions for, where appropriate, continuing to operate that tunnel or re-opening that tunnel.

NOTES
Amendment Para (2)(c): revoked by SI 2009/64.

[1086]

Administrative authority—duty to compile accident and fire reports

6 (1) The administrative authority shall, for the two year period ending on 31 March 2008 and every two year period thereafter for which it is the administrative authority, compile a report containing the information set out in paragraph (2) in respect of fires and accidents which have occurred in the road tunnel, and which affect the safety of road users of that tunnel.

(2) The report compiled under paragraph (1) shall—

(a) evaluate the frequency and causes of those fires and accidents; and
(b) provide information on the role and effectiveness of the safety facilities and measures found in the road tunnel in question including any failures of safety-critical equipment.

(3) The administrative authority shall send each report to the Secretary of State within 22 weeks of the expiry of the period to which it relates.

[1087]

Administrative authority—suspension or restriction of use of a road tunnel

7 (1) The administrative authority may, in relation to a road tunnel for which it is the administrative authority, suspend or restrict the operation of the road tunnel if safety requirements, (including any additional safety requirement drawn up pursuant to regulation 5(2)(b), and any risk reduction measures permitted pursuant to regulation 17), or minimum operating requirements have not been met in relation to that tunnel.

(2) The administrative authority may, in relation to a road tunnel for which it is the administrative authority suspend or restrict the operation of a road tunnel in order to carry out periodic exercises pursuant to Annex II.

(3) In relation to a road tunnel located in Great Britain, sections 14 and 16 of the Road Traffic Regulation Act 1984 and the Road Traffic (Temporary Restrictions) Procedure Regulations 1992, subject to the modifications set out in paragraph (7), shall apply to an order made under paragraphs (1) or (2) as if it were an order made under section 14(1) of that Act.

(4) In relation to a road tunnel located in Northern Ireland, Article 7 of, and Schedule 3 to, the Road Traffic Regulation (Northern Ireland) Order 1997, subject to the modifications set out in paragraph (8), shall apply to a suspension or restriction made under paragraphs (1) or (2) as if it were a restriction or prohibition made under Article 7 of that Order.

(5) Where the administrative authority suspends or restricts the operation of a road tunnel pursuant to paragraph (1), it shall specify the conditions to be met in order for the suspension or restriction to be lifted and shall—

- (a) ensure that those conditions have been met before the suspension or restriction is lifted; and
- (b) when those conditions have been met, in relation to—
  - (i) an order relating to a road tunnel made in Great Britain, revoke that order, or
  - (ii) a suspension or restriction relating to a road tunnel made in Northern Ireland, lift the suspension or restriction.

(6) The administrative authority shall only suspend the operation of a road tunnel pursuant to paragraph (2) if satisfied that suitable arrangements can be made to divert traffic from that tunnel.

(7) In relation to an order made in relation to a road tunnel in Great Britain under paragraph (1) or (2), the Road Traffic (Temporary Restrictions) Procedure Regulations 1992 shall have effect subject to the following modifications—

- (a) in regulation 2(1) after the definition of ""the 1991 Act"" insert the following definition ""the 2007 Regulations" means the Road Tunnel Safety Regulations 2007";
- (b) in regulation 3—
  - (i) at the end of paragraph (1) insert "or regulation 7 of the 2007 Regulations",
  - (ii) in paragraph (3)(a) after "section 14(1) of the 1984 Act" insert "or regulation 7(1) or (2) of the 2007 Regulations",
  - (iii) in paragraph (3)(c) after "and its maximum duration" insert " or the conditions to be met before the order will be revoked",
  - (iv) in paragraph (6)(a) after "section 14(1) of the 1984 Act" insert "or regulation 7(1) or (2) of the 2007 Regulations", and
  - (v) in paragraph (6)(c) after "and its maximum duration" insert "or the conditions to be met before the order will be revoked"; and
- (c) in regulation 15—
  - (i) in paragraph (2)(d) after "shall state the reason or purpose mentioned in section 14(1) of the 1984 Act" insert "or regulation 7(1) or (2) of the 2007 Regulations", and
  - (ii) in paragraph 2(d) after "and its maximum duration" insert "or the conditions to be met before the order will be revoked".

(8) In relation to a suspension or a restriction made under paragraph (1) or (2) in relation to a road tunnel in Northern Ireland, Article 7(5) of the Road Traffic Regulation (Northern Ireland) Order 1997 shall have effect with the substitution of the words "when the conditions imposed pursuant to regulation 7(5) of the Road Tunnel Safety 2007 Regulations have been met" for the words "at the end of the period of 18 months from the date on which the provision comes into force".

NOTES

Road Traffic (Temporary Restrictions) Procedure Regulations 1992
SI 1992/1215.

Road Traffic Regulation (Northern Ireland) Order 1997 SI 1997/276 (NI 2) (outside the scope of this work).

[1088]

Designation of the Tunnel Manager

8 (1) The administrative authority shall, in relation to every road tunnel for which it is the administrative authority, designate a person to be the Tunnel Manager for (as appropriate) the design stage, the construction stage, and the operating stage.

(2) The administrative authority may undertake the role of the Tunnel Manager.

[1089]

Duties of the Tunnel Manager

9 (1) The Tunnel Manager shall, in relation to a road tunnel, for which it is the Tunnel Manager—

- (a) be responsible for that tunnel's management;
- (b) designate the Safety Officer pursuant to regulation 10;
- (c) compile the safety documentation in accordance with Annex II and ensure that in addition to the requirements of Annex II it includes—
  - (i) the operational schemes,
  - (ii) the risk analysis (if any), and
  - (iii) inspection reports prepared under regulation 13;
- (d) organise periodic exercises for tunnel staff and the emergency services in accordance with the requirements of paragraph 5 of Annex II;
- (e) prepare and forward incident reports in accordance with paragraph (3); and
- (f) forward investigation reports in accordance with paragraph (4).

(2) The Tunnel Manager for a road tunnel that has been subject to modification, shall ensure that the provisions of paragraph 4 of Annex II are complied with.

(3) The Tunnel Manager shall, within one month of an accident or significant incident occurring within a road tunnel for which it is the Tunnel Manager—

- (a) prepare a report on that accident or incident, (an incident report) that records the circumstances of the accident or incident; and
- [(b) send the incident report to the administrative authority, the safety officer and such of the emergency services as are appropriate.]

(4) If the Tunnel Manager prepares an investigation report, that analyses the circumstances of the incident or accident referred to in paragraph (3) or the conclusions that can be drawn from it, he shall forward that report to the administrative authority, Safety Officer and such of the emergency services as are appropriate within one month of the preparation or receipt of that report.

NOTES

Amendment Para (3)(b): substituted by SI 2009/64.

[1090]

Designation of the Safety Officer

10 (1) The Tunnel Manager shall, in relation to the road tunnel for which it is the Tunnel Manager, and with the prior approval of the administrative authority, designate a Safety Officer for (as appropriate) the design stage, the construction stage, and the operating stage.

(2) The Safety Officer shall be independent in respect of road tunnel safety issues and shall not be under instructions from his employer in respect of those issues.

[1091]

Duties of Safety Officers

11 The Safety Officer shall, in respect of a road tunnel for which it is the Safety Officer—

- (a) ensure there is co-ordination with the emergency services, and take part in the preparation of the operational schemes;
- (b) take part in the planning, implementation and evaluation of emergency operations;
- (c) take part in the formulation of safety schemes and the specification of the structure, equipment and operation of new or modified road tunnels;
- (d) verify that operational staff and relevant emergency services are trained in relation to the operational schemes, take part in the organisation of training exercises for this purpose, and ensure that such exercises are held at regular intervals;
- (e) give advice on the commissioning of the structure, equipment and operation of that tunnel;
- (f) verify that the tunnel's structure and equipment is maintained and repaired; and

(g) take part in the evaluation of any significant incident or accident.

[1092]

Appointment of inspection entity

12 (1) The administrative authority shall, in relation to a road tunnel for which it is the administrative authority appoint a person to be the inspection entity.

(2) The person appointed as the inspection entity must be—

(a) a Chartered Engineer or headed by a Chartered Engineer;
(b) competent to carry out its functions; and
(c) functionally independent of the Tunnel Manager.

(3) …

(4) For the purpose of this regulation a "chartered engineer" means a person who has been designated a Chartered Engineer by the Engineering Council UK.

NOTES
Amendment Para (3): revoked by SI 2009/64.

[1093]

Duties of inspection entity

13 [(1) In order to verify whether the road tunnel for which it is the inspection entity complies with the provisions of these Regulations, the inspection entity shall carry out in relation to the road tunnel the following inspections, examinations and tests—

(a) a thorough visual inspection of the fabric of the road tunnel;
(b) a thorough visual inspection of the mechanical and electrical equipment of the road tunnel;
(c) a detailed examination of all the accessible parts of the road tunnel; and
(d) a detailed examination and test of the mechanical and electrical equipment of the road tunnel.

(2) The inspections, examinations and tests referred to in paragraph (1) shall be carried out at the following intervals—

(a) an inspection under paragraph (1)(a), within two years of these Regulations coming into force, or within two years of the road tunnel coming into operation, whichever is the later, and thereafter every two years;
(b) an inspection under paragraph (1)(b) annually;
(c) an examination under paragraph (1)(c), within six years of these Regulations coming into force, or within six years of the road tunnel coming into operation, whichever is the later and thereafter every six years and;
(d) an examination and test under paragraph (1)(d) within three years of these Regulations coming into force, or within three years of the road tunnel coming into operation, whichever is the later, and thereafter every three years.

(3) The inspection entity shall compile a report containing details of all inspections and examinations and tests carried out under this regulation and shall forward that report to the administrative authority, tunnel manager and safety officer.]

(4) A report compiled pursuant to paragraph (3) shall include information on whether or not the part of the road tunnel inspected comply with the provisions of these Regulations and if those parts of the road tunnel do not comply with the provisions of these Regulations—

(a) a description of how that tunnel fails to so comply; and
(b) a recommendation of the measures (if any) to be adopted in order to increase that tunnel's safety.

NOTES
Amendment Paras (1)–(3): substituted by SI 2009/64.

[1094]

Appointment and duties of the technical approval authority

14 (1) The relevant highway authority or, in relation to Scotland, the roads authority shall at the design stage of a proposed road tunnel, appoint in relation to that tunnel, such persons as they think fit to be the technical approval authority.

(2) The technical approval authority shall be the responsible authority for the purposes of approving the design of the road tunnel under Annex II.

(3) For the purpose of this regulation—

(a) "highway authority" in relation to—

(i) England and Wales has the same meaning as in the Highways Act 1980, and

(ii) Northern Ireland means the Department for Regional Development; and

(b) "roads authority" has the same meaning as in section 151 of the Roads (Scotland) Act 1984.

NOTES

Highways Act 1980 As to highway authorities under the 1980 Act, see ss 1–3 thereof.

[1095]

Road Tunnels already in operation

15 (1) This regulation only applies to road tunnels that were open to public traffic prior to 30th April 2006.

(2) The administrative authority shall ensure that the road tunnel has been assessed by means of an inspection, in order to ascertain whether the requirements of these Regulations have been met.

(3) Where necessary, the Tunnel Manager for a road tunnel shall ensure that proposals have been put to the administrative authority for a plan for adapting the road tunnel to the provisions of these Regulations, including the remedial measures so required.

(4) The administrative authority shall—

(a) approve the plan and remedial measures proposed under paragraph (3) or request changes to the plan and remedial measures proposed under paragraph (3), and then if satisfied with those changes approve the plan and measures; and

(b) ensure that the approved plan or remedial measures are followed and any works required by the plan or remedial measures are completed by 30th April 2014.

(5) If the remedial measures approved by the administrative authority under paragraph (4) result in modification to the construction or operation of the road tunnel, the administrative authority shall ensure that once the measures have been adopted the commissioning procedure and the requirements of paragraph 4 of Annex II have been followed.

(6) The administrative authority shall by 20th July 2007 provide the Secretary of State with a report in respect of the road tunnel that provides information on—

(a) how the requirements of these Regulations will be met;

(b) the measures and plans approved under paragraph (4); and

(c) the consequences (if any) of opening or closing the main access roads to that tunnel.

(7) The administrative authority shall provide the Secretary of State with a plan, including a timetable, for the gradual compliance of the road tunnel to the requirements of these Regulations as soon as practicable, and report on the state of the plan and any changes to it by [1st October 2010] and by 1st October in every second year thereafter until 2014.

NOTES

Amendment Para (7): words in square brackets substituted by SI 2009/64.

[1096]

Safety Requirements to be met by road tunnels

16 Except where a risk reduction measure is to be used pursuant to regulation 17 or where a derogation has been granted pursuant to regulation 19 or permitted pursuant to paragraph 1.2.1 of Annex 1, the administrative authority shall ensure that a road tunnel that was—

(a) put into operation for the first time on or after the coming into force of these Regulations, meets the safety requirements; or
(b) in operation prior to 30th April 2006 meets the safety requirements by 30th April 2014.

[1097]

Risk Reduction Measures

17 (1) Where the safety requirements specify a structural requirement that can only be satisfied by means of a technical solution that is not possible to achieve, or only achievable at disproportionate cost, the Tunnel Manager may apply to the administrative authority for authority to use a risk reduction measure.

(2) Where the same body is both the administrative authority and the Tunnel Manager, an application referred to in paragraph (1) shall be considered by a person who is functionally independent from the persons acting on behalf of the body in its capacity as Tunnel Manager.

(3) The administrative authority shall not permit the use of a risk reduction measure unless a risk analysis demonstrates that the measure will result in equivalent or improved protection for users of the road tunnel, compared to the relevant structural requirement in the safety requirements.

(4) Where the administrative authority permits the use of a risk reduction measure it shall—

(a) specify a timetable for implementation of that measure; and
(b) notify the Secretary of State of the risk reduction measure to be used and the structural requirement that it replaces.

(5) This Regulation does not apply in relation to a road tunnel that is at the design stage but the design of which had not been approved by the technical approval authority by 1st May 2006.

[1098]

Risk Analysis

18 (1) A risk analysis shall be carried out by a person that is functionally independent from the Tunnel Manager.

(2) The person carrying out the risk analysis shall produce a report in relation to the proposed risk reduction measure which includes the following matters—

(a) consideration of the risks for the safety of users of the road tunnel taking into account all design factors and traffic conditions that affect safety, including traffic characteristics and type, the length of the road tunnel, that tunnel's geometry and the forecast of the number of heavy goods vehicles which are likely to use that tunnel each day;
(b) evaluation of whether the proposed measure will result in equivalent or improved protection for users of the road tunnel, to the safety requirement that it is to replace;
(c) identification of the potential hazards arising from the use of the proposed risk reduction measure;
(d) identification of the users of the road tunnel who could be affected by the hazards referred to in sub paragraph (c);
(e) evaluation of the probabilities of harm occurring to the persons identified in sub paragraph (d); and
(f) evaluation of the adequacy of the safety requirement that the proposed measure is to replace.

(3) The risk analysis shall be included in the safety documentation.

[1099]

Derogations for innovative techniques

19 (1) The Tunnel Manager may at any time during the design, construction or operation of a road tunnel make a request in writing to the administrative authority for a derogation from the requirements of these Regulations in relation to the—

(a) installation and use of innovative safety equipment; or
(b) use of innovative safety procedures,

which provide an equivalent or higher level of protection than current technologies as prescribed in these Regulations.

(2) A request made pursuant to paragraph (1) shall be accompanied by the following information—

(a) a description of the road tunnel in relation to which the derogation is sought including a description of any physical or operational features relevant to the request;

(b) a description of the proposed procedure or equipment;

(c) an explanation of why the proposed procedures or equipment are innovative;

(d) a description, and where appropriate a demonstration, of—

(i) how the proposed procedure or equipment will provide equivalent or higher level of protection than the procedures or equipment required by these Regulations, and

(ii) why the procedures or equipment required by these Regulations cannot or should not be used in the road tunnel; and

(e) a written report prepared by the inspection entity setting out its opinion of the request and stating whether or not the proposed procedure or equipment will provide an equivalent or higher level of protection than that provided by the procedures or equipment prescribed by these Regulations.

(3) If the administrative authority considers that the information provided by the Tunnel Manager with a request made under paragraph (1) is insufficient to enable it to make a decision the administrative authority shall notify the Tunnel Manager in writing of the additional information it requires in order to make that decision.

(4) On receiving a notification under paragraph (3) the Tunnel Manager shall provide the administrative authority with such of the additional information specified in that notification as the Tunnel Manager is reasonably able to supply and, where any of that additional information so specified is not provided, a written explanation as to why the Tunnel Manager is unable to provide it.

(5) If the administrative authority considers that the use or installation of the proposed innovative safety equipment or the use of the proposed innovative safety procedures will not provide equivalent or higher level of protection to users of the road tunnel it shall refuse the request.

(6) If the administrative authority decides that the request for a derogation should not be granted it shall give the Tunnel Manager reasons for that decision in writing.

(7) If the administrative authority decides that a derogation should, subject to the view of the Commission, be granted it shall forward the request made and information sent under paragraphs (1) (2) and (4) to the Secretary of State.

(8) The Secretary of State shall forward the information sent under paragraph (7) to the Commission within one month of receiving that information.

(9) On receipt of confirmation from the Commission that in relation to the request made under this regulation—

(a) no objection has been made to the Commission under Article 14 of the Road Tunnel Directive, or an objection has been made to the Commission under Article 14 of the Road Tunnel Directive, and following the procedure prescribed by that Article, a positive decision has been made by the Article 17 committee, the Secretary of State shall notify the administrative authority that it may grant the request made under paragraph (1); or

(b) an objection has been made to the Commission under Article 14 of the Road Tunnel Directive and, following the procedure prescribed by that Article, a negative decision has been made by the Article 17 committee, the Secretary of State shall notify the administrative authority that it may not grant the request made under paragraph (1).

(10) The administrative authority shall notify the Tunnel Manager, within 2 weeks of receipt of the confirmation set out in paragraph (9) whether the request made under paragraph (1) has been granted or refused.

(11) For the purpose of this regulation—

(a) "innovative" in relation to safety equipment and safety procedures means safety equipment or safety procedures that are not provided for in these Regulations; and

(b) "Article 17 Committee" means the Committee set up pursuant to Article 17 of the Road Tunnel Directive.

[1100]

Application of Regulations where the same person undertakes functions of different authorities

20 [(1) Where these Regulations impose on one of the authorities specified in paragraph (2) any obligation to send information or documentation to another such authority, and the same person acts as both authorities, that person shall instead ensure that a complete set of records is maintained in relation to each role.]

(2) Those authorities are—

(a) an administrative authority;

(b) a Tunnel Manager; and

(c) the Secretary of State.

NOTES

Amendment Para (1): substituted by SI 2009/64.

[1101]

Notification to the Commission

21 The Secretary of State shall send to the Commission—

(a) notification of the name and address of the administrative authorities designated under regulation 4;

(b) notification of the risk reduction measures permitted by the administrative authority pursuant to regulation 17;

(c) by 30th September 2008, and by 30th in every second year thereafter, a consolidated copy of the reports sent to him pursuant to regulation 6;

(d) by 17th August 2007 a consolidated copy of the reports sent to him pursuant to regulation 15(6); and

(e) on 30th October 2008 and on 30th October in every second year thereafter until 2014 a consolidated copy of the plans sent to him pursuant to regulation 15(7).

[1102]

SCHEDULE
SIGNING FOR TUNNELS

Regulation 2, Annex I (2.12)

1	General requirements The following are road signs and symbols to be used for road tunnels. In order to facilitate international understanding of signs, the system of signs and signals prescribed in this Schedule is based on the use of shapes and colours characteristic of each class of sign and, wherever possible, on the use of graphic symbols rather than words.
1.1	Road signs shall be used to designate the following safety facilities in tunnels (where they have been provided): —lay-bys, —emergency exits: the same sign shall be used for all kinds of emergency exits, —escape routes: the two nearest emergency exits shall be signed on the sidewalls at distances of no more than 25 metres, at a height of 1.0 to 1.5 metres above escape route level, with an indication of the distances to the exits, —emergency stations: signs to indicate the presence of emergency phones and fire extinguishers.
1.2	Radio: In road tunnels where users can receive information via their radio, appropriate signs placed before the entrance shall inform users on how to receive this information.

1.3	Signs and markings shall be designed and positioned so that they are clearly visible.
2	Description of signs and panels Appropriate signs shall be used, if necessary, in the advance warning area of the road tunnel, inside the tunnel and after the end of the tunnel. When designing the signs for a road tunnel, local traffic and construction conditions as well as other local conditions shall be considered.
2.1	Road Tunnel Sign The traffic sign shown in diagram 529.1 in Schedule 1 to the TSRGD shall be used in combination with the traffic sign shown in diagram 570 in Schedule 1 to the TSRGD (with the distance varied as appropriate) at the entrance to the road tunnel. For road tunnels over 3,000 metres in length, the remaining length of the tunnel shall be indicated approximately every 1,000 m. The name of the tunnel may be indicated in the manner shown below. *(Diagram (not printed): see the note to para 2.1 below.)*
2.2	Horizontal signing Horizontal delineation should be used at the roadside edge. In the case of bi-directional road tunnels, clearly visible means should be used along the median line (single or twin) separating the two directions.
2.3	Signs and panels for signing of facilities:
2.3.1	Emergency stations Emergency stations shall bear informative signs which indicate the equipment available to road users, such as:
	(a) For an emergency telephone: the traffic signs to be used shall be those shown in diagrams 2714 and 2715 in Schedule 7 to the TSRGD;
	(b) The symbol to be used for a fire extinguisher shall be that shown in diagram F001 in International Standard ISO 7010:2003 relating to safety colours and safety signs—safety signs used in workplaces and public areas; and
	(c) In emergency stations which are separated from the road tunnel by a door, a clearly legible text, written in appropriate languages, shall indicate that the emergency station does not ensure protection in case of fire. An example is given below: "THIS AREA DOES NOT PROVIDE PROTECTION FROM FIRE Follow signs to emergency exits"
2.3.2	Lay-bys The signs to indicate lay-bys shall be the traffic sign shown in diagram 2713.1 in Schedule 7 to the TSRGD with the "P" symbol omitted. Telephones and fire extinguishers shall be indicated by an additional panel or incorporated in the sign itself.
2.3.3	Emergency exits The signs to be used to indicate "Emergency exits" shall be the sign shown in diagram 2711 of Schedule 7 to the TSRGD; and The sign shown in diagram 2711 in of Schedule 7 to the TSRGD shall also be used to sign the two nearest exits on the sidewalls, with the distance to those exits shown below the arrow where appropriate. This sign shall be internally illuminated.
2.3.4	[Lane signal The signs shown in diagrams 5001.1, 5001.2, 5003, 5003.1, 5005 and 5005.1 in Schedule 10 to the TSRGD shall be used for lane signals.]
2.3.5	Variable message signing Any variable message signs shall have clear indications to inform tunnel users of congestion, breakdown, accident, fire or any other hazards.
3	In this Schedule "the TSRGD" means the Traffic Signs Regulations and General Directions.
3.1	For the purposes of the application of these Regulations to Northern Ireland—
	(a) references in paragraphs 2.1 and 2.3.4 to the traffic signs shown in diagrams 529.1, 570, 5001.1, 5001.2, 5003, 5003.1, 5005 and 5005.1 of the TSRGD are references to signs shown in diagrams of corresponding numbers in the Traffic Signs Regulations (Northern Ireland) 1997 ("the 1997 Regulations");

	(b)	the traffic signs shown in diagrams 2711, 2713.1, 2714 and 2715 of the TSRGD shall be deemed to be incorporated with those numbers in Schedule 7 to the 1997 Regulations together with the untitled Table below each diagram, and references in these regulations to those diagrams in the TSRGD shall be deemed to be references to those diagrams as so incorporated; and
	(c)	in relation to the Tables below each diagram referred to in sub-paragraph (b)—
	(d)	items 1, 2 and 3 shall be omitted;
	(e)	items 4 and 5 shall be renumbered 3 and 4;
	(f)	in item 3 as so renumbered (permitted variants) the items in Schedule 16 to TSRGD shall be deemed to be incorporated with those numbers in Schedule 16 to the 1997 Regulations; and
	(g)	in item 4 as so renumbered (illumination requirements) the items in Schedule 17 to TSRGD shall be deemed to incorporated with those numbers in Schedule 17 to the 1997 Regulations.

NOTES
Amendment Para 2.3.4: entry in square brackets in column 2 substituted by SI 2009/64.
Para 2.1 diagram The diagram set out in para 2.1, which is not printed in this work, displays the name of a tunnel in black capital letters against a white background, within a black border.
Traffic Signs Regulations and General Directions SI 2002/3113.
Traffic Signs Regulations (Northern Ireland) 1997 SR 1997/386 (outside the scope of this work).

[1103]

COMMUNITY DRIVERS' HOURS AND RECORDING EQUIPMENT REGULATIONS 2007
SI 2007/1819

Authority Made by the Secretary of State for Transport under the Transport Act 1968, ss 95(1), (1A), 101(2), (5), 157 and the European Communities Act 1972, s 2(2), Sch 2, para 1A.
Date made 25 June 2007.
Commencement 2 July 2007.
Summary These regulations facilitate compliance with Regulation (EC) 561/2006 of the European Parliament and of the Council on the harmonisation of certain social legislation relating to road transport (OJ L102, 11.04.2006, p 1) ("the Community Drivers' Hours Regulation"), implementing the new enforcement measures contained in that Regulation. They revoke and replace the Community Drivers' Hours and Recording Equipment (Exemptions and Supplementary Provisions) Regulations 1986, SI 1986/1456, and the amending SI 1986/1669, SI 1987/805, SI 1988/760, SI 1998/2006, and revoke SI 1994/857 in so far as it amended the said SI 1986/1456. Consequential amendments are made to the Transport Act 1968, Pt VI, which sets out the drivers' hours enforcement penalties.

Reg 2 of the regulations gives effect to the discretionary national derogations allowed under Arts 13, 14 of the Community Drivers' Hours Regulation that have been adopted in Great Britain, by exempting certain vehicles from Articles 6, 7, 8 and 9 of that Regulation. Reg 3 defines "historic status" for the purpose of a new automatic exemption from the Community Drivers' Hours Regulation in Art 3(i) thereof for commercial vehicles which have a historic status according to the legislation of the member state in which they are being driven and which are used for the non-commercial carriage of passengers or goods.

Reg 4 exempts certain vehicles from the application of the whole of Council Regulation (EEC) 3821/85 on recording equipment in road transport (OJ L370, 31.12.1985, p 8).

Regs 5–8 set out amendments to the Transport Act 1968, ss 95, 96, 103.

[1104]

RAILWAY PENSIONS (TRANSFER OF PENSION SCHEMES) ORDER 2007
SI 2007/2205

Authority Made by the Secretary of State for Transport under the Railways Act 1993, Sch 11, paras 4, 12.
Date made 25 July 2007.
Commencement 1 August 2007.
Summary This order provides that on 1 August 2007 ("the transfer date") members of specified pension schemes ("transferor schemes") become members of the 1994 Pensioners Section of the Railways Pension Scheme ("the transferee scheme") and cease to be members of any transferor scheme. All of the pension rights of the transferring members under the transferor schemes become pension rights under the transferee scheme. Provision is made for the transfer of the assets and liabilities of the transferor schemes, with special provision being made in relation to one transferor scheme, the BR (1974) Pension Fund ("the 1974 Fund").

The order modifies the operation of arts 6(2), 7(4) of SI 1994/1432 in relation to the transfer of pension rights or liabilities under the 1974 Fund. The transferor schemes, other than the 1974 Fund, are treated as fully wound up, from the transfer date.

[1105]

DRIVERS' HOURS (GOODS VEHICLES) (MILK COLLECTION) (TEMPORARY EXEMPTION) REGULATIONS 2007
SI 2007/2370

Authority Made by the Secretary of State for Transport under the Transport Act 1968, s 96(10).
Date made 10 August 2007.
Commencement 11 August 2007.
Summary These regulations extend the permissible maximum working day of a driver engaged in the collection and transportation of milk, when at least one of the specified conditions applies. The conditions are that the driver spends time driving or on duty during any working day either: (a) to meet special needs occasioned by the outbreak of foot-and-mouth disease in Great Britain, or (b) to deal with effects or consequences of the outbreak. In such cases, the working day of a driver, as specified by the Transport Act 1968, s 96(3)(a), is increased from a maximum of eleven to thirteen hours.

[1106]

CONCESSIONARY BUS TRAVEL ACT 2007 (COMMENCEMENT AND TRANSITIONAL PROVISIONS) ORDER 2007
SI 2007/2799

Authority Made by the Secretary of State for Transport under the Concessionary Bus Travel Act 2007, s 15(1), (2).
Date made 23 September 2007.
Summary This order, which applies subject to transitional provisions, brings the Concessionary Bus Travel Act 2007 into force for specified purposes on 17 October 2007. For all other purposes the order brings the 2007 Act into force on 1 April 2008.

The 2007 Act comes into force on 17 October 2007 for the purposes of:

(a) permitting the Secretary of State to issue guidance pursuant to the Transport Act 2000, s 145A(6), (8) and the Greater London Authority Act 1999, s 240(5C);
(b) permitting the Secretary of State to make regulations under s 145A(5) of the 2000 Act and s 243(7) of the 1999 Act;
(c) permitting a travel concession authority in England, any London authority and the Council of the Isles of Scilly to issue statutory travel concession permits in accordance with the provisions made by the 2007 Act on or before 1 April 2008 to those persons who will be entitled to make use of such permits from that date;
(d) pursuant to the Transport Act 2000, ss 149, 150, permitting:
    (1) a travel concession authority in England, any London authority and the Council of the Isles of Scilly to determine the arrangements or variations to apply with respect to the reimbursement of operators in relation to concessions exercised on or after 1 April 2008 as a consequence of the issue and use of statutory travel concession permits;
    (2) an operator affected by such arrangements or variations to apply for the modification of them;
    (3) the Secretary of State to take such steps as are necessary to determine any such application; and
    (4) for any direction to be given in relation to the application pursuant to s 150(8) of the 2000 Act; and
(e) pursuant to the Greater London Authority Act 1999:
    (1) requiring Transport for London to take into account, when forming its view under s 241(1) of the 1999 Act, the requirement that from 1 April 2008 travel concessions be provided for all eligible England residents and that additional travel concessions be provided for all eligible London residents;
    (2) permitting any London authority and Transport for London to make all arrangements necessary to enable the travel concession specified in s 242(8) of the 1999 Act and the additional travel concession mentioned in s 242(8A) thereof to be provided to those entitled to those concessions from 1 April 2008;
    (3) permitting London authorities to make arrangements pursuant to s 244 of the 1999 Act for the joint discharge of their functions under the Transport Act 2000, ss 148–150; and
    (4) requiring Transport for London, when notifying each London authority of the charge to be paid by the authority pursuant to para 5 of Sch 16 to the 1999 Act, to take into account any service outside Greater London which, but for s 179(2) of that Act, would be part of the London bus network.

The order also makes transitional provision in relation to statutory travel concession permits issued by a travel concession authority in England pursuant to s 145 of the 2000 Act prior to the commencement of the 2007 Act. Such permits continue to have effect until whichever is the earlier of 30 September 2008 or the expiry date shown on the face of the permit (if any). The provisions of the 2000 Act (including those relating to reimbursement of operators) continue to apply to any such permit in their unamended form.

[1107]

CIVIL ENFORCEMENT OF PARKING CONTRAVENTIONS (ENGLAND) REPRESENTATIONS AND APPEALS REGULATIONS 2007

SI 2007/3482

Authority Made by the Lord Chancellor under the Road Traffic Regulation Act 1984, s 101B and the Traffic Management Act 2004, ss 80, 89.
Date made 10 December 2007.
Commencement 31 March 2008; see reg 1(1).
Interpretation See reg 2, Schedule, Pt 1, para 1.
General The Traffic Management Act 2004, Pt 6 (ss 72–93 and Schs 7–11) enables regulations to be made providing for a single framework for the civil enforcement of road traffic contraventions (i e parking contraventions, bus lane contraventions, London lorry ban contraventions and moving traffic contraventions) by local authorities. These regulations (which should be read in conjunction with SI 2007/3483) implement Pt 6 of the 2004 Act in so far as it relates to the civil enforcement of parking contraventions in England.

These regulations entitle persons who are or may be liable to pay penalty charges in respect of parking contraventions, or who pay charges to secure the release of vehicles which have been immobilised or removed on account of such contraventions, to make representations to enforcement authorities regarding their liability for the charges and to appeal to an adjudicator if the representations are not accepted.

Pt 1 of the regulations contains preliminary provisions. Pt 2 concerns representations and appeals against penalty charge notices and notices to owner given under SI 2007/3483. Pt 3 provides for representations and appeals in relation to vehicles which have been immobilised in accordance with SI 2007/3483. Pt 4 provides for the making of representations and appeals in relation to vehicles which have been removed and stored or disposed of in accordance with the Road Traffic Regulation Act 1984 and regulations made under that Act. Pt 5 relates to offences and procedure.
Wales The following regulations make similar provision in relation to Wales as SI 2007/3482 makes in relation to England:

(a) SI 2008/608 (made by the Lord Chancellor under the Traffic Management Act 2004, ss 80, 89 and in force on 31 March 2008), provides for representations and appeals against penalty charge notices and notices to owner given under SI 2008/609 and SI 2008/1214 (formerly SI 2008/614 (revoked)), and for representations and appeals in relation to vehicles which have been immobilised under SI 2008/1214;
(b) SI 2008/615 (made by the Welsh Ministers under the Road Traffic Regulation Act 1984, s 101B and in force on 31 March 2008), provides for representations and appeals in relation to vehicles which have been removed in accordance with the Road Traffic Regulation Act 1984, s 99.

[1108]

PART 1
PRELIMINARY

Citation, commencement and application

1 (1) These Regulations may be cited as the Civil Enforcement of Parking Contraventions (England) Representations and Appeals Regulations 2007 and shall come into force on 31st March 2008.

(2) These Regulations apply only to England.

[1109]

Interpretation

2 (1) In these Regulations—

"the 1984 Act" means the Road Traffic Regulation Act 1984;
"the 2004 Act" means the Traffic Management Act 2004;
"appellant", in relation to an appeal under these Regulations or any process connected with such an appeal, means the person bringing the appeal;
"the General Regulations" means the Civil Enforcement of Parking Contraventions (England) General Regulations 2007;
"notice of rejection" means a notice served by an enforcement authority rejecting, or not accepting, representations made to it under regulation 4, 8 or 11;
"notice to owner" has the meaning given in paragraph (2);
"penalty charge" and "penalty charge notice" have the same meanings as in the General Regulations (see regulation 2(1) of those Regulations);
"owner", in relation to a vehicle, includes any person who, by virtue of regulation 5(3) of the General Regulations, falls to be treated as the owner of the vehicle for the purposes of those Regulations;
"procedural impropriety" has the meaning given by regulation 4(5); and

"recipient" has the meaning given in paragraph (2).

(2) In these Regulations (except regulation 3)—

(a) references to a "notice to owner" shall be taken—

(i) in a case where a penalty charge notice has been served under regulation 9 of the General Regulations, as references to a notice to owner as defined by regulation 2(1) of those Regulations;

(ii) in a case where a penalty charge notice has been served under regulation 10 of the General Regulations, as references to that penalty charge notice; and

(b) references to "the recipient" in relation to a notice to owner as so defined shall be taken as references to the person on whom the notice to owner was served.

NOTES

Civil Enforcement of Parking Contraventions (England) General Regulations 2007 SI 2007/3483.

[1110]

PART 2

REPRESENTATIONS AND APPEALS IN RELATION TO NOTICES TO OWNER

Scope of Part 2 and duty to notify rights to make representations and to appeal

3 (1) Regulations 4 to 7 have effect where a penalty charge which has become payable under the General Regulations has not been paid and either—

(a) a penalty charge notice has been served by a civil enforcement officer under regulation 9 of the General Regulations, and a notice to owner served by the enforcement authority under regulation 19 of those Regulations; or

(b) a penalty charge notice has been served under regulation 10 of the General Regulations.

(2) A penalty charge notice served under regulation 9 of the General Regulations must, in addition to the matters required to be included in it under paragraph 1 of the Schedule to the General Regulations, include the following information—

(a) that a person on whom a notice to owner is served will be entitled to make representations to the enforcement authority against the penalty charge and may appeal to an adjudicator if those representations are rejected; and

(b) that, if representations against the penalty charge are received at such address as may be specified for the purpose before a notice to owner is served—

(i) those representations will be considered;

(ii) but that, if a notice to owner is served notwithstanding those representations, representations against the penalty charge must be made in the form and manner and at the time specified in the notice to owner.

(3) A notice to owner served under regulation 19 of the General Regulations must, in addition to the matters required to be included in it under that regulation, include the following information—

(a) that representations on the basis specified in regulation 4 against payment of the penalty charge may be made to the enforcement authority, but that any representations made outside the period of 28 days beginning with the date on which the notice is served ("the payment period") may be disregarded;

(b) the nature of the representations which may be made under regulation 4;

(c) the address (including if appropriate any email address or FAX telephone number, as well as the postal address) to which representations must be sent and the form in which they must be made;

(d) that if representations which have been made—

(i) within the payment period; or
(ii) outside that period but not disregarded,

are not accepted by the enforcement authority the recipient of the notice may appeal against the authority's decision to an adjudicator; and

(e) in general terms, the form and manner in which an appeal may be made.

(4) A penalty charge notice served under regulation 10 of the General Regulations must, in addition to the matters required to be included in it under paragraph 2 of the Schedule to those Regulations, include the following information—

(a) that representations on the basis specified in regulation 4 may be made to the enforcement authority against the imposition of the penalty charge but that representations made outside the period of 28 days beginning with the date on which the penalty charge notice is served ("the representations period") may be disregarded;
(b) the nature of the representations which may be made under regulation 4;
(c) the address (including if appropriate any email address or FAX telephone number, as well as the postal address) to which representations must be sent and the form in which they must be made;
(d) that if representations which have been made—

(i) within the representations period; or
(ii) outside that period but not disregarded,

are not accepted by the enforcement authority the recipient of the penalty charge notice may appeal against the authority's decision to an adjudicator;

(e) where the penalty charge notice is served by virtue of regulation 10(1)(a) of the General Regulations (evidence produced by an approved device), the effect of paragraphs (5) and (6).

(5) The recipient of a penalty charge notice served by virtue of regulation 10(1)(a) of the General Regulations may, by notice in writing to the enforcement authority, request it—

(a) to make available at one of its offices specified by him, free of charge and at a time during normal office hours so specified, for viewing by him or by his representative, the record of the contravention produced by the approved device pursuant to which the penalty charge was imposed; or
(b) to provide him, free of charge, with such still images from that record as, in the authority's opinion, establish the contravention.

(6) Where the recipient of the penalty charge notice makes a request under paragraph (5), the enforcement authority shall comply with the request within a reasonable time.

[1111]

Representations against notice to owner

4 (1) The recipient may make representations against a notice to owner to the enforcement authority which served the notice on him.

(2) Any representations under this regulation must—

(a) be made in such form as may be specified by the enforcement authority;
(b) be to either or both of the following effects—

(i) that, in relation to the alleged contravention on account of which the notice to owner was served, one or more of the grounds specified in paragraph (4) applies; or
(ii) that, whether or not any of those grounds apply, there are compelling reasons why, in the particular circumstances of the case, the enforcement authority should cancel the penalty charge and refund any sum paid to it on account of the penalty charge.

(3) In determining the form for making representations, an enforcement authority which is a London authority must act through the joint committee through which, in accordance with regulation 15 of the General Regulations, it exercises its functions relating to adjudicators.

(4) The grounds referred to in paragraph (2)(b)(i) are—

(a) that the alleged contravention did not occur;

(b) that the recipient—
   (i) never was the owner of the vehicle in question;
   (ii) had ceased to be its owner before the date on which the alleged contravention occurred; or
   (iii) became its owner after that date;

(c) that the vehicle had been permitted to remain at rest in the place in question by a person who was in control of the vehicle without the consent of the owner;

(d) that the recipient is a vehicle-hire firm and—
   (i) the vehicle in question was at the material time hired from that firm under a hiring agreement; and
   (ii) the person hiring it had signed a statement of liability acknowledging his liability in respect of any penalty charge notice served in respect of any parking contravention involving the vehicle during the currency of the hiring agreement;

(e) that the penalty charge exceeded the amount applicable in the circumstances of the case;

(f) that there has been a procedural impropriety on the part of the enforcement authority;

(g) that the order which is alleged to have been contravened in relation to the vehicle concerned, except where it is an order to which Part VI of Schedule 9 to the 1984 Act applies, is invalid;

(h) in a case where a penalty charge notice was served by post on the basis that a civil enforcement officer was prevented by some person from fixing it to the vehicle concerned or handing it to the owner or person in charge of the vehicle, that no civil enforcement officer was so prevented;

(i) that the notice to owner should not have been served because—
   (i) the penalty charge had already been paid in full;
   (ii) the penalty charge had been paid, reduced by the amount of any discount set in accordance with Schedule 9 to the 2004 Act, within the period specified in paragraph 1(h) of the Schedule to the General Regulations.

(5) In these Regulations "procedural impropriety" means a failure by the enforcement authority to observe any requirement imposed on it by the 2004 Act, by the General Regulations or by these Regulations in relation to the imposition or recovery of a penalty charge or other sum and includes in particular—

(a) the taking of any step, whether or not involving the service of any document, otherwise than—
   (i) in accordance with the conditions subject to which; or
   (ii) at the time or during the period when,

   it is authorised or required by the General Regulations or these Regulations to be taken; and

(b) in a case where an enforcement authority is seeking to recover an unpaid charge, the purported service of a charge certificate under regulation 21 of the General Regulations before the enforcement authority is authorised to serve it by those Regulations.

(6) Where the ground mentioned in paragraph (4)(b)(ii) is relied on in any representations made under this regulation, those representations must include a statement of the name and address of the person to whom the vehicle was disposed of by the person making the representations (if that information is in his possession).

(7) Where the ground mentioned in paragraph (4)(b)(iii) is relied on in any representations made under this regulation, those representations must include a statement of the name and address of the person from whom the vehicle was acquired by the person making the representations (if that information is in his possession).

(8) Where the ground mentioned in paragraph (4)(d) is relied on in any representations made under this regulation, those representations must include a statement of the name and address of the person to whom the vehicle was hired at the material time.

(9) In this regulation "hiring agreement" and "vehicle-hire firm" have the same meanings as in section 66 of the Road Traffic Offenders Act 1988.

[1112]

Duty of enforcement authority to which representations are made

5 (1) The enforcement authority may disregard any representations which are received by it after the end of the period of 28 days beginning with the date on which the relevant notice to owner was served.

(2) Where representations are made to an enforcement authority by virtue of regulation 4(1) and in accordance with regulation 4(2), it shall subject to paragraph (1) be the duty of the enforcement authority—

- (a) to consider the representations and any supporting evidence which the person making them provides; and
- (b) within the period of 56 days beginning with the date on which the representations were served on it, to serve on that person notice of its decision as to whether or not it accepts that—
  - (i) one or more of the grounds specified in regulation 4(4) applies; or
  - (ii) there are compelling reasons why, in the particular circumstances of the case, the notice to owner should be cancelled and any sum paid in respect of it should be refunded.

(3) Where the enforcement authority accepts that a ground specified in regulation 4(4) applies or that there are such compelling reasons it shall—

- (a) cancel the notice to owner; and
- (b) state in the notice served under paragraph (2)(b) that the notice to owner has been cancelled and at the same time refund any sum paid in relation to the notice.

(4) The cancellation of a notice to owner under this regulation shall not be taken to prevent the enforcement authority from serving, in accordance with the General Regulations, a fresh notice to owner on another person.

(5) If the enforcement authority fails to comply with paragraph (2)(b) within the period of 56 days there specified, it shall be deemed for the purposes of these Regulations to have accepted—

- (a) that such of the grounds referred to in paragraph (2)(b)(i) as were relied upon in the representations apply; or
- (b) in a case where paragraph (2)(b)(ii) is relied upon, that there are compelling reasons of the kind referred to in that paragraph,

and paragraph (3) shall apply accordingly.

[1113]

Rejection of representations against notice to owner

6 (1) Where representations are made under regulation 4 and the enforcement authority serves a notice of rejection under regulation 5(2)(b), that notice shall—

- (a) state that a charge certificate may be served unless before the end of the period of 28 days beginning with the date of service of the notice of rejection—
  - (i) the penalty charge is paid; or
  - (ii) the person on whom the notice is served appeals to an adjudicator against the penalty charge;
- (b) indicate the nature of an adjudicator's power to award costs; and
- (c) describe in general terms the form and manner in which an appeal to an adjudicator must be made.

(2) A notice of rejection served in accordance with paragraph (1) may contain such other information as the enforcement authority considers appropriate.

[1114]

Appeals to an adjudicator in relation to decisions under regulation 5

7 (1) Where an authority serves a notice of rejection under regulation 5(2)(b) in relation to representations made under regulation 4, the person who made those representations may appeal to an adjudicator against the authority's decision—

- (a) before the end of the period of 28 days beginning with the date of service of the notice of rejection; or
- (b) within such longer period as an adjudicator may allow.

(2) If, on an appeal under this regulation, the adjudicator after considering the representations in question together with any other representations made to the effect referred to in regulation 4(2)(b) and any representations made by the enforcement authority, concludes that a ground specified in regulation 4(4) applies, he shall allow the appeal and may give such directions to the enforcement authority as he may consider appropriate for the purpose of giving effect to his decision, and such directions may in particular include directions requiring—

- (a) the cancellation of the penalty charge notice;
- (b) the cancellation of the notice to owner; and
- (c) the refund of such sum (if any) as may have been paid to the enforcement authority in respect of the penalty charge.

(3) It shall be the duty of an enforcement authority to which such a direction is given to comply with it forthwith.

(4) If the adjudicator does not allow the appeal but is satisfied that there are compelling reasons why, in the particular circumstances of the case, the notice to owner should be cancelled he may recommend the enforcement authority to cancel the notice to owner.

(5) It shall be the duty of an enforcement authority to which a recommendation is made under paragraph (4) to consider afresh the cancellation of the notice to owner taking full account of all observations made by the adjudicator and, within the period of thirty-five days beginning with the date on which the recommendation was given ("the 35-day period"), to notify the appellant and the adjudicator as to whether or not it accepts the adjudicator's recommendation.

(6) If the enforcement authority notifies the appellant and the adjudicator that it does not accept the adjudicator's recommendation, it shall at the same time inform them of the reasons for its decision.

(7) No appeal to the adjudicator shall lie against the decision of the enforcement authority under paragraph (6).

(8) If the enforcement authority accepts the adjudicator's recommendation it shall forthwith cancel the notice to owner and refund to the appellant any sum paid in respect of the penalty charge.

(9) If the enforcement authority fails to comply with the requirements of paragraph (5) within the 35-day period, the authority shall be taken to have accepted the adjudicator's recommendation and shall cancel the notice to owner and refund to the appellant any sum paid in respect of the penalty charge immediately after the end of that period.

[1115]

PART 3
REPRESENTATIONS AND APPEALS IN RELATION TO THE IMMOBILISATION OF VEHICLES

Right to make representations

8 (1) This regulation applies to the owner or person in charge of a vehicle where—

- (a) in accordance with regulation 12 of the General Regulations an immobilisation device has been fixed to a vehicle found in a civil enforcement area; and
- (b) he secures the release of the vehicle from the device on payment of an amount in accordance with regulation 14 of those Regulations.

(2) A person to whom paragraph (1) applies shall immediately upon the release of the vehicle be informed—

- (a) of his right to make representations to the enforcement authority in accordance with this regulation; and
- (b) of his right to appeal to an adjudicator if his representations are not accepted,

and that information must include a statement of the effect of paragraphs (4) and (5).

(3) The enforcement authority shall give that information, or cause it to be given, in writing.

(4) A person to whom paragraph (1) applies may make representations to the effect—

(a) that one or more of the grounds specified in paragraph (5) apply; or

(b) that, whether or not any of those grounds apply, there are compelling reasons why, in the particular circumstances of the case, the enforcement authority should refund some or all of the amount paid to secure the release of the vehicle,

and any such representations shall be in such form as may be specified by the enforcement authority.

(5) The grounds are—

(a) that the vehicle had not been permitted to remain at rest in a civil enforcement area in circumstances in which a penalty charge was payable under regulation 4 of the General Regulations;

(b) that the vehicle had been permitted to remain at rest in the place where it was by a person who was in control of the vehicle without the consent of the owner;

(c) that the place where the vehicle was at rest was not in a civil enforcement area;

(d) that, in accordance with regulation 13 (limitations on the power to immobilise vehicles) of the General Regulations, there was in the circumstances of the case no power under those Regulations to immobilise the vehicle at the time at which it was immobilised or at all;

(e) that the penalty charge or other charge paid to secure the release of the vehicle exceeded the amount applicable in the circumstances of the case; or

(f) that there has been a procedural impropriety on the part of the enforcement authority.

(6) In determining the form for making representations an enforcement authority which is a London authority must act through the joint committee through which, in accordance with regulation 15 of the General Regulations, it exercises its functions relating to adjudicators.

[1116]

Duty of enforcement authority to which representations are made

9 (1) The enforcement authority may disregard any representations which are received by it after the end of the period of 28 days beginning with the date on which the person making them is informed under regulation 8(2) of his right to make representations.

(2) Subject to paragraph (1), it shall be the duty of the enforcement authority, if representations are made to it in accordance with regulation 8(4), before the end of the period of 56 days beginning with the date on which it receives the representations—

(a) to consider them and any supporting evidence which the person making them provides; and

(b) to serve on that person notice of its decision as to whether or not it accepts that—

(i) a ground specified in regulation 8(5) applies; or

(ii) there are compelling reasons why, in the particular circumstances of the case, some or all of the sums paid to secure the release of the vehicle should be refunded.

(3) Where an authority serves notice under paragraph (2)(b)(i) that it accepts that such a ground applies it shall (when serving that notice) refund any sums that the person to whom the vehicle was released was required to pay under regulation 14 of the General Regulations, except to the extent (if any) to which those sums were properly paid.

(4) Where an authority serves notice under paragraph (2)(b)(ii) that it accepts that there are such compelling reasons, it shall refund the sums referred to in paragraph (3) or such of them as it considers appropriate.

(5) Where an authority serves a notice of rejection under paragraph (2)(b), that notice shall—

(a) inform the person on whom it is served of his right to appeal to an adjudicator under regulation 10;
(b) indicate the nature of an adjudicator's power to award costs; and
(c) describe in general terms the form and manner in which such an appeal is required to be made.

(6) Where an authority fails to comply with paragraph (2) before the end of the period of 56 days mentioned there—

(a) it shall be deemed to have accepted the representations and to have served notice to that effect under paragraph (2)(b); and
(b) it shall immediately after the end of that period refund all such sums as are mentioned in paragraph (3).

[1117]

Appeals to an adjudicator in relation to decisions under regulation 9

10 (1) Where an authority serves a notice of rejection under regulation 9(2)(b) in relation to representations made under regulation 8(4), the person making those representations may, before the end of—

(a) the period of 28 days beginning with the date of service of that notice; or
(b) such longer period as an adjudicator may allow,

appeal to a adjudicator against the authority's decision.

(2) On an appeal under this regulation, the adjudicator shall consider the representations in question and any additional representations which are made by the appellant together with any representations made to him by the enforcement authority.

(3) If the adjudicator concludes—

(a) that any of the grounds referred to in regulation 8(5) apply; and
(b) that the enforcement authority would have been under the duty imposed by regulation 9(3) to refund any sum if it had served notice that it accepted that the ground in question applied,

he shall direct that authority to refund that sum.

(4) It shall be the duty of an enforcement authority to which a direction is given under paragraph (3) to comply with it forthwith.

(5) If the adjudicator gives no direction under paragraph (3) but is satisfied that there are compelling reasons why, in the particular circumstances of the case, some or all of the sums paid to secure the release of the vehicle should be refunded, he may recommend the enforcement authority to make such a refund.

(6) It shall be the duty of an enforcement authority to which a recommendation is made under paragraph (5) to consider afresh the making of a refund of those sums taking full account of any observations by the adjudicator and, within the period of thirty-five days beginning with the date on which the direction was given ("the 35-day period"), to notify the appellant and the adjudicator as to whether or not it accepts the adjudicator's recommendation.

(7) If the enforcement authority notifies the appellant and the adjudicator that it does not accept the adjudicator's recommendation it shall at the same time inform them of the reasons for its decision.

(8) No appeal to the adjudicator shall lie against the decision of the enforcement authority under paragraph (7).

(9) If the enforcement authority accepts the adjudicator's recommendation it shall make the recommended refund within the 35-day period.

(10) If the enforcement authority fails to comply with the requirements of paragraph (6) within the 35-day period, the authority shall be taken to have accepted the adjudicator's recommendation and shall make the recommended refund immediately after the end of that period.

[1118]

PART 4
REPRESENTATIONS AND APPEALS IN RELATION TO REMOVED VEHICLES

Right to make representations about a removed vehicle

11 (1) This regulation applies to a person where, as respects a vehicle which has been found in a civil enforcement area for parking contraventions and removed under regulations made under section 99 of the 1984 Act—

(a) he is required to pay an amount on recovery of the vehicle under section 101A of that Act;
(b) he receives a sum in respect of the vehicle under section 101A(2) of that Act;
(c) he is informed that the proceeds of sale of the vehicle did not exceed the aggregate amount mentioned in that provision; or
(d) he is informed that the vehicle was disposed of without there being any proceeds of sale.

(2) A person to whom paragraph (1) applies shall immediately upon the happening of an occurrence referred to in paragraph (1) be informed—

(a) of his right to make representations to the enforcement authority in accordance with this regulation; and
(b) of his right to appeal to an adjudicator if his representations are not accepted,

and that information must include a statement of the effect of paragraphs (4) and (5).

(3) The enforcement authority shall give that information, or cause it to be given, in writing.

(4) A person to whom paragraph (1) applies may make representations to the effect—

(a) that one or more of the grounds specified in paragraph (5) apply; or
(b) that, whether or not any of those grounds apply, there are compelling reasons why, in the particular circumstances of the case, the enforcement authority should—
    (i) refund some or all of the amount paid to secure the release of the vehicle or deducted from the proceeds of sale; or
    (ii) waive its right to recover all or any of the sums due to it on account of the removal or disposal of the vehicle,

and any such representations shall be in such form as may be specified by the enforcement authority.

(5) The grounds referred to in paragraph (4)(a) are—

(a) that the vehicle had not been permitted to remain at rest in a civil enforcement area for parking contraventions in circumstances in which a penalty charge was payable by virtue of regulation 4 of the General Regulations;
(b) that a civil enforcement officer had not, in accordance with regulation 9 of the General Regulations, fixed a penalty charge notice to the vehicle or handed such a notice to the person appearing to him to be in charge of the vehicle, before the vehicle was removed;
(c) that, at the time the vehicle was removed, the power to remove the vehicle conferred by paragraph (2) of regulation 5C of the Removal and Disposal of Vehicles Regulations 1986 was, by virtue of paragraph (3) of that regulation, not exercisable;
(d) that the vehicle had been permitted to remain at rest in the place where it was by a person who was in control of the vehicle without the consent of the owner;
(e) that the place where the vehicle was at rest was not in a civil enforcement area for parking contraventions;
(f) that the penalty charge or other charge paid to secure the release of the vehicle exceeded the amount applicable in the circumstances of the case; or
(g) that there has been a procedural impropriety on the part of the enforcement authority.

(6) In determining the form for making representations the London authorities must act through the joint committee through which, in accordance with regulation 15 of the General Regulations, they exercise their functions relating to adjudicators.

NOTES

Regulations made under s 99 of the 1984 Act See SI 1986/183, in the title Highways, Streets and Bridges.

Removal and Disposal of Vehicles Regulations 1986 SI 1986/183, in the title Highways, Streets and Bridges.

[1119]

Duty of enforcement authority to which representations are made

12 (1) The enforcement authority may disregard any representations under regulation 11 which are received by it after the end of the period of 28 days beginning with the date on which the person making them is informed under regulation 11(2) of his right to make representations.

(2) Subject to paragraph (1), if representations are made to it in accordance with regulation 11(4), it shall be the duty of the enforcement authority, before the end of the period of 56 days beginning with the date on which it receives the representations—

(a) to consider them and any supporting evidence which the person making them provides; and

(b) to serve on that person notice of its decision as to whether or not it accepts that—

(i) a ground specified in regulation 11(5) applies; or

(ii) there are compelling reasons of the kind referred to in regulation 11(4)(b).

(3) Where an authority serves notice under paragraph (2)(b)(i) that it accepts that a ground specified in regulation 11(5) applies it shall (when serving that notice)—

(a) refund any sums that—

(i) the person to whom the vehicle was released was required to pay under section 101A(1) of the 1984 Act; or

(ii) were deducted from the proceeds of sale of the vehicle in accordance with section 101A(2) of that Act,

except to the extent (if any) to which those sums were properly paid or deducted; and

(b) inform the person making representations that it has waived the right to recover any sum which might otherwise have been due to it by way of a penalty charge or on account of the removal, storage or disposal of the vehicle.

(4) Where an authority serves notice under paragraph (2)(b)(ii) that it accepts that there are such compelling reasons, it shall (when serving that notice)—

(a) refund the sums referred to in paragraph (3)(a) or such of them as it considers appropriate in the circumstances of the case; and

(b) inform the person making representations that it has waived the right to recover any sum which might otherwise have been due to it by way of a penalty charge or on account of the removal, storage or disposal of the vehicle.

(5) An authority which has waived its right to recover a sum loses its right to do so.

(6) Where an authority serves notice under paragraph (2)(b) that it does not accept that paragraph (2)(b)(i) or (ii) is fulfilled, that notice shall—

(a) inform the person on whom it is served of his right to appeal to an adjudicator under regulation 13;

(b) indicate the nature of an adjudicator's power to award costs; and

(c) describe in general terms the form and manner in which such an appeal is required to be made.

(7) Where an authority fails to comply with paragraph (2) before the end of the period of 56 days mentioned there it shall be treated as having accepted the representations and as having served notice to that effect under paragraph (2)(b) and paragraph (3) shall apply accordingly.

[1120]

Appeals to an adjudicator in relation to decisions under regulation 12

13 (1) Where an authority serves a notice of rejection under regulation 12(2)(b) in relation to representations under regulation 11(4), the person making those representations may, before—

(a) the end of the period of 28 days beginning with the date of service of that notice; or

(b) such longer period as an adjudicator may allow,

appeal to an adjudicator against the authority's decision.

(2) On an appeal under this regulation, the adjudicator shall consider the representations in question and any additional representations that are made by the appellant.

(3) If the adjudicator concludes—

(a) that any of the grounds referred to in subparagraphs (a) to (g) of regulation 11(5) applies; and

(b) that the enforcement authority would have been under the duty imposed by regulation 12(3) to refund any sum if it had served notice that it accepted that the ground in question applied,

he shall direct that authority to refund that sum.

(4) It shall be the duty of an enforcement authority to which a direction is given under paragraph (3) to comply with it forthwith and the enforcement authority shall cease to have any right to recover any sum which might otherwise have been due to it by way of a penalty charge or on account of the removal, storage or disposal of the vehicle.

(5) If the adjudicator gives no direction under paragraph (3) but is satisfied that there are compelling reasons why, in the particular circumstances of the case, some or all of the sums paid to secure the release of the vehicle, or deducted from the proceeds of sale, should be refunded, he may recommend the enforcement authority to make such a refund.

(6) It shall be the duty of an enforcement authority to which a recommendation is made under paragraph (5) to consider afresh the making of a refund of those sums taking full account of any observations by the adjudicator and, within the period ("the 35-day period") of thirty-five days beginning with the date on which the direction was given, to notify the appellant and the adjudicator as to whether or not it accepts the adjudicator's recommendation.

(7) If the enforcement authority notifies the appellant and the adjudicator that it does not accept the adjudicator's recommendation, it shall at the same time inform them of the reasons for its decision.

(8) No appeal to the adjudicator shall lie against the decision of the enforcement authority under paragraph (7).

(9) If the enforcement authority accepts the adjudicator's recommendation it shall make the recommended refund within the 35-day period.

(10) If the enforcement authority fails to comply with the requirements of paragraph (6) within the 35-day period, the authority shall be taken to have accepted the adjudicator's recommendation and shall make the recommended refund immediately after the end of that period.

[1121]

PART 5
OFFENCES AND PROCEDURE

False representations

14 (1) A person who makes any representation under Part 2 or 3 of these Regulations, or under the Schedule so far as it relates to an appeal under Part 2 or 3, which is false in a material particular, and does so recklessly or knowing it to be false, is guilty of an offence.

(2) A person convicted of an offence under paragraph (1) shall be liable on summary conviction to a fine not exceeding level 5 on the standard scale.

[1122]

Procedure to be followed by adjudicators, service of documents and recovery of sums payable

15 (1) The Schedule to these Regulations shall have effect as to procedure and the service of documents in adjudication proceedings.

(2) Subject to the provisions of that Schedule, an adjudicator may regulate his own procedure.

(3) Any amount which is payable—

(a) under an adjudicator's adjudication;

(b) by virtue of any other provision of these Regulations which requires an enforcement authority to refund any sum,

shall, if a county court so orders, be recoverable by the person to whom the amount is payable as if it were payable under a county court order.

(4) Paragraph (3) does not apply to a penalty charge which remains payable following an adjudication under regulation 7.

[1123]

SCHEDULE
PROCEDURE IN ADJUDICATION PROCEEDINGS

Regulation 15

PART 1
INTERPRETATION

Interpretation of Schedule

1 (1) In this Schedule—

"appeal" means an appeal under regulation 7(1), 10(1) or 13(1);

"document exchange" means a document exchange providing a system of delivery of documents by reference to numbered boxes at document exchanges;

"fax" means the making of a facsimile copy of a document by the transmission of electronic signals;

"hearing" means an oral hearing;

"proper officer" means a member of the administrative staff provided under section 81(4)(a) of the 2004 Act appointed to perform the functions of the proper officer under this Schedule;

"register" means the register required to be kept under paragraph 21;

"registered keeper" means the person in whose name a vehicle is registered under the Vehicle Excise and Registration Act 1994; and

"working day" means any day except a Saturday, a Sunday, Good Friday, Christmas Day or a bank holiday in England by virtue of the Banking and Financial Dealings Act 1971.

(2) In this Schedule in relation to an appeal or any process connected with an appeal—

"disputed decision" means the decision appealed against;

"the enforcement authority" means the enforcement authority which made the disputed decision; and

"the original representations" means the representations to the enforcement authority under regulation 4(1), 8(4) or 11(4).

[1124]

PART 2
PROCEDURE RELATING TO APPEALS

Initiating an appeal

2 (1) An appeal shall be made by delivering a notice of appeal to the proper officer.

(2) A notice of appeal—

(a) must be in writing signed by the appellant or someone authorised by him to sign on his behalf;

(b) must state the name and address of the appellant;

(c) may specify some other address as being the address to which the appellant wishes documents to be sent to him in connection with the appeal;

(d) must state the date and any reference number of the disputed decision and the name of the enforcement authority; and

(e) may include any representations which the appellant desires to make in addition to the original representations.

(3) If the notice of appeal is delivered to the proper officer later than the time limit specified in regulation 7(1)(a), 10(1)(a) or 13(1)(a) (as the case may be), the appellant must include in the notice a statement of the reasons on which he relies for justifying the delay, and the adjudicator shall treat any such statement of reasons for delay as a request for extending that time limit.

Action upon receipt of notice of appeal and copy of such notice

3 (1) Upon receiving a notice of appeal the proper officer shall—

(a) send an acknowledgement of its receipt to the appellant; and
(b) enter particulars of the appeal in the register.

(2) If he is satisfied that the notice is in accordance with paragraph 2, the proper officer shall send to the enforcement authority a copy of the notice of appeal and any directions extending the time limit for appealing.

(3) Upon receipt of a copy of the notice of appeal sent to it under subparagraph (2), the enforcement authority shall within 7 days deliver to the proper officer copies of—

(a) the original representations;
(b) the relevant penalty charge notice (if any); and
(c) the relevant notice of rejection.

(4) If a notice of appeal is received by the proper officer and he considers that it may not be in accordance with paragraph 2, he shall refer the issue of its validity to an adjudicator.

(5) If the adjudicator determines that a notice of appeal referred to him under subparagraph (4) is in accordance with paragraph 2, the proper officer shall deal with it in accordance with subparagraph (2).

(6) If—

(a) a notice of appeal is delivered outside the appeal period with a request to extend the appeal period and the adjudicator declines to direct that the period be extended; or
(b) the adjudicator determines that a notice of appeal is not in accordance with paragraph 2,

the proper officer shall inform the appellant that the adjudicator has declined the request for an extension or, as the case may be, of the reasons why the adjudicator considers that the notice does not accord with paragraph 2 and shall record the action taken in the register.

Further representations

4 (1) Any party may deliver representations in relation to the matters referred to in regulation 4(2)(b), 8(4) or 11(4), as appropriate in the circumstances, to the proper officer at any time before the appeal is determined.

(2) The adjudicator may invite a party to deliver to the proper officer representations dealing with such matters relating to the appeal as may be specified and any such representations shall be so delivered within the time and in the manner specified.

(3) Where a party fails to respond to an invitation under subparagraph (2), the adjudicator may draw such inferences as appear to him proper.

(4) Any representations delivered under this paragraph shall be signed by the party in question or someone authorised by him to sign on his behalf.

(5) Where the appellant delivers representations to the proper officer under this paragraph, the proper officer shall send a copy of the representations to the enforcement authority.

(6) Where the enforcement authority delivers representations to the proper officer under this paragraph, it shall at the same time send a copy of the representations to the appellant.

(7) This paragraph is without prejudice to the powers of an adjudicator under paragraph 10.

Adjudicator's power to require attendance of witnesses and production of documents

5 (1) The adjudicator may, by notice in writing sent to any person (including a party to the proceedings), require that person—

(a) to attend, at a time and place specified by the adjudicator, to give evidence at the hearing of an appeal; and
(b) to produce any documents in his custody or under his control, relating to any matter in the proceedings,

and any such notice shall contain a statement of the effect of subparagraphs (2) to (6) below.

(2) A person in respect of whom a requirement has been made under subparagraph (1) may apply to the adjudicator to vary or set aside the requirement.

(3) A person shall not be bound to comply with a requirement under subparagraph (1) unless he has been given at least 7 days' notice of the hearing or, if less than 7 days, he has informed the adjudicator that he accepts such notice as he has been given.

(4) No person, other than the appellant, shall be bound to comply with a requirement under subparagraph (1) unless the necessary expenses of his attendance are paid or tendered to him.

(5) No person shall be required to give any evidence or produce any documents under subparagraph (1) which he could not be required to give or produce in the trial of an action in a court of law.

(6) Any person who fails to comply with a requirement made under subparagraph (1) is guilty of an offence and shall be liable on summary conviction to a fine not exceeding level 2 on the standard scale.

Disposal of an appeal without a hearing

6 (1) Subject to the following provisions of this paragraph, the adjudicator may dispose of an appeal without a hearing.

(2) The adjudicator shall not dispose of an appeal without a hearing if, in his opinion, the appeal raises issues of public importance such as to require that a hearing be held.

(3) The adjudicator shall not dispose of an appeal without a hearing if either party has requested a hearing unless—

- (a) the party who made the request withdraws the request before notice of a hearing has been sent to the other party under paragraph 7;
- (b) both parties have subsequently consented to the appeal being disposed of without a hearing; or
- (c) the party requesting the hearing having been sent a notice of the hearing of an appeal in accordance with paragraph 7, fails to attend or be represented at the hearing.

(4) Where the adjudicator is minded to dispose of an appeal without a hearing, he shall not do so unless and until either—

- (a) there has elapsed a period of 28 days beginning with the date on which an acknowledgement is sent in accordance with paragraph 3(1) during which neither party has requested a hearing; or
- (b) both parties have consented to its disposal without a hearing.

Notice of time and place of hearing

7 (1) This paragraph shall have effect where a hearing is to be held for the purpose of disposing of an appeal.

(2) The proper officer shall—

- (a) fix the time and place of the hearing; and
- (b) not less than 21 days before the time so fixed, or such shorter time as the parties agree—
  - (i) send to each party a notice that the hearing is to be at that time and place; or
  - (ii) inform them of those matters in such other manner as he thinks fit.

(3) The adjudicator may alter the time and place of any hearing, and the proper officer shall, not less than 7 days before the date on which the hearing is then to be held, or such shorter time as the parties agree—

- (a) send to each party notice of the new time and place of the hearing; or
- (b) inform them of those matters in such other manner as he thinks fit.

(4) This paragraph applies to an adjourned hearing; but, if before the adjournment the time and place of the adjourned hearing are notified to all persons expected to attend, no further notice shall be required.

Admission to a hearing

8 (1) Subject to the provisions of this paragraph, a hearing shall be held in public.

(2) The adjudicator may direct that the whole or any part of a hearing be held in private if he is satisfied that it is just and reasonable for him so to do by reason of—

- (a) the likelihood of disclosure of intimate personal or financial circumstances;
- (b) the likelihood of disclosure of commercially sensitive information or information obtained in confidence; or
- (c) exceptional circumstances not falling within paragraph (a) or (b).

(3) The following persons shall be entitled to attend the hearing of an appeal which is held in private—

- (a) any other adjudicator; and
- (b) (for the purpose of discharging his functions as a member of that Council) a member of the Council on Tribunals.

(4) The adjudicator, with the consent of the parties, may permit any other person to attend the hearing of an appeal which is held in private or, where part of it is so held, that part.

(5) Without prejudice to any other powers he may have, an adjudicator may exclude from the hearing of an appeal, or part of it, any person whose conduct has disrupted or is likely, in the opinion of the adjudicator, to disrupt the hearing.

Appearances at a hearing

9 (1) The appellant and the enforcement authority shall be entitled to appear at the hearing of an appeal.

(2) Any other person may appear at a hearing at the discretion of the adjudicator.

(3) At the hearing of an appeal, the appellant may conduct his case himself (with assistance from any person if he wishes) or may be represented, by a solicitor, counsel or any other person.

(4) If in any particular case the adjudicator is satisfied that there are sufficient reasons for doing so, he may prohibit a particular person from assisting or representing either party at the hearing.

Procedure at a hearing

10 (1) At the beginning of the hearing of an appeal the adjudicator shall explain the order of proceedings which he proposes to adopt.

(2) Subject to the provisions of this paragraph, the adjudicator shall conduct the hearing of an appeal in such manner as he considers most suitable to the clarification of the issues before him and generally to the just handling of the proceedings; he shall so far as appears to him appropriate seek to avoid formality in the proceedings.

(3) At the hearing of an appeal—

(a) the parties shall be entitled to give evidence, to call witnesses and to address the adjudicator both on the evidence and generally on the subject matter of the appeal;

(b) the adjudicator may receive evidence of any fact which appears to him to be relevant notwithstanding that such evidence would be inadmissible in proceedings before a court of law.

(4) Without prejudice to paragraph 6(3)(c), where a party who has been sent a notice of the hearing of an appeal or has otherwise been notified of the hearing in accordance with paragraph 7 fails to attend the hearing, the adjudicator may dispose of the appeal in his absence.

Decisions on appeals

11 (1) The adjudicator must give the reasons for his decision on an appeal.

(2) Where an appeal is disposed of at a hearing, the adjudicator may give his decision and the reasons orally at the end of the hearing, or may reserve his decision and give it and his reasons subsequently in writing.

(3) Upon the decision being given (whether at a hearing or otherwise), the proper officer shall—

(a) as soon as practicable record the decision in the register, together with the adjudicator's reasons and any directions given; and

(b) send a copy of the register entry to each party.

Review of adjudicator's decision

12 (1) The adjudicator may, on the application of a party, review—

(a) any interlocutory decision; or

(b) any decision to determine that a notice of appeal does not accord with paragraph 2 or to dismiss or allow an appeal, or any decision as to costs, on one or more of the following grounds—

(i) the decision was wrongly made as the result of an administrative error;

(ii) the adjudicator was wrong to reject the notice of appeal;

(iii) a party who failed to appear or be represented at a hearing had good and sufficient reason for his failure to appear;

(iv) where the decision was made after a hearing, new evidence has become available since the conclusion of the hearing, the existence of which could not reasonably have been known of or foreseen;

(v) where the decision was made without a hearing, new evidence has become available since the decision was made, the existence of which could not reasonably have been known of or foreseen; or

(vi) the interests of justice require such a review.

(2) An application under subparagraph (1) must—

(a) be delivered to the proper officer within the period of 14 days beginning with the date on which the copy of the register entry is served on the parties; and

(b) state the grounds in full.

(3) The parties shall have the opportunity to be heard on any application for review under subparagraph (1).

(4) Having reviewed the decision the adjudicator may direct that it be confirmed, that it be revoked or that it be varied.

(5) If, having reviewed a decision, the adjudicator directs that it be revoked, he shall substitute a new decision or order a re-determination by himself, the original adjudicator or a different adjudicator.

(6) Paragraph 11 shall apply to the confirmation, revocation or variation of a decision under this paragraph as it applies to a decision made on the disposal of an appeal.

Costs

13 (1) The adjudicator shall not normally make an order awarding costs and expenses, but may, subject to subparagraph (2) make such an order—

(a) against a party (including an appellant who has withdrawn his appeal or an enforcement authority which has consented to an appeal being allowed) if he is of the opinion that that party has acted frivolously or vexatiously or that his conduct in making, pursuing or resisting an appeal was wholly unreasonable; or

(b) against an enforcement authority where he considers that the disputed decision was wholly unreasonable.

(2) An order shall not be made under subparagraph (1) against a party unless that party has been given an opportunity of making representations against the making of the order.

(3) An order under subparagraph (1) shall require the party against whom it is made to pay to the other party a specified sum in respect of the costs and expenses incurred by that other party in connection with the proceedings.

Consolidation of proceedings

14 (1) Where there are pending two or more appeals and at any time it appears to an adjudicator that—

(a) some common question of law or fact arises in both or all appeals; or

(b) for some other reason it is desirable to make an order under this paragraph,

the adjudicator may order that all of the appeals or those specified in the order shall be considered together and may give such consequential directions as may appear to him to be necessary.

(2) An order shall not be made under this paragraph unless all parties concerned have been given an opportunity of making representations against the making of the order.

Miscellaneous powers of adjudicators

15 (1) An adjudicator may, if he thinks fit—

(a) extend the time appointed by or under this Schedule for the doing of any act notwithstanding that the time appointed has expired;

(b) if an appellant at any time gives notice of the withdrawal of his appeal, dismiss the proceedings;

(c) if an enforcement authority consents to an appeal being allowed, allow the appeal;

(d) if both or all of the parties agree in writing on the terms of a decision to be made by an adjudicator, decide accordingly; or

(e) adjourn a hearing.

(2) An adjudicator may exercise the powers conferred by this Schedule (other than paragraph 12) on his own motion or on the application of a party.

Clerical errors

16 Clerical mistakes in any document recording a direction or decision of the adjudicator, or errors in such a document arising from an accidental slip or omission, may be corrected by the proper officer on the direction of the adjudicator.

NOTES

Council on Tribunals Abolished by the Tribunals, Courts and Enforcement Act 2007, s 45(1), as from 1 November 2007 (see SI 2007/2709, in the title Courts and Legal Services). S 44 of, and Sch 7 to, the 2007 Act establish the Administrative Justice and Tribunals Council (the AJTC) to replace the Council on Tribunals, and provide for the AJTC to keep under review, consider and report on matters relating to listed tribunals. SI 2007/2951, in the title Courts and Legal Services, designates as a listed tribunal for the purposes of Sch 7 to the 2007 Act adjudicators appointed under the Traffic Management Act 2004, s 81 for the purposes of Pt 6 of the 2004 Act.

[1125]

PART 3
SERVICE OF DOCUMENTS AND NOTICES

Service of documents on the parties

17 (1) This paragraph has effect in relation to any notice or other document required or authorised by these Regulations to be sent to a party to an appeal.

(2) Any document shall be regarded as having been sent to that party if it is—

(a) delivered to him;

(b) left at his proper address;

(c) sent by first class post to him at that address; or

(d) transmitted to him by fax or other means of electronic data transmission in accordance with subparagraph (3).

(3) A document may be transmitted to a party by fax or by other means of electronic data transmission where—

(a) the party has indicated in writing to the party sending the notice or document that he is willing to regard a document as having been duly sent to him if it is transmitted to a specified fax telephone number or, as the case may be, a specified electronic address; and

(b) the document is transmitted to that number or address.

(4) In the case of an enforcement authority, an indication under subparagraph (3)(a) may be expressed to apply in relation to any appeal to which it is the respondent.

(5) Where the proper address includes a box number at a document exchange, the delivery of such a document may be effected by leaving the document addressed to that box number—

(a) at that document exchange; or

(b) at a document exchange which transmits documents every working day to that exchange,

and any such document so left shall, unless the contrary is proved, be taken to have been delivered on the second working day after the day on which it was left.

(6) For the purposes of this Schedule, and of section 7 (references to service by post) of the Interpretation Act 1978 ("the 1978 Act") in its application to this paragraph—

(a) the proper address of the appellant is the address for service specified pursuant to paragraph 2(2)(c) or, if no address is so specified, the address specified pursuant to regulation 2(2)(b), and

(b) the proper address of an enforcement authority in proceedings in which it is the respondent is such address as the authority may from time to time specify in a notice delivered to the proper officer as being the authority's address for service in all such proceedings.

(7) If no address for service has been specified, the proper address for the purposes of this Schedule, and section 7 of the 1978 Act, shall be—

(a) in the case of an individual, his usual or last known address;

(b) in the case of a partnership, the principal or last known place of business of the firm within the United Kingdom;

(c) in the case of an incorporated or unincorporated body, the registered or principal office of the body.

(8) A party may at any time, by notice in writing delivered to the proper officer, change his proper address for the purposes of this Schedule and section 7 of the 1978 Act.

(9) A party may, by notice in writing delivered to the other party and the proper officer, vary or revoke any indication given under subparagraph (3)(a).

(10) Unless the contrary is proved, a notice or document—

(a) left at the proper address of a party shall be taken to have been delivered on the second working day after the day on which it was left;

(b) sent by fax or other means of electronic data transmission shall be taken to have been delivered on the second working day after the day on which it was transmitted.

Delivery of notices or documents to the proper officer

18 (1) This paragraph has effect in relation to any notice or other document required or authorised by or under this Schedule to be delivered to the proper officer.

(2) Any such notice or document may be delivered to the proper officer by being transmitted to the proper officer by fax or other means of electronic data transmission, but only to a telephone number or, as the case may be, electronic address for the time being published by the proper officer for the purpose of receiving such notices or documents.

(3) Any notice or document so transmitted shall, unless the contrary is proved, be taken to have been delivered on the second working day after the day on which it was transmitted.

(4) Where the address of the proper officer includes a box number at a document exchange the delivery of such a document may be effected by leaving the document addressed to that box number—

(a) at that document exchange; or

(b) at a document exchange which transmits documents every working day to that exchange,

and any such document so left shall be taken, unless the contrary is proved, to have been delivered on the second working day after the day on which it was left.

(5) Paragraphs 2(2)(a) and 4(4)—

(a) shall, in the case of a document transmitted by fax, be satisfied if a copy of the signature of the relevant person appears on the transmitted copy; and

(b) shall not apply in relation to a document transmitted by other means of electronic data transmission.

[1126]

PART 4
DIRECTIONS AS TO INVALID NOTICES

Scope of Part 4

19 Paragraph 20 applies to a case where—

(a) the order of a county court which has been made against a person ("a relevant person") is deemed under regulation 23 of the General Regulations to have been revoked following the making of a witness statement; and

(b) the enforcement authority has referred the case to the adjudicator for directions.

Procedure

20 (1) Where a case to which this paragraph applies is referred to the adjudicator—

(a) the proper officer shall enter particulars of the case in the register; and

(b) the adjudicator shall give directions as to the conduct of the proceedings unless he decides that no such directions are necessary.

(2) The adjudicator may, in particular—

(a) if it appears to him that no appeal has been made by the relevant person in relation to the subject matter of the case, direct that the case proceed as an appeal and, in that event, this Schedule (except paragraphs 2 and 3) shall apply as if an appeal had been duly made by the relevant person; or

(b) if it appears to him that an appeal has been made by the relevant person in relation to the subject matter of the case and that the appeal has been dismissed, direct that the case proceed as an application under paragraph 12 to review that decision.

[1127]

PART 5
THE REGISTER

The register

21 (1) The proper officer shall establish and maintain, in accordance with the following provisions of this paragraph, a register for the purpose of recording proceedings conducted under these Regulations.

(2) The register shall be kept open for inspection by any person without charge at all reasonable hours at the principal office of the adjudicators.

(3) The register may be kept in electronic form.

(4) If the register is kept in electronic form, the duty to allow inspection is to be treated as a duty to allow inspection of a reproduction in legible form of the recording of the entry the inspection of which is being sought.

(5) A document purporting to be certified by the proper officer to be a true copy of any entry of a decision in a register shall be evidence of the entry and of the matters contained in it.

[1128]

CIVIL ENFORCEMENT OF PARKING CONTRAVENTIONS (ENGLAND) GENERAL REGULATIONS 2007
SI 2007/3483

Authority Made by the Secretary of State for Transport under the Traffic Management Act 2004, ss 72, 73(3), 79, 88, 89, Sch 9, para 6 and by the Lord Chancellor under ss 78, 81, 82, 89 of that Act.
Date made 10 December 2007.
Commencement 31 March 2008; see reg 1(1).
Amendment Printed as amended by SI 2009/478. Previously amended by SI 2008/1513 (revoked).
Interpretation See reg 2.
General The Traffic Management Act 2004, Pt 6 (ss 72–93 and Schs 7–11) enables regulations to be made providing for a single framework for the civil enforcement of road traffic contraventions (ie parking contraventions, bus lane contraventions, London lorry ban contraventions and moving traffic contraventions) by local authorities. These regulations (together with SI 2007/3482) implement Pt 6 of the 2004 Act in so far as it relates to the civil enforcement of parking contraventions in England (including Greater London).

Pt 1 of the regulations provides for preliminary matters. Pts 2 and 3 relate respectively to penalty charges and the immobilisation of vehicles. Pt 4 provides for the appointment of adjudicators by enforcement authorities. Pt 5 concerns the enforcement of penalty charges. Pt 6 contains financial provisions.

As to representations and appeals against penalty charge notices and notices to owner given under these regulations, and in relation to immobilised vehicles, see SI 2007/3482. As to guidelines to enforcement authorities outside Greater London on the level of charges for parking contraventions, see SI 2007/3487.

Wales The following regulations make similar provision in relation to Wales as SI 2007/3483 makes in relation to England:

(a) SI 2008/609 (made by the Lord Chancellor under the Traffic Management Act 2004, ss 78, 81, 82, 89 and in force on the 31 March 2008), as amended by SI 2008/913, makes provision relating to penalty charge notices, the appointment of adjudicators by enforcement authorities, and the enforcement of penalty charges;

(b) SI 2008/1214 (made by the Welsh Ministers under the Traffic Management Act 2004, ss 72, 73(3), 79, 88, 89 and in force on 22 May 2008), makes provision relating to the imposition of penalty charges, the immobilisation of vehicles and financial matters (modifying the Road Traffic Regulation Act 1984, s 55); it also revokes and replaces the Civil Enforcement of Parking Contraventions (General Provisions) (Wales) Regulations 2008, SI 2008/614.

As to representations and appeals against penalty charge notices and notices to owner given under SI 2008/609 and SI 2008/1214, and in relation to vehicles which have been immobilised, see SI 2008/608 (noted under the head "Wales" to SI 2007/3482). As to guidelines to enforcement authorities in Wales on the level of charges for parking contraventions, see SI 2008/613 (noted under the head "Wales" to SI 2007/3487).

[1129]

PART 1
PRELIMINARY

Citation, commencement and application

1 (1) These Regulations may be cited as the Civil Enforcement of Parking Contraventions (England) General Regulations 2007 and shall come into force on 31st March 2008.

(2) These Regulations apply only to England.

[1130]

Interpretation

2 (1) In these Regulations—

"the 2004 Act" means the Traffic Management Act 2004;

"the 28-day period" has the meaning given by regulation 10(4);

"adjudicator" means an adjudicator appointed under Part 4 of these Regulations;

"applicable discount" and "applicable surcharge" mean the amount of any discount or, as the case may be, surcharge set in accordance with Schedule 9 to the 2004 Act;

"charge certificate" has the meaning given by regulation 21(1);

"enforcement authority" in relation to a penalty charge or the immobilisation of a vehicle means the enforcement authority in relation to the alleged contravention in consequence of which the charge was incurred or the vehicle was immobilised;

"notice to owner", subject to regulations 21(4) and 23(9) has the meaning given by regulation 19;

"outstanding" in relation to a penalty charge shall be construed in accordance with paragraphs (2) to (4);

"owner" in relation to a vehicle includes any person who falls to be treated as the owner of the vehicle by virtue of regulation 5(3);

"pedestrian crossing contravention" means a parking contravention consisting of an offence referred to in paragraph 3(2)(c), 3(2)(h)(i), 4(2)(c) or 4(2)(i)(i) of Schedule 7 to the 2004 Act (prohibition on stopping of vehicles on or near pedestrian crossings);

"penalty charge" means a penalty charge relating to a parking contravention and payable in accordance with regulation 4;

"penalty charge notice" has the meaning given by regulation 8(1);

"regulation 10 penalty charge notice" has the meaning given by regulation 10;

"the English enforcement authorities" means Transport for London and those enforcement authorities which are London authorities or other local authorities in England and "the non-London enforcement authorities" means the English enforcement authorities other than Transport for London and the London authorities; and

"the Representations and Appeals Regulations" means the Civil Enforcement of Parking Contraventions (England) Representations and Appeals Regulations 2007.

[(1A) …]

(2) For the purposes of these Regulations a penalty charge is outstanding in relation to a vehicle if—

(a) the charge has not been paid and the enforcement authority to which the charge is payable has not waived payment, whether by cancellation of the penalty charge notice or notice to owner or otherwise;

(b) the owner of the vehicle when it was immobilised was also the owner of the vehicle when the penalty charge was imposed; and

(c) either—

  (i) a notice to owner or regulation 10 penalty charge notice has been served in respect of the charge and the conditions in paragraph (3) are satisfied; or

  (ii) no notice to owner or regulation 10 penalty charge notice has been served in respect of the charge and the conditions in paragraph (4) are satisfied.

(3) The conditions referred to in paragraph (2)(c)(i) are that—

(a) the penalty charge was imposed, in accordance with these Regulations, by an enforcement authority in respect of a parking contravention;

(b) the penalty charge is the subject of a charge certificate served under regulation 21 which has not been set aside in accordance with regulation 23.

(4) The conditions referred to in paragraph (2)(c)(ii) are that—

(a) the penalty charge related to a vehicle which, when the penalty charge became payable,—

(i) was not registered under the Vehicle Excise and Registration Act 1994; or

(ii) was so registered, but without the inclusion in the registered particulars of the correct name and address of the keeper of the vehicle;

(b) having taken all reasonable steps, the enforcement authority to which the penalty charge was payable was unable to ascertain the name and address of the keeper of the vehicle and was consequently unable to serve a notice to owner under regulation 19 or a regulation 10 penalty charge notice; and

(c) the period of 42 days beginning with the date on which the penalty charge became payable has expired.

NOTES

Amendment Para (1A): revoked by SI 2009/478 (originally inserted by SI 2008/1513 (revoked)).
Civil Enforcement of Parking Contraventions (England) Representations and Appeals Regulations 2007 SI 2007/3482.

[1131]

Service by post

3 (1) Subject to paragraph (5), any notice (except a penalty charge notice served under regulation 9) or charge certificate under these Regulations—

(a) may be served by first class (but not second class) post; and

(b) where the person on whom it is to be served is a body corporate, is duly served if it is sent by first class post to the secretary or clerk of that body.

(2) Service of a notice or charge certificate contained in a letter sent by first class post which has been properly addressed, pre-paid and posted shall, unless the contrary is proved, be taken to have been effected on the second working day after the day of posting.

(3) In paragraph (2), "working day" means any day except—

(a) a Saturday or a Sunday;

(b) New Year's Day;

(c) Good Friday;

(d) Christmas Day;

(e) any other day which is a bank holiday in England and Wales under the Banking and Financial Dealings Act 1971.

(4) A document may be transmitted to a vehicle hire firm (as defined in regulation 5(4)) by a means of electronic data transmission where—

(a) the vehicle hire firm has indicated in writing to the person sending the notice or document that it is willing to regard a document as having been duly sent to it if it is transmitted to a specified electronic address; and

(b) the document is transmitted to that address.

(5) Nothing in this regulation applies to the service of any notice or order made by a county court.

[1132]

PART 2
PENALTY CHARGES

Imposition of penalty charges

4 Subject to the provisions of these Regulations a penalty charge is payable with respect to a vehicle where there has been committed in relation to that vehicle—

(a) a parking contravention within paragraph 2 of Schedule 7 to the 2004 Act (contraventions relating to parking places in Greater London);

(b) a parking contravention within paragraph 3 of that Schedule (other parking contraventions in Greater London) in a civil enforcement area in Greater London; or

(c) a parking contravention within paragraph 4 of that Schedule (parking contraventions outside Greater London) in a civil enforcement area outside Greater London.

[1133]

Person by whom a penalty charge is to be paid

5 (1) Where a parking contravention occurs, the person by whom the penalty charge for the contravention is to be paid shall be determined in accordance with the following provisions of this regulation.

(2) In a case not falling within paragraph (3), the penalty charge shall be payable by the person who was the owner of the vehicle involved in the contravention at the material time.

(3) Where—

(a) the vehicle is a mechanically propelled vehicle which was, at the material time, hired from a vehicle-hire firm under a hiring agreement;

(b) the person hiring it had signed a statement of liability acknowledging his liability in respect of any penalty charge notice served in respect of any parking contravention involving the vehicle during the currency of the hiring agreement; and

(c) in response to a notice to owner served on him, the owner of the vehicle made representations on the ground specified regulation 4(4)(d) of the Representations and Appeals Regulations and the enforcement authority accepted those representations,

the penalty charge shall be payable by the person by whom the vehicle was hired and that person shall be treated as if he were the owner of the vehicle at the material time for the purposes of these Regulations.

(4) In this regulation—

(a) "hiring agreement" and "vehicle-hire firm" have the same meanings as in section 66 of the Road Traffic Offenders Act 1988; and

(b) "the material time" means the time when the contravention giving rise to the penalty charge is said to have occurred.

[1134]

[Evidence of contravention

6 A penalty charge shall not be imposed except on the basis of—

(a) a record produced by an approved device; or

(b) information given by a civil enforcement officer as to conduct observed by that officer.]

NOTES

Amendment Substituted by SI 2009/478.

Approved devices See SI 2007/3486.

[1135]

Criminal proceedings for parking contraventions in civil enforcement areas

7 (1) No criminal proceedings may be instituted and no fixed penalty notice may be served in respect of any parking contravention occurring in a civil enforcement area, except a pedestrian crossing contravention.

(2) A penalty charge shall not be payable in relation to a pedestrian crossing contravention where—

(a) the conduct constituting the contravention is the subject of criminal proceedings; or

(b) a fixed penalty notice, as defined by section 52 of the Road Traffic Offenders Act 1988, has been given in respect of that conduct.

(3) Where, notwithstanding the provisions of paragraph (2)—

(a) a penalty charge has been paid in respect of a pedestrian crossing contravention; and

(b) the circumstances are as mentioned in paragraph (2)(a) or (b),

the enforcement authority shall, as soon as reasonably practicable after those circumstances come to its notice, refund the amount of the penalty charge.

[1136]

Penalty charge notices

8 (1) In these Regulations a "penalty charge notice" means a notice which—

(a) was served in accordance with regulation 9 or 10 in relation to a parking contravention; and

(b) complies with the requirements of the Schedule which apply to it as well as those of regulation 3 of the Representations and Appeals Regulations which so apply.

(2) The Schedule has effect with regard to penalty charge notices.

[1137]

Penalty charge notices—service by a civil enforcement officer

9 Where a civil enforcement officer has reason to believe that a penalty charge is payable with respect to a vehicle which is stationary in a civil enforcement area, he may serve a penalty charge notice—

(a) by fixing it to the vehicle; or

(b) giving it to the person appearing to him to be in charge of the vehicle.

[1138]

Penalty charge notices—service by post

10 (1) An enforcement authority may serve a penalty charge notice by post where—

(a) on the basis of a record produced by an approved device, the authority has reason to believe that a penalty charge is payable with respect to a vehicle which is stationary in a civil enforcement area;

(b) a civil enforcement officer attempted to serve a penalty charge notice in accordance with regulation 9 but was prevented from doing so by some person; or

(c) a civil enforcement officer had begun to prepare a penalty charge notice for service in accordance with regulation 9, but the vehicle concerned was driven away from the place in which it was stationary before the civil enforcement officer had finished preparing the penalty charge notice or had served it in accordance with regulation 9,

and references in these Regulations to a "regulation 10 penalty charge notice" are to a penalty charge notice served by virtue of this paragraph.

(2) For the purposes of paragraph (1)(c), a civil enforcement officer who observes conduct which appears to constitute a parking contravention shall not thereby be taken to have begun to prepare a penalty charge notice.

(3) A regulation 10 penalty charge notice shall be served on the person appearing to the enforcement authority to be the owner of the vehicle involved in the contravention in consequence of which the penalty charge is payable.

(4) Subject to paragraph (6), a regulation 10 penalty charge notice may not be served later than the expiration of the period of 28 days beginning with the date on which, according to a record produced by an approved device, or information given by a civil enforcement officer, the contravention to which the penalty charge notice relates occurred (in these Regulations called "the 28-day period").

(5) Paragraph (6) applies where—

(a) within 14 days of the appropriate date the enforcement authority has requested the Secretary of State to supply the relevant particulars in respect of the vehicle involved in the contravention and those particulars have not been supplied before the expiration of the 28-day period;

(b) an earlier regulation 10 penalty charge notice relating to the same contravention has been cancelled under regulation 23(5)(c); or

(c) an earlier regulation 10 penalty charge notice relating to the same contravention has been cancelled under regulation 5 of the Representations and Appeals Regulations.

(6) Where this paragraph applies, notwithstanding the expiration of the 28-day period, an enforcement authority shall continue to be entitled to serve a regulation 10 penalty charge notice—

(a) in a case falling within paragraph (5)(a), for a period of six months beginning with the appropriate date; or

(b) in a case falling within paragraph (5)(b) or (c), for a period of 4 weeks beginning with the appropriate date.

(7) In this regulation—

(a) "the appropriate date" means—

(i) in a case falling within paragraph (5)(a), the date referred to in paragraph (4);

(ii) in a case falling within paragraph (5)(b), the date on which the district judge serves notice in accordance with regulation 23(5)(d); or

(iii) in a case falling within paragraph (5)(c) the date on which the previous regulation 10 penalty charge notice was cancelled; and

(b) "relevant particulars" means particulars relating to the identity of the keeper of the vehicle contained in the register of mechanically propelled vehicles maintained by the Secretary of State under the Vehicle Excise and Registration Act 1994.

[1139]

Removal of or interference with a penalty charge notice

11 (1) A penalty charge notice fixed to a vehicle in accordance with regulation 9(a) shall not be removed or interfered with except by or under the authority of—

(a) the owner or person in charge of the vehicle; or

(b) the enforcement authority.

(2) A person contravening paragraph (1) shall be guilty of an offence and liable on summary conviction to a fine not exceeding level 2 on the standard scale.

[1140]

PART 3
IMMOBILISATION OF VEHICLES

Power to immobilise vehicles

12 (1) Subject to regulation 13 (limitations on the power to immobilise vehicles), where a penalty charge notice has been served in accordance with regulation 9, a civil enforcement officer or a person acting under his direction may fix an immobilisation device to the vehicle concerned while it remains in the place where it was found.

(2) On any occasion when an immobilisation device is fixed to a vehicle in accordance with this regulation, the person fixing the device shall also fix to the vehicle a notice—

(a) indicating that such a device has been fixed to the vehicle and warning that no attempt should be made to drive it or otherwise put it in motion until it has been released from that device;

(b) specifying the steps to be taken in order to secure its release; and

(c) warning that unlawful removal of an immobilisation device is an offence.

(3) A notice fixed to a vehicle in accordance with this regulation shall not be removed or interfered with except by or under the authority of—

(a) the owner, or person in charge, of the vehicle; or

(b) the enforcement authority.

(4) A person contravening paragraph (3) shall be guilty of an offence and liable on summary conviction to a fine not exceeding level 2 on the standard scale.

(5) Any person who, without being authorised to do so in accordance with these Regulations, removes or attempts to remove an immobilisation device fixed to a

vehicle in accordance with this regulation shall be guilty of an offence and shall be liable on summary conviction to a fine not exceeding level 3 on the standard scale.

[1141]

Limitations on the power to immobilise vehicles

13 (1) An immobilisation device must not be fixed to a vehicle if there is displayed on the vehicle—

(a) a current disabled person's badge; or
(b) a current recognised badge.

(2) If, in a case in which an immobilisation device would have been fixed to a vehicle but for paragraph (1)(a), the vehicle was not being used—

(a) in accordance with regulations under section 21 of the Chronically Sick and Disabled Persons Act 1970; and
(b) in circumstances falling within section 117(1)(b) of the Road Traffic Regulation Act 1984 (use where a disabled persons' concession would be available),

the person in charge of the vehicle shall be guilty of an offence and liable on summary conviction to a fine not exceeding level 3 on the standard scale.

(3) If, in a case in which an immobilisation device would have been fixed to a vehicle but for paragraph (1)(b), the vehicle was not being used—

(a) in accordance with regulations under section 21A of the Chronically Sick and Disabled Persons Act 1970; and
(b) in circumstances falling within section 117(1A)(b) of the Road Traffic Regulation Act 1984 (use where a disabled person's concession would be available by virtue of displaying a non-GB badge),

the person in charge of the vehicle shall be guilty of an offence and liable on summary conviction to a fine not exceeding level 3 on the standard scale.

(4) An immobilisation device must not be fixed to a vehicle which is in a parking place in respect of a contravention consisting of, or arising out of, a failure—

(a) to pay a parking charge with respect to the vehicle;
(b) properly to display a ticket or parking device; or
(c) to remove the vehicle from a parking place by the end of the period for which the appropriate charge was paid,

until the appropriate period has elapsed since the service of a penalty charge notice under regulation 9 in respect of the contravention.

(5) For the purposes of paragraph (4) the appropriate period is—

(a) in the case of a vehicle as respects which there are 3 or more penalty charges outstanding, 15 minutes;
(b) in any other case 30 minutes.

NOTES

Regulations under the Chronically Sick and Disabled Persons Act 1970, s 21
See SI 2000/682 and SI 2000/1786.

[1142]

Release of immobilised vehicles

14 (1) A vehicle to which an immobilisation device has been fixed in accordance with regulation 12 may only be released from that device by or under the direction of a person authorised by the enforcement authority to give such a direction.

(2) Subject to paragraph (1), such a vehicle shall be released from the device on payment in any manner specified in the notice fixed to the vehicle under regulation 12(2) of—

(a) the penalty charge payable in respect of the parking contravention; and
(b) such charge in respect of the release as may be required by the enforcement authority.

NOTES

Such charge in respect of the release as may be required by the enforcement authority
In the case of enforcement authorities in England outside Greater London, the charge payable under reg 14(2)(b) must be £40; see SI 2007/3487, Schedule, para 4.

[1143]

PART 4
ADJUDICATORS

Discharge of functions relating to adjudicators in Greater London

15 (1) The functions of the London local authorities and Transport for London relating to adjudicators under section 81 of the 2004 Act and under regulations 17 and 18 shall be discharged jointly, under arrangements made under section 101(5) of the Local Government Act 1972, by a single joint committee appointed by those authorities and Transport for London under section 102(1)(b) of that Act.

(2) The arrangements for the discharge of functions by a single joint committee under section 73 of the Road Traffic Act 1991 which were—

(a) made between the London local authorities and Transport for London; and

(b) subsisting immediately before the coming into force of these Regulations,

shall continue in force and have effect as if made under this regulation, until such time as they are varied or replaced.

NOTES

Road Traffic Act 1991, s 73 Repealed by the Traffic Management Act 2004, s 98, Sch 12, Pt 1, as from 31 March 2008 in relation to England (see SI 2007/2053).

[1144]

Discharge of functions relating to adjudicators outside Greater London

16 (1) The functions of the non-London enforcement authorities relating to adjudicators under section 81 of the 2004 Act and under regulations 17 and 18 shall be discharged jointly, under arrangements made under section 101(5) of the Local Government Act 1972, by a joint committee or joint committees appointed under section 102(1)(b) of that Act of which at least three of the non-London enforcement authorities are constituent authorities.

(2) The constituent authorities of a joint committee may include county or county borough councils in Wales.

(3) Any arrangements for the discharge of functions by a joint committee under section 73 of the Road Traffic Act 1991, as that section was applied to local authorities outside Greater London, which were—

(a) made between local authorities outside Greater London; and

(b) subsisting immediately before the coming into force of these Regulations,

shall continue in force and shall have effect as if made under this regulation, until such time as those arrangements are varied or replaced.

NOTES

Road Traffic Act 1991, s 73 Repealed by the Traffic Management Act 2004, s 98, Sch 12, Pt 1, as from 31 March 2008 in relation to England (see SI 2007/2053).

[1145]

Appointment of adjudicators

17 (1) The relevant enforcement authorities shall appoint such number of adjudicators for the purposes of Part 6 of the 2004 Act on such terms as they may decide.

(2) Any decision by those authorities to appoint a person as an adjudicator shall not have effect without the consent of the Lord Chancellor.

(3) Any decision by those authorities—

(a) not to re-appoint a person as an adjudicator; or

(b) to remove a person from his office as an adjudicator,

shall not have effect without the consent of the Lord Chancellor and of the Lord Chief Justice.

(4) The Lord Chief Justice may nominate a judicial office holder (as defined in section 109(4) of the Constitutional Reform Act 2005) to exercise his functions under paragraph (3).

(5) Adjudicators who—

(a) were appointed under section 73 of the Road Traffic Act 1991, whether by the London local authorities and Transport for London or by local authorities outside Greater London; and

(b) held office immediately before the coming into force of this regulation,

shall be treated as having been appointed under this regulation on the same terms as those on which they held office at that time.

(6) Each adjudicator shall make an annual report to the relevant enforcement authorities in accordance with such requirements as may be imposed by those authorities.

(7) The relevant authorities shall make and publish an annual report to the Secretary of State on the discharge by the adjudicators of their functions.

NOTES

Road Traffic Act 1991, s 73 Repealed by the Traffic Management Act 2004, s 98, Sch 12, Pt 1, as from 31 March 2008 in relation to England (see SI 2007/2053).

[1146]

Expenses of the relevant authorities

18 (1) In default of a decision by any of the enforcement authorities under section 81(9)(a) of the 2004 Act as to the proportions in which their expenses under section 81 of that Act are to be defrayed, the authorities concerned shall refer the issue to an arbitrator nominated by the Chartered Institute of Arbitrators for him to determine.

(2) Where the Secretary of State is satisfied that there has been a failure on the part of any of the relevant enforcement authorities to agree those proportions, he may give to the relevant joint committee such directions as are in his opinion necessary to secure that the issue is referred to arbitration in accordance with paragraph (1).

(3) In this regulation "the relevant joint committee" means the joint committee constituted under regulation 15 or 16 of which the enforcement authorities in default are constituent authorities.

[1147]

PART 5
ENFORCEMENT OF PENALTY CHARGES

The notice to owner

19 (1) Subject to regulation 20, where—

(a) a penalty charge notice has been served with respect to a vehicle under regulation 9; and

(b) the period of 28 days specified in the penalty charge notice as the period within which the penalty charge is to be paid has expired without that charge being paid,

the enforcement authority concerned may serve a notice ("a notice to owner") on the person who appears to them to have been the owner of the vehicle when the alleged contravention occurred.

(2) A notice to owner served under paragraph (1) must, in addition to the matters required to be included in it under regulation 3(3) of the Representations and Appeals Regulations, state—

(a) the date of the notice, which must be the date on which the notice is posted;

(b) the name of the enforcement authority serving the notice;

(c) the amount of the penalty charge payable;

(d) the date on which the penalty charge notice was served;

(e) the grounds on which the civil enforcement officer who served the penalty charge notice under regulation 9 believed that a penalty charge was payable with respect to the vehicle;

(f) that the penalty charge, if not already paid, must be paid within "the payment period" as defined by regulation 3(3)(a) of the Representations and Appeals Regulations;

(g) that if, after the payment period has expired, no representations have been made under regulation 4 of the Representations and Appeals Regulations and the penalty charge has not been paid, the enforcement authority may increase the penalty charge by the applicable surcharge; and

(h) the amount of the increased penalty charge.

[1148]

Time limit for service of a notice to owner

20 (1) A notice to owner may not be served after the expiry of the period of 6 months beginning with the relevant date.

(2) The relevant date—

(a) in a case where a notice to owner has been cancelled under regulation 23(5)(c) of these Regulations, is the date on which the district judge serves notice in accordance with regulation 23(5)(d);

(b) in case where a notice to owner has been cancelled under regulation 5 of the Representations and Appeals Regulations, is the date of such cancellation;

(c) in a case where payment of the penalty charge was made, or had purportedly been made, before the expiry of the period mentioned in paragraph (1) but the payment or purported payment had been cancelled or withdrawn, is the date on which the enforcement authority is notified that the payment or purported payment has been cancelled or withdrawn;

(d) in any other case, is the date on which the relevant penalty charge notice was served under regulation 9.

[1149]

Charge certificates

21 (1) Where a notice to owner is served on any person and the penalty charge to which it relates is not paid before the end of the relevant period, the authority serving the notice may serve on that person a statement (a "charge certificate") to the effect that the penalty charge in question is increased by the amount of the applicable surcharge.

(2) The relevant period, in relation to a notice to owner, is the period of 28 days beginning—

(a) where no representations are made under regulation 4 of the Representations and Appeals Regulations, with the date on which the notice to owner is served;

(b) where—

(i) such representations are made;

(ii) a notice of rejection is served by the authority concerned; and

(iii) no appeal against the notice of rejection is made,

with the date on which the notice of rejection is served;

(c) where an adjudicator has, under regulation 7(4) of the Representations and Appeals Regulations, recommended the enforcement authority to cancel the notice to owner, with the date on which the enforcement authority notifies the appellant under regulation 7(5) of those Regulations that it does not accept the recommendation; or

(d) in a case not falling within subparagraph (c) where there has been an unsuccessful appeal to an adjudicator under the Representations and Appeals Regulations against a notice of rejection, with the date on which notice of the adjudicator's decision is served on the appellant.

(3) Where an appeal against a notice of rejection is made but is withdrawn before the adjudicator serves notice of his decision, the relevant period in relation to a notice to owner is the period of 14 days beginning with the date on which the appeal is withdrawn.

(4) In this regulation—

(a) references to a "notice to owner" include a regulation 10 penalty charge notice; and

(b) "notice of rejection" has the meaning given by regulation 2 of the Representations and Appeals Regulations.

[1150]

Enforcement of charge certificate

22 Where a charge certificate has been served on any person and the increased penalty charge provided for in the certificate is not paid before the end of the period of 14 days beginning with the date on which the certificate is served, the enforcement authority may, if a county court so orders, recover the increased charge as if it were payable under a county court order.

[1151]

Invalid notices

23 (1) This regulation applies where—

(a) a county court makes an order under regulation 22;

(b) the person against whom it is made makes a witness statement complying with paragraph (2); and

(c) that statement is served on the county court which made the order, before the end of—

(i) the period of 21 days beginning with the date on which notice of the county court's order is served on him; or

(ii) such longer period as may be allowed under paragraph (4).

(2) The witness statement must state one and only one of the following—

(a) that the person making it did not receive the notice to owner in question;

(b) that he made representations to the enforcement authority under regulation 4 of the Representations and Appeals Regulations but did not receive from that authority a notice of rejection in accordance with regulation 6 of those Regulations;

(c) that he appealed to an adjudicator under regulation 7 of those Regulations against the rejection by the enforcement authority of representations made by him under regulation 4 of those Regulations but—

(i) he had no response to the appeal;

(ii) the appeal had not been determined by the time that the charge certificate had been served; or

(iii) the appeal was determined in his favour; or

(d) that he has paid the penalty charge to which the charge certificate relates.

(3) Paragraph (4) applies where it appears to a district judge, on the application of a person on whom a charge certificate has been served, that it would be unreasonable in the circumstances of his case to insist on his serving his witness statement within the period of 21 days allowed for by paragraph (1).

(4) Where this paragraph applies, the district judge may allow such longer period for service of the witness statement as he considers appropriate.

(5) Where a witness statement is served under paragraph (1)(c)—

(a) the order of the court shall be deemed to have been revoked;

(b) the charge certificate shall be deemed to have been cancelled;

(c) in the case of a statement under paragraph (2)(a), the notice to owner to which the charge certificate relates shall be deemed to have been cancelled; and

(d) the district judge shall serve written notice of the effect of service of the statement on the person making it and on the enforcement authority concerned.

(6) Subject to regulation 20, service of a witness statement under paragraph (2)(a) shall not prevent the enforcement authority from serving a fresh notice to owner.

(7) Where a witness statement has been served under paragraph (2)(b), (c) or (d), the enforcement authority shall refer the case to the adjudicator who may give such directions as he considers appropriate and the parties shall comply with those directions.

(8) A witness statement under this regulation may be served on the county court by email in accordance with Section I of Practice Direction 5B in Part 5 of the Civil Procedure Rules 1998.

(9) In this regulation—

(a) references to a "notice to owner" include a regulation 10 penalty charge notice; and

(b) "witness statement" means a statement which is a witness statement for the purposes of the Civil Procedure Rules 1998 and which is supported by a statement of truth in accordance with Part 22 of those Rules.

NOTES

Civil Procedure Rules 1998 SI 1998/3132, printed in full in the title Courts and Legal Services (Vol 5(3)).

[1152]

PART 6
FINANCIAL PROVISIONS

Setting the levels of charges applicable in Greater London

24 (1) The functions conferred on the London local authorities by Part 2 of Schedule 9 to the 2004 Act (charges applicable in Greater London) in relation to parking contraventions shall be exercised by those authorities jointly by means of the single joint committee set up in pursuance of regulation 15 ("the Joint Committee").

(2) No person who represents Transport for London on that joint committee shall take any part in any proceedings of the Joint Committee so far as they relate to the discharge by the Joint Committee of functions conferred on the London local authorities by Part 2 of Schedule 9 to the 2004 Act.

(3) Any arrangements in force immediately before the coming into force of these Regulations for the discharge of functions under sections 74 and 74A of the Road Traffic Act 1991 by means of the joint committee set up under section 73 of that Act shall continue in force and have effect as if made under this regulation, until such time as they are varied or replaced.

NOTES

Road Traffic Act 1991, ss 73, 74, 74A Repealed by the Traffic Management Act 2004, s 98, Sch 12, Pt 1, as from 31 March 2008 in relation to England (see SI 2007/2053).

[1153]

Modification of section 55 of the Road Traffic Regulation Act 1984

25 (1) Section 55 of the Road Traffic Regulation Act 1984 shall apply to enforcement authorities subject to the following modifications.

(2) For subsection (1) there shall be substituted—

"(1) An enforcement authority which is a London authority shall keep an account of—

(a) their income and expenditure under this Part of this Act in respect of designated parking places;

(b) their income and expenditure as an enforcement authority in relation to parking contraventions within paragraph 2 of Schedule 7 to the 2004 Act (parking places); and

(c) their income and expenditure as an enforcement authority in relation to parking contraventions within paragraph 3 of that Schedule (other parking matters).

(1A) An enforcement authority which is not a London authority shall keep an account of—

(a) their income and expenditure under this Part of this Act in respect of designated parking places in their area which are not in a civil enforcement area for parking contraventions;

(b) their income and expenditure under this Part of this Act in respect of designated parking places in their area which are in a civil enforcement area for parking contraventions; and

(c) their income and expenditure as an enforcement authority in relation to parking contraventions within paragraph 4 of Schedule 7 to the 2004 Act (contraventions outside London)."

(3) After subsection (3A) there shall be inserted—

"(3ZA) An enforcement authority which is a London authority shall, after each financial year, send a copy of the account kept by them under subsection (1) to the Mayor of London.

(3ZB) A copy of an account required to be sent under subsection (3ZA) shall be sent as soon as is reasonably practicable after the conclusion of the audit of the authority's accounts for the financial year in question."

(4) In subsection (10) before the definition of "London authority" there shall be inserted—

""the 2004 Act" means the Traffic Management Act 2004;

"enforcement authority" means an authority which is an enforcement authority for the purposes of paragraph 1(2), 2(5) or 8(5) of Schedule 8 to the 2004 Act (parking contraventions);".

(5) After subsection (10) there shall be inserted the following subsections—

"(11) A reference in this section to the income and expenditure of an authority as an enforcement authority is to their income and expenditure in connection with their functions under Part 6 of the 2004 Act (civil enforcement).

(12) A reference in this section to a civil enforcement area for parking contraventions is to be construed in accordance with Schedule 8 to the 2004 Act."

[1154]

Surpluses to be carried forward

26 Where, immediately before the coming into force of these Regulations there is a surplus in an account which is—

(a) kept under section 55 of the Road Traffic Regulation Act 1984 as modified in relation to that authority by an order made under Schedule 3 to the Road Traffic Act 1991; and

(b) kept by a local authority which is not a London authority,

the surplus shall be carried forward and treated as a surplus arising under section 55 as it is modified by regulation 25.

NOTES

Road Traffic Act 1991, Sch 3 Repealed by the Traffic Management Act 2004, s 98, Sch 12, Pt 1, as from 31 March 2008 in relation to England (see SI 2007/2053).

[1155]

SCHEDULE
PENALTY CHARGES NOTICES

Regulation 8

Contents of a penalty charge notice served under regulation 9

1 A penalty charge notice served under regulation 9 must, in addition to the matters required to be included in it by regulation 3(2) of the Representations and Appeals Regulations, state—

(a) the date on which the notice is served;

(b) the name of the enforcement authority;

(c) the registration mark of the vehicle involved in the alleged contravention;

(d) the date and the time at which the alleged contravention occurred;

(e) the grounds on which the civil enforcement officer serving the notice believes that a penalty charge is payable;

(f) the amount of the penalty charge;

(g) that the penalty charge must be paid not later than the last day of the period of 28 days beginning with the date on which the penalty charge notice was served;

(h) that if the penalty charge is paid not later than the last day of the period of 14 days beginning with the date on which the notice is served, the penalty charge will be reduced by the amount of any applicable discount;

(i) the manner in which the penalty charge must be paid; and

(j) that if the penalty charge is not paid before the end of the period of 28 days referred to in subparagraph (g), a notice to owner may be served by the enforcement authority on the owner of the vehicle.

Contents of a regulation 10 penalty charge notice

2 A regulation 10 penalty charge notice, in addition to the matters required to be included in it by regulation 3(4) of the Representations and Appeals Regulations, must state—

(a) the date of the notice, which must be the date on which it is posted;
(b) the matters specified in paragraphs 1(b), (c), (d), (f) and (i);
(c) the grounds on which the enforcement authority believes that a penalty charge is payable;
(d) that the penalty charge must be paid not later than the last day of the period of 28 days beginning with the date on which the penalty charge notice is served;
(e) that if the penalty charge is paid not later than the applicable date, the penalty charge will be reduced by the amount of any applicable discount;
(f) that if after the last day of the period referred to in subparagraph (d)—
  (i) no representations have been made in accordance with regulation 4 of the Representations and Appeals Regulations; and
  (ii) the penalty charge has not been paid,

  the enforcement authority may increase the penalty charge by the amount of any applicable surcharge and take steps to enforce payment of the charge as so increased;
(g) the amount of the increased penalty charge; and
(h) that the penalty charge notice is being served by post for whichever of the following reasons applies—
  (i) that the penalty charge notice is being served by post on the basis of a record produced by an approved device;
  (ii) that it is being so served, because a civil enforcement officer attempted to serve a penalty charge notice by affixing it to the vehicle or giving it to the person in charge of the vehicle but was prevented from doing so by some person; or
  (iii) that it is being so served because a civil enforcement officer had begun to prepare a penalty charge notice for service in accordance with regulation 9, but the vehicle was driven away from the place in which it was stationary before the civil enforcement officer had finished preparing the penalty charge notice or had served it in accordance with regulation 9.

3 In paragraph 2 for the purposes of subparagraph (e) the "applicable date" is—
(a) in the case of a penalty charge notice served by virtue of regulation 10(1)(a) (on the basis of a record produced by an approved device), the last day of the period of 21 days beginning with the date on which the notice was served;
(b) in any other case, the last day of the period of 14 days beginning with that date.

[1156]

CIVIL ENFORCEMENT OFFICERS (WEARING OF UNIFORMS) (ENGLAND) REGULATIONS 2007
SI 2007/3485

Authority Made by the Secretary of State for Transport under the Traffic Management Act 2004, s 76(4).
Date made 10 December 2007.
Commencement 31 March 2008.
Summary The Traffic Management Act 2004, Pt 6 (ss 72–93 and Schs 7–11) enables regulations to be made providing for a single framework for the civil enforcement of parking and other types of road traffic contraventions by local authorities. Under s 76(1) of the 2004 Act, a local authority may provide for the enforcement of road traffic contraventions for which it is the enforcement authority by civil enforcement officers.

These regulations, which apply to parking contraventions in England, specify functions which, under s 76(3) of the 2004 Act, may only be exercised by civil enforcement officers when in uniform. The specified functions are all functions conferred on such officers by or under ss 78(2)(a), (b), 79 of the 2004 Act (notification of penalty charge in respect of stationary vehicles and the immobilisation of stationary vehicles) and the Road Traffic Regulation Act 1984, s 99 (removal of vehicles).
Wales SI 2008/616 (made by the Welsh Ministers under the Traffic Management Act 2004, s 76(4), and in force on 31 March 2008), applies to parking contraventions in Wales. It specifies the same functions which, under s 76(3) of the 2004 Act, may only be exercised by civil enforcement officers when in uniform as SI 2007/3485 specifies in relation to England.

[1157]

CIVIL ENFORCEMENT OF PARKING CONTRAVENTIONS (APPROVED DEVICES) (ENGLAND) ORDER 2007
SI 2007/3486

Authority Made by the Secretary of State for Transport under the Traffic Management Act 2004, ss 89(1), (3), 92(1).
Date made 10 December 2007.
Commencement 31 March 2008.
Summary The Traffic Management Act 2004, Pt 6 (ss 72–93 and Schs 7–11) enables regulations to be made providing for a single framework for the civil enforcement of parking and other types of road traffic contraventions by local authorities; as to such regulations, see, in particular, SI 2007/3482 and SI 2007/3483. Reg 6(a) of SI 2007/3483 prohibits, in accordance with s 72(4) of the 2004 Act, the

imposition of a penalty charge for a parking contravention except on the basis of: (a) a record produced by an approved device, or (b) information given by a civil enforcement officer as to conduct observed by that officer.

This order, which applies only to England, specifies approved devices for the purposes of reg 6(a) of SI 2007/3483 (made under s 72(4)(a) of the 2004 Act). A device is an approved device if it is of a type which has been certified by the Secretary of State as one which meets the scheduled requirements (see below). A device is taken to meet the scheduled requirements if there has been produced to the Secretary of State evidence which satisfies him that it has been found by a competent authority in an EEA state to be one which meets the requirements of an EEA standard which requires a level of performance equivalent to that required by the scheduled requirements.

"EEA standard" means: (a) a standard or code of practice of a national standards body or equivalent body of any EEA state; (b) any international standard recognised for use as standard or code of practice by any EEA state; or (c) a technical specification recognised for use as a standard by a public authority of any EEA state.

The scheduled requirements are as follows:

(a) the device must include a camera which is:
   (1) securely mounted on a vehicle, a building, a post or other structure;
   (2) mounted in such a position that vehicles in relation to which parking contraventions are being committed can be surveyed by it;
   (3) connected by secure data links to a recording system; and
   (4) capable of producing, in one or more pictures, a legible image or images of the vehicle in relation to which a parking contravention was committed which show its registration mark and enough of its location to show the circumstances of the contravention;

(b) the device must include a recording system in which:
   (1) recordings are made automatically of the output from the camera or cameras surveying the vehicle and the place where a contravention is occurring;
   (2) there is used a secure and reliable recording method that records at a minimum rate of 5 frames per second;
   (3) each frame of all captured images is timed (in hours, minutes and seconds), dated and sequentially numbered automatically by means of a visual counter; and
   (4) where the device does not occupy a fixed location, it records the location from which it is being operated;

(c) the device and visual counter must:
   (1) be synchronised with a suitably independent national standard clock; and
   (2) be accurate within plus or minus 10 seconds over a 14-day period and re-synchronised to the suitably independent national standard clock at least once during that period;

(d) where the device includes a facility to print a still image, that image when printed must be endorsed with the time and date when the frame was captured and its unique number;

(e) where the device can record spoken words or other data simultaneously with visual images, the device must include a means of verifying that, in any recording produced by it, the sound track is correctly synchronised with the visual image.

The order also makes transitional provision whereby a device which is not an approved device under the order, but which was in use in Greater London immediately before 31 March 2008 for the purpose of parking enforcement in accordance with the London Local Authorities Act 2000, s 4 (service of penalty charge notice on the basis of camera-derived information), is to be treated as an approved device for a transitional period of 12 months beginning on 31 March 2008. S 4 of the 2000 Act has been repealed by the Traffic Management Act 2004, s 98, Sch 12, Pt 1 as from 31 March 2008 (see SI 2007/2053).

Wales SI 2008/1215 (made by the Welsh Ministers under the Traffic Management Act 2004, s 92(1), and in force on 22 May 2008), applies to Wales only. The order specifies approved devices of the purposes of regulations relating to the civil enforcement of parking contraventions in Wales made under s 72(4)(a) of the 2004 Act (see reg 5(a) of SI 2008/1214, noted under "Wales" to SI 2007/3483). The approved devices correspond with those specified in relation to England by SI 2007/3486 above. SI 2008/1215 also revokes and replaces the Civil Enforcement of Parking Contraventions (Approved Devices) (Wales) Order 2008, SI 2008/620.

[1158]

CIVIL ENFORCEMENT OF PARKING CONTRAVENTIONS (GUIDELINES ON LEVELS OF CHARGES) (ENGLAND) ORDER 2007

SI 2007/3487

Authority Made by the Secretary of State for Transport under the Traffic Management Act 2004, Sch 9, para 8.

Date made 10 December 2007.

Commencement 20 January 2008; see art 1(1).

General The Traffic Management Act 2004, Pt 6 (ss 72–93 and Schs 7–11) enables regulations to be made providing for a single framework for the civil enforcement of road traffic contraventions (ie parking contraventions, bus lane contraventions, London lorry ban contraventions and moving traffic contraventions) by local authorities. Pt 3 (paras 7–9) of Sch 9 to the 2004 Act provides for the setting by each enforcement authority outside Greater London of the level of charges under Pt 6 of the

Act in respect of such contraventions. The level of charges must accord with guidelines made by the appropriate national authority, except where that authority permits an enforcement authority to depart from the guidelines.

This order, which applies to England only, sets out the guidelines given by the Secretary of State for Transport for the setting by enforcement authorities outside Greater London of the level of charges for parking contraventions.

Wales SI 2008/613 (made by the Welsh Ministers under the Traffic Management Act 2004, Sch 9, para 8 and in force on 31 March 2008), applies to Wales only. The order sets out the guidelines given by the Welsh Ministers for the setting by enforcement authorities in Wales of the level of charges for parking contraventions.

[1159]

Citation, commencement, interpretation and application

1 (1) This Order may be cited as the Civil Enforcement of Parking Contraventions (Guidelines on Levels of Charges) (England) Order 2007 and shall come into force on 20th January 2008.

(2) In this Order "the General Regulations" means the Civil Enforcement of Parking Contraventions (England) General Regulations 2007.

(3) This Order applies only to England.

NOTES

Civil Enforcement of Parking Contraventions (England) General Regulations 2007 SI 2007/3483.

[1160]

Guidelines

2 The guidelines given by the Secretary of State, as appropriate national authority for England, for the setting by enforcement authorities outside Greater London of the level of charges for parking contraventions are those set out in the Schedule.

[1161]

SCHEDULE
GUIDELINES FOR THE SETTING BY ENFORCEMENT AUTHORITIES OUTSIDE GREATER LONDON OF CHARGES FOR PARKING CONTRAVENTIONS

Article 2

Scope of guidelines

1 These guidelines apply to the setting by enforcement authorities outside Greater London—

(a) of penalty charges and charges for release from immobilisation devices to be imposed by such authorities under the General Regulations; and

(b) of charges for removal, storage and disposal to be made by such authorities under section 102 of the Road Traffic Regulation Act 1984,

in respect of vehicles found on or after 31st March 2008 in civil enforcement areas for parking contraventions.

Penalty charges

2 (1) Penalty charges for parking contraventions must be set—

(a) for higher level contraventions, at the level specified in column (2) of one of the bands in table 1; and

(b) for all other contraventions, at the level specified in column (3) of the band selected for higher level contraventions.

(2) The discounted level for a penalty charge which is paid early (that is within 21 days in the case of penalty charges imposed on the basis of a record produced by an approved device under regulation 10(1)(a) of the General Regulations and 14 days in all other cases) must be set—

(a) for higher level contraventions, at the level specified in column (4);

(b) for all other contraventions, at the level set in column (5),

of the band specifying the levels of the penalty charges.

(3) The surcharged level for payment of a penalty charge after a charge certificate has been issued must be set—

(a) for higher level contraventions at the level specified in column (6);

(b) for all other contraventions at the level specified in column (7),

of the band specifying the levels of the penalty charges.

TABLE 1

(1) *Band*	*(2)* *Higher level penalty charge*	*(3)* *Lower level penalty charge*	*(4)* *Higher level penalty charge paid early*	*(5)* *Lower level penalty charge paid early*	*(6)* *Higher level penalty charge paid after service of charge certificate*	*(7)* *Lower level penalty charge paid after service of charge certificate*
1	£60	£40	£30	£20	£90	£60
2	£70	£50	£35	£25	£105	£75

(4) An enforcement authority may set penalty charges in accordance with different bands in the table in different parts of its area, provided that all the charges in each part of its area are set in accordance with the same band.

(5) "Higher level contraventions" are those falling within one or more of the descriptions of contravention listed in column (2) of table 2 (on street contraventions) or table 3 (off street contraventions), being descriptions based on Version 6.5 of the Standard PCN Codes used by local authorities engaged in parking enforcement and have the code number shown in column (1) of that table.

TABLE 2

(1) Code	*(2) Description*
01	Parked in a restricted street during prescribed hours
02	Parked or loading/unloading in a restricted street where waiting and loading/unloading restrictions are in force
12	Parked in a residents' or shared use parking place without clearly displaying either a permit or voucher or pay and display ticket issued for that place
14	Parked in an electric vehicles' charging place during restricted hours without charging
16	Parked in a permit space without displaying a valid permit
18	Using a vehicle in a parking place in connection with the sale or offering or exposing for sale of goods when prohibited
20	Parked in a loading gap marked by a yellow line
21	Parked in a suspended bay/space or part of bay/space
23	Parked in a parking place or area not designated for that class of vehicle
25	Parked in a loading place during restricted hours without loading
26	Vehicle parked more than 50 centimetres from the edge of the carriageway and not within a designated parking place
27	Parked adjacent to a dropped footway
40	Parked in a designated disabled person's parking place without clearly displaying a valid disabled person's badge
41	Parked in a parking place designated for diplomatic vehicles
42	Parked in a parking place designated for police vehicles
45	Parked on a taxi rank
46	Stopped where prohibited (on a red route or clearway)
47	Stopped on a restricted bus stop or stand
48	Stopped in a restricted area outside a school
49	Parked wholly or partly on a cycle track
55	A commercial vehicle parked in a restricted street in contravention of an overnight waiting ban
56	Parked in contravention of a commercial vehicle waiting restriction
57	Parked in contravention of a coach ban
61	A heavy commercial vehicle wholly or partly parked on a footway, verge or land between two carriageways

(1) Code	*(2) Description*
62	Parked with one or more wheels on any part of an urban road other than a carriageway (footway parking)
99	Stopped on a pedestrian crossing and/or crossing area marked by zig-zags

TABLE 3

(1) Code	*(2) Description*
70	Parked in a loading area during restricted hours without reasonable excuse
74	Using a vehicle in a parking place in connection with the sale or offering or exposing for sale of goods when prohibited
81	Parked in a restricted area in a car park
85	Parked in a permit bay without clearly displaying a valid permit
87	Parked in a disabled person's parking space without clearly displaying a valid disabled person's badge
89	Vehicle parked exceeds maximum weight and/or height and/or length permitted in the area
91	Parked in a car park or area not designated for that class of vehicle
92	Parked causing an obstruction

Charges for the removal, storage and disposal of vehicles

3 Charges for the removal, storage and disposal of vehicles found in a civil enforcement area must be those in table 4.

TABLE 4

(1) *Item*	*(2)* *Type of charge*	*(3)* *Amount of charge*
1	Vehicle removal charge	£105.00
2	Vehicle storage charge	£12 for each day, or part of day, during which the vehicle is impounded
3	Vehicle disposal charge	£50.00

Release of vehicle from an immobilisation device under Section 79 of the Traffic Management Act 2004

4 The charge payable under regulation 14(2)(b) of the General Regulations for the release of a vehicle from an immobilisation device must be £40.

Saving for powers of the Secretary of State

5 Nothing in these guidelines prejudices or affects the power of the Secretary of State, under paragraph 8(3) of Schedule 9 to the Traffic Management Act 2004, to permit an enforcement authority to depart from these guidelines.

[1162]

CHANNEL TUNNEL (SAFETY) ORDER 2007

SI 2007/3531

Authority Made by the Secretary of State for Transport under the Channel Tunnel Act 1987, s 11(1)(a), (g), (2)(a), (b), (3)(a), (b), (f).

Date made 13 December 2007.

Commencement 4 July 2008; see the *London, Edinburgh and Belfast Gazettes*, 14 July 2008.

Summary This order brings into effect, for the Channel Tunnel, Directive 2004/49/EC of the European Parliament and of the Council on safety on the Community's railways (OJ L164, 30.04.2004, p 44; corrected version published at OJ L220, 21.06.2004, p 16) ("the Railway Safety Directive"). It does so by giving the force of law to a Regulation of the Intergovernmental Commission on the Safety of the Channel Fixed Link ("the Regulation") made on 24 January 2007 on behalf of the Governments of the United Kingdom of Great Britain and Northern Ireland and the French Republic. The key provisions of the Regulation (the text of which is set out in the Schedule to the order) concern the following matters:

(a) the duties and responsibilities of the Intergovernmental Commission (the safety authority for the Channel Tunnel), the Concessionaires (the infrastructure manager for the Channel Tunnel), and railway undertakings;
(b) safety management systems, safety authorisation for the Concessionaires, and certification for railway undertakings;
(d) the training of train drivers and staff performing vital safety tasks;
(e) the authorisation of railway undertakings' rolling stock; and
(f) investigation into accidents and incidents in the Channel Tunnel.

Art 3 of the order provides that the Regulation has the force of law. Subject to certain exceptions, art 4 requires the Office of Rail Regulation to make adequate arrangements for the enforcement of the Regulation, and applies various enforcement provisions of the Health and Safety at Work etc Act 1974 for this purpose.

Article 5 provides rights of appeal to the Office of Rail Regulation for the benefit of railway undertakings, or train drivers or staff performing vital safety tasks, if they are denied any entitlement conferred on them by arts 56–60 of the Regulation (access to training facilities).

Art 6 concerns civil liability. In particular, it provides that breach of a duty, requirement or prohibition imposed by certain articles of the Regulation is, in so far as it causes damage, actionable. By art 7, nothing in this order or the Regulation prejudices or affects the provisions of the Railways and Transport Safety Act 2003, Pt 1 or SI 2005/1992. Art 8 empowers the Intergovernmental Commission to impose charges reflecting its administrative costs of processing applications for certain certificates and authorisations under the Regulation. Art 9 amends SI 2005/3207, in the titles Criminal Law and Nationality and Immigration. Art 10 amends SI 2006/599, in this title.

[1163]

CONCESSIONARY BUS TRAVEL (PERMITS) (ENGLAND) REGULATIONS 2008
SI 2008/417

Authority Made by the Secretary of State for Transport under the Greater London Authority Act 1999, ss 243(7), 420(1) and the Transport Act 2000, ss 145A(5), 160.
Date made 20 February 2008.
Commencement 21 March 2008.
Amendment Amended by SI 2008/2091.
Summary These regulations make provision relating to the free concessionary travel permits to be issued to elderly persons and disabled persons by a travel concession authority in England under the Transport Act 2000, s 145A(4), and by a London authority under the Greater London Authority Act 1999, Pt IV, Chapter VIII.

Reg 2 prescribes the form of a permit, and requires it to contain an electronic chip. The period of validity of a permit must not exceed five years from the date on which the permit starts to have effect. Reg 3 makes transitional provision enabling an authority in Greater London, on or before 31 March 2010, to issue a permit in the form of an adhesive sticker, fixed to an existing concessionary permit, which does not contain an electronic chip. The expiry date on such a permit may not be later than 31 March 2010. Reg 4 makes transitional provision enabling an authority outside Greater London to issue a temporary permit in a prescribed form which does not include an electronic chip. The expiry date of such permit must be 30 September 2008. Reg 5 sets out the manner in which a date required to be included in a permit must be expressed.

[1164]

CROSS-BORDER RAILWAY SERVICES (WORKING TIME) REGULATIONS 2008
SI 2008/1660

Authority Made by the Secretary of State for Transport under the European Communities Act 1972, s 2(2).
Date made 25 June 2008.
Commencement 27 July 2008; see reg 1(1).
Interpretation See reg 2, Sch 1, para 2, Sch 2, para 8(1).
General These regulations implement Council Directive 2005/47/EC on the Agreement between the Community of European Railways (CER) and the European Transport Workers' Federation (ETF) on certain aspects of the working conditions of mobile workers engaged in interoperable cross-border services in the railway sector (OJ L195, 27.07.2005, p 15). They apply to workers ("cross-border workers") whose daily shift includes more than one hour on train services going through the Channel Tunnel, in respect of which at least two network safety requirement certifications are required.

Under the regulations cross-border workers are entitled to rests and breaks from work, and limits are imposed on driving time. The employer of a cross-border worker is required to keep and retain records which show whether the requirements of the regulations are being complied with. Further provisions concern the enforcement of the regulations and offences. The regulations also amend certain primary legislation (see Sch 3) and SI 1998/1833, in the title Employment.

[1165]

Citation, commencement and extent

1 (1) These Regulations may be cited as the Cross-border Railway Services (Working Time) Regulations 2008 and come into force on 27th July 2008.

(2) These Regulations extend to Great Britain only.

[1166]

Interpretation

2 In these Regulations—

"collective agreement" means a collective agreement within the meaning of section 178 of the Trade Union and Labour Relations (Consolidation) Act 1992, the trade union parties to which are independent trade unions within the meaning of section 5 of that Act;

"cross-border worker" means any worker who is a member of a train crew and who is assigned to interoperable cross-border services for more than one hour on a daily shift basis;

"driver" means a cross-border worker in charge of operating a traction unit;

"employer", in relation to a cross-border worker, means the person by whom the worker is (or where the employment has ceased, was) employed;

"employment", in relation to a cross-border worker, means employment under the worker's contract, and "employed" is to be construed accordingly;

"inspector" means a person appointed under paragraph 1 of Schedule 2;

"interoperable cross-border services" are services through the tunnel system, as defined by section 1(7) of the Channel Tunnel Act 1987, in respect of which at least two network safety requirement certifications are required, as stipulated by Article 10(2)(b) and (4) of Directive 2004/49/EC of the European Parliament and the Council of 29th April 2004;

"leave year" for a cross-border worker is the year beginning on—

(a) such date as is provided for in a relevant agreement, or
(b) if there are no provisions of a relevant agreement which apply, on 1 January;

"relevant agreement", in relation to a cross-border worker, means—

(a) a workforce agreement which applies to the worker,
(b) any provision of a collective agreement which forms part of a contract between the worker and the worker's employer, or
(c) any other agreement in writing which is legally enforceable as between the worker and the employer;

"relevant training" means work experience provided pursuant to a training course or programme, training for employment, or both, other than work experience or training—

(a) the immediate provider of which is an educational institution or a person whose main business is the provision of training, and
(b) which is provided on a course run by that institution or person;

"rest period" means any period which is not working time;

"week" means a period of seven days which starts at such time as is determined for the purposes of these Regulations by a relevant agreement, or in default of such a determination at midnight at the beginning of Monday;

"workforce agreement" means an agreement between an employer and workers employed by the employer or their representatives in respect of which the conditions set out in Schedule 1 to these Regulations are satisfied; and

"working time", in relation to a cross-border worker, means—

(a) any period during which the worker is working, at the employer's disposal and carrying out the worker's activities or duties,
(b) any period during which the worker is receiving relevant training, and
(c) any additional period which is to be treated as working time for the purpose of these Regulations under a relevant agreement.

NOTES

Directive 2004/49/EC OJ L164, 30.04.2004, p 44.

[1167]

Daily rest

3 (1) A cross-border worker is entitled in each 24 hour period to a rest period that is a minimum number of consecutive hours ("a daily rest period").

(2) In the case of a daily rest period that can be taken at the cross-border worker's normal place of residence ("a daily rest period at home") the minimum period is twelve hours, but this is subject to paragraphs (3) and (4).

(3) Once a week a daily rest period at home may be reduced by the employer of a cross-border worker to a minimum period of nine hours, but this is subject to paragraph (7).

(4) If a daily rest period at home is reduced by the employer below twelve hours, the minimum period for the next daily rest period at home is increased by the number of hours, including any part of an hour, by which the earlier period was less than twelve hours.

(5) In the case of a daily rest period that cannot be taken at the cross-border worker's normal place of residence ("a daily rest period away from home") the minimum period is eight hours.

(6) When there is a daily rest period away from home the cross-border worker is entitled to work that is scheduled to enable the worker to take the next daily rest period as a daily rest period at home.

(7) If a daily rest period at home is scheduled to be between two daily rest periods away from home, the daily rest period at home must not be reduced under paragraph (3) below ten hours.

[1168]

Break for sole driver

4 (1) Where there is only one driver and the driver's scheduled daily working time is six or more hours the driver is entitled to a break, but this paragraph and paragraphs (2) to (4) are subject to paragraphs (5) to (7).

(2) The minimum length of the scheduled break must be 30 minutes, but this is subject to paragraph (3).

(3) In the case of a driver whose daily scheduled working time is more than eight hours the minimum length of the scheduled break must be 45 minutes.

(4) At least 15 minutes of the break must be scheduled to be between the third and sixth hour of the working time.

(5) If a train service is delayed the time and duration of a driver's entitlement to a break under this regulation may be adapted during the working day.

(6) If possible under the timetable for the train service the total time of the adapted break entitlement must be at least equal to the minimum scheduled break entitlement under the relevant paragraph of this regulation.

(7) The time and duration of the break entitlement must be sufficient to ensure the effective recuperation of the worker.

[1169]

Breaks for drivers

5 (1) A driver who is not entitled to a break under regulation 4 but whose scheduled daily working time is more than six hours is entitled to a break, but this paragraph and paragraphs (2) and (3) are subject to paragraph (4).

(2) The details of the break to which a driver is entitled under paragraph (1), including its duration and the terms on which it is granted, must be in accordance with any provisions for the purposes of this regulation which are contained in a collective agreement or a workforce agreement.

(3) Subject to the provisions of any applicable collective agreement or workforce agreement, the break provided for in paragraph (1) is an uninterrupted period of not less than 20 minutes.

(4) The employer of a driver may require the driver to work during a period that would, but for this paragraph, be a time when the driver is entitled to a break under this regulation; and when a driver is required to do so—

(a) the employer must wherever possible allow the driver to take an equivalent period of compensatory rest, and

(b) in exceptional cases in which it is not possible, for objective reasons, to grant such a period of rest, the employer must afford the driver such protection as may be appropriate to safeguard the driver's health and safety.

[1170]

Breaks for other workers

6 (1) A cross-border worker who is not a driver and whose scheduled daily working time is more than six hours is entitled to a break.

(2) The minimum length of the scheduled break must be 30 minutes.

[1171]

Weekly rest

7 (1) A cross-border worker is entitled every week to an uninterrupted rest period of 24 hours (a "rest day") in addition to the minimum daily rest entitlement under regulation 3 and any days taken as part of the worker's entitlement to annual leave.

(2) A cross-border worker is entitled to 104 rest days each leave year, but this paragraph and paragraphs (3) and (5) are subject to paragraph (6).

(3) A cross-border worker is entitled each leave year on at least 24 occasions to take a rest day that is immediately followed by another rest day (a "two-day rest period"), but this is subject to paragraph (4).

(4) If there are more than two consecutive rest days, each rest day only counts towards one two-day rest period.

(5) A cross-border worker is entitled each leave year on at least twelve occasions to take a two-day rest period over a week-end, so that the period includes a part or the whole of a Saturday and a part or the whole of a Sunday.

(6) Paragraphs (2), (3) and (5) apply only to a person who is a cross-border worker throughout a complete leave year that begins after 26th July 2008, but this is subject to paragraphs (8) to (11).

(7) If a leave year of a person who was a cross-border worker on 27th July 2008 begins before that date, but has not ended by that date, the entitlements under paragraphs (2), (3) and (5) apply proportionately to the relevant part year, but this is subject to paragraphs (10) and (11).

(8) If a person's employment as a cross-border worker begins after 26th July 2008 and part way through a leave year, the entitlements under paragraphs (2), (3) and (5) apply proportionately to the relevant part year, but this is subject to paragraphs (10) and (11).

(9) The "relevant part year" means—

- (a) in paragraph (7), the period beginning on 27th July 2008 and ending when the leave year ends; and
- (b) in paragraph (8), the period beginning on the date that the person's employment as a cross-border worker begins and ending when the leave year ends.

(10) If applying paragraphs (2), (3) and (5) proportionately would, but for this paragraph, result in an entitlement to a number of rest days or a number of two-day rest periods that is not a whole number, the entitlement is to the number rounded to the nearest whole number, but if the number is exactly half-way between the two nearest whole numbers the number is rounded up.

(11) Paragraphs (7) and (8) apply only if the person is a cross-border worker throughout the relevant part year.

[1172]

Driving time

8 (1) Between two daily rest periods taken in accordance with regulation 3 a driver's scheduled driving time must not exceed—

- (a) in the case of a shift that is scheduled to include at least three hours of night time, eight hours; and
- (b) in any other case, nine hours.

(2) In any period of two weeks a driver's scheduled driving time must not exceed 80 hours.

(3) The employer of the driver must take all reasonable steps to ensure that this regulation is complied with.

(4) In this regulation—

"night time" means a period which—

(a) is not less than seven hours,
(b) includes the period between midnight and 5 am, and
(c) is determined for the purposes of this regulation by a relevant agreement, or, in default of such a determination, the period which is between 11 pm and 6 am; and

"scheduled driving time" means the time scheduled for the driver to be in charge of the traction unit, excluding the scheduled time to prepare or shut down the unit, but including any scheduled interruptions when the driver is to remain in charge.

[1173]

Records

9 (1) The employer of a cross-border worker must—

(a) keep records which are adequate to show whether these Regulations are being complied with in respect of that worker, including information as to actual hours worked; and
(b) retain those records for at least one year after the end of the period covered by those records.

(2) The employer of a cross-border worker must, upon request, provide to—

(a) a cross-border worker, or (as the case may be)
(b) the Office of Rail Regulation,

a copy of the records retained in accordance with paragraph (1) in respect of that cross-border worker.

[1174]

Enforcement

10 (1) It is the duty of the Office of Rail Regulation to make adequate arrangements for the enforcement of regulations 8(3) and 9.

(2) The provisions of Schedule 2 apply in relation to the enforcement of regulations 8(3) and 9.

[1175]

Offences

11 (1) An employer of a cross-border worker who fails to comply with regulation 8(3) or regulation 9 is guilty of an offence.

(2) The provisions of paragraph (3) apply where an inspector is exercising or has exercised any power conferred by Schedule 2.

(3) It is an offence for a person—

(a) to contravene any requirement imposed by the inspector under paragraph 2 of Schedule 2;
(b) to prevent or attempt to prevent any other person from appearing before the inspector or from answering any question to which the inspector may by virtue of paragraph 2(2)(e) of Schedule 2 require an answer;
(c) to contravene any requirement or prohibition imposed by an improvement notice or a prohibition notice (including any such notice as is modified on appeal);
(d) intentionally to obstruct the inspector in the exercise or performance of his powers or duties;
(e) to use or disclose any information in contravention of paragraph 8 of Schedule 2;
(f) to make a statement which the person knows to be false or recklessly to make a statement which is false, where the statement is made in purported compliance with a requirement to furnish any information imposed by or under these Regulations.

(4) An employer guilty of an offence under paragraph (1) is liable—

(a) on summary conviction, to a fine not exceeding the statutory maximum;
(b) on conviction on indictment, to a fine.

(5) A person guilty of an offence under paragraph (3) is liable to the penalty prescribed in relation to that provision by paragraphs (6), (7) or (8) as the case may be.

(6) A person guilty of an offence under paragraph (3)(a), (b) or (d) is liable on summary conviction to a fine not exceeding level 5 on the standard scale.

(7) A person guilty of an offence under paragraph (3)(c) is liable—

(a) on summary conviction, to imprisonment for a term not exceeding three months, or a fine not exceeding the statutory maximum;

(b) on conviction on indictment, to imprisonment for a term not exceeding two years, or a fine, or both.

(8) A person guilty of an offence under paragraph (3)(e) or (f), is liable—

(a) on summary conviction, to a fine not exceeding the statutory maximum;

(b) on conviction on indictment—

(i) if the offence is under paragraph (3)(e), to imprisonment for a term not exceeding two years or a fine or both;

(ii) if the offence is under paragraph (3)(f), to a fine.

(9) The provisions set out in regulations 12 to 16 apply in relation to the offences provided for in paragraphs (1) and (3).

[1176]

Offences due to fault of other person

12 Where the commission by any person of an offence is due to the act or default of some other person, that other person is guilty of the offence, and a person may be charged with and convicted of the offence by virtue of this paragraph whether or not proceedings are taken against the first-mentioned person.

[1177]

Offences by bodies corporate

13 (1) Where an offence committed by a body corporate is proved to have been committed with the consent or connivance of, or to have been attributable to any neglect on the part of, any director, manager, secretary or other similar officer of the body corporate or a person who was purporting to act in any such capacity, that person as well as the body corporate is guilty of that offence and liable to be proceeded against and punished accordingly.

(2) Where the affairs of a body corporate are managed by its members, the preceding paragraph apply in relation to the acts and defaults of a member in connection with the member's functions of management as if the member were a director of the body corporate.

[1178]

Restriction on institution of proceedings in England and Wales

14 Proceedings for an offence must not, in England and Wales, be instituted except by an inspector or by or with the consent of the Director of Public Prosecutions.

[1179]

Prosecutions by inspectors

15 (1) An inspector, although not of counsel or a solicitor, may prosecute before a magistrate's court proceedings for an offence under these Regulations if authorised in that behalf by the Office of Rail Regulation.

(2) This regulation does not apply to Scotland.

[1180]

Power of court to order cause of offence to be remedied

16 (1) Where a person is convicted of an offence in respect of any matters which appear to the court to be matters which it is in the person's power to remedy, the court may, in addition to or instead of imposing any punishment, order the person, within such time as may be fixed by the order, to take such steps as may be specified in the order for remedying the matters.

(2) The time fixed by an order under paragraph (1) may be extended or further extended by order of the court on an application made before the end of that time as originally fixed or as extended under this paragraph, as the case may be.

(3) Where a person is ordered under paragraph (1) to remedy any matters, that person shall not be liable under these Regulations in respect of those matters in so far as they continue during the time fixed by the order or any further time allowed under paragraph (2).

[1181]

Remedies

17 (1) A cross-border worker may present a complaint to an employment tribunal that his employer has refused to permit the worker to exercise any right the worker has under regulations 3 to 7.

(2) An employment tribunal may not consider a complaint under this regulation unless it is presented—

- (a) before the end of the period of three months beginning with the date on which it is alleged that the exercise of the right should have been permitted (or in the case of a rest period extending over more than one day, the date on which it should have been permitted to begin);
- (b) within such further period as the tribunal considers reasonable in a case where it is satisfied that it was not reasonably practicable for the complaint to be presented before the end of that period of three months.

(3) Where the period within which a complaint must be presented in accordance with paragraph (2) is extended by regulation 15 of the Employment Act 2002 (Dispute Resolution) Regulations 2004, the period within which the complaint must be presented is the extended period rather than the period in paragraph (2).

(4) Where an employment tribunal finds a complaint under paragraph (1) well-founded, the tribunal—

- (a) must make a declaration to that effect, and
- (b) may make an award of compensation to be paid by the employer to the cross-border worker.

(5) The amount of the compensation is to be such as the tribunal considers just and equitable in all the circumstances having regard to—

- (a) the employer's default in refusing to permit the worker to exercise the worker's right, and
- (b) any loss sustained by the worker which is attributable to the matters complained of.

NOTES

Employment Act 2002 (Dispute Resolution) Regulations 2004 SI 2004/752 (lapsed). The statutory dispute resolution procedures formerly contained in the Employment Act 2002, Pt III (ss 29–40 and Schs 2–4), under which SI 2004/752 was made, have largely been repealed by the Employment Act 2008, ss 1, 20, Schedule, Pt 1 (for transitional provisions and savings, see SI 2008/3232, in the title Employment). Provision is made instead for the Advisory, Conciliation and Arbitration Service to issue a Code of Practice under the Trade Union and Labour Relations (Consolidation) Act 1992, Pt IV relating exclusively or primarily to procedure for the resolution of disputes.

[1182]

Restrictions on contracting out

18 (1) Any provision in an agreement (whether a contract of employment or not) is void in so far as it purports—

- (a) to exclude or limit the operation of any provision of these Regulations, save in so far as these Regulations provide for an agreement to have that effect, or
- (b) to preclude a person from bringing proceedings under these Regulations before an employment tribunal.

(2) Paragraph (1) does not apply to—

- (a) any agreement to refrain from instituting or continuing proceedings where a conciliation officer has taken action under section 18 of the Employment Tribunals Act 1996 (conciliation); or
- (b) any agreement to refrain from instituting or continuing proceedings under regulation 17, if the conditions regulating compromise agreements under these Regulations are satisfied in relation to the agreement.

(3) For the purposes of paragraph (2)(b) the conditions regulating compromise agreements under these Regulations are that—

(a) the agreement must be in writing,

(b) the agreement must relate to the particular complaint,

(c) the cross-border worker must have received advice from a relevant independent adviser as to the terms and effect of the proposed agreement and, in particular, its effect on the worker's ability to pursue the worker's rights before an employment tribunal,

(d) there must be in force, when the adviser gives the advice, a contract of insurance, or an indemnity provided for members of a profession or a professional body, covering the risk of a claim by the cross-border worker in respect of loss arising in consequence of the advice,

(e) the agreement must identify the adviser, and

(f) the agreement must state that the conditions regulating compromise agreements under these Regulations are satisfied.

(4) A person is a relevant independent adviser for the purposes of paragraph (3)(c)—

(a) if the person is a qualified lawyer,

(b) if the person is an officer, official, employee or member of an independent trade union who has been certified in writing by the trade union as competent to give advice and as authorised to do so on behalf of the trade union, or

(c) if the person works at an advice centre (whether as an employee or as a volunteer) and has been certified in writing by the centre as competent to give advice and as authorised to do so on behalf of the centre.

(5) But a person is not a relevant independent adviser for the purposes of paragraph (3)(c)—

(a) if the person is employed by or is acting in the matter for the employer or an associated employer,

(b) in the case of a person within paragraph (4)(b), if the trade union is the employer or an associated employer, or

(c) in the case of a person within paragraph (4)(c), if the cross-border worker makes a payment for the advice received from the adviser.

(6) In paragraph (4)(a), "qualified lawyer" means—

(a) as respects England and Wales, a barrister (whether in practice as such or employed to give legal advice), a solicitor who holds a practising certificate, or a person other than a barrister or solicitor who is an authorised advocate or authorised litigator (within the meaning of the Courts and Legal Services Act 1990); and

(b) as respects Scotland, an advocate (whether in practice as such or employed to give legal advice), or a solicitor who holds a practicing certificate.

(7) A person is to be treated as being a qualified lawyer within paragraph (6)(a) if the person is a Fellow of the Institute of Legal Executives employed by a solicitors' practice.

(8) For the purposes of paragraph (5) any two employers are to be treated as associated if—

(a) one is a company of which the other (directly or indirectly) has control; or

(b) both are companies of which a third person (directly or indirectly) has control;

and "associated employer" is to be construed accordingly.

NOTES

Authorised advocate or authorised litigator within the meaning of the Courts and Legal Services Act 1990 See s 119(1) of the 1990 Act. The definitions of these expressions in s 119(1) are repealed by the Legal Services Act 2007, ss 208(1), 210, Sch 21, paras 83, 97(1), (2), Sch 23, as from a day to be appointed by order.

[1183]

Amendments to legislation

19 Schedule 3 has effect.

[1184]

SCHEDULE 1
WORKFORCE AGREEMENTS

Regulation 2

1 An agreement is a workforce agreement for the purposes of these Regulations if the following conditions are satisfied—

(a) the agreement is in writing;
(b) it has effect for a specified period not exceeding five years;
(c) it applies either—
 (i) to all of the relevant members of the workforce, or
 (ii) to all of the relevant members of the workforce who belong to a particular group;
(d) the agreement is signed—
 (i) in the case of an agreement of the kind referred to in sub-paragraph (c)(i), by the representatives of the workforce, and in the case of an agreement of the kind referred to in sub-paragraph (c)(ii) by the representatives of the group to which the agreement applies (excluding, in either case, any representative not a relevant member of the workforce on the date on which the agreement was first made available for signature), or
 (ii) if the employer employed 20 or fewer workers on the date referred to in sub-paragraph (d)(i), either by the appropriate representatives in accordance with that sub-paragraph or by the majority of the workers employed by him;
(e) before the agreement was made available for signature, the employer provided all the workers to whom it was intended to apply on the date on which it came into effect with copies of the text of the agreement and such guidance as those workers might reasonably require in order to understand it fully.

2 In this Schedule—

"a particular group" is a group of the relevant members of a workforce who undertake a particular function, work at a particular workplace or belong to a particular department or unit within their employer's business;

"relevant members of the workforce" are all of the workers employed by a particular employer, excluding any worker whose terms and conditions of employment are provided for, wholly or in part, in a collective agreement;

"representatives of the workforce" are workers duly elected to represent the relevant members of the workforce;

"representatives of the group" are workers duly elected to represent the members of a particular group, and representatives are "duly elected" if the election at which they were elected satisfied the requirements of paragraph 3 of this Schedule.

3 The requirements concerning elections referred to in paragraph 2 are that—

(a) the number of representatives to be elected is determined by the employer;
(b) the candidates for election as representatives of the workforce are relevant members of the workforce, and the candidates for election as representatives of a group are members of the group;
(c) no worker who is eligible to be a candidate is unreasonably excluded from standing for election;
(d) all the relevant members of the workforce are entitled to vote for representatives of the workforce, and all the members of a particular group are entitled to vote for representatives of the group;
(e) the workers entitled to vote may vote for as many candidates as there are representatives to be elected;
(f) the election is conducted so as to secure that—
 (i) so far as is reasonably practicable, those voting do so in secret, and
 (ii) the votes given at the election are fairly and accurately counted.

[1185]

SCHEDULE 2
ENFORCEMENT

Regulation 10

Appointment of inspectors

1 (1) The Office of Rail Regulation may appoint as inspectors (under whatever title it may from time to time determine) such persons having suitable qualifications as it thinks necessary for carrying into effect these Regulations within its field of responsibility, and may terminate any appointment made under this paragraph.

(2) Every appointment of a person as an inspector under this paragraph must be made by an instrument in writing specifying which of the powers conferred on inspectors by these Regulations are to be exercisable by the person appointed; and an inspector in right of an appointment under this paragraph—

(a) is entitled to exercise only such of those powers as are so specified; and
(b) is entitled to exercise the powers so specified only within the field of responsibility of the Office of Rail Regulation.

(3) So much of an inspector's instrument of appointment as specifies the powers which the inspector is entitled to exercise may be varied by the Office of Rail Regulation.

(4) An inspector must, if so required when exercising or seeking to exercise any power conferred on the inspector by these Regulations, produce the inspector's instrument of appointment or a duly authenticated copy of it.

Powers of inspectors

2 (1) Subject to the provisions of paragraph 1 and this paragraph, an inspector may, for the purpose of carrying into effect these Regulations within the field of responsibility of the Office of Rail Regulation, exercise the powers set out in sub-paragraph (2).

(2) The powers of an inspector referred to in sub-paragraph (1) are the following, namely—

(a) at any reasonable time (or, in a situation which in the inspector's opinion is or may be dangerous, at any time) to enter any premises which the inspector has reason to believe it is necessary for the inspector to enter for the purpose mentioned in sub-paragraph (1);
(b) to take with the inspector a constable if the inspector has reasonable cause to apprehend any serious obstruction in the execution of his duty;
(c) without prejudice to Paragraph (b), on entering any premises by virtue of Paragraph (a) to take with the inspector—
  (i) any other person duly authorised by the Office of Rail Regulation; and
  (ii) any equipment or materials required for any purpose for which the power of entry is being exercised;
(d) to make such examination and investigation as may in any circumstances be necessary for the purpose mentioned in sub-paragraph (1);
(e) to require any person whom the inspector has reasonable cause to believe to be able to give any information relevant to any examination or investigation under Paragraph (d) to answer (in the absence of persons other than a person nominated by the inspector to be present and any persons whom the inspector may allow to be present) such questions as the inspector thinks fit to ask and to sign a declaration of the truth of the person's answers;
(f) to require the production of, inspect, and take copies of or of any entry in—
  (i) any records which by virtue of these Regulations are required to be kept, and
  (ii) any other books, records or documents which it is necessary for the inspector to see for the purposes of any examination or investigation under Paragraph (d);
(g) to require any person to afford the inspector such facilities and assistance with respect to any matters or things within that person's control or in relation to which that person has responsibilities as are necessary to enable the inspector to exercise any of the powers conferred on the inspector by this paragraph;
(h) any other power which is necessary for the purpose mentioned in sub-paragraph (1).

(3) No answer given by a person in pursuance of a requirement imposed under sub-paragraph (2)(e) above is admissible in evidence against that person or the husband or wife of that person in any proceedings.

(4) Nothing in this paragraph is to be taken to compel the production by any person of a document of which the person would on grounds of legal professional privilege be entitled to withhold production on an order for discovery in an action in the High Court or, as the case may be, on an order for the production of documents in an action in the Court of Session.

Improvement notices

3 If an inspector is of the opinion that a person—

(a) is contravening one or more of these Regulations;
(b) has contravened one or more of these Regulations in circumstances that make it likely that the contravention will continue or be repeated,

the inspector may serve on the person a notice (in this Schedule referred to as "an improvement notice") stating that the inspector is of that opinion, specifying the provision or provisions as to which the inspector is of that opinion, giving particulars of the reasons why the inspector is of that opinion, and requiring that person to remedy the contravention or, as the case may be, the matters occasioning it within such period (ending not earlier than the period within which an appeal against the notice can be brought under paragraph 6) as may be specified in the notice.

Prohibition notices

4 (1) This paragraph applies to any activities which are being or are likely to be carried on by or under the control of any person, being activities to or in relation to which any of these Regulations apply or will, if the activities are so carried on, apply.

(2) If as regards any activities to which this paragraph applies an inspector is of the opinion that, as carried on or likely to be carried on by or under the control of the person in question, the activities involve or, as the case may be, will involve a risk of serious personal injury, the inspector may serve on that person a notice (in this Schedule referred to as "a prohibition notice").

(3) A prohibition notice must—

(a) state that the inspector is of that opinion;

(b) specify the matters which in the inspector's opinion give or, as the case may be, will give rise to that risk;

(c) where in the inspector's opinion any of those matters involves or, as the case may be, will involve a contravention of any of these Regulations, state that the inspector is of that opinion, specify the regulation or regulations as to which the inspector is of that opinion, and give particulars of the reasons why the inspector is of that opinion; and

(d) direct that the activities to which the notice relates must not be carried on by or under the control of the person on whom the notice is served unless the matters specified in the notice in pursuance of Paragraph (b) and any associated contraventions of provisions so specified in pursuance of Paragraph (c) have been remedied.

(4) A direction contained in a prohibition notice in pursuance of sub-paragraph (3)(d) takes effect—

(a) at the end of the period specified in the notice; or

(b) if the notice so declares, immediately.

Provisions supplementary to paragraphs 3 and 4

5 (1) In this paragraph "a notice" means an improvement notice or a prohibition notice.

(2) A notice may (but need not) include directions as to the measures to be taken to remedy any contravention or matter to which the notice relates; and any such directions—

(a) may be framed to any extent by reference to any approved code of practice; and

(b) may be framed so as to afford the person on whom the notice is served a choice between different ways of remedying the contravention or matter.

(3) Where an improvement notice or a prohibition notice which is not to take immediate effect has been served—

(a) the notice may be withdrawn by an inspector at any time before the end of the period specified in the notice in pursuance of paragraph 3 or paragraph 4(4) as the case may be; and

(b) the period so specified may be extended or further extended by an inspector at any time when an appeal against the notice is not pending.

Appeal against improvement or prohibition notice

6 (1) In this paragraph "a notice" means an improvement or a prohibition notice.

(2) A person on whom a notice is served may within 21 days from the date of its service appeal to an employment tribunal; and on such an appeal the tribunal may either cancel or affirm the notice and, if it affirms it, may do so either in its original form or with such modifications as the tribunal may in the circumstances think fit.

(3) Where an appeal under this paragraph is brought against a notice within the period allowed under sub-paragraph (2), then—

(a) in the case of an improvement notice, the bringing of the appeal has the effect of suspending the operation of the notice until the appeal is finally disposed of or, if the appeal is withdrawn, until the withdrawal of the appeal;

(b) in the case of a prohibition notice, the bringing of the appeal shall has the like effect if, but only if, on the application of the appellant the tribunal so directs (and then only from the giving of the direction).

(4) One or more assessors may be appointed for the purposes of any proceedings brought before an employment tribunal under this paragraph.

Power to indemnify inspectors

7 Where an action has been brought against an inspector in respect of an act done in the execution or purported execution of these Regulations and the circumstances are such that the inspector is not legally entitled to require the Office of Rail Regulation to indemnify the inspector, the Office of Rail Regulation may, nevertheless, indemnify the inspector against the whole or part of any damages and costs or expenses which the inspector may have been ordered to pay or may have incurred, if the Office of Rail Regulation is satisfied that the inspector honestly believed that the act complained of was within the inspector's powers and that the inspector's duty as an inspector required or entitled the inspector to do it.

Restrictions on disclosure of information

8 (1) In this paragraph—

"the 1974 Act" means the Health and Safety at Work etc Act 1974;

"the Executive" means the Health and Safety Executive referred to in section 10(1) of the 1974 Act;

"the recipient", in relation to any relevant information, means the person by whom that information was so obtained or to whom that information was so furnished, as the case may be;

"relevant information" means information obtained by an inspector in pursuance of a requirement imposed under paragraph 2(2)(e) or (f); and "relevant statutory requirement" means—

(a) the provisions of the 1974 Act and any regulations made under powers contained in that Act; and

(b) while and to the extent that they remain in force, the provisions of the Acts mentioned in Schedule 1 to the 1974 Act and which are specified in the third column of that Schedule and the regulations, orders and other instruments of a legislative character made or having effect under a provision so specified.

(2) Subject to the sub-paragraph (3), no relevant information must be disclosed without the consent of the person by whom it was furnished.

(3) Sub-paragraph (2) does not apply to—

(a) disclosure of information to the Executive, a government department or the Office of Rail Regulation;

(b) without prejudice to Paragraph (a), disclosure by the recipient of information to any person for the purpose of any function conferred on the recipient by or under any of the relevant statutory provisions or under these Regulations;

(c) without prejudice to Paragraph (a), disclosure by the recipient of information to a constable authorised by a chief officer of police to receive it; or

(d) disclosure by the recipient of information in a form calculated to prevent it from being identified as relating to a particular person or case.

(4) In sub-paragraph (3) any reference to the Executive, a government department or the Office of Rail Regulation includes respectively a reference to an officer of that body (including in the case of the Office of Rail Regulation, any inspector appointed by it), and also, in the case of a reference to the Executive, includes a reference to—

(a) a person performing any functions of the Executive by virtue of section 13(3) of the 1974 Act;

(b) an officer of a body which is so performing any such functions; and

(c) an adviser appointed in pursuance of section 13(7) of the 1974 Act.

(5) A person to whom information is disclosed in pursuance of sub-paragraph (3) must not use the information for a purpose other than—

(a) in a case falling within sub-paragraph (3)(a), a purpose of the recipient in question in connection with these Regulations or with the relevant statutory provisions, as the case may be;

(b) in the case of information given to a constable, the purposes of the police in connection with these Regulations, the relevant statutory provisions or any enactment whatsoever relating to working time, public health, public safety or the safety of the State.

(6) A person must not disclose any information obtained by the person as a result of the exercise of any power conferred by paragraph 2 (including in particular any information with respect to any trade secret obtained by the person in any premises entered by the person by virtue of any such power) except—

(a) for the purposes of the person's functions;

(b) for the purposes of any legal proceedings; or

(c) with the relevant consent.

In this sub-paragraph "the relevant consent" means the consent of the person who furnished it, and, in any other case, the consent of a person having responsibilities in relation to the premises where the information was obtained.

(7) Notwithstanding anything in sub-paragraph (6) an inspector must, in circumstances in which it is necessary to do so for the purpose of assisting in keeping persons (or the representatives of persons) employed at any premises adequately informed about matters affecting their health, safety and welfare or working time, give to such persons or their representatives the following descriptions of information, that is to say—

(a) factual information obtained by the inspector as mentioned in sub-paragraph (6) which relates to those premises or anything which was or is in the premises or was or is being done in them; and

(b) information with respect to any action which the inspector has taken or proposes to take in or in connection with those premises in the performance of the inspector's functions;

and, where an inspector does this, the inspector must give the same information to the employer of the persons employed at the premises.

(8) Notwithstanding anything in sub-paragraph (6), a recipient who has obtained such information as is referred to in sub-paragraph (6) may furnish to a person who appears to the recipient to be likely to be a party to any civil proceedings arising out of any accident, occurrence, situation or other matter, a written statement of the relevant facts observed by the recipient in the course of exercising any of the powers conferred by paragraph 2.

[1186]

SCHEDULE 3

(Amends the Employment Tribunals Act 1996, ss 18, 21, the Employment Rights Act 1996, ss 45A, 101A, 104, the Employment Act 2002, Schs 3, 4, 5, and SI 1998/1833, in the title Employment.)

VEHICLES CRIME (REGISTRATION OF REGISTRATION PLATE SUPPLIERS) REGULATIONS 2008
SI 2008/1715

Authority Made by the Secretary of State for Transport under the Vehicles (Crime) Act 2001, ss 17(3), 18(2), 19(1), 24(1), (3), 25(1), (2), 41(2).
Date made 30 June 2008.
Commencement 1 August 2008; see reg 1.
Interpretation See reg 2.
General These regulations, which revoke and replace the Vehicles Crime (Registration of Registration Plate Suppliers) (England and Wales) Regulations 2002, SI 2002/2977 and the amending SI 2003/228, SI 2005/2981, make provision for the registration of registration plate suppliers under the Vehicles (Crime) Act 2001, s 17.

[1187]

Citation and commencement

1 These Regulations may be cited as the Vehicles Crime (Registration of Registration Plate Suppliers) Regulations 2008 and shall come into force on 1st August 2008.

[1188]

Interpretation

2 (1) In these Regulations—

"the Act" means the Vehicles (Crime) Act 2001;
"company" means a body corporate but does not include a limited liability partnership or a Scottish partnership;
"fixed" in relation to a registration plate, means fixed in accordance with regulations made under section 22(2) or 23(2) of the 1994 Act;
"insurer" means a person who is an "authorised insurer" within the meaning of Part VI of the Road Traffic Act 1988;
"limited liability partnership" has the same meaning as that expression bears in the Limited Liability Partnerships Act 2000 (or the Limited Liability Partnerships Act (Northern Ireland) 2002, as appropriate;
"limited partnership" has the same meaning as that expression bears in the Limited Partnerships Act 1907;
"partnership" includes a partnership under the Partnership Act 1890 and a limited partnership registered in England and Wales but does not include a limited liability partnership or a Scottish partnership;
"the register" means the register maintained by the Secretary of State under section 18 of the Act;
"registration certificate" has the same meaning as that expression bears in Council Directive 1999/37/EC on the registration documents for vehicles;
"registration document" means a registration certificate issued in accordance with regulations under section 22(1) of the 1994 Act;
"relevant policy" means an insurance policy issued by an insurer in respect of a vehicle which has sustained damage;
"relevant repairer" means a person carrying on the business of a vehicle repairer who, in respect of the sale of a registration plate, is acting under the instruction or direction of an insurer;
"Scottish partnership" means a firm within the meaning of section 4(2) of the Partnership Act 1890 or, where a firm is registered in Scotland, within the meaning of section 3 of the Limited Partnerships Act 1907;
"sole trader" includes a representative of an unincorporated association other than a partnership.

(2) In these Regulations a reference to a document in terms of the letter V and a number is a reference to the document issued by the Secretary of State bearing that letter and number and a reference to such document includes any equivalent of that document issued in Northern Ireland or Wales, as appropriate.

NOTES

Council Directive 1999/37/EC OJ L138, 01.06.1999, p 57.
Limited Liability Partnerships Act 2000 As to the meaning of "limited liability partnership" in the 2000 Act, see s 1(2) thereof.

Limited Partnerships Act 1907 As to the meaning of "limited partnership" in the 1907 Act, see s 4 thereof.
Road Traffic Act 1988 As to the meaning of "authorised insurer" in Pt VI of the 1988 Act, see s 145(5) thereof.
The 1994 Act It is thought that this is a reference to the Vehicle Excise and Registration Act 1994.

[1189]

Exempted activity

3 The transfer of possession of a registration plate in consequence of the sale or other transfer of the vehicle to which it is fixed and to which the registration mark which is displayed on that registration plate has been assigned shall be treated for the purposes of Part 2 of the Act as not being an activity which consists in selling registration plates where the seller or transferor, as the case may be, of the vehicle is a dealer in vehicles and—

(a) he has arranged the first registration in the United Kingdom of the vehicle on behalf of the intended purchaser or keeper; or
(b) the registration plate was not fixed to the vehicle by him or on his behalf.

[1190]

Prescribed particulars of register

4 The register shall contain the following particulars as respects each registered person's entry—

(a) in the case of a sole trader—
  (i) the full name and residential address of the trader;
  (ii) any other name under which he trades;
  (iii) the address of all premises where he carries on business as a registration plate supplier;
(b) in the case of a partnership in England and Wales or Northern Ireland—
  (i) the firm name;
  (ii) the name and address of each partner;
  (iii) the address of the firm's principal place of business and, in the case of a limited partnership, this address shall be that which is registered as such under the Limited Partnerships Act 1907;
  (iv) the address of any other premises where the firm carries on business as a registration plate supplier;
(c) in the case of a Scottish partnership—
  (i) the firm name;
  (ii) the name and address of each partner;
  (iii) the address of the firm's principal place of business;
  (iv) the address of any other premises where the firm carries on business as a registration plate supplier;
(d) in the case of a limited liability partnership—
  (i) the name and number under which it is registered pursuant to the Limited Liability Partnerships Act 2001 or the Limited Liability Partnerships Act (Northern Ireland) 2002;
  (ii) its registered office for the purposes of the Act pursuant to which it is registered;
  (iii) the address of its principal place of business if different from its registered office;
  (iv) the address of any other premises where it carries on business as a registration plate supplier;
(e) in the case of a company—
  (i) the name and number under which it is registered pursuant to the Companies Act 2006;
  (ii) its registered office for the purposes of that Act;
  (iii) the address of its principal place of business if different from its registered office;
  (iv) the address of any other premises where it carries on business as a registration plate supplier; and
(f) in all cases—

(i) a telephone number for the registered person or firm;
(ii) the date of registration and of any suspension of registration;
(iii) details of any conviction of that person, or any partner in that firm, for an offence under Part 2 of the Act where less than five years or, in the case of any natural person aged under eighteen years at the date of his conviction, less than thirty months has elapsed since the date of that conviction;
(iv) the identification number allocated to the person or firm upon registration under Part 2 of the Act.

NOTES

Erratum It is thought that the reference to "the Limited Liability Partnerships Act 2001" in reg 4(d)(i) of the Queen's Printer's copy of these regulations should be to the Limited Liability Partnerships Act 2000.

[1191]

Application for registration

5 An application for registration under section 19 of the Act shall—

(a) contain the particulars which an entry in the register in respect of that applicant would be required to contain under regulation 4, save for sub-paragraphs (ii) to (iv) of paragraph (f), were the applicant to be registered; and
(b) be accompanied by a fee of £40 in respect of each of the premises to be entered in the register as the principal place of business or one at which the business of supplying registration plates is to be carried on.

[1192]

Information on sale of registration plates

6 (1) Subject to paragraphs (4) and (5), a registered person (other than a relevant repairer in circumstances where paragraph (9) applies) shall obtain from the prospective purchaser of a registration plate the information referred to in paragraph (2) before the sale takes place.

(2) The information is—

(a) where the prospective purchaser is the partnership or is one or more partners of a partnership purchasing on behalf of the partnership, the firm name and the address of the principal place of business or that firm;
(b) where the prospective purchaser is a Scottish partnership, the firm name and the address of the principal place of business of that firm;
(c) where the prospective purchaser is a limited liability partnership, its name and office as registered under the Limited Liability Partnerships Act 2001 or the Limited Liability Partnerships Act (Northern Ireland) 2002 and its principal place of business if different from its registered office;
(d) where the prospective purchaser is a company, its name and office as registered under the Companies Act 2006 and its principal place of business if different from its registered office;
(e) where the prospective purchaser is not within sub-paragraph (a), (b), (c) or (d), the purchaser's name and residential or other address;
(f) where a person is acting as agent for a prospective purchaser, the name and address of that agent;
(g) the registration mark to be displayed on the plate; and
(h) the connection of the prospective purchaser with the registration mark or the vehicle on which the registration plate is intended to be fixed.

(3) Subject to paragraph (4), where a registered person is a relevant repairer and paragraph (9) applies he shall, before the sale takes place, obtain from the prospective purchaser—

(a) the information referred to in—
   (i) paragraph (2)(a), (b), (c), (d) or (e), as appropriate; and
   (ii) paragraph (2)(f) and (h); and
(b) the number of the relevant policy and the name of the insurer who issued it.

(4) The information referred to in paragraph (2) is not required to be obtained where the prospective purchaser is a registered person or a dealer in vehicles who has arranged the first registration of the vehicle as mentioned in regulation 3(a).

(5) The information referred to in paragraph (2)(g) and (h) is not required to be obtained where paragraph (9) applies and the registered person is not a relevant repairer.

(6) Save where paragraph (9) applies, the information referred to in paragraph (2)(a), (b), (c), (d), (e) or (f) which is obtained by the registered person shall be verified by him using one or more of the documents referred to in Part I of the Schedule.

(7) The information referred to in paragraph (2)(h) which is obtained by a registered person, other than a relevant repairer, shall be verified by him using one or more of the documents referred to in Part II of the Schedule.

(8) Where the registered person is a relevant repairer the information referred to in paragraph (2) (h) which is obtained by him shall be verified by him using one or more of the documents referred to in Part II of the Schedule unless that information is verified using the information referred to in paragraph (3)(b).

(9) This paragraph applies where the registration plate is fixed to the vehicle to which there has been assigned the registration mark displayed on the registration plate and that vehicle is to be sold or transferred with the registration plate fixed to it.

(10) Section 25(3) of the Act shall apply to the provisions of this regulation.

NOTES

Erratum It is thought that the reference to "the Limited Liability Partnerships Act 2001" in reg 6(2)(c) of the Queen's Printer's copy of these regulations should be to the Limited Liability Partnerships Act 2000.

[1193]

Keeping of records by registered persons

7 (1) A registered person shall keep at his principal place of business, or at any other premises at which he carries on business as a registration plate supplier, records which meet the requirements of paragraphs (2) to (4).

(2) Each sale of a registration plate shall be recorded by date and the record relating to that sale shall be kept for a period of at least three years after such date.

(3) In respect of each sale there shall be recorded—

- (a) the information obtained in accordance with regulation 6;
- (b) the registration mark displayed on the registration plate (where not recorded under sub-paragraph (a)); and
- (c) details of all documents used for verification in accordance with regulation 6(6), (7) or (8).

(4) The details referred to in paragraph (3)(c) shall include—

- (a) in the case of a document used for verification in accordance with regulation 6(6), such particulars or numbers (if any) appearing on the document as purport to make it, or those particulars or numbers (or both), unique to the purchaser and which in the case of a document referred to in paragraph 1(a) or 2(a) of the Schedule shall be the driver number;
- (b) in the case of a document referred to in paragraph 1(c) or 4(a) of the Schedule the reference number of that document and in the case of the document referred to in paragraph 4(g) of the Schedule, the reference number referred to in that document.

(5) The record of the details of a document used for verification may consist of a copy of that document.

(6) Section 24(4) of the Act shall apply to the provisions of this regulation.

[1194]

8 *(Revokes the Vehicles Crime (Registration of Registration Plate Suppliers) (England and Wales) Regulations 2002, SI 2002/2977, and the amending SI 2003/228, SI 2005/2981.)*

THE SCHEDULE
VERIFICATION DOCUMENTS

Regulation 6

PART 1
NAME OR ADDRESS

1 The documents to be used for verification under regulation 6(6) are—

(a) a valid driving licence which bears a photograph of its holder (whether or not issued in the United Kingdom);
(b) one (or more) of the documents mentioned in paragraph 2 or 3; or
(c) a registration document or registration certificate provided that such document or certificate is also used to verify the information referred to in regulation 6(2)(h).

2 The documents referred to as being mentioned in this paragraph are—

(a) a driving licence (whether or not issued in the United Kingdom),
(b) a passport (whether or not issued in the United Kingdom,
(c) a national identity card issued by the government of a state or of a territory other than the United Kingdom,
(d) a debit card or a credit card issued by a bank or a building society,
a police warrant card, or
(e) an armed forces identity card,

which in each case is valid at the time when used for the purpose of validation.

3 The documents referred to as being mentioned in this paragraph are—

(a) a bill or statement of account issued in respect of the supply of gas, electricity, water or telecommunications services to premises at a specified address,
(b) a bill or statement of account issued in respect of council tax,
(c) a bill or statement of account issued in respect of rates payable in Northern Ireland, or
(d) a statement relating to an account held at a bank or building society,

which in each case is dated, or relates to a period ending, no earlier than six months before its use for the purpose of validation.

[1195]

PART 2
CONNECTION WITH REGISTRATION MARK OR VEHICLE

4 The documents to be used for verification under regulation 6(7) or (8) are—

(a) a registration document or registration certificate or that part of such document or certificate as is required by regulations made under section 22(1)(d) of the 1994 Act to be furnished to a new keeper of the vehicle upon its sale or disposal;
(b) Form V750 (certificate of entitlement to a registration mark);
(c) Form V778 (retention document relating to a right of retention in a registration mark);
(d) Form V11 (vehicle licensing reminder issued to a registered keeper);
(e) Form V379 (temporary registration certificate);
(f) Form V948 (authorisation to purchase a number plate); or
(g) an authorisation to purchase the number plate, issued by a company owning more than one vehicle, stating that it holds the registration document or the registration certificate and giving the reference number of that document or certificate.

NOTES

The 1994 Act It is thought that this is a reference to the Vehicle Excise and Registration Act 1994.

[1196]

RAIL VEHICLE ACCESSIBILITY EXEMPTION ORDERS (PARLIAMENTARY PROCEDURES) REGULATIONS 2008
SI 2008/2975

Authority Made by the Secretary of State for Transport under the Disability Discrimination Act 1995, ss 67(2), (3)(b), 67A(3).
Date made 14 November 2008.
Commencement 15 November 2008; see reg 1(1).
Interpretation See reg 1(2).
General These regulations set out the basis on which the Secretary of State will decide which parliamentary procedure is to be followed when making a rail vehicle accessibility exemption order under the Disability Discrimination Act 1995, s 47(1) (such orders are noted to SI 1998/2456).

The regulations set out the circumstances in which the negative resolution procedure would normally be adopted in making an order, so that it is subject to annulment in pursuance of a resolution of either House of Parliament. They also set out the circumstances in which the draft affirmative resolution procedure is to be adopted, requiring an order to be laid and approved by a resolution of both Houses of Parliament before being made and brought into force. The Secretary of State may adopt a different procedure for an order having regard to representations by the Disabled Persons Transport Advisory Committee.

[1197]

Citation, commencement and interpretation

1 (1) These Regulations may be cited as the Rail Vehicle Accessibility Exemption Orders (Parliamentary Procedures) Regulations 2008 and shall come into force on the day after the day on which they are made.

(2) In these Regulations—

"the 1995 Act" means the Disability Discrimination Act 1995;

"draft affirmative resolution procedure", in relation to an order, means the procedure under which the order is only made if a draft of the statutory instrument containing the order has been laid before, and approved by a resolution of, each House of Parliament;

"exemption" means an authority given under section 47(1)(a) or (b) of the 1995 Act by an order;

"negative resolution procedure", in relation to an order, means the procedure under which a statutory instrument containing the order is subject to annulment in pursuance of a resolution of either House of Parliament;

"network" means any permanent way or other means of guiding or supporting vehicles to which the provisions of RVA Regulations apply;

"network order" means an order—

(a) which only applies to vehicles which are used on a specified network or on networks of a specified description (or which are used on both); and

(b) the application of which is not limited to specified vehicles;

"RVA Regulations" means rail vehicle accessibility regulations made under section 46(1) of the 1995 Act.

NOTES

Rail vehicle accessibility regulations made under s 46(1) of the 1995 Act
See SI 1998/2456.

[1198]

Orders under section 47 of the 1995 Act which are normally subject to the negative resolution procedure

2 (1) When the Secretary of State comes to make an order under section 47(1) of the 1995 Act in any of the circumstances referred to in paragraph (3), the Secretary of State will decide that the negative resolution procedure is to be adopted in connection with the making of the order.

(2) But having regard to representations by the Disabled Persons Transport Advisory Committee in response to consultation under section 67A(1) of the 1995 Act, the Secretary of State may decide that the draft affirmative resolution procedure is to be adopted instead.

(3) The circumstances referred to in paragraph (1) are where—

(a) the order meets any of the qualification criteria listed in regulation 3(1) (which relates to existing vehicles and minor amendments etc) but does not meet any of the disqualification criteria listed in regulation 3(2),

(b) the order meets either of the qualification criteria listed in regulation 4(1) (which relates to vehicles used on exempt networks and historical vehicles etc) but does not meet any of the disqualification criteria listed in regulation 4(2),

(c) the order is made solely to revoke an order, to remove an exemption or to reduce the scope of an exemption, or

(d) the effects of the order could be achieved by one or more orders (each an "alternative order"), and each alternative order would fall within sub-paragraph (a), (b) or (c).

NOTES

Order under s 47(1) of the 1995 Act These orders are noted to SI 1998/2456.

[1199]

Criteria relating to existing vehicles, and minor amendments etc

3 (1) The qualification criteria referred to in regulation 2(3)(a) are that—

(a)

(i) the only vehicles to which the order applies are ones to which RVA Regulations do not apply prior to the coming into force of the amendment of section 46(6) of the 1995 Act by the Disability Discrimination Act 2005, or ones which belong to a class of vehicle to which RVA Regulations do not so apply; and

(ii) the reason, or one of the reasons, for RVA Regulations not applying is that the vehicles were first brought into use, or belong to a class of vehicle which were first brought into use, before 1st January 1999;

(b)

(i) the only vehicles to which the order applies are ones to which RVA Regulations do not apply prior to the coming into force of the repeal of section 46(10) of the 1995 Act by the Disability Discrimination Act 2005; and

(ii) the reason, or one of the reasons, for RVA Regulations not applying is that the vehicles are not used for the carriage of members of the public for hire or reward at separate fares;

(c) the only vehicles to which the order applies are ones to which RVA Regulations do not apply prior to the making of these Regulations, and the reason for RVA Regulations not applying is that the vehicles are not ones which were constructed or adapted to carry passengers on—

(i) a railway or tramway, or

(ii) a system which uses magnetic levitation or monorail, or which is track-based with side guidance;

(d) the order applies only to a unique vehicle;

(e) the order contains only one or more minor amendments to an order;

(f) the exemption to which the order relates is for specified vehicles and for a specified period of time during which—

(i) the vehicles are to be used solely for testing;

(ii) no fares are to be charged to any passenger in the vehicles; and

(iii) the vehicles are not to be available for use by members of the general public;

(g) the exemption to which the order relates is granted for a period not exceeding six months.

(2) The disqualification criteria referred to in regulation 2(3)(a) are that—

(a) the order creates or extends the scope of an exemption with no expiry date or an expiry date later than 31st December 2019;

(b) other than where the sole purpose is to amend a typographical error, the order amends an order by extending the period of time for which the exemption applies;

(c) the order is a network order creating or extending the scope of an exemption.

(3) In paragraph (1)(c) "railway" and "tramway" have the same meaning as in section 67(1) of the Transport and Works Act 1992 and "magnetic levitation", "monorail" and "tracked-based with side guidance" have the same meaning as in article 3(1) of the Transport and Works (Guided Transport Modes) Order 1992;

(4) In paragraph (1)(e), a "minor amendment" means any of the following—

(a) the correction of a typographical error,

(b) the elucidation or correction of an order that has been drawn to the special attention of both Houses of Parliament in a report by the Joint Committee on Statutory Instruments,

(c) an amendment made solely for the purpose of extending to additional vehicles an exemption which was previously granted to more than one specified vehicle, and the additional vehicles are of an identical type to the specified vehicles,

(d) an amendment which does not create or extend the scope of an exemption.

NOTES

Transport and Works (Guided Transport Modes) Order 1992 SI 1992/3231.

[1200]

Criteria relating to vehicles used on exempt networks, and historical vehicles etc

4 (1) The qualification criteria referred to in regulation 2(3)(b) are that—

(a) the order only applies to a vehicle which—

(i) was first brought into use on or after 1st January 1999;

(ii) is used for carriage on a network on which one or more of the vehicles brought into use before that date are the subject of a network order (an "exempt network"); and

(iii) if used also on one or more networks which are not exempt networks, is not used on them for more than 20 days in total in any calendar year;

(b) the order only applies to a vehicle which—

(i) is used to demonstrate or operate a historical or special type of railway service; and

(ii) is used exclusively or primarily for tourist, educational or recreational purposes.

(2) The disqualification criteria referred to in regulation 2(3)(b) are that—

(a) the order applies to a vehicle first brought into use on or after 1st January 1999 and the order creates or extends the scope of an exemption with no expiry date or an expiry date later than 31st December 2019;

(b) other than where the sole purpose is to amend a typographical error, the order amends an order by extending the period of time for which the exemption applies;

(c) the order is a network order creating or extending the scope of an exemption.

[1201]

Orders under the 1995 Act which are normally subject to the draft affirmative resolution procedure

5 (1) When the Secretary of State comes to make an order under section 47(1) of the 1995 Act otherwise than in any of the circumstances referred to in regulation 2(3), the Secretary of State will decide that the draft affirmative resolution procedure is to be adopted in connection with the making of the order.

(2) But having regard to representations by the Disabled Persons Transport Advisory Committee in response to consultation under section 67A(1) of the 1995 Act, the Secretary of State may decide that the negative resolution procedure is to be adopted instead.

NOTES

Order under s 47(1) of the 1995 Act These orders are noted to SI 1998/2456.

[1202]

MUTUAL RECOGNITION OF DRIVING DISQUALIFICATIONS (GREAT BRITAIN AND IRELAND) REGULATIONS 2008
SI 2008/3010

Authority Made by the Secretary of State for Transport under the Crime (International Co-operation) Act 2003, ss 57(2)(b), (4)(b), 72(3).

Date made 19 November 2008.

Commencement These regulations come into force on the date specified in SI 2008/3009, art 2(1); see the summary below.

Summary The Crime (International Co-operation) Act 2003, Pt 3, Chapter 1 (ss 54–75) provides for the mutual recognition of driving disqualifications between member states, so as to implement the European Union Convention on Driving Disqualifications (signed by the United Kingdom and other member states on 17 June 1998).

Chapter 1 of Pt 3 of the 2003 Act has been brought into force by SI 2008/3009, in the title Criminal Law, in relation to the mutual recognition of driving disqualifications as between the United Kingdom and Ireland. Under art 2 of SI 2008/3009, Chapter 1 comes into force on the date on which the Convention on Driving Disqualifications applies to both the United Kingdom and Ireland, which will be: (a) 90 days after the date on which the United Kingdom and Ireland make declarations under

Art 15(4) of the Convention, or (b) if they are not made on the same date, 90 days after the later of the dates on which those declarations are made. This commencement date will be notified in the *London, Edinburgh and Belfast Gazettes*.

Under s 57 of the 2003 Act, the appropriate minister must give the offender a notice under that section if the unexpired period of the foreign disqualification is not less than one month, and may give him a notice if that period is less than one month (s 57(1)). By s 57(2), the unexpired period of the foreign disqualification is the period of the foreign disqualification, less any period of that disqualification which is treated by regulations as having been served in the state in which the offender was convicted. Reg 2 of these regulations provides that, for the purpose of calculating the unexpired period of foreign disqualification under s 57(2), the period to be treated as having been served in Ireland: (a) commences on the day the disqualification came into operation in Ireland, and (b) ends on the day immediately before the beginning of the relevant period of disqualification specified in s 57(5)(a). In determining the period to be treated as having been served in Ireland, any time during which the operation of the disqualification imposed in Ireland is suspended is to be disregarded.

By s 57(4) of the 2003 Act, if the appropriate minister gives the offender a notice under that section, the offender is disqualified in each part of the United Kingdom: (a) for the relevant period, and (b) if the foreign disqualification is also effective until a condition is satisfied, until the condition or a corresponding prescribed condition is satisfied. Under reg 3 of these regulations, where the disqualification in Ireland is effective until a driving test condition is satisfied, the corresponding condition for the purposes of s 57(4)(b) is the passing of a prescribed test of competence to drive under the Road Traffic Act 1988, s 89(3).

[1203]

CHANNEL TUNNEL RAIL LINK (NOMINATION) ORDER 2008 SI 2008/3076

Authority Made by the Secretary of State for Transport under the Channel Tunnel Rail Link Act 1996, s 34(1), (4).
Date made 28 November 2008.
Commencement 30 November 2008.
Summary This order specifies HS1 Limited (previously named Union Railways (North) Limited) as the nominated undertaker:

(a) for the purposes of the Channel Tunnel Rail Link Act 1996, Pt I, except for s 14(1)(b), so far as connected with or in any way relating to specified works on the rail link; and
(b) for the purposes of s 14(1)(b) of the 1996 Act, so far as concerns the provision of any services in connection with the construction or maintenance of those works.

The order revokes the Channel Tunnel Rail Link (Nomination) Order 1999, SI 1999/391 (the amending SI 2003/2306, SI 2003/2834, SI 2007/2920 are accordingly spent), which specified Union Railways (North) Limited and CTRL (UK) Limited as nominated undertakers for the purposes specified in the 1999 order. Provision is made by this order for the transfer of rights and liabilities of CTRL (UK) Limited in connection with its former role as a nominated undertaker under the 1996 Act to HS1 Limited.

Previous order SI 1999/1985, as amended by SI 1999/2198, was made under the Channel Tunnel Rail Link Act 1996, s 34(1), (4). It specifies London Underground Limited and Union Railways (North) Limited as the nominated undertakers for the purposes of certain of the provisions of Pt I of the 1996 Act in relation to works at St Pancras station in London. It also provides that Union Railways (North) Limited is to cease to be the nominated undertaker for certain works for which it was made nominated undertaker by SI 1999/391 (revoked by SI 2008/3076 above).

[1204]

LOCAL TRANSPORT ACT 2008 (COMMENCEMENT NO 1 AND TRANSITIONAL PROVISIONS) ORDER 2009 SI 2009/107

Authority Made by the Secretary of State for Transport under the Local Transport Act 2008, s 134.
Date made 26 January 2009.
Summary This order brought into force provisions of the Local Transport Act 2008, as noted in the table below. Transitional provisions made by the order are set out in full at the end of the table. Note that any power under or by virtue of the 2008 Act to make regulations or orders came into force on 26 November 2008 (date of royal assent); see s 134(1)(c) of the Act.
Further commencement orders SI 2009/579 (made by the Welsh Ministers under the Local Transport Act 2008, s 134(6)) brought into force provisions of the 2008 Act, subject to transitional provisions, as noted in the table below.

Provision	*Date and extent (if any)*
s 1	9 February 2009 (in so far as not already in force) (SI 2009/107)
s 3(1)	4 March 2009 (in so far as inserts the Public Passenger Vehicle Act 1981, ss 4A, 4C, 4D) (SI 2009/107)
s 3(2)–(4)	4 March 2009 (SI 2009/107)

Provision	*Date and extent (if any)*
s 6	9 February 2009 (in so far as not already in force) (SI 2009/107)
s 7(1)–(4)	9 February 2009 (England only) (SI 2009/107) 1 April 2009 (Wales only) (SI 2009/579)
s 7(5)	See Sch 1 below
s 8	9 February 2009 (England only) (SI 2009/107) 1 April 2009 (Wales only) (SI 2009/579)
s 9(1)	1 April 2009 (Wales only) (SI 2009/579) 1 April 2011 (England only) (SI 2009/107)
s 9(2)	See sub-ss (3)–(5) below
s 9(3)	1 April 2009 (Wales only) (SI 2009/579) 1 April 2011 (England only) (SI 2009/107)[1]
s 9(4), (5)	9 February 2009 (England only) (SI 2009/107) 1 April 2009 (Wales only) (SI 2009/579)
ss 10–12	9 February 2009 (England only) (SI 2009/107) 1 April 2009 (Wales only) (SI 2009/579)
s 13(1)	See sub-ss (2)–(7) below
s 13(2)	9 February 2009 (England only) (SI 2009/107) 1 April 2009 (Wales only) (SI 2009/579)
s 13(3)–(7)	6 April 2009 (England only) (SI 2009/107)
ss 14–18	6 April 2009 (England only) (SI 2009/107)
s 46(1), (2)	9 February 2009 (England only) (SI 2009/107) 1 April 2009 (Wales only) (SI 2009/579)
s 46(3)	See Sch 2 below
s 47(1)	9 February 2009 (SI 2009/107)
s 47(2)	See Sch 3 below
s 48	6 April 2009 (in so far as not already in force) (SI 2009/107)
ss 50–52	9 February 2009 (in so far as not already in force) (SI 2009/107)
s 53	6 April 2009 (SI 2009/107)
s 54(1)–(7)	6 April 2009 (SI 2009/107)
s 54(8)	6 April 2009 (in so far as not already in force) (SI 2009/107)
ss 57–59	6 April 2009 (SI 2009/107)
s 60	6 April 2009 (in so far as not already in force) (SI 2009/107)
s 61	6 April 2009 (SI 2009/107)
ss 62, 63	9 February 2009 (SI 2009/107)
s 64	9 February 2009 (England only) (SI 2009/107) 1 April 2009 (Wales only) (SI 2009/579)
s 65(1)	9 February 2009 (England only) (SI 2009/107) 1 April 2009 (Wales only) (SI 2009/579)
s 65(2)–(4)	9 February 2009 (in so far as not already in force) (SI 2009/107)
ss 66, 67	9 February 2009 (SI 2009/107)
s 68(1)	See sub-ss (2), (3) below
s 68(2)	9 February 2009 (England only) (SI 2009/107)
s 68(3)	9 February 2009 (England only) (SI 2009/107) 1 April 2009 (Wales only) (SI 2009/579)
ss 69–71	9 February 2009 (England only) (SI 2009/107)

Provision	*Date and extent (if any)*
	1 April 2009 (Wales only) (SI 2009/579)
s 72	6 April 2009 (SI 2009/107)
s 74	9 February 2009 (in so far as not already in force) (SI 2009/107)
s 75	9 February 2009 (England only) (in so far as not already in force) (SI 2009/107) 1 April 2009 (Wales only) (in so far as not already in force) (SI 2009/579)
s 76	9 February 2009 (SI 2009/107)
s 77(1)–(4)	9 February 2009 (SI 2009/107)
s 77(5)	See Sch 4 below
s 77(6)–(9), (11)	9 February 2009 (SI 2009/107)
s 78	9 February 2009 (in so far as not already in force) (SI 2009/107)
ss 79–83	9 February 2009 (SI 2009/107)
s 84	9 February 2009 (in so far as not already in force) (SI 2009/107)
s 85	9 February 2009 (SI 2009/107)
ss 86–88	9 February 2009 (in so far as not already in force) (SI 2009/107)
s 89	9 February 2009 (SI 2009/107)
ss 90, 91	9 February 2009 (in so far as not already in force) (SI 2009/107)
s 92	9 February 2009 (SI 2009/107)
s 93	9 February 2009 (in so far as not already in force) (SI 2009/107)
ss 94–99	9 February 2009 (SI 2009/107)
ss 100, 101	9 February 2009 (in so far as not already in force) (SI 2009/107)
s 102	9 February 2009 (SI 2009/107)
ss 103–111	9 February 2009 (England only) (in so far as not already in force) (SI 2009/107) 1 April 2009 (Wales only) (in so far as not already in force) (SI 2009/579)
s 112(1)	9 February 2009 (England only) (SI 2009/107) 1 April 2009 (Wales only) (SI 2009/579)
s 112(2)	9 February 2009 (in so far as not already in force) (SI 2009/107)
s 113(1)–(4)	9 February 2009 (England only) (in so far as not already in force) (SI 2009/107) 1 April 2009 (Wales only) (SI 2009/579)
s 113(5), (6)	9 February 2009 (SI 2009/107)
s 113(7)	9 February 2009 (in so far as not already in force) (SI 2009/107)
s 114	9 February 2009 (England only) (SI 2009/107) 1 April 2009 (Wales only) (SI 2009/579)
s 115(1), (2)	9 February 2009 (England only) (in so far as not already in force) (SI 2009/107) 1 April 2009 (Wales only) (SI 2009/579)
s 115(3)–(5)	9 February 2009 (SI 2009/107)
s 116(1)–(3)	9 February 2009 (England only) (in so far as not already in force) (SI 2009/107) 1 April 2009 (Wales only) (SI 2009/579)
s 116(4)–(8)	9 February 2009 (SI 2009/107)
s 117(1)	9 February 2009 (England only) (SI 2009/107) 1 April 2009 (Wales only) (SI 2009/579)
s 117(2)	9 February 2009 (SI 2009/107)

Provision	*Date and extent (if any)*
s 118(1)–(5)	9 February 2009 (England only) (SI 2009/107) 1 April 2009 (Wales only) (SI 2009/579)
s 118(6)–(9)	9 February 2009 (SI 2009/107)
s 119	9 February 2009 (SI 2009/107)
s 120	9 February 2009 (in so far as not already in force) (SI 2009/107)
s 121	See Sch 6 below
ss 125, 126	9 February 2009 (in so far as not already in force) (SI 2009/107)
ss 128–130	9 February 2009 (SI 2009/107)
s 131	See Sch 7 below
Sch 1	9 February 2009 (England only) (SI 2009/107) 1 April 2009 (Wales only) (SI 2009/579)
Sch 2	9 February 2009 (England only) (SI 2009/107) 1 April 2009 (Wales only) (SI 2009/579)
Sch 3	9 February 2009 (in so far as not already in force) (SI 2009/107)
Sch 4	9 February 2009 (SI 2009/107)
Sch 5	9 February 2009 (England only) (SI 2009/107) 1 April 2009 (Wales only) (SI 2009/579)
Sch 6, Pt 1	9 February 2009 (England only) (SI 2009/107) 1 April 2009 (Wales only) (SI 2009/579)
Sch 6, Pt 2	9 February 2009 (SI 2009/107)
Sch 7, Pt 1	9 February 2009 (repeals of or in Transport Act 1968, s 9A(7); Transport Act 1985, ss 63(8), (8A), 89; Transport Act 2000) (England only) (SI 2009/107)
Sch 7, Pt 2	9 February 2009 (repeals of or in Transport Act 2000, Sch 10; Enterprise Act 2002) (England only) (SI 2009/107) 6 April 2009 (repeal in Transport Act 2000, s 116) (England only) (SI 2009/107)
Sch 7, Pt 3	9 February 2009 (repeals of or in Transport Act 1968, ss 10, 24; Transport Act 1985, ss 9, 60; Constitutional Reform Act 2005, Sch 9, para 42) (SI 2009/107) 9 February 2009 (repeals of or in Transport Act 1985, ss 74, 75, 79; Transport Act 2000) (England only) (SI 2009/107) 6 April 2009 (repeals of or in Transport Act 1985, ss 22, 23) (SI 2009/107)
Sch 7, Pt 4	9 February 2009 (SI 2009/107)
Sch 7, Pt 5	9 February 2009 (repeals in Greater London Authority Act 1999, Sch 23) (SI 2009/107) 9 February 2009 (repeals in Transport Act 2000) (England only) (SI 2009/107)

1 The Transport Act 2000, s 109(2) (replacement of local transport plans) continues to apply to a local transport authority without the amendments made by s 9(3) of the 2008 Act until that local transport authority has wholly replaced the local transport plan which is taken to be its local transport plan on 9 February 2009

Transitional provisions

SI 2009/107: England and Wales Pt 2 of Sch 1 to SI 2009/107 contains the following transitional provisions in relation to certain provisions of the Local Transport Act 2008 ("the Act") brought into force in England and Wales on 9 February 2009:

(a) notwithstanding the coming into force of s 51 of the Act, the Transport Act 1985, s 9 (appeals against traffic regulation conditions) is to continue to apply without the amendments made by s 51 of the Act as respects appeals made before 9 February 2009;

(b) notwithstanding the coming into force of s 62 of the Act, the powers of traffic commissioners conferred by the Transport Act 1985, s 26 (conditions attached to PSV operator's licence) are to continue to apply without the amendments made by s 62 of the Act as respects any failure to comply with requirements listed in that section which took place before 9 February 2009;

(c) notwithstanding the coming into force of s 63 of the Act, the powers of traffic commissioners conferred by the Transport Act 1985, s 27A (additional powers where service not operated as registered) are not available to a traffic commissioner in any case where it appears to a traffic commissioner that an operator:

(1) has, or may have, failed to operate a local service registered under s 6 of the 1985 Act; or

(2) has, or may have, failed to operate such a service in accordance with the particulars registered under that section,

and that failure, or alleged failure, took place before 9 February 2009.

SI 2009/107: England only Pt 2 of Sch 2 to SI 2009/107 contains the following transitional provisions in relation to certain provisions of the Act brought into force on 9 February 2009 in relation to England only:

(a) notwithstanding the coming into force of s 8 of the Act, local transport policies developed, and local transport plans prepared and published, by a local transport authority before 9 February 2009 continue to have effect until 1 April 2011 as though the Transport Act 2000, s 108 (local transport plans) had not been amended by s 8 (this does not apply to the extent that the local transport policies and plans of a local transport authority are altered by that authority before 1 April 2011);

(b) notwithstanding the coming into force of s 10 of the Act, a bus strategy prepared by a local transport authority in accordance with the Transport Act 2000, s 110 (bus strategies) continues to have effect as respects s 124(1)(a) of that Act (quality contracts schemes);

(c) local transport policies and plans developed and prepared jointly for an integrated transport area by an Integrated Transport Authority and the councils for the metropolitan districts comprised in the area, in accordance with the Transport Act 2000, ss 108(1)(a), (3), 113(1) (role of metropolitan district councils), are treated, from 9 February 2009, as local transport policies and plans developed and prepared by the Integrated Transport Authority in accordance with s 108(1)(a) of the 2000 Act, including for the purposes of SI 2009/107;

(d) notwithstanding the coming into force of s 64 of the Act, the Transport Act 2000, s 155 (penalties) continues to apply in England without the amendments made by s 64 of the Act in respect of penalties imposed by a traffic commissioner against an operator of a local service where that traffic commissioner is satisfied that the operator had, before 9 February 2009:

(1) failed to operate a local service registered under the Transport Act 1985, s 6,

(2) operated a local service in contravention of that section or s 118(4) or 129(1)(b) of the 2000 Act, or

(3) failed to comply with s 138 or 140(3) of the 2000 Act;

(e) notwithstanding the coming into force of s 71 of the Act, any application which is made before 9 February 2009 and which seeks the consent of the Secretary of State under any of the Transport Act 1985, s 75(3), 79(3), (7) or (8) but which has not been determined by that date, is to be dealt with as if that application had been made on a date on or after 9 February 2009;

(f) notwithstanding the coming into force of ss 110, 111 of the Act, the Transport Act 2000, ss 169, 170 (charging schemes) continue to apply without the amendments made by s 110, 111 in respect of any charging scheme under Pt III of the 2000 Act which was submitted to the Secretary of State in accordance with s 169 of that Act before 9 February 2009.

SI 2009/579: Wales only SI 2009/579 contains transitional provisions in relation to certain provisions of the Act brought into force on 1 April 2009 in relation to Wales only. It makes the same provision in relation to Wales as SI 2009/107 makes in relation to England, as set out in the immediately preceding heads (b), (d), (e) (referring to "1 April 2009" in place of "9 February 2009", and "the Welsh Ministers" in place of "the Secretary of State").

[1205]

SECTION 19 PERMIT REGULATIONS 2009
SI 2009/365

Authority Made by the Secretary of State for Transport under the Transport Act 1985, ss 21, 23A(1), 134, the Local Transport Act 2008, s 60(2), (7), and the Public Passenger Vehicles Act 1981, ss 52(1), 60.
Date made 21 February 2009.
Commencement 6 April 2009.
Summary These regulations, which revoke and replace, the Minibus and Other Section 19 Permit Buses Regulations 1987, SI 1987/1230, and the amending SI 1996/3088, SI 1997/2916, SI 2007/691, apply to any vehicle used under a permit granted under the Transport Act 1985, s 19 ("a section 19 permit") and to the drivers of such vehicles. Under a section 19 permit, certain educational and other bodies may carry their members and certain other people on a public service vehicle without having to satisfy the usual public service vehicle operator licensing requirements; such vehicles may not be used for the carriage of members of the general public nor with a view to profit.

S 19 of the 1985 Act has been amended by the Local Transport Act 2008, s 57 so as to enable public service vehicles with not more than 8 passenger seats to be used under a section 19 permit. As a result of these amendments there are two classes of permit under these regulations: (a) a large bus permit granted in accordance with reg 8, which authorises the use of a large bus (a vehicle adapted to carry more than 16 passengers); and (b) a standard permit granted in accordance with reg 8, which authorises the use of a small bus (a vehicle adapted to carry more than 8 but not more than 16 passengers) or a public service vehicle other than a bus (a vehicle adapted to carry not more than 8 passengers).

Reg 3 sets out the conditions to be fulfilled by the driver of a large bus. Such a person must hold a licence to drive a passenger-carrying vehicle, a PCV Community licence, or a corresponding Northern Ireland licence, which authorises the driving of that vehicle. Reg 4 sets out the conditions to be fulfilled by the driver of a small bus, who does not hold a licence of a type specified in reg 3, which authorises the driving of a small bus. If such a driver does not fulfil the conditions in reg 4(2), he must fulfil the alternative conditions in reg 4(3) and abide by the restrictions in reg 4(4). Reg 4(2)–(4) of these regulations correspond with reg 4(2)–(4) of SI 2009/366 below.

Reg 5 sets out the conditions to be fulfilled by the driver of a public service vehicle other than a bus, who does not hold a licence of a type specified in reg 3, which authorises the driving of that vehicle. The conditions are that the driver must:

(a) hold a valid full licence granted under the Road Traffic Act 1988, Pt III authorising the driving of motor vehicles in category B (excepting a licence which only authorises the driving of vehicles in sub-category B1);
(b) have held such a licence for a period of, or periods amounting in aggregate to, not less than 2 years; and
(c) be aged 21 years or over.

Reg 6 provides that a small bus used under a permit must comply with the conditions of fitness specified in SI 1986/1078, regs 41–43 (or if the vehicle was first used before 1 April 1988, with the conditions specified in SI 1981/257, regs 6–33, 35–44, 45A). Reg 7 prescribes a fee of £20 for the grant of a large bus permit and £11 for a standard permit. Reg 8 provides that a permit granted on or after 6 April 2009 must be for a period not exceeding five years; it also prescribes the information which a permit must contain. Where an issuing body (i e the traffic commissioner or a body designated by the Secretary of State) grants a permit, it must, at the same time, issue a corresponding disc, containing the information set out in reg 9. The disc must be displayed in a vehicle whilst it is being used under the corresponding permit. Regs 10–12 set out the procedure to be followed where permits or discs are lost or destroyed, and where permits and discs must be surrendered to the issuing body. Reg 13 contains transitional provisions.

[1206]

COMMUNITY BUS REGULATIONS 2009
SI 2009/366

Authority Made by the Secretary of State for Transport under the Transport Act 1985, ss 23(2), (3), (8), 23A(1), 134, the Local Transport Act 2008, s 60(2), (7) and the Public Passenger Vehicles Act 1981, ss 52(1), 60.

Date made 21 February 2009.

Commencement 6 April 2009.

Summary These regulations, which revoke and replace the Community Bus Regulations 1986, SI 1986/1245, and the amending SI 1996/3087, SI 1997/2917, SI 2008/1465, apply to any vehicle used under a community bus permit (granted under the Transport Act 1985, s 22) and to the drivers of such vehicles. "Community bus service" is defined by s 22(1) as a local service provided by a body concerned for the social and welfare needs of one or more communities, without a view to profit, and by means of a vehicle adapted to carry more than eight passengers. S 23 relates to the conditions which apply to every community bus permit. Both ss 22, 23 of the 1985 Act have been amended by the Local Transport Act 2008, ss 59, 131, Sch 7, Pt 3 so as to relax the restrictions applying to the provision of community bus services by removing: (a) the restriction on the use of vehicles adapted to carry more than 16 passengers; and (b) the prohibition on certain drivers of such vehicles from being paid.

Reg 3 sets out the conditions to be fulfilled by the driver of a large bus (i e a vehicle adapted to carry more than 16 passengers). Such a person must hold a licence to drive a passenger-carrying vehicle, a PCV Community licence, or a corresponding Northern Ireland licence, which authorises the driving of that vehicle. Reg 4 sets out the conditions to be fulfilled by the driver of a small bus (a vehicle adapted to carry more than eight but not more than sixteen passengers) who does not hold a licence of a type specified in reg 3, which authorises the driving of a small bus. If such a driver does not fulfil the conditions in reg 4(2), he must fulfil the alternative conditions in reg 4(3) and abide by the restrictions in reg 4(4). The conditions in reg 4(2) are that the driver:

(a) was first granted a full licence under the Road Traffic Act 1988, Pt III authorising the driving of motor vehicles in category B (excepting a licence which only authorises the driving of vehicles in sub-category B1) before 1 January 1997; and
(b) is the holder of a valid full licence under Pt III of the 1988 Act authorising the driving of motor vehicles in category B (excepting a licence which only authorises the driving of vehicles in sub-category B1) and sub-category D1 (not for hire or reward).

The alternative conditions in reg 4(3) are that the driver:

(a) is the holder of a valid full licence granted under Pt III of the 1988 Act, a valid corresponding Northern Ireland licence, or a valid Community licence, authorising the driving of motor vehicles included in category B (excepting a licence which only authorises the driving of vehicles in sub-category B1);
(b) has held such a licence for a period of, or periods amounting in aggregate to, not less than 2 years;
(c) is 21 years of age or over;
(d) if aged 70 years or over, is not suffering from a relevant disability in respect of which the Secretary of State would be bound to refuse to grant him a licence authorising the driving of a class of vehicles in sub-category D1; and
(e) receives no payment or other consideration for driving the vehicle other than out-of-pocket expenses.

The restrictions in reg 4(4) are that the driver:

(a) must not have a trailer attached;
(b) must, in a case where the driver's licence only authorises the driving of vehicles with automatic transmission, be fitted with automatic transmission; and

(c) must satisfy the weight restrictions specified in the Transport Act 1985, s 18(4).

Reg 5 provides that a small bus used under a permit must comply with the conditions of fitness specified in SI 1986/1078, regs 41–43 (or if the vehicle was first used before 1 April 1988, with the conditions specified in SI 1981/257, regs 6–33, 35–44, 45A). Reg 6 empowers a traffic commissioner to attach conditions to a permit restricting the use of a large bus under a permit. Reg 7 prescribes the procedure for permits to be returned to a traffic commissioner so that certain conditions can be attached to the permit.

The fee to be paid for the grant of a permit is £55 (reg 8). Reg 9 provides that a permit granted on or after 6 April 2009 must be for a period not exceeding five years; it also prescribes the information which a permit must contain. Where a traffic commissioner grants a permit, he must, at the same time, issue a corresponding disc containing the information set out in reg 10. The disc must be displayed in a vehicle whilst it is being used under the corresponding permit. Regs 11–13 set out the procedure to be followed where permits or discs are lost or destroyed, and where permits and discs must be surrendered to the traffic commissioner.

[1207]

PUBLIC SERVICE VEHICLES (REGISTRATION RESTRICTIONS) (ENGLAND AND WALES) REGULATIONS 2009
SI 2009/443

Authority Made by the Secretary of State for Transport under the Transport Act 1985, ss 6(9)(b), (c), 6A(3)(b), (11) and the Public Passenger Vehicles Act 1981, s 5(1).
Date made 28 February 2009.
Commencement 6 April 2009; see reg 1(1).
Interpretation See reg 2.
General These regulations prescribe the procedure to be followed under the Transport Act 1985, s 6A (inserted by the Local Transport Act 2008, s 48(1), (3)) where an application is received by a traffic commissioner under s 6 of the 1985 Act (registration of local services) in respect of local services in an area where a quality partnership scheme containing registration restrictions has been made. Consequential amendments are made to SI 1986/1629 and SI 1986/1671.

A quality partnership scheme is a scheme made under the Transport Act 2000, s 114 by a local transport authority, or two or more such authorities acting jointly, under which the authority (or authorities) provides particular facilities on routes used by local bus services, and operators of local services wishing to use those facilities undertake to provide local services of a particular standard when using them (see generally s 114(1), (2) of the 2000 Act). As part of a quality partnership scheme, local transport authorities may impose restrictions on the registration of local services within the area of a scheme where it is considered necessary or expedient to prevent or restrict the registration of new services, or the variation or withdrawal of existing services, where such changes might be detrimental to the provision of services under the scheme (see generally s 114(3A), (3B)).

[1208]

Citation, commencement and extent

1 (1) These Regulations may be cited as The Public Service Vehicles (Registration Restrictions) (England and Wales) Regulations 2009 and come into force on 6th April 2009.

(2) These Regulations extend to England and Wales.

[1209]

Interpretation

2 (1) In these Regulations—

"the 1985 Act" means the Transport Act 1985;

"decision" means the decision of a traffic commissioner under subsection (5) of section 6A of the 1985 Act (applications for registration etc where restrictions are in force);

"notice" means, except in regulation 6 and paragraph (1) of the Schedule, the notice given by the traffic commissioner to relevant authorities and relevant operators under subsection (2) of section 6A of the 1985 Act.

(2) Except in regulation 6, any period of days prescribed in these Regulations is to be calculated excluding any day which is Christmas Day, Good Friday or a day which is a bank holiday in England and Wales under the Banking and Financial Dealings Act 1971.

[1210]

Procedure for giving notice

3 (1) Subject to paragraph (3), a notice must be given in writing as soon as reasonably practicable after the date of receipt of the relevant application, and in any event no more than 14 days after that date.

(2) For the purposes of section 6A(3)(b) of the 1985 Act, a notice must include all of the following—

(a) a copy of the relevant application to which the notice relates;
(b) information about the procedure prescribed in regulation 4 for relevant authorities and relevant operators to make relevant representations to the traffic commissioner;
(c) the address to which relevant representations should be sent;
(d) where the service of relevant representations in electronic format is accepted, the fax number, e-mail address or other electronic address to which relevant representations may be sent;
(e) the date by which relevant representations must be made, which must be not less than 21 days after the date of the notice; and
(f) a list of the relevant authorities and relevant operators to whom the notice has been sent.

(3) Paragraph (1) does not apply if a relevant application does not contain all of the particulars prescribed for the purposes of section 6(2)(a) of the 1985 Act which are applicable to the application.

[1211]

Procedure for making relevant representations

4 (1) Relevant representations must—

(a) be made in writing;
(b) be served on the traffic commissioner who gave the notice no later than the date specified in accordance with regulation 3(2)(e); and
(c) state the reasons why the relevant authority or, as the case may be, the relevant operator believes that the effect of accepting the relevant application would be detrimental to the provision of local services under the quality partnership scheme.

(2) Relevant representations may, where the notice includes any of the information described in regulation 3(2)(d), be served by fax or electronic communication.

(3) The relevant authority or, as the case may be, the relevant operator must, at the same time as they submit relevant representations to the traffic commissioner, send a copy of those representations to—

(a) the person who made the relevant application; and
(b) the persons listed in the notice in accordance with regulation 3(2)(f).

(4) Where a relevant authority or, as the case may be, a relevant operator submits relevant representations after the date stipulated in the notice in accordance with regulation 3(2)(e), but before the traffic commissioner has made a decision in respect of the relevant application to which the relevant representations relate, the traffic commissioner may take those representations into account if satisfied that—

(a) there is an acceptable reason for the delay in submitting the representations; and
(b) taking the representations into account will not delay the making of the decision.

[1212]

Procedure to be followed in determining the application

5 (1) Where relevant representations are made to the traffic commissioner, the traffic commissioner must notify the parties described in paragraph (2) in writing, within the periods described in paragraph (3), of the decision as to whether the relevant application is to be accepted.

(2) The parties are—

(a) the person who made the relevant application;
(b) any relevant authority who made relevant representations against the application; and
(c) any relevant operator who made relevant representations against the application.

(3) The periods are—

(a) within 21 days beginning with the date stipulated in the notice in accordance with regulation 3(2)(e); or

(b) where the traffic commissioner holds an inquiry under section 54 of the Public Passenger Vehicles Act 1981 (inquiries held by traffic commissioners) in respect of a relevant application, within 14 days beginning with the date of the conclusion of the inquiry.

(4) Where the decision is to accept the relevant application, the notification referred to in paragraph (1) must specify the date, determined in accordance with regulation 6, on which the registration or, as the case may be, variation or cancellation of an existing registration, will take effect.

(5) Where the traffic commissioner considers it to be necessary in order for a particular case to be dealt with fairly and justly, the traffic commissioner may, in accordance with paragraph (6), extend either of the periods prescribed in paragraph (3).

(6) A period may be extended by virtue of paragraph (5) only for such period as the traffic commissioner considers appropriate in the circumstances of the case.

[1213]

Period of notice for purposes of section 6 of the 1985 Act

6 (1) Where a relevant application is accepted by the traffic commissioner, the period of notice referred to in section 6(2)(b) or, as the case may be, the date described in section 6(8)(a) of the 1985 Act is such period or date as the traffic commissioner may determine in accordance with this regulation.

(2) Unless the traffic commissioner decides that a shorter period should apply in accordance with paragraph (4), the date on which the period of notice expires must not be earlier than the later of the dates referred to in paragraph (3).

(3) The dates are—

(a) 28 days after the date on which the traffic commissioner notified the applicant of the decision in accordance with regulation 5(1); and

(b) the date cited in the relevant application as the date on which the applicant proposes to start to provide the new service or, as the case may be, to bring into effect the variation or cancellation of the registration of the service.

(4) The traffic commissioner may provide for the period of notice referred to in section 6(2)(b) or, as the case may be, section 6(8)(a) of the 1985 Act to be shorter than 28 days where the traffic commissioner considers that—

(a) due to exceptional circumstances, a shorter period would be appropriate; and

(b) it is reasonable to expect the operator to implement the new or, as the case may be, the revised particulars of the service within the shorter period.

(5) Where an application is made under section 6(7) of the 1985 Act to vary a registration to which registration restrictions imposed under section 114(3A) of the Transport Act 2000 have effect, and that application is made in either of the cases described in paragraph (6), section 6(8) of the 1985 Act is modified to exclude the requirement of the expiry of a period.

(6) The cases are—

(a) where the registration is varied only to enable the operator of the service to comply with a traffic regulation condition or any other provision made by or under an enactment prohibiting or restricting the use of any road by vehicular traffic; or

(b) where the registration is varied only in respect of a change in the operator's address.

[1214]

Consequential amendments

7 The amendments in the Schedule have effect.

[1215]

SCHEDULE

(*Para 1 amends SI 1986/1629; para 2 amends SI 1986/1671.*)

QUALITY PARTNERSHIP SCHEMES (ENGLAND) REGULATIONS 2009
SI 2009/445

Authority Made by the Secretary of State for Transport under the Transport Act 2000, ss 122, 160(1)(b), (c).

Date made 28 February 2009.

Commencement 6 April 2009; see reg 1(1).

Interpretation See reg 2.

General A quality partnership scheme is a scheme made under the Transport Act 2000, s 114 by a local transport authority, or two or more such authorities acting jointly, under which the authority (or authorities) provides particular facilities on routes used by local bus services, and operators of local services wishing to use those facilities undertake to provide local services of a particular standard when using them (see generally s 114(1), (2) of the 2000 Act). These regulations, which apply in relation to England only, make provision about quality partnership schemes, including requirements as to frequencies, timings and maximum fares as a standard of services.

Pt 1 of the regulations contains general provisions. Pt 2 defines "admissible objection" and "relevant operator" for the purposes of ss 114(6B), 122(3)(c) of the 2000 Act. Pt 3 prescribes the procedure under which requirements as to frequencies, timings and maximum fares may be reviewed.

[1216]

PART 1
GENERAL

Citation, commencement and extent

1 (1) These Regulations may be cited as The Quality Partnership Schemes (England) Regulations 2009 and come into force on 6th April 2009.

(2) These Regulations apply to England only.

[1217]

Interpretation

2 (1) In these Regulations—

"the Act" means the Transport Act 2000;

"the 1981 Act" means the Public Passenger Vehicles Act 1981;

"the 1985 Act" means the Transport Act 1985;

"admissible objection" has the meaning given in regulation 7;

"authority" means a local transport authority;

"lead authority" means—

(a) the authority which has made, or is proposing to make, a scheme; or

(b) where regulation 3 applies, the authority named as the lead authority in the notice of a proposed scheme given under section 115(1) of the Act;

"objector" means an operator who has made an objection in accordance with regulation 8;

"relevant operator" has the meaning given in regulations 5 and 6;

"scheme" means a quality partnership scheme;

"traffic commissioner" means, except for the purposes of regulations 5 and 7—

(a) where the area to which the scheme, or proposed scheme, relates falls entirely within one traffic area, the traffic commissioner for that traffic area; or

(b) where the area to which the scheme, or proposed scheme, relates falls within two or more traffic areas, the traffic commissioner for the traffic area in which the lead authority's area is situated.

(2) Any period of days prescribed in these Regulations is to be calculated excluding any day which is Christmas Day, Good Friday, or a day which is a bank holiday in England and Wales under the Banking and Financial Dealings Act 1971.

(3) In these Regulations, where a person is required to consider whether an operator could be expected to secure an "appropriate rate of return" for operating

services of a particular standard specified in any proposed or existing scheme, that person must have regard to the typical rates of return for operating local services of a comparable nature elsewhere in England.

[1218]

Identification of lead authority

3 (1) This regulation applies to any scheme containing a standard of services which includes requirements as to—

(a) the frequency or timing of services, or

(b) the maximum fares that may be charged for particular journeys, or for journeys of particular descriptions,

which is made, or is proposed to be made, by two or more authorities acting jointly.

(2) Where this regulation applies, the authorities referred to in paragraph (1) must specify in the notice of the proposed scheme given in accordance with section 115(1) of the Act which of them is to act as the lead authority for the purposes of these Regulations.

(3) Where this regulation applies the lead authority must, before exercising powers in relation to any of the duties and responsibilities assigned by virtue of these Regulations—

(a) consult and seek representations from, and

(b) wherever appropriate, act in accordance with the representations of,

the other authority or other authorities by whom the scheme is made, or is proposed to be made, jointly with the lead authority.

[1219]

Services to be excluded from the application of section 114(6B) of the Act

4 (1) This regulation applies where a local service is provided in accordance with a service subsidy agreement, or series of such agreements taken together, and that agreement or series of agreements has the effect described in paragraph (2).

(2) The effect is that by virtue of a requirement of the agreement or series of agreements, an operator provides services which would meet one or more relevant requirements.

(3) Where this regulation applies the restriction contained in section 114(6B) of the Act does not apply in respect of any relevant requirements.

(4) For the purposes of this regulation—

(a) a "service subsidy agreement" means an agreement made under section 9A(4) of the Transport Act 1968 or section 63(5) of the 1985 Act; and

(b) a "relevant requirement" means a requirement specified in a scheme, or proposed scheme, as to the standard of services to be provided in relation to the frequency or timing of services, or as to the maximum fares that may be charged for particular journeys, or for journeys of particular descriptions.

[1220]

PART 2
DETERMINATION OF RELEVANT OPERATOR AND ADMISSIBLE OBJECTION

Definition of "relevant operator"

5 (1) For the purposes of sections 114(6B) and 122(3)(c) of the Act, "relevant operator" has the meaning given to it by this regulation and regulation 6.

(2) Subject to paragraphs (3) and (4) a "relevant operator" is an operator who, on the day on which an authority or authorities first give notice under section 115(1) of the Act of the proposal to make a scheme—

(a) is operating one or more local services in accordance with particulars registered under section 6 of the 1985 Act, or

(b) is eligible under section 6(4) of the 1985 Act to have an application for registration accepted, and has made such an application to the traffic commissioner to register the particulars of one or more local services,

and the local service to which the registration or, as the case may be, application relates has one or more stopping places in the area to which the proposed scheme relates.

(3) Paragraph (2) does not apply to an operator when—

(a) the operator has, in respect of a local service to which paragraph (2)(a) applies, submitted an application to the traffic commissioner under section 6(7) of the 1985 Act to vary or cancel the registration of that local service, or

(b) the operator has, in respect of an application to which paragraph (2)(b) applies, withdrawn that application,

and the effect of either sub-paragraph (a) or (b) is that the operator would not, at such time as the variation, cancellation or withdrawal takes effect, be operating any local services with one or more stopping places in the area to which the proposed scheme relates.

(4) Paragraph (2) does not apply to an operator of local services if the only services which that operator provides, or proposes to provide, and to which that paragraph would otherwise apply are services which, under the scheme as proposed by the authority or authorities in the notice given under section 115(1) of the Act, would be excluded from the scheme under section 116(3) of the Act.

[1221]

Definition of "relevant operator" following modification of proposed scheme

6 (1) This regulation applies where an authority or authorities, following consultation under section 115 of the Act, make a scheme under section 116(1) of the Act with modifications and those modifications have the effect described in paragraph (2).

(2) The effect is that an operator who did not, on the day referred to in regulation 5(2), satisfy the definition of a relevant operator in that paragraph would have satisfied that definition if the proposed scheme referred to in the notice given under section 115(1) of the Act had instead been the scheme as modified.

(3) Where this regulation applies the lead authority must, as soon as reasonably practicable, serve notice on any operator to whom paragraph (2) may apply informing that operator of the modifications to the proposed scheme.

(4) Regulations 8 to 15 apply to any operator on whom notice is required to have been served in accordance with paragraph (3) as if the reference in regulation 8(1) to the publication of a notice under section 115(1) of the Act was a reference to the service of a notice under paragraph (3) of this regulation.

[1222]

Definition of "admissible objection"

7 (1) For the purposes of sections 114(6B) and 122(3)(c) of the Act "admissible objection" has the meaning given to it in this regulation.

(2) An "admissible objection" is an objection—

(a) made in accordance with the procedure prescribed in regulation 8; and

(b) which satisfies either or both of the grounds described in paragraph (3).

(3) The grounds are that—

(a) for either or both of the reasons listed in paragraph (4), it would not be practicable for the objector to provide particular relevant services, or relevant services of a particular description, to a specified standard which would apply to those relevant services if the scheme as proposed in the notice given under section 115(1) of the Act were to be made; or

(b) taking into account the matters listed in paragraph (5), it would not be commercially viable for the objector, acting in a competent and efficient manner, to provide relevant services to a specified standard which would apply to those relevant services if the scheme as proposed in the notice given under section 115(1) of the Act were to be made.

(4) The reasons referred to in paragraph (3)(a) are that—

(a) additional vehicles would need to be procured by the objector, or existing vehicles upgraded, to provide the service to the particular standard specified in the proposed scheme and it would not be practicable for the objector to procure the additional vehicles, or to upgrade existing vehicles, by the date specified in the proposed scheme; or

(b) additional staff would need to be employed by the objector to provide the service to the particular standard specified in the proposed scheme and it would not be practicable for the objector to employ the additional staff by the date specified in the proposed scheme.

(5) The matters referred to in paragraph (3)(b) are—

(a) the likely cost to the objector of providing relevant services to the particular standard which would apply to those services if the scheme as proposed in the notice given under section 115(1) of the Act were to be made;

(b) the income which the objector would be likely to receive from operating the relevant services, taking into account any additional fare revenue which is likely to accrue as a result of the—

(i) provision of facilities by the authority, and

(ii) improvements to the standard of services,

if the scheme as proposed in the notice given under section 115(1) of the Act were to be made; and

(c) whether, taking into account the matters described in sub-paragraphs (a) and (b), the objector could be expected to secure an appropriate rate of return from the operation of the relevant services in the area to which the proposed scheme relates.

(6) Subject to paragraphs (7) and (8), for the purposes of this regulation "relevant services" means, in relation to a particular operator—

(a) all local services registered under section 6 of the 1985 Act in the name of that operator which have one or more stopping places in the area to which the scheme relates and in respect of which, on the day on which the authority or authorities first gave notice under section 115(1) of the Act, the registration was extant; or

(b) all proposed local services with one or more stopping places in the area to which the scheme relates in respect of which the operator had made an application to the traffic commissioner to register particulars under section 6 of the 1985 Act, and that application was made on or before the day on which the authority or authorities first gave notice under section 115(1) of the Act.

(7) A local service is not a relevant service for the purposes of this regulation if, after the day on which the authority or authorities first gave notice under section 115(1) of the Act—

(a) in respect of a local service to which paragraph (6)(a) applies, the operator submits an application to the traffic commissioner under section 6(7) of the 1985 Act to vary or cancel the registration of the service, and the effect is as described in paragraph (8); or

(b) in respect of a proposed local service to which paragraph (6)(b) applies, the operator withdraws the application to register the service.

(8) The effect is that, at such time as the variation or cancellation takes effect the local service or, as the case may be, proposed local service, which, but for paragraph (7) and this paragraph, would be a relevant service, has no stopping places in the area to which the scheme relates.

[1223]

Procedure for making an objection

8 (1) An operator who wishes to object to a requirement falling within section 114(6)(b) or (6A) of the Act must make the objection in writing and serve it on the lead authority within a period of 28 days beginning with the day on which the notice given under section 115(1) of the Act in relation to that requirement is published.

(2) A copy of the objection made under paragraph (1) must, at the same time as the objection is served on the lead authority, be sent by the objector to the traffic commissioner.

(3) An objection made under paragraph (1) must contain—

(a) a statement describing the basis on which the objector considers that the objector is a relevant operator for the purposes of sections 114(6B) and 122(3)(c) of the Act;

(b) a statement describing the basis on which the objector considers that either or both of the grounds specified in regulation 7(3) is or are satisfied; and

(c) evidence to support the statements described in sub-paragraphs (a) and (b).

[1224]

Request for further information by lead authority

9 (1) Subject to paragraph (2) the lead authority may, within a period of 14 days beginning with the day on which an objection described in regulation 8 is received, request such further information or evidence from the objector as that authority considers necessary in order to reach a decision as to whether the objection is an admissible objection or the objector is a relevant operator.

(2) The lead authority may, with the written consent of the objector, extend the 14 day period specified in paragraph (1).

(3) If the lead authority requests information or evidence in accordance with paragraph (1) the authority must specify the period within which such information or evidence is to be submitted by the objector and that period must—

(a) be of sufficient length, taking into account the nature and complexity of the request, to provide the objector with a reasonable period within which to respond; and

(b) be not less than 14 days beginning with the day on which the request is issued by the authority.

(4) If the objector fails to respond to a request under paragraph (1) within the period specified in the request in accordance with paragraph (3) the lead authority may nevertheless proceed to make a decision under regulation 10.

[1225]

Decision of lead authority

10 (1) Subject to paragraph (2), within a period of 28 days beginning with the day on which an objection is received or, as the case may be, the end of the period within which such further information or evidence requested under regulation 9 must be submitted, the lead authority must make a decision as to whether—

(a) the objector is a relevant operator, and

(b) the objection is an admissible objection,

and issue a written notice to inform the objector of that decision.

(2) The lead authority may, with the written consent of the objector, extend the 28 day period specified in paragraph (1).

(3) Where the decision of the lead authority is that—

(a) the objector is a relevant operator, and

(b) the objection is an admissible objection,

the written notice issued in accordance with paragraph (1) must satisfy the requirement described in paragraph (4).

(4) The requirement is that the written notice must either—

(a) describe the modifications that the lead authority proposes to make to the standard of services to be specified in the scheme as a consequence of the decision; or

(b) describe when and in what manner the lead authority will issue a supplementary notice to inform the objector of the proposed modifications.

(5) The lead authority must send a copy of the written notice issued in accordance with paragraph (1) and, where appropriate, the supplementary notice issued in accordance with paragraph (4)(b) to the traffic commissioner.

[1226]

Referral to the traffic commissioner

11 (1) The objector may, within a period of 14 days beginning with the day on which the written notice is issued under regulation 10(1) or, where appropriate, the supplementary notice described in regulation 10(4)(b) is issued, refer either of the matters described in paragraph (2) to the traffic commissioner for a determination under regulation 14.

(2) The matters are—

- (a) an objection to the decision of the lead authority under regulation 10(1) that an objector is not a relevant operator or that an objection is not an admissible objection; or
- (b) an objection to the modified standard of services that the lead authority proposes to specify in the scheme as a consequence of a decision as described in regulation 10(3).

(3) When a matter is referred to the traffic commissioner in accordance with this regulation the objector must at the same time send to the traffic commissioner—

- (a) a copy of the objection as submitted to the lead authority;
- (b) a copy of any further information or evidence submitted to the lead authority in response to any request under regulation 9(1);
- (c) where the matter is an objection described in paragraph (2)(a) a statement describing why, in the opinion of the objector, the decision of the lead authority made under regulation 10 is incorrect; and
- (d) where the matter is an objection described in paragraph (2)(b) a statement describing why, in the opinion of the objector, either or both of the grounds specified in regulation 7(3) are satisfied in relation to the modified standard of services proposed to be specified in a scheme.

(4) The objector must, at the same time as submitting the information described in paragraph (3) to the traffic commissioner, submit a copy of that information to the lead authority.

[1227]

Provision of information to traffic commissioner

12 (1) Where a matter is referred to the traffic commissioner under regulation 11 for a determination the lead authority must, within a period of 14 days beginning with the day on which the information provided by virtue of regulation 11(4) is received, submit to the traffic commissioner—

- (a) a statement describing the basis on which the decision under regulation 10 was taken; and
- (b) any additional evidence or information which that authority considers to be relevant to the determination.

(2) The lead authority must, at the same time as it submits the statement described in paragraph (1)(a), send to the objector a copy of that statement and such additional evidence or information which the lead authority is submitting to the traffic commissioner in accordance with paragraph (1)(b).

(3) If the lead authority fails to submit the material described in paragraph (1)(a) and (b) within the period specified in that paragraph, the traffic commissioner may nevertheless proceed to make a determination under regulation 14.

(4) The traffic commissioner may, within a period of 14 days beginning with the end of the period for the submission of the material described in paragraph (1)(a) and (b), request such further information or evidence from the objector or the lead authority as the traffic commissioner considers necessary in order to make a determination.

(5) Where such information or evidence is requested in accordance with paragraph (4) the objector or, as the case may be, the lead authority must submit that information or evidence within a period of 14 days beginning with the day on which the request is received.

(6) The objector or, as the case may be, the lead authority must, at the same time as it submits any information or evidence requested under paragraph (4) to the traffic commissioner, send a copy of that information or evidence to the lead authority or, as the case may be, the objector.

(7) If the objector or, as the case may be, the lead authority fails to respond to a request under paragraph (4) within the period specified in paragraph (5) the traffic commissioner may nevertheless proceed to make a determination under regulation 14. **[1228]**

Assessors to assist traffic commissioners

13 (1) This regulation applies where the traffic commissioner, in considering any matter referred under regulation 11, is required to determine whether the ground specified in regulation 7(3)(b) has been satisfied.

(2) In making such a determination the traffic commissioner may be assisted by an assessor selected from a panel of persons appointed by the Secretary of State for the purposes of section 17A of the 1981 Act.

(3) Where a traffic commissioner seeks the assistance of a person described in paragraph (2), the traffic commissioner must pay that person such remuneration as may be determined by the Secretary of State. **[1229]**

Determination of the traffic commissioner

14 (1) Within a period of 28 days beginning with the date of the later of the following—

(a) the end of the period for submission of the material described in regulation 12(1)(a) and (b), or

(b) the end of the period within which such further information or evidence requested under regulation 12(4) must be submitted,

the traffic commissioner must make a determination of the matter referred under regulation 11 and issue a written notice to the objector and the lead authority informing them of the determination.

(2) Where the determination of the traffic commissioner is that the objection should be upheld, the traffic commissioner may recommend to the lead authority such modifications to the requirements specified in the proposed scheme as to frequencies, timings or maximum fares as the traffic commissioner considers appropriate.

(3) Where the traffic commissioner makes recommendations to the lead authority in accordance with paragraph (2), and the authority either—

(a) modifies the scheme in accordance with those recommendations, or

(b) removes the requirement to which the admissible objection relates,

the objection is no longer an admissible objection for the purposes of section 114(6B) of the Act.

(4) Where either—

(a) the traffic commissioner does not make recommendations to the lead authority in relation to a determination described in paragraph (2), or

(b) the authority proposes modifications to the scheme which are different to those recommended by the traffic commissioner under paragraph (2),

paragraphs (5) to (9) apply.

(5) Where this paragraph applies the lead authority must, within a period of 28 days beginning with the day on which the determination made under paragraph (1) is received, send a written notice to the objector describing the modifications that the authority proposes to make to the standard of services to be specified in the scheme as a consequence of a determination described in paragraph (2).

(6) The lead authority may, with the written consent of the objector, extend the 28 day period specified in paragraph (5).

(7) If within a period of 14 days beginning with the day on which the notice under paragraph (5) is received the objector has not withdrawn the objection, the lead authority may refer the matter back to the traffic commissioner for a determination.

(8) Where any matter is referred back to the traffic commissioner by virtue of paragraph (7), the traffic commissioner must make a determination within a period of 14 days beginning with the date on which the matter is referred.

(9) Where the determination of the traffic commissioner in response to a referral under paragraph (7) is that the objection is not an admissible objection, the objection is no longer an admissible objection for the purposes of section 114(6B) of the Act.

[1230]

Extension of time

15 (1) Where the traffic commissioner considers it to be necessary in order for a particular case to be dealt with fairly and justly the traffic commissioner may, in accordance with paragraph (2), extend any of the periods described in paragraph (3).

(2) A period described in paragraph (3) may only be extended for such period as the traffic commissioner considers appropriate in the circumstances of the case.

(3) The periods are those specified in—

- (a) regulation 11(1);
- (b) regulation 12(1);
- (c) regulation 12(4);
- (d) regulation 12(5);
- (e) regulation 14(1); and
- (f) regulation 14(8).

[1231]

PART 3
REVIEW OF REQUIREMENTS AS TO FREQUENCIES, TIMINGS OR MAXIMUM FARES

Interpretation of Part 3

16 For the purposes of this Part—

- (a) a review is "completed" on the latest of the following dates—
  - (i) where an objection to the whole or any part of the outcome of the review has been submitted by virtue of regulation 25(2), the date on which that objection is finally determined,
  - (ii) the date on which the time for the submission of an objection under regulation 25(2) expires without any such objection having been made, or
  - (iii) the date on which an objection made in accordance with regulation 25(2) is abandoned or withdrawn,

  and "objection" includes a reference to any further referral to a traffic commissioner for a determination under regulation 11, as applied by regulation 25;
- (b) a request for a review of a requirement as to frequencies, timings or maximum fares is an "excepted request" if the lead authority is of the opinion that, since the relevant date, there has not been a change in market conditions which materially affects the ability of the operator or operators making the request, acting in a competent and efficient manner, to secure an appropriate rate of return from continuing to operate existing services to the standard specified in the scheme;
- (c) "existing services" means, in relation to a particular operator, all local services registered under section 6 of the 1985 Act in the name of that operator—
  - (i) which have one or more stopping places in the area to which the scheme relates; and
  - (ii) in respect of which, on the day on which the lead authority, without a request from a relevant participating operator, decides to start a review or, as the case may be, a request for a review is made by a relevant participating operator, the registration is extant;
- (d) "maximum fares requirement period" has the meaning given in regulation 17(2);

(e) "participating operator" means, in relation to a particular scheme, an operator—
   (i) who has given a written undertaking to the traffic commissioner in accordance with section 118(4)(a) of the Act in respect of that scheme; and
   (ii) who is, at the relevant time, operating local services in accordance with the terms of that undertaking;

(f) "relevant date", in relation to a requirement as to frequencies, timings or maximum fares, means either—
   (i) the date on which the requirement or, where a requirement as to maximum fares is varied in accordance with a formula, that formula was first introduced; or
   (ii) where there has been a previous review of that requirement or formula, the date on which that review was completed;

(g) "relevant participating operator" means, in relation to any requirement as to frequencies, timings or maximum fares specified in a scheme, a participating operator to whom that requirement applies; and

(h) "review notice" means a notice issued by a lead authority to start a review of requirements as to frequencies, timings or maximum fares under these Regulations.

[1232]

Review of requirements as to maximum fares by lead authority

17 (1) Except where regulation 20 applies, where an authority or authorities make a scheme which specifies a standard of services which includes requirements as to the maximum fares that may be charged for particular journeys, of for journeys of particular descriptions, that scheme must specify a maximum fares requirement period in accordance with paragraphs (2) and (3).

(2) A maximum fares requirement period is, as the case may be, the period—

(a) between the date on which the requirements as to maximum fares first come into effect, and the latest date by which it is specified that the first review of those requirements must start; or

(b) between the completion of a review of the requirements as to maximum fares, and the latest date by which it is specified that the next review of those requirements must start.

(3) The maximum fares requirement period must be no greater than 12 months.

(4) Prior to the end of the maximum fares requirement period the lead authority must start a review by issuing a written review notice to participating operators to whom the requirements as to maximum fares apply.

(5) The review notice must propose—

(a) that requirements as to the maximum fares that may be charged for particular journeys, or for journeys of particular descriptions, contained in the scheme, or any part of the scheme, should cease to have effect;

(b) that the existing maximum fares that may be charged for particular journeys, or for journeys of particular descriptions, should continue to have effect until the next review; or

(c) revised requirements as to the maximum fares that may be charged for particular journeys, or for journeys of particular descriptions.

(6) Provided the lead authority issues a review notice prior to the end of the maximum fares requirement period, the existing requirements as to maximum fares contained in the scheme continue to have effect, unless paragraph (7) applies, until that authority makes a decision in accordance with regulation 24(2).

(7) Where the decision made in accordance with regulation 24(2) is that revised requirements as to maximum fares should be incorporated into the scheme, the existing requirements as to maximum fares contained in the scheme continue to have effect until such time as those revised requirements take effect in accordance with the timetable specified in accordance with regulation 24(5)(b).

(8) If the lead authority considers that either or both of the conditions in paragraph (9) are met in relation to some or all of the requirements as to the maximum

fares that may be charged for particular journeys, or for journeys of particular descriptions, it may, at any time prior to the end of the maximum fares requirement period, start a review of those requirements by issuing a written review notice to relevant participating operators.

(9) The conditions are that—

(a) there has, since the relevant date, been a change in market conditions which materially affects the ability of relevant participating operators, acting in a competent and efficient manner, to secure an appropriate rate of return from continuing to operate existing services in accordance with the requirements as to maximum fares specified in the scheme; or

(b) the existing requirements are no longer consistent with the local transport policies of the lead authority or of the other authority or of any of the other authorities (as the case may be) by whom the scheme is made.

[1233]

Failure of lead authority to review requirements as to maximum fares

18 (1) If a lead authority fails to issue a review notice before the end of the maximum fares requirement period, any participating operator to whom requirements as to maximum fares apply may request a review of the requirements.

(2) An operator who wishes to make a request under paragraph (1) must make the request in writing and serve it on the lead authority within a period of 28 days beginning with the day on which the maximum fares requirement period ends.

(3) A copy of the request made under paragraph (1) must, at the same time as the request is served on the lead authority, be sent to the traffic commissioner.

(4) If, within a period of 14 days beginning with the day on which a request made in accordance with paragraph (1) is received, the lead authority has not issued a review notice, any requirements as to the maximum fares that may be charged for particular journeys, or for journeys of particular descriptions, cease to have effect.

(5) If a lead authority fails to issue a review notice before the end of the maximum fares requirement period, and no request is made under paragraph (1), any requirements as to the maximum fares that may be charged for particular journeys, or for journeys of particular descriptions, remain in force until—

(a) revised requirements come into effect following a subsequent review, or

(b) the requirements cease to have effect following a subsequent review,

whichever is the earlier.

[1234]

Request for review of requirements as to maximum fares by operator

19 (1) At any time prior to the end of the maximum fares requirement period a review of any requirement or requirements as to maximum fares may be requested by—

(a) three or more relevant participating operators, or

(b) at least 50% of relevant participating operators,

(whichever is the lesser).

(2) Where a review is requested in accordance with paragraph (1) the operator or operators making the request must—

(a) specify to which requirement or requirements as to maximum fares the request relates;

(b) submit representations and evidence in support of the request; and

(c) propose revised requirements as to the maximum fares that may be charged for particular journeys, or for journeys of particular descriptions.

(3) Except where the request for a review is an excepted request the lead authority must, within a period of 28 days beginning with the day on which a request submitted in accordance with paragraph (1) is received, issue a written review notice to relevant participating operators.

[1235]

Review of formula for varying maximum fares by lead authority

20 (1) This regulation applies where a scheme includes requirements as to the maximum fares that may be charged for particular journeys, or for journeys of particular descriptions, and that scheme includes a mechanism under which those maximum fares are varied at least every 12 months in accordance with a formula.

(2) If the lead authority considers that the conditions in paragraph (3) are met in relation to any or all of the requirements as to maximum fares that may be charged for particular journeys, or for journeys of a particular description, which are varied in accordance with a formula the lead authority may, at any time, start a review of that formula by issuing a written review notice to relevant participating operators in accordance with paragraph (4).

(3) The conditions are that—

(a) there has, since the relevant date, been a change in market conditions which materially affects the ability of relevant participating operators, acting in a competent and efficient manner, to secure an appropriate rate of return from continuing to operate existing services in accordance with the requirements as to maximum fares specified in the scheme if the fares are varied in accordance with the formula; or

(b) the effect of the formula is no longer consistent with the local transport policies of the lead authority or of the other authority or of any of the other authorities (as the case may be) by whom the scheme is made.

(4) The review notice must propose—

(a) that the requirements as to the maximum fares that may be charged for particular journeys, or for journeys of particular descriptions, contained in the scheme, or any part of the scheme, should cease to have effect;

(b) one or more revisions to the formula referred to in paragraph (1); or

(c) replacing the formula with specified maximum fares that may be charged for particular journeys, or for journeys of particular descriptions.

[1236]

Request for review of formula varying maximum fares by operators

21 (1) At any time during a period in which a formula described in regulation 20(1) applies a review of the formula may be requested by—

(a) three or more relevant participating operators, or

(b) at least 50% of relevant participating operators,

(whichever is the lesser).

(2) Where a review of the formula is requested in accordance with paragraph (1), the operator or operators making that request must—

(a) specify to which part of the formula the request relates;

(b) submit representations and evidence in support of the request; and

(c) propose a revised formula for the variation of maximum fares.

(3) Except where paragraph (4) applies the lead authority must, within a period of 28 days beginning with the day on which the request submitted in accordance with paragraph (1) is received, issue a written review notice to relevant participating operators.

(4) The obligation in paragraph (3) does not apply where the request submitted in accordance with paragraph (1)—

(a) is received less than 12 months after the relevant date; and

(b) is an excepted request.

[1237]

Review of requirements as to frequencies or timings by lead authority

22 (1) Where an authority or authorities make a scheme which specifies a standard of services which includes requirements as to the frequency or timing of services the lead authority may, if they consider that either or both of the conditions in paragraph (2) are met in relation to any or all of those requirements, start a review of those requirements by issuing a written review notice to relevant participating operators.

(2) The conditions are that—

(a) there has, since the relevant date, been a change in market conditions which materially affects the ability of relevant participating operators, acting in a competent and efficient manner, to secure an appropriate rate of return from continuing to operate existing services in accordance with the requirements as to the frequency or timing of services specified in the scheme; or

(b) the existing requirements are no longer consistent with the local transport policies of the lead authority or of the other authority or of any of the other authorities (as the case may be) by whom the scheme is made.

(3) The review notice must propose either—

(a) that the requirements as to the frequency or timing of services contained in the scheme, or any part of the scheme, should cease to have effect; or

(b) that those requirements should be revised.

[1238]

Request for review of requirements as to frequencies and timings by operator

23 (1) At any time a review of any requirement or requirements as to the frequency or timing of services may be requested by—

(a) three or more relevant participating operators, or

(b) at least 50% of relevant participating operators,

(whichever is the lesser).

(2) Where a review is requested in accordance with paragraph (1) the operator or operators making that request must—

(a) specify to which requirement or requirements as to the frequency or timing of services the request relates;

(b) submit representations and evidence in support of the request; and

(c) propose revised requirements as to frequencies and timings.

(3) Except where paragraph (4) applies the lead authority must, within a period of 28 days beginning with the day on which the request submitted in accordance with paragraph (1) is received, issue a written review notice to relevant participating operators.

(4) The obligation in paragraph (3) does not apply where the request submitted in accordance with paragraph (1)—

(a) is received less than 12 months after the relevant date; and

(b) is an excepted request.

[1239]

Procedure for reviews

24 (1) A review notice must specify the last date for the receipt of representations from relevant participating operators in response to that notice, and that date must be—

(a) not less than 28 days, and

(b) not more than 42 days,

after the date on which the review notice is issued.

(2) The lead authority must, within a period of 35 days beginning with the date specified in the review notice in accordance with paragraph (1), decide whether the requirements as to frequencies, timings or maximum fares or, as the case may be, the formula used to vary maximum fares, should—

(a) continue to have effect until the next review,

(b) cease to have effect, or

(c) be revised.

(3) The lead authority must, once a decision is made by virtue of paragraph (2), issue a written notice to all relevant participating operators.

(4) The lead authority may, with the written consent of all of the relevant participating operators, extend the period specified in paragraph (2).

(5) Where the decision referred to in paragraph (2) is that the requirements as to frequencies, timings or maximum fares, or the formula used to vary maximum fares, should be revised, the notice issued under paragraph (3) must—

(a) set out the details of the proposed revisions; and

(b) subject to paragraph (6), set out the timetable for the proposed implementation of the revisions.

(6) The timetable specified in accordance with paragraph (5)(b) must—

(a) provide for any revision of requirements as to maximum fares, or the formula used to vary maximum fares, to take effect as soon as reasonably practicable after the review is completed;

(b) provide for any revision of requirements as to frequencies or timings to take effect as soon as reasonably practicable after the review is completed, taking into account the need for operators, as appropriate, to register a new local service, or vary or cancel the registration of an existing local service, in accordance with section 6 of the 1985 Act; and

(c) take into account, where the lead authority is aware that a relevant participating operator is party to a voluntary partnership agreement, as defined in section 153(2) of the Act, or any other agreement with operators of local services, any conditions which that agreement might contain restricting the implementation of changes to requirements as to frequencies, timings or maximum fares to particular dates or times in the year.

[1240]

Objections to the outcome of a review

25 (1) Revised requirements as to frequencies, timings or maximum fares (including any revision to a formula described in regulation 20(1)) may come into effect only if there are no admissible objections to the revised requirements from relevant participating operators.

(2) Where, following receipt of the notice described in regulation 24(3), a relevant participating operator wishes to submit an objection to the whole or any part of the outcome of the review, the procedures in regulations 8 to 15 apply as if the reference to a notice given under section 115(1) of the Act was a reference to a notice given under regulation 24(3).

[1241]

ROAD SAFETY (FINANCIAL PENALTY DEPOSIT) ORDER 2009 SI 2009/491

Authority Made by the Secretary of State for Transport under the Road Traffic Offenders Act 1988, ss 90A(2)(b), 90B(1)(a), 90C(11), 90E(3).

Date made 5 March 2009.

Commencement 31 March 2009; see art 1.

Interpretation See art 2.

General The Road Traffic Offenders Act 1988, Pt 3A (ss 90A–90F) (inserted by the Road Safety Act 2006, s 11(1)) provides for a constable or vehicle examiner to impose a financial penalty deposit requirement on a person without a satisfactory United Kingdom address if he reasonably believes that: (a) the person is committing or has committed an offence relating to a motor vehicle, and (b) the person, the offence and the circumstances in which the offence is committed are of a description specified by order (see s 90A).

This order specifies persons, offences and circumstances in which a financial penalty deposit requirement may be imposed for the purposes of s 90A. It also specifies the manner of payment of the appropriate amount (as to which, see SI 2009/492) for the purposes of s 90B of the 1988 Act, and the appropriate steps to be taken by the Secretary of State when making an appropriate refund under s 90C.

Financial penalty deposit: interest The Road Traffic Offenders Act 1988, s 90C applies where a person on whom a financial penalty deposit requirement is imposed in respect of an offence makes a payment of the appropriate amount in accordance with s 90B(1). S 90C sets out the circumstances in which the Secretary of State must take steps to make an appropriate refund to the person concerned. Under s 90C(12), "the appropriate refund" is any amount by which the financial penalty deposit exceeds the fixed penalty or any court fine payable, or the whole of the financial penalty deposit where no fixed penalty or fine is payable, together with interest calculated in accordance with provision made by order.

SI 2009/498 (made by the Treasury under s 90C(12) of the 1988 Act and in force on 31 March 2009), provides that the rate of interest payable is the Bank of England base rate at the beginning of the day that the payment of the appropriate amount was made. "Bank of England base rate" means:

(a) the rate announced from time to time by the Monetary Policy Committee of the Bank of England as the official dealing rate, being the rate at which the Bank is willing to enter into transactions for providing short term liquidity in the money markets, or

(b) where an order under the Bank of England Act 1998, s 19 is in force, any equivalent rate determined by the Treasury under that section.

[1242]

Citation and commencement

1 This Order may be cited as the Road Safety (Financial Penalty Deposit) Order 2009 and shall come into force on 31st March 2009.

[1243]

Interpretation

2 In this Order—

"the Act" means the Road Traffic Offenders Act 1988;

"credit card" means a card or similar thing issued by any person, use of which enables the holder to defer the payment by the holder of the charge for the appropriate amount; and

"debit card" means a card or similar thing issued by any person, use of which by the holder causes the charge for the appropriate amount to be paid by the electronic transfer of funds from any current account of the holder at a bank or other institution providing banking services.

[1244]

The specified person

3 The specified person for the purposes of section 90A(2)(b) of the Act is the person in charge of the motor vehicle at the time at which the constable or vehicle examiner has reason to believe that a person is committing, or has on that occasion committed an offence specified in this Order relating to that vehicle.

[1245]

The specified offences

4 The specified offences for the purposes of section 90A(2)(b) of the Act are set out in column one of the tables in the Schedule (the general nature of the offence is also indicated in column two).

[1246]

The specified circumstances

5 (1) The specified circumstances for the purposes of section 90A(2)(b) of the Act are that the offence is being committed, or has on that occasion been committed, on a road or other public place.

(2) In this article, "road" has the meaning given in section 192(1) of the Road Traffic Act 1988.

[1247]

Manner of payment

6 Payment of the appropriate amount shall be made—

(a) in person to the vehicle examiner or the constable, by cash or credit or debit card, if the vehicle examiner or constable has the necessary means to accept payment in that manner;

(b) by telephone by credit or debit card, to the number given on the document referred to in section 90A(3) of the Act, if a number is so given; or

(c) by any other means specified on the document referred to in section 90A(3) of the Act.

[1248]

Appropriate steps to make an appropriate refund

7 (1) The appropriate steps to trace the person and to make an appropriate refund, for the purposes of section 90C(11) of the Act are set out in paragraphs (2) and (3).

(2) The Secretary of State shall—

(a) attempt to contact the person (on whom the financial penalty requirement was imposed) at any address given in any response or in any document provided to a vehicle examiner or constable;

but if the attempt to contact that person is unsuccessful, and if a person other than that person made the payment,

(b) attempt to contact that other person, at any address or contact details given when the person made the payment.

(3) The means by which an appropriate refund can be made by the Secretary of State are—

(a) by cheque;
(b) by refund to any credit or debit card used to make the financial penalty payment; or
(c) by any other means agreed with the person to whom the appropriate refund is to be made.

[1249]

SCHEDULE

Article 4

PART 1
ACTS OF PARLIAMENT

Table 1

Transport Act 1968

Provision creating offence	*General nature of offence*
Section 96(11)	Contravention of any requirement of the domestic drivers' hours code
Section 96(11A)	Contravention of any requirement of applicable Community rules as to periods of driving, etc
Section 97(1)	Using vehicle in contravention of any requirement of applicable Community rules as to periods of driving, etc
Section 97AA(1)	Forgery, etc, of seals on recording equipment
Section 98(4)	Contravention of regulations made under section 98 or any requirement as to books, records or documents of applicable Community rules
Section 99(4)	Failing to comply with requirements relating to inspection of records or obstructing an officer
Section 99(5)	Making false entry in book, register or document, etc
Section 99ZD(1)	Failing to comply with requirements relating to inspection of recording equipment or records (whether electronic or hard copy) made by or stored on recording equipment
Section 99ZE(1)	Making or permitting, false record or entry, etc
Section 99ZE(3)	Recording or causing or permitting to be recorded false data on recording equipment or driver card, etc
Section 99ZE(6)	Producing, supplying or installing device to interfere with recording equipment or falsify, etc, data
Section 99C	Failure to comply with prohibition or direction in relation to driving vehicle.

Table 2

Road Traffic (Foreign Vehicles) Act 1972

Provision creating offence	*General nature of offence*
Section 3(1)	Driving a foreign goods or foreign public service vehicle in contravention of a prohibition, etc

Table 3

Public Passenger Vehicles Act 1981

Provision creating offence	*General nature of offence*
Section 6(2)	Using a vehicle without certificate of initial fitness (or equivalent)
Section 12(5)	Using public service vehicle except under PSV operators' licence
Section 18(4)	Using a vehicle without displaying operator's disc
Section 65(2)	Forgery and misuse of documents, etc

Table 4

Road Traffic Regulation Act 1984

Provision creating offence	*General nature of offence*
Section 5(1)	Using a vehicle in contravention of a traffic regulation order outside Greater London
Section 8(1)	Breach of traffic regulation order in Greater London
Section 11(1)	Breach of experimental traffic order
Section 16(1)	Using a vehicle in contravention of temporary prohibition or restriction of traffic in case of execution of works, etc
Section 17(4)	Wrongful use of special road
Section 18(3)	Using a vehicle in contravention of provision for one-way traffic on trunk road
Section 20(5)	Driving a vehicle in contravention of order prohibiting or restricting driving vehicles on certain classes of roads
Section 25(5)	Breach of pedestrian crossing regulations
Section 88(7)	Contravention of minimum speed limit
Section 89(1)	Exceeding speed limit

Table 5

Road Traffic Act 1988

Provision creating offence	*General nature of offence*
Section 3	Careless, and inconsiderate, driving
Section 4(1)	Driving or attempting to drive when unfit to drive through drink or drugs
Section 4(2)	Being in charge of a mechanically propelled vehicle when unfit to drive through drink or drugs
Section 5(1)(a)	Driving or attempting to drive with excess alcohol in breath, blood or urine

Provision creating offence	*General nature of offence*
Section 5(1)(b)	Being in charge of a motor vehicle with excess alcohol in breath, blood or urine
Section 12(1)	Motor racing and speed trials on public ways
Section 13(1)	Other unauthorised or irregular competitions or trials on public ways
Section 14(3)	Breach of regulations requiring wearing of seat belts
Section 15(2)	Driving motor vehicle with child not wearing seat belt or with child in a rear-facing child restraint front seat with an active air bag
Section 15(4)	Driving motor vehicle with child in rear not wearing seat belt
Section 16(4)	Driving or riding motor cycles in contravention of regulations requiring wearing of protective headgear
Section 18(3)	Contravention of regulations with respect to use of head-worn appliances (eye protectors) on motor cycles
Section 19(1)	Prohibition of parking of heavy commercial vehicles on verges, etc
Section 22	Leaving vehicle in dangerous position
Section 33(3)	Unauthorised motor vehicle trial on footpaths or bridleways, etc
Section 34(1)	Driving mechanically propelled vehicles elsewhere than on roads
Section 35(1)	Failing to comply with traffic directions given by constable or traffic officer engaged in the regulation of traffic in a road
Section 35(2)	Failing to comply with traffic directions given by constable or traffic officer where a traffic survey is being carried out
Section 36(1)	Failing to comply with traffic signs
Section 40A	Using a vehicle in dangerous condition etc
Section 41A	Breach of requirement as to brakes, steering-gear or tyres
Section 41B	Breach of requirement as to weight: goods and passenger vehicles
Section 41D	Breach of requirements as to control of vehicle, mobile telephone, etc
Section 42	Breach of other construction and use requirements
Section 47(1)	Using etc, vehicle without required test certificate being in force
Section 53(1)	Using, etc, goods vehicle without required plating certificate being in force
Section 53(2)	Using, etc, goods vehicle without required goods vehicle test certificate being in force
Section 53(3)	Using, etc, goods vehicle where Secretary of State is required by regulations under section 49 to be notified of an alteration to the vehicle or its equipment but has not been notified
Section 63(1)	Using, etc, goods vehicle without required certificate being in force showing that the vehicle, etc, complies with type approval requirements applicable to it

Provision creating offence	*General nature of offence*
Section 63(2)	Using, etc, certain goods vehicles for drawing trailer when plating certificate does not specify maximum laden weight for vehicle and trailer
Section 63(3)	Using, etc, goods vehicle where Secretary of State is required to be notified under section 59 of alteration to it or its equipment but has not been notified
Section 64(2)	Using goods vehicle with unauthorised weights as well as unauthorised weights marked on it
Section 67(9)	Obstructing testing of vehicle by examiner on road or failing to comply with requirements of Road Traffic Act 1988 section 67 or Schedule 2
Section 68(3)	Obstructing inspection, etc, of vehicle by examiner
Section 68(5)	Failing to comply with requirement to take vehicle for inspection
Section 71(1)	Driving, etc, vehicle in contravention of prohibition on driving it as being unfit for service, or failing to comply with direction to remove a vehicle found overloaded
Section 76(1)	Fitting of defective or unsuitable vehicle parts
Section 78(3)	Failing to comply with requirement about weighing motor vehicle or obstructing authorised person
Section 87(1)	Driving otherwise than in accordance with a licence
Section 94A(1)	Driving after refusal or revocation of licence etc
Section 96(1)	Driving with uncorrected defective eyesight
Section 103(1)(b)	Driving while disqualified
Section 114(1)	Failing to comply with conditions of LGV or PCV driver's licence
Section 114(2)	Causing or permitting a person under 21 to drive LGV or PCV in contravention of conditions of licence
Section 143(2)	Using, etc, motor vehicle while uninsured or unsecured against third party risks
Section 163(3), insofar as it relates to section 163(1)	Failing to stop mechanically propelled vehicle when required
Section 164(6)	Failing to produce driving licence or counterpart, etc, or to state date of birth, etc
Section 165(3)	Failing to give certain names and addresses or produce certain documents on request when driving a motor vehicle, etc
Section 165(6)	Failing to give certain names and addresses while supervising a provisional licence-holder, etc
Section 168 (insofar as it relates to the case referred to in paragraph (a) of that section)	Refusing to give, or giving false, name and address in case of reckless, careless or inconsiderate driving of a mechanically propelled vehicle
Section 170(4)	Failing to stop after accident and give particulars or report accident
Section 181(3)	Obstructing inspection of vehicles after accident

Table 6

Road Traffic Offenders Act 1988

Provision creating offence	*General nature of offence*
Section 62(2)	Removing or interfering with fixed penalty notice fixed to vehicle
Section 90D(6)	Driving a vehicle in contravention of a prohibition on driving, etc, on failure to make a financial penalty deposit payment

Table 7

Vehicles Excise and Registration Act 1994

Provision creating offence	*General nature of offence*
Section 42(1)	Driving or keeping a vehicle without required registration mark
Section 43(1)	Driving or keeping a vehicle with registration mark obscured etc
Section 44(1)	Forgery and fraudulent use, etc, of a registration mark etc

Table 8

Goods Vehicles (Licensing of Operators) Act 1995

Provision creating offence	*General nature of offence*
Section 2(5)	Using goods vehicle on road for carriage of goods except under operator's licence
Section 3(6)	Using a vehicle on a restricted operator's licence whilst carrying goods for hire or reward
Section 3(7)	Using a vehicle on an international journey carrying goods for hire or reward whilst holding a licence for national transport operations only
Section 38(1)	Forgery of documents, etc

Table 9

Disability Discrimination Act 1995

Provision creating offence	*General nature of offence*
Section 40(3)	Failure to comply with PSV accessibility regulations made under section 40(1) etc
Section 41(3)	Using a regulated public service vehicle on the road where no accessibility certificate or approval certificate has been issued

[1250]

PART 2
SECONDARY LEGISLATION

Table 1

The Road Transport (International Passenger Services) Regulations 1984

Provision creating offence	*General nature of offence*
Regulation 19(1)	Using vehicle for Community regulated carriage of passengers otherwise than in accordance with the Council Regulations or the Commission Regulation
Regulation 19(2)	Using vehicle for ASOR regulated or Community regulated carriage by road without passenger waybill

Table 2

The Goods Vehicles (Community Authorisations) Regulations 1992

Provision creating offence	*General nature of offence*
Regulation 3	Use of goods vehicle without Community authorisation
Regulation 7	Failure to comply with conditions governing use of Community authorisation

Table 3

The Public Service Vehicles (Community Licences) Regulations 1999

Provision creating offence	*General nature of offence*
Regulation 3	Use of public service vehicles without Community licence
Regulation 7	Failure to comply with conditions governing use of Community licence

Table 4

The Road Transport (Passenger Vehicles Cabotage) Regulations 1999

Provision creating offence	*General nature of offence*
Regulation 3(1)	Use of vehicle for UK cabotage operations without Community licence
Regulation 4(1)	Use of vehicle for UK cabotage operations without control document
Regulation 7(1)	Failure to produce Community licence when requested
Regulation 7(3)	Failure to produce control document when requested

Table 6

The Vehicle Drivers (Certificate of Professional Competence) Regulations 2007

Provision creating offence	*General nature of offence*
Regulation 10(1)	Driving on road without completing appropriate initial Certificate of Professional Competence (CPC) test, or driving on road if more than five years have elapsed since obtaining relevant CPC
Regulation 10(2)	Causing or permitting another person to drive in breach of regulation 10(1)

Provision creating offence	*General nature of offence*
Regulation 11(1)	Failing to carry evidence of initial CPC
Regulation 11(3)	Failing to carry evidence of periodic CPC
Regulation 11(5)	Failing to carry National Vocational Training Certificate in the vehicle in which the person is driving
Regulation 11(7)	Failing to produce evidence of CPC or National Vocational Training Certificate when required
Regulation 13(1)	Forgery, alteration, etc of certain documents

NOTES

Erratum It is thought that Table 6 in Pt 2 of the Schedule in the Queen's Printer's copy of these regulations should be numbered Table 5.
Goods Vehicles (Community Authorisations) Regulations 1992 SI 1992/3077.
Public Service Vehicles (Community Licences) Regulations 1999 SI 1999/1322.
Road Transport (International Passenger Services) Regulations 1984 SI 1984/748.
Road Transport (Passenger Vehicles Cabotage) Regulations 1999 SI 1999/3413.
Vehicle Drivers (Certificate of Professional Competence) Regulations 2007 SI 2007/605.

[1251]

ROAD SAFETY (FINANCIAL PENALTY DEPOSIT) (APPROPRIATE AMOUNT) ORDER 2009
SI 2009/492

Authority Made by the Secretary of State for Transport under the Road Traffic Offenders Act 1988, ss 90B(2), 90E(3).
Date made 5 March 2009.
Commencement 31 March 2009; see art 1(1).
Interpretation See art 1(2).
General The Road Traffic Offenders Act 1988, Pt 3A (ss 90A–90F) (inserted by the Road Safety Act 2006, s 11(1)) provides for a constable or vehicle examiner to impose a financial penalty deposit requirement on a person without a satisfactory United Kingdom address if he reasonably believes that a specified offence has been committed relating to a motor vehicle in specified circumstances (see s 90A and SI 2009/491). S 90B defines a financial penalty deposit requirement as a requirement to make a payment of the appropriate amount to the Secretary of State, in a manner specified by order (see SI 2009/491) either immediately or within the relevant period. This order specifies the appropriate amount of a financial penalty deposit in relation to an offence for the purposes of s 90B.

[1252]

Citation, commencement and interpretation

1 (1) This Order may be cited as the Road Safety (Financial Penalty Deposit) (Appropriate Amount) Order 2009 and shall come into force on 31st March 2009.

(2) In this Order—

"the AETR" means the European Agreement concerning the Work of Crews of Vehicles engaged in International Road Transport of 1 July 1970, as amended, as applied by article 2(3) of the EC Regulation;

"the Community Recording Equipment Regulation" has the meaning given in section 97(7) of the Transport Act 1968;

"the EC Regulation" means the Community Drivers Hours Regulation as defined in section 103(1) of the Transport Act 1968;

"fixed penalty offence" means an offence listed in Schedule 1; and

"graduated fixed penalty offence" means an offence listed in Schedule 2.

NOTES

European Agreement concerning the Work of Crews of Vehicles engaged in International Road Transport of 1 July 1970 Cmnd 7401.
"Community Recording Equipment Regulation" has the meaning given in the Transport Act 1968, s 97(7) Ie Council Regulation (EEC) 3821/85 on recording equipment in road transport (OJ L370, 31.12.1985, p 8) as it has effect in accordance with the Community Regulations and other provisions listed in s 97(7) of the 1968 Act.

Community Drivers Hours Regulation as defined in the Transport Act 1968, s 103(1) Ie Regulation (EC) 561/2006 of the European Parliament and of the Council on the harmonisation of certain social legislation relating to road transport (OJ L102, 11.04.2006, p 1) as amended from time to time.

[1253]

The appropriate amount

2 (1) Subject to paragraph (2), the appropriate amount of a financial penalty deposit shall be—

- (a) in relation to a fixed penalty offence for which a person has been given a fixed penalty notice or handed a conditional offer, the amount indicated in relation to that offence in the third column of Schedule 1;
- (b) in relation to a graduated fixed penalty offence for which a person has been given a fixed penalty notice or handed a conditional offer, the amount indicated in relation to that offence in Schedule 2, by reference to the circumstances of the offence, those being the nature of the contravention and, where specified, its seriousness; and
- (c) in relation to an offence for which a person has been given notification that it appears likely that proceedings will be brought against him, £300.

(2) The appropriate amount shall not, in respect of any single occasion on which more than one financial penalty deposit requirement has been imposed, exceed £900.

[1254]

SCHEDULE 1
DEPOSITS FOR FIXED PENALTY OFFENCES

Article 2(1)(a)

PART 1
PRIMARY LEGISLATION

Table 1

Transport Act 1968

(1) Provision creating offence	*(2) General nature of offence*	*(3) Deposit*
1 Section 98(4)	Contravention of regulations made under section 98 or any requirement as to books, records or documents of applicable Community rules	£200
2 Section 99(4)	Failing to comply with requirements relating to inspection of records or obstructing an officer	£200
3 Section 99ZD(1)	Failing to comply with requirements relating to inspection of recording equipment or records (whether electronic or hard copy) made by or stored on recording equipment	£200
4 Section 99C	Failure to comply with prohibition or direction in relation to driving vehicle.	£200

Table 2

Road Traffic (Foreign Vehicles) Act 1972

(1) Provision creating offence	*(2) General nature of offence*	*(3) Deposit*
1 Section 3(1)	Driving a foreign goods or foreign public service vehicle in contravention of a prohibition, etc	£200

Table 3

Public Passenger Vehicles Act 1981

(1) Provision creating offence	*(2) General nature of offence*	*(3) Deposit*
1 Section 12(5)	Using public service vehicle except under PSV operators' licence	£200

Table 4

Road Traffic Regulation Act 1984

(1) Provision creating offence	*(2) General nature of offence*	*(3) Deposit*
1 Section 5(1)	Using a vehicle in contravention of a traffic regulation order outside Greater London	£30
2 Section 8(1)	Breach of traffic regulation order in Greater London	£30
3 Section 11(1)	Breach of experimental traffic order	£30
4 Section 16(1)	Using a vehicle in contravention of temporary prohibition or restriction of traffic in case of execution of works, etc	£30, but £60 if committed in respect of a speed restriction
5 Section 17(4)	Wrongful use of special road	£30, but £60 if committed otherwise than by unlawfully stopping or allowing the vehicle to remain at rest on a part of a special road on which vehicles are in certain circumstances permitted to remain at rest
6 Section 18(3)	Using a vehicle in contravention of provision for one-way traffic on trunk road	£30
7 Section 20(5)	Driving a vehicle in contravention of order prohibiting or restricting driving vehicles on certain classes of roads	£30
8 Section 25(5)	Breach of pedestrian crossing regulations	£60
9 Section 88(7)	Contravention of minimum speed limit	£30
10 Section 89(1)	Exceeding speed limit	£60

Table 5

Road Traffic Act 1988

(1) Provision creating offence	*(2) General nature of offence*	*(3) Deposit*
1 Section 14(3)	Breach of regulations requiring wearing of seat belts	£30
2 Section 15(2)	Driving motor vehicle with child not wearing seat belt or with child in a rear-facing child restraint front seat with an active air bag	£30
3 Section 15(4)	Driving motor vehicle with child in rear not wearing seat belt	£30
4 Section 16(4)	Driving or riding motor cycles in contravention of regulations requiring wearing of protective headgear	£30
5 Section 18(3)	Contravention of regulations with respect to use of head-worn appliances (eye protectors) on motor cycles	£30
6 Section 19(1)	Prohibition of parking of heavy commercial vehicles on verges, etc	£30
7 Section 22	Leaving vehicle in dangerous position	£60
8 Section 34(1)	Driving mechanically propelled vehicles elsewhere than on roads	£30
9 Section 35(1)	Failing to comply with traffic directions given by constable or traffic officer engaged in the regulation of traffic in a road	£30, but £60 if committed in respect of a motor vehicle by failure to comply with a direction of a constable, traffic officer or traffic warden
10 Section 35(2)	Failing to comply with traffic directions given by constable or traffic officer where a traffic survey is being carried out	£60
11 Section 36(1)	Failing to comply with traffic signs	£30, but £60 if committed by failure to comply with an indication given by a sign specified in regulation 10(2) of the Traffic Signs Regulations and General Directions 2002
12 Section 40A	Using a vehicle in dangerous condition etc	£60
13 Section 41D	Breach of requirements as to control of vehicle, mobile telephone, etc	£60
14 Section 47(1)	Using etc, vehicle without required test certificate being in force	£60
15 Section 71(1)	Driving, etc, vehicle in contravention of prohibition on driving it as being unfit for service, or failing to comply with direction to remove a vehicle found overloaded	£200

(1) Provision creating offence	(2) General nature of offence	(3) Deposit
16 Section 87(1)	Driving otherwise than in accordance with a licence	£30, but £60 in the case where the driving would not have been in accordance with any licence that could have been granted to the driver
17 Section 143(2)	Using, etc, motor vehicle while uninsured or unsecured against third party risks	£200
18 Section 163(3), insofar as it relates to section 163(1)	Failing to stop mechanically propelled vehicle when required	£30

Table 6

Road Traffic Offenders Act 1988

(1) Provision creating offence	(2) General nature of offence	(3) Deposit
1 Section 90D(6)	Driving a vehicle in contravention of a prohibition on driving, etc, on failure to make a financial penalty deposit payment	£200

Table 7

Vehicles Excise and Registration Act 1994

(1) Provision creating offence	(2) General nature of offence	(3) Deposit
1 Section 42(1)	Driving or keeping a vehicle without required registration mark	£30
2 Section 43(1)	Driving or keeping a vehicle with registration mark obscured etc	£30

Table 8

Goods Vehicles (Licensing of Operators) Act 1995

(1) Provision creating offence	(2) General nature of offence	(3) Deposit
1 Section 2(5)	Using goods vehicle on road for carriage of goods except under operator's licence	£200

[1255]

PART 2
SECONDARY LEGISLATION

Table 1

The Road Transport (International Passenger Services) Regulations 1984

(1) Provision creating offence	(2) General nature of offence	(3) Deposit
1 Regulation 19(1)	Using vehicle for Community regulated carriage of passengers otherwise than in accordance with the Council Regulations or the Commission Regulation	£30

(1) Provision creating offence	*(2) General nature of offence*	*(3) Deposit*
2 Regulation 19(2)	Using vehicle for ASOR regulated or Community regulated carriage by road without passenger waybill	£30

Table 2

The Goods Vehicles (Community Authorisations) Regulations 1992

(1) Provision creating offence	*(2) General nature of offence*	*(3) Deposit*
1 Regulation 3	Use of goods vehicle without Community authorisation	£60
2 Regulation 7	Failure to comply with conditions governing use of Community authorisation	£30

Table 3

The Public Service Vehicles (Community Licences) Regulations 1999

(1) Provision creating offence	*(2) General nature of offence*	*(3) Deposit*
1 Regulation 3	Use of public service vehicles without Community licence	£60
2 Regulation 7	Failure to comply with conditions governing use of Community licence	£30

Table 4

The Road Transport (Passenger Vehicles Cabotage) Regulations 1999

(1) Provision creating offence	*(2) General nature of offence*	*(3) Deposit*
1 Regulation 3(1)	Use of vehicle for UK cabotage operations without Community licence	£60
2 Regulation 4(1)	Use of vehicle for UK cabotage operations without control document	£60
3 Regulation 7(1)	Failure to produce Community licence when requested	£30
4 Regulation 7(3)	Failure to produce control document when requested	£30

Table 5

The Vehicle Drivers (Certificate of Professional Competence) Regulations 2007

(1) Provision creating offence	*(2) General nature of offence*	*(3) Deposit*
1 Regulation 11(7)	Failing to produce evidence of CPC or National Vocational Training Certificate when required	£30

NOTES

Goods Vehicles (Community Authorisations) Regulations 1992 SI 1992/3077.
Public Service Vehicles (Community Licences) Regulations 1999 SI 1999/1322.
Road Transport (International Passenger Services) Regulations 1984 SI 1984/748.
Road Transport (Passenger Vehicles Cabotage) Regulations 1999 SI 1999/3413.

Vehicle Drivers (Certificate of Professional Competence) Regulations 2007
SI 2007/605.

[1256]

SCHEDULE 2
DEPOSITS FOR GRADUATED FIXED PENALTY OFFENCES

Article 2(1)(b)

Table 1

Section 96(11) Transport Act 1968

(1) Nature of contravention or failure constituting the offence	*(2) Seriousness of offence and applicable level of deposit*		
	£60	*£120*	*£200*
1 Driving a vehicle or vehicles for more than 10 hours, contrary to section 96(1)	More than 10 hours but less than 11 hours driving	11 hours or more but less than 12 hours driving	12 hours or more driving
2 Failure to take an interval for rest and refreshment, contrary to section 96(2)	Being on duty for up to 1 hour beyond the required break	Being on duty for 1 hour or more, but less than 2 hours, beyond the required break	Being on duty for 2 hours or more beyond the required break
3 Exceeding working day of 11 hours, contrary to section 96(3)(a)	More than 11 hours but less than 12 hours working	12 hours or more but less than 13 hours working	13 hours or more working
4 Failing to take a daily rest period between two successive working days, contrary to section 96(4)	Less than 11 hours but more than 10 hours daily rest	10 hours or less but more than 9 hours daily rest	9 hours or less daily rest
5 Failing to take a weekly rest period of 24 hours, contrary to section 96(6)	Less than 24 hours but more than 23 hours rest	23 hours or less but more than 22 hours rest	22 hours or less rest
6 Exceeding the daily working limit of 16 hours in respect of a passenger vehicle to which the Drivers' Hours (Passenger and Goods Vehicles) (Modifications) Order 1971 apply, contrary to section 96(3)(c) as modified by that Order in relation to such vehicles	More than 16 hours, but less than 17 hours working	17 hours or more but less than 18 hours working	18 hours or more working

(1) Nature of contravention or failure constituting the offence	*(2) Seriousness of offence and applicable level of deposit*		
	£60	*£120*	*£200*
7 Failing to take a daily rest period between two successive working days by a driver of a passenger vehicle to which the Drivers' Hours (Passenger and Goods Vehicles) (Modifications) Order 1971) apply, contrary to section 96(4) , as modified by that Order in relation to such vehicles	Less than 10 hours but more than 9 hours daily rest (or, in the case of a reduced daily rest period, less than 8.5 hours but more than 7.5 hours daily rest)	9 hours or less but more than 8 hours daily rest (or, in the case of a reduced daily rest period, 7.5 hours or less but more than 6.5 hours daily rest)	8 hours or less daily rest (or, in the case of a reduced daily rest period, 6.5 hours or less daily rest)
8 Failing to take a rest period of 24 hours in each successive two week period by a driver of a passenger vehicle to which the Drivers' Hours (Passenger and Goods Vehicles) (Modifications) Order 1971) apply, contrary to section 96(6), as modified by that Order in relation to such vehicles	Less than 24 hours but more than 23 hours weekly rest	23 hours or less but more than 22 hours weekly rest	22 hours or less weekly rest
9 In all other cases	£30		

Table 2

Section 96(11A) Transport Act 1968

(1) Nature of contravention or failure constituting the offence	*(2) Seriousness of offence and applicable level of deposit*		
	£60	*£120*	*£200*
1 Exceeding 9 hours daily driving, in contravention of paragraph 1 of Article 6(1) of the EC Regulation	More than 9 hours but less than 10 hours driving	10 hours or more but less than 11 hours driving	11 hours or more driving
2 Exceeding 10 hours daily driving, in contravention of paragraph 2 of Article 6(1) of the EC Regulation	More than 10 hours but less than 11 hours driving	11 hours or more but less than 12 hours driving	12 hours or more driving
3 Exceeding the weekly driving time of 56 hours, in contravention of Article 6(2) of the EC Regulation	More than 56 hours but less than 58 hours driving	58 hours or more but less than 59 hours driving	59 hours or more driving

(1) Nature of contravention or failure constituting the offence	*(2) Seriousness of offence and applicable level of deposit*		
	£60	*£120*	*£200*
4 Exceeding 90 hours accumulated driving time in any two consecutive weeks, in contravention of Article 6(3) of the EC Regulation	More than 90 hours but less than 93 hours driving	93 hours or more but less than 94 hours driving	94 hours or more driving
5 Exceeding 4.5 hours driving without a break, in contravention of Article 7 of the EC Regulation	More than 4.5 hours but less than 5.5 hours driving	5.5 hours or more but less than 6.5 hours driving	6.5 hours or more driving
6 Insufficient regular daily rest period in 24 hour period, in contravention of Articles 8(1) and 8(2) of the EC Regulation	Less than 11 hours but more than 10 hours daily rest	10 hours or less but more than 9 hours daily rest	9 hours or less daily rest
7 Insufficient reduced daily rest period in 24 hour period, in contravention of Articles 8(1) and 8(2) of the EC Regulation	Less than 9 hours but more than 8 hours daily rest	8 hours or less but more than 7 hours daily rest	7 hours or less daily rest
8 Failure to take first rest of at least 3 consecutive hours where daily rest period is split, as required by the first indent of Article 4(g) of the EC Regulation and in contravention of Articles 8(1) and 8(2) of that Regulation	Less than 3 hours but more than 2 hours rest	2 hours or less but more than 1 hours rest	1 hour or less rest
9 Failure to take second rest of at least 9 consecutive hours where daily rest period is split, as required by the first indent of Article 4(g) of the EC Regulation, and in contravention of Articles 8(1) and 8(2) of that Regulation	Less than 9 hours but more than 8 hours rest	8 hours or less but more than 7 hours rest	7 hours or less rest

(1) Nature of contravention or failure constituting the offence	*(2) Seriousness of offence and applicable level of deposit*		
	£60	*£120*	*£200*
10 Failure to take daily rest period of at least 12 hours in total, where regular daily rest period is split, as required by the first indent of Article 4(g) of the EC Regulation and in contravention of Articles 8(1) and 8(2) of that Regulation	Less than 12 hours but more than 11 hours rest	11 hours or less but more than 10 hours rest	10 hours or less rest
11 Insufficient rest in 30 hour period by a driver engaged in multi-manning, in contravention of Articles 8(1) and 8(5) of the EC Regulation	Less than 9 hours but more than 8 hours rest	8 hours or less but more than 7 hours rest	7 hours or less rest
12 Insufficient regular weekly rest period, in contravention of Articles 8(1) and (6) of the EC Regulation	Less than 45 hours but more than 43 hours weekly rest	43 hours or less but more than 42 hours weekly rest	42 hours or less weekly rest
13 Insufficient reduced weekly rest period, in contravention of Articles 8(1) and (6) of the EC Regulation	Less than 24 hours but more than 22 hours rest	22 hours or less but more than 21 hours rest	21 hours or less rest
14 Failure to take equivalent period of compensatory rest before the end of the third week where reduced weekly rest period has been taken, as required by the second indent of Article 8(6) of the EC Regulation	Up to 3 hours less rest than required	3 hours or more but less than 4 hours less rest than required	4 hours or more less rest than required
15 Exceeding 9 hours daily driving, in contravention of the first sub-paragraph of Article 6.1 of the AETR	More than 9 hours but less than 10 hours driving	10 hours or more but less than 11 hours driving	11 hours or more driving
16 Exceeding 10 hours daily driving (where permitted), in contravention of the first sub-paragraph of Article 6.1 of the AETR	More than 10 hours but less than 11 hours driving	11 hours or more but less than 12 hours driving	12 hours or more driving

(1) Nature of contravention or failure constituting the offence	*(2) Seriousness of offence and applicable level of deposit*		
	£60	*£120*	*£200*
17 Exceeding 90 hours total period of driving in any one fortnight, in contravention of Article 6.2 of the AETR	More than 90 hours but less than 93 hours driving	93 hours or more but less than 94 hours driving	94 hours or more driving
18 Exceeding 4.5 hours driving without a break, in contravention of Article 7.1 of the AETR	More than 4.5 hours but less than 5.5 hours driving	5.5 hours or more but less than 6.5 hours driving	6.5 hours or more driving
19 Insufficient daily rest period in 24 hour period in contravention of the first sub-paragraph of Article 8.1 of the AETR	Less than 11 hours but more than 10 hours rest	10 hours or less but more than 9 hours rest	9 hours or less rest
20 Insufficient reduced daily rest period (where permitted) in 24 hours period in contravention of the first sub-paragraph of Article 8.1 of the AETR	Less than 9 hours but more than 8 hours rest	8 hours or less but more than 7 hours rest	7 hours or less rest
21 Failure to take equivalent period of compensatory rest before the end of the following week, in accordance with Article 8.1 of the AETR, where reduced daily rest periods taken	Up to 3 hours less rest than required	3 hours or more but less than 4 hours less rest than required	4 hours or more less rest than required
22 Failure to take rest of at least 8 consecutive hours, in accordance with Article 8.1 of the AETR, where daily rest period is split	Less than 8 hours but more than 7 hours rest	7 hours or less but more than 6 hours rest	6 hours or less rest
23 Failure to take daily rest period of 12 hours in total, in accordance with Article 8.1 of the AETR, where regular daily rest period is split	Less than 12 hours but more than 11 hours rest	11 hours or less but more than 10 hours rest	10 hours or less rest

(1) Nature of contravention or failure constituting the offence	*(2) Seriousness of offence and applicable level of deposit*		
	£60	*£120*	*£200*
24 Insufficient consecutive rest period of 8 hours in 30 hour period where vehicle is manned by at least two drivers, in contravention of Article 8.2 of the AETR	Less than 8 hours but more than 7 hours rest	7 hours or less but more than 6 hours rest	6 hours or less rest
25 Insufficient regular weekly rest period, in contravention of Articles 6.1 and 8.3 of the AETR	Less than 45 hours but more than 43 hours rest	43 hours or less but more than 42 hours rest	42 hours or less rest
26 Insufficient reduced weekly rest period if taken where the vehicle is normally based or where the driver is based, in contravention of Articles 6.1 and 8.3 of the AETR	Less than 36 hours but more than 34 hours rest	34 hours or less but more than 33 hours rest	33 hours or less rest
27 Insufficient reduced weekly rest period of 24 hours if taken elsewhere than where the vehicle is normally based or where the driver is based, in contravention of Articles 6.1 and 8.3 of the AETR	Less than 24 hours but more than 22 hours rest	22 hours rest or less but more than 21 hours rest	21 hours or less rest
28 Failure to take sufficient compensatory rest for reductions in weekly rest period before the end of the third week in question, in contravention of Articles 6.1 and 8.3 of the AETR	Up to 3 hours less rest than required	3 hours or more but less than 4 hours less rest than required	4 hours or more less rest than required
29 In all other cases	£30		

Table 3

Section 97(1) Transport Act 1968

(1) Nature of contravention or failure constituting the offence	*(2) Applicable level of deposit*
1 Failure to ensure recording equipment installed in accordance with article 3(1) of the Community Recording Equipment Regulation	£200
2 Failing to ensure correct functioning of recording equipment or driver card, in accordance with article 13 of that Regulation	£60

(1) Nature of contravention or failure constituting the offence	*(2) Applicable level of deposit*
3 Failing to ensure the proper use of the recording equipment, in accordance with article 13 of that Regulation	£120
4 Failing to ensure the proper use of the driver card, in accordance with article 13 of that Regulation	£200
5 Failure to ensure that printing can be carried out correctly in the event of an inspection (other than a failure to provide sufficient printing material), in accordance with article 14(1) of that Regulation	£120
6 Failure to ensure that printing can be carried out correctly in the event of an inspection by a failure to provide sufficient printing material, in accordance with article 14(1) of that Regulation	£60
7 Using driver card of which the driver is not the holder, contrary to article 14(4)(a) of that Regulation	£200
8 Using a defective driver card, contrary to article 14(4)(a) of that Regulation	£60
9 Failure, at the start of the journey, to print out information required, etc, in accordance with article 15(1)(a) of that Regulation	£120
10 Failure, at the end of the journey, to print out the information required, etc, in accordance with article 15(1)(b) of that Regulation	£120
11 Failure to use record sheets or driver card, in accordance with article 15(2) of that Regulation	£200
12 Unauthorised withdrawal of record sheet or driver card, contrary to article 15(2) of that Regulation	£120
13 Failure to enter legibly on the record sheet, when away from the vehicle, periods of time, in accordance with article 15(2) of that Regulation	£120
14 Failure to amend record sheet or driver card as necessary when more than one driver on board the vehicle, in accordance with article 15(2) of that Regulation	£120
15 In all other cases	£30

Table 4

Section 41A Road Traffic Act 1988

(1) Nature of contravention or the failure constituting the offence	*(2) Applicable level of deposit*
1 Contravention of regulation 27(1)(g)(failure to have a tread pattern of at least 1 millimetre) of the Road Vehicles (Construction and Use) Regulations 1986	£120
2 In all other cases	£60

Table 5

Section 41B Road Traffic Act 1988

(1) Nature of contravention or failure constituting the offence	*(2) Applicable level of deposit*		
	£60	*£120*	*£200*
1 Exceeding maximum authorised weight of vehicle, contrary to regulation 4(1)(a) of, and Schedule 1 to, the Road Vehicles (Authorised Weight) Regulations 1998	Exceeding weight by up to 10%	Exceeding weight by 10% or more, but less than 15%	Exceeding weight by 15% or more
2 Exceeding maximum authorised weight of vehicle combination, contrary to regulation 4(1)(b) of, and Schedule 2 to, the Road Vehicles (Authorised Weight) Regulations 1998	Exceeding weight by up to 10%	Exceeding weight by 10% or more, but less than 15%	Exceeding weight by 15% or more
3 Exceeding maximum authorised weight of axle, contrary to Regulation 4(1)(c) of, and Schedule 3 to, the Road Vehicles (Authorised Weight) Regulations 1998)	Exceeding weight by up to 10%	Exceeding weight by 10% or more, but less than 15%	Exceeding weight by 15% or more
4 Exceeding maximum permitted laden weight of a vehicle, contrary to regulation 75(1) of, and Parts I, IA and II of Schedule 11 to, the Road Vehicles (Construction and Use) Regulations 1986	Exceeding weight by up to 10%	Exceeding weight by 10% or more, but less than 15%	Exceeding weight by 15% or more
5 Exceeding maximum permitted laden weight of trailer, contrary to regulation 75(3) of the Road Vehicles (Construction and Use) Regulations 1986	Exceeding weight by up to 10%	Exceeding weight by 10% or more, but less than 15%	Exceeding weight by 15% or more
6 Exceeding maximum permitted laden weight of a vehicle and trailer, other than an articulated vehicle, contrary to regulation 76(1) of the Road Vehicles (Construction and Use) Regulations 1986	Exceeding weight by up to 10%	Exceeding weight by 10% or more, but less than 15%	Exceeding weight by 15% or more

(1) Nature of contravention or failure constituting the offence	*(2) Applicable level of deposit*		
	£60	*£120*	*£200*
7 Exceeding any weights shown on the plate fitted in accordance with regulation 66 of the Road Vehicles (Construction and Use) Regulations 1986, contrary to regulation 80(1)(a) of those Regulations	Exceeding weight by up to 10%	Exceeding weight by 10% or more, but less than 15%	Exceeding weight by 15% or more
8 Exceeding any weight shown in column (2) of the plating certificate, contrary to regulation 80(1)(b) of the Road Vehicles (Construction and Use) Regulations 1986)	Exceeding weight by up to 10%	Exceeding weight by 10% or more, but less than 15%	Exceeding weight by 15% or more
9 Exceeding maximum gross weight in respect of an agricultural trailed appliance, contrary to regulation 80(1)(c) of the Road Vehicles (Construction and Use) Regulations 1986	Exceeding weight by up to 10%	Exceeding weight by 10% or more, but less than 15%	Exceeding weight by 15% or more
10 Exceeding sum of weights in respect of axles fitted with a compensating arrangement, contrary to regulation 80(2) of the Road Vehicles (Construction and Use) Regulations 1986	Exceeding weight by up to 10%	Exceeding weight by 10% or more, but less than 15%	Exceeding weight by 15% or more
11 In all other cases	£30		

Table 6

Section 42 Road Traffic Act 1988

(1) Nature of contravention or failure constituting the offence	*(2) Applicable level of deposit*
1 Failure to meet requirements regarding speed limiters, in accordance with regulation 36A(4) of those Regulations	£120
2 Failure to meet requirements regarding speed limiters, in accordance with regulation 36B(6) of the Road Vehicles (Construction and Use) Regulations 1986	£120
3 Failure to maintain vehicle, etc, or to carry, etc, passengers in accordance with regulation 100(1) of those Regulations, so as not to be a danger	£60

(1) Nature of contravention or failure constituting the offence	*(2) Applicable level of deposit*
4 Failure to carry load in a secure manner, etc, in accordance with regulation 100(2) of those Regulations, so as not to be a danger or nuisance	£60
5 Failure to use vehicle for suitable purposes, in accordance with regulation 100(3) of those Regulations, so as not to cause or be likely to cause a danger or nuisance	£60
6 In all other cases	£30

NOTES
Drivers' Hours (Passenger and Goods Vehicles) (Modifications) Order 1971 SI 1971/818.
Road Vehicles (Authorised Weight) Regulations 1998 SI 1998/3111.
Road Vehicles (Construction and Use) Regulations 1986 SI 1986/1078.

[1257]

ROAD SAFETY (IMMOBILISATION, REMOVAL AND DISPOSAL OF VEHICLES) REGULATIONS 2009
SI 2009/493

Authority Made by the Secretary of State for Transport under the Road Safety Act 2006, s 11(3), Sch 4.
Date made 5 March 2009.
Commencement 31 March 2009; see reg 1.
Interpretation See reg 2.
General These regulations provide for the immobilisation, removal and disposal of vehicles which have been prohibited from being driven under specified provisions relating to drivers' hours, foreign goods vehicles and foreign public service vehicles, unfit or overloaded vehicles, and the financial penalty deposit requirement (see reg 3). The regulations do not apply if the vehicle is displaying a current disabled person's badge or current recognised badge.

[1258]

PART 1
PRELIMINARY

Citation and commencement

1 These Regulations may be cited as the Road Safety (Immobilisation, Removal and Disposal of Vehicles) Regulations 2009 and shall come into force on 31st March 2009.

[1259]

Interpretation

2 In these Regulations—

"identified person" has the meaning given in regulation 10(2);
"immobilisation notice" means a notice given in accordance with regulation 4(2);
"owner" means, in relation to a vehicle—
(a) the person in whose name the vehicle is then registered under the Vehicle Excise and Registration Act 1994; or
(b) if the vehicle is not so registered, the person appearing to the authorised person to own that vehicle;
"recognised badge" has the meaning given by section 21A(1) of the Chronically Sick and Disabled Persons Act 1970; and
"release fee" has the meaning given by regulation 4(7).

[1260]

Application

3 (1) These Regulations apply with respect to any case where the driving of a vehicle has been prohibited under—

(a) section 99A(1) of the Transport Act 1968 (powers to prohibit driving of vehicles in connection with contravention of provisions about drivers' hours);
(b) section 1 of the Road Traffic (Foreign Vehicles) Act 1972 (powers to prohibit driving of foreign goods vehicles and foreign public service vehicles);
(c) section 69 or 70 of the Road Traffic Act 1988 (powers to prohibit driving of unfit or overloaded vehicles); or
(d) section 90D of the Road Traffic Offenders Act 1988 (power to prohibit driving of vehicle on failure to make payment in compliance with financial penalty deposit requirement).

(2) These Regulations do not apply in relation to a vehicle if a current disabled person's badge or current recognised badge is displayed on that vehicle.

[1261]

PART 2
IMMOBILISATION OF VEHICLES

Power to immobilise vehicles

4 (1) An authorised person or a person acting under the direction of the authorised person may, in relation to any vehicle in a case where these Regulations apply—
(a) fix an immobilisation device to the vehicle; and
(b) move the vehicle, or direct the driver or the person appearing to be in charge of the vehicle to move the vehicle, for the purpose of enabling an immobilisation device to be fitted to it.

(2) On any occasion when an immobilisation device is fixed to a vehicle in accordance with these Regulations, the person fixing the device must also fix to the vehicle a notice ("an immobilisation notice")—
(a) indicating that the device has been fixed to the vehicle and warning that no attempt should be made to drive it or otherwise put it in motion until it has been released from the device;
(b) specifying the steps to be taken to secure its release, including—
  (i) how payment of any release fee should be made; and
  (ii) the evidence to be produced to show that the prohibition under which the driving of the vehicle was prohibited has been removed; and
(c) giving any other relevant information, including the consequences of not securing release of the vehicle.

(3) A vehicle to which an immobilisation device has been fixed in accordance with these Regulations—
(a) may only be released from the device by or under the direction of an authorised person; but
(b) subject to sub-paragraph (a), must be released from the device if the first and second requirements specified below are met.

(4) The first requirement is that a charge of £80 in respect of the release is paid in any manner specified in the immobilisation notice.

(5) The second requirement is that, in accordance with instructions specified in the immobilisation notice, there is produced—
(a) in the case of a prohibition issued under section 99A(1) of the Transport Act 1968 (powers to prohibit driving of vehicles in connection with contravention of provisions about drivers' hours), the notice referred to in section 99B(3) of that Act (notice to driver of the vehicle that the prohibition has been removed), or evidence that that prohibition has expired;
(b) in the case of a prohibition issued under section 1 of the Road Traffic (Foreign Vehicles) Act 1972 (powers to prohibit driving of foreign goods vehicles and foreign public service vehicles), the notice referred to in section 2(3) of that Act (notice to driver of the vehicle that the prohibition has been removed), or evidence that that prohibition has expired;

(c) In the case of a prohibition issued under sections 69 or 70 of the Road Traffic Act 1988 (powers to prohibit driving of unfit or overloaded vehicles), the notice referred to in section 72(7) of that Act (notice to owner that the prohibition has been removed); and

(d) in the case of a prohibition issued under section 90D of the Road Traffic Offenders Act 1988 (power to prohibit driving of vehicle on failure to make payment in compliance with financial penalty deposit requirement), evidence that one of the events referred to in section 90D(4) of that Act has occurred.

(6) An immobilisation notice may not be removed or interfered with except by an authorised person or a person acting on the authority of an authorised person.

(7) In this regulation, the "release fee" means the charge referred to in paragraph (4).

[1262]

Offence of failing to move vehicle

5 A person who fails to comply within a reasonable time with a direction under regulation 4(1)(b) is guilty of an offence and liable on summary conviction to a fine not exceeding level 5 on the standard scale.

[1263]

Offence of removing or interfering with immobilisation notice

6 A person, other than an authorised person or a person acting on the authority of an authorised person, who removes or interferes with an immobilisation notice is guilty of an offence and liable on summary conviction to a fine not exceeding level 2 on the standard scale.

[1264]

Offence of removing or interfering with immobilisation device, etc

7 A person, other than an authorised person or a person acting under the direction of an authorised person, who removes or attempts to remove an immobilisation device fixed to a vehicle in accordance with these Regulations is guilty of an offence and liable on summary conviction to a fine not exceeding level 3 on the standard scale.

[1265]

False or misleading statements, etc

8 (1) Where—

(a) a person makes a declaration with a view to securing the release of a vehicle from an immobilisation device purported to have been fixed in accordance with these Regulations;

(b) the declaration is that the prohibition has been removed; and

(c) the declaration is to the person's knowledge either false or in any material respect misleading,

that person is guilty of an offence.

(2) A person guilty of an offence under paragraph (1) is liable—

(a) on summary conviction, to a fine not exceeding the statutory maximum; or

(b) on conviction on indictment, to imprisonment for a term not exceeding two years, or to a fine, or both.

[1266]

PART 3
REMOVAL AND DISPOSAL OF VEHICLES

Power to remove vehicles

9 (1) Where any of the conditions specified in paragraph (2) are met, an authorised person, or a person acting under the direction of an authorised person, may remove the vehicle or direct the driver or the person appearing to be in charge of the vehicle to remove the vehicle.

(2) The conditions are that the authorised person considers that the vehicle should be removed—

- (a) for the safety of traffic, the vehicle, its occupants or its load;
- (b) because there is insufficient space for the vehicle to remain at the location at which the vehicle was inspected; or
- (c) because it appears to the authorised person that the vehicle has been abandoned.

[1267]

Delivery of vehicles

10 (1) An authorised person, or a person acting under the direction of an authorised person, may deliver a vehicle removed under regulation 9, or direct it to be delivered, into the custody of an identified person if—

- (a) the identified person agrees to accept delivery; and
- (b) a receipt is provided by the identified person to the authorised person, or the person acting under the direction of an authorised person, to confirm that the identified person has taken safe custody of the vehicle.

(2) An "identified person" is a person who—

- (a) is capable of accepting delivery of the vehicle; and
- (b) has agreed arrangements with the Secretary of State for accepting custody of vehicles, including arrangements regarding security and access.

(3) The arrangements made by virtue of sub-paragraph (2)(b) may include provision as to the payment of a sum to the identified person.

[1268]

Notice of removal of vehicle

11 (1) Subject to paragraph (3), where a vehicle has been removed and delivered into the custody of an identified person under regulation 10, the authorised person must provide a notice to the person referred to in paragraph (2) specifying—

- (a) the statutory power under which the vehicle has been removed;
- (b) the particulars of the place to which the vehicle has been removed;
- (c) the identity of the person to whom the vehicle has been delivered;
- (d) the steps to be taken to reclaim the vehicle, including—
  - (i) how payment of any release fee should be made; and
  - (ii) the evidence to be produced to show that the prohibition under which the driving of the vehicle was prohibited has been removed or has expired;
- (e) the steps to be taken, in accordance with regulation 18, in the event of a dispute; and
- (f) any other relevant information, including the consequences of not reclaiming the vehicle.

(2) The notice shall be provided by the authorised person to the person who was the driver of the vehicle when the driving of the vehicle was prohibited.

(3) If it is not reasonably practicable to give the notice to the person referred to in paragraph (2), then the authorised person shall take reasonable steps to locate the owner of the vehicle and to give the notice to the owner in writing by post.

[1269]

Taking possession of a vehicle

12 A person ("the claimant") may take possession of the vehicle if the claimant—

- (a) claims it before it is disposed of;
- (b) claims it not more than three months from the date on which the vehicle was removed or the direction to remove it was given;
- (c) produces evidence to the satisfaction of the authorised person that the claimant—
  - (i) is either the owner of the vehicle; or
  - (ii) was the person in charge of the vehicle at the time it was removed or was directed to be removed;

(d) pays the charges specified in the Schedule for the release, removal and custody of the vehicle, as applicable; and
(e) produces such evidence as is required by regulation 4(5).

[1270]

Compensation

13 (1) An amount calculated in accordance with paragraph (2) may be paid to a person if—

(a) he claims after the vehicle's disposal to be or to have been its owner or to have been the person in charge of the vehicle when it was removed; and
(b) the claim is made within three months of the date on which the vehicle was removed or the direction to remove the vehicle was given.

(2) The amount payable under paragraph (1) shall be calculated by deducting from any proceeds of sale the charges specified in the Schedule in respect of the release, removal, custody and disposal of the vehicle, as applicable.

[1271]

Power to dispose, etc, of vehicles

14 The person into whose custody the vehicle is delivered pursuant to regulation 10 may dispose, sell or destroy the vehicle as that person sees fit if the vehicle has not been claimed in accordance with regulation 12 within three months from the date on which the vehicle was removed or the direction to remove the vehicle was given.

[1272]

Recovery of prescribed charges

15 Whether or not a claim is made under regulation 12 or 13—

(a) the Secretary of State; or
(b) a person into whose custody the vehicle is delivered in accordance with regulation 10

may recover from the vehicle's owner or the person in charge of the vehicle the charges specified in the Schedule in respect of the release, removal, custody and disposal of the vehicle, as applicable.

[1273]

Offences of failing to remove or deliver vehicles

16 A person who fails to comply within a reasonable time with a direction under regulation 9(1) or 10(1) is guilty of an offence and liable on summary conviction to a fine not exceeding level 5 on the standard scale.

[1274]

False or misleading statements, etc

17 (1) Where—

(a) a person makes a declaration with a view to securing possession of a vehicle purported to have been delivered into the custody of an identified person;
(b) the declaration is that the prohibition has been removed; and
(c) the declaration is to the person's knowledge either false or in any material respect misleading,

that person is guilty of an offence.

(2) A person guilty of an offence under paragraph (1) is liable—

(a) on summary conviction, to a fine not exceeding the statutory maximum; or
(b) on conviction on indictment, to imprisonment for a term not exceeding two years, or to a fine, or both.

[1275]

PART 4
GENERAL

Disputes

18 (1) A person may apply to the appropriate court on the grounds that the authorised person, or person acting under his direction, did not comply with any of the requirements of any of regulations 4(1), 9, 10(1), 11, 12, or 13 ("the specified requirements").

(2) If the appropriate court finds that an authorised person, or person acting under his direction, did not comply with any of the specified requirements, it may order the Secretary of State to pay a sum to the person applying to the court to reflect any financial loss directly attributable to that failure to comply.

(3) In this regulation, "appropriate court" means—

(a) in England and Wales, a magistrates' court; or
(b) in Scotland, the sheriff court in the sheriffdom—
  (i) in which the claimant resides, in the case of an individual;
  (ii) where the principal or last known place of business of the claimant is situated, in the case of a partnership; or
  (iii) where the registered or principal office of the claimant is situated, in the case of an incorporated or unincorporated body.

[1276]

Application of Road Traffic Offenders Act 1988

19 The following provisions of the Road Traffic Offenders Act 1988 shall apply to the offences created by these Regulations—

(a) section 1 (requirement of warning etc of prosecutions for certain offences);
(b) section 6 (time within which summary proceedings for certain offences must be commenced);
(c) section 11 (evidence by certificate as to driver, user or owner); and
(d) section 12(1) (proof, in summary proceedings, of identity of driver of vehicle).

[1277]

SCHEDULE
THE PRESCRIBED CHARGES

Regulations 12, 13 and 15

The prescribed charges for any matter referred to in column (1) of the Table shall be the sum specified in column (2) of the Table.

TABLE

(1) Matter for which charge may be made	*(2) Amount of charge (£)*
Release of vehicle from immobilisation device	80
Removal of vehicle	160
Custody of vehicle – for each period of 24 hours or part thereof	35
Disposal of vehicle	50

[1278]

FIXED PENALTY (PROCEDURE) (VEHICLE EXAMINERS) REGULATIONS 2009
SI 2009/495

Authority Made by the Secretary of State for Transport under the Road Traffic Offenders Act 1988, ss 84, 88(4).
Date made 5 March 2009.
Commencement 1 April 2009; see reg 1(1).
General These regulations set out the procedure to be followed where a fixed penalty notice is given by a vehicle examiner in accordance with the Road Traffic Offenders Act 1988, s 54 (notices

on-the-spot etc) (as to fixed penalty notices issued other than by a vehicle examiner, see SI 1986/1330). See further the Preliminary Note "Penalties" (under the main head "Road traffic").

[1279]

Citation, commencement and extent

1 (1) These Regulations may be cited as the Fixed Penalty (Procedure) (Vehicle Examiners) Regulations 2009 and shall come into force on 1st April 2009.

(2) These Regulations do not extend to Scotland.

[1280]

Interpretation

2 In these Regulations, "the Act" means the Road Traffic Offenders Act 1988.

[1281]

Application

3 These Regulations apply in cases where a fixed penalty notice is given by a vehicle examiner in accordance with section 54 (notices on-the-spot etc) of the Act.

[1282]

Documents or information to be provided

4 The documents described in column 1 of the Schedule to these Regulations (as referred to in the provisions of the Act specified in column 2 of the Schedule) shall contain the information, or, as the case may be, further information prescribed in column 3 of the Schedule.

[1283]

Remittance

5 If payment of the fixed penalty is made by a person otherwise than as required by the fixed penalty notice, the Secretary of State shall return the remittance to that person.

[1284]

Return of driving licence (if so held)

6 Where—

(a) the person to whom the fixed penalty notice was given holds a driving licence;

(b) the suspended enforcement period has expired;

(c) the fixed penalty has not been paid; and

(d) either that person has requested a hearing under section 55(2) or no registration certificate has been issued under section 70(2) of the Act;

the Secretary of State shall, in the case of an endorseable offence, return the driving licence to that person.

[1285]

Notification of registration of sum

7 Where, in a case involving an endorseable offence, any sum is registered under section 71 of the Act for enforcement against that person as a fine, the designated officer for the court where the sum is registered shall notify the Secretary of State that the sum has been registered.

[1286]

Receipt for payment

8 Where a fixed penalty is paid within the suspended enforcement period the Secretary of State shall send a receipt for the payment, if requested, to the payer.

[1287]

Licence receipts

9 For the purposes of section 56(3)(a) of the Act, there is prescribed a period of two months beginning with the same date of issue.

[1288]

SCHEDULE
INFORMATION OR FURTHER INFORMATION TO BE PROVIDED IN CERTAIN DOCUMENTS MENTIONED IN PART 3 OF THE ACT

Regulation 4

Document	*Provision of the Act*	*Information or further information to be provided*
1 Fixed Penalty Notice	Section 52	(i) the name of the vehicle examiner giving the notice (ii) the serial number of the fixed penalty notice (iii) whether the notice relates to an endorseable offence (iv) the name, date of birth and address of the person to whom the notice is given (v) the date, time and place of the alleged offence (vi) the details of the vehicle including the registration number (vii) the documents, if any, to be provided to the Secretary of State and the period within which they must be provided and the address to which they must be sent (viii) an explanation of the action to be taken by the driver where (a) the driver has not or (b) the driver has, surrendered the licence, if the driver holds such a licence (ix) the fact that the person to whom the notice is given may opt for trial (x) the method of paying the fixed penalty (xi) guidance to the driver as to the legal consequences of a fixed penalty notice
2 Receipt for driving licence (if the offender holds a driving licence)	Section 56	(i) whether the driving licence is full or provisional (ii) the driver number as shown on the licence (iii) the groups of vehicles which the driver is entitled to drive (iv) the expiry date of the licence (v) the duration of the validity of the licence receipt

Document	*Provision of the Act*	*Information or further information to be provided*
		(vi) the method of obtaining a new receipt on expiry of an old receipt (vii) the name of the vehicle examiner issuing the fixed penalty notice
3 Registration certificate	Section 70	(i) the serial number and date, time and place of issue of the fixed penalty notice (ii) the vehicle registration number (iii) the driver number (either as shown on the licence or as allocated by the Secretary of State) (iv) the amount of the appropriate fixed penalty (iv) the amount of the appropriate fixed penalty (v) the sum to be registered in default of payment of the fixed penalty

[1289]

ROAD VEHICLES (APPROVAL) REGULATIONS 2009
SI 2009/717

Authority Made by the Secretary of State for Transport under the European Communities Act 1972, s 2(2).
Date made 24 March 2009.
Commencement 29 April 2009.
Summary These regulations revoke and replace the Motor Vehicles (EC Type Approval) Regulations 1998, SI 1998/2051, and the amending SI 1999/778, SI 1999/2324, SI 2000/869, SI 2000/2730, SI 2001/2809, SI 2002/1835, SI 2002/2743, SI 2003/1019, SI 2003/2428, SI 2004/73, SI 2004/2186, SI 2005/2454, SI 2006/142, SI 2006/1695, SI 2006/2409, SI 2006/2816, SI 2007/855, SI 2007/3135, SI 2008/2844. The primary purpose of the regulations is to implement Directive 2007/46/EC of the European Parliament and of the Council establishing a framework for the approval of motor vehicles and their trailers, and of systems, components and separate technical units intended for such vehicles (OJ L263, 09.10.2007, p 1) ("the Framework Directive"), as amended.

Pt 1 (regs 1–5 and Schs 1, 2, Sch 3, Pt 1) of the regulations provides for preliminary matters. Reg 2 provides for the revocation of the Motor Vehicles (EC Type Approval) Regulations 1998, SI 1998/2051, as amended (listed in Sch 1). Regs 3 and 4 define terms used in the regulations. Reg 3 introduces Sch 2, which provides for the interpretation of references in the regulations to requirements contained in a regulatory act (i e certain Community instruments listed in Pt I of Annex IV or in Annex XI to the Framework Directive, and any UNECE Regulation listed in Pt II of Annex IV to the Framework Directive).

Reg 5 sets out the scope of the regulations. In general, the regulations apply to: (a) vehicles designed and constructed in one or more stages for use on a road; (b) systems, components and separate technical units designed and constructed for those vehicles; and (c) parts and equipment intended for those vehicles. This is subject to several exceptions, including: (a) agricultural or forestry tractors, and trailers and interchangeable towed machinery designed and constructed specifically to be towed by them (including their systems, components and separate technical units); (b) quadricyles; (c) tracked vehicles; (d) old vehicles (including systems, components and separate technical units designed and manufactured specifically for them). Reg 5 introduces Pt 1 of Sch 3, which determines the date on which, and the circumstances in which, the regulations apply to vehicles of different categories and classes.

Pt 2 (regs 6–11 and Sch 3, Pt 2) prescribes conditions relating to vehicle approval which must be satisfied before a vehicle may be registered or put into service on a road in the United Kingdom. Reg 6 provides that a motor vehicle may not be registered or granted a first licence under the Vehicle Excise and Registration Act 1994, s 21 unless a relevant condition is satisfied or the temporary exemption applies. A "relevant condition" is one of the principal conditions, or where the alternative conditions may be satisfied, any of those conditions. The principal conditions are that:

(a) an appropriate EC certificate of conformity has effect with respect to the vehicle;
(b) an appropriate national small series certificate of conformity has effect with respect to the vehicle;
(c) an appropriate individual approval certificate has effect with respect to the vehicle.

Pt 2 of Sch 3 specifies when the alternative conditions may be satisfied, prescribes those conditions, and specifies when the temporary exemption applies.

Regs 7–10 prescribe the conditions to be satisfied by suppliers of trailers in respect of the first use of such vehicles. By reg 7, a large trailer may not be put into service unless the supplier first notifies the approval authority (the Secretary of State), furnishes the approval authority with pertinent information (defined by reg 10) about the trailer, and obtains the consent of the approval authority. The approval authority must give consent if the principal conditions are satisfied, or when the alternative conditions apply, those conditions are satisfied. The principal conditions are that:

(a) an appropriate approval or certificate of conformity has effect with respect to the trailer,

(b) where the application for consent is in consequence of the importation of the trailer from a place outside the United Kingdom, any value added tax or customs duty charged on or arising from its removal into the United Kingdom has been paid or remitted (or the approval authority is satisfied that it will be paid or remitted), and

(c) there is otherwise no lawful reason for refusing to give consent.

Pt 3 of Sch 3 specifies when the alternative conditions apply and prescribes those conditions.

Regs 8, 9 provide for the records to be kept in respect of large trailers and small trailers. Reg 10 sets out in detail the meaning of"pertinent information". Reg 11 creates offences relating to supplying and using trailers without complying with prescribed conditions.

Pt 3 (regs 12–23) makes provision for EC type approvals. Reg 12 provides for applications for EC type approval by a manufacturer in respect of a relevant vehicle, or a system, component or separate technical unit for a relevant vehicle, by reference to the Framework Directive. Reg 13 provides for the procedure to be followed by the approval authority and prescribes the requirements which must be fulfilled for the grant of EC type approval (also by reference to the Framework Directive). Reg 14 provides for amendment to EC type approvals. Reg 15 requires the holder of an EC type approval to comply with the requirements of the Framework Directive regarding the issue of certificates of conformity and type approval marks. Reg 16 relates to the tests and associated checks to verify conformity of production to be carried out by the holder of a type approval. Reg 17 requires the holder of a type approval to co-operate with the approval authority in relation to specified matters. Reg 18 relates to the technical and safety information to be provided by a manufacturer to users of vehicles and other manufacturers.

Reg 19 provides for the withdrawal or suspension of EC type approval in the event of failure to conform to the approved type or failure to comply with requirements imposed by or under regs 12, 14–17. Reg 20 makes special provision for EC type approval of vehicles produced in small numbers ("small series"). Regs 21–23 relate to unsafe or harmful vehicles and vehicle parts. Reg 21 sets out the powers of the approval authority where a vehicle is a serious risk to road safety. Reg 22 applies where parts and equipment may pose a significant risk to the correct functioning of essential systems. Reg 23 provides for the recall of vehicles which are a risk to public safety or the environment.

Pt 4 (regs 24–28 and Schs 4–6) makes provision for vehicle approvals which are valid in the United Kingdom only. Reg 24 provides for applications by a vehicle manufacturer for a national small series type approval (broadly, national type approval of vehicles produced in small numbers). Reg 25 provides for the grant of national small series type approval and prescribes, with Sch 4, the technical requirements which must be fulfilled for the grant of such approval. It also makes provision for conformity of production and the issue of certificates of conformity. Reg 26 sets out the procedure for recognition of national small series type approvals granted in other member states. Reg 27 provides for the individual approval of particular vehicles by the approval authority, including the recognition of vehicles covered by approval under the national regime of other member states. It also prescribes the technical requirements which must be fulfilled for the grant of an individual approval (in connection with which, see Sch 5). (As to the fees payable in connection with applications for individual approval under reg 27, see SI 2009/718.) Reg 28 prescribes the form of national small series type approval certificate and individual approval certificate, set out in Sch 6.

Pt 5 (regs 29–32) makes provision about the validity of type approvals and end-of-series vehicles. Reg 29 specifies the circumstances in which an EC type approval ceases to be valid and reg 30 specifies the circumstances in which a national small series type approval ceases to be valid. Regs 31 and 32 provide for "end-of-series" vehicles, i e vehicles which satisfy the following conditions:

(a) the vehicle is manufactured in conformity with a valid EC type approval or national small series type approval which has since ceased to be valid; and

(b) the EC certificate of conformity or national small series certificate of conformity issued in respect of the vehicle bears a date not less than 3 months earlier than the date on which the type approval ceases to be valid.

In such cases, the approval authority may direct that an EC certificate of conformity or a national small series certificate of conformity issued under the approval in respect of an end-of-series vehicle has effect for the purposes of Pt 2 of the regulations for the relevant period from the date when the type approval ceases to be valid (12 or 18 months according to the number of stages of manufacture).

Pt 6 (regs 33–42) makes provision for miscellaneous matters, including enforcement and the review of approval authority decisions. Reg 33 creates offences relating to forgery of type approvals and certificates of conformity and making false statements, supplying false information or using a false document for the purposes of the regulations. Reg 34 confers powers of entry and inspection, and other related powers, on the approval authority. Reg 35 requires the approval authority to give reasons when issuing notice of specified decisions; reg 36 provides for the review of the authority's decisions on type approval applications; and reg 37 provides for appeals against decisions on applications for individual approvals under reg 27 (fees payable in connection with such appeals are prescribed by SI 2009/718). Further provisions concern the issue of duplicate certificates to replace lost or defaced certificates (reg 38) (the fee for a duplicate certificate is prescribed by SI 2009/718); the service of notices under the regulations (reg 39); the provision of testing stations (reg 40); and the designation of technical services (reg 41). Reg 42 contains a saving for applications for an EC type approval made under the Motor Vehicles (EC Type Approval) Regulations 1998, SI 1998/2051 (revoked) before 29 April 2009.

[1290]

ROAD VEHICLES (INDIVIDUAL APPROVAL) (FEES) REGULATIONS 2009
SI 2009/718

Authority Made by the Secretary of State for Transport under the Finance Act 1973, s 56(1), (2) and by virtue of SI 1988/643, and the Finance Act 1990, s 128.
Date made 24 March 2009.
Commencement 29 April 2009.
Summary These regulations prescribe the fees payable in respect of applications, appeals and the issue of documents relating to the individual approval of particular vehicles under reg 27 of SI 2009/717. Reg 2 provides for the interpretation of these regulations, by reference to SI 2009/717. The regulations prescribe fees for original applications (reg 4) and further applications (reg 5). Reg 6 sets out the circumstances in which no fee is payable in respect of a further application where a vehicle will be further examined before the end of the fifth day after the original examination.

Reg 7 prescribes the fee payable in specified circumstances where notice has been given to the approval authority that a vehicle is not to be submitted for examination. Reg 8 prescribes the fees payable for an appeal against the refusal of an original or further application under reg 37 of SI 2009/717. Reg 9 enables appeal fees to be repaid by the approval authority where, after completion of a re-examination of a vehicle, it appears that the appellant had substantial grounds for making the appeal; reg 9 also prescribes the fee payable by an appellant where notice has been given to the approval authority that a vehicle is not to be submitted for re-examination. Reg 10 prescribes the fee payable where a vehicle is not submitted for examination or re-examination and the approval authority has not been notified or has received insufficient notice.

Reg 11 prescribes the fee for a duplicate certificate under reg 38 of SI 2009/717. Reg 12 prescribes the fee in respect of a type approved vehicle which has been the subject of minor modification before its first registration.

[1291]

MOTOR CYCLES ETC (REPLACEMENT OF CATALYTIC CONVERTERS) REGULATIONS 2009
SI 2009/1896

Authority Made by the Secretary of State for Transport under the European Communities Act 1972, s 2(2).
Date made 14 July 2009.
Commencement 13 August 2009.
Summary These regulations impose requirements and prohibitions in relation to the supply and installation of replacement catalytic converters for vehicles subject to an EC certificate of conformity (within the meaning of reg 3 of SI 1999/2920). "Replacement catalytic converter" is defined by reference to Annex I to Chapter 5 of Directive 97/24/EC of the European Parliament and of the Council on certain components and characteristics of two or three-wheel motor vehicles (OJ L226, 18.08.1997, p 1) ("the Vehicle Emissions Chapter"). The regulations do not apply to a catalytic converter which is second-hand (reg 3).

Reg 4 prohibits the supply for installation on a relevant vehicle of a catalytic converter intended as a replacement part unless it is an original replacement which has been clearly and indelibly marked in accordance with provisions of Annex I or Annex VII to the Vehicle Emissions Chapter, and is accompanied by information which is specified in the relevant provisions of Annex I or Annex VII to that Chapter. "Relevant vehicle" means a vehicle which is subject to an EC certificate of conformity where that certificate was issued in consequence of the vehicle satisfying the requirements of the Vehicle Emissions Chapter.

Reg 5 prohibits the installation on a relevant vehicle of a catalytic converter intended as a replacement part unless it is an original replacement which:

(a) has been clearly and indelibly marked in accordance with provisions of Annex I to the Vehicle Emissions Chapter, and is covered by section 4a of the component type-approval certificate (referred to in Annex VI to that Chapter) issued in respect of the type of vehicle on which it is being installed; or

(b) it has been clearly and indelibly marked in accordance with provisions of Annex VII to the Vehicle Emissions Chapter, and is being installed on a vehicle of a type covered by point 5 of the type-approval certificate (referred to in Appendix 2 to Annex VII to that Chapter) issued in respect of that replacement catalytic converter.

Reg 6 provides for the enforcement of the regulations, and introduces the Schedule, which has effect with regard to offences, enforcement and other related matters.

[1292]

MOTOR VEHICLES (REPLACEMENT OF CATALYTIC CONVERTERS AND POLLUTION CONTROL DEVICES) REGULATIONS 2009

SI 2009/1899

Authority Made by the Secretary of State for Transport under the European Communities Act 1972, s 2(2).

Date made 14 July 2009.

Commencement 13 August 2009.

Interpretation In the summary below:

(a) "the Vehicle Emissions Directive" means Council Directive 70/220/EEC on the approximation of the laws of the Member States relating to measures to be taken against air pollution by gases from positive-ignition engines of motor vehicles (OJ L76, 06.04.1970, p 1);

(b) "ECE Regulation 103" means Regulation 103 which is an annex to the UNECE Agreement (the Agreement of the United Nations Economic Commission for Europe concluded at Geneva on 20 March 1958, as amended) and contains uniform provisions concerning the approval of replacement catalytic converters for power-driven vehicles (as in force on 4th April 2005).

Summary These regulations impose requirements and prohibitions in relation to the installation on certain vehicles of replacement catalytic converters and replacement pollution control devices. "Replacement catalytic converter" is defined by reference to: (a) the Vehicle Emissions Directive (if approved pursuant to the requirements set out in that Directive) or ECE Regulation 103 (if approved pursuant to the requirements set out in that Regulation). "Replacement pollution control device" is defined by reference to Regulation (EC) 715/2007 of the European Parliament and of the Council (OJ L171, 29.06.2007, p 1). The regulations do not apply to a catalytic converter or pollution control device which is second-hand (reg 3).

Reg 4 prohibits the supply of a catalytic converter for installation on a 220 relevant vehicle (as defined) unless certain marking and information requirements of the Vehicle Emissions Directive or ECE Regulation 103 are met in connection with that converter. Reg 5 imposes a similar prohibition on the installation of a catalytic converter on a 220 relevant vehicle. Regs 4 and 5 do not apply to a replacement catalytic converter of a type approved before 31 October 2002.

Reg 6 prohibits the supply of a pollution control device for installation on a 715 relevant vehicle (as defined) unless certain marking and information requirements of Commission Regulation (EC) 692/2008 (OJ L199, 28.07.2008, p 1) are met in connection with that device. Reg 7 imposes a similar prohibition on the installation of a pollution control device on a 715 relevant vehicle.

Reg 8 prohibits the supply of a non-type approved catalytic converter or pollution control device (as defined), which is a replacement part capable of being fitted to a 220 relevant vehicle or a 715 relevant vehicle, unless it is marked or labelled in accordance with reg 8, and is accompanied by specified information.

Reg 9 provides for the enforcement of the regulations, and introduces the Schedule, which has effect with regard to offences, enforcement and other related matters.

[1293]

PUBLIC SERVICE VEHICLES (ENFORCEMENT POWERS) REGULATIONS 2009

SI 2009/1964

Authority Made by the Secretary of State for Transport under the Public Passenger Vehicles Act 1981, Sch 2A.

Date made 16 July 2009.

Commencement 1 October 2009.

Summary These regulations empower an authorised person to detain a vehicle adapted to carry more than eight passengers which is being, or has been, used on a road in contravention of the public service vehicle operator licensing requirements in the Public Passenger Vehicles Act 1981, s 12.

Reg 3 empowers an authorised person to detain a vehicle and its contents where that person has reason to believe that the vehicle is being, or has been, used on a road in contravention of s 12(1) of the 1981 Act. Where, at the time of the detention, passengers are travelling on the vehicle, the authorised person must make provision for the passengers and their personal effects to be transported in safety to their destination, or to a suitable place from which to continue their journey (reg 4). Reg 5 provides that an authorised person may fix an immobilisation device to a detained vehicle and, if he does so, must fix an immobilisation notice to the vehicle. Reg 6 creates offences relating to the unauthorised removal of, or attempt to remove, an immobilisation device from a vehicle, or the unauthorised removal of, or interference with, an immobilisation notice. Where a vehicle is detained, the authorised person must take such steps as are reasonably practicable to return the contents and any personal effects remaining on the vehicle to the person entitled to their return (reg 7). Reg 8 provides for a detained vehicle or any detained contents or personal effects to be delivered into the custody of a nominated custodian. Reg 9 sets out the steps to be taken to inform a person that his vehicle and any other property has been detained.

Reg 10 provides that a detained vehicle must be returned to the owner, without the need for an application under reg 11, where one or more of the following grounds is or are made out:

(a) at the time the vehicle was detained, the person using the vehicle held a valid operator's licence (whether or not authorising the use of the vehicle);

(b) at the time the vehicle was detained, the vehicle was not being, and had not been, used in contravention of s 12(1) of the 1981 Act;

(c) although at the time the vehicle was detained it was being, or had been, used in contravention of s 12(1) of the 1981 Act, the owner did not know that it was being, or had been, so used;
(d) although knowing at the time the vehicle was detained that it was being, or had been, used in contravention of s 12(1) of the 1981 Act, the owner had taken steps with a view to preventing that use and has taken steps with a view to preventing any further such use.

Regs 11–15 prescribe the procedure under which the owner of a detained vehicle may apply to the traffic commissioner for the area in which the vehicle was detained for its return. Provision is made for the form of application to the traffic commissioner (reg 11); the conduct of a hearing by the traffic commissioner (reg 12); notification of the traffic commissioner's determination (reg 13); the consequences of a determination (reg 14); and appeals to the Upper Tribunal against a determination of the traffic commissioner (reg 15).

Provision is made for the procedure to be followed in connection with the sale or destruction of a detained vehicle by the nominated custodian in specified circumstances (reg 16); the return or disposal of any contents or personal effects in the custody of the nominated custodian by virtue of reg 8 (reg 17); and the disposal of any contents or personal effects where the authorised person considers that their condition is such that they must be disposed of without delay (reg 18). Reg 19 requires the nominated custodian to take such steps as are necessary for the safe custody of detained vehicles, contents or personal effects. Reg 20 provides for the application of the proceeds of sale of any property sold under reg 16 or 18.

Reg 21 provides for the resolution of disputes arising in relation to:
(a) the return or disposal of any contents of, or personal effects on, a detained vehicle; or
(b) the application of the proceeds of sale of any detained vehicle, contents or personal effects.

Regs 22 and 23 provide that it is an offence intentionally to obstruct an authorised person in the exercise of his powers, or to make a false or misleading declaration with a view to securing the return of a vehicle. Reg 24 relates to the service of notices and applications under the regulations. Reg 25 empowers a traffic commissioner to extend certain time limits under the regulations where it is considered necessary in order for a case to be dealt with fairly and justly.

As to the detention of heavy goods vehicles operated in contravention of the licensing requirements in the Goods Vehicles (Licensing of Operators) Act 1995, s 2, see SI 2001/3981.

[1294]

WORKPLACE PARKING LEVY (ENGLAND) REGULATIONS 2009 SI 2009/2085

Authority Made by the Secretary of State for Transport under the Transport Act 2000, ss 178(2), 184(2), 189(1)–(3), 197(1) and by the Lord Chancellor under ss 189(4), 195(1), 197(1) of the 2000 Act.
Date made 28 July 2009.
Commencement 1 October 2009; see reg 1(1).
Interpretation See reg 2.
General The Transport Act 2000, Pt III, Chapter II (ss 178–190) (workplace parking levy) concerns licensing schemes for imposing charges in respect of the provision of workplace parking places. These regulations, which apply in England (except Greater London), make provision in relation to such licensing schemes. Pt 2 of the regulations exempts certain licensing scheme orders from the requirement to be confirmed by the Secretary of State under s 184(1) of the 2000 Act and provides for the payment of licence charges. Pt 3 of the regulations provides for the imposition of penalty charges for breach of licensing requirements and for the enforcement of penalty charges.

[1295]

PART 1
PRELIMINARY

Citation, commencement and application

1 (1) These Regulations may be cited as the Workplace Parking Levy (England) Regulations 2009 and come into force on 1st October 2009.

(2) These Regulations apply in England except Greater London.

[1296]

Interpretation

2 (1) In these Regulations—

"charge certificate" has the meaning given in regulation 13(1);
"chargee" has the meaning given in regulation 8(4);
"licence charge" means the charge for the grant of a licence;
"licensed premises", in the case of any licence, means the premises in respect of which the licence is granted;
"notice of rejection" means a notice served under regulation 11(1);
"penalty charge" means a charge imposed under regulation 5;
"penalty charge notice" means a notice served under regulation 8.

(2) In these Regulations, where an arrangement has been made for any function under a joint local licensing scheme to be discharged by one of the licensing authorities, "licensing authority" means the authority on which the function has been conferred by the arrangement.

[1297]

PART 2
LICENSING SCHEMES AND LICENCE CHARGES

Exemption of licensing scheme orders from confirmation requirement

3 (1) Section 184(1) of the Transport Act 2000 (confirmation of licensing schemes) does not apply to a licensing scheme order if—

- (a) the order varies a licensing scheme, and
- (b) its sole purpose is to provide for licence charges to be altered in line with alterations in the retail prices index.

(2) In this regulation "retail prices index" has the meaning given in section 21(4) of the Statistics and Registration Service Act 2007.

[1298]

Liability to pay licence charge

4 (1) This paragraph applies where the occupier of any premises has—

- (a) entered into arrangements with another person (P) for the provision by P of a parking place at those premises (whether or not for P's own use), and
- (b) provided the licensing authority with such evidence of those arrangements as that authority may reasonably require.

(2) Where paragraph (1) applies, the licence charge imposed in respect of those premises by a licensing scheme must be paid by P.

[1299]

PART 3
PENALTY CHARGES

Imposition of penalty charges

Imposition of penalty charges

5 (1) A licensing scheme may provide for the imposition of a penalty charge in any of the following circumstances—

- (a) where a person is providing a workplace parking place at any premises in the area covered by a licensing scheme and there is no licence in force in respect of those premises;
- (b) where a person is providing a workplace parking place at licensed premises in circumstances where the number of vehicles (excluding exempt vehicles) occupying workplace parking places at those premises exceeds the maximum number of workplace parking places covered by the licence;
- (c) if a condition in a licence (other than a condition as to the number of vehicles which may occupy workplace parking places at licensed premises) has been contravened.

(2) Where a licensing scheme provides for the imposition of a penalty charge it must specify the period within which the charge must be paid and may specify different periods for different circumstances.

(3) A licensing scheme may not specify under paragraph (2) a period of less than 28 days beginning on the date on which the penalty charge notice is served.

[1300]

Rates of penalty charges

6 (1) A licensing scheme which provides for penalty charges must specify the amount of the penalty charge and may specify different amounts in different circumstances.

(2) A licensing scheme may provide for the amount of the penalty charge to be reduced if it is paid before the expiry of a specified period.

[1301]

Liability to pay penalty charges

7 (1) This paragraph applies where the occupier of any premises has—

- (a) entered into arrangements with another person (P) for the provision by P of a parking place at those premises (whether or not for P's own use), and
- (b) provided the licensing authority with such evidence of those arrangements as that authority may reasonably require.

(2) Where paragraph (1) applies, any penalty charge imposed in respect of those premises must be paid by P.

[1302]

Enforcement of penalty charges

Penalty charge notices

8 (1) Where a licensing authority believes that a penalty charge is payable under the terms of a licensing scheme, the authority may serve notice of that fact ("a penalty charge notice").

(2) A penalty charge notice must be served on the person liable to pay the penalty charge.

(3) A penalty charge notice must state—

- (a) the amount of the penalty charge to which it relates;
- (b) all the circumstances in which a penalty charge is payable and the date and time at which each of those circumstances occurred;
- (c) the period specified in the licensing scheme within which the penalty charge must be paid;
- (d) the manner in which the penalty charge must be paid;
- (e) if the licensing scheme so provides, the amount of the reduced penalty charge if it is duly paid in the time specified in the notice;
- (f) the grounds on which the chargee may make representations under regulation 9;
- (g) the amount of the increased penalty charge if, before the end of the relevant period determined under regulation 13—
  - (i) the penalty charge is not paid, or
  - (ii) no representations are made under regulation 9, and
- (h) the address to which payment of the penalty charge must be sent.

(4) In this regulation and regulations 9 to 15 "chargee" means—

- (a) the person on whom the penalty charge notice is served; or
- (b) where it is alleged that the penalty charge notice was sent but never received, the person to whom the licensing authority sent that notice.

[1303]

Representations against penalty charge notices

9 (1) Where it appears that any of the grounds mentioned in paragraph (2) are satisfied, the chargee may make representations in writing to that effect to the licensing authority which served the penalty charge notice.

(2) The grounds are that—

- (a) the circumstances stated in the penalty charge notice—
  - (i) did not occur, or
  - (ii) did not occur at the date or time or in the manner specified in the notice;
- (b) the penalty charge exceeded the amount applicable in the circumstances of the case.

(3) The licensing authority may disregard any representations received after the end of the period of 28 days beginning with the date on which the penalty charge notice is served.

(4) It is the duty of a licensing authority to which representations are duly made under this regulation—

(a) to consider them and any supporting evidence which is provided with them, and

(b) to serve on the chargee notice of its decision as to whether or not it accepts that the ground in question has been established (and, if it accepts that it has, whether completely or partially).

[1304]

Cancellation of penalty charge notices

10 (1) Where representations are made under regulation 9 and the licensing authority accepts that the ground in question has been established it shall—

(a) cancel the penalty charge notice; and

(b) state in the notice served under regulation 9(4)(b) that the notice has been cancelled.

(2) The cancellation of a penalty charge notice does not prevent the licensing authority from serving a fresh penalty charge notice on the chargee or another person.

[1305]

Rejection of representations against penalty charge notices

11 (1) Where representations are made under regulation 9 and the licensing authority decides that none of the grounds in regulation 9(2) has been established, the notice served under regulation 9(4)(b) must be a notice of rejection stating that—

(a) a charge certificate may be served under regulation 13 unless—

(i) the penalty charge is paid, or

(ii) the chargee appeals against the licensing authority's decision, and

(b) the chargee has a right of appeal to a county court.

(2) A notice of rejection may contain such other information as the licensing authority thinks appropriate.

[1306]

Appeals

12 (1) Where a licensing authority has served a notice of rejection, the chargee may appeal to a county court against the licensing authority's decision.

(2) An appeal under this regulation—

(a) is a re-hearing of the licensing authority's decision to impose a charge, and

(b) may be determined having regard to matters of which the licensing authority was unaware.

(3) On an appeal the court may either—

(a) quash the notice of rejection and substitute such decision of its own as it thinks fit for the decision of the licensing authority under regulation 9(4), or

(b) dismiss the appeal.

(4) If the court makes an order under paragraph (3)(a), the penalty charge notice to which the notice of rejection relates is cancelled but the cancellation does not prevent the licensing authority from serving a fresh penalty charge notice on the chargee or another person if that is consistent with the decision which the court has substituted.

[1307]

Charge certificates

13 (1) Where a chargee has not paid the penalty charge specified in a penalty charge notice before the end of the relevant period, the licensing authority may serve on the chargee a statement (a "charge certificate") to the effect that the penalty charge is increased to such an amount as is provided in the licensing scheme.

(2) The licensing authority may—

(a) cancel a charge certificate, and

(b) if the authority thinks fit in such a case, serve a further charge certificate.

(3) For the purposes of paragraph (1), the relevant period in relation to a penalty charge notice is—

(a) where no representations are made, the period specified in the licensing scheme within which the penalty charge must be paid;

(b) where—

(i) representations are made,

(ii) a notice of rejection is served, and

(iii) no appeal against the notice of rejection is made,

the period of 28 days beginning with the date on which the notice of rejection is served;

(c) where an appeal against a notice of rejection is dismissed, the period of 28 days beginning with the date of service of the order dismissing the appeal; and

(d) where an appeal against a notice of rejection is made but is withdrawn before a county court makes an order under regulation 12(3), the period of 14 days beginning with the date on which the appeal is withdrawn.

[1308]

Payment of increased penalty charge

14 The chargee must pay the increased penalty charge specified in the charge certificate before the end of the period of 14 days beginning with the date on which the charge certificate is served.

[1309]

Recovery of unpaid penalty charges

15 The licensing authority may, if a county court so orders, recover a penalty charge as if it were payable under a county court order—

(a) in a case where the authority has served a charge certificate, if the chargee has not paid the increased penalty charge provided for in the charge certificate before the end of the period specified in regulation 14, or

(b) in a case where the authority has not served a charge certificate, if the chargee has not paid the penalty charge specified in the penalty charge notice before the end of the relevant period specified in regulation 13(3).

[1310]

Service of notices etc

16 (1) Any penalty charge notice, charge certificate or other notice to be served by the licensing authority under these Regulations ("a relevant notice") may be served—

(a) by delivering it to that person or by leaving it at that person's proper address,

(b) by sending it by first class (but not second class) post to that person at that address, or

(c) if the person is a body corporate, by serving it in accordance with sub-paragraph (a) or (b) on the secretary, clerk or principal officer of that body,

(d) if the person is a partnership, by serving it in accordance with sub-paragraph (a) or (b) on a partner or a person having the control or management of the partnership business, or

(e) by means of any form of electronic communication which is agreed with the person to whom it is to be sent.

(2) For the purposes of paragraph (1), and of section 7 of the Interpretation Act 1978 (service of documents by post) in its application to this regulation, the proper address of a person is—

(a) in the case of an individual, that person's last known address,

(b) in the case of the secretary, clerk or principal officer of a body corporate, the address of the registered office of the body or its principal office in the United Kingdom,

(c) in the case of a partner in, or a person having the control or management of, a partnership, it is the address of the principal office of the partnership in the United Kingdom,

but subject to paragraph (3).

(3) If a person to be served with a relevant notice has notified the licensing authority of an address within the United Kingdom other than that person's proper address at which that person, or another acting on that person's behalf, will accept service of a relevant notice, that address is the person's proper address.

(4) Unless the contrary is proved, service of a relevant notice sent by a form of electronic communication shall, if sent to an agreed fax telephone number or electronic address, be taken to have been effected on the first working day after the day on which it was transmitted.

(5) In paragraph (4), "working day" means any day except—

(a) a Saturday or a Sunday;
(b) New Year's Day;
(c) Good Friday;
(d) Christmas Day; and
(e) any other day which is a bank holiday in England under the Banking and Financial Dealings Act 1971.

[1311]

MOTOR VEHICLES (REFILLING OF AIR CONDITIONING SYSTEMS BY SERVICE PROVIDERS) REGULATIONS 2009 SI 2009/2194

Authority Made by the Secretary of State for Transport under the European Communities Act 1972, s 2(2).

Date made 9 August 2009.

Commencement 7 September 2009.

Summary These regulations implement Art 6(3) of Directive 2006/40/EC of the European Parliament and of the Council relating to emissions from air conditioning systems in motor vehicles (OJ L161, 14.06.2006, p 12).

Regs 1 and 2 provide for preliminary matters, including interpretation of the regulations. Reg 3 provides that a service provider must not fill an air conditioning system with fluorinated greenhouse gases (as defined by Art 3 of Directive 2006/40/EC) where an abnormal amount of refrigerant has leaked from that system, and the necessary repair to the system has not been completed. It also specifies the matters to be taken into account in determining whether the amount of refrigerant that has leaked from an air conditioning system is abnormal.

Reg 4 provides that a person commits an offence if he contravenes any of regs 3(1) (servicing and repairing of air conditioning systems), 7 (obstructing etc an officer) and 8(9) (purporting to act as an officer), and is liable on summary conviction to a fine not exceeding level 3 on the standard scale. By reg 5, it is a defence in proceedings for any offence under the regulations for the person charged to show that he took all reasonable steps and exercised all due diligence to avoid committing the offence. Reg 6 extends liability for an offence under the regulations to a party whose act or default in the course of his business or employment has resulted in the principal offender committing the offence. Reg 7 makes it an offence to obstruct the officer of an enforcement authority when acting in pursuance of the regulations or to provide a false statement to the officer.

Reg 8 confers various powers on the officer of an enforcement authority, including powers to inspect an air conditioning system or equipment used to service such a system or to fill it with refrigerant; to enter and search premises; and to seize and detain such equipment and certain records. Reg 9 provides for applications for the release of detained equipment and records. Reg 10 requires an enforcement authority to pay compensation to a person in respect of any loss or damage caused where an officer exercises any power under reg 8 to seize and detain equipment or records if there has been no contravention of the regulations. Where a person is convicted of an offence in relation to equipment or records, reg 11 enables an enforcement authority to recover any expenditure incurred by it in connection with the seizure or detention of equipment or records (in addition to other costs and expenses).

Regs 12 and 13 make savings for certain privileges and civil rights.

[1312]

Trustee

See the title Trusts

Trustee in Bankruptcy

See the title Bankruptcy and Insolvency

Trustee Savings Banks

See the title Savings Banks

Trusts

CHRONOLOGICAL LIST OF INSTRUMENTS

SR & O	*Description*	*Remarks*	*Page*
SR & O 1912/348	Public Trustee Rules 1912	—	780
SR & O 1916/489	Public Trustee Rules 1916	Amend SI 1912/348	—

SI	*Description*	*Remarks*	*Page*
SI 1962/658	Trustee Investments (Additional Powers) Order 1962	See Preliminary Note "Trustee investments"	—
SI 1962/2611	Trustee Investments (Additional Powers) (No 2) Order 1962	See Preliminary Note "Trustee investments"	—
SI 1964/703	Trustee Investments (Additional Powers) Order 1964	See Preliminary Note "Trustee investments"	—
SI 1964/1404	Trustee Investments (Additional Powers) (No 2) Order 1964	See Preliminary Note "Trustee investments"	—
SI 1966/401	Trustee Investments (Additional Powers) Order 1966	See Preliminary Note "Trustee investments"	—
SI 1968/470	Trustee Investments (Additional Powers) Order 1968	See Preliminary Note "Trustee investments"	—
SI 1972/1818	Trustee Investments (Additional Powers) Order 1972	See Preliminary Note "Trustee investments"	—
SI 1973/1332	Trustee Investments (Additional Powers) Order 1973	See Preliminary Note "Trustee investments"	—
SI 1975/1189	Public Trustee (Custodian Trustee) Rules 1975	Amend SI 1912/348	—
SI 1975/1710	Trustee Investments (Additional Powers) Order 1975	See Preliminary Note "Trustee investments"	—
SI 1976/836	Public Trustee (Custodian Trustee) Rules 1976	Amend SI 1912/348	—
SI 1977/831	Trustee Investments (Additional Powers) Order 1977	See Preliminary Note "Trustee investments"	—
SI 1977/1878	Trustee Investments (Additional Powers) (No 2) Order 1977	See Preliminary Note "Trustee investments"	—
SI 1981/358	Public Trustee (Custodian Trustee) Rules 1981	Amend SI 1912/348	—
SI 1982/1086	Trustee Investments (Additional Powers) Order 1982	See Preliminary Note "Trustee investments"	—
SI 1983/370	Judicial Trustee Rules 1983	—	793
SI 1983/772	Trustee Investments (Additional Powers) Order 1983	See Preliminary Note "Trustee investments"	—
SI 1983/1050	Public Trustee (Amendment) Rules 1983	Amend SI 1912/348	—
SI 1983/1525	Trustee Investments (Additional Powers) (No 2) Order 1983	See Preliminary Note "Trustee investments"	—
SI 1984/109	Public Trustee (Custodian Trustee) Rules 1984	Amend SI 1912/348	—
SI 1985/132	Public Trustee (Custodian Trustee) (Amendment) Rules 1985	Amend SI 1912/348	—
SI 1985/1780	Trustee Investments (Additional Powers) Order 1985	See Preliminary Note "Trustee investments"	—
SI 1986/601	Trustee Investments (Additional Powers) Order 1986	See Preliminary Note "Trustee investments"	—
SI 1987/1177	Recognition of Trusts Act 1987 (Commencement) Order 1987	Made under s 3(2) of the 1987 Act; brought the Act into force on 1 August 1987	—
SI 1987/1891	Public Trustee (Custodian Trustee) Rules 1987	Amend SI 1912/348	—
SI 1987/2249	Public Trustee (Amendment) Rules 1987	Amend SI 1912/348	—

SI	*Description*	*Remarks*	*Page*
SI 1988/2254	Trustee Investments (Additional Powers) Order 1988	See Preliminary Note "Trustee Investments	—
SI 1989/673	Recognition of Trusts Act 1987 (Overseas Territories) Order 1989	—	798
SI 1991/999	Trustee Investments (Additional Powers) Order 1991	See Preliminary Note "Trustee Investments"	—
SI 1991/2684	Solicitors' Incorporated Practices Order 1991	See title Courts and Legal Services; modifies SI 1912/348	—
SI 1992/1738	Trustee Investments (Additional Powers) Order 1992	See Preliminary Note "Trustee Investments"	—
SI 1994/265	Trustee Investments (Additional Powers) Order 1994	See Preliminary Note "Trustee Investments"	—
SI 1994/1908	Trustee Investments (Additional Powers) (No 2) Order 1994	See Preliminary Note "Trustee Investments"	—
SI 1994/2519	Public Trustee (Custodian Trustee) Rules 1994	Amend SI 1912/348	—
SI 1995/768	Trustee Investments (Additional Powers) Order 1995	See Preliminary Note "Trustee Investments"	—
SI 1995/1330	Public Trustee (Notices Affecting Land) (Title on Death) Regulations 1995	See title Executors and Administrators	—
SI 1996/845	Trustee Investments (Division of Trust Fund) Order 1995	See Preliminary Note "Trustee Investments"	—
SI 1996/2974	Trusts of Land and Appointment of Trustees Act 1996 (Commencement) Order 1996	Made under s 27(2) of the 1996 Act; brought the Act into force on 1 January 1997	—
SI 2000/215	Powers of Attorney (Welsh Language Forms) Order 2000	—	798
SI 2000/216	Trustee Delegation Act 1999 (Commencement) Order 2000	Made under s 13(1) of the 1999 Act; brought ss 1–12 of, and the Schedule to, the Act into force on 1 March 2000	—
SI 2001/49	Trustee Act 2000 (Commencement) Order 2001	Made under s 42(2) of the 2000 Act; brought the whole Act, in so far as not already in force, into force on 1 February 2001	—
SI 2002/2469	National Health Service Reform and Health Care Professions Act 2002 (Supplementary, Consequential etc Provisions) Regulations 2002	See title National Health Service; amend SI 1912/348	—
SI 2008/611	Public Trustee (Fees) Order 2008	—	799

[1313]

INSTRUMENTS NO LONGER IN OPERATION

The following instruments, formerly included in this title, are no longer in operation:

SI 1986/2261	lapsed[1]	
SI 1999/855	revoked by	SI 2008/611
SI 2002/2232	revoked by	SI 2008/611
SI 2003/690	revoked by	SI 2008/611
SI 2004/799	revoked by	SI 2008/611
SI 2005/351	revoked by	SI 2008/611
SI 2007/681	revoked by	SI 2008/611

1 Lapsed on repeal of enabling power by the Statute Law (Repeals) Act 2004, s 1(1), Sch 1, Pt 1, Group 4

CROSS REFERENCES

Administration of estates	Executors and Administrators
Charities	Charities
Court rules	Courts and Legal Services
Exchange of government securities	Money

Income tax	Taxation
Inheritance tax	Taxation
Public Guardian	Mental Health
Real property	Real Property
Solicitors	Courts and Legal Services
Superannuation trust funds	Social Security (Pt 2)
Trustee in bankruptcy	Bankruptcy and Insolvency
Trusts of land	Real Property
Wills	Wills
Statutory instruments generally, their validity, effect and termination	Statutory Instruments, Vol 1 of this work

PRELIMINARY NOTE

The instruments in this title mainly concern the Public Trustee, judicial trustees and custodian trustees, and trustee investments. Since the Public Trustee may act in the capacity of a judicial trustee or of a custodian trustee (as well as in other capacities), judicial trustees and custodian trustees are considered before the office of Public Trustee.

[1314]

Judicial trustees

A judicial trustee is a trustee appointed by the court under the Judicial Trustees Act 1896, s 1. The person appointed a judicial trustee is an officer of the court, and is therefore subject to its control and supervision. The purpose of appointing a judicial trustee is to ensure the proper execution of the trust, but without incurring the full expense of having the trust administered by the court. The power to appoint a judicial trustee under s 1(1) of the 1896 Act is discretionary. Any fit and proper person may be appointed a judicial trustee; if the court is not satisfied of the fitness of the person nominated as judicial trustee it may appoint an official of the court (s 1(1), (3)). S 1(5) provides that the court may direct that the judicial trustee be remunerated for his services from the trust property.

SI 1983/370 concerns the appointment of judicial trustees, the preparation and examination of accounts, remuneration and disbursements of judicial trustees, default by judicial trustees, and other related matters.

[1315]

Custodian trustees

In a custodian trust the custodian trustees hold the legal title to the trust assets, but the management of the trust property and the exercise of any power or discretion exercisable by the trustees under the terms of the trust remain vested in the other trustees (who are called the managing trustees). The provisions of the Public Trustee Act 1906, s 4, which govern the appointment, powers, duties and liabilities of custodian trustees, apply to any banking or insurance company or other corporate body entitled by rules made under the Act to act as custodian trustees (s 4(3) of the 1906 Act); the companies and other corporate bodies so entitled are specified in SR & O 1912/348, r 30.

[1316]

Public Trustee

The Public Trustee is a trust corporation established by the Public Trustee Act 1906. SR & O 1912/348, made under the 1906 Act, concerns the authorised trusts and duties of the Public Trustee and other related matters. Further provisions relating to the Public Trustee are made by the Public Trustee and Administration of Funds Act 1986, ss 1, 3.

Under the provisions mentioned above, the Public Trustee can act as executor or administrator of estates of small value and as the appointed trustee of settlements or when requested to take over these responsibilities by retiring trustees (see generally ss 2, 3, 5, 6 of the 1906 Act), and may exercise the functions of a deputy appointed by the

Court of Protection established by the Mental Capacity Act 2005, Pt 2 (see s 3(1) of the 1986 Act). The mental health functions (protection, receivership and enduring powers of attorney) of the Public Trustee were taken over by the Public Guardianship Office, but those functions have now been taken over by the Public Guardian, a new official established under the Mental Capacity Act 2005, ss 57–60; see further the title Mental Health.

Under the Law of Property (Miscellaneous Provisions) Act 1994, s 18, notices affecting land which would have been served on a person but for his death must be served on the Public Trustee. As to the filing of documents so served, the keeping of a register of details taken from them, and searches of the register, see SI 1995/1330, in the title Executors and Administrators; and as to the fees payable to the Public Trustee in respect of his functions relating to notices affecting land, see SI 2008/611, art 29.

In April 2000, the Government stated its intention to modernise the Public Trust Office (*"Making Changes—the Future of the Public Trust Office"*). On 1 April 2001, the offices of the Public Trustee and the Official Solicitor were merged and housed in one building at 81 Chancery Lane, London WC2A 1DD. The Offices of Court Funds, Official Solicitor and Public Trustee was created on 1 April 2007, when the Court Funds Office merged with the Official Solicitor and Public Trustee. As to the division of estates and trusts work between the Official Solicitor and the Public Trustee, see http://www.officialsolicitor.gov.uk/estates/estates.htm.

Other functions of the Public Trustee relate to the investigation and audit of the accounts of any trust, pursuant to r 31 of SR & O 1912/348.

[1317]

Fees The fees payable to the Public Trustee in respect of his duties are prescribed by SI 2008/611. The order indicates, as required by the Public Trustee (Fees) Act 1957, s 1(2), whether a fee is to be payable out of capital or out of income. Note that a fee is prescribed by Pt 9 of the order for the purpose of reimbursing the Public Trustee in respect of value added tax.

[1318]

Trustee investments

Trustees without specific powers of investment were limited to specified "authorised investments" in the Trustee Investments Act 1961. There are separate lists of authorised investments for trustees of settled land (Settled Land Act 1925, s 73) and there are some special provisions for charitable trusts (Charities Act 1993, ss 24, 25, 25A) and pension fund trustees (Pensions Act 1995, ss 34–36, 36A). The Trustee Investments Act 1961 divides investments into two principal groups: narrower-range and wider-range (s 1, Sch 1). Narrower-range investments are further subdivided into those requiring advice from a person having practical experience of financial matters and those not requiring advice (s 6(2), (4), Sch 1, Pts I, II). No wider-range investment may be made unless the trust fund has been divided into two parts, the narrower-range part and the wider-range part (s 2(1)). The parts are to be equal in value at the date of division (s 2(1)), but this ratio may be altered by an order made by the Treasury to a ratio of up to three to one in favour of the wider-range part (s 13): it is directed by SI 1996/845, made under s 13, that the ratio be altered to a ratio of three to one.

S 12 of the 1961 Act enables Orders in Council to add investments to those set out in Sch 1. By the orders cited in brackets, made under this power, the following investments have been added:

(a) to Sch 1, Pt I (narrower-range investments in which a trustee may invest without being required to take advice):
   - Ulster Development Bonds (SI 1962/2611);
   - National Development Bonds (SI 1964/703);
   - British Savings Bonds (SI 1968/470);
   - National Savings Income Bonds (SI 1982/1086);
   - National Savings Deposit Bonds (SI 1983/1525);
   - National Savings Indexed-Income Bonds (SI 1985/1780);
   - National Savings Capital Bonds (SI 1988/2254);
   - National Savings FIRST Option Bonds (SI 1992/1738); and

— National Savings Pensioners Guaranteed Income Bonds (SI 1994/265);

(b) to Sch 1, Pt II (narrower-range investments in which a trustee may not invest without advice):

— certain loans to, and securities issued by, the former Great Ouse Water Authority (SI 1962/658);

— fixed-interest securities issued by the Inter-American Development Bank (SI 1964/1404);

— Bank of Ireland 7 per cent Loan Stock 1986/91 (SI 1966/401);

— fixed-interest securities issued by the European Investment Bank or by the European Coal and Steel Community (SI 1972/1818);

— certain loans to, and securities issued by, any district council in Northern Ireland (SI 1973/1332);

— certificates of tax deposit (SI 1975/1710);

— variable interest Government Stock (SI 1977/831);

— certain variable interest securities, issued by Commonwealth governments, by certain international banks and by certain local authorities and bodies (SI 1977/1878);

— certain fixed and variable interest securities issued by certain international organisations (SI 1983/772);

— certain loans to and securities issued by the Inner London Education Authority or any residuary body established by the Local Government Act 1985, s 57 (SI 1986/601);

— certain fixed interest securities and variable interest securities issued in the United Kingdom by the European Bank for Reconstruction and Development (SI 1991/999);

— units of a gilt unit trust scheme, certain fixed interest securities and variable interest securities issued by the government of a relevant state (ie Austria, Finland, Iceland, Liechtenstein, Norway, Sweden or a member state other than the United Kingdom) or by specified bodies in a relevant state, debentures issued in a relevant state by a company incorporated in that state, loans to local authorities etc in a relevant state, deposits with a mutual investment society whose head office is located in a relevant state and loans secured on certain interests in property in a relevant state (SI 1994/1908, SI 1995/768); and

(c) to Sch I, Pt III (the authorised wider-range investments):

— certain securities issued in a relevant state by a company incorporated in that state or by any unincorporated body constituted under the law of that state, shares in a mutual investment society whose head office is located in a relevant state and units of certain recognised schemes (SI 1994/1908).

The Trustee Act 2000, Pts II (ss 3–7) and III (ss 8–10) enable trustees to invest, or acquire land for any purpose, including as an investment, as if they were absolutely entitled to the trust assets. The 2000 Act came into force partly (ss 41–43) on 23 November 2000 and fully on 1 February 2001 (SI 2001/49). Pts II, III of the 2000 Act do not apply to occupational pension schemes (s 36(1), (3)), authorised unit trusts (s 37) or common investment schemes or common deposit schemes under the Charities Act 1993, s 24 or 25 (s 38 of the 2000 Act).

Pt II (ss 3–7) of the 2000 Act replaces the provisions relating to the manner in which trustees may invest in the Trustee Investments Act 1961. S 3 of the 2000 Act creates the general power of investment for trustees. This power applies to the extent that the investment powers of the trustees are not expressed in the instrument creating the trust. It does not extend to investments in land other than by way of loans secured on land (s 3(3)–(6); but see s 8). Ss 4, 5 impose additional duties on the trustees to consider standard investment criteria and to obtain and consider proper advice in exercising any power of investment. Pt III (ss 8–10) introduces a new power allowing trustees to acquire and deal with land on behalf of a trust. The standard of care which is to be expected of trustees when carrying out their investment function is defined in Pt I (ss 1, 2 and Sch 1) of the 2000 Act. S 41 of the Act empowers a Minister of the Crown to amend by order any Act, including an Act extending to places outside England and Wales, in consequence of or in connection with Pt II or III.

The Trustee Investments Act 1961, ss 1, 2, 5, 6, 12, 13, 15, which are replaced by the new power of investment in Pt II of the 2000 Act, are repealed by s 40(1), (3) of, and para 1(1) of Pt I of Sch 2 and Pt I of Sch 4 to, that Act, except in so far as they are applied by or under any other enactment. Consequently, where an enactment continues to operate by reference to the 1961 Act, its effect is preserved. For this purpose, it will still be possible (under s 12 of the 1961 Act) for additions to be made to the list of investments specified in Sch 1 to that Act (which is not specifically repealed).

[1319]

Recognition of trusts

The Recognition of Trusts Act 1987 incorporates into the law of the United Kingdom most of the Convention on the Law Applicable to Trusts and on their Recognition, adopted in draft at the Hague on 20 October 1984 and signed by the United Kingdom on 10 January 1986. The Convention:

(a) provides for the determination of the law applicable to any trust which is governed by the Convention;

(b) sets out the effect of recognition of a trust; and

(c) makes general provision limiting the effect of the Convention in particular circumstances.

The 1987 Act was brought into force on 1 August 1987 by SI 1987/1177. See further SI 1989/673.

[1320]

Trusts of land etc

A new system of holding land on trust, replacing the existing systems of the trust for sale and the strict settlement, was introduced by the Trusts of Land and Appointment of Trustees Act 1996. The 1996 Act was brought into force on 1 January 1997 by SI 1996/2974. Under Pt I of the Act, trustees are provided with enhanced powers of delegation to achieve substantially the same results as a settlement without bringing into operation the complex provisions of the Settled Land Act 1925. Pt II of the 1996 Act (which applies to trusts of personalty as well as to trusts of land) deals with the appointment and retirement of trustees at the direction of the beneficiaries.

[1321]

Delegation of trustee functions

The Trustee Delegation Act 1999 amends the law relating to the delegation of trustee functions by power of attorney and makes provision in relation to the exercise of such delegated functions so as to implement the recommendations of the Law Commission in its report *The Law of Trusts: Delegation by Individual Trustees*. The Act came into force partly (s 13) on 15 July 1999 and fully on 1 March 2000 (SI 2000/216). The Trustee Act 2000, Pt IV (ss 11–27) contains a wide range of measures relating to collective delegation by trustees. Pt IV of the 2000 Act was brought into force on 1 February 2001 (SI 2001/49).

[1322]

PUBLIC TRUSTEE RULES 1912
SR & O 1912/348

Authority Made by the Lord Chancellor, with the concurrence of the Treasury, in pursuance of the Public Trustee Act 1906; power to make such rules is conferred by s 14 of that Act.
Date made 15 April 1912.
Commencement 15 April 1912; see r 46.
Amendment Printed as amended by SR & O 1916/489, SI 1975/1189, SI 1976/836, SI 1981/358, SI 1983/1050, SI 1984/109, SI 1985/132, SI 1987/1891, SI 1987/2249, SI 1994/2519, SI 2002/2469, and by virtue of the Constitutional Reform Act 2005, s 59(4).
Previously amended by SR & O 1925/1269 (revoked by SR & O 1926/1423), SR & O 1941/1534, SI 1948/2188, SI 1957/2201, SI 1962/1001 (all revoked by SI 1971/1894), SI 1971/1894 (revoked by SI 1975/1189), and SI 1974/595 (superseded so far as amended these rules). Also amended by virtue of the Coal Industry Act 1987, s 1(3) (repealed by the Coal Industry Act 1994, s 67(8), Sch 11, Pt IV).
Modification Modified by SI 1991/2684, so that references to a solicitor or solicitors (except in r 30) are to be construed as including references to a body corporate recognised by the Council of the Law Society under the Administration of Justice Act 1985, s 9.

Interpretation See rr 1, 2.
General See the Preliminary Note "Public Trustee".

[1323]

Interpretation

1 In these Rules the expression "the Act" means the Public Trustee Act 1906, and unless there is anything in the context or in the Act inconsistent therewith—

The expression "trust" includes any trust duty or office which the Public Trustee is authorised by the Act or these Rules to accept; and the expression "trustee" shall be construed accordingly.

The expression "trust instrument" includes any instrument, Act of Parliament, or Order of Court by which a trust is created or declared.

The expression "trust property" includes all property subject to a trust, or comprised in an estate, which is proposed to be administered by the Public Trustee.

NOTES
Authorised ... to accept See the Public Trustee Act 1906, s 2 and rr 6, 7.

[1324]

2 The Interpretation Act 1889, applies for the purpose of the interpretation of these Rules as it applies for the purpose of the interpretation of an Act of Parliament.

NOTES
Interpretation Act 1889 Repealed and replaced by the Interpretation Act 1978, printed in the title Statutory Instruments (Pt 2), Vol 1 of this work.

[1325]

Offices

3 (1) The Central Office of the Public Trustee shall be situate in London.

(2) Branch Offices may from time to time be established as may be prescribed by the Lord Chancellor by notice in the *London Gazette*.

NOTES
Central Office of the Public Trustee The Public Trustee and Official Solicitor merged on 1 April 2001 and the Offices of Court Funds, Official Solicitor and Public Trustee was created on 1 April 2007, when the Court Funds Office merged with the Official Solicitor and Public Trustee. The address of the Public Trustee is 81 Chancery Lane, London WC2A 1DD. See further the Preliminary Note "Public Trustee".

[1326]

Deputy Public Trustees

4 There shall be Deputy Public Trustees at any branch offices so established who shall be officers of the Public Trustee, and shall have the powers and perform the duties assigned to them by or under these Rules. Their number shall be such as the Lord Chancellor, with the sanction of the Treasury, may from time to time prescribe, and every such appointment shall be notified in the *London Gazette*.

NOTES
Deputy Public Trustees See the Preliminary Note "Public Trustee".

[1327]

Security

5 Security shall be given by such persons employed under the Act as the Treasury may direct for the due performance of their duties, and for the due accounting for and payment of all moneys received by them in pursuance of the Act and these Rules. The security shall be for such sum and shall be given in such manner and form as the Treasury shall order in the case of each such person, and the Treasury may at any time require that the amount or nature of any such security be varied.

[1328]

Authorised Trusts and Duties

6 Subject to the Act and these Rules the Public Trustee is authorised—

(a) to accept any trust created or declared by any trust instrument or arising upon an intestacy;

(b) to accept any duty incident to, and to act in, any of the following offices, *viz*:

(i) as incident to the office of Trustee of any trust accepted by him the office of guardian of any infant beneficiary,

(ii) the office (where the execution of any trust is involved therein) of agent or attorney for any person;

(c) to accept by the name of the Public Trustee probate or letters of administration of any kind and either as principal or as agent for any person;

(d) to accept as custodian Trustee any trust created or declared by any trust instrument;

(e) to receive any money or damages paid to him in pursuance of the Rules of the Supreme Court, Order 22, Rule 15, or any rule which may be substituted therefor, and to apply the same in accordance with such rule or any directions of the Court or a Judge thereunder.

Provided that he shall not accept the trusts of any instrument made solely by way of security for money.

NOTES

Rules of the Supreme Court The Rules of the Supreme Court 1883, Ord 22, r 15 was replaced by the Rules of the Supreme Court 1965, Ord 80, r 10. See now the Civil Procedure Rules 1998, SI 1998/3132, Pt 21, r 21.10(1) (which relates to the compromise of claims by or on behalf of a child or protected party), in the title Courts and Legal Services, Vol 5(3).

Cases relating to this rule *Re Bass, Bass v Public Trustee* [1914] WN 368.

[1329]

7 The Public Trustee may if he thinks fit—

(1) act as custodian trustee of a trust which involves the management or carrying on of any business, but upon the conditions that

(a) he shall not act in the management or carrying on of such business, and

(b) he shall not hold any property of such a nature as will expose the holder thereof to any liability except under exceptional circumstances and when he is satisfied that he is fully indemnified or secured against loss; and

(2) accept as ordinary trustee, under exceptional circumstances, a trust which involves the management or carrying on of any business, but upon the conditions that, except with the consent of the Treasury, he shall only carry on the same

(a) for a short time not exceeding eighteen months, and

(b) with a view to sale disposition or winding-up, and

(c) if satisfied that the same can be carried on without risk of loss.

[1330]

Trusteeships

8 (1) A testator may appoint the Public Trustee to be trustee or custodian trustee under any testamentary instrument without previously applying to him for his consent to act as such.

(2) No such appointment by a testator shall have effect, and no appointment of the Public Trustee to be trustee or custodian trustee shall be made except by a testator, unless and until (in either case) the consent of the Public Trustee to act as such trustee shall have been obtained in accordance with these Rules. Provided that in the case of any such appointment by a testator the Public Trustee shall at any time after the fact of his appointment shall have come to his knowledge be at liberty to act as if an application for his consent had been received by him.

(3) It shall be the duty of any person appointed by a testator to be co-trustee with the Public Trustee, and not renouncing or disclaiming the trust, to give to the Public Trustee notice in writing of such appointment as soon as practicable after the same has come to his knowledge.

NOTES

Cases relating to this rule *Re Shaw, Public Trustee v Little* [1914] WN 141, 110 LT 924, CA.

[1331]

9 Upon receiving an application for his consent to act as trustee or as custodian trustee the Public Trustee may require to be produced to him the trust instrument (if any), and may require to be supplied to him a copy of that instrument, and of any other document affecting the trust, and such particulars as to the nature and value of any trust property, and the liabilities (if any) attaching to such property, or the holder thereof, and the names and places of abode of any beneficiaries and trustees under the trust, and such other information relating to the trust as he may consider it desirable to obtain in any particular case.

[1332]

10 As soon as may be after receiving any such application the Public Trustee shall take into consideration upon such evidence as may appear to him sufficient—

(a) the gross capital value of the trust property;
(b) the mode of investment and the condition of the trust property;
(c) the situation, tenure, and character of any land comprised in the trust property;
(d) any liabilities attaching to the trust property or the holder thereof;
(e) the duties incident to the office of trustee of the trust;
(f) the places of abode and circumstances of any beneficiaries; and
(g) all the circumstances of the case;

and shall decide whether the application ought to be accepted or refused, and shall give notice to the applicant of such acceptance or refusal, and in case of acceptance shall in writing under his ... official seal signify his consent to act in the trust.

NOTES
Amendment Words omitted revoked by SR & O 1916/489.

[1333]

11 Upon the appointment of the Public Trustee being completed, the Public Trustee shall consider and determine whether the trust shall be administered from his Central Office or from a Branch Office, and shall give directions accordingly, and any such directions may at any time be rescinded or varied by the Public Trustee at his discretion.

NOTES
Central Office of the Public Trustee See the note to r 3.

[1334]

Administration of Small Estates

12 Upon receiving an application under section 3(1) of the Act the Public Trustee shall require to be supplied to him such evidence as to the value of the estate, and the circumstances of the persons beneficially entitled, and such other information relating thereto as he may consider it desirable to obtain in any particular case.

NOTES
Cases relating to this rule *Re Devereux, Toovey v Public Trustee* [1911] 2 Ch 545, [1911–13] All ER Rep 641.

[1335]

13 (1) If it is not proved to the satisfaction of the Public Trustee that the gross capital value of the estate is less than £1,000, or if it does not appear to him that the persons beneficially entitled are persons of small means, or if he sees any other good reason for refusing the application, he shall refuse the same, and shall forthwith give notice to the applicant of such refusal.

(2) In any other case the Public Trustee shall make in respect of the estate the declaration mentioned in section 3(2) of the Act, and shall give notice to the applicant that the application is accepted, and shall take such other steps as may be necessary or proper to enable him to administer the estate; and any person having the custody of the probate or letters of administration, or other document relating to the estate, shall, upon the request in writing of the Public Trustee, deliver the same to him, or as he shall direct.

(3) A refusal under this Rule shall not prevent the Public Trustee from exercising, with respect to the estate, any powers (other than powers under section 3 of the Act) exerciseable by him with respect thereto under the Act or these Rules, if duly appointed to exercise the same.

(4) Upon the acceptance of any application the Public Trustee shall consider and determine whether the estate shall be administered from his Central Office or from a Branch Office, and shall give directions accordingly, and any such directions may at any time be rescinded or varied by the Public Trustee at his discretion.

NOTES

Central Office of the Public Trustee See the note to r 3.

[1336]

14 For the purposes of the administration the Public Trustee shall (subject as hereinafter provided) have all the administrative powers and authorities exercisable by a Master of the [Senior Courts] acting in the administration of an estate.

NOTES

Amendment Words in square brackets substituted by virtue of the Constitutional Reform Act 2005, s 59(4).

Powers … exercisable by a Master of the Senior Courts As to the jurisdiction and powers of Masters generally, see the Civil Procedure Rules 1998, SI 1998/3132, Pt 2, r 2.4, in the title Courts and Legal Services, Vol 5(3).

[1337]

15 (1) The Public Trustee may, … without judicial proceedings, take the opinion of the High Court upon any question arising in the course of an administration.

[(2) Any such question shall be submitted—

- (a) to such Judge of the Chancery Division as the Vice-Chancellor may specify; and
- (b) in such manner as that judge may direct.]

(3) …

(4) The Judge may, before giving his opinion, require the attendance of, or communicate with any person interested in the estate as trustee or beneficiary, but no such person shall have a right to be heard by the Judge unless he otherwise directs.

(5) The Judge shall give his opinion to the Public Trustee, and the Public Trustee shall act in accordance with such opinion, and shall, upon the request in writing of any such interested person, communicate to him the effect of such opinion.

NOTES

Amendment Para (1): words omitted revoked by SI 1983/1050.
Para (2): substituted by SI 1983/1050.
Para (3): revoked by SI 1983/1050.

[1338]

Administration of Trusts and Estates

16 There shall be kept at the Central Office in London of the Public Trustee such registers and other books as shall be required for recording or entering in a convenient form as to each trust or estate which the Public Trustee is administering the particulars following:—

- (a) the date of the acceptance of the trust or of the declaration made under section 3(2) of the Act;
- (b) particulars of the trust property from time to time;
- (c) the names and place of abode of the person in receipt of the income of the trust property;
- (d) a reference to any notice received of any dealing with any beneficial interest in the trust property, and of any exercise or release of any power relating to the trust or estate;
- (e) an entry of any decision or opinion of the High Court in respect of the trust or estate;
- (f) such entries of his decisions and such other particulars as the Public Trustee may think fit;

and such particulars shall be recorded or entered accordingly.

NOTES

Central Office of the Public Trustee See the note to r 3.

[1339]

[**17** The Public Trustee may—

(a) invest or retain invested money belonging to any trust or estate and coming into his hands in any mode of investment—

  (i) expressly or implicitly authorised by the trust instrument, or

  (ii) if there is no trust instrument, authorised by law for the investment of trust funds,

(b) pay and deposit such money in court for investment in any manner authorised by rules made under section 38(7) of the Administration of Justice Act 1982,

(c) if authorised by the trust instrument or otherwise by law, retain any investment existing at the date of the commencement of the trust.

Provided that he shall not invest in or hold any investment in such manner as to expose him to liability as the holder thereof, unless he is satisfied that he is fully indemnified or secured against loss.]

NOTES

Amendment Substituted by SI 1987/2249.

May invest or retain invested Temporary cash balances awaiting investment or distribution may be included in the general deposit fund maintained by the Public Trustee under the Public Trustee (General Deposit Fund) Act 1939.

Authorised by law for the investment of trust funds See the Preliminary Note "Trustee investments".

Rules made under the Administration of Justice Act 1982, s 38(7) See SI 1987/821, in the title Courts and Legal Services.

[1340]

18 (1) The securities and documents belonging or relating to a trust or estate which the Public Trustee is administering shall, if under his control, be kept at the bank to the trust or estate or at some other safe place of deposit allowed generally or specially by the Treasury, so far as the convenience of business will admit.

(2) All orders for the withdrawal of securities or documents from any such bank or other place of deposit shall be signed by not less than two persons, *viz*.: (a) by the Public Trustee and a co-trustee, or (b) by the Public Trustee and an officer of the Public Trustee authorised in writing by him to act in that behalf, either generally or in any particular case, or (c) by a co-trustee and one such duly authorised officer, or (d) by two such duly authorised officers.

[1341]

19 (1) Separate accounts shall be kept for every trust or estate.

(2) A separate account shall be kept of the capital of the trust property and of the mode in which it is from time to time invested, and all dealing with such capital shall be entered in such account.

(3) A separate account shall be kept of the income of the trust property (if received by the Public Trustee), and of the mode in which it is from time to time dealt with by the Public Trustee.

[1342]

20 All payments of money to or from the capital of the trust property shall be made through the bank to the trust or estate.

[1343]

[**21** In all cases where any deed or other instrument requires to be executed by the Public Trustee under his Official Seal, the affixing of the Seal may be authenticated by the signature either of the Public Trustee or of some officer of the Public Trustee duly authorised by the Public Trustee in that behalf under his Seal, and any deed or other instrument purporting to be a deed or instrument executed by the Public Trustee and to be sealed with his seal authenticated in manner provided by this Rule shall be received in evidence and be deemed to be a deed or instrument so executed without further proof unless the contrary is shown.]

NOTES
Amendment Substituted by SR & O 1916/489.

[1344]

22 All sums payable out of the income or capital of the trust property shall be made by a cheque [on the Bank of England bearing a signature or a facsimile signature of an officer of the Public Trustee authorised in writing by him to act in that behalf or a cheque] on a bank signed by not less than two persons, *viz*:

(a) by the Public Trustee and a co-trustee, or
(b) by the Public Trustee and an officer of the Public Trustee authorised in writing by him to act in that behalf either generally or in any particular case, or
(c) by a co-trustee and one such duly authorised officer, or
(d) by two such duly authorised officers.

Provided that in any particular case the Public Trustee may authorise the payment of income by the person liable to pay the same direct to the person entitled to receive the same, or to his bank.

NOTES
Amendment Words in square brackets inserted by SI 1983/1050.

[1345]

23 (1) The income of the trust property may be paid to the person for the time being entitled to receive the same either through a bank or direct, and where such person is a married woman may be so paid notwithstanding any restraint on anticipation.

(2) Where authority is given to any Corporation or bank to pay any income to any person, the books of that Corporation or bank showing the payment of that income in accordance with the authority shall be a sufficient discharge to the Public Trustee.

(3) Where authority is given to any person to pay any income to the bank of the person entitled, the certificate of that bank stating the receipt of that income shall be a sufficient discharge to the Public Trustee.

(4) Where any person is solely entitled to receive any income, the Public Trustee may, on the request in writing of that person, and notwithstanding any restraint on anticipation, authorise that person for such period as the Public Trustee may think fit to collect or arrange for the collection of such income. During the continuance of any such authority such request in writing shall be a sufficient discharge to the Public Trustee in respect of such income.

NOTES
Restraint on anticipation Restraints on anticipation (other than those that can be attached to the enjoyment of property by a man) were abolished as from 16 December 1949 by the Married Women (Restraint upon Anticipation) Act 1949.

[1346]

24 The Public Trustee may, if the special circumstances of the case appear to him to render it desirable, pay to any other trustee of the trust or allow him to receive, the income of the trust property or any part thereof, on such trustee undertaking to apply it in manner directed by the trust.

[1347]

25 The Public Trustee may make advances for the purposes of any trust or estate in course of administration, or about to be administered, by him, out of any moneys which may be placed at his disposal by the Treasury for that purpose, and upon such terms as he may think proper.

[1348]

26 Subject to the provisions of the Act and of these rules and to the terms of any particular trust, the Public Trustee may, in the administration of any trust or estate, take and use professional advice and assistance in regard to legal and other matters, and may act on credible information (though less than legal evidence) as to matters of fact.

[1349]

27 The Public Trustee may at any time require a statutory declaration or other sufficient evidence that a person is alive and is the person to whom any money or property is payable or transferable, and may refuse payment or transfer until such declaration or evidence is produced.

NOTES
Statutory declaration Ie a declaration made by virtue of the Statutory Declarations Act 1835.
Cases relating to this rule *Re Wilson* [1964] 1 All ER 196, [1964] 1 WLR 214.

[1350]

28 Where a person appearing to be beneficially entitled to any sum of money under the trust or to be interested in the trust property cannot be found, or it is not known whether he is living or dead, the Public Trustee may apply to the Court for directions as to the course to be taken with reference to such person, and until an Order of the Court is made shall keep any sum payable to such person, and if it is kept for more than six months shall invest the same or deposit the same at interest and shall accumulate the dividends or interest thereof.

NOTES
Apply to the Court for directions See the Civil Procedure Rules 1998, SI 1998/3132, Pts 26, 27, 28, 29 (and supplementary Practice Directions), in the title Courts and Legal Services, Vol 5(3).
Cases relating to this rule *Re Wilson* [1964] 1 All ER 196, [1964] 1 WLR 214.

[1351]

29 (1) Upon an application in writing by or with the authority of any person interested in the trust property the Public Trustee—

- (a) shall permit the applicant or his Solicitor or other authorised agent to inspect and take copies of any entry in any Register or book relating to the trust or estate and (so far as the interest of the applicant in the trust property is or may be affected thereby) of any account notice or other document in the custody of the Public Trustee;
- (b) shall at the expense of the applicant supply him or his Solicitor or other authorised agent with a copy of any such entry, account notice or document as aforesaid, or with any extract therefrom;
- (c) shall give to the applicant or his Solicitor or other authorised agent such information respecting the trust or estate and the trust property as shall be reasonably requested in the application and shall be within the power of the Public Trustee.

(2) Subject as aforesaid the Public Trustee shall observe strict secrecy in respect of every trust or estate in course of administration by him.

NOTES
Solicitor See the note "Modification" at the beginning of these rules.

[1352]

[Corporate Bodies as Custodian Trustees

30 [(1)] The following corporations shall be entitled to act as custodian trustees:

- (a) the Treasury Solicitor;
- (b) any corporation which:
  - (i) is constituted under the law of the United Kingdom or of any part thereof, or under the law of any other Member State of the European Economic Community or of any part thereof;
  - (ii) is empowered by its constitution to undertake trust business (which for the purpose of this rule means the business of acting as trustee under wills and settlements and as executor and administrator) in England and Wales;
  - (iii) has one or more places of business in the United Kingdom; and
  - (iv) is—

a company incorporated by special Act of Parliament or Royal Charter, or

a company registered (with or without limited liability) in the United Kingdom under the Companies Act 1948 or under the Companies Act (Northern Ireland) 1960 or in another Member State of the European Economic Community and having a capital (in stock or shares) for the time being issued of not less than £250,000 (or its equivalent in the currency of the State where the company is registered), of which not less than £100,000 (or its equivalent) has been paid up in cash, or

a company which is registered without limited liability in the United Kingdom under the Companies Act 1948 or the Companies Act (Northern Ireland) 1960 or in another Member State of the European Economic Community and of which one of the members is a company within any of the classes defined in this sub-paragraph;

(c) any corporation which is incorporated by special Act or Royal Charter or under the Charitable Trustees Incorporation Act 1872 which is empowered by its constitution to act as a trustee for any charitable purposes, but only in relation to trusts in which its constitution empowers it to act;

(d) any corporation which is constituted under the law of the United Kingdom or of any part thereof and having its place of business there, and which is either:

(i) established for the purpose of undertaking trust business for the benefit of Her Majesty's Navy, Army, Air Force or Civil Service or of any unit, department, member or association of members thereof, and having among its directors or members any persons appointed or nominated by the Defence Council or any Department of State or any one or more of those Departments, or

(ii) authorised by the Lord Chancellor to act in relation to any charitable, ecclesiastical or public trusts as a trust corporation, but only in connection with any such trust as is so authorised;

[(e)

(i) any [Strategic Health Authority, Health Authority] or special health authority, but only in relation to any trust which the authority is authorised to accept or hold by virtue of section 90 of the National Health Service Act 1977;]

(ii) any preserved Board as defined by section 15(6) of [The National Health Service Reorganisation Act 1973], but only in relation to any trust which the Board is authorised to accept or hold by virtue of an order made under that section;

(f) the British Gas Corporation [or any subsidiary of the British Gas Corporation], but only in relation to a pension scheme or pension fund established or maintained by the Corporation by virtue of section 36 of the Gas Act 1972;

(g) the London Transport Executive, but only in relation to a pension scheme or pension fund—

(i) which is established or administered by the Executive by virtue of section 6 of the Transport (London) Act 1969, or

(ii) in relation to which rights, liabilities and functions have been transferred to the Executive by an order under section 74 of the Transport Act 1962 as applied by section 18 of the Transport (London) Act 1969;

(h) any of the following, namely:—

(i) the Greater London Council,

(ii) the corporation of any London borough (acting by the council),

(iii) a county council, district council, parish council or community council,

(iv) the Council of the Isles of Scilly,

[(v) the Common Council of the City of London,

but only in relation to charitable or public trusts (and not trusts for an ecclesiastical charity or for a charity for the relief of poverty) for the benefit of the inhabitants of the area of the local authority concerned and its neighbourhood, or any part of that area.]

[(i) any of the following, namely:—

(i) a metropolitan district council or a non-metropolitan county council,

(ii) the corporation of any London borough (acting by the council),

(iii) the Common Council of the City of London,

(iv) the Council of the Isles of Scilly,

but only in relation to any trust under which property devolves for the sole benefit of a person who occupies residential accommodation provided under section 21(1)(a) of the National Assistance Act 1948 by the local authority concerned or is in the care of that authority; and a corporation acting as a custodian trustee by virtue of this paragraph in relation to any trust shall be entitled to continue so to act in relation to that trust until a new custodian trustee is appointed, notwithstanding that the person concerned ceases to occupy such accommodation or to be in the care of that authority, as the case may be.]

[(j) The [British Coal Corporation] or any subsidiary of the [British Coal Corporation], but only in relation to a scheme or arrangements established under regulations made under section 37 of the Coal Industry Nationalisation Act 1946;]

[(k) any corporation acting as trustee of the trusts of any pension scheme or pension fund established or maintained by the British Broadcasting Corporation, but only in relation to those trusts];

[(l) any corporation appointed by the Secretary of State as a trustee of any scheme having effect by virtue of regulations made under section 37 of the Coal Industry Nationalisation Act 1946 for purposes relating to pensions, gratuities or other like benefits and in relation to which provision is, or has been, made by regulations made under paragraph 2(1) of Schedule 5 to the Coal Industry Act 1994 for the scheme to continue in force notwithstanding the repeal by the Coal Industry Act 1994 of section 37 of the Coal Industry Nationalisation Act 1946 and of the enactments modifying that section, but only in relation to such a scheme].

[(2) In this rule "subsidiary" has the same meaning as in section 154 of the Companies Act 1948.]

NOTES

Amendment Text of this rule substituted by SI 1975/1189; substituted text subsequently renumbered as para (1) by SI 1981/358.
Para (1)(e)(i): substituted by SI 1984/109; words in square brackets substituted by SI 2002/2469.
Para (1)(e)(ii): words in square brackets substituted by SI 1984/109.
Para (1)(f): words in square brackets inserted by SI 1985/132.
Para (1)(h): sub-para (v) and final paragraph inserted by SI 1976/836.
Para (1)(i): inserted by SI 1976/836.
Para (1)(j): inserted by SI 1981/358; words in square brackets substituted by virtue of the Coal Industry Act 1987, s 1(3) (repealed).
Para (1)(k): inserted by SI 1987/1891.
Para (1)(l): inserted by SI 1994/2519.
Para (2): inserted by SI 1981/358.

Health Authority Provision for the establishment of Health Authorities in Wales was made by the National Health Service Act 1977, s 8, Sch 5, Pt I (repealed). The functions of Health Authorities in Wales were transferred to the National Assembly for Wales by order made under the Government of Wales Act 1998, s 27 (repealed) and were subsequently transferred to Local Health Boards.

British Gas Corporation This body, which was originally known as the Gas Council, was constituted under the Gas Act 1972, s 1 (repealed). The Corporation was dissolved on 28 February 1990 by SI 1990/147 (lapsed) in accordance with the Gas Act 1986, s 57 (repealed), and its undertaking was transferred to British Gas plc, by virtue of the Gas Act 1986, s 49.

London Transport Executive Notwithstanding the repeal by the London Regional Transport Act 1984 of the provisions of the Transport (London) Act 1969, s 4, under which the Executive was established, the Executive continued to exist, but was known as London Regional Transport (ss 1(2), 67(1) of the 1984 Act). The 1984 Act was itself repealed by the Greater London Authority Act 1999, s 423, Sch 34, Pt II, and the former functions of the London Transport Executive, which were exercisable by London Regional Transport, are now exercisable by Transport for London (established by

Chapter II (ss 154–169) of Pt IV of the 1999 Act); see s 301 of the 1999 Act. Provision for the dissolution of London Regional Transport on 16 July 2003 was made by s 302 of the 1999 Act and SI 2003/1913, in the title Transport.
Greater London Council The council was abolished by the Local Government Act 1985, s 1, and its functions were transferred mainly to the London borough councils and the Common Council of the City of London by Pt II of the 1985 Act.
British Coal Corporation The Corporation was dissolved on 27 March 2004 in accordance with the Coal Industry Act 1994, s 23 (see SI 2004/144, in the title Mines, Minerals and Quarries), and the Corporation's successor body, the Coal Authority, is established by s 1 of, and Sch 1 to, that Act.
Charitable Trustees Incorporation Act 1872 Repealed; see now the Charities Act 1993, Pt VII (ss 50–62).
Coal Industry Nationalisation Act 1946, s 37 Repealed as from a day to be appointed by the Coal Industry Act 1994, s 67(8), Sch 11, Pt III. As to the continuance in force of regulations made under the said s 37, see the title Mines, Minerals and Quarries.
Companies Act 1948 Repealed, and replaced by the Companies Act 1985, itself largely repealed and replaced by the Companies Act 2006. As to the commencement of the 2006 Act, see SI 2006/3428, and the further orders noted thereto, in the title Companies. "Subsidiary" is now defined by the Companies Act 2006, s 1159.
Companies Act (Northern Ireland) 1960 Repealed.
Gas Act 1972, s 36 Repealed by the Gas Act 1986, s 67(4), Sch 9, Pt II.
National Health Service Act 1977, s 90 Repealed by the National Health Service (Consequential Provisions) Act 2006, s 6, Sch 4. See now the National Health Service Act 2006, Sch 2, para 12, Sch 6, para 8 and the National Health Service (Wales) Act 2006, Sch 2, Pt 3, para 13, Sch 5, para 8.
National Health Service Reorganisation Act 1973, s 15(6) Repealed by the Health Authorities Act 1995, ss 2(1), 5(1), Sch 1, Pt III, para 98, Sch 3.
Transport Act 1962, s 74 Provisions in the Transport Act 1962, ss 73, 74 as regards pensions and pension schemes and the power of the Secretary of State to make orders about pensions were applied to London Regional Transport (now dissolved; see above) with modifications (London Regional Transport Act 1984, ss 25, 71(2), Sch 5, para 6 (repealed by the Greater London Authority Act 1999, s 423, Sch 34, Pt II)). As regards pensions and pension schemes and the power to make orders for or in respect of persons who are or have been employees of, or of subsidiaries of, London Regional Transport, see the Greater London Authority Act 1999, s 411 and SI 2000/3386, in the title Transport.
Transport (London) Act 1969, ss 6, 18 Repealed by the London Regional Transport Act 1984, ss 71(3), Sch 7.
Cases relating to this rule *Re Bigger (deceased)* [1977] Fam 203, [1977] 2 All ER 644; *Re Skinner* [1958] 3 All ER 273, [1958] 1 WLR 1043.

[1353]

Investigation and Audit of Trust Accounts

31 Any application under section 13(1) of the Act shall be made to the Public Trustee, and notice thereof shall (unless the Public Trustee otherwise directs) be given by the applicant to every other person being a trustee or beneficiary under the trust.

NOTES

Application ... shall be made to the Public Trustee As to service, see r 40.

[1354]

32 (1) Upon receiving any such application the Public Trustee may in his absolute discretion by notice to the applicant require that before a day to be specified in the notice such security (by deposit of a sum of money) as he shall deem sufficient shall be given to him by the applicant for the payment of any expenses of the investigation and audit which may be ordered by the Public Trustee to be paid by the applicant personally.

(2) Where any such requirement is made no further proceedings shall be taken upon the application until the security has been given, and if the same is not given before the day specified in the notice the application shall be disallowed unless under special circumstances the Public Trustee thinks fit to extend the time for giving the security or to dispense therewith.

(3) Any sum so deposited shall be kept by the Public Trustee on deposit in his name and to a separate account at a Bank until all proceedings in connection with the investigation and audit have been concluded, and thereupon the deposited sum and the interest (if any) allowed thereon by the Bank shall be applied in or towards payment of any expenses of the investigation and audit which may be so ordered to be paid by the applicant personally and the balance (if any) shall be paid to the applicant.

[1355]

33 The Public Trustee may in his absolute discretion upon the application of any trustee or beneficiary direct that the investigation and audit shall extend only to a specified period of time or to a specified part of the trust property or shall be otherwise restricted.

[1356]

34 If within one month from the date of the application under section 13(1) of the Act no Solicitor or public accountant shall have been appointed by the applicant and the trustees to conduct the investigation and audit, there shall be deemed to be a default of agreement within the meaning of the said section 13(1) and the applicant may apply to the Public Trustee accordingly.

NOTES
Solicitor See the note "Modification" at the beginning of these rules.

[1357]

35 The remuneration of the auditor and the other expenses of the investigation and audit shall be such as may be determined by the Public Trustee. Provided that the Public Trustee may refer the costs of any Solicitor (being part of such expenses) for taxation to a Taxing Master of the [Senior Courts], and in such case the amount of the said costs when taxed shall be included in such expenses.

NOTES
Amendment Words in square brackets substituted by virtue of the Constitutional Reform Act 2005, s 59(4).
Solicitor See the note "Modification" at the beginning of these rules.

[1358]

36 (1) Where any investigation or audit has been made, copies of the report and certificate of the auditor under section 13(2) of the Act and such copies of accounts and other documents as the Public Trustee may require shall be forwarded to him by the auditor, and shall be considered by the Public Trustee before giving any direction or making any order under section 13(5) of the Act.

(2) The expense of making and forwarding any such copies as aforesaid and the fee of the Public Trustee (within the limits prescribed by or in pursuance of any order relating to the fees of the Public Trustee for the time being in force) shall for the purpose of section 13(5) of the Act be part of the expenses of the investigation and audit.

NOTES
Fee of the Public Trustee See SI 2008/611, art 23.

[1359]

37 (1) Before making any order under section 13(5) of the Act the Public Trustee shall, if any of the parties interested so desire, hear the said parties in such manner as he shall think fit.

(2) Any such order shall specify the person by or to whom any sum is to be paid and the amount of such sum provided that such an order may direct payment of the taxed costs of any solicitor employed in connection with the investigation and audit, and such costs shall be taxed by a Taxing Master of the [Senior Courts], and the amount of such costs when taxed shall be paid as if such amount had been specified in the Order.

(3) Any such Order may be enforced in the same manner as a judgment or order of the Court to the same effect.

NOTES
Amendment Para (2): words in square brackets substituted by virtue of the Constitutional Reform Act 2005, s 59(4).
Solicitor See the note "Modification" at the beginning of these rules.
Enforce in the same manner as a judgment or order of the Court See generally the Civil Procedure Rules 1998, SI 1998/3132, Pt 70 and Sch 1, RSC Ord 45, in the title Courts and Legal Services, Vol 5(3).
S 13(5) of the Act Under the Public Trustee Act 1906, s 13(5), the remuneration of the auditor and other expenses of the investigation and audit are borne by the estate unless the Public Trustee otherwise directs. Para (1) of this rule follows the decision in *Re Oddy* [1911] 1 Ch 532, [1911–13] All ER Rep

744. If an investigation and audit are applied for unreasonably, the applicant will have to bear the costs; see *Re Utley, Russell v Cubin* (1912) 106 LT 858, 56 Sol Jo 518 (application after consulting solicitors and accountants, who were satisfied).

[1360]

Miscellaneous

38 The accounts of the Public Trustee shall be audited and the securities held by him verified from time to time by such person or persons as the Treasury may appoint in accordance with regulations made by the Treasury.

NOTES

Regulations made by the Treasury These regulations are not printed in the SR & O/SI series presumably owing to their executive character (see SI 1948/1, r 2(1), printed in the title Statutory Instruments (Pt 2), Vol 1 of this work). The accounts of the Public Trustee are audited by the National Audit Office.

[1361]

39 Any Officer of the Public Trustee who shall be authorised by him in writing in that behalf may take any oath, make any declaration, verify any account and give personal attendance at any Court or place.

[1362]

40 (1) Any notice or application required to be given or made for the purposes of the Act or these Rules to the Public Trustee may be addressed to the Public Trustee at his Office in London, or if the same relates to a trust or estate in course of administration or proposed to be administered from a Branch Office then at that Branch Office.

(2) Any notice or application required to be given or made for the purpose of the Act or these Rules to any person other than the Public Trustee may be addressed to that person at his last known place of abode or place of business.

(3) Any such notice or application may be delivered at the place to which it is addressed or may be served by post.

[1363]

41 Where any person who (if not under disability) might have made any application, given any consent, done any act, or been party to any proceeding in pursuance of these Rules is an infant, idiot, or lunatic, the guardian or (as the case may require) the committee or receiver of the estate of such person may make such application, give such consent, do such act, and be party to such proceedings as such person if free from disability might have made, given, done or been party to, and shall otherwise represent such person for the purposes of these Rules. Where there is no guardian or committee or receiver of the estate of any such infant, idiot, or lunatic, or where any person is of unsound mind, or incapable of managing his affairs but has not been found lunatic under any inquisition, it shall be lawful for the Court to appoint a guardian of such person for the purpose of any proceedings under these Rules and from time to time to change such guardian.

NOTES

General This rule must be read in the light of the Mental Capacity Act 2005, which now governs the management of the property and affairs of a person lacking capacity.

[1364]

42 (1) The Public Trustee may in writing authorise any Deputy Public Trustee to exercise and perform (either generally or in relation to any particular case and subject to such conditions and restrictions (if any) as the Public Trustee may impose) all or any of the powers and duties of the Public Trustee under any of the foregoing Rules except—

- (a) the power or duty of determining whether a trust or estate shall be administered from his Central Office or from a Branch Office; and
- (b) the power of authorising officers of the Public Trustee to transfer securities or assure land or to sign cheques;
- (c) the power of making advances for the purposes of any trust or estate.

(2) Any such authority conditions or restrictions may at any time in like manner be withdrawn or varied by the Public Trustee at his discretion.

NOTES
Central Office of the Public Trustee See the note to r 3.

[1365]

43 No Deputy Public Trustee and no firm or member of a firm of Solicitors of which such Deputy is a member shall, except with the consent in writing of the Public Trustee and subject to such conditions as he may impose, act as Solicitor or Solicitors to a trust or estate which is in course of administration by such Deputy.

NOTES
Solicitor See the note "Modification" at the beginning of these rules.

[1366]

44 The Public Trustee may frame and cause to be printed and circulated or otherwise promulgated such forms and directions and regulations as he may deem requisite or expedient for facilitating proceedings under the Act and these Rules.

[1367]

45 (*Rescinds the Public Trustee Rules 1907, SR & O 1907/938.*)

46 These Rules may be cited as "The Public Trustee Rules 1912", and shall come into operation on the 15th day of April, 1912.

[1368]

JUDICIAL TRUSTEE RULES 1983
SI 1983/370

Authority Made by the Lord Chancellor under the Judicial Trustees Act 1896, s 4, with the consent of the Treasury and the authority for making orders under the Solicitors Act 1974, s 56.
Date made 8 March 1983.
Commencement 1 April 1983; see r 1.
Amendment Amended by virtue of the Courts and Legal Services Act 1990, s 74(1)(b), (3), and of the Constitutional Reform Act 2005, s 59(4), (5), Sch 11, Pt 1, para 1(2).
Interpretation See r 2(1). In addition, the word "trust", which is defined neither by these rules nor by the 1896 Act, is to be given its ordinary meaning, and includes a trust the trustees of which are trustees for the purposes of the Settled Land Act 1925; see *Re Marshall's Will Trusts* [1945] Ch 217, [1945] 1 All ER 550.
General See the Preliminary Note "Judicial trustees".

[1369]

Citation and commencement

1 These Rules may be cited as the Judicial Trustee Rules 1983 and shall come into operation on 1st April 1983.

[1370]

Interpretation

2 (1) In these Rules, unless the context otherwise requires—

"the Act" means the Judicial Trustees Act 1896;

"the Court" has the same meaning as in the Rules of the Supreme Court;

"Corporate Trustee" means the Official Solicitor, the Public Trustee or a corporation either appointed by the Court in any particular case to be a trustee or entitled by rules made under section 4(3) of the Public Trustee Act 1906 to act as custodian trustee;

"judicial trustee" means a sole judicial trustee or two or more judicial trustees appointed to act together;

"master" means a master of the [Senior Courts] other than a master of the [Senior Courts] (Taxing Office) and includes a [district judge] of a district registry of the High Court;

"official of the Court" means the holder of any paid office in or connected with the [Senior Courts] and includes the Official Solicitor to the [Senior Courts];

"Official Solicitor" means the Official Solicitor to the [Senior Courts];

"qualified accountant" means a person who is a member or a firm all the partners in which are members of the Institute of Chartered Accountants in England and Wales or of the Association of Certified and Corporate Accountants;

"Rules of the Supreme Court" has the same meaning as in section 151(4) of the [Senior Courts Act 1981].

(2) Subject to the provisions of these Rules and of any enactment, the Rules of the Supreme Court shall apply with the necessary modification to proceedings under the Act and these Rules.

NOTES

Amendment Para (1): in definition "master" words in first and second pairs of square brackets substituted by virtue of the Constitutional Reform Act 2005, s 59(4); words in third pair of square brackets substituted by virtue of the Courts and Legal Services Act 1990, s 74(1)(b), (3);
in definitions "official of the Court" and "Official Solicitor", words in square brackets substituted by virtue of the Constitutional Reform Act 2005, s 59(4);
in definition "Rules of the Supreme Court", words in square brackets substituted by virtue of the Constitutional Reform Act 2005, s 59(5), Sch 11, Pt 1, para 1(2).

Senior Courts Act 1981, s 151(4) The definition "Rules of the Supreme Court" in s 151(4) of the 1981 Act has been repealed by the Civil Procedure Act 1997, s 10, Sch 2, para 1(1), (7).

Rules of the Supreme Court SI 1965/1776. These rules have generally been replaced, as from 26 April 1999, by the Civil Procedure Rules 1998, SI 1998/3132, in the title Courts and Legal Services, Vol 5(3). The Chancery Division of the High Court exercises jurisdiction with regard to judicial trustees; see the Judicial Trustees Act 1896, s 2.

[1371]

APPOINTMENT OF JUDICIAL TRUSTEE

Making of application

3 (1) An application to the Court for the appointment of a judicial trustee must be made by originating summons or, if it is made in a pending cause or matter, by summons or motion in the cause or matter.

(2) An application for an injunction ancillary or incidental to an order appointing a judicial trustee may be joined with the application for such order.

(3) The Court hearing an application under paragraph (2) may grant an injunction restraining any trustee or person entitled to any interest in the property of which a judicial trustee is sought from assigning, charging or otherwise dealing with that property until after the hearing of a summons for the appointment of the judicial trustee and may require such summons returnable on such date as the Court may direct, to be issued.

(4) The evidence in support of such an application must include an affidavit by the applicant containing the following particulars so far as the applicant can gain information with regard to them:—

(a) a short description of the trust and instrument by which it is, or is to be, created;

(b) short particulars of the trust property, with an approximate estimate of its income, and capital value;

(c) short particulars of the incumbrances (if any) affecting the trust property;

(d) particulars as to the persons who are in possession of the documents relating to the trust;

(e) the names and addresses of the beneficiaries and short particulars of their respective interests; and

(f) the name, address and description of the proposal judicial trustee (if any) together with any proposal the applicant may make for his remuneration.

(5) Where the applicant cannot gain the information required on any point he must mention his inability in the affidavit.

NOTES

General For the mode of making applications to a district registry, see r 17.

Cases relating to this rule *Re Jones, Jones v Pickett* [1934] WN 77, 177 LT Jo 274.

[1372]

Service of summons and notice

4 (1) Subject to any direction of the Court—

(a) the summons shall be served on every existing trustee who is not an applicant and on such of the beneficiaries as the applicant thinks fit; but

(b) a summons issued by or on behalf of a person creating or intending to create a trust need not be served on any person.

(2) The Court may give such directions as it thinks fit for the service of the summons or the dispensing with service of the summons on any person.

(3) Where an applicant has no nomination for a judicial trustee he may, if he thinks fit, give not less than four days notice of the hearing of the application to any official of the Court who may be appointed judicial trustee.

(4) Where an official of the Court receives notice under paragraph (3) of this rule he shall not be a party to the proceedings but shall be entitled to attend the hearing.

[1373]

Service of order

5 (1) A copy of the order appointing a judicial trustee shall be served by the party having conduct of the proceedings on the judicial trustee, such beneficiaries, former trustees and other persons as the Court may direct.

[1374]

Security

6 (1) This rule shall apply where the judicial trustee is not an official of the Court.

(2) Subject to paragraph (3) below, an order appointing a judicial trustee may include such directions as the Court thinks fit for the giving of security by the person appointed.

(3) The Court shall not, except for special reasons, require security to be given when the application is made by a person creating or intending to create a trust.

(4) Where, by virtue of paragraph (2), a person is required to give security in accordance with this rule he must give security approved by the Court duly to account for what he receives as judicial trustee and to deal with it as the Court directs.

(5) Unless the Court otherwise directs, the security shall be by guarantee.

(6) Any guarantee or undertaking ordered to be filed as security shall be filed in Chancery Chambers or, if the cause or matter is proceeding in a district registry, that registry.

NOTES

General As to proceedings in a district registry, see r 17.

[1375]

Custody of trust funds, property and documents

7 The Court may give such directions as it thinks fit as to the manner in which and the conditions subject to which—

(a) the trust fund is to be held;

(b) any title deeds, certificates or other documents which are evidence of the title to the trust property are to be held or disposed of;

(c) trust property may be vested in the judicial trustee; and

(d) any payments received or made on behalf of the trust are to be dealt with and accounts thereof are to be kept.

[1376]

Applications for directions

8 (1) A judicial trustee or any person interested in the trust may at any time request the Court to give directions as to the trust or its administration, including a direction that there shall cease to be a judicial trustee, and such request shall state in writing the matters with regard to which directions are required.

(2) The Court may require the trustee or any other person to attend at chambers (if it appears that such attendance is necessary or convenient) or may direct a summons to be issued in the proceedings, or direct an issue or issues to be tried.

NOTES

Cases relating to this rule *Re Ridsdel, Ridsdel v Rawlinson* [1947] Ch 597, [1947] 2 All ER 312.

[1377]

ACCOUNTS AND EXAMINATION

Preparation of accounts

9 Unless the Court otherwise orders a judicial trustee shall make up his accounts (in such form as the Court shall require) in each year to the anniversary of his appointment and shall deliver them in accordance with rules 12 or 13, as the case may be, within one calendar month after such anniversary.

[1378]

10 A judicial trustee shall endorse on his accounts a certificate of the approximate capital value of the trust property at the commencement of the year of account.

[1379]

Remuneration and disbursements

11 (1) A person appointed judicial trustee shall be allowed on the examination of his accounts—

(a) by way of remuneration, if any, such reasonable amount in respect of work reasonably performed as may be authorised by the Court and the Court may direct that such remuneration shall be fixed by reference to such scales or rates of professional charges as it thinks fit provided that remuneration authorised under this rule shall not, in any year of account, exceed 15 per cent of the capital value of the trust property.

(b) such disbursements as have actually and properly been expended in his trusteeship.

(2) For the purpose of sub-paragraph (1)(a) of this rule:—

(a) the capital value shall be ascertained from the certificate under rule 10 in respect of the year of account, or, if the Court sees fit in the case of a final account, from the certificate in respect of the preceding year.

(b) The Court may, if it thinks fit, indicate to a judicial trustee upon his appointment the scale or rate of professional charges that it considers would be appropriate in relation to the appointment.

[1380]

Filing, examination and inspection of accounts

12 (1) This rule shall apply where the judicial trustee is not a corporate trustee.

(2) Unless the Court otherwise directs a judicial trustee must submit his accounts to the Court.

(3) The accounts shall be examined by the Court unless it considers that the accounts are likely to involve questions of difficulty and refers them to a qualified accountant for report, in which case the Court may order payment to him out of the trust of such reasonable amount in respect of his report as it thinks fit.

(4) Following examination by or on behalf of the Court, the result of such examination must be certified by a master and an order may thereupon be made as to the incidence of any costs or expenses incurred.

(5) The judicial trustee shall send a copy of the accounts, or if the Court thinks fit, a summary of the accounts, of the trust to such beneficiaries or other persons as the Court may direct.

(6) If an application is made by any person to inspect the filed accounts, the Court may, if it thinks fit, having regard to the nature of the relation of the applicant to the trust, allow them to be inspected on giving reasonable notice.

(7) Any person who is served with a copy of the accounts, or a summary of the accounts under paragraph (5), or, after inspection of the accounts under paragraph (6), remains dissatisfied with them, may apply to the Court for directions.

NOTES

Cases relating to this rule *Re Ridsdel, Ridsdel v Rawlinson* [1947] Ch 597, [1947] 2 All ER 312.

[1381]

13 (1) This rule shall apply where the judicial trustee is a corporate trustee.

(2) A judicial trustee shall submit for examination such accounts to such persons as the Court may direct.

(3) Any person to whom a judicial trustee is required to submit accounts may, on giving reasonable notice to the judicial trustee, inspect, either personally or by an agent, the books and other papers relating to such accounts.

(4) Any person to whom the judicial trustee is required to submit accounts, or any beneficiary, who is dissatisfied with them may give notice specifying the item or items as to which objection is taken and requiring the judicial trustee within not less than 14 days to lodge his accounts with the Court and a copy of such notice shall be lodged in Chancery Chambers or, if the cause or matter is proceeding in a district registry, that registry.

(5) Following an examination by or on behalf of the Court of an item or items in an account to which objection is taken the result of such examination must be certified by a master and an order may thereupon be made as to the incidence of any costs or expenses incurred.

NOTES

General The Judicial Trustees Act 1896, s 4(1A) allows different provision to be made for different classes of trust, trustees, beneficiaries or trust property. By this rule and the previous rule corporate trustees are distinguished from other trustees in relation to the examination and inspection of accounts.

[1382]

Default by judicial trustee

14 (1) Where a judicial trustee fails to submit his account in the prescribed manner or do any other thing which he is required to submit, provide or do, he and any or all of the beneficiaries and such other persons as the Court may direct may be required to attend in chambers to show cause for the failure and the Court may, either in chambers or after adjourning into Court, give such directions as it thinks proper, including if necessary, directions for the discharge of the judicial trustee and the appointment of another and the payment of costs.

(2) Without prejudice to paragraph (1) of this Rule, where the judicial trustee has failed to comply with the Act or with these Rules or with any direction of the Court made in accordance with these Rules or has otherwise misconducted himself in relation to the trust the Court may disallow any remuneration claimed in any subsequent account.

(3) If the Court is satisfied that the judicial trustee has failed to pay any sum into the trust account within a reasonable period of time it may charge him with interest at the rate currently payable in respect of judgment debts on that sum while in his possession.

[1383]

Special Provisions Relating to Officials of the Court

15 An official of the Court shall not be appointed or act as judicial trustee—

(a) for any persons in their capacity as members or debenture holders of, or being in any other relation to, any corporation or unincorporated body, or any club, or

(b) of a trust which involves the carrying on of any trade or business unless the Court, with or without special conditions to ensure the proper supervision of the trade or business, specifically directs.

[1384]

16 (1) The appointment of an official of the Court as a judicial trustee shall be an appointment of the holder of that office for the time being, and no further order or appointment shall be necessary by reason only of the person appointed dying or ceasing to hold office.

(2) Any property vested in an official of the Court as a judicial trustee shall, on his dying or ceasing to hold office, vest in the person appointed to succeed him without any conveyance, assignment or transfer.

[1385]

District Registries

17 (1) Notwithstanding any provisions contained in the Rules of the Supreme Court, an originating summons may be issued out of a district registry for the purpose of an application to appoint a judicial trustee.

(2) Where a judicial trustee is appointed on a summons or motion or in a cause or matter proceeding in a district registry all proceedings with respect to the trust and the administration thereof under the Act or these Rules shall, subject to paragraph (3) of this rule, be taken in the district registry.

(3) The Court may transfer any trust of which there is a judicial trustee from a district registry to Chancery Chambers or from Chancery Chambers to a district registry, or from one district registry to another, according as it appears convenient for the administration of the trust.

NOTES

District registry As to the places in which district registries are situated, see SI 1983/713, in the title Courts and Legal Services.

Rules of the Supreme Court See the note to r 2.

[1386]

Fees

18 Where in any matter proceeding under these Rules a fee would be payable under the Order for the time being in force relating to [Senior Courts] Fees, that fee shall be paid.

NOTES

Amendment Words in square brackets substituted by virtue of the Constitutional Reform Act 2005, s 59(4).

Senior Courts Fees These are currently prescribed by SI 2008/1053, in the title Courts and Legal Services.

[1387]

Revocations

19 (1) The Judicial Trustee Rules 1972 are hereby revoked.

(2) The provisions of the rules in force immediately before the commencement of the Judicial Trustee Rules 1972 shall continue to apply to proceedings taken before that date in a county court.

NOTES

Judicial Trustee Rules 1972 SI 1972/1096.

[1388]

RECOGNITION OF TRUSTS ACT 1987 (OVERSEAS TERRITORIES) ORDER 1989

SI 1989/673

Authority Made under the Recognition of Trusts Act 1987, s 2(2), (3).

Date made 18 April 1989.

Commencement 1 June 1989.

Summary This Order in Council provides that the Recognition of Trusts Act 1987, and the Schedule thereto, as modified in this Order in Council, are to form part of the law of the following specified territories: Bermuda, British Antarctic Territory, the Falkland Islands, St Helena and Dependencies, South Georgia and the South Sandwich Islands, the Sovereign Base Areas of Akrotiri and Dhekelia and the Virgin Islands.

[1389]

POWERS OF ATTORNEY (WELSH LANGUAGE FORMS) ORDER 2000

SI 2000/215

Authority Made by the Lord Chancellor under the Welsh Language Act 1993, s 26(2).

Date made 1 February 2000.
Commencement 1 March 2000.
Summary This order prescribes two Welsh language forms for powers of attorney. The first form allows a trustee to delegate the exercise of his powers and may be used instead of that set out in the Trustee Act 1925, s 25(6). The second form confers a general power of attorney in accordance with the Powers of Attorney Act 1971, s 10 and may be used instead of that set out in Sch 1 to the 1971 Act.

[1390]

PUBLIC TRUSTEE (FEES) ORDER 2008
SI 2008/611

Authority Made by the Lord Chancellor under the Public Trustee Act 1906, s 9(1).
Date made 5 March 2008.
Commencement 1 April 2008; see art 1.
Interpretation See art 2.
General This order, which revokes and replaces the Public Trustee (Fees) Order 1999, SI 1999/855, as amended, makes provision in connection with the fees chargeable in respect of the duties of the Public Trustee, for the purposes of the Public Trustee Act 1906.

[1391]

PART 1
CITATION, COMMENCEMENT AND INTERPRETATION

Citation and commencement

1 This Order may be cited as the Public Trustee (Fees) Order 2008 and shall come into force on 1st April 2008.

[1392]

Interpretation

2 In this Order—

"acceptance valuation date" in respect of any trust property means the date selected by the public trustee in relation to that property under article 11(1) or 15(1);

"executor" means the executor of a will or the administrator of an estate however appointed;

"financial year" means the year ending on 31st March;

"gross capital value" means the value of the estate or trust property (excluding any annuity or other terminable payment purchased by any person in the name of, transferred to or covenanted to be paid to the public trustee for the benefit of some other person) without deduction for debts, incumbrances, funeral expenses or inheritance tax.

[1393]

PART 2
GENERAL

Payment of fees from capital or income

3 (1) Subject to paragraph (2), all fees must be paid out of capital.

(2) The following fees must be paid out of income—

(a) fees which the public trustee has directed to be paid out of income under section 1(3) of the Public Trustee (Fees) Act 1957;
(b) the administration fee in cases to which article 18 applies;
(c) the insurance fee provided for by article 21;
(d) the income collection fee provided for by article 24;
(e) the management fee provided for by article 30; and
(f) the value added tax fee provided for by article 31, in cases where the fee in respect of which the value added tax fee is payable is itself payable out of income.

[1394]

Calculation

4 In ascertaining the amount payable in respect of any fee the public trustee—

(a) will take the value of any estate or trust property to be the price which it is estimated that the estate or property would fetch in the open market; and

(b) may treat the value of any estate or trust property as being that multiple of £100 which is nearest to the estimate of its exact value.

[1395]

Postponement of payment of fee

5 The public trustee may postpone any payment due in respect of any fee.

[1396]

Commutation

6 Liability to pay all or any part of any sums which may become due in respect of any fee may be commuted by the public trustee in consideration of a payment which represents the capital value of that liability.

[1397]

Power to remit fees and settle disputes

7 (1) The public trustee may remit so much as appears equitable of any fee payable in respect of any estate or trust where the whole or any part of the property is in another estate or trust in which the public trustee is acting.

(2) The public trustee may remit the whole or part of any fee where it is equitable to do so having regard to—

(a) the nature and character of the estate, trust or other matter;

(b) the work in respect of which the fee is charged; or

(c) the impact of the fee on a beneficiary or beneficiaries.

[1398]

PART 3
EXECUTORSHIP FEE

When executorship fee payable

8 An executorship fee is payable, in accordance with articles 9 to 11, on acceptance by the public trustee of any executorship.

[1399]

Property subsequently received

9 If additional property becomes part of an estate of which the public trustee is executor an executorship fee is payable in respect of the gross capital value of the additional property on its acceptance valuation date of such amount as would have been payable if the additional property had formed part of the estate at the date of acceptance of the executorship and this Order had been in force at that date.

[1400]

Postponement of payment of executorship fee

10 Where an executorship fee becomes payable under article 8 or 9 in respect of an estate any part of which is not in possession or not readily realisable, the public trustee will exclude the value of that part from the value of the remainder of the estate for the purpose of ascertaining the amount of the executorship fee then payable.

[1401]

Amount of executorship fee

11 (1) Subject to paragraphs (3) and (4), the executorship fee is calculated in accordance with paragraph (2) as a percentage of the gross capital value of the estate on the date of acceptance or on such convenient date as the public trustee may select.

(2) The rate of executorship fee is—

(a) in respect of the first £50,000, 12.5 per cent;

(b) in respect of any excess over £50,000 up to £75,000, 10 per cent;

(c) in respect of any excess over £75,000 up to £100,000, 5 per cent;

(d) in respect of any excess over £100,000, 3.8 per cent

but so that the fee payable is not less that £1,250.

(3) Where the main asset of an estate to be vested in one or more beneficiaries is an unencumbered property which was the principal private residence of the deceased and the public trustee's executorship duties have been exceptionally simple, a reduction may be made in the amount of the fee payable.

(4) Where the public trustee is acting as personal representative of a deceased statutory owner or tenant for life and is not acting otherwise in the trust a fee of £150 only will be payable.

(5) In this article, "statutory owner" and "tenant for life" have the meanings given by section 117(1) of the Settled Land Act 1925.

[1402]

PART 4
ACCEPTANCE FEE

When acceptance fee payable

12 (1) Subject to paragraph (2), an acceptance fee is payable, in accordance with articles 13 to 15, on acceptance by the public trustee of any trust other than a trust consisting entirely of an annuity or other terminable payment purchased by any person in the name of, transferred to or covenanted to be paid by the public trustee for the benefit of some other person.

(2) An acceptance fee is not payable in respect of any estate which the public trustee accepts as executor on or after 1st April 1977 during the period in which the public trustee so acts.

[1403]

Property subsequently coming into trust

13 If additional property becomes subject to a trust (other than an executorship accepted by the public trustee on or after 1st April 1977) which is administered by the public trustee as executor or as trustee, and such property is not an accumulation of the income of the property already subject to the estate or the trust, an acceptance fee is payable in respect of the gross capital value of the additional property on its acceptance valuation date of such amount as would have been payable if—

(a) the additional property had formed part of the estate or the trust property at the date of acceptance of the estate or the trust; and

(b) this Order had been in force at that date.

[1404]

Postponement of payment of acceptance fee

14 Where an acceptance fee becomes payable in accordance with article 12 or 13 in respect of estate or trust property, any part of which is not in possession or not readily realisable, the public trustee—

(a) will exclude the value of the property not in possession or not readily realisable from the value of the remainder of the estate or trust property for the purpose of ascertaining the amount of the acceptance fee then payable; and

(b) will, when the property so excluded falls into possession or is realised, as the case may be, charge an acceptance fee in respect of the gross capital value of the excluded property of such amount as would have been payable if—

(i) the excluded property had formed part of the estate or of the trust property at the date of acceptance of the estate or of the trust; and

(ii) this Order had been in force at that date.

[1405]

Amount of acceptance fee

15 (1) The acceptance fee is calculated in accordance with paragraph (2) as a percentage of the gross capital value of the estate or the trust property on the date of acceptance or on such convenient date as the public trustee may select.

(2) Subject to paragraph (3), where the public trustee is acting—

(a) under a declaration of trust in favour of one beneficiary only; or

(b) as original, substituted or additional trustee of property to which an infant is absolutely entitled under a will (or other testamentary disposition) or on an intestacy,

the rate of the acceptance fee is—

(i) in respect of the first £50,000, 1.25 per cent;

(ii) in respect of any excess over £50,000, 0.5 per cent

but so that the fee payable is not less than £175.

(3) No acceptance fee will be charged in respect of property to which paragraph (2) applies if that property is immediately and directly derived from an estate or a trust in which the public trustee is acting.

(4) In all other cases in which the public trustee is acting as trustee the rate of the acceptance fee is one half the rate of the executorship fee but so that the fee payable is not less than £550.

[1406]

PART 5
ADMINISTRATION FEE

When administration fee payable

16 (1) Subject to paragraph (3), an administration fee is payable, in accordance with articles 17 and 18, at the beginning of each financial year.

(2) An administration fee is payable in full even if the public trustee ceases to act in the estate or the trust, or any part of the estate or trust, in the course of that year.

(3) An administration fee is not payable—

(a) in respect of the period between the date of the acceptance of a trust or any part of a trust and the commencement of the next financial year; or

(b) in respect of any estate or part of an estate which the public trustee accepts as executor during the period in which the public trustee so acts.

[1407]

Amount of administration fee

17 (1) Subject to paragraphs (5) to (9), the administration fee is the relevant percentage of that multiple of £100 which is nearest to the net capital value of the estate or the trust fund as certified by the public trustee after such value has been estimated in accordance with paragraph (2).

(2) The net capital value of an estate or a trust fund is A + B – C where—

"A" is the value on the appropriate valuation date of the estate or the trust property other than interests not in possession and annuities or other terminable payments to which article 18 applies;

"B" is the value, on its acceptance valuation date, of any additional property becoming part of the estate or subject to the trust during the relevant period; and

"C" is such sum as the public trustee considers to be a reasonable deduction in respect of any estate or trust property distributed or disbursed by the public trustee during the relevant period.

(3) In valuing any property for the purposes of this article no deduction will be made for any debt specifically charged on it.

(4) The relevant percentage of the net capital value of the estate or the trust fund is—

(a) in respect of the first £30,000, 5 per cent;

(b) in respect of any excess over £30,000 up to £150,000, 3 per cent;

(c) in respect of any excess over £150,000 up to £375,000, 2 per cent;

(d) in respect of any excess over £375,000 up to £2,500,000, 1.25 per cent;

(e) in respect of any excess over £2,500,000 up to £3,000,000, 0.6 per cent; and

(f) in respect of any excess over £3,000,000, 0.3 per cent,

but so that the fee payable is not less than £375.

(5) Where the public trustee is acting exclusively as custodian trustee, the fee payable will be reduced by one half where the trust was accepted before 1st April 1980.

(6) Where the public trustee is acting exclusively as trustee of a settlement under the Settled Land Act 1925, the fee payable will be reduced by three quarters in respect of any part of the trust property which at the date on which the fee becomes payable is represented by land.

(7) Where the public trustee is acting as trustee under a declaration of trust for one beneficiary only, the fee payable will be reduced by five eighths.

(8) Where the public trustee is acting in a trust or an estate where an asset is represented by either—

(a) the principal private residence of a beneficiary who discharges all outgoings but pays no rent to the estate or trust; or

(b) a mortgage secured on the principal private residence of a beneficiary,

the fee payable will be reduced by three quarters in respect of that asset provided that in the event of a beneficiary occupying part only of a building such reduction will apply only to the value of that part of the building.

(9) Where the trust or estate has a net capital value of less than £3,000 (calculated in accordance with paragraph (2)) the fee payable will be 10 per cent of the net capital value.

(10) In this article—

"appropriate valuation date" means whichever of the following dates next precedes the date on which the fee is payable—

(a) 30th September 2006, in the case of any estate or trust in which the public trustee was acting on that date; and

(b) in any other case, the acceptance valuation date of the estate or trust;

"relevant period" means the period between the appropriate valuation date and the date on which the fee is payable.

[1408]

Annuities

18 Where trust property includes an annuity or other terminable payment purchased by any person in the name of, transferred to or covenanted to be paid to the public trustee for the benefit of some other person, the administration fee in respect of that annuity or other payment is charged at the rate of 5 per cent of the gross income without deduction of income tax or other outgoings, and no other fee is payable under this Part.

[1409]

PART 6
WITHDRAWAL FEE

When withdrawal fee payable

19 A withdrawal fee is payable—

(a) on the public trustee ceasing to act—

(i) as trustee or manager of any scheme or funds under Part 8 whether on retirement or otherwise; or

(ii) other than on retirement, in any estate or trust; or

(b) on the withdrawal or distribution of any part of the estate or the trust property, or, as the case may be, of the capital of a scheme or fund under Part 8, except where—

(i) the public trustee ceases to act as executor of an estate in respect of which an executorship fee is payable;

(ii) trust property held on a declaration of trust in favour of one beneficiary only is withdrawn for the purpose of transfer to a new executorship or a new trust accepted by the public trustee;

(iii) the public trustee is acting other than as trustee or manager of any scheme or fund under Part 8 and the trust or estate has, in the opinion of the public trustee, a total value of £30,000 or less on 31st March 2004; or

(iv) trust property or, as the case may be, capital of a scheme or fund under Part 8, is withdrawn for the purpose of paying any fees prescribed by this Order.

[1410]

Amount of withdrawal fee

20 (1) Subject to paragraph (4), the withdrawal fee is charged at a relative percentage of the gross capital value of the property withdrawn or distributed.

(2) Subject to paragraph (3), the relative percentage is—

(a) one half of the effective rate of administration or management fee charged on that property on the assessment date immediately prior to withdrawal, other than where the public trustee ceases to act on retirement, in any estate or trust; and

(b) equivalent to the effective rate of administration or management fee charged on that property on the assessment date immediately prior to withdrawal or distribution, in any other case.

(3) Where the property did not form part of the estate or trust on the assessment date prior to withdrawal or distribution the value of that property on its acceptance valuation date will be used to determine the effective rate of the administration fee as if it had formed part of the estate or trust on the assessment date prior to withdrawal or distribution.

(4) Where the public trustee ceases to act as trustee or manager of any scheme or fund under Part 8—

(a) the withdrawal fee is such amount as may be agreed between the public trustee and the other trustees of the scheme or society as commensurate with the amount of work involved in the cessation and the capital value of the fund; or

(b) where no such agreement is reached, the withdrawal fee will be charged as a relative percentage of the gross capital value of the property withdrawn or distributed equivalent to the effective rate of administration or management fee charged on that property on the assessment date immediately prior to the withdrawal or distribution.

(5) In this article—

"assessment date" means whichever of the following dates next precedes the date on which the fee is payable—

(a) 1st April, in the case of any estate or trust subject to administration fee under Part 5, or

(b) the accounting date in the case of any scheme or fund subject to management fee under Part 8;

"effective rate" means the percentage rate determined by the formula *(a/b) x 100* where—

"a" equals the amount of administration or management fee charged, or deemed to have been charged, on the property on the assessment date prior to withdrawal or distribution; and

"b" equals the value on which that fee was, or was deemed to have been, assessed.

(6) Where some or all of a fee has been remitted, the references in this article to administration or management fee charged mean such fee as would have been charged but for the remission.

[1411]

PART 7
FEES FOR SPECIAL SERVICES

Insurance fee

21 If the public trustee is paid commission when effecting or renewing a policy of insurance on any trust property, a fee is payable in an amount equal to the amount of the commission paid.

[1412]

Commission fee

22 (1) On any dealing in securities, a fee is payable equal to the amount of any stockbroker's commission refunded to the public trustee.

(2) Where a commission is received by the public trustee on any deposit of money, a fee is payable equal to the amount of the commission received.

[1413]

Supervision of investigation or audit fee

23 A fee of £750 is payable to the public trustee for the supervision of any investigation or audit under section 13 of the Public Trustee Act 1906.

[1414]

Income collection fee

24 (1) Subject to the following paragraphs, an income collection fee at the rate of 7.5 per cent is payable at such time or times as the public trustee may direct in respect of the gross income of any estate or trust received by the public trustee.

(2) Where the public trustee receives income from dividends or interest after deduction of tax, the income collection fee is payable in respect of the income so received.

(3) Where the public trustee is acting exclusively under a declaration of trust for one beneficiary only, the income collection fee is payable at one-half of the rate payable under paragraph (1).

(4) No fee is payable under this article in respect of an annuity or other terminable payment to which article 18 applies.

(5) The public trustee may remit so much as appears equitable of any fee payable under this article where—

(a) the public trustee's duties have been or are likely to be exceptionally simple; or

(b) the circumstances are otherwise exceptional.

[1415]

Investigation fee

25 (1) On being asked to act as trustee of an existing trust, the public trustee may demand the deposit of such fee or fees as is deemed sufficient to cover the cost of examining and considering relevant documents and accounts whether or not the public trustee subsequently accepts appointment as trustee.

(2) If the public trustee is subsequently appointed, the public trustee may set off all or part of the fee or fees deposited under paragraph (1) against fees then due under Parts 3 or 4.

(3) When the public trustee renounces probate of any will (or other testamentary disposition) of which the public trustee has been appointed executor, the public trustee may charge a fee commensurate with the work involved in the public trustee's investigation of the assets and liabilities of the estate.

[1416]

Fee for agency work

26 On acting as agent, the public trustee is entitled to make such a charge commensurate with the amount of work involved as the public trustee may determine.

[1417]

Fee for additional work

27 The public trustee is entitled to make a reasonable additional charge according to the work involved in—

(a) dealing with a business;
(b) dealing with assets situated outside the United Kingdom;
(c) supplying information for the purpose of any proposed dealing with a beneficial interest or for registering a notice of charge;
(d) dealing with freehold or leasehold property or a mortgage;
(e) supplying copies of documents and additional copies of accounts;
(f) an administration following the cessation of a life or other interest in property in circumstances in which no withdrawal fee is payable;
(g) work incidental to any application to the court in connection with the administration of an estate or trust;
(h) conducting a hearing in accordance with rule 37 of the Public Trustee Rules 1912; or
(i) dealing with duties of an unusual, complex or exacting nature.

NOTES

Public Trustee Rules 1912 SR & O 1912/348.

[1418]

Registration and enquiry fees

28 A fee is payable in respect of trusts or estates in which the public trustee is nominated to receive notices under section 138 of the Law of Property Act 1925—

(a) for accepting nomination, a fee of £100;
(b) for the entry of each notice, a fee of £35 (such fee to cover any necessary acknowledgement of the notice);
(c) for permitting any authorised person to inspect and take copies of the register and of any notices, a fee of £35 for each inspection in respect of each trust or estate; and
(d) for replying to an enquiry respecting notices, a fee not exceeding £85 for each reply in respect of each trust.

[1419]

Fees for registration of documents in respect of deceased persons and searches of the register

29 The following fees are payable in respect of the functions of the public trustee under section 19 of the Law of Property (Miscellaneous Provisions) Act 1994 (functions of public trustee in relation to notices etc)—

(a) for entering details of documents on the register, £40 for each deceased person against whose name the details are registered, payable in relation to each property in respect of which registration is made; or
(b) for causing a search of the register to be made, £20 for each name or variation of a name against which the search is made.

[1420]

PART 8
SUPERANNUATION SCHEMES AND FRIENDLY SOCIETIES

Management fee

30 (1) A management fee is payable where the public trustee is acting as trustee of a superannuation scheme or is managing funds on behalf of the trustees of a friendly society.

(2) The management fee is payable annually on the accounting date and is charged at an amount commensurate with the amount of work involved and, subject to paragraph (3), the capital value of the Fund on the relevant accounting date as the public trustee may agree with the trustees.

(3) In the event that agreement is not reached in accordance with paragraph (2), the management fee will be 1.25 times the annual fee last charged or, if not actually charged, chargeable, before 1st April 2005.

(4) In this article—

"friendly society" means a society registered as a friendly society under the Friendly Societies Act 1974; and

"superannuation scheme" means any scheme established for the provision of superannuation or other benefits for persons entitled to or eligible for such benefits under the scheme.

[1421]

PART 9
VALUE ADDED TAX

Amount of fee

31 For the purposes of reimbursing the public trustee in respect of value added tax payable on the supply of services in relation to which a fee (other than a fee payable under article 21 or 22) is charged, an additional fee equal to the amount of the tax is payable.

[1422]

PART 10
REVOCATIONS

32 (*Revokes the Public Trustee (Fees) Order 1999, SI 1999/855 and the amending SI 2002/2232, SI 2003/690, SI 2004/799, SI 2005/351, SI 2007/681.*)

INDEX